American Casebook Series
Hornbook Series and Basic Legal Texts
Nutshell Series

of

WEST PUBLISHING COMPANY
P.O. Box 3526
St. Paul, Minnesota 55165
July, 1981

ACCOUNTING

Fiflis and Kripke's Teaching Materials on Accounting for Business Lawyers, 2nd Ed., 684 pages, 1977 (Casebook)

ADMINISTRATIVE LAW

Davis' Cases, Text and Problems on Administrative Law, 6th Ed., 683 pages, 1977 (Casebook)

Davis' Basic Text on Administrative Law, 3rd Ed., 617 pages, 1972 (Text)

Davis' Police Discretion, 176 pages, 1975 (Text)

Gellhorn and Boyer's Administrative Law and Process in a Nutshell, 2nd Ed., approx. 440 pages, 1981 (Text)

Mashaw and Merrill's Introduction to the American Public Law System, 1095 pages, 1975, with 1980 Supplement (Casebook)

Robinson, Gellhorn and Bruff's The Administrative Process, 2nd Ed., 959 pages, 1980 (Casebook)

ADMIRALTY

Healy and Sharpe's Cases and Materials on Admiralty, 875 pages, 1974 (Casebook)

AGENCY—PARTNERSHIP

Crane and Bromberg's Hornbook on Partnership, 695 pages, 1968 (Text)

Fessler's Alternatives to Incorporation for Persons in Quest of Profit, 258 pages, 1980 (Casebook)

Henn's Cases and Materials on Agency, Partnership and Other Unincorporated Business Enterprises, 396 pages, 1972 (Casebook)

AGENCY—PARTNERSHIP—Continued

Reuschlein and Gregory's Hornbook on the Law of Agency and Partnership, 625 pages, 1979, with 1981 pocket part (Text)

Seavey's Hornbook on Agency, 329 pages, 1964 (Text)

Seavey and Hall's Cases on Agency, 431 pages, 1956 (Casebook)

Seavey, Reuschlein and Hall's Cases on Agency and Partnership, 599 pages, 1962 (Casebook)

Selected Corporation and Partnership Statutes and Forms, 777 pages, 1980

Steffen and Kerr's Cases and Materials on Agency-Partnership, 4th Ed., 859 pages, 1980 (Casebook)

Steffen's Agency-Partnership in a Nutshell, 364 pages, 1977 (Text)

AMERICAN INDIAN LAW

Canby's American Indian Law in a Nutshell, 288 pages, 1981 (Text)

Getches, Rosenfelt and Wilkinson's Cases on Federal Indian Law, 660 pages, 1979 (Casebook)

ANTITRUST LAW

Gellhorn's Antitrust Law and Economics in a Nutshell, 2nd Ed., 425 pages, 1981 (Text)

Oppenheim, Weston and McCarthy's Cases and Comments on Federal Antitrust Laws, 4th Ed., approximately 1200 pages, 1981 (Casebook)

LAW SCHOOL PUBLICATIONS—Continued

ANTITRUST LAW—Continued

Oppenheim and Weston's Price and Service Discrimination Under the Robinson-Patman Act, 3rd Ed., 258 pages, 1974 (Casebook—reprint from Oppenheim and Weston's Cases and Comments on Federal Antitrust Laws, 3rd Ed., 1968)

Posner and Easterbrook's Cases and Economic Notes on Antitrust, 2nd Ed., 1077 pages, 1981 (Casebook)

Sullivan's Hornbook of the Law of Antitrust, 886 pages, 1977 (Text)

See also Regulated Industries, Trade Regulation

BANKING LAW

See Regulated Industries

BUSINESS PLANNING

Epstein and Scheinfeld's Teaching Materials on Business Reorganization Under the Bankruptcy Code, 216 pages, 1980 (Casebook)

Painter's Problems and Materials in Business Planning, 791 pages, 1975, with 1980 Supplement (Casebook)

CIVIL PROCEDURE

Casad's Res Judicata in a Nutshell, 310 pages, 1976 (Text)

Cound, Friedenthal and Miller's Cases and Materials on Civil Procedure, 3rd Ed., 1147 pages, 1980 with 1980 Supplement (Casebook)

Cound, Friedenthal and Miller's Cases on Pleading, Joinder and Discovery, 643 pages, 1968 (Casebook)

Ehrenzweig, Louisell and Hazard's Jurisdiction in a Nutshell, 4th Ed., 232 pages, 1980 (Text)

Federal Rules of Civil-Appellate-Criminal Procedure—West Law School Edition, 344 pages, 1981

Hodges, Jones and Elliott's Cases and Materials on Texas Trial and Appellate Procedure, 2nd Ed., 745 pages, 1974 (Casebook)

Hodges, Jones and Elliott's Cases and Materials on the Judicial Process Prior to Trial in Texas, 2nd Ed., 871 pages, 1977 (Casebook)

Kane's Civil Procedure in a Nutshell, 271 pages, 1979 (Text)

Karlen's Procedure Before Trial in a Nutshell, 258 pages, 1972 (Text)

Karlen and Joiner's Cases and Materials on Trials and Appeals, 536 pages, 1971 (Casebook)

Karlen, Meisenholder, Stevens and Vestal's Cases on Civil Procedure, 923 pages, 1975 (Casebook)

CIVIL PROCEDURE—Continued

Koffler and Reppy's Hornbook on Common Law Pleading, 663 pages, 1969 (Text)

McBaine's Cases on Introduction to Civil Procedure, 399 pages, 1950 (Casebook)

McCoid's Cases on Civil Procedure, 823 pages, 1974 (Casebook)

Park's Computer-Aided Exercises on Civil Procedure, 118 pages, 1976 (Coursebook)

Shipman's Hornbook on Common-Law Pleading, 3rd Ed., 644 pages, 1923 (Text)

Siegel's Hornbook on New York Practice, 1011 pages, 1978 with 1979-80 Pocket Part (Text)

See also Federal Jurisdiction and Procedure

CIVIL RIGHTS

Abernathy's Cases and Materials on Civil Rights, 660 pages, 1980 (Casebook)

Cohen's Cases on the Law of Deprivation of Liberty: A Study in Social Control, 755 pages, 1980 (Casebook)

Lockhart, Kamisar and Choper's Cases on Constitutional Rights and Liberties, 5th Ed., 1298 pages plus Appendix, 1981, with 1981 Supplement (Casebook)—reprint from Lockhart, et al. Cases on Constitutional Law, 5th Ed., 1980

Vieira's Civil Rights in a Nutshell, 279 pages, 1978 (Text)

COMMERCIAL LAW

Bailey's Secured Transactions in a Nutshell, 2nd Ed., 391 pages, 1981 (Text)

Epstein and Martin's Basic Uniform Commercial Code Teaching Materials, 599 pages, 1977 (Casebook)

Henson's Hornbook on Secured Transactions Under the U.C.C., 2nd Ed., 504 pages, 1979 with 1979 P.P. (Text)

Murray's Commercial Law, Problems and Materials, 366 pages, 1975 (Coursebook)

Nordstrom and Clovis' Problems and Materials on Commercial Paper, 458 pages, 1972 (Casebook)

Nordstrom and Lattin's Problems and Materials on Sales and Secured Transactions, 809 pages, 1968 (Casebook)

Nordstrom's Hornbook on Sales, 600 pages, 1970 (Text)

Selected Commercial Statutes, 1367 pages, 1981

LAW SCHOOL PUBLICATIONS—Continued

COMMERCIAL LAW—Continued

Speidel, Summers and White's Teaching Materials on Commercial and Consumer Law, 3rd Ed., approximately 1490 pages, 1981 (Casebook)

Stockton's Sales in a Nutshell, 2nd Ed., 370 pages, 1981 (Text)

Stone's Uniform Commercial Code in a Nutshell, 507 pages, 1975 (Text)

Uniform Commercial Code, Official Text with Comments, 994 pages, 1978

UCC Article 8, 1977 Amendments, 249 pages, 1978

UCC Article 9, Reprint from 1962 Code, 128 pages, 1976

UCC Article 9, 1972 Amendments, 304 pages, 1978

Weber's Commercial Paper in a Nutshell, 2nd Ed., 361 pages, 1975 (Text)

White and Summers' Hornbook on the Uniform Commercial Code, 2nd Ed., 1250 pages, 1980 (Text)

COMMUNITY PROPERTY

Huie's Texas Cases and Materials on Marital Property Rights, 681 pages, 1966 (Casebook)

Verrall's Cases and Materials on California Community Property, 3rd Ed., 547 pages, 1977 (Casebook)

COMPARATIVE LAW

Langbein's Comparative Criminal Procedure: Germany, 172 pages, 1977 (Casebook)

CONFLICT OF LAWS

Cramton, Currie and Kay's Cases-Comments-Questions on Conflict of Laws, 3rd Ed., approximately 1027 pages, 1981 (Casebook)

Ehrenzweig's Conflicts in a Nutshell, 3rd Ed., 432 pages, 1974 (Text)

Scoles and Weintraub's Cases and Materials on Conflict of Laws, 2nd Ed., 966 pages, 1972, with 1978 Supplement (Casebook)

CONSTITUTIONAL LAW

Engdahl's Constitutional Power in a Nutshell: Federal and State, 411 pages, 1974 (Text)

Ginsburg's Constitutional Aspects of Sex-Based Discrimination, 129 pages, 1974 (Casebook)—reprint from Davidson, Ginsburg and Kay's Cases on Sex-Based Discrimination, 1974

Lockhart, Kamisar and Choper's Cases-Comments-Questions on Constitutional Law, 5th Ed., 1705 pages plus Appendix, 1980, with 1981 Supplement (Casebook)

CONSTITUTIONAL LAW—Continued

Lockhart, Kamisar and Choper's Cases-Comments-Questions on the American Constitution, 5th Ed., 1185 pages plus Appendix, 1981, with 1981 Supplement (Casebook)—reprint from Lockhart, et al. Cases on Constitutional Law, 5th Ed., 1980

Lockhart, Kamisar and Choper's Cases and Materials on Constitutional Rights and Liberties, 5th Ed., 1298 pages plus Appendix, 1981, with 1981 Supplement (Casebook)—reprint from Lockhart, et al. Cases on Constitutional Law, 5th Ed., 1980

Manning's The Law of Church-State Relations in a Nutshell, 305 pages, 1981 (Text)

Miller's Presidential Power in a Nutshell, 328 pages, 1977 (Text)

Nowak, Rotunda and Young's Handbook on Constitutional Law, 974 pages, 1978, with 1979 pocket part (Text)

Rotunda's Modern Constitutional Law: Cases and Notes, approximately 1035 pages, 1981, with 1981 Supplement (Casebook)

Vieira's Civil Rights in a Nutshell, 279 pages, 1978 (Text)

Williams' Constitutional Analysis in a Nutshell, 388 pages, 1979 (Text)

CONSUMER LAW

Epstein and Nickles' Consumer Law in a Nutshell, 2nd Ed., 418 pages, 1981 (Text)

McCall's Consumer Protection, Cases, Notes and Materials, 594 pages, 1977, with 1977 Statutory Supplement (Casebook)

Schrag's Cases and Materials on Consumer Protection, 2nd Ed., 197 pages, 1973 (Casebook)—reprint from Cooper, et al. Cases on Law and Poverty, 2nd Ed., 1973

Selected Commercial Statutes, 1367 pages, 1981

Spanogle and Rohner's Cases and Materials on Consumer Law, 693 pages, 1979 (Casebook)

See also Commercial Law

CONTRACTS

Calamari & Perillo's Cases and Problems on Contracts, 1061 pages, 1978 (Casebook)

Calamari and Perillo's Hornbook on Contracts, 2nd Ed., 878 pages, 1977 (Text)

CONTRACTS—Continued

Corbin's Text on Contracts, One Volume Student Edition, 1224 pages, 1952 (Text)

Freedman's Cases and Materials on Contracts, 658 pages, 1973 (Casebook)

Friedman's Contract Remedies in a Nutshell, approx. 325 pages, 1981 (Text)

Fuller and Eisenberg's Cases on Basic Contract Law, 4th Ed., approximately 1200 pages, 1981 (Casebook)

Jackson and Bollinger's Cases on Contract Law in Modern Society, 2nd Ed., 1329 pages, 1980 (Casebook)

Keyes' Government Contracts in a Nutshell, 423 pages, 1979 (Text)

Reitz's Cases on Contracts as Basic Commercial Law, 763 pages, 1975 (Casebook)

Schaber and Rohwer's Contracts in a Nutshell, 307 pages, 1975 (Text)

Simpson's Hornbook on Contracts, 2nd Ed., 510 pages, 1965 (Text)

COPYRIGHT

Nimmer's Cases and Materials on Copyright and Other Aspects of Law Pertaining to Literary, Musical and Artistic Works, Illustrated, 2nd Ed., 1023 pages, 1979 (Casebook)

See also Patent Law

CORPORATIONS

Hamilton's Cases on Corporations—Including Partnerships and Limited Partnerships, 2nd Ed., 1108 pages, 1981, with 1981 Statutory Supplement (Casebook)

Hamilton's Law of Corporations in a Nutshell, 379 pages, 1980 (Text)

Henn's Cases on Corporations, 1279 pages, 1974, with 1980 Supplement (Casebook)

Henn's Hornbook on Corporations, 2nd Ed., 956 pages, 1970 (Text)

Jennings and Buxbaum's Cases and Materials on Corporations, 5th Ed., 1180 pages, 1979 (Casebook)

Selected Corporation and Partnership Statutes, Regulations and Forms, 777 pages, 1980

CORRECTIONS

Krantz's Cases and Materials on the Law of Corrections and Prisoners' Rights, 2nd Ed., 735 pages, 1981 (Casebook)

Krantz's Law of Corrections and Prisoners' Rights in a Nutshell, 353 pages, 1976 (Text)

CORRECTIONS—Continued

Model Rules and Regulations on Prisoners' Rights and Responsibilities, 212 pages, 1973

Popper's Post-Conviction Remedies in a Nutshell, 360 pages, 1978 (Text)

Rubin's Law of Criminal Corrections, 2nd Ed., 873 pages, 1973, with 1978 Supplement (Text)

CREDITOR'S RIGHTS

Epstein's Debtor-Creditor Law in a Nutshell, 2nd Ed., 324 pages, 1980 (Text)

Epstein and Landers' Debtors and Creditors: Cases and Materials, 722 pages, 1978, with 1979 Supplement (Casebook)

Epstein and Sheinfeld's Teaching Materials on Business Reorganization Under the Bankruptcy Code, 216 pages, 1980 (Casebook)

Riesenfeld's Cases and Materials on Creditors' Remedies and Debtors' Protection, 3rd Ed., 810 pages, 1979 with 1979 Statutory Supplement and 1981 Case Supplement (Casebook)

Selected Bankruptcy Statutes, 351 pages, 1979

CRIMINAL LAW AND CRIMINAL PROCEDURE

Cohen and Gobert's Problems in Criminal Law, 297 pages, 1976 (Problem book)

Davis' Police Discretion, 176 pages, 1975 (Text)

Dix and Sharlot's Cases and Materials on Criminal Law, 2nd Ed., 771 pages, 1979 (Casebook)

Federal Rules of Civil-Appellate-Criminal Procedure—West Law School Edition, 344 pages, 1981

Grano's Problems in Criminal Procedure, 2nd Ed., 176 pages, 1981 (Problem book)

Heymann and Kenety's The Murder Trial of Wilbur Jackson: A Homicide in the Family, 340 pages, 1975 (Case Study)

Israel and LaFave's Criminal Procedure in a Nutshell, 3rd Ed., 438 pages, 1980 (Text)

Johnson's Criminal Law: Cases, Materials and Text on Substantive Criminal Law in its Procedural Context, 2nd Ed., 956 pages, 1980 (Casebook)

Kamisar, LaFave and Israel's Cases, Comments and Questions on Modern Criminal Procedure, 5th ed., 1635 pages plus Appendix, 1980 with 1981 Supplement (Casebook)

CRIMINAL LAW AND CRIMINAL PROCEDURE—Continued

Kamisar, LaFave and Israel's Cases, Comments and Questions on Basic Criminal Procedure, 5th Ed., 869 pages, 1980 with 1981 Supplement (Casebook)—reprint from Kamisar, et al. Modern Criminal Procedure, 5th ed., 1980

LaFave's Modern Criminal Law: Cases, Comments and Questions, 789 pages, 1978 (Casebook)

LaFave and Scott's Hornbook on Criminal Law, 763 pages, 1972 (Text)

Langbein's Comparative Criminal Procedure: Germany, 172 pages, 1977 (Casebook)

Loewy's Criminal Law in a Nutshell, 302 pages, 1975 (Text)

Saltzburg's American Criminal Procedure, Cases and Commentary, 1253 pages, 1980 with 1981 Supplement (Casebook)

Uviller's The Processes of Criminal Justice: Investigation and Adjudication, 2nd Ed., 1384 pages, 1979 with 1979 Statutory Supplement and 1980 Update (Casebook)

Uviller's The Processes of Criminal Justice: Adjudication, 2nd Ed., 730 pages, 1979. Soft-cover reprint from Uviller's The Processes of Criminal Justice: Investigation and Adjudication, 2nd Ed. (Casebook)

Uviller's The Processes of Criminal Justice: Investigation, 2nd Ed., 655 pages, 1979. Soft-cover reprint from Uviller's The Processes of Criminal Justice: Investigation and Adjudication, 2nd Ed. (Casebook)

Vorenberg's Cases on Criminal Law and Procedure, 2nd Ed., approximately 1000 pages, 1981 (Casebook)

See also Corrections, Juvenile Justice

DECEDENTS ESTATES

See Trusts and Estates

DOMESTIC RELATIONS

Clark's Cases and Problems on Domestic Relations, 3rd Ed., 1153 pages, 1980 (Casebook)

Clark's Hornbook on Domestic Relations, 754 pages, 1968 (Text)

Kay's Sex-Based Discrimination in Family Law, 305 pages, 1974 (Casebook)—reprint from Davidson, Ginsburg and Kay's Cases on Sex-Based Discrimination, 1974

Krause's Cases and Materials on Family Law, 1132 pages, 1976, with 1978 Supplement (Casebook)

Krause's Family Law in a Nutshell, 400 pages, 1977 (Text)

EDUCATION LAW

Morris' The Constitution and American Education, 2nd Ed., 992 pages, 1980 (Casebook)

EMPLOYMENT DISCRIMINATION

Cooper, Rabb and Rubin's Fair Employment Litigation: Text and Materials for Student and Practitioner, 590 pages, 1975 (Coursebook)

Player's Cases and Materials on Employment Discrimination Law, 878 pages, 1980 (Casebook)

Player's Federal Law of Employment Discrimination in a Nutshell, 2nd Ed., 402 pages, 1981 (Text)

Sovern's Cases and Materials on Racial Discrimination in Employment, 2nd Ed., 167 pages, 1973 (Casebook)—reprint from Cooper et al. Cases on Law and Poverty, 2nd Ed., 1973

See also Women and the Law

ENERGY AND NATURAL RESOURCES LAW

Rodgers' Cases and Materials on Energy and Natural Resources Law, 995 pages, 1979 (Casebook)

Selected Environmental Law Statutes, 681 pages, 1981

Tomain's Energy Law in a Nutshell, 338 pages, 1981 (Text)

See also Environmental Law, Oil and Gas, Water Law

ENVIRONMENTAL LAW

Currie's Cases and Materials on Pollution, 715 pages, 1975 (Casebook)

Federal Environmental Law, 1600 pages, 1974 (Text)

Findley and Farber's Cases and Materials on Environmental Law, 738 pages, 1981 (Casebook)

Hanks, Tarlock and Hanks' Cases on Environmental Law and Policy, 1242 pages, 1974, with 1976 Supplement (Casebook)

Rodgers' Hornbook on Environmental Law, 956 pages, 1977 (Text)

Selected Environmental Law Statutes, 681 pages, 1981

See also Energy and Natural Resources Law, Water Law

EQUITY

See Remedies

ESTATES

See Trusts and Estates

ESTATE PLANNING

Casner and Stein's Estate Planning under the Tax Reform Act of 1976, 2nd Ed., 456 pages, 1978 (Coursebook)

ESTATE PLANNING—Continued

Lynn's Introduction to Estate Planning, in a Nutshell, 2nd Ed., 378 pages, 1978 (Text)

See also Taxation

EVIDENCE

Broun and Meisenholder's Problems in Evidence, 2nd Ed., 304 pages, 1981 (Problem book)

Cleary and Strong's Cases, Materials and Problems on Evidence, 3rd Ed., approximately 1125 pages, 1981 (Casebook)

Federal Rules of Evidence for United States Courts and Magistrates, 325 pages, 1979

Graham's Federal Rules of Evidence in a Nutshell, 429 pages, 1981 (Text)

Kimball's Programmed Materials on Problems in Evidence, 380 pages, 1978 (Problem book)

Lempert and Saltzburg's A Modern Approach to Evidence: Text, Problems, Transcripts and Cases, 1231 pages, 1977 (Casebook)

Lilly's Introduction to the Law of Evidence, 486 pages, 1978 (Text)

McCormick, Elliott and Sutton's Cases and Materials on Evidence, 5th Ed., 1212 pages, 1981 (Casebook)

McCormick's Hornbook on Evidence, 2nd Ed., 938 pages, 1972, with 1978 pocket part (Text)

Rothstein's Evidence, State and Federal Rules in a Nutshell, 2nd Ed., 514 pages, 1981 (Text)

Saltzburg's Evidence Supplement: Rules, Statutes, Commentary, 245 pages, 1980 (Casebook Supplement)

FEDERAL JURISDICTION AND PROCEDURE

Currie's Cases and Materials on Federal Courts, 2nd Ed., 1040 pages, 1975, with 1978 Supplement (Casebook)

Currie's Federal Jurisdiction in a Nutshell, 2nd Ed., 258 pages, 1981 (Text)

Federal Rules of Civil-Appellate-Criminal Procedure—West Law School Edition, 344 pages, 1981

Forrester and Moye's Cases and Materials on Federal Jurisdiction and Procedure, 3rd Ed., 917 pages, 1977 with 1981 Supplement (Casebook)

Merrill and Vetri's Problems on Federal Courts and Civil Procedure, 460 pages, 1974 (Problem book)

Wright's Hornbook on Federal Courts, 3rd Ed., 818 pages, 1976 (Text)

FUTURE INTERESTS

See Trusts and Estates

HOUSING AND URBAN DEVELOPMENT

Berger's Cases and Materials on Housing, 2nd Ed., 254 pages, 1973 (Casebook)—reprint from Cooper et al. Cases on Law and Poverty, 2nd Ed., 1973

See also Land Use

INDIAN LAW

See American Indian Law

INSURANCE

Dobbyn's Insurance Law in a Nutshell, 281 pages, 1981 (Text)

Keeton's Cases on Basic Insurance Law, 2nd Ed., 1086 pages, 1977

Keeton's Basic Text on Insurance Law, 712 pages, 1971 (Text)

Keeton's Case Supplement to Keeton's Basic Text on Insurance Law, 334 pages, 1978 (Casebook)

Keeton's Programmed Problems in Insurance Law, 243 pages, 1972 (Text Supplement)

INTERNATIONAL LAW

Henkin, Pugh, Schachter and Smit's Cases and Materials on International Law, 2nd Ed., 1152 pages, 1980, with Documents Supplement (Casebook)

Jackson's Legal Problems of International Economic Relations, 1097 pages, 1977, with Documents Supplement (Casebook)

Kirgis' International Organizations in Their Legal Setting, 1016 pages, 1977, with 1981 Supplement (Casebook)

Weston, Falk and D'Amato's International Law and World Order—A Problem Oriented Coursebook 1195 pages, 1980, with Documents Supplement (Casebook)

Wilson's International Business Transactions in a Nutshell, 393 pages, 1981 (Text)

INTRODUCTION TO LAW

Dobbyn's So You Want to go to Law School, Revised First Edition, 206 pages, 1976 (Text)

Kinyon's Introduction to Law Study and Law Examinations in a Nutshell, 389 pages, 1971 (Text)

See also Legal Method and Legal System

JUDICIAL ADMINISTRATION

Carrington, Meador and Rosenberg's Justice on Appeal, 263 pages, 1976 (Casebook)

LAW SCHOOL PUBLICATIONS—Continued

JUDICIAL ADMINISTRATION—
Continued

Leflar's Appellate Judicial Opinions, 343 pages, 1974 (Text)

Nelson's Cases and Materials on Judicial Administration and the Administration of Justice, 1032 pages, 1974 (Casebook)

JURISPRUDENCE

Christie's Text and Readings on Jurisprudence—The Philosophy of Law, 1056 pages, 1973 (Casebook)

JUVENILE JUSTICE

Fox's Cases and Materials on Modern Juvenile Justice, 2nd Ed., approx. 971 pages, 1981 (Casebook)

Fox's Juvenile Courts in a Nutshell, 2nd Ed., 275 pages, 1977 (Text)

LABOR LAW

Gorman's Basic Text on Labor Law-Unionization and Collective Bargaining, 914 pages, 1976 (Text)

Leslie's Labor Law in a Nutshell, 403 pages, 1979 (Text)

Nolan's Labor Arbitration Law and Practice in a Nutshell, 358 pages, 1979 (Text)

Oberer, Hanslowe and Andersen's Cases and Materials on Labor Law—Collective Bargaining in a Free Society, 2nd Ed., 1168 pages, 1979, with 1979 Statutory Supplement (Casebook)

See also Employment Discrimination, Social Legislation

LAND FINANCE—PROPERTY SECURITY

Bruce's Real Estate Finance in a Nutshell, 292 pages, 1979 (Text)

Maxwell, Riesenfeld, Hetland and Warren's Cases on California Security Transactions in Land, 2nd Ed., 584 pages, 1975 (Casebook)

Nelson and Whitman's Cases on Real Estate Transfer, Finance and Development, 2nd Ed., 1114 pages, 1981 (Casebook)

Osborne's Cases and Materials on Secured Transactions, 559 pages, 1967 (Casebook)

Osborne, Nelson and Whitman's Hornbook on Real Estate Finance Law, 3rd Ed., 885 pages, 1979 (Text)

LAND USE

Hagman's Cases on Public Planning and Control of Urban and Land Development, 2nd Ed., 1301 pages, 1980 (Casebook)

LAND USE—Continued

Hagman's Hornbook on Urban Planning and Land Development Control Law, 706 pages, 1971 (Text)

Wright and Gitelman's Cases and Materials on Land Use, 3rd Ed., approx. 915 pages, 1981 (Casebook)

Wright and Webber's Land Use in a Nutshell, 316 pages, 1978 (Text)

See also Housing and Urban Development

LAW AND ECONOMICS

Manne's The Economics of Legal Relationships—Readings in the Theory of Property Rights, 660 pages, 1975 (Text)

See also Antitrust, Regulated Industries

LAW AND MEDICINE—PSYCHIATRY

Cohen's Cases and Materials on the Law of Deprivation of Liberty: A Study in Social Control, 755 pages, 1980 (Casebook)

King's The Law of Medical Malpractice in a Nutshell, 340 pages, 1977 (Text)

Shapiro and Spece's Problems, Cases and Materials on Bioethics and Law, 892 pages, 1981 (Casebook)

Sharpe, Fiscina and Head's Cases on Law and Medicine, 882 pages, 1978 (Casebook)

LEGAL CLINICS

See Office Practice

LEGAL HISTORY

Presser and Zainaldin's Cases on Law and American History, 855 pages, 1980 (Casebook)

See also Legal Method and Legal System

LEGAL METHOD AND LEGAL SYSTEM

Aldisert's Readings, Materials and Cases in the Judicial Process, 948 pages, 1976 (Casebook)

Bodenheimer, Oakley and Love's Readings and Cases on an Introduction to the Anglo-American Legal System, 161 pages, 1980 (Casebook)

Dvorkin, Himmelstein and Lesnick's Becoming a Lawyer: A Humanistic Perspective on Legal Education and Professionalism, 211 pages, 1981 (Text)

Fryer and Orentlicher's Cases and Materials on Legal Method and Legal System, 1043 pages, 1967 (Casebook)

LEGAL METHOD AND LEGAL SYSTEM—Continued

Greenberg's Judicial Process and Social Change, 666 pages, 1977 (Coursebook)

Kempin's Historical Introduction to Anglo-American Law in a Nutshell, 2nd Ed., 280 pages, 1973 (Text)

Kimball's Historical Introduction to the Legal System, 610 pages, 1966 (Casebook)

Mashaw and Merrill's Introduction to the American Public Law System, 1095 pages, 1975, with 1980 Supplement (Casebook)

Murphy's Cases and Materials on Introduction to Law—Legal Process and Procedure, 772 pages, 1977 (Casebook)

Reynolds' Judicial Process in a Nutshell, 292 pages, 1980 (Text)

See also Legal Research and Writing

LEGAL PROFESSION

Aronson's Problems in Professional Responsibility, 280 pages, 1978 (Problem book)

Aronson and Weckstein's Professional Responsibility in a Nutshell, 399 pages, 1980 (Text)

Mellinkoff's The Conscience of a Lawyer, 304 pages, 1973 (Text)

Mellinkoff's Lawyers and the System of Justice, 983 pages, 1976 (Casebook)

Pirsig and Kirwin's Cases and Materials on Professional Responsibility, 3rd Ed., 667 pages, 1976, with 1981 Supplement (Casebook)

Smith's Preventing Legal Malpractice, 142 pages, 1981 (Text)

LEGAL RESEARCH AND WRITING

Cohen's Legal Research in a Nutshell, 3rd Ed., 415 pages, 1978 (Text)

Dickerson's Materials on Legal Drafting, approximately 425 pages, 1981 (Casebook)

Felsenfeld and Siegel's Writing Contracts in Plain English, approx. 230 pages, 1981 (Text)

Gopen's Writing From a Legal Perspective, 225 pages, 1981 (Text)

How to Find the Law With Special Chapters on Legal Writing, 7th Ed., 542 pages, 1976. Problem book available (Coursebook)

Mellinkoff's Legal Writing Sense and Nonsense, approx. 320 pages, 1981 (Text)

Rombauer's Legal Problem Solving—Analysis, Research and Writing, 3rd Ed., 352 pages, 1978 (Coursebook)

LEGAL RESEARCH AND WRITING—Continued

Statsky's Legislative Analysis: How to Use Statutes and Regulations, 216 pages, 1975 (Text)

Statsky and Wernet's Case Analysis and Fundamentals of Legal Writing, 576 pages, 1977 (Text)

Weihofen's Legal Writing Style, 2nd Ed., 332 pages, 1980 (Text)

LEGISLATION

Davies' Legislative Law and Process in a Nutshell, 279 pages, 1975 (Text)

Nutting and Dickerson's Cases and Materials on Legislation, 5th Ed., 744 pages, 1978 (Casebook)

Statsky's Legislative Analysis: How to Use Statutes and Regulations, 216 pages, 1975 (Text)

LOCAL GOVERNMENT

McCarthy's Local Government Law in a Nutshell, 386 pages, 1975 (Text)

Michelman and Sandalow's Cases-Comments-Questions on Government in Urban Areas, 1216 pages, 1970, with 1972 Supplement (Casebook)

Stason and Kauper's Cases and Materials on Municipal Corporations, 3rd Ed., 692 pages, 1959 (Casebook)

Valente's Cases and Materials on Local Government Law, 2nd Ed., 980 pages, 1980 (Casebook)

MASS COMMUNICATION LAW

Gillmor and Barron's Cases and Comment on Mass Communication Law, 3rd Ed., 1008 pages, 1979 (Casebook)

Ginsburg's Regulation of Broadcasting: Law and Policy Towards Radio, Television and Cable Communications, 741 pages, 1979 (Casebook)

Zuckman and Gayne's Mass Communications Law in a Nutshell, 431 pages, 1977 (Text)

MILITARY LAW

Shanor and Terrell's Military Law in a Nutshell, 378 pages, 1980 (Text)

MORTGAGES

See Land Finance—Property Security

NATURAL RESOURCES LAW

See Energy and Natural Resources Law, Environmental Law, Oil and Gas, Water Law

OFFICE PRACTICE

Binder and Price's Legal Interviewing and Counseling: A Client-Centered Approach, 232 pages, 1977 (Text)

Edwards and White's Problems, Readings and Materials on the Lawyer as a Negotiator, 484 pages, 1977 (Casebook)

Hegland's Trial and Practice Skills in a Nutshell, 346 pages, 1978 (Text)

Shaffer's Legal Interviewing and Counseling in a Nutshell, 353 pages, 1976 (Text)

Strong and Clark's Law Office Management, 424 pages, 1974 (Casebook)

OIL AND GAS

Hemingway's Hornbook on Oil and Gas, 486 pages, 1971, with 1979 pocket part (Text)

Huie, Woodward and Smith's Cases and Materials on Oil and Gas, 2nd Ed., 955 pages, 1972 (Casebook)

See also Energy and Natural Resources Law

PARTNERSHIP

See Agency—Partnership

PATENT LAW

Choate and Francis' Cases and Materials on Patent Law, 2nd Ed., 1110 pages, 1981 (Casebook)

See also Copyright

POVERTY LAW

Brudno's Poverty, Inequality, and the Law: Cases-Commentary-Analysis, 934 pages, 1976 (Casebook)

Cooper, Dodyk, Berger, Paulsen, Schrag and Sovern's Cases and Materials on Law and Poverty, 2nd Ed., 1208 pages, 1973 (Casebook)

LaFrance, Schroeder, Bennett and Boyd's Hornbook on Law of the Poor, 558 pages, 1973 (Text)

See also Social Legislation

PRODUCTS LIABILITY

Noel and Phillips' Cases on Products Liability, 836 pages, 1976 (Casebook)

Noel and Phillips' Products Liability in a Nutshell, 2nd Ed., 341 pages, 1981 (Text)

PROPERTY

Aigler, Smith and Tefft's Cases on Property, 2 volumes, 1339 pages, 1960 (Casebook)

PROPERTY—Continued

Bernhardt's Real Property in a Nutshell, 2nd Ed., approx. 440 pages, 1981 (Text)

Boyer's Survey of the Law of Property, 766 pages, 1981 (Text)

Browder, Cunningham, Julin and Smith's Cases on Basic Property Law, 3rd Ed., 1447 pages, 1979 (Casebook)

Burby's Hornbook on Real Property, 3rd Ed., 490 pages, 1965 (Text)

Chused's A Modern Approach to Property: Cases-Notes-Materials, 1069 pages, 1978 with 1980 Supplement (Casebook)

Cohen's Materials for a Basic Course in Property, 526 pages, 1978 (Casebook)

Donahue, Kauper and Martin's Cases on Property, 1501 pages, 1974 (Casebook)

Hill's Landlord and Tenant Law in a Nutshell, 319 pages, 1979 (Text)

Moynihan's Introduction to Real Property, 254 pages, 1962 (Text)

Phipps' Titles in a Nutshell, 277 pages, 1968 (Text)

Uniform Land Transactions Act, Uniform Simplification of Land Transfers Act, Uniform Condominium Act, 1977 Official Text with Comments, 462 pages, 1978

See also Housing and Urban Development, Land Finance, Land Use

REAL ESTATE

See Land Finance—Property Security

REGULATED INDUSTRIES

Morgan's Cases and Materials on Economic Regulation of Business, 830 pages, 1976, with 1978 Supplement (Casebook)

Pozen's Financial Institutions: Cases, Materials and Problems on Investment Management, 844 pages, 1978 (Casebook)

White's Teaching Materials on Banking Law, 1058 pages, 1976, with 1980 Case and Statutory Supplement (Casebook)

See also Mass Communication Law

REMEDIES

Cribbet's Cases and Materials on Judicial Remedies, 762 pages, 1954 (Casebook)

Dobbs' Hornbook on Remedies, 1067 pages, 1973 (Text)

LAW SCHOOL PUBLICATIONS—Continued

REMEDIES—Continued

Dobbs' Problems in Remedies, 137 pages, 1974 (Problem book)

Dobbyn's Injunctions in a Nutshell, 264 pages, 1974 (Text)

Friedman's Contract Remedies in a Nutshell, approx. 325 pages, 1981 (Text)

Leavell, Love and Nelson's Cases and Materials on Equitable Remedies and Restitution, 3rd Ed., 704 pages, 1980 (Casebook)

McClintock's Hornbook on Equity, 2nd Ed., 643 pages, 1948 (Text)

McCormick's Hornbook on Damages, 811 pages, 1935 (Text)

O'Connell's Remedies in a Nutshell, 364 pages, 1977 (Text)

York and Bauman's Cases and Materials on Remedies, 3rd Ed., 1250 pages, 1979 (Casebook)

REVIEW MATERIALS

Ballantine's Problems

Smith's Review Series

West's Review Covering Multistate Subjects

SECURITIES REGULATION

Ratner's Securities Regulation: Materials for a Basic Course, 2nd Ed., 1050 pages, 1980 with 1980 Statutory Supplement (Casebook)

Ratner's Securities Regulation in a Nutshell, 300 pages, 1978 (Text)

SOCIAL LEGISLATION

Brudno's Income Redistribution Theories and Programs: Cases-Commentary-Analyses, 480 pages, 1977 (Casebook)—reprint from Brudno's Poverty, Inequality and the Law, 1976

LaFrance's Welfare Law: Structure and Entitlement in a Nutshell, 455 pages, 1979 (Text)

Malone, Plant and Little's Cases on Workers' Compensation and Employment Rights, 2nd Ed., 951 pages, 1980 (Casebook)

See also Poverty Law

TAXATION

Chommie's Hornbook on Federal Income Taxation, 2nd Ed., 1051 pages, 1973 (Text)

Dodge's Federal Taxation of Estates, Trusts and Gifts: Principles and Planning, approximately 785 pages, 1981 (Casebook)

TAXATION—Continued

Gunn's Cases and Materials on Federal Income Taxation of Individuals, 785 pages, 1981 (Casebook)

Hellerstein and Hellerstein's Cases on State and Local Taxation, 4th Ed., 1041 pages, 1978 (Casebook)

Kahn's Handbook on Basic Corporate Taxation, 3rd Ed., Student Ed., 614 pages, 1981 (Text)

Kahn and Gann's Corporate Taxation and Taxation of Partnerships and Partners, 1107 pages, 1979, with 1981 Supplement (Casebook)

Kragen and McNulty's Cases and Materials on Federal Income Taxation, Vol. I: Taxation of Individuals, 3rd Ed., 1283 pages, 1979 (Casebook)

Kragen and McNulty's Cases on Federal Income Taxation, Vol. II: Taxation of Corporations, Shareholders, Partnerships and Partners, 3rd Ed., 989 pages, 1981 (Casebook)

Kramer and McCord's Problems for Federal Estate and Gift Taxes, 206 pages, 1976 (Problem book)

Lowndes, Kramer and McCord's Hornbook on Federal Estate and Gift Taxes, 3rd Ed., 1099 pages, 1974 (Text)

McCord's 1976 Estate and Gift Tax Reform-Analysis, Explanation and Commentary, 377 pages, 1977 (Text)

McNulty's Federal Estate and Gift Taxation in a Nutshell, 2nd Ed., 488 pages, 1979 (Text)

McNulty's Federal Income Taxation of Individuals in a Nutshell, 2nd Ed., 422 pages, 1978 (Text)

Rice's Problems and Materials in Federal Estate and Gift Taxation, 3rd Ed., 474 pages, 1978 (Casebook)

Rice and Solomon's Problems and Materials in Federal Income Taxation, 3rd Ed., 670 pages, 1979 (Casebook)

Rose and Raskind's Advanced Federal Income Taxation: Corporate Transactions—Cases, Materials and Problems, 955 pages, 1978 (Casebook)

Selected Federal Taxation Statutes and Regulations, 1307 pages, 1981

Sobeloff and Weidenbruch's Federal Income Taxation of Corporations and Stockholders in a Nutshell, 362 pages, 1981 (Text)

TORTS

Green, Pedrick, Rahl, Thode, Hawkins, Smith and Treece's Cases and Materials on Torts, 2nd Ed., 1360 pages, 1977 (Casebook)

TORTS—Continued

Green, Pedrick, Rahl, Thode, Hawkins, Smith, and Treece's Advanced Torts: Injuries to Business, Political and Family Interests, 2nd Ed., 544 pages, 1977 (Casebook)—reprint from Green, et al. Cases and Materials on Torts, 2nd Ed., 1977

Keeton's Computer-Aided and Workbook Exercises on Tort Law, 164 pages, 1976 (Coursebook)

Keeton and Keeton's Cases and Materials on Torts, 2nd Ed., 1200 pages, 1977, with 1981 Supplement (Casebook)

Kionka's Torts in a Nutshell: Injuries to Persons and Property, 434 pages, 1977 (Text)

Malone's Torts in a Nutshell: Injuries to Family, Social and Trade Relations, 358 pages, 1979 (Text)

Prosser's Hornbook on Torts, 4th Ed., 1208 pages, 1971 (Text)

Shapo's Cases on Tort and Compensation Law, 1244 pages, 1976 (Casebook)

See also Products Liability

TRADE REGULATION

Oppenheim and Weston's Cases and Materials on Unfair Trade Practices and Consumer Protection, 3rd Ed., 1065 pages, 1974, with 1981 Supplement (Casebook)

See also Antitrust, Regulated Industries

TRIAL AND APPELLATE ADVOCACY

Appellate Advocacy, Handbook of, 249 pages, 1980 (Text)

Bergman's Trial Advocacy in a Nutshell, 402 pages, 1979 (Text)

Hegland's Trial and Practice Skills in a Nutshell, 346 pages, 1978 (Text)

Jeans' Handbook on Trial Advocacy, Student Ed., 473 pages, 1975 (Text)

McElhaney's Effective Litigation, 457 pages, 1974 (Casebook)

Nolan's Cases and Materials on Trial Practice, 518 pages, 1981 (Casebook)

TRUSTS AND ESTATES

Atkinson's Hornbook on Wills, 2nd Ed., 975 pages, 1953 (Text)

Averill's Uniform Probate Code in a Nutshell, 425 pages, 1978 (Text)

TRUSTS AND ESTATES—Continued

Bogert's Hornbook on Trusts, 5th Ed., 726 pages, 1973 (Text)

Clark, Lusky and Murphy's Cases and Materials on Gratuitous Transfers, 2nd Ed., 1102 pages, 1977 (Casebook)

Gulliver's Cases and Materials on Future Interests, 624 pages, 1959 (Casebook)

Gulliver's Introduction to the Law of Future Interests, 87 pages, 1959 (Casebook)—reprint from Gulliver's Cases and Materials on Future Interests, 1959

Halbach (Editor)—Death, Taxes, and Family Property: Essays and American Assembly Report, 189 pages, 1977 (Text)

Mennell's Cases and Materials on California Decedent's Estates, 566 pages, 1973 (Casebook)

Mennell's Wills and Trusts in a Nutshell, 392 pages, 1979 (Text)

Powell's The Law of Future Interests in California, 91 pages, 1980 (Text)

Simes' Hornbook on Future Interests, 2nd Ed., 355 pages, 1966 (Text)

Turrentine's Cases and Text on Wills and Administration, 2nd Ed., 483 pages, 1962 (Casebook)

Uniform Probate Code, 5th Ed., Official Text With Comments, 384 pages, 1977

Waggoner's Future Interests in a Nutshell, 361 pages, 1981 (Text)

WATER LAW

Trelease's Cases and Materials on Water Law, 3rd Ed., 833 pages, 1979 (Casebook)

See also Energy and Natural Resources Law, Environmental Law

WILLS

See Trusts and Estates

WOMEN AND THE LAW

Kay's Text, Cases and Materials on Sex-Based Discrimination, 2nd Ed., approx. 1030 pages, 1981 (Casebook)

See also Employment Discrimination

WORKMEN'S COMPENSATION

See Social Legislation

TAX PROCEDURE

AND

TAX FRAUD

CASES AND MATERIALS

By

MARVIN J. GARBIS

Garbis and Schwait, Baltimore, Maryland and Washington, D.C.
Adjunct Faculty, University of Maryland School of Law

and

STEPHEN C. STRUNTZ

Garbis and Schwait, Baltimore, Maryland and Washington, D.C.
Adjunct Faculty, University of Maryland School of Law

with the assistance of
Jeffrey I. Margolis

AMERICAN CASEBOOK SERIES

ST. PAUL, MINN.
WEST PUBLISHING CO.
1982

COPYRIGHT © 1982 By WEST PUBLISHING CO.

50 West Kellogg Boulevard
P.O. Box 3526
St. Paul, Minnesota 55165

Printed in the United States of America

Library of Congress Cataloging in Publication Data

Garbis, Marvin Joseph.
  Tax procedure and tax fraud, cases and materials.

  (American casebook series)
  Includes index.
  1. Tax administration and procedure—United States
—Cases. 2. Tax protests and appeals—United States
—Cases. 3. Tax evasion—United States—Cases. I.
Struntz, Stephen G. II. Margolis, Jeffrey I. III. Title.
IV. Series.

KF6320.A7G37   343.7304'2   81–13080
                      347.30342   AACR2

ISBN 0-314-61180-0

DEDICATION

IN MEMORY OF:
Samuel Garbis,
Leslie H. Wald,
Esther Warshaw,
Nathan Warshaw,
and
David A. Wilson
M.J.G.

To my parents
S.C.S.

*

PREFACE

This casebook was prepared to meet the need presented by an increasing number of courses in federal tax procedure and tax fraud being taught at law schools throughout the country. This work is designed as a single, comprehensive source of cases and materials from which the professor can design a graduate or undergraduate level course covering the civil, criminal and/or collection aspects of tax practice and procedure.

This work provides both an introduction to tax practice and a depository of many of the cases and materials which constitute the intellectual heritage of those who engage in the practice of tax law. However, this casebook (and presumably the course in which it is being used) is not designed solely for those who will spend their professional lives exclusively as "tax lawyers." As the tax laws become more complex and pervasive, virtually every attorney must confront tax issues in the course of his or her practice. Indeed, from the most routine of domestic relations cases to the most complex of corporate reorganizations, one will find the tax law being applied, misapplied or ignored in blissful ignorance. Moreover, almost every lawyer, during the course of his or her career, will represent clients whose tax affairs are being scrutinized by the Internal Revenue Service. Hence, most attorneys will need some introduction to, and some will require a comprehensive indoctrination in, the procedural aspects of tax practice.

Throughout this book, cases and statute citations, as well as footnotes, of the courts and commentators have been omitted without so specifying. Numbered footnotes are from the original materials and retain the original numbering; lettered footnotes within the cases and other materials are those of the authors. Deletions from the text of cases and other materials are indicated by asterisks. The occasional use of the masculine gender alone in the authors' text is intended to include the feminine gender as well, unless the context indicates to the contrary.

In the interest of comprehensiveness, the authors have prepared two appendices which reflect changes and developments which occurred subsequent to preparation of the page proofs. Appendix A (the text of Formal Opinion 346 of the ABA Standing Committee on Ethics and Professional Responsibility) is an extremely important development relating to tax practitioners' ethical responsibilities in issuing tax law opinions for tax shelter investment offerings, and should be read in conjunction with Chapter II, Section 2. Appendix B is a synopsis of the procedural changes enacted as part of the Economic Recovery Tax

PREFACE

Act of 1981 (August 13, 1981). The majority of the procedural changes made by the Act involve topics treated in Chapter IV, and the authors have indicated by asterisked footnotes those portions of Chapter IV which are affected by the new Act.

The authors express their appreciation to those in the law firm of Garbis and Schwait who aided them in their work on this book. In particular, the authors wish to thank Allen L. Schwait for his aid in the overall organization of the book; Jeffrey I. Margolis for his invaluable efforts in research, editing and preparation; Paula M. Junghans for critically reviewing the manuscript as it progressed; Peter Driscoll for his help in proofreading and preparation of the Index; and Jean DeFrank, Mary Bedingfield and Teresa Thommen for their patient assistance with the production of the manuscript.

Finally, the authors wish to acknowledge a number of distinguished authorities in the tax field for offering their consultation and advice in their particular fields of expertise. Special thanks are due to N. Jerold Cohen, James T. Fuller, Gerald Feffer, M. Carr Ferguson, Daniel I. Halperin, Patricia Ann Metzer, Jerome S. Hertz, Michael I. Saltzman, Martin A. Schainbaum and the Honorable Theodore Tannenwald, Jr.

MARVIN J. GARBIS
STEPHEN C. STRUNTZ

Baltimore, Maryland
October, 1981

ACKNOWLEDGMENTS

The authors wish to thank the following authors and publishers for their permission to reprint the materials listed below.

American Bar Association, A.B.A. Committee on Professional Ethics, Opinion 314, 51 A.B.A.J. 671 (1965). Reprinted with permission from American Bar Association Journal.

American Bar Association, Guidelines to Tax Practice, Report of the Committee on Standards of Tax Practice, Section of Taxation, 31 Tax Lawyer 551 (1978). Copyright © 1978, The Tax Lawyer and the American Bar Association; reprinted by permission.

American Bar Association, Proposals for a New National Court of Tax Appeals, Panel Discussion, 33 Tax Lawyer 7 (1979). Copyright © 1979, The Tax Lawyer and the American Bar Association; reprinted by permission.

J. Borison, Comment—Section 6901: Transferee Liability, 30 Tax Lawyer 433 (1977). Copyright © 1977, The Tax Lawyer and the American Bar Association. Reprinted with permission from The Tax Lawyer, the American Bar Association and Jerome Borison, J.D., Gonzaga School of Law; Attorney, I.R.S. Chief Counsel's Office; Adjunct Professor, Golden Gate Law School.

F. Corneel, Ethical Guidelines for Tax Practice, 28 Tax L.Rev. 1 (1972). Copyright © 1972 by New York University School of Law. All rights reserved. Reprinted with permission.

G. Crowley and R. Manning, Criminal Tax Fraud—Representing the Taxpayer Before Trial. Copyright © 1976, Practising Law Institute.

T. Gallagher, Jr., The Tax Legislative Process, 3 The Review of Taxation of Individuals 203 (1979). Reprinted by permission from The Review of Taxation of Indivuduals, Volume 3, Number 3, Summer 1979. Copyright © 1979, Warren, Gorham and Lamont, Inc., 210 South Street, Boston, Mass. All rights reserved.

M. Garbis, What Can a Taxpayer Do When a Case Has Been Turned Over for Collection: Administrative and Legal Remedies: Powers of the Agent, 29 N.Y.U. Institute on Federal Taxation 909 (1971). Copyright © 1971, N.Y.U. Institute on Federal Taxation; used by permission.

M. Garbis and S. Sack, Diagnosis of Tax Fraud Investigations, 55 A.B.A.J. 441 (1969). Reprinted with permission from American Bar Association Journal.

ACKNOWLEDGMENTS

M. Garbis, A. Schwait and P. Junghans, Tax Court Practice (1974, 1980 Supp.). Reprinted by permission from Tax Court Practice by Marvin J. Garbis and Allen L. Schwait, Copyright © 1974, Warren, Gorham and Lamont, Inc., 210 South Street, Boston, Mass. All rights reserved.

Internal Revenue Service, Income Tax Audit Procedure. Reproduced with permission from CCH Standard Federal Tax Reports, published and copyrighted by Commerce Clearing House, Inc., 4025 W. Peterson Avenue, Chicago, Illinois 60646.

Internal Revenue Service, Statement of Chief Counsel, 8 P-H Fed. Tax ¶41,360. Reproduced with permission of Prentice-Hall, from the Fed. Tax Service, Englewood Cliffs, N.J. 07632.

A. Johnson, An Inquiry Into the Assessment Process, 35 Tax Law Review 285 (1980). Copyright © 1980 by New York University School of Law. All rights reserved. Reprinted with permission.

M. Nash, Effective Internal Revenue Service Appellate Division Practice, 35 N.Y.U. Inst. Fed. Tax. 325 (1977). Copyright © 1977, N.Y.U. Institute on Federal Taxation; reprinted by permission.

Note, Federal Tax Rulings: Procedure and Policy, 21 Vanderbilt Law Review 78 (1967). Copyright © 1967, Vanderbilt Law Review. Reprinted with permission.

J. Piper and J. Jerge, Shifting the Burden of Proof in Tax Court, 31 Tax Lawyer 303 (1978). Copyright © 1978, The Tax Lawyer and the American Bar Association; reprinted by permission.

J. Rowen, When May a Lawyer Advise a Client That He May Take a Position on His Tax Return?, 29 Tax Lawyer 237 (1976). Copyright © 1976, The Tax Lawyer and the American Bar Association; reprinted by permission.

M. Saltzman, Tax Procedure and Internal Revenue Service Practice (1981). Reprinted by permission from Tax Procedure and Internal Revenue Service Practice. Copyright © 1981, Warren, Gorham and Lamont, Inc., 210 South Street, Boston, Mass. All rights reserved.

S. Sisson, The Sandman Cometh: Conspiracy Prosecutions and Tax Practitioners, 31 Tax Lawyer 805 (1978). Copyright © 1978, The Tax Lawyer and the American Bar Association; reprinted by permission.

T. Tannenwald, Jr., Tax Court Trials: A View From the Bench, 59 A.B.A.J. 295 (1973). Reprinted with permission from the American Bar Association Journal.

SUMMARY OF CONTENTS

APPENDICES

*

TABLE OF CONTENTS

TABLE OF CONTENTS

TABLE OF CONTENTS

TABLE OF CONTENTS

XXVIII

TABLE OF CONTENTS

TABLE OF CONTENTS

TABLE OF CONTENTS

APPENDICES

TABLE OF CASES

Principal cases are in italic type. Nonprincipal cases are in roman type.
References are to Pages.

TABLE OF CASES

TABLE OF CASES

TABLE OF CASES

TABLE OF CASES

*

TABLE OF INTERNAL REVENUE CODE SECTIONS

In general, only those sections of the Internal Revenue Code of 1954 which pertain to procedural matters are cited. References are to Pages.

TABLE OF INTERNAL REVENUE CODE SECTIONS

TABLE OF INTERNAL REVENUE CODE SECTIONS

TABLE OF INTERNAL REVENUE CODE SECTIONS

TABLE OF INTERNAL REVENUE CODE SECTIONS

TABLE OF INTERNAL REVENUE CODE SECTIONS

TABLE OF INTERNAL REVENUE CODE SECTIONS

TABLE OF INTERNAL REVENUE CODE SECTIONS

TABLE OF INTERNAL REVENUE CODE SECTIONS

TABLE OF INTERNAL REVENUE CODE SECTIONS

TAX PROCEDURE

AND

TAX FRAUD

CASES AND MATERIALS

*

Chapter I

ORGANIZATION AND FUNCTION
OF THE GOVERNMENT

Scope Note: Representing taxpayers before revenue authorities requires a working knowledge of the internal organization of those government agencies involved in the creation and administration of the internal revenue laws. The administration of the federal tax system in the United States is focused primarily in the Internal Revenue Service, the largest component of the Treasury Department. Substantial roles are played also by senior Treasury Department officials in setting tax policy, by the congressional staff (and, of course, Congress itself) in connection with tax legislation, and by the Department of Justice in connection with litigation. The materials in this chapter are intended to provide a general description of the various components of the government which contribute to the administration of the tax laws, and to serve as an introduction to the tax legislative process.

SECTION 1. DEPARTMENT OF THE TREASURY

The Secretary of the Treasury possesses the ultimate authority for the administration and enforcement of the internal revenue laws. Pursuant to § 7802(a) of the Code, the bulk of this authority has been delegated to the Commissioner of Internal Revenue, who directs the operations of the Internal Revenue Service. A few revenue related functions have not been delegated to the Commissioner; these relate primarily to alcohol, tobacco and firearms taxes, and to the legislation-making process. Advising the Secretary of the Treasury in legal matters are the General Counsel for the Treasury and several Assistant General Counsel. One Assistant General Counsel also serves as chief legal officer of the Internal Revenue Service in his capacity as Chief Counsel for the IRS.

A. INTERNAL REVENUE SERVICE

The Internal Revenue Service is the largest component of the Department of the Treasury. The Service consists of a National Office in Washington, D.C. and a field organization. The latter consists of seven internal revenue regions, each headed by a Regional Commissioner; fifty-eight internal revenue districts, each headed by a District Director; and ten service centers. In communities where the concentration of workload requires, the Service maintains area,

zone or local offices below the district level. The overall organization
of the Internal Revenue Service is depicted in Figure 1, and the geo-

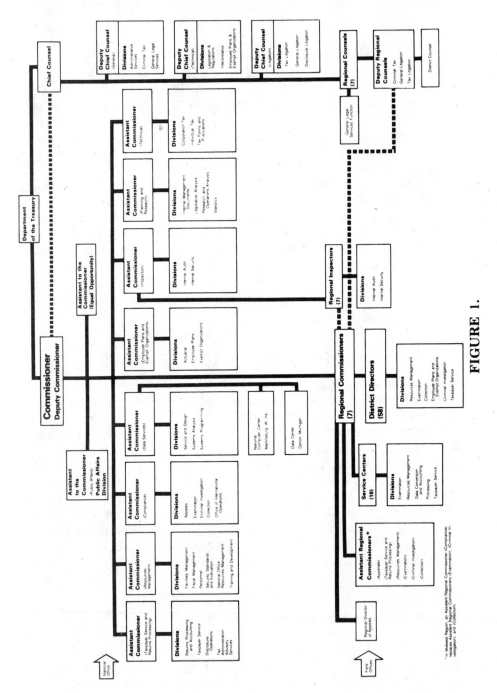

FIGURE 1.

graphical distribution of internal revenue regions and districts is shown in Figure 2.

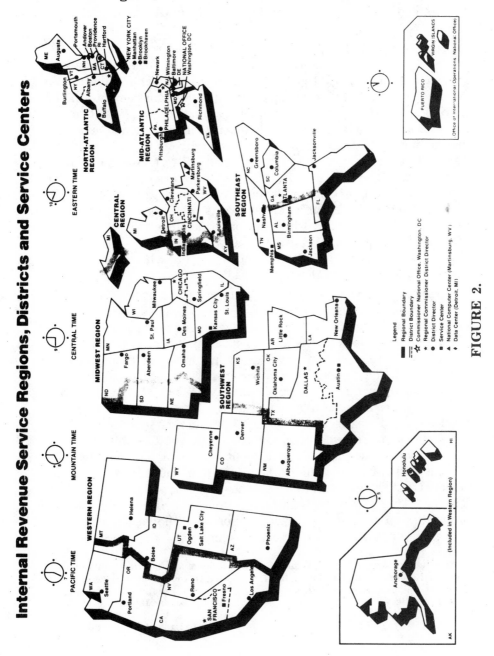

FIGURE 2.

(1) NATIONAL OFFICE

The National Office, located in Washington, D.C., develops broad nationwide policies and programs to guide field personnnel in administering and enforcing the internal revenue laws. At the head of the National Office is the Commissioner of Internal Revenue. Assisting him are eight Assistant Commissioners and the Chief Counsel of the IRS.

The National Office is organized functionally into various divisions. The Assistant Commissioner (Compliance) oversees the operations and compliance activities of the Service. The Office of the Assistant Commissioner (Compliance) is subdivided further into the Examination Division, the Collection Division and the Criminal Investigation Division. There is also an Appeals Division which supervises the administrative appeals procedure whereby taxpayers can appeal district level determinations of their tax liability to the regional Appeals Office. The Office of International Operations, within the Office of the Assistant Commissioner (Compliance), is responsible for administering the internal revenue laws as they relate to citizen taxpayers residing or doing business abroad (including United States territories and possessions),[a] foreign taxpayers deriving income from sources within the United States, and taxpayers who are required to withhold tax on income flowing abroad.

Taxpayer service and returns processing are under the ambit of the Assistant Commissioner (Taxpayer Service and Returns Processing). Matters pertaining to the tax treatment of pension plans and exempt organizations are handled exclusively by the Office of the Assistant Commissioner (Employee Plans and Exempt Organizations). The Office of the Assistant Commissioner (Technical) provides technical advice for the guidance of taxpayers and service personnel. This office promulgates Revenue Rulings, Revenue Procedures, Announcements, Releases and other advisory statements.[b] Internal support functions are supervised by the Assistant Commissioners for Data Services, Resources Management and Planning and Research. The Inspection Division, under the direction of the Assistant Commissioner (Inspection), functions as the internal policing unit of the Service. This unit investigates allegations of bribery and other improprieties on the part of Service personnel. The basic organization of the National Office is depicted in Figure 3.

a. The tax returns of foreign subsidiaries of domestic corporations and of resident aliens are processed by the district offices.

b. Rulings and advisory statements relating to the tax treatment of pension plans and exempt organizations are promulgated by the Office of the Assistant Commissioner (Employee Plans and Exempt Organizations).

Basic Organization of the National Office

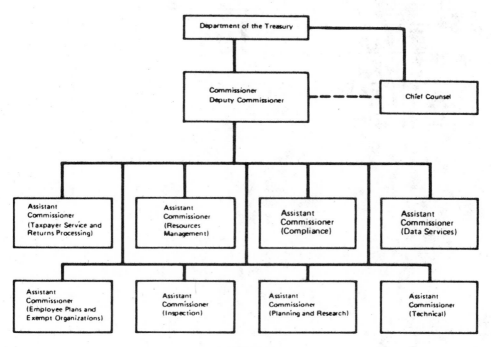

FIGURE 3.

(2) OFFICE OF REGIONAL COMMISSIONER

Each of the seven regional offices is headed by a Regional Commissioner. The Office of Regional Commissioner directs and coordinates the activities of the district and service center offices within the region. The Regional Commissioner also evaluates the effectiveness of Service policies and procedures, and advises the National Office as to the need for their revision.

The organization of the regional offices parallels that of the National Office. There are five Assistant Regional Commissioners: Examination, Collection, Criminal Investigation, Resources Management and Taxpayer Service and Returns Processing. A Regional Director of Appeals supervises the administration of the appeals program at the district and regional levels. The organization of the regional offices is depicted in Figure 4.

Organization of the Office of Regional Commissioner

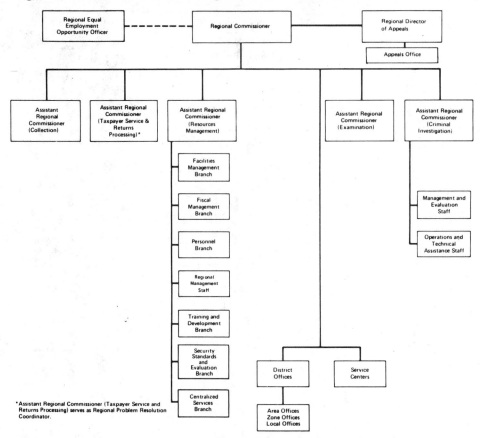

FIGURE 4.

In the Midwest Region, the Service is testing a new concept of regional organization. The components of that office are the immediate Office of the Regional Commissioner, the Offices of Assistant Regional Commissioners (Compliance, Taxpayer Service and Returns Processing, and Resources Management) and the Regional Director of Appeals. The Assistant Regional Commissioner (Compliance), which is a position unique to the Midwest Region, has the same functions in that region as the Assistant Regional Commissioners (Examination, Criminal Investigation and Collection) have in the other regions. The staff of the Assistant Regional Commissioner (Compliance) includes an Executive Assistant for each of these major programs. This concept is being tested before determining applicability to other regions.

Although the Office of International Operations is a Division of the Office of the Assistant Commissioner (Compliance) in the National Office, most OIO functions are performed directly by the various Assistant Regional Commissioners of the Mid-Atlantic Region.

(3) SERVICE CENTERS

There are ten internal revenue service centers dispersed throughout the country. Each service center is headed by a Director who functions under the supervision of a Regional Commissioner. The service centers process the returns they receive, verify their correctness and store tax return information. They are also called upon to use their data processing capabilities to perform a variety of examination, criminal investigation and collection related functions.

In addition to the ten service centers, the IRS maintains a National Computer Center in Martinsburg, West Virginia (where some centralized returns processing functions are performed) and a Data Center in Detroit, Michigan (where statistical data are compiled for use by the Service). Both the National Computer Center and the Data Center are under the jurisdiction of the Assistant Commissioner (Data Services), in the National Office.

(4) OFFICE OF DISTRICT DIRECTOR

The district offices, each headed by a District Director, are charged with the responsibility for administering the internal revenue laws within an internal revenue district in conformance with the policies and programs of the National Office and the regional offices. The typical district office is organized functionally into the following divisions: Examination, Collection, Criminal Investigation, Taxpayer Service and Resources Management. There is also an Employee Plans and Exempt Organizations Division in some districts. The organization of a typical district office is shown in Figure 5.

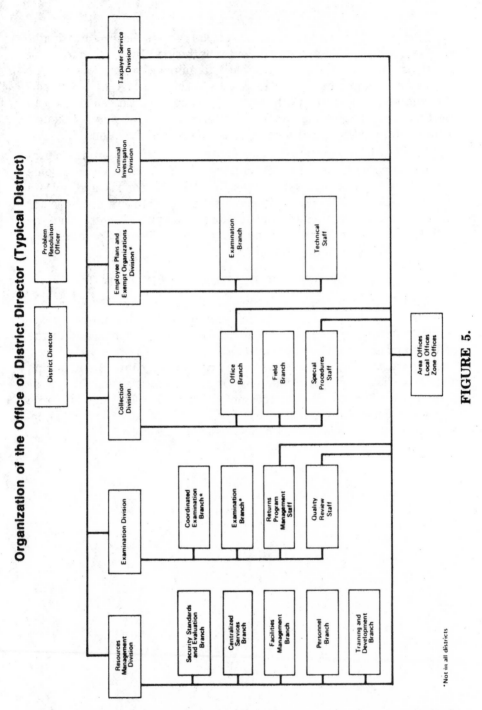

Organization of the Office of District Director (Typical District)

FIGURE 5.

*Not in all districts

As the tax practitioner is likely to have his most frequent contacts with the Service at the district office level, the functions of the various district office personnel will be considered in some detail in the material that follows.

The Examination Division administers a district-wide program involving the selection for examination and actual examination of all types of tax returns and related documents (other than those relating to employee plans and exempt organizations) including income, estate and gift tax returns, claims for refund, offers in compromise and informants' claims for reward. Examination employees select returns for examination and perform field or office audits to determine the correctness of the taxpayer's liability for tax and penalties.

The Collection Division is responsible for the collection of delinquent accounts, the taking of distraint action, the securing of delinquent returns and the receipt and transmittal of tax returns and related documents received within the district. The Collection Division also reviews offers in compromise of 100% penalties and offers in compromise based on doubt as to the collectability of taxes. Collection personnel cause the filing of notices of tax lien and levy and provide assistance to U.S. Attorneys, District and Regional Counsel on all collection matters.

The Criminal Investigation Division enforces the criminal statutes applicable to income, estate, gift, employment and excise tax laws by developing information concerning alleged criminal violations thereof, evaluating allegations and indications of such violations to determine whether investigations should be undertaken, and recommending prosecution when warranted. Sometimes, Criminal Investigation Division personnel will assist IRS and Justice Department attorneys in grand jury proceedings and in the trial of criminal tax cases.

The Taxpayer Service Division manages the district's disclosure, public affairs and taxpayer service activities. This division assists taxpayers in preparing returns and in responding to notices of deficiency and other communications received by the taxpayer from the Service. Through the Disclosure Officer, the Taxpayer Service Division evaluates and processes Freedom of Information, Privacy Act and other disclosure matters within the district. The district office also contains a Resources Management Division and, in some districts, an Employee Plans and Exempt Organizations Division.

The IRS has designated twelve of its districts as "streamlined" districts, with smaller staffs and fewer of the intermediate levels of management common to the typical district structure. In the streamlined districts the District Director functions not only in the traditional broad tax administration role, but also exercises more direct supervision of the front line activities of Examination, Collection, Criminal Investigation and Taxpayer Service. Certain larger, nearby ("prime") districts perform the Examination Quality Review function and Resources Management services for the streamlined districts.

Seventeen "key" districts have also been designated for the management of Computer Examination, Engineering and International

Enforcement Programs, as well as for the management of Employee Plans and Exempt Organizations Programs. A key district is responsible for the entire management of an activity within the key district itself and in the neighboring districts associated with it.

Offices below the district headquarters (area, zone and local offices) perform one or more of certain Collection, Taxpayer Service, Examination and Criminal Investigation functions as the workload warrants. These offices range in size from large area offices containing all of the principal functioning elements of the district office to small, one or two person local offices set up in the town post office.

B. OFFICE OF CHIEF COUNSEL

The Chief Counsel of the Internal Revenue Service, formally an Assistant General Counsel of the Treasury Department, is counsel and legal advisor to the Commissioner of Internal Revenue on all matters pertaining to the administration and enforcement of the tax laws (and some matters that are not strictly tax related). This includes representing the Service in connection with the formulation of tax legislation and regulations; legal review of certain proposed private letter rulings, technical advice memoranda and published rulings; preparation and review of recommendations to the Department of Justice for criminal prosecution of taxpayers; recommendations and coordination with Justice concerning refund suits in the district courts and the Court of Claims; recommendations to Justice concerning certiorari and appeals of all tax litigation matters; assistance to the Department of Justice in summons enforcement, injunctions, Freedom of Information Act and Privacy Act matters; legal advice to the Service in connection with assessment and collection matters; and representation of the Commissioner before the United States Tax Court.

The key officials under the supervision of the Chief Counsel are the Deputy Chief Counsel (Technical), who manages a large staff of Washington-based attorneys involved mainly in National Office matters, and two Deputy Chief Counsel (General and Litigation), who supervise and coordinate the activities of District Counsel lawyers under the direction of Regional Counsel. The organization of the Office of Chief Counsel is depicted in Figure 6.

Organization of the Office of the Chief Counsel

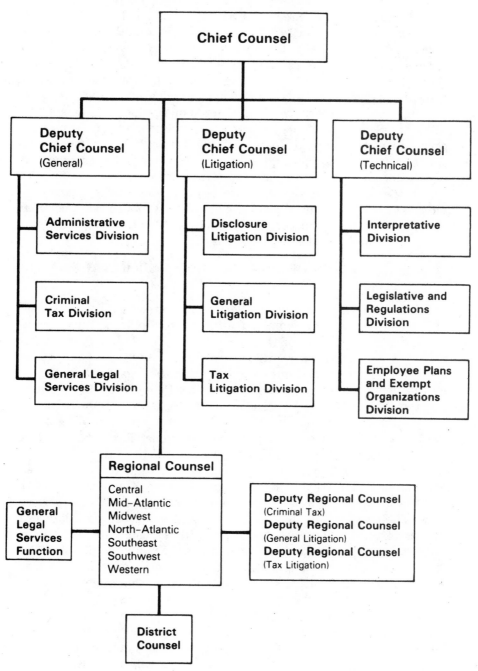

FIGURE 6.

C. OFFICE OF THE DIRECTOR OF PRACTICE

The Office of the Director of Practice was created in 1953 to replace the Committee on Practice and the Office of Attorney for the Government. Originally, the Director of Practice was under the supervision of the Commissioner, but in 1963, pursuant to T.D.O. No. 175–1 (1963–2 C.B. 731), the Office of the Director of Practice was transferred from the Internal Revenue Service to the Office of the Secretary of the Treasury. The Director of Practice is now appointed by the Secretary of the Treasury and is under the immediate supervision of the General Counsel of the Treasury Department. His duties include acting upon appeals from decisions of the Commissioner of Internal Revenue denying application for enrollment to practice before the Internal Revenue Service; instituting and providing for the conduct of disciplinary proceedings relating to attorneys, certified public accountants, and enrolled agents; and making inquiries with respect to matters under his jurisdiction.

D. OFFICE OF THE ASSISTANT SECRETARY FOR TAX POLICY

While the Internal Revenue Service is charged with the responsibility for the day-to-day administration of the tax laws, the Office of the Assistant Secretary of the Treasury for Tax Policy is concerned mainly with matters of overall tax policy. The Office of the Assistant Secretary is divided into two branches, the legal branch, headed by the Deputy Assistant Secretary for Tax Policy (Tax Legislation), and the economic branch, headed by the Deputy Assistant Secretary for Tax Policy (Tax Analysis).[c] The legal staff, under the direction of the Tax Legislative Counsel and the International Tax Counsel, works in conjunction with the responsible officials of the Internal Revenue Service on the development of new and revised regulations; final regulations are signed by both the Commissioner of Internal Revenue and the Assistant Secretary for Tax Policy. The legal staff also reviews published rulings to determine whether the Service's interpretations of the tax laws are consistent with Treasury's overall policy direction and with developing regulations. Finally, as discussed below, the legal staff of the Office of the Assistant Secretary plays an important role in the legal aspects of the formulation of new tax legislation. The economic branch of the Office of the Assistant Secretary is staffed by economists and statisticians and is also heavily involved in the development of new legislation, through the process of "revenue estimating," the evaluation of the revenue producing potential of proposed tax legislation. The Office of Tax Analysis is also engaged in the study and analysis of the present tax system, potential changes in it, and of the tax systems of other countries.

c. See generally F. Hickman, Aspects of Tax Policy, 50 Taxes 722 (1972).

SECTION 2. DEPARTMENT OF JUSTICE

The Tax Division of the Department of Justice, under the direction of an Assistant Attorney General, represents (or coordinates the representation of) the United States and its officers in most civil and criminal litigation arising under the internal revenue laws in the state and federal courts (with the exception of the Tax Court).

The Tax Division is divided into eight sections. The Criminal Section supervises the prosecution of criminal tax cases by United States Attorneys throughout the country. Normally, the Criminal Section's task is limited to a review of criminal tax cases referred to the Division with recommendations for prosecution by the Internal Revenue Service. However, attorneys of the Criminal Section often try a number of the more important or difficult cases, conduct grand jury investigations in some such cases, and assist United States Attorneys in the trial of others. In addition, a senior member of the Criminal Section is assigned to maintain liaison with each interdepartmental Organized Crime Strike Force which comes into existence, often participating actively in the conduct of Strike Force investigations.

The four Civil Trial Sections handle (or supervise) all refund suits in the district courts and all other civil tax litigation in federal and state trial courts, including collection and injunction matters, Freedom of Information Act suits involving the Internal Revenue Service, and other miscellaneous matters arising under the Internal Revenue Code. The Court of Claims Section is responsible for all cases filed with that court and participates in both stages of Court of Claims proceedings—the trial of the case before the trial judge and the appeal of the trial judge's findings and proposed conclusions of law.

The Appellate Section represents the government in appeals of most civil and criminal tax cases in the United States courts of appeals, and participates with the Solicitor General in proceedings taken to the Supreme Court. The Appellate Section is also charged with reviewing adverse Tax Court and district court decisions and preparing recommendations as to whether an appeal should be taken. The final decision on appeal is made by the Solicitor General, to whom the Tax Division and the Chief Counsel of the Internal Revenue Service submit recommendations.

The Review Section is responsible for coordinating the settlement policies of the Division and for conducting research on general legal matters including proposed legislation on which the Division has been asked to comment.

SECTION 3. CONGRESS

THE TAX LEGISLATIVE PROCESS

Thomas J. Gallagher, Jr.
3 The Review of Taxation of Individuals 203 (1979).

* * *

The Constitution grants Congress the power "to lay and collect Taxes, Duties, Imposts and Excises," and provides further that "all Bills for raising Revenue shall originate in the House of Representatives; but the Senate may propose or concur with Amendments * * *." Generally, this tax legislative power is limited only by the presidential veto power, which, of course, can be overridden by a two-thirds vote of each House.

The Committee on Ways and Means has primary jurisdiction over tax matters. It consists of six standing subcommittees and occasionally of various task forces assigned to examine particular problems or subjects. Members of the Committee are designated by their respective parties, and total membership may vary. The allocation of seats to the Democratic and Republican parties depends, in part, upon the ratio of party members in the House.

Although revenue raising measures must originate in the House, various executive communications frequently provide a source of legislative proposals. Such communications may be in the form of a letter, draft, or bill from the President, a cabinet member, or an agency head to the speaker of the House and the president of the Senate. Indeed, the Constitution requires the President to report to Congress on the state of the union, and to recommend measures considered to be necessary and expedient. Often other proposals may accompany the annual presidential message on the transmission of the budget. These, and other executive communications, are referred to the Committee which has jurisdiction over the subject matter contained in the proposal. Since only a member may introduce a bill, the chairman of the committee to which the proposal is referred usually will introduce the proposal in bill form by placing it in the "hopper." (The bill may indicate that it was introduced "by request.") However, there is no requirement that a bill be introduced to effectuate its recommendations.

Hearings by the Ways and Means Committee

Normally, the tax legislative process actually begins with hearings by the Ways and Means Committee. Generally, the committee must announce the time, place, and subject matter of any hearing at least one week in advance. Witnesses, who may be scheduled in panels, ordinarily must file a written statement of their proposed testimony with the committee in advance of the hearing, and only may summarize their argument at the oral presentation.

The House rules require that all committee hearings and business meetings, including those for the markup of legislation, be open to the public. If, however, a majority of the Committee members authorize it by roll-call vote, a one-day closed business meeting may be held. Only Committee members and authorized staff and Treasury representatives may attend a business or markup session which has been closed.

Prior to the commencement of the hearings, the Staff of the Joint Committee on Taxation generally prepares a pamphlet which describes present law and the proposal on which the hearings are scheduled. It also may contain a description of the issues involved, and various factors which the Committee may wish to consider during its deliberations.

If an executive communication forms the basis of the measure under consideration, administration representatives generally will be the first witnesses to appear. Ordinarily, the Secretary of the Treasury broadly outlines the contents of, and the reasons for, the administration's proposals. The Assistant Secretary of the Treasury for Tax Policy normally provides a more detailed description of the proposals. Other administration representatives frequently follow the Treasury Department's presentation. These officials may include presidential advisers in the Office of Management and Budget, the Council of Economic Advisors, the Internal Revenue Service, and the Federal Reserve Board. Various cabinet or agency heads also may testify if the measures are shaped to effect a goal or objective within their jurisdiction. Witnesses from the general public normally follow these governmental spokespersons. Throughout the course of the public hearings, the Committee's staff, Treasury representatives, and members of the Staff of the Joint Committee usually are present to answer any member's questions.

Following the conclusion of the hearings, the Committee generally considers ("marks up") the proposed legislation on a conceptual basis, rather than with direct reference to a bill. Decisions made during these deliberations usually are tentative, that is, subject to reconsideration prior to final approval of a bill. The markup session generally is coordinated by the Chief of Staff of the Joint Committee. The Committee's staff, Treasury representatives, and members of the Joint Committee's Staff usually are present to state their veiws, respond to questions, and furnish the Committee with various data, analyses, and estimates.

The House Bill

Once the Committee's policy decisions are finalized, House Legislative Counsel, in conjunction with staff members of the Joint Committee, Ways and Means, and the Treasury, translate them into bill form. Simultaneously, the Joint Committee Staff prepares a report which accompanies and describes the bill, and which also sets forth the reasons for the legislation. To comply with both the requirements of the House Rules and the congressional Budget Act, the report must contain (1) the Committee's recorded vote, and oversight findings and recommendations, (2) a statement explaining how any new or increased "tax expenditures," or budget authority, affects the level of those amounts as set forth in the concurrent budget resolution, together with the projected cost for each of the present and succeeding four fiscal years, (3) an estimate and comparision prepared by the Congressional Budget Office, (4) a summary of any oversight findings and recommendations made by the Government Operations Committee, and (5) a detailed analytical statement as to the bill's potential inflationary impact on prices and costs. If the reported bill repeals or amends any statute, the report must contain a section (the Ramseyer) which shows the proposed deletions and insertions. (The Senate counterpart of this section is required under the "Condon Rule.")

Consideration on the House Floor

After the bill and report are approved and reported by the Committee, it decides upon the rule to be requested for consideration of the bill on the House floor. Generally, tax bills are considered by the House under a "closed" rule which permits amendments to be offered only by the Committee. However, the Committee may agree to seek a "modified" closed rule pursuant to which a specified amendment could be offered to the reported bill. This procedure is adopted most frequently at the request of a Committee member whose proposal failed to garner enough votes to be included in the reported bill. In any event, the rule sought by the Committee must be approved by the Rules Committee after the bill and report are filed with the House clerk.

As a practical matter, a closed rule generally cannot be granted until four legislative days after the Committee's notice of its intention to seek such a rule appears in the *Congressional Record*. If, within that period, fifty Democratic members serve notice that they wish to offer a germane amendment to the bill, the chairman may not seek, and the Democratic members of the Rules Committee may not support, a closed rule until the Democratic Caucus meets and decides whether the amendment should be considered by the House. If the Caucus decides to support the amendment, it will instruct the Democratic members of the Rules Committee to do the same.

Once a rule (together with a specified period for debate) is granted, the bill is scheduled for consideration on the House floor. The deliberation time allotted is divided evenly between the two parties, and controlled on the floor by each party's manager for the bill (generally the Committee's chairman and the ranking member of the minority). When the deliberation time has expired, opponents may move to recommit the bill to the Committee with instructions to report it back to the House with specified changes. If such a motion prevails, the bill effectively is amended; if it fails to carry, then the bill is unchanged. A complete transcript of these proceedings is reported in the *Congressional Record*.

Once the bill is approved by the House it is forwarded to the House's enrolling clerk. (At this point, the measure technically is an Act of one body of Congress rather than a bill.) The engrossed and certified bill then is delivered to the Senate, the President of which refers it to the appropriate standing committee.

Consideration by the Senate

The tax legislative process in the Senate is substantially similar to that of the House, and generally begins with hearings before the Committee on Finance. While Senate hearings invariably proceed with reference to, and focus upon, the House-passed bill, the Finance Committee may or may not call that bill from the Senate desk. In any event, the Committee's decisions may range from altering the House bill in minor detail to "stripping" the bill entirely of the House-approved provisions. The Committee, in particular, and the Senate, in general, traditionally have felt free to exercise the constitutionally granted power to "propose or concur with Amendments" to House tax bills.

Once reported by the Finance Committee, the Senate rules generally allow both unlimited debate and unrestricted amendment of the bill. In fact, an amendment does not have to be germane unless cloture has been invoked. However, amendments may be subject to various procedural and parliamentary objections. Since Senate floor amendments are not explained in the report of the Finance Committee, their legislative history may be contained largely in the *Congressional Record*.

Conference Committee

After approval by the Senate, the bill, and the Senate amendment, is returned for consideration by the House. (Where the Senate and House versions are identical, this procedure is not necessary.) While the House may accept the Senate changes, it generally requires a Committee of Conference of the House and Senate to reconcile the differences between the two versions. The House and Senate conferees, who are the ranking members, by party, of the Ways and Means and Finance Committees, vote separately as a unit (with a majority governing) on each of the differences between the two versions of the bill. (Provisions which are identical in both bills ordinarily are not "in conference," and therefore are not subject to adjustment by the conferees.) Conference meetings, like those of the Ways and Means and Finance Committees, are required to be open. Generally, the two versions are reconciled by compromise. In some instances, however, the conferees may be unable to reach an agreement with respect to one or more items. This is most likely to occur when a significant amendment was added by the Senate and a similar item never had been approved, or considered, by the House. In such a case, the conferees report back their inability to agree on the amendment to their respective bodies. Such a "technical disagreement" then can be acted upon separately.

The action of the Conference is contained in a Conference Report. This document explains the decision made with respect to each Senate amendment, and also contains the language of the Conference Agreement. The Report, in addition, contains a Joint Explanatory Statement of the Conference Committee by the Managers on the part of the House and the Senate, which explains the final actions taken by the conferees. This part of the document essentially functions as a committee report.

Once the Report is completed, it is submitted to the House and Senate for approval. The enrolled bill then is forwarded to the President for action. Although tax bills generally are approved, some have been vetoed, some have become law without the President's signature, and some presidential vetoes have been overridden.

Minor Revenue Bills

While minor tax bills generally follow these same procedures, they ordinarily receive much less detailed attention. In fact, in many instances no Conference Committee action is necessary because the provisions are identical, the House simply recedes from its disagreement to Senate amendments, or the Senate recedes from its amendments to the House bill. However, minor revenue bills easily may be forgotten, and thus die, in an end-of-the-Congress rush.

Due to this general lack of public scrutiny of minor tax bills, such proposals may tend to provide substantial benefits for a limited number of persons. However, incident to an informal arrangement between the committees and the Joint Committee staff, the descriptive hearing pamphlets generally indicate whether any minor or technical bills are retroactive, or directed to any particular taxpayer(s). Thus, to the extent of the staff's information, "private-interest" tax bills can be examined, by the Committee and the public, both for their content and as to any particular potential beneficiary.

General Explanation

Ordinarily, the Staff of the Joint Committee prepares a postenactment General Explanation of major revenue measures. While this document has neither the weight nor the legislative history status of a committee report, it usually contains more detailed description and analysis of the various new or changed provisions.

NOTES

1. Upon final Congressional approval, the President has ten days to approve or veto the tax bill. During this time, various government agencies will submit their views on the legislation to the Office of Management and Budget, which then summarizes their opinions and reports to the President. Once signed, the legislation may take effect immediately, retroactively, or at some future date as specified in the legislation itself. The considerations involved in determining the effective date of tax legislation are discussed in Note, Setting Effective Dates for Tax Legislation: A Rule of Prospectivity, 84 Harv.L.Rev. 436 (1970).

2. The Joint Committee on Taxation is a joint congressional committee charged with the general responsibility for overseeing the administration and operation of the Federal system of internal revenue taxation. IRC §§ 8021–8023. It is composed of the five ranking members of each of the House Committee on Ways and Means and the Senate Finance Committee and is supported by a staff of experts and other assistants appointed by the Joint Committee and under the direction of its Chief of Staff. IRC §§ 8001–8005.

   Congress has given the Joint Committee rather wide-ranging oversight responsibilities and, by virtue of IRC § 6405, requires the Joint Committee to review all claims for refunds or credits for taxes in excess of $200,000. Section 6405(a) of the Code provides that no payment on such a claim may be made until after the expiration of thirty days from the date upon which a report giving the name of the person to whom the refund or credit is to be made, the amount of the refund or credit and a summary of the facts and decision of the appropriate Treasury official, is made to the Joint Committee on Taxation. The Joint Committee's review procedure is outlined in D. Alexander, New IRS Procedures for Handling Joint Committee Cases, 138 Journal of Accountancy No. 4, 93 (1974).

Chapter II

RESPONSIBILITIES OF THE TAX PRACTITIONER

Scope Note: The tax practitioner operates under the constraints of several, sometimes conflicting, obligations. He must serve his client's interests to the extent permissible. However, he is restricted in his zeal by ethical and legal rules under which he has duties vis-a-vis others, including the IRS. Moreover, the tax practitioner often finds himself in a position in which there are two clients who have conflicting interests. The purpose of this chapter is to sensitize future practitioners to the ethical dimension of tax practice, for quite often the error that the practitioner makes is in the failure to recognize an ethical problem at the outset and to take immediate steps to reach a resolution. The chapter covers the basic requirements for practice before the IRS as well as some recurring ethical problems and dilemmas faced in the course of tax practice. A portion of the chapter is devoted to the statutory regulation of income tax return preparers brought into the law by the Tax Reform Act of 1976.

SECTION 1. REGULATIONS GOVERNING PRACTICE BEFORE THE IRS

TAX PROCEDURE AND INTERNAL REVENUE SERVICE PRACTICE

Michael I. Saltzman

* * *

Standards governing admission to practice as well as duties of those practicing before the Service are designed to protect taxpayers and the quality of representation. The Secretary of the Treasury is authorized to prescribe rules and regulations governing the recognition of persons representing claimants before his department and may disbar or suspend any person from practice if the person refuses to comply with these rules. The Treasury Department has adopted rules governing the recognition and conduct of persons representing taxpayers before the Internal Revenue Service. These rules have been promulgated in 31 Code of Federal Regulations, Part 10, and are commonly referred to as T.D. Circular 230. Circular 230 is divided into four parts: (1) rules relating to authority to practice before the IRS; (2) the duties and restrictions relating to such practice; (3) rules relating to disciplinary proceedings; and (4) general rules, such as provisions relating to the availability of records. In addition, conference and practice requirements applying to all offices of the IRS have been promulgated as 26 Code of Federal Regulations, Part 601. The Secretary has appointed a Director of Practice in his office to carry out his functions relating to admission to practice and the conduct of disciplinary proceedings.

What constitutes "practice" before the Service.

Every person who on behalf of a taxpayer, transferee or fiduciary appears before the IRS must meet the practice requirements the Treasury has established in Circular 230, unless the person is not engaged in "practice" before the IRS. Practice occurs, in general, when a person makes an advocate's presentation of a client-taxpayer's rights, privileges or liabilities under IRS-administered laws or regulations. A "presentation" includes the preparation and filing of necessary documents, correspondence with and communications to the Service, and the representation of a client at conferences, hearings and meetings. But neither the preparation and signing of a tax return, claim or election nor an appearance before the Service as a witness or the furnishing of information at its request constitutes "practice" before the IRS. Consequently, a return preparer may answer questions and supply information to an IRS agent as a witness without having to satisfy the requirements prerequisite to practice and without obtaining a power of attorney. It is only when the return preparer becomes an advocate representing his client's position before the Service (usually after the agent has proposed adjustments and the matter is at the Appeals Office conference stage) that he is considered to be engaged in "practice before the Service."

Who may practice before the Service.

Three broad classes of persons may practice before the Service: attorneys, certified public accountants and enrolled agents. Enrolled actuaries and others in specific situations may engage in limited practice before the Service without enrollment.[1]

* * *

When powers of attorney and tax information authorizations are required.

The Service's conference and practice regulations require an individual appearing as an advocate to file (1) an instrument authorizing the holder to perform certain acts or to receive confidential tax information (a power of attorney or tax information authorization) and (2) a declaration that the person is recognized to practice before the Service (a practice declaration). Even if the person appearing is merely to act as a witness who may receive or inspect confidential tax information, a tax information authorization must be filed. * * *

* * * The power [of attorney] or authorization is a prerequisite to representation. Unless the representative has on file a power

1. Circular 230 § 10.3. * * *

or authorization, he will not be heard as the taxpayer's representative, and with [only a] few exceptions [2] * * * cannot receive confidential tax information, and no notice or other written communication (or copy of one) that contains confidential information about a filed tax return will be sent to the representative.

* * *

Duties and restrictions on practice.

Circular 230 imposes a number of duties and restrictions on practice before the IRS. These are as follows:

1. A person authorized to practice before the IRS may not interfere with an effort by the IRS to obtain information unless the person believes in good faith and on reasonable grounds that the information is privileged or the effort of doubtful legality.

2. A person authorized to practice before the IRS must, on request, supply the Director of Practice with information about violations of the regulations and must testify in any disbarment or suspension proceeding unless the person believes in good faith and on reasonable grounds that the information is privileged or that the request is of doubtful legality.

3. A person authorized to practice retained by a client who has not complied with the revenue laws or has made an error in or omission from a return or other document the client is required by law to execute, must advise the client promptly of the noncompliance, error, or omission. It appears that no obligation beyond this advice is necessary, and presumably the final decision to comply or correct the error or omission is the client's. This result is consistent with the American Bar Association's position that a lawyer has a duty to urge his client to correct the error but only states that the lawyer "may" have to withdraw if the client refuses.[3] The American Institute of Certified Public Accountants takes a similar view: the CPA has the responsibility of advising the taxpayer of the error and the measures to be taken, but if the client does not correct the error, the CPA only "should consider the implications of this refusal on his future relationship with the client." [4]

4. A person authorized to practice must exercise due diligence in preparing and filing returns, documents and other papers relating to internal revenue matters and in determining the

---

2. Under the confidentiality and disclosure rules of § 6103, returns and return information may be disclosed to a designee of the taxpayer.

3. ABA Comm. on Professional Ethics, Opinion No. 314 (1965), 51 ABA J. 671 (1965). A duty to withdraw may become more definite if continued

representation will require him to use false evidence or to make a false statement. ABA Code of Professional Responsibility, Canon 7, DR 7–102(A) (3)–(7). * * *

4. AICPA Statements of Responsibilities in Tax Practice, No. 6 (1970).

correctness of representations to the Treasury Department and to a client. This duty is to a substantial degree enforced by the return preparer rules and penalties provided by the Code * * *. However, it has been held that the regulation "suggests a principal concern with making representatives accountable for negligence" and "connotes loyalty and devotion" to the client.[5] Consequently, when a representative deceives his client in a matter before the IRS, the representative violates the regulation and may be disbarred.[6]

5. A person authorized to practice must not unreasonably delay the prompt disposition of a matter before the IRS.

6. A person authorized to practice may not knowingly and directly or indirectly employ a person disbarred or suspended from practice or accept employment from such a person, or accept assistance from a former government employee prohibited by regulations or law from providing assistance.

7. Special rules apply to practice by former government officials or partners of government employees.

8. A person authorized to practice may not notarize papers in a matter in which he is also counsel, attorney or agent.

9. A person authorized to practice may not charge an unconscionable fee.

10. A person authorized to practice may not represent conflicting interests, except by express consent of all directly interested parties after full disclosure has been made. * * *

11. Persons admitted to practice may not solicit employment in matters before the IRS, except (a) from an existing or former client in a related matter; (b) by way of a mailing designed for the general public. Advertising disclosing factual data, such as a description of the services offered, membership in professional organizations and fee information is permitted.

12. Persons admitted to practice may not negotiate a refund check [in violation of IRC § 6695(f)].

Disciplinary proceedings: disbarment and suspension from practice.

The Secretary of the Treasury has the power to disbar or suspend any person recognized to practice before the Service who (1) is shown to be incompetent or disreputable, (2) who refuses to comply with the rules and regulations in Circular No. 230, or (3) who, with

5. Harary v. Blumenthal, 555 F.2d 1113 (2d Cir. 1977).

6. In Harary v. Blumenthal, supra, a CPA who was acquitted of bribing an IRS agent had told his client the agent had to be paid $2,000, but paid the agent $1,250, pocketing the $750 for himself.

intent to defraud, willfully and knowingly deceives, misleads or threatens a prospective client by oral or written solicitation.

There are nine examples of disreputable conduct for which a representative may be disbarred or suspended: [7]

    1.   Conviction of any tax crime or a crime involving dishonesty or a breach of trust;

    2.   Knowingly giving false or misleading information to the Service in a matter currently or to be pending before the Service;

    3.   Soliciting employment;

    4.   Willful failure to file a tax return or tax evasion or participating in any way in evading or attempting to evade a tax [liability of the representative or of the] client;

    5.   Misappropriation or failure to remit properly and promptly funds received from a client for payment of tax and other federal obligations;

    6.   Bribery of IRS officials;

    7.   Disbarment or suspension from practice as an attorney, CPA or public accountant by a state;

    8.   Assisting a disbarred or suspended person in practicing before the IRS; and

    9.   Contemptuous conduct.

In addition, a person recognized to practice may be disbarred or suspended for willful violation of any of the regulations contained in Circular No. 230, including, presumably, the standards of and restrictions on practice.

If Service personnel have reason to believe a person admitted to practice or any other person has information of violation of the rules of Circular No. 230, a report is made to the Director of Practice in the Treasury Department on the basis of which the Director may reprimand or commence disbarment or suspension proceedings. Generally, however, a proceeding will not be commenced until the person involved is notified of the facts and conduct complained of. The Director may, but is not required to, offer the person a conference at which he has the opportunity to convince the Director no violation has occurred, or to consent to a voluntary suspension or resignation which the Director may, but again is not required to, accept. After the conference (if it is offered), the Director may reprimand the representative, accept the offer of consent to voluntary suspension or resignation or proceed to file a complaint commencing the disciplinary proceedings.

    7. Circular 230 § 10.51.

Formal proceedings are heard by a hearing examiner, and, after the filing of an answer, motions, trial and submission of proposed findings, the hearing examiner makes findings of fact and law and [issues an] appropriate order for filing with the Director of Practice. An appeal must be filed with the Secretary of the Treasury within 30 days after the decision, but, in any event, the Secretary will make the agency's decision.

A disbarred or suspended person may not practice before the Service until reinstated or the period of suspension expires and notice of disbarment or suspension is given not only to Service personnel, but also to other federal and state authorities. Notices of disbarment or suspension are published in Internal Revenue Bulletins.

NOTES

1.   Subpart E of the Statement of Procedural Rules (Proc. Rules §§ 601.501–601.509—Conference and Practice Requirements) sets forth additional requirements concerning practice before the Internal Revenue Service.   Included among these are the Service's rules regarding conferences with representatives of the IRS (§§ 601.502(a), 601.507); requirements concerning the necessity and proper execution and filing of powers of attorney and/or tax information authorizations (§§ 601.502(c), 601.503, 601.-504); requirements for changing representation (§ 601.505); and regulations regarding delivery of notices and refund checks to a taxpayer's recognized representative (§ 601.506).

2.   During the past decade the IRS has become increasingly concerned about the problem of abusive tax shelters.   In addition to stepping up enforcement in that area by the use of special shelter audit programs and more frequent recommendations for criminal prosecution and civil fraud penalties, the Service has begun to concentrate on the tax practitioner's involvement in such shelters.   The Treasury Department has recently proposed amendments to Circular 230 which would regulate writers of tax shelter opinions and subject them to disciplinary action for violations of the proposed regulations.   See 45 Fed.Reg. 58,594, 58,597 (Sept. 4, 1980). See also, P. Sax, Lawyer Responsibility in Tax Shelter Opinions, 34 Tax Lawyer 5 (1980).

SECTION 2.   ETHICS OF TAX PRACTICE *

ETHICAL GUIDELINES FOR TAX PRACTICE

Frederic G. Corneel
28 Tax Law Review 1 (1972).

Introduction

This article is intended as a primer for young attorneys entering upon tax practice regarding the outer limits to which they may properly let themselves be carried by their desire to help their clients and

* Section 2 should be read in conjunction with A.B.A. Opinion 346, (Appendix A), entitled Tax Law Opinions in Tax Shelter Investment Offerings.

thereby, indirectly, themselves. A primer of this type may be useful since there is not available any brief authoritative guide for lawyers in tax practice and little, if any, time in the schools is devoted to the subject.

Even experienced lawyers are often puzzled by the questions discussed in this article. Too many believe that professional ethics is chiefly a matter of individual conscience and therefore individual choice. In fact, there is a good deal of relevant authority which can be summarized into rules of general application. Familiarity with these rules may not only solve vexing problems but may function as a support and guide to the conscience when there is strong pressure to depart from the rules of good practice. No attempt will be made in this article to summarize all rules of good practice applicable to a tax lawyer, for the canons applicable to every lawyer apply equally to him. Rather the discussion will confine itself to those aspects of the prelitigation stage where the tax specialist may encounter problems different at least in degree from those faced by the general practitioner.

Is tax practice ethical? Many a layman—and unfortunately many a law school student—are amused by the notion that private tax practice can ever be ethical. Their position can be stated simply: The tax lawyer assists clients solely with their selfish monetary concerns. He helps them in their unchristian endeavor to shift their tax burden to their neighbors. He deprives the government of revenue needed for the common good.

In light of these indictments, all of which are true, how can the tax lawyer return at night to his innocent children without "cheeks incarnadined by a blush of shame?" The answer lies in a very different view of the profession: The basic decision of how much wealth shall remain in the private sector and how much shall pass to the public is made not by tax practitioners but by Congress. Equally it is Congress and not the practitioner which determines how the tax burden shall be shared among the various segments of the population. Nearly all so-called loopholes have been specifically approved by Congress and are reflected in the Code.

Accordingly, while tax lawyers work for those who have or would like to have money, they do not generally speaking provide them with more than their representative government has decided is proper. But given the complexities of our tax law—complexities both astonishing and unfortunate for a law of such wide application—expert advice is essential to assure both that the taxes which should be paid are in fact paid and that the taxes which need not be paid are avoided.

Further, the size of the tax bite is such that ignorance of how the law applies to a particular transaction can turn profit into loss or deprive the intended beneficiary of the contemplated gift. Expert advice is necessary to permit the planning and completion of an almost limitless range of economic activity: organizing a business, selling a residence, making a charitable contribution, compensating an employee, supporting a child, dealing in securities and so on. One would have to condemn all such private activities to classify the tax adviser's work as evil.

Finally, the tax practitioner affords his client the protection of the law: He assures that tax payments are made, not pursuant to the views of the auditing agent, but in accordance with the provisions of the Code.

All of this does not mean that in terms of Judeo-Christian ethics the work of a tax lawyer ranks with nursing in a leper colony. But it is a socially necessary and demanding task of which no one need be ashamed *if* he does his work well. The caveat is important. It may be "more ethical" to make blue jeans than to make a mink coat. But once one undertakes to make a mink coat there is an ethical obligation to make it in a workmanlike manner.

This brings us to "professional ethics"—which generally speaking means a code of conduct intended to assure that the community will get good service from the profession. The most frequent violation of this code by lawyers results not from their dishonesty, but from lack of care. A principal ethical obligation of the tax lawyer, therefore, is to devote the necessary time, energy and attention to tax law and its development and to his clients' affairs.

THE CONFLICT OF PRINCIPLES

The basic source of difficulties in finding the right course is not so much the need to know and apply a large number of intricate rules of conduct, rather, it is the need to resolve the conflicting demands of different underlying principles.

In the ethical problems facing a tax lawyer, two sets of competing principles are likely to demand attention. On the one side, the lawyer owes it to his client to represent him with zeal and loyalty within the bounds of the law, and he must not without authority disclose the secrets and confidences of his client. On the other side, the lawyer has an obligation to see that the law is upheld and to be "honest" with his adversaries in general and governmental agencies in particular. We will examine the resolution of the conflict between these principles at four stages of tax practice: the return, postreturn developments, tax audit and tax planning.

It is important to remember that "professional ethics" is a composite of (1) rules designed to provide society with a service it has a right to expect, that is, the service generally provided by members of the profession, and (2) aspirations for improvement in the level of professional conduct. Both of these aspects are important. Let us assume, for instance, that it is present professional practice not to disclose voluntarily to the Service evidence adverse to the client's position. If a tax practitioner concludes that he wishes to adhere to what he believes to be a "higher" ethical standard and present all information whether favorable or unfavorable, is it not clear that he owes his client the obligation of cautioning him in advance, so that the client may then choose whether that is the type of representation he desires?

Ethical problems should be widely discussed, both for the development of ethical standards in tax practice and as a guide to the individual practitioner. After years of agonizing over questions of this kind in the privacy of his office, the author resolved to make an attempt to determine the standards of the community in which he practices. He circulated to approximately 100 Boston tax practitioners, lawyers and accountants—herein referred to as "the Bostonians"—a questionnaire posing a variety of ethical problems. Thirty-eight replies were received. In some cases there were substantial disagreements. But in most there was so clear a concensus as to provide a useful guide to the present views of the profession. Accordingly, some of the questions and answers will be noted below even though they do not constitute "authority" in the usual sense.

Preparation of Returns

The execution of a return is a good point from which to start consideration of the ethical aspects of tax practice. Most of the problems revolve around the extent to which the Service must be told the truth and, since returns are signed both by the taxpayer and the preparer under the penalties of perjury, this is the ideal point to test the extent to which the ethical obligations interact with the legal obligations.

PREPARATION AND SIGNATURE OF RETURNS

The Incorrect Return

The regulations require the person who prepares a return for compensation to verify it.[16] Obviously, a lawyer cannot verify a return which he knows to be incorrect. Further, the lawyer's signature on the return as a preparer may be taken as evidence by the Service that he has made at least some effort to insure that the return is correct and complete. Thus it would be improper for him to sign the return unless that effort has been made.

Closely related to the incorrect return is the return which is incomplete or which intentionally deviates from the accepted form—perhaps through use of a "statement attached"—in order to prevent the Service from noting a fact that might prove troublesome to the client.

---

16.   Reg. § 1.6065–1(b)(1).

While this practice is probably not uncommon, in most cases it would be difficult to find any support for it as conforming to professional standards. It is one thing to decide that a taxpayer need not volunteer information disadvantageous to his position, it is quite another intentionally to fail to supply information the government has a right to demand.

Return That May Be Incorrect

What should the lawyer do when confronted with a return in which the taxpayer is giving himself the benefit of the doubt but the lawyer is unable to do likewise?

A corporation was formed with a view to a reorganization carried out shortly thereafter. In the opinion of counsel the transaction clearly does not meet the [Service] requirements for a reorganization and probably, but less certainly, would not receive court approval.

The client intends to report the transaction as a reorganization exchange.

Would you as attorney sign the return?

It seems a strong argument can be made for the proposition that a lawyer's signature of a return signifies that he believes it to be correct and, if there are doubts, the lawyer before signing the return should satisfy himself the chances are at least even that the taxpayer would prevail if the matter were decided by the Supreme Court. The appropriate organs of both the legal and the accounting professions have indicated, however, that it is proper for members of these professions to sign returns if they believe there is a reasonable basis for the position taken. This is in line with the general proposition that a lawyer should not attempt to act as judge of his client's case and can properly proceed if there is reasonable support for his client's position.

One argument in favor of permitting execution of returns which may be wrong as long as they are not known to be wrong, is that doubtful questions could otherwise be tested only by claims for refund. A stronger consideration is that it is often easier to say there is a respectable argument for a particular position than to determine whether in the particular case it outweighs a contrary argument. Even here difficult problems may arise, for instance, where an inconsistent position was taken on a prior return, or on another taxpayer's return or was agreed to in connection with a prior audit.

In sum, the accepted view is that the taxpayer, or the preparer, may sign a return as "correct" if he believes there is a reasonable possibility the return is not incorrect. One tax practitioner informed the author that he would sign a return if he felt that the taxpayer has a 15 per cent chance of being right. Of course, a 15 per cent chance is no easier to estimate than a 50 per cent chance. Thus the more general test of reasonable support of the taxpayer's position suggested by the professional associations appears preferable.

DISCLOSURE OF WEAKNESSES

The attorney's decision to sign a return even though he recognizes that another view is reasonable and would probably be asserted by the Service, leads to the next question:

Relevant Facts

Is there an ethical obligation to disclose the relevant facts?

A family corporation redeems a part of the stock of a family member under circumstances which may make the payment essentially equivalent to a dividend.

Is it sufficient that the client's capital gain schedule merely reports the basis, sales price and gain or should it go further and at least disclose that the purchaser was the issuer?

There are strong arguments for disclosure: The taxpayer's view, though reasonable, may well be wrong and nondisclosure would permit the taxpayer to pay less tax than Congress intended. Further, there is a national interest to have doubtful questions brought to light and litigated in order to help settle the law for the future. Finally, for those who view the return as part of a contest between taxpayers and the Service, fairness seems to require the Service be given at least a sporting chance by being alerted to the problem.

The contrary argument is that the "flagging" of a problem is likely to lead to a time-consuming and expensive controversy with the Service, possibly involving more costs than the taxes at issue. The government has an obligation to provide clear rules of law and such obligation, by hypothesis, has not been met in these cases. Many doubts arise from mixed questions of law and fact—such as the reasonableness of compensation—which could not usefully be dealt with in a statement. The normal course of audit will bring up sufficient cases to permit clarification of the law. Would it really help the growth of jurisprudence if every recipient of a payment on a note rushed forward with facts indicating the note might be "thin" and the payment a dividend rather than a return of capital? Finally, equality of treatment among taxpayers is much more likely to be promoted by requiring answers to specific questions on the return rather than by reliance on the ethics of those tax advisers sufficiently competent to recognize the problem.

Both lines of argument have merit and in any actual case must be weighed against each other. The concensus of opinion appears to be that the smaller the amount involved and the greater the likelihood that the taxpayer will ultimately prevail, the less is the obligation to disclose the weakness. On the other hand, where the amount involved is large and the taxpayer's ultimate chance of success substantially less than even, most Bostonians feel some disclosure is required. Rarely however, will the disclosure be a large red flag. Usually it will be a relatively inconspicuous reference to a fact—just enough to preclude any claim of fraud, but not enough to stimulate further inquiry by any but the most astute of agents.

Valuation Problems

A peculiar problem exists in the valuation of stock of closely held corporations since in the experience of most practitioners the Service virtually never accepts the value reported. The Bostonians were asked to respond to the following question:

> You are preparing the return for an estate, which includes a minority stock interest in a closely held company. In your opinion, a "fair value" would be $50 a share. However, you believe that the [Service] will settle at this amount only if you report the value at not more than $40 a share. The book value of the stock is $30 a share, and if you apply a 25% discount because it is a minority interest, you could report the stock at $22.50. Would you:
>
> 1. Report the stock at
>
>   a) $50 b) $40 c) $30 d) $22.50 e) $......
>
>   (Please check one of the above even though you also check 2 or 3)
>
> 2. Request an appraiser whom you informed of the purpose of the appraisal to set the price.
>
> 3. Request an appraiser whom you did not inform of the purpose to set the price.

A majority of the Bostonians would be inclined to report the value at $30 or less, about one third at $40 and virtually none at $50. The amount most frequently chosen was $22.50.

That this approach is practically necessary is clear to experienced practitioners. In support of ethics it may be said that a question as to fair market value of stock which in fact has no market can be truthfully answered only by saying that it falls somewhere within a broad range; and neither the client nor the lawyer is unethical in reporting at the lower end of this range since there is a reasonable basis for this position.

I do not mean to imply that it is unreasonable for the Service to add a "mendacity premium" to the values reported. It clearly does so in response to the practice of taxpayers and advisers to be more than conservative in gift and estate tax valuations, just as the taxpayers' practice is clearly in response to the Service custom to increase reported values no matter what the facts. Thus evil begets evil.

In my personal view, the business of fixing estate and gift tax al-
ues by a process of Near Eastern bargaining is degrading to both the
profession and the Service. A better way of taxing closely held businesses should be devised. In the interim a lawyer should probably
make every effort to reduce the Service's incentive to bargain by obtaining well substantiated appraisals from competent appraisers.
However, he fools himself and does his client no favor if he assumes
that on audit a mendacity premium will not be added to the reported
value. [See Appendix B re new valuation overstatement penalty.]

REVIEW OF RETURNS

The discussion so far has concerned the rules applicable to returns prepared by attorneys. Usually, the number of returns prepared by an attorney is small in comparison to the number he reviews. However, the applicable rules of ethics are no different: He
should never advise a client to complete a return in such manner that
the attorney would not be prepared to sign it if he himself had prepared it. Moreover, it is clear that lawyers have an ethical obligation
to urge clients to file "correct" returns, or more accurately stated, returns not known to be wrong. Many lawyers find it difficult to deliver homilies on the moral aspects of obeying law for the sake of obedience. In many cases, however, the taxes saved by chicanery are small
when compared to the time, money and reputation that may be lost if
the omission from income or improper deduction is discovered.

Postreturn Developments

UNINTENTIONAL ERROR

A taxpayer may become aware some time after he has filed his
return that he has unintentionally underpaid his tax. The underpayment may be due to a mistake of law, as where a contribution to the
League of Women Voters was deducted in ignorance of the rule that
political action organizations do not qualify as charities. It may be
due to a mistake of fact, as where a work of art is included in an estate at a nominal value in ignorance of the fact that it is the work of
a famous artist. There may have been a mistake of computation or a
change in the law, as where an installment sale is retroactively disqualified by the exclusion of the amount allocable to imputed interest.
Let us assume that in all these cases the taxpayer acted in good faith
when he filed his return. Now he becomes aware of his mistake.
What should he do? What must he do?

Taxpayer's Obligation

Unless the statute of limitations has expired, it is clear that the
tax is owing and the taxpayer *should* pay the tax. However, there is
virtually no legal authority requiring the taxpayer to file an amended
return and pay the tax. While there are regulations to the effect

that the taxpayer "should" file an amended return [36] and the Service provides special forms for the purpose, there are no Code provisions in support of these regulations and no action has ever been brought for failure to comply with these regulations. The very words used: "should * * * file an amended return," appear to indicate that the regulations are aspirational rather than mandatory in character.

While it is desirable that mistakes be rectified when they are discovered, the desirability of imposing negligence or fraud penalties for failure to report discovered mistakes is not clear. At the time the return is signed under penalties of perjury, the taxpayer presumably reviews the facts and law known to him to make sure that his return is honest. If the jurat were amended to give it prospective effect, difficult problems of proof might result. Clearly the mere discovery of previously unknown facts should not be enough for imposition of a penalty. Recognition of the effect on the return and an awareness of a legal obligation to correct it should be necessary. In many cases proof of such recognition and awareness would depend upon evidence of advice from the taxpayer's accountant or lawyer and, even where such advice is not privileged, it is clearly undesirable that professional advice become an important enforcement tool.

Lawyer's Obligation

The lawyer's obligation when a prior mistake comes to his attention is simple: He must call the mistake to his client's attention and he should urge his client to correct the mistake, particularly where he himself has participated in the preparation of the return. The taxpayer's situation is really no different from that of a shopper who buys a handkerchief and upon coming home finds that he has by mistake taken two handkerchiefs or has received too much change. When the situation is explained in these terms, many taxpayers will wish to rectify the prior mistake. On the other hand, the need to urge correction is less when the amount involved is small and the time and effort needed to carry out the correction are out of proportion to the amount of tax involved. In such a case it may be adequate to make the adjustment on the next return. It must be recalled, however, that a return found to contain one error may also contain others. Accordingly, any recommendation to report an error should be preceded by the suggestion that the entire return and supporting material be carefully reviewed to determine the precise extent of the problem.

Client Refusal to Correct Return

Urging a correction is pretty much the end of the lawyer's ethical obligation. He cannot inform the Service without his client's permission. Of course, if the error in the prior year has a bearing on a

36. Reg. §§ 1.451–1(a) and 1.461–1(a)(3).

current return, as in the case of a loss carryover, the attorney cannot sign the current year's return if it reflects the error of the prior year. A lawyer may also have to consider, just as accountants are urged to do, whether he wishes to continue to represent a client who does not pay all his taxes. Where the lawyer has signed the prior incorrect return himself, a termination of the relationship may be desirable in order to preserve the lawyer's reputation with the Service.

INTENTIONAL ERROR

The error on the return may have been intentional rather than inadvertent. However, the rules applicable to both the taxpayer (to report the error) and to his lawyer (to urge correction) are the same in either case. We are now, however, in an area which may give rise to criminal charges. And if the Service cannot, without violating the fifth amendment, require filing of returns which incriminate gamblers under applicable state law,[46] it is difficult to see that the lawyer must in fact insist upon disclosure of prior fraud.[47] On the other hand, it is clear that fear of criminal punishment does not excuse filing of further false returns in order to hide the original wrong.

The question has been raised whether it would be proper to sign returns which intentionally overstate income in order to make amends for prior intentional omissions without disclosing the same. Most of the Boston lawyers consulted were reluctant to sign such a return. To this writer, who has had little practical experience with the correction of fraudulent underpayments, it seems that half a loaf is better than none.

The Audit

PROCEEDINGS INVOLVING PENALTIES

In one sense, the audit is merely one type of postreturn development and most of the rules discussed above are applicable. However, at the audit stage we have reached a truly adversary proceeding, even though the Service representative, like a prosecuting attorney, should be guided not only by the importance of winning but also by the need to achieve a correct result. The lawyer's obligation to the Service may depend upon the nature of the proceeding. Where negligence or fraud penalties may be involved, the lawyer's position may not be much different from that of the lawyer in a criminal case who must defend his client even though he knows him to be guilty so that his client may not be deprived of life, liberty or property except by operation of law. Thus, the lawyer's obligation to see that the law is

46. See Marchetti v. United States, 390 U.S. 39, 88 S.Ct. 697, 19 L.Ed.2d 889 (1968); Grosso v. United States, 390 U.S. 62, 88 S.Ct. 709, 19 L.Ed.2d 906 (1968).

47. For the problems of lawyers who paid a taxpayer's tax without disclosing the name of the taxpayer, see Tillotson v. Boughner, 350 F.2d 663 (7th Cir. 1965); Baird v. Koerner, 279 F.2d 623 (9th Cir. 1960).

carried out relates only to that part of the law which provides that taxes be paid or that people not be murdered, but not to that part of the law which imposes the punishment. The lawyer cannot advise or cooperate in any way in a violation of the former, must urge obedience to it and may even be required to disclose his client's confidential information if necessary to prevent the commission of a crime. But there is no similar obligation to that part of the law which imposes punishment. In a case involving fraud or negligence the lawyer's obligation to the Service may be limited to extending the usual courtesies in matters not going to the substance and never to make any statement of fact or law which is known to be incorrect.

PROCEEDINGS NOT INVOLVING PENALTIES

Disclosure of Facts

In areas not involving penalties, the ethical obligations to the Service and the law may be broader. While the lawyer is instructed to observe "candor and fairness" in his dealings with other lawyers and the court, the illustrations in the canons make it clear that these words are given an exceedingly restricted meaning: A lawyer cannot intentionally misquote a document or cite an authority which he knows has been repealed or overruled. Does the requirement of candor go further and require disclosure to the Service of facts adverse to the client's position? The Bostonians were asked the following question:

> A. You are retained to represent an estate before the Appellate Division [a] [of the Service] in a proceeding in which the sole question is whether a particular series of gifts was made in contemplation of death. In going through the file of the decedent's correspondence with her investment adviser, you find a letter from the adviser recommending the gifts that were in fact made and setting out in detail the computations as to the savings that might result both from an income tax and estate tax point of view. You show the letter to the decedent's daughter and she says (you believe sincerely) "It may be that this letter caused my mother to think about the matter, but she was never particularly interested in taxes and I am sure that she made the gifts to my brother and me only because we were having financial difficulties and she wanted us to have the money when we needed it." You believe personally that the gift was not made in contemplation of death, but you are also of the opinion that because of the decedent's age and health, the case will have to be settled by including at least some of the gifts and that if this letter were disclosed to the [Service] neither a settlement nor a favorable court decision could be expected.

---

a. The Appellate Division is now referred to as the Appeals Office.

1. Would you disclose the letter to the [Service]?

2. Would you request your client's permission to disclose the letter, warning her that you will not continue to act in the matter unless you are given permission to disclose?

3. Would you not disclose the letter but be careful not to make any positive misstatements such as "We know of no evidence that would indicate that the gifts were motivated by tax considerations."

4. Would you destroy the letter?

B. Would your answer to the foregoing questions be any different if you believed that the gifts were in fact made in contemplation of death but that if you failed to disclose the letter the estate could obtain a favorable settlement to which it really is not entitled?

Only a very small minority would disclose the letter: There is no ethical obligation to show the Service cards they have not asked to see. It is equally clear that it would be unethical for the lawyer to destroy the letter or advise its destruction. Since, in dealing with the Service the lawyer has an obligation not to misstate the facts, the answer under number 3 was the one given by most of the Bostonians. Somewhat surprisingly, in almost no case would the answer be different if the lawyer believed that the gifts were made in contemplation of death.

While it is true that the taxpayer rather than the Service tends to have possession of the relevant facts, this situation should not be corrected by volunteering information adverse to the client. Rather, the Service should request whatever information it may deem relevant either informally or by means of summons, and the taxpayer will then be required to produce the necessary information.

Disclosure of "Primary Facts"

While there is no ethical obligation to volunteer evidence adverse to the client's position, the situation is different where the fact unknown to the Service is a "primary fact"—a fact which by itself is dispositive of the matter in controversy. For instance, if a lawyer, negotiating on audit the rate of depreciation applicable to a particular business property, were to learn that the property had been disposed of prior to the beginning of the taxable year, he would have to advise his client to drop the case. If the client refused to do so, the lawyer might be under an ethical obligation to withdraw from the case. The rule involved here is related to the rule which precludes a lawyer from presenting a frivolous case to the court. Although the lawyer need not believe in the merits of his case there must be, at least in civil cases, some reasonable basis for the position that he is taking.

Disclosure of Adverse Law

The duty to disclose adverse law to the Service may be even weaker than the duty to disclose adverse facts. None of the canons require a disclosure of legal authority that casts doubt on the client's case. There is a duty to disclose *to a court* authority directly in point which has been overlooked by the other side. The clear implication would appear to be that there is no duty to call such adverse authority to the attention of opposing counsel prior to the time the matter is submitted to court.

Nevertheless, where as a result of a particular Code provision the taxpayer's position is known to be wrong beyond any question, maintenance of the taxpayer's position would appear to fly in the face of the rule that an attorney should not advance an entirely indefensible argument on behalf of his client. Moreover, failure to disclose adverse law which is dispositive of a particular point would be contrary to the rule which requires the lawyer to urge compliance with the law. Nevertheless, in my view the final decision as to disclosure must remain with the client and, if he vetoes disclosure, the lawyer's only option is to consider whether to continue the representation.

An interesting question arises in this connection where the provision of law unknown to the Service becomes applicable only because of an audit adjustment. The Bostonians were asked the following question:

> You are representing an individual taxpayer in connection with an audit. The principal point raised by the Service is that the pass-through to your client of a loss from a subchapter S company should be reduced because the payments on two notes received by the subchapter S company were really dividends rather than return of capital. The agent has indicated that he is willing to close out the matter if you will agree to dividend treatment with respect to one of the notes. You think that this result would be favorable to the client. The agent has not noted that dividend treatment even with respect to one of the notes would cause the subchapter S company to have too much passive income so that it would be disqualified and there would be no pass-through of losses at all. Would you:
>
> 1. Settle on the basis of a reduction in the pass through of the loss?
>
> 2. Call the attention of the Service to the fact that pass through will not be available?
>
> 3. Request your client's permission to inform the Service?
>
>   (a) Would you continue to represent your client if he failed to give permission?

A majority of the Bostonians would not feel an ethical obligation to disclose the legal problem. This is probably due to the common experience that settlements often do not make sense as a matter of law, but reflect merely the parties' overall appraisal of the situation, including matters such as the time and costs of litigation which clearly have no bearing on the legal merits. Based upon personal experience in a litigation involving a plea of guilty to a lesser offense, the author believes that a tax settlement is in truth only an agreement as to the dollar amount to be paid. The parties at times, and as in the problem just cited, construct a fact situation to justify the result, but this fact situation is hypothetical and there is no ethical basis for concern as to the legal implications of these hypothetical facts.

In settlement negotiations generally, it is my view (which seems to have little support from published authorities) that the obligation to report adverse law or adverse facts varies with concessions made or exactions demanded by the Service on other points. Where the agent has insisted upon a point which in fact has no merit and which was conceded by the taxpayer only to terminate the controversy, rough justice, as contrasted with "the punctilio * * * the most sensitive" of professional ethics, would seem to excuse a reluctance on the part of the taxpayer and his counsel to volunteer information leading to additional taxes.

Disclosure of Subsequent Developments

Frequently there are developments subsequent to the filing of a return which may have a bearing on the matter under audit. The Bostonians were asked the following question:

> At the time of the audit of an estate tax return you are approached by a potential buyer who indicates an interest at $100 a share. You are certain that if the agent, who has indicated a willingness to settle for $50, were to hear of this offer he would insist on at least $80 for estate tax purposes. Assuming the estate tax rates are substantially in excess of the capital gains rates, would you:
>
> 1. Settle as quickly as you can with the agent, then sell the stock.
>
> 2. Inform the agent of the pending offer.
>
> Do you think it would be proper to make an agreement to sell the stock with a closing date postponed until after probable completion of the audit?
>
> Do you think it would be proper to sell the stock and not tell the agent about it?

Most of the Bostonians were inclined to settle the tax audit quickly without disclosure to the agent of the pending offer. Many would be embarrassed to sign an agreement to sell the stock without disclosing the fact to the agent even though it is clear that the sale, particularly if it takes place a substantial time after the date of death, is really only limited evidence of value at the time of death. On the other hand, it must be admitted that if the offer was low, every lawyer would urge it as proof positive in support of his low estate tax valuation.

Disclosure of Mistakes in Computation

In the normal course, after a settlement has been agreed upon in the audit, the Service will compute the additional tax due and send a bill to the taxpayer or his counsel. At times, such bills will contain mistakes in favor of the client. What should a lawyer do when he receives a bill containing a substantial mistake in favor of his client? The Bostonians were given choices between the following courses of action:

1. Inform the [Service] of its mistake.

2. Pass the bill on to the client
    (a) without comment

    (b) with the recommendation that the [Service] be advised of its mistake

    (c) with the recommendation that nothing be done about the matter

    (d) with the advice that it is entirely at the client's option whether or not to inform the Service.

A substantial number would inform the Service of its mistake. Most of the others would pass the bill on to the client with a recommendation that the Service be advised of its mistake. When this problem confronted me in practice, I requested the client's permission to inform the Service of the mistake and fortunately received permission. Clearly, if permission is refused, the lawyer would be under an obligation to consider withdrawal from the case. Indeed, relevant authority would indicate that a computation mistake favorable to the client may have to be called to the adverse party's attention even though the client declines to give permission to make the disclosure.

Disclosure of Unrelated Issues

Not infrequently an attorney or accountant retained to represent a client with respect to a particular issue raised on audit will notice that his client has made a clear error with respect to quite a different matter which has gone unnoticed.

In substance the situation is no different from that discussed already, where without an audit a mistake is discovered in a prior return: Here as there it is the lawyer's obligation to urge his client to permit disclosure of the error to the Service. This obligation is particularly strong where the Service appears to assume that the lawyer is satisfied that the return is correct.

The Bostonians were asked whether in deciding to urge disclosure and how strongly to urge it, they would be influenced by the fact that the disposition of other matters on the audit had been relatively favorable or unfavorable for their client. Nearly all indicated that they would urge disclosure regardless of the result on other issues. However, no matter how strong the desire of the attorney to see the law carried out or, more likely, to clear his name with the Service, nothing would permit the attorney, without his client's permission, to disclose the error. The most the attorney can do in such a situation is to make a written record of his recommendation and to withdraw from further work for the client.

Tax Planning

While tax planning may chronologically be the first step in a chain which includes reporting, audit and litigation, it has been left to the end because at the time the plan is formulated the adviser must ask himself: "How will this transaction be reported? What questions will have to be answered and what arguments will have to be met in the event of audit or litigation?"

It should be emphasized again that the discussion here is limited to the question of what is ethical tax planning rather than what is good tax planning. While any number of plans may save or postpone taxes and be perfectly ethical, they may be undesirable either from a personal or a business point of view or because they are likely to lead to difficult, time-consuming and expensive audit or litigation proceedings.

Certainly one of the obligations of a lawyer who assists a client in devising a plan to reduce taxes is to give him his best estimate of the chances of success and the costs of failure. For the client's sake as well as the lawyer's it is advisable in most cases for the lawyer to put in writing the facts and assumptions on which the plan is based and a frank description of any inherent problems. Failure to do so may prove expensive both for the lawyer and his client.

INCORRECT RETURNS

General

Since the attorney cannot collaborate in a clearly incorrect return, he cannot advise or collaborate in a transaction which will save taxes only if an incorrect return is filed. To take an obvious case, a lawyer cannot advise a client who is a church usher to exchange his personal check for the cash on the collection plate each Sunday (with the explanation that this avoids the risk of having the rectory carry cash over the weekend) when the true purpose of the plan is to file a return on which the check will be claimed as a charitable contribution deduction.

The rule is no different where the contemplated return might not be fraudulent but would clearly be incorrect. Suppose, for instance, the client intends to buy a piece of machinery with a long useful life. The lawyer cannot advise that the machinery be acquired through a short-term lease with an option to purchase for one dollar at the end of the term with a view to deducting the rent as it is paid. If all that may be said for a plan is that it may not be caught on audit and that in any case the client has been able to borrow from the government at 6 per cent, the plan is not ethical.

Client's State of Mind

The above examples involved the creation of evidence to support an incorrect return—the checks for the church "plate" to support the charitable contribution deduction, the lease to support the rental deduction. Is the situation any different when the evidence relates to the client's state of mind?

A client has just been advised by his doctor that he only has a limited time to live and the client asks how he can reduce estate taxes on the transfer of his property to his children.

The lawyer can properly advise the making of inter vivos gifts, since even gifts made in contemplation of death will save taxes.

But can the lawyer ethically say "Pay your doctor in cash and tell him not to bill you. Buy yourself a new wardrobe. Make arrangements for a cruise around the world next year. Send the checks to your children with a covering letter that you are making the gift in order to let them have some experience in the management of money and to reduce your own time and attention to financial matters, etc."

The answer to this question is that it is just as unethical to manufacture misleading evidence relative to the client's state of mind as it is unethical to suggest any other misleading evidence.

Agreement With Others

Not infrequently a taxpayer will be asked to become involved in some plan to save taxes for another. The seller of a business does not care whether a large portion of the sales price is allocated to goodwill or to a building, since both will result in capital gain to him. The buyer, however, cares a great deal since only that part of the price allocated to the building results in a depreciation deduction. Here again it would seem unethical for the seller's lawyer to permit his client to cooperate in a plan under which the buyer will file an incorrect tax return by allocating an unreasonably high portion of the purchase price to the building.

BOLSTERING THE PLAN

The above discussion focused on situations where if all the facts were known to the Service or a court, the taxpayer could not possibly succeed. The situation is quite different where if all the facts were known, the taxpayer would succeed. Thus, for example, there is nothing unethical in advising a taxpayer who has business needs justifying an accumulation of earnings to make a detailed contemporaneous record of those needs.

Given the complexities and uncertain standards of many parts of our tax law, the more frequent case is one where if all the facts were known the result would be uncertain. Is it ethical to structure the transaction in such a way as to reduce the chances of an audit or to improve the taxpayer's position if there is an audit?

A grandfather has created a trust for the benefit of his grandson. The father is the trustee. The law is not clear whether if the income of the trust is used to pay the son's college education the income will be taxed to the father because it discharges his support obligation. Can the lawyer ethically advise that income be currently distributed to the son, placed by the son into a savings account and then used by him from time to time later on, if he so wishes, to pay his college expenses?

The author fervently hopes this advice is not unethical since he himself has given it. However, care is needed in such a situation to prevent the client from extending the arrangement. If, for instance, the payments were made into a bank account for the son, but the father had physical custody of the bankbook and refused to let the son have it except to make withdrawals for college payments, the question might well be raised whether there had in fact been distributions to the son prior to payment of the expenses.

SUBSTANCE VERSUS FORM

The foregoing is related to the familiar doctrine that substance rather than form must govern taxation, a rule frequently applied to defeat complicated avoidance plans. Of course, the Code itself and many reported cases often look to form rather than substance, so that like Latin maxims of statutory construction, "substance over form" tends to be a label given to the result, rather than a guide to it. Precedent, therefore, is the only sound basis for judging elaborate tax reduction plans. If, based upon precedent, form may be recognized, there would seem to be no ethical inhibition against proposing or collaborating in such a plan. If, on the other hand, the plan is unsound, there seems no greater justification for it than for some other less complicated scheme which likewise rests merely on the hope that the truth will not be discovered. Nevertheless, while there are numerous cases in which the court's decision rests on the basis that the transaction was a sham, the author is not familiar with any which in this connection question the ethics of the inventor.

Correcting Prior Mistakes

One area where the problem of form becomes particularly difficult is where the taxpayer has overlooked, innocently enough, one of the myriad of hidden traps in the Code and regulations. To what extent can omissions and commissions be corrected prior to the time the return is filed? The Bostonians were given two problems in this area:

> You are the senior tax partner of your firm. After a business trip you return to your office on March 16 and are told by an associate in the tax department that yesterday he had advised the president of a substantial, closely-held corporation which is a client of your firm, that this was the last day for payment of a dividend that would be taken into account for accumulated earnings tax purposes, that he had urged the payment of such a dividend, but that the president has replied "You are probably right and we will write the checks for payment of the dividend, but we won't distribute the checks until your boss confirms that this is actually necessary." You know that a dividend paid deduction is not available unless the checks have actually been distributed to the shareholders within the two and one-half month period following the close of the fiscal year. The company is very closely held, most of the stock being owned by the top management. You are convinced that if the dividend is not paid a substantial accumulated earnings tax will be imposed on the company. Would you:

> 1. Call your client and advise distribution of the checks.

> 2. Inform the client that is is too late for payment of the dividend for the prior year (realizing that you may subject your firm to liability because an associate failed to advise the client that the technique suggested by the client was not workable).

> 3. Advise the client of the problem, tell him "Technically the [Service] may question the dividend, but chances are they will never raise the question" and that it is up to him what action to take.

Most Bostonians were of the opinion that unless a case could be made for the proposition that the shareholders had constructively received the dividend when the checks were written, the only correct answer is to advise the client it is too late to pay the dividend.

> Suppose that your office has prepared the draft of an irrevocable trust for a client; the intended beneficiaries are the grantor's children and grandchildren but the grantor's wife is also named as a potential beneficiary just in case a quite unforeseen need should arise. You have computed the size of the gift tax assuming that the grantor's wife agrees to gift splitting. Immediately following delivery of the check at the closing, while all are still

present, it occurs to you that unless the wife's interest is strictly limited she will not be able to consent to the gift splitting and the tax will be substantially higher than the grantor had planned. Would it be unethical to say right at the closing "Stop. We made a mistake. Let us substitute a page with the proper language." ?

> Would it be unethical to correct the mistake if it did not come to light until the next day? Or if it was not noticed until immediately prior to filing the return? Does it make a difference if in the interim the trust instrument has been filed with the registry of probate?

Both of these examples involved situations where the mistake was wholly or partly the lawyer's fault. In such cases the pressure on the lawyer to extricate his client and thereby himself is, of course, particularly strong.

In my view, the question of whether in any particular case the correction of an error or the avoidance of an unintended result is ethical, must begin with a determination of whether both as a matter of state law and tax law an "annulment" is possible; and the lawyer must be aware that here the tax law does not necessarily follow state law. Where there is a reasonable possibility that if all of the facts were known to a court, it would not hold the taxpayer to the error, a correction should not be unethical. Of course, the more time that has passed and the more people that have become involved, the more difficult it will be to take the position that what was done in fact was not done in the contemplation of the tax law, because it was unintended or done in error.

LAWYER AS A WITNESS

Occasionally the most important evidence may be that of the lawyer who assisted in the planning or carrying out of a transaction. This may relate to a gift in contemplation of death or to the allocation of a fee between deductible and nondeductible items. The Bostonians were asked to wrestle with the following:

> A client, the President and principal shareholder of a closely held corporation asks you to include in your bill to the corporation services your firm has performed for him personally. You assume that he does so because he plans to have the corporation deduct the fee which would be non-deductible if he paid it himself. Would you a) Agree b) Insist on charging a nominal amount to client c) Insist on charging the client with a full fee d) Say "We will just forget about it" and really forget about it e) Say "We will just forget about it" but in fact take the matter into consideration when fixing the bill to the corporation.

It seems clear that if there are no other shareholders or if it is known they would not object, the bill can be rendered to the corporation as well as to the president. The real question is whether the bill can just hide the personal service under some heading like "miscellaneous other matters" or whether the attorney is bound to identify the work sufficiently to alert an agent, should the bill be reviewed on audit.

The ethically correct answer here is clear and the answers of most Bostonians indicate that they would not feel comfortable helping the president hide a substantial item of income. Most would explain to the president the need to bill him directly but would only bill him a minimum amount. I suspect, however, in many cases the allocation of fees between deductible and nondeductible charges reflects to an excessive degree the personal interest of lawyers to improve client acceptance of the bill by allocating charges in a manner and to entities most helpful to the client.

OBLIGATION TO THIRD PARTIES

Tax planning for the client may also have tax consequences to others. The principal ethical obligation of the attorney in such a situation is to assure the others are also represented by counsel or at least are made aware that their own tax situation is also being affected. Thus, where the chief executive of a company which is represented by a lawyer requests the lawyer's advice how best to structure a deferred compensation arrangement for himself, the lawyer should realize there is a potential conflict of interest between the executive and his company and suggest appropriate arrangements.

If the other party is represented by counsel, is there any obligation to point out the tax consequences to the other party of the actions proposed by you? The Bostonians were asked their reaction to the following:

Your client is purchasing an interest in a partnership carrying on a construction business on the basis of the selling partner's pro rata share of book value of the partnership assets other than equipment with respect to which the price is based upon its appraised value which is substantially in excess of its depreciated book value. In your presence the seller's tax adviser confirms to seller his prior advice that since there are no unrealized receivables or substantially appreciated inventory, all of his gain will be capital gain. You know this advice is unsound because the statute provides that to the extent the gain is due to depreciation recapture it is treated as an unrealized receivable. It is clear that if the seller were aware of this fact he would insist upon and could probably obtain a higher price for his interest. Would you:

1) Advise the seller or his counsel of the mistake.

2) Inform your client of the mistake and

        (a) Tell him it is entirely at his option whether seller should be informed.

        (b) Tell him that you will withdraw if he refuses permission to inform seller.

3) Do nothing.

4) Request the advice of _____

                            (fill in blank)

From the answers it is clear that most Bostonians would feel uncomfortable to see a brother lawyer make a mistake of the type that could well make him liable in a malpractice suit. However, most doubted that they were ethically obligated to inform opposing counsel of his mistake and would not do so without their client's permission. Many would withdraw if they were not given permission to point out the error, particularly if the negotiations were being conducted in a friendly and cooperative manner where the other side might in a sense rely on the opposing tax specialist. Given less than amicable negotiations, few felt an obligation to go further than to point out the error to their client. This is different, of course, from the attitude taken with respect to errors of law in dealings with the Service, where the client's obligation to pay any tax due results in an ethical duty on his counsel to urge compliance with that obligation.

Conclusion

Nearly all tax practitioners if asked whether they wish in their practice to adhere to the standards of professional ethics would answer in the affirmative. However, far too many think of professional ethics as something nebulous and vague to which there is no guide other than their own consciences. The difficulty with this "situation ethics" approach is that it leaves the practitioner unprepared for temptation: Where the need to build a practice or to retain a client are on one side of the balance, it is easy for unguided conscience to throw in the sponge with the thought "Everybody does it. Why should I be a sucker?"

PREPARING YOUR OWN CODE

In the field of professional conduct, we can improve upon situation ethics in at least two respects. The first is to put down in black and white and circulate to every tax practitioner in the office a code of conduct in tax matters.   * * *

        * * *

CONSULTATION WITH OTHERS

The other improvement upon letting our conscience be the guide 's to be aware that our livelihood depends in the first place upon our ˙lients. Under these circumstances our judgment as to what is ethically permissible may well be affected. In case of doubt, therefore, the lawyer should make it a point to consult another—where the matter is important to the firm as a whole, someone outside the firm. Not only will consultation with an unprejudiced outsider prevent what might otherwise be a misstep, but I have found I sleep better when advised by one not directly involved that my course of action is proper.

IMPROVING GENERAL STANDARDS

So far we have referred only to what a lawyer can do to improve his own professional standards. However, neither from the lawyer's nor from the client's point of view is it desirable for an individual lawyer to adhere to standards substantially different from those of the profession as a whole—even if they are believed to be better. Accordingly, tax lawyers should make more of an effort to establish and improve their rules of conduct, perhaps in a manner similar to that followed by the American Institute of Certified Public Accountants.[b]

Finally, I have found that in my own practice the most difficult ethical problems arise where, due to inadvertence either by the client or his lawyer, a transaction which is not in any way tax motivated has quite unexpected and potentially disastrous tax consequences. This is a direct result of the complications of the tax law and creates a conflict of true ethics with professional ethics: A law so filled with special rules, elections, exceptions and exceptions to exceptions which hide its true import and cause it to operate as an ex post facto law is not a just law. To close the discussion of one subject by opening another: Tax lawyers can make no greater contribution to the ethical aspects of tax practice than by working for improvement and simplification of the tax laws.

GUIDELINES TO TAX PRACTICE

Report of the Committee on Standards of Tax Practice,
Section of Taxation, American Bar Association

31 Tax Lawyer 551 (1978).

The Committee on Standards of Tax Practice urges law firms to adopt guidelines to assist particularly their younger lawyers in observing ethical standards in tax practice. A sample of such guideline prepared by the Committee follows.

* * *

Many who are not themselves experienced tax practitioners believe that in tax practice "Everybody Does It": Everyone inflates his charitable deductions; everyone claims as a business need for accu-

---

b. See the various Statements on Responsibilities in Tax Practice issued by the American Institute of Certified Public Accountants.

mulated earnings tax purposes an expansion plan dreamed up solely by the tax adviser; every closely-held company deducts the car used by the president's wife as a business expense; everyone puts his minor children or his aged mother on the corporate payroll; everyone backdates his instruments when it helps save taxes.

Experienced tax practitioners know that in fact Everybody doesn't do it. But the general impression that sham and corner cutting are an acceptable and customary part of tax practice constitutes a threat to the way in which most of us want to live and work. Particularly for the sake of younger lawyers, it is important for a firm to be very clear what it will and will not do in helping clients reduce their tax burden.

For this reason alone, it may be helpful for a firm to establish guidelines for the conduct of its tax practice. Such guidelines may also help make clear to everyone in the firm that right and wrong in tax practice is more than a feel of the seat of the pants, or as it is now more elegantly expressed, "situation ethics"; that there is in fact a substantial body of established rules. The adoption of guidelines may assist younger lawyers in developing a proper approach to their own work and in providing the necessary guidance to their clients.

For all of these reasons we believe that it would be useful for law firms generally to adopt guidelines for dealing with ethical problems commonly arising in their tax practice. We recognize that the content of these guidelines must vary from firm to firm, depending upon the size of the firm and its tax department and particularly the nature of its tax practice. A firm largely engaged in criminal work will need different guidelines than a firm principally engaged in tax planning. What follows is an adaptation of a guideline used by a medium-sized law firm engaged largely in the non-litigious aspects of tax practice.

* * *

GUIDELINES TO TAX PRACTICE OF A, B & C

There is nothing in any way unethical in assisting clients in arranging their affairs so as to reduce their tax obligations. However, any system of law, and particularly one which involves self-assessment, can operate only if citizens as a whole, and lawyers in particular, respect the law. As all of us know, questions of professional ethics arise frequently in tax practice. They result from a conflict between two basic principles:

(1) The lawyer owes to his client a duty of "warm zeal" within the bounds of the law and, without authority, he cannot disclose his client's confidences and secrets.

(2) The lawyer has an obligation to support the law and the administration of the law, which at times may require disclosure, and,

further, he must not seek to deceive his adversaries in general and government agencies in particular.

Every attorney should adhere to accepted standards of professional ethics: This firm insists upon adherence. Questions of professional ethics should not be resolved merely on the basis of individual conscience, but on the basis of clear and accessible rules applicable to the entire office. With this in mind, we are publishing and circulating to every attorney in our firm the guidelines set forth below to promote familiarity with our approach and to assist everyone in the continuing conduct of the kind of practice we can enjoy and of which we can be proud. The firm expects each attorney involved in tax matters to adhere to these guidelines.

Return Preparation

(1) Reasonable doubts in connection with the preparation of a return may be resolved in favor of a client, and the existence of such doubts need not generally be flagged by explanatory statements or riders. However, this office will not sign a return which contains any item that we believe to lack reasonable basis, either in the law or the facts. For instance, on an estate tax return, while it is entirely proper to use a "conservative" valuation, it must be within the limits of what is reasonable and defensible.

(2) We will not include clearly erroneous items merely in order to "have points that we can give to the agent on audit" or in the hope that the matter may not be discovered, or because the client needs the cash and wants to defer payment.

(3) We have no obligation to audit the taxpayer and we normally assume that the tax return information supplied by clients is correct and complete. However, where a comparison with the prior year's return or other information indicates that the material supplied to us may be incorrect or incomplete, we must make further inquiry.

(4) We will not suggest to clients that they file returns we would not be prepared to sign.

(5) If a client refuses to accept our advice and insists upon filing a return we believe to be erroneous, we should not sign the return and should advise the client in writing of the reason for our disagreement. The lawyer concerned should also consider with a partner in the Tax Department and a senior partner outside the Department whether the firm should continue other representation of the client.

(6) Section 6694(a) of the Internal Revenue Code imposes a penalty upon anyone who prepares an income tax return or refund claim containing an understatement of liability, any part of which is due to negligent or intentional disregard of rules and regulations. Under the regulations, if a preparer in good faith and with reasonable basis determines that a rule or regulation does not accurately reflect

the Code, he will not be deemed to have been negligent. Therefore, any return preparation involving a failure to follow a revenue ruling or regulation must be fully documented in the firm's files. Further, any action which may expose the firm to the risk of negligence penalty must be approved by the senior partner in the Tax Department.

(7) If we discover a clear and substantial mistake in a prior year's return not barred by the statute of limitations, whether made by us or not, we must advise the client of the error. T.D. Cir. 230 ¶ 10.21. In doing so we should explain that present law does not make mandatory the filing of an amended return but that a tax that is owing is a debt that should be paid and therefore in general an amended return should be filed to correct all but minor errors.

If correction seems to give rise to a risk of penalty, we must describe the risk and explore ways of paying the tax due that will minimize exposure to the penalty. However, in any situation involving potential fraud charges we should carefully explain to the taxpayer the benefits and hazards of the various options available, including any constitutional right not to cooperate with the Service.

Audit Representation

(1) We are not under any obligation in an audit to volunteer to the Service evidence or law adverse to our client's position. However, where the fact or authority involved is clearly dispositive of the matter, we should generally urge the client to permit disclosure. Also, mathematical mistakes favorable to the client, whether made by the client or the Service, should, with the client's permission, be disclosed.

(2) We do not knowingly make any misstatements of fact or law to the Service or continue to handle a case where a client insists on lying. We make reasonable efforts to satisfy ourselves as to the facts in each case.

(3) If we find that in the course of an audit a client has affirmatively misled the Internal Revenue Service, we must advise the client to correct the misleading statement. If the client refuses, we should normally withdraw from the matter. If we continue the representation, we must make sure that our continuing representation is handled in such a way as not to corroborate the misleading statement of the client.

Tax Planning

(1) We will counsel against any tax plans that are bound to fail if all of the facts become known to the Service. We will not participate in transactions entirely lacking in economic substance and intended solely to conceal or mislead.

(2) We will not assist in the offering of a "tax shelter" program unless in our judgment there is a substantial likelihood that the tax consequences will be resolved in favor of the taxpayer. Even though

we may have disclosed in our legal opinion all of the risks and possible adverse tax consequences of a tax shelter program, the fact that we gave an opinion may be taken by the public as our endorsement of the program.

(3) We should generally counsel against borderline plans since borders in taxation frequently shift sufficiently that a transaction just on the right side when planned is just on the wrong side when audited. If we do advise with respect to such plan—and at times such plans are justifiable on the basis that the client has much to gain and little to lose—we should point out the risks before the plan is implemented.

Resolving Ethical Questions

(1) Ethical problems in practice are best resolved by a combination of research and discussion with others. A good place to begin research is the A.B.A. Opinion 314 and B. Bittker's, Professional Responsibility in Federal Tax Practice (1970). See also Sellin, Professional Responsibility of the Tax Practitioner, 52 Taxes, 584 (1974); Corneel, Ethical Guidelines for Tax Practice, 28 Tax L.Rev. 1 (1972) and Rowen, When May a Lawyer Advise a Client That He May Take a Position on His Tax Return, 29 Tax Lawyer 237 (1976). Note, however, that none of the foregoing reflect the most recent revisions in Circular 230 or the impact of the return preparers' negligence penalty under section 6694. In connection with return preparation, the AICPA Statements on Responsibilities in Tax Practice are helpful.

(2) We want all lawyers working here to feel comfortable with the standards observed in our tax practice. Anyone who has any question concerning the propriety of any actual or proposed action, whether involving him or another lawyer in the firm, should promptly discuss the question with one or more partners in the firm.

(3) The foregoing guidelines must be applied to all of our clients alike, without reference to their monetary importance to the firm. However, we must recognize that our financial interest in a matter may affect our judgment as to whether a contemplated course is proper. Accordingly, if we have serious doubt as to the propriety of a particular action and the matter is material from the point of view of the firm, either by risking the loss of an important client or by exposing the firm to the charge that it made a mistake in a substantial matter, it may be advisable to obtain the opinion of another lawyer outside the firm. In such an instance the partner in charge of the Tax Department will be responsible for seeking such an opinion.

                                        The Management Committee

ABA COMMITTEE ON PROFESSIONAL ETHICS OPINION 314

51 A.B.A.J. 671 (1965).

The Committee has received a number of specific inquiries regarding the ethical relationship between the Internal Revenue Service and lawyers practicing before it. Rather than answer each of these separately, the Committee, believing this to be a matter of general interest, has formulated the following general principles governing this relationship.

Canon 1 says: "It is the duty of the lawyer to maintain towards the Courts a respectful attitude." Canon 15 says that the lawyer owes "warm zeal" to his client and that "The office of attorney does not permit, much less does it demand of him for any client, violation of law or any manner of fraud or chicane." Canon 16 says: "A lawyer should use his best efforts to prevent his clients from doing those things which the lawyer himself ought not to do, particularly with reference to their conduct towards Courts * * *." Canon 22 says: "The conduct of the lawyer before the Court and with other lawyers should be characterized by candor and fairness."

All of these canons are pertinent to the subject here under consideration, for Canon 26 provides: "A lawyer openly, and in his true character, may render professional services * * * in advocacy of claims before departments of government, upon the same principles of ethics which justify his appearance before the Courts * * *."

Certainly a lawyer's advocacy before the Internal Revenue Service must be governed by "the same principles of ethics which justify his appearance before the Courts". But since the service, however fair and impartial it may try to be, is the representative of one of the parties, does the lawyer owe it the same duty of disclosure which is owed to the courts? Or is his duty to it more nearly analogous to that which he owes his brother attorneys in the conduct of cases which should be conducted in an atmosphere of candor and fairness but are admittedly adversary in nature? An analysis of the nature of the Internal Revenue Service will serve to throw some light upon the answer to these questions.

The Internal Revenue Service is neither a true tribunal, nor even a quasi-judicial institution. It has no machinery or procedure for adversary proceedings before impartial judges or arbiters, involving the weighing of conflicting testimony of witnesses examined and cross-examined by opposing counsel and the consideration of arguments of counsel for both sides of a dispute. While its procedures provide for "fresh looks" through departmental reviews and informal and formal conference procedures, few will contend that the service provides any truly dispassionate and unbiased consideration to the taxpayer. Although willing to listen to taxpayers and their representatives and obviously intending to be fair, the service is not designed and does not purport to be unprejudiced and unbiased in the judicial sense.

It by no means follows that a lawyer is relieved of all ethical responsibility when he practices before this agency. There are certain things which he clearly cannot do, and they are set forth explicitly in the canons of ethics.

Canon 15 scorns the false claim that it is the duty of the lawyer to do whatever may enable him to succeed in winning his client's cause no matter how unscrupulous, and after making it clear that the lawyer owes entire devotion to the interest of his client, Canon 15 concludes as follows:

> * * * But it is steadfastly to be borne in mind that the great trust of the lawyer is to be performed within and not without the bounds of the law. The office of attorney *does not permit,* much less does it *demand* of him for any client, violation of law or any manner of fraud or chicane. He must obey his own conscience and not that of his client [emphasis supplied].

Canon 22, relating to candor and fairness, states that

> It is unprofessional and dishonorable to deal other than candidly with the facts * * * in the presentation of causes.
>
> These and all kindred practices are unprofessional and unworthy of an officer of the law charged, as is the lawyer, with the duty of aiding in the administration of justice.

Canon 29 provides in part that a lawyer

> should strive at all times to uphold the honor and to maintain the dignity of the profession and to improve not only the law but the administration of justice.

Canon 32 states that

> No client * * * is entitled to receive nor should any lawyer render * * * any advice involving disloyalty to the law whose ministers we are * * *. [He] advances the honor of his profession and the best interests of his client when he * * * gives advice tending to impress upon the client and his undertaking exact compliance with the strictest principles of moral law * * *. [A] lawyer will find his highest honor in a deserved reputation for fidelity to private trust and to public duty, as an honest man and as a patriotic and loyal citizen.

In addition, the preamble to the canons concludes as follows:

> No code or set of rules can be framed, which will particularize all the duties of the lawyer * * * in all the relations of professional life. The following canons of ethics are adopted by the American Bar Association as a general

guide, yet the enumeration of particular duties should not be construed as a denial of the existence of others equally imperative, though not specifically mentioned.

The problem arises when, in the course of his professional employment, the attorney acquires information bearing upon the strength of his client's claim. Although a number of canons have general bearing on the problem (Canons 15, 16, 22 and 26), Canon 37 regarding client confidences and Canons 29, 41 and 44 regarding perjury, fraud and deception and the withdrawal of an attorney are most relevant.

For example, what is the duty of a lawyer in regard to disclosure of the weaknesses in his client's case in the course of negotiations for the settlement of a tax case?

Negotiation and settlement procedures of the tax system do not carry with them the guarantee that a correct tax result necessarily occurs. The latter happens, if at all, solely by reason of chance in settlement of tax controversies just as it might happen with regard to other civil disputes. In the absence of either judicial determination or of a hypothetical exchange of files by adversaries, counsel will always urge in aid of settlement of a controversy the strong points of his case and minimize the weak; this is in keeping with Canon 15, which does require "warm zeal" on behalf of the client. Nor does the absolute duty not to make false assertions of fact require the disclosure of weaknesses in the client's case and in no event does it require the disclosure of his confidences, unless the facts in the attorney's possession indicate beyond reasonable doubt that a crime will be committed. A wrong, or indeed sometimes an unjust, tax result in the settlement of a controversy is not a crime.

Similarly, a lawyer who is asked to advise his client in the course of the preparation of the client's tax returns may freely urge the statement of positions most favorable to the client just as long as there is reasonable basis for those positions. Thus where the lawyer believes there is a reasonable basis for a position that a particular transaction does not result in taxable income, or that certain expenditures are properly deductible as expenses, the lawyer has no duty to advise that riders be attached to the client's tax return explaining the circumstances surrounding the transaction or the expenditures.

The foregoing principle necessarily relates to the lawyer's ethical obligations—what he is *required* to do. Prudence may recommend procedures not required by ethical considerations. Thus, even where the lawyer believes that there is no obligation to reflect a transaction in or with his client's return, nevertheless he *may*, as a tactical matter, advise his client to disclose the transaction in reasonable detail by way of a rider to the return. This occurs when it is to the client's advantage to be free from either a *claim* of fraud (albeit unfounded) or to have the protection of a shorter statute of limitations (which might be available by the full disclosure of such a transaction in detail by way of a rider to the return).

In all cases, with regard both to the preparation of returns and negotiating administrative settlements, the lawyer is under a duty not to mislead the Internal Revenue Service deliberately and affirmatively, either by misstatements or by silence or by permitting his client to mislead. The difficult problem arises where the client has in fact misled but without the lawyer's knowledge or participation. In that situation, upon discovery of the misrepresentation, the lawyer must advise the client to correct the statement; if the client refuses, the lawyer's obligation depends on all the circumstances.

Fundamentally, subject to the restrictions of the attorney-client privilege imposed by Canon 37, the lawyer may have the duty to withdraw from the matter. If for example, under all the circumstances, the lawyer believes that the service relies on him as corroborating statements of his client which he knows to be false, then he is under a duty to disassociate himself from any such reliance unless it is obvious that the very act of disassociation would have the effect of violating Canon 37. Even then, however, if a direct question is put to the lawyer, he must at least advise the service that he is not in a position to answer.

But as an advocate before a service which itself represents the adversary point of view, where his client's case is fairly arguable, a lawyer is under no duty to disclose its weaknesses, any more than he would be to make such a disclosure to a brother lawyer. The limitations within which he must operate are best expressed in Canon 22:

> It is not candid or fair for the lawyer knowingly to misquote the contents of a paper, the testimony of a witness, the language or the argument of opposing counsel, or the language of a decision or a textbook; or with knowledge of its invalidity, to cite as authority a decision that has been overruled, or a statute that has been repealed; or in argument to assert as a fact that which has not been proved, or in those jurisdictions where a side has the opening and closing arguments to mislead his opponent by concealing or withholding positions in his opening argument upon which his side then intends to rely.

> It is unprofessional and dishonorable to deal other than candidly with the facts in taking the statements of witnesses, in drawing affidavits and other documents, and in the presentation of causes.

So long as a lawyer remains within these limitations, and so long as his duty is "performed within and not without the bounds of the law", he "owes 'entire devotion to the interest of the client, warm zeal in the maintenance and defense of his rights and the exertion of his utmost learning and ability', to the end that nothing be taken or be withheld from him, save by the rules of law, legally applied" in his practice before the Internal Revenue Service, as elsewhere (Canon 15).

WHEN MAY A LAWYER ADVISE A CLIENT THAT HE MAY TAKE A POSITION ON HIS TAX RETURN?

James R. Rowen
29 Tax Lawyer 237 (1976).

* * *

Opinion 314 of the American Bar Association's Committee on Professional Ethics, promulgated in 1965 [unqualifiedly holds]:

* * *

(1) An attorney may advise a client that he may take a position on his tax return if there is a "reasonable basis" for the position. There is no requirement that the attorney or the client believe that the position will ultimately prevail.

(2) If such a "reasonable basis" exists, there is no need to put a rider on the return explaining the circumstances.

Opinion 314 represents as authoritative a statement on the ethical standards in this situation as one can find. On the premise that a lawyer may adhere to prevailing ethical standards, rather than follow what he personally considers to be ethical, he should be able to follow Opinion 314 until it is modified by the American Bar Association or by statute, or rejected by the courts.

* * *

* * * The premise of Opinion 314 is that the Service generally takes an adversary attitude in auditing returns, and that "few will contend that the Service provides any truly dispassionate and unbiased consideration to the taxpayer." * * * The Opinion notes that it is not necessary to cite adverse authority to opposing counsel in an adversary proceeding and suggests that the taxpayer has no greater obligation of disclosure in a tax return than an attorney has in dealing with such opposing counsel. * * *

Even if one accepts the premise of Opinion 314 that a tax return is like a brief in an adversary proceeding, one may question whether the ordinary rules of adversary litigation should apply to the tax return. The rationale of the adversary system is that justice may best be reached between contending parties when each contending party, represented by counsel, presents his argument to an independent tribunal. As applied to the tax return system, the premise would be that the taxpayer is presenting his position as to his tax liability. The government then has an opportunity to audit the taxpayer's return and to present its position on the tax liability. When there is a conflict, each side, more or less equally represented by counsel, can then present its position to an independent tribunal, which can then make a rationale decision. This is fine in theory, but in practice the government is not able to audit most returns effectively * * *. The premise of the adversary system, that the two adversaries will be in an equal position to uncover and present the facts, is unrealistic as applied to the current tax system. While the government's disadvantage is overcome somewhat by the rule that places the burden of proof on the taxpayer, this rule only applies when an issue has been raised; it does not help the government to uncover the issue.

* * *

* * * Even if one rejects (as I do) the rationale of Opinion 314 that a tax return is like a brief in an adversary proceeding, it may nevertheless be possible to justify the holding of Opinion 314 that a reasonable basis is sufficient for taking a position on a tax return.

[There are] certain policy arguments for permitting a taxpayer to take a position on his return where there is a reasonable basis therefore, i. e., the difficulty of applying an "honest belief" standard, the disadvantage that the "honest belief" standard imposes on the intellectually honest taxpayer, and the fact that the "honest belief" standard does not give taxpayer the opportunity to litigate doubtful questions. A further point is that filing a tax return is a special type of conduct; a tax return is an information return that a taxpayer is required to file with the government. It may be argued that in such a return the taxpayer should not be asked to be impartial and should not be held liable for penalties when he takes a position for which there is a reasonable basis. * * *

* * *

A rule that permits a taxpayer to take a "reasonable basis" position on his return would not seriously impede the fair administration of the tax laws if there were sufficient legal incentives to encourage taxpayers to disclose doubtful items. If a taxpayer takes a "reasonable basis" position on his return and does not disclose the doubtful item, it is less likely that an agent will uncover the item and assert additional tax. Accordingly, unless there are other legal incentives to a taxpayer to disclose doubtful items, the taxpayer often does not want to do it. Current legal incentives to disclose doubtful items seem inadequate * * *.

* * *

As Opinion 314 itself points out, it may be desirable to attach a rider to a return disclosing doubtful issues in order to avoid danger of the mere claim of fraud. The mere claim of fraud by an agent, even though it is defeated, would be very disturbing to most taxpayers. Accordingly, this danger is an incentive to many taxpayers to disclose material items when the taxpayer has a reasonable basis for his position but believes that the Service would have strong authority for a contrary position.

However, the cases in the tax area hold that a taxpayer cannot be held liable for criminal or civil fraud, which require proof of willfulness, if he prepares his return in good faith reliance on the advice of counsel. I have not found any discussion in the criminal cases of a "reasonable basis" opinion. However, if, as Opinion 314 states, counsel may advise a client to take a position on his return when there is a "reasonable basis" for the position, it should follow that the client may rely on such opinion, and that such reliance will be a defense to a criminal indictment. Opinion 314 seems to assume this point.

*   *   *

*   *   * The American Bar Association or Congress could change the rule of Opinion 314. For example, in appropriate language, Congress could provide that an adviser may only advise a client to take a position on a tax return if (a) the adviser believes the position to be correct, or (b) the adviser believes that there is a reasonable basis for the position and advises the client to disclose the issue and the facts relating to the issue on the return.

Such a rule would not be subject to some of the objections that have been made to a rule that a taxpayer can only take a position if he "honestly believes" that his position is correct. In particular, the intellectually honest taxpayer would not be foreclosed from raising a debatable issue. While such a reformulated rule might still encourage the aggressive tax adviser to stretch his opinion, the adviser would at least have to be consistent in his advice to clients in similar situations. If he advised one client that the law provided a certain result X, he could not advise another client to take a contrary position without advising him to disclose the issue and the facts on his return. Opinion 314 does not now hold the adviser to any standard of consistency.

*   *   * To make a suggestion, the following provision, which uses some of the language of section 6501, might be added to the penalty provisions of the Code:

> If part of any underpayment is attributable to an erroneous omission, deduction, credit, or classification of any item of income, deduction, or credit where
>
>> (a) the item is not described in the return, or in a statement to the return, in a manner adequate to apprise the Secretary or his delegate of the nature and amount of such item, and
>>
>> (b) the taxpayer's treatment of the item is contrary to
>>
>>> (i) a regulation or published ruling of the Internal Revenue Service;

(ii) a determination upon audit of a prior return of taxpayer or a related person (as defined in section ——);

(iii) a position taken by taxpayer or a related person in another return; or

(iv) a position taken by another party to the transaction to which the item relates where taxpayer has reason to believe that such other person has taken or intends to take such a position;

there shall be added to the tax an amount equal to 25 percent of such part.

While this provision does not cover a large area of doubtful items, particularly those involving the categorization of facts, it is difficult to draft a broader provision that is sufficiently definite.

This provision would differ from section 6653 (the negligence penalty) in two important respects. First, the penalty is increased to 25 percent, which is much more meaningful than a five percent penalty, but still less than the 50 percent fraud penalty. Second, the penalty would apply irrespective of whether there is negligence or intentional disregard of rules and regulations; the penalty could not be avoided by a legal opinion.

The argument may be made that a 25 percent penalty could operate unfairly on taxpayers who do not have good tax advice. A defense to the penalty could be provided where the taxpayer establishes that he did not have reason to believe that the item was of a type that required disclosure. However, the standards for avoiding the penalty should be tighter than the obtaining of a "reasonable basis" opinion.

UNITED STATES v. YORKE

(Unpublished Opinion, D. Md., July 19, 1976).

[YOUNG, J.:] [The taxpayer was prosecuted for failing to report as income $400 per week of advances denominated as "loans" in documents prepared by his employer's tax counsel. These advances were subject to forgiveness in the event that the taxpayer did not realize sufficient income from certain speculative stock purchases to finance the repayment from capital gains. The defendant contended that he attempted to avoid rather than evade his tax liability.]

* * *

The key to the application of the distinction [between avoidance and evasion] should be the taxpayer's state of mind. An honest belief that a particular scheme is legal negates the element of willfulness, and perforce renders the conduct non-criminal. Some authorities have gone even further and suggested that a tax practitioner need not have a genuine belief that a particular scheme will succeed. His ethical obligation is satisfied when he can find a reasonable basis in the law for the scheme, regardless of whether or not he believes it will ultimately succeed. See Opinion 314 of the A.B.A. Committee on Professional Ethics, 51 A.B.A.J. 671 (1965).

Surely, it would be unfair to judge the client's criminal liability on a stricter standard than his lawyer's ethical obligation. The question of a client's criminal liability for following such so-called "reasonable basis" advice is briefly posed by James R. Rowen in his article "When May A Lawyer Advise A Client That He May Take A Position On His Tax Return?" 29 Tax Lawyer 237 (1976). The author criticizes the A.B.A.'s position on the lawyer's duty, but his research disclosed no criminal case in which a "reasonable basis" opinion had resulted in liability.

The scheme in the instant case is a very aggressive one. The Court is somewhat shocked that it was approved by competent counsel * * *. Indeed, the literature in the entire area of tax avoidance planning, particularly the A.B.A. opinion, tends to take a rather cavalier attitude toward obviously questionable schemes.

The instant case, however, is a criminal matter. This Court's attitude toward the ethics of some tax planners should not affect its views herein. Regardless of what position is taken on the avoidance-evasion distinction, the Government has not produced a *prima facie* case of criminal liability. It is clear that the Defendant, while perhaps excessively aggressive in his planning, had both an honest belief in the legality of his plan and a reasonable basis in the law for it, as well. His implementation of that plan included full documentation, and no attempt to conceal.

Accordingly, the Defendant's motion for judgment of acquittal is this day granted.

SECTION 3.   THE MULTIPLE REPRESENTATION ISSUE

BACKER v. COMMISSIONER

275 F.2d 141 (5th Cir. 1960).

TUTTLE, Circuit Judge.

This action covers a very narrow compass. Appellant is a Certified Public Accountant who had been employed in connection with preparation of the tax returns of one Walter D. Williams, Jr. In the course of investigation of Williams' tax affairs for five years numerous consultations were had between the Internal Revenue agents and special agents and appellant. Appellant fully answered all questions asked, produced all papers requested during the many interviews conducted both with and without the presence of an attorney for taxpayer.

In this posture of affairs, after appellant had disclosed all the information sought from him touching on Williams' tax affairs, he was subpoenaed to appear and testify under oath before the Special Agent at a prescribed time and place. He did appear, accompanied by counsel, Cubbedge Snow, Esquire. Mr. Snow had previously filed a power of attorney to represent the taxpayer, Williams, in the investigation of his tax matters. The Special Agent stated that Mr. Snow could not be present at the investigation of appellant, whereupon appellant, on the advice of his counsel, declined to submit to the interrogation; counsel based this action on the provisions of the Administrative Procedure Act which says:

> "Any person compelled to appear in person before any agency or representative thereof shall be accorded the right to be accompanied, represented, and advised by counsel
> *   *   *" 5 U.S.C.A. § 1005.

Thereupon the Commissioner of Internal Revenue filed his petition with the United States District Court to require the attendance of Backer "without the presence of counsel retained by or connected with the said Walter D. Williams, Jr."

The trial court expressly found that counsel was employed by Backer at his own expense and without any suggestion from the taxpayer.[1] It also found that both appellant and his counsel were "of unquestioned and unquestionable character" and that neither of them had attempted in any manner to impede the investigation.

Nevertheless, the court held that Backer must appear to give his testimony without being represented by Mr. Snow. The trial court said:

> "*   *   * Whether or not the Commissioner is correct in contending that the mere presence of taxpayer's counsel at the investigation while taxpayer's accountant is being questioned serves as a damper upon the voluntary testimony

1. The findings included the following: "In this case both respondent and his counsel are unquestionably able, reputable and highly ethical practitioners in their respective professions. Each has furnished to the investigators all information requested. The respondent has permitted the investigators to photostat his work papers and has not refused to put anything in writing. Taxpayer did not suggest that respondent retain taxpayer's counsel and respondent did not consult taxpayer about it. Respondent retained taxpayer's counsel in this case because he had confidence in him and because of said counsel's familiarity with the entire matter. Respondent has paid said counsel a retainer and does not look to taxpayer for reimbursement thereof. Both respondent and counsel have concluded that there is no conflict of interest. Neither respondent nor his counsel sees any necessity of respondent's testimony being taken under oath but neither of them has attempted in any manner to impede this investigation unless it can be said, as the Commissioner argues, that the mere presence of taxpayer's counsel at the investigation, even though he refrains from obstructive tactics, serves as a damper on the voluntary testimony of taxpayer's accountant."

of taxpayer's accountant, I think the correct solution to this problem was pointed out in United States v. Smith, D.C. Conn.1949, 87 F.Supp. 293, 294, where the Court said:

> " 'While no harm seems likely from such a situation in this case, since the knowledge of these witnesses is necessarily also the knowledge of the taxpayer, any possibility of prejudice to the investigation should be obviated by requiring that counsel be not connected with, or retained by, the taxpayer.' "

The Commissioner does not base his right to exclude any particular counsel from such representation of the appellant on any Regulations of the Internal Revenue Service. He acts under a policy established by him prior to the adoption of the Administrative Procedure Act. The policy is stated in a Manual of Instructions for Special Agents, Intelligence Unit, July 10, 1945, which gave a witness the right stated as follows:

> "The right to have an attorney present at the time of his questioning for the purpose of advising the witness relevant to his right to refuse to give any answers which might incriminate him under the laws of the United States. Under this policy, however, a third party witness is entitled to the attendance of his own counsel, but not the counsel for taxpayer."

It is clear that the right to counsel guaranteed under the Administrative Procedure Act is much broader than the right to have an attorney to advise him relative to his rights under the Fifth Amendment. The Act says such counsel may accompany, represent and advise the witness, without any limitation. Moreover, it seems quite doubtful that the policy statement itself, even if it were valid under the new act, covers the situation where the counsel is in fact counsel for the witness, even though he is also counsel for the taxpayer. It draws the distinction between counsel for the witness and counsel for the taxpayer. It does not seem to deal with the situation where one lawyer is both.

In any event, we are not here dealing with an attempted limitation on the generality of the right guaranteed under the Administrative Procedure Act by a formally adopted department regulation. We, therefore, do not come to the question whether, if under formal rule-making procedures the Treasury Department had adopted regulations purporting to qualify the right of a witness to be represented by a lawyer who is also counsel for the person under investigation, such regulation would warrant the ruling of the court below. Certain it is that in the absence of any such regulation the Commissioner cannot put limitations on the general authority to have counsel as granted by the statute by saying that the witness's choice cannot include one who also represents the taxpayer.

We recognize that what is in issue here is not the constitutional right to counsel. It is, however, a statutory right. The term "right to counsel" has always been construed to mean counsel of one's choice. We think this is the plain and necessary meaning of this provision of the law. When Congress used the terms "right to be accompanied, represented, and advised by counsel," it must have used the language in the regularly accepted connotation, even though the language of the courts in using it was in connection with the right to counsel guaranteed by the Sixth Amendment to the Constitution.

Nor do we have a case in which the Commissioner is complaining to a trial court that counsel is in fact obstructing the orderly inquiry process by improper conduct or tactics.

None of the harm which the Commissioner here apprehends will result from letting taxpayer's counsel represent a witness as his own selected counsel will result except upon the failure of counsel to conduct himself in accord with his sworn duty to the court. If he does so fail then is the time for remedial action to be taken. Such action is not permissible when, as here, the trial court and government counsel reject any suggestion that either the witness or counsel will violate either the law or the ethics of their profession in the proposed investigation.

We hold that under the circumstances of this case the action of the District Court was not authorized.

The order of the District Court is reversed and vacated and the case remanded for further proceedings not inconsistent with this opinion.

DUAL REPRESENTATION

IRS Handbook for Special Agents, § 343.6 (April 13, 1981).

(1) Treasury Department Circular No. 230 (Rev. 6–79), which covers the practice of attorneys, certified public accountants, enrolled agents, and enrolled actuaries before the Internal Revenue Service, provides the following with respect to dual representation:

§ 10.29 Conflicting Interests

No attorney, certified public accountant, or enrolled agent shall represent conflicting interests in his practice before the Internal Revenue Service, except by express consent of all directly interested parties after full disclosure has been made.

(2) Dual representation exists when a summoned third-party witness is represented by an attorney, certified public accountant, enrolled agent, or other person who also represents the taxpayer or another interested party. It may also occur where an attorney under investigation represents a third-party witness in that investigation or

where an attorney-witness seeks to represent another witness in the same investigation. An interested party is one who has a significant pecuniary interest in the testimony of the witness or who, by virtue of the nature of the investigation and the known facts, may be incriminated by the witness.

(3) Except as provided below, the mere existence of a dual representation situation which may potentially have an adverse impact on the investigation will not, without some action by the attorney to impede or obstruct the investigation, provide a sufficient basis for seeking a disqualification. However, where an attorney's representation has substantially prejudiced the questioning of a third-party witness and, as a result, has significantly impaired the progress of the investigation, the Service will request the Department of Justice to seek a court order, as part of the summons enforcement proceeding, to disqualify that attorney as counsel for that witness.

(4) In view of the well-established principle granting a person the right to counsel of one's choice, this disqualification procedure will only be used in extreme circumstances, such as where an attorney has taken some action to improperly or unlawfully impede or obstruct the investigation. It is essential that the interviewing officer have sufficient facts to support such allegations.

* * *

(7) Obstruction of interview

* * *

(d) Unjustifiable obstruction by an attorney may take a variety of forms. It is, therefore, impossible to set forth the precise factual circumstances under which the Government would ask a court to disqualify an attorney as counsel for a third-party witness.

(e) The following is an example of a circumstance which may provide the basis for a recommendation for the institution of litigation to seek the disqualification of an attorney:

Taxpayer and third-party witness are both represented by the same attorney. The witness is summoned to testify. The attorney refuses to permit the witness to answer questions for other than legitimate reasons or disrupts the questioning by repeatedly making frivolous objections to the questions, or asserts frivolous claims of privilege or defenses on behalf of the witness to delay the investigation, or so disrupts the interview that the interviewing officer, with due diligence and perseverance, is unable to proceed with the interview. [*Backer v. Commissioner*].^c This is not intended to suggest that there is anything inherently wrong in claiming the Fifth Amendment privilege.

A careful distinction must be drawn between situations in which the proper remedy is to compel the witness to answer and those in which the attorney may be disqualified because of this conduct. The

---

c. 275 F.2d 141 (5th Cir. 1960). Reprinted above.

latter is an extreme remedy which will only be sought in very unusual circumstances, as courts are reluctant to deprive a person of his/her choice of attorney. District Counsel, therefore, will make a considered determination on a case-by-case basis prior to seeking disqualification of an attorney.

* * *

(9) Procedures where an attorney will be excluded prior to interviewing witness are:

(a) Where an individual taxpayer under investigation attempts to appear with a summoned witness as the witness' attorney, the witness should be told that the taxpayer/attorney is the person under investigation and that he/she will not be allowed to be present during the questioning. The witness should be given the opportunity of either proceeding with the interview without the taxpayer present or adjourning the interview to a specific future date in order to afford the witness an opportunity to secure the services of another attorney. If the witness refuses to either proceed with the interview without the attorney's representation or to adjourn for the purpose of obtaining a new representative, the interview will be terminated and a request will be made to District Counsel for judicial enforcement of the summons and exclusion of the taxpayer from representing the witness.

(b) A witness may appear pursuant to a summons accompanied by an attorney who also represents the taxpayer (or other interested party) where the taxpayer (or other interested party) has already made exculpatory statements to the Service alleging that the witness was criminally responsible for circumstances to be discussed during the interview. In this case, the witness will be told that the attorney also represents the taxpayer (or other interested party) and that the agent believes that an irreconcilable conflict of interest exists which could prejudice the investigation. The witness should then be given the opportunity of either proceeding with the interview without the attorney present or adjourning the interview to secure the services of another attorney. If the witness insists upon retaining the same attorney despite the assertion of a conflict of interest, the interviewing officer will terminate the interview and a request will be made to District Counsel for judicial enforcement of the summons and exclusion of the attorney.

(c) Where a witness appears pursuant to a summons and is accompanied by a person (other than the taxpayer) who does not represent the individual witness, such person may be excluded from the interview. An example of a situation in which a person may be excluded from the interview is where a corporate official (witness) is summoned in his/her individual capacity regarding an examination of the corporation and an attorney representing the corporation, who does not also represent the witness, attempts to attend the interview. However, if the witness refuses to be interviewed if that person is excluded and the person is a designee of the taxpayer within the meaning of IRC 6103(c) and its regulations, the interview will proceed unless the interviewing officer makes a determination that continuation of the interview will impede development of the case. If such a determination is made, the interview will be terminated and a request will be made to District Counsel for a recommendation for judicial enforcement of the summons by the Department of Justice and exclusion of the person from any future interviews pursuant to the court's order.

NOTES

1. The attorney who represents clients with potentially conflicting interests must carefully consider whether he will be able to maintain his undivided loyalty with respect to each client. Although a lawyer may be justified in representing clients with differing interests, it is essential that he first discuss the implications of common representation with the clients and obtain their consent before undertaking or continuing employment on their behalf. See A.B.A. Code of Professional Responsibility EC 5–14 through 5–20 and DR 5–105.

2. The multiple representation issue is often raised at the grand jury stage of a criminal investigation by a motion to disqualify the attorney (or law firm) seeking to represent both target and witness before the grand jury. In re Grand Jury, 446 F.Supp. 1132 (N.D.Tex.1978), involving the ability of third-party witnesses to waive potential and actual conflicts arising from multiple representation, contains an excellent discussion of the law in this area.

SECTION 4. STATUTORY REGULATION OF INCOME TAX RETURN PREPARERS

The tax return preparer provisions of the Code impose obligations upon persons who participate in the preparation of income tax returns and claims for refunds. These provisions impose disclosure and recordkeeping requirements and provide penalties for the negligent and willful understatement of the taxpayer's tax liability. Moreover, in appropriate circumstances the preparer can be enjoined from engaging in practice before the IRS and from the preparation of tax returns. These provisions were added to the Code by the Tax Reform Act of 1976 in order to improve the accountability of commercial tax return preparers and to upgrade the quality of their work. Unfortunately for tax professionals, these requirements were made applicable to attorneys and accountants who prepare their clients' returns as well as to commercial tax return preparers. Although generally regarded as a nuisance by professional tax advisers, the preparer regulations are accompanied by significant penalty provisions which require strict internal office controls to ensure compliance with their requirements.

Who is an "income tax return preparer"? The income tax return preparer regulations are applicable to any person who prepares, for compensation, all or a substantial portion of an income tax return or claim for refund.[d] Only a person who prepares a substantial portion of a return or claim for refund will be considered an income tax return preparer. The regulations state that "[w]hether a schedule, entry, or other portion of a return or claim for refund is a substantial portion is determined by comparing the length and complexity of, and tax liability or refund involved in, that portion to the length and complexity of, and tax liability or refund involved in, the return or claim for refund as a whole."[e] Regs. § 301.7701–15(b)(2) establishes a safe harbor—an objective means of determining when the preparation of only a portion of a return or claim for refund will be considered insubstantial and the preparer need not, therefore, comply with the recordkeeping and disclosure requirements of the preparer regulations. Generally, if the portion prepared for compensation by someone other than the taxpayer involves amounts of gross income, deductions, or amounts determining credits which are either less than $2,000 in the absolute, or less than $100,000 *and* also less than 20 percent of the taxpayer's adjusted gross income, then the portion prepared will not be considered "substantial". A person who does not physically prepare the return but who furnishes the taxpayer or other preparer with sufficient advice so that completion of the return is largely a mechanical or clerical matter is deemed to be a tax return preparer. Under the regulations, both the physical preparer of the return and off-return advisers may be income tax return preparers; a single return may subject several persons to the income tax return preparer requirements.

A tax adviser who provides his client with advice on a specific issue subjects himself to the preparer regulations if the advice is given with respect to a completed transaction and if the advice is directly relevant to the existence, characterization, or amount of an entry on a return or claim for refund.[f] Of course, the entry must also constitute a substantial portion of the return. A preparer of an income tax return may be deemed to be an income tax return preparer of a related income tax return where the entries reported in the first return are directly reported in the second return. Thus, an accountant who prepares a partnership's income tax return will be considered to be a preparer of the individual partners' returns where the entries from

d. IRC § 7701(a)(36). A person who prepares an income tax return or a claim for refund as a fiduciary for another, or for his regular employer, or in response to any notice of deficiency issued to a taxpayer, is not deemed to be an income tax return preparer subject to the tax preparer regulations. IRC § 7701(a)(36)(B).

Neither is a person who furnishes merely typing, reproducing, or mechanical assistance a tax return preparer. Id.

e. Reg. § 301.7701–15(b)(1).

f. Regs. § 301.7701–15(a)(2).

the partnership return constitute substantial portions of the partners' returns.   Note that the preparer regulations are not applicable to preparers of excise, estate and gift tax returns; neither are they applicable to applications for tentative carrybacks.

Disclosure and recordkeeping requirements—penalty provisions. An income tax return preparer must personally sign the completed return,[g] note the preparer's place of business, and include his identification or social security number on the return.[h]   The failure to satisfy these requirements subjects the preparer to immediate assessment of a penalty through the Service Center computers.   After receiving the assessment notice, the preparer may seek abatement of the penalty by providing the Service with a written explanation of why he believes there was reasonable cause for his noncompliance.[i]

Preparers also must provide the taxpayer with a copy of the return or claim for refund, and retain a completed copy of the return or of a listing of the taxpayer's name and identification number. These records must be retained for three years after the close of the return period to which the return relates.   Violations of preparer regulations which are not apparent from the face of the return are assessed through the district office.   The penalty provisions will not be applied if the preparer can prove that the violations were due to reasonable cause and not willful neglect.

Employers of tax return preparers, and self-employed preparers, are required to file an annual information return, setting forth the name, identification number and principal place of business of each preparer under their employ.[j]   The regulations also contain a prohibition against the negotiation, by tax return preparers, of refund checks issued to a taxpayer.[k]

Sections 6694(a) and (b) of the Code impose penalties for the negligent and intentional understatement of the taxpayer's tax liability.   The preparer is not required to verify information provided by the taxpayer; however, the preparer may not ignore the implications of the information furnished.   To contest preparer penalties assessed under § 6694 for the willful or negligent understatement of tax liability, the preparer must pay 15% of the penalty assessed, file a claim for refund, and seek review of the Service's decision in the district court.[l]

g. Regs. § 1.6695–1(b).

h. IRC § 6109(a)(4).

i. See Regs. § 1.6695–1(b)(5); see also Regs. § 1.6696–1 (relating to claims for credit or refund by tax return preparers of penalties assessed under IRC §§ 6694, 6695).

j. IRC § 6060.

k. IRC § 6695(f).

l. Regs. § 6696–1.

Tax return preparers are also subject to the general criminal provisions of the Code. Especially relevant is IRC § 7206(2), dealing with willfully assisting in the preparation or presentation of a false document to revenue authorities. Additionally, IRC § 7216 makes it a misdemeanor for any preparer to use or disclose tax return information without authorization from the taxpayer except as specifically provided in the statute.

Chapter III

ADMINISTRATIVE RULEMAKING AND RULINGS

Scope Note: In order to provide taxpayers with an understanding of the meaning and application of the internal revenue laws, the Service promulgates Treasury Regulations and responds to taxpayer requests for rulings interpreting the tax laws and applying them to specific factual situations. The regulations are afforded substantial weight by the courts in applying the Code to a specific set of facts. This chapter discusses those factors which influence a court to give more or less weight to the applicable Treasury Regulations and outlines the nature of the Service's rulings program. The section on Confidentiality and Disclosure considers the usefulness of the Freedom of Information Act, the Privacy Act and Sections 6103 and 6110 of the Code in obtaining access to agency records and in protecting taxpayers from damaging disclosure of confidential information by revenue authorities.

SECTION 1. TREASURY REGULATIONS

LEGISLATIVE AND INTERPRETATIVE REGULATIONS

The regulations published by the Treasury Department constitute the single most authoritative source for guidance in interpreting the Internal Revenue Code. Regulations promulgated pursuant to a specific Congressional delegation of rule-making power, referred to as legislative regulations, are accorded the force of law unless they are outside the scope of delegated authority, contrary to statute, or unreasonable.[a]

Interpretative regulations, i. e., those promulgated pursuant to the general authorization by Congress that the Secretary of the Treasury may "prescribe all needful rules and regulations" for the enforcement of the internal revenue laws, IRC § 7805(a), have been treated with less deference by the courts. To buttress the force and effect of interpretative regulations, several rationales have been developed by the courts. First, an interpretative regulation which has been in effect for a long period of time is considered to be more persuasive than a recently enacted one. Second, if the underlying statute was reenacted by Congress while the regulation was in effect, the reenactment is often deemed to be a tacit approval of the interpretative regulation. Third, an interpretative regulation is accorded great-

---

a. See M. Rogovin, The Four R's: Regulations, Rulings, Reliance and Retroactivity—A View from Within, 43 Taxes 756, 759 (1965).

er legal effect if it was developed contemporaneously with the statute it interprets.[b]

Although the courts have distinguished interpretative regulations from legislative ones, no such distinction has been drawn by Congress. As both interpretative and legislative regulations generally are promulgated in accordance with the procedural requirements of the Administrative Procedure Act, 5 U.S.C.A. § 553, the continuing validity of this distinction is open to question.[c]

THE REGULATION–MAKING PROCESS

After deciding to develop a regulation to implement a newly enacted statute, or to revise an old regulation, an attorney in the Legislation and Regulations Division of the Chief Counsel's Office begins the drafting process.[d] When substantive matters of tax policy are involved, the drafter may receive policy guidance from the Assistant Secretary for Tax Policy, the Commissioner, the Chief Counsel, and the Assistant Commissioner (Technical).

Upon approval by the appropriate Treasury officials, the proposed regulation is published in the Federal Register pursuant to the terms of the Administrative Procedure Act. (Although the A.P.A. procedures are required only for legislative regulations, and not for interpretative ones, the Treasury Department generally follows the A.P.A. procedures for both types of regulations). Written comments and suggestions from the public are encouraged to be submitted to the Treasury Department within sixty days of the regulation's publication in proposed form. A public hearing may be scheduled at which time oral comments are received. The public comments are then considered by the Treasury staff, and the regulation frequently is revised. Generally, these revisions will benefit the taxpayer. If the revisions are minor in character, the regulation is published in the Federal Register in final form. If the proposed rule has undergone substantial alteration, and the final rule imposes a greater burden on taxpayers than did its predecessor, the regulation must be republished in proposed form, with comments again solicited from the public.

In certain circumstances the Treasury may issue regulations without adhering to the A.P.A. procedure. When immediate interpretations of a newly enacted statute are required, the Treasury may issue temporary regulations, which are effective until superseded by permanent ones. Also, when a revision of an existing regulation only

b. Id. at 759–760.

c. See W.D. Popkin, A Critique of the Rule-Making Process in Federal Income Tax Law With Special Reference to Conglomerate Acquisitions, 45 Ind.L.J. 453, 510–512 (1970).

d. See generally P.F. Schmid, The Tax Regulations Making Process—Then and Now, 24 Tax Lawyer 541, 543 (1971).

serves to benefit taxpayers, the Treasury need not follow the A.P.A. rule-making procedure. Both of these exceptions to the normal rule-making procedure are based upon 5 U.S.C.A. § 553(b)(3)(B), which allows an agency to dispense with the notice and public participation procedures when the rule-making agency "for good causes finds * * * that notice and public procedure thereon are impracticable, unnecessary, or contrary to the public interest."

Regulations promulgated under the A.P.A. become effective thirty days after the date of final publication. However, once adopted, a regulation may have retroactive effect. Congress has delegated to the Secretary of the Treasury the power to decide whether to apply a regulation retroactively so as to avoid undue hardship to the taxpayers affected thereby. IRC § 7805(b).

A. EFFECT OF LEGISLATIVE REENACTMENT

HELVERING v. R. J. REYNOLDS TOBACCO CO.

Supreme Court of the United States, 1939.
306 U.S. 110, 59 S.Ct. 423, 83 L.Ed. 536.

Mr. Justice ROBERTS delivered the opinion of the Court.

The sole question for decision is whether gain accruing to a corporation consequent on the purchase and resale of its own shares constitutes gross income within the meaning of Section 22(a) of the Revenue Act of 1928.

* * *

The Commissioner determined a deficiency in the tax paid * * *. He based his claim upon Treasury Regulation 74, Article 66, as amended by a Treasury decision of May 2, 1934, which states "where a corporation deals in its own shares as it might in the shares of another corporation, the resulting gain or loss is to be computed in the same manner as though the corporation were dealing in the shares of another."

The Board, after finding the facts in detail, sustained the Commissioner. The Circuit Court of Appeals reversed the Board's ruling. * * *

Section 22(a) is: "General definition. 'Gross income' includes gains, profits, and income derived from salaries, wages, or compensation for personal service, of whatever kind and in whatever form paid, or from professions, vocations, trades, businesses, commerce, or sales, or dealings in property, whether real or personal, growing out of the ownership or use of or interest in such property; also from interest, rent, dividends, securities, or the transaction of any business carried on for gain or profit, or gains or profits and income derived from any source whatever." Section 62 e directs the Commissioner,

e. The predecessor to § 7805(a) of the 1954 Code.

"with the approval of the Secretary" of the Treasury, to "prescribe and publish all needful rules and regulations for the enforcement of this title [chapter]." Article 66 of Treasury Regulations 74, promulgated under the Act of 1928, so far as material, is: "If * * * the corporation purchases any of its stock and holds it as treasury stock, the sale of such stock will be considered a capital transaction and the proceeds of such sale will be treated as capital and will not constitute income of the corporation. A corporation realizes no gain or loss from the purchase or sale of its own stock."

Petitioner contends that, as Congress must be taken to have exercised its constitutional power to the fullest extent in laying the tax, Section 22(a) should be held to include the gain realized from sales of a corporation's own stock, and the quoted regulation cannot restrict the scope of the statutory definition. The respondent replies that such gain is capital gain and not income, as is demonstrated by the theory and practice of accounting and by court decisions. The court below found it unnecessary to decide this issue, holding that whether the increment is income is at least a debatable question and the regulation was, therefore, proper as an interpretation of the meaning of the section. We agree that Section 22(a) is so general in its terms as to render an interpretative regulation appropriate.

The administrative construction embodied in the regulation has, since at least 1920, been uniform with respect to each of the revenue acts from that of 1913 to that of 1932, as evidenced by Treasury rulings and regulations, and decisions of the Board of Tax Appeals. In the meantime successive revenue acts have reenacted, without alteration, the definition of gross income as it stood in the Acts of 1913, 1916, and 1918. Under the established rule Congress must be taken to have approved the administrative construction and thereby to have given it the force of law.

The petitioner concedes that if nothing further appeared he would be bound to apply the statute in conformity to the regulation. He asserts, however, that the amendment adopted by the Treasury May 2, 1934, while this cause was pending before the Board, is controlling. By the amendment Article 66 is made to read: "Whether the acquisition or disposition by a corporation of shares of its own capital stock gives rise to taxable gain or deductible loss depends upon the real nature of the transaction, which is to be ascertained from all its facts and circumstances. * * *

"But where a corporation deals in its own shares as it might in the shares of another corporation, the resulting gain or loss is to be computed in the same manner as though the corporation were dealing in the shares of another. * * * Any gain derived from such transactions is subject to tax, and any loss sustained is allowable as a deduction where permitted by the provisions of applicable statutes."

Petitioner urges that the amendment operates retroactively and governs the ascertainment of gross income for taxable periods prior to the date of its promulgation, and, further, since Congress has reenacted Section 22(a) in the Revenue Acts of 1936 and 1938 it has approved the regulation as amended. We hold that the respondent's tax liability for the year 1929 is to be determined in conformity to the regulation then in force.

Section 605 of the Revenue Act of 1928 [f] provides that "In case a regulation or Treasury decision relating to the internal revenue laws is amended by a subsequent regulation or Treasury decision, made by the Secretary or by the Commissioner with the approval of the Secretary, such subsequent regulation or Treasury decision may, with the approval of the Secretary, be applied without retroactive effect." It is clear from this provision that Congress intended to give to the Treasury power to correct misinterpretations, inaccuracies, or omissions in the regulations and thereby to affect cases in which the taxpayer's liability had not been finally determined, unless, in the judgment of the Treasury, some good reason required that such alterations operate only prospectively. The question is whether the granted power may be exercised in an instance where, by repeated reenactment of the statute, Congress has given its sanction to the existing regulation.

Since the legislative approval of existing regulations by reenactment of the statutory provision to which they appertain gives such regulations the force of law, we think that Congress did not intend to authorize the Treasury to repeal the rule of law that existed during the period for which the tax is imposed. We need not now determine whether, as has been suggested, the alteration of the existing rule, even for the future, requires a legislative declaration or may be shown by reenactment of the statutory provision unaltered after a change in the applicable regulation. As the petitioner points out, Congress has, in the Revenue Acts of 1936 and 1938, retained Section 22(a) of the 1928 Act in haec verba. From this it is argued that Congress has approved the amended regulation. It may be that by the passage of the Revenue Act of 1936 the Treasury was authorized thereafter to apply the regulation in its amended form. But we have no occasion to decide this question since we are of opinion that the reenactment of the section, without more, does not amount to sanction of retroactive enforcement of the amendment, in the teeth of the former regulation which received Congressional approval, by the passage of successive Revenue Acts including that of 1928.

The judgment is affirmed.

f. The predecessor to § 7805(b) of the 1954 Code.

NOTE: RETROACTIVE APPLICATION OF TREASURY REGULATIONS

The general rule is that the Commissioner always may retroactively apply the first regulations interpreting a particular Code provision. Helvering v. Reynolds, 313 U.S. 428, 61 S.Ct. 971, 85 L.Ed. 1438 (1941); Manhattan Gen. Equipment Co. v. Commissioner, 297 U.S. 129, 56 S.Ct. 397, 80 L. Ed. 528 (1936). As stated by Rogovin in The Four R's: Regulations, Rulings, Reliance and Retroactivity—A View from Within, 43 Taxes 756, 762 (1965):

> [T]he Supreme Court has questioned whether it is even proper to characterize the relation-back of the first regulation to the effective date of the interpreted Code section as being a retroactive application of the regulation. [Manhattan Gen. Equipment Co. v. Commissioner, supra]. Absent a regulation, the taxpayer must rely upon the particular Code section for guidance. Accordingly, no question of reliance as a bar to retroactivity can arise; regulations do not alter the statute, they explain its meaning.

The doctrine of legislative reenactment, as espoused in the *R. J. Reynolds* case excerpted above, constitutes the major inroad upon the Commissioner's power of retroactive application. This doctrine has been applied to situations involving the retroactive application of *amended* Treasury Regulations. Occasionally taxpayers have argued, without success, that the doctrine of legislative reenactment applies to published Treasury Department rulings, general counsel memoranda and uniform lower court interpretations of the underlying Code provision, thereby rendering the retroactive application of the *original* interpretative regulation improper. See, e. g., Helvering v. Reynolds, supra. More recently, however, the Supreme Court has suggested that the doctrine of legislative reenactment may be applicable to situations involving a long-standing administrative practice and a consistent and uniform judicial construction of the underlying Code provision. See, Commissioner v. Estate of Noel, excerpted below; Corn Products Refining Co. v. Commissioner, 350 U.S. 46, 76 S.Ct. 20, 100 L.Ed. 29 (1955).

QUESTION

Is it possible to reconcile the holding in the *R. J. Reynolds* case as to the nonretroactive effect of the 1934 amendment to the regulations under § 22(a) with the holding in Manhattan Gen. Equipment Co. v. Commissioner, 297 U.S. 129, 56 S.Ct. 397, 80 L.Ed. 528 (1936)? The facts of the latter case, as summarized in Rogovin, The Four R's: Regulations, Rulings, Reliance and Retroactivity—A View from Within, 43 Taxes 756 (1965), were that the taxpayers had sold certain shares of stock acquired in a reorganization at a loss, the amount of which they determined under the regulation which was in force in 1926. The regulation in question was a legislative regulation, being required by the language of § 204(a)(9) of the Revenue Act of 1926. In 1928 the Commissioner amended this regulation, and applied the amended regulation to the taxpayer's 1926 transaction. In upholding the Commissioner's right to apply the change in position retroactively the court stated:

> The power of an administrative officer or board to administer a federal statute and to prescribe rules and regulations to that end

is not the power to make law, for no such power can be delegated by Congress, but the power to adopt regulations to carry into effect the will of Congress as expressed by the statute. A regulation which does not do this, but operates to create a rule out of harmony with the statute, is a mere nullity. * * * The original regulation as applied to a situation like that under review is both inconsistent with the statute and unreasonable.

The contention that the new regulation is retroactive is without merit. Since the original regulation could not be applied, the amended regulation in effect became the primary and controlling rule in respect of the situation presented. It pointed the way for the first time, for correctly applying the antecedent statute to a situation which arose under the statute. The statute defines the rights of the taxpayer and fixes the standard by which such rights are to be measured. The regulation constitutes only a step in the administrative process. It does not, and could not alter the statute. It is no more retroactive in its operation than is a judicial determination construing and applying a statute to a case in hand.

297 U.S. at 134–135, 56 S.Ct. at 399–400, 80 L.Ed. 528. See also, Helvering v. Reynolds, 313 U.S. 428, 61 S.Ct. 971, 85 L.Ed. 1438 (1941); Dixon v. United States, 381 U.S. 68, 85 S.Ct. 1301, 14 L.Ed.2d 223 (1965); Rogovin, supra.

B. EFFECT OF LONG–STANDING REGULATION

COMMISSIONER v. ESTATE OF NOEL

Supreme Court of the United States, 1965.
380 U.S. 678, 85 S.Ct. 1238, 14 L.Ed.2d 159.

Mr. Justice BLACK delivered the opinion of the Court.

This is a federal estate tax case * * *. The questions presented in this case are whether certain flight insurance policies payable upon the accidental death of the insured were policies "on the life of the decedent" and whether at his death he had reserved any of the "incidents of ownership" in the policies.

* * * The Commissioner of Internal Revenue determined that the proceeds of the policies should have been included [in the decedent's gross estate] and the Tax Court sustained that determination, holding that the flight accident policies were insurance "on the life of the decedent"; that Mr. Noel has possessed exercisable "incidents of ownership" in the policies at his death; and that the $125,000 paid to Mrs. Noel as beneficiary was therefore includable in the gross estate. Although agreeing that decedent's reserved right to assign the policies and to change the beneficiary amounted to "exercisable incidents of ownership within the meaning of the statute," the Court of Appeals nevertheless reversed, holding that given "its ordinary, plain and generally accepted meaning," the statutory phrase "policies on the life of the decedent" does not apply to insurance paid on account

of accidental death under policies like those here. The court's reason for drawing the distinction was that under a life insurance contract an insurer "agrees to pay a specified sum upon the occurrence of an *inevitable* event," whereas accident insurance covers a risk "which is *evitable* and not likely to occur." (Emphasis supplied.)　＊　＊　＊

In 1929, 36 years ago, the Board of Tax Appeals, predecessor to the Tax Court, held in Ackerman v. Commissioner, 15 B.T.A. 635, that "amounts received as accident insurance" because of the death of the insured were includable in the estate of the deceased.　＊　＊　＊ This view of the Board of Tax Appeals is wholly consistent with the language of the statute　＊　＊　＊. Even were the statutory language less clear, since the Board of Tax Appeals' *Ackerman* case it has been the settled and consistent administrative practice to include insurance proceeds for accidental death under policies like these in the estates of decedents. The Treasury Regulations remain unchanged from the time of the *Ackerman* decision and from that day to this Congress has never attempted to limit the scope of that decision or the established administrative construction of § 2042(2), although it has re-enacted that section and amended it in other respects a number of times. We have held in many cases that such a longstanding administrative interpretation, applying to a substantially re-enacted statute, is deemed to have received congressional approval and has the effect of law. We hold here that these insurance policies, whether called "flight accident insurance" or "life insurance," were in effect insurance taken out on the "life of the decedent" within the meaning of § 2042(2).

＊　＊　＊

C.　DETERMINING THE VALIDITY OF LEGISLATIVE REGULATIONS

AMERICAN STANDARD, INC. v. UNITED STATES

602 F.2d 256 (Ct.Cl.1979).

BENNETT, Judge.

The plaintiff, American Standard, Inc., seeks to recover overpayments of federal income taxes and interest for the taxable year ending December 31, 1966, and the taxable period ending May 31, 1968. The case concerns the proper methods for computing the deduction for Western Hemisphere Trade Corporations (WHTC), I.R.C. §§ 921–922, when such corporations are members of an affiliated group which files a consolidated income tax return, I.R.C. §§ 1501–1563. This case is before the court on the parties' stipulations of facts. We hold for plaintiff.

Plaintiff is the successor by merger to Westinghouse Air Brake Company (WABCO). During the tax years in issue, WABCO and its affiliates filed consolidated income tax returns. The group claimed a deduction based on the portion of "consolidated taxable income" (as defined in Treas.Reg. § 1.1502–11 (1966)) allocable to the WHTCs multiplied by the fraction provided in I.R.C. § 922. The group calculated the amount of consolidated taxable income allocable to the WHTCs by the *fractional method with losses*. In determining the fraction, the group took into consideration all members in the particular class including those whose taxable income was a net loss. This included one WHTC and several non-WHTCs which had net losses. Upon audit, the Internal Revenue Service (Service) determined, under its interpretation of Treas.Reg. § 1.1502–25, that the group's calculation of the deduction was improper because corporations whose taxable incomes resulted in a loss were not to be considered in either the numerator or denominator of the fraction.

Though plaintiff has argued that the Service's interpretation of its own regulation is incorrect, we find no merit to this contention. Thus, plaintiff's method is clearly incorrect and plaintiff is not entitled to recover if Treas.Reg. § 1.1502–25 is valid law controlling in this case.

Plaintiff, however, advances two major theories under which, it contends, the regulation is invalid. Plaintiff's primary theory, which is directed to the substance of the regulation, is that the regulation is invalid because it is an arbitrary and unreasonable exercise of the Secretary of the Treasury's power to promulgate regulations governing consolidated income tax returns. Plaintiff's second theory, which is based on procedural grounds, is that the regulation is invalid because it was not promulgated in accordance with the Administrative Procedure Act (APA). We conclude that the regulation is invalid under both standards.

I

The concept of dealing with separate affiliated corporations on a consolidated return basis goes back as far as 1917. The process by which income tax liability could be determined on the basis of consolidated returns subject to legislative regulations was inaugurated by section 141 of the Revenue Act of 1928.

The rationale for Congress' delegation of legislative rulemaking powers was expressed by the Senate Committee report to the 1928 Act as follows:

> * * * The committee believes it to be impracticable to attempt by legislation to prescribe the various detailed and complicated rules necessary to meet the many differing and complicated situations. Accordingly, it has found it necessary to delegate power to the commissioner to prescribe regulations legislative in character covering them. The standard prescribed by the section keeps the delegation from being a delegation of pure legislative power, and is well

within the rules established by the Supreme Court. * * *
[S.Rep.No.960, 70th Cong., 1st Sess. 15 (1928)].

As noted in the committee report, the promulgation of consolidated return regulations is a legislative function. This court recognized this in Union Elec. Co. of Mo. v. United States, 305 F.2d 850, 854, 158 Ct.Cl. 479, 486 (1962), where the court concluded that consolidated return regulations "unlike ordinary Treasury Regulations, are legislative in character and have the force and effect of law." Though legislative regulations are law, they are good law only if enacted in accordance with the authority vested in the Treasury by the enabling Act. A consolidated return regulation is invalid if it be inconsistent with the Act.

The delegation of rulemaking power is presently found in I.R.C. § 1502, as follows:

> The Secretary shall prescribe such regulations as he may deem necessary in order that the tax liability of any affiliated group of corporations making a consolidated return and of each corporation in the group, both during and after the period of affiliation, may be returned, determined, computed, assessed, collected, and adjusted, in such manner as clearly to reflect the income-tax liability and the various factors necessary for the determination of such liability, and in order to prevent avoidance of such tax liability.

Thus, the Code grants to the Secretary broad legislative authority governing the manner in which a group's tax liability is determined when a consolidated return is filed. But this power must be construed in terms of Congress' purpose that both the group's and its individual member's actual tax liability be found under the regulations "in such manner as clearly to reflect the income-tax liability * * * and in order to prevent avoidance of such tax liability." I. R.C. § 1502. Income tax liability is not imposed by the Secretary's regulations, but by the Internal Revenue Code. Thus, the purpose of the delegation of power to the Secretary can be stated more broadly as the power to conform the applicable income tax law of the Code to the special, myriad problems resulting from the filing of consolidated income tax returns. Though there may be many reasonable methods to determine a group's tax liability and the Secretary's authority is absolute when it represents a choice between such methods, the statute does not authorize the Secretary to choose a method that imposes a tax on income that would not otherwise be taxed.

We note that, as discussed in part II, infra, the Secretary did not provide any statement of the basis and purpose of the regulation. We are thus unaware of any special factual or legal problem caused by the filing of consolidated returns with which the method adopted by the regulation was meant to deal. Defense counsel has added nothing to enlighten us. All we have is the obvious inference from Treas.Reg. § 1.1502–25 and the statute under which it was promulgated that the regulation represents the Secretary's choice of a reasonable method to determine a group's tax liability or to prevent avoidance of that liability. We acknowledge that the Secretary is the expert in this complex field and that the regulation must be sustained unless it is clearly unreasonable. We must determine, however, the question of reasonableness for ourselves.

Our analysis must begin with an examination of the purposes and policy of the statute and regulations. The basic purpose behind allowing corporations to file consolidated returns is to permit affiliated corporations, which may be separately incorporated for various business reasons, to be treated as a single entity for income tax purposes as if they were, in fact, one corporation. Therefore, as provided by regulation, Treas.Reg. § 1.1502–2(a), the tax is computed solely on the basis of consolidated taxable income.

* * *

The deduction granted by section 922 was designed to foster American business within the Western Hemisphere. The purpose of the legislation "was to ameliorate somewhat the unfavorable situation in which domestic corporations had to compete with foreign corporations in the Western Hemisphere. S.Rep.No.1631, 77th Cong., 2d Sess. 32 (1942)." A corporation had to meet the rigid requirements of section 921 to qualify. Arm's-length pricing was required between a related party and a WHTC in order that the benefit of the statute be strictly conferred on income earned by the WHTC. It is clear that the purpose of the deduction was to ensure that WHTCs' products and services were competitively priced in Western Hemisphere trade.

Treas.Reg. § 1.1502–25 clearly defeats this intended inducement to American business. Sharing the losses of non-WHTC corporations with the profits of WHTC corporations for purposes of the deduction directly decreases the profitability of Western Hemisphere trade and concomitantly the price for which goods and services are provided. Congress specifically conferred both the privilege of filing consolidated returns and the special deduction on WHTCs, and reduced the onus on a taxpayer for having to incorporate its Western Hemisphere business separately. The regulation penalizes WHTCs which are affiliated with a group that desires to file consolidated returns. Congress granted a deduction to the earnings of WHTCs; the regulation changes this concept by reducing WHTC earnings by the losses of domestic or non-WHTC enterprises. In doing this, it is in direct conflict with sections 922 and 1502.

* * *

II

Plaintiff's alternative argument is that the regulation was not promulgated in compliance with the Administrative Procedure Act

(APA), and is, therefore, invalid. Plaintiff alleges that the requirement of notice 30 days before the promulgation of the regulation and a statement of the basis and purpose of the regulation were not provided, in violation of the APA.

5 U.S.C. § 553(b), (c) and (d) requires that notice of proposed rulemaking be published in the Federal Register 30 days prior to the adoption of a regulation. Such notice includes "either the terms or substance of the proposed rule or a description of the subjects and issues involved." 5 U.S.C. § 553(b)(3). The purpose of this procedure is "to assure fairness and mature consideration of rules of general application," NLRB v. Wyman-Gordon Co., 394 U.S. 759, 764, 89 S.Ct. 1426, 1429, 22 L.Ed.2d 709 (1969), and to give affected members of the public an opportunity to comment. A substantive rule is invalid if it is not promulgated in accordance with the notice requirements of the APA.

On September 8, 1966, notice of proposed rulemaking and a regulation covering the consolidated WHTC deduction were published in the Federal Register, 31 Fed.Reg. 11845, 11848 (1966). The problem presented for resolution is whether this proposed regulation gave the public adequate notice of the regulation which was adopted on December 30, 1966. To analyze this problem properly, some background information is necessary.

[The September 8, 1966 notice of proposed rulemaking supplanted an earlier notice of a proposed regulation (October 1, 1965) which would have taken into account corporations with net losses in computing the WHTC deduction. The second proposal was worded in an extremely confusing manner and did not explicitly note the change from the prior version.]

* * * In light of the fact that the first proposal (Oct. 1, 1965) clearly took losses into account, it is unlikely that the public would have been put on notice by the second proposal that the Treasury intended to change diametrically its substantive approach. * * * [T]he proposal did [not] give the public fair notice of the intendment of the final form of the regulation. Therefore, we hold that the notice provision of the APA was violated in this case and the regulation is invalid.

The APA also requires that when a rule is adopted, a statement of its basis and purpose shall accompany its publication. 5 U.S.C. § 553(c). No such statement accompanied the promulgation of Treas. Reg. § 1.1502–25. Plaintiff contends that the regulation is thus invalid.

The purpose of requiring a statement of the basis and purpose is to enable courts, which have the duty to exercise review, to be aware of the legal and factual framework underlying the agency's action. Derived from the very rationale of the requirement is an exception to its overtechnical application, and that is, when the basis and purpose of the rule is inherent in the rule and the enabling statute, then no separate statement is required. Defendant contends it is obvious why the regulation was promulgated; it was promulgated to adjust the Code provisions to the special problems incurred with consolidated returns.

The reason the lack of a rationale renders a regulation invalid is that a court cannot evaluate the reasonableness of a regulation without a statement of the purpose and basis. Consolidated return regulations differ from some legislative rules in that they clarify and establish a uniform system for reporting tax liability on a consolidated basis. Unlike some legislative rules that are promulgated pursuant to vague statutory commands and within a vague statutory framework which make review difficult, if not impossible, consolidated return regulations are reviewed in terms of a large, comprehensive code and sizeable body of decisional law.

Though determining the reasonableness of the regulation is difficult in this context, and a challenge to its reasonableness by plaintiff must overcome significant obstacles, it is not impossible in our situation, as demonstrated by part I of our opinion. Therefore, we conclude that the purpose and basis requirements of the APA were not violated in this case but the notice requirement was.

CONCLUSION

In view of all the circumstances, we hold that part of Treas.Reg. § 1.1502–25(c) which excludes all corporations with net losses from the fraction determining the portion of consolidated taxable income is invalid in violation of the delegation of rulemaking power and of the notice requirement of the Administrative Procedure Act. Accordingly, judgment is entered for plaintiff with interest as provided by law and the case is remanded to the trial division for proceedings under Rule 131(c) to determine the amount of recovery.

SECTION 2. REQUESTS FOR RULINGS AND DETERMINATION LETTERS

A. IRS POLICY AND PROCEDURE

The Internal Revenue Service rulings function, described in the following Note, is an important policy implementing tool. It may well be that the basic purpose of the rulings function is to advise all taxpayers in general (through published rulings) and those making specific requests particularly (through unpublished but not generally available private letter rulings) of the Service's interpretation and application of the tax laws. However, in many circumstances the power to provide an unfavorable ruling or to decline to rule at all is the power to influence the activities of taxpayers to a significant extent.

In some circumstances (for example, in the case of a transfer to a foreign entity under §§ 1491 and 1492 of the Code) a ruling is required as a legal matter. In other circumstances, (such as a major corporate acquisition) a ruling may be a practical necessity to insure the tax treatment to be afforded the corporations and shareholders. Moreover, with regard to such matters as the status of a putative tax exempt entity or the qualification of a retirement plan, an administrative determination is both a practical necessity and a legal requirement. To an extent, the final decision-making power of the IRS with respect to rulings has been ameliorated in some areas by provisions for judicial review through declaratory judgment actions.[g]

In most circumstances, however, taxpayers are free to choose whether to submit a proposed transaction for an advance ruling, and are limited only by the Service's "no-ruling" policy as to certain types of transactions involving important legal issues and as to other matters in which the determination requested is primarily one of fact.[h]

It is important to note the effect of a ruling or a determination letter. A published ruling is intended to be notice to the public of the Service's interpretation of the law and its application to the facts set forth in the ruling, and may be relied upon by all taxpayers. A private (officially unpublished) ruling or determination letter is intended solely for the use of the particular taxpayer to whom it is directed and may not be relied upon by another. Moreover, a ruling or determination letter is only as valid as the statement of facts upon which it is based. Hence, the factual underpinning of a ruling or determination letter is subject to verification on audit. In addition, except to the extent incorporated in a closing agreement under IRC § 7121, a ruling may be revoked or modified at any time under appropriate circumstances.[i]

g. See pages 303–305, below.

h. See Rev.Proc. 80–22, 1980–1 C.B. 654. The "no ruling" list contained in Rev.Proc. 80–22 is not comprehensive, and the Service may decline to issue a ruling or determination letter on other questions whenever warranted.

i. See Rev.Proc. 80–20, 1980–1 C.B. 633, § 17.01. If a ruling is revoked or modified, the revocation or modification applies to all open years unless the Commissioner or his delegate exercises the discretionary authority under § 7805(b) to limit the retroactive effect of the revocation or modification. Id.

A ruling found to be in error or not in accord with the current views of the IRS may be modified or revoked by: a notice to the taxpayer to whom the ruling was issued; an enactment of legislation or ratification of a tax treaty; a decision of the Supreme Court; the issuing of temporary or final regulations; or the issuing of a revenue ruling, a revenue procedure, or other statement published in the Internal Revenue Bulletin. Id. § 1704.

Section 17.05 of Rev.Proc. 80–20, supra, states:

Essentially, the procedure for obtaining a ruling or determination requires the taxpayer to submit a request together with pertinent facts, documents and legal discussion to the appropriate office of the Internal Revenue Service. Various specific disclosures (for example whether the same issue is, or has been, involved in an audit or litigation concerning the same or a related taxpayer) are required.[j] There may then follow informal discussion and conferences prior to the issuance of the final ruling or determination letter.[k]

It should be noted that rulings and determination letters (and certain documents submitted by the taxpayer) are open to public inspection subject to statutorily permitted deletions of identification data. The taxpayer has the burden of supplying a statement identifying and supporting the desired deletions when making the request for a ruling or determination letter.[l]

NOTE, FEDERAL TAX RULINGS: PROCEDURE AND POLICY

21 Vanderbilt Law Review 78 (1967).

I. INTRODUCTION

Although we have developed a highly sophisticated judicial mechanism for ultimately resolving tax disputes, such a

Except in rare or unusual circumstances, the revocation or modification of a ruling will not be applied retroactively to the taxpayer for whom the ruling was issued or to a taxpayer whose tax liability was directly involved in the ruling if (1) there has been no misstatement or omission of material facts, (2) the facts developed later are not materially different from the facts on which the ruling was based, (3) there has been no change in the applicable law, (4) the ruling was originally issued with respect to a prospective or proposed transaction, and (5) the taxpayer directly involved in the ruling acted in good faith in reliance upon the ruling and the retroactive revocation would be to the taxpayer's detriment. * * *

j. See Rev.Proc. 80–20, supra § 9, for details. Section 9.08 of Rev.Proc. 79–45, 1979–2 C.B. 508, the predecessor to Rev.Proc. 80–20, stated that if the taxpayer asserted a particular determination in the request, he was *required* to inform the Service of all authorities contrary to the position advanced in the request. If the taxpayer determined that there were no contrary authorities, a statement to that effect had to be included in the ruling request. The tax bar vehemently opposed these requirements, and they were abandoned in the 1980 revision of the Rev.Proc. Compare the language of Rev.Proc. 79–45, § 9.-08, with the almost apologetic language of § 9.08 of Rev.Proc. 80–20, supra.

k. See Rev.Proc. 80–20, supra §§ 10 and 11.

l. IRC § 6110(f) requires the Service to mail a "notice of intention to disclose" to any person to whom a given disclosure pertains, and to prescribe regulations establishing administrative remedies with respect to both requests for additional disclosures and requests to restrain disclosure. Section 9.19 of Rev.Proc. 80–20, supra, sets forth the administrative remedies available to a person who is dissatisfied with the deletions which the IRS agrees to make. If the matter cannot be settled administratively, the person affected may institute an action in the Tax Court to restrain disclosure, pursuant to § 6110(f)(3). For more on the interrelation between the Freedom of Information Act, § 6110, and rulings and determination letters, see pages 105–114, below.

system fails to meet the needs of the most industrialized nation on earth. A taxing statute of one quarter of a million words cannot be complied with solely through the results of litigation. Proper tax administration requires that the Service provide reliable and timely information to aid taxpayers in interpreting this complex statute.[1]

The rulings program of the Internal Revenue Service was designed to meet the need for predictability of the tax consequences of any given financial transaction. Though the rulings program is not particularly important to the average taxpayer, it has become increasingly crucial both to the financial community [2] and to the Service itself. As the tax laws become more complex and tax risks become increasingly important to the success of business ventures, the need for confirmation before entering into a transaction is intensified. Thus parties to a transaction will generally request a ruling

> whenever the answer is uncertain or when the transaction involves substantial sums of money, even when the uncertainty may not be very great. In such circumstances the availability of a ruling in advance of the transaction has become almost as important as the financing or the know-how involved.[4]

* * *

II. DEFINITIONS

Before beginning a discussion of "rulings," it is necessary to define the exact types of communication embodied by that term—the "letter ruling" and the "Revenue Ruling"—and to compare them to other forms of communication between the Internal Revenue Service and the taxpayer.

"A 'ruling' is a written statement issued to a taxpayer * * * by the National Office which interprets and applies the tax laws to a specific state of facts." [m] This is an expression of an official interpretation by the Commissioner, and may not be given orally by any-

1. Rogovin, The Four R's: Regulations, Rulings, Reliance and Retroactivity, 43 Taxes 756–57 (1965).

2. Redman, New Procedures Re Letter Rulings; Request for Washington Assistance, 15 U.So.Cal.1963 Tax Inst. 411. "Perhaps the most popular phrase in many complicated * * * business transactions is—'subject to favorable rulings of the Internal Revenue Service.' There is barely a corporate merger, reorganization, or liquidation that rates notice on the fi-

nancial pages that does not include that phrase among the mountains of paperwork that reflect the terms of the transaction."

4. Redman, supra note 2, at 413.

m. See Rev.Proc. 80–20, 1980–1 C.B. 633, § 4.04. This Rev.Proc. sets forth the Service's general policies and procedures for the issuance of rulings and determination letters.

one employed by the Service.[6]   Rulings are applicable both to prospective transactions and to completed transactions for which a return has not yet been filed; they "serve the purpose of establishing principles and procedures of the Service in the interpretation and application of substantive tax law." [8]

In contrast to a ruling:

> [a] 'determination letter' is a written statement issued by a District Director in response to an inquiry * * * which applies to the particular facts involved the principles and precedents previously announced by the National Office.   Determination letters are issued only where a determination can be made on the basis of clearly established rules as set forth in the statutes, Treasury Decisions or regulations, or by rulings, opinions, or court decisions published in the Internal Revenue Bulletin."

The determination letter generally applies only to completed transactions and appears more limited in scope than the ruling, since the District Director is restricted to determinations based upon "clearly established" rules.[11]   Thus, the National Office, in its rulings, "makes" law, while the District Director is limited to applying that law to the facts according to the sharply defined patterns established by the superior branch.   This seems a wise limitation since the various District Directors, if allowed total freedom to interpret the tax laws as they saw fit, might destroy the uniformity so necessary to the national tax structure.

> An 'information letter' is a statement issued either by the National Office or by a District Director which does no more than call attention to a well established interpretation or principle of tax law, without applying it to a specific set of facts.[o]

The information letter is usually extremely general in nature, and does not give a solution based on the application of the law to specific facts.   Its primary purpose is to impart general knowledge which the Service feels will be of assistance to taxpayers requesting information.

"A 'Revenue Ruling' is an official interpretation by the Service which has been published in the Internal Revenue Bulletin * * *

6. Marshall, Recent Developments in Ruling Procedures: The New Two-Part Procedure; Requests for Technical Advice, N.Y.U. 24th Inst. on Fed. Tax. 83 (1966).

8. Marshall, supra note 6, at 84.

n. See Rev.Proc. 80–20, supra § 4.05.

11. "Where such a determination cannot be made, e. g. where the question

presented involves a novel issue, a determination letter will not be issued by a District Director.   A determination letter * * * is similar to a ruling in that it is an interpretation of facts submitted by the taxpayer.   It differs in that it does not normally venture into untried issues." Marshall, supra note 6, at 84.

o. See Rev.Proc. 80–20, supra § 4.06.

for the information and guidance of taxpayers, Internal Revenue Service officials, and others concerned." [p]   Published rulings concern questions which the National Office considers important both to taxpayers and Service officials, and are generally derived from letter rulings, determination letters, and requests for technical advice.   The Service takes the position that if the taxpayer's factual situation is "substantially the same" as that proposed in the Revenue Ruling, he may consummate his transaction without requesting a letter ruling; [17] however, practitioners feel that the wiser course is to obtain a letter ruling whenever there is uncertainty about the outcome.

*   *   *

Of the various forms of communication, the private ruling is the most significant to the taxpayer who desires advance assurance of the tax consequences of a proposed transaction.   The closing agreement, though attractive in its finality, is too slow and would be of little value if a relatively quick determination is needed.   The information letter is too general to aid in determining the specific tax results which will flow from given facts, and the determination letter, though often useful, will generally not issue in response to a novel tax question which requires interpretation.   Though the Revenue ruling is often helpful, there are hidden dangers if the taxpayer's factual situation is not "substantially the same," or if the Ruling is later superseded and the taxpayer consummates a transaction without this knowledge.   Thus, the wise course demands an individual ruling which interprets the law according to the taxpayer's specific factual situation.

III.   HISTORY OF THE RULINGS PROGRAM

Under the original Revenue Act of 1913, the policy of the Service was to answer all questions, whether related to proposed or consummated transactions.   These answers were considered purely advisory, and the Service could change its mind without warning, even though the taxpayer had relied upon its opinion.   In 1919, however, the Service began to restrict its rulings to completed transactions, except in those areas in which rulings were commanded by statute before a proposed transaction might be closed.

This restrictive policy was continued through 1937, when taxpayer concern over the lack of reliable advice resulted in legislation which authorized the Commissioner to enter into formal closing agreements with regard to proposed transactions.   It soon became ob-

p. Id. § 4.07. The standards for publication of private letter rulings as Revenue Rulings are set forth in Rev.Proc. 78–24, 1978–2 C.B. 503.

17. Caplin, Taxpayer Rulings Policy of the Internal Revenue Service: A Statement of Principles, N.Y.U. 20th Inst. on Fed.Tax. 1, 18 (1962). Caplin goes on to caution the taxpayer to give "careful consideration * * * to subsequent legislation and subsequently published rulings, regulations and court decisions, for any one of them may change the results of the original published position."

vious that the closing agreement was too formal and cumbersome to handle the number of requests submitted, and this method was recognized as unsatisfactory both to the taxpayer and to the Service. In answer to this problem, the Service began to treat each request for a ruling concerning the tax consequences of a proposed transaction as a *potential* request for a closing agreement, and responded to these requests with letter rulings. This policy was formally publicized by the Service in 1953, in Revenue Ruling 10.[30]

In 1954, through Revenue Ruling 54–172, the Service clearly stated that its policy would be

> to answer inquiries of individuals and organizations, whenever appropriate in the interest of sound tax administration, as to their status for tax purposes and as to the tax effects of their acts or transactions, prior to their filing of returns
> * * * * [31]

The ruling went on to point out that taxpayers who relied upon rulings would generally be protected from retroactive change—a clear shift from the prior practice of regarding rulings as mere advisory opinions. Ruling 54–172 has been supplemented on several occasions, but it still is a valid statement of the Service's position that rulings are purely a matter of discretion, and that in numerous instances they will not be granted.

A. *The No-Ruling List*

The rulings program grew as an answer to the consistent taxpayer plea for a convenient method of obtaining advance assurance in tax questions. This growth, if taken to its logical extreme, would lead to a policy of answering any and all questions, whether based on hypothetical or actual facts, whether attempting to solve a serious business problem or attempting to use the Service's information to establish a tax avoidance scheme. Furthermore, if the Service seriously attempted to answer all questions presented to it, it is doubtful whether any would be answered within sufficient time to be useful to the taxpayer. Thus, the policy favoring easily accessible advance advice was balanced against the administrative feasibility of attempting to rule upon every request submitted. The scope of the rulings program was limited by excluding certain questions, first under the discretionary power of the Commissioner and later through the published "no-ruling" lists.[q]

* * *

30. 1953–1 Cum.Bull. 488; Redman, supra note 2, at 424.

31. Rev.Rul. 172, § 2.01, 1954–1 Cum. Bull. 395.

q. The current "no-ruling" list may be found at Rev.Proc. 80–22, 1980–1 C.B. 654.

B. *Effect of "No-Ruling"*

Although the no-ruling lists were instituted to save taxpayers time and money, it is possible that they have taken on the character of indirect economic controls, due to the adverse effects which the addition of an item to the no-ruling list may have on proposed transactions. This economic control has been illustrated by several commentators in discussions of the Warwick Fund, and its demise after a refusal to rule upon its tax consequences.[48] The Warwick Fund was a "swap-fund" which was to have been organized in partnership form so as to avoid the no-ruling policy which was already in force with respect to corporate funds. A favorable private ruling was obtained by the Fund, but this ruling was quickly revoked. The Service did not rule adversely to the plan; it merely refused to rule at all, thus chilling any plans for continuation of the project due to the "contemplated difficulty of convincing a sufficient number of individuals holding highly appreciated stocks to subscribe [to the Fund] without the final assurance of the Commissioner that this would not be a taxable exchange." [52] Thus, the power to refuse to act gives the Commissioner a key influence upon the success or failure of economic ventures, even though the plan in question is arguably within the express language of the Code. It is this "propriety of refusing to rule when the Service could not, in good conscience, rule unfavorably" [53] which has been questioned by the tax bar in situations such as the Warwick Fund.

The Commissioner explains the no-ruling policy by pointing out that

> [c]ertain plans have tax attractiveness if a narrow reading
> of a Code provision is assumed. In fact, the correct tax in-
> terpretation may be uncertain or borderline in light of the
> total legislative history. Others may appear to be designed
> solely, or at least primarily, for tax avoidance purposes—or
> fall into the category of what is commonly called a 'tax gim-
> mick.' In these situations where the correct tax result is in
> doubt, it does not appear to be 'wise administration' for the

48. See Goldman, Warwick Fund Ruling Withdrawn; IRS Policy Questioned, 19 J.Tax. 197 (1963); Note, The Availability and Reviewability of Rulings of the Internal Revenue Service, 113 U.Pa.L.Rev. 81, 93 (1964).

52. Note, supra note 48, at 85. The Commissioner has pointed out that the mere addition of an item to the no-ruling list is not to be construed as "*necessarily* reflecting a hostile attitude towards the transaction."

(emphasis added). Caplin, supra note 17, at 15. It is difficult to comprehend the Commissioner's statement in view of the realities of the situation. If a specific transaction is added to the no-ruling list, it will always be construed, and probably accurately, as subject to hostility from the Service, because the Commissioner has expressly refused to grant a favorable ruling in the matter.

53. Goldman, supra note 48, at 198.

Service to give its official blessing by issuing a favorable advance ruling.[54]

* * *

* * *

IV.   PRACTICAL CONSIDERATIONS IN OBTAINING A RULING

Clearly a practice which affords advance information concerning the tax consequences of a proposed transaction is quite advantageous to the taxpayer. Indeed, it has been recognized by Mortimer Caplin (then Commissioner of Internal Revenue) that the present rulings policy is most helpful to the Service as well. Mr. Caplin points out that the present policy provides:

(1) Uniformity in the application of the laws and regulations * * * through centralized interpretation.

(2) [F]air and economical tax administration * * *.

(3) [V]aluable information to the Service by advising it in advance of audit or litigation, on the kinds of transactions being consummated or considered by taxpayers.[57]

The advantages of such a program apply to taxpayers as a group; but before the individual taxpayer decides to obtain a ruling, there are numerous other factors to be considered. In essence, the taxpayer must balance "the desirability of obtaining a high degree of tax certainty against the time and expense involved in obtaining a ruling and against the consequences of obtaining an adverse ruling or no ruling at all." [58] This broad statement must be sub-divided before it can provide meaningful guidance to the tax practitioner faced with the problem of obtaining a ruling.

A.   *Is a Favorable Ruling Likely To Be Obtained?*

A tax practitioner should not request a ruling if he is not fairly optimistic about the Service's potential response to his request. Thus, he must attempt to ascertain the basic position of the Service with regard to the type of transaction in question before he ever asks for the ruling. One method by which this may be accomplished is the so-called "telephone practice," whereby tax practitioners call individuals in the National Office and determine the Service's position on a particular issue without the need for a formal request. In addition, the practitioner must consider the language of the Code sections involved and the general policy against ruling on any transaction which seems to lack a bona fide business purpose. If the Code language indicates a restrictive policy, or if the transaction is subject to an inter-

---

54. Caplin, supra note 17, at 16.

57. Caplin, supra note 17, at 7.

58. Clark, Practical Considerations in Obtaining Rulings and in Filing Claims for Refund, Tulane 6th Tax Inst. 257, 268 (1957). * * *

pretation which points towards tax motivation as a primary purpose, there will be little chance that the Service will rule formally.

B.　*Time Factor*

If time is of the essence to the success of the transaction, it is best to act without the assurance of a ruling. Although the average ruling request (65%) takes approximately sixty days, this average is of no value to the individual taxpayer with a complex problem, as his request may take three months or longer to process. If the taxpayer is forced to make a binding decision within two months of the request, it is probably unwise to request a ruling.

C.　*Possibility of Raising Collateral Issues*

In every ruling request there is a possibility that the submission of facts to the Commissioner will raise additional issues which the taxpayer would rather avoid at that time. As one commentator points out the request for a ruling always places the tax practitioner

> in the extraordinary position of seeking a judicial response from an opposing litigant. This fact has certain significant consequences; it means that counsel must always take into account the dangers of (1) disclosing unnecessary facts to this adversary and (2) calling the attention of the latter's investigative and auditing arm to this particular transaction.[66]

Thus the request for ruling on one transaction may result in audit or litigation on a tangential problem which was not clearly brought to the tax advisor's attention.

D.　*Nature of the Transaction*

If the transaction is established in such an inflexible form that it cannot be changed if an unfavorable ruling is returned, and the taxpayer is not confident that the reply will be favorable, it might be best to undertake the transaction without requesting a ruling. If the taxpayer receives an adverse ruling, and consummates the transaction despite it, he can be positive that the district office will take an adverse position since "the field almost always follows the conclusions of the National Office * * *."[67]

It is also somewhat unwise to request a ruling on a consummated transaction. The facts upon which tax liability will be based have already been irrevocably established, and if an unfavorable ruling were then issued, the taxpayer would be hard-pressed indeed in trying to change the mind of a District Director armed with an adverse opinion from the National Office.

66.　Clark, supra note 58, at 272–273.　　**67.**　Ellentuck, How and When to Use the Advance Ruling, 21 J.Tax. 52, 55 (1964).

It is best not to request a ruling in a transaction which is frowned upon by the Service but acceptable to the courts. Here it might be wise to take the calculated risk of litigation and proceed, rather than to evoke an immediate negative response from the Service.

Assuming, however, that the tax practitioner errs and submits a ruling request, what alternatives will be open to him, or to the Service?

1. *Withdrawal of Ruling Requests.*—The taxpayer has the right to withdraw a ruling request until the ruling letter is signed at the National Office.

> However, in such a case, the National Office may furnish its views to the District Director in whose office the return * * * will be filed. The District Director will consider the information submitted in a subsequent audit or examination * * *.[r]

Thus, the withdrawal, although motivated by fear of an unfavorable ruling, may be ineffectual. This problem is indicative of the need for extreme care on the part of the practitioner before submitting the request for advice.

2. *Receipt of an Adverse Ruling.*—Some commentators suggest that the receipt of an adverse ruling is not a major disaster, since it allows the taxpayer to mold his transaction to meet the objections of the Service. If, however, the transaction is inflexible, the taxpayer must either abandon it, consummate it and pay the additional taxes, or litigate. The District Office will not be amenable to compromise on the results of the transaction since it will follow the already stated position of the National Office.

3. *Refusal To Rule.*—Other than the feeling of uncertainty which is created by a refusal to rule, the taxpayer is in no worse position than if he had withdrawn his request. If the Commissioner believes that the transaction has been or will be consummated in the same form as suggested in the request, he will send the information to the District Office.

In each of the three situations above, it is clear that no result of an unwise request will materially benefit the taxpayer, and the tax practitioner must carefully analyze each possible result before submitting the ruling request.

* * *

QUESTIONS

1. In recent years, as part of the war against what it categorizes as "abusive" tax shelters, the IRS has utilized as a weapon the issuance of unsolicited (unfavorable) rulings directly pertinent to currently marketed tax

---

r. See Rev.Proc. 80–20, supra § 15.

shelters. Is this practice fair to the promoters? To the prospective participants? Would it be any more fair for the Service to keep its position secret until the audit stage? Should rulings be the vehicle for the IRS to announce its hostility to specific tax shelters?

2. What will be the long range effects of the commercial publication of private letter rulings?

B. REVOCATION, RELIANCE AND RETROACTIVITY

The IRS, in the course of issuing rulings and determination letters, necessarily causes reliance to be placed upon its statements as to the interpretation and application of the tax law. All taxpayers may rely upon published rulings. The particular taxpayers receiving private letter rulings or determination letters may rely upon such rulings to the extent that the facts upon which they are issued are correct. However, the tax law is highly volatile. New legislation, court decisions and other developments can cause the Service in perfectly good faith to change a position set forth in a ruling. The following cases discuss the extent to which the Service is able to change a position set forth in a ruling or determination letter, and the limits upon the Commissioner's exercise of the discretionary authority contained in IRC § 7805(b) to prescribe the extent to which such a change may be applied without retroactive effect.

LESAVOY FOUNDATION v. COMMISSIONER

238 F.2d 589 (3d Cir. 1956).

GOODRICH, Circuit Judge.

This case raises the question of (1) the liability to taxation of a corporation organized for charitable, educational and philanthropic purposes,[1] which the Commissioner claims departed from its exempt purpose and was used in part as a means of furthering business enterprises in which the donor of the foundation of the charitable trust was interested and (2) the limits, if any, of the power of the Commissioner to make a revocation of an exemption retroactive.

The foundation on July 31, 1945, upon application was granted a certificate of exemption from taxation under the statute just referred to. Six years later, on December 19, 1951, the Commissioner revoked the certificate of exemption alleging the reason just mentioned and assessed a deficiency against the petitioner along with penalties. The revocation was made retroactive to 1946 during which year the foundation acquired Clover Spinning Mills, an enterprise which manufactured cotton yarn and cloth. This imposed a deficiency on the taxpayer for the years 1946 to 1948 and 1950. The taxpayer claims the

---

1. Int.Rev.Code of 1939, § 101(6) (now Int.Rev.Code of 1954, § 501(c)(3)) exempts organizations for "religious, charitable, scientific, literary or educational purposes."

resulting deficiency thus assessed will completely wipe out the assets of the foundation. This statement seems to be borne out by the last report we have for the year ending December 31, 1949   *   *   *.

*   *   *

*   *   * [W]e think the Commissioner went beyond his authority in revoking the certificate of exemption retroactively. We quite realize that the Commissioner may change his mind when he believes he has made a mistake in a matter of fact or law. Our own decision in Keystone Automobile Club v. Commissioner, 3 Cir. 1950, 181 F.2d 420, recognizes this point fully and that point is sustained by abundant authority. But it is quite a different matter to say that having once changed his mind the Commissioner may arbitrarily and without limit have the effect of that change go back over previous years during which the taxpayer operated under the previous ruling.

Although there is ample authority that the Commissioner may change retroactively a ruling of general application, there is a dearth of cases involving individualized taxpayer's rulings. This is so because the Commissioner has almost invariably followed a policy of honoring his rulings and making changes prospective only   *   *   *. Indeed, this policy has been codified by one of the Commissioner's own rulings.[6]

The few authorities that there are concerning individualized rulings are not unanimous. The point has had the most attention in the Sixth Circuit. The latest decision of that Court in Automobile Club of Michigan v. Commissioner, 6 Cir., 1956, 230 F.2d 585, certiorari granted, 352 U.S. 817, discusses previous rulings and comes out with elaborate opinions both supporting and against the Commissioner's action. The result of that case, another one concerning an automobile club, was to permit a two-year retroactive effect to a revocation of the certificate under which the club was exempt as a social club. Note, however, that the majority found, 230 F.2d at pages 588 and 590, that the ruling was not arbitrary or oppressive since the retroactive effect was limited to two years though it could have been extended back eleven, and there was no element of estoppel since the tax-

---

6. Rev.Rul. 54–146, 1954–1 Cum.Bull. 88, 91 provides:

"It is the general policy of the Internal Revenue Service to limit the revocation of a ruling with respect to an organization previously held to qualify under section 101 to a prospective application only, if the organization has acted in good faith in reliance upon the ruling issued to it and a retroactive revocation of such ruling would be to its detriment. Any ruling issued as to the exempt status of an organization will not be considered controlling where there has been a misstatement or omission of a material fact or where the operations of the organization are conducted in a manner materially different from that represented. A revocation may be effected by a notice to the organization or by a ruling or other statement published in the Internal Revenue Bulletin applicable to the type of organization involved. *   *   * "

[Compare § 13 of Rev.Proc. 80–25, 1980–1 C.B. 667 and § 17.05 of Rev. Proc. 80–20, supra.]

payer did not assert that it acted in reliance on the certificate. On the other hand, there is respectable authority that the Commissioner may not retroactively change an individualized taxpayer's ruling, unless the taxpayer is himself estopped from relying on the ruling in good faith because he has concealed the facts, or because of some other fraud or misrepresentation.

We, therefore, turn our attention to the question of whether this taxpayer has done anything to estop itself from relying on the certificate. In arguing that it has, the government urges that the taxpayer was not frank in the manner in which it filled out its 1946 information return. The income tax form asks: "Have you any sources of income or engaged in any activities which have not previously been reported to the Bureau? If so, attach detailed statement." Taxpayer answered, "Yes" in the blank provided after the question. In the margin directly under the question was typed, "Purchased Clover Spinning Mills Co., Clover, So. Carolina, March 18, 1946." A balance sheet attached to the 1946 return listed such assets as mill buildings, machinery and equipment, accounts receivable and under inventory listed cotton, work in progress, finished yarn and manufacturing supplies. Under liabilities were items for accounts payable and payroll. Another question on the form asked for gross receipts from business activities and the taxpayer reported substantial sales of yarn and cloth. Taken as a whole, we think that the return fully and fairly disclosed that taxpayer was engaged in an active textile spinning enterprise. We see nothing more that the form called for. The taxpayer did not misstate anything it told the Commissioner, nor did it omit to disclose anything it should have told him. In fact, a schedule attached to the 1946 return indicated a close connection between the foundation and other textile enterprises by listing as contributors Fabrics Corporation of America, Rayon Corporation of America and two other businesses which contain "Mills" as part of their names.

The taxpayer fully disclosed the information required by the informational return. The original exemption certificate imposed upon the foundation a duty to inform the Commissioner of any relevant changes in the facts and, as already stated, taxpayer gave the information. The taxpayer did not bring to the Commissioner's attention the fact that Clover sold yarn to the donor's mills. We do not find this fact any evidence of lack of frankness for the information would have been irrelevant at the time the return was made. The Commissioner's theory is a debatable one at best even today and some of the cases he relies on most heavily were not decided until the end of the taxable years involved.

The statutory section on retroactivity is found in section 3791(b) of the 1939 Code (now Int.Rev.Code of 1954, § 7805(b)). The section reads as follows:

> "Retroactivity of regulations or rulings. The Secretary, or the Commissioner with the approval of the Secretary,

may prescribe the extent, if any, to which any ruling, regulation, or Treasury Decision, relating to the internal revenue laws, shall be applied without retroactive effect."

As the Sixth Circuit points out, the provision gives the Commissioner discretionary power to determine the extent of retroactivity in a given case. The usual rule in such case is that an official vested with discretionary power is not to be interfered with unless it can be found that his action in a given case goes beyond the bounds of discretion. We think that usual rule should be applicable here.

We think further that the bounds of permissible discretion were exceeded when the Commissioner changed his mind as to the exemption to be granted this foundation and made it liable for a tax bill so large as to wipe it out of existence. As already indicated the people in charge of it committed no fraud and made no misstatement. Whether there was any basis for holding that it departed from the facts which would entitle it to a charitable exemption is at least an arguable question of law. We, therefore, see no grounds for sustaining such a harsh result as the ruling of the Commissioner, if enforced, would involve.

The judgment of the Tax Court will be reversed.

AUTOMOBILE CLUB OF MICHIGAN v. COMMISSIONER

Supreme Court of the United States, 1957.
353 U.S. 180, 77 S.Ct. 707, 1 L.Ed.2d 746.

Mr. Justice BRENNAN delivered the opinion of the Court.

In 1945, the Commissioner of Internal Revenue revoked his 1934 and 1938 rulings exempting the petitioner from federal income taxes, and retroactively applied the revocation to 1943 and 1944. The Commissioner also determined that prepaid membership dues received by the petitioner should be taken into income in the year received, rejecting the petitioner's method of reporting as income only that part of the dues as was recorded on petitioner's books as earned in the tax year. The Tax Court sustained the Commissioner's determinations, and the Court of Appeals for the Sixth Circuit affirmed. * * *

The Commissioner had determined in 1934 that the petitioner was a "club" entitled to exemption under provisions of the internal revenue laws corresponding to § 101(9) of the Internal Revenue Code of 1939, notifying the petitioner that " * * * future returns, under the provisions of section 101(9) * * * will not be required so long as there is no change in your organization, your purposes or methods of doing business." In 1938, the Commissioner confirmed this ruling in a letter stating: " * * * as it appears that there has been no change in your form of organization or activities which would affect your status the previous ruling of the Bureau holding you to be exempt from filing returns of income is affirmed * * *."

Accordingly the petitioner did not pay federal taxes from 1933 to 1945. The Commissioner revoked these rulings in 1945, however, and directed the petitioner to file returns for 1943 and subsequent years.[5] Pursuant to this direction, the petitioner filed, under protest, corporate income and excess profits tax returns for 1943, 1944 and 1945.

The Commissioner's earlier rulings were grounded upon an erroneous interpretation of the term "club" in § 101(9) and thus were based upon a mistake of law. It is conceded that in 1943 and 1944 petitioner was not, in fact or in law, a "club" entitled to exemption within the meaning of § 101(9), and also that petitioner is subject to taxation for 1945 and subsequent years. It is nevertheless contended that the Commissioner had no power to apply the revocation retroactively to 1943 and 1944 * * *.

The petitioner argues that, in light of the 1934 and 1938 rulings, the Commissioner was equitably estopped from applying the revocation retroactively. This argument is without merit. The doctrine of equitable estoppel is not a bar to the correction by the Commissioner of a mistake of law. * * *

Petitioner's reliance on H. S. D. Co. v. Kavanagh, 6 Cir., 191 F. 2d 831, and Woodworth v. Kales, 6 Cir., 26 F.2d 178, is misplaced because those cases did not involve correction of an erroneous ruling of law. Reliance on Lesavoy Foundation v. Commissioner, 3 Cir., 238 F.2d 589, is also misplaced because there the court recognized the power in the Commissioner to correct a mistake of law, but held that in the circumstances of the case the Commissioner had exceeded the bounds of the discretion vested in him under § 3791(b) of the 1939 Code.

The Commissioner's action may not be disturbed unless, in the circumstances of this case, the Commissioner abused the discretion vested in him by § 3791(b) of the 1939 Code. * * * The petitioner contends that this section forbids the Commissioner taking retroactive action. On the contrary, it is clear from the language of the section and its legislative history that Congress thereby confirmed the authority of the Commissioner to correct any ruling, regulation or Treasury decision retroactively, but empowered him, in his discretion, to limit retroactive application to the extent necessary to avoid inequitable results.

The petitioner, citing Helvering v. R. J. Reynolds Tobacco Co., 306 U.S. 110, 59 S.Ct. 423, 83 L.Ed. 536, argues that resort by the

5. The letter of revocation stated that in order to qualify as a club under § 101(9), the " * * * organization should be so composed and its activities be such that fellowship among the members plays a material part in the life of the organization * * *." It was then stated that the previous rulings were revoked because "[t]he evidence submitted shows that fellowship does not constitute a material part of the life of * * * [petitioner's] organization and that * * * [petitioner's] principal activity is the rendering of commercial services to * * * [its] members."

Commissioner to § 3791(b) was precluded in this case because the re-peated re-enactments of § 101(9) gave the force of law to the provi-sion of the Treasury regulations relating to that section. These regu-lations provided that when an organization had established its right to exemption it need not thereafter make a return of income or any further showing with respect to its status unless it changed the char-acter of its operations or the purpose for which it was originally cre-ated. Helvering v. R. J. Reynolds Tobacco Co. is inapplicable to this case. As stated by the Tax Court: "The regulations involved there [Helvering v. R. J. Reynolds Tobacco Co.] * * * purported to determine what did or did not constitute gain or loss. The regula-tions here * * * in no wise purported to determine whether any organization was or was not exempt." [11] These regulations did not provide the exemption or interpret § 101(9), but merely specified the necessary information required to be filed in order that the Commis-sioner might rule whether or not the taxpayer was entitled to exemp-tion. This is thus not a case of " * * * administrative construc-tion embodied in the regulation[s] * * * " which, by repeated re-enactment of § 101(9), " * * * Congress must be taken to have approved * * * and thereby to have given * * * the force of law." Helvering v. R. J. Reynolds Tobacco Co., 306 U.S. at pages 114, 115, 59 S.Ct. at page 425.

We must, then, determine whether the retroactive action of the Commissioner was an abuse of discretion in the circumstances of this case. The action was the consequence of the reconsideration by the Commissioner, in 1943, of the correctness of the prior rulings ex-empting automobile clubs, initiated by a General Counsel Memoran-dum interpreting § 101(9) to be inapplicable to such organizations. The Commissioner adopted the General Counsel's interpretation and proceeded to apply it, effective from 1943, indiscriminately to auto-mobile clubs. We thus find no basis for disagreeing with the conclu-sion, reached by both the Tax Court and the Court of Appeals, that the Commissioner, having dealt with petitioner upon the same basis as other automobile clubs, did not abuse his discretion. Nor did the two-year delay in proceeding with the petitioner's case, in these cir-cumstances, vitiate the Commissioner's action.

* * *

Affirmed.

NOTE

See Dixon v. United States, excerpted below at page 291, where the Su-preme Court relies upon *Automobile Club of Michigan* in holding that the Commissioner is empowered to correct a mistake of law by withdrawing retroactively a published acquiescence in an "erroneous" Tax Court decision, even though the taxpayer acted to his detriment in reliance upon the acqui-escence.

11. 20 T.C. at page 1041.

C. DISCRIMINATORY TREATMENT

It would appear to be axiomatic that all taxpayers should receive equal treatment from the Internal Revenue Service. Certainly, one would expect that all taxpayers similarly situated would have the tax law interpreted by the Internal Revenue Service in the same manner. Yet, for valid reasons, one taxpayer generally is not permitted to rely upon a private letter ruling issued to another taxpayer regardless of the identity of the circumstances of the two taxpayers. The following case considers the ability of one taxpayer to obtain the favorable tax treatment afforded another by virtue of a private letter ruling.

BOOKWALTER v. BRECKLEIN

357 F.2d 78 (8th Cir. 1966).

VOGEL, Circuit Judge.

The question in this case is whether the taxpayer, plaintiff-appellee herein, is entitled to refunds for tax deductions not previously taken by him in 1957 [for certain special assessments paid to the city of Kansas City, Missouri for the construction of parking facilities] on the grounds that private letter rulings issued to other taxpayers in 1958 erroneously allowed such other taxpayers to take similar deductions. The said letter rulings were eventually revoked but were revoked prospectively rather than retroactively. The District Court * * * allowed appellee to recover for years prior to the time the private letter rulings were revoked. We reverse.

* * *

In 1958 the City of Bismarck, North Dakota, sought a ruling relating to the deductibility for income tax purposes of special assessments levied by that city against some 500 property owners with land located in and benefitted by parking improvement districts in Bismarck's central business area. Such deductions were made permissible in a May 21, 1958, letter sent to the Commissioners of the City of Bismarck by Dan J. Ferris, the Acting Director of the Tax Rulings Division (this will hereafter be referred to as the Bismarck letter). * * * The Bismarck letter was never published in the Internal Revenue Bulletin but it was picked up and published by the Commerce Clearing House, a private tax service. The Bismarck letter was revoked prospectively in an April 4, 1960, letter from Dana Latham, the Commissioner of Internal Revenue, to the Bismarck Commissioners. * * * The revocation of the Bismarck letter was published in the Internal Revenue Bulletin as Rev.Rul. 60–327, 1960–2, Cum.Bull. 65.

After the issuance, but before the revocation, of the Bismarck letter, a Bismarck type of ruling was sought by a partnership owning business rental property known as the Wirthman Building in Kansas

City, Missouri. * * * In response to their request, the Wirthman partners were informed in a letter dated June 18, 1959, * * * (hereafter this will be referred to as the Wirthman determination letter) that in the future a deduction for the assessment payments would be allowed. * * * For the fiscal years ending in 1959 and 1960, the Wirthman partners deducted the installments paid as ordinary and necessary business expenses pursuant to the Wirthman determination letter. However, the Wirthman determination letter was revoked "henceforth" in a letter, dated January 12, 1961, sent to the Wirthman partners * * *.

Following the prospective repudiations of the Bismarck letter and the Wirthman determination letter, appellee, on March 23, 1961, filed suit to recover an overpayment of taxes for 1957 resulting from a failure to deduct the benefit district assessments paid by him in one lump sum in 1957. After an evidentiary hearing, the District Court entered judgment for appellee, holding that the taxpayer was

"* * * entitled as a matter of law to equality of treatment with the 500 Bismarck taxpayers, the Wirthman partners, and any others who were accorded the benefit of the Commissioner's modification provision of no retroactive application of the modification ruling of April 4, 1960.

The authority for making the revocation of the Bismarck and Wirthman letters prospective only is derived from 26 U.S.C.A. § 7805(b) * * *.

Appellee argues that:

"The Unlawful Discrimination Between Similarly-Situated Taxpayers, As Found by the District Court, Was Such That the Judgment of the District Court Was Not Erroneous."

We do not agree. Ordinarily, the Commissioner of Internal Revenue or his duly authorized subordinates act within their power when revoking an erroneous private ruling with or without retroactive effect. The evidence does not show that the appellee herein is being treated any worse or any differently from other taxpayers in his position who did not request or receive private letter rulings. Taxpayers without rulings are entitled only to be taxed the same as other taxpayers without rulings. See, e. g., Bornstein v. United States, Ct.Cl., 1965, 345 F.2d 558, 563–564; Goodstein v. Commissioner, 1 Cir., 1959, 267 F.2d 127, 132.

The fact that the private Bismarck letter was published by the Commerce Clearing House is not of decisive consequence. In *Goodstein,* supra, the taxpayer had seen other private but officially unpublished rulings and this factor was not enough to allow him (and, inferentially, all other taxpayers in his position) to rely on the said private rulings. As a practical matter, officials of the Internal Revenue Service are themselves not bound for precedent purposes by rulings or decisions not officially published. This fact is not unknown to the public since the policy of the Internal Revenue Service is set out in the introduction to the Internal Revenue Bulletins. In any event, the appellee did not rely either on the Bismarck letter or the Wirthman determination letter for he had paid his taxes on the assessment prior to when those letters were issued. There is no showing that appellee ever incurred expense or arranged his affairs in reliance on the Bismarck or Wirthman determinations. Even if such reliance had been shown, this is not necessarily decisive.

Certain cases relied on by the court below and by the appellee in his brief are inapposite to the instant situation. Each case must be viewed on its facts to determine if the Commissioner has abused his discretion under 26 U.S.C.A. § 7805(b). We will deal with these cases individually below.

International Business Machines Corp. v. United States, Ct.Cl., 1965, 343 F.2d 914, certiorari denied, 86 S.Ct. 647, (hereafter referred to as the *I.B.M.* case), a three to one decision, involved two competitors, I.B.M. and Remington Rand, in the manufacturing, selling and leasing of large electronic computer systems. On April 13, 1955, Remington requested a ruling from the Commissioner of Internal Revenue to permit it to avoid existing tax liabilities arising out of the sale and rental of its computers. A favorable ruling was issued by the Commissioner in a telegram sent to Remington on April 15, 1955. On July 13, 1955, I.B.M., having learned of the Remington ruling, sought a similar ruling on its sale and leasing of comparable computers. I.B.M.'s letter to the Commissioner was marked "Urgent! Please Expedite" and closed as follows:

> "In view of the extreme urgency of this matter, your immediate ruling, wire collect, is respectfully requested."

I.B.M.'s request was not acted upon for over two years, and then in a negative manner. Both I.B.M. (on July 29, 1955) and Remington (in September 1955) also sought refunds for taxes paid on the sale and leasing of computers in the past. I.B.M.'s claim covered the period from June 1, 1951, to May 31, 1955, and Remington's from January 1, 1952, to April 30, 1955. Remington's refund was allowed in July of 1956. I.B.M.'s refund claim, however, was rejected. The favorable tax ruling as to Remington was finally revoked prospectively as of February 1, 1958. In other words, Remington enjoyed six years of paying no tax on the selling and leasing of its computers, while I.B.M. did not share in such advantages for the selling and leasing of an almost identical product, even though both companies made similar requests of the Commissioner. This amounted to a comparative loss of over $13,000,000 to I.B.M. The Court of Claims allowed I.B.M. to recover the taxes paid by it on income derived from the rental and sale of computers for the period that Remington was not subjected to the tax.

Clearly, the facts of the *I.B.M.* case are entirely different from those in the instant situation. In *I.B.M.* there are clear and uncontradicted indications that the Commissioner abused his discretion in granting Remington tax-free treatment to the detriment of I.B.M. Unlike the instant appeal, the *I.B.M.* case involved a situation where one competitor was being favored unjustifiably over the only other competitor in the computer industry. Thus, the only members of the only logical class therein—the computer industry—were being treated in exactly opposite ways to the great detriment of I.B.M. Herein the situation is entirely different since appellee was treated no differently from many other similarly situated taxpayers who also had not sought rulings. In *I.B.M.* no reason was shown as to why Remington was not taxed retroactively. Here rational explanations were set forth as to why the Wirthman partners were not taxed retroactively—e. g., Mr. Jack U. Hiatt, a group supervisor for the Field Audit Branch of the Internal Revenue Service, testified that it was not feasible to collect a relatively small tax liability from a large number of taxpayers (the 22 members of the Wirthman partnership) located in different collection districts. There is a great contrast between the relatively small amounts involved herein and the $13,000,000 involved in *I.B.M.* Furthermore, there was a much greater reliance factor in *I.B.M.* since I.B.M. was, at the time it was paying the disputed taxes, aware of the ruling made to Remington and within three months after the private ruling to Remington had made an urgent request for a similar ruling. Herein appellee paid his assessment *before* either the Bismarck or Wirthman determination letters were issued.

In *I.B.M.* Judge Davis, writing for the three-man majority, stated:

> "Implicit, too, in the Congressional award of discretion to the [Internal Revenue] Service, through Section 7805(b), is the power as well as the *obligation to consider the totality of the circumstances surrounding the handing down of a ruling—including the comparative or differential effect on the other taxpayers in the same class. 'The Commissioner cannot tax one and not tax another without some rational basis for the difference.'* United States v. Kaiser, 363 U.S. 299, 308, 80 S.Ct. 1204, 1210, 4 L.Ed.2d 1233 (1960) (Frankfurter, J., concurring). This factor has come to be recognized as central to the administration of the section. Equality of treatment is so dominant in our understanding of justice that discretion, where it is allowed a role, must pay the strictest heed.
>
> *   *   *
>
> " *   *   * *When we examine the agreed facts,* we cannot escape holding that there was a clear abuse, that the circumstances compelled the Service to confine its ruling ·(when it was finally given) to the future period for which

Remington Rand's computers were to be held taxable.
* * *

* * *

"*This history* exposes a manifest and unjustifiable discrimination against the taxpayer." (Emphasis supplied.)

As is apparent from the italicized portions of the above quotation, the Court of Claims was limiting itself in *I.B.M.* to the "totality of the circumstances" there involved. That *I.B.M.* was not intended to be a blanket ruling is clearly evidenced in two later cases decided by the Court of Claims. Those decisions are Knetsch v. United States, Ct. Cl., 1965, 348 F.2d 932, certiorari denied 86 S.Ct. 1221, and Bornstein v. United States, supra. In *Knetsch*, that court stated:

"As the court pointed out in *Bornstein*, supra, *our decision in International Business Machines Corp. v. United States, Ct.Cl., 343 F.2d 914, decided April 16, 1965, rested in section 7805(b) of the Internal Revenue Code, of 1954, and was based on the court's evaluation of the particular circumstances in that case.*" (Emphasis supplied.)

In *Bornstein* the Court of Claims stated:

"There are also controlling factual differences between these cases [*Bornstein*] and International Business Machines Corp. v. United States. In that case the court applied Section 7805(b) of the Internal Revenue Code of 1954 in behalf of a taxpayer who had made prompt application to obtain a private ruling to the same effect as a ruling issued to another taxpayer, which manufactured and sold business machines that were similar in all material respects to the machines manufactured by plaintiff. *In these cases, none of the taxpayers nor the corporations in which they are shareholders asked for rulings.*" (Emphasis supplied.)

Herein, as in *Bornstein*, the appellee had not requested a ruling prior to paying his assessment and was clearly not discriminated against in the manner that I.B.M. was in the *I.B.M.* case. In *I.B.M.* the evidence was very strong that the Commissioner abused his discretion under 26 U.S.C.A. § 7805(b) but, under the facts of the instant case, the evidence is at least just as strong that there was no abuse of administrative discretion in prospectively withdrawing the Bismarck and Wirthman letters.

The other authorities relied on by appellees i. e., City Loan & Savings Co. v. United States, N.D.Ohio, 1959, 177 F.Supp. 843, aff'd 6 Cir., 1961, 287 F.2d 612; Exchange Parts Co. of Fort Worth v. United States, 1960, 279 F.2d 251, 150 Ct.Cl. 538; Connecticut Ry. & Lighting Co. v. United States, 1956, 142 F.Supp. 907, 135 Ct.Cl. 538—are also of no avail to the appellee herein. In *Exchange Parts Co.* and *Connecticut Ry. & Lighting Co.*, as pointed out in *Bornstein*, supra, " * * * This court [the Court of Claims] held that it was an abuse of discretion for the Commissioner to apply his ruling retroactively, *solely* on the basis that plaintiffs had paid the taxes in question." (Emphasis supplied.)   Herein, as we have already noted and as the record clearly indicates, the Commissioner's decision was based on rational administrative considerations and was not intended to be nor actually was discriminatory to appellee in regard to others in his situation—i. e., those who had not desired to nor actually did not receive private rulings prior to paying taxes on the assessments.   In the *City Loan & Savings Co.* case there was a strong reliance factor not present herein since there the Commissioner, after some fourteen years, had attempted to retroactively revoke as to the taxpayer there involved his (the Commissioner's) official published acquiescence in a certain Tax Court case previously relied on by the taxpayer.

We would not be remiss to point out that a favorable ruling to appellee herein could open the proverbial floodgates of litigation as suits could feasibly be brought by all other similarly situated taxpayers who did not deduct special assessments from their returns during the years in question.   Not allowing the Commissioner some proper discretion in prospectively or retroactively revoking private rulings could cause the elimination of private letter rulings and any and all benefits to be derived therefrom.   Private letter rulings are issued to certain private parties and are not intended to be relied on by the general public as a whole.   It is only when the Commissioner abuses his discretion under 26 U.S.C.A. § 7805(b) that remedial action should be taken.   The instant case is no such situation.

We also note that to allow appellee to recover herein would arguably prejudice other taxpayers—e. g., the Wirthman partners—since appellee could deduct his entire assessment, whereas other taxpayers could deduct only that portion paid prior to the revocation of the private letter rulings.   The shoe would then be on the other foot and appellee would have a windfall merely because he chose to pay his entire assessment in one lump sum.   This could give rise to even more undesirable litigation.   In the absence of cogent reasons to the contrary, no court should overturn a discretionary ruling by the Commissioner under 26 U.S.C.A. § 7805(b) which could lead to wholesale and time-consuming litigation.   As already noted, such cogent reasons are not present herein.

We reverse and remand for further proceedings not inconsistent with the foregoing.

SECTION 3.   CONFIDENTIALITY AND DISCLOSURE

A.   THE FREEDOM OF INFORMATION ACT

The Freedom of Information Act, 5 U.S.C.A. § 552, enacted in 1966 as an amendment to the public disclosure section of the Administrative Procedure Act, provides the public with an effective means of access to a broad spectrum of government information and records. By opening up vast stores of agency information to the public, the Freedom of Information Act has become a valuable resource tool for individuals and businesses who find themselves subject to government regulation. Not surprisingly, the Act has had a significant impact upon tax practice. FOIA suits have triggered the disclosure of private letter rulings,[s] large portions of the Internal Revenue Manual,[t] and numerous other types of internal IRS memoranda.[u] Disclosed material provides tax practitioners with valuable insights into IRS positions and policies. FOIA disclosures may also be used to supplement discovery procedures prior to and during tax litigation.

Agency records obtained through FOIA disclosures may be utilized in subsequent tax proceedings in a variety of ways. Inconsistent rulings by the IRS can show an abuse of discretion by the Service in the retroactive revocation of rulings or the good faith of a taxpayer's position in a penalty or criminal context.[v] Differential treatment of similarly situated taxpayers may also tend to indicate intentionally discriminatory conduct on the part of the IRS.[w]

Information Subject to Disclosure

The FOIA requires each federal agency to make various categories of official information available to the public. Disclosable material is classified into three broad categories according to the manner in which the information is to be made available to the public:

 1.   Materials that must be published in the Federal Register, including substantive rules of general applicability, state-

---

s. Tax Analysts and Advocates v. IRS, 362 F.Supp. 1298 (D.D.C.1973), aff'd in pertinent part, 505 F.2d 350 (D.C. Cir. 1974).

t. Hawkes v. IRS, 467 F.2d 787 (6th Cir. 1972), appeal after remand, 507 F.2d 481 (1974).

u. See, e. g., Taxation With Representation Fund v. IRS, 485 F.Supp. 263 (D.D.C.1980); aff'd in part and remanded in part, 47 AFTR 2d 81–1026 (D.C.Cir. 1981).

v. In United States v. Wahlin, 384 F. Supp. 43 (W.D.Wis.1974), a defendant charged with evasion of manufacturer's excise taxes used FOIA procedures to obtain access to private letter rulings (and correspondence relating thereto) in order to construct his defense that the taxing provision which he allegedly violated was unduly vague, confusing, indefinite and inconsistent.

w. See discussion in D. Walter, The Battle for Information: Strategies of Taxpayers and the IRS to Compel (or Resist) Disclosure, 56 Taxes 740 (1978).

ments of general policy, and interpretations of general applicability which have been formulated and adopted by the agency. 5 U.S.C.A. § 552(a)(1).

2. Material that must be made available for public inspection and copying, including final orders and opinions resulting from agency adjudications, statements of policies and interpretations which have been adopted by the agency but not published in the Federal Register, and administrative staff manuals and agency instructions that affect the public. 5 U.S.C.A. § 552(a)(2).

3. Other information, not subject to disclosure by the above-described methods, and not specifically exempted from disclosure, must be made available upon a request "reasonably describing" the desired records. 5 U.S.C.A. § 552(a)(3).

In an attempt to balance the public's right to know about the function and operation of its government against the government's legitimate need for secrecy, the Act specifically exempts nine categories of information from public disclosure.[x] The presence of some exempt material in a document does not justify the withholding of the entire document. When exempt and non-exempt material are present in the same record, the Act requires the agency to disclose any "reasonably segregable" portion of the requested records. 5 U.S.C.A. § 522(b).[y]

In addition to the segregation requirement, the Act contains several incentives to assure the agency's voluntary compliance with the

---

x. 5 U.S.C.A. § 552(b)(1)–(9). The nine categories are as follows:

1. Classified information relating to the national defense and foreign policy.

2. Materials relating solely to the internal rules and policies of the agency.

3. Information specifically exempted by statutes other than the FOIA itself.

4. Trade secrets and commercial or financial information obtained from a person and privileged or confidential.

5. Inter-agency and intra-agency memoranda which would not be available to a party in litigation with the agency.

6. Personnel, medical, and similar files, the disclosure of which would constitute a "clearly unwarranted invasion of personal privacy".

7. Investigatory records compiled for law enforcement purposes, but only to the extent that disclosure would (A) interfere with enforcement proceedings, (B) deprive a person of a fair trial, (C) constitute an unwarranted invasion of personal privacy, (D) reveal the identity of a confidential source, (E) disclose investigative techniques and procedures, or (F) endanger the safety of law enforcement personnel.

8. Information relating to agency supervision and regulation of financial institutions.

9. Geological and geophysical data concerning wells.

y. Treasury regulations define "reasonably segregable portions" to be "any portion of the record which is not exempt * * * and which after deletion of the exempt material still conveys meaningful and nonmisleading information." 31 CFR § 1.-2(c)(3) (1977).

Act's disclosure provisions. First, the FOIA provides that no person shall be "adversely affected" by material required to be published in the Federal Register but not so published. 5 U.S.C.A. § 522(a)(1). Failure to comply with the publication requirement may estop the agency from invoking an unpublished "rule of general applicability" against an individual.[z] A further incentive to disclose is found in § 522(a)(2), which provides that no agency can rely on or cite as precedent any final order, opinion, or statement of policy which has not previously been made available to the public. Finally, the Act authorizes the allowance of attorneys' fees and other costs in actions in which the complainant "substantially prevails". 5 U.S.C.A. § 522(a)(4)(E).

Scope of the Act's Exemptions

Litigation under the FOIA has generally focused upon the scope of the nine exemptions. The exemptions of particular relevance to the tax practitioner are discussed below.

Exemption 3: Information Specifically Exempted By Other Statutes. Exemption 3 permits the withholding of information the confidentiality of which is assured by some other (non-FOIA) statute. To qualify as an Exemption 3 statute, the statute which purportedly requires non-disclosure must either: (1) leave no discretion to the agency as to its duty to withhold, or (2) establish particular criteria for agency guidance in determining which material is to be withheld. 5 U.S.C.A. § 552(b)(3)(A) and (B). Section 6103 of the Internal Revenue Code, relating to the confidentiality of returns and return information, has been held to be an Exemption 3 statute.[a]

Under § 6103, tax returns and "tax return information" (defined so as to include all information collected to determine a taxpayer's tax liability) may not be disclosed to persons other than the taxpayer about whom the information was compiled.[b] Tax return information

---

z. See, e. g., Morton v. Ruiz, 415 U.S. 199, 232–236, 94 S.Ct. 1055, 1073–1074, 39 L.Ed.2d 270 (1974); W. G. Cosby Transfer & Storage Corp. v. Froehlke, 480 F.2d 498 (4th Cir. 1973).

a. Chamberlain v. Kurtz, 589 F.2d 827 (5th Cir.), cert. denied, 444 U.S. 842, 100 S.Ct. 82, 62 L.Ed.2d 54 (1979); Belisle v. Commissioner, 462 F.Supp. 460 (W.D.Okl.1978). See also Zale Corp. v. IRS, 481 F.Supp. 486 (D.D.C.1979).

b. In Conway v. IRS, 447 F.Supp. 1128 (D.D.C.1978), a taxpayer seeking disclosure of IRS memoranda regarding third parties' attempts to obtain tax credits for foreign tax payments was unable to view the relevant docu-

ments until all identifying information had been excised. See also, Lobosco v. IRS, 42 AFTR 2d 78–5630 (E.D.N.Y.1978) (complainant not entitled to records regarding investigation of tax liability of third parties).

It should be noted that § 6103(b)(2) excepts from the definition of "return information" data which "cannot be associated with, or otherwise identify, directly or indirectly, a particular taxpayer." This exception allows the IRS to perform statistical studies and to release the results of those studies. See Long v. IRS, 596 F.2d 362 (9th Cir. 1979), cert. denied, 446 U.S. 917, 100 S.Ct. 1851, 64 L.Ed.2d 271 (1980), where this exception was used by the court to require the production of appropriately excised source data under-

may be released to the individual about whom the information pertains unless the Secretary of the Treasury determines that the disclosure would "seriously impair Federal tax administration." [c]

Exemption 4: Trade Secrets and Certain Commercial or Financial Information. Exemption 4 prohibits the disclosure of "trade secrets and commercial or financial information obtained from a person and privileged or confidential." This exemption has been narrowly construed by the courts. Information is not exempted from disclosure merely because the information is not customarily provided to the public by the person from whom it was obtained. Rather, the courts generally require the agency to demonstrate that disclosure is likely to impair the government's ability to obtain necessary information in the future, or to cause substantial competitive harm to the person from whom the information was obtained.[d] The Trade Secrets Act, 18 U.S.C.A. § 1905, which imposes criminal penalties for the unauthorized disclosure of trade secrets by federal employees, appears to afford no independent basis to withhold information; neither does it qualify as an Exemption 3 statute.[e]

Exemption 5: Certain Inter-Agency and Intra-Agency Memoranda. Exemption 5 permits the withholding of internal memoranda which would not be available to a party in litigation with an agency under the rules of discovery. This exemption preserves the traditional common law evidentiary privileges including the attorney-client and governmental privileges, as well as material unavailable under the attorney work-product doctrine.[f] This exemption is routinely raised by the IRS to justify the withholding of internal agency memoranda.

The pertinent inquiry in determining the scope of Exemption 5 is whether the disclosure sought would be injurious to the consultative

lying an IRS study of taxpayer compliance where disclosure would not entail a significant risk of indirect identification of particular taxpayers. See also Cliff v. IRS, 46 AFTR 2d 80–5789 (S.D.N.Y.1980).

c. IRS § 6103(c) and (e)(6). In Chamberlain v. Kurtz, supra, a taxpayer was denied access to various investigatory files compiled in the course of an audit and fraud inquiry concerning him on the grounds that disclosure would "seriously impair Federal tax administration." The Fifth Circuit sustained the Secretary's determination that the documents were not subject to release, as disclosure was likely to impair the federal government in collecting back taxes and penalties from the plaintiff and would tend to assist the taxpayer in defend-

ing himself from those claims currently being leveled against him by the government.

d. National Parks & Conservation Ass'n v. Kleppe, 547 F.2d 673 (D.C. Cir. 1976).

e. See National Parks & Conservation Ass'n v. Kleppe, supra, at 686; Grumman Aircraft Engineering Corp. v. Renegotiation Bd., 425 F.2d 578, 580, n. 5 (D.C.Cir. 1970). See also Chrysler Corp. v. Brown, 441 U.S. 281, 99 S.Ct. 1705, 60 L.Ed.2d 208 (1979).

f. See generally E.P.A. v. Mink, 410 U.S. 73, 93 S.Ct. 827, 35 L.Ed.2d 119 (1975); Pope v. United States, 424 F. Supp. 962 (S.D.Tex.1977), aff'd per curiam, 585 F.2d 802 (5th Cir. 1978).

and decision-making processes of government.[g] Generally, agency memoranda must be both predecisional and of a deliberative nature to be subject to withholding under Exemption 5.[h] The courts have held that the disclosure of intra-agency memoranda containing purely factual material does not threaten the deliberative and consultative functions of government.[i]

The applicability of Exemption 5 to a wide variety of internal IRS memoranda was considered recently in Taxation With Representation Fund v. IRS.[j] The plaintiff challenged the Service's failure to make available General Counsel Memoranda, Technical Memoranda and Actions on Decisions for public inspection pursuant to 5 U.S.C.A. § 552(a)(2).[k] The District Court rejected the government's contention that these memoranda were within the purview of Exemption 5, noting that the documents were postdecisional interpretations of existing law, and were frequently referred to by IRS officials in the course of their settlement and rulemaking activities. The continued use of these memoranda by revenue officials indicated that the memoranda constituted policy interpretations which had been adopted by the Service. Hence, the release of these memoranda was required by the FOIA, their disclosure being entirely consistent with the FOIA's primary objective of providing public access to hitherto secret interpretations of administrative law.[l]

g. See NLRB v. Sears Roebuck & Co., 421 U.S. 132, 150–152, 95 S.Ct. 1504, 1516–1517, 44 L.Ed.2d 29 (1975); E. P.A. v. Mink, supra.

h. Falcone v. IRS, 479 F.Supp. 985 (E. D.Mich.1979) (appeal pending); Dick v. IRS, 41 AFTR 2d 78–639 (D.D.C. 1978). In *Dick*, a taxpayer sought disclosure of an IRS memorandum which allegedly recommended that IRS agents discontinue accepting intelligence information from Bahamian banks. Reasoning that disclosure of this type of recommendation would discourage frank discussions between IRS officials and their superiors on matters of sensitive investigative policy, the court held the memorandum to be within the ambit of Exemption 5.

i. E.P.A. v. Mink, supra, 410 U.S. at 89–92, 93 S.Ct. at 836–838, 35 L.Ed.2d 119. See also Conway v. IRS, supra (IRS may delete emphasis remarks and other indications of its deliberative process from documents otherwise subject to disclosure).

j. 485 F.Supp. 263 (D.D.C.1980); aff'd in part and remanded in part, 47 AFTR 2d 81–1026 (D.C.Cir. 1981).

k. General Counsel Memoranda, prepared by the Office of Chief Counsel, contain legal analyses of substantive issues raised in proposed private letter rulings, technical advice memoranda and revenue rulings. Technical Memoranda, prepared in connection with proposed Treasury Decisions, generally explain the proposed rule and discuss the controversial legal and policy issues involved. An Action on Decision is prepared by Chief Counsel whenever the government loses an issue in a tax case. It recommends whether the Commissioner should acquiesce in the court's decision.

l. On appeal, the Court of Appeals for the District of Columbia affirmed the decision of the District Court *except* with respect to General Counsel Memoranda that are never distributed; Technical Memoranda pertaining to proposed Treasury decisions or regulations that have never been approved; and Actions on Decisions recommending appeals of pending cases. The question of whether Actions on Decisions recommending appeals of pending cases were required to be disclosed was remanded to the District Court for further consideration and appropriate findings of fact. 47 AFTR 2d 81–1026, at 81–1038.

Exemption 7: Certain Investigatory Records Compiled for Law Enforcement Purposes.   Exemption 7, relating to investigatory records compiled for law enforcement purposes, is frequently important in tax practice.   The Supreme Court, in NLRB v. Robbins Tire & Rubber Co., 437 U.S. 214, 98 S.Ct. 2311, 57 L.Ed.2d 159 (1979) adopted a broad construction of Exemption 7.   In *Robbins*, an employer sought to obtain statements of potential witnesses collected by the NLRB for use in a pending labor practices dispute.   The NLRB resisted disclosure on the grounds that release of these statements would interfere with pending enforcement proceedings.   The district court ordered disclosure of the statements upon the NLRB's failure to make a particularized showing that the requested disclosures were likely to interfere with administrative enforcement proceedings.   In reversing the lower court's decision, the Supreme Court held that an agency's claim of interference with a pending enforcement proceeding need not be shown on a case-by-case basis.   A sufficient showing of interference is made when disclosure would give the requestor "earlier and greater" access to the agency's case than it would otherwise have.

Exemption 7 has been invoked successfully by the IRS to prevent disclosure of IRS files to the subject of an ongoing tax fraud investigation.[m]   Information gathered for law enforcement purposes is protected from disclosure even before there is an actual prosecution.[n]   Exemptions 7(C) and 7(D) are typically raised to shield from disclosure the identity of informants and other individuals who have provided the Service with information in the course of a tax investigation.[o]

Exemption 7 also applies even though the records were compiled in the course of a law enforcement investigation with little or no possibility of eventual enforcement.[p]   However, there is respectable authority that Exemption 7 is inapplicable where the underlying investigation was unauthorized or illegal.[q]

---

m. Bryan v. IRS, 38 AFTR 2d 76–5643 (D.Me.1976).

n. Id.

o. See Maroscia v. Levi, 569 F.2d 1000 (7th Cir. 1977) (reports of interviews and the names of interviewees resulting from FBI investigation not subject to disclosure).   See also Lobosco v. IRS, supra; Luzaich v. United States, 435 F.Supp. 31 (D.Minn.), aff'd without opinion 564 F.2d 101 (8th Cir. 1977); Bast v. IRS, 42 AFTR 2d 78–5078 (D.D.C.1978).

p. Irons v. Bell, 596 F.2d 468 (1st Cir. 1979).

q. Kanter v. IRS, 433 F.Supp. 812, 822 (D.C.Ill.1977).   However, in Providence Journal Co. v. FBI, 602 F.2d 1010 (1st Cir. 1979), cert. denied, 444 U.S. 1071, 100 S.Ct. 1015, 62 L.Ed.2d 752 (1980), the First Circuit held that information gathered as a result of illegal electronic surveillance, in violation of Title III of the Omnibus Crime Control and Safe Streets Act of 1968, 18 U.S.C.A. §§ 2510–2520, was exempt from disclosure as an unwarranted invasion of personal privacy, 5 U.S.C.A. § 552(b)(7)(C).

Exemption 7, by its own terms, does not prevent the disclosure of administrative staff manuals, the disclosure of which would significantly impede the law enforcement process, as such materials are not investigatory records compiled for law enforcement purposes. However, the courts need not require disclosure of such documents when the government demonstrates that disclosure would "significantly impede" the law enforcement process.ʳ

NOTES

1. Any person may request disclosure of records which have not been published in the Federal Register or made available for public inspection and copying. However, strict compliance with the agency's published rules relating to FOIA disclosure is required. The IRS regulations relating to FOIA requests are contained in Proc. Rules §§ 601.701 and 601.702. These sections also set forth internal IRS rules for processing requests for information.

2. After pursuing one's administrative remedies, an unsuccessful requestor may apply to a district court for an order enjoining the agency from withholding agency records and to order the production of records improperly withheld. For details as to the procedure to be followed in the district court action, see 5 U.S.C.A. § 552(a)(4).

B. THE PRIVACY ACT OF 1974

The Privacy Act of 1974, codified at 5 U.S.C.A. § 552a (1976), provides individuals with a right of access to agency records concerning them. The Privacy Act also contains various restrictions on the collection and dissemination of personal information by federal agencies. It is important to note, however, that the Act's provisions apply only to information compiled concerning *individuals*, and not information relating to corporations or other artificial entities. 5 U.S.C.A. § 552a(a)(2).

The Privacy Act protects individuals against the unauthorized disclosure of personal information by administrative agencies. The Act forbids the disclosure of personal records by an agency unless the agency has obtained the prior consent of the individual to whom the records relate. 5 U.S.C.A. § 552a(b). The Act's general proscription against unauthorized disclosures is subject to several exceptions that are of interest to the tax practitioner. Agency records may be disclosed, upon request, to federal, state and local law enforcement authorities without the prior consent of the individual whose records are at issue. 5 U.S.C.A. § 552a(b)(7). Personal information may also be disclosed without prior consent pursuant to a court order. 5 U.S.C.A. § 552a(b)(11). Disclosure is also permitted for routine

---

r. Hawkes v. IRS, supra. Similarly, in Caplan v. Bureau of Alcohol, Tobacco and Firearms, 445 F.Supp. 699 (S.D. N.Y.1978), the court exercised its equitable discretion in declining to order the disclosure of a government manual on "Raids and Searches".

agency uses, provided that notice of such uses has been furnished by publication in the Federal Register. 5 U.S.C.A. § 552a(a)(7).[s] An example of a routine agency use is when the IRS discloses information pursuant to its policy of providing notice to interested parties of the Service's referral of cases to the Justice Department for criminal prosecution.[t]

Agency records which are subject to mandatory disclosure under the FOIA are also exempted from the Privacy Act's consent requirement. 5 U.S.C.A. § 552a(b)(2). Material which is not subject to mandatory disclosure under the FOIA, but which the agency nevertheless chooses to disclose, would appear to implicate the consent requirements of § 552a(b).[u] The difficulty in determining when FOIA disclosures are mandatory as opposed to permissive, combined with the potential liability of agency officials for improper disclosure, is likely to inhibit agency officials from exercising their discretionary authority to disclose material exempted from the mandatory disclosure requirements of the FOIA.

An individual's rights under the Privacy Act are enforceable in the district courts in proceedings closely resembling FOIA suits. After exhausting one's administrative remedies, an individual seeking access to agency records concerning him, or seeking damages for unauthorized disclosure of private information, may apply to the district court for relief. 5 U.S.C.A. § 552a(g).

C. THE CONFIDENTIALITY PROVISIONS OF THE TAX REFORM ACT OF 1976

In response to the strongly felt need to protect the confidentiality of tax returns and tax return information, Congress enacted §§ 1201(a) and 1202(a) of the Tax Reform Act of 1976, extensively amending section 6103 of the Code and adding a new section 6110. The amendments to § 6103 create a comprehensive regulatory scheme for the release of tax returns and "tax return information" which arguably preempts FOIA regulations in this area.[v] New § 6110 creates a separate category of records (written determinations and background file documents relating to such written determinations), and establishes a special set of rules for disclosure of such records. Section 6110 has been held to provide the exclusive means of public access to records falling within the definition of "written determination" or "background file document", ruling out resort to the regular FOIA procedures.[w]

s. See Ryan v. Department of Justice, 595 F.2d 954 (4th Cir. 1979).

t. Harper v. United States, 423 F.Supp. 192 (D.S.C.1976).

u. See Providence Journal Co. v. IRS, 460 F.Supp. 762, 767–768 (D.R.I.1978), rev'd on other grounds, 602 F.2d 1010

(1st Cir. 1979), cert. denied, 444 U.S. 1071, 100 S.Ct. 1015, 62 L.Ed.2d 752 (1980).

v. Zale Corp. v. IRS, 481 F.Supp. 486 (D.D.C.1979).

w. Fruehauf Corp. v. IRS, 566 F.2d 574 (6th Cir. 1977) (Fruehauf II).

Section 6103 establishes the general rule that tax returns and tax return information shall be confidential. The section then goes on to identify those requesting parties to whom tax return information may be released, including particular government officials, presidential designees, taxpayers or their representatives, and others with a material interest. The statute also vests in the Secretary of the Treasury the discretion to withhold information from the taxpayer whose records are at issue, where the Secretary determines that such disclosure "would seriously impair Federal tax administration". IRC § 6103(c) and (e)(6). Thus, in Zale Corp. v. IRS, supra, the court sustained the Service's discretionary determination to withhold a Special Agent's Report from the taxpayer to whom it related.

In contrast to the general obligation of secrecy imposed by § 6103, section 6110 provides that all written determinations, including rulings, determination letters, technical advice memoranda, and background file documents relating thereto, shall be made available to the public. In the case of rulings, determination letters and technical advice memoranda, disclosure is an automatic procedure. Background file documents, however, are disclosed only upon a written request.[x] The routine disclosure of written determinations generally occurs within 75 to 90 days after their issuance. The statute allows for the postponement of disclosure when the transaction which is the subject of the determination has not yet been completed. IRC § 6110(g)(3) and (4).

Several mechanisms are provided by § 6110 to protect the privacy interests of taxpayers who apply to the IRS for written determinations. Most significantly, the statute requires the IRS to delete identifying details from written determinations prior to their disclosure. IRC § 6110(c). To facilitate this process, the Service has promulgated regulations which require taxpayers who make requests for written determinations to provide the IRS with redacted versions of their requests.[y] Section 6110 also requires the Service to notify any persons to whom a written determination pertains of its intention to disclose. Should disputes arise regarding the proper scope of the Service's proposed deletions, any person to whom the determination pertains may apply to the Tax Court for relief after exhausting his administrative remedies. IRC § 6110(f)(3). In situations where the

---

x. IRC § 6110(f)(4) vests the Tax Court and the District Court for the District of Columbia with jurisdiction to entertain suits to compel the disclosure of written determinations and background file documents (or portions thereof). The procedure is analogous to an FOIA action, except that § 6110(f)(4)(B) allows intervention by any person to whom the determination or background file document at issue pertains. The right to intervene is very important, since these documents are often extremely valuable for planning purposes, and may contain copies of the contracts and other papers which are the subject of the written determination as well as trade secrets and other confidential financial information.

y. See, e. g., Rev.Proc. 80–20, § 9.09, 1980–1 C.B. 633, 640.

Service fails to make deletions required by law, or to follow the statutorily prescribed procedure, an injured party may vindicate his rights in the Court of Claims, where he is entitled to actual damages (not less than $1,000) and attorney's fees.[z]

CHAMBERLAIN v. KURTZ

589 F.2d 827 (5th Cir.), cert. denied,
444 U.S. 842, 100 S.Ct. 82, 62 L.Ed.2d 54 (1979).

AINSWORTH, Circuit Judge:

* * * Bart W. Chamberlain brought this action under the FOIA to obtain from the IRS various documents compiled in the course of criminal and civil fraud investigations of Chamberlain's federal income tax returns for 1965 and 1966. The IRS resisted disclosure of most of the documents sought by plaintiff. * * * The case comes before us on cross-appeals, the Government challenging the district court's order insofar as it mandates the disclosure of six specific documents and Chamberlain challenging the order to the extent that it permits any documents to be withheld in whole or in part.

* * *

* * *

* * * The Government contends that amended section 6103 of the Internal Revenue Code satisfies the requirements of Exemption 3 of the FOIA and that it exempts from disclosure all but five of the documents at issue in this appeal. In deciding this question we must determine which provisions of section 6103 govern this case, whether those provisions are the sort contemplated by Exemption 3, and whether the documents here fall within the ambit of section 6103.

* * *

New section 6103 of the Internal Revenue Code was enacted primarily to regulate and restrict access to tax returns and return information by the many government bodies and agencies that routinely had access to such information under former section 6103. Subsection 6103(a) states the general rule that "returns and return information shall be confidential" and shall not be disclosed except as authorized by the section; "return" and "return information" are defined in subsection 6103(b).

There is dispute as to which of the substantive disclosure provisions of section 6103 is properly applicable to the instant litigation. The Government contends that subsections 6103(c) and 6103(e)(6) control this case, while Chamberlain argues that subsection 6103(h)(4) is the proper provision. Although each of these subsections accords the Secretary discretion to withhold information, the criteria to be applied are different. Subsections (c) and (e)(6) di-

z. IRC § 6110(i).

rect the Secretary not to disclose return information to the taxpayer or his designee if he determines that such disclosure "would seriously impair Federal tax administration"; subsection (h)(4) provides more narrowly for nondisclosure only if the Secretary determines that disclosure would "identify a confidential informant or seriously impair a civil or criminal tax investigation."

* * *

Chamberlain argues   *   *   *   that subsection (h)(4) which authorizes disclosure "in judicial and administrative tax proceedings" applies to this case since the instant litigation is "a Federal or State judicial or administrative proceeding pertaining to tax administration."   He contends that this provision mandates disclosure to him unless the Secretary determines that "such disclosure would identify a confidential informant or seriously impair a civil or criminal tax investigation."   We reject this interpretation.   The provision must be read in context; subsection (h) deals with disclosure to federal officials for purposes of tax administration.   Subsection (h)(4) merely describes the circumstances in which these officials may disclose confidential information in a judicial or administrative proceeding. Without subsection (h)(4) officials could not use the information as evidence in such proceedings.   There is nothing to indicate that the provision was designed to accord a taxpayer automatic access to all information pertaining to his tax liability immediately upon the initiation of such a proceeding.

It is not reasonable to believe that Congress enacted subsections 6103(c) and (e)(6) which specifically address a taxpayer's right to his own tax files, intending that these provisions cease to operate as soon as the taxpayer's tax information becomes either directly or indirectly involved in a judicial or administrative tax proceeding.   Such an interpretation would effectively nullify subsections (c) and (e)(6) since they could be circumvented merely by initiating a judicial or administrative proceeding.

* * *

We, therefore, conclude that subsections 6103(c) and 6103(e)(6) are applicable in this case, and that the proper criterion for the Secretary's exercise of discretion in withholding documents from disclosure is whether "such disclosure would seriously impair Federal tax administration."   The next question is whether these subsections are sufficiently specific to satisfy the requirements of Exemption 3 of the FOIA.   This provision exempts from disclosure matters which are "specifically exempted from disclosure by statute   *   *   *   provided that such statute   *   *   *   (B) establishes particular criteria for withholding or refers to particular types of matters to be withheld." Both the language and legislative history of Exemption 3, as amended, indicate that subsections 6103(c) and 6103(e)(6) qualify for the statutory exemption to the FOIA.

Part B of Exemption 3 requires only that a statute either establish particular criteria or refer to particular types of matters. Subsections 6103(c) and 6103(e)(6) satisfy both of these tests. The criterion for the withholding of information is whether disclosure would "seriously impair Federal tax administration," and these subsections apply only to a particular type of matter, return information, which is carefully defined by the statute. Subsections 6103(c) and 6103(e)(6) are, therefore, drawn narrowly enough to avoid the evils of unfettered agency discretion with which Congress was trying to deal when it amended Exemption 3. * * *

It is a well-settled and sensible principle of statutory interpretation that statutes should be reconciled where possible. Congress enacted the Government in the Sunshine Act [which amended the language of Exemption 3 of the FOIA] and the Tax Reform Act of 1976 within a month of each other in September and October of 1976. It is difficult to believe that Congress enacted a comprehensive scheme for releasing information to taxpayers with the intention that it have no further applicability once the taxpayer files an FOIA suit. Accordingly, we conclude that the provisions of section 6103 dealing with the disclosure of return information to a taxpayer with a material interest therein satisfy the requirements of Exemption 3.

Having decided that Exemption 3 and section 6103 permit the IRS to withhold return information from the taxpayer where the release of the information would seriously impair federal tax administration, we now determine whether the exemption is applicable to the contested documents in this case. * * *

[The court concluded that all of the documents in dispute constituted "return information" pertaining to either Chamberlain or to third-party taxpayers. The information pertaining to third-parties was held to be strictly confidential, and the Secretary had no discretionary authority to disclose it to Chamberlain. The return information pertaining to Chamberlain was disclosable, however, subject to the Secretary's authority to withhold it upon a determination that such disclosure "would seriously impair Federal tax administration".]

We next consider whether the Secretary has adequately demonstrated that the release of this return information to Chamberlain would "seriously impair Federal tax administration." The FOIA, of course, places the burden of sustaining a decision to withhold information on the agency. In this case, we find that the IRS has sustained its burden by demonstrating that the release of the documents would result in serious impairment of the effort to collect back taxes and penalties from Chamberlain. Virtually all of the documents sought discuss either the facts or law relating to the fraud claim against Chamberlain or the computation of tax deficiencies for the years 1962 to 1968.   Release of this information would doubtless be of benefit to him in the preparation of his defense to the various claims against him.   Subsections 6103(c) and (e)(6) were designed precisely to avoid the damage to tax collection that would result from the untimely disclosure of the IRS' files, while allowing the taxpayer to gain access to return information after the Secretary has determined that release of this information would not interfere with tax administration.   Accordingly, we find that the Government has established that the disclosure of these documents would seriously impair tax administration.   They are, therefore, exempted from disclosure by section 6103 of the Code in conjunction with Exemption 3 of the FOIA.

* * *

Affirmed in part and reversed in part.

ZALE CORP. v. INTERNAL REVENUE SERV.

481 F.Supp. 486 (D.D.C.1979).

GESELL, District Judge.

This is another Freedom of Information Act ("FOIA") suit arising out of an effort to inspect government documents relating to an on-going law enforcement investigation.   In this instance, FOIA's preference for the public disclosure of governmental information must be reconciled with a necessity for confidentiality in federal tax administration recognized in the Tax Reform Act of 1976.

* * *

The FOIA requests—there were four—covered more than 500,000 pages of documents and 350,000 computer cards.   *   *   * About one-half of the dispute concerns Zale's request for the IRS Special Agents' Report itself.   This enormously detailed document is at the core of the Service's major tax enforcement effort that may well involve civil deficiencies in excess of $100,000,000 and as many as 1,000 separate notices of deficiency, as well as possible criminal charges now being examined by a grand jury.

* * *

Both Zale and the Service have approached this case as a pure FOIA action, apparently in the belief that the sole issue for decision is whether or not the contested documents are protected under exemptions 3 or 7(A) of that Act.   The Court's analysis, however, raises an important consideration of statutory interpretation that must first be resolved, namely the meaning and effect of section 6103(e)(6) of the Internal Revenue Code of 1954, as amended. *   *   *

The Court must determine whether section 6103(e)(6) was intended by Congress to be the sole standard governing the disclosure or non-disclosure of tax return information or whether it is only of significance here to the extent it may be said to provide support for a claim of exception under exemption 3 of FOIA. This question must be answered at the outset since, among other things, it affects the standard by which IRS's refusal to disclose documents must be reviewed in this Court.

The same Congress that amended exemption 3 by narrowing its scope later enacted § 6103(e)(6) as part of the Tax Reform Act. Indeed the tax legislation was enacted three weeks after approval of the FOIA changes. Under accepted principles of statutory interpretation, courts have an obligation to construe statutes harmoniously where it is reasonable to do so. * * *

* * *

Courts confronted with an exemption 3 claim frequently have been forced to extremes of analysis in order to reconcile conflicting statutory provisions without benefit of any useful legislative history. While statutory analysis is, of course, a proper function for the courts, it has too often, in the context of FOIA, required judges to abandon established rules of statutory construction and, in effect, to surmise what Congress intended. This case fortunately calls for the Court to apply more straightforward canons of statutory interpretation. If Congress meant something more or different from what is stated in § 6103, it must make this meaning known. It has not done so and accordingly the section must be viewed as the sole standard governing release of tax return information. Applicable review criteria under the Administrative Procedure Act, 5 U.S.C. § 701 et seq. (1976), control the judicial assessment of IRS's action in withholding the documents sought by Zale.[13]

In determining whether or not the Service has correctly construed its discretionary disclosure obligations, the standard of review

---

13. Although the Court concludes that Congress did not intend to apply the revised standards of exemption three to section 6103(e)(6), it is apparent that the tax reform provision would in any event be fully qualified for exemption under those standards. As discussed above, the enactment of § 6103 reflects clear congressional appreciation of the need to protect certain types of data. "Return information," the type of matter referred to, is sufficiently particularized in the careful and thorough definition found at 26 U.S.C. § 6103(b)(2). The particular criteria for withholding, a finding by the Secretary that disclosure "would not seriously impair federal tax administration," allows the Secretary to determine with adequate precision "whether disclosure in any instance would pose the hazard that Congress foresaw." American Jewish Cong. v. Kreps, 187 U.S.App.D.C. 413, 574 F.2d 624, 628–29 (D.C.Cir. 1978). Thus both prongs of the exemption are satisifed. See Chamberlain v. Kurtz, 589 F.2d 827 (5th Cir. 1978), cert. denied, 444 U.S. 842, 100 S.Ct. 82, 62 L.Ed.2d 54 (1979). See also Fruehauf Corp. v. IRS, 566 F.2d 574 (6th Cir. 1977).

* * *

is a highly deferential one. The Court finds no basis for overcoming the heavy presumption favoring reviewability of agency action. Congress neither expressed nor implied that judicial review should be foreclosed and the standard governing IRS's action is well set out in the applicable statute. Once the possibility of discretionary judgment has been recognized, however, the discretion vested in the agency in this instance is quite broad. The Court must accept the Service's determination in this area of its acknowledged experience and technical competence so long as that determination is rational and has support in the record. *De novo* review is neither necessary nor desirable under such circumstances.

In its earlier exercise of administrative discretion, the Service elected to turn over thousands of pages of records, and prepared an index and detailed sworn justification for withholding the remaining documents. The task that remains for the Court is simply to assure itself that the decision to withhold was not an arbitrary or unconscionable abuse of discretion.

[The affidavits submitted to this Court indicate that, i]n the Service's view, further disclosure would damage the investigation by prematurely revealing transactions being investigated, the scope and limits of the government's knowledge, and specific evidence against plaintiff, including statements of witnesses and informers and agency work papers. The Court's review of the documents themselves suggests no reason to disturb the agency's considered judgment in this matter.

Defendant has established that its action in withholding was neither arbitrary nor an abuse of discretion. The Court must therefore grant defendant's motion for summary judgment and deny plaintiff's motion for partial summary judgment. The action is dismissed.

So Ordered.

QUESTIONS

1. Do you agree with the holding in *Zale Corp.*, that § 6103 "must be viewed as the sole standard governing release of tax return information"? Or is Exemption 3 of the FOIA still relevant, as the Fifth Circuit holds in *Chamberlain*? If an analysis under the FOIA is appropriate, do you agree that § 6103 qualifies as an Exemption 3 statute? I. e., does the language of §§ 6103(c) and (e)(6), which allows the IRS to withhold tax return information from taxpayers if disclosure "would seriously impair Federal tax administration", establish sufficiently particular criteria for withholding such information?

2. Brady v. Maryland, 373 U.S. 83, 83 S.Ct. 1194, 10 L.Ed.2d 215 (1963), requires the government, in a criminal case, to disclose exculpatory information to the defendant upon his request. What effect, if any, do the provisions of § 6103(h)(4) have upon the *Brady* requirement?

3. Section 6103(k)(6) allows IRS employees to disclose return information to third-parties in connection with a civil or criminal tax investiga-

tion "to the extent that such disclosure is necessary in obtaining information, which is not otherwise reasonably available *   *   *." Return information often contains trade secrets or other confidential commercial or financial data which, if disclosed to third-parties who are competitors of the taxpayer under investigation, might result in substantial financial loss to the taxpayer. Does § 6103(k)(6) thus authorize a deprivation of property without due process, in violation of the Fifth Amendment? Do the regulations under § 6103(k)(6), Reg. § 301.6103(k)(6)–1(b), provide for adequate due process notice and hearing rights? Do you think a predeprivation hearing is constitutionally required before the IRS may disclose trade secrets to a competitor? What other mechanisms are available to protect the taxpayer's interests in this situation? See IRC §§ 7213 and 7217.

Chapter IV

ADMINISTRATIVE DETERMINATION OF
LIABILITY FOR TAX, PENALTIES
AND INTEREST

Scope Note: Chapter IV traces the path of a tax dispute from the selection of a return for audit to the issuance of a demand for payment of a tax deficiency, penalties (if any) and interest. Besides describing agency practice at the examination and appeal level stages, and the many legal issues related thereto, this chapter discusses such associated topics as requests for technical advice; reopening of closed cases by the Service; the various settlement forms and their effect on subsequent attempts to litigate the correctness of an asserted deficiency; and the statute of limitations on the assessment of deficiencies. The final two sections of the chapter are devoted to an analysis of the civil penalty provisions of the Internal Revenue Code and a discussion of the rules applicable to the payment of interest on deficiencies and overpayments.

SECTION 1.   EXAMINATION OF TAX RETURNS

A.   SELECTION OF RETURNS FOR EXAMINATION

A tax controversy begins when the subject tax return is selected for examination or when the absence of a required return is detected by the Internal Revenue Service. If the return is not selected there is, perforce, no possible adjustment to the tax liability reported by the taxpayer. In practical terms, a taxpayer wins the audit lottery when his ticket is not pulled from the barrel. The Service cannot examine every taxpayer's liability; hence, there will always be winners in the audit lottery. However, the IRS tries to insure that no taxpayer can be certain that he will escape examination. Moreover, the Service can, and does, select returns for examination based upon the probability of finding tax deficiencies and thereby encouraging voluntary compliance.

The IRS does not publicize the standards it employs to select returns for examination, which may vary from year to year and, sometimes, from area to area. In addition, in every selection process some factor of randomness is introduced so that there is at least some chance that any given return will be the subject of an examination. Probably the majority of those returns selected are chosen through the DIF (discriminant function) system. In essence, the IRS computers analyze each return in terms of various formulas [a] designed to detect variations from normal relationships among items on the return and between return information and other data (perhaps including industry standards, specific information items, or prior returns and audit results).

Obviously, the "size" of a tax return will affect its chances for selection. "Size" can be defined in various ways, including gross income, total positive income (before deductions), net income, balance sheet assets and liabilities, etc. Moreover, from time to time particular professions or industries are chosen for intensive audit coverage.

Returns may be selected for examination by a process of "infection." Thus, the audit of a corporation may trigger the audit of its principal shareholders. The examination of a partnership may result not only in adjustments to the partnership return, but also to those of the individual partners.

An examination may be caused by an informant's accusations, by an inconsistent position being taken by another taxpayer (for example, two taxpayers claiming the same dependents), or perhaps even due to actions taken by the taxpayer which attract attention to the subject return. It is said that an audit will often result from the filing of a refund claim, a request for ruling or determination letter, or some other special action requested from the Service. Almost certainly, the discovery of a substantial deficiency on one audit will lead to another.

There cannot be a comprehensive list or precise statement of the criteria utilized for the selection of returns for audit. Moreover, assuming honest reporting, a taxpayer can do little (if anything) to shape his return to avoid an audit selection profile. Should there be less than honest reporting, the taxpayer still must be concerned with the inevitable random selection component of the process.

B. EXAMINATION PROCEDURES

The original examination of returns is normally the function of Revenue Agents in the Examination Division of the office of each District Director, although some individual income tax return adjustments are handled entirely by correspondence between the taxpayer and the Examination Division of regional service centers. There are two general types of district office examinations, commonly called "office examinations" (conducted in the IRS office) and "field examinations" (conducted in the field).

The examination is the primary (but not exclusive) issue raising stage of a tax controversy. Should the examination conclude with an

a. DIF formulas are revised from time to time, based upon the results of TCMP (Taxpayer Compliance Measurement Program) audits, which are in-depth, random audits of a statistical sample of all classes of taxpayers.

agreement as to the taxpayer's liability, the case will be closed with a "no change" determination, an agreed deficiency assessment or even an agreed refund. However, should the liability be unagreed, the case will proceed to administrative and/or judicial procedures for the resolution of tax disputes. See Figure 7 for a flow chart of the procedures incident to the examination of income tax returns.

INCOME TAX AUDIT PROCEDURE
Internal Revenue Service

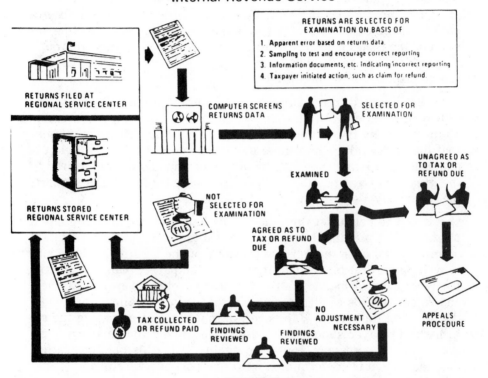

RETURNS ARE SELECTED FOR
EXAMINATION ON BASIS OF

1. Apparent error based on returns data.
2. Sampling to test and encourage correct reporting
3. Information documents, etc. indicating incorrect reporting
4. Taxpayer initiated action, such as claim for refund.

RETURNS FILED AT
REGIONAL SERVICE CENTER

COMPUTER SCREENS
RETURNS DATA

SELECTED FOR
EXAMINATION

UNAGREED AS
TO TAX OR
REFUND DUE

EXAMINED

RETURNS STORED
REGIONAL SERVICE CENTER

NOT
SELECTED FOR
EXAMINATION

AGREED AS TO
TAX OR REFUND
DUE

TAX COLLECTED
OR REFUND PAID

FINDINGS
REVIEWED

FINDINGS
REVIEWED

NO
ADJUSTMENT
NECESSARY

APPEALS
PROCEDURE

FIGURE 7.

PREPARING FOR THE EXAMINATION

When a taxpayer's representative learns of a forthcoming examination he should have his client execute a power of attorney authorizing the representative to appear and act on his behalf before the Service.[b] Naturally, preparations for an examination will vary depending on the facts and circumstances of the particular case, such as the type of taxpayer, return, and examination involved. The following are general guidelines and procedures that may be helpful in many cases although inappropriate in others. In considering the desirability of preparatory procedures, the effort and expense of prepa-

---

b. For the requirements relating to powers of attorney and tax informa- tion authorizations, see Proc. Rules §§ 601.502(c) and 601.503–601.505.

ration must be weighed against the likelihood that an item will be questioned and the amounts involved.

In the case of a field examination the initial examination may be followed by a conference with the taxpayer or his representative to discuss the issues raised. In these cases the taxpayer may utilize the initial meeting with the agent to delineate the issues and defer a substantial portion of the preparation for the period between the meeting and the conference. Advance knowledge of the issues will permit efficient preparation, although experienced practitioners can often recognize most issues prior to the examination and prepare accordingly. In the case of an office examination the taxpayer will be advised of the issues prior to the examination. Consequently, thorough preparation can be completed in advance in the hope that the case can be disposed of at the initial meeting.

The first step in preparing for an examination is analysis of the return in question. In an office examination the taxpayer's representative should try, in reviewing the return, to anticipate any issues that may arise other than those indicated. In the case of a field examination the items that may be questioned should be anticipated to the greatest extent possible. Then, the factual information supporting the taxpayer's position should be assembled.

It will be helpful at this stage if the likelihood of an examination has been kept in mind during the preparation of the return. Mindful of an eventual examination, the preparer of the return should reduce to writing all oral facts submitted by the taxpayer, maintain a written record indicating how all items on the return were determined, and retain records of all information that may be utilized to support the items on the return. Moreover, in the course of preparing the return the taxpayer should be advised of all items that may be questioned and, if necessary, cautioned against using his opinions rather than factual data in determining what to report on the return.

The task of gathering the necessary proof generally should be performed by the client under the supervision of his adviser. The organization and presentation of the proof should be done by the latter. In advising the taxpayer as to necessary proof, it is desirable that instructions be written, detailed and specific. Thus in a case involving an entertainment deduction, a request for diaries, memoranda, bills, vouchers, receipts and checks for each item of expense together with a statement naming the individual entertained, his occupation and/or title, the business relationship to the taxpayer, the date, duration, time, place and nature of the business which preceded, followed or accompanied the expense, etc., is much more useful than a request merely for all information supporting entertainment deductions.

After all the factual data has been gathered and organized, the taxpayer's representative should be in a position to furnish proof necessary to support the taxpayer's position on any item on the return that may be questioned by the agent.

At this point, a decision must be made as to whether there is any question of law involved. If a legal question is likely to arise, appropriate research should be done and legal authority for the taxpayer's position obtained. If the taxpayer's adviser is not a lawyer and the legal problem is significant, consideration should be given to obtaining counsel.

Finally, the likelihood that the taxpayer's position will be sustained and his overall vulnerability (including the effect on prior and subsequent years) should be estimated. After the foregoing is done, the taxpayer's representative will be in a position to represent the taxpayer effectively and decide what would constitute a desirable outcome of the examination.

CONDUCT OF THE EXAMINATION

Office Examination. In the examination of most nonbusiness returns, where the records to be examined are not extensive or only minor adjustments are necessary, a form letter will be forwarded to the taxpayer requesting that he furnish additional information by mail or that he appear at an office interview. Generally, the letter requesting an office conference also will request proof to support certain items on the return. In these instances the taxpayer's representative will be able to prepare thoroughly for the interview. Proof as to any of the questioned items and favorable legal authority should be organized for effective presentation. Generally, the objective should be to dispose of the matter in a single interview.

Field Examination. Field examinations generally are performed in connection with a return filed by a business with extensive records to be examined. In these instances the taxpayer will not know which issues will be raised until the examination is completed. Accordingly, preparation of evidence and legal authority relevant to potential issues will be less extensive than in the case of an office examination. Some effort, however, should be made to anticipate the issues and to gather the necessary information and, where necessary, favorable legal authority, before the field examination.

Generally, notification of a field examination will be received by a phone call or letter from the agent. The appointment will then be arranged. When the agent arrives, his credentials should be requested. The taxpayer should ascertain whether the agent is from the Examination Division or a special agent from the Criminal Investigation Division. If there are two agents, the taxpayer should be sure that neither is a special agent from the Criminal Investigation Division. The presence of a special agent indicates that a criminal investigation is being made. In these cases the examination should not proceed until counsel has been consulted and the advisability of permitting an examination is considered in light of the taxpayer's right not to incriminate himself. Where it is ascertained that the examination is routine, it should proceed.

In conducting the examination the agent should be given a comfortable place to work—preferably a private office or semi-private work area. Only one person should be assigned to work with the agent. The agent should be provided with the information and records he requests. Answers to his questions should be candid and complete and be given by someone qualified to answer. If the agent detects an attempt to be devious or evasive or to conceal something, he is apt to extend his examination to be certain he is getting the full story. In providing the agent with the information he requests the taxpayer should, however, be mindful of the fact that it is neither necessary nor desirable to volunteer more than the information requested. After the agent has completed his examination of the taxpayer's records, the first phase of the examination is complete.

It is desirable to utilize this first phase to determine what items on the return the agent is questioning, to provide the agent with the information he needs, and to avoid any detailed discussion of the issues. From the taxpayer's standpoint it is desirable to discuss the issues in detail at a second conference. This generally will prevent the agent from extending his examination to find added issues or at least make it inconvenient for him to do so, although he may find at the second conference that certain issues are seriously disputed or that most issues are being resolved in the taxpayer's favor.

The taxpayer's representative may use the time between the first and second conferences and his knowledge of the items questioned by the agent to gather and organize additional proof and to research any technical legal questions involved.

Working with the Agent. Obviously, an important element in arriving at a successful disposition of the issues raised during an examination is the development of a sound relationship with the agent. Perhaps the first step in establishing this relationship is the adoption of the attitude that both the taxpayer's representative and the agent are professionals, and that neither of them is personally or emotionally involved in the case. Toward this end the taxpayer's representative should start with the assumption that the agent is doing a job and will be fair and open-minded. It is important also that the taxpayer's representative have the respect of the agent—respect not only for his knowledgeability but more significantly for his integrity. The acknowledgment of the validity of the agent's points when they are clearly valid, as well as the volunteering of information as to any obvious errors or omissions, will help establish this respect. Of course general friendliness, cordiality and consideration will help create the desired relationship with the agent. The creation of this relationship will also be fostered by providing the agent with favorable working conditions, assisting him effectively, and facilitating his conduct of the examination.

PRESENTING PROOF TO THE SERVICE

Establishing a case before the Service is much like presenting a case to any other fact-finding forum. Evidence is introduced by means of testimony or documents that support the taxpayer's conclusions. The major distinction between administrative proof and judicial proof is that the rules of evidence are not applicable before the Service, and the proceedings themselves are informal.

The degree of formality increases as the taxpayer proceeds up the administrative ladder, but requirements as to evidence and admissible proof are flexible. Accordingly, the Service will accept as proof not only the taxpayer's business records, but also documents, letters, contemporaneous memoranda, diaries, and similar items. Unlike a judicial proceeding, these items need not be sworn to or formally authenticated.[c]

The presentation of proof at a settlement conference or office examination should be carefully planned. Thorough preparation is critical: all evidence must be collected and organized concisely and comprehensibly. In cases where the factual situation is complex, summaries and diagrams may be useful.

AGREEMENT WITH THE AGENT

As indicated above, when the examination is concluded, the taxpayer will have the opportunity to reach an agreement with the agent as to the amount of tax due. Agreement at this point may be the simplest and most desirable means of disposing of the dispute, particularly if the agent's approach indicates that he is willing to recognize the validity of the taxpayer's position to some extent and a compromise seems possible. Once the examination has been completed, the agent will prepare what is known as the Revenue Agent's Report. If the agent and the taxpayer have reached a tentative agreement, the report will outline the nature of the agreement and the reasons for making the agreement, and will indicate the proposed computations. The taxpayer eventually will receive a copy of portions of this report. When the tentative agreement is reached, the taxpayer will be asked to sign a settlement form, Form 870.

If no agreement has been reached with the taxpayer, the agent's report will serve as a summary of the case and will be passed on for use by the agent's superiors at the next administrative level. If such is the case, the report will include a statement of the arguments ad-

c. See, however, Proc.Rules § 601.507, which states, in part: "All evidence, except that of a supplementary or incidental character, may be required to be submitted over the signed declaration of the taxpayer, made under penalties of perjury, that such evidence is true."

vanced, the settlements proposed, the reasons for rejecting them, all facts, documents and chronological events relating to the case, and a summary of the agent's own opinion of the case.

Review of the Agreement. An agent's agreement with a taxpayer is only tentative pending a number of steps of review. When the agent submits his report, it will be reviewed first by his group supervisor and then forwarded to the Quality Review Staff in the office of the Examination Division.[d] At either point the report may be returned to the agent with the request that he supply additional information or ask the taxpayer to supply additional information, or with instructions to continue the examination in order to resolve newly raised legal issues. If the Quality Review Staff accepts the report, the settlement may proceed. If the report is not accepted, the taxpayer is left with the alternative of making a settlement satisfactory to the reviewers or proceeding to the next administrative level for further negotiations.

Processing the Settlement. Assuming that there is agreement between the taxpayer and the agent, and that the agreement has not been disturbed upon review, the settlement will be forwarded for processing. The Accounting Branch will perform a thorough check of the mathematics of the computations and will investigate whether any other taxes are owed or refunds are due, and what effect the settlement may have on any other matters affecting the taxpayer that are still pending. All deficiencies and overassessments will be offset against one another, and the Collection Division finally will issue a bill for a deficiency, or a refund for overassessment will be made from Washington or through the local office. The above procedure may take anywhere from two months to over a year, depending on the complexity of the issues involved in the case. There may be an additional delay if the taxpayer's case has come up for post examination review.

Post Examination Review Procedure. Each year, certain cases selected at random are subjected to what is known as a post examination review. The standards for choosing cases for such a review are established in Washington, but there is much discretion on the part of the Regional Commissioner, who carries out the review. Generally, the post examination review functions merely as a psychological deterrent to inappropriate activity by the agent as well as to insure uniformity in application of the provisions of the Code.

---

d. For the procedures involved in cases where the settlement calls for a refund in excess of $200,000, see page 19, above.

C. CLOSINGS, REOPENINGS AND SECOND INSPECTIONS

COUNCIL OF BRITISH SOCIETIES IN SOUTHERN CALIFORNIA v. UNITED STATES

42 AFTR 2d 78–6014 (C.D.Cal.1978).

KELLEHER, District Judge:

*   *   *

Plaintiff [hereinafter cited as "CBSSC"] was formed as an incorporated association in 1932 for the primary purpose of incorporating the activities of various British organizations in Southern California. The IRS granted CBSSC tax exempt status in 1966 as a social and recreational club pursuant to 26 U.S.C. § 501(c)(7). Since 1958, CBSSC has sponsored charter air flights to and from Europe for its members, for whom annual membership fees are $1.00 per person. In December 1972, IRS Agent Nyberg issued a report recommending retroactive revocation of CBSSC's tax exempt status. That report concluded:

> Your nominal membership fee ($1.00 annually), your fluctuating membership (6,000 to 15,000) and the limited number of other social activities (5 to 6 annual dances) indicates [sic] that most individuals are members of your Council for the primary purpose of enjoying reduced rates on your charter flights. It has been concluded that in substance you are a federation of clubs whose primary activity is the operation of charter flights and in accordance with Revenue Ruling 67–428, you do not qualify for exemption from Federal income tax as an organization described in section 501(c)(7) of the Code.

Notwithstanding this recommendation, upon filing of an appeal with the District Director and hearing with District Conferee Lacher of the District Director's Office, the Conferee did not sustain the revocation so proposed:

> It is the opinion of the conferee based on the information in the case file and from the information secured from the National Office and from other information that any form of revocation is improper on the grounds that CBSSC was always a social club organized and operated exclusively within the intendment of Section 501(c)(7).

Despite this rejection of the recommendation to revoke tax exempt status, the IRS determined that CBSSC was liable for filing certain tax forms:

> *   *   *   Accordingly, under the 1969 Tax reform act, it was determined that the organization was liable for filling

[sic] forms 990–T on its interest income for the years 1970 and 1971. (* * * Liability for filing forms 990–T was not an issue which was determined at the district conference.)

* * *

On February 14, 1974, the IRS sent a "thirty-day letter" to plaintiff proposing deficiencies for unrelated business income received in 1970 and 1971. * * * The IRS made the determination that CBSSC's interest income for 1970 and 1971 was "unrelated business income."

On March 12, 1974, Thomas Barrett, CBSSC President, sent a letter to the IRS District Director objecting to the February 14, 1974 report:

> On January 8, 1974, a determination letter L–251 Code 421 covering tax years 1971 and 1972 for the Council of British Societies in Southern California, Inc, [sic] was issued by the District Director, in which the tax returns were accepted as filed * * *.
>
> As we understand it, the acceptance by the District Director of the tax returns for said years indicates that the returns are no longer in question. Therefore, we believe the report by Agent Robbins [dated February 14, 1974] is not applicable at this time.

On March 14, 1974, the IRS sent a statutory notice of deficiency (Form L–21) for the years 1970 and 1971. * * *

Hence, as framed by the parties, this action presents two issues: (1) Did the IRS erroneously reopen an audit involving plaintiff's tax obligations for 1970 and 1971? (2) Did plaintiff realize unrelated business income during the calendar years 1970 and 1971, and if so, were the assessments of tax for such income valid?

A. *Reopening Issue.* Plaintiff contends that the District Director reopened the return without using the proper reopening procedure. 26 U.S.C. § 7605(b) is cited by plaintiff and provides:

> No taxpayer shall be subject to unnecessary examination or investigations, and only one inspection of a taxpayer's books of account shall be made for each taxable year unless the taxpayer requests otherwise or unless the Secretary or his delegate, after investigation, notifies the taxpayer in writing that an additional inspection is necessary.

Each party refers to Rev.Proc. 72–40, 1972–2 Int.Rev.Cum.Bull. 819, which sets forth the rules governing the reopening of cases closed after examination in the office of a District Director. Section 3.01(1) of Rev.Proc. 72–40, 1972–2 Int.Rev.Cum.Bull. at 820 provides the applicable definition of "closed case:"

A case agreed at the district level is considered closed when the taxpayer is notified in writing, after district conference, if any, of adjustments to tax liability or acceptance of his return without change.

Plaintiff contends that it was notified in writing that the returns for 1970 and 1971 were "accepted as filed," which would mean that the interest reported on the Form 990 had been so accepted. In section 4.02 of Rev.Proc. 72–40, supra, it is provided:

All reopenings must be approved by the District Director or by the Director of International Operations for cased [sic] under his jurisdiction. If an additional inspection of the taxpayer's books of account is necessary, the notice to the taxpayer required by section 7605(b) of the Code must be signed by the District Director, or by the Director of International Operations for cases under his jurisdiction.

Plaintiff contends that this case was reopened because Statutory Notices of Deficiency were issued without approval or authorization of the District Director of Internal Revenue, as required in this section. Because the returns were accepted as filed, plaintiff contends that all income, including all interest income, reported on Form 990–T, "should be closed by the closing letter of the District Director."

* * *

The government contends (1) the audit involving the 990–T liabilities was never closed so that a reopening never occurred, thus rendering Rev.Proc. 72–40 inapplicable, and (2) even if Rev.Proc. 72–40 is applicable, failure to adhere to the procedures for reopening the case would not invalidate the assessments. As the government points out, the revenue procedure is inapplicable in this case because there had been no prior closing of the audit of taxpayer's unrelated business income under section 512(a)(3), and no reopening therefore occurred. Plaintiff's argument ignores the fact that two distinct aspects of the audit were involved: a Form 990 audit (dealing with qualification for exemption under section 501(c)(7)) and a Form 990–T audit (dealing with the section 512(a)(3) issue). The prior audit, which was closed by the January 8, 1974 letter, dealt only with the exemption issue, and taxpayer was aware of this. The subsequent Form 990–T audit did not constitute a reopening.

Even if Rev.Proc. 72–40 were applicable, the assessments would not be invalid. Tax determinations are not invalidated because they involve a violation of an internal procedural rule. Brown v. Comm'r, T.C.M. 1968–29, aff'd per curiam, 418 F.2d 574 (9th Cir. 1969). See also, Collins v. Comm'r, 61 T.C. 693, 701 (1974):

It is too well settled for discussion that procedural rules, such as Rev.Proc. 68–28, [superseded by Rev.Proc. 72–40] are merely directory, not mandatory, "and compliance with them is not essential to the validity of a notice of deficiency." Luhring v. Glotzbach, 304 F.2d 560, 563 (C.A.4).

The Court finds that the IRS did not erroneously reopen the audit involved herein.

*   *   *

Accordingly, judgment is entered for defendant and against plaintiff on all issues.

NOTE

Rev.Proc. 74–5, 1974–1 C.B. 416, which superseded Rev.Proc. 72–40, referred to in the *CBSSC* case, states that the IRS will not reopen any case closed after examination by a district office to make an adjustment unfavorable to the taxpayer unless: (1) there is evidence of fraud, malfeasance, collusion, concealment or misrepresentation of a material fact; or (2) the prior closing involved a clearly defined substantial error based on an established Service position existing at the time of the previous examination; or (3) other circumstances exist which indicate failure to reopen would be a serious administrative omission. See also Proc.Rules § 601.105(j)(1).

CLEVELAND TRUST CO. v. UNITED STATES

421 F.2d 475 (6th Cir. 1970).

JOHN W. PECK, Circuit Judge.

These combined appeals arose out of an action for the refund of federal estate tax deficiencies of $565,980.20, assessed and collected by the Internal Revenue Service against the Estate of Helen Wade Greene. The deficiencies were based on the determination of the Internal Revenue Service that a transfer of property to an irrevocable trust by the decedent, Helen Wade Greene, some sixteen months prior to her death, was made in contemplation of death and thus includable in her gross estate.

*   *   *

The estate and the IRS initially attempted to use informal conference procedures to settle the dispute concerning whether the gift in trust was made in contemplation of death. For reasons more fully discussed below, the dispute was not thus settled at the administrative level; instead additional disputes outside the original contemplation of death issue arose out of the attempted settlement procedure. After that attempt disintegrated the estate paid the deficiency and filed a four-count suit for a refund. The last three counts, more fully discussed below, alleged that the estate was entitled to recover the deficiency independently of the merits of the contemplation of death issue because the IRS violated its own procedures in the course of the attempted settlement of the issue at the administrative level. The District Court granted the government's motion for summary judgment on the last three counts.   *   *   *

*   *   *

Upon the initial examination of the estate tax return the IRS determined that the transfer to the irrevocable trust was a gift in contemplation of death and that therefore the amount of that transfer was includable in the decedent's gross estate. However, following an informal conference, as provided for by Treasury Regulations, an informal conference agreement was reached between the IRS and the estate. The agreement provided for certain concessions by both sides. The IRS agreed not to raise the contemplation of death issue in return for the estate's agreement to the increased valuation of some securities held by it and payment of additional estate tax and interest in the sum of $86,089.24. Pursuant to this agreement the estate executed a Form 890–B, Waiver of Restrictions on Assessment and Collection of Deficiency and Acceptance of Overassessment. The executors and the beneficiaries of the estate also executed a "collateral agreement" which established their cost basis for the securities held by the estate at the increased valuation. Finally, the executors paid the additional assessed tax and interest of $86,089.24.

Approximately three months thereafter, the IRS informed the estate that it had rejected the informal conference agreement. The IRS again asserted that the irrevocable trust was executed in contemplation of death and includable in the gross estate. There then followed a great deal of correspondence between the estate and various levels of the IRS, with the estate seeking an explanation of the "clearly defined error" in the informal conference agreement for which the IRS exercised its power to reject the agreement. The most enlightening response came from the Commissioner of Internal Revenue, who stated:

> " *   *   * I do believe that it was reasonable for the review staff to find that, in your case, there was involved 'a clearly defined error having a substantial effect on the tax liability.' The legal presumption in favor of the Government, as provided by Section 2035 of the Code, was not adequately considered by the conferee, particularly in the light of the evidence indicating testamentary motive."

The estate then paid the deficiency and filed this four-count suit for a refund. *   *   *

*   *   *   [T]he estate contends that the IRS was bound by its own procedures to limit its rejection of informal conference agreements to circumstances involving "clearly defined error." Rev.Proc. 60–24(5)(.04), 1960 Cum.Bull. 60–24. While recognizing that the informal conference agreement is not binding on the IRS by statute such as a closing agreement authorized by § 7121 of the Internal Revenue Code or a compromise agreement authorized by § 7122 of the Code, the estate contends that the failure to identify the "clearly defined error" prevents the IRS from rejecting the agreement. In examining the estate's argument, we note first that there is no require-

ment in the Treasury Regulations establishing the informal confer-ence procedures that the IRS must identify or explain the error upon which it rejects an informal conference agreement. The Regulations, after providing for review of the informal conference agreements by regional commissioners, states:

> "In certain circumstances, such as where substantial errors are found or where there is evidence of fraud or collusion, the regional commissioner has authority to reopen the case." Treas.Reg. 601.105(i).

Thus the estate's argument must stand or fall on the Revenue Proce-dure which provides:

> "Occasionally, in cases where an agreement is reached at an informal conference, review of the case will disclose that the conferee's decision was *based on a clearly defined error* hav-ing a substantial effect on the tax liability. In such in-stances, if the change necessary to correct the error is ad-verse to the taxpayer, he will be offered another informal conference in the matter with the Conference Coordinator." Rev.Proc. 60–24(5) (.04), 1960 Cum.Bull. 60–24. (Emphasis supplied.)

Without reaching the question of whether the responses by the IRS to the estate's requests for identification of the "clearly defined er-ror" were in fact sufficient, we must hold that the IRS was not re-quired by the Revenue Procedures to identify the error for which the informal conference agreement was rejected. It is clear that the above quoted Revenue Procedure is directory, not mandatory, and the IRS's alleged failure to sufficiently identify the error can not affect its right to assert a deficiency against the estate. See Luhring v. Glotzbach, 304 F.2d 560 (4th Cir. 1962). Whatever deficiencies there may have been in the identification of the "clearly defined error" for which the agreement was rejected, the IRS was not foreclosed from rejecting the agreement by its own Revenue Procedures.

*　*　*

NOTES

1. The prohibition against second inspections contained in § 7605(b) was designed to prevent abusive and unnecessary inspections of a taxpayer's *books and records.* Hence, the reexamination of a taxpayer's *return alone* does not constitute a second inspection within the meaning of § 7605(b). See Gardner v. Commissioner, 45 P–H Memo TC ¶76, 337 (1976).

2. The usual context in which a reopening/second inspection issue arises is in defense to the production of documents in response to an admin-istrative summons. See pages 418–422, below. There was one case, how-ever, in which a surreptitious second inspection of a taxpayer's books for a previously examined year was held to render an assessment based upon the

examination improper, and, therefore, the assessment was set aside. See Reineman v. United States, 301 F.2d 267 (7th Cir. 1962).

SECTION 2.   ADMINISTRATIVE APPEALS

A.   THE "30–DAY LETTER"

At the conclusion of Examination Division consideration of a return the taxpayer normally will be issued a "30-day letter"—so denominated because the document provides thirty days in which the taxpayer must respond.   There are a number of different forms of 30-day letters for use in cases concerning various types of taxes and various procedural and substantive situations.   However, in essence, the 30-day letter puts the taxpayer on notice that there has been a conclusion of the Examination Division consideration of the return at issue, and that there are proposed adjustments to the return.   The taxpayer may, at that point, agree with the adjustments or take one of a number of alternative routes to obtain administrative and/or judicial review of the issues.

ALTERNATIVE RESPONSES TO THE 30-DAY LETTER

When a 30-day letter is received, the taxpayer has four alternatives: he can pay the deficiency asserted, make partial payment, ignore the letter, or protest it and request further administrative proceedings in the hope of disposing of or settling the case.ᵉ

Payment.   If payment of the deficiency asserted in the 30-day letter is made, such payment will be assessed and will waive, in effect, the taxpayer's right to petition the Tax Court.   He will be able, however, to file a claim for refund and institute suit in a United States District Court or the Court of Claims for recovery of the taxes paid, if he wishes to contest the issues raised by the 30-day letter in one of those tribunals.

Partial Payment.   Some taxpayers will make partial payment of the deficiency asserted in order to stop the running of interest.   Yet, they will still be hopeful of utilizing further administrative procedures with respect to the balance of the asserted deficiency, or they may wish to file a petition in the Tax Court to contest all issues relative to the year in question.   Payment with respect to some issues generally will impede subsequent administrative proceedings because the taxpayer, by such payment, gives up in advance concessions that might be of value in the give-and-take of a settlement conference.

---

e. No written protest is required to obtain an Appeals Office conference in an office examination case. However, in a field examination case, a written protest is required to obtain an Appeals Office conference if the total amount of proposed additional tax, proposed overassessment, or claimed refund (or, in the case of an offer in compromise, the total amount of assessed tax, penalty, and interest sought to be compromised) exceeds $2,500 for any taxable period. Proc.Rules § 601.105(d)(2).

Unless the interest that can be saved is extremely significant, partial payment is inadvisable because it may result in a waiver of the taxpayer's right to petition the Tax Court. This waiver may occur because a Tax Court petition may be filed only during the 90 days following the issuance of a deficiency notice. If the Service accepts the taxpayer's payment and does not issue a deficiency notice, the taxpayer will not be able to petition the Tax Court. If, however, a deficiency notice is issued with respect to the unpaid portion of the deficiency, the taxpayer can allege overpayment and collect any sums erroneously paid. Expectancy that a deficiency notice will issue despite the partial payment (enabling the filing of a Tax Court petition and litigation of all issues) encourages taxpayers to make partial payment and stop the running of interest.

No Protest. If the taxpayer chooses to ignore the 30-day letter, a statutory notice of deficiency ("90-day letter") will be issued. The taxpayer will then have 90 days to file a petition in the Tax Court. If a petition is filed, the deficiency may not be assessed or collected until the litigation is completed. If no petition is filed, the deficiency asserted may be assessed and collected forthwith. However, the taxpayer is not foreclosed from pursuing post-payment administrative and judicial review via a claim for refund.

Protest. If the taxpayer believes he can dispose of the case administratively, he can respond to the 30-day letter by filing a protest (when required) and requesting a conference with the Office of Regional Director of Appeals.[f]

FACTORS INFLUENCING RESPONSE TO THE 30-DAY LETTER

If the taxpayer does not wish to concede that the agent's determinations set forth in the 30-day letter are correct, his basic decision is whether to litigate the issues or make further attempts to resolve them administratively by filing a protest. If litigation is being given serious consideration and the taxpayer's representative does not intend to prosecute the litigation himself, he should at this point suggest that the taxpayer retain counsel. Counsel will be able to determine the impact that continued settlement efforts before the Service may have on ultimate litigation and advise as to which of the three tax litigation tribunals would be the most desirable for the taxpayer.

If the decision to litigate is made, the taxpayer must decide whether to (1) ignore the 30-day letter or request a deficiency notice and litigate in the Tax Court, or (2) pay the asserted deficiency, file a claim for refund, and litigate in the appropriate United States District Court or the Court of Claims.

---

f. Prior to October 1, 1978, the taxpayer had a right to appeal the Revenue Agent's proposed adjustments to a District Conference Staff prior to reaching the regional Appeals Office (then called the Appellate Division). The District Conference level of appeal was eliminated in 1978.

Current precedents, possibility of claims for increased liabilities in the Tax Court, available defenses, desire for a jury trial, and necessity of prompt decision are just a few of the many factors that will influence the choice of how to proceed.

If the decision is to continue efforts to resolve the issues with the Service, the taxpayer must protest the 30-day letter, usually in writing, and request a meeting with the Appeals Office. Naturally, the decision as to how to proceed will vary depending on the circumstances in each case. It may be helpful, however, to discuss some of the procedures used to arrive at the decision and the considerations influencing it.

The taxpayer's representative should analyze the return in question and the 30-day letter to determine the proof necessary to support the taxpayer's position, the extent to which the available proof provides the needed support, and the extent to which the relevant legal authorities favor the taxpayer. On the basis of this information, an estimate of a fair and desirable disposition, as well as a judgment as to the probable outcome of a lawsuit, can be made. With this in mind, the amount of the deficiency asserted by an agent can be weighed against the expense and risks involved in continuing settlement efforts or proceeding to litigation, and a choice can be made accordingly.

In deciding how to proceed, at least three other important factors must be considered. First is the impact of the disposition on years not involved in the examination. An issue resolved by litigation or in certain settlements (depending on the settlement form used) will be binding in other years. Second, the taxpayer's representative must be mindful of his client's vulnerability on doubtful items on the return that have not been raised by the agent or in the review of his report. While the Service professes that no intensive effort is made to find additional issues once the examination is completed, if an issue that has not been raised previously is evident to the Appeals Office conferee, it will of course be explored. If the vulnerability on these issues is substantial, it may dictate an early and even an unfavorable disposition foregoing all post-examination procedures. If the taxpayer wishes, he may reopen the conceded issues without vulnerability on undiscovered issues by making a claim for refund after the statute of limitations on assessment has expired. He may then sue for a refund on the claim if the likelihood of recovery and the amounts involved warrant the suit. The government in this case will then be able to raise new issues only to offset the claim. However, the government will not be able to create additional liability.

Another consideration in deciding whether to continue in the administrative process or go directly to court is the likelihood of settlement and added proof available. Generally, any additional proof will not be significant, but in unusual cases the taxpayer may have information that will be valuable at trial and that the government has not inquired about and will not know about. This is more likely in a Tax Court case, where there are limited discovery procedures. If effective presentation of his case before an Appeals Office conferee requires disclosure of such information (as it generally will), continuing in the administrative process may damage the taxpayer at trial. Accordingly, these circumstances may favor bypassing the conference and proceeding directly to litigation.

THE PROTEST

Contents of the Protest. If the taxpayer decides that additional administrative proceedings probably will result in a desirable disposition of the dispute, he must file a protest in response to the 30-day letter.[g] No particular form is required for the protest that must be filed, but certain information is essential to presenting a clear and precise statement of the taxpayer's arguments. These requirements are set out in Publication No. 5, which accompanies the 30-day letter. Basically, the protest should include:

1. The name and address of the taxpayer.

2. Designation of the year or years involved and the type and amount of tax in dispute for each year.

3. A detailed list of each finding in the Revenue Agent's Report to which an exception is taken. Each exception should be followed by the taxpayer's own contentions. Excessive length should be avoided, but the material facts should be presented and, if unfavorable, explained, not deleted.

4. In conclusion, a request for an Appeals Office conference.

All protests must be executed by the taxpayer. The execution must contain a statement that the taxpayer is subject to the penalties for perjury for any false statement in the protest.[h]

g. Except in the cases described in note e, above.

h. See Proc.Rules § 601.507. That section also provides as follows:
    * * * In lieu of a declaration of the taxpayer made under penalties of perjury, every claim, written argument, brief, or recitation of the facts, prepared or filed by the taxpayer's representative in any matter pending before the Revenue Service, should have endorsed thereon a declaration signed by such representative as to whether or not he prepared such document and whether or not he knows of his own knowledge that the facts contained therein are true and correct. In any case in which the taxpayer's representative is unable or unwilling to declare of his own knowledge that the facts are true and correct, the Revenue Service may request the taxpayer to make such a declaration under penalties of perjury.

B.   ARE ADMINISTRATIVE APPEALS REQUIRED?

LUHRING v. GLOTZBACH

304 F.2d 560 (4th Cir. 1962).

SOPER, Circuit Judge.

Separate suits were filed August 9, 1961 in the District Court against the District Director of Internal Revenue at Richmond, Virginia, by Henry G. Luhring, Jr., and wife, and by Lawrence R. Luhring and wife, and on August 10th by Henry G. Luhring, Sr. and wife, seeking to enjoin the collection of income taxes assessed against them in excess of the taxes reported by them on their several joint income tax returns for the taxable years 1957, 1958 and 1959.   *   *   *

The gravamen of the complaints is that the deficiencies claimed for the taxable years were illegally assessed because the District Director, before sending deficiency notices to the taxpayers, failed to follow certain general procedural rules set forth in 26 C.F.R.—Internal Revenue Part 601 of Subchapter H, Internal Revenue Practice, prescribing the actions to be followed by agents of the Internal Revenue Service under the direction of the Commissioner of Internal Revenue, unless the procedure is interrupted by the imminent expiration of the statutory period for the assessment of the tax.   *   *   *

*   *   *

The taxpayers complain that the agents of the District Director ignored and violated the procedural rules set out in § 601.105 which were promulgated under the authority of 5 U.S.C.A. § 22.[i] Particularly, it is charged that the taxing authorities failed to comply with the provisions set forth in Subsection (b)(1), (3) and (4), and in Subsections (c) and (d) of § 601.105, as follows:

1.   The agents did not examine, at the taxpayers' premises, the taxpayers' returns for the years 1957, 1958 and 1959, or their books and papers bearing on the matters required to be included in the returns, and did not afford the taxpayers an opportunity to agree with the findings of the examining agents.

2.   The taxpayers were deprived of the right to an informal conference in the Auditing Department of the District Director, as provided by Subsection (c), which a taxpayer may have if he applies for it within 10 days after he is advised in writing that he may present his objections to the findings of the examining agent.

3.   The taxpayer was deprived of the benefit of the provisions of Subsection (d) which directs the District Director to send to the taxpayer a 30-day letter setting out the agent's determination and advising the taxpayer of his right to file a written

i.   The predecessor to 5 U.S.C.A. § 301.

protest within 30 days and to have a hearing in the Appellate Division of the region.

The taxpayers contend that these procedural rules were promulgated under the authority of Section 7805(a) of the Internal Revenue Code of 1954 and the Administrative Procedure Act, 5 U.S.C.A. § 1011,[j] and were published in the Federal Register in accordance with 5 U.S.C.A. § 1002(a) [k] of the latter act. They contend in effect that the rules have the force and effect of law and are mandatory in their operation and unless they are observed no valid assessment and collection of taxes can be made.

In our view the procedural rules do not have this weight; and compliance with them is not essential to the validity of a notice of deficiency. The Statement of Procedural Rules, part of which is pertinent here, was promulgated and published in the Federal Register of June 30, 1955, 20 F.R. 4621, now 26 C.F.R., part 600, et seq. It was signed only by the Commissioner, Internal Revenue, and purports to be issued under R.S. § 161; 5 U.S.C.A. § 22, which reads: "The head of each department is authorized to prescribe regulations, not inconsistent with law, for the government of his department, the conduct of its officers and clerks, the distribution and performance of its business, and the custody, use, and preservation of the records, papers, and property appertaining to it." This statute was originally passed in 1789 and codified in 1875 as section 161 of the Revised Statutes. Its purpose was to enable General Washington to get his administration under way by spelling out the authority of Government officers to set up offices and to file Government documents.

The significance of the promulgation of the rules without the approval of the Secretary should not be overlooked. Section 7805, I.R. C., gave to the Secretary, or his delegate, authority to prescribe needful rules and regulations for the enforcement of the statute. Section 7802 provides for the appointment of a Commissioner of Internal Revenue by the President with such duties and powers as may be prescribed by the Secretary. Section 301.7085–1 of Part 301, Procedure and Administration, 26 C.F.R.—Internal Revenue, empowers the Commissioner, with the approval of the Secretary, to prescribe all rules and regulations for the enforcement of the Code. Since the procedural rules now under examination were promulgated without the approval of the Secretary they constitute rules laid down by the Commissioner for the regulation of the affairs of his office rather than formal regulations with the force and effect of law; and they have no added authority by reason of the terms of the Administrative Procedure Act, 5 U.S.C.A. § 1001 et seq.,[l] as the taxpayers contend. Section 1002 of that statute requires the publication of the rules of an

---

j. The predecessor to 5 U.S.C.A. § 559.

k. The predecessor to 5 U.S.C.A. § 553(b).

l. The predecessor to 5 U.S.C.A. § 551 et seq.

agency adopted according to law for guidance of the public, and Section 1011 grants every agency the authority to comply with the requirements of the statutes through the issuance of rules or otherwise. It is obvious, however, that the latter provision merely enables the agencies to comply with the statute and does not take the place of or modify Section 7805 from which the Secretary of the Treasury or his delegate derives authority to prescribe needful rules for the enforcement of the Internal Revenue laws.

Even if it should be supposed that the procedural rules have the same authority as if they had been issued by the Commissioner with the approval of the Secretary in strict conformity to Section 7805, their directory character would still be apparent. Obviously, they are rules to govern the conduct of the agents of the Internal Revenue Service in the performance of their duty to determine the correctness of the income tax returns of the taxpayers. They are carefully devised to avoid litigation in disputed cases by affording an opportunity to the taxpayer to agree with examining agents in adjustments of the tax shown on the return and by authorizing the representatives of the Commissioner to enter into compromises and settlements when complete agreement cannot be had. To this end, if a return has been audited and found to be incorrect the taxpayer is notified and given an opportunity to agree to the changes suggested by the agent and, if no agreement is reached, further informal conferences between the taxpayer and the Government agents may be had in the auditing office of the District Director and later with the Appellate Board of the District. Obviously, this pretrial procedure is of great value both to the taxpayer and to the Government in composing disputed questions of fact and law and avoiding the delay and expense of litigation; and it is so much to the interest of the parties that it is customarily employed. We think, however, that the rules are directory and not mandatory in legal effect, and they do not curtail the power conferred upon the Secretary of the Treasury or his delegate by § 6212, I.R.C. to send a notice of deficiency if he determines that there is a deficiency in the tax shown on the taxpayer's return.

* * *

Affirmed.

C. THE APPEALS OFFICE

EFFECTIVE INTERNAL REVENUE SERVICE APPELLATE DIVISION PRACTICE

Martin J. Nash
35 N.Y.U. Institute on Federal Taxation 325 (1977).

INTRODUCTION

The Appellate Division of the Regional Commissioner's Office [renamed the Office of Regional Director of Appeals in the 1978 reorganization of the IRS| has been designed by the Internal Revenue Service to serve as its main arm in resolving tax controversies. It is the only division of the Internal Revenue Service that may settle tax cases based upon judgment, or as the Internal Revenue Service calls it: "hazards of litigation." Accordingly, the great majority of tax controversies are disposed of at the Appellate Division level. The strategy to be utilized by the tax practitioner to the best advantage of his client in a tax controversy depends to a significant degree on his ability to evaluate the settlement potential of his case. A thorough knowledge of the role of the Appellate Division as well as those techniques which may be utilized in handling tax controversies before the Appellate Division is indispensible in aiding the practitioner in the settlement of controversies on a favorable basis for his client.

THE APPELLATE FUNCTION

The Appellate Division's function is to resolve tax controversies without litigation on a basis that is fair and impartial to both the taxpayers and the Internal Revenue Service. In order to achieve this result, the Appellate Division is delegated the authority to represent the Regional Commissioner exercising that authority in disposing of cases involving income, profits, estate and gift taxes, employment taxes and certain excise taxes.

Cases within the jurisdiction of the Appellate Division are generally divided into two broad categories: docketed and nondocketed.

Nondocketed cases include those involving income, estate and gift taxes prior to the issuance of the statutory notice, claims for refund and overpayment, employment taxes, (including Section 6672 cases) and certain excise taxes. Docketed cases are those which are pending before the United States Tax Court and involve income, estate and gift taxes.'"

* * *

PRACTITIONER'S ROLE IN THE APPELLATE PROCEEDINGS

The practitioner's role in the Appellate proceedings is to represent the taxpayer in achieving for him the most favorable disposition

---

m. A nondocketed case reaches the Appeals Office by virtue of a protest directly from a proposed adjustment (i. e., 30-day letter) issued by the Examination Division of the District Director's office. Where the taxpayer fails to file a protest, the District Director's office will automatically issue a notice of deficiency. If, thereafter, the taxpayer petitions the Tax Court for a redetermination of the deficiency, the matter will be forwarded to Appeals after the case is entered on the Tax Court's docket by the Clerk. Appeals then has exclu-

sive settlement jurisdiction for a period of four months. Where a protest is filed, but a settlement cannot be reached with Appeals, then Appeals officials will issue the notice of deficiency and any post-docketing settlement negotiations in that event are within the exclusive jurisdiction of District Counsel's office. See Rev. Proc. 79–59, 1979–2 C.B. 573. See pages 274–277, below, for a further discussion of the settlement of docketed cases in the Tax Court, and the division of jurisdiction between the Appeals Office and District Counsel.

of the tax controversy without the necessity of litigation and with the minimum amount of exposure to adverse future tax consequences. Not every case is susceptible of settlement at the Appellate Division level. Some cases that may be settled at the Appellate level may nevertheless create a risk of adverse tax exposure for the same or future tax periods.

The practitioner, in evaluating whether or not he wishes to avail himself of the opportunity for an Appellate conference, should consider: the probability of settlement based upon the facts and the application of the law to his case; the timing of Appellate consideration; and the effect of settlement of the case on tax exposure for past or future periods. If an Appellate conference is requested, the tax practitioner should be prepared to discuss openly and frankly the issues and law involved and to present such evidence as may be reasonably requested by the Appellate appeals officer in order to support the taxpayer's position. Caution, however, dictates that the practitioner be alert to those rare situations when the Appellate appeals officer becomes an advocate and attempts to strengthen the Government's case while weakening the taxpayer's position, rather then trying to reach a basis for settlement.

Restrictions and Limitations on Appellate Authority

In evaluating the probability of a settlement, the tax practitioner should be aware of certain restrictions and limitations on the authority of the Appellate Division to resolve the matter.

Prime Issues

The Internal Revenue Service, including the Appellate appeals officer, is not authorized to concede, in whole or in part, any cases or issues of a case which have been denominated as "Prime Issues." A settlement discussion involving a "Prime Issue" may be fruitless, and moreover, the practitioner who pursues the settlement of such issues runs the risk of exposing the theory and facts of the taxpayer's case.

Ruling Positions

The Appellate appeals officer is required to follow the Regulations promulgated under the Internal Revenue Code and the published Ruling positions of the Internal Revenue Service. Accordingly, if settlement of the matter would conflict with a published Revenue Ruling, the probability of settlement is substantially reduced although not completely diminished. Generally, settlement of this type of matter is more likely when the case has reached docketed status rather than when it is nondocketed.

Joint Committee Cases

In the event a tax matter involves a refund or overpayment in excess of $200,000, a report must be made to the Joint Committee on

G. & S. Cs. Tax Proc. & Fraud ACB—7

Internal Revenue Taxation of the United States Congress before the refund or credit can be made.[16] * * *

Whipsaw Cases

Appellate appeals officers are required to protect the Government's interest in so-called "whipsaw cases." These cases arise when taxpayers take inconsistent legal positions on the same factual matters: for example, the issue of alimony payments versus support payments, goodwill payments versus payments for covenants not to compete, dependency exemptions, and 100 percent penalty cases where each alleged responsible corporate officer defends by alleging that the other was the responsible officer. In such cases, the Internal Revenue Service generally will not dispose of the matter even though a basis for settlement has been reached. Accordingly, unless a settlement can be reached with all of the taxpayers with inconsistent positions, they will find themselves in court in a consolidated matter with the Government on the sidelines in the position of a stakeholder.

Fraud Penalties

The Appellate Division is required to secure the consent of the Regional Counsel before it may concede or eliminate the ad valorem fraud penalty for a year in which a recommendation had been made to criminally prosecute the taxpayer,[18] even though the taxpayer may have been acquitted in the criminal trial. In this type of situation, the ability of the Appellate appeals officer to reach a basis or settlement is more difficult. Accordingly, less difficulty will be encountered if the case is immediately docketed, since all settlement conferences in docketed cases are conducted in the presence of a representative of Regional Counsel.

Coordination Problems

Occasionally, related matters involving the same taxpayer or different taxpayers and the same issues may be pending in different courts. Where a matter is pending in the district court, the Appellate Division will be required to coordinate with the Department of Justice. In such instances, it is most difficult to effect a settlement with the Appellate Division if that action is contrary to the desires and trial strategy of the Department of Justice.

There are other areas where the Appellate Division is required to coordinate its activities with other branches of the Internal Revenue Service. For example, in view of the new declaratory relief afforded to taxpayers in the pension and exempt organization areas it is anticipated that the Appellate Division will be granted jurisdiction but will be required to coordinate its activities with other branches of the Internal Revenue Service. By its very nature, the problem of coordination subjects the taxpayer to the risk of having to disclose his en-

---

16. Reg. § 601.106(g); I.R.C. § 6405. **18.** Reg. § 601.106(a)(2)(iii).

tire case in order to achieve a settlement while at the same time having that settlement rejected for reasons other than the merits of the matter in litigation.

TIMING OF THE APPELLATE REVIEW

In point of fact very few cases cannot be settled, if properly evaluated by both the taxpayer's representative and the Internal Revenue Service. Most of the barriers to settlement deal with restrictions and limitations on the exclusive authority of the Appellate Division to settle the matter rather than a complete denial of that authority. Accordingly, it generally behooves the taxpayer to attempt an expeditious and fair disposition of the matter at the Appellate Division level. However, even if he believes the case is capable of being settled, the tax practitioner should not automatically attempt to secure Appellate Division's consideration at the nondocketed stage in every case. He should first consider the risks to his client's case as a consequence of Appellate Division consideration before requesting such consideration when the case is in a nondocketed status.

Appellate Division consideration may be received at several stages. It may be secured upon protest of the case after receipt of a 30-day letter in income, estate or gift tax matters. However, if the taxpayer chooses to ignore the 30-day letter and initially contest the case in the Tax Court, the case subsequently will be referred to the Appellate Division for purposes of exploring settlement possibilities. After assessment and payment of a tax, a claim for refund may be filed, and a protest of the proposed disallowance of the claim for refund by the examining agent may be made to the Appellate Division.

Tax Exposures

In evaluating the timing of the Appellate review, the tax practitioner should keep in mind the tax exposure at each stage of that review.

Statute of Limitations

The statute of limitations for assessment is required to be maintained in open status during the entire period of the Appellate Division's consideration. Therefore, a protest at the nondocketed stage always creates the exposure to additional deficiencies determined by the Appellate Division. A change in the theory of the case, the creation of a new issue, or the referral of the matter back to the revenue agent for further development of the case or further audit may lead to the proposal of additional deficiencies. If a statutory notice is eventually issued by the Appellate Division raising new issues and proposing additional deficiencies, the taxpayer will have the burden of proof on those issues as well as the protested issues and deficiencies proposed by the Internal Revenue Service. A petition to the Tax Court tolls the statute of limitations, and increased deficiencies may be proposed by the Internal Revenue Service. The significant advantage of filing a petition to the Tax Court is that the Internal Revenue Service must sustain the burden of proof in alleging and proving increased deficiencies and new issues.[20] Accordingly, there appears to be a greater reluctance on the part of the Internal Revenue Service to raise new issues at the docketed level as contrasted with the nondocketed level. However, Regional Counsel will raise such issues if they are readily apparent from the facts of the case or necessary to properly plead and prove an alternative issue in order to protect the theory of the Government's case.

New Issues

A great concern of most tax practitioners is the raising of new issues by the Appellate Division at the nondocketed stage. There is no guarantee that such issues will not be raised, particularly when the failure to raise such issue will be a serious administrative omission. The experience of this writer in this area is that the definition of "a serious administrative omission" depends in large part upon the individual Appellate appeals officer and his predilection toward being an adversary. If the practitioner believes that the tax exposure of a new issue or an alternative theory of the case creating a greater deficiency is real, then, he ought to follow the procedure of paying the tax, awaiting the expiration of the statute of limitations before filing a claim for refund, and then securing the Appellate Division's consideration. Although a new issue may be raised to offset the potential claim for refund, an increased deficiency cannot be assessed or collected from the taxpayer after the tax year is barred by the statute of limitations.[22] This course of action of the taxpayer's representative is in large part dictated by the taxpayer's ability to pay the amount of the proposed deficiency plus interest. If the taxpayer cannot or is not desirous of paying the deficiency, it is preferable to proceed with a petition to the Tax Court, since the Government will then be required to assume the burden of proof in the event it desires to raise a new issue.

New Theory

Appellate appeals officers are, on balance, more sophisticated tax practitioners than revenue agents. Occasionally, revenue agents utilize a certain theory of law in their Revenue Agent's Reports when there may be alternative and more persuasive theories which give the Commissioner a better litigating position. In evaluating his choice of action the practitioner should be aware that in refund litigation the taxpayer must prove his entitlement to a refund, while the Government may defend on any theory. In the Tax Court the taxpayer's

---

20. Tax Court Rules of Practice and Procedure, Rule 142; I.R.C. § 6214(a).

22. Lewis v. Reynolds, 284 U.S. 281, 52 S.Ct. 145, 76 L.Ed. 293 (1932), mod., 284 U.S. 599, 52 S.Ct. 264, 76 L.Ed. 514.

burden is merely to prove that the Government's determination is erroneous. Accordingly, the tax practitioner should consider the alternative of filing a petition in a Tax Court in order to fix the Government's position, thereby requiring the Internal Revenue Service to amend its pleadings and take the burden to proof on a new or alternative theory. The Appellate appeals officer will generally take the opportunity to modify and correct the Government's theory of the case in the statutory notice so that the burden of proof will still remain with the taxpayer.

Disclosure of Evidence

In order to secure a settlement, the practitioner must disclose the taxpayer's evidence in support of his legal position. If oral testimony is to be utilized, the Internal Revenue Service may use its summons power to secure evidence partly rebutting or contradicting the taxpayer's evidence or, at the very minimum, destroying the credibility of the witness. If documentary and demonstrative evidence is presented, the practitioner may find a shift in the Government's theory of a case in order to avoid the damaging effect of the evidence that has been presented for purposes of settlement. Part of this risk may be eliminated by requiring the Internal Revenue Service to explore settlement possibilities in the framework of a docketed matter so that discovery proceeds in accordance with the rules of procedure of the appropriate tribunal. Fortunately, most Appellate appeals officers understand that they are not advocates nor are they adversaries seeking solely to strengthen the Government's case. However, judgment dictates that the tax practitioner properly evaluate the effect on his case of failure to achieve settlement at the Appellate Division level.

Additional Development

If the Internal Revenue Service's case has been poorly developed, the Appellate appeals officer either will request additional information from the taxpayer in order to develop the matter, or he may refer the matter back to the Audit Division for further development. He may also refer the matter back to the examining agent to verify additional information presented by the taxpayer. The appeals officer is under operating instructions to refer new material back to the District Director for his verification and comment if it would have a significant impact on an important issue in a case, or if the verification by the appeals officer of the evidence submitted would be a time-consuming process. At the audit level the Internal Revenue Service may continue its audit using all of its summons power to build and improve its case. Psychologically, a revenue agent will attempt to improve his position in the case rather than concede the error of his original action. Practitioners should always keep in mind, if the matter is petitioned directly to the Tax Court, that although the Internal Revenue Service may still develop its case including the use of third-party summons, it will be restricted to the discovery procedures of the Tax Court as to discovery directly from the taxpayer. Furthermore, some advantage may be gained if the revenue agent is called as a witness in the trial of the matter and has previously taken an inconsistent position in his report.

Admission Against Interest

The protest is a statement of facts made by the taxpayer and may be utilized as evidence in any trial as an admission against interest. A common mistake made by some practitioners is to file a protest based upon an assumed set of facts which later prove to be in error, thus jeopardizing factual presentation of the case at trial.

Summary

A majority of tax practitioners accept the risks and exposures of Appellate Division consideration in the nondocketed stage, because of the overall fairness of the Appellate Division and the opportunity to settle the case at the Appellate Division level or at least to narrow the legal and factual disputes between the parties at a relatively low cost. Most Appellate appeals officers understand their settlement function and do not attempt to be adversaries at the expense of the tax practitioner. Nevertheless, the practitioner must carefully weigh the advantages of Appellate Division consideration against the potential tax exposures to his client of such consideration.

* * *

SECTION 3. REQUESTS FOR TECHNICAL ADVICE

"Technical advice" means advice or guidance furnished by the National Office of the IRS upon request of a District Director or an Appeals Office in response to any technical or procedural question that develops during any stage of administrative proceedings on the interpretation and proper application of the tax laws to a specific set of facts. The Assistant Commissioner (Technical) and the Assistant Commissioner (Employee Plans and Exempt Organizations) act as the primary assistants to the Commissioner in the rendering of technical advice to field personnel.

The proceedings with respect to which technical advice may be requested include the examination of a taxpayer's return, claim for refund or credit, and any other matter involving a specific taxpayer under the jurisdiction of the Chief, Examination Division of any district office. They also include processing and consideration of nondocketed cases in any Appeals Office. Technical advice is furnished as a way of helping Service personnel close cases and establish and maintain consistent holdings throughout the Internal Revenue Service. To justify a request for technical advice it must be demonstrated that a lack of uniformity exists on the disposition of the issue or that the issue is unusual or complex enough to warrant consideration by the National Office. Obviously, a request for technical advice is desirable only in extraordinary cases. It is of little effect when there is simply a disagreement as to interpretation of legal principles. It is most useful when the Service concedes that there is a substantial doubt as to the existing law.

The District Director or Chief, Appeals Office is responsible for determining whether to request technical advice on any issue being considered. However, while the case is under the consideration of the District Director or the Chief, Appeals Office, a taxpayer may request that an examining agent or Appeals conferee refer an issue to the National Office for technical advice. Regardless of whom initiates the request, the taxpayer is given an opportunity to present his version of the statement of facts and specific points at issue. If the examining agent or Appeals conferee declines the taxpayer's request to submit the issue for technical advice, the taxpayer may protest the refusal to the appropriate district or Appeals Office officials. Where the referral is made, but it appears that advice adverse to the taxpayer will be given, the taxpayer is entitled to a conference in the National Office.

Rev.Proc. 80–21, 1980–1 C.B. 646, governs most situations in which requests for technical advice are made. It sets forth the taxpayer's rights and the procedures to be followed by the taxpayer, the internal IRS procedures, the effect of technical advice and various other matters relating to the processing of requests. Rev.Proc. 80–26, 1980–1 C.B. 671, provides the same information with respect to requests from key District Directors and Appeals Offices in cases involving employee plans and exempt organization matters.

SECTION 4. SETTLEMENT AND CLOSING AGREEMENTS

A. FORM 870 (CONSENT TO ASSESSMENT)

If the taxpayer and the Service reach an agreement at a stage in the examination process prior to an Appeals Office conference, the taxpayer will execute a consent to assessment without deficiency notice on Form 870 (income tax), Form 890 (estate or gift tax) or a similar form for other tax liabilities.[n] Form 870 (or 890) may also

---

n. The operative language of Form 870 is as follows:

I consent to the immediate assessment and collection of any deficiencies (increase in tax and penalties) and accept any overassessments (decrease in tax and penalties) shown below, plus any interest allowed by law. I understand that by signing this waiver, I will not be able to contest these years in the United States Tax Court, unbe used when the government makes no concession in reaching agreement as to the tax due at an Appeals Office conference.

By executing Form 870 (or 890), the taxpayer waives the statutory notice requirement that the Service formally notify him that it has determined, and intends to assess, a deficiency at least 90 days prior to the actual assessment.[o] Since a petition may be filed in the Tax Court only after a formal notice has been received by the taxpayer, the execution of either form results in relinquishment of the taxpayer's right to petition the Tax Court for a redetermination of the deficiency. Filing the waiver, in addition to allowing immediate assessment, suspends the running of interest for the period beginning on the 31st day after such filing and ending on the date the Service makes notice and demand on the taxpayer for payment of the deficiency.[p]

Although the execution of Form 870 (or 890) usually results in final disposition of the case, it does not (as the form itself indicates) prevent the assertion of an additional deficiency by the government, nor does it prevent a suit for refund by the taxpayer. Therefore, Form 870 (or 890) is often utilized by taxpayers to consent to immediate assessment at the conclusion of an examination with a view to the later filing of a claim for refund and the possible prosecution of a tax refund suit.

QUESTION

The normal statute of limitations on assessments expires three years after the filing of the pertinent tax return. The limitations period for filing a refund claim will not run until two years after the payment of the amount to be refunded. How might the interplay of these two limitations periods operate to preserve a taxpayer's ability to contest a tax issue without fear of an increased deficiency contention from the IRS?

less additional deficiencies are determined for these years.

In a note on the form, it is provided further:

* * * Your consent will not prevent you from filing a claim for refund (after you have paid the tax) if you later believe you are so entitled; nor prevent us from later determining, if necessary, that you owe additional tax; nor extend the time allowed by law for either action.

If you later file a claim and the Service disallows it, you may file suit for refund in a district court or in the United States Court of Claims, but you may not file a petition with the United States Tax Court.

We will consider this waiver a valid claim for refund or credit of any overpayment due you resulting from any decrease in tax and penalties determined by the Internal Revenue Service, shown above, provided you sign and file it within the period established by law for making such a claim.

o.   See IRC § 6213(d).

p.   IRC § 6601(c).

PAYSON v. COMMISSIONER

166 F.2d 1008 (2d Cir. 1948).

SWAN, Circuit Judge.

This proceeding involves a deficiency in the petitioner's income tax liability for the year 1941. Two questions are presented for decision. The first is whether the Commissioner was precluded from determining the deficiency in suit by reason of the taxpayer having paid a previously determined deficiency for the same year, after signing a waiver of restrictions on the assessment and collection of that deficiency. After an audit of his 1941 return the taxpayer was notified of an additional tax of $6,900.70. In July 1944 he signed Form 870 of the Treasury Department, Internal Revenue Service, which is a "Waiver of Restrictions on Assessment and Collection of Deficiency in Tax"; and thereafter he paid said additional tax with interest thereon. Such a waiver is provided for by section 272(d) of the Internal Revenue Code.[q] After payment of this deficiency the taxpayer was notified of an additional deficiency resulting from disallowance of a capital loss claimed in his return. This item had not been disallowed in the determination of the first deficiency. In contesting the additional deficiency, the taxpayer contended before the Tax Court, and reasserts here, that the Commissioner's acceptance of the waiver and of payment of the first deficiency estops him from assessing and collecting the second. The argument, as we understand it, is that where the United States has received the consideration due it under an agreement it cannot refuse to perform its own obligations thereunder. But the cases relied upon are inapposite because the waiver imposed no obligation on the United States. On the contrary it expressly gave the taxpayer notice that it was not a final closing agreement and did not preclude the assertion of a further deficiency. By his waiver the taxpayer surrendered his right to appeal that particular deficiency to the Tax Court, but not his right to claim a refund of the tax, and in return he obtained relief from the running of interest on the deficiency, as stated in Internal Revenue Code § 282(a).[r] The Tax Court rightly held that the claim of estoppel is groundless.

* * *

Finding no error in the Tax Court's decision, we affirm it.

B. FORM 870–AD (AGREEMENT TO ASSESSMENT)

If the taxpayer and the IRS reach a settlement at the Appeals Office level, the settlement usually is documented by an agreement to assessment on Form 870–AD (income tax), 890–AD (estate tax) or a similar form for other taxes.[s] These forms are often used rather

---

q. The predecessor to § 6213(d) of the 1954 Code.

r. The predecessor to § 6601(c) of the 1954 Code.

s. The operative language of the Form 870–AD is as follows:

Pursuant to the provisions of section 6213(d) * * * the unthan the statutory closing agreements (Forms 866 and 906). In the past, the procedures within the Service necessary to obtain execution of a statutory closing agreement were arduous and complicated. The IRS has recently simplified the procedures for execution of the statutory closing agreements, evidently to encourage more frequent use of the closing agreement.

In effect, the Form 870–AD (or 890–AD) is an offer by the taxpayer to waive the restrictions on assessments and collection in return for concessions by the Service. The Forms indicate that, if the offer is accepted by the IRS, " * * * the case shall not be reopened in the absence of fraud * * *." In keeping with this language, the government does not assert additional deficiencies (absent fraud or other malfeasance by the taxpayer) once the Form 870–AD (or 890–AD) "settlement" has been consummated. In a number of instances, however, taxpayers have sought to violate the Form 870–AD agreement, typically, but not always, by waiting until the statute of limitations on further assessments has expired and then filing claims for refunds for years covered by the agreement.

UINTA LIVESTOCK CORP. v. UNITED STATES

355 F.2d 761 (10th Cir. 1966).

HILL, Circuit Judge.

This is an income tax refund suit to recover $88,330.27 of taxes paid for 1948.

The facts are largely undisputed. The Rees Land and Livestock Company, a large family owned corporation, conducted a sheep operation in Wyoming and a cattle operation in Utah. The sheep portion of the corporation comprised approximately 57% of the assets and

dersigned offers to waive the restrictions provided in section 6213(a) * * * and to consent to the assessment and collection of the following deficiencies with interest as provided by law. The undersigned offers also to accept the following overassessments as correct * * *.

This offer is subject to acceptance for the Commissioner of Internal Revenue. It shall take effect as a waiver of restrictions on the date it is accepted. Unless and until it is accepted, it shall have no force or effect.

If this offer is accepted for the Commissioner, the case shall not be reopened in the absence of fraud, malfeasance, concealment or misrepresentation of material fact, an important mistake in mathematical calculation, or excessive tentative allowances of carrybacks provided by law; and no claim for refund or credit shall be filed or prosecuted for the year(s) stated above other than for amounts attributed to carrybacks provided by law.

In a note on the form, it is provided further:

The execution and filing of this offer will expedite the above adjustment of tax liability. This offer, when executed and timely submitted, will be considered a claim for refund for the above overassessments, as provided in Revenue Ruling 68–65, C.B. 1968–1, 555. It will not, however, constitute a closing agreement under section 7121 of the Internal Revenue Code.

was operated by William Rees and certain members of his family. For various reasons, it was decided to split the company. The idea conceived was for the William Rees group of shareholders to form a new corporation (Uinta) by transferring their Rees stock to it for Uinta stock. Uinta Corporation would then exchange the Rees stock it now owned for the sheep assets of the Rees Company. The end result was that the Raymond Rees group of shareholders were left with all the 274 outstanding shares of Rees Company and the cattle business and the William Rees group owned all the stock of Uinta whose assets were the sheep business. All this transpired in 1948. Uinta Corporation did not file a tax return for 1948, nor did the shareholders of Uinta report any gain on their transfers of Rees stock to Uinta for Uinta stock.

[After an audit of Uinta's 1948 income tax return the IRS proposed a deficiency resulting from (1) the treatment of the exchange of the Rees stock for the sheep assets as taxable, (2) the valuation of the sheep assets at $387,662.22, (3) the denial of a claimed net operating loss and (4) the imposition of a delinquency (late filing) penalty.]

Uinta protested the deficiency and conferences with the Appellate Division were had and various affidavits filed, etc. As a result of this, taxpayer gained in some areas and lost ground in others. Appellate Division dropped the $21,991.31 delinquency penalty but denied the $28,210.16 net operating loss. The Appellate Division did agree to a lesser value on the sheep assets coming down from $387,662.22 to $305,352.65.

Uinta finally gave in and agreed to a $67,386.61 deficiency and signed a Form 870–AD waiving restrictions on time for assessment and agreed not to seek a refund for the year in question. Also in the 870–AD the Commissioner agreed not to reopen 1948 absent fraud, etc. At the bottom of the 870–AD it states that it is not a final closing agreement under § 7121. The Form 870–AD as signed by Uinta was received by the Appellate Division on June 12, 1956, and was accepted on behalf of the Commissioner on August 23, 1956.

* * *

The government contends that the taxpayer may not maintain this action by virtue of having executed the Treasury Form 870–AD agreement relating to waiver of restrictions on assessment. True, the agreement does recite that the taxpayer will not seek a refund for the year in question. However, the form also carefully states it is not a closing agreement in accordance with section 7121 of the 1954 Internal Revenue Code. Neither is it a valid compromise of a tax deficiency as prescribed by section 7122 for it was not executed in full compliance with the requirements of that code provision. We believe the Supreme Court answered the question here years ago in Botany Worsted Mills v. United States, 278 U.S. 282, 49 S.Ct. 129, 73 L.Ed.

379, when it said in this regard: "We think that Congress intended by the statute to prescribe the exclusive method by which tax cases could be compromised, * * * and did not intend to intrust the final settlement of such matters to the informal action of subordinate officials in the Bureau. When a statute limits a thing to be done in a particular mode, it includes the negative of any other mode." This Circuit has subscribed to that position in Sanders v. Commissioner of Internal Revenue, 10 Cir., 225 F.2d 629. Furthermore, a sizeable number of courts that have considered the matter are in agreement, although there are differences of opinion. We have no alternative but to hold on these facts that mere execution of a Form 870–AD like the one in question does not in and of itself preclude a taxpayer from filing a claim for refund. We do not sound the death knell on this form of settlement agreement lightly for we recognize the need to effectuate administrative settlements of tax disputes. All we say is that at the present time Congress has specified how tax matters may be settled either by a closing agreement or by compromise. Any changes in that procedure will have to be made by Congress.

The next issue the government raises to defeat the taxpayer's action is the defense of equitable estoppel. * * *

The crux of the government's estoppel argument is this: That it made several concessions of tax liability in order to secure the Form 870–AD agreement and, as a result of the agreement, it declined to seek deficiency assessments against the individual shareholders of Uinta and allowed the statute of limitations to run against those shareholders.

It is true that the government conceded the delinquency penalty and it did agree to a reduced value for the sheep assets received. However it is also true that it denied the taxpayer a net operating loss of $28,210.16. On balance, the government's concessions for the agreement would not appear to be all one sided. However, the strongest argument made is that by virtue of its reliance on this agreement, the government allowed the statute of limitations to run against the individual shareholders of Uinta Corporation for 1948 and hence it may not deal with that situation further. Even if this factor was enough to invoke the defense of estoppel, we doubt that the government has proved the point which it was incumbent upon it to do. It is impossible for us to say conclusively how the Uinta shareholders affected this whole transaction. The individual shareholders apparently filed timely returns in March of 1949. Under ordinary circumstances, § 275 of the 1939 Code would provide a three year statute of limitations or five years if over 25% of gross income was omitted. Five of the six shareholders of Uinta did sign waivers extending the statute of limitations to June 30, 1956, but not until January of 1954. Therefore, if the three year limitation was applicable to them, the extensions were a nullity for the statute had already run when the waivers were signed. Of course, the waivers extending the statute would have been timely if over 25% of gross income was omitted but the answer to this depends in large part on whether the creation of Uinta was a tax free exchange under § 112(b)(5). If it was, and the government took that position with Uinta, then of course the shareholders had no recognized gain on Uinta's creation. One more factor in this regard bears comment. The Form 870–AD agreement was not executed by the government until August 23, 1956. Even assuming the statute of limitations for the individual shareholders was extended until June 30, 1956, it had expired before the 870–AD was executed by the government and the form very carefully states that it has no effect until accepted by the government.

The subject of equitable estoppel in tax matters is not clear by any means. It has been suggested that to constitute such a defense there must be (1) false representation or wrongful misleading silence, (2) the error must originate in a fact statement not in an opinion or statement of law, (3) the person claiming estoppel must be ignorant of the true facts, and (4) must be adversely affected by the person against whom the estoppel is claimed. Van Antwerp v. United States, 9 Cir., 92 F.2d 871. Furthermore, the burden of proving each of these elements is upon the party asserting it. Van Antwerp, supra.

The cases considering the question of equitable estoppel in a situation similar to this do not yield much conformity owing perhaps to different factual situations. Yet we are unable to distinguish the cases purely on a factual basis. However, a considerable number of courts have adhered to a more strict reading of the previously mentioned estoppel elements and found one or more of these elements missing in a situation similar to this, particularly either the lack of detrimental reliance or the lack of false representation. The Tax Court seems to sanction this line of cases believing it necessary to at least find false representation before denying taxpayer's claim. Arthur V. Davis, 29 T.C. 878 and Badger Materials, Inc., 40 T.C. 725, where it noted quite correctly we believe that mutual mistakes of law do not give rise to estoppel.

On the other hand, a respectable number of courts seem to favor a liberal quasi type of estoppel. See Guggenheim v. United States, 77 F.Supp. 186, 111 Ct.Cl. 165; Cain v. United States, 8 Cir., 255 F.2d 193; and Daugette v. Patterson, 5 Cir., 250 F.2d 753. Their position can perhaps best be summed up if at all in the words of the Eighth Circuit in the *Cain* case where the court said at page 199 of 255 F.2d, " * * * We think it is sufficient to preclude a taxpayer from claiming refund, in relation to an executed settlement agreement, that the statute of limitations has run against the right of the Commissioner to deal with the situation further." The court also indicated it was concerned there because the agreement also effected the tax status of other parties since a partnership was involved. In Daugette v. Patterson, the Fifth Circuit followed the *Guggenheim* case and the language therein which stated, "It would obviously be inequitable to allow the plaintiff to renounce the agreement when the Commissioner cannot be placed in the same position he was when the agreement was executed."

One of the most recent cases to examine the issue confronting us is an opinion by Judge Dawson in Morris White Fashions, Inc. v. United States, D.C.S.D.N.Y., 176 F.Supp. 760 (1959). In a lengthy review, Judge Dawson concludes that the cases applying estoppel overlook one factor; that is the government can always plead recoupment to a refund suit like this. The doctrine of recoupment announced in Bull v. United States, 295 U.S. 247, 55 S.Ct. 695, 79 L.Ed. 1421, allows the government to offset a barred deficiency against a valid refund. Whatever effect the recoupment doctrine still has, we decline to rest our decision based upon its applicability for it may be possible in cases like this that the government has no barred deficiency to raise and then the issue remains of whether or not to allow the refund suit. Also, recoupment could not be used against the corporate shareholders in any event for they are different parties from the taxpayer here.

The answer is by no means an easy one, but we believe after weighing the matter carefully that we must subscribe to the ordinary rules of equitable estoppel. The government has not pointed to any action of the taxpayer that was misleading and certainly we can find no false representation. In fact, the taxpayer has done nothing except pay an asserted deficiency the Commissioner contended was correct and it is the Commissioner's misfortune if he mistakenly went after the wrong taxpayer. Furthermore, the facts do not indicate a strong case of reliance and detriment especially when the Commissioner should have been aware of the doubtful validity of an agreement which is neither a closing agreement nor a compromise signed by the Secretary. By applying some kind of estoppel to a situation like this where the true elements of estoppel are not present, we would be breathing life into the Form 870–AD agreement where the Supreme Court said in the *Botany* case, supra, there should be none.

* * *

The judgment appealed from is reversed with directions to enter judgment in favor of the appellant taxpayer as prayed for in its complaint.

STAIR v. UNITED STATES

516 F.2d 560 (2d Cir. 1975).

IRVING R. KAUFMAN, Chief Judge.

We are presented in this case with a rather interesting illustration of tax gamesmanship. The taxpayers' essential contention is "Heads I win, tails you lose." The dispute arises from a filing by Arthur and Bernice Stair for a refund of taxes paid for the taxable year ended December 31, 1964, seeking to undo an informal settlement agreement embodied in a Form 870–AD.

I

[The facts stipulated before the district court disclosed that, in an audit, the IRS raised the issue of whether the condemnation of certain real estate owned by Arthur Stair should have been treated as ordinary income or as capital gains, and proposed a deficiency of $83,065.69 for the year 1964.   There was a conference with the Appellate Division (now Appeals Office) and an agreement for a deficiency of roughly 50% of the amount proposed.   A Form 870–AD was executed and in December, 1966, the tax was paid.   Purportedly because of the intervening decision in Commissioner v. Tri-S Corp., 400 F.2d 862 (10th Cir. 1968), supporting the taxpayers' claim for long-term capital gains treatment, a refund claim was filed after limitations had run against the IRS with respect to assessments for the year in issue.]

II

Although the Internal Revenue Code has long provided procedures for definitive settlement [1] or compromise [2] of tax disputes, limitations on the authority to execute such agreements [3] have necessitated the use of less formal methods for resolving controversy short of litigation.   Chief among those used for the enforcement of the income tax laws is the Form 870–AD, the Offer of Waiver of Restrictions on Assessment and Collection of Deficiency in Tax and of Acceptance of Overassessment.   In addition to providing a waiver of the restrictions set forth in the Internal Revenue Code of 1954, § 6213(a), see id. at § 6213(d), that form contains clear representations that the taxpayer shall file no claim for a refund, and that the Commissioner will not reopen the case absent certain enumerated circumstances not here relevant.

The binding force of such an agreement upon each of the parties is generally no stronger than their adherence to the maxim that *"pacta sunt servanda."*   For the Supreme Court, considering the predecessor of the current provision for closing agreements, Rev.Stat. § 3229, concluded that

> Congress intended by the statute to prescribe the exclusive method by which tax cases could be compromised, requiring therefor the concurrence of the Commissioner and the Sec-

1. Int.Rev.Code   of   1954,   §   7121 * * *.

2. Int.Rev.Code   of   1954,   §   7122 * * *.

3. Section 7121(a) provides that "The Secretary or his delegate is autho-

rized to enter into an agreement in writing with any person relating to the liability of such person * * * in respect of any internal revenue tax for any taxable period."   Similar restrictions were imposed by the predecessors of the present section.

retary, and prescribing the formality with which * * * it should be attested * * *.

Botany Worsted Mills v. United States, 278 U.S. 282, 288, 49 S.Ct. 129, 131, 73 L.Ed. 379 (1929). A similar construction has been applied without disagreement to § 7121, presently in force. See e. g., Uinta Livestock Corp. v. United States, 355 F.2d 761, 765 (10th Cir. 1966). *Botany Mills,* however, left open the question whether an informal settlement agreement, "though not binding in itself, may when executed become, under some circumstances, binding on the parties by estoppel * * *." 278 U.S. at 289, 49 S.Ct. at 132. The Court found it unnecessary to consider that issue since the Government conceded in its brief that "[n]o ground for the United States to claim estoppel is disclosed in the findings." Id. at 288, 49 S.Ct. at 131.

The Government here bases its claim of estoppel on the fact that it may no longer assert its claim to that portion of the deficiency which it conceded in the settlement embodied in the Form 870–AD, since Internal Revenue Code of 1954, § 6501(a) bars assessments after three years from the due date of the return. The argument cannot, of course, rest merely on the fact that the taxpayer may have a longer time to seek a refund, for the Code itself permits such a result by authorizing claims for a credit or refund within two years from the date of payment. Internal Revenue Code of 1954, § 6511(a).[6] Recognizing this fact the Government points to an additional circumstance not presented in the ordinary case. It asserts with some vigor that it was lulled into accepting the December 30, 1966 payment as a final resolution of the controversy, by the taxpayers' promise that "no claim for refund or credit shall be filed or prosecuted."

Although this question has been presented on other occasions, the variety of answers which have been given are inconsistent, unclear in some instances, and certainly not dispositive of this case because of the unusual facts presented. Some circuits have refused to allow claims for a refund which would have the effect of undoing settlement agreements involving several taxpayers, or more than one disputed claim made by a single taxpayer. These cases, however, might seem to present more appealing grounds for estoppel, since the Government's right to assess deficiencies against other taxpayers or on taxable items not involved in the suit, although time-barred, was unquestioned. In this case, it is argued, the Government has only lost a claim—to ordinary income treatment of all the revenues received upon condemnation of the Stairs' property—whose very merit has been put in issue by the filing of suit.

Several courts have refused to apply the doctrine of equitable estoppel, holding that the Government is sufficiently protected by its

---

6. Thus, for example, a taxpayer will have more than three years to file his claim whenever an audit is completed —and payment made—more than one year after the due date of the return.

ability to set off uncollected deficiencies against the claim made by the taxpayer. But these cases followed upon settlement agreements compromising several claims, not all of which were in issue. In the instant case, the only item which has ever been in dispute is the subject of the litigation. Thus, the Government would have no further claim to set off against a victorious taxpayer.

Other cases have either flatly accepted or flatly rejected the contention that the mere running of the statute of limitations on assessments is sufficient to preclude a taxpayer's action for refund. The considerations upon which the stricter view of estoppel rests were set forth in Lignos v. United States, 439 F.2d 1365, 1368 (2d Cir. 1971);

> (1) there must be a false representation or wrongful misleading silence; (2) the error must originate in a statement of fact, not in opinion or a statement of law; (3) the one claiming the benefits of estoppel must not know the true facts; and (4) that same person must be adversely affected by the acts or statements of the one against whom an estoppel is claimed.

In *Lignos* we found the proof that the Government had been adversely affected much too uncertain to warrant summary judgment in its favor. For according to the plaintiffs' affidavits, the proposed tax deficiencies and civil fraud penalties for 1962 and 1963 had been reduced because the taxpayers had been "able to substantiate items of deductions and refute assertion of additional income * * * and not because of any concession on the part of the Internal Revenue Service * * *." Id. Thus even if the "settlement" for those two years were permitted to be undone after the statute of limitations on assessments had run, the Government might have lost no claim which it could not assert in the suit for a refund. Proof of the taxpayers' claim that the Government had made no concession was, of course, a matter for the determination of the district court on remand.

Here, the adverse effect on the Government is crystal clear. Contrary to the Stairs' claim that Commissioner v. Tri–S Corp., supra, is dispositive of the merits of their refund claim, the proper tax treatment of condemned property held by a real estate developer is far from uncontroverted and still the subject of considerable doubt. By its reliance on the taxpayers' promise not to file for a refund, the Government lost its opportunity to litigate the issue of capital gain or ordinary income treatment, and to collect the full deficiency originally assessed if successful.

The Stairs assert that equitable estoppel is improper in any event, since no misrepresentation was made at the time they signed the Form 870–AD. Rather, the argument proceeds, their intention to file for a refund did not crystallize until after *Tri–S Corp.* was decided in August of 1968, several months after the period of limitations on assessments had expired. We may note preliminarily that that decision did little but reinforce the advice which [the taxpayers' attorney] offered after meeting with the appellate conferee in August of 1966 [suggesting that the taxpayers litigate the issue]. We note also that the Tax Court opinion which was affirmed in *Tri-S Corp.* had been handed down on June 15, 1967, long before the statute of limitations had run against the government.

Quite apart from such considerations, however, we conclude that the statement that no refund claim would be filed—once the taxpayer has reneged—is misrepresentation of a kind sufficient to ground estoppel. To insist that the Government must fail since it cannot establish that the statement was a misrepresentation at the time it was made, ignores the reality of the situation. For the misrepresentation in fact inheres in the failure to state—at the time the settlement is made—that the representation is only conditional, and that there are circumstances under which the promise may be revoked. We may be sure that, had the Stairs explicitly reserved the right to seek a refund in the event of a later favorable decision on the condemnation issue, the Commissioner would have been considerably less willing to forego his right to assess a full deficiency.

We feel constrained to note that prudential considerations dictate the same result as we reach today. It requires little elaboration to demonstrate that a contrary outcome would arm the taxpayer with both a shield and a sword, and permit him to enter the lists with no chance of losing. The Stairs, if allowed to proceed, could fare no worse than the compromise they have already succeeded in negotiating. If victorious on the merits, they would be freed even from the obligation of sustaining their half of that bargain. Given such a state of affairs, it would be an imprudent taxpayer indeed who did not resort to litigation even after compromise. We see little purpose in straining *Botany Mills* to the breaking point in order to accommodate such a result.

Affirmed.

McGRAW–HILL, INC. v. UNITED STATES

623 F.2d 700 (Ct.Cl.1980).

PER CURIAM:

*   *   *

There is a long-standing conflict about the federal courts as to whether a taxpayer can be estopped from suing for a refund by an agreement less formal than the closing agreement or compromise statutorily described in sections 7121 and 7122 of the Code. However, the Court of Claims has consistently adhered to a more "liberal" view of estoppel. It has applied the doctrine of equitable estoppel whenever the IRS cannot be placed in the same position it was in when the agreement was executed. Guggenheim v. United States, 77

F.Supp. 186, 111 Ct.Cl. 165 (1948), cert. denied, 335 U.S. 908, 69 S.Ct. 411, 93 L.Ed. 441 (1949). Estoppel has been applied if the statute of limitations on assessments against the taxpayer had expired or if the statute had expired against other parties not before the court who were part of a "package deal." While the "liberal" view of estoppel first espoused in *Guggenheim,* supra, has not been followed in many circuits, most circuits will apply the doctrine of equitable estoppel against a taxpayer despite the absence of a formal closing agreement. Furthermore, the Supreme Court opinion in Botany Worsted Mills v. United States, 278 U.S. 282, 49 S.Ct. 129, 73 L.Ed. 379 (1929), deliberately leaves open the possibility of estopping a taxpayer in such circumstances. In any event, it is clear that the doctrine of equitable estoppel is available in this court in circumstances far less formal than those in which the statutorily prescribed closing agreements have been utilized.

* * *

Notwithstanding the fact that some courts may permit a taxpayer to sue for a refund even though a Form 870–AD "settlement" has been reached, a practitioner should not advise a client to execute the form with an intent to file a claim for refund. As a practical matter, one cannot be sure that the taxpayer will not be held to be estopped from pursuing the refund claim. More important, perhaps, is the fact that the execution of a Form 870–AD in this situation may be perceived as an implicit misrepresentation to the Appeals Office of the IRS, because of the agency's view that refund claims are forbidden once the agreement is accepted. It is perfectly acceptable, and far better practice, to provide on the Form 870–AD itself that the taxpayer expressly reserves the right to file and pursue refund claims with respect to specified issues.

C. FORMS 866 AND 906 (CLOSING AGREEMENTS)

Forms 866 and 906 are the closing agreements that comply with § 7121 of the Internal Revenue Code. The Code states, with respect to the finality of these agreements:

> (b) FINALITY—If such agreement is approved by the Secretary (within such time as may be stated in such agreement, or later agreed to) such agreement shall be final and conclusive, and, except upon a showing of fraud or malfeasance, or misrepresentation of a material fact—
>
>> (1) the case shall not be reopened as to the matters agreed upon or the agreement modified by any officer, employee, or agent of the United States, and
>>
>> (2) in any suit, action, or proceeding, such agreement, or any determination, assessment, collection, pay-

ment, abatement, refund, or credit made in accordance therewith, shall not be annulled, modified, set aside or disregarded.

Thus, execution of these forms results in a final settlement or closing which may not be disturbed by the government or the taxpayer.

Form 866 (Agreement as to Final Determination of Tax Liability) is used to effect the final closing of the total tax liability of the taxpayer. Form 906 (Closing Agreement as to Final Determination Covering Specific Matters) is used to effect the final closing as to one or more separate issues affecting the tax liability of a taxpayer.

Thus, Form 866 is used to close conclusively the total tax liability for a period ending prior to the date of the agreement. This form is not only useful in resolving disputes, but may also be desirable for a fiduciary seeking discharge of his obligations, or in making final distributions, or in the case of a corporate liquidation or sale of a corporate business. Form 906 may be used not only as to prior years, but also with respect to subsequent taxable periods. With regard to prior years' items, such as the amount of gross income, a particular deduction or valuation may be agreed upon; and with respect to future years, matters such as basis and depreciation may be agreed upon.

QUESTION

Closing agreements may be approved and entered into on behalf of the Commissioner by the persons authorized in Delegation Order No. 97 (Revision 18), 1980–1 C.B. 574 (effective February 28, 1980). In view of the fairly extensive delegation of authority (down to Appeals Team Chiefs) contained in Delegation Order No. 97, is there really any need for Appeals Offices to continue to use Forms 870–AD to close out routine nondocketed cases?

D. COLLATERAL AGREEMENTS

The term "collateral agreement" can be defined as an agreement secured from a taxpayer under examination (or related parties) to clarify or resolve a matter other than the particular tax liability at issue, but corollary to the disposition of the pending case.

A typical example of the use of a collateral agreement is found in the context of the settlement of the valuation, for estate tax purposes, of an item of property. Assume that the estate under examination reported the property in question at $100,000 and that the agent proposes a value of $200,000. The Appeals Office conferee and the estate's representative reach accord on a $150,000 valuation for estate tax purposes, and the estate's deficiency is computed using that figure. The Appeals conferee will often condition settlement with the estate upon the obtaining of a collateral agreement with the heirs, binding them to use the estate tax valuation as their basis in the asset.

Collateral agreements also are used frequently to bind a taxpayer with respect to a matter for future years, or to prevent a taxpayer whose tax liability is not currently at issue from placing the Service in a "whipsaw" situation by taking a position inconsistent with that of the taxpayer whose liability is at issue.

A collateral agreement is an administrative device which is not expressly provided for in the Code. It is, therefore, distinctly different from a closing agreement, which binds both the IRS and the taxpayer. Thus, at least in a theoretical sense, a collateral agreement does not bind the Service to the terms of the collateral agreement. Hence, in the estate tax example discussed above, the basic substantive agreement as to the estate tax deficiency would be effected on a Form 890–AD, which binds the Service vis-a-vis the estate, absent specified exceptions for fraud, etc. The collateral agreement would bind the heirs and require them to value their basis in the property at $150,000, but might not be binding on the IRS. As a practical matter, the likelihood that the Service, having finally accepted an estate tax valuation of $150,000, would subsequently contend that the valuation (hence the heirs' basis) was excessive, is remote indeed. Moreover, in most cases, the effect of the collateral agreement is to restrict the nongovernmental parties from claiming tax treatment of an item which would be more favorable to them than treatment consistent with the settlement embodied in the underlying agreement. Nevertheless, in circumstances in which the terms of the collateral agreement are favorable to the nongovernmental parties, the possibility of a statutorily authorized closing agreement in lieu of a collateral agreement should be considered.

The term "collateral agreement" is also used to describe the agreement customarily required by the Service when compromising an assessed tax liability based upon considerations of collectibility. This type of collateral agreement, which is connected to the settlement of a tax liability for payment of less than 100 cents on the dollar, requires the taxpayer to make payments in excess of the compromised amount if his income (and certain other receipts) exceed specified levels during the term of the agreement. See pages 684–686, below, for a discussion of offers in compromise.

SECTION 5. STATUTE OF LIMITATIONS ON THE ASSESSMENT OF DEFICIENCIES

A. BASIC RULES

The following is a discussion of the *basic* rules governing limitations on assessments of taxes under the Internal Revenue Code. It does not cover the many circumstances in which special limitations rules may be applicable in the case of a particular type of tax or of a particular type of adjustment.[t]

The Basic Three-Year Period. The tax collector is allowed a three-year period to make assessments against taxpayers absent circumstances deemed (under § 6501 of the Code) sufficient to justify additional time. The limitations period begins with the later of the date the subject tax return is due or is filed. Thus, if a 1981 federal income tax return which is due on April 15, 1982 is filed timely (or early) and there are no special circumstances causing an extension of the period, limitations expire on April 15, 1985. If the return was filed June 15, 1982 (regardless of whether it was timely because of an extension obtained by the taxpayer) limitations would run June 15, 1985. Where no tax return is ever filed, the period of limitations never commences and, hence, never expires.[u]

The Double (Six-Year) Period for 25% Omissions. The basic three-year period is doubled to six years if there has been a 25% omission (defined below) from the subject return. The policy of the law is to provide a longer period for assessment if the omitted amount is above the statutorily set proportion. The requisite omission is specifically defined as gross income in excess of 25% of the amount stated in the return for income taxes, and total gifts or gross estate assets in excess of 25% of the amount stated in the return for gift or estate tax purposes.[v]

The Open-Ended Period for Fraud. If the taxpayer has engaged in a willful attempt in any manner to evade tax or has filed a false or fraudulent return with the intent to evade tax, an assessment may be made at any time.[w] Hence, in many cases, the basic tax liability is not debated but the deficiency stands or falls on the existence *vel non* of an attempt to evade.

Extended Period by Consent. Except in the case of estate taxes, the taxpayer may enter into an agreement with the IRS to extend the period of limitations for assessment.[x]

Suspension of Period by Deficiency Notice. Certain taxes, particularly income, estate and gift taxes, cannot be assessed prior to the issuance of a statutory notice of deficiency [y] and, if a timely petition is filed, the conclusion of Tax Court proceedings in which the liability is determined.[z] Therefore, the running of the period of limitations

---

t. For example, certain carryback adjustments receive special treatment under IRC §§ 6501(h)–(j).

u. IRC § 6501(c)(3), perhaps superfluously, states expressly that where there is a failure to file a return, an assessment may be made at any time.

v. IRC §§ 6501(e)(1) and (2).

w. IRC §§ 6501(c)(1) and (2).

x. IRC § 6501(c)(4). See discussion on pages 180–182, below.

y. However, in a jeopardy situation, the IRS may assess any tax without issuing a notice of deficiency. See pages 709–729, below.

z. IRC § 6213(a).

on assessments is suspended once a deficiency notice is issued. The suspension is in effect during the period assessment is prohibited and for 60 days thereafter.[a] Hence, if a deficiency notice (providing 90 days to petition the Tax Court) is ignored, limitations are suspended for a total of 150 days. But, if a timely petition is filed, limitations are suspended until 60 days after the decision of the Tax Court becomes final—which might not occur until years after the deficiency notice is issued.

Reopening of Closed Periods. In the tax law there are situations in which periods of limitations long closed may be reopened for a particular purpose. As discussed more fully below,[b] in some circumstances the doctrine of equitable recoupment or the statutory mitigation provisions[c] will permit a closed period to be reopened to avoid an inequitable result of a party's taking inconsistent positions for closed and opened years.

B. COMMENCEMENT OF RUNNING OF LIMITATIONS PERIOD

The period of limitations on assessments commences with the later of the date the subject tax return is either due or filed. In some circumstances there can be an issue as to whether the subject tax return was in fact filed but not recorded as received by the Service. There can also be an issue as to whether a particular putative tax return is properly characterized as a tax return for purposes of commencing the period of limitations.

ZELLERBACH PAPER CO. v. HELVERING

Supreme Court of the United States, 1934.
293 U.S. 172, 55 S.Ct. 127, 79 L.Ed. 264.

Mr. Justice CARDOZO delivered the opinion of the Court.

The controversy in these cases hinges upon the date when the statute of limitations began to run against deficiency assessments by the Commissioner of Internal Revenue.

On July 16, 1921, Zellerbach Paper Company filed a consolidated income and profits tax return on behalf of itself and a subsidiary, National Paper Products Company, for the fiscal year beginning May 1, 1920 and ending April 30, 1921 [pursuant to the Revenue Act of 1918].

[A new statute, the Revenue Act of 1921, required the taxpayer to file a new or supplemental return for the year ending in 1921 re-

a. IRC § 6503(a)(1).   c. IRC §§ 1311–1314.

b. See pages 182–188.

porting an additional tax liability mathematically derived from amounts reported on the original return.]

* * *

The Act of 1921 in its application to the petitioners made one change and one only. If the net income of the taxpayer was more than $25,000, there was to be a denial of the credit or exemption of $2,000 otherwise allowable. The fiscal year of the petitioners ran, as we have seen, from May 1, 1920, to April 30, 1921, and of this period one-third was in the calendar year 1921. The net income being largely in excess of $25,000, the effect of the new law was to cut down the permissible credit by one-third of $2,000, thus increasing the tax by little more than a nominal amount. What that amount was could be ascertained by a simple computation, dependent upon data fully supplied by the return already filed, and calling only for application of the statutory rule.

The petitioners did not make a new or supplemental return correcting the computation in the one on file. The change was so trivial and so obvious as perhaps to lead them to believe that no amendment was expected. Be that as it may, they heard nothing more from the Bureau of Internal Revenue with reference to their taxes till May 11, 1928, an interval of nearly seven years, when they received from the Commissioner notices of deficiency assessments in large amounts upon grounds unrelated (except for the deduction already mentioned) to any changes in the law. The Revenue Act of 1921 provides that income and profits taxes shall be determined and assessed by the Commissioner within four ^d years after a return is filed. If the return filed by the petitioners or in their behalf in July, 1921, served to set in motion the term of limitation, the assessments were too late. The Board of Tax Appeals, however, upheld the action of the Commissioner, and ruled (two members dissenting) that the return on file was a nullity, and hence that the statute of limitations had never been set running. The Court of Appeals for the Ninth Circuit affirmed. * * *

* * *

[The conclusion of the courts below] would lead in practice to complications and injustice. Many taxpayers filing returns under the Act of 1918 were unaffected by the changes wrought by the Act of 1921. Their returns, if made over again, would have been an exact reproduction of those they had made already. A statute would have to be very plain to justify a holding in such circumstances that there was an obligation to report anew. Certainly the average man would be slow to suspect that he was subject to such a duty. If he looked into the Treasury Decisions, he would learn that the Commissioner agreed with him. In these he was told by the plainest implication that unless he had an additional tax to pay, his return would stand as

---

d. Now three years. See IRC §
6501(a).

filed, without supplement or correction. Now, the Commissioner of Internal Revenue is without dispensing power. If a return under the old act is not good under the new one, but, instead, is an utter nullity, he may not relieve the taxpayer of making a return over again. To this the government assents, and on it builds the argument that the first returns are to be disregarded altogether, whether more is due or nothing. In that view, hundreds of taxpayers, perhaps thousands, though innocent of willful wrong, have been deprived of the protection of any rule of limitation, not to speak of other penalties unwittingly incurred. A statute of uncertain meaning will not readily be made an instrument for so much of hardship and confusion.

* * *

From [the] administrative history the inference is compelling that a second return, reporting an additional tax, is an amendment or supplement to a return already upon the files, and being effective by relation does not toll a limitation which has once begun to run. Perfect accuracy or completeness is not necessary to rescue a return from nullity, if it purports to be a return, is sworn to as such, and evinces an honest and genuine endeavor to satisfy the law. This is so though at the time of filing the omissions or inaccuracies are such as to make amendment necessary. Even more clearly is it so when the return is full and accurate in the beginning under the statutes then in force, but is made inaccurate or incomplete by supervening changes of the law, unforeseen and unforeseeable. Supplement and correction in such circumstances will not take from a taxpayer, free from personal fault, the protection of a term of limitation already running for his benefit. * * *

* * *

UNITED STATES v. MOORE

627 F.2d 830 (7th Cir. 1980).

LARSON, Senior District Judge.

Defendant David Moore was charged with failing to file income tax returns for the years 1972, 1973, and 1974, in violation of 26 U.S. C. § 7203. Defendant was tried in June 1979 and the jury found him guilty on all counts. Defendant was a businessman whose income in each of the years he failed to file was in excess of $30,000. He had filed valid tax returns for at least five years prior to 1972.

In April 1973 defendant and his wife submitted a joint return for the 1972 year to the I.R.S. This form contained only their names, occupations, social security numbers and number of dependents. Fifth Amendment objections were written across the form and a packet of tax protest literature was attached. The form was signed by the defendant and his wife, but the verification was scratched out. The I.R.S. notified defendant in August 1973 that the forms were not sufficient returns. In a rather contentious January 1974 letter, defendant replied to the I.R.S., stating that he considered dollars to be worthless and his tax return to be adequate.

In May 1974, however, defendant submitted an amended 1040 form for the 1972 year. This form was filed for himself only. On the amended form defendant filled in the various blanks calling for numerical information with "none," except that under interest income he put $41 and under dividend income he placed the figure $22. The Fifth Amendment objections were retained and more tax protest material was appended. Although signed, the certification on the form was again marked over.

In 1974 defendant also filed a return for the year 1973 which was substantially the same as his amended form for 1972. It contained a small amount in interest income and the certification was scratched out. The I.R.S. notified defendant by letter in July 1974 that it did not consider this to be a return. In 1975 defendant filed a similar return for the 1974 year. The I.R.S. again informed him that it did not consider this to be a return.

* * *

* * * [D]efendant contends that what he filed was a return and that the district court erred in taking this issue from the jury. The determination of what is an adequate return is a legal question and it was proper for the district court to decide that question.

Defendant asserts that he filed an acceptable return because he did provide some figures, although incomplete and inaccurate, from which a tax could be computed. He argues that his return is therefore unlike those which contain blanket objections and no income figures at all. This is a difficult problem and one which we fortunately do not have to decide. The forms defendant supplied to the I.R.S. were not returns for another reason: they were not verified.

26 U.S.C. § 6001 states that "every person liable for any tax imposed by this title * * * shall * * * make such returns, and comply with such rules and regulations as the Secretary (of the Treasury) may from time to time prescribe." Section 6011(a) requires taxpayers to make returns "according to the forms and regulations prescribed by the Secretary." Section 6061 provides that returns "shall be signed in accordance with forms or regulations prescribed by the Secretary." Section 6065 (section 6065(a) at the time defendant filed his returns) states that "any return * * * required to be made under any provision of the internal revenue laws or regulations shall contain or be verified by a written declaration that it is made under the penalties of perjury." In 26 C.F.R. § 1.6065–1(a) the Secretary of the Treasury has by regulation also required income taxpayers to verify their returns. Defendant had a duty by statute and regulation to file tax returns with a verified signature. The forms he submitted to the I.R.S. were not returns because the decla-

ration that the forms were completed and signed under penalty of perjury was obliterated.

Even if the forms had been verified, the I.R.S. could have properly rejected them as insufficient returns. The tax protestor cases have forced courts to grapple with the definition of a "return." The tax code and regulations provide little guidance. In United States v. Porth, [426 F.2d 519 (10th Cir. 1970)], the Tenth Circuit held that a return "which does not contain any information relating to the taxpayer's income from which the tax can be computed is not a return within the meaning of the Internal Revenue Code." The return in *Porth* had no information at all on income. The *Porth* test has been adopted by almost all courts, including this one. It is not clear, however, what the result should be when the form does include some income figures, even if incomplete or inaccurate.

Varying positions have been taken by the Courts of Appeals. The Tenth Circuit has held that a form giving some small income amounts in "constitutional" dollars was tantamount to one giving no information, and would be treated as such. United States v. Brown, 600 F.2d 248, 251 (10th Cir.), cert. denied, 444 U.S. 917, 100 S.Ct. 233, 62 L.Ed.2d 172 (1979). The Third Circuit appears to have taken a similar approach in United States v. Edelson, 604 F.2d 232, 234 (3rd Cir. 1979). The form had only a total income figure, and that was in "constitutional" dollars. In United States v. Smith, 618 F.2d 280, 281 (5th Cir. 1980), the taxpayer put zeroes in some of the income blanks. The court said the "return" did not purport to disclose the required information and would not be treated as a return. Most recently, in United States v. Farber, 630 F.2d 569, (8th Cir. 1980), the Eighth Circuit upheld the failure-to-file conviction of a taxpayer who had reported a small amount of income. In all of these cases it was apparent from Fifth Amendment objections written on the forms and from accompanying literature that the filer was a tax protestor.

The Ninth Circuit, however, has taken the opposite position. In United States v. Long, 618 F.2d 74, 75 (9th Cir. 1980), the taxpayer submitted a form with zeroes in all the blanks. The court held that even if this information was false, a tax liability could be computed from it and it was therefore an adequate return. Part of the court's rationale appeared to be that a different penalty could be levied against those who took the chance of supplying false information.
* * *

The Ninth Circuit is clearly correct in stating that a tax liability could be computed from zeroes, or from small amounts. The fact that the information is inaccurate only means that the tax owed, if any, will be wrong, not that it cannot be calculated. When the income information is incomplete, a more difficult problem is presented, but as long as a total income figure is given, the I.R.S. could compute the tax. Certainly a bright line rule that even a form with inaccurate or incomplete income information is a return would be easier to enforce.

The mere fact that a tax could be calculated from information on a form, however, should not be determinative of whether the form is a return. *Porth* relied in part on earlier Supreme Court cases which considered the definition of a return in another context. These cases indicate that it is not enough for a form to contain some income information; there must also be an honest and reasonable intent to supply the information required by the tax code. In Zellerbach Paper Co. v. Commissioner, 293 U.S. 172, 180, 55 S.Ct. 127, 131, 79 L. Ed. 264 (1934), it was said that:

> "Perfect accuracy or completeness is not necessary to rescue a return from nullity, if it purports to be a return, is sworn to as such, and evinces an honest and genuine endeavor to satisfy the law." (citation omitted.)

In the tax protestor cases, it is obvious that there is no "honest and genuine" attempt to meet the requirements of the code. In our self-reporting tax system the government should not be forced to accept as a return a document which plainly is not intended to give the required information.

It is important to harmonize the various tax crime laws. The government apparently prefers to charge tax protestors with failure to file—§ 7203, a misdemeanor, rather than tax evasion—§ 7201, or making false returns—§ 7206, both felonies. A serious problem might be presented if the government took the position that any form with false information on it is not a return. That is not our situation. It is not the false data which makes these returns defective, but the fact that there is no real attempt to comply with the requirement of filing a return.

The government should not have to guess whether it should take the position that a form is not a return and charge the taxpayer with failure to file, or that the form is a return and charge him with filing a false return or tax evasion. If the Courts of Appeals continue to disagree the Supreme Court will eventually have to decide the question, but it is our view that when it is apparent that the taxpayer is not attempting to file forms accurately disclosing his income, he may be charged with failure to file a return.

The conviction is affirmed.

QUESTION

If a fraudulent tax return is filed with intent to evade tax, an assessment may be made at any time. Suppose, however, an original return is in fact fraudulent with intent to evade tax, but that a non-fraudulent amended return is filed. Is there no period of limitations because of the original fraudulent return? Is the fraud cured in some fashion by the amended return? If so, when does the statute of limitations begin to run?

DOWELL v. COMMISSIONER

614 F.2d 1263 (10th Cir. 1980).

SETH, Chief Judge.

This an appeal from a ruling of the United States Tax Court against appellants. The facts are undisputed. Taxpayers filed fraudulent income tax returns for calendar years 1963, 1964, 1965, and 1966. On September 13, 1968, taxpayers filed nonfraudulent amended returns for 1965 and 1966, and on November 25, 1968 they filed nonfraudulent amended returns for 1963 and 1964.

The Government used the amended returns in its fraud investigation, and also used them to convict taxpayers of willfully filing fraudulent returns for 1963–1966.

The Government apparently also used the amended returns to determine additional taxes due for all four years plus penalties and interest. Taxpayers received a notice of deficiency issued December 11, 1974, and filed a petition in the Tax Court which sought a refund and a bar against further assessments.

The taxpayers' position is that the nonfraudulent amended returns satisfied the requirements of 26 U.S.C. § 6501(a), and accordingly started the three-year period of limitation. Thus they assert that the Government failed to assess within the three-year period. The Tax Court held in substance that there was no limitation period for assessment of the 1963–1966 taxes because the original returns were fraudulent, and the matter was governed only by § 6501(c)(1) which entitled the Government to assess tax "at any time." Thus it held that the taxpayers could not start the period provided in § 6501(a). For the reasons that follow we must disagree with the ruling of the Tax Court.

The general statute of limitations, 26 U.S.C. § 6501(a), provides "any tax imposed by this title shall be assessed within 3 years after the return was filed." However, it is often difficult to determine whether certain filings are "returns." The Supreme Court in Zellerbach Paper Co. v. Helvering, 293 U.S. 172, 55 S.Ct. 127, 79 L.Ed. 264 held:

> "Perfect accuracy or completeness is not necessary to rescue a return from nullity, if it purports to be a return, is sworn to as such * * *, and evinces an honest and genuine endeavor to satisfy the law. This is so though at the time of filing the omissions or inaccuracies are such as to make amendment necessary."

Thus once the taxpayer has evinced an honest and genuine effort to satisfy the law by filing such a return, the § 6501(a) period begins to run.

In John D. Alkire Inv. Co. v. Nicholas, 114 F.2d 607 (10th Cir.), this court held that a subsequent corrective filing to a *deficient return* started the three-year limitations period. Taxpayer had filed returns from 1926 to 1935 that "not only failed to disclose requisite information but were misleading and calculated to prevent discovery of material facts." In late 1936, taxpayer filed amended returns for each year in question. These contained the required information, and we held they started the limitations period. There was no holding of fraud in *Alkire* but the original returns were totally deficient and misleading.

In Bennett v. Commissioner, 30 T.C. 114, *acq.* 1958–2 C.B. 3, taxpayer originally failed to file any return. The Tax Court found as fact the "failure to file was deliberate and fraudulent with intent to evade tax." Taxpayer eventually filed a return which satisfied the requirements of the three-year statute of limitations. The Tax Court held the subsequent filing of an honest return triggered the three-year limitations period notwithstanding the previous applicability of § 6501(c)(3). The court reasoned:

> "For, once a nonfraudulent return is filed, putting the Commissioner on notice of a taxpayer's receipts and deductions, there can be no policy in favor of permitting assessment thereafter at any time without limitation. We think that the statute of limitations begins to run with the filing of such returns."

This reasoning is equally compelling in this case. Furthermore, the Internal Revenue Service adopted the *Bennett* holding in Rev.Rul. 79–178, 1979–23 I.R.B. 16. The Tax Court did not here follow its *Bennett* opinion because it reasoned the *Bennett* court applied the three-year limitation to "an original, although delinquent return," and therefore "[t]his is different from petitioners' situation." The distinction thus was made between a fraudulent failure to file and a fraudulent return.

The question would seem to be whether taxpayers have filed a return that meets the requirements of § 6501(a) and *Zellerbach,* not whether the return was "original" or "amended." The fraudulent returns filed in the first instance here were really not "returns" within the meaning of § 6501(a) or *Zellerbach.* They started no statute of limitations; they simply entitled the Government to make its assessment "at any time" as provided in § 6501(c)(1). This "at any time" does not mean regardless of what may take place. It is not, as the Government argues, some sort of period of limitation or "statute of limitations." We are thus not concerned with an act which stops the running of a period of limitations. We are concerned instead with something which *starts* the period. Section 6501(c) represents the antithesis of a limitations concept, and in the absence of anything else the commencement of any period of repose for fraudulent or evasive "returns" is put in limbo.

The purpose of § 6501(c) is to provide the Government time to unearth information the taxpayer did not furnish and to file an assessment. Once the Government has the information from a *Zellerbach* filing or as in *Alkire* or as said in *Bennett,* "there can be no policy in favor of permitting assessment thereafter at any time without limitation." *   *   *

The original returns in the case before us are in many respects comparable to those in John D. Alkire Inv. Co. v. Nicholas, 114 F.2d 607 (10th Cir.). In the cited case there was found to be no fraud, but we said, as mentioned above:

> "The returns not only failed to disclose requisite information but were misleading and calculated to prevent discovery of material facts. Returns of that kind are not effective to start the period of limitation running."

The amended returns were held to be sufficient to start the period of limitations. We consider that the *Alkire* decision is not necessarily controlling, but is sufficiently similar to indicate the conclusion to be reached in this appeal.

The position of the Government also fails to recognize that §§ 6501(c)(1) and 6501(c)(3) are in *pari materia* and accordingly should be construed consistently with one another. The Revenue Act of 1921 extended the unlimited assessment period to include failure-to-file situations, and also included this in the same subsection with fraudulent filings. These two situations were so included in the same subsection through the Internal Revenue Code of 1939, § 276(a). The 1954 Code retained them in the same subsection, but for some undisclosed reason placed the two situations into separate subdivisions, §§ 6501(c)(1) and 6501(c)(3). Congress provided no indication that it intended statute of limitations treatment to differ between taxpayers who filed fraudulent returns, and those who fraudulently failed to file.

The Government raises the additional argument that the statute governing failure to file a return, § 6501(c)(3), would be rendered superfluous by taxpayers' reading of § 6501(c)(1) (fraudulent filing). This argument is not persuasive, and it has carried little weight through the decades of litigation on this point. It is a better reading of § 6501 to conclude that Congress foresaw the need for express exceptions to the general statute of limitations in at least two situations—fraudulent filing and failure to file. The fraud penalties and criminal prosecution take care of the fraud problem. The "at any time" assessment is not a further penalty. Once the taxpayer has filed a *Zellerbach-Alkire* return the "at any time" reason is removed, and the matter proceeds as in any tax case. No irrevocable forfeiture of the benefits of limitation periods is contemplated as an additional punishment or penalty. That the "case" may be in one division of the IRS or in another division can make no difference.

* * *

The judgment of the Tax Court is REVERSED and the case is REMANDED.

C. SPECIAL SIX–YEAR LIMITATIONS PERIOD FOR 25% OMISSIONS

THE COLONY, INC. v. COMMISSIONER

Supreme Court of the United States, 1958.
357 U.S. 28, 78 S.Ct. 1033, 2 L.Ed.2d 1119.

Mr. Justice HARLAN delivered the opinion of the Court.

The sole question in this case is whether assessments by the Commissioner of two asserted tax deficiencies were barred by the three-year statute of limitations provided in the Internal Revenue Code of 1939.

* * * A special five-year [now six-year] period of limitations is provided when a taxpayer, even though acting in good faith, "omits from gross income an amount properly includible therein which is in excess of 25 per centum of the amount of gross income stated in the return * * *." § 275(c).ᵉ * * *

[In this case there was a nonfraudulent overstatement of the basis of certain lots which were sold, resulting in a greater than 25% understatement of gross income. The assessments were made more than three but less than five years after the subject returns were filed. The Commissioner argued that the extended statute was applicable because of the 25% understatement of gross income. The taxpayer argued that the extended statute was available only where there was a *complete* omission of *specific items* of gross income. |

Although we are inclined to think that the statute on its face lends itself more plausibly to the taxpayer's interpretation, it cannot be said that the language is unambiguous. In these circumstances we turn to the legislative history of § 275(c). We find in that history persuasive evidence that Congress was addressing itself to the specific situation where a taxpayer actually omitted some income receipt or accrual in his computation of gross income, and not more generally to errors in that computation arising from other causes.

* * *

e. The predecessor to § 6501(e) of the
1954 Code.

The Commissioner also suggests that in enacting § 275(c) Congress was primarily concerned with providing for a longer period of limitations where returns contained relatively large errors adversely affecting the Treasury, and that effect can be given this purpose only by adopting the Government's broad construction of the statute. But this theory does not persuade us. For if the mere size of the error had been the principal concern of Congress, one might have expected to find the statute cast in terms of errors in the total tax due or in total taxable net income. We have been unable to find any solid support for the Government's theory in the legislative history. Instead, * * * this history shows to our satisfaction that the Congress intended an exception to the usual three-year statute of limitations only in the restricted type of situation already described.

We think that in enacting § 275(c) Congress manifested no broader purpose than to give the Commissioner an additional two years to investigate tax returns in cases where, because of a taxpayer's omission to report some taxable item, the Commissioner is at a special disadvantage in detecting errors. In such instances the return on its face provides no clue to the existence of the omitted item. On the other hand, when, as here, the understatement of a tax arises from an error in reporting an item disclosed on the face of the return the Commissioner is at no such disadvantage. And this would seem to be so whether the error be one affecting "gross income" or one, such as overstated deductions, affecting other parts of the return. To accept the Commissioner's interpretation and to impose a five-year limitation when such errors affect "gross income," but a three-year limitation when they do not, not only would be to read § 275(c) more broadly than is justified by the evident reason for its enactment, but also to create a patent incongruity in the tax law.

Finally, our construction of § 275(c) * * * is in harmony with the unambiguous language of § 6501(e)(1)(A) of the Internal Revenue Code of 1954.[3]

3. "§ 6501. Limitations on assessment and collection.

* * *

"(e) Omission from gross income—Except as otherwise provided in subsection (c)—

"(1) Income taxes.—In the case of any tax imposed by subtitle A—

"(A) General rule.—If the taxpayer omits from gross income an amount properly includible therein which is in excess of 25 percent of the amount of gross income stated in the return, the tax may be assessed, or a proceeding in court for the collection of such tax may be begun without assessment, at any time within 6 years after the return was filed. For purposes of this subparagraph—

"(i) In the case of a trade or business, the term 'gross income' means the total of the amounts received or accrued from the sale of goods or services (if such amounts are required to be shown on the return) prior to diminution by the cost of such sales or services; and

"(ii) In determining the amount omitted from gross income, there shall not be taken into account any amount which is omitted from gross income stated in the return if such amount is disclosed in the return, or in a statement attached to the return, in a manner adequate to apprise the Secretary or his delegate of the nature and amount of such item."

We hold that both tax assessments before us were barred by the statute of limitations.

Reversed.

ESTATE OF KLEIN v. COMMISSIONER

537 F.2d 701 (2d Cir. 1976).

MESKILL, Circuit Judge:

Bebe Klein, individually and as co-executor of the estate of Herman Klein, deceased, and Malcolm B. Klein and Ira K. Klein, the remaining co-executors of that estate, appeal from a judgment of the United States Tax Court, Dawson, *J.,* which held that Bebe Klein was not entitled to the benefits of the "innocent spouse" provisions of Section 6013(e) of the Internal Revenue Code of 1954. The tax court * * * concluded that the "innocent spouse" protection was not available because the amount of gross income which was omitted from Herman and Bebe Klein's joint tax return for the taxable year 1955 did not exceed twenty-five percent of the amount of gross income "stated in the return" as is required by Section 6013(e)(1)(A) of the Code. We agree with the result reached by the tax court and affirm.

Section 6013(e) is designed to relieve the co-signer of a joint income tax return from liability for certain deficiencies caused by the omission from the return of a significant amount of gross income attributable to the other spouse. The applicability of this section, however, does not depend entirely on the equities of each particular situation. Rather, the "innocent spouse" must meet specific criteria in order to qualify for this statutory protection. First, the "innocent spouse" must show that in the joint return for the tax year in question "there was omitted from gross income an amount properly includable therein which is attributable to [the other] spouse and which is in excess of 25 percent of the amount of gross income stated in the return." 26 U.S.C. § 6013(e)(1)(A). It is this requirement that the tax court determined had not been met by appellant Bebe Klein.[f] * * *

The essential facts were stipulated and so found by the tax court. During the tax year involved here, 1955, Herman Klein, who died in 1964, owned a thirty percent interest in two dress manufacturing partnerships, Miss Smart Frocks and C & S Dress Company. Those partnerships filed a partnership return for the taxable year beginning May 1, 1954 and ending April 29, 1955, using the accrual method of accounting and showing gross sales receipts in the amount of $3,545,911.95 and income from contracting in the amount of

---

f. The two additional requirements for "innocent spouse" treatment are discussed at pages 777–781, below.

$141,457.40. The partnership return further reported the partnerships' net income to be in the amount of $311,594.62, and, in Schedule K thereof, Herman Klein's distributive share of that net income to be in the amount of $90,845.89.

Herman and Bebe Klein timely filed a joint income tax return for the taxable year 1955. In that return they reported interest income in the amount of $191.21, royalty income in the amount of $494.05 and partnership income in the amount of $90,845.89, which components totalled $91,531.15. The $90,845.89 figure reported as partnership income on the joint income tax return, of course, represented Herman's distributive share of the partnerships' net income as reported on the partnership return. Herman and Bebe Klein's joint income tax return omitted * * * a total of $45,733.28, all of which was attributable solely to Herman Klein.

The question put squarely before us then, is whether or not the $45,733.28 concededly omitted from gross income on the joint income tax return exceeded twenty-five percent of the amount of gross income stated in the return. Appellants contend that the gross income stated in Herman and Bebe Klein's joint income tax return was $91,531.15, the actual amount reported on the Form 1040, including, insofar as the partnership income is concerned, only Herman's distributive share of the partnerships' net profits. Since the amount of gross income omitted from the return, $45,733.28, exceeds twenty-five percent of $91,531.15, they assert that the requirements of § 6013(e)(1)(A) have been met.

The tax court and the appellee Commissioner of Internal Revenue, however, reading the joint income tax return, Form 1040, as if it included the partnership return, Form 1065, concluded that the gross income reported by Herman and Bebe Klein was $1,106,896.07, which figure includes Herman's thirty percent distributive share, $1,106,210.81, of the partnerships' reported gross receipts income. There can be no doubt that if the tax court's approach is correct, the amount omitted from gross income does not even approach the twenty-five percent threshold required by § 6013(e)(1)(A).

It is beyond dispute that the statutory definition of gross income includes a partner's distributive share of the partnership's gross income. Sections 61(a)(13) and 702(c) of the Code, specifically so state. These definitions, however, provide only a starting point from which to determine whether or not a partner's distributive share of the partnership's gross income is his gross income "stated" in his return for the purposes of § 6013(e)(1)(A). Appellants argue that regardless of the general statutory definition of gross income, the only gross income "stated" in the return for the purposes of § 6013(e) is that which is actually entered on the joint income tax return, Form 1040. They argue that if the legislation had been meant to include a partner's distributive share of the partnership's gross income, which

is generally and properly reported only on the partnership return, §
6013(e)(1)(A) would have provided that the amount omitted must
be in excess of twenty-five percent of the amount of gross income
"stated in the *returns*." However logical that argument may seem in
the abstract, it ignores both the function of the particular return
forms used in a partnership situation and the consistent line of tax
court decisions which have held that, in other situations, the partnership return must be read as an adjunct to a partner's individual or
joint income tax return.   *   *   *

*   *   *

As the tax court pointed out, § 6013(e)(2)(B) itself provides
convincing support for the Commissioner's position. That part of the
innocent spouse section directs that the determination of "the amount
omitted from gross income" should be made in "the manner provided
by section 6501(e)(1)(A)   *   *   *," the section which determines
whether or not the Commissioner will be able to extend to six years
the general three year statute of limitations. The purpose of §
6501(e)(1)(A) is to extend the statute of limitations for the assessment or collection of income taxes in situations literally identical to
those required in the innocent spouse provision, namely, where the
taxpayer "omits from gross income an amount properly includible
therein which is in excess of 25 percent of the amount of gross income stated in the return   *   *   *." According to subparagraph (ii)
of § 6501(e)(1)(A), an amount is not "omitted from gross income
stated in the return" if it is "disclosed in the return, or in a statement attached to the return, in a manner adequate to apprise the
Secretary or his delegate of the nature and amount of such item."
Essentially, § 6501(e)(1)(A)(ii) directs that anything that is "disclosed" in the return is not "omitted" from the return. It would
seem to be a truism that if an amount is "disclosed" in the return, it
is somehow "stated" in the return. To that effect, it seems only logical that one must read the partnership return in order to discover
whether or not an item of a partner's gross income has been "disclosed," i. e., not "omitted." If one could not look at the partnership
return for that purpose, a partner's actual gross income (his distributive share of the partnership's gross income) would always be "omitted" from his return since that figure appears only on the partnership return. Such a result could not have been intended by Congress.
Congress could not have intended that the statute of limitations be
extended against a taxpayer when that taxpayer has properly reported all of his items of gross income. Yet that would be the technical
result if the partnership return were to be isolated from examination
in determining what gross income was "disclosed" in the partner's return for the purposes of § 6501(e)(1)(A)(ii). We fail to see why
something which must be considered to have been "disclosed" and
therefore not "omitted" from the return for purposes of §
6501(e)(1)(A)(ii), should not also be considered "stated" in the re-

turn for the purposes of both that section and, through §
6013(e)(2)(B)'s reference, the "innocent spouse" provision.

As mentioned at the outset, since the enactment of the 1954
Code, the tax court has consistently rejected the specific construction
urged by the appellants in this case. Compare L. Glenn Switzer, 20
T.C. 759, 766–68 (1953) (accepting such an argument under the 1939
Code), with Jack Rose, 24 T.C. at 768–70 (apparently, again under
the 1939 Code, rejecting the argument in dictum and noting that the
Court of Appeals for the Ninth Circuit had vacated *Switzer* upon the
stipulation of the parties). [In cases] after *Switzer*, the tax court
has recognized that one must look to the partnership return to determine the amount of a partner's gross income not only "omitted" from
his return but also "stated" in his return. We see no reason to overrule this reasoned line of cases indirectly by holding that what is
"stated" in the return for "innocent spouse" purposes, is only the figure actually entered on the Form 1040.

Finally the tax court, in supporting the conclusion that the partnership return must be read together with the personal return and in
computing the amount of the partnership's gross income, relied upon
the definition of gross income from a trade or business as "gross receipts," which definition is contained in subparagraph (i) of §
6501(e)(1)(A). The appellants have challenged the applicability of
that particular subparagraph by arguing, inter alia, that since the innocent spouse section, § 6013(e)(2)(B), refers to the statute of limitations section, § 6501(e)(1)(A), only for the purpose of determining
what is "omitted" from gross income, the reference is limited to subparagraph (ii) of § 6501(e)(1)(A). They argue that subparagraph
(i) is irrelevant in determining what is "omitted." Although appellants' argument is persuasive, we feel no need to entertain it here.
Since, as we have shown above, it is not necessary to rely upon subparagraph (i) in order to conclude that the partnership return must
be read as an adjunct to a partner's personal return, and since appellants have not demonstrated any independent prejudice resulting
from the use of the "gross receipts" definition,[11] we shall leave the

---

11. The appellants cannot be heard to
complain that the tax court's use of §
6501(e)(1)(A)(i)'s "gross receipts" definition of gross income in this case
resulted in any prejudice to Bebe
Klein's attempt to fit within the innocent spouse provisions. Section
6501(e)(1)(A)(i) defines gross income
from a trade or business to include
gross receipts from sales prior to
diminution by the cost of the goods
sold. In the instant case, even if we
were to accept appellants' argument,
which never alleges any particular
prejudice, and subtract the cost of
the goods sold as reported by Miss

Smart Frocks, see Treas.Reg. § 1.61–
3, its gross income on the return
would have been $585,422.19, which
added to C & S Dress Co.'s "contracting" income of $141,547.40, results in
a total partnership gross income of
$726,969.59. Herman Klein's thirty
percent distributive share of that
partnership gross income is then
$218,090.88, and twenty-five percent
of that gross income stated in the return is $54,522.72. Since the parties
stipulated that only $45,733.25, which
is obviously less than $54,522.72, was
"omitted" from gross income stated
in the return, appellants have simply

resolution of this difficult question to some future case where its resolution will affect the outcome.

Accordingly, the order of the tax court denying the benefits of "innocent spouse" status to appellant Bebe Klein is affirmed.

D. EXTENSION OF LIMITATIONS BY AGREEMENT

Under normal circumstances the IRS must assess a tax deficiency within three years of the date the subject tax return was filed. Frequently, three years are not sufficient for the Service to commence and complete an examination and provide internal reviews and administrative appeal. The Code permits taxpayers and the Service to agree to extend limitations except as to estate taxes.[g] These agreements, commonly referred to as "Consents", usually are solicited by the Service sufficiently in advance of the expiration of limitations to permit the issuance of a deficiency notice [h] if the taxpayer declines to execute the Consent.

The agreement to extend limitations is entered into on a Form 872—Consent to Extend the Time to Assess Tax—or its equivalent. There are two types of Consents utilized. The "regular" Consent (Form 872) [i] extends limitations to the earlier of a specified date or

not demonstrated that Bebe Klein has been harmed by the tax court's use of the "gross receipts" definition of gross income contained in § 6501(e)(1)(A)(i). She would have failed to meet the twenty-five percent requirement even if that definition had not been used.

g. IRC § 6501(c)(4).

h. Or the making of an assessment in the case of certain taxes for which no deficiency notice is required.

i. The operative provisions of the Form 872 are as follows:

(1) The amount of any Federal *(Kind of tax)* tax due on any return(s) made by or for the above taxpayer(s) for the period(s) ended ——— may be assessed at any time on or before *(Expiration date)*. However, if a notice of deficiency in tax for any such period(s) is sent to the taxpayer(s) on or before that date, then the time for assessing the tax will be further extended by the number of days the assessment was previously prohibited, plus 60 days.

(2) This agreement ends on the earlier of the above expiration date or the assessment date of an increase in the above tax that reflects the final determination of tax and the final administrative appeals consideration. An assessment for one period covered by this agreement will not end this agreement for any other period it covers. Some assessments do not reflect a final determination and appeals consideration and therefore will not terminate the agreement before the expiration date. Examples are assessments of: (a) tax under a partial agreement; (b) tax in jeopardy; (c) tax to correct mathematical or clerical errors; (d) tax reported on amended returns; and (e) advance payments. In addition, unassessed payments, such as amounts treated by the Service as cash bonds and advance payments not assessed by the Service, will not terminate this agreement before the expiration date.

This agreement ends on the above expiration date regardless of any assessment for any period includible in a report to the Joint Committee on Taxation submitted under section 6405 of the Internal Revenue Code.

the assessment date of an increase in tax reflecting the final IRS determination of tax. The Special Consent (Form 872–A) [j] keeps the period of limitations open until 90 days after either the taxpayer or the Service decides to end activity on the case in the Examination, Appeals, or Employee Plans and Exempt Organizations Division.[k]

It is not absolutely essential that a Consent keep limitations open for all purposes. Subject, of course, to IRS agreement, a Consent can be restricted to a specified matter. The effect of a restricted Consent is to allow limitations to expire except for assessments arising from specific adjustments. The Service may balk at entering into a restricted Consent for fear of getting involved in a future controversy over precisely what is the scope of the extension of limitations. However, in some circumstances, for example a Consent in which the only unsettled issue relates to the taxpayer's reporting of a share of a partnership loss, a restricted Consent may be acceptable.

It must be recalled that the taxpayer always has the option to refuse to provide a requested Consent altogether, or to refuse to execute a Consent unless it has the expiration date or other terms the taxpayer wishes. However, the Service can always reject the taxpayer's proposal and issue a deficiency notice.[l] Therefore, the duration and the restrictions (if any) on a Consent are very much negotiable items. The taxpayer's representative should consider carefully whether some variation from the solicited Consent is appropriate, particularly with regard to the length of time given the Service. Hence, it often will be advisable at the examination level to give extensions of three or six months rather than the year or more usually requested by the Service. The three or six month extension will give

(3) The taxpayer(s) may file a claim for credit or refund and the Service may credit or refund the tax within 6 months after this agreement ends.

j. The operative provisions of the Form 872–A which differ from those included in the Form 872 are as follows:

(1) The amount(s) of any Federal *(Kind of tax)* tax due on any return(s) made by or for the above taxpayer(s) for the period(s) ended —— may be assessed on or before the 90th (ninetieth) day after: (a) the Internal Revenue Service office considering the case receives Form 872–T, Notice of Termination of Special Consent to Extend the Time to Assess Tax, from the taxpayer(s); or (b) the Internal Revenue Service mails Form 872–T to the taxpayer(s); or (c) the Internal Revenue Service mails a notice of deficiency for such period(s).

However, if a notice of deficiency is sent to the taxpayer(s), the time for assessing the tax for the period(s) stated in the notice of deficiency will be further extended by the number of days the assessment was previously prohibited, plus 60 days. A final adverse determination subject to declaratory judgment under sections 7428, 7476, or 7477 of the Internal Revenue Code will not terminate this agreement.

* * *

(3) This agreement will not reduce the period of time otherwise provided by law for making such assessment.

k. See Rev.Proc. 79–22, 1979–1 C.B. 563 regarding the pertinent procedures for using the Form 872–A.

l. Or make an assessment in the case of taxes for which no deficiency notice is required.

the taxpayer a chance to reconsider how long he wishes the examination to continue. On the other hand, at the Appeals Office level the effect of failing to provide a reasonable time for administrative review will mean the abandonment of the opportunity for an administrative resolution of the controversy.

E. EQUITABLE RECOUPMENT AND THE MITIGATION PROVISIONS

In the tax law the pertinent statutes of limitations are applied strictly. In the specific context of tax refunds, the Internal Revenue Code provides that the government may not offset against a taxpayer's overpayment of taxes for a given taxable period his underpayment for another period as to which collection or assessment is barred by the statute of limitations. That is, a credit of an overpayment against an asserted tax liability for a period for which assessment or collection is barred by the statute of limitations is void.[m] Thus, for example, a taxpayer who has established a $25,000 overpayment of his income taxes for 1982 normally is entitled to a full refund even though he may, in fact, have underpaid his income taxes for 1972 (a year as to which assessment and collection is barred) by $50,000. However, in very limited situations, where the strict application of the statutes of limitations would enable a party to gain an unfair advantage by assuming inconsistent positions for closed and open taxable periods, an inequitable result will not be permitted. In effect, the law sometimes permits the opening of a closed taxable period in order to make corrections normally barred by the statute of limitations. The narrowly applied judicial doctrine of equitable recoupment provides for relief from a party's attempt to "burn the candle at both ends" of a transaction.

In Rothensies v. Electric Storage Battery Co., 329 U.S. 296, 67 S.Ct. 271, 91 L.Ed. 296 (1946), the Supreme Court stated the doctrine of equitable recoupment in the following terms:

> The essence of the doctrine of recoupment is stated in the *Bull* case; "recoupment is in the nature of a defense arising out of some feature of the transaction upon which the plaintiff's action is grounded." 295 U.S. 247, 262. It has never been thought to allow one transaction to be offset against another, but only to permit a transaction which is made the subject of suit by a plaintiff to be examined in all its aspects, and judgment to be rendered that does justice in view of the one transaction as a whole.[n]

This defense, which allows the government an offset against the refund to which a taxpayer would otherwise be entitled, is to be distin-

---

m. IRC § 6514(b).

n. 329 U.S. 296 at 299, 67 S.Ct. 271 at 272, 91 L.Ed. 296.

guished from the defense of lack of overpayment, which also can give rise to an offset. In the words of the United States Court of Claims:

> * * * the defense of recoupment in a refund suit should not be confused with the broader and more funda-mental defense of lack of overpayment of the particular tax involved in the suit for refund, traceable to the landmark de-cision by the Supreme Court in Lewis v. Reynolds, 284 U.S. 281, 52 S.Ct. 145, 76 L.Ed. 293 (1932). The former involves attempts to set off tax liability from one year against that for another year after the statute of limitations has run or where attempts are made to set off the tax liability of one taxpayer against that of a second taxpayer. This type of defense has been commonly referred to as "equitable recoup-ment." In these situations where the challenged item arose in a year other than in suit or where different parties are involved, the defense may only be maintained where a single or same transaction is involved.
>
> On the other hand, where both the taxpayer's claim and the government's setoff concern the same tax for the same year by the same taxpayer, the government's right to raise such a defense is unconditional and need not meet the "same transaction" requirement of the equitable recoupment de-fense. Here the right of the government is based on the broader principle that a taxpayer is not entitled to a refund unless he has in fact overpaid the particular tax, while in "equitable recoupment" the right to raise such a defense is based on the more limited principle that a party should not gain the protection of the statute of limitations where he has given a different tax treatment to the same transaction in different years.[o]

The application of the doctrine of equitable recoupment is illus-trated by the case of Stone v. White, 301 U.S. 532, 57 S.Ct. 851, 81 L.Ed. 1265 (1937), in which trustees paid (under protest) taxes that should have been paid by the beneficiary. After the statute of limi-tations had run, barring collection from the beneficiary, the trustees sued for a refund on the ground that income was properly taxable to the beneficiary and not to them. They contended that they were en-titled to a refund even though their recovery would be paid over to the beneficiary and the net result would be that no tax at all would be collected on the income in question. The trustees argued that statutory provisions barred the collection of the tax from the benefi-ciary and also prohibited the government from using an underpay-ment for a closed year as an offset against an overpayment for an open year. The Supreme Court, relying upon the basically equitable

o. Dysart v. United States, 340 F.2d 624, 627 (Ct.Cl.1965).

nature of a tax refund suit, answered the trustees' contentions as follows:

> These provisions limit the collection of a tax, and prevent the retention of one paid after it is barred by the statute. They preclude, in a suit by the taxpayer against the collector or the government, reliance on a claim against the taxpayer, barred by statute, as a set-off, or counterclaim. But the demand made upon the trustees was not barred by limitation and it would be an unreasonable construction of the statute, not called for by its words, to hold that it is intended to deprive the government of defenses based on special equities establishing its right to withhold a refund from the demanding taxpayer. The statute does not override a defense based on the estoppel of the taxpayer. R. H. Stearns Co. v. United States, 291 U.S. 54, 61, 62, 54 S.Ct. 325, 328, 78 L.Ed. 647 (1933). The statutory bar to the right of action for the collection of the tax does not prevent reliance upon a defense which is not a set-off or a counterclaim, but is an equitable reason, growing out of the circumstances of the erroneous payment, why petitioners ought not to recover.
>
> Here the defense is not a counter demand on petitioners, but a denial of their equitable right to undo a payment which, though effected by an erroneous procedure, has resulted in no unjust enrichment to the government, and in no injury to petitioners or their beneficiary. The government, by retaining the tax paid by the trustees, is not reviving a stale claim. Its defense, which inheres in the cause of action, is comparable to an equitable recoupment or diminution of petitioners' right to recover. "Such a defense is never barred by the statute of limitations so long as the main action itself is timely." Bull v. United States, 295 U.S. 247, 55 S.Ct. 695, 700, 79 L.Ed. 1421 (1935); Williams v. Neely, 134 F. 1, 13 (8th Cir. 1904).ᴾ

In §§ 1311–1314 of the Internal Revenue Code of 1954 Congress has codified, in part, the doctrine of equitable recoupment and to an extent expanded the ability of the government and taxpayers to avoid the unfair effects that can sometimes result from a strict application of the statutes of limitation. These complex statutory provisions, applicable in specified situations only, will permit adjustments in spite of normally applicable statutes of limitations to correct errors of the following types:

1. Double inclusion of an item of gross income.

2. Double allowance of a deduction or credit.

p.   301 U.S. 532 at 538–39, 57 S.Ct. 851
at 854, 81 L.Ed. 1265.

3. Double exclusion of an item of gross income.

4. Double disallowance of a deduction or credit.

5. Correlative deductions and inclusions for trusts or estates and legatees, beneficiaries, or heirs.

6. Correlative deductions and credits for related corporations.

7. Erroneous basis of property resulting from erroneous treatment of a prior transaction.[q]

It has been held that Congress, in establishing the detailed mitigation provisions of §§ 1311–1314 of the 1954 Code, superseded any common law recoupment remedies formerly available with regard to those categories of situations described in § 1312.[r] When used as a defense in a tax refund suit, the net result of §§ 1311–1314 is that of an equitable recoupment. In effect, the "deficiency" for the closed taxable period is used to eliminate or reduce the refund due as a result of the overpayment for the open taxable period in suit in the refund case.[s] Achieving the correct result can require the assessment of an adjustment for the closed year as if it were a deficiency, followed by a credit of the "deficiency" against the overpayment for the open years.[t]

It should be noted that the doctrine of equitable recoupment and the statutory mitigation provisions, although discussed above as government defenses in a tax refund suit, may be used by the government in certain circumstances to "reopen" a closed year for the purpose of issuing a statutory notice of deficiency where no refund suit is involved. Moreover, in appropriate circumstances, they could provide the foundation for a refund action by the taxpayer.[u]

B. C. COOK & SONS, INC. v. COMMISSIONER

65 T.C. 422 (1977), aff'd per curiam, 584 F.2d 53 (5th Cir. 1978).

STERRETT, Judge.

The respondent determined deficiencies in petitioner's Federal income taxes for the fiscal years ended September 30, 1958, September 30, 1959, September 30, 1960, and September 30, 1961. The only issue in controversy is whether respondent is entitled to adjust petitioner's Federal income tax liability for those years pursuant to sections 1311 through 1314.

* * *

q. IRC § 1312.

r. Gooding v. United States, 326 F.2d 988, 995–96 (Ct.Cl.1964).

s. IRC § 1314.

t. IRC § 1314(b).

u. E. g., Bull v. United States, 295 U.S. 247, 55 S.Ct. 695, 79 L.Ed. 1421 (1935); Boyle v. United States, 355 F.2d 233 (3d Cir. 1965). Note that the same special limitations period applicable to the government for the issuance of statutory notices for closed years applies to a taxpayer's claim for refund. IRC § 1314(b).

The facts may be briefly summarized. From 1958 through 1965 one of petitioner's employees embezzled from it substantial sums of money by writing checks for fictitious fruit purchases. Petitioner's cost of goods sold was correspondingly overstated, and its gross income and taxable income were correspondingly understated for each of the fiscal years herein involved. In 1965 the scheme was discovered and petitioner claimed the embezzlement losses as a deduction under section 165(a) and (e). Our earlier decision in B. C. Cook & Sons, Inc., 59 T.C. 516 (1972), allowed the deduction. On November 15, 1973,[v] respondent mailed his statutory notice of deficiency for the fiscal years 1958, 1959, 1960, and 1961. On that date he was barred from assessing and collecting any additional taxes by section 6501, except as may be provided by sections 1311 through 1314.

Section 1311(a) provides:

> (a) GENERAL RULE.—If a determination (as defined in section 1313) is described in one or more of the paragraphs of section 1312 and, on the date of the determination, correction of the effect of the error referred to in the applicable paragraph of section 1312 is prevented by the operation of any law or rule of law, * * * then the effect of the error shall be corrected by an adjustment made in the amount and in the manner specified in section 1314.

Section 1311(b) sets forth conditions necessary for an adjustment. Subparagraph (1) permits an adjustment only if the party who was successful in the "determination" maintained a position inconsistent with the erroneous treatment which position was adopted in the "determination."

The parties agree that our prior decision in *B. C. Cook & Sons, Inc.*, supra, is a "determination" on the date of which correction of the overstatements in cost of goods sold in 1958, 1959, 1960, and 1961 was barred by section 6501. The controverted points are (1) whether the facts presented fall within any of the circumstances described in section 1312, and (2) whether petitioner has maintained an inconsistent position. Our resolution of the former makes it unnecessary to decide the latter issue.

Respondent's position is that section 1312(2) encompasses the factual setting before us.[2] He argues that the legislative history demonstrates that Congress intended the words, "double allowance of a deduction or credit" in section 1312(2) to include any position tak-

---

v. Which date was prior to the expiration of the special 1-year period of limitations set forth in § 1314(b).

2. Sec. 1312. Circumstances of Adjustment.

The circumstances under which the adjustment provided in section 1311 is authorized are as follows:

* * *

(2) Double allowance of a deduction or credit.—The determination allows a deduction or credit which was erroneously allowed to the taxpayer for another taxable year * * *

en by a taxpayer which would result in a double reduction of tax. He urges that a broad interpretation is necessary to effectuate the purpose of the mitigation provisions.

* * * We do not agree.

* * *

We conclude that the instant facts are not within the scope of section 1312(2). Concededly, our "determination" in *B. C. Cook & Sons, Inc.,* supra, allowed a deduction for petitioner's 1965 taxable year. It is not, however, a *deduction* "which was erroneously allowed to the taxpayer for another taxable year."

In the fiscal years involved, petitioner erroneously overstated its cost of goods sold and consequently understated its gross income and taxable income. It is true that the same result would have obtained had petitioner erroneously claimed an itemized deduction for costs of goods sold. However, there is a crucial distinction between the treatment of either basis or cost of goods sold and deductible expenses. Both basis and cost of goods sold are offsets employed in the computation of gross income, section 1001(a); sec. 1.61–3(a), Income Tax Regs. Itemized deductions, on the other hand, are subtracted from gross income in arriving at taxable income.

* * *

The mitigation provisions are extremely complex and are written with great precision. "Deduction" appears several times in section 1312, but nowhere is it used in connection with errors relating to gross income. Rather, the terms "inclusion," "exclusion," and "omission," are used to describe such errors. We also note that the language of section 1312(2) parallels the language of section 161 which reads: "In computing taxable income under section 63(a), there shall be *allowed as deductions* the items specified in this part." (Emphasis supplied.) Where a phrase is used in different parts of the same statute it will be presumed to have the same meaning throughout. It is apparent that Congress used the word "deduction" as a term of art. This proves to us that Congress intended "deduction" in section 1312(2) to include deductions from gross income in arriving at taxable income and only that.

* * *

* * * The precise terminology of section 1312 makes clear that Congress is cognizant of this distinction. * * * Had Congress intended section 1312(2) to include reductions in arriving at gross income it would have so indicated in clear, unambiguous terms. Absent such a statement, we are convinced that the word "deduction" in section 1312(2) refers only to deductions subtracted from gross income in arriving at taxable income.

It may be fairly said that petitioner has not turned the appropriate square corner with its Government. It has availed itself of a situation which slips between the statutory cracks to gain an unwarranted tax advantage. Nonetheless, it is entitled to our unprejudiced interpretation of the law in issue.

Reviewed by the Court.

DRENNEN, J., dissenting:

* * *

In my opinion respondent will be justifiably confused by the result reached by the majority. In the earlier *B. C. Cook & Sons, Inc.,* case in which this Court allowed the loss deduction for 1965, 59 T.C. 516, the majority opinion repeatedly referred to the increases in cost of goods sold by the fictitious invoices as though they were tantamount to deductions. Respondent's argument was that where the taxpayer has previously derived a tax benefit through an erroneous *deduction* or otherwise, he may not deduct the same amount in a subsequent year after the Commissioner is barred by the statute of limitations from adjusting the tax for the prior year. Our majority opinion stated: "But the key to the decision here lies in the fact that the petitioner *erroneously* deducted nonexistent purchases in computing its cost of goods sold for prior years." Petitioner asserted in its reply brief that the proper procedure for respondent to follow if he believed that petitioner had received a double benefit was under the mitigation provisions. And finally our opinion stated that *"the deduction must be allowed in its proper year and that the Commissioner's recourse is through the correction procedures set forth in sections 1311 through 1315."* (Emphasis added.) Certainly the majority of this Court was equating the increase in costs of goods sold as a deduction similar to that allowed for 1965, and I fail to understand why the present majority relies on technical distinctions to deny the recourse suggested to respondent in our opinion in the prior case. Probably in reliance thereon, respondent did not appeal the prior case. He must now feel that he was enticed out on to a limb which we now saw off.

RAUM and WILBUR, JJ., agree with this dissent.

NOTE

The mitigation provisions are not the only area in which the difference between a deduction from gross income and a deduction to reach gross income is highly relevant. In the *Pittsburgh Milk Co.* case, 26 T.C. 707 (1956), illegal sales discounts were paid to customers, while, in order to conceal the true nature of the transactions from local authorities, the sales were entered on the books at list price and the discounts charged to advertising. Although the adjustments were not proper "deductions" (as they were not deductible under § 162), the Tax Court allowed the taxpayer to take the "above the line" adjustments into account in computing the cost of goods sold in arriving at gross income. See also Max Sobel Wholesale Liquors v. Commissioner, 69 T.C. 477, aff'd, 46 AFTR 2d 80–5799 (9th Cir. 1977).

SECTION 6.   CIVIL PENALTIES

A.   THE CIVIL PENALTY FRAMEWORK *

The Internal Revenue Code provides civil penalties in the form of additions to tax for a hierarchy of civil offenses.[w]   The most commonly encountered of these are the penalties for fraud, negligence or intentional disregard of rules and regulations, failure to file and late payment.[x]

* Note that the Economic Recovery Tax Act of 1981 added a new civil penalty for income tax valuation overstatements and an additional "negligence" penalty, and affected various other penalty provisions.   See discussion in Appendix B.

w.   See generally, IRC Chapter 68 (§§ 6651–6699).

x.   These "routine" penalties are set forth in §§ 6651 and 6653 of the Code, the pertinent portions of which read as follows:

Sec. 6651.   Failure to File Tax Return or to Pay Tax.

(a) Addition to the Tax.—In case of failure—

(1) to file any return required under authority of subchapter A of chapter 61 (other than part III thereof), subchapter A of chapter 51 (relating to distilled spirits, wines, and beer), or of subchapter A of chapter 52 (relating to tobacco, cigars, cigarettes, and cigarette papers and tubes), or of subchapter A of chapter 53 (relating to machine guns and certain other firearms), on the date prescribed therefor (determined with regard to any extension of time for filing), unless it is shown that such failure is due to reasonable cause and not due to willful neglect, there shall be added to the amount required to be shown as tax on such return 5 percent of the amount of such tax if the failure is for not more than 1 month, with an additional 5 percent for each additional month or fraction thereof during which such failure continues, not exceeding 25 percent in the aggregate;

(2) to pay the amount shown as tax on any return specified in paragraph (1) on or before the date prescribed for payment of such tax (determined with regard to any extension of time for payment), unless it is shown that such failure is due to reasonable cause and not due to willful neglect, there shall be added to the amount shown as tax on such return 0.5 percent of the amount of such tax if the failure is for not more than 1 month, with an additional 0.5 percent for each additional month or fraction thereof, during which such failure continues, not exceeding 25 percent in the aggregate; or

(3) to pay any amount in respect of any tax required to be shown on a return specified in paragraph (1) which is not so shown (including an assessment made pursuant to section 6213(b)) within 10 days of the date of the notice and demand therefor, unless it is shown that such failure is due to reasonable cause and not due to willful neglect, there shall be added to the amount of tax stated in such notice and demand 0.5 percent of the amount of such tax if the failure is for not more than 1 month, with an additional 0.5 percent for each additional month or fraction thereof during which such failure continues, not exceeding 25 percent in the aggregate.

(b) Penalty Imposed on Net Amount Due.—For purposes of—

(1) subsection (a)(1), the amount of tax required to be shown on the return shall be reduced by the amount of any part of the tax which is paid on or before the date pre-

scribed for payment of the tax and by the amount of any credit against the tax which may be claimed on the return.

(2) subsection (a)(2), the amount of tax shown on the return shall, for purposes of computing the addition for any month, be reduced by the amount of any part of the tax which is paid on or before the beginning of such month and by the amount of any credit against the tax which may be claimed on the return, and

(3) subsection (a)(3), the amount of tax stated in the notice and demand shall, for the purpose of computing the addition for any month, be reduced by the amount of any part of the tax which is paid before the beginning of such month.

(c) Limitations and Special Rule—

(1) Additions under more than one paragraph.—

(A) With respect to any return, the amount of the addition under paragraph (1) of subsection (a) shall be reduced by the amount of the addition under paragraph (2) of subsection (a) for any month to which an addition to tax applies under both paragraphs (1) and (2).

(B) With respect to any return, the maximum amount of the addition permitted under paragraph (3) of subsection (a) shall be reduced by the amount of the addition under paragraph (1) of subsection (a) which is attributable to the tax for which the notice and demand is made and which is not paid within 10 days of notice and demand.

(2) Amount of tax shown more than amount required to be shown. —If the amount required to be shown as tax on a return is less than the amount shown as tax on such return, subsections (a)(2) and (b)(2) shall be applied by substituting such lower amount.

* * *

Sec. 6653. Failure to Pay Tax.

(a) Negligence or Intentional Disregard of Rules and Regulations With Respect to Income, Gift, or Windfall Profit Taxes.—If any part of any underpayment (as defined in subsection (c)(1)) of any tax imposed by subtitle A, by chapter 12 of subtitle B (relating to income taxes and gift taxes), or by chapter 45 (relating to windfall profit tax) is due to negligence or intentional disregard of rules and regulations (but without intent to defraud), there shall be added to the tax an amount equal to 5 percent of the underpayment.

(b) Fraud.—If any part of any underpayment (as defined in subsection (c)) of tax required to be shown on a return is due to fraud, there shall be added to the tax an amount equal to 50 percent of the underpayment. In the case of income taxes and gift taxes, this amount shall be in lieu of any amount determined under subsection (a). In the case of a joint return under section 6013, this subsection shall not apply with respect to the tax of a spouse unless some part of the underpayment is due to the fraud of such spouse.

(c) Definition of Underpayment. —For purpose of this section, the term "underpayment" means—

(1) Income, estate, gift, and certain excise taxes.—In the case of a tax to which section 6211 (relating to income, estate, gift, and certain excise taxes) is applicable, a deficiency as defined in that section (except that, for this purpose, the tax shown on a return referred to in section 6211(a)(1)(A) shall be taken into account only if such return was filed on or before the last day prescribed for the filing of such return, determined with regard to any extension of time for such filing),

* * *

(d) No Delinquency Penalty if Fraud Assessed.—If any penalty is assessed under subsection (b) (relating to fraud) for an underpayment of tax which is required to be shown on a return, no penalty under section 6651 (relating to failure to file such return or pay tax) shall be assessed with respect to the same underpayment.

* * *

The "fraud" penalty of 50% of the underpayment on a return is imposed if any part of the underpayment is due to fraud.[y] The "negligence" penalty of 5% of the underpayment [*] is imposed if any part of the underpayment is due to negligence or intentional disregard of rules and regulations (but without intent to defraud).[z]

The failure to file penalty of 5% [a] per month [b] (25% maximum) of the amount due is imposed if a return is not timely filed, unless it is shown that the failure to file timely was due to reasonable cause and not willful neglect.[c]

The late payment penalty of ½% per month [d] (25% maximum) of the amount underpaid is imposed for the late payment of tax shown due on a return or assessed, unless the failure to pay on time is due to reasonable cause and not willful neglect.[e] This nondeductible penalty runs concurrently with interest once a return is filed or an assessment is made. However, during the period between the filing of a return and the assessment of a deficiency, only interest accrues on the deficiency; the failure to pay penalty accrues only after assessment and demand for payment are made.

B. THE FAILURE TO FILE PENALTY—THE REASONABLE CAUSE EXCEPTION

The failure to file penalty essentially involves two basic issues. First, was there in fact a failure to timely file a required tax return? Second, if there was a failure to file a timely return, was the failure due to reasonable cause and not willful neglect?

The first of the two issues most frequently involves the question of whether for a given year the taxpayer was required to file an income tax return under the provisions of § 6012 of the Code (or whether some other type of return was required to be filed by some other section of the Code). However, this issue can also turn upon the question of whether a document which was filed timely will be held to be a tax return. See pages 165–174, above, for a discussion of this matter in the context of the commencement of the period of limitations on assessments.

The second of the issues, whether the failure to file timely returns was due to reasonable cause and not willful neglect, is discussed in the following cases.

y. IRC § 6653(b).

* See Appendix B re additional "negligence" penalty added by 1981 Tax Act.

z. IRC § 6653(a).

a. Reduced to 4½% for any month as to which the ½% failure to pay penalty is also applicable. IRC § 6651 (c)(1).

b. I. e., for each month or fraction of a month.

c. IRC § 6651(a)(1).

d. I. e., for each month or fraction of a month.

e. IRC §§ 6651(a)(2) and (3).

HAYWOOD LUMBER & MINING CO. v. COMMISSIONER

178 F.2d 769 (2d Cir. 1950).

SWAN, Circuit Judge.

The taxpayer is a personal holding company. The Commissioner determined deficiencies in personal holding company surtaxes for the years 1941 and 1942 and added thereto a 25% penalty, pursuant to § 291 [f] of the Internal Revenue Code, for petitioner's failure to file personal holding company returns for those years. The sole question presented to the Tax Court and likewise here is whether the taxpayer's failure to file personal holding company returns for the years in suit was "due to reasonable cause and not due to willful neglect". The Tax Court held that it was not due to reasonable cause.

"Reasonable cause" has been defined by the Regulations to mean that the taxpayer exercised ordinary business care and prudence. In the case at bar Mr. Sprague, the taxpayer's secretary-treasurer, requested a certified public accountant, Mr. Wolcott, who was competent to advise on tax matters, to prepare the proper corporate tax returns for the years 1941 and 1942. Sprague fully disclosed to Wolcott all necessary information about the corporation and Wolcott knew that the taxpayer was a personal holding company but "through inadvertence" did not inform Sprague of this fact nor submit to him a personal holding company surtax return. Sprague was aware of the personal holding company surtax statute but he had never studied its application and it did not occur to him that the petitioner was a personal holding company. He filed on behalf of the corporation only the returns prepared by Wolcott. Because Sprague did not "specifically inquire" of Wolcott "concerning the personal holding company status of petitioner" but "merely awaited passively for such tax advice as Wolcott might volunteer to give," the Tax Court held, one judge dissenting, that petitioner had not sustained the burden of proving that ordinary business care and prudence were exercised in failing to file the personal holding company surtax returns.

With this conclusion we disagree. When a corporate taxpayer selects a competent tax expert, supplies him with all necessary information, and requests him to prepare proper tax returns, we think the taxpayer has done all that ordinary business care and prudence can reasonably demand. Sprague had not "awaited passively for such tax advice" as Wolcott "might volunteer to give" ; he affirmatively requested the preparation by his consultant of proper returns. To require Mr. Sprague to inquire specifically about the personal holding company act nullifies the very purpose of consulting an expert. We doubt if anyone would suggest that a client who stated the facts of

f. The predecessor to § 6651(a)(1) of the Internal Revenue Code of 1954.

his case to his lawyer must, in order to show ordinary business care and prudence, inquire specifically about the applicability of various legal principles which may be relevant to the facts stated. The courts have recognized that reliance on the advice of counsel or of expert accountants, sought and received in good faith is "reasonable cause" for failing to file a tax return. We think those cases are correctly decided and in principle control the case at bar. The Tax Court relies on Hermax Co. v. Commissioner, 3 Cir., 175 F.2d 776, affirming 11 T.C. 442. There the accountant was not qualified to advise about tax matters and the corporation's president testified to no reason why he relied on him. Here the undisputed evidence showed that Wolcott had had over twenty years of extensive tax experience with a prominent accounting firm in Binghamton and had advised the petitioner on tax matters in previous years.

The respondent contends that where all responsibility for the preparation of tax returns is delegated to an agent, the taxpayer should be held to accept its agent's efforts *cum onere* and be chargeable with his negligence. That was the rationale suggested by this court in Berlin v. Commissioner, 59 F.2d 996. Further reflection convinces us that that proposition is not sound. The standard of care imposed by section 291 is personal to the taxpayer. To impute to the taxpayer the mistakes of his consultant would be to penalize him for consulting an expert; for if he must take the benefit of his counsel's or accountant's advice *cum onere,* then he must be held to a standard of care which is not his own and one which, in most cases, would be far higher than that exacted of a layman. The cases which hold that advice sought and received in good faith from a competent adviser constitutes reasonable cause for failure to file the required return are inconsistent with the *cum onere* doctrine suggested in the Berlin case.

In Paymer v. Commissioner, 2 Cir., 150 F.2d 334, 337 we said that reasonable cause was a question of fact and "therefore presents no reviewable issue." This abbreviated statement does not state the whole principle, which is better expounded in Hatfried, Inc. v. Commissioner, 3 Cir., 162 F.2d 628, 635. As there pointed out, whether the elements which constitute "reasonable cause" are present is a question of fact, but what elements must be present to constitute "reasonable cause" is a question of law. The Tax Court erred in our opinion upon this question of law. Accordingly the decision must be modified to strike out the penalties in personal holding company surtax for the years 1941 and 1942 in the respective amounts of $567.77 and $923.83.

UNITED STATES v. KROLL

547 F.2d 393 (7th Cir. 1977).

MOORE, Senior Circuit Judge.

The United States of America (the "Government") plaintiff-appellant, brought this suit to reduce to judgment a penalty of $16,414.-

69 which had been assessed against Richard L. Kroll, as Executor of
the Estate of Gertrude O'Reilly ("Kroll"), defendant-appellee, for
failure to file an estate tax return within the period provided by law.
* * *

The decedent died on July 13, 1967. Her son-in-law, Richard L.
Kroll, was appointed the executor on July 18, 1967. His wife, decedent's daughter, was the sole heir of the estate, which was substantial. The bulk of the estate consisted of realty (apartment buildings), the management of which Kroll supervised, both before and
after decedent's death. Filing of the federal estate tax return was
due fifteen (15) months after death, or October 13, 1968.

Although Kroll was a college graduate with one year of law
school added, had experience both with a large industrial company
and a brokerage firm and had prepared and filed his own income tax
returns for many years, he entrusted the preparation of the estate
tax return to an attorney, William C. Dill, who had had some experience in this field.

The return which was due by October 13, 1968, was ultimately
filed on October 27, 1969. The law provides in substance for a penalty for failure to timely file "unless" it can be shown "that such failure is due to reasonable cause and not due to willful neglect." Regulations define an acceptable excuse for non-compliance as a showing
that the taxpayer "exercised ordinary business care and prudence and
was nevertheless unable to file the return within the prescribed time."

The sole issue before this Court is whether the taxpayer has
shown "reasonable cause" and "ordinary business care and prudence."

Kroll takes the position that he relied on his attorney to file the
return and this reliance "CONSTITUTED REASONABLE CAUSE
AS A MATTER OF LAW FOR THE FAILURE TO FILE THE RE-
TURN TIMELY."

The District Court in a conclusory way found that Kroll "was
entitled to rely and did rely in good faith on his attorney." This conclusion, in our opinion, is not supported by the facts. Insofar as any
question of tax law, complicated or otherwise, might have been involved, there is little doubt that Kroll would have been entitled to en-
trust these problems to an attorney for resolution. The intricacies of
the Internal Revenue Code with its sections, sub-sections, paragraphs
and sub-paragraphs, cross-references, etc. often require the tax expertise of the most skilled, and on occasion, a soothsayer or attorney
able to divine the ultimate result in some appellate court. But no
such problems were here presented to Kroll or Dill. Their only task
with respect to filing was to read a calendar and to jot down on their
desk or office records a single date. Nothing would be found in the
tax treatises to inform Kroll that he had to sign the return and draw
a check. This task was exclusively his and was one which he had
done for his own affairs and for the estate as to income tax. Ob-

viously, Dill could not have handled these matters for him. As the executor, Kroll was burdened with the responsibilities imposed on him by law, namely, to file a return. And quite apart from the law, the fact that his wife was the sole beneficiary of a large sum of money to become available through his stewardship, could not have been totally absent from his thoughts.

The District Court found that there was "no evidence that he [Kroll] failed to make a full disclosure to his lawyer" and that "Mr. Kroll was not an expert in the field of tax or estate reporting." Neither fact plays a role here. It may be assumed that Kroll made full disclosure of the facts necessary for tax calculation and that he was not a tax expert, but disclosure and tax expertise are not in issue. The sole issue is Kroll's knowledge of the filing date and his failure to file on time.

Even assuming, contrary to fact, that Kroll had planned, in retaining Dill, not to give the estate another thought, the Internal Revenue Service did not permit this euphoric status to remain unnoticed. Charged with the collection of the revenue, it had noticed the O'Reilly estate's dereliction but with forebearance allowed a two and a half months period to elapse before calling this omission to Kroll's specific attention. By letter dated January 9, 1969 the Service advised Kroll that no return had been filed when due and even disclosed the method by which he might be able to avoid a penalty—if the facts so warranted. Kroll opened and read the letter and straightaway took it to Dill for an explanation. Dill's explanation was that the estate needed more time to liquidate property to pay the tax. Nevertheless, Dill, by letter (copy to Kroll) assured the Service that the return would be filed no later than April 1, 1969. Here was another date entry to be noted on Kroll's records. No return was filed by this date and the record discloses no effort or even inquiry on Kroll's part to check as to whether that deadline had been met. And at least Kroll must have known that he had not signed a return as executor nor had he drawn an estate check for the tax. Despite this uncontradicted proof of Kroll's awareness of the facts, the District Court concluded that Kroll was entitled to rely on Dill and he did so in good faith. With this conclusion we must disagree as completely unsupported by the facts and accordingly reverse the judgment below.

Whether or not the taxpayer is liable for taxes is a question of tax law which often only an expert can answer. The taxpayer not only can, but must, rely on the advice of either an accountant or a lawyer. This reliance is clearly an exercise of ordinary business care and prudence.

Such a situation is exemplified in this Circuit by the case of Commissioner of Internal Revenue v. American Ass'n of Engineers Employment, Inc., 204 F.2d 19 (7th Cir. 1953). In that case, the taxpayer corporation failed to file federal tax returns for five years, in reliance on the written opinion of a tax attorney that it was an exempt corporation. The Tax Court disapproved the 25% penalty imposed by the Commissioner, and this Court affirmed, stating:

> "We think that this is a case where the taxpayer did all that it was required to do and that it should not be penalized for an error made by its expert tax counsel in deciding a close question of law." 204 F.2d at 21.

An entirely different situation is presented where a penalty is assessed because a return, although filed, is filed after the due date. This situation often arises where the taxpayer knows that he must file a return, but entrusts the preparation and filing of the return to an attorney or an accountant. Any layman with the barest modicum of business experience knows that there is a deadline for the filing of returns and knows that he must sign the return before it is filed. If, in addition, the taxpayer in a given case knows the exact date of the deadline, then the failure of his attorney or accountant to present him with the return for his signature before that date must put him on notice that reliance on the attorney or accountant is not an exercise of ordinary business care and prudence.

This situation is exemplified in the Fifth Circuit case, Logan Lumber Co. v. Commissioner of Internal Revenue, 365 F.2d 846 (5th Cir. 1966). In that case, the Fifth Circuit upheld the assessment of a penalty for a late filing, over the taxpayer corporation's claim of reliance on its accountant. The Court held that this reliance was unfounded in light of the fact that the company's treasurer had signed a "tentative return" two days before the due date, indicating that he was aware of the deadline. The instant case is indistinguishable. Whether or not Kroll knew the date of the deadline (October 13, 1968) before it passed, he was apprised on January 9, 1969 that the deadline had passed three months previously. His reliance on Dill from this date onwards was not an exercise of ordinary business care and prudence.

Thus, we hold that, when there is no question that a return must be filed, the taxpayer has a personal, nondelegable duty to file the tax return when due. This view accords with that of the Fifth and Ninth Circuits. In the cases holding that no penalty may be imposed because of good-faith reliance on counsel, the question was whether a return had to be filed. The advice relied on related to that question. Those cases do not sanction an abdication of responsibility for the timely filing of a return admittedly due.

For the reasons above-stated, the judgment appealed from should be reversed, except as to interest in the sum of $4,505.27, and judgment should be entered in favor of the Government for the penalty of $16,414.69.

ESTATE OF DiPALMA v. COMMISSIONER

71 T.C. 324 (1978).

TANNENWALD, Judge.

*   *   *

We deal first with the question of the addition to tax for late filing. The estate tax return was due December 14, 1970. Sec. 6075(a). There is no question but that it was not timely filed and that the addition to tax for late filing applies unless petitioner, who has the burden of proof, establishes that the failure to file within the prescribed time was due to reasonable cause and not willful neglect.

Respondent's position herein is that, since this case does not involve any question *whether* a return had to be filed, Constance, as executrix, had a nondelegable duty which, as a matter of law, she could not discharge by reliance on the attorney for the estate. Admittedly, there are statements in some of the decided cases which tend to support respondent's position. See, e. g., United States v. Kroll, 547 F.2d 393, 396 (7th Cir. 1977). But such statements have usually been articulated in situations where the taxpayer did no more than delegate responsibility to a lawyer or accountant and thereafter made no effort to ascertain whether the necessary steps to discharge that responsibility had been, or should have been, taken. In any event, they do no more than set forth a general rule and do not abrogate the principle that whether the failure to file on time was due to reasonable cause is primarily a question of fact to be determined from all of the circumstances in a particular case. *   *   *

Although the record herein is not as neat and tidy as we would have preferred, we are satisfied that petitioner has carried its burden of proof that the delay in filing of the estate tax return was due to reasonable cause and not to willful neglect. The executrix did not sit supinely by and leave everything to Dallacasa. She made inquiry of him. Compare Estate of Lammerts v. Commissioner, 456 F.2d 681 (2d Cir. 1972), affg. on this issue 54 T.C. 420, 445–447 (1970). She was led to believe by the attorney for the estate that the pending dispute with Florence [her daughter] justified the delay in the filing of the return. Inexperienced as she was in such matters, we think that she was justified in relying on her belief, albeit that such belief was, in point of fact, erroneous. We hold that the addition to tax under section 6651(a) should not be imposed.

*   *   *

QUESTIONS

1. The applicability of the failure to pay penalty also turns upon whether the failure was due to reasonable cause and not willful neglect. Is there any reason for there to be a difference in the interpretation of these criteria in the payment as distinct from the filing context? See Internal

Revenue Manual—Audit §§ 4563.3(6) and 4562.2. Should the penalty be imposed in situations in which:

a. The taxpayer did not get actual timely notice of the assessment and demand of a liability for a deficiency, but pays promptly upon learning of the assessment?

b. The taxpayer does not have the funds to make the demanded payment? Should the cause for the absence of available funds make a difference? See Reg. § 301.6651–1(c)(1) and (2).

c. Can advice from an adviser that an assessment is defective and, hence, not subject to payment, eliminate the penalty? Would it make a difference if the taxpayer brought an injunction action in good faith alleging that the assessment was improper?

C. PENALTY FOR NEGLIGENCE OR INTENTIONAL DISREGARD OF RULES AND REGULATIONS *

BENNETT v. COMMISSIONER

139 F.2d 961 (8th Cir. 1944).

THOMAS, Circuit Judge.

* * *

The Tax Court sustained the Commissioner's determination of a 5% negligence penalty under § 293 of the Revenue Act of 1936,[g] and petitioners object.

Section 293(a) of the Act provides that "If any part of any deficiency is due to negligence, or intentional disregard of rules and regulations but without intent to defraud, 5 per centum of the total amount of the deficiency * * * shall be assessed, collected, and paid * * *."

Under the statute the imposition of the penalty is dependent upon a finding that some part of the deficiency is due (1) to negligence or (2) to intentional disregard of rules and regulations. A finding that the return is incorrect, or that the taxpayer did not keep proper or complete books of account, or that his calculations are confusing is not enough.

The Commissioner based his action upon a finding that the taxpayers failed to keep sufficient records in regard to income and expenditures; claimed a loss on a mortgage without reporting the income derived; and failure to report various items pertaining to income and deductions in the correct amounts; and that such failures constituted negligence or intentional disregard of rules and regulations.

The Tax Court found that Bennett "kept no books and records which would properly reflect his transactions entered into for profit

* See Appendix B re additional "negligence" penalty added by 1981 Tax Act.

g. The predecessor to § 6653(a) of the 1954 Code.

or the results of any business conducted by him and that in making his income tax return he made no serious effort to assemble or organize facts and data essential to making of a proper return", and sustained the penalty.

The record shows that the deficiency found to exist resulted from claimed deductions not allowed and from failure to report as income gains from a trading account and dividends paid to a broker. All these items are clearly the result of a mistaken conception of the taxpayers' legal rights. While ignorance of the law is not an excuse for wrongful acts, we think it is distinguishable from negligence within the meaning of § 293. Had the taxpayers been better advised as to their legal rights, and had they kept correct accounts of their business transactions, they might have taken deductions in the proper years for whatever losses were actually sustained by them on the $10,000 and the $4,200 mortgage loans in Florida. We think the Commissioner and the Tax Court erred in respect of the penalty under § 293.

*   *   *

The decision of the Tax Court is modified by the elimination of the penalty imposed under § 293 of the Act, and as so modified it is affirmed.

BURGLASS v. COMMISSIONER

48 P–H Memo TC ¶ 79,246 (1979).

STERRETT, Judge.

*   *   *

The * * * question with which we must deal is whether or not petitioner is chargeable with the section 6653(a) 5 percent addition to tax for negligence or intentional disregard of rules and regulations for either or both of the taxable years before us. Petitioner bears the burden of proving that the imposition of this penalty is improper. Both the section 6651(a) failure to timely file addition to tax and the section 6653(a) addition to tax may be imposed for the same taxable year. Further, the section 6653(a) addition to tax may be imposed for the same reasons that the section 6651(a) addition to tax is imposed. Petitioner has already conceded the section 6651(a) addition to tax for both the taxable years before us.

The 5 percent addition to tax is computed on the amount of the "underpayment" of tax for that taxable year. Section 6653(c)(1) defines "underpayment" for section 6653 purposes in terms of a modification of the general section 6211 definition of "deficiency". Specifically, section 6653(c) defines an underpayment for section 6653(a) purposes to be the same as a "deficiency" as defined in sections 6211 "except that, for this purpose, the tax shown on a return referred to in section 6211(a)(1)(A) shall be taken into account only if such return was filed on or before the last day prescribed for the filing of such return, determined with regard to any extension of time for such filing   *   *   *."

Clearly, since the returns for the taxable years before us were not timely filed and were not filed within the time specified in any extension of time for filing, and since there has been no "amount previously assessed" or "rebates"—it follows that the entire amount of tax we find to be due for the years in issue are "underpayments" for section 6653(a) purposes. It is our task, therefore, to determine whether any part of these underpayments was due to negligence or intentional disregard of rules and regulations. Since at least part of these section 6653(a) "underpayments" stem from petitioner's failure to file timely returns, this final issue resolves itself into the question of whether or not petitioner failed to file timely returns due to negligence or intentional disregard of rules and regulations.

We think it clear that petitioner's nonfeasance was the product of an intentional disregard of rules and regulations. Petitioner has been an attorney since 1953. He testified repeatedly that he was well aware of his obligation to file timely Federal returns of income. He testified that he had many times advised his own clients, some of whom had failed to file returns for many years, of their obligation to file and that it was his practice in such a case immediately to take his clients down to the local Internal Revenue Service office. Corroborating petitioner's candid confession of his knowledge of his legal duty to file timely returns of income was the fact that he filed an application for extension of time to file for his taxable years 1968, 1969, and 1970. Finally, petitioner's decision to stop filing timely income tax returns after 1962 was a volitional policy choice he made "when I couldn't file an accurate return with my brother."

The Fifth Circuit has already spoken on this issue:

> The authorities indicate that the taxpayer also has the burden to show that he did not intentionally disregard rules and regulations. The latter segment of the disjunctive clause is usually brought into play when a taxpayer who is aware or should be aware of a rule or regulation chooses to ignore its requirements. The taxpayer can avoid the penalty by showing no intent to disregard the rule or regulations involved. [Marcello v. Commissioner, 380 F.2d 499, 506 (5th Cir. 1967).]

We think it clear that petitioner deliberately made an informed choice to ignore his legal obligation to file timely Federal income tax returns. That such a choice should be made by an attorney-at-law is rendered even more surprising by the clear testimony of one of petitioner's accountants that there was sufficient information in petitioner's cardboard boxes from which accurate returns could be constructed. At the least, therefore, petitioner has failed to show that he had no intent to disregard the rules and regulations requiring timely and accurate filings of returns. We find that part of petitioner's "underpayments" for both the taxable years before us were due to his intentional disregard of the rules and regulations requiring timely filing of returns.

Since we have found that the section 6653(a) addition to tax must be imposed herein due to petitioner's intentional disregard of rules and regulations, we find it unnecessary to determine whether or not petitioner was also negligent.

Decision will be entered under Rule 155.

QUESTION

Is it intellectually sound to impose both the failure to file penalty (§ 6651(a)) and the "negligence" penalty (§ 6653(a)) for the same year? Is it not true that virtually every late filing (or failure to file) without reasonable cause is due to either negligence or intentional disregard of rules and regulations? Hence, is the Tax Court in *Burglass* not, in effect, imposing a 30% penalty for failure to file the tax returns in issue?

D. THE CIVIL FRAUD PENALTY

(1) IMPOSITION OF THE PENALTY

CARTER v. CAMPBELL

264 F.2d 930 (5th Cir. 1959).

JOHN R. BROWN, Circuit Judge:

* * *

[The Court addressed the issue of "what is and what is not fraud" as follows:]

* * * We have recently given our approval to the strong language of Davis v. Commissioner, 10 Cir., 1950, 184 F.2d 86, 87. "Fraud implies bad faith, intentional wrongdoing and a sinister motive. It is never imputed or presumed and the Courts should not sustain findings of fraud upon circumstances which at most create only suspicion." Equally emphatic is that stated for us by Judge Sibley in Mitchell v. Commissioner, 5 Cir., 1941, 118 F.2d 308, 310. "Negligence, whether slight or great, is not equivalent to the fraud with intent to evade tax named in the statute. The fraud meant is actual, intentional wrongdoing, and the intent required is the specific purpose to evade a tax believed to be owing. Mere negligence does not establish either." These principles have been restated frequently and recently with no recession either from emphatic language or like application.

Added to this is the burden placed upon the Commissioner. The Code [h] places it expressly upon the Commissioner. "The burden is upon the Commissioner to prove affirmatively by clear and convincing evidence actual and intentional wrongdoing on the part of the petitioner with a specific intent to evade the tax." Eagle v. Commissioner, 5 Cir., 1957, 242 F.2d 635, 637.

Where the case involves both a deficiency and a civil fraud penalty, each party has its own peculiar burden of proof. The result is, as we once pointed out, the case may end in a standoff from the failure of each party to go ahead with his evidence. The taxpayer fails on the deficiency. The Government fails on the fraud penalty. Failure of the taxpayer to overcome the deficiency does not create a presumption of fraud.

* * *

It is not difficult to articulate the legal standard for tax fraud and to state the burden of proof which the IRS must meet to succeed in imposing the civil fraud penalty under § 6653(b). However, as illustrated by the following case, it is another matter to predict the outcome of a particular case. How would you decide the *Candela* case, below?

CANDELA v. UNITED STATES

635 F.2d 1272 (7th Cir. 1980).

CAMPBELL, Senior District Judge:

This appeal presents two issues: whether the taxpayers successfully overcame the Commissioner of Internal Revenue's determination of a tax deficiency; and whether the Commissioner established, by clear and convincing evidence, that these deficiencies were the result of fraud. The plaintiffs-taxpayers have the burden of proof on the first issue, the Commissioner on the latter. The District Court, after a bench trial, concluded that the taxpayers had failed to rebut the deficiency determinations, and that the deficiencies were the product of fraud. While we concur with the District Court's finding as to the deficiencies, we do not believe that the record supports a finding of fraud. We, therefore, reverse.

The plaintiffs, Filippo Candela and Providenza Candela, reside in Lomira, Wisconsin. They were married in 1925 and emigrated to this country from Italy the following year. The Candelas lived in Ohio at first and then moved to Wisconsin in 1939. In April of 1941 Filippo started working at the Grande Cheese Company. The Candelas and their two children, Antoinette and John, lived in a house owned by the cheese company. They paid no rent. Since there was

h. See IRC § 7454(a).

no hotel in town, they would provide lodging for customers and suppliers of the cheese company, for which they were compensated by the company.

The Candelas apparently lived very frugally. Filippo worked seven days a week, and they did not mix socially with other members of the community. They grew their own vegetables which served as a major source of their food. The Candelas did send their two children to parochial schools, and then on to college. Their daughter, Antoinette, testified that for seven years after she graduated from college and was working, she lived either at home or with relatives, and routinely sent a portion of her income home to her father.

In 1967 Filippo and his son John, who was approximately twenty-one years old, purchased the Grande Cheese Company from the Di Bella family for $60,000. Filippo paid for the stock of the company with a money order in the amount of $46,004.78, and a check from the Gourmay Cheese Company in the amount of $13,995.22. The check from Gourmay was a partial payment of a $20,000 debt owed by the Grande Cheese Company to Filippo. The money order was purchased with a $40,000 withdrawal from Filippo's checking account at the Brownsville State Bank, and the remaining $6,004.78 was in cash.

Filippo Candela never learned to read or write, nor did he learn much English. His daily contact was limited to his family and fellow workers at the cheese company. Thus, there was little need for English in his daily life. The preparation of Filippo's annual tax returns was handled by his barber until 1968. In 1968 the barber died, and his return for that year and subsequent years was prepared by Herbert Hauptman, the accountant for the cheese company.

In April of 1975 the Commissioner sent the Candelas notice of a tax deficiency for the years 1967, 1968 and 1969. They paid the deficiencies together with penalties for fraud and, on November 29, 1976, instituted this action for a refund. The deficiencies asserted by the Commissioner were for $6,280.71 in 1967, $12,561.02 in 1968, and $13,547.00 in 1969. In addition, fraud penalties of 50% of deficiencies were assessed. The entire amount at issue, including interest, is $60,606.88.

It should be noted at the outset that the finding of fraud is crucial to the outcome of this case. Normally, the Commissioner is barred from assessing a tax deficiency more than three years after any part of such tax was paid. 26 U.S.C. § 6501(a). However, the three year limitation does not apply in cases where the taxpayer files a "fraudulent return with the intent to evade tax." 26 U.S.C. § 6501(c)(1). Thus, the Commissioner is barred from collecting anything unless he can establish the requisite fraudulent intent of the taxpayer. The standard by which fraud must be established is one of clear and convincing evidence.

In the instant case, the Commissioner does not rely on any direct evidence to establish an understatement of income for the years in question. Rather, the Internal Revenue Service has employed a net worth method of determining income. Under that method a taxpayer's net worth is established as of the beginning of the period under scrutiny. This is done by subtracting the value of the taxpayer's liabilities from the value of his assets. Once the taxpayer's net worth for the beginning of the taxable period is determined, that figure is subtracted from his net worth for the following year. The difference is the taxpayer's income for that year. To determine income for subsequent years, the Commissioner simply subtracts the taxpayer's net worth at the beginning of the year from the end of the year. Using this method the Commissioner determined that Candela's adjusted gross income for 1967 was $40,870.89 rather than the reported amount of $11,796.28; $54,421.19 for 1968 rather than $16,111.81; and $58.526.86 in 1969, rather than the $31,485.15 reported on that year's return.

The taxpayers' primary attack on the use of the net worth theory is that the initial figure for their net worth is erroneous, thus rendering each successive determination of annual income incorrect. The taxpayers claim that the Commissioner's initial net worth figure of $96,807.13 failed to take into account approximately $70,000 in cash on hand as of December 31, 1966. This cash was allegedly kept in a safe deposit box at the National Exchange Bank in Fond du Lac, Wisconsin; in another safe deposit box at the Brownsville State Bank in Lomira; and in a milk can in the basement of the Candelas' home. The source of the cash was allegedly savings over the years and money sent home by their daughter Antoinette prior to her marriage. According to the testimony of his son John, Filippo Candela kept large amounts of cash in his home out of a general distrust of banks based on his first hand experience of the 1929 depression.

In support of their cash hoard argument, the Candelas rely on Filippo's own testimony and the testimony of their son John regarding the large sums of money kept in the basement and in the safe deposit boxes; the testimony of Antoinette describing her contribution to the family income; the Commissioner's failure to consider additional income from providing room and board to visitors of the cheese company; and the fact that Filippo had over six thousand dollars in cash when he purchased the Grande Cheese Company in April of 1967. The Commissioner argues that based on the Candelas' income and expenditures between 1945 and 1967, they could not have saved $40,000 in that period.[1]

The District Court's finding that the taxpayers had failed to overcome the deficiency assessments is based largely on credibility

1. $70,000 less the $30,000 allegedly contributed by Antoinette.

determinations. With the exception of Filippo Candela whose deposition was introduced, the District Judge had the benefit of observing the witnesses testify, and made findings as to their credibility. Credibility determinations are clearly within the province of the trier of fact. We find nothing in the record to suggest that the finding of deficiencies for the years in question is clearly erroneous.

Had this case been brought within the three-year period for civil tax deficiency suits, our review of the proceedings below would go no further. However, because the Commissioner's deficiency assessment is time barred unless fraud is established, we must focus on evidence relied upon to sustain the Court's finding of fraud.

The Commissioner contends that an understatement of income is "by itself indicative of fraud." However, the District Court did not rely on the understatements as demonstrated by the use of the net worth theory, and we believe rightly so. The Court found that the understatements of income had been established by the net worth theory to a "reasonable certainty." Yet, clear and convincing evidence of fraud requires more than that. While a consistent pattern of understatements can be persuasive evidence of fraud, the quantum of evidence which establishes those understatements must also meet the clear and convincing standard if they are to sustain a finding of fraud.

The Court below did rely on three "indicators" in support of the finding of fraud. First, the District Court concluded that Filippo Candela possessed a "high degree of business acumen" sufficient to understand his tax obligations. While Filippo Candela may well have been knowledgeable about the production and sale of cheese, his acumen was limited to that field. The record before the District Court strongly suggests that Candela lacked any business expertise outside of the operation of a cheese factory. He was illiterate and could not speak English very well. Up until the time he acquired the cheese company he retained his barber to prepare his tax returns for five dollars. He kept his money in milk cans and safe deposit boxes rather than in interest bearing accounts or investments. Candela had no formal education, and testified that he had no knowledge of mathematics. Candela appears to have had little knowledge or understanding of the tax laws. While this does not absolve him of his obligations under the law, it does suggest that the failure to report certain portions of his income was due to negligence or ignorance of the law rather than fraud.

Perhaps the most significant evidence of a possible fraudulent intent is Candela's sales of cheese purchased from the company. For several years prior to his acquiring Grande Cheese Company Candela would purchase significant quantities of Romano cheese from Grande which he would age and then sell to various retailers. He apparently kept no record of his profit or loss on these sales, though each sale was documented by a purchaser's invoice and a check for payment. Candela would deposit the checks received from these sales in his account at the Brownsville State Bank. He would occasionally make disbursements from that account to cover expenses such as his children's tuition and life insurance premiums. These sales took place in 1966 and 1967, though no profit or loss was reported on Candela's tax returns for those years.

The District Court relied heavily on this second indicator in finding fraud. The Court found that these sales occurred during "at least three of the years in question." Yet evidence introduced by the Government suggests that the sales of cheese stopped in mid-1967, or, at the latest, early 1968. Candela's bank account records on which the District Court specifically relied indicate that the deposits ceased in September 1967, and the account became inactive at that time. While the record reflects that Candela received a check for $2,500 in January 1968, and for $500 in June 1969, from the Costa Grocery, the corresponding statements indicate that these payments were for prior sales of cheese.

Candela's failure to keep adequate records and failure to report any profits or losses from his sales of cheese was clearly improper. However, the significant issue is whether his actions reflect an intent to evade taxes or ignorance of his obligations under the law. Several factors in the record indicate that Candela's practice of selling cheese on his own is not probative of any intent to evade or defeat his tax obligations.

First, we note that Candela received checks from cheese purchasers rather than cash. He opened a bank account in the name of Filippo Candela & Co. at the Brownsville State Bank where he regularly deposited any checks he received. His purchases of cheese were documented on the books of Grande Cheese Company, and on the books of the retailers to whom he sold. Such documentation would not suggest a scheme to evade taxes. When Candela's lack of education and formal business training is considered in conjunction with his actions, it is difficult for us to conclude that he possessed the requisite intent to deceive and evade the tax collector.

The record also discloses that at the time these unreported sales of cheese were ongoing, Candela's tax returns were still being prepared by his barber. Since the barber died in 1968, and did not testify at trial, we cannot say whether the subject of income in addition to Candela's salary was ever discussed. Yet, it seems unlikely that the barber would know of these sales of cheese.

The final "indicator" relied on by the District Court is that Candela kept money in an out-of-state bank account. Specifically, the Court was referring to $18,000 held in a savings account in Toledo, Ohio. This money was a repayment to Candela of a mortgage note on property in Ohio. The interest earned in that account was not reported on Candela's income tax return of the years in question. The form 1099s indicating the interest earned in the account were sent to the attorney who handled the sale of the property. He was located in Toledo. For some reason, the attorney returned the forms to the Toledo bank, rather than forward them to Candela.

We fail to see how keeping funds in an out-of-state bank would indicate fraud. The failure to report the income from the account would be indicative of fraud had the Form 1099s been sent to Candela. However, the taxpayer's failure to determine his interest income by contacting the bank and securing the appropriate forms was no more than negligence, particularly in light of his limited understanding of English.

As we noted at the outset, the government has the burden to establish fraud by clear and convincing evidence in this case. We find little evidence in the record to support a finding of fraud. The Government's net worth analysis, while reasonable, is not convincing evidence of fraud. Aside from Candela's practice of selling cheese purchased from the company, the record is devoid of any affirmative act which would indicate an intent to evade taxes. Given Candela's background and limited education, we cannot conclude that this alone rises to the level of clear and convincing evidence of fraud. Rather, our perception of Filippo Candela from this record is that of a man who was successful in his own field, but lacking even the most basic understanding of other aspects of the business world. His poor record keeping and failure to report income from his cheese sales was negligent and improper. But the Commissioner has failed to establish that it was the result of fraud.

The dissent finds the government's characterization of Candela's activities more convincing. While there is some evidentiary support for that view, we believe the clear and convincing standard requires a greater quantum of evidence to support a finding of fraud. The District Court's finding of fraud is clearly erroneous, and must be reversed. Accordingly, the Commissioner's assessment of a deficiency is time barred, and the taxpayers are entitled to a refund as a matter of law. Reversed.

WOOD, Circuit Judge, dissenting:

The majority, in my opinion, gives the taxpayers an undeserved pass for the income taxes they fraudulently avoided paying.

It appears that Mr. Candela lived in this country for forty years without learning English, but he did learn how to make cheese and money. It is said that the taxpayers were frugal. That is ordinarily a worthy characteristic, but not if you are being frugal by not paying your income taxes.

Taxpayers' assets rose from about $99,000 to $228,000 between 1966 and 1969. Those assets included various bank accounts, a cheese inventory, savings bonds, accounts receivables, loans, a mortgage, a stockbroker deposit, real estate stocks, and farm machinery. Even though he could not speak English, Mr. Candela was obviously no babe in the economic woods.

Critical to the case is taxpayers' claim of $70,000 cash on hand for which the government gave them no credit in the net worth analysis. However, the taxpayers themselves have considerable difficulty trying to explain it. It is admitted by taxpayers in their brief that "[t]he source of the $70,000.00 cash on hand of the plaintiffs cannot be demonstrated with exactness." "Doubtless," it is argued, "plaintiffs saved some cash over a period of forty years." The plaintiffs sum up their case by arguing that they have "shown a likely source of at least $30,000.00 from their daughter in the years prior to 1967, and a distinct possibility that plaintiffs may have saved or accumulated an additional $40,000.00 in the forty years prior to 1967, due to their abstemious ways." Those are not very strong or satisfying statements. Taxpayers claim, incidentally, that their cash hoard was kept in a can in the basement, plus in two safe deposit boxes. I am surprised that taxpayers by now have not thought up something original to claim besides just having a can full of money in the basement. These particular taxpayers at least distinguish their explanation by saying that their can full of money in the basement was a milk can, a container of impressive dimensions.

Let us also look at the $30,000 portion of that cash hoard which they attribute to their daughter. It is claimed that the daughter routinely sent a portion of her wages home to her father. Such filial assistance to aging parents can be most laudable. This, however, appears to be an exceptional case. The daughter claims that over a six-year period she sent home $30,000 of her total income of $38,000. It is also exceptional that she was able to exist on what little she would have had left. The parents were doing very well without the need for such extreme sacrifices by their daughter. I wonder if the daughter realized that her wages were only headed for deposit in the milk can in the basement.

"Dutifully," it is argued, Mr. Candela took his records to his barber to do his tax returns. What he dutifully delivered, however, were incomplete records which did not reveal at least his additional income from cheese sales on the side and the interest received.

Judge Warren who heard taxpayers' story firsthand didn't believe it when weighed against the net worth analysis, and I don't either.

————

The IRS often will assert the civil fraud penalty in a situation in which the taxpayer failed to file required tax returns. As illustrated by the following case, a failure to file tax returns (even a willful failure to file for which criminal prosecution is appropriate) does not necessarily justify the imposition of the civil fraud penalty.

CIRILLO v. COMMISSIONER

314 F.2d 478 (3d Cir. 1963).

HASTIE, Circuit Judge.

In June 1957, Joseph Cirillo and his wife, Martha, jointly filed their first income tax returns for the years 1945 to 1954, inclusive. They acted after having learned that revenue agents were investigating the husband's tax liability.

* * *

Before the Tax Court, Joseph Cirillo, whom we shall call the taxpayer, testified that he had failed to file timely returns, not because of any intent to defraud, but because he believed, on the basis of a summary mental calculation made at the end of each year, that the withholdings from his salary alone were enough to cover all income taxes payable on both his salary and his small net income from private law practice. However, he concedes that he kept no systematic records of receipts and expenditures in the course of his practice and made no detailed computation of his tax liability at the end of each taxable year. In the absence of such records, he urges that the good faith and reasonableness of his asserted belief that his taxes were covered by salary withholdings are substantiated by the subsequent detailed computations which appear in the delinquent returns filed in 1957. * * *

The taxpayer does not challenge the existence of deficiencies or their amounts as found by the Tax Court. Therefore, we have to consider only whether and to what extent fraud penalties were justified.

The evidence in this case strongly indicates that the taxpayer's failure to file returns was a willful neglect of a statutory duty. As a lawyer, he must have been aware that one who earns several thousand dollars a year is obligated to file income tax returns. Each year he was reminded of his duty to file a return by the standard W–2 Form which he received from his employer. Moreover, he has been convicted of the misdemeanor of willful failure to file income tax returns for the years 1953 and 1954.

But willful failure to file a timely return, which may create both criminal liability and an additional civil liability, does not in itself and without more establish liability for a fraud penalty, though it may be relevant in that connection. This is true because a fraud penalty can be imposed only where proof of a deficiency is supplemented by proof that the "deficiency is due to fraud with intent to evade tax". The critical question is whether the circumstances attending a particular failure to file warrant an inference of intention to evade taxes. Moreover, the evidence must be evaluated in the light of the settled rule that fraud can be established only by clear and convincing proof or, as we have put it, "by something impressively more than a slight preponderance of evidence". Valetti v. Commissioner, 3d Cir., 1958, 260 F.2d 185, 188. To justify a fraud penalty the circumstances surrounding the failure to file returns must strongly and unequivocally indicate an intention to avoid the payment of taxes.

Taxpayer contends that his willful failure to file was not and could not have been the result of a scheme to cheat the government out of taxes which he was obligated to pay, because he did not believe that he owed any taxes. We are aware that the Tax Court disbelieved this testimony and that it is not for this appellate court to assess taxpayer's credibility as a witness. However, the Commissioner's heavy burden of proof on the issue of fraud cannot be satisfied by mere disbelief of taxpayer's testimony. The record must contain some convincing affirmative indication of the required specific intent.

Taxpayer's delinquent returns lend considerable credibility to his testimony concerning the years from 1945 through 1951. Taking into account the expenses which he believed he was entitled to deduct plus the credit for income taxes withheld, taxpayer calculated that he had overpaid his taxes for each of those years by amounts in the order of fifty to one hundred seventy-five dollars. These delinquent returns were not fraudulent, and there is no showing or argument that any of the deductions claimed but disallowed were fictitious. Only because taxpayer was unable to substantiate them with the kind of records which the Commissioner properly demanded was it determined that he owed additional taxes for each of these years except 1948. And for that year it is agreed that he owes nothing. All of this corroborates taxpayer's testimony that at the end of each of these years he believed that he owed the government no taxes beyond what had already been withheld from his salary.

In the face of this evidence, the Commissioner offered little to sustain his burden of proving fraud for the years 1945 to 1951. Apart from evidence which, as already pointed out, builds a very strong case of willful failure to file without demonstrating the intent which accompanied that failure, the only evidence offered by the Commissioner was the taxpayer's failure to keep systematic and detailed records of income and expenditures of his law practice. The significance of this omission is minimized by the fact that from 1945 through 1951, taxpayer's practice was very small, never yielding receipts in excess of $2200 in any year and, in several years, yielding less than $1000. Indeed, government agents conceded that, even without such records, they were able to determine the amount of taxpayer's earnings from bank deposit statements retained by him, and that there was no indication that taxpayer had received additional income not reflected in these statements. Thus, the only needed information which was lacking because of the taxpayer's failure to keep books was a record of the expenditures which he made in the regular course of his law practice. In these circumstances, any inference that taxpayer's unbusinesslike procedure was intended to conceal tax liability is too weak to achieve the clear and convincing character which proof of fraud must exhibit.

The years 1952, 1953 and 1954 present a different picture. In 1952, taxpayer's gross income from his law practice increased very substantially to $4,169.70, four times as much as it had been in any year before 1951 and twice as much as it had been in 1951, while his deductible expenses did not increase proportionately. Moreover, withholdings did not increase substantially. As a consequence, the tax withheld from taxpayer's salary in 1952 was more than $500 short of covering his total tax liability. Even his own calculations for 1952, made several years later, failed to disclose an overpayment such as those he consistently claimed for the years before 1952. And for 1953 and 1954, taxpayer's delinquent returns admitted substantial deficiencies. Thus, the record indicates that at the end of 1952 and thereafter, even a rough calculation, honestly made, would at least have shown the taxpayer that there was need for a more careful analysis of income and expenditures to substantiate or dissipate his hope that no additional taxes were due. His disingenuous avoidance of accurate knowledge when the need for such knowledge must have been apparent was in itself a substantial indication of fraudulent intent.

We conclude, therefore, that the evidence of fraud was sufficiently clear and convincing to justify the imposition of fraud penalties for the years 1952, 1953 and 1954. Not so, however, for the years from 1945 through 1951.

* * *

NOTE

The civil fraud penalty of § 6653(b) is not applicable to a spouse who signs a joint return unless some part of the underpayment is due to the fraud of such spouse. Moreover, a spouse qualifying as an "innocent spouse" within the meaning of IRC § 6013(e), will not be liable for tax deficiencies resulting from the omission from a joint return of income of the other spouse. IRC § 6013(e). See pages 777–781, below, for a discussion of the innocent spouse provisions.

(2) COMPUTATION OF THE PENALTY

LEVINSON v. UNITED STATES

496 F.2d 651 (3d Cir. 1974).

JAMES HUNTER, III, Circuit Judge:

The sole issue on this appeal is the determination of the proper method by which civil tax fraud penalties are to be assessed under 26

U.S.C. § 6653. The Internal Revenue Service ("IRS") assessed a 50% fraud penalty on the difference between taxpayers' true tax liability and the tax liability shown on taxpayers' original tax returns. The district court upheld this method of computation and we affirm.

Taxpayers' returns for 1967 through 1959 were timely filed and the taxes shown thereon timely paid. When the IRS subsequently conducted routine examinations of these returns, adjustments were made resulting in the assessment of additional taxes. Subsequent to this, taxpayers filed amended returns reporting income which had not been included in the original tax returns. The IRS then began an investigation which uncovered further unreported income of taxpayers and which eventually resulted in the bringing of fraud charges against taxpayers. On this appeal taxpayers do not contest their tax liability or the finding of fraud.

Taxpayers do contend, however, that the fraud penalty should not be applied to those deficiencies assessed because of adjustments made to the original tax return at the time routine audits were conducted. The additional taxes assessed at this time resulted from adjustments to inventories and business deductions. These adjustments apparently were not the subject of the subsequent fraud investigation which was based on omitted income. Thus the taxpayers suggest that the fraud penalty should have been computed by the following formula:

50% × [correct tax—(tax shown on original timely filed return + additional tax assessed because of routine audit on original return)]

The fraud penalty was actually computed on the basis of this formula:

50% × [correct tax—tax shown on original timely filed return]

Taxpayers argue that the decisional law and applicable statute supports their view that the fraud penalty should not apply to nonfraudulent deficiencies assessed as a result of routine adjustments made to their original returns. We do not agree.

Under the Internal Revenue Code of 1939, the fraud penalty provision, section 293(b), provided that "if *any part* of any deficiency is *due to fraud* * * * then 50 per centum of the *total amount of the deficiency* * * * shall be so assessed * * *." (Emphasis added.) "Deficiency" was defined under section 271(a) by the following formula:

deficiency = correct tax—(tax shown on return + amounts previously assessed or collected without assessment—rebates)

Where there have been several deficiencies, this definition quite logically requires that, in computing the amount of any new deficiency, credit should be given for deficiencies previously assessed or collected.

In computing the fraud penalty under the 1939 Code, however, courts consistently refused to apply the penalty to only this narrowly defined deficiency. Since the fraud penalty provision referred to "the total amount of the deficiency," courts consistently reasoned that where more than one deficiency had been assessed, the penalty applied to all of the deficiencies; thus, the total deficiency was held to be the difference between the correct tax and the tax shown on the original return.

Contrary to what taxpayers suggest, we have found no decision under the 1939 Code which deviated from this method of computing the fraud penalty or even suggested that in certain situations a different method of computation would apply. Taxpayers rely heavily on J. S. McDonnell v. Commissioner, 6 B.T.A. 685 (1927) as support for the proposition that in computing the fraud penalty the IRS should allow taxpayers "legitimate adjustments" to the tax as reported on the original return.

Taxpayers, however have misread *McDonnell*. The 50% fraud penalty in that case was applied to the difference between the correct tax and the tax shown on the original return. The court specifically held that no error had been committed in the method of computation of the penalty. What the court did say, which is far different from that contended by the taxpayers, is that in computing the total tax liability and hence the correct deficiency, the IRS had failed to give credit for legitimate deductions and losses. Taxpayers, however, have not contested the final tax liability determined by the IRS and therefore *McDonnell* does not support taxpayers' position. It is also significant that *McDonnell* was specifically cited by the same court in Wilson v. Commissioner, 7 T.C. 395, 398 (1942) when it noted that,

"[S]ince the Revenue Act of 1918, the [IRS] has consistently computed the [fraud] penalty upon the *total amount understated on the return* and in every instance in those cases coming before us of which we are aware, we have approved the computation." (Emphasis added.)

We therefore conclude that under the Internal Revenue Code of 1939, it was the court-sanctioned practice of the IRS to compute fraud penalties on the difference between the correct tax and the tax shown on the original return. The only question remaining then is whether the enactment of the Internal Revenue Code of 1954 affected changes in this substantive policy. We think not.

The present fraud penalty provision, 26 U.S.C. § 6653(b), differs from its predecessor only in its use of the word "underpayment" rather than deficiency:

"If *any part* of any underpayment * * * of tax required to be shown on a return *is due to fraud,* there shall
be added to the tax an amount equal to 50 percent of the underpayment." (Emphasis added.)

"Underpayment" is defined in section 6653(c) [6] by reference to the
definition of deficiency in 26 U.S.C. § 6211 [7] which is virtually identical to its predecessor, section 271(a). Section 6653(c), however,
states that for purposes of defining deficiency, only the tax shown on
the original timely filed return is to be considered.

On their face these changes appear minor and at most appear to
merely clarify what the practice had been under the 1939 Code.
That this was the Congressional intent is unquestionably clear from
the legislative history. We thus agree with the Second Circuit that
the Internal Revenue Code of 1954 did not change the method of
computing the fraud penalty and that the method by which the IRS
has computed the penalty in the present case is proper under 26 U.S.
C. § 6653.

In view of taxpayers' insistence that deficiencies assessed as a result of the routine audit of their returns must be applied as a credit
pursuant to 26 U.S.C. § 6211(a)(1)(B), a few further observations
appear necessary. First, section 6211(a)(1)(B) is identical to its
predecessor under the 1939 Code, section 271(a)(1)(B), and as noted
previously, prior deficiencies were never applied under the 1939 Code
as a credit in determining the "total" deficiency subject to the fraud
penalty.

Second, taxpayers suggest that previously assessed deficiencies
should be applied as credit under section 6211(a)(1)(B) *just in some
circumstances.* Yet, there is no support in the statute, its legislative

---

6. 26 U.S.C. § 6653(c) provides, *inter
alia:*
> "For purposes of this section, the
> term 'underpayment' means—
> "(1) *Income, estate, and gift tax-
> es.*—In the case of a tax to which
> section 6211 (relating to income,
> estate, and gift taxes) is applicable,
> a deficiency as defined in that sec-
> tion (except that, for this purpose,
> the tax shown on a return referred
> to in section 6211(a)(1)(A) shall be
> taken into account only if such re-
> turn was filed on or before the last
> day prescribed for the filing of
> such return, determined with re-
> gard to any extension of time for
> such filing) * * *."

7. 26 U.S.C. § 6211 provides, *inter
alia:*
> *"Definition of a deficiency*

> "(a) *In general.*—For purposes of
> this title in the case of income, es-
> tate, and gift taxes, imposed by
> subtitles A and B, the term 'defi-
> ciency' means the amount by
> which the tax imposed by subtitles
> A or B exceeds the excess of—
> "(1) the sum of
> "(A) the amount shown as the
> tax by the taxpayer upon his re-
> turn, if a return was made by
> the taxpayer and an amount was
> shown as the tax by the taxpay-
> er thereon, plus
> "(B) the amounts previously
> assessed (or collected without as-
> sessment) as a deficiency, over—
> "(2) the amount of rebates, as
> defined in subsection (b)(2),
> made."

history or in the case law for applying section 6211(a)(1)(B) selectively.

Third, the inequities of taxpayers' position is manifest. Had there been only one deficiency assessed coupled with a finding that at least a part of the underpayment was due to fraud, then there would not have been any previously assessed deficiency for which taxpayers could claim a credit under section 6211(a)(1)(B). The fraud penalty quite clearly would have been applied to the total underpayment, *i. e.*, the difference between the correct tax and the tax shown on the original timely filed return. It does not seem likely that Congress would have conditioned the severity of the fraud penalty on such a fortuity as whether or not a routine audit had been conducted prior to the assessment giving rise to the fraud charge.

Lastly, if there is ambiguity in the statutory language, we think the clear Congressional purpose must prevail. Since Congress unquestionably did not intend to modify the substantive law under the 1939 Code, we agree with the Second Circuit that the fraud penalty under 26 U.S.C. § 6653 is properly computed on the basis of the difference between the correct tax and the tax shown on the original timely filed return.

The order of the district court of August 29, 1973 will be affirmed.

CIRILLO v. COMMISSIONER

314 F.2d 478 (3d Cir. 1963).

[The facts of the *Cirillo* case, and that portion of the opinion holding that imposition of the fraud penalty was proper for certain of the years in issue, appear at pages 209–211, above.]

    * * * In this case the Tax Court added 50% to the taxpayer's total liability for each year as a fraud penalty, without having subtracted either the amount withheld from salary or the amount of tax reported on the delinquent return.

In section 271(a) "deficiency" is defined as "the amount by which the tax imposed by this chapter exceeds * * * the amount shown as the tax by the taxpayer upon his return, if a return was made * * *." Section 271(b)(1) explicitly provides that "[t]he tax imposed by this chapter and the tax shown on the return shall both be determined * * * without regard to the credit under section 35 [for amounts withheld from wages] * * *." This language makes it clear that neither the existence nor the amount of the "deficiency" of a taxpayer who has failed to file a return is affected in any way by the existence of a withholding credit partially or fully offsetting his tax liability. Moreover, in the circumstances of this case the "total amount of the deficiency", upon which the fraud penalty is based, must be the entire amount of the "tax imposed" for the year unless, under the section 271 definition of deficiency, it is permissible to deduct from that total tax liability the amount of tax shown on the delinquent return filed several years after the due date. We think this is not permissible.

1952 is the first year as to which we have concluded that fraud was proved. When the deadline for filing a 1952 tax return passed, a "deficiency" in the amount of "the tax imposed" came into existence. Because no return had then been filed, there simply was no "amount shown as the tax by the taxpayer upon his return" to be deducted from the total tax liability in computing the "deficiency". And since the failure to file was fraudulent the taxpayer's liability at that time included a fraud penalty measured by that deficiency. * * * The parties recognize that section 6653(c)(1) of the 1954 Code, which is applicable to the 1954 fraud penalty, has now explicitly provided that only a timely return is to be considered in determining the existence and amount of the underpayment which is the measure of the fraud penalty.

* * *

QUESTION

Suppose a taxpayer files a fraudulent 1980 tax return reflecting no tax liability. On examination it is established that a deficiency of $20,000 exists for 1980, but that due to the effect of a net operating loss carryback from 1983 no tax is actually due for 1980. May the IRS assess a fraud penalty for 1980 and, if so, in what amount? See Rev.Rul. 173, 1963–2 C. B. 227; Simon v. Commissioner, 248 F.2d 869, 877 (8th Cir. 1957).

SECTION 7. INTEREST ON DEFICIENCIES AND OVERPAYMENTS

Absent an agreement or a specific prohibition, interest must be paid to the IRS on underpayments of tax and to the taxpayer on overpayments of tax.[i] As stated in Rev.Proc. 60–17, 1960–2 C.B. 942:

Under the general rule, interest is paid on a tax overpayment for the time the government has the use of the taxpayer's money. Interest is collected, similarly, for the time the taxpayer has the use of the government's money. The underlying objective is to determine in a given situation whose money it is and for how long the other party had the use of it.

Interest on Underpayments. As to tax deficiencies, the taxpayer is considered to have the use of the government's money starting with the due date of the subject tax return. Therefore, for a 1981 income tax return due April 15, 1982, interest on an underpayment

i. IRC §§ 6601, 6611.

shown on the return or on a deficiency assessed many years later commences running on April 15, 1982. However, interest on penalties commences only after assessment is made and payment is demanded.[j] Moreover, there is no accrual of interest on an obligation to pay interest.[k] Thus, interest to the IRS is simple interest which runs without compounding from the commencement date to the termination date.

Interest on amounts due to the IRS ceases running on the date the underlying liability is paid.[l] However, if a deficiency is assessed and payment is made within ten days of demand, the interest termination date is the date of demand.[m]

The basic rules pertinent to interest on underpayments can be illustrated by the following example:

The taxpayer files a 1981 income tax return on April 15, 1982, reporting $10,000 tax due on the return and making no payment. On April 15, 1984 there is assessed a $15,000 tax deficiency and a $7,500 fraud penalty. On April 15, 1985, the taxpayer finally pays his full liability for 1981, which consists of the following [n] (assuming, for simplicity, a 10% per annum interest rate):

$10,000	Tax due per return.
3,000	Interest (3 years) on tax due per return.
15,000	Deficiency assessment.
4,500	Interest (3 years) on tax deficiency.
7,500	Civil fraud penalty.
750	Interest (1 year) on fraud penalty.

Hence, the total interest paid would be $8,250.

Interest on Overpayments. As to overpayments, the IRS is considered to have the use of the taxpayer's money starting with the date of payment.[o] Interest in favor of the taxpayer runs from the date of overpayment on all liabilities (whether tax, penalty or interest). Hence, as to taxpayer overpayments, there is what might be considered a compounding of interest.

Interest on amounts due taxpayers which are refunded ceases running on a date preceding the issuance of a refund check by not more than thirty days.[p] If the overpayment is credited against a tax

j. IRC § 6601(e)(3).

k. IRC § 6601(e)(2).

l. IRC § 6601(a).

m. IRC § 6601(e)(4).

n. The failure to pay penalty will also be imposed unless there was reasonable cause for the failure to pay. See pages 191–198, above.

o. IRS § 611(b). A payment made early is deemed paid on the due date of the subject tax return.

p. IRC § 6611(b)(2).

debt due by the taxpayer, interest in effect runs to the date of application of the credit.[q]

The basic rules pertinent to interest on overpayments can be illustrated by continuing with the prior example as follows:

> The taxpayer files a refund claim on April 15, 1986, claiming that there was no deficiency, that in fact there was a $2,000 overpayment with the return, and that the fraud penalty should not have been assessed. The taxpayer prevails, and April 15, 1988 is the date utilized to compute interest for a refund check issued within 30 days of that date. Assuming, for simplicity, a 10% per annum interest rate, the refund check will consist of the following amounts: [r]

$ 2,000	Overpayment on original return.
1,200	Interest (6 years) on the original return overpayment.
15,000	Deficiency overpayment.
4,500	Interest (3 years) on the deficiency overpayment.
7,500	Fraud penalty overpayment.
2,250	Interest (3 years) on the fraud penalty overpayment.
8,250	Overpayment of interest.
2,475	Interest (3 years) on overpayment of interest.

Hence, the total interest refunded by the IRS would be $10,425.

Rates of Interest. The rate of interest on underpayments is the same as the rate on overpayments.[s] Prior to July 1, 1975, that rate had remained constant at 6%. However, the interest rate has fluctuated since July 1, 1975 under amendments to IRC § 6621. Section 6621, as amended by the Economic Recovery Tax Act of 1981, provides that the interest rate on deficiencies and overpayments is 9% or such adjusted rate as may be established by the Secretary of the Treasury under the formula prescribed in § 6621(b). In essence, that formula allows the Secretary to adjust the interest rate on January 1 of each year to equal the "adjusted prime rate" charged by banks during the preceding September, if the adjusted prime rate for the preceding September is at least a full percentage point more or less than the tax interest rate which was then in effect.[t]

---

q. IRC § 6611(b)(1). The statute is written in terms of the payment of interest to the due date of the amount against which the credit is due.

r. If there had been an overpayment of the failure to pay penalty, the amount of the penalty, plus interest thereon, would also be refunded to the taxpayer.

s. IRC § 6621(a).

t. See IRC §§ 6621(b) and (c). Interest rates in effect over the years have been as follows:
Up to and including June 30, 1975...6%.
July 1, 1975 to January 31, 1976... 9%.
Feb. 1, 1976 to January 31, 1978... 7%.

Restricted Interest. There are special provisions in the tax law which limit or prohibit interest under certain conditions. These give rise to the term "restricted interest." The application of the many, sometimes overlapping, restricted interest rules is among the most complex tasks in the field of taxation. For extensive coverage of this subject see Rev.Proc, 60–17, supra.ᵘ By way of illustration, however, consider the restricted interest rules pertinent to net operating loss carrybacks:

> Assume a taxpayer has 1981 taxable income of $100,000, with a tax liability of $25,000 reported on a tax return filed March 15, 1982 and paid with the return. For 1984 the taxpayer had a $100,000 net loss reported on the return filed March 15, 1985. Under § 172(b) of the Code, the NOL is carried back 3 years, and would eliminate the tax liability for 1981. Hence, the taxpayer is entitled to a refund of the $25,-000 of 1981 income taxes timely paid on March 15, 1982.

Under normal rules, the taxpayer would receive interest from March 15, 1982 (the date of overpayment). However, the Code contains a special restricted interest rule which, in effect, provides that the right to the NOL deductions arose at the end of the year in which the operating loss occurred—in the example, at the end of 1984.ᵛ Therefore, in the example, interest on the $25,000 overpayment would commence running on December 31, 1984, rather than March 15, 1982.

MOTOR FUEL CARRIERS, INC. v. UNITED STATES

420 F.2d 702 (Ct.Cl.1970).

DAVIS, Judge.

We have to decide, on undisputed facts submitted by joint stipulation, a narrow but prickly issue emerging from the accumulated earnings tax imposed by § 531 of the Internal Revenue Code of 1954. Taxpayer, a Florida corporation, was assessed income tax deficiencies for 1958–1962, including accumulated earnings taxes. Within ten days of notice and demand by the Government, the company paid the entire amount of the tax alleged to be due, with interest from the return due date of the years in question. It then sued to recover the amount thus paid under § 531. Judgment for the Government for the entire amount was finally rendered in the spring of 1965. Thereafter, plaintiff made claim with the District Director of Internal Revenue for return of the interest paid on the accumulated earnings tax, $34,381.09. The theory was that this tax is a penalty or additional

Feb. 1, 1978 to January 31, 1980... 6%.
Feb. 1, 1980 to January 31, 1982... 12%.

u. As modified by Rev.Proc. 62–27, 1962–2 C.B. 495 and Rev.Proc. 65–20, 1965–2 C.B. 1003.

v. IRC § 6611(f)(1).

tax, interest upon which must be assessed under § 6601(f)(3),[2] prescribing that interest on assessable penalties or additions to the tax begins ten days after notice and demand. Upon failure of the District Director to allow the claim,[3] plaintiff filed suit for refund in this court.

The case presents two related questions: (1) Is the accumulated earnings tax an "assessable penalty, additional amount, or addition to the tax" within § 6601(f)(3); and (2) if the interest on the § 531 tax is not covered by § 6601(f)(3), what, for the purposes of § 6601(a), is the "last date prescribed for payment"? Since we find for the taxpayer on alternative grounds, we discuss both of these issues in the matrix of the accumulated earnings tax.

The accumulated earnings tax: [The court noted that the accumulated earnings tax (or penalty) is imposed on a corporation which is found to have accumulated its earnings beyond the reasonable needs of the business. The liability is not required to be reported on any tax return.]

Section 6601(f)(3): Section 6601(f)(3) (supra, note 2), headed "Interest on penalties, additional amounts, or additions to the tax", allows interest "in respect of any assessable penalty, additional amount, or addition to the tax" only if that sum is not paid within 10 days of notice and demand. Literally read, this section covers the accumulated earnings tax. That impost may or may not be a "penalty" within this section's coverage, but it can easily be characterized as an "additional amount" or an "addition to the tax." * * * [T]hat was how Congress expressly described it, in terms, until 1934 and, again, in the 1954 Code. In ordinary English, moreover, that is just what this tax appears to be—an addition to the regular income tax.

* * *

Given the breadth of the phrasing of § 6601(f)(3), we think that the proper way to interpret the provision is to seek the reason why —for this subsection, in contrast to other interest provisions—interest is allowed to run only after notice and demand, and not from an earlier time. It seems plain that the answer lies in the need, in these

2. "Except as otherwise provided in this title—

* * *

Interest shall be imposed under subsection (a) in respect of any assessable penalty, additional amount, or addition to the tax only if such assessable penalty, additional amount, or addition to the tax is not paid within 10 days from the date of notice and demand therefor, and in such case interest shall be imposed only for the period from the date of the notice and demand, to the date of payment."

[Sec. 6601(f)(3) was redesignated as § 6601(e)(3) by Sec. 7(b)(1) of P.L. 93–625, Jan. 3, 1975, effective July 1, 1975.]

3. The Government's position is that interest is controlled by § 6601(a) of the 1954 Code which, according to the Government, puts the interest back to the dates of the returns for the various taxable years. § 6601(a) speaks in terms of interest running from "the last date prescribed for payment" of the tax.

instances, for an administrative determination by the Service. The factor common to the chapter 68 items which § 6601(f)(3) admittedly covers is that a Service determination precedes the imposition of those penalties and additions. The taxpayer knows that he has to pay because the Service tells him so; these are not items which are treated as self-assessable or which the taxpayer is expected to remit before demand is made. In other words, we infer that § 6601(f)(3) covers those "extra" payments or sanctions which the taxpayer can properly wait for the Service to determine and to invoke, and which he need not himself include in his tax return.

As we have indicated, the accumulated earnings tax falls into this class of additional payments. A taxpayer can properly file its corporate return without paying any attention to this tax; in so doing it will not make any erroneous or false statement nor will it leave its return with any omission or gap. The taxpayer can then pay all the sums shown due on this accurate and complete return and still be held liable, later, for an amount of tax under § 531, as subsequently determined by the Service. The reason is, of course, that an administrative decision is the normal precondition. The situation is the same as with the sanctions for civil fraud, negligence, under-estimation of the estimated tax, and for failure to file a timely return—all of which require administrative determination and all of which defendant admits to be governed by § 6601(f)(3).

* * *

The Government stresses, in response, that this § 531 tax is part of the income tax—and has always been—and is to be collected in the same manner. But that is an insufficient reply since the additional amounts and penalties specified in chapter 68—to which § 6601(f)(3) admittedly applies—are also regarded as part of the tax and collected as such. * * *

We hold, therefore, that § 6601(f)(3) applies and that plaintiff, having paid its accumulated earnings tax within 10 days of demand, should not have been charged interest.

Section 6601(a): Even if § 6601(a) applies, as the Government contends, taxpayer is nevertheless entitled to recover. Under that section, interest accrues from the "last date prescribed for payment." § 6601(c) ʷ states that

> For purposes of this section the last date prescribed for payment of the tax shall be determined under chapter 62 [with the application of certain rules].

Chapter 62 "Time and Place for Paying Tax" §§ 6151–6166, details the time and place for payment. Since, as we have pointed out, the

---

w. Section 6601(c) was redesignated as § 6601(b) by section 7(b)(1) of P.L. 93–625, effective July 1, 1975.

accumulated earnings tax is not reportable on any return, but rather "result[s] from the initiative of the tax collector and not, as is more usual with other income taxes, from the initiative of the taxpayer", it follows that this tax becomes payable only upon notice and demand by the Internal Revenue Service. For that reason, the part of chapter 62 we deem applicable is § 6155, which states that:

> Upon receipt of notice and demand from the Secretary or his delegate, there shall be paid at the place and time stated in such notice the amount of any tax (including any interest, additional amounts, additions to tax, and assessable penalties) stated in such notice and demand.

Because § 6155 prescribes the last date for payment of the accumulated earnings tax, none of the subdivisions of subsection 6601(c), giving rules for determining the date prescribed for payment, is applicable. Under § 6601(a), accordingly, taxpayer is liable for interest on the unpaid § 531 levy only between the receipt of notice-and-demand and payment.

Taxpayer has made timely payment under either § 6601(a) or § 6601(f)(3), and it is entitled to recover that amount of its payment which represents the interest charged upon the assessed accumulated earnings tax. Judgment is entered for plaintiff to that effect. The amount of recovery will be determined under Rule 131(c).

*   *   *

Chapter V

CIVIL TAX LITIGATION

Scope Note: Chapter V discusses those factors which must be taken into account by the tax practitioner in making an intelligent decision as to the most favorable forum in which to litigate a civil tax dispute. Considered below are the subject matter jurisdiction, applicable precedent, trial and settlement procedures, burden of proof considerations and the jurisdictional prerequisites of each of the tax litigation forums. Collateral topics which frequently arise in civil tax litigation are also discussed, including: the application of the doctrines of res judicata and collateral estoppel, the suppression of evidence in civil tax controversies and the recovery of attorney's fees. Brief consideration is also given to the action for recovery of taxes paid based upon the theory of an account stated.

SECTION 1. TAXPAYERS' CHOICE OF FORUM

TAX COURT PRACTICE

Marvin J. Garbis, Allen L. Schwait
and Paula M. Junghans

IMPORTANCE OF FORUM SELECTION

Perhaps the greatest oddity of our system for the adjudication of tax disputes lies in the area of forum selection. For, in our system a taxpayer engaged in a tax dispute, subject to certain practical and legal restrictions, actually has the opportunity to select from among three different courts the forum which will determine the case. Each court has a different procedure, each provides judges of different backgrounds, and each may be governed by a different body of precedents. [A simplified diagram of the alternative procedures for civil tax litigation is set forth in Figure 8.]

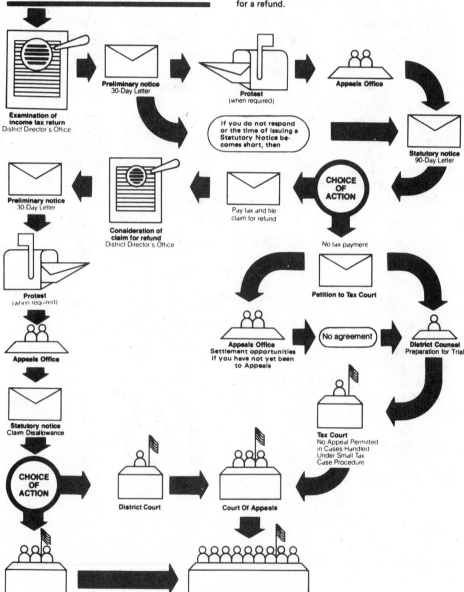

FIGURE 8.

Whether forum selection should exist in our system at all is, of course, highly debatable. Indeed, on occasion Congress reexamines the question with a view toward revising our entire tax litigation system. Nevertheless, now and in the foreseeable future, the taxpayer will continue to have three independent courts from which to choose. Accordingly, a taxpayer who does not take advantage of this choice would be remiss indeed:

"A recovery which results from the careful choice of a favorable court to decide the case may at first seem difficult to justify, but such pre-trial strategy is an everyday occurrence. In the tax area, (forum) shopping appears to be a natural consequence of the court system established by Congress * * *. The taxpayer's notorious exercise of this choice without objection suggests that it is not an accidental characteristic of the system." [1]

A startling lesson in the value of choosing the best court is provided by the case of the Sam Berger Investment Company, a partnership.

Several partners sold their respective interests in this partnership and sought capital gains treatment for their profits. The IRS claimed that ordinary income treatment was appropriate. Two partners chose the Tax Court to litigate their disputes while one selected the Court of Claims. Both courts concluded that the issue depended on whether certain land was held by the partnership for sale in the ordinary course of business. The two partners who litigated in the Tax Court received their decision first, the court concluding that the land was held for sale to customers in the ordinary course of business, so that the gain was taxable as ordinary income.[2] Three weeks later, the partner who chose the Court of Claims obtained a decision that the land was not held for sale in the ordinary course of business, so that the gain was capital gain.[3]

When still another partner took his case to the Court of Claims, that court could only shrug its judicial shoulders and say:

"Though unfortunate perhaps, the different tax consequences for [the previous partners] are the result of the * * * taxpayers having had their rights adjudicated in two different forums, each of which has the primary fact-finding responsibilities." [4]

The selection of the forum is the single most important decision which must be made in planning for the litigation of a tax case. In

1. "Mistake and Forum Shopping in Suits for Refund of Federal Tax," 114 Pa.L.Rev. 1244, 1248 (1966).

2. Freeland's Estate v. Commissioner, 35 P–H T.C. Mem. ¶ 66,283 aff'd 393 F.2d 573 (9th Cir. 1968).

3. Morse v. United States, 371 F.2d 474, 482 (Ct.Cl.1967).

4. Ginsburg v. United States, 396 F.2d 983, 986 (Ct.Cl.1968).

making the selection it is imperative to be familiar with the three tribunals available and their essential characteristics.

AVAILABLE FORUMS

A civil tax case may be heard in any one of three courts, the United States Tax Court, the United States Court of Claims, or the United States District Court. In determining, in a given case, which of the forums is best for the taxpayer, it is necessary to consider the specific characteristics and procedures in each of these courts as applied to the particular nature of the taxpayer's case. A great number of factors must be weighed and, in each instance, a judgment made —generally on all the factors together, as only rarely does one factor so predominate as to make the decision obvious or easy. As discussed more fully below, the considerations to take into account would include such matters as the presumed expertise of the particular court in tax matters, the availability of a jury trial, the extent of discovery proceedings, the location of trial proceedings, the settlement possibilities, the taxpayer's ability to pay the taxes in issue so as to be able to choose freely, and other factors as well. The starting point for the decision lies on a consideration of the basic characteristics of the tax tribunals and of the process of a tax case in these courts.

United States Tax Court

The United States Tax Court is a Washington based tribunal which hears only tax cases. The Tax Court's jurisdiction includes income, estate, gift, and excess profits taxes as well as certain excise tax matters arising under Chapter 42 of the Internal Revenue Code (pertaining to private foundations).

The Tax Court also has been given jurisdiction over declaratory judgment actions with regard to the initial or continuing qualification of certain retirement plans, the initial or continuing qualification of certain exempt organizations, the initial or continuing classification of certain private foundations, with regard to exchanges described in Section 367(a)(1) of the Internal Revenue Code, with regard to the status of certain governmental obligations, and with regard to certain public disclosure matters arising under the Code.

Created to provide a forum in which a taxpayer could contest tax liability *before payment*, the Tax Court is the only one of the three tax forums which does not make payment of the taxes in question a prerequisite to filing suit.

The Tax Court consists of [nineteen, prior to 1981 sixteen] judges who hear cases and motions in most of the major cities of the United States. Geographically, the Tax Court's jurisdiction is nationwide. Judges of the Tax Court hear only tax cases and thus are well versed in the complexities of the Internal Revenue Code. If the legal issue is highly technical and intricate, and the taxpayer wishes to have the matter decided by a court accustomed to wending its way through the labyrinthian maze of the tax law, the Tax Court is the forum in which to obtain consideration of the case by a tax specialist.

Although the Tax Court maintains its headquarters in Washington, individual judges travel at regularly scheduled intervals to most of the principal cities in the United States to hear tax dockets. Hence, the trial of the case is likely to be as geographically convenient in the Tax Court as it would be in the district court for the taxpayer's home district.

Trial by jury is not available in the Tax Court, and until the promulgation of the new Tax Court rules [in 1974], discovery was completely lacking in this court. The new rules now permit discovery by interrogatories directed to parties to the litigation, and requests for production. Discovery depositions are available in the Tax Court only to the extent the parties agree that a specific deposition may be taken. * * *

To the extent that a general statement may be made, it appears that the discovery provisions of the Tax Court Rules are being utilized with restraint in the vast majority of cases. Hence, the fear of some practitioners that there would be interrogatories (often burdensome) issued as a matter of course has not been realized * * *.

Trial procedure in the Tax Court is much the same as trial procedure in the district court in nonjury cases. Enforcement of the rules of evidence in the Tax Court sometimes is more lenient than in the district courts and in the Court of Claims. If the taxpayer's case rests on a piece of evidence the admissibility of which may be doubtful, the chances of "getting it in" before the Tax Court are better than elsewhere (although the Court of Claims may also be less than technical in this respect). Needless to say, if the taxpayer's case rests on keeping certain government evidence out, this may not be the best court.

The Tax Court is seldom in the public limelight. If the taxpayer has reason to be shy of a courtroom or of publicity, this may be the safest and quietest of the available tax forums. Indeed, the fact that, as a practical matter, a taxpayer, no matter where situated, can select a Washington trial in most instances adds to the ability to avoid publicity.

Unlike the district court and the Court of Claims, the Tax Court permits the representation by taxpayers of individuals who are not attorneys. Accountants and others can qualify to practice before the Tax Court by passing an examination. However, since nonlawyers, generally, have little experience in pretrial and trial procedures and tactics, motion practice, rules of evidence, and other requisites for adequate presentation of clients in court, it is usually in the client's best interest to retain an attorney experienced in tax matters.

The Commissioner of Internal Revenue is always the defendant (called the "respondent") in a Tax Court case. The Commissioner is represented by an attorney from the Office of [District] Counsel of the Internal Revenue Service.   *   *   *

[The settlement of Tax Court cases is within the exclusive jurisdiction of the Service's Appeals Office (if the case has not previously been considered by that office) for a period of four months. Thereafter, exclusive settlement jurisdiction lies with the Office of District Counsel (as the Chief Counsel's delegate). If the case has already undergone Appeals Office review, the Office of District Counsel has exclusive settlement jurisdiction from the outset.] [a]

The Tax Court's decisional process is unique. The Tax Court judge who hears a case will, after considering the evidence and submissions of the parties, write an opinion which is then referred to the Chief Judge for consideration. The Chief Judge either permits the trial judge's opinion to constitute the decision of the Tax Court or refers the case to the full court, which then decides the suit en banc (resulting in a decision "reviewed by the Court").

The losing party in this court has the right to appeal the decision to a United States Court of Appeals.

United States District Courts

The United States District Courts are the general trial courts of the federal judicial system. They are local courts. In contrast to the Tax Court and Court of Claims, which hear cases from all over the country, the district court's geographical scope is that of a single federal district, the size of no more than a single state. Therefore, one can expect the district court to be well aware of local conditions and circumstances that may bear upon a tax case. Similarly the local district judge, being close to the local business and professional community, may be in a better position to judge the credibility of local lay and expert witnesses than a judge or trial commissioner from Washington.

The district courts are bound by the decisions of the Supreme Court and of the court of appeals for the circuit in which the district is located.

The district court is the only tax trial court in which a jury trial is available, and thus, the only tax tribunal in which the facts of a case may be determined by the commonsense approach of a lay person.

In view of the number and diversity of federal district courts, one cannot speak accurately of an "attitude" toward tax cases on the part of the district judges. However, by and large, district judges are well-rounded lawyers and not tax specialists. In all districts, the

a. See Rev.Proc. 79–59, 1979–2 C.B. 573.

judges hear cases involving all fields of federal (and often state) law. Therefore, generally speaking, it is reasonable to expect a broader approach to a tax case heard in a district court than one heard in the Tax Court or even in the Court of Claims. In the district courts the technical niceties of the Internal Revenue Code are frequently tempered with a view toward practicality and equity, particularly in jury cases. On the other hand, the rules of evidence are most strictly construed in the district courts, especially in jury trials.

The district court handles tax refund litigation in much the same manner as any other civil action. Both parties have available to them all the extensive discovery tools found in the Federal Rules of Civil Procedure. There are occasions where these discovery provisions can be most helpful in the preparation of a tax case. However, it is important to note that the government can, and almost always does, use the discovery provisions fully. Therefore, the taxpayer will make ample pretrial disclosures in the district courts, and may be put to substantial expense to comply with the government's request for discovery. On the other hand, when it is needed, access to the government's evidence before trial is equally available to the taxpayer.

The proper defendant in a district court tax refund suit is the United States. Attorneys from the Tax Division of the Justice Department represent the government in district court tax refund cases, except in the Southern District of New York and in two California districts, where Assistant United States Attorneys handle tax cases. This fact may influence the choice of forum if settlement is desired. Tax Division attorneys are principally trial lawyers and their primary interest is litigation more often than taxes. Therefore, their approach to a case is likely to be the traditional one of the advocate: What are my chances of success in court? Moreover, neither they nor their agency has passed upon the case prior to litigation. A taxpayer who desires a compromise but has reached a stalemate at the administrative level, may have more luck at settling the case with the Tax Division in a refund suit than with * * * the Internal Revenue Service in a Tax Court case.

A factor that will influence the decision on where to litigate, but which will vary from district to district, is the length of time it will take the case to reach the trial list. In some larger cities the dockets in the district courts may be so clogged that years can pass before a case is reached. * * *

* * *

Insofar as comparative time is concerned, a district court tax refund case (in most districts) will probably reach decision faster than a Court of Claims tax suit. The specific comparison of speed of action can only be made, however, in the light of the situation in the particular district court under consideration.

Appeals from district court decisions in tax refund suits lie to the respective courts of appeals.

United States Court of Claims

The United States Court of Claims is a Washington based tribunal, which has jurisdiction to hear cases involving claims against the United States, including suits based upon claims for tax refunds. The Court of Claims has seven [active] judges, [two senior judges] and a staff of [seventeen] trial judges formerly called commissioners. The Court of Claims trial judges travel throughout the country to conduct proceedings at locations convenient for the parties and witnesses. The trial judge assigned to a case decides motions, takes evidence, holds conferences, reads the parties' trial briefs and hears arguments. At the conclusion of the trial, the trial judge writes an opinion containing recommended findings of fact and conclusions of law. The parties are permitted at this time to submit briefs and arguments to the judges of the Court of Claims in what is, in effect, an appeal from the decision by the trial judge. This unique trial procedure, which incorporates the elements of a trial and an appellate proceeding in one forum, is one of the unusual features of the Court of Claims.[b]

*   *   *

Another noteworthy aspect of trial procedures in the Court of Claims, made possible by the extensive use of trial judges, is the amount of attention which can be paid to the convenience of the parties and the witnesses. The trial judge sometimes will hear evidence at several locations if the circumstances warrant such action. Moreover, where appropriate, the trial judge may schedule several trial sessions in the same case, permitting a significant interval between witnesses. In the Tax Court or in a district court the trial of a case is much more likely to be continuous. In a complex case the spacing of witnesses can afford essentially needed time for reflection and further preparation during the course of a trial. In addition, where the transportation of widely scattered witnesses to one trial location at one given time can present serious logistic problems, Court of Claims procedures can ease the way. Since the trial judge will travel to a location convenient for the witnesses, testimony which otherwise might have to be presented through an evidentiary deposition can often be given by the witness in person.

b. It is possible that the Court of Claims will be restructured in the 1980's by virtue of a merger with the Court of Customs and Patent Appeals and the transfer of trial level jurisdiction to a separate claims court. This restructuring would formally divide the present trial and appellate procedures in tax refund suits between two separate courts rather than between the two levels of the present Court of Claims. However, the essential characteristics of the Court of Claims as a forum for tax refund litigation are not likely to change.

The Court of Claims considers itself bound only by its own precedents and the decisions of the Supreme Court of the United States.

Tax refund suits account for approximately one-third of the docket in the Court of Claims. Therefore, although this court clearly is considerably less specialized than the Tax Court, its judges and trial commissioners may be presumed to have more expertise in the tax field than can the average district judge.

Discovery is available in the Court of Claims almost as extensively as in the district courts. In addition attorneys from the Tax Division of the Justice Department, with their traditional penchant for taking the greatest possible advantage of discovery techniques, are the government's advocates before the Court of Claims. So, with reference to discovery—in both its favorable and unfavorable aspects —the Court of Claims can be said to be the approximate equivalent of the district courts. As in district courts, the defendant in a Court of Claims tax refund action is the United States.

Unlike the district court, however, the Court of Claims does not afford a local forum for the taxpayer, despite the fact that the trial may be held in the taxpayer's home city. The trial judge and the judges are based in Washington and cannot be as familiar with local conditions as a district judge. In addition, there is no trial by jury in the Court of Claims, and hence, no opportunity for a factual decision by the taxpayer's peers.

Speaking broadly, the Court of Claims tends to be more liberal in admitting evidence than the district courts. And many practitioners in the Court of Claims divine a more liberal attitude toward the law in this forum than in the Tax Court. Therefore, it is believed by some that the Court of Claims has a tendency to disregard technical rules and evidentiary restrictions to reach a result based on the equities of a case. But generalities regarding the "attitude" of the Court of Claims, although frequently expressed, are unreliable indicators of the probable outcome of a given case.

Two additional facets of litigation in the Court of Claims should be included in the decision of where to sue. First, the more complicated trial procedure of this court makes an action in the Court of Claims somewhat more expensive than an action either in the Tax Court or in the district court. Second, review of a decision by the Court of Claims is only available upon a writ of certiorari to the Supreme Court, which is very rarely granted. This second aspect of litigation in the Court of Claims means that for planning purposes any decision by this court can be considered virtually free from further review. The relative unavailability of appeal from a decision by the Court of Claims may act as a deterrent from commencing a doubtful case there; on the other hand, it helps to eliminate the difference in the cost of an action in the three forums. The cost of a trial in the

Tax Court or in a district court plus the cost of an appeal will be just as great as—if not more than—the cost of bringing a refund action in the Court of Claims. In addition, many Court of Claims practitioners feel that a dual hearing of the case permits a more thorough presentation by the parties and a more careful consideration by the court.

LEGAL RESTRICTIONS ON CHOICE OF FORUM

Not every tax case necessarily provides the taxpayer with a choice among all three tax tribunals. The courts have jurisdictional requirements that can legally, and practically, narrow the selection available in a given case.

In the first place, the Tax Court, as noted previously, has jurisdiction only over income, estate, gift, and excess profits taxes, and excise taxes arising under Chapter 42 of the Code. Therefore, in a controversy involving any other type of tax, e. g., ordinary excise taxes or employer's taxes, this forum is not available. In addition, the Tax Court's jurisdiction begins only after the Commissioner has determined that a deficiency exists and has issued a statutory deficiency notice. Therefore, the Tax Court is unavailable in cases arising from the taxpayer's discovery of a right to a refund, e. g., where the taxpayer erred in the government's favor on a tax return. A third limitation on suits in the Tax Court is the jurisdictional prerequisite of a timely petition. A taxpayer who misses the court's deadline for filing the petition has no choice but to pay the tax assessed and to seek a refund.

The Court of Claims and the United States District Courts have jurisdiction over suits for refund of all internal revenue taxes. Therefore, regardless of the type of tax in question, the refund forums are available. However, as a practical matter, a taxpayer may not be able to use either of these forums, since a refund suit must be preceded by the full payment of the tax alleged by the IRS to be due with respect to a full taxable period. In the case of annual taxes, such as income taxes, this can be burdensome and can, as a practical matter, bar the taxpayer from a refund suit.

Exclusive jurisdiction has been given the United States Tax Court with regard to certain types of declaratory judgment actions involving tax matters. [For example,] it is only the Tax Court which may hear declaratory judgment actions with regard to the initial or continuing qualification of retirement plans, with regard to the reasonablness of the Commissioner of Internal Revenue's determinations with regard to Section 367(a)(1) exchanges, and with regard to the status of certain governmental obligations. However, concurrent jurisdiction has been given to each of the tax forums [with regard to certain other types of declaratory judgment actions.] c

c. See pages 303–305, below.

ABILITY TO PAY AS A FACTOR IN FORUM SELECTION

Unfortunately, the financial condition of the taxpayer can become an important aspect of forum selection. The jurisdictional prerequisites for a tax refund suit (in a district court or the Court of Claims) require that the taxpayer make full payment of the deficiency asserted for each taxable year (in the case of income and gift taxes) or for each taxable estate (in the case of estate taxes) in which there is a dispute before bringing an action in these courts. Some taxpayers will simply be unable to raise the money needed to make the required payments and will be forced to litigate in the Tax Court. Others, although theoretically able to make the payment, may feel that the difficulty of payment makes the Tax Court, with its "free admission," a more desirable forum. Still other taxpayers may feel that, all things being equal, they would prefer to go to the Tax Court and use the money during the interim for other purposes, paying interest on any deficiency that may be determined. * * *

Obviously, it is inequitable to have a procedure whereby the doors of certain courts are open to those who have the financial resources to pay their putative tax liability in advance while closed to those who cannot raise the money required. This aberration in our system is indefensible. Yet, it exists, and until the day when our tax litigation system is given its long needed overall revision, the full payment rule will be with us.

* * *

Effect of Payment on Interest

A taxpayer who desires to pay the tax assessed and thereby stop the running of interest is not compelled to litigate in one of the refund forums. Payment of the deficiency after the filing of a petition in the Tax Court will not deprive that court of jurisdiction.

The taxpayer who elects to pay the tax and sue for a refund in either a district court or the Court of Claims, or who elects to pay the deficiency after filing a Tax Court petition, normally will be entitled to receive interest on account of tax, penalty, and assessed (paid) interest ultimately refunded as a result of a compromise or a judicial determination. * * *

PRECEDENTS

Legal Issues

The most significant single factor in selecting the forum for a tax case is a determination of which tribunal will be governed by the most favorable body of precedents. This can be resolved only after thorough research of the cases decided in the three trial forums as well as in the U.S. Courts of Appeals and the Supreme Court, with an understanding of the precedents deemed binding by the respective tax trial courts.

Of course, where the Supreme Court has spoken on a particular issue, all courts are bound to treat the decision as "the law of the land."

The Court of Claims considers itself bound to follow its own decisions and those of the Supreme Court, but, because it is a court of national scope, it does not follow decisions of the courts of appeals. Thus, appellate decisions have far less influence in this forum than specific precedents or discernible trends in the decisions of the Court of Claims itself.

The district courts are bound by precedents in the court of appeals for the circuit in which they are located as well as by decisions of the Supreme Court. Furthermore, there is a tendency for district courts to give somewhat greater weight to a decision from a court of appeals of a different circuit than to a decision of the Court of Claims.

In determining which precedents to consider binding, the Tax Court has had the difficult task of reconciling its role as a national tribunal with the practical fact that its decisions are subject to review by the courts of appeals in the various circuits. The Tax Court initially rejected the idea that it was bound by the decisions of the courts of appeals, but this led to certain jurisdictional problems. For example, it was possible for two taxpayers in different circuits, with cases involving identical issues, to appeal identical Tax Court decisions to the courts of appeals in their respective circuits—and to end up with completely opposite results if their circuits held opposing views. For this reason, the Tax Court in 1970, changed its position and agreed to follow decisions of the appellate circuit to which an appeal would lie.[9] By so doing, the Tax Court has eliminated the possibility of unnecessary appeals in those cases where the Tax Court disagrees with the view of the law pronounced by the Court of Appeals to which venue for an appeal would lie.

However, it is still possible for two taxpayers, in identical cases, to receive inconsistent results from the same tribunal by virtue of appellate venue. For example, note the identical cases of Kenneth W. Doehring [9a] and Paul E. Puckett,[9b] in which interest income from the same loan company was deemed passive investment income as to Puckett (Fifth Circuit appellate venue) but not as to Doehring (Eighth Circuit appellate venue). These inconsistent decisions are an inevitable consequence of our regional appellate system and would, presumably, have occurred if each taxpayer had proceeded in his

9. Jack E. Golsen, 54 T.C. 742 (1970). The Tax Court will not, however, consider itself bound to follow actions of the court of appellate venue which do not have precedential value. Paul Ruegsegger, 68 T.C. 463 (1977) (affirmance of a prior case in open court without opinion not a precedent in Second Circuit and not binding on Tax Court).

9a. T.C. Memo. 1974–234, rev'd 527 F. 2d 945 (8th Cir. 1975).

9b. T.C. Memo. 1974–235, aff'd 522 F. 2d 1385 (5th Cir. 1975).

home federal district court. However, had they both proceeded in the Court of Claims, then by virtue of their both being before the same court and subject to the same precedents, consistent results would have been obtained.

In summary, therefore, the following guidelines should be kept in mind:

(a) If the taxpayer's home circuit has spoken on an issue, then, at least as to that issue, both the Tax Court and the district courts will apply the law as pronounced by that circuit.

(b) If the taxpayer's home circuit has decided an issue one way and the Court of Claims has reached a contrary result, the Court of Claims will follow its own precedents, and not the precedents of the court of appeals.

(c) If the taxpayer's home circuit has not ruled on the issue involved, then the Tax Court will be guided by its own precedents, the Court of Claims (as always) will follow its previous decisions, but the district courts will tend to give the heaviest weight to decisions in other circuits.

Factual Issues

In tax law as in any other area of the law, the application of legal principles often turns upon the resolution of factual questions. The existence of three different trial-level tribunals in the tax field provides the taxpayer an opportunity to choose the forum with the most sympathetic attitude toward the facts of his or her individual case. The three courts have a history of treating certain factual questions differently. An example may help to illustrate this phenomenon.

A corporate employer not infrequently will make a payment to the widow of a deceased employee shortly after the death of the employee. The employer usually treats such payments as compensation, claiming a deduction on its tax return. The widow almost always treats the payment as a gift and pays no income tax on it. The Internal Revenue Service regularly makes the claim that "widow payments" must be treated as compensation by the recipient.

The answer to the question posed by the so-called "widow payment" cases—Is the payment compensation or gift?—is a matter of fact which must be determined on a case-by-case basis.[10] Tax Court decisions on this question consistently have found that such payments constituted compensation. District court results have been more even-handed. This difference in viewing the facts makes the most favorable forum in a widow-payment case obvious. Trends often can be discerned with reference to other factual matters, and the taxpay-

---

10. E. g. Commissioner v. Duberstein, 363 U.S. 278, 80 S.Ct. 1190, 4 L.Ed.2d 1218 (1960).

er's representative should take full advantage of these tendencies in choosing the forum for litigation.

Statistical Results

A word of caution should be added at this point. When examining the case law for factual and legal precedents, the taxpayer's representative should be guided by results in individual fact situations. The Attorney General and the Commissioner of Internal Revenue publish annual reports containing statistical analyses of the overall results of tax cases litigated in the three tax tribunals. Impressive though these statistics may be, they are of no importance in the taxpayer's selection of a forum for litigation. General figures cannot give a very precise answer to the way a given court will decide a given issue. Careful study of the precedents is a much more reliable index of a particular court's point of view for the purpose of choice of forum. It is far better to consider the treatment by the respective forums of cases similar to the taxpayer's case than to be concerned with overall percentages of government "wins" or "losses," as the terms may be defined for government statistical reporting purposes.

Where there is a significant difference in the state of the precedents in the tax forums, the taxpayer's choice of forum should be largely governed by this factor. Where the precedential differences are not compelling, other factors must be weighed.

GOVERNMENT'S POWER TO ASSERT NEW ISSUES

One hazard of litigating a tax dispute is the possibility that the Internal Revenue Service will, at some point, assert issues in addition to those presented at the administrative level. The taxpayer's choice of forum has a very definite effect upon the IRS's ability to assert tax deficiencies during the course of litigation.

The basic principles are relatively simple. Filing a Tax Court petition suspends the running of the statute of limitations on assessments for the duration of the litigation and for sixty days thereafter.[12] Therefore, a taxpayer who proceeds to the Tax Court is vulnerable to an additional deficiency (over and above that proposed by the deficiency notice) if the IRS should raise the new issues in the course of litigation. While the IRS must sustain the burden of proof on these issues, this burden is often surmountable. An illustration of the effect of this principle of law is provided by the *Raskob* case [13] in which the taxpayer decided to litigate a $16,000 deficiency. The government raised a new issue and was sustained. The result was a final deficiency in the amount of $1,026,000.

---

12. I.R.C. § 6503(a).

13. John J. Raskob, 37 B.T.A. 1283 (1938), aff'd sub nom. Dupont v.

Commissioner, 118 F.2d 544 (3d Cir.), cert. denied, 314 U.S. 623, 62 S.Ct. 79, 86 L.Ed. 501 (1941).

The statute of limitations is not suspended by suit in a refund forum, and the government cannot assess any deficiency more than three years after the filing of the relevant tax return, unless the assessment is for fraud or one of the other events which extends the normal limitations period. Since the taxpayer almost always can delay the commencement of a refund suit until after the expiration of the limitations period on assessments, this shield is normally available to any taxpayer in the refund forums. The government, of course, can raise new issues in tax refund suits. However, if the statute of limitations on assessments has run, these new issues may only be used to offset the taxpayer's eventual recovery.[14] The new (postlimitations) issues cannot result in a net recovery for the government against the taxpayer. If the taxpayer in *Raskob,* had taken advantage of this feature of refund litigation, he could not have lost more than the original $16,000 assessment. As the case turned out, his error in choosing a forum was a million dollar mistake.

SECTION 2.   BURDEN OF PROOF IN CIVIL TAX LITIGATION

LEWIS v. REYNOLDS

Supreme Court of the United States, 1932.
284 U.S. 281, 52 S.Ct. 145, 76 L.Ed. 293.

Mr. Justice McREYNOLDS delivered the opinion of the Court.

*   *   *

" *   *   * [T]he ultimate question presented for decision, upon a claim for refund, is whether the taxpayer has overpaid his tax. This involves a redetermination of the entire tax liability. While no new assessment can be made, after the bar of the statute has fallen, the taxpayer, nevertheless, is not entitled to a refund unless he has overpaid his tax. The action to recover on a claim for refund is in the nature of an action for money had and received and it is incumbent upon the claimant to show that the United States has money which belongs to him."

*   *   *

While the statutes authorizing refunds do not specifically empower the Commissioner to reaudit a return whenever repayment is claimed, authority therefor is necessarily implied. An overpayment must appear before refund is authorized. Although the statute of limitations may have barred the assessment and collection of any additional sum, it does not obliterate the right of the United States to

14.   Lewis v. Reynolds, 284 U.S. 281,
52 S.Ct. 145, 76 L.Ed. 293 (1932),
aff'g 48 F.2d 515 (10th Cir. 1931).

retain payments already received when they do not exceed the amount which might have been properly assessed and demanded.

* * *

HELVERING v. TAYLOR

Supreme Court of the United States, 1935.
293 U.S. 507, 55 S.Ct. 287, 79 L.Ed. 623.

Mr. Justice BUTLER delivered the opinion of the Court.

The Commissioner determined a deficiency of $9,156.69 on account of respondent's 1928 income tax. The Board of Tax Appeals [d] made the same determination. The court [of appeals] held it excessive and that the evidence did not show the correct amount, reversed the order of the Board, and remanded the case for further proceedings in accordance with the opinion. The petition for our writ states the question: "Whether the Circuit Court of Appeals erred in remanding this case to the Board of Tax Appeals for a new hearing on the ground that the Commissioner's determination of the amount of income was incorrect, although the taxpayer had failed to prove facts from which a correct determination could be made."

[The factual dispute involved the proper allocation of basis between the taxpayer's holdings of preferred and common stock, and the gain subsequently recognized upon the sale of the preferred shares. |

* * *

The only question for consideration is that stated in the petition for the writ of certiorari. That question in effect assumes, and here it is taken as granted, that the court rightly held the evidence sufficient to require a finding that the Commissioner's apportionment of total cost as between preferred and common stock was unfair and erroneous and that therefore the Commissioner's determination was excessive. We also assume that the total purchase price is susceptible of fair apportionment and that upon another hearing the correct amount may be found. The point to be considered is whether, the taxpayer having failed to establish the correct amount to be assigned to the preferred stock as its costs to him, the court erred in reversing and remanding for further proceedings in accordance with its opinion.

The Commissioner does not contend that, in cases where Circuit Courts of Appeals properly reverse determinations of the Board, they are without power to remand for further hearing in the nature of a new trial. His contention is that in this case the burden on the taxpayer was not only to prove that the Commissioner's determination is erroneous, but to show the correct amount of the tax. In substance

d. Now called the Tax Court.

he says that, because of the taxpayer's failure to establish facts on which a fair apportionment may be made, the Board's redetermination at the Commissioner's erroneous figure was valid, and, there being no error of law, should have been sustained by the court. And he maintains that, in the absence of error on the part of the Board, the court was without power to remand for further hearing.

* * *

The Commissioner cites United States v. Anderson, 269 U.S. 422, 443, 46 S.Ct. 131, 70 L.Ed. 347; [and] Reinecke v. Spalding, 280 U.S. 227, 232, 233, 50 S.Ct. 96, 74 L.Ed. 385. * * * Each was an action to recover taxes paid. Obviously the burden was on the plaintiff, in order to establish a basis for judgment in his favor, specifically to show not merely that the assessment was erroneous, but also the amount to which he was entitled. For like reason the burden is upon the taxpayer to establish the amount of a deduction claimed.

We find nothing in the statutes, the rules of the Board or our decisions that gives any support to the idea that the Commissioner's determination shown to be without rational foundation and excessive will be enforced unless the taxpayer proves he owes nothing or, if liable at all, shows the correct amount. * * *

Unquestionably the burden of proof is on the taxpayer to show that the Commissioner's determination is invalid. Frequently, if not quite generally, evidence adequate to overthrow the Commissioner's finding is also sufficient to show the correct amount, if any, that is due. But, where as in this case, the taxpayer's evidence shows the Commissioner's determination to be arbitrary and excessive, it may not reasonably be held that he is bound to pay a tax that confessedly he does not owe, unless his evidence was sufficient also to establish the correct amount that lawfully might be charged against him. On the facts shown by the taxpayer in this case, the Board should have held the apportionment arbitrary and the Commissioner's determination invalid. Then, upon appropriate application that further hearing be had, it should have heard evidence to show whether a fair apportionment might be made and, if so, the correct amount of the tax. The rule for which the Commissioner here contends is not consonant with the great remedial purposes of the legislation creating the Board of Tax Appeals. The Circuit Court of Appeals rightly reversed and remanded the case for further proceedings in accordance with its opinion.

Affirmed.

COMPTON v. UNITED STATES

334 F.2d 212 (4th Cir. 1964).

BOREMAN, Circuit Judge.

Plaintiff, Nannie V. Compton, brought this action seeking a refund of $194.19 alleged to have been illegally assessed and collected as federal taxes. She joined with her claim for refund prayers for certain injunctive relief and for abatement of the balance of a $75,167.39 assessment for taxes and penalties alleged to have been unlawfully made. From the judgment of the District Court dismissing the action on the merits she appeals.

The relevant facts are not in controversy. On October 21, 1957, members of the Arlington County Police Department, armed with a search warrant, entered and searched the premises of the plaintiff in Arlington, Virginia. Indicia of gambling or wagering operations, including adding machines, tapes, numbers slips and a large amount of cash, were seized. Plaintiff and one Joseph A. Chase were arrested and charged with violating Virginia's lottery laws. On November 7, 1957, plaintiff and Chase entered separate pleas of guilty in the County Court of Arlington County, Virginia, to charges of operating a lottery and possessing lottery slips. Plaintiff was given a suspended sentence of nine months and placed on probation for a period of five years. Subsequently, Chase was prosecuted on charges of failure to file federal gambing excise tax returns and failure to purchase a wagering tax stamp as required by law. He was convicted in the District Court but, on appeal on Government's motion, the judgment of conviction was reversed and the cause remanded, the Government conceding before this court that the warrant under which plaintiff's home was searched and the property seized was invalid, and that the evidence upon which Chase had been convicted was obtained in violation of the constitutional protection against unreasonable search and seizure. That prosecution was subsequently dismissed in the District Court on Government's motion.

Prior to the criminal proceedings mentioned above, agents of the Internal Revenue Department, having learned from newspapers of the raid, were permitted by the police to inspect the seized property. From information gained through their inspection and from helpful and revealing discussions with the Arlington police, the agents estimated the gross receipts of the lottery business. On the basis of these estimates the District Director, pursuant to 26 U.S.C.A. § 6862, made a joint jeopardy assessment of excise and occupational taxes owed by plaintiff and Chase which, together with penalties and interest, totaled $75,167.39. * * * In an effort to collect the assessment, the District Director filed liens against property of the plaintiff, including her automobile and her home, and levied upon a bank account in plaintiff's name. The balance in the bank account, $194.-19, was paid by the bank to the District Director and credited to the total joint assessments against plaintiff and Chase.

In her complaint plaintiff alleged that at no time had she engaged in the State of Virginia in any of the activities that would require her to file a return of wagering taxes or to "apply for an occupational stamp to accept wagers." * * * Before the District Court, plaintiff testified that she had never been engaged in the business of accepting wagers or operating a lottery and contended that, in any event, the assessment, being based upon illegally seized evidence, was void. The District Court held that she had not sustained the burden of showing that she was entitled to the relief requested and dismissed her action on the merits. We think the decision of the District Court should be affirmed.

* * *

We turn first to plaintiff's contention that illegally seized evidence is inadmissible in federal tax proceedings. Plaintiff makes this argument as an abstract proposition of law without in any manner demonstrating that unlawfully obtained evidence was introduced in the District Court. In fact, no physical or tangible evidence obtained as a result of the illegal search was introduced by the Government. The only evidence introduced by the Government which could possibly be deemed a product of the unlawful search was offered for the purpose of impeachment only and * * * we think the evidence was properly admitted for that purpose. Obviously the thrust of plaintiff's argument here, as in the court below, is that the assessment itself is invalid because it was based on illegally obtained evidence. Apparently she seeks to press that issue by broadly insisting that illegally obtained evidence is inadmissible in a civil proceeding. At trial, plaintiff introduced the testimony of three agents of the Internal Revenue Department to show the manner in which the assessment was made. From their testimony, it is clear that the assessment was based almost entirely upon the fruits of the illegal search but that fact is not decisive of the issues here. The difficulty with plaintiff's position is that she apparently misconceives the burden of proof imposed upon her and which she must sustain in order to establish her claim of entitlement to a refund.

It is a well established principle that in every case, whether in a proceeding in the Tax Court to contest a deficiency assessment or in a District Court in a suit for refund, the assessment of the Commissioner is presumed to be correct. To be sure, this presumption is not evidence in itself and may be rebutted by competent evidence. It operates merely to place upon the opposing party the burden of going forward with the evidence. However, to prevail in an action for refund, the taxpayer must not only overcome this presumption but must assume and discharge the added burden of demonstrating the correct amount of the tax due or that he owes no tax at all. See Helvering v. Taylor, 293 U.S. 507, 55 S.Ct. 287, 79 L.Ed. 623 (1935).

An action for refund of taxes paid is in the nature of an action of assumpsit for money had and received and the plaintiff's right to recover must be measured by equitable standards. Here, taxpayer's entire liability is at issue and if, under any state of facts, the Government is entitled to the money claimed, she cannot prevail. Consequently, it is not enough merely to show that the assessment was invalid or that the Commissioner erred; the plaintiff must go further and produce evidence from which another and proper determination can be made. The extent of the taxpayer's burden in a refund action was aptly stated by Judge Learned Hand in Taylor v. Commissioner, 70 F.2d 619, 620 (2 Cir. 1934), aff'd sub. nom. [Helvering v. Taylor,] 293 U.S. 507, 55 S.Ct. 287, 79 L.Ed. 623 (1935):

> "* * * If the burden of proof goes so far as to demand not only that the taxpayer show that the deficiency assessed against him is wrong, but what is the proper deficiency, or that there should be none at all, the decision was right, even though we know that the tax is too high. In an action to recover taxes unlawfully collected the burden does go so far. * * * But the reason for this is obvious; a plaintiff, seeking an affirmative judgment measured in dollars, must prove how much is due. His claim is for money paid and he must show that every dollar he recovers is unjustly withheld. So it is not enough merely to prove that the tax as a whole was unlawful; some of the dollars he paid may nevertheless have been due. * * *"

To put it another way, the ultimate question in a suit for refund is not whether the Government was wrong, but whether the plaintiff can establish that taxes were in fact overpaid. The plaintiff, to prevail, must establish the exact amount which she is entitled to recover.

* * *

* * * The burden was on the plaintiff to prove that she was not engaged in accepting wagers during the period in question and the [admission of the illegally seized] evidence, offered only to impeach her testimony, was proper. Also, in view of our conclusions with respect to plaintiff's burden of proof, we need not decide whether the assessment was vitiated by the manner in which it was achieved. Even assuming that the assessment was thereby rendered invalid, plaintiff could not recover without a further showing that she did not in fact owe all or some part of the amount collected. Her attempt to do so failed when the District Court rejected her testimony that she had not been engaged in the numbers business during the period in question. Her proof clearly fell short of meeting her obligation to show that she, in fact, owed *no* tax and that the money collected by the Government was unjustly withheld.

Two cases, United States v. Harris, 216 F.2d 690 (5 Cir. 1954), and Roybark v. United States, 218 F.2d 164 (9 Cir. 1954), illustrate the proper application of the burden of proof rule. In *Harris*, the plaintiff was an automobile dealer against whom the Commissioner had made a deficiency assessment based upon his disallowance of claimed deductions for purchase prices of automobiles in excess of the legal ceiling. The plaintiff paid the assessment and brought suit in the District Court for refund. In its answer the Government admitted that the original assessment was erroneously based on the theory, subsequently discredited, that amounts paid in excess of lawful ceiling prices could not be deducted, but denied generally that the overceiling prices had actually been paid. The District Court granted summary judgment for the plaintiff and the Government appealed. The Court of Appeals for the Fifth Circuit reversed, emphasizing that in an action for refund the burden is on the taxpayer to establish that the tax he paid was not in fact due. Thus, even though the assessment was based on an erroneous conclusion of law, the plaintiff was required to prove that above legal ceiling prices had actually been paid and that plaintiff did not owe the money which had been paid to the Government.

Roybark v. United States, supra, involved facts almost identical to those in *Harris*. The Court of Appeals for the Ninth Circuit similarly held that, although the tax had been assessed under an erroneous view of the law, the plaintiffs had the burden, which they had not met, of establishing facts from which a proper determination could be made.

* * *

For the reasons stated above, the decision of the District Court is

Affirmed.

UNITED STATES v. JANIS

Supreme Court of the United States, 1976.
428 U.S. 433, 96 S.Ct. 3021, 49 L.Ed.2d 1046.

Mr. Justice BLACKMUN delivered the opinion of the Court.

[In this case there was an unconstitutional seizure of evidence upon which an assessment of wagering excise taxes was based. The taxpayer effected a partial payment on the assessment and brought a refund suit in which the government filed a counterclaim for the unpaid balance of the assessment. The following discussion of burden of proof considerations arose in the context of a decision as to the applicability of the exclusionary rule to civil tax litigation. See pages 363–366, below, for the exclusionary rule aspect of the *Janis* case.]

* * *

Some initial observations about the procedural posture of the case in the District Court are indicated. If there is to be no limit to the burden of proof the respondent, as "taxpayer," must carry, then, even though he were to obtain a favorable decision on the inadmissibility-of-evidence issue, the respondent on this record could not possibly defeat the Government's counterclaim. The Government notes, properly we think, that the litigation is composed of two separate elements: the refund suit instituted by the respondent, and the collection suit instituted by the United States through its counterclaim. In a refund suit the taxpayer bears the burden of proving the amount he is entitled to recover. Lewis v. Reynolds, 284 U.S. 281, 52 S.Ct. 145, 76 L.Ed. 293 (1932). It is not enough for him to demonstrate that the assessment of the tax for which refund is sought was erroneous in some respects.

This Court has not spoken with respect to the burden of proof in a tax collection suit. The Government argues here that the presumption of correctness that attaches to the assessment in a refund suit must also apply in a civil collection suit instituted by the United States under the authority granted by §§ 7401 and 7403 of the Code. Thus, it is said, the defendant in a collection suit has the same burden of proving that he paid the correct amount of his tax liability.

The policy behind the presumption of correctness and the burden of proof, see Bull v. United States, 295 U.S. 247, 259–260, 55 S.Ct. 695, 699–700, 79 L.Ed. 1421 (1935), would appear to be applicable in each situation. It accords, furthermore, with the burden-of-proof rule which prevails in the usual preassessment proceeding in the United States Tax Court. In any event, for purposes of this case, we assume that this is so and that the burden of proof may be said technically to rest with respondent Janis.

Respondent, however, submitted no evidence tending either to demonstrate that the assessment was incorrect or to show the correct amount of wagering tax liability, if any, on his part. In the usual situation one might well argue, as the Government does, that the District Court then could not properly grant judgment for the respondent on either aspect of the suit. But the present case may well not be the usual situation. What we have is a "naked" assessment without *any* foundation whatsoever if what was seized by the Los Angeles police cannot be used in the formulation of the assessment. The determination of tax due then may be one "without rational foundation and excessive," and not properly subject to the usual rule with respect to the burden of proof in tax cases. Helvering v. Taylor, 293 U.S. 507, 514–515, 55 S.Ct. 287, 290–291, 79 L.Ed. 623 (1935).[8] See 9 J. Mertens, Law of Federal Income Taxation § 50.65 (1971).

There appears, indeed, to be some debate among the Federal Courts of Appeals, in different factual contexts, as to the effect upon the burden of proof in a tax case when there is positive evidence that an assessment is incorrect. Some courts indicate that the burden of showing the amount of the deficiency then shifts to the Commissioner. Others hold that the burden of showing the correct amount of the tax remains with the taxpayer. However that may be, the debate does not extend to the situation where the assessment is shown to be naked and without *any* foundation. The courts then appear to apply the rule of the *Taylor* case. See Pizzarello v. United States,

---

8. *Taylor,* although decided more than 40 years ago, has never been cited by this Court on the burden-of-proof issue. The Courts of Appeals, the Court of Claims, the Tax Court, and the Federal District Courts, however, frequently have referred to that aspect of the case.

408 F.2d 579 (CA2), cert. denied, 396 U.S. 986, 90 S.Ct. 481, 24 L. Ed.2d 450 (1969); Suarez v. Commissioner of Internal Revenue, 58 T.C. 792, 814–815 (1972). But cf. Compton v. United States, 334 F. 2d 212, 216 (CA4 1964).

Certainly, proof that an assessment is utterly without foundation is proof that it is arbitrary and erroneous. For purposes of this case, we need not go so far as to accept the Government's argument that the exclusion of the evidence in issue here is insufficient to require judgment for the respondent or even to shift the burden to the Government. We are willing to assume that if the District Court was correct in ruling that the evidence seized by the Los Angeles police may not be used in formulating the assessment (on which both the levy and the counterclaim were based), then the District Court was also correct in granting judgment for Janis in both aspects of the present suit. * * *

* * *

SECTION 3.   TAX COURT LITIGATION

A.   JURISDICTIONAL PREREQUISITES

TAX COURT PRACTICE

Marvin J. Garbis, Allen L. Schwait and Paula M. Junghans

STATUTORY SOURCE OF JURISDICTION

The United States Tax Court was created by Congress with one purpose only: To resolve certain controversies between the Internal Revenue Service and taxpayers with regard to the payment of particular classes of tax.[1] The Tax Court is not a common law court. Its subject matter jurisdiction is limited to the interpretation of the Internal Revenue Code's provisions on income tax, estate and gift taxes, and certain taxes imposed by Chapter 42 of the Internal Revenue Code upon foundations and foundation managers who attempt to use tax-exempt funds for non-tax-exempt purposes.[2] The Tax Court's specific jurisdictional prerequisites have been created by statute.

Before the adoption of the 1969 Tax Reform Act the Tax Court had been in an anomolous position. As stated by then Chief Judge Drennen,[3] "[a]lthough the Tax Court has been considered *de facto* a court for many years, it is technically constituted as 'an independent agency in the Executive Branch.'" By virtue of its status at that

---

1. I.R.C. §§ 7441–7448.

2. I.R.C. § 6211.

3. Hearings on Tax Litigation Before the Subcommittee on Improvements in Judicial Machinery of the Senate Committee on the Judiciary, 91st Cong., 1st Sess. 428, 430 (1969).

time, the Tax Court, although denominated a court and performing an essentially judicial function, was powerless to take many actions traditionally within the power of courts of law. For example, if the Tax Court found it necessary to issue a contempt citation it was unable to do so. Instead, the Tax Court had to apply to a United States District Court for an order of court which, at that point, had to be followed at risk of contempt, not of the Tax Court, but of the district court issuing the order.

The 1969 Tax Reform Act granted the Tax Court constitutional status and changed its name from the "Tax Court of the United States" to the "United States Tax Court." The Tax Court derives its constitutional authority from Article I of the Constitution of the United States, the legislative article, as distinguished from Article III, the judicial article. This distinction has little, if any, bearing upon the conduct of litigation in the court. Rather, it has its principal significance with respect to such matters as judicial tenure.

The new status of the Tax Court provides the court with the authority to enforce its own rules and orders. Moreover, the Internal Revenue Code now specifically provides that a judge of the Tax Court has the power to punish, by fine or imprisonment, anyone in contempt of its authority.[5]

However, despite the fact that the Tax Reform Act of 1969 did clarify to some extent the status of the Tax Court in the federal judicial system, it did not give the Tax Court the power to go beyond its statutory mandate in order to exercise jurisdiction. Therefore, the Tax Court must follow its jurisdictional prerequisites to the letter. It may never enlarge its jurisdiction for equitable reasons to hear a case which does not meet all the statutory requirements for Tax Court jurisdiction.

JURISDICTIONAL PREREQUISITES

The Tax Court has jurisdiction to decide tax controversies with respect to which the Internal Revenue Service has determined that a deficiency exists, if the IRS has sent a formal notice of the deficiency to the taxpayer and if the taxpayer has filed a timely petition with the Tax Court requesting redetermination of the deficiency. The foregoing are all the essential prerequisites of the Tax Court's long-standing jurisdiction to redetermine tax "deficiencies." However, [since 1975 the Tax Court has had certain declaratory judgment jurisdiction].[e] * * * As to the various declaratory judgment

e. See pages 303–305, below.   e. See pages —— – ——, below.

matters, jurisdiction depends upon the issuance of notices of determination or failure to make such determinations within specified periods.

Deficiency Determination

The term deficiency applies only to certain kinds of taxes—income, estate, and gift taxes and the excise tax imposed upon private foundations and foundation managers by Chapter 42 of the Internal Revenue Code. "Deficiency" is a word of art, and although, as a practical matter, the amount of a deficiency will often be the difference between the tax which the taxpayer has paid and the tax which the government claims to be due, technically the definition of "deficiency" is more complex than this.

In order to determine the "deficiency" the Internal Revenue Service first determines the total amount of tax due from the taxpayer for the items or period in question. Then, the amount of tax shown on the taxpayer's return is added to any amounts already assessed or collected without assessment (this does not include sums which the taxpayer has simply paid voluntarily). This sum is reduced by the amount of any rebates from the government to the taxpayer. The "deficiency" is the amount by which the total tax due exceeds this result.

* * *

Notice of Deficiency Requirement

The issuance of a notice of deficiency is a statutory prerequisite to Tax Court jurisdiction. The notice of deficiency has been called the ticket to the Tax Court. The issuance of a notice of deficiency is also in most situations a statutory prerequisite to assessment and collection of those taxes for which the Tax Court can have jurisdiction, i. e., income, estate, gift, excess profits, and certain private foundation excise taxes. There are specific situations in which the Internal Revenue Service is allowed to assess and collect deficiencies on taxes of these types without issuing a deficiency notice. In these circumstances f * * * the taxpayer may be unable to proceed to the Tax Court.

It should be noted that the absence of an adequate, timely, and properly mailed deficiency notice will render an assessment based upon that notice invalid. In those cases where the defect is determined to exist after the period of limitations on an assessment has expired, no deficiency assessment may be made. Where limitations have not run, the Service is free to issue a new notice of deficiency correcting the defective one. * * *

* * *

f. For example, where a Form 870 (waiving the right to a deficiency notice) has been executed by the taxpayer as part of an administrative settlement.

In the normal case involving taxes within the jurisdiction of the Tax Court, a deficiency notice will be issued at the conclusion of administrative procedures following an audit. The notice is commonly referred to as a "90-day letter" because it provides notice that within ninety days after its receipt a petition must be filed in the Tax Court or an immediate assessment will be made. It advises the taxpayer of the deficiency determined and gives more or less notice of the specific findings on which the asserted deficiency is based. Upon receipt of the deficiency notice the taxpayer has ninety days (150 days for a deficiency notice addressed to a person outside the United States) in which to petition the Tax Court. The taxpayer may obtain access to the Tax Court simply by filing a timely petition in response to the deficiency notice.

While, as noted above, a deficiency notice is normally issued at the conclusion of administrative procedures following an audit, there is no requirement that the notice be preceded by a completed audit or by administrative review procedures. Indeed, except in rare and exceptional circumstances involving allegations of extraordinary misconduct, the Tax Court will not "go behind" a deficiency notice to examine allegations of procedural irregularity. For, the focus of the case in the Tax Court is the correctness of the deficiency determined in the statutory notice and not the procedure by which the notice was issued.

*   *   *

Form of Notice of Deficiency

No particular form of deficiency notice is required by statute. However, the Internal Revenue Service has evolved a standard letter, called alternately a deficiency notice or a ninety-day letter, which informs the taxpayer of the amount of the deficiency and some of the options available if the taxpayer wants to contest the determination. Accompanying the letter will be a statement showing the IRS's computations, giving a brief explanation of the reason for the deficiency, and a waiver which the taxpayer may return to the IRS if he or she does not intend to contest the deficiency.

Because no formal requirements govern the content of a deficiency notice, any letter which adequately informs the taxpayer of the assertion of a deficiency will be deemed adequate, and it is seldom worthwhile to contest the substance of the deficiency notice unless the document purporting to be a deficiency notice cannot fairly be said to warn the taxpayer of the fact that an assessment is proposed and state the amount of such assessment. It has been held that so long as these minimal requirements are met, the purported notice will satisfy the statutory requirements and is as effective as the standard printed form.[21]   *   *   *

*   *   *

21. Cooper Agency, Inc. v. McLeod, 235 F.Supp. 276 (E.D.S.C.1964), aff'd   per curiam, 348 F.2d 919 (4th Cir. 1965).

Mailing Requirements

The Internal Revenue Code requires that the deficiency notice be sent to the taxpayer by registered or certified mail.[22] If a deficiency notice is properly mailed to a correct address, it is validly issued even if the taxpayer never actually receives the notice. The deficiency notice must be sent to the taxpayer's last known address.   *   *   *

*   ⁂   ⁂

(1) TIMELY FILED PETITION

Once a deficiency notice is issued and mailed to the taxpayer's last known address, the taxpayer must file a timely petition to invoke the jurisdiction of the Tax Court. "Timely" means within 90 days of the date of mailing of the deficiency notice or 150 days for a deficiency notice addressed to a taxpayer outside the United States.[g] However, there can also be a debate as to whether, in a given case, a petition was filed within the pertinent time limit; for in Tax Court litigation the date of filing is not necessarily determined by the date a petition is actually received by the Clerk of the Tax Court. For example, a Tax Court petition will be deemed filed on the date of mailing (i. e., the date of certification, registration or postmark) if placed in a properly addressed envelope.[h] As might be expected, there has been considerable litigation in the Tax Court as to whether there was a timely and proper mailing, avoidable by the simple expedient of careful attention to time limits and the absence of procrastination. This has led to a body of jurisprudence on such issues as the effect of an illegible postmark,[i] the effect of a foreign postmark,[j] the effect of a postmark dated later than delivery to the post office due to a change in post office procedure,[k] the effect of the absence of any postmark,[l] the effect of a postmark from a private postage meter,[m] etc.

22. I.R.C. § 6212(a).

g. IRC § 6213(a). There can be significant issues raised as to whether the 90-day or the 150-day period is applicable. See, e. g., Lewy v. Commissioner, 68 T.C. 779 (1978); Estate of Lombard v. Commissioner, 66 T.C. 1 (1976); Looper v. Commissioner, 73 T.C. 690 (1980).

h. IRC § 7502.

i. Mason v. Commissioner, 68 T.C. 354 (1977) (if timely mailing proven, petition is timely).

j. Electronic Automation Systems, Inc. v. Commissioner, ¶ 76,270 P–H Memo TC (1976) (petition late, only U.S. postmark effective).

k. Drake v. Commissioner, 554 F.2d 736 (5th Cir. 1977) (date of postmark governs, not date of delivery to post office).

l. Sylvan v. Commissioner, 65 T.C. 548 (1975) (treated as if there were an illegible postmark, but see dissenting opinions).

m. If timely private postmark, taxpayer must still prove delivery to Tax Court within normal delivery time, Stotter v. Commissioner, 69 T.C. 896 (1978), or must prove timely deposit in mail, delay of transmission of mail

Absent the most unusual circumstances,[n] a taxpayer should be able to avoid an issue as to the date of filing a petition either by filing at the Tax Court or by obtaining a certified or registered mail receipt evidencing timely mailing.

However, there can be problems relating to timely filing in which the deficiency notice is not actually received by the taxpayer until after the specified time for filing a petition has expired. If the deficiency notice was properly addressed, the fact that it was not received is of no aid to the taxpayer. The absence of a timely filed petition permits the assessment and collection of the tax alleged to be due, although the taxpayer can obtain judicial review of the merits of the assessment in a post payment refund suit. However, if the deficiency notice was not properly addressed, then an assessment would be improper. The issue whether there was proper mailing could be raised in an injunction action which, in this particular instance, is expressly permitted by the Code.[o] However, in the case of a possibly misaddressed deficiency notice, the taxpayer may also file a petition in the Tax Court. The fact that the petition is filed later than the specified date will establish, in the Tax Court, a situation in which there will be cross motions for dismissal for lack of jurisdiction. The IRS will contend that dismissal should be granted due to the absence of a timely filed petition. The taxpayer will argue for dismissal for lack of jurisdiction due to the absence of a properly mailed deficiency notice. The Tax Court's determination of which ground upon which to dismiss for lack of jurisdiction will determine the validity of an assessment based on the deficiency notice at issue.[p]

O'BRIEN v. COMMISSIONER

62 T.C. 543 (1974).

DRENNEN, Judge.

* * *

This case is before the Court on remand from the U.S. Court of Appeals for the Ninth Circuit. Respondent mailed two notices of deficiency to petitioner on May 7, 1969, one in care of an attorney in Los Angeles, the other in care of a bail bondsman in the same city. Neither address had been given as his own by petitioner, who was at

and cause of the delay, Lindemood v. Commissioner, 566 F.2d 646 (9th Cir. 1977).

n. E. g., Curry v. Commissioner, 571 F.2d 1306 (4th Cir. 1978) (divided panel held timely deposit by prisoner in prison mail system adequate although there was untimely placement in U.S. mail system).

o. IRC § 6213(a).

p. The taxpayer should file the petition, if at all possible, within 90 days of its actual receipt to preserve the argument that the date of actual receipt should be substituted for the date of mailing in computing the deadline for filing the petition. See Reddock v. Commissioner, 72 T.C. 21 (1979); Kennedy v. United States, 403 F.Supp. 619 (W.D.Mich.1975), aff'd without opinion, 556 F.2d 581 (6th Cir. 1977).

the time incarcerated in the Los Angeles County Jail. Petitioner received one of the notices in June 1970; there is nothing in the record to suggest that he ever received the other. Petitioner filed a petition in this Court on September 13, 1971. On November 17, 1971, we entered an order of dismissal for lack of jurisdiction, on the ground that the petition was not filed in the time prescribed by statute. Petitioner appealed to the Ninth Circuit Court of Appeals which first dismissed the appeal, then vacated its dismissal order, vacated our order of dismissal, and remanded to us for reconsideration in light of Robinson v. Hanrahan, 409 U.S. 38, 93 S.Ct. 30, 34 L.Ed.2d 47 (1972). *Robinson* concerned the notice requirements of the due process clause of the 14th amendment * * *.

* * *

We doubt that petitioner was denied due process of law by the fact that notice of deficiency was not sent to his place of incarceration, even though that place was known to respondent. In Robinson v. Hanrahan, and the cases relied upon by it, the effect of inadequate notice was to deny interested parties the opportunity to appear, in the only trial-level proceeding open to them for the purpose, and present objections to a taking of property by a governmental unit and of the final settling of rights to property as between private parties. Failure to issue, or defect in the issuance of, notice of deficiency does not deprive a taxpayer of opportunity to appear and contest the Commissioner's determination that additional tax is owed: After assessment and collection the taxpayer may still file a claim for refund and, if denied, sue in a Federal District Court or the U. S. Court of Claims. Cohen v. United States, 297 F.2d 760, 772 (C.A.9, 1962). Indeed, Congress could dispense altogether with the procedure by which notice of deficiency is issued and opportunity for review by this Court is granted. Robinson v. Hanrahan and the cases relied upon by it "deal with the cutting off of all rights [to appear and present objections], not of one of two alternative remedies provided to the taxpayer by the Congress as a matter of grace." Cohen v. United States, supra at 772. In this context, we think the requirements of due process of law are satisfied, even if notice of deficiency be not issued at all so long as adequate notice is given of assessment of tax and/or seizure of property to alert the taxpayer to the need to make a claim, and if necesseary file suit, for refund; there is no claim in the present case that petitioner did not receive such notice.

However, we need not decide here whether petitioner's constitutional rights have been infringed, for we find that as a statutory matter, the notices of deficiency issued by respondent are insufficient to confer jurisdiction upon this Court.

Because the petition before the Court was not timely filed, we must in any event dismiss for lack of jurisdiction. Where jurisdiction is also lacking for respondent's failure to issue a proper statutory notice of deficiency, we will dismiss on that ground, rather than for lack of timely filing of a petition. The distinction is not without significance. Where notice of deficiency is found inadequate under the statute, the effect may be to vitiate the notice and any assessment of tax related to it, sec. 6213(a), whereas dismissal for lack of timely filing does not affect the validity of the underlying notice and assessment, if any.

Section 6212(b)(1) authorizes respondent to send notice of deficiency to a taxpayer "at his last known address." This Court stated in Daniel Lifter, 59 T.C. 818, 821 (1973), that—

> for purposes of section 6212(b)(1), a taxpayer's last known address must be determined by a consideration of all relevant circumstances; it is the address which, in the light of such circumstances, the respondent reasonably believes the taxpayer wishes to have the respondent use in sending mail to him.

Where notice of a deficiency is sent other than to a taxpayer's "last known address," there is a split of authority as to whether it may nonetheless qualify as a proper statutory notice for purposes of conferring jurisdiction upon the Court. Some decisions have stated the defect to be jurisdictional in nature. DeWelles v. United States, 378 F.2d 37, 39 (C.A.9, 1967); Gennaro A. Carbone, 8 T.C. 207, 212 (1947). Others have stated that even though notice is not sent to taxpayer's "last known address," it nonetheless satisfies the statute if actually received by the taxpayer "within ample time to file a timely petition." Clement Brzezinski, 23 T.C. 192, 195 (1954); *Daniel Lifter,* supra.

We find, however, that respondent's notice of deficiency in this case is invalid under either line of authority.

Normally, a taxpayer's "last known address" is that shown on his tax returns filed with respondent. Respondent is required to use a different address if he learns, or is advised by the taxpayer, that the taxpayer has changed his address; but if the taxpayer is merely—

> temporarily sojourning elsewhere, as in a hotel or hospital or vacation resort or jail, or even abroad, while still retaining the same "permanent" address * * * [respondent] is not required to treat the address of temporary sojourn as the "last known address." To so require would place an impossible administrative burden on the Commissioner. * * * The Commissioner can hardly make a daily check to see when the taxpayer may leave such temporary address. [Cohen v. United States, supra at 773.]

Here, however, a somewhat different situation is presented, in that petitioner did not file a return for the year at bar; nor does the record indicate that respondent otherwise had an address for petitioner on file which could qualify as his "last known address." In this context, we think our inquiry must be whether respondent took adequate steps to determine an address petitioner would want used to send mail to him and where respondent could reasonably expect petitioner to receive it.

Our findings of fact relate the circumstances and the efforts made by respondent's agents to determine where to send the notice of deficiency. Two copies of the notice were mailed to petitioner but neither of them was sent to an address given by petitioner. Nor were they sent to addresses respondent had reason to believe petitioner would want used in mailing documents to him. We have no evidence about why one copy of the notice was sent to the attorney who did not represent petitioner. And there is no evidence that petitioner gave the agents any reason to believe he should be contacted through the bondsman. The revenue agents apparently made some effort to find petitioner's correct address by examining various police records, but neither of the notices was sent to any of the addresses they found. We believe the agents could have obtained an address from petitioner when they interviewed him. And when they made their report and found confusion as to petitioner's address, we believe they should have made some further effort to contact petitioner at the jail, where they last saw him, or by tracing him through the Los Angeles police.

If the mailing of a notice of deficiency to a taxpayer is to be any more than an empty gesture, there should be some reasonable expectation that the taxpayer will receive it. Section 6212(b)(1) provides that the notice shall be sufficient if mailed to the taxpayer "at his last known address." If this is done the notice is sufficient even though the taxpayer may not actually receive it. But here respondent apparently had no "last known address" for petitioner, although his agents had been in contact with petitioner. Thus, section 6212(b)(1) does not serve to validate this notice of deficiency.

The purpose of the notice of deficiency is to notify the taxpayer of the determination of a deficiency in tax and the proposed assessment of that deficiency within time for petitioner to file a timely petition in this Court. *Clement Brzezinski*, supra. Under the circumstances here present, we think it was incumbent upon respondent to either obtain a usable address from petitioner or to make a reasonable effort to see to it that petitioner received a copy of the notice within time to file a timely petition in this Court. This could have been done by either attempting to deliver a copy of the notice to petitioner in jail or by attempting to determine which of the various addresses they had for petitioner would be the address at which petitioner would most reasonably be calculated to receive the notice.

Here respondent had no reason to believe that petitioner wanted him to use either of the addresses used to send mail to him, see *Dan-*

iel Lifter, supra; nor could the notice of deficiency, so mailed, be reasonably calculated to apprise petitioner of the action respondent proposed to take so petitioner could file a timely petition in this Court, see Robinson v. Hanrahan, supra. The defect in mailing of the notice was not merely technical, see *Daniel Lifter,* supra at 823, and petitioner did not receive a copy of the notice of deficiency in time to file a timely petition in this Court.

We recognize that the respondent should not be required to go to unreasonable lengths to be certain that the taxpayer receives the notice of deficiency where the taxpayer has not filed returns and respondent has no readily accessible "last known address," and we make no effort here to lay down any rules as to what the respondent should do in all such cases. Each case will have to be decided on its own facts, using as possible guidelines the criteria set forth in *Daniel Lifter,* supra, and/or Robinson v. Hanrahan, supra, mentioned in the preceding paragraph. We do say that the actions taken by respondent in this case do not meet the requirements to comply with the congressional intent in providing for notices of deficiency or the criteria mentioned in either of those cases. Respondent's failure to make a determined effort to conform to section 6212(b)(1) cannot be excused.

We conclude that the notice of deficiency here involved was a nullity and invalid and that it did not serve to give this Court jurisdiction in this case.

GRUBART v. COMMISSIONER

48 P–H Memo TC ¶ 79,409 (1979).

WILBUR, Judge. On April 14, 1978, respondent filed a motion to dismiss this case for lack of jurisdiction on the ground that the petition was not filed within the 90-day statutory period prescribed by sections 6213(a) and 7502. * * *

* * *

* * * [I]n response to respondent's motion to dismiss for lack of jurisdiction, petitioner, in a "Memorandum of Law" in opposition to respondent's motion, and in support of petitioner's motion to dismiss, stated:

> The petitioner alleges that he did not receive the subject notice of deficiency *although he resides at 155 East 38th Street, New York City,* but that same came to his attention only accidentally in the early part of February 1978 while he was unpacking his furnishings in his new apartment, after having removed from his former apartment. * * *

From the record it appears that the deficiency notice was sent to petitioner's legal residence, 155 East 38th Street, New York, New

York. However, petitioner had used his business address, 9 East 46th Street, New York, New York, as his address for the taxable years at issue herein, as he had for numerous other years. Hence, petitioner claims, the notice of deficiency was not sent to his last *known* address. Petitioner asserts that:

> It cannot be denied [by respondent] that the 90-day letter was not sent to petitioner's last known address, i. e., 9 East 46th Street, New York City 10017, where he had maintained his office for a period of almost 40 years. * * *

We find petitioner's argument, although original, to be totally without merit.

First, we find that where the taxpayer, in his petition or on brief, states that he resided at the address to which the statutory notice was sent, he can hardly complain that the notice was not mailed to the taxpayer at his last known address. Petitioner places great emphasis on the fact that he found the deficiency notice only after unpacking during a move from his personal residence. However, he ultimately admitted that the *address* of his personal residence is still the same—155 East 38th Street, New York, New York—because he merely moved from one apartment to another in the same building. Hence there could have been no delay in the mails due to a change of address.

Petitioner also surmised that the deficiency was mislaid by a maid or household member and thus argues that he should not be held accountable for not receiving personal, actual notice of the deficiency. Petitioner is an attorney, and surely must realize the necessity of keeping both business and personal records in order. It is clear that the statutory notice arrived at his personal residence, while he was residing there, by certified mail, and this is sufficient to constitute notice for purposes of the statute. "Actual" notice of a subjective, personal nature is not required, and would render the statute impossible to administer.

In addition, petitioner relies heavily on his assertion that the telephone calls regarding the audit by the Commissioner were made to and from his business phone at his business address, and that numerous other communications from the Commissioner were sent to that address. However, it is well understood that there may be more than only one correct "last known" address upon which the Commissioner may reasonably rely. In Delman v. Commissioner, 384 F.2d 929 (3d Cir. 1967), affg. a Memorandum Opinion of this Court, the Commissioner had two addresses for the taxpayer, both of which were equally suitable. In speaking of the purpose of section 6212(b)(1), the court stated:

> Section 6212(b)(1) was intended to apply only in situations where the Secretary did not have the taxpayer's correct ad-

dress because of the failure or inability of the taxpayer to notify him of a change. *This section was enacted to protect the Secretary in this circumstance and is not a sword to be used by the taxpayer.* The language "shall be sufficient" is the first key to this analysis. It immediately suggests that *although other means may be equally suitable and, perhaps, even better,* the Government is protected if the notice is sent to the last known address. * * * [Delman v. Commissioner, supra at 932. Emphasis added.]

Thus, there may be more than one address which the Commissioner may reasonably believe is an address where the taxpayer will receive the notice of deficiency.

In the instant case, petitioner himself used his personal residence address in at least one of his communications with respondent. Petitioner's consent form fixing the period of limitation upon assessment of income tax was mailed to the Commissioner in an envelope bearing a postmark of September 28, 1976 and a return of address of 155 East 38th Street, petitioner's personal residence. In addition on the consent form itself, signed by petitioner on or about September 24, 1976, petitioner gave his personal residence address as his address. From these instances, we find that respondent was reasonable in mailing a notice of deficiency to petitioner's personal address, even though it was not the address given on his Federal income tax returns for the years in issue.

As stated in Lifter v. Commissioner, 59 T.C. 818 (1973), "It might have been reasonable for [the Commissioner] to adopt a different course * * * but surely it must be recognized that there was reason for the course that he adopted." *Lifter,* supra at 822.

Although petitioner herein apparently did not learn of the asserted deficiency until after the 90-day statutory period had expired, that was clearly the result of his own negligence or carelessness.

Both parties cite numerous cases to support their respective positions, and, indeed, there is a myriad of cases concerning a taxpayer's "last known address." However, none of the cases we found are exactly on point.

To hold, in effect, that the Commissioner must *choose,* and choose correctly, from several of what he knows, or has reasonable basis to believe, to be taxpayer's actual addresses (such as taxpayer's home and business addresses), would place an undue administrative burden upon the Commissioner, and result in an absurd application of the last known address statutory standard.

Accordingly, respondent's motion will be granted and,

An appropriate order will be issued.

(2) PROPER PARTY PETITIONER

FLETCHER PLASTICS, INC. v. COMMISSIONER

64 T.C. 35 (1975).

DAWSON, Chief Judge.

This matter is before the Court on respondent's motion to dismiss for lack of jurisdiction on the ground that the petition in this case was not filed by a proper party.

In a notice of deficiency dated June 20, 1974, respondent determined * * * Federal income tax deficiencies * * *. This notice of deficiency was addressed to "Atlas Tool Co. Inc., Successor to Fletcher Plastics, Inc." * * *

* * *

There is no dispute that the petition captioned "Fletcher Plastics, Inc., Stephan Schaffan, Transferee, Petitioner" was timely filed. However, respondent asserts in his motion that neither Fletcher Plastics, Inc., nor Stephan Schaffan is the party to whom a notice of deficiency was sent nor are they legally entitled to institute a case on behalf of Atlas Tool Co., Successor to Fletcher Plastics, Inc., based on the notice of deficiency mailed in this case.

The only issue for our decision is whether Atlas Tool Co., Inc., the taxpayer to whom the notice of deficiency was sent, can ratify and amend, after the 90-day statutory period has expired, a petition filed on its behalf and signed by its counsel which was intended to contest the deficiencies determined in that notice, but incorrectly captioned.

The jurisdiction of the Tax Court is specifically limited by statute, section 7442, and the statutory requirements must be satisfied for us to acquire jurisdiction. See Cincinnati Transit, Inc., 55 T.C. 879, 882 (1971), affd. per curiam 455 F.2d 220 (6th Cir. 1972); Oklahoma Contracting Corp., 35 B.T.A. 232, 236 (1937).

To invoke our jurisdiction, section 6213(a) requires that "the taxpayer" to whom a notice of deficiency is addressed must file a timely petition with this Court for a redetermination of the deficiency determined in such notice.

A review of the cases decided prior to the adoption of our new Rules of Practice and Procedure on January 1, 1974, indicates that the general rule is that a petition must be filed by the taxpayer against whom the deficiency was determined or his duly authorized representative, except in cases of transferee liability, see *Cincinnati Transit, Inc.,* supra at 882–883; and except where a party is permitted to ratify an imperfect petition, after proving that the original filing was made on his behalf by one authorized to do so. Norris E. Carstenson, 57 T.C. 542 (1972).

Section 7453 provides that proceedings in this Court "shall be conducted in accordance with such rules of practice and procedure * * * as the Tax Court may prescribe." The conflict here arises because respondent believes that language in selected portions of the Notes accompanying the new Rules reflects a change in our attitude toward amendments to pleadings, even though the Note to Rule 41(a),[2] which deals with amendments to pleadings, expressly states that the new Rule does "not represent a change in present practice."

Respondent notes that Rule 60(a) provides that a petition should be filed by and in the name of the person against whom the Commissioner determined a deficiency. He contends that since that was not done here, Rule 41(a) bars amendment of the petition. The pertinent part of that Rule reads as follows:

> No amendment shall be allowed after expiration of the time for filing the petition, however, which would involve conferring jurisdiction on the Court over a matter which otherwise would not come within its jurisdiction under the petition as then on file * * *

* * *

To the contrary, petitioner argues that this is a procedural, not a jurisdictional problem. After noting that Rules 23(a)(1) and 32(a) require that a proper caption be placed on all pleadings filed with this Court, petitioner cites Rule 41(a) which provides, in relevant part, that a party may amend his pleadings either "by leave of court or by written consent of the adverse party; *and leave shall be given freely when justice so requires*." (Emphasis added.) Petitioner argues that this reflects a liberal attitude toward amendment of pleadings.

In further support of his position, petitioner refers to Rule 60(a) which provides, in relevant part, that:

> A case timely brought shall not be dismissed on the ground that it is not properly brought on behalf of a party until a reasonable time has been allowed after objection for ratification by such party of the bringing of the case; and such ratification shall have the same effect as if the case had been properly brought by such party. * * *

The Note following this Rule further shows a liberal attitude toward amendment and/or correction of pleadings in a case like that presently before us:

> Where the intention is to file a petition on behalf of a party, the scope of this provision permits correction of errors as to the proper party or his identity made in a petition otherwise timely and correct. * * *

2. Unless otherwise noted, all references to a Rule or Rules are to the Tax Court Rules of Practice and Procedure.

After careful examination of the record and the law, we will deny respondent's motion to dismiss and grant petitioner's motion to amend the caption and the pleadings. Atlas Tool clearly intended to file a petition to contest the deficiencies determined in a notice of deficiency sent to it and this petition was signed by its duly authorized counsel, as permitted by Rule 34(b)(7). Rule 60(a) expressly permits a party to timely ratify a defective petition filed on its behalf. The Note states that this Rule permits the correction of errors as to the proper party to be made where there was an intent to file a petition on behalf of a party.

Our holding here is consistent with Rule 34(a) which provides that "Failure of the petition to satisfy applicable requirements *may* be ground for dismissal of the case." (Emphasis added.) The Note to this Rule explains the emphasized language as follows:

> The dismissal of a petition, for failure to satisfy applicable requirements, depends on the nature of the defect, and therefore is put in the contingent "may" rather than the mandatory "shall" of present T.C.Rule 7(a)(2).   *   *   *

In so acting, we are not taking jurisdiction of a matter which is outside our jurisdiction as determined by the petition originally filed. See Rule 41(a). A review of the cases cited in the Note to that Rule shows that most deal with untimely amendments relating to taxable years or categories of taxes different than those contained in the original petition. Motions to make such amendments are generally not granted since they would confer jurisdiction over a matter which otherwise would not be within our jurisdiction as determined by the petition as then on file. Miami Valley Coated Paper Co. v. Commissioner, 211 F.2d 422 (6th Cir. 1954), and Citizens Mutual Investment Assn., 46 B.T.A. 48 (1942), are cases where the petitioner attempted to question for the first time, in his proffered amendment, the propriety of a different kind of tax than that raised in the original timely petition. Most of the other cited cases were untimely attempts to contest a determination for a taxable year not questioned in the original petition.   *   *   *

*   *   *

This situation is also distinguishable from those cases where a petition has been brought by a nonexistent party, see Great Falls Bonding Agency, Inc., 63 T.C. 304 (1974), since Atlas Tool was in existence when the petition and amendment were filed. Finally, this case is to be distinguished from *Cincinnati Transit, Inc.,* supra, and *Oklahoma Contracting Corp.,* supra, where a party to whom a statutory notice of deficiency was not sent attempts to join, as a party-petitioner, the taxpayer to whom the notice of deficiency was sent. Here the statutory notice was sent to Atlas Tool on whose behalf a petition was filed. Atlas Tool has ratified that filing and seeks to amend that petition here.

Accordingly, we conclude that although the original defective petition was not filed in the name of a proper party as required by Rule 60, and did not have a proper caption as required by Rules 23(a)(1) and 32(a), the clear language of Rule 60(a) bars dismissal under these particular facts. We hold that this is a proper case for amendment of the pleadings under Rule 41(a); and under Rule 41(d) the amendment will relate back to the date of the filing of the original petition.

HOLT v. COMMISSIONER

67 T.C. 829 (1977).

DAWSON, Chief Judge.

* * *

Ernest B. Holt and Lessie L. Holt filed joint Federal income tax returns for 1971, 1972, and 1973. On October 17, 1975, a joint statutory notice of deficiency was mailed to them by the Commissioner determining deficiencies for those years * * *.

On January 15, 1976, this Court received the following handwritten letter in an envelope postmarked January 13, 1976:

1/13/76
U. S. TAX COURT
400 Second St. N.W.
Wash. D.C. 20217

DEAR SIR:
I would like to file a petition to the U.S. Tax Court, as I do not agree with the findings of I.R.S. Commissioner, Donald C. Alexander. Inclosed is a letter dated Oct. 17, 1975. I am also enclosing 10.00 check for your consideration of this case.

> Sincerely Yours,
> ERNEST B. HOLT
> Rt. One
> Asher, Okla. 74826

The joint notice of deficiency was attached to the letter which was filed as a "petition" in the name of Ernest B. Holt, and an "Order for Proper Petition" was sent to him on January 16, 1976. That order required him to file a proper amended petition by March 16, 1976.

On March 17, 1976, the Court received a petition in an envelope postmarked March 15, 1976. The petition was captioned in the names of both Ernest B. and Lessie L. Holt and was signed by both of them. On March 26, 1976, the Court ordered that the latter petition be filed as an amended petition and that the caption of the case be amended to include both names.

After filing an answer to the amended petition, the Commissioner filed a motion to dismiss as to Lessie L. Holt on the grounds that the January 13 letter did not purport to be an appeal on behalf of Lessie L. Holt, and that the amended petition filed 152 days after the statutory notice of deficiency was mailed cannot confer jurisdiction as to her.

In response to such motion to dismiss, the Court received an affidavit which provides in part:

> Ernest B. Holt and Lessie L. Holt, being duly sworn upon oath depose and state:

> That since Ernest B. Holt and his wife, Lessie L. Holt filed a joint return, Mr. Holt considers that anything filed by him is filed by both; that by Mrs. Holt signing this Memorandum, she indicates that she wants to be embraced therein; that since they wish to represent themselves and have the matter heard in a more convenient location other than Washington, D.C., they are asking the Court to give them a chance to have the matter heard on substance and merit rather than on form.

Such affidavit was signed by both parties.

In John L. Brooks, 63 T.C. 709 (1975), the facts were essentially the same, with one exception. In *Brooks,* the original document which was filed as a petition bore a caption in the joint names of the parties. The *Brooks* opinion discussed and analyzed the applicable portions of the Tax Court Rules of Practice and Procedure, particularly Rule 34(a), Rule 34(b)(7), Rule 41(a), and Rule 60(a). We do not think it necessary here to repeat that analysis. The essence of the *Brooks* opinion is the statement that "in the light of the explanatory Notes to such Rules, we think the 'intent test' should continue to be applied to cases such as this under the new Rules." The "intent" which we seek to ascertain in this particular type of case is whether the nonsigning spouse (typically the wife) intended that the signing spouse (typically the husband) act on her behalf and with her approval when he filed a timely imperfect petition with this Court.

In determining this Court's jurisdiction we think a distinction which turns upon the presence or absence of a caption in an imperfect petition could deservedly be labeled as a "captious distinction." We do not believe that the intent which the *Brooks* opinion directs us to ascertain can, in any realistic sense, be gleaned so mechanically. Certainly, lack of knowledge should not be equated with lack of intent, and Ernest Holt obviously was not sophisticated enough to place a caption on his letter which we accepted and filed as an imperfect petition. That letter was a response, in the best way he knew how to respond, to a notice of deficiency addressed to both spouses. The realistic presumption of intent, based upon the letter and the attached joint notice of deficiency and upon the totality of circumstances herein, is that the petitioner-husband was acting as agent for his wife as well as for himself in filing such imperfect petition in response to the joint notice of deficiency.

Accordingly, in situations where there is a joint notice of deficiency, a timely filed imperfect petition, the Court's "Order for Proper Petition," and the filing of a timely amended petition signed by both spouses, it is our view that the spouse who did not sign the imperfect petition should be given the opportunity to confirm the correctness of that presumption of intent. In this case the presumed intent was confirmed by filing, within the time specified in our "Order for Proper Petition," the amended petition captioned in the names of both spouses and signed by both. To rule otherwise would be wholly inconsistent with the liberal and salutary policy which we followed in accepting and filing as an imperfect petition the original and inartfully drawn letter which is quoted above. Such a shifting between realism and hypertechnicality cannot be justified in these circumstances.

Since the facts of this case sufficiently establish to our satisfaction that Ernest B. Holt was acting both for himself and Lessie L. Holt in sending the letter which was filed herein as the timely imperfect petition, we will deny the Commissioner's motion to dismiss for lack of jurisdiction as to Lessie L. Holt and to change the caption.

An appropriate order will be entered.

Reviewed by the Court.

STERRETT, J., dissenting: It is an article of faith of this Court that a taxpayer shall be given an opportunity to have his tax liability judicially determined before paying any portion thereof if the statute granting jurisdiction can be reasonably interpreted to permit it. In the instant case the majority has, in my opinion, gone beyond the bounds of statutory reason to reach a desired result.

* * *

I would go no further than the doctrine laid down in John L. Brooks, 63 T.C. 709 (1975). There must be some objective indication within the four corners of the documents timely filed that fairly raises the question as to whether the filing spouse was authorized to speak for the other. Once fairly raised we should accept a subsequent ratification of the intent.

I respectfully submit that, rather than establishing any rule, the majority has in fact, in any joint notice situation, established an open-end situation where only one spouse need file a timely petition, and the other spouse can have such additional time to determine whether to join in the petition as the Court in its sole discretion decides. No matter how nobly motivated, judicial legislation remains just that.

DRENNEN, QUEALY, and GOFFE, JJ., agree with this dissent.

(3) IRREVOCABILITY OF TAX COURT JURISDICTION

ESTATE OF MING, JR. v. COMMISSIONER

62 T.C. 519 (1974).

DRENNEN, Judge.

Respondent, by notice of deficiency dated October 8, 1970, determined deficiencies in petitioners' income taxes for the years 1964, 1965, and 1966 in the total amount of $2,714.07, and additions to tax under section 6653(b) in the total amount of $8,992.17. Petitioners filed a timely petition in the Tax Court for redetermination of those deficiencies on January 6, 1971. The case was set for trial on a trial calendar of the Tax Court starting February 4, 1974, in Chicago, Ill. On January 25, 1974, petitioners filed a motion to continue the case and a motion for leave to withdraw the petition without prejudice.
* * *

* * *

* * * We assume the motion means that petitioners may withdraw their petition in the Tax Court, pay the deficiencies, and sue for refund in the United States District Court.

In the recent case of Emma R. Dorl, 57 T.C. 720, 721–722 (1972), this Court held that a taxpayer's motion for removal of her case to the United States District Court, after issuance of a notice of deficiency and filing a petition in the Tax Court, must be denied; and also that the taxpayer was not entitled to a jury trial in the Tax Court. In our opinion in that case, we said:

> Where, as here, a taxpayer receives a notice of an income tax deficiency and files a timely petition with the United States Tax Court, he gives the Tax Court exclusive jurisdiction. See sec. 6512(a). Thereafter, a refund suit in the U. S. District Court for the same tax and the same taxable year is barred. The mere filing of the petition in the Tax Court is enough to deprive a U.S. District Court of jurisdiction for years as to which the petition was filed. This is the rule even where the Tax Court petition was dismissed, or the issue sought to be litigated was not presented in the Tax Court. It is significant that it is the taxpayer's action in filing a valid petition in the Tax Court, under circumstances which give the Tax Court jurisdiction, and not any action taken by the Court, that bars a subsequent refund suit in the U.S. District Court.

It is now a settled principle that a taxpayer may not unilaterally oust the Tax Court from jurisdiction which, once invoked, remains unimpaired until it decides the controversy.

Our opinion in the *Dorl* case is supported not only by the cases cited therein, but also by the legislative history of sections 6512(a) and 7459(d), which had their origins in sections 284(d) and 906(c) of the Revenue Act of 1926, respectively. The significance of those provisions is explained in the Senate Finance Committee Report (S. Rept. No. 52, 69th Cong., 1st Sess., 1939–1 C.B. (Part 2) 351), as follows:

> But if he [the taxpayer] does elect to file a petition with the Board his entire tax liability for the year in question (except in case of fraud) is finally and completely settled by the decision of the Board when it has become final, whether the decision is by findings of fact and opinion, *or by dismissal,* as in case of lack of prosecution, insufficiency of evidence to sustain the petition, *or on the taxpayer's own motion.* The duty of the Commissioner to assess the deficiency thus determined is mandatory, and no matter how meritorious a claim * * * for refund he cannot entertain it, nor can suit be maintained against the United States * * *. Finality is the end sought to be attained by these provisions of the bill, and the committee is convinced that to allow the reopening of the question of the tax for the year involved either by the taxpayer or by the Commissioner (save in the sole case of fraud) would be highly undesirable. [Emphasis added.]

While we were concerned in the *Dorl* case with petitioner's motion to remove the case to the District Court, and here we have petitioners' motion to withdraw without prejudice, the reasoning in the *Dorl* opinion applies with equal force to require us to deny petitioners' motion in this case. Under section 7459(d), if a petition has been filed by the taxpayer in the Tax Court and the Court dismisses the case for any reason other than lack of jurisdiction, the Court must enter an order finding the deficiency in tax to be the amount determined by the Commissioner in his notice of deficiency, unless the Commissioner reduces the amount of his claim. See also Rule 123(d) of the Tax Court Rules. Thus, if we were to grant petitioners' motion, we would be required to enter a decision finding deficiencies in petitioners' taxes for the years involved in the amounts determined by respondent in the notice of deficiency. This would clearly negate the objective of petitioners' motion to withdraw without prejudice and would preclude petitioners' efforts to litigate this case on its merits in a District Court.

* * *

Furthermore, respondent has been prejudiced by the filing of a petition in this Court in that he has been precluded from assessing and collecting the additional taxes he claims to be owing by petitioners. See sec. 6212. We do not believe the law intended to permit a taxpayer to avoid payment of deficiencies determined by the Commissioner by filing a petition in this Court and then later withdrawing it without prejudice to his right to litigate the merits of his case by the refund route in the District Court or the Court of Claims. Accordingly, the motion will be denied.

B. DECISION–MAKING AUTHORITY OF THE TAX COURT

TAX COURT PRACTICE

Marvin J. Garbis, Allen L. Schwait and Paula M. Junghans

Once the threshold requirements which confer jurisdiction upon the Tax Court have been met, the court has the authority to resolve the issues in any way which the facts justify. It may find that the taxpayer owes less than the government asserts, or that the taxpayer owes nothing at all.[29]

Once the Tax Court has acquired jurisdiction over the subject matter of a case, even the respondent's concession of no deficiency for the period in issue does not deprive the court of jurisdiction. Hence, once a petition is properly filed, the Tax Court has jurisdiction to render a decision as to the absence of, or the amount of, any deficiency for the period in issue. However, the court does not have jurisdiction to render a decision which affects tax liability for other periods and has no effect on the existence *vel non* of a deficiency for the period in issue. But, it may be necessary to determine the correct income for a year not in issue in order to determine the net operating loss carryover to the year in issue so as to determine the tax liability for the year in issue.

* * *

The Tax Court may also find that the taxpayer owes more than the IRS has asserted to be due,[30] although the Commissioner must assume the burden of proof on deficiencies resulting from issues asserted after the petition has been filed. Once the court's jurisdiction has been established, the Tax Court may even find that there has been an overpayment for the period in issue.[31] Indeed, it has been held that if there is the possibility of a refund or offset (even due to a net operating loss carryback from a subsequent year) for a year over which the Tax Court has jurisdiction, the claim for refund or offset must be pleaded in the Tax Court or it will be lost. This determination by the Tax Court is res judicata as to the fact of overpayment or the absence of an overpayment. However, as a technical matter, the Tax

29. I.R.C. § 6214(a).

30. I.R.C. § 6214(a).

31. I.R.C. § 6512(b)(1). * * *

Court does not have jurisdiction to order a refund in spite of the language of the Internal Revenue Code providing that such an overpayment shall, after the Tax Court decision becomes final, "be credited or refunded to the taxpayer." [31c]

It should be noted that there may be litigable issues which may be raised by the Internal Revenue Service in regard to a refusal to refund or credit an overpayment. For example, there might be issues as to which of several claimants is entitled to the refund; who was the "taxpayer" who should get the refund or credit; whether an offer in compromise provision bars a refund to the petitioners; etc. The petitioner who feels that a refund or credit of an overpayment determined by the Tax Court is being wrongfully withheld should file an action to recover the determined refund in the United States Court of Claims or a federal district court to litigate the issue.

* * *

LTV CORP. v. COMMISSIONER

64 T.C. 589 (1975).

WILBUR, Judge.

Respondent has determined deficiencies in petitioner's income tax for the taxable years 1965 and 1966 of $3,735,081.11 and $7,622,261.09. In its petition for redetermination, petitioner alleged numerous errors on the part of respondent, including the disallowance of consolidated net operating losses of $16,981,402, for petitioner's taxable year 1968 and of $62,354,518, for petitioner's taxable year 1969. Respondent's answer denied the existence of any net operating loss for 1968 and 1969.

While the parties continue to disagree on the magnitude of the 1968 and 1969 losses, respondent now admits that there are sufficient consolidated net operating losses from 1968 and 1969 to completely eliminate any deficiency for 1965 and 1966, and has unequivocally conceded that there are no deficiencies due for these years.

Respondent contends that in view of his concession, this Court's jurisdiction is limited to entering a decision of no deficiency in accordance with the agreement of the parties, and that section 6214 deprives this Court of jurisdiction to consider facts relating to the 1968 or 1969 consolidated net operating losses. Additionally, even if it should be determined that his concession is without jurisdictional significance, respondent argues that his concession of no deficiency for 1965 and 1966 (the only years for which a deficiency notice has been issued) eliminates any controversy relating to the redetermina-

31c. I.R.C. § 6512(b)(1). Morse v. United States, 494 F.2d 876 (2d Cir. 1974). * * *

tion of a deficiency, and that we should simply enter a decision of no deficiency for petitioner.

Petitioner argues that the filing of a timely petition for the redetermination of a deficiency gives this Court jurisdiction, and that subsequent actions of the parties, including a concession on all or some of the issues, does not deprive this Court of jurisdiction. Additionally, petitioner argues that respondent's concession of no deficiency for the years before the Court, does not eliminate the controversy dividing the parties. Petitioner notes that the impact of the present controversy on future years, as well as the substantial interest associated with the pre-carryback deficiencies, provides the parties with a real stake in a present controversy involving concrete issues ripe for decision. Petitioner also emphasizes the adverse impact on financial planning and access to the financial markets that continued uncertainty over substantial tax liabilities imposes.

Petitioner filed a motion for a pretrial conference and order sustaining this Court's jurisdiction to avoid extensive preparation for a trial that may, if the Court sustains the position of the respondent, be unnecessary. Subsequent to the pretrial conference the parties filed briefs in support of their respective positions.

We agree with petitioner that respondent's concession of no deficiency does not deprive us of jurisdiction over the subject matter. It would be anomalous in the extreme if respondent's concession on the merits deprived the Court of jurisdiction to enter a decision in favor of petitioner. As we said in Daniel E. Hannan, 52 T.C. 787, 791 (1969):

> it is not the *existence* of a deficiency but the Commissioner's *determination* of a deficiency that provides a predicate for Tax Court jurisdiction. * * * Indeed, were this not true, then the absurd result would be that in every case in which this Court determined that no deficiency existed, our jurisdiction would be lost.

Having acquired jurisdiction, this Court has the authority and responsibility to enter a decision on the merits.

It is true that section 6214, after directing us to redetermine the deficiency before us by referring, to the extent necessary, to facts relating to other years, specifically denies us "jurisdiction to determine whether or not the tax for any other year * * * has been overpaid or underpaid." But section 6214(b) simply makes unmistakably clear what is contemplated by the jurisdiction conferred in section 6214(a) and the two preceding sections: that this Court's jurisdiction is limited to a redetermination of the correct amount of the deficiency, if any, for the years for which the deficiency notice specified in section 6212 has determined a deficiency as defined in section 6211.

We must look at the facts relevant to the years before us even if these facts relate to taxes for other taxable years. Respondent's concession as to the facts bearing on the correct amount of the tax liability does not diminish our jurisdiction, but goes only to the merits of the controversy, even where the facts involved relate to the taxes of other taxable years. In this, as in other instances involving concessions by either party, the Court retains jurisdiction to redetermine the correct amount of the deficiency.

Having decided that our jurisdiction is unimpaired by respondent's concession of no deficiency (which we accept), we must decide whether we should simply enter a decision for petitioner, or whether we should nevertheless determine the correct amount of the pre-carryback deficiencies, if any, for 1965 and 1966, the precise amount of the consolidated net operating losses attributable to 1968 and 1969, and the amount of the 1968 and 1969 losses that must be used to eliminate any such deficiencies.

Petitioner argues that the 1968 and 1969 losses, not absorbed by the 1965 and 1966 deficiencies, will be carried to the years 1973 and 1974, thus requiring a determination of all the issues currently before the Court at some future date. Petitioner emphasizes the convenience of resolving these issues now when witnesses are available and memories fresh, rather than in connection with 1973 and 1974, which (given the complexity of the returns involved) may not reach the litigation stage until 1980. Petitioner urges that the parties have a real stake in a concrete controversy in view of the impact any decision is likely to have on future years, and also because of the substantial interest associated with any pre-carryback deficiency for 1965 and 1966. Petitioner notes that if we do not resolve the issues for 1965 and 1966, they will be resolved in a refund suit over restricted interest, resulting in a multiplicity of litigation in different forums. Finally, petitioner points out that the failure to resolve the issues now is inconsistent with the mechanical steps for computing a net operating loss carryover and will impose substantial uncertainties undermining corporate financial planning.

Respondent argues that in view of his concession of no deficiency, resolution of these issues will have no impact on the years before the Court, but will be merely an advisory opinion concerning the amount of a deduction (that may or may not be needed) for future years over which the Court has no present jurisdiction. He argues that any existing controversy over the pre-carryback deficiencies or the size of the losses for 1968 and 1969 has been mooted by his concession. While he acknowledges that interest computations are predicated on the deficiency redetermined by the Court, he points out that this is an indirect consequence of the exercise of our jurisdiction over deficiencies, and that we clearly do not have jurisdiction over interest.

Although the issue is not as free from doubt as it at first appears, we have determined that we should enter a decision in favor of petitioner rather than continue these proceedings. Our responsibility is limited to redetermining the deficiency asserted for the years before us. If the respondent predicates a deficiency on understated income or overstated deductions (or some combination of the two) and the taxpayer claims that either additional depreciation, interest, or business expenses eliminate the asserted deficiency, the respondent's concession that any of these deductions (either alone or in combination) exist in sufficient magnitude to eliminate the deficiency results in a decision of no deficiency (if we accept respondent's concession, as we do here). We do not nevertheless determine whether all of the claimed deductions are available, or whether the claimed deductions (either alone or in combination) are actually in excess of the deficiency determined.

Since the net operating loss deduction provided by section 172 is simply one of the deductions provided by chapter 1 of subtitle A, it is difficult to see why the decision should be different here. It is unnecessary to determine which of the parties is correct as to specific deduction and income items making up their respective computations. The result is the same in either case: the deficiency as redetermined for the years before us is zero.

* * *

We, of course, do not have jurisdiction to render a monetary judgment, but simply determine the amount of the deficiency or overpayment. The only issue before us is the deficiency determined by respondent for 1965 and 1966. A decision of no deficiency in accordance with respondent's concession provides a complete victory for petitioner; a continuation of the proceedings "cannot affect the result as to the thing in issue" in this case, and can add nothing other than an advisory opinion declarative of the size of a deduction petitioner may be able to use in some future years.

* * *

The size of the 1968 net operating loss is relevant to the differences the parties have over interest.[12] Yet it is clear that section 6214(b) directs us to look at "the taxes of other years" only to the extent it is "necessary to correctly determine the amount of [the] *deficiency*" (emphasis added) before us.[13] There is no reason for us to

---

12. Petitioner received interest on the refund attributable to the 1968 loss from the end of the loss year (Dec. 31, 1968) until the refund was paid. If the correct amount of the 1968 loss is less than claimed, a portion of this interest must be repaid. Additionally, the size of the 1968 loss will affect the amount of pre-carryback interest due on any 1966 deficiency between Dec. 31, 1968 (the year of the 1968 loss), and Dec. 31, 1969 (the year of the 1969 loss).

13. While the jurisdictional bar of sec. 6214(b) relates only to determining an underpayment or overpayment for years not before us, the section nevertheless expresses a policy that, even aside from the jurisdictional bar, supports our analysis. Petitioner's right to litigate the size of the 1968 and 1969 losses as to future years is fully protected. See sec. 6511(d)(2)(B).

look at 1968 to determine the 1965 and 1966 deficiencies before us. These deficiencies are zero in any event. We would be deciding issues relative to 1968 solely for purposes of interest computation, a subject over which we clearly have no jurisdiction. Standard Oil Co. v. McMahon, 244 F.2d 11 (2d Cir. 1957); Commissioner v. Kilpatrick's Estate, 140 F.2d 887 (6th Cir. 1944). We believe that it would be clearly inappropriate to look at 1968, not for purposes of redetermining the deficiency before us, but for purposes of determining interest.

* * *

We recognize that this may be far from a perfect solution to the problems confronting petitioner. It might be more convenient for the parties if we had jurisdiction over restricted interest. We are not without sympathy relative to the practical problems petitioner has so ably detailed in its brief, but we take the statute as we find it.

Decision will be entered for the petitioner.

McGOWAN v. COMMISSIONER

67 T.C. 599 (1976).

DAWSON, Chief Judge.

[The sole substantive issue for decision was whether withholdings from an employee's wages, paid over to the State of Rhode Island's temporary disability fund, were deductible by the employees as either taxes or medical expenses. The IRS filed a notice of concession of the case which the taxpayers were unwilling to accept because they wished an opinion on the merits of the issue. |

* * *

* * * Respondent's position is that the Court must honor his tendered concession and cannot thereafter act upon the case in any fashion other than to enter a decision of no deficiency in accordance with the terms of that concession.

* * *

[In LTV Corp., 64 T.C. 589 (1975),] we ruled that a concession by the Commissioner did not impair our ability to *enter decision* for the taxpayer because we retained jurisdiction over the subject matter of the controversy, but that the existence of an *accepted, bilateral* agreement of no deficiency covering the years in issue rendered the factual controversies moot. Therefore, we declined to proceed further and entered decision for the taxpayer.

The most salient distinguishing feature between *LTV Corp.* and the instant case is the type of judicial discretion in issue. We are concerned with the question whether judicial discretion to accept or reject an offered concession exists, while in *LTV Corp.* we had to decide whether judicial discretion could be exercised during the postacceptance period to give the Court jurisdiction over nonessential matters. *LTV Corp.* provides us with no guidance concerning whether we must accept a tendered concession.

Respondent's contentions predicated upon the Court's lack of general declaratory judgment powers and our admitted policy of declining to rule on years not before us or our refusal to consider issues that may never be litigated are not persuasive. By virtue of our failure to accept this tendered concession we have a bona fide question before us arising out of a taxable year properly placed in issue. Only our acceptance of either the concession or an agreed joint stipulated decision would remove the matter from issue.

* * * Neither party can forcibly remove a case from the Court's jurisdiction through the mere act of filing a concession once our jurisdiction has been properly invoked. All concessions, including stipulated settlement agreements, are subject to the Court's discretionary review. Only through this process can the interests of justice be protected. If we were to adopt respondent's position as our own, the Court's role as a viable, independent arbiter of Federal Tax disputes would be undermined. * * *

* * *

* * * Many taxpayers in Rhode Island will be affected by the outcome herein and the time for filing another year's return is rapidly approaching for most of them. We continuously have emphasized our desire to reach a speedy determination from the moment petitioner's motion for summary judgment was filed on October 15, 1976. * * * Therefore, we conclude that our rejection of respondent's Notice of Concession represents a valid exercise of judicial discretion.

* * *

All in all, we perceive no sound or rational legal basis for sustaining the validity of [respondent's position, as stated in] Rev.Rul. 75–148, 1975–1 C.B. 64. In our judgment the ruling is invalid and, in fairness to thousands of Rhode Island employees, it should be revoked immediately. To let linger the uncertainty created by respondent's inaction would show a careless and callous disregard of the rights of these individuals. They seek a definitive answer. They are entitled to have it.

G. & S. Cs. Tax Proc. & Fraud ACB—11

* * *

C. SOME ASPECTS OF TAX COURT PROCEDURE

(1) DISCOVERY

TAX COURT PRACTICE

Marvin J. Garbis, Allen L. Schwait and Paula M. Junghans

With the [1974] rules the Tax Court has experimented with formal discovery procedures for the first time. This is not to say that before the adoption of the new rules there was no "discovery" in the sense that neither party had the opportunity to obtain information from the other. Indeed, under prior practice such procedures as settlement conferences, required stipulation sessions, and occasional pretrial conferences did tend to open channels of communication between the parties. However, these communications were voluntary to a large degree. Rarely was a party required to divulge information to the adversary except in furtherance of his or her own purposes, for example, to obtain a more favorable settlement.

In addition, discovery, which in effect was compulsory, was available to the IRS under prior practice. During the audit stage of a tax controversy the IRS was entitled to examine the taxpayer's books and records, if need be, under the compulsion of an administrative summons. Indeed, it has even been held that an IRS summons can be used to gather evidence during the pendency of a Tax Court case.[1] However, it must be noted that the oft stated policy of Chief Counsel is to eschew the use of the administrative summons for purposes of discovery in Tax Court litigation. Nevertheless, at least in the audit stage, under prior practice the IRS did have the power in the course of a tax controversy to compel the adversary to produce evidence. However at no point—save perhaps in an unusual case in which a Tax Court judge might issue an anomalous order—could the taxpayer compel the IRS to produce evidence prior to the trial of a case in the Tax Court.

* * *

The discovery provisions of the Tax Court Rules will work to absolute perfection if not a single interrogatory is asked and not a single request for production is filed. The discovery provisions are not designed to be used, rather they are designed to be available. It is the expectation of the court, as expressed in Tax Court Rule 70(a)(1), that the parties will make every good faith attempt to attain the objectives of discovery through informal consultation or communication before utilizing the discovery procedures provided in

---

1. Bolich v. Rubel, 67 F.2d 894 (2d Cir. 1933).

the rules. It is to the advantage of all concerned in Tax Court litigation to fulfill to the utmost the Tax Court's expectations.

* * *

The kind of information which can be obtained from the adversary under the Tax Court's new discovery provisions is much the same as the kind of information available to the district court litigant under the Federal Rules of Civil Procedure.

Essentially, any matter which is not privileged is subject to discovery if it is "relevant to the subject matter involved in the pending case * * *." The fact that information is sought which will not be admissible at trial is no ground for objection if the information desired is "reasonably calculated" to lead to admissible evidence.

* * *

The revised Tax Court Rules include almost verbatim the 1970 amendment to the Federal Rules of Civil Procedure which relates to interrogatories, by providing that information which is otherwise properly obtainable through discovery may not be refused by the responding party "merely because the information or response involves an opinion or contention that relates to fact or to the application of law to fact." [11]

* * *

[The specific discovery devices available in the Tax Court include interrogatories,[q] requests for production of documents or entry on property,[r] depositions (but only by consent of all parties),[s] requests for admissions [t] (which are not, strictly speaking, discovery devices) and, in transferee cases, the examination of the records of a nonparty.] [u]

(2) STIPULATIONS

TAX COURT PRACTICE

Marvin J. Garbis, Allen L. Schwait and Paula M. Junghans

The use of extensive stipulations is characteristic of Tax Court litigation. Indeed, as stated by the court in one of the first decisions issued under the [1974] rules [1a]:

"For many years the bedrock of Tax Court practice has been the stipulation process, now embodied in Rule 91

---

11. T.C.R. 70(b).

q. T.C.R. 71.

r. T.C.R. 72.

s. T.C.R. 74(a).

t. T.C.R. 90.

u. T.C.R. 73.

1a. Branerton Corp., 61 T.C. 691, 692 (1974), later proceeding, 64 T.C. 191 (1975).

* * * The recently adopted discovery procedures were not intended in any way to weaken the stipulation process."

The parties to a Tax Court case may not decide themselves whether or not they want to enter into a stipulation regarding undisputed areas of the case. Tax Court Rule 91 (a) (1) requires them:

"to stipulate, to the fullest extent to which complete or qualified agreement can or fairly should be reached, all matters not privileged which are relevant to the pending case, regardless of whether such matters involve fact or opinion or the application of law to fact."

In case any Tax Court practitioners are left in doubt as to the required content of stipulations, the rule further explains its intent, stating that stipulations should include "all facts, all documents and papers or content, or aspects thereof, and all evidence which fairly should not be in dispute."

The rules of the Tax Court leave the process of stipulation largely to the parties. It is anticipated that the same spirit of cooperation in working out areas of agreement which was evident in practice under the prior rules will carry over into practice under the new rules. In this regard, it is anticipated that there will be early meetings between opposing counsel to work out the exchanges of information and views requisite to the formalization of a stipulation. Certainly it is expected that the parties will make every effort to stipulate and to exchange data informally before any resort to the formal discovery procedures or to the formal procedures attendant to the process of stipulation. In addition, the establishment of candid communications between opposing counsel, and a mutual consideration of the facts of the case may be of material assistance in settlement efforts.

* * *

(3) SETTLEMENT

TAX COURT PRACTICE

Marvin J. Garbis, Allen L. Schwait and Paula M. Junghans

[The settlement of a Tax Court case may be reached with the Appeals Office or with District Counsel. | v

The Appeals [Office]

The Appeals [Office] has exclusive settlement jurisdiction for a period of four months over any case docketed in the Tax Court in which the deficiency notice was issued other than:

v. See Rev.Proc. 79–59, 1979–2 C.B. 573.

    (1) By Appeals Officials;

    (2) After appellate consideration by the Employee Plans/Exempt Organizations function;

    (3) By a District Director based upon a National Office ruling or technical advice involving the qualification of a plan, entity, and/or foundation status.

In those cases in which the Appeals [Office] is not given jurisdiction, District Counsel has exclusive settlement jurisdiction from the time the case is docketed.

Speaking generally, where there have been no predocketing Appeals [Office] proceedings, Appeals will have the first crack at working out a settlement. The Appeals [Office] has been directed to arrange settlement conferences within forty-five days of receipt of case. Settlement negotiations will conclude at the Appeals [Office] at such time as it is determined that the case is not susceptible of settlement or at the end of the four-month period. This period of Appeals exclusive jurisdiction may be extended *by District Counsel* for a period of not more than sixty days (but not beyond the date of receipt of trial status order or calendar) if at the end of the four-month period there is substantial likelihood that a settlement of the entire case can be effected in a reasonable period of time.

While the case is within the jurisdiction of the Appeals [Office], it may be possible to settle some but not all of the issues. In this event, Appeals will provide District Counsel with the agreement, and District Counsel will prepare the appropriate documents for filing with the Tax Court. The unsettled issues will be referred to District Counsel for disposition.

In the event of a complete settlement with the Appeals [Office], Appeals will prepare the necessary computations and forward them to District Counsel who will prepare the settlement documents for execution by the parties and filing with the Tax Court.

District Counsel

Following the period, if any, during which the Appeals [Office] has exclusive settlement jurisdiction, the authority to settle the Tax Court case passes to District Counsel. It is important to be aware that the Internal Revenue Service views this phase as a new look at the case. Hence, it is the announced position of the Service that settlement offers and counteroffers made between Appeals and the taxpayer are not binding on District Counsel.

When District Counsel obtains sole jurisdiction of the case, it will take steps to develop fully all of the relevant facts and legal positions before determining whether to proceed with settlement negotiations. Conferences will be set within forty-five days to request informally any additional information felt to be needed. And, if any requested information is not forthcoming within a reasonable period of time, the Tax Court's discovery procedures will be utilized, as appropriate.

* * *

BASIS FOR SETTLEMENT

Tax Court settlements are somewhat more complex than settlements in the typical civil suit, where the settlement agreement usually results in a flat reduction of the plaintiff's claim for damages. A tax settlement may take this form, with the government settling for a reduced liability across the board. However, where several issues are involved, the settlement may take the form of an agreement that each party concede totally on certain issues, or that some issues be conceded and others be settled by means of an adjustment. For example, in a situation where the Internal Revenue Service claims that a taxpayer was not entitled to use an accelerated form of depreciation on certain property, that certain expenses claimed as business deductions were really personal, and that the taxpayer should have been taxed on certain receipts received by a family member, the IRS might abandon the claim with reference to depreciation, the taxpayer might concede that the income was really taxable to him or herself, and the parties might agree that some of the claimed business deductions were really for business purposes and make a partial adjustment of this issue. Settlement of some tax claims may also affect other issues which are not in dispute. For example, a settlement with regard to depreciation will affect previous and future years' tax liabilities. The parties should include in the settlement an agreement regarding the effect that the resolution of disputed items will have on items or periods not currently at issue.

The question of the basis for settlement of a Tax Court case should be approached with an attitude of flexibility. It is, of course, necessary that the settlement provide for some agreed resolution of the Tax Court case itself. However, the settlement need not be limited to the mere agreement upon a Tax Court judgment. Rather, it is possible, and sometimes necessary, to agree upon various matters which are not included on the face of the Tax Court judgment. For example, in a gift tax case, it may be appropriate or required, in valuing the gift, to establish the basis which the subject matter will have in the hands of donees who are not parties to the Tax Court case. In such a situation it may be appropriate to have a collateral agreement between the IRS and the donees regarding the basis of the property.

Although the IRS may not compromise a claim merely because of the effort which will be involved in defending its position, it is specifically authorized to consider collectability in deciding whether to settle a claim.[3] Nevertheless, it has been the practice of the IRS not

3. Treas.Reg. § 301.7122–1(a).

to consider collectability in the process of settlement of a Tax Court case. * * *

* * *

(4) SPECIAL BURDEN OF PROOF RULES

TAX COURT PRACTICE

Marvin J. Garbis, Allen L. Schwait and Paula M. Junghans

The Tax Court Rules provide that the burden of proof is on the petitioner except with regard to new matters, increases in deficiency, affirmative defenses, fraud, and certain other matters discussed below.[1] Except where a higher standard of proof is required by specific rule or statute, the burden imposed is that of producing a preponderance of the evidence.

There is a subtle, and possibly academic, difference between the nature of the burden of proof imposed on a taxpayer in the Tax Court and the burden placed on a taxpayer in a tax refund litigation forum. It is said that in the Tax Court all the taxpayer need do is to overcome the presumption of correctness which applies to the determination of the Commissioner of Internal Revenue as expressed in the deficiency notice. On the other hand, in a tax refund suit "the taxpayer must not only overcome this presumption but must assume and discharge the added burden of demonstrating the correct amount of the tax due or that he owes no tax at all."[2] * * *

* * *

New Matters and Arbitrary Determinations

The Commissioner of Internal Revenue must sustain the burden of proof on all new matters.[3] The major problem which arises in applying this rule in practice lies in the determination of what is, and what is not, a "new matter" in the context of the case. [For a discussion of the "new matter" issue see Piper and Jerge, Shifting the Burden of Proof in Tax Court, 31 Tax Lawyer 303 (1978), excerpted at pages 278–282, below.]

Fraud

Fraud is an affirmative defense which must be proven by the Commissioner and as is the case where fraud is alleged in most courts, proof of the existence of fraud must be shown by "clear and

1. T.C.R. 142.

2. Compton v. United States, 334 F.2d 212, 216 (4th Cir. 1964). See also Helvering v. Taylor, 293 U.S. 507, 55

S.Ct. 287, 79 L.Ed. 623 (1935), aff'g Taylor v. Commissioner, 70 F.2d 619 (2d Cir. 1934).

3. T.C.R. 142(a).

convincing evidence." [7]   This is a higher standard of proof than the normally applicable preponderance of the evidence.

Foundation Manager Issues

Where the IRS alleges that the manager of a foundation has knowingly engaged in wrongful conduct, the burden is upon the Commissioner to prove by clear and convincing evidence the existence of such knowing conduct. This provision is intended to make the burden the same in this situation as it is in cases of alleged fraud.[8]

Transferee Liability

The liability of a "transferee" of property for tax relating to the property asserted against the transferor is a question which must be proven by the Commissioner by a preponderance of the evidence. If the transferee contests the merits of the assessment against the original taxpayer, however, the burden is upon the transferee as to the assessment.[9] On the issue of transferee liability the burden remains with the Commissioner of Internal Revenue in any event.

Accumulated Earnings Tax

The burden of proof with respect to accumulated earnings tax is determined by I.R.C. § 534. When the Internal Revenue Service imposes this tax upon a corporation, it is required to send to the taxpayer, before mailing the deficiency notice, a certified or registered letter explaining that the asserted deficiency includes an amount imposed because of the taxpayer's failure properly to distribute earnings.[10] If this notice is not sent, the burden of proof is on the Commissioner with respect to this issue.[11] Even if the IRS sends the required notice, the taxpayer may shift the burden to the Commissioner by submitting a statement setting forth the grounds upon which the taxpayer relies to establish that earnings are being retained to meet reasonable business expenses.[12]

* * *

SHIFTING THE BURDEN OF PROOF IN TAX COURT

John T. Piper and James M. Jerge
31 Tax Lawyer 303 (1978).

* * *

Most taxpayers who win suits in the Tax Court do so by proving facts from which the correct tax can be ascertained. They show that

7. See I.R.C. § 7454(a); T.C.R. 142(c).

8. See I.R.C. §§ 4941, 4944, & 4945 for the definition of foundation manager. See also I.R.C. § 7574(b) for the statutory burden of proof requirement and T.C.R. 142(c).

9. See I.R.C. § 6902(a); T.C.R. 142(d).

10. I.R.C. § 534(b).

11. I.R.C. § 534(a)(1).

12. I.R.C. § 534(c).

the Commissioner is wrong by proving the amount of tax that is correct.

There are opportunities, however, for prevailing in the Tax Court without meeting the burden of proving the correct tax by *shifting* the burden to the Commissioner.

*   *   *

MEANING OF "BURDEN OF PROOF"

*   *   *

"Burden of proof" can mean the burden of *ultimate persuasion*. Under that definition, the party with the burden bears the risk of nonpersuasion; he loses if there is insufficient evidence in the record or if the evidence is in equipoise.

The phrase "burden of proof" is also used by courts when they appear to mean merely the burden of *going forward*. It is likely that, in some situations to be discussed, the taxpayer who "shifts the burden of proof" in the court's phraseology *is really shifting only the burden of going forward*. The difference may be academic when the problem of presenting persuasive evidence is such that the Commissioner is unable to go forward. If the burden of going forward shifts to the Commissioner and he is unable to do so, the taxpayer will prevail. But if the Commissioner does go forward, the taxpayer may still bear the risk of nonpersuasion, including the risk that the evidence may be found in equipoise. *   *   *

TAX COURT RULE 142

Tax Court Rule 142 reads in part:

Burden of proof. (a) General. The burden of proof shall be upon the petitioner, except as otherwise provided by statute or determined by the Court; and except that, in respect of any new matter, increases in deficiency, and affirmative defenses, pleaded in his answer, it shall be upon the respondent *   *   *.

*   *   *

A. *New Matter*

Neither the Tax Court rules nor Tax Court decisions are explicit about what constitutes "new matter." Inferences about the meaning of "new matter" must be drawn from the facts of decided cases, which do not present a clear pattern.

The most cited case on "new matter" is *Sheldon Tauber*.[6] The Commissioner treated payment of notes by a corporation to its share-

---

6. 24 T.C. 179 (1955).

holders as a dividend. In his ninety-day letter, the Commissioner asserted that promissory notes were equity in a thin corporation.

This theory was destroyed in the Tax Court by the taxpayers' showing that the initial capital of the corporation was much more than that shown on its books. At that point, the Commissioner was "left with nothing to support the deficiencies he determined." The Commissioner then filed an amended answer, asserting that the taxpayers had recognized taxable gain on transfer of assets to the corporation in exchange for the notes. The Tax Court, citing Rule 32, said that "[t]he Commissioner must properly plead and prove any such alternative issue as the one he has in mind, which is upon a new theory different from and inconsistent with his determination of the deficiencies." The court held that the Commissioner failed to meet his burden under the new theory. Although the taxpayer offered no evidence to disprove the Commissioner's alternative theory, the taxpayer prevailed. Thus, in *Tauber,* the risk of nonpersuasion shifted. It is clear that Rule 142 can be used to shift the ultimate burden of proof (the risk of failing to persuade the court) to the Commissioner when the Commissioner is forced to plead new matter.

* * *

However, the more closely related the Commissioner's new position is to his original determination, the harder it is to say whether it should be deemed "new matter." The position taken in the ninety-day letter can sometimes be construed broadly enough to cover a new argument that will not be deemed "new matter." In that case the burden will not shift. * * *

* * *

B. *The Taylor Rule*

A principal limitation on Rule 142 is that *it operates only after the Commissioner has amended his answer.* When Rule 142 is not by its terms applicable, the taxpayer may find useful the rule of *Helvering v. Taylor.*[41] The rule, simply stated, is that the taxpayer is required to show only that the Commissioner is wrong; he does not have to produce evidence from which the correct tax can be determined. * * *

The Court [in *Taylor*] held:

On the facts shown by the taxpayer in this case, the Board [of Tax Appeals] should have held the [basis] apportionment arbitrary and the Commissioner's determination invalid. Then, upon appropriate application that further hearing be had, it should have heard evidence to show whether a fair

41. 293 U.S. 507, 55 S.Ct. 287, 79 L.Ed.
623 (1935).

apportionment might be made, and if so, the correct amount of the tax.[46]

* * *

There have been many cases applying the *Taylor* rule, consistently providing the taxpayer a rehearing at which the Commissioner is expected to produce a reasonable determination. Most cases are silent on who bears the burden of *proof* (risk of nonpersuasion) at the hearing. Thus, the cases in the *Taylor* line generally support an inference that its doctrine shifts only the burden of *going forward* to the Commissioner. Despite some statements about the presumption of correctness "disappearing" and that the "burden of proof will shift," it seems likely that the courts mean only a shifting of the burden of going forward.

If *Taylor* shifts only the burden of going forward, it will be most useful when the state of available evidence makes having the burden of going forward tantamount, for practical purposes, to having the burden of proof. When the Commissioner has the burden of going forward with a new determination (one that is not arbitrary and excessive) and is unable to do so for want of sufficient records or another satisfactory basis for a new determination, the consequences to the Commissioner's case would presumably be the same as if he had the burden of persuasion. He should lose.

* * *

Surprisingly, although the *Taylor* rule applies only in the Tax Court, the Tax Court has not itself applied the rule. [Those cases applying the *Taylor* rule] are decisions by the courts of appeals reversing and remanding to the Tax Court. In a reviewed decision, the Tax Court seemed to justify its refusal to apply the *Taylor* rule in part by the blame that it fixed on the taxpayers for failure to maintain accurate records.[61]

The *Taylor* rule applies on an item-by-item basis. A showing that the Commissioner has acted arbitrarily as to one item of income will shift the burden of going forward to the Commissioner as to that item only. Other items in the determination require independent showings pertaining specifically to those items.

Another limitation on the application of the *Taylor* rule is that it apparently does not apply to deductions. While that limitation is of questionable logic, and occasionally may be overlooked by the courts, it seems firmly fixed in the law. The rationale, originating in the *Taylor* case itself, appears to be that deductions are a matter of legislative grace. Just why the "legislative grace" rationale should excuse arbitrary conduct by the Commissioner has not been explained satisfactorily. After distinguishing Tax Court cases from refund cases

---

46. 293 U.S. 507 at 514, 55 S.Ct. 287 at 291, 79 L.Ed. 623.

61. Anthony DelSanter, 28 T.C. 845, 849 (1957).

(where taxpayers must prove the correct tax), the Court in *Taylor* went on to state: "for like reason the burden is upon the taxpayer to establish the amount of a deduction claimed." [64] While the language seems to be dictum and may not have been compelled by the citations given, it generally has been followed by the courts that refused to apply the *Taylor* rule to deductions.[65] Occasionally, however, courts have applied the *Taylor* rule to deductions, overlooking its apparent inapplicability.[66] In other cases, courts have refused to apply *Taylor*, but have discussed its possible application as though it might properly apply to deductions.[67]

The *Taylor* rule, in any event, does apply to basis deductions.[68] They apparently are not considered a matter of legislative grace.

* * *

(5) TRIAL AND DECISION

TAX COURT TRIALS: A VIEW FROM THE BENCH

Judge Theodore Tannenwald, Jr.
59 A.B.A.J. 295 (1973).

Justice Cardozo wrote in *The Nature of the Judicial Process* that there may be "the grandeur of conception that lifts [judges] into the realm of pure reason, above and beyond the sweep of perturbing and deflecting forces. Nonetheless, * * * they do not stand aloof on these chill and distant heights; and we shall not help the cause of truth by acting and speaking as if they do. The great tides and currents which engulf the rest of man do not turn aside in their course, and pass the judges by."

Clearly, what this statement means is that the trial of a case is a human process and that judges, as well as litigants, are human beings, with all the concomitant attributes—plus and minus. This is why, to use the words of the Supreme Court, decisions on many tax issues "must be based ultimately on the application of the fact-find-

---

64. 293 U.S. 507 at 514, 55 S.Ct. 287 at 290, 79 L.Ed. 623.

65. See Rockwell v. Commissioner, 512 F.2d 882 (9th Cir.), cert. denied 423 U.S. 1015, 96 S.Ct. 448, 46 L.Ed.2d 386 (1975); Nor-Cal Adjusters v. Commissioner, 503 F.2d 359 (9th Cir. 1974); Herbert v. Commissioner, 377 F.2d 65 (9th Cir. 1966); Welch v. Commissioner, 297 F.2d 309 (4th Cir. 1961).

66. See Welch v. Commissioner, 297 F.2d 309 (4th Cir. 1961); Cohen v. Commissioner, 266 F.2d 5 (9th Cir. 1959).

67. See Bernuth v. Commissioner, 470 F.2d 710 (2d Cir. 1972); United Aniline Co. v. Commissioner, 316 F.2d 701 (1st Cir. 1963).

68. Welch v. Commissioner, 297 F.2d 309, 311–312 (4th Cir. 1961); Caldwell v. Commissioner, 234 F.2d 660, 661 (6th Cir. 1956) (per curiam).

ing tribunal's experience with the mainsprings of human conduct"[1] and "common understanding and experience are touchstones for the interpretation of the revenue laws."[2]

If one accepts the premise that judges have many of the same instincts and traits as other human beings, one's concept of the trial of a tax case may change considerably. Most tax cases do not involve —as many people seem to assume—highly complicated and technical legal questions. Rather, they often involve many of the mundane problems of everyday life: Which of two divorced parents provided the required support for the children so as to be entitled to claim a dependency deduction? When is an expenditure for education deductible as an ordinary and necessary business expense? To what extent is an expenditure for travel a deductible business rather than a nondeductible commuting expense? What is the liability of a wife who dutifully signs a joint tax return with her husband and later discovers the return was fraudulent? The list is endless, and occasionally high drama is involved.

Some lawyers view the trial of a case in the United States Tax Court as the modern version of the feudal trial by battle, with mental instead of physical weapons. Victory is thought to go to the side scoring the most points, which is sometimes achieved through an incomplete disclosure of material facts. Other lawyers see the trial merely as a continuation of the informal procedures of the Internal Revenue Service. They believe victory will go to the one who talks (at trial) and writes (on brief) with an appearance of persuasiveness, irrespective of the facts or the efforts at trial to bring those facts to the court's attention.

Not only are these approaches insulting to the judge, in that they assume that he can either be ignored or deceived, but they are wrong. The object of a tax trial is to find out whether the taxpayer should properly be required to pay the taxes claimed. The taxpayer has a direct interest in the outcome—his money is at stake, and he is entitled to assurance that he will not be required to pay a penny more than he legally owes. But, unlike the ordinary tort or contract case, the other real party in interest is the taxpaying public. If the taxpayer gets off the hook for what he really should be required to pay, the pockets of all have been depleted. Thus, the public equally is entitled to assurance that the taxpayer will not be permitted to "eat, drink, and be merry" at the expense of the federal fisc.[4]

* * *

1. Commissioner v. Duberstein, 363 U.S. 278, 289, 80 S.Ct. 1190, 1198, 4 L.Ed.2d 1218, 1227 (1960).

2. Helvering v. Horst, 311 U.S. 112, 118, 61 S.Ct. 144, 147, 85 L.Ed. 75, 79 (1940).

4. See Friendly, J., concurring, Burde v. Commissioner, 352 F.2d 995, 1003 (2d Cir. 1965).

The two principal pretrial activities in a Tax Court case are settlement negotiations and preparation of a stipulation of facts. As to settlements, it is rare that the trial of a tax case is inevitable. Most cases can and should be settled. Outstanding examples are cases in which the question is merely substantiation of the amount of an otherwise concededly deductible item or the valuation of property. Particularly in valuation cases, litigants should frankly recognize that a precise determination is impossible and that the most that can be hoped for is that the judge will make an intelligent guess. If this recognition occurs, the imperative as well as the desirability of settlement will become obvious. But whatever the issue, no litigant should expect to obtain an undue advantage in a settlement. In fact, the best settlement is one which leaves both sides dissatisfied.

A bona fide effort to stipulate as many facts as possible is essential under Rule [91] of the Rules of Practice of the Tax Court and serves a variety of purposes. First, the stipulation process will force counsel to face the realities of the issues involved and as a consequence will often encourage partial, if not complete, settlements. Second, careful attention to the preparation of a stipulation of facts will enable the parties to state undisputed subsidiary facts with a degree of precision that in many cases will not be reflected in the oral testimony of witnesses with its inherent uncertainties. Finally, the more complete the stipulation of facts, the less the time required for the trial itself and the more meaningful the trial will be.

In most situations the judge probably will be receptive to receiving a copy of the stipulation in advance of trial. This will give him an opportunity to familiarize himself with the case, facilitate his understanding of the testimony, and afford him the opportunity to have gaps in that testimony filled—gaps counsel may have inadvertently overlooked. To the extent that written material is stipulated, needless expenditure of time in marking exhibits and offering them into evidence is avoided.

* * *

The actual trial in the Tax Court is, for the most part, an uncomplicated affair. The taxpayer, who usually has the burden of proof under Rule [142] of the Tax Court's Rules of Practice is generally expected to present his case first. Often, the respondent (the government) will offer no witnesses of its own. If the essential documentary evidence has been stipulated, the trial can be completed expeditiously.

* * *

* * * The development of a satisfactory record is critical. The more complete it is, the better the basis for decision. Counsel for the parties will be able to provide more complete analyses and arguments on brief. The trial judge will have a fuller understanding of the case and will be able to concentrate on the issues requiring decision without having his energies and attention diverted in a frustrating struggle with gaps in the record.

But the printed record is only a part—albeit an important part —of the trial. Judge Frank once stated: "The best and most accurate record is like a dehydrated peach. It has neither the substance nor the flavor of the fruit before it was dried. It resembles a pressed flower." [6]

This statement reflects the hard fact that the trial judge's memory will have dimmed when he reads the record at the time he is deciding the case and preparing his opinion. A well-tried case, with the lawyers prepared to ask all pertinent questions and to obtain coherent and complete answers from the witnesses, is likely to be etched in the trial judge's memory. He will tend to remember this kind of trial much more than a perfunctory or sloppy performance.

* * *

Once a case has been submitted, the trial judge, after he has prepared his findings of fact and an opinion, submits them to the chief judge of the Tax Court. The chief judge exercises a co-ordinating function in order to avoid inconsistencies between a proposed decision and prior or concurrent decisions of the court. He decides whether the proposed opinion should be published in the bound volume of Tax Court opinions, thereby conferring precedential status upon it. He may decide that in view of the factual content of a particular case or because it merely applies a well-established legal principle, no precedential value attaches and it should be released as a memorandum decision. Beyond this, the chief judge has a statutory responsibility under Section 7460(b) of the code to determine whether a case should be the subject of court review.

There are many factors that influence the chief judge to direct court review, and he has complete and exclusive discretion. The case may be one of first impression. It may involve a factual pattern of widespread interest because of the probability of recurrence. The trial judge may be proposing to overrule a prior Tax Court decision; he may be refusing to follow a court of appeals decision; [9] he may be distinguishing district court or prior Tax Court decisions on a basis the chief judge considers doubtful; or the chief judge may question the validity of the legal approach the trial judge has adopted. Each of these factors influences, but does not necessarily control the chief judge's action.

6. Broadcast Music v. Havana Madrid Restaurant Corporation, 175 F.2d 77, 80 (2d Cir. 1949).

9. Of course, if that decision is squarely in point and an appeal lies to the same circuit, it will be deemed controlling on the Tax Court. Jack E. Golsen, 54 T.C. 742, 756–758 (1970), aff'd 455 F.2d 985 (10th Cir. 1971). Compare Estate of George I. Speer, 57 T.C. 804, 812 (1972), on appeal (3d Cir., June 12, 1972).

The Tax Court meets in conference on most Fridays from September through June and during the summer months as the occasion requires. Proposed opinions are usually circulated a week in advance in order to give each judge an opportunity to do his own independent investigation. Often there is a good deal of discussion among the judges during that period. Sometimes, if a judge thinks he will dissent or concur in result, he will prepare an opinion and circulate it in advance. But his failure to do so will not preclude him from publishing his opinion if and when the trial judge's proposed opinion is adopted.

If the opinion is not adopted, the findings of fact and the opinion are not part of the record and are not available to the parties or others. If this happens, the trial judge may elect to rewrite the opinion the other way (which he may sometimes do if the issue is a close one and he is not certain of his position) or he may request that the case be reassigned to another judge. In either situation the rewritten opinion is submitted to the court conference for another vote. In a controversial case a vote may be so close as to cause the chief judge to hold an opinion until it can be voted on by a full complement of the judges of the court—a process that can sometimes delay final action for a substantial period of time.

The Tax Court plays a critical role in the development of the law of federal taxation. As a national court, it has an enormous responsibility to exert a "steady influence toward a systematic body of tax law" [10] and to try to introduce "some certitude in a landscape of shifting sands." [11] Its members are of varying ages. All have had prior tax law experience, either with the government or in private practice. As trial judges, their conduct is inevitably influenced by their personalities and backgrounds. There is a human element that practitioners before the court must take into account, along with the established rules of practice that govern the trial of the case.

(6) SMALL CASE PROCEDURE

TAX COURT PRACTICE

Marvin J. Garbis, Allen L. Schwait and Paula M. Junghans

The Tax Reform Act of 1969 created a new class of Tax Court cases which have come to be known as small tax cases.[1] The informal procedures followed in the trial of these cases are designed to provide a forum for the taxpayer whose alleged deficiency is too

---

10. See Justice Jackson dissenting in Arrowsmith v. Commissioner, 344 U. S. 6, 12 (1952). See also Dobson v. Commissioner, 320 U.S. 489 (1944).

11. See United States v. Rhode Island Hospital Trust Company, 355 F.2d 7, 10 (1st Cir. 1966).

1. See generally I.R.C. § 7463 and T. C.R. 170–179.

small to make the expensive and time-consuming process of ordinary Tax Court litigation practicable. A taxpayer is permitted to represent him or herself in any case tried before the Tax Court.[2] However, the complexities of most cases make an attempt at self-representation a risky venture. In small tax cases on the other hand, legal issues are de-emphasized, the rules of evidence are relaxed, and the court has discretion to act in such a manner as to make it feasible for the taxpayer to try a small case by him or herself with some reasonable possibility of success.

The assignment of trial commissioners to hear small tax cases, a practice which the court has followed since the implementation of the small case procedures, enables the court to hear these cases in cities where the Tax Court does not ordinarily sit. In addition, the trial commissioners enable the Tax Court to schedule special small case trial calendars as needed in those larger cities in which the Tax Court regularly holds sessions.

As of June 1, 1979, the amount in controversy in a small tax case may not exceed $5,000 in any taxable year where the controversy involves gift or income taxes, nor $5,000 for any single taxable estate where the controversy involves estate taxes.[3]　*　*　*

*　*　*

D.　TREATMENT OF DIVERSE COURTS OF APPEALS PRECEDENTS

(1) TAX COURT

LAWRENCE v. COMMISSIONER

27 T.C. 713 (1957).

MURDOCK, Judge.

*　*　*

One of the difficult problems which confronted the Tax Court, soon after it was created in 1926 as the Board of Tax Appeals, was what to do when an issue came before it again after a Court of Appeals had reversed its prior decision on that point. Clearly, it must thoroughly reconsider the problem in the light of the reasoning of the reversing appellate court and, if convinced thereby, the obvious procedure is to follow the higher court. But if still of the opinion that its original result was right, a court of national jurisdiction to avoid confusion should follow its own honest beliefs until the Supreme Court

2.　T.C.R. 24(b).　　　　3.　I.R.C. § 7463(a).

decides the point. The Tax Court early concluded that it should decide all cases as it thought right.

This was not too difficult if appeal in the later case would not lie to the reversing circuit. The difficulty increased when the Tax Court adhered to its own opinion when appeal would lie to the reversing circuit. The pressure increased in situations where more than one Court of Appeals differed with the Tax Court, but was relieved if one or more agreed with the Tax Court. * * *. Several Courts of Appeals have affirmed the Tax Court on the point decided in the present case.

The Tax Court and its individual Judges have always had respect for the 11 Courts of Appeals, have had no desire to ignore or lightly regard any decisions of those courts, and have carefully considered all suggestions of those courts. The Tax Court not infrequently has been persuaded by the reasoning of opinions of those courts to change its views on various questions being litigated.

* * *

The Tax Court has always believed that Congress intended it to decide all cases uniformly, regardless of where, in its nationwide jurisdiction, they may arise, and that it could not perform its assigned functions properly were it to decide one case one way and another differently merely because appeals in such cases might go to different Courts of Appeals. Congress, in the case of the Tax Court, "inverted the triangle" so that from a single national jurisdiction, the Tax Court appeals would spread out among 11 Courts of Appeals, each for a different circuit or portion of the United States. Congress faced the problem in the beginning as to whether the Tax Court jurisdiction and approach was to be local or nationwide and made it nationwide. Congress expected the Tax Court to set precedents for the uniform application of the tax laws, insofar as it would be able to do that.

The Tax Court feels that it is adequately supported in this belief not only by the creating legislation and legislative history but by other circumstances as well. The Tax Court never knows, when it decides a case, where any subsequent appeal from that decision may go, or whether there will be an appeal. It usually, but not always, knows where the return of a taxpayer was filed and, therefore, the circuit to which an appeal could go, but the law permits the parties in all cases to appeal by mutual agreement to any Court of Appeals. Sec. 7482(b)(2), I.R.C.1954. Furthermore, it frequently happens that a decision of the Tax Court is appealable to two or even more Courts of Appeals. A few examples will illustrate. A corporation, having stockholders scattered over the United States, makes a distribution to all. The Commissioner holds it taxable as a dividend from accumulated earnings. The stockholders join in a trial before the Tax Court which decides the issue as to all petitioning stockholders, contrary to a decision of Court of Appeals A, which reversed a prior Tax Court decision, but perhaps in line with an affirming decision of Court of Appeals B. If it had rendered a separate different decision for those stockholders in Circuit A, what amount of accumulated earnings would remain for future distribution? * * *

The Commissioner of Internal Revenue, who has the duty of administering the taxing statutes of the United States throughout the Nation, is required to apply these statutes uniformly, as he construes them. The Tax Court, being a tribunal with national jurisdiction over litigation involving the interpretation of Federal taxing statutes which may come to it from all parts of the country, has a similar obligation to apply with uniformity its interpretation of those statutes. That is the way it has always seen its statutory duty and, with all due respect to the Courts of Appeals, it cannot conscientiously change unless Congress or the Supreme Court so directs.

* * *

GOLSEN v. COMMISSIONER

54 T.C. 742 (1970).

RAUM, Judge.

* * *

The precise question relating to the deductibility of "interest" like that involved herein has been adjudicated by two Courts of Appeals. In one case, Campbell v. Cen-Tex., Inc., 377 F.2d 688 (C.A.5), decision went for the taxpayer; in the other, Goldman v. United States, 403 F.2d 776 (C.A.10), affirming 273 F.Supp. 137 (W.D.Okla.), the Government prevailed. *Goldman* involved the same insurance company, the same type of policies, and the same financial arrangements as are before us in the present case. *Cen-Tex.* involved a different insurance company but dealt with comparable financing arrangements. Despite some rather feeble attempts on the part of each side herein to distinguish the case adverse to it, we think that both cases are in point. It is our view that the Government's position is correct.

Moreover, we think that we are in any event bound by *Goldman* since it was decided by the Court of Appeals for the same circuit within which the present case arises. In thus concluding that we must follow *Goldman*, we recognize the contrary thrust of the oft-criticized case of Arthur L. Lawrence, 27 T.C. 713. Notwithstanding a number of the considerations which originally led us to that decision, it is our best judgment that better judicial administration requires us to follow a Court of Appeals decision which is squarely in point where appeal from our decision lies to that Court of Appeals and to that court alone.

Section 7482(a), I.R.C.1954, charges the Courts of Appeals with the primary responsibility for review of our decisions, and we think that where the Court of Appeals to which appeal lies has already passed upon the issue before us, efficient and harmonious judicial administration calls for us to follow the decision of that court. Moreover, the practice we are adopting does not jeopardize the Federal interest in uniform application of the internal revenue laws which we emphasized in *Lawrence*. We shall remain able to foster uniformity by giving effect to our own views in cases appealable to courts whose views have not yet been expressed, and, even where the relevant Court of Appeals has already made its views known, by explaining why we agree or disagree with the precedent that we feel constrained to follow.

To the extent that *Lawrence* is inconsistent with the views expressed herein it is hereby overruled. We note, however, that some of our decisions, because they involve two or more taxpayers, may be appealable to more than one circuit. This case presents no such problem, and accordingly we need not decide now what course to take in the event that we are faced with it.

* * *

———

(2) THE IRS ACQUIESCENCE AND NONACQUIESCENCE PROGRAM

The following statement, published on page 1 of each volume of the Internal Revenue Cumulative Bulletin, sets forth the Service's policy regarding acquiescence or nonacquiescence in decisions of the Tax Court:

It is the policy of the Internal Revenue Service to announce in the Internal Revenue Bulletin at the earliest practicable date the determination of the Commissioner to acquiesce or not acquiesce in a decision of the Tax Court which disallows a deficiency in tax determined by the Commissioner to be due.

Notice that the Commissioner has acquiesced or nonacquiesced in a decision of the Tax Court relates only to the issue or issues decided adversely to the Government.

Actions of acquiescences in adverse decisions shall be relied on by revenue officers and others concerned as conclusions of the Service only to the application of the law to the facts in the particular case. Caution should be exercised in extending the application of the decision to a similar case unless the facts and circumstances are substantially the same, and consideration should be given to the effect of new legislation, regulations, and rulings as well as subsequent court decisions and actions thereon.

Acquiescence in a decision means acceptance by the Service of the conclusion reached, and does not necessarily mean acceptance and approval of any or all of the reasons assigned by the court for its conclusions.

No announcements are made in the Bulletin with respect to memorandum opinions of the tax court.

The announcements published in the weekly Internal Revenue Bulletins are consolidated semiannually and annually. The semiannual consolidation appears in the first Bulletin for July and in the Cumulative Bulletin for the first half of the year and the annual consolidation appears in the first Bulletin for the following January and in the Cumulative Bulletin for the last half of the year.

DIXON v. UNITED STATES

Supreme Court of the United States, 1965.
381 U.S. 68, 85 S.Ct. 1301, 14 L.Ed.2d 223.

Mr. Justice BRENNAN delivered the opinion of the Court.

* * *

In Automobile Club of Michigan v. Commissioner of Internal Revenue, 353 U.S. at 183–184, 77 S.Ct. at 709, we held that the Commissioner is empowered retroactively to correct mistakes of law in the application of the tax laws to particular transactions. He may do so even where a taxpayer may have relied to his detriment on the Commissioner's mistake. This principle is no more than a reflection of the fact that Congress, not the Commissioner, prescribes the tax laws. The Commissioner's rulings have only such force as Congress chooses to give them, and Congress has not given them the force of law. Consequently it would appear that the Commissioner's acquiescence in an erroneous decision, published as a ruling, cannot in and of itself bar the United States from collecting a tax otherwise lawfully due.

But petitioners point to prefatory statements in the Internal Revenue Bulletins for 1952 and other years stating that Tax Court decisions acquiesced in "should be relied upon by officers and employees of the Bureau of Internal Revenue as precedents in the disposition of other cases." These are merely guidelines for Bureau personnel, however, and hardly help the petitioners here. The title pages of the same Revenue Bulletins give taxpayers explicit warning that rulings

"* * * are for the information of taxpayers and their counsel as showing the trend of official opinion in * * * the Bureau of Internal Revenue; the rulings other than Treasury Decisions have none of the force or effect of Treasury Decisions and *do not commit the Department to any interpretation of the law which has not been formally approved and promulgated by the Secretary of the Treasury.*" [6]

(Emphasis added.)

This admonition, together with the language of § 7805(b)'s predecessor, § 3791(b) of the 1939 Code, gave ample notice that the Commissioner's acquiescence * * * was not immune from subsequent retroactive correction to eliminate a mistake of law.

* * *

We cannot agree with petitioners that Automobile Club of Michigan v. Commissioner of Internal Revenue, supra, supports a finding that the Commissioner abused his discretion in giving retroactive effect to the withdrawal of the acquiescence. In that case the Commissioner had issued general pronouncements according exempt status to all automobile clubs similarly situated, following letter rulings to that effect in favor of the taxpayer. The Commissioner then corrected his erroneous view and, in 1945, specifically revoked the taxpayer's exemption for 1943 and subsequent years. We rejected the taxpayer's claim that the Commissioner had abused the discretion given him by § 7805(b)'s predecessor. The Commissioner's action had been forecast in a General Counsel Memorandum in 1943, and the corrected ruling had been applied to all automobile clubs for tax years back to 1943. 353 U.S., at 185–186, 77 S.Ct. at 710–711.

* * *

Although we mentioned certain facts in support of our conclusion in Automobile Club that there had not been an abuse of discretion in that case, it does not follow that the absence of one or more of these facts in another case wherein a ruling or regulation is applied retroactively establishes an abuse of discretion. Automobile Club merely examined all the circumstances of the particular case to determine whether the Commissioner had there abused his discretion. 353 U.S., at 185, 77 S.Ct. at 711. In the present case it cannot be said that the

---

6. Compare the current Internal Revenue Bulletins, wherein, with specific regard to acquiescences, it is stated:

"Actions of acquiescences in adverse decisions shall be relied on by Revenue officers and others concerned as conclusions of the Service only to the application of the law to the facts in the particular case. Caution should be exercised in extending the application of the decision to a similar case unless the facts and circumstances are substantially the same * * *." And the introduction to Revenue Rulings now expressly warns that "Except where other-

wise indicated, published rulings and procedures apply retroactively." See also Rev.Proc. 62–28, 1962–2 Cum.Bull. 496, which states at 504:

"A ruling * * * may be revoked or modified at any time in the wise administration of the taxing statutes. * * * If a ruling is revoked or modified, the revocation or modification applies to all open years under the statutes, unless the Commissioner exercises the discretionary powers given to him under section 7805(b) of the Code to limit the retroactive effect of the ruling."

Commissioner abused his discretion in either of the respects urged by petitioners. The absence of notice does not prove an abuse, since, for the reasons we have stated, the petitioners were not justified in relying on the acquiescence as precluding correction of the underlying mistake of law and the retroactive application of the correct law to their case. Since no reliance was warranted, no notice was required.

* * *

Insofar as petitioners' arguments question the policy of empowering the Commissioner to correct mistakes of law retroactively when a taxpayer acts to his detriment in reliance upon the Commissioner's acquiescence in an erroneous Tax Court decision, their arguments are more appropriately addressed to Congress. Congress has seen fit to allow the Commissioner to correct mistakes of law, and in § 7805(b) has given him a large measure of discretion in determining when to apply his corrections retroactively. In the circumstances of this case we cannot say that this discretion was abused.

Affirmed.

STATEMENT OF CHIEF COUNSEL

P–H Federal Taxes ¶ 41,360.w

* * *

It should be pointed out that usually the Government's position, once it has been fairly tested and rejected by one or more courts of appeals will be conformed to such adverse decision, provided they lay down a rule capable of fair and equitable administration on a nationwide basis and one likely to be acceptable to taxpayers in courts across the country. In fact, where the adverse decision, even of a trial court, is found to satisfy this standard it will frequently be accepted without circuit-court test.

* * *

While a course of litigation involving more than two circuits has in some instances resulted in a final resolution favorable to the Government, and in others favorable to the taxpayer, a number of recent instances emphasize why it may be unwise, as a policy matter, to conform office position too quickly to adverse decisions of a court of appeals or the Court of Claims.

* * *

There appear sound reasons upon occasion for pursuing the Service position in more than one circuit. To illustrate the broader administrative considerations, the reasoning of the court of appeals in the particular case may, while leading to a result favorable to the

w. Excerpted from the Report of Hearings before Subcommittee of the House Committee on Appropriations (p. 463), 84th Congress, 2d Session; in full at ¶ 76,379 P–H Fed.1956.

taxpayer in the given case, still if applied to taxpayers for purposes of other provisions of the Internal Revenue Code may redound to the benefit not of the taxpayer but of the Government. So that acceptance by the Internal Revenue Service * * * of the circuit court's reasoning will not be acceptable to taxpayers in all situations and the law will not therefore be settled nor will further litigation necessarily be prevented by the Government's acceptance of the circuit court's decision in such situations.

* * *

This office is well aware of the limited jurisdiction which the Supreme Court can and will assume in the Federal tax field. Every effort is made to confine recommendations for certiorari to those instances in which the need for final resolution by the Court is believed greatest from an overall administrative standpoint. As previously indicated, the great majority of adverse decisions are accepted as a matter of office policy. Where believed appropriate, legislative remedy is considered and recommended.

In pursuing such a course of litigation, this office is sensitive to the inconvenience to which some taxpayers may be put in protecting their rights pending final resolution of an issue. The problem of the Internal Revenue Service is a practical one of attempting to administer tax laws with consistency and uniformity, while at the same time avoiding resort to the processes of litigation where no useful purpose will be served. The examples [given in complete text of the statement] serve to illustrate in small measure why it would not be consistent with these fundamental objections for the Government to follow each and every adverse court of appeals decision, inasmuch as such a policy applied on a nationwide basis could only lead to confusion, unfairness, and complete lack of uniformity.

* * *

---

(3) THE SOLUTION: A NATIONAL COURT OF TAX APPEALS?

PROPOSALS FOR A NEW NATIONAL COURT OF TAX APPEALS * * *

Meeting of the Section of Taxation, American Bar Association—Panel Discussion held May 19, 1979
33 Tax Lawyer 7 (1979).

Mr. Redman: Interest has been revived within the last year in an old subject, namely the procedures for litigating tax cases. Various proposals have been under discussion in different circles since last Fall. These have now culminated in the form of two bills introduced by Senator Kennedy, namely S. 677 and S. 678.

Our prime interest today is the latter bill and more particularly those of its provisions dealing with the concept of a National Court of Tax Appeals. First, does the concept make sense under any circumstances, regardless of how it is done; and secondly, assuming it is to be done, how best should it be done in terms of staffing the court. S. 678 proposes a unique technique in the latter regard. It calls for authorizing the Chief Justice to appoint members of this court for three-year terms from among the sitting judges of the federal circuit courts of appeals. * * *

* * *

Our participants today are Mr. Carr Ferguson, Assistant Attorney General, Tax Division, Mr. Jerome Kurtz, Commissioner of Internal Revenue, Mr. Kenneth Feinberg, Senator Kennedy's legislative assistant with particular responsibility for S. 678, and Marvin Garbis, Chairman of the Section's Committee on Court Procedures.

* * *

With that introduction we will go first to our initial topic, the concept of a national court of tax appeals. The basic position in favor of that concept will be presented by Mr. Feinberg, and arguments to the contrary will be presented by Mr. Garbis.

Mr. Feinberg: * * * Although there will be various issues raised this afternoon, I must defer at the outset to some fifty years of academic and practical discussion and debate concerning the issue of a centralized court of tax appeals. Erwin Griswold, Henry Friendly, and others have made the arguments for a national court of tax appeals; I can do little more than second their words.

We must deal with two problems that plague both our existing federal judiciary and the administration of the tax law. One is the uncertainty that surrounds tax decision-making today. Whether one talks about forum shopping, the race to the courthouse, administrative inconvenience, or cost, there is a feeling on the part of many that we must do something about this unseemly situation in the area of tax law and tax jurisdiction. That is what Senator Kennedy's proposal is designed to accomplish.

The real and interesting issues surrounding this new tax court proposal do not relate to whether or not we need the tax court. It seems to me that issue has long been resolved. Is it feasible, however, to develop and create a court that will meet the objections and concerns that have been targeted against such a proposal over the years? We think we've done that in S. 678.

The second issue does not concern the question of certainty needed in the development of tax law, but, rather, is what Judge Friendly has raised time and time again—that the existing system is a luxury that the federal courts can no longer afford.

Quantitatively, tax cases are not a particular burden on the federal courts. Qualitatively, in terms of time—man hours and time spent in deciding tax cases—they are a major burden on the existing federal judiciary. Thus, whether one looks at the new court in terms of tax law—the development of certainty—or in terms of the quality of judicial administration, there is a feeling by many that something should be done. S. 678 is designed to address these problems.

*   *   *

Mr. Garbis: If I might be a little flippant, I am concerned about one who says (which Mr. Feinberg hasn't directly) "I can't do it as well as you've been doing it, but I can do it faster." I want to know how much not as well, how much faster, and what else will happen to us when you develop this new system.

Essentially, the proposers of this concept say (1) there will be greater efficiency, (2) there will be a shorter period of uncertainty, (3) we will eliminate different tax laws in different circuits, and (4) we will reduce the volume of litigation, both administrative and judicial.

Those who propose this acknowledge some of the costs. They concede that the new system will provide quickness, but that quality will suffer "somewhat." They argue "Better a fast and certain answer than a slower, more sifted and ventilated one." They claim there is a balance, and I agree. But I think it is too easy to overstate the benefits from this concept and to understate the costs.

I think the question is this: Are the removal (or the shortening) of a period of uncertainty and the corresponding reduced delay in getting an answer worth the added uncertainty that I submit this court will add to our overall legal system and the disruption that we're going to face.

First, how big a problem do we really have? A lot of people traverse the country giving speeches on forum selections. Like Judge Smith, they cite the Sam Berger Investment Company case [3] and other cases in which there have been different results for members of the same partnership.

I submit to you there aren't very many such examples. There are the "horribles," but they are few indeed. I don't think there are very many issues, although there are some, in which we have uncertainty and divided circuits. Although there is some of that, it's a very, very small percentage of the tax cases.

The new court is supposed to eliminate all that, but I am prompted to ask this: Will creation of this new court really remove from our vocabulary that dirty word, non-acquiesce? In short, will the

---

3. See Ginsburg v. United States, 396 F.2d 983, 986 (Ct.Cl.1968); Morse v. United States, 371 F.2d 474, 482 (Ct. Cl.1968); Freeland v. Commissioner, 35 P–H T.C. Memo ¶ 66,283, aff'd, 393 F.2d 573 (9th Cir. 1968).

Service accept and follow every decision of this new court and not preserve the issue for reconsideration, even though, in the Service's view, the decision is clearly wrong, the argument was not presented properly, and so forth.

I submit that it won't. I ask you to consider that. If my claim is correct, there will not be as much elimination of uncertainty as supposed. We've all had experience with the Service during our professional lifetimes and we know it is not likely that the Service will abandon a position because of a decision that they think is wrong or should be limited to its facts.

The Service is not the only advocate in our system. I submit that taxpayers will not sit quietly and accept a decision that they "know" is wrong. And, although slightly off of this subject, I further ask what will happen with regard to reconsideration if we create a court with rotating judicial assignments, so that the whole court changes every few years and a majority changes every year or two. I submit that uncertainty may take on a new dimension.

If the proposed system functions properly, the first case will be of tremendous importance on every issue. I submit that the Service will be in a position to control selection of the first case to a greater extent than is now possible. Those who lived through the litigation on the recognition of professional associations recall what happened in that area. I don't blame government lawyers. They're advocates. They want to press their point in the best possible context. When the first case came up, however, and it was under the wrong set of regulations, they conceded the case. The taxpayer was helpless. The government waited for the best case. They tried to get the "right" precedent. That can still be done and I don't blame anyone for trying to do it. But it is a fact that it will be far easier for the Service to "program" the timing of cases under the proposed system.

The proposed court would be composed, whether it has temporary or permanent judges, of what we presume will be good judges. They too will be aware that the first case is the biggest decision they will issue. They will be aware of the fact that they haven't had the sifting and ventilating process that now goes on before a case comes to the Supreme Court. I think you will see, and I ask to you to contemplate, what I would call the "Supreme Court syndrome." That is, an inclination to decide cases very carefully and as narrowly as possible, so that even in the single court there can be a very gradual development of law in an area. If you consider what has happened in the summons enforcement action in one court over a long period of time from Reisman v. Caplin [4] to *LaSalle*,[5] I think you can see that,

4. 375 U.S. 440, 84 S.Ct. 508, 11 L.Ed. 2d 459 (1964).

5. United States v. LaSalle Nat'l Bank, 437 U.S. 298, 98 S.Ct. 2357, 57 L.Ed. 2d 221 (1978).

even in one court, taking substantial and regular bites at a tough issue, there will remain a long period of uncertainty.

Another element of concern to me appears crystal clear. Every important case, the case that is the reason for this court to exist, should be heard en banc. That means in Washington, D.C.

Most of the cases (as admitted by the advocates) will be heard by panels because they won't be important. I submit that we can't measure the effectiveness of the proposed court by the majority of these cases. Well over ninety percent of the cases can be referred to panels. There's no reason to take those away from the present circuits. They are routine. Thus in every case that is important, all the litigants must argue the case en banc in Washington.

Another cost that is less theoretical and more practical and emotional, is the impact on the Tax Court. I think the proposal will change the character of the Tax Court. Perhaps one can say it would be a more efficient tribunal because it won't have to waste time with court-reviewed decisions or with the care it now takes in issuing at the trial level, theoretically earlier than the proposed court would, a decision that impacts, if not binds, every taxpayer in the country.

The Tax Court won't have to do that. After a period of time, I presume, it won't have to carefully review its decisions because its function will be that of preparing its cases for review by what will then be the national tribunal declaring the tax law.

I also think, there will be a cost in the creation of uncertainty and problems. First, I would mention the transition. It's easy to "pooh-pooh" this because there's always a transition problem with any change. If the new court is created, every issue that has not been decided by the Supreme Court is now wide open; even those issues that have been settled in a circuit are fair game for relitigation. And, as has been pointed out, pity the person who planned his transaction relying on the settled law of the Ninth Circuit, but who now faces an audit after the creation of a new court.

Beyond the transition there is another problem worthy of attention. What will be transferred to the new court are not tax *issues* but tax *cases*. This means that the court of tax appeals must decide procedural and substantive issues outside of the Code. This creates a tremendous problem, particularly in district court appeals.

I also put on the table something that the court must face almost immediately. Is there going to be a "reverse *Golsen* rule"? [6] That is, for an issue not within the Code, will the case be decided as it would have been decided by the circuit in which the appeal would otherwise lie? I submit that the new court might have to reach that position. If it does, then there will be the same number of, if not

6. Jack E. Golsen, 54 T.C. 742 (1970).

more, cases that must be decided on identical facts, differently for different taxpayers, depending on their circuits.

But suppose the court doesn't go that way. Suppose they say "No, we are going to decide the entire case our way." In that case we have separate procedural and substantive areas of law applicable to the same taxpayer, depending upon whether they arise in a tax case or in another type of case.

You can think about this in terms of property rights, in terms of other federal statutes, and so forth. Let me give a clear example. We are now going through a transition period in the scope of the attorney-client privilege in a corporate context. Some courts adopt the scope of employment test. A communication within the scope of employment of an employee may be privileged. Other courts have adopted the control-group test. The privilege applies to communication for a narrow group at the top.

Put yourself in a district court. You're the attorney, and you're either asked to produce documents in response to a summons or you're asked questions. The district court says, "Well, the Fourth Circuit has the scope of employment test." But this is a tax case, and the Court of Tax Appeals has the control group test. Therefore, you've got to answer the question or produce the documents because the appeal to the Court of Tax Appeals means that under its known test it affirms and orders you to produce.

But if you don't produce the documents (and risk contempt) and if you could appeal to the Fourth Circuit, they will reverse because they reject the control group test and follow the scope of employment test.

Another problem area relates to the summons context. The new tax court would have jurisdiction over summons enforcement action. It's going to develop law relating to enforcement of summonses. But under the *Genser* [7] case (which I hope all the circuits will follow), after a criminal prosecution, you can move to suppress any evidence gathered by any summons. Therefore, you can have a case in which a summons that was duly enforced on appeal yields evidence that is nevertheless suppressed because the law of the circuit is not the same as the law of the national court of tax appeals.

Finally, it is impossible to provide that every tax issue go to the new court. Criminal cases, bankruptcy cases, and so forth, will go to the circuits. The circuit courts of appeals are not known to be retiring violets that will defer unquestioningly to a national court of tax appeals. I believe differences will remain a part of our system even with the new court.

Mr. Redman: I think it's fair to say that the bottom line choice is quicker certainty at the cost of less quality. Is that the price we

7. United States v. Genser, 582 F.2d 292 (3rd Cir. 1978).

would be paying, and is it worth it? Mr. Commissioner, perhaps you would like to respond.

Commissioner Kurtz: I'd like to put this in a somewhat different context. I don't think it's a question of whether this court favors the taxpayer or the tax administrator. If you talk about decisions that came out one way and then, after being relitigated, go another way, my feeling is that there are as many that turned against the government later on as turned against the taxpayer.

The issue is not who will gain an advantage from this court— taxpayers or tax administrators—but whether the court will produce a better system for both. On this, I think we're on the same side.

* * *

Thinking about it that way, I believe the question is a very close one and the answer is not at all obvious. I think the tradeoff is exactly the one that Mr. Redman described. It is a tradeoff of earlier certainty, against the sense that when cases are relitigated the law has a tendency to move toward a better answer.

I'm not sure that's completely demonstrable, but we probably all agree that it is so, having faith in our profession to move toward ultimate justice.

Sitting where I do, I am in favor of the single court because I put a heavy value on certainty. It is not healthy for the Service to continue litigating cases and requiring taxpayers to go through the courts after other courts have already decided that the taxpayers should win.

It is something we don't like to do. It is a burden on taxpayers and there's little to justify it, except that, given the present system and our faith that the law will move in the right direction, we have some obligation to litigate further when we feel decisions are clearly wrong.

On the other hand, I think the uncertainty is more of a burden on government than it is on taxpayers who may have to litigate issues already decided. When the government wins a case, even in a court of appeals, it does not in any realistic way bind taxpayers in the way they report transactions. This is particularly true if the taxpayer is not in that circuit and the lawyer or accountant has some feeling that the deciding circuit is wrong.

Thus we have little opportunity to get issues clearly resolved for reporting purposes. Recognizing that only a relatively small percentage of returns are audited, I believe there is a substantial sacrifice, in terms of even-handed tax administration, in not having an authority that can decide cases and issues early.

Of course there will be questions of whether the resolution of an issue against a particular factual background will cover a similar issue under different facts. Cases will always be litigated on both sides to test the scope of the earlier decision. It seems to me, however, that at least we won't have the kind of diversity that exists today. For decisions that are obviously bad, either for the taxpayer or the tax administrator, there is, of course, recourse to Congress. That's not always a satisfactory way to solve issues, but it does give a safety valve and, my guess is, we would be there in particular cases six or eight years sooner.

Mr. Redman: Thank you Mr. Kurtz. Let's move now to Mr. Ferguson, whose recent testimony before the Senate Judiciary Committee indicates the closeness of the question and his own difficulty in making a choice.

Mr. Ferguson: I must confess I still suffer from split vision on this issue. I don't think participation in litigation, even as intensively as Mr. Garbis and I have been fortunate enough to do, gives one a clear answer to this very difficult question.

I have a couple of observations that perhaps many of you would second. The arguments in favor of a centralized court of tax appeals are much more obvious and much more easily and quickly grasped than are the arguments against. That's true of many issues of reform, whether in tax or other fields. We can easily see the appeal of a change in the law before we begin to discover the problems that attend any proposed change.

The opportunities for speedier resolution on a national basis of tax issues, which the court of tax appeals would clearly provide, is a plus. While I personally have little problem with forum shopping at the trial level, and believe that it may be beneficial in some cases, I find forum shopping at the appellate level very troublesome. The present circuit system keeps this to a minimum by restricting appellate venue to place of residence or principal place of business. Nonetheless, discrepancies in the way taxpayers are treated from one circuit to another do exist.

I think that the depth of one's reaction to what Mr. Feinberg called the "unseemly uncertainty" of the tax law, caused by these conflicts, depends upon the proximity of one's practice to the courtroom. Those of us who have engaged in office practice without recourse to the courts find much uncertainty in the tax law that has very little to do with circuit conflicts. In my experience in planning I was rarely—almost never—deeply concerned about a planning issue being poised upon a conflict between judicial opinions of two circuit courts. If that kind of uncertainty in the law exists, one tends to plan around the problem.

If, on the other hand, one's practice tends to issues that arise on audit or forensically later on, the proliferation of cases caused by a lack of commanding authority at the appellate level is troublesome, and there is a waste both to the courts and to taxpayers in the multiplicity of lawsuits that frequently result.

In summary, I believe that S. 678 would reduce the amount of tax litigation and would provide speedier resolution of doubtful issues. These are clear benefits.

On the other side, I am persuaded that the concerns that Mr. Garbis expressed are valid. Very frequently, in my experience, an issue raised for the first time on appeal is not raised in a vacuum. It is raised in a matrix of other questions, and in the focus and bias of a particular fact pattern.

The significance of that issue and the way it is articulated when it is resolved by the Court of Appeals may not be apparent until after the initial decision is made. The development of the considerations for and against a particular issue frequently is given insufficient attention in both the government's and the taxpayers' brief, and these considerations may not be fully appreciated by a court in resolving an issue for the first time. Part of the genius of the circuit system is that it permits reanalysis in other settings of the same issue free of the numbing effect of *stare decisis*.

Another concern, which has less to do with the shaping or improving of the quality of the tax law, is to assure all taxpayers an impartial, open, and concerned decision by an independent judiciary.

A perhaps inexact, but nonetheless easily understood, analogy in a field outside the tax law is the litigation during the 1950s and 1960s on busing and integration. How likely is it that the federal court system would have been able to withstand the agonizing pressures and problems that Brown v. Board of Education [8] placed on many parts of the country 25 years ago, were it not for the fact that the magistrates, the decision-makers in the federal district courts and courts of appeals, were sons and daughters of the soil from which the problems arose?

I believe there is still a sense of value in regionalism that we as a group may not appreciate, but that our clients, particularly individual clients, do. There is a sense of comfort and satisfaction with a system that permits resolution by lawyers who are from the same states as the parties, and who appreciate local problems, local economic situations, and local customs and differences in the substantive laws of our various states.

I mean no disrespect to the arguments for centralism or to the very beneficial unifying influence of the United States Tax Court and the marvelous job that court has done in dealing every day with issues of local law and their impact on our federal system. But I think the opportunity for review of that court's decision by the eleven circuits has allowed taxpayers and those of us who are also concerned to feel that the tax law has continued to grow sturdily and well as part of the balance of the *corpus juris* of this country.

8.   347 U.S. 483, 74 S.Ct. 686, 93 L.Ed. 873 (1954), supplemented, 349 U.S. 294, 75 S.Ct. 753, 99 L.Ed. 1083 (1955).

And while I think that this impression could survive in the context of a specialized court of tax appeals, whether centered in Washington or not, I think it would necessarily result from a significant amount of public education, sophistication, and acceptance of the circumstance of having the tax system sifted out from the rest of our judicial system.

As I say, I have split vision on this issue and would feel more comfortable with a firm conviction one way or the other. Nevertheless, I feel that those urging change have not carried the burden of proving that the change would clearly outweigh the adjustments necessary to implement it.

*   *   *

E. DECLARATORY JUDGMENTS AND DISCLOSURE ACTIONS

The vast majority of cases in the Tax Court are those brought by taxpayers for a redetermination of deficiencies determined by the Commissioner of Internal Revenue. This "deficiency" jurisdiction has been provided to the Tax Court since its creation as the Board of Tax Appeals. The *raison d'etre* of the court is to provide a prepayment forum for the litigation of a taxpayer's substantive tax liability. However, since 1975 the Tax Court also has exercised jurisdiction over several types of tax-related declaratory judgment and disclosure actions.

Initially, the Tax Court was authorized to render declaratory judgments as to the initial or continuing qualification of employer (and self-employed) retirement plans.[x] The Tax Reform Act of 1976 added to the declaratory judgment jurisdiction of the Tax Court, authorizing the rendition of judgments as to the following:

(a) The initial or continuing qualification of an organization as exempt under section 501(a) or as a qualified charitable gift recipient under section 170(c)(2).[y]

(b) The initial or continuing classification of an organization as a private foundation under section 509(a) or as a private operating foundation under section 4942(j)(3).[z]

(c) Determinations under section 367,[a] concerning transfers of

---

x. IRC § 7476.

y. IRC § 7428.

z. Id.

a. Section 367 of the Code provides that where a United States person transfers property to a foreign corporation, in connection with an ex-
change described in section 332, 351, 354, 355, 356 or 361, the foreign corporation shall not be recognized as a corporation for purposes of determining recognition of gain on the transfer, unless there has been a determination that the exchange is not part of a plan to avoid federal income taxes. IRC § 367(a)(1).

property to foreign corporations in connection with certain
types of exchanges.[b]

In 1978, the Congress added once more to the declaratory judgment
jurisdiction of the Tax Court. For determinations made after 1978,
the Tax Court was authorized to issue declaratory judgments regarding the tax exempt status of interest on certain governmental obligations under section 103(a).[c]

The Tax Reform Act of 1976 also added to the Tax Court's jurisdiction several types of disclosure actions. These are actions:

(a) To restrain disclosure by the Internal Revenue Service of information contained in written determinations and background file documents relating thereto.[d]

(b) To require additional disclosure from the Internal Revenue
Service of information contained in written determinations
and background file documents relating thereto.[e]

(c) To obtain the identity of certain third-parties making contact with the Internal Revenue Service regarding pending requests for written determinations.[f]

The Tax Court procedures in declaratory judgment and disclosure actions are governed largely by special rules designed for these
types of cases.[g] Those actions which involve solely a review of an Internal Revenue Service determination made upon materials submitted
by a taxpayer, such as the initial qualification of a retirement plan or
of an alleged charitable organization, normally would be decided upon
the administrative record. Other actions, for example, whether revocation of an organization's tax exempt status was proper in light of
events occuring subsequent to the organization's initial qualification,
may require pre-trial and trial procedures similar to those in a tax
deficiency case. In any event, these declaratory judgment and disclosure actions can raise procedural and practical problems. The potential existence of multiple parties, the possibility that the taxpayer and
the Internal Revenue Service may be aligned against a third party
(protesting qualification, for example), the possibility of the Labor
Department and/or the Pension Benefit Guaranty Corporation as a
litigant (and possibly as a litigant opposed to the IRS) and other
complexities can be features of these types of actions.

---

b. IRC § 7477.

c. IRC § 7478.

d. IRC § 6110(f)(3).

e. IRC § 6110(f)(4). Jurisdiction is
concurrent with the United States
District Court for the District of Columbia.

f. IRC § 6110(d)(3). This provision
enables taxpayers to investigate alle-

gations of undue influence or other
improprieties relating to the issuance
of a written determination. Jurisdiction is concurrent with the United
States District Court for the District
of Columbia.

g. T.C.R. 210 et seq. (declaratory judgment actions), 220 et seq. (disclosure
actions). For a complete discussion
of the details of these procedures see
Garbis and Schwait, Tax Court Practice, Chs. 14, 15 (1974, 1980 Supp.).

NOTE

Although the wisdom of declaratory judgments in tax matters can be debated, there was a sound rationale for each type of action currently permitted. In each case there was concern that the inability to obtain judicial review of an adverse IRS determination would prevent taxpayers from undertaking legitimate and socially useful activities. An organization cannot operate effectively or solicit contributions if it has not been determined exempt, even if it, or its contributors, could receive vindication (in litigation occurring years after the fact) as to the deductibility and tax exempt status of the contributions. An employer would be most unwise to proceed to make substantial contributions to a retirement plan which, at the administrative level, has been determined to be unqualified. A township can hardly sell bonds if it must represent to investors that, although the IRS takes the position that the interest is taxable, counsel for the township feels strongly that, if the investor will take the matter to court, it is more likely than not that the interest will be declared exempt.

Persuasive arguments can thus be made for providing declaratory judgment jurisdiction with respect to the qualification of exempt organizations and retirement plans, and of the taxability of interest on government obligations as well as with respect to determinations involving transfers to foreign corporations. However, apparently equally effective arguments can be made in other contexts in which taxpayers are required to accept IRS dictates and forego transactions or take substantial tax risks. It could be argued that in every case of denial of a private ruling request the taxpayer should be able to obtain a declaratory judgment. However, this would overwhelm the resources of the Tax Court. Obviously, Congress cannot overload the Tax Court or the other tax litigation forums with declaratory judgment cases. In all but the most essential areas taxpayers must perform their own analyses of tax effects and bear the risk if they choose to take steps which will be challenged by the IRS. Further expansion of the declaratory judgment jurisdiction of the Tax Court should be undertaken, if at all, most carefully.

QUESTION

What would you add to, or subtract from, the declaratory judgment jurisdiction of the Tax Court?

SECTION 4. TAX REFUND LITIGATION

A. JURISDICTIONAL PREREQUISITES

Tax refund suits are actions in which the sovereign has waived immunity and consented to be sued by taxpayers who wish to contest their tax liability.[h] This waiver of sovereign immunity has been conditioned upon the taxpayer's complying with a number of prerequi-

h. United States v. Michel, 282 U.S. 656, 51 S.Ct. 284, 75 L.Ed. 598 (1931).

sites to the bringing of his or her suit.[i] These jurisdictional prerequisites are strictly construed. As stated by Justice Holmes, speaking for the Supreme Court of the United States:

> Men must turn square corners when they deal with the Government. If it attaches even purely formal conditions to its consent to be sued, those conditions must be complied with. *Lex non praecipit inutilia* [j] expresses rather an ideal than an accomplished fact.[k]

In order to bring a tax refund suit before a court, a taxpayer must take all of the required steps in the required order. He must:

1. Pay the tax of which refund is sought;

2. File a proper and timely claim for refund;

3. Wait until six months pass or the claim for refund is denied; and

4. File a timely and proper complaint with the court.

B. THE FULL PAYMENT RULE

The case of Flora v. United States, excerpted below, should be read not only for its holding espousing what has come to be known as the "full payment rule", but also for its detailed discussion of the history and structure of our system for the resolution of civil tax controversies.

FLORA v. UNITED STATES

Supreme Court of the United States, 1960.
362 U.S. 145, 80 S.Ct. 630, 4 L.Ed.2d 623;
aff'g on reh., 357 U.S. 63, 78 S.Ct. 1079, 2 L.Ed.2d 1165 (1958).

Mr. Chief Justice WARREN delivered the opinion of the Court.

The question presented is whether a Federal District Court has jurisdiction under 28 U.S.C.A. § 1346(a)(1) of a suit by a taxpayer for the refund of income tax payments which did not discharge the entire amount of his assessment.

THE FACTS

[The IRS assessed a deficiency of $28,908.60 against the taxpayer. The taxpayer paid $5,058.54 and then filed a claim for refund of that amount. The lower court dismissed the refund claim for lack of jurisdiction due to the absence of a full payment on the amount as-

---

i. United States v. Chicago Golf Club, 84 F.2d 914 (7th Cir. 1936); Lipsett v. United States, 37 F.R.D. 549 (S.D.N.Y.1965), appeal dism'd, 359 F.2d 956 (2d Cir. 1966).

j. The law does not require a useless act.

k. Rock Island, A. & L. R. R. Co. v. United States, 254 U.S. 141, 143, 41 S.Ct. 55, 56, 65 L.Ed. 188 (1920).

sessed. The Court of Appeals for the Tenth Circuit affirmed the decision of the district court, and the Supreme Court granted certiorari to resolve a conflict among the Courts of Appeals.]

* * *

THE STATUTE

* * *

Section 1346(a)(1) provides that the District Courts shall have jurisdiction, concurrent with the Court of Claims, of

"(1) Any civil action against the United States for the recovery of *any internal-revenue tax* alleged to have been erroneously or illegally assessed or collected, or *any penalty* claimed to have been collected without authority or *any sum* alleged to have been excessive or in any manner wrongfully collected under the internal-revenue laws * * *." (Emphasis added.)

It is clear enough that the phrase "any internal-revenue tax" can readily be construed to refer to payment of the entire amount of an assessment. Such an interpretation is suggested by the nature of the income tax, which is "*A* tax * * * imposed for each taxable year," with the "amount of *the* tax" determined in accordance with prescribed schedules. (Emphasis added.) But it is argued that this reading of the statute is foreclosed by the presence in § 1346(a)(1) of the phrase "any sum." This contention appears to be based upon the notion that "any sum" is a catchall which confers jurisdiction to adjudicate suits for refund of part of a tax. A catchall the phrase surely is; but to say this is not to define what it catches. The sweeping role which petitioner assigns these words is based upon a conjunctive reading of "any internal-revenue tax," "any penalty," and "any sum." But we believe that the statute more readily lends itself to the disjunctive reading which is suggested by the connective "or." That is, "any sum," instead of being related to "any internal-revenue tax" and "any penalty," may refer to amounts which are neither taxes nor penalties. Under this interpretation, the function of the phrase is to permit suit for recovery of items which might not be designated as either "taxes" or "penalties" by Congress or the courts. One obvious example of such a "sum" is interest. And it is significant that many old tax statutes described the amount which was to be assessed under certain circumstances as a "sum" to be added to the tax, simply as a "sum," as a "percentum," or as "costs." Such a rendition of the statute, which is supported by precedent, frees the phrase "any internal-revenue tax" from the qualifications imposed upon it by petitioner and permits it to be given what we regard as its more natural reading—the full tax. Moreover, this construction, under which each phrase is assigned a distinct meaning, imputes to

Congress a surer grammatical touch than does the alternative interpretation, under which the "any sum" phrase completely assimilates the other two. Surely a much clearer statute could have been written to authorize suits for refund of any part of a tax merely by use of the phrase "a tax or any portion thereof," or simply "any sum paid under the internal revenue laws." This Court naturally does not review congressional enactments as a panel of grammarians; but neither do we regard ordinary principles of English prose as irrelevant to a construction of those enactments.

We conclude that the language of § 1346(a)(1) can be more readily construed to require payment of the full tax before suit than to permit suit for recovery of a part payment. But * * * the statutory language is not absolutely controlling, and consequently resort must be had to whatever other materials might be relevant.

LEGISLATIVE HISTORY AND HISTORICAL BACKGROUND

Although frequently the legislative history of a statute is the most fruitful source of instruction as to its proper interpretation, in this case that history is barren of any clue to congressional intent.

* * *

Thus there is presented a vexing situation—statutory language which is inconclusive and legislative history which is irrelevant. This, of course, does not necessarily mean that § 1346(a)(1) expresses no congressional intent with respect to the issue before the Court; but it does make that intent uncommonly difficult to divine.

It is argued, however, that the puzzle may be solved through consideration of the historical basis of a suit to recover a tax illegally assessed. The argument proceeds as follows: A suit to recover taxes could, before the Tucker Act,[l] be brought only against the Collector. Such a suit was based upon the common-law count of assumpsit for money had and received, and the nature of that count requires the inference that a suit for recovery of part payment of a tax could have been maintained. Neither the Tucker Act nor the 1921 amendment indicates an intent to change the nature of the refund action in any pertinent respect. Consequently, there is no warrant for importing into § 1346(a)(1) a full-payment requirement.

For reasons which will appear later, we believe that the conclusion would not follow even if the premises were clearly sound. But in addition we have substantial doubt about the validity of the premises. As we have already indicated, the language of the 1921 amendment does in fact tend to indicate a congressional purpose to require full payment as a jurisdictional prerequisite to suit for refund. Moreover, we are not satisfied that the suit against the Collector was identical to the common-law action of assumpsit for money had and re-

_____

l. 24 Stat. 505 (1887), as amended, 28
U.S.C.A. §§ 1346, 1491.

ceived. One difficulty is that, because of the Act of February 26, 1845, which restored the right of action against the Collector after this Court had held that it had been implicitly eliminated by other legislation, the Court no longer regarded the suit as a common-law action, but rather as a statutory remedy which "in its nature [was] a remedy against the Government." On the other hand, it is true that none of the statutes relating to this type of suit clearly indicate a congressional intention to require full payment of the assessed tax before suit. Nevertheless, the opinion of this Court in Cheatham v. United States, 92 U.S. 85, 23 L.Ed. 561, prevents us from accepting the analogy between the statutory action against the Collector and the common-law count. In this 1875 opinion, the Court described the remedies available to taxpayers as follows:

> "So also, in the internal-revenue department, the statute which we have copied allows appeals from the assessor to the commissioner of internal revenue; and, if dissatisfied with his decision, *on paying the tax* the party can sue the collector; and, if the money was wrongfully exacted, the courts will give him relief by a judgment, which the United States pledges herself to pay.

> * * *

> " * * * While a free course of remonstrance and appeal is allowed within the departments before the money is finally exacted, the general government has wisely made *the payment of the tax claimed,* whether of customs or of internal revenue, a condition precedent to a resort to the courts by the party against whom the tax is assessed. * * * If the compliance with this condition [that appeal must be made to the Commissioner and suit brought within six months of his decision] requires the party aggrieved to pay the money, he must do it. He cannot, after the decision is rendered against him, protract the time within which he can contest that decision in the courts by his own delay in paying the money. It is essential to the honor and orderly conduct of the government that its taxes should be promptly paid, and drawbacks speedily adjusted; and the rule prescribed in this class of cases is neither arbitrary nor unreasonable. * * *

> "The objecting party can take his appeal. He can, if the decision is delayed beyond twelve months, rest his case on that decision; or he can *pay the amount claimed,* and commence his suit at any time within that period. So, after the decision, he can pay at once, and commence suit within the six months * * *." 92 U.S. at pages 88–89, 23 L.Ed. 561. (Emphasis added.)

Reargument has not changed our view that this language reflects an understanding that full payment of the tax was a prerequisite to suit. Of course * * * the *Cheatham* statement is dictum; but we reiterate that it appears to us to be "carefully considered dictum." 357 U.S. at page 68, 78 S.Ct. at page 1083. Equally important is the fact that the Court was construing the claim-for-refund statute from which, as amended, the language of § 1346(a)(1) was presumably taken. Thus it seems that in *Cheatham* the Supreme Court interpreted this language not only to specify which claims for refund must first be presented for administrative reconsideration, but also to constitute an additional qualification upon the statutory right to sue the Collector. It is true that the version of the provision involved in *Cheatham* contained only the phrase "any tax." But the phrases "any penalty" and "any sum" were added well before the decision in *Cheatham*; the history of these amendments makes it quite clear that they were not designed to effect any change relevant to the *Cheatham* rule; language in opinions of this Court after *Cheatham* is consistent with the *Cheatham* statement; and in any event, as we have indicated, we can see nothing in these additional words which would negate the full-payment requirement.

If this were all the material relevant to a construction of § 1346(a)(1), determination of the issue at bar would be inordinately difficult. Favoring petitioner would be the theory that, in the early nineteenth century, a suit for recovery of part payment of an assessment could be maintained against the Collector, together with the absence of any conclusive evidence that Congress has ever intended to inaugurate a new rule; favoring respondent would be the *Cheatham* statement and the language of the 1921 statute. There are, however, additional factors which are dispositive.

We are not here concerned with a single sentence in an isolated statute, but rather with a jurisdictional provision which is a keystone in a carefully articulated and quite complicated structure of tax laws. From these related statutes, all of which were passed after 1921, it is apparent that Congress has several times acted upon the assumption that § 1346(a)(1) requires full payment before suit. Of course, if the clear purpose of Congress at any time had been to permit suit to recover a part payment, this subsequent legislation would have to be disregarded. But, as we have stated, the evidence pertaining to this intent is extremely weak, and we are convinced that it is entirely too insubstantial to justify destroying the existing harmony of the tax statutes. The laws which we consider especially pertinent are the statute establishing the Board of Tax Appeals (now the Tax Court), the Declaratory Judgment Act, 28 U.S.C.A. § 2201 et seq., and § 7422(e) of the Internal Revenue Code of 1954.

THE BOARD OF TAX APPEALS

The Board of Tax Appeals was established by Congress in 1924 to permit taxpayers to secure a determination of tax liability before payment of the deficiency. The Government argues that the Congress which passed this 1924 legislation thought full payment of the tax assessed was a condition for bringing suit in a District Court; that Congress believed this sometimes caused hardship; and that Congress set up the Board to alleviate that hardship. Petitioner denies this, and contends that Congress' sole purpose was to enable taxpayers to prevent the Government from collecting taxes by exercise of its power of distraint.

We believe that the legislative history surrounding both the creation of the Board and the subsequent revisions of the basic statute supports the Government. The House Committee Report, for example, explained the purpose of the bill as follows:

> "The committee recommends the establishment of a Board of Tax Appeals to which a taxpayer may appeal *prior to the payment* of an additional assessment of income, excess-profits, war-profits, or estate taxes. *Although a taxpayer may, after payment of his tax, bring suit for the recovery thereof* and thus secure a judicial determination on the questions involved, he can not, in view of section 3224 of the Revised Statutes, which prohibits suits to enjoin the collection of taxes, secure such a determination prior to the payment of the tax. The right of appeal after payment of the tax is an incomplete remedy, and does little to remove the hardship occasioned by an incorrect assessment. The payment of a large additional tax on income received several years previous and which may have, since its receipt, been either wiped out by subsequent losses, invested in non-liquid assets, or spent, sometimes forces taxpayers into bankruptcy, and often causes great financial hardship and sacrifice. These results are not remedied by permitting the taxpayer *to sue for the recovery of the tax after this payment.* He is entitled to an appeal and to a determination of his liability for the tax prior to its payment." (Emphasis added.)

Moreover, throughout the congressional debates are to be found frequent expressions of the principle that payment of the full tax was a precondition to suit * * *.

Petitioner's argument falls under the weight of this evidence. It is true, of course, that the Board of Tax Appeals procedure has the effect of staying collection, and it may well be that Congress so provided in order to alleviate hardships caused by the long-standing bar against suits to enjoin the collection of taxes. But it is a considerable leap to the further conclusion that amelioration of the hardship of prelitigation payment as a jurisdictional requirement was not another important motivation for Congress' action. To reconcile the legislative history with this conclusion seems to require the presumption that all the Congressmen who spoke of payment of the assessment before suit as a hardship understood—without saying—that suit could be brought for whatever part of the assessment had been paid, but believed that, as a practical matter, hardship would nonetheless arise because the Government would require payment of the balance of the tax by exercising its power of distraint. But if this was in fact the view of these legislators, it is indeed extraordinary that they did not say so. Moreover, if Congress' only concern was to prevent distraint, it is somewhat difficult to understand why Congress did not simply authorize injunction suits. It is interesting to note in this connection that bills to permit the same type of prepayment litigation in the District Courts as is possible in the Tax Court have been introduced several times, but none has ever been adopted.

In sum, even assuming that one purpose of Congress in establishing the Board was to permit taxpayers to avoid distraint, it seems evident that another purpose was to furnish a forum where full payment of the assessment would not be a condition precedent to suit. The result is a system in which there is one tribunal for prepayment litigation and another for post-payment litigation, with no room contemplated for a hybrid of the type proposed by petitioner.

THE DECLARATORY JUDGMENT ACT

The Federal Declaratory Judgment Act of 1934 was amended by § 405 of the Revenue Act of 1935 expressly to except disputes "with respect to Federal taxes." The Senate Report explained the purpose of the amendment as follows:

> "Your committee has added an amendment making it clear that the Federal Declaratory Judgments Act of June 14, 1934, has no application to Federal taxes. The application of the Declaratory Judgments Act to taxes would constitute a *radical departure* from the long-continued policy of Congress (as expressed in Rev.Stat. 3224 and other provisions) with respect to the determination, assessment, and collection of Federal taxes. Your committee believes that the orderly and prompt determination and collection of Federal taxes should not be interfered with by a procedure designed to facilitate the settlement of private controversies, and that existing procedure both in the Board of Tax Appeals and the courts affords ample remedies for the correction of tax errors." (Emphasis added.)

It is clear enough that one "radical departure" which was averted by the amendment was the potential circumvention of the "pay first and litigate later" rule by way of suits for declaratory judgments in tax cases. Petitioner would have us give this Court's imprimatur to precisely the same type of "radical departure," since a suit for recovery of but a part of an assessment would determine the legality of the balance by operation of the principle of collateral estoppel. With respect to this unpaid portion, the taxpayer would be securing what is in effect—even though not technically—a declaratory judgment. The frustration of congressional intent which petitioner asks us to endorse could hardly be more glaring, for he has conceded that his argument leads logically to the conclusion that payment of even $1 on a large assessment entitles the taxpayer to sue—a concession amply warranted by the obvious impracticality of any judicially created jurisdictional standard midway between *full* payment and *any* payment.

SECTION 7422(e) OF THE 1954 CODE

One distinct possiblity which would emerge from a decision in favor of petitoner would be that a taxpayer might be able to split his cause of action, bringing suit for refund of part of the tax in a Federal District Court and litigating in the Tax Court with respect to the remainder. In such a situation the first decision would, of course, control. Thus if for any reason a litigant would prefer a District Court adjudication, he might sue for a small portion of the tax in that tribunal while at the same time protecting the balance from distraint by invoking the protection of the Tax Court procedure. On the other hand, different questions would arise if this device were not employed. For example, would the Government be required to file a compulsory counterclaim for the unpaid balance in District Court under Rule 13 of the Federal Rules of Civil Procedure, 28 U.S.C.A.? If so, which party would have the burden of proof?

Section 7422(e) of the 1954 Internal Revenue Code makes it apparent that Congress has assumed these problems are nonexistent except in the rare case where the taxpayer brings suit in a District Court and the Commissioner then notifies him of an additional deficiency. Under § 7422(e) such a claimant is given the option of pursuing his suit in the District Court or in the Tax Court, *but he cannot litigate in both.* Moreover, if he decides to remain in the District Court, the Government may—but seemingly is not required to —bring a counterclaim; and if it does, the taxpayer has the burden of proof. If we were to overturn the assumption upon which Congress has acted, we would generate upon a broad scale the very problems Congress believed it had solved.

* * *

[The Court noted that of the approximately 40,000 tax refund suits litigated between 1900 and 1940, the full payment issue was present only 9 times. In 6 cases it was the basis for a government objection to jurisdiction; the failure of the government to contest the issue in 3 cases was held not significant. The small number of cases presenting the issue reinforced the Court's conclusion that there was a uniform pre-1940 belief that full payment was required prior to suit.]

A word should also be said about the argument that requiring taxpayers to pay the full assessments before bringing suits will subject some of them to great hardship. This contention seems to ignore entirely the right of the taxpayer to appeal the deficiency to the Tax Court without paying a cent. If he permits his time for filing such an appeal to expire, he can hardly complain that he has been unjustly treated, for he is in precisely the same position as any other person who is barred by a statute of limitations. On the other hand, the Government has a substantial interest in protecting the public purse, an interest which would be substantially impaired if a taxpayer could sue in a District Court without paying his tax in full. * * * It is quite true that the filing of an appeal to the Tax Court normally precludes the Government from requiring payment of the tax, but a decision in petitioner's favor could be expected to throw a great portion of the Tax Court litigation into the District Courts. Of course, the Government can collect the tax from a District Court suitor by exercising its power of distraint—if he does not split his cause of action—but we cannot believe that compelling resort to this extraordinary procedure is either wise or in accord with congressional intent. Our system of taxation is based upon voluntary assessment and payment, not upon distraint. A full-payment requirement will promote the smooth functioning of this system; a part-payment rule would work at cross-purposes with it.

In sum, if we were to accept petitioner's argument, we would sacrifice the harmony of our carefully structured twentieth century system of tax litigation, and all that would be achieved would be a supposed harmony of § 1346(a)(1) with what might have been the nineteenth century law had the issue ever been raised. Reargument has but fortified our view that § 1346(a)(1), correctly construed, requires full payment of the assessment before an income tax refund suit can be maintained in a Federal District Court.

Affirmed.

QUESTIONS

1. What do you think would be the present judicial procedure for the resolution of civil tax disputes had the *Flora* decision gone the other way and permitted refund suits after only partial payments?

2. Is there any rationale to support the inevitable effect of the full payment rule, which renders a trial by jury (in the district courts) or a different body of precedents (in the Court of Claims) available only to those taxpayers with sufficient funds to make a full payment of the tax asserted to be due prior to litigation?

(1) THE DIVISIBLE TAX CONCEPT

JONES v. FOX

162 F.Supp. 449 (D.Md.1957).

R. DORSEY WATKINS, District Judge.

This is an action to recover fifty dollars paid by the plaintiff under protest in partial satisfaction of a cabaret excise tax assessment levied by the defendant in the amount of One Thousand, Five Hundred Fifty-eight Dollars and Ten Cents ($1,558.10) for the fourth quarter of 1954. The answer of the defendant District Director, which challenged the jurisdiction of this court, was coupled with a counterclaim for the unpaid balance of the assessment plus interest. * * * The United States then moved to intervene and the defendant district director's counterclaim was amended so as to permit its being treated as the complaint in intervention of the United States.

The first question presented is one of jurisdiction, the defendant and the intervenor contending that the court lacks jurisdiction of a suit for refund of taxes when only a part of the tax assessed has been paid.

* * *

It should be noted that the cabaret tax is an excise tax. The Tax Court has not been granted jurisdiction over excise taxes. The fact that, if this court does not have jurisdiction, the plaintiff is denied a judicial determination of his liability for the tax prior to payment in full of the amount assessed, a determination to which those challenging asserted deficiencies in income, estate, or gifts taxes are expressly entitled through recourse to the Tax Court, is, of course, not determinative of the legal soundness of his position but it does render inapposite the reasoning of cases [involving taxes within the subject matter jurisdiction of the Tax Court].

[The court concluded that partial payment on an assessment was adequate for purposes of district court jurisdiction over an excise tax refund suit. Subsequent to its original decision, the court issued an addendum in order to clarify its decision in light of the Supreme Court's holding in Flora v. United States.^m |

ADDENDUM

* * *

The *Flora* case dealt with a deficiency in income tax. The instant case deals with a deficiency assessment of excise taxes. Without elaborating upon what has already been said in this opinion regarding the lack of jurisdiction in the Tax Court over excise taxes with con-

---

m. The original *Flora* decision, 357 U. S. 63, 78 S.Ct. 1079, 2 L.Ed.2d 1165 (1958).

comitant hardship to the taxpayer and the absence of alternative remedies, such as the Supreme Court indicated would be present in the case of suit for recovery of income tax, it is necessary to reexamine the divisible nature of the excise tax.

> "Income taxes and estate taxes flow from calculations involving complicated considerations of credits, exemptions, etc. The resulting tax has been influenced by and reflects these considerations. They are not naturally separable as in the case of the stamp tax. It is a wise law that governs their prepayment before suit can be brought. Otherwise, the power of collection of taxes would be continuously impeded and rendered practically useless. But in the case of these separable items the issue is clear-cut. There can be no complicated questions of credits, exemptions, and the like. It is simply an issue of whether or not the stamp should be applied and in what amount." Friebele v. United States, D. C.N.J.1937, 20 F.Supp. 492, 493.

Relying on Friebele v. United States, this court holds that if prepayment of a cabaret tax "deficiency" is a prerequisite to suit, this requirement is met by payment in full of the tax on any independent taxable item or event even although this payment may constitute but a partial payment of the entire assessment.

* * *

Accordingly, the court holds that the payment by the taxpayer of fifty dollars, whether the proper taxable item or event be considered one day's gross taxable receipts or the total amount received from any one patron, thus entitling him to be present during any portion of a public performance, constituted payment in full of the cabaret tax imposed thereon.

NOTE

In Steele v. United States, 280 F.2d 89 (8th Cir. 1960), the government conceded that the full payment rule of *Flora* was inapplicable to penalties imposed under sections 6671 and 6672 of the Code for the willful failure of responsible persons to pay over withholdings of income and social security taxes taken by the employer corporation from the wages of its employees. Thus, the corporate officers in *Steele* were entitled to make payment of the amount of the penalty applicable to the withheld taxes of any individual employee and then bring suit for recovery of that amount in the district court as a means of litigating the issue of whether they were "responsible persons" within the meaning of IRC § 6671(b).

QUESTION

In Kell-Strom Tool Co. v. United States, 205 F.Supp. 190, 194 (D. Conn.1962), the court held:

It is not a condition precedent to the jurisdiction of the [district court] that the interest upon the tax deficiency assessed shall be paid. The full amount of the tax has been paid. A suit to obtain a refund of it will lie in this court.

Would it ever be to the taxpayer's advantage to pay the interest component of a deficiency assessment prior to the filing of a refund suit?

(2) PAYMENT ON AN ASSESSMENT

The payment jurisdictionally required is one made on a tax assessment.[n] It is not enough for a taxpayer voluntarily to advance a payment in the amount of an anticipated assessment. Hence, an attempt to create a tax refund suit in court prior to assessment will not succeed. This procedure is sometimes attempted by taxpayers seeking to obtain the benefits of civil discovery against the Government during the pendency of a criminal investigation or prosecution.[o]

Should a taxpayer wish to make an advance payment prior to assessment in order to stop the running of interest against him, he may do so without relinquishing his right ultimately to sue for a refund. He should wait until after the anticipated assessment is made, however, before he files his claim for refund with respect to the advance payment.

C. THE CLAIM FOR REFUND

---

(1) FORMAL REQUIREMENTS

Section 7422(a) of the Code provides that no tax refund suit may be brought in any court until a claim for refund has been filed with the IRS in accordance with the applicable law and regulations. The pertinent regulations are those promulgated pursuant to § 6402 of the Code,[p] which authorizes the Service to credit the amount of any overpayment (including interest) against "any outstanding tax liability for any tax [including interest and penalties] owed by the person making the overpayment," and mandates the refund of any balance to the person who made the overpayment.

As a general rule, claims for refund are to be filed with the Service Center serving the internal revenue district in which the tax was paid. The claim must set forth in detail each ground upon which a credit or refund is claimed and facts sufficient to apprise the Commissioner of the exact basis thereof. The statement of the grounds and facts must be verified by a written declaration that it is made under the penalties of perjury. A claim which does not comply with

---

n. Farnsworth & Chambers Co. v. Phinney, 279 F.2d 538 (5th Cir. 1960), aff'g, 178 F.Supp. 330 (S.D.Tex.1959).

o. E. g., Campbell v. Eastland, 307 F. 2d 478 (5th Cir. 1962), cert. denied, 371 U.S. 955, 83 S.Ct. 502, 9 L.Ed.2d 502 (1963).

p. Regs. §§ 301.6402–1 et seq.

the foregoing requirements will not be considered. In the case of income, gift and Federal unemployment taxes, a separate claim must be made for each type of tax for each taxable year or period. If a return is filed by an individual and, after his death, a refund claim is filed by his or her legal representative, certified copies of the letters testamentary or other similar evidence must be annexed to the claim, to show the authority of the legal representative to file the claim.

All claims except those for the refund of overpaid income taxes must be made on Form 843. In the case of income taxes the claim for refund or credit is made on the appropriate income tax return. A great number of taxpayers, of course, automatically claim the excess of estimated taxes paid or taxes withheld by employers over actual tax liability when they file their yearly return. In this situation the service center will credit or refund the overpayment as a matter of course, without awaiting examination of the completed return and without awaiting filing of a separate claim for refund. Where a claim is made with respect to income tax overpaid in a prior year, however, a separate amended return must be filed. In the case of individuals who have filed either a Form 1040 or 1040A, the claim is made on Form 1040X. Corporations make claims for refund on Form 1120X and all other claims (for example for taxes overpaid by a fiduciary or an exempt organization) must be made on the appropriate tax return, which should be clearly marked to indicate that it is an amended return.

After the claim is filed with the service center, it will be forwarded to the appropriate district office for examination. When claims are examined by the Examination Division of the district office, substantially the same procedure is followed (including appeal rights afforded to taxpayers) as when taxpayers' returns are originally examined. If the claim is allowed, a refund will be made or a credit given by the service center. If it is disallowed, a statutory notice of claim disallowance will be issued pursuant to § 6532(a)(1) of the Code, and the stage will be set for the filing of a refund suit. If the Service fails to take any action with respect to the claim, the taxpayer may bring suit at any time after the expiration of six months from the date of filing the claim. See Figure 8, page 224, above.

(2) WAIVER OF REQUIREMENTS

TUCKER v. ALEXANDER

Supreme Court of the United States, 1927.
275 U.S. 228, 48 S.Ct. 45, 72 L.Ed. 253.

Mr. Justice STONE delivered the opinion of the Court.

Petitioner, from March 1, 1913, and in 1920, was the owner of shares of stock in a corporation which in the latter year was dissolved and liquidated. A distribution of some portion of its assets to the stockholders had been made in May, 1913. The Commissioner of Internal Revenue taxed as income on dissolution the difference between the value of the property received by petitioner as a liquidating dividend, and the value of his stock on March 1, 1913, less the value of the distribution of May, 1913, which was treated as a return of capital. Petitioner paid the tax under protest, setting up that it was excessive, and after filing a claim for refund brought the present suit in the District Court for Western Oklahoma to recover the excess. In his claim for refund petitioner assigned as reasons for it (1) the Commissioner's erroneous computation of the value of the stock on March 1, 1913, and (2) his failure to deduct from the capital and surplus of the company at the date of liquidation the amount of certain outstanding debts which were assumed by the stockholders, but no explicit statement was made that the Commissioner had erred in decreasing the March 1, 1913, value by the value of the property distributed in May, 1913, nor was that point raised by the petition in the district court which in effect merely repeated the allegations of the claim for refund.

In the course of the trial petitioner without objection by the government abandoned the grounds of recovery stated in the petition and attacked only the Commissioner's deduction of the return of capital from the March 1, 1913, value. That issue alone was litigated. At the close of the trial counsel stipulated that, if the court found the deduction to have been erroneously made, the petitioner should have judgment in the sum named. The District Court's judgment for petitioner was reversed by the Circuit Court of Appeals for the Eighth Circuit which held that a recovery on grounds different from those set up in the claim for refund was precluded by [the predecessor to § 7422(a) of the Code and the regulations promulgated thereunder, which require a claim for refund to set forth all the facts relied upon in support thereof].

* * *

* * * During the entire course of the trial no question was raised as to the sufficiency of the claim for refund. The only substantial issue litigated was the correctness of the Commissioner's deduction of the distribution of May, 1913. All other questions were taken out of the case by stipulation.

If the collector and counsel for the government had power to waive an objection to the sufficiency of the description of the claim filed it was waived here, and we need not consider the precise extent of the requirements prescribed by statute and regulations, nor whether petitioner's claim for refund fell short of satisfying them. The Solicitor General does not urge that the government's possible objection could not be waived, but submits the question for our decision.

Literal compliance with statutory requirements that a claim or appeal be filed with the Commissioner before suit is brought for a tax refund may be insisted upon by the defendant, whether the collector or the United States. But no case appears to have held that such objections as that urged here may not be dispensed with by stipulation in open court on the trial. The statute and the regulations must be read in the light of their purpose. They are devised, not as traps for the unwary, but for the convenience of government officials in passing upon claims for refund and in preparing for trial. Failure to observe them does not necessarily preclude recovery. If compliance is insisted upon, dismissal of the suit may be followed by a new claim for refund and another suit within the period of limitations. If the Commissioner is not deceived or misled by the failure to describe accurately the claim, as obviously he was not here, it may be more convenient for the government and decidedly in the interest of an orderly administrative procedure that the claim should be disposed of upon its merits on a first trial without imposing upon government and taxpayer the necessity of further legal proceedings. We can perceive no valid reason why the requirements of the regulations may not be waived for that purpose. We are not unmindful of those cases holding that in suits against the government no officer of the government may waive statutes of limitations. Such waivers if allowed would defeat the only purpose of the statute and impose a liability upon the United States which otherwise would not exist—consequences which do not attach to the waiver here.

Reversed.

UNITED STATES v. FELT & TARRANT MFG. CO.

Supreme Court of the United States, 1931.
283 U.S. 269, 51 S.Ct. 376, 75 L.Ed. 1025.

Mr. Justice STONE delivered the opinion of the Court.

[Felt & Tarrant filed what amounted to a "protective" claim for refund on Form 843, with respect to taxes paid for the year 1917. The sole ground stated in the claim was that it had previously filed with the Commissioner an application for special relief from the amount of its excess profits tax under § 210 of the Revenue Act of 1917. The government conceded that the company was entitled to a deduction for 1917 on account of exhaustion or obsolescence of patents under § 203 of the 1917 Act which, if allowed, would have resulted in the refund demanded. The government contended, however, that the claim for refund did not comply with the regulations under the predecessor to § 7422(a) of the Code, which required that claims for refund be made on Form 843, and that "all the facts relied upon in support of the claim should be clearly set forth under oath." The section cited by the company in its claim had no relation to deductions on account of exhaustion or obsolescence of patents. In support of its claim, the company filed a brief and had a conference in the office of the Commissioner; but neither in its claim, its brief, nor at the conference, was mention made of the deduction which was at issue in the Court of Claims. Nevertheless, the Court of Claims allowed recovery, and the government appealed.]

The filing of a claim or demand as a prerequisite to a suit to recover taxes paid is a familiar provision of the revenue laws, compliance with which may be insisted upon by the defendant, whether the collector or the United States. Tucker v. Alexander, 275 U.S. 228, 48 S.Ct. 45, 72 L.Ed. 253.

One object of such requirements is to advise the appropriate officials of the demands or claims intended to be asserted, so as to insure an orderly administration of the revenue, a purpose not accomplished with respect to the present demand by the bare declaration in respondent's claim that it was filed "to protect all possible legal rights of the taxpayer." The claim for refund, which section 1318 makes prerequisite to suit, obviously relates to the claim which may be asserted by the suit. Hence, quite apart from the provisions of the Regulation, the statute is not satisfied by the filing of a paper which gives no notice of the amount or nature of the claim for which the suit is brought; and refers to no facts upon which it may be founded.

The Court of Claims, in allowing recovery, relied upon Tucker v. Alexander, supra, and upon the fact that, at the time when respondent filed its return and its claim for refund, the Treasury had consistently refused to allow deductions from gross income for exhaustion of patents. Consequently it held that the filing of a demand which was certain to be refused was a futile and unnecessary act. But in Tucker v. Alexander the right of the government to insist upon compliance with the statutory requirement was emphasized. Only because that right was recognized was it necessary to decide whether it could be waived. The Court held that it could, and that in that case it had been waived by the stipulation of the collector filed in court. Here there was no compliance with the statute, nor was there a waiver of its condition, since the Commissioner had no knowledge of the claim and took no action with respect to it.

The necessity for filing a claim such as the statute requires is not dispensed with because the claim may be rejected. It is the rejection which makes the suit necessary. An anticipated rejection of the claim, which the statute contemplates, is not a ground for suspending its operation. Even though formal, the condition upon which the consent to suit is given is defined by the words of the statute, and "they mark the conditions of the claimant's right." Rock Island R. R. Co. v. United States, 254 U.S. 141, 143, 41 S.Ct. 55, 56, 65 L.Ed. 188. Compliance may be dispensed with by waiver, as an administrative act, Tucker v. Alexander, supra; but it is not within the judicial province to read out of the statute the requirement of its words.

Reversed.

ANGELUS MILLING CO. v. COMMISSIONER

Supreme Court of the United States, 1945.
325 U.S. 293, 65 S.Ct. 1162, 89 L.Ed. 1619.

Mr. Justice FRANKFURTER delivered the opinion of the Court.

This is a suit * * * for a refund of processing taxes paid under the Agricultural Adjustment Act of 1933. The problem of the case derives from the procedural requirements of a claim for such a refund.

The petitioner, Angelus Milling Company, known until June, 1933 as the Middleport Flour Mills, Inc., was a processor of wheat, with its principal office in Niagara Falls, New York. During the years for which the refund is claimed—1933 to 1936—its processing operations were closely connected with those of the Niagara Falls Milling Company. The two companies had the same officers, employees, and majority stockholder, and a joint bank account. They also had a common set of books, but the respective transactions of the two companies—purchases, costs of manufacture, sales—were entered in their separate accounts on the books. Between July 9, 1933, and January 31, 1935, the companies filed joint processing tax returns. Between February 1, 1935, and November 30, 1935, Niagara filed returns in its name on behalf of itself and petitioner.

After United States v. Butler, 297 U.S. 1, 56 S.Ct. 312, 80 L.Ed. 477, 102 A.L.R. 914, invalidated the processing tax, three claims were filed with the Commissioner on June 22, 1936, all stating the name of the taxpayer and claimant as "Niagara Falls Milling Co., Inc., and/or Middleport Flour Mills, Inc." Each of these claims is for only part of the period during which the tax was paid, and their total is $434,045.-27. Admittedly the form of these claims did not satisfy the requirements of the statute [1] or the authorized Treasury Regulations.[2] They were filed on an old Form 843 and not on the required Form P. T. 79. While these claims were still undetermined, Niagara, on June 30, 1937, filed a claim in the sum of $436,231.73. This claim was in due form but was filed by Niagara on its own behalf alone. Thereafter, on August 15, 1938, petitioner filed a claim, designated "Amendment to Claim", for itself alone for the refund of $145,839.12. While this claim was submitted on Form P. T. 79, it failed to give the informa-

1. Section 903 of Title VII of the 1936 Revenue Act, 49 Stat. 1648, 1747, 7 U.S.C.A. § 645, requires that no refund be made or allowed "unless * * * a claim for refund has been filed * * * in accordance with regulations prescribed by the Commissioner with the approval of the Secretary. All evidence relied upon in support of such claim shall be clearly set forth under oath."

2. The applicable regulations provide for the making of claims on prescribed forms, presentation of the grounds urged, and submission of evidence, etc. The only information furnished in these claims is the name and address of the joint claimants, and a statement of the dates and amounts of the tax payments made by the Niagara Milling Company.

tion required by the form and the regulations, containing merely an apportionment between Angelus and Niagara of the three earlier claims. An attached affidavit stated that this claim "was originally filed on the 22nd day of June 1936 in the name of the Niagara Falls Milling Company and/or Middleport Flour Mills, Inc." The Commissioner, on May 23, 1941, denied this claim.

* * *

Petitioner's claim for recovering processing taxes paid by it was properly rejected by the Commissioner if it did not satisfy the conditions which Congress directly and through the rule-making power given to the Treasury laid down as a prerequisite for such refund. Insofar as Congress has made explicit statutory requirements, they must be observed and are beyond the dispensing power of Treasury officials. Tucker v. Alexander, 275 U.S. 228, 231, 232, 48 S.Ct. 45, 46, 72 L.Ed. 253; United States v. Memphis Cotton Oil Co., 288 U.S. 62, 71, 53 S.Ct. 278, 281, 77 L.Ed. 619. Without needless elaboration, we conclude that there is nothing in what Congress has explicitly commanded to bar the claim. The effective administration of these modern complicated revenue measures inescapably leads Congress to authorize detailed administrative regulations by the Commissioner of Internal Revenue. He may insist upon full compliance with his regulations. It is hardly contended that the confusing series of petitioner's claims which we have summarized, whether singly or in conjuction, obeyed the regulations. For such default the Commissioner could have rejected the claims out of hand. He did not do that, and by what he did do he has given rise to the contention that he waived the requirement of his regulations. The basis of this claim of waiver is that the Commissioner through his agents dispensed with the formal requirements of a claim by investigating its merits.

Candor does not permit one to say that the power of the Commissioner to waive defects in claims for refund is a subject made crystal-clear by the authorities. The question has been somewhat complicated by cases involving amendments of claim. Thus, in United States v. Memphis Cotton Oil Co., supra, a claimant's amendment was allowed because filed before his original claim was rejected on formal grounds. According to what was there said there can be no amendment after a rejection though the Commissioner had examined the claimant's books and tentatively found an overpayment. It smacks too much of the strangling niceties of common law pleading to find no existing claim to which a curative amendment may be attached, although there has been an examination of the merits, simply because of the prior rejection of a formally defective claim and yet find waiver of a formal defect merely because an examination of the merits by the Commissioner manifests consideration of the claim.

Treasury Regulations are calculated to avoid dilatory, careless, and wasteful fiscal administration by barring incomplete or confusing claims. Tucker v. Alexander, supra. But Congress has given the Treasury this rule-making power for self-protection and not for self-imprisonment. If the Commissioner chooses not to stand on his own formal or detailed requirements, it would be making an empty abstraction, and not a practical safeguard, of a regulation to allow the Commissioner to invoke technical objections after he has investigated the merits of a claim and taken action upon it. Even tax administration does not as a matter of principle preclude considerations of fairness.

Since, however, the tight net which the Treasury Regulations fashion is for the protection of the revenue, courts should not unduly help disobedient refund claimants to slip through it. The showing should be unmistakable that the Commissioner has in fact seen fit to dispense with his formal requirements and to examine the merits of the claim. It is not enough that in some roundabout way the facts supporting the claim may have reached him. The Commissioner's attention should have been focused on the merits of the particular dispute. The evidence should be clear that the Commissioner understood the specific claim that was made even though there was a departure from form in its submission. We do not think that the petitioner has made out such a case here.

The evidence of waiver largely rests upon a letter from a General Deputy Collector requesting an examination of certain books, and upon affidavit of two accountants, one an officer of the company, to the effect that the Commissioner examined petitioner's books in order to consider the claim. We agree with the Tax Court that the evidence is insufficient to establish waiver. The letter from the General Deputy Collector requesting petitioner's president to allow examination of the "records of the Middleport Flour Mills, Inc., and Angelus Flour Mills, Inc." was in connection with the claim which had been filed by the Niagara Milling Company. In view of the confusing identify of interest of the two companies, it is not unreasonable to attribute this inquiry, as did the Tax Court, to Niagara's claim and not to petitioner's. For similar reasons, the affidavits regarding the purpose of the Commissioner's representatives bear interpretation of a like significance.

In the *Memphis Cotton Oil case,* where an amendment was allowed out of time, the Deputy Commissioner, after an audit of the taxpayer's books, notified the taxpayer in writing that its refund claims had been considered and that its taxes had been readjusted in accordance with a proven overassessment. Similar evidence of preoccupation by the Commissioner with the particular claim and controversy has been offered in cases where waiver was recognized. To be sure, it is not essential for the establishment of a waiver that the Commissioner communicate his ruling on the merits to the taxpayer. But in the absence of such explicitness the implication that formal requirements were dispensed with should not be tenuously argumentative. No more than that can be squeezed out of the materials in this record. Thus it is claimed that the Commissioner offered a refund, subject to offsets, to the Niagara Falls Milling Company. But this rather confirms the indication the Commissioner was bent on Niagara's claim. The Commissioner may have acquired knowledge of petitioner's affairs but only by the way, incidentally to his investigation of Niagara's claims. Petitioner has failed to sustain his burden of showing that the Commissioner, by examining the facts of petitioner's claim in order to determine the merits, dispensed with the exactions of the regulations.

An additional argument of the petitioner need not detain us long. It urges that taking the claims filed by Niagara and petitioner together, they furnish all the data required by the regulations. But it is not enough that somewhere under the Commissioner's roof is the information which might enable him to pass on a claim for refund. The protection of the revenue authorizes the Commissioner to demand information in a particular form, and he is entitled to insist that the form be observed so as to advise him expeditiously and accurately of the true nature of the claim.

Affirmed.

(3) INFORMAL CLAIMS

AMERICAN RADIATOR & STANDARD SANITARY CORP. v. UNITED STATES

318 F.2d 915 (Ct.Cl.1963).

DAVIS, Judge, delivered the opinion of the court:

The only contested point in this suit for refund of income and excess profits taxes is the timeliness of plaintiff's refund claim. The defendant does not deny that the taxes were overpaid, but it contends that recovery is now barred because the formal claim for refund came some months too late. We reject the defense and hold that plaintiff made a seasonable demand.

* * *

Plaintiff did not file formal claims for refund of the overpayments of its taxes for 1942, 1943, and 1945 [resulting from its excess cost of replacement, in 1949, of goods inventoried under the LIFO method,] until May 1953 and January 1954—more than three years after March 15, 1950 [the due date for the tax return covering the year of replacement]. In 1958, these claims were finally rejected by the Internal Revenue Service as untimely.

* * *

[A] basis for deciding that plaintiff is not barred is that it made a timely *informal* claim for refunds for the liquidation years (1942, 1943, and 1945) within three calendar years of the filing of its tax return for 1949 (the year of replacement). Informal refund claims have long been held valid. But they must have a written component and should adequately apprise the Internal Revenue Service that a refund is sought and for certain years. It is not enough that the Service have in its possession information from which it might deduce that the taxpayer is entitled to, or might desire, a refund; nor is it sufficient that a claim involving the same ground has been filed for another year or by a different taxpayer. On the other hand, the writing should not be given a crabbed or literal reading, ignoring all the surrounding circumstances which give it body and content. The focus is on the claim as a whole, not merely the written component. In addition to the writing and some form of request for a refund, the only essential is that there be made available sufficient information as to the tax and the year to enable the Internal Revenue Service to commence, if it wishes, an examination into the claim.

Under these standards, and in the light of the particular circumstances, this court has found informal refund claims based upon an objection on the back of a check paying the tax; written protests prior to payment; a letter of transmittal accompanied by an executed waiver of restrictions on assessment; and on an executed waiver subject to special conditions.

On what can our plaintiff rely to demonstrate that it made an informal claim prior to March 15, 1953 (i. e., "within three years after the date of the filing of the income tax return for the year of replacement")? The chief written component consisted of various notations and figures on its income tax return for 1949. One schedule of that return listed an item of $750,000 as "Estimated Refund Federal Taxes —Re: 'Lifo' Inventory"; another schedule listed the sum of $965,193.72 for "Excess Cost of Replacements—Re: 'Lifo' Inventory"; and still another schedule indicated that the increase during 1949 in "Federal Taxes Refundable" was $750,000 (the same figure as the taxes refundable "Re 'Lifo' Inventory"). These parts of the return were sufficient to satisfy the requirement that there be a written element in the informal demand. If there were nothing else, perhaps these notations would not have been adequate by themselves to create a valid informal claim, but with their explicit references to tax refunds, "Lifo" inventory, and excess cost of replacements they certainly supplied enough of an underpinning.

For the rest, plaintiff can properly rely on the very specific knowledge gained by the revenue agent in auditing its returns for 1949 and 1950. This agent was thoroughly familiar with plaintiff's tax problems; he audited its returns for each year prior to 1949, beginning with 1940 or 1941. Significantly, he completed his audit of 1942, 1943, and 1945 (the liquidation years for which refunds are now sought) before March 15, 1953; he likewise finished his audit of 1949 and 1950 and made his reports before that critical date. Our detailed findings show that, in the course of his thorough examination of the 1949 and 1950 returns, the agent clearly came to know that plaintiff had had involuntary liquidations in 1942, 1943, and 1945 (among other years); that it had elected to come under Section 22(d)(6) of the 1939 Code for those years; and that it believed itself entitled to, and expected, a certain sum in refunds for those (and other) years on account of replacements made in 1949. The agent's reports of his examination of the 1949 and 1950 returns plainly revealed, in computations and breakdown of items, his recognition that plaintiff affirmatively anticipated such refunds. Headings in both reports referred expressly to expected refunds for earlier years due to replacements in 1949; the agent also made adjustments in the 1950 tax which were affected by his acceptance of these anticipated refunds. In addition, he thought that formal refund claims would be filed and that he would consider them. There can therefore be no doubt that, before the expiration of the three-year period, a responsible employee of the Internal Revenue Service had "notice fairly advising the Commissioner of the nature of the taxpayer's claim." United States v. Kales, 314 U.S. at 194, 62 S.Ct. at 218.

The defendant objects that this informal claim—reflected in plaintiff's returns for 1949 and 1950, taken together with the revenue agent's knowledge—did not give the Service such important prerequisites as the years for, or the amounts in, which the refunds were being sought, or the costs of the various inventories for each year. * * * An informal claim which is partially informative may be treated as valid even though "too general" or suffering from a "lack of specificity"—at least where those defects have been remedied by a formal claim filed after the lapse of the statutory period but before the rejection of the informal request. Plaintiff's formal refund claims (in May 1953 and January 1954) were admittedly complete and they were filed well before the rejections of all claims in 1955 and 1958. Any irregularities in the informal claim were thus cured retroactively. It is irrelevant that the formal demands did not refer to the informal claim and were not designated as amendments. Whatever the nomenclature, they supplied the missing information before the Revenue Service had rejected the informal claim, and were therefore equivalent to amendments in substance.

* * *

QUESTION

Obviously, no one should plan to rely upon an informal rather than a formal claim for refund. However, if there has been no formal submission of a claim, one can only scrutinize all written communications between the taxpayer (or his representative) and the Service to find the basis for an argument that an informal claim has been made. The result cannot always be predicted. For example, would you find that the following exchange of correspondence constituted an informal claim for refund?

To the Internal Revenue Service:

"The taxpayers agree to pay the assessment in installments. It is our intention, as soon as the entire amount is paid, to file claims for refund for what amounts we consider proper. The taxpayers do not have a formal set of books and considerable work will have to be done before the refund claims are filed."

From the Internal Revenue Service:

"With the issuance of statutory notices of deficiencies the jurisdiction of this office ceased in the matter. However, it is noted that claim is to be filed by the taxpayers and accordingly your letter is being retained in the records of this office for association with any claims which may be filed."

See Crenshaw v. Hrcka, 237 F.2d 372 (4th Cir. 1956).

(4) LIMITATIONS ON FILING REFUND CLAIMS

GENERAL RULES

A claim for refund is timely filed if filing occurs within whichever of the following periods expires later:

1. Three years from the date the return in question was filed.

2. Two years from the date the payments were made that are sought to be refunded.[q]

In the event that no tax return was filed, the period for filing a claim expires two years after the payment in question was made.[r]

The limitations period applicable to the filing of claims for refund are statutorily imposed and cannot be waived by the government.[s] Therefore, where a claim is not filed within three years of the time the subject return is filed but is filed within two years of the date some of the payments in question are made, the refund allowable on the claim is limited to the amount paid during the two years immediately preceding the filing of the claim.[t] Where the claim is filed within three years of the date the return was filed, the claim is effective only as to payments made during a period immediately preceding the filing of the claim for refund equal to three years plus the period of any extension or extensions of time granted for the filing of the subject return.[u] It should be noted that where a claim for refund is timely as to only a part of the payments made on the subject assessment it is not invalid. A refund suit can be based upon the

---

q. IRC § 6511(a). For a stamp tax, the statute of limitations expires 3 years after the tax is paid. Ibid.

r. Ibid.

s. Garbutt Oil Co. v. United States, 302 U.S. 528, 58 S.Ct. 320, 82 L.Ed. 405 (1938).

t. IRC § 6511(b)(2)(B). vance payments of taxes are considered to have been paid on the date the return was due. IRC § 6513(a).

u. IRC § 6511(b)(2)(A). Note that ad-

claim. However, the taxpayer's recovery in the suit will be limited to the payments with respect to which the claim for refund was timely.[v]

The limitation on recovery relates only to the *amount* recoverable, not the grounds for refunds that can be asserted. Therefore, if the only payment "covered" by a claim was made on an assessment based upon the disallowance of travel expenses, a refund could still be claimed on the ground, for instance, that the taxpayer was entitled to a depreciation deduction larger than had been taken on the originally filed return. The following example illustrates operation within the limitation rules:

April 15, 1980	Return filed and reported taxes paid ($10,-000) by prepaid estimated taxes.
May 3, 1982	Deficiency assessed ($5,000 plus interest).
June 1, 1982	First payment ($2,000 plus interest).
September 1, 1982	Second payment ($2,000 plus interest).
December 1, 1982	Final payment ($1,000 plus interest).

A claim filed before April 16, 1983 would be filed within three years of the date the return was filed. Thus, it would be timely and effective to support a claim for all payments made including a claim for a refund of a portion of the taxes shown due on the original return.

A claim filed on April 20, 1983 would be outside the three year period. However, it would be timely with regard to all deficiency payments made. Hence, it would be effective only to the extent of the $5,000 plus interest paid within two years of the date it was filed.

A claim filed in August, 1984 would be timely only as to the second and final payments; the maximum allowable refund would be the $3,000 plus interest paid two years prior to the claim.

Finally, a claim filed after December 3, 1984[w] would be too late as to all payments and completely ineffective.

EFFECT OF EXTENDING STATUTE OF LIMITATIONS ON ASSESSMENTS

As noted in the discussion of prelitigation administrative procedures, pages 180–182, above, there are occasions when the IRS requests a taxpayer to agree to extend the period during which assessments may be made. Section 6511(c)(1) of the Code provides that where such a § 6501(c)(4) agreement has been made, the period for

---

v. Hutchens Metal Products, Inc. v. Bookwalter, 174 F.Supp. 338 (W.D. Mo.1959), rev'd on other grounds, 281 F.2d 174 (8th Cir. 1960); San Joaquin Light & Power Corp. v. McLaughlin, 65 F.2d 677 (9th Cir. 1933).

w. Since December 1, 1984 falls on a Saturday, the limitations period does not expire until the following Monday. IRC § 7503.

filing a claim for refund (and the period within which the Service can make a refund or credit without a claim) shall not expire prior to six months after the expiration of the period within which an assessment could have been made pursuant to the agreement and any extensions thereof. Furthermore, as to any claim filed after the § 6501(c)(4) agreement is made and prior to six months after the end of the extended assessment period, the normal rules limiting the amount refundable pursuant to the claim are also extended. Finally, § 6511(c)(2) provides that the claim will be effective to obtain a refund of all amounts paid between the date the agreement is executed and the date the claim is filed, plus all amounts that would be refundable under the normal rules if a claim had been filed on the date the agreement was executed.

The limitations benefits given to a taxpayer who agrees to extend the assessment period do not shorten any longer period otherwise available to him. Section 6511(c)(1) states that where an agreement is made, the limitation period for filing claims "shall not expire prior to" the end of the extended period. Therefore, the normal rule permitting a claim to be filed within two years after payment is made is still applicable. The following example illustrates operation within the extension rules:

April 15, 1982	Return filed and reported taxes paid by prepaid estimated taxes.
April 1, 1985	Form 872 agreement executed, extending statute of limitations for assessment to April 15, 1986.
April 1, 1986	Deficiency assessment made.
August 1, 1986	Deficiency assessment paid.

By virtue of the Form 872 agreement a claim for refund filed not later than October 15, 1986 would be timely since it would have been filed within six months after the extended period for assessments expired. Moreover, the October 15, 1986 claim would be valid even if it sought a refund of all taxes paid by the taxpayer on the subject return, since a claim filed on the date the agreement was made would have been filed within three years of the date the return was filed. A claim filed on or before August 1, 1988 but after October 15, 1986 would still be valid insofar as it sought a refund of the amount paid on August 1, 1986. That is, the claim, which would be filed within two years of the date of the payment in question, would be timely (as to that payment only) under the normally applied limitations rules.

SPECIAL CIRCUMSTANCES

Recognizing that there are circumstances in which it would be difficult, or impossible, for a taxpayer to file a claim for refund within the normal limitations period, the Code provides lengthened periods for filing claims based upon certain specified grounds enumerated in § 6511(d) of the Code, such as claims based on bad debt losses, worthless securities, various carrybacks, etc. Whereas the general rule requires a claim to be filed within three years after the return in question was filed or within two years after the taxes in question were paid, the special rules set out in § 6511(d) lengthen the three-year period. In other words, the taxpayer retains the ability to file a claim within two years of a tax payment and also receives the right to file a timely claim within a period greater than three years after the subject tax return was filed. Where a claim is filed within the lengthened period, the amount recoverable is not limited by the normally applicable rules to the extent the claim is based upon the special grounds for which the lengthened period is provided.

(5) AMENDMENT OF CLAIMS

UNITED STATES v. ANDREWS

Supreme Court of the United States, 1938.
302 U.S. 517, 58 S.Ct. 315, 82 L.Ed. 398.

Mr. Justice ROBERTS delivered the opinion of the Court.

* * *

* * * Where a claim which the Commissioner could have rejected as too general, and as omitting to specify the matters needing investigation, has not misled him but has been the basis of an investigation which disclosed facts ncessary to his action in making a refund, an amendment which merely makes more definite the matters already within his knowledge, or which, in the course of his investigation, he would naturally have ascertained, is permissible. On the other hand, a claim which demands relief upon one asserted fact situation, and asks an investigation of the elements appropriate to the requested relief, cannot be amended to discard that basis and invoke action requiring examination of other matters not germane to the first claim.

With these settled principles in mind we turn to the circumstances disclosed in the present case. The claim here was not general but specific. It did not assert generally that income, gross or net, had been overappraised or, generally, that the taxpayer was entitled to deductions not taken or granted. On the contrary, it pointed to two specific items of deduction which had not been taken and to which the taxpayer claimed to be entitled. It stated that during the taxable year the taxpayer's holdings of stock in two named corporations had become worthless, entailing a deductible loss of $995. While the claim added the phrase that the taxpayer claimed the sum named, or any greater sum which might be ascertained to be due, this did not call upon the Commissioner to make a complete reaudit of the taxpayer's return. The fact that he might have done so is immaterial. He could have acted on the claim, as apparently he did, by investigating the affairs of the two corporations. It was ascertained that litigation was in process upon the outcome of which would depend a decision as to the alleged worthlessness of some of the shares in question. He, therefore, naturally postponed action on the claim until the termination of that litigation. While matters were in this posture, and after the period of limitation had expired, the respondent presented a so-called amendment of her claim having no relation whatever to the items set forth in the original claim but dealing with a wholly distinct item of $36,750 reported as dividends received and asking that it be eliminated from that category and that the transaction be reclassified as capital gain upon a basis which would result in a reduction of tax by some $6,000. This is not a case where the Commissioner waived the regulation with respect to the particularity with which the grounds of the claim must be set forth. There was no need for him to do so. The claim was not general like that in the *Memphis Cotton Oil* Case and the others following in its train. It was as specific as it could be made and pointed unerringly to the items the Commisioner must consider. It called for no general audit of the taxpayer's affairs and apparently none was made. An investigation of the items designated could not have the least relation to that attempted to be opened in the untimely amendment. The respondent urges that these considerations are of no legal significance, since the claim not only called for redress of a specified grievance but demanded general relief as well. She insists we have likened a claim for refund to an action for money had and received and have required the Commissioner to accept and act upon a bill of particulars furnished him before actual rejection of the claim although the period of limitation has expired. But, as we said in United States v. Henry Prentiss & Co., Inc., 288 U.S. 73, at 84, 53 S.Ct. 283, 285, 77 L.Ed. 626, "This does not mean that a pleader who abandons the common count and states the particular facts out of which his grievance has arisen retains unfettered freedom to change the statement at his pleasure."

Were it not for the presence in the original claim of the demand for refund of any other or greater sum which might be found due the taxpayer, we think it could not even be suggested that the claim was a general one for money had and received. Save for that clause the demand was of a specific amount based upon a specific transaction. Whether adjudication in strict analogy to the rules of pleading would permit the amendment we need not determine, for the necessities and realities of administrative procedure preclude any such result. The very specification of the items of the complaint would tend to confine the investigation to those items and there is no evidence that the examination was more extended.

* * *

[Thus, there was no timely claim filed to provide the court below with jurisdiction to consider the issues raised by the amendment.]

The judgment is reversed.

UNITED STATES v. GARBUTT OIL CO.

Supreme Court of the United States, 1938.
302 U.S. 528, 58 S.Ct. 320, 82 L.Ed. 405.

Mr. Justice ROBERTS delivered the opinion of the Court.

* * *

[On] March 30, 1929, within the four-year period of limitations prescribed by the applicable statute,[1] the respondent filed a claim for the return of the additional tax so paid, based upon two grounds * * *. While this claim was pending, but subsequent to the expiration of the period of limitation, the respondent filed a "Statement of Garbutt Oil Company * * * for the purpose of perfecting and completing claim for refund covering alleged overpayment of income tax for the calendar year 1919." Therein the respondent asserted that it "now develops that a further reason exists in support of" the pending claim since, by distribution of oil in kind, the respondent realized no taxable income during 1919, and that "it therefore follows that even though the specific grounds set forth in the claim for refund are denied said claim should, nevertheless, be allowed in full," for the reasons set forth in the statement. * * *

* * *

The respondent urges that, although the amendment was not timely, the Commissioner, in considering the merits of the position taken therein, waived any objection which might have been available to him that this position was not disclosed in the original claim. The contention is bottomed upon the fact that, in his letter of August 12, 1929, the Commissioner refers to the reasons advanced in the untimely statement. The argument confuses the power of the Commissioner to disregard a statutory mandate with his undoubted power to waive the requirements of the Treasury regulations. The distinction was pointed out in United States v. Memphis Cotton Oil Co., 288 U.S. 62, 71, 53 S.Ct. 278, 281, 77 L.Ed. 619, wherein it was said: "The line of division must be kept a sharp one between the function of a statute requiring the presentation of a claim within a given period of time, and the function of a regulation making provision as to form. The function of the statute, like that of limitations generally, is to give protection against stale demands. The function of the regulation is to facilitate research." In the cited case, and others decided at about the same time, we held that, while the Commissioner might have enforced the regulation and rejected a claim for failure to comply with

1. Revenue Act of 1926, c. 27, §
284(a)(b)(1)(2), 44 Stat. 9, 66.

it in omitting to state with particularity the grounds on which the claim was based, he was not bound to do so, but might waive the requirement of the regulation and consider a general claim on its merits. This was far from holding that after the period set by the statute for the filing of claims he had power to accept and act upon claims that complied with or violated his regulations. Tucker v. Alexander, 275 U.S. 228, 48 S.Ct. 45, 46, 72 L.Ed. 253, cited by the respondent, is clearly distinguishable. There a timely claim was filed and disallowed. [In that case the waiver of objection at trial to a new ground for recovery took place within the period of limitation for filing a refund claim.] * * *

The statement filed after the period for filing claims had expired was not a permissible amendment of the original claim presented. It was a new claim untimely filed and the Commissioner was without power, under the statute, to consider it.

The judgment is reversed.

UNITED STATES v. IDEAL BASIC INDUS., INC.

404 F.2d 122 (10th Cir. 1968).

HICKEY, Circuit Judge.

[The taxpayer initially filed timely refund claims for the years 1951 through 1954 contending that it was entitled to greater deductions for percentage depletion than it had claimed on its original returns for the reason that gross income from mining should be computed on the basis of the sales price of the finished cement. After the running of the limitations period, the taxpayer determined that materials previously identified as calcium carbonate and shale, subject to depletion percentages of 10% and 5%, respectively, were in reality chemical grade limestone and clay, both subject to a 15% depletion percentage. On this basis the taxpayer submitted amended claims for refund.]

The test applied to determine, "[w]hether a new ground of recovery may be introduced after the statute has run by amending a pending claim filed in time depends upon the facts which an investigation of the original claim would disclose. Where the facts upon which the amendment is based would necessarily have been ascertained by the Commissioner in determining the merits of the original claim, the amendment is proper." Pink v. United States, 105 F.2d 183, 187 (2d Cir. 1939). "The test is one which affords the government ample protection against the filing of stale claims * * * while at the same time providing no arbitrary limit on the amendment of claims previously filed." St. Joseph Lead Co. v. United States, 299 F.2d 348, 350 (2d Cir. 1962).

The trial court found the contested mineral identification issues in favor of the taxpayer. When the initial claim was filed it was incumbent upon the Commissioner to identify the minerals upon which depletion was claimed. The findings clearly indicated the identity of the minerals as limestone and clay, entitled to the 15% depletion rate. Therefore, the Commissioner could not have been misled nor did the amendment introduce a new ground for recovery.

* * *

D. TIMELY FILING OF REFUND SUIT

Premature Filing. After all other administrative prerequisites have been met, a taxpayer must still refrain from filing his tax refund suit until either (1) six months have elapsed from the date he filed his refund claim or (2) his claim has been disallowed by the Internal Revenue Service.[x]

A suit brought prematurely is properly subject to a motion to dismiss for lack of jurisdiction. A dismissal due to premature filing would be without prejudice, thus enabling the taxpayer to file a new action as soon as the administrative prerequisites have been met.

Late Filing. Section 6532(a)(1) of the Code provides that a tax refund suit may not be commenced:

> * * * before the expiration of 6 months from the date of filing the claim [for refund] unless the Secretary renders a decision thereon within that time, nor after the expiration of 2 years from the date of mailing by certified mail or registered mail by the Secretary to the taxpayer of a notice of the disallowance of the part of the claim to which the suit or proceeding relates.

This statute prescribes a condition under which the United States has consented to suit by taxpayers for a refund of taxes. Commencing suits within the statutory period, therefore, is a jurisdictional prerequisite to a tax refund suit.[y]

The two-year limitation period commences on the date of mailing of the formal notice of disallowance of the subject claim.[z] If a claim is never formally rejected, the statutory period may never commence running. Hence, the cause of action could theoretically remain alive indefinitely.[a]

x. IRC § 6532(a)(1); Regs. § 301.-6532–1(a).

y. Garbutt Oil Co. v. United States, 302 U.S. 528, 58 S.Ct. 320, 82 L.Ed. 405 (1938); Bell v. Gray, 287 F.2d 410 (6th Cir. 1960), aff'g on the decision of the district court, 191 F.Supp. 328 (E.D.Ky.1960).

z. One court has alluded to the possibility that a 30-day letter referring to the claim for refund could constitute a statutory notice of rejection. Register Pub. Co. v. United States, 189 F.Supp. 626 (D.Conn.1960).

a. See Detroit Trust Co. v. United States, 130 F.Supp. 815 (Ct.Cl.1955), where suit was timely, though filed almost thirty years after the original claim.

The two-year limitation period may begin without the issuance of a formal notice of disallowance where the taxpayer has filed a written waiver of the requirement of a formal notice (Form 2297). On the day a written waiver of the formal notice requirement is filed, the two-year limitation period for commencing a tax refund suit begins to run.[b]

The two-year statutory period may be extended by agreement between the taxpayer and the IRS.[c] Such an agreement (Form 907) must be signed by the taxpayer and is not effective until signed by a District Director, an Assistant Regional Commissioner, or a Regional Director of Appeals.

The statutory period for filing a refund suit cannot be enlarged except by the aforementioned specific agreement. Thus, once a formal notice of disallowance has been mailed, further action (such as reconsideration) by the IRS on the claim for refund will not extend the period within which suit may be begun.[d] Therefore, the period of limitations for filing a refund suit cannot be extended by the device of filing a second or further timely claim for refund raising the same grounds as an earlier filed claim. A notice of disallowance (or a waiver of notice of disallowance) of the first filed claim raising the grounds on which the suit is based will commence the statutory period of limitations. Later rejection, or consideration without rejection, of the second or later filed claim will not operate to enlarge the time within which the suit may be brought.[e]

E. THE ANTI–ASSIGNMENT STATUTE

Assignments of claims against the United States, including tax refund claims, are limited by the "Anti-assignment" Statute.[f] This statute provides, in pertinent part:

> All transfers and assignments made of any claim upon the United States, or of any part or share thereof, or interest therein, whether absolute or conditional, and whatever may be the consideration therefor, and all powers of attorney, orders, or other authorities for receiving payment of any such claim, or of any part of share thereof * * * shall be absolutely null and void, unless they are freely made and executed in the presence of at least two attesting wit-

b. IRC § 6532(a)(3).

c. IRC § 6532(a)(2). See Regs. § 301.-6532–1(b), stating the formal requirements for such an agreement.

d. IRC § 6532(a)(4).

e. 18th Street Leader Stores v. United States, 142 F.2d 113 (7th Cir. 1944);

Einson-Freeman Co. v. Corwin, 112 F.2d 683 (2d Cir. 1940); Cf. W. A. Schemmer Limestone Quarry, Inc. v. United States, 240 F.Supp. 356 (S.D. Iowa 1964) (if the later claim raises new grounds, the date of its disallowance will commence the statutory period).

f. 31 U.S.C.A. § 203.

nesses, after the allowance of such a claim, the ascertainment of the amount due, and the issuing of a warrant for the payment thereof.

The statutory ban on assignment of claims does not apply to assignments that take place "by operation of law." [g]

Tax refund suits are, of course, actions to recover on claims against the United States. The tax refund claims on which the suits are based have not been allowed by the government. Accordingly, their assignment, other than by operation of law, is prohibited by the Anti-assignment Statute. Where suit on a claim for refund is brought by an assignee, if the assignment should be held void, the action is subject to dismissal for want of the proper plaintiff. For example, consider the situation of an individual who sells all his stock in his wholly owned corporation at a time when it had a claim for refund pending before the IRS. If, as part of the deal, the corporation transferred the pending claim for refund to the seller, the Anti-assignment Statute would be violated. Therefore, a tax refund suit by the seller (transferee) based on the claim for refund that had been transferred to him would be subject to dismissal.[h]

The exemption from the Anti-assignment Statute of assignments or transfers of claims that take place by operation of law was read into the statute by the courts to prevent manifest unfairness. As noted by Judge Graven:

> Where a just claim against the United States passes by operation of law from the party to whom the claim accrued to another, if the Anti-assignment Statute were to be held to interdict such assignee from bringing action on the claim, then the result would be that a just claim would go unpaid since the party to whom the claim accrued could not bring an action on it because he was no longer the owner of it. The exception was based on the necessity.[i]

The judicially created exception allows transferees to bring actions on claims for refund where they became the owner of the claim by "devolutions of title by force of law." [j] Thus, the personal representative of a deceased taxpayer may pursue the decedent's claims for refund,[k] and the trustee of a bankrupt may prosecute the bank-

g. United States v. Aetna Sur. Co., 338 U.S. 366, 70 S.Ct. 207, 94 L.Ed. 171 (1949).

h. Lane, Assignment of Claims for Refund, 19 J.Tax. 362 (1963).

i. Kinney-Lindstrom Foundation, Inc. v. United States, 186 F.Supp. 133, 138 (N.D.Iowa 1960).

j. Id.

k. United States v. Aetna Sur. Co., supra note g, at 375; Erwin v. United States, 97 U.S. 392, 397, 24 L.Ed. 1065 (1878); Kinney-Lindstrom Foundation, Inc. v. United States, supra note i.

rupt's claims.[l] The claims of estate are considered to pass by operation of law to the beneficiaries upon the final distribution of the assets of the estate.[m] However, an attempt to assign claims owned by an estate prior to final distribution will violate the Anti-assignment Statute.[n] Similarly, transfers of claims from a corporation to its shareholders in connection with the complete liquidation of the business,[o] or assignments by virtue of corporate merger, dissolution, or consolidation are considered to occur by operation of law and do not violate the Anti-assignment Statute.[p]

SECTION 5. TAXPAYER'S SUIT ON ACCOUNT STATED

A consideration of civil tax litigation would not be complete without some reference to the taxpayer's action on the theory of an account stated. This theory, in essence, is that there exists an implied contract between the government and the taxpayer whereby a stipulated refund is to be made to the taxpayer.[q]

Usually, a suit on an account stated arises in a context in which a taxpayer has not met the jurisdictional prerequisites to a tax refund suit but can contend that the government has agreed to make a refund to him. The courts require all three of the following to have occurred:

1. The government and the taxpayer have agreed that the taxpayer has overpaid his taxes for a given taxable period.

2. Accord has been reached with regard to the amount of the overpayment.

3. The government has proposed, and the taxpayer has agreed, that a refund of the stated amount will be made and accepted to close the account.

If there was, in fact, an account stated the taxpayer would be able to recover on contractual grounds without having to satisfy the stringent prerequisites to the bringing of a tax refund suit.

Jurisdiction over account stated suits is based solely upon the statutes by means of which the United States has consented to be

l. Erwin v. United States, supra note k, at 397. Cf. United States v. Rochelle, 363 F.2d 225, 233 (5th Cir. 1966).

m. Pettengill v. United States, 253 F. Supp. 321 (N.D.Ill.1966).

n. Kinney-Lindstrom Foundation, Inc. v. United States, supra note i.

o. Novo Trading Corp. v. Commissioner, 113 F.2d 320 (2d Cir. 1940).

p. Seaboard Air Line Ry. v. United States, 256 U.S. 655, 41 S.Ct. 611, 65 L.Ed. 1149 (1921). Cf. Western Pac. R. R. v. United States, 268 U.S. 271, 45 S.Ct. 503, 69 L.Ed. 951 (1925).

q. Bonwit Teller & Co. v. United States, 283 U.S. 258, 51 S.Ct. 395, 75 L.Ed. 1018 (1931).

sued on contractual claims.[r] The pertinent statute of limitations provisions, 28 U.S.C.A. §§ 2401 and 2501, require account stated suits to be commenced within six years after the cause of action "first accrues." The cause of action "first accrues" when the implied contract first comes into existence. This generally occurs when the critical document, the District Director's Notice of Adjustment [s] (advising the taxpayer that an overassessment has been determined with regard to his tax liability), is delivered to the taxpayer and he accepts it.

WEST PUB. CO. EMPLOYEES' PREFERRED STOCK ASS'N v. UNITED STATES

198 Ct.Cl. 668 (1972).

ON DEFENDANT'S MOTION TO DISMISS

DAVIS, Judge, delivered the opinion of the court:

The plaintiff-taxpayer is an unincorporated association, formed in 1913 as a mutual savings bank for West Publishing Company employees. It lost its tax-exempt status in 1952 with the repeal of § 101(2) of the 1939 Internal Revenue Code (which exempted non-stock mutual savings banks), but nevertheless continued from 1953 to 1965 to file returns as a tax-exempt organization under a good-faith mistake that it still retained the immunity. On audit, the Internal Revenue Service discovered the error and proposed deficiencies for various years totalling $82,139 in income tax and $566,017 of accumulated earnings tax. The taxpayer protested both sets of deficiencies, but compromised with the Appellate Division of the Service on July 29, 1966, and signed a Form 870–AD, requiring it to pay only the corporate income tax plus $27,526 assessed interest.

On January 28, 1971—four and one-half years after payment, and without making a claim for refund—plaintiff filed this suit seeking rescission of its Form 870–AD and recovery in full of the $109,665 paid under that agreement. The basis for the claim is an alleged mutual mistake of fact arising out of an incorrect mathematical calculation; if this error is corrected, plaintiff says, it will owe no income taxes at all for the years involved.

Defendant has moved to dismiss maintaining that the court lacks jurisdiction because of plaintiff's failure to file a timely claim for refund under § 7422(a) of the Internal Revenue Code of 1954 and

r. 28 U.S.C.A. §§ 1346(a)(2) and 1491. The United States district courts and the Court of Claims have concurrent jurisdiction over these actions.

s. The Notice of Adjustment, issued pursuant to IRC § 6402, discloses to the taxpayer the amount of the overassessment determined by the District Director and his disposition of it, i. e., the amount to be credited to the outstanding tax liabilities of the taxpayer and the amount to be refunded.

§ 3772 of the Internal Revenue Code of 1939; the Government says, in addition, that it is far too late to remedy this defect since a refund claim must be filed under § 6511(a) of the 1954 Code within three years of the return or two years from payment of the tax, whichever is later.

Plaintiff's response is to insist that its claim does not fall under 26 U.S.C. §§ 6511 and 7422, but that it is merely seeking to rescind an agreement with the Government and can avail itself of the ordinary six-year limitations period generally applicable to such contractually-founded claims.[4]

The agreement taxpayer signed, Form 870–AD, is used by the Appellate Division of the Internal Revenue Service in place of the statutory closing agreement.[5] The document is, on its face, an offer by the taxpayer to waive the statutory restrictions on assessments and collection and to consent to the assessment and collection of the stated deficiencies. Once accepted by the Service, no further deficiencies will be assessed (absent fraud, malfeasance, mathematical error and certain other equitable exceptions) and interest will no longer run. In exchange, the taxpayer agrees not to file a claim for refund for the taxable period to which the form relates. * * * The form also provides: "The execution and filing of this offer will expedite the adjustment of your tax liability. It is not, however, a final closing agreement under Section 7121 of the Internal Revenue Code of 1954, nor does it extend the statutory period of limitations for refund, assessment, or collection of the tax."

I.

At bottom this is indisputably an action to recover taxes paid on its own behalf by West Publishing Company Employees' Preferred Stock Association in which the basic ground for recovery is that the taxes were not owed. The general rule for demands for return of taxes improperly paid is, of course, that a refund claim must be filed with the Internal Revenue Service and suit must be initiated within the special shortened limitations period Congress has established for tax refund claims (26 U.S.C. § 6532). * * *

* * *

[A] long line of decisions, as well as the whole history of the mechanism of refund-claim-plus-shorter-limitations for tax refunds, manifests a potent policy in favor of fidelity to this particular tax pattern where Congress has not made an express departure.

---

4. 28 U.S.C. §§ 2401(a), 2501.

5. On Form 870–AD generally, see Garbis and Frome, Procedures in Fed-

eral Tax Controversies, 1.24–1.27 and 12.10–12.12 (1968) * * *.

II.

Some rare non-statutory exceptions to the general rule do exist, however, and our precise problem is whether taxpayer fits or should be put into that narrow class.

The major qualification of the normal refund prerequisites is the so-called suit on an "account stated", which does not require a refund claim and can be brought within the over-all six-year limitations span.   To constitute such an account the Government must have agreed with the taxpayer that he has overpaid his taxes in a definite amount, and must have communicated to him its intention to repay. The action is based on the common law concept that an implied contract arises when a debtor (the Service) submits to a creditor (the taxpayer) a statement of the final balance due on an account and the creditor agrees to accept the proposed balance to close the account. See Garbis and Frome, supra [n.5] at 12.22–25. The Government has already had the chance to pass on the plaintiff's claim and has made a definite decision in his favor; this previous opportunity for the Service to correct its error—an opportunity which it has used— makes a refund claim meaningless, and accordingly the courts have dispensed with it.

But the components of an account stated are plainly not present in this case. The Government has never agreed that it owes plaintiff the sum for which suit is brought, or any sum at all. If plaintiff is right that the Form 870–AD agreement incorporated a mathematical error, the most that the agreement provides is that plaintiff may ask for a reopening of its tax liability for the covered years. The Government has not said or intimated, either in the Form 870–AD or otherwise, that on reopening it would mechanically concede the recovery now sought; it might, for instance, find other grounds for offsetting the mathematical error (as it would have a right to do), including, perhaps, some of the accumulated earnings tax which it gave up when it acceded to the Form 870–AD agreement. There has been, in a word, no acknowledgment at all by the Service that it owes plaintiff the amount sued for (or any part of it).

We are warranted in looking closely to see whether the Service has definitively and finally agreed to refund the precise amount claimed. The Supreme Court has been very strict in insisting that, before the concept of an account stated can be used, it be shown beyond peradventure that the Government has in fact agreed with, and communicated to, the taxpayer its intention to pay a stated sum. See Daube v. United States, 289 U.S. 367, 372 (1933) * * *.

In the same vein the Supreme Court has also admonished against expanding the concept of account stated beyond the narrow confines that Court has framed for it. The *Daube* opinion says (289 U.S. at 372–73):

High public interests make it necessary that there be stability and certainty in the revenues of Government. These ends are not susceptible of attainment if periods of limitation may be disregarded or extended. By the ruling in the *Bonwit Teller* case [283 U.S. 258 (1931)] a specific limitation applicable to claims for the recovery of taxes is set aside and superseded whenever the statement of an account sustains the inference of an agreement that the tax shall be repaid. As soon as this appears, a fresh term of limitation is born and set in motion. It is a ruling not to be extended through an enlargement of the concept of an account stated by latitudinarian construction.

The other recognized exception to the refund-claim requirements of §§ 7422 and 6511 is a suit in implied contract to recover a sum not collected as the plaintiff's own taxes but applied to the tax debts of others. Kirkendall v. United States, 90 Ct.Cl. 606, 31 F.Supp. 766 (1940); Ralston Steel Corp. v. United States, 169 Ct.Cl. 119, 340 F. 2d 663 (1965), cert. denied, 381 U.S. 950 (1965). Obviously, this type of action is altogether different from what we have here. In *Kirkendall,* for example, where money belonging to plaintiff was wrongfully confiscated by the Government and applied as a credit against a tax assessment alleged to be due by a third party, it was held that a claim for refund by the plaintiffs (the rightful owners) was not an appropriate step since defendant did not say that the plaintiffs had paid (or had assessed against them) any taxes.

* * *

For these reasons, defendant's motion to dismiss is granted and the petition is dismissed as barred by 26 U.S.C. §§ 7422 and 6511 (and, where applicable, the comparable sections of the 1939 Code).

SECTION 6.   RES JUDICATA AND
COLLATERAL ESTOPPEL

A.   GOVERNMENT A PARTY IN FIRST CASE

COMMISSIONER v. SUNNEN

Supreme Court of the United States, 1948.
333 U.S. 591, 68 S.Ct. 715, 92 L.Ed. 898.

Mr. Justice MURPHY delivered the opinion of the Court.

* * *

The respondent taxpayer was an inventor-patentee and the president of the Sunnen Products Company, a corporation engaged in the manufacture and sale of patented grinding machines and other tools.
* * *

The taxpayer had entered into several non-exclusive agreements whereby the corporation was licensed to manufacture and sell various devices on which he had applied for patents. In return, the corporation agreed to pay to the taxpayer a royalty equal to 10% of the gross sales price of the devices. * * *

The taxpayer at various times assigned to his wife all his right, title and interest in the various license contracts. She was given exclusive title and power over the royalties accruing under these contracts. All the assignments were without consideration and were made as gifts to the wife, those occurring after 1932 being reported by the taxpayer for gift tax purposes. The corporation was notified of each assignment.

In 1937 the corporation, pursuant to this arrangement, paid the wife royalties in the amount of $4,881.35 on the license contract made in 1928; no other royalties on that contract were paid during the taxable yers in question. The wife received royalties from other contracts totaling $15,518.68 in 1937, $17,318.80 in 1938, $25,243.77 in 1939, $50,492.50 in 1940, and $149,002.78 in 1941. She included all these payments in her income tax returns for those years, and the taxes she paid thereon have not been refunded.

Relying upon its own prior decision in Estate of Dodson v. Commissioner, 1 T.C. 416, the Tax Court held that, with one exception, all the royalties paid to the wife from 1937 to 1941 were part of the taxable income of the taxpayer. The one exception concerned the royalties of $4,881.35 paid in 1937 under the 1928 agreement. In an earlier proceeding in 1935, the Board of Tax Appeals dealt with the taxpayer's income tax liability for the years 1929–1931; it concluded that he was not taxable on the royalties paid to his wife during those years under the 1928 license agreement. This prior determination by the Board caused the Tax Court to apply the principle of *res judicata* to bar a different result as to the royalties paid pursuant to the same agreement during 1937.

* * * We * * * brought the case here on certiorari, the Commissioner alleging that the result below conflicts with prior decisions of this Court.

If the doctrine of *res judicata* is properly applicable so that all the royalty payments made during 1937–1941 are governed by the prior decision of the Board of Tax Appeals, the case may be disposed of without reaching the merits of the controversy. We accordingly cast our attention initially on that possibility, one that has been explored by the Tax Court and that has been fully argued by the parties before us.

It is first necessary to understand something of the recognized meaning and scope of *res judicata,* a doctrine judicial in origin. The general rule of *res judicata* applies to repetitious suits involving the same cause of action. It rests upon considerations of economy of judicial time and public policy favoring the establishment of certainty in legal relations. The rule provides that when a court of competent jurisdiction has entered a final judgment on the merits of a cause of action, the parties to the suit and their privies are thereafter bound "not only as to every matter which was offered and received to sustain or defeat the claim or demand, but as to any other admissible matter which might have been offered for that purpose." Cromwell v. County of Sac, 94 U.S. 351, 352, 24 L.Ed. 195. The judgment puts an end to the cause of action, which cannot again be brought into litigation between the parties upon any ground whatever, absent fraud or some other factor invalidating the judgment.

But where the second action between the same parties is upon a different cause or demand, the principle of *res judicata* is applied much more narrowly. In this situation, the judgment in the prior action operates as an estoppel, not as to matters which might have been litigated and determined, but "only as to those matters in issue or points controverted, upon the determination of which the finding or verdict was rendered." Cromwell v. County of Sac, supra, 353 of 94 U.S. Since the cause of action involved in the second proceeding is not swallowed by the judgment in the prior suit, the parties are free to litigate points which were not at issue in the first proceeding, even though such points might have been tendered and decided at that time. But matters which were actually litigated and determined in the first proceeding cannot later be relitigated. Once a party has fought out a matter in litigation with the other party, he cannot later renew that duel. In this sense, *res judicata* is usually and more accurately referred to as estoppel by judgment, or collateral estoppel.

These same concepts are applicable in the federal income tax field. Income taxes are levied on an annual basis. Each year is the origin of a new liability and of a separate cause of action. Thus if a claim of liability or non-liability relating to a particular tax year is litigated, a judgment on the merits is *res judicata* as to any subsequent proceeding involving the same claim and the same tax year. But if the later proceeding is concerned with a similar or unlike claim relating to a different tax year, the prior judgment acts as a collateral estoppel only as to those matters in the second proceeding which were actually presented and determined in the first suit. Collateral estoppel operates, in other words, to relieve the government and the taxpayer of "redundant litigation of the identical question of the statute's application to the taxpayer's status." Tait v. Western Md. R. Co., 289 U.S. 620, 624, 53 S.Ct. 706, 707, 77 L.Ed. 1405.

But collateral estoppel is a doctrine capable of being applied so as to avoid an undue disparity in the impact of income tax liability. A taxpayer may secure a judicial determination of a particular tax matter, a matter which may recur without substantial variation for some years thereafter. But a subsequent modification of the significant facts or a change or development in the controlling legal principles may make that determination obsolete or erroneous, at least for future purposes. If such a determination is then perpetuated each succeeding year as to the taxpayer involved in the original litigation, he is accorded a tax treatment different from that given to other taxpayers of the same class. As a result, there are inequalities in the administration of the revenue laws, discriminatory distinctions in tax liability, and a fertile basis for litigious confusion. Such consequences, however, are neither necessitated nor justified by the principle of collateral estoppel. That principle is designed to prevent repetitious lawsuits over matters which have once been decided and which have remained substantially static, factually and legally. It is not meant to create vested rights in decisions that have become obsolete or erroneous with time, thereby causing inequities among taxpayers.

And so where two cases involve income taxes in different taxable years, collateral estoppel must be used with its limitations carefully in mind so as to avoid injustice. It must be confined to situations where the matter raised in the second suit is identical in all respects with that decided in the first proceeding and where the controlling facts and applicable legal rules remain unchanged. If the legal matters determined in the earlier case differ from those raised in the second case, collateral estoppel has no bearing on the situation. And where the situation is vitally altered between the time of the first judgment and the second, the prior determination is not conclusive. As demonstrated by Blair v. Commissioner, 300 U.S. 5, 9, 57 S.Ct. 330, 331, 81 L.Ed. 465, a judicial declaration intervening between the two proceedings may so change the legal atmosphere as to render the rule of collateral estoppel inapplicable. But the intervening decision need not necessarily be that of a state court, as it was in the *Blair* case. While such a state court decision may be considered as having changed the facts for federal tax litigation purposes, a modification or growth in legal principles as enunciated in intervening decisions of this Court may also effect a significant change in the situation. Tax inequality can result as readily from neglecting legal modulations by this Court as from disregarding factual changes wrought by state courts. In either event, the supervening decision cannot justly be ignored by blind reliance upon the rule of collateral estoppel. It naturally follows that an interposed alteration in the pertinent statutory provisions or Treasury regulations can make the use of that rule unwarranted. Tait v. Western Md. R. Co., supra, 625.

Of course, where a question of fact essential to the judgment is actually litigated and determined in the first tax proceeding, the parties are bound by that determination in a subsequent proceeding even though the cause of action is different. And if the very same facts and no others are involved in the second case, a case relating to a different tax year, the prior judgment will be conclusive as to the same legal issues which appear, assuming no intervening doctrinal change.

But if the relevant facts in the two cases are separable, even though they be similar or identical, collateral estoppel does not govern the legal issues which recur in the second case. Thus the second proceeding may involve an instrument or transaction identical with, but in a form separable from, the one dealt with in the first proceeding. In that situation, a court is free in the second proceeding to make an independent examination of the legal matters at issue. It may then reach a different result or, if consistency in decision is considered just and desirable, reliance may be placed upon the ordinary rule of *stare decisis*. Before a party can invoke the collateral estoppel doctrine in these circumstances, the legal matter raised in the second proceeding must involve the same set of events or documents and the same bundle of legal principles that contributed to the rendering of the first judgment.

It is readily apparent in this case that the royalty payments growing out of the license contracts which were not involved in the earlier action before the Board of Tax Appeals and which concerned different tax years are free from the effects of the collateral estoppel doctrine. That is true even though those contracts are identical in all important respects with the 1928 contract, the only one that was before the Board, and even though the issue as to those contracts is the same as that raised by the 1928 contract. For income tax purposes, what is decided as to one contract is not conclusive as to any other contract which is not then in issue, however similar or identical it may be. In this respect, the instant case thus differs vitally from Tait v. Western Md. R. Co., supra, where the two proceedings involved the same instruments and the same surrounding facts.

A more difficult problem is posed as to the $4,881.35 in royalties paid to the taxpayer's wife in 1937 under the 1928 contract. Here there is complete identity of facts, issues and parties as between the earlier Board proceeding and the instant one. The Commissioner claims, however, that legal principles developed in various intervening decisions of this Court have made plain the error of the Board's conclusion in the earlier proceeding, thus creating a situation like that involved in Blair v. Commissioner, supra. This change in the legal picture is said to have been brought about by such cases as Helvering v. Clifford, 309 U.S. 331, 60 S.Ct. 554, 84 L.Ed. 788; Helvering v. Horst, 311 U.S. 112, 61 S.Ct. 144, 85 L.Ed. 75, 131 A.L.R. 655; Commissioner v. Tower, 327 U.S. 280, 66 S.Ct. 532, 90 L.Ed. 670; and Lusthaus v. Commissioner, 327 U.S. 293, 66 S.Ct. 539, 90 L.Ed. 679. These cases all imposed income tax liability on transferors who had assigned or transferred various forms of income to others within their family groups, although none specifically related to the assignment of patent license contracts between members of the same family. It must therefore be determined whether this *Clifford-Horst* line of cases represents an intervening legal development which is pertinent to the problem raised by the assignment of the 1928 agreement and which makes manifest the error of the result reached in 1935 by the Board. If that is the situation, the doctrine of collateral estoppel becomes inapplicable. A different result is then permissible as to the royalties paid in 1937 under the agreement in question. But to determine whether the *Clifford-Horst* series of cases has such an effect on the instant proceeding necessarily requires inquiry into the merits of the controversy growing out of the various contract assignments from the taxpayer to his wife. To that controversy we now turn.

[After reviewing the *Clifford-Horst* line of cases, the Court concluded:] The principles which have thus been recognized and developed by the *Clifford* and *Horst* cases, and those following them, are directly applicable to the transfer of patent license contracts between members of the same family. They are guideposts for those who seek to determine in a particular instance whether such an assignor retains sufficient control over the assigned contracts or over the receipt of income by the assignee to make it fair to impose income tax liability on him.

Moreover, the clarification and growth of these principles through the *Clifford-Horst* line of cases constitute, in our opinion, a sufficient change in the legal climate to render inapplicable in the instant proceeding, the doctrine of collateral estoppel relative to the assignment of the 1928 contract. True, these cases did not originate the concept that an assignor is taxable if he retains control over the assigned property or power to defeat the receipt of income by the assignee. But they gave much added emphasis and substance to that concept, making it more suited to meet the "attenuated subtleties" created by taxpayers. So substantial was the amplification of this concept as to justify a reconsideration of earlier Tax Court decisions reached without the benefit of the expanded notions, decisions which are now sought to be perpetuated regardless of their present correctness. Thus in the earlier litigation in 1935, the Board of Tax Appeals was unable to bring to bear on the assignment of the 1928 contract the full breadth of the ideas enunciated in the *Clifford-Horst* series of cases. And, as we shall see, a proper application of the principles as there developed might well have produced a different result, such as was reached by the Tax Court in this case in regard to the assignments of the other contracts. Under those circumstances collateral estoppel should not have been used by the Tax Court in the instant proceeding to perpetuate the 1935 viewpoint of the assignment.

* * *

The judgment below must therefore be reversed and the case remanded for such further proceedings as may be necessary in light of this opinion.

Reversed.

TOMLINSON v. LEFKOWITZ

334 F.2d 262 (5th Cir. 1964).

TUTTLE, Chief Judge.

*   *   *

The major issue raised on this appeal is whether the lower court correctly held that the criminal conviction of Sidney Lefkowitz for felonious evasion of income taxes in the years in question collaterally estopped taxpayers from seeking a refund of civil fraud penalties assessed for the same taxable years. * * * [T]axpayers argue that the doctrine of collateral estoppel by judgment was improperly invoked since the necessary elements in a prosecution under Internal Revenue Code of 1939, § 145(b),[2] under which the husband was convicted, differ from those required to impose a fraud penalty under § 293(b).[3]

This Court made a thorough analysis of collateral estoppel in Hyman v. Regenstein, 258 F.2d 502, 509–11 (5th Cir. 1958), cert. denied, 359 U.S. 913, 79 S.Ct. 589, 3 L.Ed.2d 575 (1959). The general principle was stated to be that "a fact decided in an earlier suit is conclusively established between the parties and their privies, provided it was necessary to the result in the first suit." Id. at 510 of 258 F.2d. In setting the limits of its application, the Court observed * * * that only facts essential to the judgment, as opposed to the evidentiary facts on which the facts in issue depend, are subject to collateral estoppel. Once the issue is actually determined, however, it cannot be relitigated between the parties even in a suit on a different cause of action. Moreover, an issue resolved in favor of the United States in a criminal prosecution may not be contested by the same defendants in a civil suit brought by the Government. The converse is not true, however; the Government is not estopped to raise in a civil proceeding an issue on which it lost in a criminal case because the burden of proof beyond a reasonable doubt is greater than in a civil case. Since, in the case at bar, the issue on which collateral es-

---

2. *"Failure to Collect and Pay Over Tax, or Attempt to Defeat or Evade Tax.* Any person required under this chapter to collect, account for, and pay over any tax imposed by this chapter, who willfully fails to collect or truthfully account for and pay over such tax, and any person who willfully attempts in any manner to evade or defeat any tax imposed by this chapter or the payment thereof, shall, in addition to other penalties provided by law, be guilty of a felony and, upon conviction thereof, be fined not more than $10,000, or imprisoned for not more than five years, or both, together with the costs of prosecution." [The predecessor to §§ 7201 and 7202 of the 1954 Code.]

3. *"Fraud.* If any part of any deficiency is due to fraud with intent to evade tax, then 50 per centum of the total amount of the deficiency (in addition to such deficiency) shall be so assessed, collected, and paid, in lieu of the 50 per centum addition to the tax provided in section 3612(d)(2)." [The predecessor to § 6653(b) of the 1954 Code.]

toppel was invoked was one on which the Government succeeded, there can be no objection that the former case was a criminal one whereas this one is civil.

We thus come to the critical question whether a criminal conviction for willfully attempting to evade a tax necessarily carries with it a determination that the resulting deficiency was due to fraud with intent to evade the tax.   *   *   *

We conclude that the term "willfully," as used in section 145(b), must necessarily include the elements of "fraud," as used in section 293(b).   The term "willfully" as it is used in the criminal statute is "a specific intent involving the bad purpose and evil motive to evade or defeat the payment of   *   *   *   income tax."   Bloch v. United States, 221 F.2d 786, 788 (9th Cir. 1955).   On the other hand, the fraud necessary for the imposition of the 50% penalty is a specific purpose to avoid a tax known to be owing.   Or, as this Court has said, there must be "actual and intentional wrong-doing on the part of the [taxpayer]   *   *   *   with a specific intent to evade the tax." Eagle v. Commissioner, 242 F.2d 635, 637 (5th Cir. 1957).   From examining the components of the two it can readily be seen that "willful" includes all the elements of "fraud."   The difference, if any, is in the greater degree of bad motive or evil purpose required under the criminal provision;   both require a wrongful intent to deprive the Government of taxes owing it.

*   *   *   We therefore find that the issue of the existence of a fraudulent intent is foreclosed by collateral estoppel arising from Sidney's conviction under section 145(b).   Since it is not challenged that deficiencies existed for the years 1951–1953, we hold that imposition of the section 293(b) fraud penalties is proper.

*   *   *

NOTE

The *Lefkowitz* case discusses the collateral estoppel effects of a conviction at trial.   The same effects would result from a conviction based upon a guilty plea.   However, it should be noted that there are no collateral estoppel effects flowing from a plea of *nolo contendere,* even though a conviction upon such a plea renders the defendant liable for the same criminal penalties as a conviction upon a guilty plea or after a trial.   See H. Balter, Tax Fraud and Evasion ¶ 12.08 (4th ed. 1976).   The plea of *nolo contendere* (literally, "I will not contest it,") can be entered only with the approval of the court, Fed.R.Crim.P. 11(b), and almost always is opposed by the prosecution in a tax case.

MOORE v. UNITED STATES

360 F.2d 353 (4th Cir. 1966).

SOBELOFF, Circuit Judge:

* * *

Jerome H. Moore and his wife, Mildred V. Moore, filed joint income tax returns for the years 1955–1958. In 1961 the husband was convicted after trial, pursuant to 26 U.S.C.A. § 7201, for willful evasion of taxes in those years. Subsequently a fraud assessment was made against both taxpayers pursuant to 26 U.S.C.A. § 6653(b), and when they sued in the District Court for a refund of certain taxes paid, the Government counter-claimed for the unpaid fraud penalties. In our original opinion, issued December 7, 1965, we agreed with the Government's contention that the existence of fraud on Mr. Moore's part was necessarily determined in his prior criminal trial and that as to him the issue of fraud was therefore foreclosed in the civil proceeding, adopting the view of the Fifth Circuit in Tomlinson v. Lefkowitz, 334 F.2d 262 (1964), cert. denied, 379 U.S. 962, 85 S.Ct. 650, 13 L.Ed.2d 556 (1965). * * *

[The taxpayer * * * contended in the District Court that the Government itself was collaterally estopped from redetermining the amount of taxes owed for the years in question, since it had stipulated in the earlier criminal proceeding the exact amount owed. The District Judge ruled that the Government was not estopped because the determination of an exact liability was not "essential to the judgment," a prerequisite to the application of the doctrine of collateral estoppel. Commissioner of Internal Revenue v. Sunnen, 333 U.S. 591, 601, 68 S.Ct. 715, 92 L.Ed. 898 (1948). With this ruling we agree. As stated by the District Judge, "a conviction under 26 U.S.C.A. § 7201 does not require the proving of any definite sum of taxable income beyond a substantial amount." Moore v. United States, 235 F.Supp. 387, 391 (W.D.Va.1964). There is therefore no basis here for the application of the estoppel doctrine against the Government in respect to the amount of taxes due.] t

* * *

NOTE

The preceding case, in addition to the issue discussed in the foregoing excerpt, involved the question of whether (under the pre-1971 Code) the wife who signed the joint income tax returns in issue was estopped to deny the existence of her husband's fraud in a civil proceeding following the conviction of the husband. Under the version of § 6653(b) then in effect, the fraud of the husband would render the wife (although nonparticipating) liable for the civil fraud penalty. The Fourth Circuit held, in Moore, that

---

t. From text of original opinion of December 7, 1965.

the wife was not estopped to deny the husband's fraud because she had not been a party to the husband's criminal tax prosecution. This issue was mooted in 1971 when § 6653(b) was amended to provide that the civil fraud penalty cannot be imposed upon a spouse signing a joint income tax return unless the spouse participated in the fraud. See pages 176–180, above, and 777–781, below for additional materials on the "innocent spouse" provisions of the Code.

QUESTIONS

1. The *Moore* case holds that the government is not estopped to vary, in future civil litigation, from the amount of the tax deficiency established in a criminal prosecution for attempted evasion. It should be noted that this conclusion results from the fact that the amount of the deficiency (as long as it is more than insubstantial) is not essential to a successful prosecution for attempted evasion. Should not the defendant-taxpayer, as well, be free to contest the amount of the deficiency in a civil tax controversy following a conviction? In any event, if a taxpayer pleads guilty to criminal tax charges, should he not be careful to avoid inadvertent admissions as to the amount of tax deficiencies by noting on the record in the criminal case the fact (if it is true) that the precise amounts charged are not conceded?

2. What do you think should be the result in a case in which the majority shareholder of a corporation is convicted of causing the corporation to file false and fraudulent returns? Should the corporation, which was not a party to the criminal case, be estopped to deny fraud for civil tax purposes? See C.B.C. Supermarkets, Inc. v. Commissioner, 54 T.C. 882 (1970).

GOODWIN v. COMMISSIONER

73 T.C. 215 (1979).

SCOTT, Judge.

* * *

Respondent takes the position that petitioner is estopped by reason of his conviction on a plea of guilty of violation of section 7206(1) for each of the years 1968, 1969 and 1970 from denying that his returns for each of these years was false and fraudulent in that he knew and believed that his correct total income for each of these years was an amount substantially in excess of the income reported on his return for the year.

Respondent argues, based on the decisions in Arctic Ice Cream Co. v. Commissioner, 43 T.C. 68 (1964), and Plunkett v. Commissioner, 465 F.2d 299 (7th Cir. 1972), affg. a Memorandum Opinion of this Court, that for the purposes of applying the doctrine of collateral estoppel there is no difference between a conviction based upon a plea of guilty and a conviction entered after a trial on the merits. Both of these cases specifically so hold and we follow the holdings of those cases in the instant case.

In support of his position that because of his conviction petitioner is estopped to deny that his return for each of the years 1968, 1969 and 1970 is fraudulent and to deny that he omitted substantial amounts of income from his return in each of those years, respondent relies on Considine v. Commissioner, 68 T.C. 52 (1977).

In the *Considine* case we held that the taxpayer was estopped by his conviction after a jury trial of violating section 7206(1) from denying that his return for the year there involved was fraudulent in that it failed to report a specific item of capital gain income. We pointed out that estoppel applies only with respect to those facts actually litigated in the first case which were essential to the judgment in that case. In the instant case, therefore, we must decide what facts were litigated and essential to the judgment in the criminal case since the conviction was on a guilty plea.

In Arctic Ice Cream Co. v. Commissioner, supra, we stated (at 75):

> It is well settled that a plea of guilty means "guilty as charged in the indictment," and that such a plea is a conclusive judicial admission of all of the essential elements of the offense which the indictment charges.

The essential element of the indictment in the instant case, to which petitioner pleaded guilty, was that in each of the years here in issue he subscribed under penalties of perjury a joint Federal income tax return which was filed with the Internal Revenue Service, which return he did not believe to be true and correct in that he well knew and believed that his correct total income for the year was substantially in excess of the income he reported.

The indictment for violation of section 7206(1) in the instant case to which petitioner pleaded guilty, as was the indictment in Considine v. Commissioner, supra, was for willfully subscribing under penalties of perjury a Federal income tax return known or believed to be incorrect in that income was omitted therefrom. It was essential to petitioner's conviction that it be shown that he willfully subscribed to a return which he knew and believed to be false in that income was omitted therefrom. As discussed in the *Considine* case, the willful subscribing to a false return is the filing of a fraudulent return. In fact, the judgment here convicted petitioner of filing "false and fraudulent income tax returns." In our view, here, as in *Considine,* petitioner is estopped to deny that his return for each of the years here in issue was false and fraudulent and that he omitted substantial amounts of income from his return in each of these years.

* * *

In order for collateral estoppel to apply with respect to the issue raised under section 6653(b), it must be shown as stated in Considine v. Commissioner, supra at 64, that the facts to which the estoppel applies are "ultimate facts with respect to which an identical issue is presented under section 6653(b)." As stated in Sunnen v. Commissioner, 333 U.S. 591, 599–600 (1948), where a question of fact essential to the judgment in the first case is actually litigated and determined in that proceeding, the parties are bound by the determination in a subsequent proceeding even though the cause of action is different. In order for the judgment in the prior proceeding to be given conclusive effect, it must establish "one of the ultimate facts in issue in the subsequent proceeding." Yates v. United States, 354 U.S. 298, 338 (1957); The Evergreens v. Nunan, 141 F.2d 927–928, 931 (2d Cir. 1944), affg. 47 B.T.A. 815 (1942), cert. den. 323 U.S. 720 (1944). In The Evergreens v. Nunan, supra at 928, the term ultimate fact in the collateral estoppel context is defined as " * * * one of those facts, upon whose combined occurrence the law raises the duty, or the right, in question * * *." Such an ultimate fact is distinguished in that case from an evidentiary fact, "from whose existence may be rationally inferred the existence of one of the facts upon whose combined occurrence the law raises the duty, or the right."

A conclusion that a taxpayer has filed a false and fraudulent return from which substantial income is omitted is a finding of an ultimate fact. This is one of the ultimate facts required to be shown in order to sustain an addition to tax under section 6653(b) even though it is necessary under that section, in order to find the addition to tax to be due, to make a further ultimate finding of fact that there is an underpayment of tax due to the fraudulent omission of income from the return.[7] While section 6653(b) does not include the phrase "with intent to evade tax" as did section 293(b), I.R.C. 1939, this difference in wording was not a change in the proof necessary to show that a taxpayer is liable for an addition to tax for fraud. If an underpayment of tax is due to fraud, it is this fraud which comprises the intent to evade tax. Therefore, to find the further ultimate fact that an underpayment of tax results from the fraudulent omission of income from the return is to find that the underpayment is due to fraud with intent to evade tax.

While, as heretofore pointed out, an "ultimate fact" is defined in The Evergreens v. Nunan, supra at 928, for purposes of collateral estoppel as one of the facts "upon whose combined occurrence the law raises the duty, or the right, in question," we have found no case specifically discussing what is an "ultimate fact" in a case involving an addition to tax under section 6653(b) other than the *Considine* case,

---

7. In the case of Considine v. Commissioner, 68 T.C. 52, 59 (1977), we discussed at some length the fact that willful, as used in sec. 7206(1) and sec. 7201, has the same meaning and that the bad faith or evil intent referred to in cases discussing the meaning of the word, willful, in the context of these statutes "simply means a voluntary, intentional violation of a known legal duty." See United States v. Pomponio, 429 U.S. 10, 12 (1976). See also Amos v. Commissioner, 43 T.C. 50, 55 (1964), affd. 360 F.2d 358 (4th Cir. 1965).

the *Amos* case and cases similar to the *Amos* case. We have therefore analyzed cases applying collateral estoppel in other situations to determine the nature of the facts considered in those cases to be ultimate facts in relation to the issues involved in those cases. From this analysis we can compare the facts in those cases to which collateral estoppel was held to apply in relation to the issues therein to the fact of fraudulent omission of income from a Federal tax return to the issue of whether there is an underpayment of tax, a part of which is due to fraud.

* * *

From these cases, it is clear that uniformly courts have held that a fact which by its nature is an ultimate fact, such as the omission of substantial income from a false and fraudulent return which has been decided in a prior case, collaterally estops the person involved in the prior case from denying in a later action that ultimate fact even though other facts must be found to dispose of the issue involved in the second case. In our view, petitioner in this case is estopped by his conviction in the prior criminal case from denying that he filed a fraudulent Federal income tax return from which was omitted substantial income for each of the years here involved.

Having concluded that petitioner is estopped to deny that his returns for the years here in issue were false and fraudulent in that he knowingly failed to report substantial income, it is necessary for us to decide whether respondent has shown by clear and convincing evidence that a part of the underpayment of tax in each of these years was due to this fraud with intent to evade tax. It is not necessary to a conviction under section 7206(1) that the false statement or omission on the return result in an underpayment of tax. However, a necessary part of the showing of an addition to tax under section 6653(b) is that there is an underpayment due to fraud.

The record here contains petitioner's tax returns showing all the deductions claimed by petitioner. None of the deductions claimed by petitioner on these returns has been disallowed by respondent. Petitioner's returns, therefore, constitute a statement of petitioner as to the deductions to which he is entitled in each of the years here in issue. This is clear evidence of petitioner's deductions. Petitioner's only business in the years here in issue was that of being an employee, a state employee and a township committeeman and mayor. The only deductible business expenses petitioner could have from his employment were employee business expenses. Petitioner produced no evidence and made no claim that he was entitled to any deductions other than those claimed on his return. From petitioner's returns respondent has shown the amount of his deductible expenses in each year here in issue.

* * *

On the basis of this record as a whole, we conclude that respondent has shown by clear and convincing evidence that part of the underpayment in tax in each of the years here in issue was due to petitioner's failure to report substantial amounts of income on his false and fraudulent returns.   In our opinion, this is sufficient to show that part of the underpayment of tax by petitioner in each year here in issue was due to fraud with intent to evade tax.

*   *   *

Reviewed by the Court.

FEATHERSTON, J., dissenting: I disagree with that portion of the majority opinion which estops petitioner from showing that he did not file a fraudulent return for each of the years in controversy. Estopping petitioner in this respect, in my opinion, has led the majority to apply an erroneous standard in finding that some part of the deficiency for the years in issue was "due to fraud" within the meaning of Code section 6653(b).

*   *   *

*   *   *   [I]n my opinion, to hold that a conviction of "willfully" making a false statement in an income tax return within the meaning of section 7206(1) estops a taxpayer from denying that any underpayment of tax he may have made for the year of the return was "due to fraud" misapplies the principle of collateral estoppel. Conviction under section 7206(1) establishes that petitioner willfully, or voluntarily and intentionally, violated the legal duty not to make a false statement as to any material matter on his income tax return. It does not establish that he violated that duty with an intent, or in an attempt, to evade tax.

I am aware that the finding and judgment entered by the district court states:

Defendant has been convicted as charged of the offense(s) of filing false and fraudulent income tax returns. 26:7206(1).

But, in entering this minute order, the court simply paraphrased the heading of section 7206, "Fraud and False Statements."   Paragraphs (2), (3), and (4) of section 7206 describe crimes involving fraud, but, *   *   * section 7206(1) does not.

While I disagree with the majority position that petitioner is estopped from denying fraud, I think petitioner is estopped to deny the question actually litigated and determined in the criminal action—in the words of the indictment, that he—

willfully and knowingly *   *   * [filed an income tax return for each of the 3 years for which he was convicted which] he did not believe to be true and correct as to every material matter, in that *   *   * he then and there well knew and believed *   *   * the correct total income for the period reported was an amount substantially in excess of the reported total sum [in each such year].

*   *   *

In resolving the issue of whether any part of petitioner's underpayments of tax were "due to fraud," it will be important to weigh his failure to show he had deductions to offset these judicially-established omissions of income. I do not think, however, such failure establishes fraud as a matter of law. Petitioner is entitled to litigate the fraud issue without regard to the principle of collateral estoppel. In other words, the Court must decide, in the light of all the evidence, whether the underpayments of tax were "due to fraud," i. e., whether petitioner made the income omissions with "the specific purpose to evade a tax believed to be owing." Carter v. Campbell, 264 F.2d 930, 936 (5th Cir. 1959). I respectfully dissent because it is not clear that the evidence has been weighed under this standard.

CHABOT, J, dissenting: Petitioner was indicted on five counts of extortion and three counts of willfully filing false Federal income tax returns. Nine months later, he "copped a plea"; he pled guilty on the three false return counts. Four months after that, all five extortion counts were dismissed and petitioner got probation and a $2,000 fine.

On the basis of the foregoing, the majority refuse to allow petitioner to deny that his tax return for each of the years before the Court was false and "fraudulent", within the meaning of section 6653(b). Having thus foreclosed petitioner from denying fraud and omission of substantial amounts of income, the majority then conclude that petitioner is liable for the civil fraud addition to tax for each of the three years.

From this conclusion I respectfully dissent, because—

(1) petitioner's conviction under section 7206(1) was not a conviction of "fraud";

(2) collateral estoppel is not applicable; and

(3) in the absence of collateral estoppel, respondent has not borne his heavy burden of proving petitioner's liability for civil tax fraud.

*   *   *

The willful filing of an income tax return omitting income is a fact which if true may, together with further facts, be a basis from which an intent to evade tax may be inferred. It is not an "ultimate" fact in a section 6653(b) proceeding.

The majority correctly recognize that, in order for the judgment in the prior proceeding to be given conclusive effect, it must establish one of the ultimate facts *   *   * in issue in the subsequent proceeding. The majority then state "[a] conclusion that a taxpayer has filed a false and fraudulent return from which substantial income is omitted is a finding of an ultimate fact" in a section 6653(b) proceeding. The latter statement may well be the law, but its application here is based on the assumption that the fact essential to the section 7206(1) proceeding (the willful subscribing to a return from which substantial amounts of income have been omitted) is a conclusion that petitioner has filed a fraudulent return. * * * [T]hat assumption is unfounded.

Therefore, I would hold that collateral estoppel does not apply to estop petitioner from denying fraud, nor from denying he willfully filed income tax returns from which substantial amounts of income have been omitted for the years before the Court.

* * *

An additional comment may be in order.

Under Arctic Ice Cream Co. v. Commissioner, 43 T.C. 68 (1964), a guilty plea in a criminal tax case can be the basis for collateral estoppel. However, in a civil tax case—

if petitioner had conceded the matter out of court, then there would be no collateral estoppel;

if petitioner had contested the matter, but stipulated as to a point, then there would be no collateral estoppel as to that point (United States v. International Building Co., 345 U.S. 502, 505 (1953)); and

if petitioner had contested the matter and had gone to trial, but conceded the matter on brief, then there would be no collateral estoppel (Coors v. Commissioner, 60 T.C. 368, 389–392 (1973), affd. 519 F.2d 1280, 1283 (CA10 1975)).

I find it hard to distinguish between the civil cases and the matter now before us.

A wag has defined the law as "common sense, as modified by the legislature". But nothing in the statute commands the results reached by the majority.[14] The concept—and the distinctions drawn by the foregoing cases—have been designed by the courts in part for the convenience of the courts. At least as to the distinctions discussed above, the modifications of common sense may not properly be charged to the legislature.

---

14. The term "collateral estoppel" appears neither in the Internal Revenue Code nor in any other part of the United States Code that provides the Congress' instructions to the courts as to the Internal Revenue Code.

B. GOVERNMENT NOT A PARTY IN FIRST CASE

COMMISSIONER v. ESTATE OF BOSCH

Supreme Court of the United States, 1967.
387 U.S. 456, 87 S.Ct. 1776, 18 L.Ed.2d 886.

Mr. Justice CLARK delivered the opinion of the Court.

These two federal estate tax cases present a common issue for our determination: Whether a federal court or agency in a federal estate tax controversy is conclusively bound by a state trial court adjudication of property rights or characterization of property interests when the United States is not made a party to such proceeding.

* * *

* * * We hold that where the federal estate tax liability turns upon the character of a property interest held and transferred by the decedent under state law, federal authorities are not bound by the determination made of such property interest by a state trial court.

* * *

[In * * * *Estate of Bosch*, the decedent created in 1930 a revocable *inter vivos* trust in favor of his wife, which also granted to her a general testamentary power of appointment over the corpus. In 1951, the decedent's wife, in order to take advantage of the Powers of Appointment Act of 1951, executed an instrument which purportedly converted the general power into a special power of appointment. Upon the decedent's death in 1957, his executor sought a marital deduction for the amount of the *inter vivos* trust; under § 2056(b)(5), the trust would qualify for the deduction only if the decedent's wife held at his death a general power of appointment over the corpus.

The Commissioner, on the basis of the release signed in 1951 by the widow, disallowed the deduction, but the executor sought from the Tax Court a redetermination of the resulting deficiency. While the Tax Court proceeding was still pending, the executor petitioned in the New York Supreme Court for a determination under state law of the validity of the 1951 release. The Tax Court, with the Commissioner's assent, temporarily suspended its proceeding. In the state court, each of the three parties—the trustee, the widow, and the guardian *ad litem* of an infant who was a possible beneficiary—contended that the release was a nullity. The state court adopted their unanimous view. The Tax Court thereupon accepted the state trial court decision as an "authoritative exposition" of the requirements of state law. A divided Court of Appeals affirmed. | ᵘ

> **u.** The statement of facts is taken from the dissenting opinion of Mr. Justice Harlan.

The problem of what effect must be given a state trial court decree where the matter decided there is determinative of federal estate tax consequences has long burdened the Bar and the courts. This Court has not addressed itself to the problem for nearly a third of a century. In Freuler v. Helvering, 291 U.S. 35, 54 S.Ct. 308, 78 L.Ed. 634 (1934), this Court, declining to find collusion between the parties on the record as presented there, held that a prior *in personam* judgment in the state court to which the United States was not made a party, "[o]bviously   *   *   *   had not the effect of *res judicata*, and could not furnish the basis for invocation of the full faith and credit clause   *   *   *." At 43, 54 S.Ct. at 311. In *Freuler's* wake, at least three positions have emerged among the circuits. The first of these holds that

> "   *   *   *   if the question at issue is fairly presented to the state court for its independent decision and is so decided by the court the resulting judgment if binding upon the parties under the state law is conclusive as to their property rights in the federal tax case   *   *   *." Gallagher v. Smith, 223 F.2d 218, at 225.

The opposite view is expressed in Faulkerson's Estate v. United States, 301 F.2d 231. This view seems to approach that of Erie R. Co. v. Tompkins, 304 U.S. 64, 58 S.Ct. 817, 82 L.Ed. 1188 (1938), in that the federal court will consider itself bound by the state court decree only after independent examination of the state law as determined by the highest court of the State. The Government urges that an intermediate position be adopted; it suggests that a state trial court adjudication is binding in such cases only when the judgment is the result of an adversary proceeding in the state court.

We look at the problem differently. First, the Commissioner was not made a party to either of the state proceedings here and neither had the effect of *res judicata*; nor did the principle of collateral estoppel apply. It can hardly be denied that both state proceedings were brought for the purpose of directly affecting federal estate tax liability. Next, it must be remembered that it was a federal taxing statute that the Congress enacted and upon which we are here passing. Therefore, in construing it, we must look to the legislative history surrounding it. We find that the report of the Senate Finance Committee recommending enactment of the marital deduction used very guarded language in referring to the very question involved here. It said that "proper regard," not finality, "should be given to interpretations of the will" by state courts and then only when entered by a court "in a bona fide adversary proceeding." We cannot say that the authors of this directive intended that the decrees of state trial courts were to be conclusive and binding on the computation of the federal estate tax as levied by the Congress. If the Congress had intended state trial court determinations to have that effect on the federal actions, it certainly would have said so—which it did not do. On the contrary, we believe it intended the marital deduction to be strictly construed and applied. Not only did it indicate that only "proper regard" was to be accorded state decrees but it placed specific limitations on the allowance of the deduction as set out in § 2056(b), (c), and (d). These restrictive limitations clearly indicate the great care that Congress exercised in the drawing of the Act and indicate also a definite concern with the elimination of loopholes and escape hatches that might jeopardize the federal revenue. This also is in keeping with the long-established policy of the Congress, as expressed in the Rules of Decision Act, 28 U.S.C. § 1652. There it is provided that in the absence of federal requirements such as the Constitution or Acts of Congress, the "laws of the several states * * * shall be regarded as rules of decision in civil actions in the courts of the United States, in cases where they apply." This Court has held that judicial decisions are "laws of the * * * state" within the section. Erie R. Co. v. Tompkins, supra; King v. Order of United Commercial Travelers, 333 U.S. 153, 68 S.Ct. 488, 92 L.Ed. 608 (1948). Moreover, even in diversity cases this Court has further held that while the decrees of "lower state courts" should be "attributed some weight * * * the decision [is] not controlling * * *" where the highest court of the State has not spoken on the point. King v. Order of United Commercial Travelers, supra, at 160–161, 68 S.Ct. at 492. And in West v. American Tel. & Tel. Co., 311 U.S. 223, 61 S.Ct. 179, 85 L.Ed. 139 (1940), this Court further held that "an intermediate appellate state court * * * is a datum for ascertaining state law which is not to be disregarded by a federal court *unless it is convinced by other persuasive data that the highest court of the state would decide otherwise.*" At 237, 61 S.Ct. at 183 (Emphasis supplied.) Thus, under some conditions, federal authority may not be bound even by an intermediate state appellate court ruling. It follows here then, that when the application of a federal statute is involved, the decision of a state trial court as to an underlying issue of state law should *a fortiori* not be controlling. This is but an application of the rule of Erie R. Co. v. Tompkins, supra, where state law as announced by the highest court of the State is to be followed. This is not a diversity case but the same principle may be applied for the same reasons, viz., the underlying substantive rule involved is based on state law and the State's highest court is the best authority on its own law. If there be no decision by that court then federal authorities must apply what they find to be the state law after giving "proper regard" to relevant rulings of other courts of the State. In this respect, it may be said to be, in effect, sitting as a state court.

We believe that this would avoid much of the uncertainty that would result from the "non-adversary" approach and at the same time would be fair to the taxpayer and protect the federal revenue as well.

The judgment in [*Estate of Bosch* is therefore] reversed and remanded for further proceedings not inconsistent with this opinion. It is so ordered.

* * *

Mr. Justice DOUGLAS, dissenting.

* * *

Not giving effect to a state court determination may be unfair to the taxpayer and is contrary to the congressional purpose of making federal tax consequences depend upon rights under state law. The result will be to tax the taxpayer or his estate for benefits which he does not have under state law. * * * I cannot believe that Congress intended such unjust results.

This is not to say that a federal court is bound by all state court decrees. A federal court might not be bound by a consent decree, for it does not purport to be a declaration of state law; it may be merely a judicial stamp placed upon the parties' contractual settlement. Nor need the federal court defer to a state court decree which has been obtained by fraud or collusion. But where, absent those considerations, a state court has reached a deliberate conclusion, where it has construed state law, the federal court should consider the decision to be an exposition of the controlling state law and give it effect as such.

Mr. Justice HARLAN, whom Mr. Justice FORTAS joins, dissenting.

The central issue presented by these two cases is whether and in what circumstances a judgment of a lower state court is entitled to conclusiveness in a subsequent federal proceeding, if the state judgment establishes property rights from which stem federal tax consequences. The issue is doubly important: it is a difficult and intensely practical problem, and it involves basic questions of the proper relationship in this context between the state and federal judicial systems. For reasons which follow, I am constrained to dissent * * *.

* * *

The issue here, despite its importance in general, is essentially quite a narrow one. The questions of law upon which taxation turns in these cases are not among those for which federal definitions or standards have been provided; it is, on the contrary, accepted that federal tax consequences have here been imposed by Congress on property rights as those rights have been defined and delimited by the pertinent state laws. The federal revenue interest thus consists entirely of the expectation that the absence or presence of the rights will be determined accurately in accordance with the prevailing state rules. The question here is, however, not how state law must in the context of federal taxation ordinarily be determined; it is instead the more narrow one of whether and under what conditions a lower state court adjudication of a taxpayer's property rights is conclusive when subsequently the federal tax consequences of those rights are at issue. in a federal court.

* * *

The interests of the federal treasury are essentially narrow here; they are entirely satisfied if a considered judgment is obtained from either a state or a federal court, after consideration of the pertinent materials, of the requirements of state law. For this purpose, the Commissioner need not have, and does not now ask, an opportunity to relitigate in federal courts every issue of state law that may involve federal tax consequences; the federal interest requires only that the Commissioner be permitted to obtain from the federal courts a considered adjudication of the relevant state law issues in cases in which, for whatever reason, the state courts have not already provided such an adjudication. In turn, it may properly be assumed that the state court has had an opportunity to make, and has made, such an adjudication if, in a proceeding untainted by fraud, it has had the benefit of reasoned argument from parties holding genuinely inconsistent interests.

I would therefore hold that in cases in which state-adjudicated property rights are contended to have federal tax consequences, federal courts must attribute conclusiveness to the judgment of a state court, of whatever level in the state procedural system, unless the litigation from which the judgment resulted does not bear the indicia of a genuinely adversary proceeding. I need not undertake to define with any particularity the weight I should give to the various possible factors involved in such an assessment; it suffices to illustrate the more important of the questions which I believe to be pertinent. The principal distinguishing characteristic of a state proceeding to which, in my view, conclusiveness should be attributed is less the number of parties represented before the state court than it is the actual adversity of their financial and other interests. It would certainly be pertinent if it appeared that all the parties had instituted the state proceeding solely for the purpose of defeating the federal revenue. The taking of an appeal would be significant, although scarcely determinative. The burden would be upon the taxpayer, in any case brought either for a redetermination of a deficiency or for a refund, to overturn the presumption that the Commissioner had correctly assessed the necessary tax by establishing that the state court had had an opportunity to make, and had made, a reasoned resolution of the state law issues, after a proceeding in which the pertinent viewpoints had been presented. Proceedings in which one or more of the parties had been guilty of fraud in the presentation of the issues to the state court would, of course, ordinarily be entitled to little or no weight in the federal court's determination of state law.

I recognize, of course, that this approach lacks the precision of both the contrasting yardsticks suggested by the Court and by my

Brother DOUGLAS. Yet I believe that it reflects more faithfully than either of those resolutions the demands of our federal system and of the competing interests involved.

*   *   *

SECTION 7. SUPPRESSION OF EVIDENCE IN CIVIL TAX CASES

UNITED STATES v. JANIS

Supreme Court of the United States, 1976.
428 U.S. 433, 96 S.Ct. 3021, 49 L.Ed.2d 1046.

Mr. Justice BLACKMUN delivered the opinion of the Court.

This case presents an issue of the appropriateness of an extension of the judicially created exclusionary rule: Is evidence seized by a state criminal law enforcement officer in good faith, but nonetheless unconstitutionally, inadmissible in a civil proceeding by or against the United States?

[Based upon the affidavit of a police officer, a Los Angeles judge issued a search warrant, pursuant to which the police seized from Janis $4,940 in cash and certain wagering records. The officer advised the IRS that Janis had been arrested for bookmaking activity. Using a calculation based upon the seized evidence, the IRS assessed Janis for wagering excise taxes and levied upon the $4,940 in partial satisfaction. In the subsequent state criminal proceedings against Janis the trial court found the police officer's affidavit defective, granted a motion to quash the warrant, and ordered the seized items returned to Janis, except for the $4,940. Janis later filed a claim for refund and, after it was denied, a civil action in the United States District Court for return of the $4,940. The United States answered, and counterclaimed for a substantial unpaid balance of the assessment. In the civil action, Janis moved to suppress the evidence seized and all copies thereof, and to quash the assessment. The District Court concluded that Janis was entitled to a refund because the assessment "was based in substantial part, if not completely, on illegally procured evidence," and that under the circumstances Janis was not required to prove the extent of the claimed refund. The assessment was quashed and the Government's counterclaim was dismissed with prejudice. The Court of Appeals for the Ninth Circuit affirmed.]

The debate within the Court on the exclusionary rule has always been a warm one. It has been unaided, unhappily, by any convincing empirical evidence on the effects of the rule. The Court, however, has established that the "prime purpose" of the rule, if not the sole one, "is to deter future unlawful police conduct." United States v.

Calandra, 414 U.S. 338, 347, 94 S.Ct. 613, 619, 38 L.Ed.2d 561 (1974).
* * *

In the complex and turbulent history of the rule, the Court never has applied it to exclude evidence from a civil proceeding, federal or state.

In the present case we are asked to create judicially a deterrent sanction by holding that evidence obtained by a state criminal law enforcement officer in good faith reliance on a warrant that later proved to be defective shall be inadmissible in a federal civil tax proceeding. Clearly, the enforcement of admittedly valid laws would be hampered by so extending the exclusionary rule, and, as is nearly always the case with the rule, concededly relevant and reliable evidence would be rendered unavailable.

* * *

If the exclusionary rule is the "strong medicine" that its proponents claim it to be, then its use in the situations in which it is now applied (resulting, for example, in this case in frustration of the Los Angeles police officers' good-faith duties as enforcers of the criminal laws) must be assumed to be a substantial and efficient deterrent. Assuming this efficacy, the additional marginal deterrence provided by forbidding a different sovereign from using the evidence in a civil proceeding surely does not outweigh the cost to society of extending the rule to that situation. If, on the other hand, the exclusionary rule does not result in appreciable deterrence, then, clearly, its use in the instant situation is unwarranted. Under either assumption, therefore, the extension of the rule is unjustified.

In short, we conclude that exclusion from federal civil proceedings of evidence unlawfully seized by a state criminal enforcement officer has not been shown to have a sufficient likelihood of deterring the conduct of the state police so that it outweighs the societal costs imposed by the exclusion. This Court, therefore, is not justified in so extending the exclusionary rule.

Respondent argues, however, that the application of the exclusionary rule to civil proceedings long has been recognized in the federal courts. He cites a number of cases. But respondent does not critically distinguish between those cases in which the officer committing the unconstitutional search or seizure was an agent of the sovereign that sought to use the evidence, on the one hand, and those cases, such as the present one, on the other hand, where the officer has no responsibility or duty to, or agreement with, the sovereign seeking to use the evidence.[31]

---

31. * * * Respondent remains free on remand to attempt to prove that there was federal participation in fact. If he succeeds in that proof, he raises the question, not presented by this case, whether the exclusionary rule is to be applied in a civil proceeding involving an intrasovereign violation. * * *

* * * Only one case cited by the respondent squarely holds that there must be an exclusionary rule barring use in a civil proceeding by one sovereign of material seized in violation of the Fourth Amendment by an officer of another sovereign. In Suarez v. Commissioner, 58 T.C. 792 (1972) (reviewed by the court, with two judges dissenting), the Tax Court determined that the exclusionary rule should be applied in a situation similar to the one that confronts us here. The court concluded that

> "any competing consideration based upon the need for effective enforcement of civil tax liabilities * * * must give way to the higher goal of protection of the individual and the necessity for preserving confidence in, rather than encouraging contempt for, the processes of Government." Id., at 805.

No appeal was taken.

We disagree with the broad implications of this statement of the Tax Court for two reasons. To the extent that the court did not focus on the deterrent purpose of the exclusionary rule, the law has since been clarified. Moreover, the court did not distinguish between intersovereign and intrasovereign uses of unconstitutionally seized material. Working, as we must, with the absence of convincing empirical data, common sense dictates that the deterrent effect of the exclusion of relevant evidence is highly attenuated when the "punishment" imposed upon the offending criminal enforcement officer is the removal of that evidence from a civil suit by or against a different sovereign. In Elkins [v. United States, 364 U.S. 206, 80 S.Ct. 1437, 4 L.Ed.2d 1669 (1960),] the Court indicated that the assumed interest of criminal law enforcement officers in the criminal proceedings of another sovereign counterbalanced this attenuation sufficiently to justify an exclusionary rule. Here, however, the attenuation is further augmented by the fact that the proceeding is one to enforce only the civil law of the other sovereign.

This attenuation, coupled with the existing deterrence effected by the denial of use of the evidence by either sovereign in the criminal trials with which the searching officer is concerned, creates a situation in which the imposition of the exclusionary rule sought in this case is unlikely to provide significant, much less substantial, additional deterrence. It falls outside the offending officer's zone of primary interest. The extension of the exclusionary rule, in our view, would be an unjustifiably drastic action by the courts in the pursuit of what is an undesired and undesirable supervisory role over police officers.

In the past this Court has opted for exclusion in the anticipation that law enforcement officers would be deterred from violating Fourth Amendment rights. Then, as now, the Court acted in the absence of convincing empirical evidence and relied, instead, on its own assumptions of human nature and the interrelationship of the various components of the law enforcement system. In the situation before us, we do not find sufficient justification for the drastic measure of an exclusionary rule. There comes a point at which courts, consistent with their duty to administer the law, cannot continue to create barriers to law enforcement in the pursuit of a supervisory role that is properly the duty of the Executive and Legislative Branches. We find ourselves at that point in this case. We therefore hold that the judicially created exclusionary rule should not be extended to forbid the use in the civil proceeding of one sovereign of evidence seized by a criminal law enforcement agent of another sovereign.

The judgment of the Court of Appeals is reversed, and the case is remanded for further proceedings consistent with this opinion.

Mr. Justice STEWART, dissenting.

* * *

If state police officials can effectively crack down on gambling law violators by the simple expedient of violating their constitutional rights and turning the illegally seized evidence over to Internal Revenue Service agents on the proverbial "silver platter," then the deterrent purpose of the exclusionary rule is wholly frustrated. "If, on the other hand, it is understood that the fruit of an unlawful search by state agents will be inadmissible in a federal trial, there can be no inducement to subterfuge and evasion with respect to federal-state cooperation in criminal investigation." Elkins v. United States, supra, 364 U.S., at 222, 80 S.Ct., at 1446.

PIZZARELLO v. UNITED STATES

408 F.2d 579 (2d Cir.), cert. denied,
396 U.S. 986, 90 S.Ct. 481, 24 L.Ed.2d 450 (1969).

MOORE, Circuit Judge:

[In the context of a refund suit, the court found as a fact that the assessment at issue was based in substantial part, if not *in toto*, on evidence unlawfully obtained by agents of the United States government.]

* * *

There remains the question of whether the fact that illegally seized evidence was used to compute the assessment renders the tax illegal. Widespread uncertainty is prevalent on the issue of whether evidence, inadmissible in a criminal case, can be used for other purposes, and the Supreme Court has yet to resolve the problem.

* * *

The District Court's initial conclusion that the illegally seized evidence could not be used to assess a wagering tax was based on a statement by Mr. Justice Holmes in Silverthorne Lumber Co. v. United States, 251 U.S. 385, 40 S.Ct. 182, 64 L.Ed. 319 (1920), where he declared, "The essence of a provision forbidding the acquisition of evidence in a certain way is that not merely evidence so acquired shall not be used before this Court, but that it shall not be used at all." Id. at 392, 40 S.Ct. at 183.

* * *

When private individuals procure evidence in violation of the law, they are subject to civil and criminal liability. The existence of such liability as a deterrent is significant. Because of the resultant availability of civil and criminal remedies, some states have held evidence obtained by illegal private searches and seizures, if probative, admissible in civil suits between private litigants.

This case, however, while civil in nature is not between private parties and there are no analogous independent deterrents to, or remedies against, government violations of the Fourth Amendment. The prohibition against unreasonable searches and seizures is directed at governmental action. Absent an exclusionary rule, the Government would be free to undertake unreasonable searches and seizures in all civil cases without the possibility of unfavorable consequences. In such a situation, while the matter has not been settled by Supreme Court decision, it seems clear, even under a view of the law most favorable to the Government, that evidence so obtained would be excluded. Because Pizzarello's tax assessment was based in substantial part, if not completely, on illegally procured evidence, the assessment is invalid.

* * *

NOTES

1. In Compton v. United States, excerpted above at pages 239–243, the Fourth Circuit approached, but did not squarely face, the civil suppression issue in holding illegally obtained evidence was admissible for impeachment purposes. The court noted:

> The Supreme Court has not squarely decided whether illegally obtained evidence may be admitted in a civil proceeding. However, in Silverthorne Lumber Co. v. United States, 251 U.S. 385, 40 S.Ct. 182, 183, 64 L.Ed. 319 (1920), a criminal action, Justice Holmes, speaking for the Court, stated: "The essence of a provision forbidding the acquisition of evidence in a certain way is that not merely evidence so acquired shall not be used before the Court but that it shall not be used at all." Id. at 392. Several lower federal court cases have interpreted this language as prohibiting the use of illegally obtained evidence in civil as well as criminal cases. * * * [O]ther cases have applied the prohibition against the use of illegally obtained evidence in forfeiture proceedings which, although essentially civil in nature, have some attributes of a criminal action. * * * On the other hand, other federal courts have indicated that the exclusionary rule has no application in civil cases.

* * * In United States v. One 1956 Ford Tudor Sedan, 253 F. 2d at 727, Judge Haynsworth, speaking for this court, stated: "We deem it unnecessary to extend, beyond the suppression of evidence in the criminal jurisdiction, the overlordship of the conduct of federal law enforcement officers."

334 F.2d at 217, n. 11.

2. The Supreme Court has held that the exclusionary rule applies in quasi-criminal forfeiture proceedings. In One 1958 Plymouth Sedan v. Pennsylvania, 380 U.S. 693, 85 S.Ct. 1246, 14 L.Ed.2d 170 (1965), the Supreme Court prohibited the use of illegally seized evidence in a forfeiture proceeding resulting from the transportation of liquor into Pennsylvania without the payment of applicable state taxes. The Court stated:

> It would be anomalous indeed, under these circumstances, to hold that in the criminal proceeding the illegally seized evidence is excludable, while in the forfeiture proceeding, requiring the determination that the criminal law has been violated, the same evidence would be admissible.

380 U.S. at 701, 85 S.Ct. at 1251. Is there a sufficient parallel between a forfeiture proceeding, which requires a clear showing that the criminal law has been violated, and a civil tax controversy, (particularly a civil fraud penalty case) to justify the extension of the exclusionary rule to prevent the use in civil tax cases of evidence which was seized unconstitutionally by agents of the federal government? What if the illegal seizure was by agents of the Internal Revenue Service?

SECTION 8. RECOVERY OF ATTORNEYS' FEES

The problem of providing for the award of attorneys' fees to taxpayers successful in tax litigation has long vexed the tax bar and, more recently, the Congress. A somewhat illusory solution to the problem was reached as a result of the enactment of the Civil Rights Attorneys' Fees Awards Act of 1976.[v] While this statute clearly provides for the awarding of attorneys' fees in civil tax litigation under appropriate circumstances, it has been held inapplicable to the vast majority of civil tax cases. The reason is that in both Tax Court and tax refund litigation the action is not considered to have been brought "by or on behalf of" the United States—it is the taxpayer who is the plaintiff in the case. The fact that in virtually every civil tax case the government is the moving party by virtue of its action in

---

v. 42 U.S.C.A., § 1988, which provides as follows:

In any action or proceeding to enforce a provision of sections 1981, 1982, 1983, 1985, and 1986 of this title, title IX of Public Law 92–318, or in any civil action or proceeding, by or on behalf of the United States of America, to en-

force, or charging a violation of, a provision of the United States Internal Revenue Code, or title VI of the Civil Rights Act of 1964, the court, in its discretion, may allow the prevailing party, other than the United States, a reasonable attorney's fee as part of the costs.

issuing a notice of deficiency or initiating an audit is not sufficient for purposes of the statute. As noted in Key Buick Co. v. Commissioner, 613 F.2d 1306, 1308 (5th Cir. 1980), "if it were the intent of Congress to provide attorneys' fees in practically every instance involving government review of tax returns, we are convinced Congress would have done so in much more specific terms." Thus, the Fifth Circuit held that attorneys' fees could not be awarded in Tax Court or tax refund litigation where the government was cast in the role of defendant. Similarly, in Alfonso v. United States, 613 F.2d 1309 (5th Cir. 1980), it was held that the improper issuance of a jeopardy assessment could not lead to an award of attorneys' fees because such an action was administrative and did not constitute a "civil action or proceeding" brought "by or on behalf of" the United States within the meaning of 42 U.S.C.A. § 1988.

Section 1988 does empower a court to award attorneys' fees in instances where the taxpayer is cast in the defendant's role in Tax Court or tax refund litigation. For example, as noted in the case of Jones v. United States, excerpted below, where the government is the counter-plaintiff in a civil tax case, and appropriate circumstances exist, attorneys' fees may be awarded. Attorneys' fees also have been awarded under section 1988 after a summons enforcement proceeding in which the court found that the taxpayer was subjected to vexatious or harassing treatment, not amounting to bad faith, by the government. See United States v. Garrison Constr. Co., Inc., 40 AFTR 2d 77–5774 (N.D.Ala.1977).

JONES v. UNITED STATES

613 F.2d 1311 (5th Cir. 1980).

POLITZ, Circuit Judge.

This opinion concludes the trilogy of cases decided this date, involving the application of the Civil Rights Attorney's Fees Awards Act of 1976 to taxpayer litigation.

After an audit, the Internal Revenue Service determined that Jimmy Wayne Morton, an experienced tree cutter, was an employee rather than an independent subcontractor of logging contractor E. C. Jones. As a result the IRS concluded that amounts paid to Morton during 1973 and 1974 were subject to income tax withholding, federal unemployment (FUTA), and Social Security (FICA) taxes. Assessments were made against Jones for FUTA taxes for 1973 and 1974 in the amounts of $28.55 and $25.19. Jones paid and immediately filed refund claims asserting that Morton was an independent contractor, not an employee. Jones did not pay withholding or FICA taxes because Morton had already paid them. Sections 3402(d) and 6521(a) of the Internal Revenue Code provide that when an "employee" pays all of his withholding or FICA taxes, the "employer" is relieved of liability.

Despite the clear statutory language (and apparently despite essentially undisputed facts), the IRS counterclaimed for FICA and withholding taxes totaling $10,170.02.

Jones prevailed in his main demand and was awarded a refund of $53.74. Jones also prevailed as defendant in the government's counterclaim which was rejected with prejudice. Jones moved for an award of attorney's fees. Citing Patzkowski v. United States, 576 F. 2d 134 (8th Cir. 1978) the district court denied the motion. We reverse and remand.

In Prince [v. United States, 610 F.2d 350 (5th Cir. 1980),] and Key Buick [v. Commissioner, 613 F.2d 1306 (5th Cir. 1980),] we held that the taxpayer must be the defendant in a lawsuit involving his tax dispute with the IRS before the court is empowered to award attorney's fees. In this cause, when the IRS filed the counterclaim, as to that dimension of the tax dispute the taxpayer became a defendant eligible to seek attorney's fees under § 1988. When the government sought judgment the taxpayer was cast in the role of a party-defendant.

We must determine the standards which govern such awards. The language of the statute assists not, however, there is much succor available both in its legislative history and in the jurisprudence. Statements made during the Senate and House floor debates clearly reflect that the IRS must have acted in an unreasonable, harassing, or vexatious manner before attorney's fees may be assessed as costs. That type of conduct weighed heavily in the discussions and has long been recognized in the jurisprudence as a traditional prerequisite for the award of attorney's fees.

*   *   *

This requirement is essential. The motivating policy considerations in the award of attorney's fees in the customary civil rights action are not present in the typical tax dispute.

In addressing the issue of an attorney's fee award under Title VII, which contains language virtually identical to that in § 1988, the Supreme Court declared in Christiansburg [Garment Co. v. Equal Employment Opportunity Comm'n, 434 U.S. 412, 98 S.Ct. 694, 54 L. Ed.2d 648 (1978)]:

> In sum, a district court may in its discretion award attorney's fees to a prevailing defendant in a Title VII case upon a finding that the plaintiff's action was frivolous, unreasonable, or without foundation, even though not brought in subjective bad faith.

434 U.S. at 421, 98 S.Ct. at 700.

We have applied the *Christiansburg* standard to § 1988 cases arising in a civil rights context. We now hold that *Christiansburg* is equally applicable to § 1988 tax cases.

In adopting the *Christiansburg* test we emphasize that the taxpayer, cast as a defendant, must come forward with evidence demonstrating that the government has acted in a proscribed manner. A showing of subjective bad faith is not required but there must be a finding that the government's action was frivolous, unreasonable, or without foundation. Upon such a finding the court may award attorney's fees.

In the instant case Jones introduced income tax returns establishing that Morton had paid his own withholding and FICA taxes. Although the IRS had proof *in its own records* that Jones did not owe FICA and withholding taxes, it persisted in advancing a counterclaim that was the epitome of a frivolous and unreasonable lawsuit. The government conceded that it had posted a lien and counterclaimed for a sum far in excess of the amount it believed to be due as an "attention-getter" or bargaining wedge. The amount sought was almost seven times the amount which could have been contested in good faith. Less than $1,500 of FICA taxes was actually in dispute.

Finding that the government's counterclaim was meritless we hold that the district court erred in refusing to award attorney's fees.

*   *   *

Reversed and Remanded.

Just four years after the passage of the Civil Rights Attorneys' Fees Awards Act of 1976, Congress again considered the subject of the awarding of attorneys' fees in litigation involving the United States, and, on October 21, 1980, the Equal Access to Justice Act, H.R. 5612 (P.L. 96–481), was signed into law. The Act amended 42 U.S.C.A. § 1988 and 28 U.S.C.A. § 2412 and added a new section 504 to title 5 of the United States Code. Title II of the Act, which was opposed by the Treasury Department and other administrative agencies, provides for the awarding of attorneys' fees and other expenses to the prevailing party (other than the United States) in administrative "adversary adjudications" (defined as those in which the United States is represented by counsel) as well as actions brought in "courts of the United States" as defined in 28 U.S.C.A. § 451. In addition to the Supreme Court, courts of appeals, district courts and certain specified courts, § 451 includes "any court created by Act of Congress the judges of which are entitled to hold office during good behavior." The Tax Court, whose judges are appointed for fifteen year terms, is not covered by the Act. However, suits initiated in district courts or the Court of Claims will be subject to the attorneys' fees provisions of the Act. The new law contains no restrictions relating to whether the United States initiated the action; nor does it require the party seeking the award to show bad faith on the part of the government. Under the Act, fees and certain other expenses of a "prevailing party" are to be awarded upon application to the court or agency involved unless the *government* shows that its action was "substantially justified" (i. e., that there was a reasonable basis in law and fact for the action) or that special circumstances exist which would make the award unjust.

Although there is no overall ceiling on the amount that can be awarded, hourly rates for attorneys generally are limited to $75, and only "reasonable" fees for experts, etc. may be awarded. The law excludes from its coverage (a) any individual whose net worth exceeds $1 million, and (b) a sole owner of an unincorporated business, or a partnership, corporation or association (i) whose net worth exceeds $5 million, or (ii) which has more than 500 employees.

The new rules are effective as of October 1, 1981 and apply to any action pending on or commenced on or after that date. A sunset provision provides for automatic repeal of the new provisions on October 1, 1984, effective for actions initiated after that date.

NOTE

The effective date of the new attorneys' fees provisions was established at October 1, 1981, in order to "provide time for the committees with jurisdiction over tax matters to enact a separate bill" covering attorneys' fees in tax related matters. See H.R.Rep. No. 96–1418, 96th Cong., 2d Sess. 11, reprinted in [1980] U.S.Code Cong. & Adm.News 4984, 4991. A bill, S. 752, entitled "Taxpayer's Protection and Reimbursement Act" was introduced in the Senate in March, 1981. If enacted, S. 752 would govern the award of attorneys' fees and other costs in all tax matters.

Chapter VI

THE INTERNAL REVENUE SERVICE SUMMONS

Scope Note: The power to issue summonses to compel the production of documents and testimony constitutes the single most important investigative tool of the Internal Revenue Service. Although the power is a broad one, certain limitations have been placed upon it. The materials that follow discuss these limitations and consider the procedures used in raising objections to improper summonses. Included in this context is a discussion of the evidentiary privileges, particularly the attorney-client privilege and the privilege against self-incrimination. Also treated below are the special requirements applicable to "John Doe" and third-party recordkeeper summonses, and the procedures involved in responding to IRS summonses.

SECTION 1. THE SUMMONS POWER

The IRS has the duty to enforce compliance with the federal tax laws—in the words of the statute, to "inquire after and concerning all persons * * * who may be liable to pay any internal revenue tax * * *." [a] Although, perhaps, one can look to taxpayers for voluntary compliance [b] in terms of reporting their liability, one can hardly expect taxpayers voluntarily to assist the Service in its audits and investigations. Hence, the duty to inquire can be carried out only if the means to enforce responses to inquiries is available. The means provided by the Internal Revenue Code is the power to examine relevant data and to issue the IRS summons for documents and testimony. [c]

Every tax audit, however informally conducted, is performed pursuant to the summons authority. In the vast majority of cases audits are conducted without the use, or even mention, of an administrative summons. Informal requests for documents and for answers to questions often suffice. However, behind every request for documents or information lies the power to issue a summons.

The IRS summons clearly imposes a legal obligation upon the summoned party. However, until the decision in Reisman v. Caplin,

---

a. IRC § 7601.

b. Inasmuch as the failure to comply with reporting requirements subjects a taxpayer to a wide range of civil and criminal penalties, the term "voluntary compliance" may not be precisely accurate in describing the process by which most taxpayers report their liabilities.

c. IRC § 7602. See also IRC § 6333, which provides the Service with the right to demand access to books and records relating to property rights in connection with a levy to collect taxes.

below, the extent of that duty was not resolved. In the face of a Code provision permitting the Service to seek the arrest of anyone who "neglects or refuses to obey" a summons,[d] there was considerable concern as to the correct course of action to take if one wished to resist compliance.

REISMAN v. CAPLIN

Supreme Court of the United States, 1964.
375 U.S. 440, 84 S.Ct. 508, 11 L.Ed.2d 459.

Mr. Justice CLARK delivered the opinion of the Court.

[Reisman, an attorney representing the Bromleys in a tax investigation, had hired accountants to assist in the representation. The IRS issued a summons demanding that the accountants produce their workpapers and appear to provide testimony. Reisman, alleging that the accountants intended to comply with the summons in spite of what he contended were valid objections to compliance, filed an injunction action against the Commissioner and the accountants, in an attempt to restrain compliance.]

* * *

The case reaches us at a stage when the only affirmative action taken by the Commissioner is the issuance of the summonses for the accountants to appear before a hearing officer, i. e., a special agent of the Internal Revenue Service, to testify and produce records. The accountants have not yet refused to do so. It is therefore necessary that we first consider the statutory scheme which Congress has provided for the issuance and enforcement of the summonses.

II.

Section 7602 authorizes the Secretary of the Treasury, or his delegate, for "the purpose of ascertaining the correctness of any return * * *, determining the liability of any person for any internal revenue tax * * *, or collecting any such liability * * * [t]o summon the person liable for tax * * *, or any person having possession, custody, or care of books of account containing entries relating to the business of the person liable for tax * * *, or any other person the Secretary or his delegate may deem proper, to appear * * * and to produce such books, papers, records, or other data, and to give such testimony, under oath, as may be relevant or material to such inquiry * * *." The petitioners make no claim that this provision suffers any constitutional infirmity on its face. This Court has never passed upon the rights of a party summoned to appear before a hearing officer under § 7602. However, the Government concedes that a witness or any interested party may attack the summons before the hearing officer. There are cases among the cir-

d. IRC § 7604(b).

cuits which hold that both parties summoned and those affected by a disclosure may appear or intervene before the District Court and challenge the summons by asserting their constitutional or other claims. We agree with that view and see no reason why the same rule would not apply before the hearing officer. Should the challenge to the summons be rejected by the hearing examiner and the witness still refuse to testify or produce, the examiner is given no power to enforce compliance or to impose sanctions for noncompliance.

If the Secretary or his delegate wishes to enforce the summons, he must proceed under § 7402(b), which grants the District Courts of the United States jurisdiction "by appropriate process to compel such attendance, testimony, or production of books, papers, or other data." [4]

Any enforcement action under this section would be an adversary proceeding affording a judicial determination of the challenges to the summons and giving complete protection to the witness. In such a proceeding only a refusal to comply with an order of the district judge subjects the witness to contempt proceedings.

III.

It is urged that the penalties of contempt risked by a refusal to comply with the summonses are so severe that the statutory procedure amounts to a denial of judicial review. The leading cases on this question are Ex parte Young, 209 U.S. 123, 28 S.Ct. 441, 52 L.Ed. 714 (1908), and Oklahoma Operating Co. v. Love, 252 U.S. 331, 40 S. Ct. 338, 64 L.Ed. 596 (1920). However, we do not believe that this point is well taken here. In *Young* certain railroad rates could be tested only by a failure to comply, which occasioned a risk of both imprisonment and large fines, regardless of the willfulness of the refusal to comply. And in *Oklahoma Operating Co.* the laundry rate fixed by the Oklahoma Corporation Commission could be tested only by contempt with a penalty of $500 per day, each day being a separate violation.

On the other hand, in tax enforcement proceedings the hearing officer has no power of enforcement or right to levy any sanctions. It is true that any person summoned who "neglects to appear or to produce" may be prosecuted under § 7210 [5] and is subject to a fine not exceeding $1,000, or imprisonment for not more than a year, or both. However, this statute on its face does not apply where the witness appears and interposes good faith challenges to the summons. It

---

4. Section 7604(a) and (b) gives an additional remedy which is considered hereafter.

5. Internal Revenue Code of 1954 § 7210:

"Any person who, being duly summoned to appear to testify, or to appear and produce books, accounts, records, memoranda, or other papers, as required under sections 6420(e)(2), 6421(f)(2), 7602, 7603, and 7604(b), neglects to appear or to produce such books, accounts, records, memoranda, or other papers, shall, upon conviction thereof, be fined not more than $1,000, or imprisoned not more than 1 year, or both, together with costs of prosecution."

only prescribes punishment where the witness "neglects" either to appear or to produce. We need not pass upon the coverage of this provision in light of the facts here. It is sufficient to say that noncompliance is not subject to prosecution thereunder when the summons is attacked in good faith.[6]

Petitioners also point to § 7604(b) as posing the risk of arrest should the Commissioner proceed under that section for an "attachment * * * as for a contempt." Arguably, such a sanction, even though temporary, might be a penalty severe enough to bring the section within the rationale of *Young,* supra, but we do not so read § 7604(b). This section provides that where "any person summoned * * * neglects or refuses to obey such summons" the Commissioner may proceed before the United States Commissioner or the judge of the District Court "for an attachment against him as for a contempt." Upon a showing of "satisfactory proof," an attachment for the person so refusing is issued and he is brought before the United States Commissioner or the district judge who proceeds "to a hearing of the case." Upon the hearing the United States Commissioner or the district judge may "make such order as he shall deem proper, not inconsistent with the law for the punishment of contempts * * *." The predecessor of § 7604(b) was adopted by the Congress in 1864 at a time when Congress was greatly concerned with tax collection delay. The proponents of the bill emphasized that after arrest the witness could assert his objections to the summons. It appears to us that the provision was intended only to cover persons who were summoned and wholly made default or contumaciously refused to comply. Section 7402(b) came into the statute in 1913 and has been uniformly used since that time.[8] As we read the legislative history, § 7604(b) remains in this comprehensive procedure provided by Congress to cover only a default or contumacious refusal to honor a summons before a hearing officer. But even in such cases, just as in a criminal prosecution under § 7210, the witness may assert his objections at the hearing before the court which is authorized to make such order as it "shall deem proper." § 7604(b).

Furthermore, we hold that in any of these procedures before either the district judge or United States Commissioner, the witness

---

6. The only prosecution under § 7210 is United States v. Becker, 2 Cir., 259 F.2d 869. There the word "neglect" was equated with willfulness. The Government admits that the section is inapplicable to persons who appear and in good faith interpose defenses as a basis for noncompliance. Cf. Federal Power Comm'n v. Metropolitan Edison Co., 304 U.S. 375, 387, 58 S.Ct. 963, 968, 82 L.Ed. 1408 (1938).

8. It is true that the attachment procedure of § 7604(b) has been occasionally used even where the person summoned refused to testify because of a claimed privilege. We believe that the use of § 7604(b) in that context is inappropriate. Attachment of a witness who has neither defaulted nor contumaciously refused to comply would raise constitutional considerations, which need not be considered at this time under our reading of the statute.

may challenge the summons on any appropriate ground. This would include, as the circuits have held, the defenses that the material is sought for the improper purpose of obtaining evidence for use in a criminal prosecution, Boren v. Tucker, 9 Cir., 239 F.2d 767, 772–773, as well as that it is protected by the attorney-client privilege. In addition, third parties might intervene to protect their interests, or in the event the taxpayer is not a party to the summons before the hearing officer, he, too, may intervene. And this would be true whether the contempt be of a civil or criminal nature. Finally, we hold that such orders are appealable. It follows that with a stay order a witness would suffer no injury while testing the summons.

Nor would there be a difference should the witness indicate—as has Peat, Marwick, Mitchell & Co.—that he would voluntarily turn the papers over to the Commissioner. If this be true, either the taxpayer or any affected party might restrain compliance, as the Commissioner suggests, until compliance is ordered by a court of competent jurisdiction. This relief was not sought here. Had it been, the Commissioner would have had to proceed for compliance, in which event the petitioners or the Bromleys might have intervened and asserted their claims.

Finding that the remedy specified by Congress works no injustice and suffers no constitutional invalidity, we remit the parties to the comprehensive procedure of the Code, which provides full opportunity for judicial review before any coercive sanctions may be imposed.

Affirmed.

UNITED STATES v. SCHOEBERLEIN

335 F.Supp. 1048 (D.Md.1971).

THOMSEN, District Judge.

This is a proceeding brought by the United States and a Special Agent of the Internal Revenue Service (IRS) under §§ 7402(b) and 7604(a), I.R.C. 1954, to compel compliance with an administrative summons issued to William E. Schoeberlein, the attorney-accountant for taxpayers, J. Stewart Brinsfield and his wife, demanding the production of certain financial records and work papers in Schoeberlein's possession on the date of service of the summons and alleged to be necessary to a determination of the Brinsfields' tax liabilities for the years 1965, 1966, 1967 and 1968. The government also seeks to punish Schoeberlein for contempt under § 7604(b). * * *

[Revenue Agent Lewald met with the taxpayers' attorney/accountant, Mr. Schoeberlein, reviewed records of the taxpayers which had been provided to Mr. Schoeberlein for this purpose, and, thereafter, referred the matter for a criminal tax investigation by the Intelligence (now Criminal Investigation) Division.]

The Intelligence Division assigned the case to Special Agent Robert H. Caplan. On July 18, 1969, Caplan and another agent visited Schoeberlein's office and inquired whether Schoeberlein still had in his possession the records that had been seen by Revenue Agent Lewald. Schoeberlein replied that he did, but that he could not relinquish them to Caplan without first consulting his own lawyer. Caplan then served upon Schoeberlein an administrative summons demanding production of specified documents in connection with an investigation to determine the tax liability of the taxpayers for the years 1965, 1966, 1967 and 1968. Caplan instructed Schoeberlein not to dispossess himself of any of the summoned documents prior to the return date, August 4, 1969. On that date, Schoeberlein appeared at Caplan's office and surrendered certain corporate tax records in his possession, but stated that, on the advice of his counsel, he refused to produce the Brinsfields' personal records, including cancelled checks, check stubs and deposit slips, as well as some accountant's workpapers prepared by Schoeberlein on the ground that such production would violate the Brinsfields' privilege against self-incrimination under the Fifth Amendment. In fact, Schoeberlein had returned all of these documents to the Brinsfields between the service date and the return date of the summons.

The records in controversy have been placed in the custody of the Court by stipulation of the parties pending determination of the enforceability of the summons.

* * *

After an attorney or an accountant has received an administrative summons from the IRS to produce certain papers, it is his duty not to turn those papers over to his client or to anyone else except the IRS [12] until the Court has ruled on any objection he or his client may have to turning them over.

* * *

Although Schoeberlein's action in turning the papers over to his client was contrary to what the Court holds to have been his duty under the circumstances, and would ordinarily amount to a contempt, the Court is aware that divergent views have been expressed in the literature, and is advised that this is the first case in which the IRS has sought a citation for contempt under these circumstances. There is no suggestion that there has been any tampering with the documents involved in this case, and they are now in the custody of the

12. Except, also, he may turn them over to his own counsel, for the purpose of preparing suit papers or preparing to defend against the enforcement of the summons. Possession by counsel for the summoned party under those circumstances would be considered possession of the summoned party.

Court. The Court will not issue a citation for contempt in this instance.[15]

The summons will be enforced. Counsel should agree upon an appropriate order.

UNITED STATES v. DAUPHIN DEPOSIT TRUST CO.

385 F.2d 129 (3d Cir. 1967).

WILLIAM F. SMITH, Circuit Judge.

This appeal is from an order of the district court enforcing three summonses issued by the Internal Revenue Service pursuant to section 7602 of the Internal Revenue Code of 1954, as limited and restricted by the affidavit and exhibits attached to the Government's Petition to Enforce. The summonses required the respondent bank to produce numerous records regarding the transactions of four purported customers over a period of four years. The bank has refused to comply at all times. It has not even confirmed whether the persons named in the summonses actually are bank customers.

*   *   *

Appellant's primary argument is that the summonses are so expansive that the financial burden of locating, retrieving, and reproducing the requested material amounts to an unreasonable search and seizure in violation of the Fourth Amendment and a deprivation of property without due process of law in violation of the Fifth Amendment. The substance of appellant's Fifth Amendment claim appears to be that the financial burden constitutes a taking of private property without just compensation.

We have already concluded that the material sought by the Internal Revenue Service is relevant to a lawful investigation. Under this circumstance there can be no doubt that the recipient of a summons has a duty of cooperation and that at least up to some point must shoulder the financial burden of cooperation. Our study of the record convinces us that the district court was correct in concluding that the appellant was not requested to submit to an unreasonable burden. If the Fourth and Fifth Amendments accord any protection it could only be from the imposition of an unreasonable and excessive financial burden.

The Petition to Enforce substantially reduced the quantum of material requested in the original summonses. It is our judgment that compliance with this reduced demand would not be unduly burdensome. Furthermore, in view of appellant's adamant refusals to cooperate with the Government in the slightest degree its arguments as to the extent of the burden become plainly speculative. Appellant

15. Citations for contempt may be appropriate in future cases.

has not even verified whether the taxpayers in question are in fact customers. Yet it persists in arguing that in locating the required materials it *might* be necessary to conduct extensive searches in eighteen offices. A simple check of signature cards would have removed this contention from the realm of the merely possible.

Our determination that the summonses would not be unduly burdensome is buttressed by the fact that the bank is not required to transport any records and may fulfill its obligation either by producing the required records at any of its offices or by giving Internal Revenue Agents access to the relevant files. It is our further understanding, based on statements made by Government counsel at oral argument, that the Internal Revenue Service has portable duplicating equipment, the use of which will limit the bank's burden of making copies of its records.

One other matter should be considered. The Government is not entitled to go on a fishing expedition through appellant's records. It must identify with some precision the documents it wishes to inspect. The requirement that the summons not be indefinite is rooted in the Fourth Amendment protection against unreasonable searches and seizures.

It is our judgment that the summonses, as limited by the Petition to Enforce, are, with one exception, not unduly indefinite. The exception pertains to the demand made as to each alleged bank customer that the appellant produce, "All records relative to other accounts during the years 1961 through 1964, such as records of other securities bought or sold for said * * * [customer(s)] or other transactions of any nature handled by the bank on behalf of said * * * [customer(s)]." The request for "records of other securities bought or sold" is sufficiently precise. The balance of the request is too indefinite and will be quashed.

We also take this opportunity to note that in regard to the other demands made on the bank its only obligation is to make a diligent search based on the information supplied by the Internal Revenue Service. If that information is inaccurate or otherwise insufficient to enable it to locate the desired records, the bank of course may not be found at fault.

The order of the district court will be affirmed as modified by this opinion.

UNITED STATES v. EUGE

Supreme Court of the United States, 1980.
444 U.S. 707, 100 S.Ct. 874, 63 L.Ed.2d 141.

Mr. Justice REHNQUIST delivered the opinion of the Court.

[During an investigation of respondent's income tax liability, in an effort to determine whether deposits in certain bank accounts not registered in respondent's name represented income attributable to him, an IRS agent issued a summons requiring respondent to appear and execute handwriting exemplars of the various signatures appearing on the bank signature cards. When respondent refused to comply with the summons, the United States brought suit to enforce it. The District Court held that the summons should be enforced, but the Court of Appeals reversed, holding that the summons authority under § 7602 does not authorize the IRS to compel the execution of handwriting exemplars.

*   *   *

Through § 7602, Congress has imposed a duty on persons possessing information "relevant or material" to an investigation of federal tax liability to produce that information at the request of the Secretary or his delegate. That duty to provide relevant information expressly obligates the person summoned to produce documentary evidence and to "appear" and "give testimony." Imposition of such an evidentiary obligation is, of course, not a novel innovation attributable to § 7602. The common law has been the source of a comparable evidentiary obligation for centuries. In determining the scope of the obligation Congress intended to impose by use of this language, we have previously analogized, as an interpretive guide, to the common-law duties attaching to the issuance of a testimonial summons. See United States v. Bisceglia, 420 U.S. 141, 147–148, 95 S.Ct. 915, 919, 43 L.Ed.2d 88 (1975); United States v. Powell, 379 U.S. 48, 57, 85 S.Ct. 248, 254, 13 L.Ed.2d 112 (1964). Congress, through legislation, may expand or contract the duty imposed, but absent some contrary expression, there is a wealth of history helpful in defining the duties imposed by the issuance of a summons.

The scope of the "testimonial" or evidentiary duty imposed by common law or statute has traditionally been interpreted as an expansive duty limited principally by relevance and privilege. *   *   *

One application of this broad duty to provide relevant evidence has been the recognition, since early times, of an obligation to provide certain forms of nontestimonial physical evidence. In Holt v. United States, 218 U.S. 245, 252–253, 31 S.Ct. 2, 6, 54 L.Ed. 1021 (1910) (Holmes, J.) the Court found that the common-law evidentiary duty permitted the compulsion of various forms of physical evidence. In Schmerber v. California, 384 U.S. 757, 764, 86 S.Ct. 1826, 1832, 16 L.Ed.2d 908 (1966), this Court observed that traditionally witnesses could be compelled, in both state and federal courts, to submit to "fingerprinting, photographing, or measurements, to write or speak for identification, to appear in court, to stand, to assume a stance, to walk, or to make a particular gesture." In Gilbert v. California, 388 U.S. 263, 266–267, 87 S.Ct. 1951, 1953, 18 L.Ed.2d 1178 (1967), handwriting was held, "like the body itself" to be an "identifying physical characteristic," subject to production. In United

States v. Dionisio, 410 U.S. 1, 93 S.Ct. 764, 35 L.Ed.2d 67 (1973), and United States v. Mara, 410 U.S. 19, 93 S.Ct. 774, 35 L.Ed.2d 99 (1973), this Court again confirmed that handwriting is in the nature of physical evidence which can be compelled by a grand jury in the exercise of its subpoena power.

This broad duty to provide most relevant, nonprivileged evidence has not been considered to exist only in the common law. The Court has recognized that by statute "Congress may provide for the performance of this duty." Blackmer v. United States, 284 U.S. 421, 438, 52 S.Ct. 252, 255, 76 L.Ed. 375 (1932). By imposing an obligation to produce documents as well as to appear and give testimony, we believe the language of § 7602 suggests an intention to codify a broad testimonial obligation, including an obligation to provide some physical evidence relevant and material to a tax investigation, subject to the traditional privileges and limitations. This conclusion seems inherent in the imposition of an obligation to "appear," since an obligation to appear necessarily entails an obligation to display physical features to the summoning authority. Congress thereby authorized the Service to compel the production of some physical evidence and it is certainly possible to conclude that this authorization extended to the execution of handwriting exemplars, one variety of relevant physical evidence. This construction of the language conforms with the historical notions of the testimonial duty attaching to the issuance of a summons.

Congress certainly could have narrowed the common-law testimonial duty in enacting § 7602 and thus we do not rely solely on the common-law meaning of the statutory language. Section 7602 does not, by its terms, compel the production of handwriting exemplars, and therefore, a narrower interpretation of the duty imposed is not precluded by the actual language of the statute. A narrower interpretation *is* precluded, however, by the precedents of this Court construing that statute. * * * There is * * * a formidable line of precedent construing congressional intent to uphold the claimed enforcement authority of the Service if such authority is necessary for the effective enforcement of the revenue laws and is not undercut by contrary legislative purposes.[9]

Applying these principles, we conclude that Congress empowered the Service to seek, and obliged the witness to provide handwriting

---

9. Congressional intent to provide the Secretary with broad latitude to adopt enforcement techniques helpful in the performance of his tax collection and assessment responsibilities is expressed throughout the Act. In § 6302, for example, Congress has conferred the Secretary with discretion to devise methods of tax collection not specifically provided by statute:

"Whether or not the method of collecting any tax imposed * * * is specifically provided for by this title, any such tax may * * * be collected by * * * other reasonable devices or methods as may be necessary or helpful in securing a complete and proper collection of the tax."

exemplars relevant to the investigation. First, there is no question that handwriting exemplars will often be an important evidentiary component in establishing tax liability. The statutory framework * * * imposes on the Secretary of Treasury, and the IRS as his designate, a broad duty to enforce the tax laws. 26 U.S.C. § 7601(a). Congress has legislated that the Secretary is "required to make the inquiries, determinations, and assessments of all taxes * * * imposed by this title * * *." 26 U.S.C. § 6201(a). Under § 6301 the Secretary "shall collect taxes imposed by the internal revenue laws." In order to fulfill these duties, the Service will often need to determine whether a particular name is an alias of a taxpayer. One effective method for resolving that issue is through the use of handwriting exemplars. * * *

There is certainly nothing in the statutory language, or in the legislative history, precluding the interpretation asserted by the Service. Nor is there any constitutional privilege of the taxpayer or other parties that is violated by this construction. Compulsion of handwriting exemplars is neither a search or seizure subject to Fourth Amendment protections, United States v. Mara, supra, nor testimonial evidence protected by the Fifth Amendment privilege against self-incrimination. Gilbert v. California, supra. The compulsion of handwriting exemplars has been the subject of far less protection than the compulsion of testimony and documents. Since Congress has explicitly established an obligation to provide the more protected forms of evidence, it would seem curious had it chosen not to impose an obligation to produce a form of evidence tradition has found it less important to protect.

* * *

We accordingly reverse the judgment of the Court of Appeals refusing enforcement of the summons.

Mr. Justice BRENNAN, with whom Mr. Justice MARSHALL and Mr. Justice STEVENS join, dissenting.

The Internal Revenue Service, unlike common-law courts, has only such authority as Congress gives it. * * * The Court holds today that this authority to compel "testimony" includes authority to compel the creation of handwriting exemplars. The Court, however, is unable to point to anything in the statutory language or legislative history that even suggests that the obligation to "give testimony" includes an obligation to *create* a handwriting exemplar. Indeed, the Court concedes, as it must, that a handwriting exemplar is a kind of *nontestimonial* physical evidence. Certainly, Congress has the power to authorize the Service to compel the creation of exemplars, but it has not chosen to do so in § 7602. Accordingly, I dissent.

SECTION 2. ENFORCEABILITY OF THE SUMMONS

A. THE "*POWELL* STANDARD"

UNITED STATES v. POWELL

Supreme Court of the United States, 1964.
379 U.S. 48, 85 S.Ct. 248, 13 L.Ed.2d 112.

Mr. Justice HARLAN delivered the opinion of the Court.

In March 1963, the Internal Revenue Service, pursuant to powers afforded the Commissioner by § 7602(2) of the Internal Revenue Code of 1954, summoned respondent Powell to appear before Special Agent Tiberino to give testimony and produce records relating to the 1958 and 1959 returns of the William Penn Laundry (the taxpayer), of which Powell was president. Powell appeared before the agent but refused to produce the records. Because the taxpayer's returns had been once previously examined, and because the three-year statute of limitations barred assessment of additional deficiencies for those years except in cases of fraud (the asserted basis for this summons),[2] Powell contended that before he could be forced to produce the records the Service had to indicate some grounds for its belief that a fraud had been committed. The agent declined to give any such indication and the meeting terminated.

Thereafter the Service petitioned the District Court for the Eastern District of Pennsylvania for enforcement of the administrative summons. With this petition the agent filed an affidavit stating that he had been investigating the taxpayer's returns for 1958 and 1959; that based on this investigation the Regional Commissioner of the Service had determined an additional examination of the taxpayer's records for those years to be necessary and had sent Powell a letter to that effect; and that the agent had reason to suspect that the taxpayer had fraudulently falsified its 1958 and 1959 returns by overstating expenses. At the court hearing Powell again stated his objections to producing the records and asked the Service to show some basis for its suspicion of fraud. The Service chose to stand on the petition and the agent's affidavit, and, after argument, the District Court ruled that the agent be [allowed] to re-examine the records.

The Court of Appeals reversed. It reasoned that since the returns in question could only be reopened for fraud, re-examination of the taxpayer's records must be barred by the prohibition of §

---

2. IRC., § 6501(c)(1), which in relevant part provides:

"In the case of a false or fraudulent return with the intent to evade tax, the tax may be assessed, or a proceeding in court for collection of such tax may be begun without assessment, at any time."

7605(b) of the Code against "unnecessary examination" unless the Service possessed information "which might cause a reasonable man to suspect that there has been fraud in the return for the otherwise closed year"; and whether this standard has been met is to be decided "on the basis of the showing made in the normal course of an adversary proceeding * * *." The court concluded that the affidavit in itself was not sufficient to satisfy its test of probable cause. Consequently, enforcement of the summons was withheld.

* * *

We reverse, and hold that the Government need make no showing of probable cause to suspect fraud unless the taxpayer raises a substantial question that judicial enforcement of the administrative summons would be an abusive use of the court's process, predicated on more than the fact of re-examination and the running of the statute of limitations on ordinary tax liability.

* * *

Respondent primarily relies on § 7605(b) to show that the Government must establish probable cause for suspecting fraud, and that the existence of probable cause is subject to challenge by the taxpayer at the hearing. That section provides:

> "No taxpayer shall be subjected to unnecessary examination or investigations, and only one inspection of a taxpayer's books of account shall be made for each taxable year unless the taxpayer requests otherwise or unless the Secretary or his delegate, after investigation, notifies the taxpayer in writing that an additional inspection is necessary."

We do not equate necessity as contemplated by this provision with probable cause or any like notion. If a taxpayer has filed fraudulent returns, a tax liability exists without regard to any period of limitations. Section 7602 authorizes the Commissioner to investigate any such liability. If, in order to determine the existence or nonexistence of fraud in the taxpayer's returns, information in the taxpayer's records is needed which is not already in the Commissioner's possession, we think the examination is not "unnecessary" within the meaning of § 7605(b). Although a more stringent interpretation is possible, one which would require some showing of cause for suspecting fraud, we reject such an interpretation because it might seriously hamper the Commissioner in carrying out investigations he thinks warranted, forcing him to litigate and prosecute appeals on the very subject which he desires to investigate, and because the legislative history of § 7605(b) indicates that no severe restriction was intended.

* * *

Congress recognized a need for a curb on the investigating powers of low-echelon revenue agents, and considered that it met this need simply and fully by requiring such agents to clear any repetitive examination with a superior. For us to import a probable cause standard to be enforced by the courts would substantially overshoot the goal which the legislators sought to attain. There is no intimation in the legislative history that Congress intended the courts to oversee the Commissioner's determinations to investigate. No mention was made of the statute of limitations and the exception for fraud.

We are asked to read § 7605(b) together with the limitations sections in such a way as to impose a probable cause standard upon the Commissioner from the expiration date of the ordinary limitations period forward. Without some solid indication in the legislative history that such a gloss was intended, we find it unacceptable. Our reading of the statute is said to render the first clause of § 7605(b) surplusage to a large extent, for, as interpreted, the clause adds little beyond the relevance and materiality requirements of § 7602. That clause does appear to require that the information sought is not already within the Commissioner's possession, but we think its primary purpose was no more than to emphasize the responsibility of agents to exercise prudent judgment in wielding the extensive powers granted to them by the Internal Revenue Code.

* * *

Reading the statutes as we do, the Commissioner need not meet any standard of probable cause to obtain enforcement of his summons, either before or after the three-year statute of limitations on ordinary tax liabilities has expired. He must show that the investigation will be conducted pursuant to a legitimate purpose, that the inquiry may be relevant to the purpose, that the information sought is not already within the Commissioner's possession, and that the administrative steps required by the Code have been followed—in particular that the "Secretary or his delegate," after investigation, has determined the further examination to be necessary and has notified the taxpayer in writing to that effect. This does not make meaningless the adversary hearing to which the taxpayer is entitled before enforcement is ordered.[18] At the hearing he "may challenge the summons on any appropriate ground," Reisman v. Caplin, 375 U.S. 440, at 449, 84 S.Ct. at 513. Nor does our reading of the statutes mean that under no circumstances may the court inquire into the underlying reasons for the examination. It is the court's process which is invoked to enforce the administrative summons and a court may not permit its process to be abused. Such an abuse would take place

---

18. Because § 7604(a) contains no provision specifying the procedure to be followed in invoking the court's jurisdiction, the Federal Rules of Civil Procedure apply, Martin v. Chandis Securities Co., 9 Cir., 128 F.2d 731. The proceedings are instituted by filing a complaint, followed by answer and hearing. If the taxpayer has contumaciously refused to comply with the administrative summons and the Service fears he may flee the jurisdiction, application for the sanctions available under § 7604(b) might be made simultaneously with the filing of the complaint.

if the summons had been issued for an improper purpose, such as to harass the taxpayer or to put pressure on him to settle a collateral dispute, or for any other purpose reflecting on the good faith of the particular investigation. The burden of showing an abuse of the court's process is on the taxpayer, and it is not met by a mere showing, as was made in this case, that the statute of limitations for ordinary deficiencies has run or that the records in question have already been once examined.

The judgment of the Court of Appeals is reversed, and the case is remanded for further proceedings consistent with this opinion.

B. THE LEGITIMATE PURPOSE (GOOD FAITH)

DONALDSON v. UNITED STATES

Supreme Court of the United States, 1971.
400 U.S. 517, 91 S.Ct. 534, 27 L.Ed.2d 580.

Mr. Justice BLACKMUN delivered the opinion of the Court.

[In furtherance of an investigation of Donaldson's tax returns, respondent Grady, an Internal Revenue Service (IRS) Special Agent, issued summonses to Donaldson's putative former employer (Acme) and its accountant (Mercurio) for the production of Acme's records of Donaldson's employment and compensation during the years under investigation. Thereafter respondents filed in the District Court petitions for enforcement of the summonses. Donaldson filed motions to intervene in the enforcement proceeding, relying on Fed.R.Civ.P. 24(a)(2), which *inter alia,* provides for intervention in an action "when the applicant claims an interest relating to the property or transaction which is the subject of the action   *   *   *." Donaldson alleged that the IRS agents were investigating him solely to obtain evidence concerning criminal violations of the tax laws and that consequently the summonses were not issued for any purpose within the scope of § 7602 and could not be enforced. The court denied Donaldson's motions and ordered that the records be produced. The Court of Appeals affirmed. |

*   *   *

We emphasize initially, as did Judge Tuttle in his opinion for the Court of Appeals, that what is sought here by the Internal Revenue Service from Mercurio and from Acme is the production of *Acme's* records and not the records of the *taxpayer*. Further, as Judge Tuttle also emphasized, this is not a case where a summons has been issued to the taxpayer himself seeking access to his books and information from his mouth. Neither is it a case where the summons is directed at the taxpayer's records in the hands of his attorney or his accountant, with the attendant questions of privilege, or even in the hands of anyone with whom the taxpayer has a confidential relationship of any kind. Each of the summonses here, we repeat, was directed to a third person with respect to whom no established legal privilege, such as that of attorney and client, exists, and had to do with records in which the taxpayer has no proprietary interest of any kind, which are owned by the third person, which are in his hands, and which relate to the third person's business transactions with the taxpayer.

* * *

* * * Donaldson's only interest—and of course it looms large in his eyes—lies in the fact that those records presumably contain details of Acme-to-Donaldson payments possessing significance for federal income tax purposes.

This asserted interest, however, is nothing more than a desire by Donaldson to counter and overcome Mercurio's and Acme's willingness, under summons, to comply and to produce records.

The nature of the "interest" urged by the taxpayer is apparent from the fact that the material in question (once we assume its relevance) would not be subject to suppression if the Government obtained it by other routine means, such as by Acme's independent and voluntary disclosure prior to summons, or by way of identifiable deductions in Acme's own income tax returns, or through Mercurio's appearance as a trial witness, or by subpoena of the records for trial. This interest cannot be the kind contemplated by Rule 24(a)(2) when it speaks in general terms of "an interest relating to the property or transaction which is the subject of the action." What is obviously meant there is a significantly protectable interest. And the taxpayer, to the extent that he has such a protectable interest, as, for example, by way of privilege, or to the extent he may claim abuse of process, may always assert that interest or that claim in due course at its proper place in any subsequent trial.

We therefore hold that the taxpayer's interest is not enough and is not of sufficient magnitude for us to conclude that he is to be allowed to intervene. Were we to hold otherwise, as he would have us do, we would unwarrantedly cast doubt upon and stultify the Service's every investigatory move.

This conclusion could dispose of the case, for our main concern here is with the taxpayer's asserted right to intervene in the particular enforcement proceedings. Donaldson, however, strenuously urges, in addition, that an internal revenue summons proceeding may not be utilized at all in aid of an investigation that has the potentiality of resulting in a recommendation that a criminal prosecution be instituted against the taxpayer. He argues that a summons so used is invalid and unenforceable because it is outside the scope of § 7602. The Government naturally argues the contrary.

The argument centers in the * * * dictum in *Reisman*, 375 U.S., at 449, 84 S.Ct. at 513:

> "[T]he witness may challenge the summons on any appropriate ground. This would include, as the circuits have held, the defenses that the material is sought for the improper purpose of obtaining evidence for use in a criminal prosecution, Boren v. Tucker, 9 Cir., 239 F.2d 767, 772–773, as well as that it is protected by the attorney-client privilege,
> * * * "

We note initially that, despite the dictum, the courts of appeals in opinions issued since *Reisman* was decided, appear uniformly to approve the use of a summons in an investigation that is likely to lead to civil liability as well as to criminal prosecution. The use of a summons also has been approved, even where it is alleged that its purpose is to uncover crime, if no criminal prosecution as yet has been instituted. On the other hand, it has been said, usually citing *Reisman,* that where the sole objective of the investigation is to obtain evidence for use in a criminal prosecution, the purpose is not a legitimate one and enforcement may be denied. This, of course, would likely be the case where a criminal prosecution has been instituted and is pending at the time of issuance of the summons.

It is precisely the latter situation—where the sole object of the investigation is to gather data for criminal prosecution—that is the subject of the *Reisman* dictum. This is evident from the fact that the dictum itself embraces the citation of Boren v. Tucker, 239 F.2d 767, 772–773 (CA9 1956), an opinion in which, at the pages cited, the Ninth Circuit very carefully distinguished United States v. O'Connor, 118 F.Supp. 248 (Mass.1953), a case where the taxpayer already was under indictment. The *Reisman* dictum is to be read in the light of its citation of *Boren,* and of *Boren's* own citation of *O'Connor;* when so read, the dictum comes into proper focus as applicable to the situation of a pending criminal charge or, at most, of an investigation solely for criminal purposes.

Any other holding, of course, would thwart and defeat the appropriate investigatory powers that the Congress has placed in "the Secretary or his delegate." When Grady's summonses were issued to Mercurio and to Acme, Donaldson was not under indictment and, indeed, no recommendation had been made for his prosecution. That he might be indicted and prosecuted was only a possibility, no more and no less in his case than in the case of any other taxpayer whose income tax return is undergoing audit. Prosecution will necessarily depend on the result of that audit and on what the examination and investigation reveal.

We bear in mind that the Internal Revenue Service is organized to carry out the broad responsibilities of the Secretary of the Treasury under § 7801(a) of the 1954 Code for the administration and enforcement of the internal revenue laws. We further bear in mind that the Service has district offices, each with an audit division and a criminal division; that the Audit Division's program emphasizes the civil aspects of enforcement but embraces "participation with special agents of the Intelligence Division in the conduct of tax fraud investigations"; that the Intelligence Division enforces the criminal statutes affecting income and certain other taxes and develops information concerning alleged criminal violations; that each assistant regional commissioner for intelligence develops programs for the investigation of alleged tax frauds and "certain other civil and alleged criminal violations of tax laws" and "approves or disapproves recommendations for prosecution" ; and that recommendations for prosecution are processed through the office of regional counsel and by that office to the Department of Justice. This demonstrates that the special agent may well conduct his investigation jointly with an agent from the Audit Division; that their combined efforts are directed to both civil and criminal infractions; and that any decision to recommend prosecution comes only after the investigation is complete or is sufficiently far along to support appropriate conclusions. The fact that a full-scale tax fraud investigation is being made does not necessarily mean that prosecution ensues when tax liability becomes apparent.

Congress clearly has authorized the use of the summons in investigating what may prove to be criminal conduct. The regulations are positive. Treas. Regs. § 301.7602–1(c)(4). The underlying statutes are just as authoritative. Section 6659(a)(2) of the Code defines the term "tax," as used in the Code and, hence, in the authorizing § 7602, to include any addition or penalty. Section 7602 contains no restriction; further, it has its ascertainable roots in the 1939 Code's § 3614 and, also, § 3615(a)–(c), which, by its very language and by its proximity to § 3616 and § 3654, appears to authorize the use of the summons for investigation into criminal conduct. There is no statutory suggestion for any meaningful line of distinction, for civil as compared with criminal purposes, at the point of a special agent's appearance. To draw a line where a special agent appears would require the Service, in a situation of suspected but undetermined fraud, to forgo either the use of the summons or the potentiality of an ultimate recommendation for prosecution. We refuse to draw that line and thus to stultify enforcement of federal law.

We hold that under § 7602 an internal revenue summons may be issued in aid of an investigation if it is issued in good faith and prior to a recommendation for criminal prosecution.

Affirmed.

UNITED STATES v. LaSALLE NAT'L BANK

Supreme Court of the United States, 1978.
437 U.S. 298, 98 S.Ct. 2357, 57 L.Ed.2d 221.

Mr. Justice BLACKMUN delivered the opinion of the Court.

This case is a supplement to our decision in Donaldson v. United States. It presents the issue whether the District Court correctly refused to enforce Internal Revenue Service summonses when it specifically found that the special agent who issued them "was conducting his investigation solely for the purpose of unearthing evidence of criminal conduct."

I

In May 1975, John F. Olivero, a special agent with the Intelligence Division of the Chicago District of the Internal Revenue Service (hereinafter IRS or Service), received an assignment to investigate the tax liability of John Gattuso for his taxable years 1970–1972. Olivero testified that he had requested the assignment because of information he had received from a confidential informant and from an unrelated investigation. The case was not referred to the IRS from another law enforcement agency, but the nature of the assignment, Olivero testified, was "[t]o investigate the possibility of any criminal violations of the Internal Revenue Code." Olivero pursued the case on his own, without the assistance of a revenue agent.
* * *

* * * In order to determine the accuracy of Gattuso's income reports, Olivero proceeded to issue two summonses, under the authority of § 7602 of the Internal Revenue Code of 1954, 26 U.S.C. § 7602, to respondent bank. * * * Respondent Joseph W. Lang, a vice president of the bank, appeared in response to the summonses but, on advice of counsel, refused to produce any of the materials requested.

The United States and Olivero, pursuant to §§ 7402(b) and 7604(a) of the Code, then petitioned the United States District Court for the Northern District of Illinois for enforcement of the summonses. This was on November 11, 1975. Olivero testified that when the petition was filed he had not determined whether criminal charges were justified and had not made any report or recommendation about the case to his superiors. It was alleged in the petition and in an incorporated exhibit that the requested materials were necessary for the determination of the tax liability of Gattuso for the years in question and that the information contained in the documents was not in the possession of the petitioners. The District Court entered an order to show cause, and respondents answered through counsel, who also represented Gattuso.

At the ensuing hearing and in a post-hearing brief, respondents argued that Olivero's investigation was "purely criminal" in nature.

* * * Respondents conceded that they bore the burden of proving that enforcement of the summonses would abuse the court's process, but they contended that they did not have to show "that there is no civil purpose to the Summons." Instead, they urged that their burden was to show that the summonses were not issued in good faith because "the investigation is solely for the purpose of gathering evidence for use in a criminal prosecution."

The District Court agreed with respondents' contentions. * * *

* * *

The United States Court of Appeals for the Seventh Circuit affirmed. It concluded that the District Court correctly had included the issue of criminal purpose within the good-faith inquiry:

> "[T]he use of an administrative summons solely for criminal purposes is a quintessential example of bad faith. * * *

* * *

> "We note that the district court formulated its factual finding by use of the expression 'sole criminal purpose' rather than by a label such as 'bad faith.' We find no basis for reversible error in that verbal formulation. The district court grasped the vital core of *Donaldson* and rendered its factual finding consistently therewith."

The Court of Appeals further decided that the District Court had reached a factual, rather than a legal, conclusion when it found the summonses to have been issued solely for a criminal prosecution. Appellate review, accordingly, was limited to application of the clearly-erroneous standard. * * * The appellate court could not reverse the trial court's judgment, it said, because it was "not left with a firm and definite conviction that a mistake [had] been made."

* * *

III

The present case requires us to examine the limits of the good-faith use of an Internal Revenue summons issued under § 7602. * * * *Donaldson* does not control the facts now before us. There, the taxpayer had argued that the mere potentiality of criminal prosecution should have precluded enforcement of the summons. Here, on the other hand, the District Court found that Special Agent Olivero was investigating Gattuso "solely for the purpose of unearthing evidence of criminal conduct." The question then becomes whether this finding necessarily leads to the conclusion that the summonses were not issued in good-faith pursuit of the congressionally authorized purposes of § 7602.

A

The Secretary of the Treasury and the Commissioner of Internal Revenue are charged with the responsibility of administering and enforcing the Internal Revenue Code. 26 U.S.C. §§ 7801 and 7802. Congress, by § 7601(a), has required the Secretary to canvass revenue districts to "inquire after and concerning all persons therein who may be liable to pay any internal revenue tax." With regard to suspected fraud, these duties encompass enforcement of both civil and criminal statutes. The willful submission of a false or fraudulent tax return may subject a taxpayer not only to criminal penalties under §§ 7206 and 7207 of the Code, but, as well, to a civil penalty, under § 6653(b), of 50% of the underpayment. And § 6659(a) provides that the civil penalty shall be considered as part of the tax liability of the taxpayer. Hence, when § 7602 permits the use of a summons "[f]or the purpose of ascertaining the correctness of any return, * * * determining the liability of any person for any internal revenue tax * * *, or collecting any such liability," it necessarily permits the use of the summons for examination of suspected tax fraud and for the calculation of the 50% civil penalty. In *Donaldson*, we clearly noted that § 7602 drew no distinction between the civil and the criminal aspects; that it "contains no restriction"; that the corresponding regulations were "positive"; and that there was no significance, "for civil as compared with criminal purposes, at the point of a special agent's appearance." The Court then upheld the use of the summonses even though fraudulent conduct carried the potential of criminal liability. The Court repeated this emphasis in Couch v. United States, 409 U.S. 322, 326, 93 S.Ct. 611, 614, 34 L.Ed.2d 548 (1973):

> "It is now undisputed that a special agent is authorized, pursuant to 26 U.S.C. § 7602, to issue an Internal Revenue summons in aid of a tax investigation with civil and possible criminal consequences."

This result is inevitable because Congress has created a law enforcement system in which criminal and civil elements are inherently intertwined. When an investigation examines the possibility of criminal misconduct, it also necessarily inquires about the appropriateness of assessing the 50% civil tax penalty.

The legislative history of the Code supports the conclusion that Congress intended to design a system with interrelated criminal and civil elements. Section 7602 derives assertedly without change in meaning, from corresponding and similar provisions in §§ 3614, 3615, and 3654 of the 1939 Code. By § 3614(a) the Commissioner received the summons authority "for the purpose of ascertaining the correctness of any return or for the purpose of making a return where none has been made." Section 3615(b)(3) authorized the issuance of a summons "[w]henever any person who is required to deliver a monthly or other return of objects subject to tax delivers any return which, in the opinion of the collector, is erroneous, false, or fraudulent, or contains any undervaluation or understatement." Section 3654(a) stated the powers and duties of the collector:

> "Every collector within his collection district shall see that all laws and regulations relating to the collection of internal revenue taxes are faithfully executed and complied with, and shall aid in the prevention, detection, and punishment of any frauds in relation thereto. For such purposes, he shall have power to examine all persons, books, papers, accounts, and premises * * * and to summon any person to produce books and papers * * * and to compel compliance with such summons in the same manner as provided in section 3615."

Under § 3616 punishment for any fraud included both fine and imprisonment. The 1939 Code, therefore, contemplated the use of the summons in an investigation involving suspected criminal conduct as well as behavior that could have been disciplined with a civil penalty.

In short, Congress has not categorized tax fraud investigations into civil and criminal components. Any limitation on the good-faith use of an Internal Revenue summons must reflect this statutory premise.

B

The preceding discussion suggests why the primary limitation on the use of a summons occurs upon the recommendation of criminal prosecution to the Department of Justice. Only at that point do the criminal and civil aspects of a tax fraud case begin to diverge. We recognize, of course, that even upon recommendation to the Justice Department, the civil and criminal elements do not separate completely. The Government does not sacrifice its interest in unpaid taxes just because a criminal prosecution begins. Logically, then, the IRS could use its summons authority under § 7602 to uncover information about the tax liability created by a fraud regardless of the status of the criminal case. But the rule forbidding such is a prophylactic intended to safeguard the following policy interests.

A referral to the Justice Department permits criminal litigation to proceed. The IRS cannot try its own prosecutions. Such authority is reserved to the Department of Justice and, more particularly, to the United States Attorneys. 28 U.S.C. § 547(1). Nothing in § 7602 or its legislative history suggests that Congress intended the summons authority to broaden the Justice Department's right of criminal litigation discovery or to infringe on the role of the grand jury as a principal tool of criminal accusation. The likelihood that discovery would be broadened or the role of the grand jury infringed is substantial if post-referral use of the summons authority were permitted. For example, the IRS, upon referral, loses its ability to compromise both the criminal and the civil aspects of a fraud case. 26 U.S.C. § 7122(a). After the referral, the authority to settle rests with the Department of Justice. Interagency cooperation on the calculation of the civil liability is then to be expected and probably encourages efficient settlement of the dispute. But such cooperation, when combined with the inherently intertwined nature of the criminal and civil elements of the case, suggests that it is unrealistic to attempt to build a partial information barrier between the two branches of the executive. Effective use of information to determine civil liability would inevitably result in criminal discovery. The prophylactic restraint on the use of the summons effectively safeguards the two policy interests while encouraging maximum interagency cooperation.[15]

C

Prior to a recommendation for prosecution to the Department of Justice, the IRS must use its summons authority in good faith. Donaldson v. United States; United States v. Powell, 379 U.S. 48, 57–58, 85 S.Ct. 248, 254–255, 13 L.Ed.2d 112 (1964). In *Powell*, the Court announced several elements of a good-faith exercise:

> "[The Service] must show that the investigation will be conducted pursuant to a legitimate purpose, that the inquiry may be relevant to the purpose, that the information sought is not already within the Commissioner's possession, and that the administrative steps required by the Code have been followed * * *. [A] court may not permit its process to be abused. Such an abuse would take place if the

---

15. The Third Circuit has suggested that our reference in *Donaldson* to the recommendation for criminal prosecution ("We hold that under § 7602 and internal revenue summons may be issued in aid of an investigation if it is issued in good faith and prior to a recommendation for criminal prosecution," 400 U.S., at 536, 91 S.Ct., at 545) intended to draw a line at the recommendation to the Service's district office from the special agent, rather than at the recommendation from the Service to the Justice Department. United States v. Lafko, 520 F.2d, at 625. This misread our intent. Given the interrelated criminal/civil nature of tax fraud investigation whenever it remains within the jurisdiction of the Service, and given the utility of the summons to investigate civil tax liability, we decline to impose the prophylactic restraint on the summons authority any earlier than at the recommendation to the Department of Justice. We cannot deny that the potential for expanding the criminal discovery rights of the Justice Department or for usurping the role of the grand jury exists at the point of the recommendation by the special agent. But we think the possibilities for abuse of these policies are remote before the recommendation to Justice takes place and do not justify imposing an absolute ban on the use of the summons before that point. Earlier imposition of the ban, given the balance of policies and civil law enforcement interests, would unnecessarily hamstring the performance of the tax determination and collection functions by the Service.

summons had been issued for an improper purpose, such as to harass the taxpayer or to put pressure on him to settle a collateral dispute, or for any other purpose reflecting on the good faith of the particular investigation." Ibid.

A number of the Courts of Appeals, including the Seventh Circuit in this case, 554 F.2d, at 309, have said that another improper purpose, which the Service may not pursue in good faith with a summons, is to gather evidence solely for a criminal investigation. The courts have based their conclusions in part on *Donaldson*'s explanation of the *Reisman* dictum. The language of *Donaldson*, however, must be read in the light of the recognition of the interrelated criminal/civil nature of a tax fraud inquiry. For a fraud investigation to be solely criminal in nature would require an extraordinary departure from the normally inseparable goals of examining whether the basis exists for criminal charges and for the assessment of civil penalties.

In this case, respondents submit that such a departure did indeed occur because Special Agent Olivero was interested only in gathering evidence for a criminal prosecution. We disagree. The institutional responsibility of the Service to calculate and to collect civil fraud penalties and fraudulently reported or unreported taxes is not necessarily overturned by a single agent who attempts to build a criminal case. The review process over and above his conclusions is multilayered and thorough. Apart from the control of his immediate supervisor, the agent's final recommendation is reviewed by the district chief of the Intelligence Division. The Office of Regional Counsel also reviews the case before it is forwarded to the National Office of the Service or to the Justice Department. If the Regional Counsel and the Assistant Regional Commissioner for Intelligence disagree about the disposition of a case, another complete review occurs at the national level centered in the Criminal Tax Division of the Office of General Counsel. Only after the officials of at least two layers of review have concurred in the conclusion of the special agent does the referral to the Department of Justice take place. At any of the various stages, the Service can abandon the criminal prosecution, can decide instead to assert a civil penalty, or can pursue both goals. While the special agent is an important actor in the process, his motivation is hardly dispositive.

It should also be noted that the layers of review provide the taxpayer with substantial protection against the hasty or overzealous judgment of the special agent. The taxpayer may obtain a conference with the district Intelligence Division officials upon request or whenever the chief of the Division determines that a conference would be in the best interests of the Government. If prosecution has been recommended, the chief notifies the taxpayer of the referral to the Regional Counsel.

As in *Donaldson*, then, where we refused to draw the line between permissible civil and impermissible criminal purposes at the entrance of the special agent into the investigation, we cannot draw it on the basis of the agent's personal intent. To do so would unnecessarily frustrate the enforcement of the tax laws by restricting the use of the summons according to the motivation of a single agent without regard to the enforcement policy of the Service as an institution. Furthermore, the inquiry into the criminal enforcement objectives of the agent would delay summons enforcement proceedings while parties clash over, and judges grapple with the thought processes of each investigator.[17] This obviously is undesirable and unrewarding. As a result, the question whether an investigation has solely criminal purposes must be answered only by an examination of the institutional posture of the IRS. Contrary to the assertion of respondents, this means that those opposing enforcement of a summons do bear the burden to disprove the actual existence of a valid civil tax determination or collection purpose by the Service. After all, the purpose of the good-faith inquiry is to determine whether the agency is honestly pursuing the goals of § 7602 by issuing the summons.

Without doubt, this burden is a heavy one. Because criminal and civil fraud liabilities are coterminous, the Service rarely will be found to have acted in bad faith by pursuing the former. On the other hand, we cannot abandon this aspect of the good-faith inquiry altogether.[18] We shall not countenance delay in submitting a recommendation to the Justice Department when there is an institutional commitment to make the referral and the Service merely would like to gather additional evidence for the prosecution. Such a delay

17. We recognize, of course, that examination of agent motive may be necessary to evaluate the good-faith factors of *Powell,* for example, to consider whether a summons was issued to harass a taxpayer.

18. The dissent would abandon this aspect of the good-faith inquiry. It would permit the IRS to use the summons authority solely for criminal investigation. It reaches this conclusion because it says the Code contains no limitation to prevent such use. Its argument reveals a fundamental misunderstanding about the authority of the IRS. The Service does not enjoy inherent authority to summon production of the private papers of citizens. It may exercise only that authority granted by Congress. In § 7602 Congress has bestowed upon the Service the authority to summon production for four purposes only: for "ascertaining the correctness of any return, making a return where none has been made, determining the liability of any person for any internal revenue tax * * * or collecting any such liability." Congress therefore intended the summons authority to be used to aid the determination and collection of taxes. These purposes do not include the goal of filing criminal charges against citizens. Consequently, summons authority does not exist to aid criminal investigations solely. The error of the dissent is that it seeks a limit on the face of the statute when it should seek an affirmative grant of summons authority for purely criminal investigations. We have made that search and could uncover nothing in the Code or its legislative history to suggest that Congress intended to permit exclusively criminal use of summonses. As a result, the IRS employs its authority in good faith when it pursues the four purposes of § 7602, which do not include aiding criminal investigations solely.

would be tantamount to the use of the summons authority after the recommendation and would permit the Government to expand its criminal discovery rights. Similarly, the good-faith standard will not permit the IRS to become an information-gathering agency for other departments, including the Department of Justice, regardless of the status of criminal cases.[19]

D

In summary, then, several requirements emerge for the enforcement of an IRS summons.[20] First, the summons must be issued before the Service recommends to the Department of Justice that a criminal prosecution, which reasonably would relate to the subject matter of the summons, be undertaken. Second, the Service at all times must use the summons authority in good-faith pursuit of the congressionally authorized purposes of § 7602. This second prerequisite requires the Service to meet the *Powell* standards of good faith. It also requires that the Service not abandon in an institutional sense, as explained in Parts III–A and III–C above, the pursuit of civil tax determination or collection.

IV

On the record before us, respondents have not demonstrated sufficient justification to preclude enforcement of the IRS summonses. No recommendation to the Justice Department for criminal prosecution has been made. Of the *Powell* criteria, respondents challenge only one aspect of the Service's showing: They suggest that Olivero already may possess the evidence requested in the summonses.

Although the record shows that Olivero had uncovered the names and identities of the LaSalle National Bank land trusts, it does not show that the Service knows the value of the trusts or their income or the allocation of interests therein. Because production of the bank's complete records on the trusts reasonably could be expected to reveal part or all of this information, which would be material to the computation of Gattuso's tax liability, the *Powell* criteria do not preclude enforcement. Finally, the District Court refused en-

---

19. To the limited extent that the institutional good faith of the Service with regard to criminal purpose may be questioned before any recommendation to the Department of Justice, our position on this issue necessarily rejects the Government's argument that prerecommendation enforcement of summonses must meet only the *Powell* elements of good faith. We have concluded that the Government's contention fails to recognize the essence of the good-faith inquiry. The *Powell* elements were not intended as an exclusive statement about the meaning of good faith. They were examples of agency action not in good-faith pursuit of the congressionally authorized purposes of § 7602. The dispositive question in each case, then, is whether the Service is pursuing the authorized purposes in good faith.

20. These requirements are not intended to be exclusive. Future cases may well reveal the need to prevent other forms of agency abuse of congressional authority and judicial process.

forcement because it found that Olivero's personal motivation was to gather evidence solely for a criminal prosecution. The court, however, failed to consider whether the Service in an institutional sense had abandoned its pursuit of Gattuso's civil tax liability.[21] The Court of Appeals did not require that inquiry. On the record presently developed, we cannot conclude that such an abandonment has occurred.

The judgment of the Court of Appeals is therefore reversed with instructions to that court to remand the case to the District Court for further proceedings consistent with this opinion.

It is so ordered.

Mr. Justice STEWART, with whom The CHIEF JUSTICE, Mr. Justice REHNQUIST, and Mr. Justice STEVENS join, dissenting.

This case is here only because of judicial misreadings of a passage in the Court's opinion in Donaldson v. United States. That passage has been read by the federal courts, in this case and in others, to mean that a summons under § 7602 of the Internal Revenue Code, 26 U.S.C. § 7602, is improper if issued in aid of an investigation solely for criminal purposes. Yet the statute itself contains no such limitation, and the *Donaldson* opinion in fact clearly stated that there are but two limits upon enforcement of such a summons: It must be "issued in good faith and prior to a recommendation for criminal prosecution." I adhere to that view.

The Court concedes that the task of establishing the "purpose" of an individual agent is "undesirable and unrewarding." Yet the burden it imposes today—to discover the "institutional good faith" of the entire Internal Revenue Service—is, in my view, even less desirable and less rewarding. The elusiveness of "institutional good faith" as described by the Court can produce little but endless discovery proceedings and ultimate frustration of the fair administration of the Internal Revenue Code. In short, I fear that the Court's new criteria will prove wholly unworkable.

Earlier this year the Court of Appeals for the Second Circuit had occasion to deal with the issue now before us in the case of United States v. Morgan Guaranty Trust Co., 572 F.2d 36. Judge Friendly's perceptive opinion for his court in that case read the *Donaldson* opinion correctly: This Court was there "laying down an objective test,

---

21. Respondents argue that the District Court made a factual finding when it concluded that the summonses were issued solely to gather evidence for a criminal prosecution. They then submit that the District Court's decision may be overturned only if this Court holds this finding to be clearly erroneous. * * * Whether the issue of the Service's good faith generally poses a factual question, or a legal and factual one, or a legal question, is not necessarily presented in the case now before the Court, and we do not reach it. The lower courts employed an incorrect legal standard to measure good faith when they limited their consideration to the personal motivation of Special Agent Olivero. In this case, then, a legal error compels reversal.

'prior to a recommendation for criminal prosecution,' that would avoid a need for determining the thought processes of special agents; and * * * the 'good faith' requirement of the holding related to such wholly different matters as those mentioned in" the case of United States v. Powell. "Such a view would * * * be consistent with the only rationale that has ever been offered for preventing an otherwise legitimate use of an Internal Revenue Service third party summons, namely that Congress could not have intended the statute to trench on the power of the grand jury or to broaden the Government's right to discovery in a criminal case * * *." 572 F.2d, at 41–42.

Instead of standing by the objective and comparatively bright-line test of *Donaldson*, as now clarified, the Court today further muddies the waters. It does not even attempt to identify the source of the requirements it now adds to enforcement proceedings under §§ 7402(b) and 7604(a) of the Code. These requirements are not suggested by anything in the statutes themselves, and nobody suggests that they derive from the Constitution. They are simply imposed by the Court from out of nowhere, and they seem to me unjustified, unworkable, and unwise.

I would reverse the judgment, not for further hearings in the District Court, but with instructions to order enforcement of the summons.

QUESTIONS

1. From a practical point of view, can any taxpayer ever establish the abandonment, in an institutional sense, of the pursuit of civil tax determination or collection?

2. To what extent does the prohibition on the IRS acting as "an information gathering agency for other departments, including the Department of Justice," interfere with beneficial inter-agency cooperation?

3. Can a "bad purpose" on the part of an informant taint an IRS summons? See United States v. Cortese, 614 F.2d 914 (3d Cir. 1980).

4. Suppose a summons is issued with regard to taxpayer *A*'s liability for the purpose of obtaining *A*'s "cooperation" in connection with an investigation of taxpayer *B*, the primary target of the IRS. Should the summons be enforced? See United States v. Equitable Trust Co., 611 F.2d 492 (4th Cir. 1979); Use of the IRS Summons to Pressure One Taxpayer into Cooperating in the Investigation of Another: United States v. Equitable Trust Co., 93 Harv.L.Rev. 1574 (1980).

C. RELEVANCE

UNITED STATES v. RLC CORP.

46 AFTR 2d 80–5023 (D.Del.1980).

SCHWARTZ, District Judge.

This is an action to enforce an Internal Revenue Service summons served upon Henry Clark, Vice-President-Finance and Treasurer of defendant RLC Corporation ("RLC"). On February 7, the Court held an evidentiary hearing on this issue. For the reasons set forth below, the IRS summons will be enforced in part.

The IRS summons seeks:

> All Capital Expenditure Requests (CER's) or similar documents, prepared by or for RLC Corporation's Subsidiaries, submitted to or acted upon by RLC Corporation during the Fiscal years ended September 30, 1976 and September 30, 1977, all memorandums, attachments, or transmittals associated with CER's submitted to or acted upon by RLC Corporation during the fiscal years ended September 30, 1976 and September 30, 1977.

It is uncontested that RLC has provided the IRS with all other information requested in the form of Information Document Requests and has balked only with respect to the IRS request for CER's. CER's are internal management forms used by RLC. Originated by employees of RLC's subsidiaries, they are requests for approval of transactions which, in the view of the subsidiary employees, involve capital expenditures. Requests of less than $1000 must be approved at the subsidiary level. Requests over $1000 must be approved by Mr. Clark and the President of RLC. Requests for capital expenditures over $10,000 require the additional approval of the Executive Committee or the Chairman and Vice-Chairman of RLC. A CER form must also be submitted for proposed expense items over $10,000. No such form is required for expense items less than $10,000. CER's are normally accompanied by other documents including inter alia blueprints, drawings, quotes from contractors, leases, or terms and conditions of proposed transactions. In passing upon these requests, corporate officials either approve, modify or reject the CER's. On occasion, approval is given to a CER only if the transaction is treated for financial accounting purposes as an expense, rather than a capital, item. This is done for internal management reasons, usually to discourage the implementation of the transaction at the subsidiary level.

In seeking to enforce an IRS summons, the government has the burden of satisfying the * * * four prongs of the test established in United States v. Powell. * * *

The only prong defendant contends the government has not proved is relevancy. According to RLC, the CER's are "proposals for transactions" which "do not provide substantiation of any of the income received, the expenditures incurred, or the transactions engaged in by defendant and its subsidiaries during the taxable years under examination."

In determining relevancy in the context of proceedings to enforce IRS summons, the courts have generally required the Government to meet a "very minimal showing of relevancy." United States v. Egenberg, 443 F.2d 512, 515–16 (3d Cir. 1971). The standard most often articulated is whether the information sought "might throw light upon the correctness of the return." Id. at 515.

As noted, the IRS summons requests all CER's "submitted or acted upon" in fiscal years 1976 and 1977. This includes CER's submitted prior to those years but approved, modified or rejected in those years, CER's submitted in 1976 and 1977 but not passed upon by RLC management until after September 30, 1977, and CER's submitted and approved or modified prior to 1976 but not implemented until 1976 or 1977.

The Court finds CER's for projects approved, modified or implemented in fiscal years 1976 and 1977 to be relevant to the IRS investigation. Leon Mintz, IRS Agent, testified that CER's provided a contemporaneous account of what work was done on a project and, to some extent, why the work was done. With this information, Mintz testified, he and his fellow agents could determine whether the expense incurred in such work was a capital expenditure not immediately deductible or an expense item that could be currently deducted. The CER's would appear to be especially helpful to the IRS audit in light of the "fragmentation" of other documentation. Mintz testified that, although RLC has made available to IRS its purchase orders, invoices, cancelled checks and other similar documents, it is very difficult for the IRS to determine exactly what work has been done and whether expenditures for such work were properly expensed or capitalized. As the CER's provide an overall account of what work has been done, CER's for work actually done in fiscal years 1976 and 1977 are clearly relevant regardless of when they were submitted or approved.

The Court also finds relevant CER's for projects approved or modified in 1976 and 1977 but not actually begun until subsequent years. Clark testified that most of the RLC subsidiaries are on an accrual basis for tax purposes. John Margetich, Corporate Tax Manager of RLC, testified that RLC does not accrue items for tax purposes on the tax returns of RLC or its subsidiaries based *only* on the CER's. Mintz testified that he found no indication that RLC accrues expenses solely on the basis of approved CER's. However, GX-1-A, a memo from Clark to Larry Anderson, an employee of an RLC subsidiary, dated August 12, 1976 states:

> I enclose the CER for the installation of partition to reduce office noise in the home office building. Please note that the CER has been approved on the basis that cost of the expenses be incurred. If you decide to proceed with this CER on this basis and a cost has not been incurred by September 30, *this should be accrued.* (emphasis added)

There is no indication that, at the time this CER was approved and the directive to accrue this expense issued, there was any documentation fixing the expenditure for partitions other than this CER. In fact, the CER request from R.L. Gregg, Jr., states "I will have a purchase order issued *once* the necessary approvals are procured." (GX-1-E) (emphasis added). Although the record is silent as to whether RLC accrued expenses for this project prior to their incurrence, this Exhibit casts some doubt upon the claim that RLC does not accrue items based solely upon the approved CER's. Moreover, the testimony of Margetich and Mintz clearly does not rule out accrual of expenses for projects for which a CER has been approved based upon documentation other than the CER's. In light of GX-1 and the Clark testimony regarding the tax reporting basis used by RLC and its subsidiaries, the government has made a sufficient showing of the relevance of CER's approved or modified in 1976 and 1977 but not implemented until later years.

The government has not, however, made a sufficient showing of the relevancy of CER's not approved, modified or rejected during fiscal years 1976 and 1977. There is no evidence that RLC accrues expenses for transactions for which a CER has not yet been acted upon, and thus no showing that these CER's might "throw light upon the correctness" of RLC's tax returns has been made.

Finally, the Court must determine the relevance of CER's rejected during 1976 and 1977. When asked whether projects for which a CER has been rejected could still be implemented by a subsidiary plant manager, Clark testified, "Technically he could. I don't think in practice they would normally do that." The government must demonstrate that "the 'might' in the articulated standard, 'might throw light upon the correctness of the return,' is in the particular circumstances an indication of a realistic expectation rather than an idle hope that something may be discovered." United States v. Harrington, 388 F.2d 520, 524 (2d Cir. 1968). The Clark testimony was the sole reference made at the hearing to the effect of corporate rejection of CER's on the proposed projects. The Court finds, based on the record, that the government's interest in CER's rejected by corporate officials is based upon an "idle hope that something may be discovered" rather than "a realistic expectation."

In accordance with this Memorandum Opinion, an order will be entered enforcing the IRS summons with the exception of CER's not approved, modified or rejected during fiscal years 1976 and 1977 and CER's rejected during the same fiscal years.

UNITED STATES v. COOPERS & LYBRAND

550 F.2d 615 (10th Cir. 1977).

BARRETT, Circuit Judge.

Petitioners-appellants, United States of America and John G. Shea, Special Agent, Internal Revenue Service, appeal the denial of enforcement of an IRS summons issued pursuant to 26 U.S.C.A. § 7602, in relation to IRS examination and audit of Johns-Manville, Inc. (J–M) corporate federal income tax returns for the years 1971 and 1972.

J–M, respondent in intervention-appellee, is a major national corporation having subsidiaries and affiliates throughout the United States and abroad. The IRS has audited every federal income tax return of J–M since 1913 and does so on a continuing basis.

Coopers and Lybrand (C&L) is a national firm of certified public accountants employed by J–M who examined and reported on the consolidated statements of J–M for the years 1971 and 1972. It functioned solely in an auditing capacity and did not participate in the actual preparation and filing of J–M's federal tax returns.

During the latter part of 1974 the IRS issued a summons pursuant to § 7602 directing C&L to testify and produce its books and records relative to its examination and audit of J–M. C&L responded and produced voluminous workpapers and documents but declined to disclose its audit program or the tax pool analysis file.

The audit program is a master plan prepared by C&L, specifically tailored for auditing J–M. Included within the audit program is a listing of procedures to be followed by C&L personnel in auditing J–M records with a "check off" method of confirming that such procedures were followed, together with suggestions for future modifications of the plan. The tax pool analysis file prepared by J–M personnel contains its estimates of J–M's contingent liabilities for future income tax periods. It is utilized by J–M in preparing financial statements in compliance with Securities and Exchange Commission's (SEC) requirements and it is also utilized by C&L in verifying that J–M's financial statements have been prepared in accordance with generally accepted accounting principles. It is uncontested that neither the audit program nor the tax pool analysis file were utilized in the preparation of the 1971 and 1972 tax returns.

After C&L refused to produce the audit program and tax pool analysis file, IRS filed its petition for judicial enforcement of the summonses pursuant to 26 U.S.C.A. §§ 7402(b) and 7604(a). A show cause order was issued and a full evidentiary hearing followed. During the hearing Shea testified that the tax pool analysis file might be relevant as a source of possible inconsistent positions or improper figures and that the audit program would bear on J–M's intent and "would assist us in determining whether or not to pursue a particular area." C&L resisted production of its audit program. C&L, joined by J–M, resisted production of the tax pool analysis file. They argued that the information sought was not relevant, that the information was already available to IRS from documents then in its possession, and that strong policy reasons relative to an auditor-client relationship weighed heavily against production.

In denying enforcement of the summonses, the court found that J–M's cooperation with the IRS in relation to the investigation was extensive and that tax fraud had not been charged. The court found and/or concluded, *inter alia*:

> Initially, we conclude that the Service has failed to make the requisite showing that the Audit Program is relevant to the tax investigation pursuant to which it is sought. The evidence establishes to our satisfaction that Coopers and Lybrand has no responsibility for the preparation or review of J–M's income tax returns. J–M's returns are prepared internally by J–M's tax personnel. As a consequence, we conclude that the Audit Program was not prepared in conjunction with or connected in any manner to the preparation or filing of J–M's 1971 and 1972 income tax returns.

> * * *

> We find from the evidence presented that the Audit Program does not contain any factual data regarding any corporate transactions of J–M; rather it consists solely of a listing of procedures to be followed by C&L personnel throughout the United States in examining books and records of J–M, documentation of the extent to which such proceedings were followed, and suggestions for the future modification of such procedures.

> The Audit program was prepared prior to C&L's 1971 and 1972 audits of J–M. During the course of the 1971 and 1972 audits, the only information recorded in the Audit Program was (1) confirmation by C&L personnel that the Audit Program procedures were complied with or (2) explanations of why the procedures were inapplicable in certain instances, and (3) modifications of the Audit Program.

> * * *

> We next approach the issue of production of the Tax Pool Analysis file and related papers * * *.

> * * *

> In the instant case, the IRS has not challenged respondents' argument that the tax pool does not contain records of transactions. The evidence is clear that the Tax Pool was not prepared in connection with the preparation and filing

of J–M's tax returns. The IRS here does not seek records of corporate transactions or the data which are customarily maintained in support of company transactions, instead it seeks private thoughts and theories of the taxpayer.

Consolidated financial statements are prepared annually by Johns-Manville for inclusion in reports to stockholders and certain mandatory filings with the Securities and Exchange Commission. Coopers and Lybrand examines and reports on these consolidated financial statements (and utilizes the tax pool analysis file to that end).

* * *

* * * The uncontradicted evidence establishes to our satisfaction that the Tax Pool Analysis file and related papers were not issued or compiled in connection with the preparation or filing of J–M's income tax returns. Coopers & Lybrand has no responsibility in regard to determining or reporting on J–M's tax liability. The limited purpose for which the Tax Pool was created by J–M and communicated to C&L was unrelated and distinct from J–M's tax liability or the preparation of J–M's tax returns.

IRS does not contest or challenge the court's findings that C&L had no responsibility for the preparation or review of J–M's income tax returns; that the returns were prepared by J–M personnel; that the audit program does not contain any factual data regarding any corporate transactions of J–M; that the tax pool was not prepared in connection with the preparation and filing of J–M's tax returns; and that the tax pool analysis file was created by J–M for its usage in preparing annual consolidated financial statements and utilized by C&L in verifying that the financial statements were properly reported in accordance with generally accepted auditing procedures. These findings are therefore accepted as true and controlling for purposes of this appeal.

On appeal IRS contends the district court (1) "erred in refusing to order enforcement of IRS summonses for the production of an independent accounting firm's tax pool analysis file, containing memoranda of conversations with taxpayer's employees and the employees' memoranda, maintained by the firm for the purpose of auditing taxpayer's financial statements", and (2) erred in "refusing to order enforcement of Internal Revenue Service summonses for production of an independent accounting firm's audit program prepared and maintained by the firm for the purpose of auditing taxpayer's financial statements."

It is significant, we believe, that the IRS's delineation of the issues on appeal reemphasize that neither the tax pool analysis file nor the audit program were utilized by J–M in the preparation of federal income tax returns; that the tax pool analysis file was utilized solely for auditing J–M's financial statements; and that the audit program's usage was similarly limited. Noteworthy, too, is the fact that all of the work papers involved in the audit program for the years 1971 and 1972 have been turned over to the IRS. Also, J–M and C&L have repeatedly made their personnel available, prior to and during trial, to the IRS to respond to any questions that the Service may have. Even so, the IRS has elected not to question the employees of either company.

I.

Notwithstanding its concession that the tax pool analysis file was developed by J–M and utilized by J–M and C&L solely for the purpose of preparing annual consolidated financial statements for inclusion in reports to stockholders and for certain mandatory filings with the SEC, IRS contends that the file comes within a § 7602 summons because it *might* show tax fraud, because it *might* show substantial tax liability, and because it would be relevant to show and establish the state of mind of employees at the time the returns were filed. IRS acknowledges it has no direct or precedential substantive authority supportive of its position.

The general cases cited by IRS all deal, for the most part, with summonses issued for the production of materials utilized in the preparation and filing of tax returns. However, extending IRS contentions herein to their logical conclusion, it is hard to determine what corporate records would not fall under a § 7602 summonses if the standard endorsed the production of *any* records which *might* show tax fraud or tax liability. IRS does not, as it appears to assume on this appeal, have *carte blanche* discovery.

We have long recognized the broad investigative powers of administrative agencies * * *. Furthermore, we have heretofore endorsed the broad investigative powers of § 7602:

> The bank's final argument, that the examination purportedly authorized by the summons exceeds the statutory reach of § 7602, is also without merit. The case law history of that section makes clear that § 7602 should be "liberally construed in recognition of the vital public purposes which [it serves]." United States v. Continental Bank & Trust Company, 503 F.2d 45 (10th Cir. 1974). 503 F.2d, at 50.

However, the investigative powers of § 7602 are not without limitation. Although the IRS need not establish probable cause prior to the issuance of a summons, it must establish that the investigation is pursuant to and relevant to a legitimate purpose; that the information is not already available; that a determination has been made by the secretary or his delegate that further examination is necessary; and that the other administrative steps required by the Code have been followed. United States v. Powell. Prior to a hearing a taxpayer "may challenge the summons on any appropriate ground." Reisman v. Caplin, 375 U.S. 440 at 449, 84 S.Ct. 508 at 513, 11 L.Ed.2d 459 (1964).

Application of the *Powell* standard has been frequent in assessing the validity of a summons. See: Donaldson v. United States, 400 U. S. 517, 91 S.Ct. 534, 27 L.Ed.2d 580 (1971); * * * Couch v. United States, 409 U.S. 322, 93 S.Ct. 611, 34 L.Ed.2d 548 (1973); * * * Fisher v. United States, 425 U.S. 391, 96 S.Ct. 1569, 48 L.Ed.2d 39 (1976) * * *.

In each of the above cases, however, the documents summoned dealt directly with the taxpayer's return as filed or were a source of information for the return, and each of the summons issued had prior judicial endorsement. * * *

One of the limitations which may be properly imposed upon a judicial summons was noted in United States v. Matras, 487 F.2d 1271 (8th Cir. 1973):

> * * * Obviously, that issue must be determined on an ad hoc basis. Certainly, a taxpayer should not erect roadblocks for the purpose of frustrating or preventing the IRS from a full-scale inquiry of the liability of the taxpayer. By the same token, the government should not, for the mere sake of its convenience, impose unnecessary burdens on a taxpayer in conducting an audit or investigation for tax liability, particularly where, as here, there is no indication of a purpose to escape any tax liability. The term "relevant" connotes and encompasses more than "convenience." Consequently, we are not persuaded to fault the district judge for concluding that the government failed to sustain its burden of proof by alleging a general need for a "road map." If we were to accede to the government's view, it is difficult to imagine corporate materials that might not contribute to a more comprehensive understanding of the workings of the corporation, and thus, according to the government, be deemed relevant to the tax investigation.
> 487 F.2d, at 1274–1275.

A similar view was espoused in United States v. Theodore, 479 F.2d 749 (4th Cir. 1973):

> A summons will be deemed unreasonable and unenforceable if it is overbroad and disproportionate to the end sought. United States v. Harrington, 388 F.2d 520, 523 (2 Cir. 1968). The Government cannot go on a "fishing expedition" through appellants' records, United States v. Dauphin Trust Co., 385 F.2d 129 (3 Cir. 1967); contra United States v. Giordano, 419 F.2d 564 (8 Cir. 1969), and where it

> appears that the purpose of the summons is "a rambling exploration" of a third party's files, it will not be enforced. See United States v. Harrington, supra. Indeed, we agree with Judge Lumbard that "[t]his judicial protection against the sweeping or irrelevant order is *particularly* appropriate in matters where the demand for records is directed not to the taxpayer but to a third-party who may have had some dealing with the person under investigation." United States v. Harrington, supra. (Emphasis added.)
> 479 F.2d, at 754.

Applying these standards, we hold that the court properly found that the tax pool analysis file was not relevant and therefore not subject to production under the summons. In this respect we deem it worthy of repeating that it was uncontroverted that the tax pool analysis file was not prepared in connection with or used to facilitate the preparation and filing of J–M's tax returns and that C&L has no responsibility for any J–M tax matters.

II.

IRS contends the court erred in refusing to order enforcement of the summons for the production of C&L's audit program which C&L prepared and maintained for auditing J–M's financial statements. In its brief IRS clarified its position. IRS desires to have the audit program "not only as an index, but as a key to understanding, the audit program would be relevant to the examination of these numerous work papers and other records; the audit program is the guiding document which gives coherence, order, and logical sequence to the audit which generated the work papers." Mere convenience does not make an item producible under an IRS summons. See discussion I., supra, particularly, United States v. Matras, supra.

The trial court handled a complicated case of first impression in an exemplary manner. We find no error.

Affirmed.

UNITED STATES v. NOALL

587 F.2d 123 (2d Cir. 1978), cert. denied,
441 U.S. 923, 99 S.Ct. 2031, 60 L.Ed.2d 396 (1979).

FRIENDLY, Circuit Judge:

The United States and Felix Karul, an IRS agent, brought this proceeding in the District Court for the Southern District of New York under IRC §§ 7402(b) and 7604(a) to enforce an IRS summons directed to Roger Noall, Executive Vice-President of the taxpayer, Bunge Corporation (Bunge). The petition recited that Karul was conducting an investigation for the purpose of ascertaining the correctness of Bunge's income tax returns for the fiscal years ending March 31, 1972, 1973 and 1974. The summons required Noall to appear before the agent and produce for examination:

> All Internal audit reports and related work papers for the periods ended 3–31–72, 3–31–73, 3–31–74.

* * *

* * * Relying particularly on United States v. Coopers & Lybrand, 413 F.Supp. 942 (D.Col.1975), aff'd, 550 F.2d 615 (10 Cir. 1977), Noall contends that the Government has not established the relevance of the documents sought and that public policy considerations dictate against their compelled production. * * *

The statutory language is "may be relevant or material". Congress acted advisedly in using the verb "may be" rather than "is", since the Commissioner cannot be certain that the documents are relevant or material until he sees them. This court has consistently held that the threshold the Commissioner must surmount is very low, namely, "whether the inspection sought 'might have thrown light upon' the correctness of the taxpayer's returns". See Foster v. United States, 265 F.2d 183, 187 (2 Cir.), cert. denied, 360 U.S. 912, 79 S. Ct. 1297, 3 L.Ed.2d 1261 (1959). The threshold is particularly low when, as here, the papers at issue are the taxpayer's own and there is no question of the invasion of the privacy of third persons against their will. Cf. United States v. Harrington, 388 F.2d 520, 523 (2 Cir. 1968).

On Bunge's own statements the internal audit reports and related work papers pass the applicable test. Clearly the purposes of the internal audit include the detection of overstatements or understatements of revenues or expenses, and of identifying accounting procedures that would lead to these. If the internal auditors have ascertained an understatement of revenues or an overstatement of expenses, this plainly might throw light on the correctness of the returns. We find no significance in the point, stressed by appellant, that the internal audit reports and related work papers were not used in preparing Bunge's income tax returns. The Commissioner's interest lies in whether the tax returns correctly reflected Bunge's actual income, not simply whether they were correctly prepared from the books of account and other records used. * * *

We are similarly unpersuaded by appellant's argument that enforcement of the summons runs counter to public policy since Bunge employees would be inhibited from full and frank disclosure to the internal auditors if they knew that their statements or investigations flowing from them were subject to production at the insistence of the IRS. * * *

This brings us to the Tenth Circuit's decision in United States v. Coopers & Lybrand. The court there affirmed a district court ruling

which declined to enforce a summons requiring an independent accounting firm to produce two sets of documents—its program for
conducting the audit of the taxpayer, Johns-Manville, Inc., and a "tax
pool analysis" file, prepared by the taxpayer's personnel, which dealt
with Johns-Manville's contingent income tax liabilities. The portion
of the decision relating to Coopers & Lybrand's audit program, namely, its instructions to its auditors, affords no support to Noall. Here
the Government did not seek Bunge's internal audit *program;* rather
it sought the results. These had already been turned over by Coopers & Lybrand and were not at issue in that case. In refusing to enforce the summons in regard to the tax pool analysis, both the district
court and the court of appeals gave much weight to the fact that this
was not used in preparing the company's income tax return. To the
extent that the decision was influenced by this factor, it is not authoritative in this circuit.[5]

* * *

Affirmed.

UNITED STATES v. ARTHUR ANDERSEN & CO.

474 F.Supp. 322 (D.Mass.1979).

FREEDMAN, District Judge.

This action is brought pursuant to Sections 7402(b) and 7604(a)
of the Internal Revenue Code of 1954, seeking judicial enforcement of
an Internal Revenue summons. * * *

* * *

On November 14, 1977, Special Agent Murphy issued a summons
under 26 U.S.C. § 7602 directing respondent Arthur Andersen to appear on November 30, 1977 to testify and to produce for examination
certain statements, records, and papers allegedly relating to tax liabilities of Good Hope [Industries, Inc.]. * * * In a timely and proper manner, Good Hope directed Arthur Andersen not to comply with
the summons, temporarily staying compliance under the terms of 26
U.S.C. § 7609(b)(2). * * *

* * *

Good Hope takes this opportunity to urge that the Court recognize a privilege between accountant and client, akin to the privilege
recognized between attorney and client. In support of his proposition, both Good Hope and Arthur Andersen have submitted numerous
affidavits addressing the need for confidentiality between accountant
and client in order that frank disclosure might be fostered, the similarity of function between accountant and lawyer in the tax field, and

5. We need not and do not express
    any opinion as to what we would do
    if confronted with the precise prob-
    lem of the tax pool analysis present-
    ed to the Tenth Circuit in *Coopers &
    Lybrand.*

the similar manner in which both professions are regarded by the public. They argue that such privilege is particularly appropriate as to Audit Work Programs, Tax Accrual Workpapers and Tax Planning and Consultation Papers. While I appreciate that valid policy questions are raised by the issues presented in this case, I am not inclined to recognize an accountant/client privilege on these facts. * * * [N]oting that the Supreme Court has explicitly stated "that no confidential accountant-client privilege exists under federal law * * *," Couch v. United States, 409 U.S. 322, 335, 93 S.Ct. 611, 619, 34 L.Ed. 2d 548 (1972), I see no grounds for establishing an accountant/client privilege as to the Audit Work Programs, Tax Accrual Workpapers, and Tax Planning and Consultation Papers, or any other documents enumerated in the summons.

* * *

Respondent's strongest argument rests upon the second prong of *Powell*—the requirement of relevancy. As an initial matter, I do not understand the respondent to resist on relevancy grounds production of material actually employed in determination of income and in tax preparation. However, they strenuously urge that Audit Work Programs, Tax Accrual Workpapers, and Tax Planning and Consultation Papers fall into a different category and are not relevant. The gist of their argument is that such materials are not "factual," in that they do not form a basis for preparation of tax returns.

In reliance upon United States v. Coopers & Lybrand, 413 F. Supp. 942 (D.Colo.), aff'd 550 F.2d 615 (10th Cir. 1977), respondents consequently argue that the government has failed to establish the relevance of the contested documents to its investigation. I am not inclined to adopt the reasoning of *Coopers & Lybrand.*

I rely upon a close reading of § 7602 to determine that the summoned documents are both relevant and reachable. In furtherance of a legitimate purpose, there is authority to summon *"any * * * person * * * to produce such books, papers, records, and other data as may be relevant or material* to such inquiry." 26 U.S.C. § 7602(2). [Emphasis added]. This expansive language invites, and has generally been accorded, a liberal construction.

It is true that some of the cases cited to me by respondents have made use in tax preparation the touchstone of relevancy. Nevertheless, I do not find that such a result is compelled by the statutory language.

The commonly articulated interpretation of "may be relevant" turns upon "whether the inspection sought 'might have thrown light upon' the correctness of the taxpayer's return." Foster v. United States, 265 F.2d 183, 187 (2d Cir. 1959); see also United States v. Harrington, 388 F.2d 520, 523 (2d Cir. 1968); United States v. Matras, 487 F.2d 1271, 1274 (8th Cir. 1973); United States v. Noall, 587 F.2d 123, 125 (2d Cir. 1978). Subsequent cases have reflected a refinement of "might" expressed in terms of whether there is, in the particular circumstance, "an indication of a realistic expectation rather than an idle hope that something may be discovered." United States v. Harrington, supra at 524; accord United States v. Matras, supra at 1274. The summons was prepared by Special Agent Murphy in cooperation with another Special Agent and two Revenue agents. The Revenue agents had been conducting an examination of Good Hope books and records for some time before Special Agent Murphy entered the case. I find that the collective familiarity of the agents involved in the joint investigation as to Good Hope records will suffice to establish a "realistic expectation" of relevancy. It is clear that expectation need not rise to the level of probable cause in order to justify examination. Special Agent Murphy does not, nor does he need to guarantee relevance in fact in order to satisfy the requirement that the summoned documents "may be relevant."

Respondents have urged, on the authority of United States v. Matras, supra, that relevancy "connotes and encompasses more than 'convenience'." While this may be ture, *Matras* is readily distinguished from the case at hand. In *Matras*, IRS sought budget proposals as a "roadmap" for their investigation; the court properly noted that it was not the proposals but the actual budgets as implemented that had tax consequences. Where, as here, procedures and systems of analysis were applied directly to actual transactions, they are clearly more than "convenient" or a "roadmap" for the joint investigation. Indeed, such evidence of knowledge of potential discrepancies appears to go directly to the heart of determining whether there has been civil or criminal fraud.

There is, in fact, broad support for the position that relevancy does not turn on whether the summoned material was used in preparing tax returns. See e. g. United States v. Noall, supra (audit reports and related workpapers). I am of the opinion that the results in this set of cases better reflect a liberal interpretation of § 7602. The decision in *Noall* is instructive on this point. The Court there initially emphasized that the statutory language is "may be relevant," denoting a low threshold of relevancy. United States v. Noall, supra at 125. In the final analysis, the determination of relevancy in fact must be deferred until the documents are produced and analyzed. While the audit reports found relevant in *Noall* are not at issue here, the underlying rationale for ordering production is particularly persuasive. As expressed by that Court, the "Commissioner's interest lies in whether the tax returns correctly reflected * * * income, not simply whether they were correctly prepared from the books of accounts and other records used." United States v. Noall, supra at 126. On the facts of this case I am satisfied that the information sought "may be" relevant to the investigation, and that *Powell* is satisfied.

* * *

For the above-stated reasons, the Petition to Enforce Internal Revenue Summons is allowed, and the summons shall be enforced according to its original terms.   *   *   *

NOTE

There were two appeals taken from the district court's decision in *Arthur Andersen*. The accountant's appeal was dismissed as moot because the documents had been produced pursuant to the order of the trial court. United States v. Arthur Andersen & Co., 623 F.2d 720 (1st Cir. 1980). The taxpayer's appeal, 623 F.2d 725 (1st Cir. 1980), was based upon the theory that there was still open for decision the issue of whether the accountants could be compelled to testify regarding the documents in issue. In the taxpayer's appeal the First Circuit determined that the issue there presented was not ripe for decision. However, the Court of Appeals expressly noted that the question of whether to compel testimony relating to the documents (over the taxpayer's relevancy objection) is a most difficult one. In the words of the court:

> The importance of the interests of all concerned—taxpayers, accountants, and IRS—is clear. That a resolution sensitively reflecting the legitimate interests of all and faithful to applicable statutes would involve the most delicate and demanding analysis of facts, research of law, and reflection on policy is equally clear. Precisely because we view the issue of "relevance" as so significant, we find this case in a poor posture to serve as the matrix for a precedent.   *   *   *   [623 F.2d at 729.]

D.   INFORMATION NOT WITHIN IRS POSSESSION

UNITED STATES v. PRITCHARD

438 F.2d 969 (5th Cir. 1971).

PER CURIAM:

*   *   *

In March 1968 Vest, a Special Agent of the Internal Revenue Service, advised taxpayers' certified public accountant Hullett that the agent was investigating the Graffeos' tax liabilities for 1960 through 1966. Thereafter, Pritchard [the Graffeos' attorney] acquired possession of the taxpayers' file from Hullett. A summons directed to Pritchard was issued by Special Agent Vest. Pritchard appeared before Vest but refused to testify or produce the papers. There followed enforcement proceedings which   *   *   *   were dismissed by the court.

While it is clear that the burden is on the taxpayer to prove that the summons is being utilized for harassment or is an abuse of the court's process, the Supreme Court has held that the Commissioner

must show that the investigation will be conducted pursuant to a legitimate purpose, that the inquiry may be relevant to the purpose, *that the information sought is not already within the Commissioner's possession,* and that the administrative steps required by the Code have been followed * * *. (Emphasis supplied)

United States v. Powell, 379 U.S. at 57–58, 85 S.Ct. at 255. Neither the Government's petition nor the agent's affidavit made reference to whether the information sought was in the Commissioner's possession.

It is undisputed that prior to the service of the summons on Pritchard, accountant Hullett had met with IRS agent Adams. Hullett testified that Adams had looked at all copies of taxpayers' papers in Hullett's file; that Adams' investigation lasted for several weeks; and that together he and Adams had spent a total of three or four hours examining the file.

It is clear that the information sought by the summons was already within the Commissioner's possession. The judgment of the District Court is

Affirmed.

UNITED STATES v. FIRST NAT'L STATE BANK OF NEW JERSEY

616 F.2d 668 (3d Cir. 1980).

GARTH, Circuit Judge.

* * *

* * * I.R.S. Special Agent John Cassie was investigating the tax liabilities of Perry, Vicki, Myron, and Heidi Levey, jointly referred to as "Levey." In aid of his investigation, he issued several summonses to banks, under the authority of I.R.C. §§ 7602, 7604, for the production of records relevant to the years 1973 through 1976.

* * * The district court * * * enforced the summonses, except as to the banks' retained copies of forms 1099 and 1087.[2] * * * [T]he district court held that forms 1099 and 1087 were already in I.R.S.' possession and therefore could not be obtained by summons under United States v. Powell. While acknowledging that it might be difficult for I.R.S. to retrieve these forms from its files, it held that this burden could not, and should not, be shifted to the banks.

* * *

2. These forms, one copy of which is retained by the preparer, reflect various types of nonwage income paid to taxpayers, such as payments of interest, investment dividends, liquidation distributions, and royalties. Form 1099 is filed by the individual or institution which is the source of the payments. Form 1087 is filed by any merely nominal or record recipient of such income and records distributions from the nominee to the actual recipients of the payments.

The question whether the Internal Revenue Service may obtain by administrative summons the copies of forms 1099 and 1087 retained by third-party recordkeepers appears to be one of first impression. * * * Levey argues that on a literal reading of *Powell*, I.R. S. has "possession" of the information contained in forms 1099 and 1087, since it has already received copies of the forms. We disagree.

As we understand, forms 1099 and 1087 are required to be prepared by those from whom taxpayers have received nonwage income. See note 2 supra. Generally, as they reflect interest income paid by a bank to its depositors or account-holders, or investment dividends paid by corporate entities, at the end of each tax year, the source of the payments will prepare a form 1099 in three copies. Copy A is transmitted to one of ten Internal Revenue Service Centers, copy B is sent to the recipient of the income, and copy C is retained by the payer. A similar procedure is followed by nominees who distribute income; the form filed by nominees is form 1087. The information recorded on the forms, and the filing of the forms, are designed to aid in tax reporting by the taxpayer and tax verification by the Service. Neither form is filed with the taxpayer's income tax return, although the information shown on the forms is intended to be incorporated in the return.

The Government explained at oral argument before us that forms 1099 and 1087 are used for a limited investigative purpose. Forms filed for a randomly selected group of taxpayers are checked against returns filed by those taxpayers for accuracy. Incredibly, all the forms are stored by the Service without any indexing system or method of retrieval. While the forms at issue may technically be deemed within the physical proprietary control of the Government, it is clear that the "information sought" is, as a practical matter, neither accessible to nor available to I.R.S. The clear purpose of *Powell,* as confirmed by the other three showings that must be made by the Government to justify enforcement of a summons (legitimacy of purpose, relevance, compliance with proper procedure), is a desire to prevent abuse of the administrative summons process and harassment of the taxpayer. *Powell* does not address the subject of protection of property rights to pieces of paper. Where resort to an administrative summons is necessary to achieve a lawful goal, i. e., to obtain information not otherwise available, there can be no legitimate charge of "harassment." Thus, *Powell* is no barrier to the enforcement of summonses requiring the production by banks of their copies of forms 1099 and 1087.

This conclusion is supported by other cases that have considered analogous issues. In United States v. Berkowitz, 488 F.2d 1235 (3d Cir. 1973), cert. denied, 421 U.S. 946, 95 S.Ct. 1674, 44 L.Ed.2d 99 (1975), this court enforced an I.R.S. summons to a tax preparer for the names and addresses of all his customers for 1971. We stated:

Even if the corporate appellant had indicated its role on every form which it had prepared, from a practical standpoint those returns would not be readily available to the government since there is no method of retrieval for the 1971 documents. To require the Internal Revenue Service to review individually the millions of forms filed in 1971 is so obviously burdensome as to make the procedure prohibitive. Furthermore, the action of the Berk Tax Service in failing to sign the return secured by pretext naturally leads to suspicion that other customers' returns are similarly deficient and would not be identifiable.

488 F.2d at 1236. In United States v. Theodore, 479 F.2d 749, 755 (4th Cir. 1973), the Fourth Circuit refused to enforce summonses directed to a tax preparer for the returns of all his clients for 1969, 1970, and 1971 because, *inter alia,* there was no record evidence that I.R.S. could not readily retrieve the information:

There is nothing in the record to support the conclusion that when IRS knows the name and social security number of a taxpayer, the Service cannot readily obtain his return. The obligation is upon the Commissioner to demonstrate that the material requested is not within his possession or, that *if it is technically within his possession, he has no practical way of obtaining the desired item.*

Id. (emphasis supplied). Cf. United States v. Schwartz, 469 F.2d 977, 985 (5th Cir. 1972) (where reference would have to be made to voluminous corporate records to locate information, I.R.S. could not be said to be in possession even though an I.R.S. agent had had access to inspect records).

Thus, *Berkowitz, Theodore,* and *Schwartz* support not the taxpayer, but the position taken by the Service, with which we agree. Where the Service requires the production of the name, address, or social security number of a taxpayer and not the particular return, that information must be furnished, and it is no answer to assert, as the taxpayer here has asserted, that the Service "has" this information in its files even though it is incapable of being retrieved. It is but a logical extension, well within the parameters of the rationale of these cases, to hold that this concept similarly applies to the furnishing of retained copies of forms 1099 and 1087. The clear import of these cases is that I.R.S. may obtain such information by summons unless the facts disclose that the summons is not necessary to accomplish I.R.S.' purpose and is therefore being used to harass the taxpayer.

Nor is there any merit to the district court's discourse concerning the relative economic burdens, as between the Service and the banks, of producing the documents. *Powell* sought to prevent harassment, not to shield banks from administrative expenditures. Moreover, and of substantial significance here, no bank in this case ever objected to retrieving the documents which they had retained or to producing them in response to the summonses. Even had there been an "economic objection," I.R.S. stood ready to supply its own personnel to perform the work, at Government cost. As the Government pointed out in its brief:

> In sum, the District Court created an issue which had not been raised by the parties, decided that issue on the basis of its perceptions of the issue rather than evidence, and ignored the holding of this Court in *Berkowitz,* supra, in the process.

Government brief at 11 (footnote omitted).

Thus, we hold that the district court, by construing the *Powell* possession requirement in too literal a fashion, and without regard to the purpose intended to be served by this requirement, erred in not ordering enforcement of the retained copies of forms 1099 and 1087.

* * *

E. ADMINISTRATIVE STEPS FOLLOWED

UNITED STATES v. CRESPO

281 F.Supp. 928 (D.Md.1968).

THOMSEN, Chief Judge.

This is a proceeding brought by the United States and a Special Agent of the Internal Revenue Service (IRS) under sections 7402(b) and 7604(a), IRC, 1954, to compel compliance with two administrative summonses issued to Gustav J. Crespo, as president, and George J. Smith, Jr., as vice president, of Remington Sales Bureau, Incorporated, the taxpayer, demanding their testimony and the production of certain corporate books and records for the period April 1, 1963 through March 31, 1965, alleged to be necessary for a determination of its income tax liabilities for the years ending March 31, 1964 and March 31, 1965.

* * *

The tax returns of the corporate taxpayer for the fiscal years ending March 31, 1963, and March 31, 1964, were assigned in regular course to Henry Weider, a revenue agent, in September 1964. * * * In March 1967 Weider completed his examination for the year ending March 31, 1963, and wrote up reports on that year for the corporation and on the calendar years 1962 and 1963 for Crespo. On April 11, 1967, notices of deficiency were sent to the corporate taxpayer for the fiscal year ending March 31, 1963, and to Crespo et ux. for the calendar years 1962 and 1963. Petitions challenging those deficiencies were filed in the Tax Court by those taxpayers in July 1967; the cases are still pending in that Court.

While working on the aforesaid reports, in March 1967, Weider became aware of the possibility of fraud in connection with the returns of the corporate taxpayer and, in accordance with established practice, suspended his work and referred the matter to the Intelligence Division of the IRS.

A revenue agent, such as Weider, examines income tax returns and determines correct tax liabilities. He is not empowered to investigate criminal tax fraud, and when his examination reveals the possibility of fraud he must suspend his examination and refer the matter to the Intelligence Division for resolution of the fraud question.

When a referral is made to the Intelligence Division, a special agent is assigned to make a preliminary investigation. The primary duties of a special agent are the investigation of possible criminal violations of the income, estate, gift, employment and excise tax statutes, the development of information concerning possible criminal violations of those statutes, the evaluation of such information, and the recommendation of prosecution when warranted.

After a case is referred to a special agent, he may determine that further investigation by the Intelligence Division is not warranted. If, however, he believes that further investigation is warranted, the case becomes a joint investigation with the revenue agent. The special agent, however, is in charge of that investigation. If the investigation develops the probability of criminal fraud, the special agent submits a report recommending prosecution.

The function of the revenue agent in such an investigation is to assist the special agent by advising him of what the revenue agent has previously learned, and by participating in such further examination of the books and records of the taxpayer and others as may be necessary to determine the correct tax liability. The determination of the correct tax liability is an essential part both of the determination by the special agent whether there has been any criminal fraud, and of the determination by the revenue agent of the tax deficiency, if any, and the propriety of assessing civil fraud penalties. The special agent's report of the results of his investigation are made available to the revenue agent to assist him in computing the civil tax liability of the taxpayer under investigation. This information is transmitted to the revenue agent whether or not fraud is found, whether or not prosecution is recommended, and whether or not a conviction is ever obtained. The results of the special agent's investigation will always affect the revenue agent's computation by raising, lowering or verifying the revenue agent's computation.

The Intelligence Division referred this corporate taxpayer's case to Special Agent William N. Jackson. During the course of his investigation, Jackson determined that it was necessary to examine certain corporate books and records of corporate taxpayer pertaining to the tax years involved. On April 19, 1967, in accordance with sections 7602 and 7603, Jackson issued and personally served summonses upon respondent Crespo, as president of corporate taxpayer, and upon Smith, as vice president of the corporation, calling on them to produce certain books and records of corporate taxpayer. Crespo and Smith appeared before Special Agent Jackson pursuant to the summonses issued to them but refused to testify or produce the records demanded. None of the books, records or documents demanded by the summonses are in the possession of the United States or of Special Agent Jackson. Nor, with the exception of two or three cancelled checks, are any copies of the demanded documents in the possession of the government. Special Agent Jackson has not seen any of the books or records demanded.

Respondents contend that the IRS has already conducted one inspection for the tax years in question, so that section 7605(b) prohibits another inspection in the absence of notice from the Secretary. Respondents argue that section 7605(b) * * * contains two separate restrictions: first, "[n]o taxpayer shall be subjected to unnecessary examination or investigations"; second, "only one inspection of a taxpayer's books of account shall be made for each taxable year unless the taxpayer requests otherwise or unless the Secretary or his delegate, after investigation, notifies the taxpayer in writing that an additional inspection is necessary".

Respondents do not contend that taxpayer is being subjected to "unnecessary examinations or investigations". Such an argument would be without merit. Respondents rely only on the absence of a notice from the Secretary or his delegate.

The government argues that the intent and meaning of section 7605(b) is that such a notice is necessary only when the investigation, including a sufficient inspection of the taxpayer's books and records, has been completed and a determination of the tax liability for the year or years in question has been made. * * *

Both sides cite portions of the legislative history to support their respective contentions. However, neither the legislative history nor the few court decisions referring to section 7605(b) which have been cited or found are conclusive of the issue. Most of the cases involved factual situations quite different from that presented in the instant case.

Respondents cited In re Paramount Jewelry Co., 80 F.Supp. 375 (S.D.N.Y.1948), in which the court held that an investigation that had involved an examination of the taxpayer's books three or four times during the past two years should not be halted as unnecessary by vacating a direction that books and records be produced but that, if the taxpayer insisted, it was entitled to receive a notice that an additional inspection was necessary before being required to produce the taxpayer's books for a fourth or fifth time. That case has apparently been cited only once, in Application of Magnus, 196 F.Supp. 127, 128 (S.D.N.Y.1961), where it was summarized substantially as set out above in an opinion dealing with a different question. On appeal in the *Magnus* case, the Second Circuit did not cite the *Paramount Jewelry* case, but noted that an investigation "often requires a long period of time. There may be many ramifications which lead into many areas. Each new clue investigated is not a new investigation in a Section 7605(b) sense." 299 F.2d 335, at 337 (2 Cir. 1962). Similarly, the fact that a revenue agent has seen a cash book, journal or ledger once does not mean that he may not need to see it again for a different purpose.

This Court does not accept the government's position that a notice from the Secretary is never needed unless the investigation, including a sufficient inspection of the taxpayer's books and records, has been completed and a determination made of the tax liability for the year or years in question. When the investigation has not been completed, the question whether a further examination of the books and records would constitute a second "inspection" within the meaning of section 7605(b) depends on the circumstances. If such examination of the books and records is part of a continuing investigation, made necessary by the discovery of invoices, correspondence, or other material which requires the agent to look at the books again, such examination is not a second "inspection" within the meaning of section 7605(b).

The taxpayers and other people of the United States have an interest in seeing that income tax returns are carefully audited, and that revenue agents investigate leads which indicate that a taxpayer has understated his taxable income, intentionally or unintentionally. But taxpayers and other people also have an interest in requiring that the work be done as promptly as is practicable, and that they are not harassed by investigations which are prolonged beyond any reasonable need, or by repeated examinations of their books and records unless such further examinations are required by the discovery or development of new leads.

The Courts are not in a position to require that all agents operate with the same efficiency, or to pass on what individual books and records an agent may re-examine as the result of a new lead. But the Courts should intervene when taxpayers are able to show that agents have abused their discretion in wielding the extensive powers granted to them by the Internal Revenue Code.

In the present case respondents Crespo and Smith did not testify themselves, but rested on the testimony of the two agents. From the evidence the Court finds that by March 1967 Revenue Agent Weider had made a sufficient examination of the corporate taxpayer's books and records for the fiscal year ending March 31, 1963, to be able to complete his report for that year. On the other hand, Revenue Agent Weider has not yet completed his report for the years ending March 31, 1964 and March 31, 1965. He has examined some of taxpayer's records for those years, but has not seen other items, e. g., correspondence with M. C. Ramos, Commercial Envelope Co. and Standard Register Co., nor the purchase invoices of the latter two concerns. He desires, and the evidence shows that he needs, further information with respect to those items, because of various questions which have arisen as to the propriety of certain claimed deductions relating to those transactions.

This Court concludes that the original investigation of the corporation's tax liabilities for the years ending March 31, 1964, and March 31, 1965 is continuing and that the production of the books and records for those taxable years would not amount to a second inspection within the meaning of section 7605(b). Therefore, notice from the Secretary or his delegate to examine taxpayer's books and records for the taxable years ending March 31, 1964 and March 31, 1965 is not required.

* * *

QUESTIONS

1. In the context of an examination, the assertion of a valid second inspection objection to the production of a taxpayer's records should result in the prompt issuance of the required notification. In United States v. Gilpin, 542 F.2d 38 (7th Cir. 1976), the court recognized that the Service can readily remedy a second inspection objection by providing the taxpayer under investigation with the required written notice. (The court also criticized the Service for failing to provide such notice as a matter of course.) What possible benefit can there be to the taxpayer who raises the objection?

2. In those cases in which there is a reasonable debate as to whether there is a continuing, or new, investigation, what reasons (if any) are there for the Service's frequent refusal to issue the second inspection notice?

3. In Reineman v. United States, 301 F.2d 267 (7th Cir. 1962), the taxpayers objected to a second inspection of their 1954 records during an examination of their 1955 return. The agent, without advising that he was doing so, inspected the 1954 records and discovered a potential adjustment to the 1954 return. What remedy, if any, should have been provided to the taxpayer?

4. Although the only "administrative step" mentioned in the *Powell* decision relates to the second inspection notice required in certain cases under § 7605(b), some additional administrative steps must now be complied with under § 7609 (added to the Code by the Tax Reform Act of 1976) in cases involving "third-party recordkeeper" summonses. What remedies are (or should be) available to taxpayers where the IRS fails to follow the § 7609 requirements? See pages 471–478, below, for a general discussion of the third-party recordkeeper summons procedure.

SECTION 3.   THE EVIDENTIARY PRIVILEGES

Any privilege which may be asserted to prevent the compulsory production of testimony or documents is potentially pertinent to a consideration of the enforceability of an IRS summons.   This section covers the two privileges which are most commonly invoked in tax investigations—the attorney-client privilege and the privilege against self-incrimination.

A. THE ATTORNEY–CLIENT PRIVILEGE AND THE WORK–PRODUCT DOCTRINE

(1) ATTORNEYS

The attorney-client privilege, deeply rooted in the common law, provides absolute protection from the compulsory production to the Internal Revenue Service (or any adversary) of those communications which fall within the scope of the privilege.   The work-product doctrine, by comparison, is not a privilege.   This doctrine provides qualified protection from production to those materials which fall within the definition of attorney's work-product.   The protection afforded by the doctrine is overcome upon an adequate showing of necessity and unavailability by the party seeking production.   In many cases, see particularly Upjohn Co. v. United States, below, the same documents must be analyzed in the context of both the attorney-client and the work-product doctrine before it can be determined whether production should be ordered.

COLTON v. UNITED STATES

306 F.2d 633 (2d Cir. 1962).

LUMBARD, Chief Judge.

These appeals raise questions concerning the propriety of a virtually complete refusal by tax counsel, primarily on the ground of the attorney-client privilege, to answer questions and produce files at an examination conducted by special agents of the Internal Revenue Service concerning the tax liability of a client.   *   *   *

At some time prior to July 29, 1960, the Internal Revenue Service began an investigation into the tax liabilities of Herbert Matter and his wife, Mercedes, apparently with a view to possible criminal prosecution.   [On July 29, 1960, the Service summoned Edward Colton, an attorney, and Lillian Kaltman, an attorney associated with Mr. Colton, directing them to appear before special agent Anton Kurtzuk on August 9, 1960 to give testimony and to bring with them and produce "retained copies of income tax returns, workpapers, correspondence files, memoranda and all other data relating to the preparation and the filing of Federal Income Tax Returns for or on the behalf of [the Matters] * * * covering and including the years 1951 through 1958." Prior to the return date of the summons, Colton obtained from the district court an order requiring the government to show cause why the summons should not be quashed or modified and staying compliance. Colton alleged that "the subject matter of Mr. Kurtzuk's proposed inquiry would * * * so flagrantly induce a violation of their duty to the taxpayers arising out of the relationship of attorney and client that this petition was deemed necessary * * *." At the hearing on the petition, Colton testified only that the Matters were clients of his firm, refusing to give any substantial information as to the firm's role, if any, in preparing the tax returns in question. Virtually all of the questions asked were objected to on the basis of the attorney-client privilege. Dissatisfied with the results of the hearing, the government caused the district court to deny the petition to quash and to vacate the stay. Colton and Kaltman bring these appeals. |

* * *

At the outset, we reiterate our view, stated in In re Albert Lindley Lee Memorial Hospital, 209 F.2d 122 (2 Cir. 1953), cert. denied, 347 U.S. 960, 74 S.Ct. 709, 98 L.Ed. 1104 (1954), that questions of privilege in a federal income tax investigation are matters of federal law. See Falsone v. United States, 205 F.2d 734 (5 Cir.), cert. denied, 346 U.S. 864, 74 S.Ct. 103, 98 L.Ed. 375 (1953). For the reasons stated in our *Albert Lindley Lee Memorial Hospital* opinion, we do not agree with the Court of Appeals for the Ninth Circuit, Baird v. Koerner, 279 F.2d 623 (1960), that a hearing held by the Internal Revenue Service under § 7602 of the Internal Revenue Code of 1954 is a "civil action" governed by state evidence law under Rule 43(a) of the Federal Rules of Civil Procedure, 28 U.S.C.A., or that state law should govern for any other reason.

Those questions which pertain to the date and general nature of the legal services performed by the Colton firm for the Matters should be answered as they do not call for any confidential communication. * * * Question 80 asks, "Did you or any member of your firm cause to have prepared a 1953 income tax return for or on behalf of Herbert and Mercedes Matter in 1954?"

This court has accepted, and few if any lawyers would quarrel with, Dean Wigmore's statement of the basic principle underlying the attorney-client privilege:

> "In order to promote freedom of consultation of legal advisers by clients, the apprehension of compelled disclosure by the legal advisers must be removed; hence the law must

prohibit such disclosure except on the client's consent." 8
Wigmore, Evidence § 2291 (McNaughton rev. 1961).

It cannot be seriously argued that this policy justifies any member of
the bar from refusing to testify as to all transactions he may have
had with any person whom he chooses to designate a "client." Thus,
according to Judge Wyzanski's much quoted formulation, it must be
shown that:

> "(1) the asserted holder of the privilege is or sought to
> become a client; (2) the person to whom the communica-
> tion was made (a) is a member of the bar of a court, or his
> subordinate and (b) in connection with this communication
> is acting as a lawyer; (3) the communication relates to a
> fact of which the attorney was informed (a) by his client
> (b) without the presence of strangers (c) for the purpose of
> securing primarily either (i) an opinion on law or (ii) legal
> services or (iii) assistance in some legal proceeding, and not
> (d) for the purpose of committing a crime or tort; and (4)
> the privilege has been (a) claimed and (b) not waived by
> the client." United States v. United Shoe Mach. Corp., 89
> F.Supp. 357, 358–59 (D.Mass.1950).

There can, of course, be no question that the giving of tax advice
and the preparation of tax returns—which unquestionably constituted
a very substantial part of the legal services rendered the Matters by
the Colton firm—are basically matters sufficiently within the professional competence of an attorney to make them prima facie subject to
the attorney-client privilege. See United States v. Kovel, 296 F.2d
918 (2 Cir. 1961). But, although the word "communications" must
be broadly interpreted in this context, the authorities are clear that
the privilege extends essentially only to the substance of matters
communicated to an attorney in professional confidence. Thus the
identity of a client, or the fact that a given individual has become a
client are matters which an attorney normally may not refuse to disclose, even though the fact of having retained counsel may be used as
evidence against the client. To be sure, there may be circumstances
under which the identification of a client may amount to the prejudicial disclosure of a confidential communication, as where the substance of a disclosure has already been revealed but not its source.
See, e. g., In re Kaplan, 8 N.Y.2d 214, 203 N.Y.S.2d 836, 168 N.E.2d
660 (1960); Baird v. Koerner, 279 F.2d 623 (9 Cir. 1960).

We find, however, no such special circumstances in the case at
bar. Nor was the permissible inquiry in this regard ended when Colton stated that the Matters were his clients and had been for some
time. The principle that permits inquiry into the existence of a professional relationship obviously also permits questioning as to the
years during which the relationship has continued. * * *

For similar reasons there was no basis for Colton's refusal to state, in answer to Question 55, whether he had received any remuneration from the Matters for legal services rendered during the years 1954 through 1957. Although no question as to the relevancy of the matters inquired into is before us, we note that the government states that this question is relevant to a determination whether the attorney-client relationship actually existed, as well as to the propriety of deductions for legal fees taken by the taxpayers in their returns for those years. Such matters are surely relevant, and—in the absence of allegations as to special circumstances—we see no reason why an attorney should be any less subject to questioning about fees received from a taxpayer than should any other person who has dealt with the taxpayer. There is no further encroachment here upon any confidential relationship than there is in questioning about the existence or date of the relationship. All these matters are quite separate and apart from the substance of anything that the client may have revealed to the attorney.

Moreover, a determination whether Colton rendered legal services to the Matters in a given year is proper as a basis for obtaining further unprivileged information from him. Not all communications between an attorney and his client are privileged. Particularly in the case of an attorney preparing a tax return (as the questioning agent attempted to establish Colton did for the Matters), a good deal of information transmitted to an attorney by a client is not intended to be confidential, but rather is given for transmittal by the attorney to others—for example, for inclusion in the tax return. Such information is, of course, not priviledged.

It was also proper for agent Kurtzuk, in Questions 16 and 18, to inquire into the nature of the "legal services" rendered by Colton. Attorneys frequently give to their clients business or other advice which, at least insofar as it can be separated from their essentially professional legal services, gives rise to no privilege whatever. Indeed, Colton admitted at the Service hearing that he sometimes gave "a little investment advice" to his clients. Because Colton's work for the Matters—both legal and non-legal—may thus have involved unprivileged communications with them, it is proper for the Service in its search for unprivileged matters not only to inquire into the years during which he rendered "legal services" but also to explore, as it does in Questions 16 and 18, to some extent the nature of the services rendered. These questions are appropriate to a determination of what, if any, areas may be inquired into further and what is protected by the attorney-client privilege. * * *

The remaining questions, which pertain to documents and files, can be subdivided into two categories. The colloquy relating to Questions 22, 73, 74 and 75 reflects Colton's total refusal, on grounds of the attorney-client privilege, to produce "retained copies of income tax returns, workpapers, correspondence, memoranda and all other data pertaining to the preparation and filing of the [returns in question] * * * " and the fact that before and after the first hearing before the Service the firm had returned some of these papers to the Matters. The remaining questions inquire into the general nature of the papers presently or formerly in the firm's possession.

* * *

It is self-evident that individual documents and files may still be withheld insofar as they thus are or report confidential communications between Colton and his clients, the Matters. Documentary evidence of confidential communications is necessarily privileged as much as testimonial evidence. Moreover, if a proper showing is made, Colton will be able to raise the Matters' privilege against self-incrimination as a basis for refusing to produce any independently pre-existing records or other documents turned over to the firm by the Matters if the Matters could have refused to produce them under that privilege.

Clearly Colton's blanket refusal on the grounds of the attorney-client privilege to produce anything was unjustified. As we have noted, the attorney-client privilege protects only those papers prepared by the client for the purpose of confidential communication to the attorney or by the attorney to record confidential communications, and Colton has not made the necessary showing that the papers he refused to produce are of such nature.

Insofar as the papers include pre-existing documents and financial records not prepared by the Matters for the purpose of communicating with their lawyers in confidence, their contents have acquired no special protection from the simple fact of being turned over to an attorney. It is only if the client could have refused to produce such papers that the attorney may do so when they have passed into his possession. Any other rule would permit a person to prevent disclosure of any of his papers by the simple expedient of keeping them in the possession of his attorney.

Appellant admits in his brief that statements, correspondence, and documents received from third parties are not protected by the attorney-client privilege, and the principle is obvious. Hickman v. Taylor, 329 U.S. 495, 508, 67 S.Ct. 385, 91 L.Ed. 451 (1947). He argues, however, that in any event such papers are wholly unavailable to the government under the "work product" rule which the Supreme Court in Hickman v. Taylor, supra, held justified an attorney's refusal to permit discovery in a civil case of statements obtained by him from prospective witnesses. We need not reach the government's contention that the work-product rule is inapplicable to such administrative investigations as that conducted by the Internal Revenue Service here, because Colton has made no suggestion that any of the papers involved were collected or prepared in anticipation of litigation, as must be shown to justify invocation of this rule.

Because Colton was unjustified in his blanket refusal to produce all of his firm's papers concerning the Matters, it was, of course, appropriate for agent Kurtzuk to question him at the hearing concerning the nature of the papers in order to determine which of them were and which were not privileged. All of the remaining questions are relevant to the government's proper attempt to uncover papers not protected under the attorney-client privilege. * * * Thus these questions must be answered and the materials they refer to must be produced.

The orders of the district court are affirmed.

BAIRD v. KOERNER

279 F.2d 623 (9th Cir. 1960).

BARNES, Circuit Judge.

Appellee, as Special Agent of the United States Internal Revenue Service, sought by his petition the aid of the district court (28 U.S.C. §§ 1340, 1345) to enforce a summons and compel testimony (26 U.S.C. § 7402) at an inquiry as to the identity of a person who might be liable to pay an internal revenue tax (26 U.S.C. §§ 7601–7605). He received such aid. The district court ordered appellant Alva C. Baird to answer a certain question. Baird refused to answer.

This is an appeal from a judgment of civil contempt and an order committing Baird to custody because of his refusal to answer that question (as to the identity of his clients) * * *.

Specifically, appellant was asked, and refused to answer, as to the "identity and addresses of each and every person who employed appellant in connection with his transmittal of a cashier's check in the sum of $12,706.85 to the Director of Internal Revenue at Baltimore, Md." Appellant based his refusal on various grounds, but primarily on the privilege existing between attorney and client. As government counsel stated in oral argument, the one real issue is: *Is there here a valid claim of the attorney-client privilege?*

* * *

We conclude there is no federal body of law that *requires* the exclusion of the identity of the client from the extent of the attorney-client privilege. We believe it must be assessed on a case to case basis, depending on the particular facts of each case. We recognize that the policy of full disclosure is a "more fundamental one" than the policy of the attorney-client privilege; that the latter is not universally regarded as absolute, and is to be strictly limited to the purposes for which it exists. VIII Wigmore on Evidence § 2291, p. 557. If the identification of the client conveys information which ordinarily would be conceded to be part of the usual privileged communication between attorney and client, then the privilege should extend to such identification in the absence of other factors. Such factors are

(a) the commencing of litigation on behalf of the client where he voluntarily subjects himself to the jurisdiction of the court; (b) an identification relating to an employment by some third person, not the client nor his agent; (c) an employment of an attorney with respect to *future* criminal or fraudulent transactions; (d) the attorney himself being a defendant in a criminal matter. In none of these categories, and perhaps not in others, would the suppressing of some truth, so that the general process of administering justice may be furthered, outweigh the desirability of the rule of privilege; itself an exception to the general view "that the fullest disclosure of the facts will best lead to the truth and ultimately to the triumph of justice." In re Selser, 1954, 15 N.J. 393, 105 A.2d 395, 401.

In summation, we find (1) that because the relationship of client and attorney is created and controlled by the law of the various states; and that such creation and control is recognized, followed, and approved by the federal courts, the nature and extent of the privilege created between a lawyer and his client by the attorney-client relationship requires the federal courts to follow the state law; (2) that some considerable number of federal cases enunciate the rule that the state law governs the rule of privilege; (3) that some federal cases apply the law of the forum state, but do so without enunciating the principle under which they act; (4) that no federal statute forbids the use of the law of the forum state, and that if there is any definite rule set up by federal statute, it requires us to follow the law of the forum state, and (5) any federal "common law" which may exist does not require us to ignore the forum state law; (6) that general policy considerations applicable to the law of privilege between attorney and client support the rule of privilege in this case; (7) that each case must stand on its own facts, with the courts balancing the public policy considerations involved, and we hold the law of the forum state should, and does control—here the State of California.

We next examine the California law. Appellee asserts that while the federal "common law as to privilege" controls, were the law of California to govern, the result would be no different. This rests on the government's position that Brunner v. Superior Court, 1959, 51 Cal.2d 616, 335 P.2d 484, overrules Ex parte McDonough, 1915, 170 Cal. 230, 149 P. 566, L.R.A.1916C, 593. We think not.

* * *

We hold that Ex parte McDonough, supra, states the law of California,[18] and Brunner v. Superior Court, supra, does not, under

18. "However desirable it may be to obtain proofs sufficient to insure the conviction of all persons who commit crimes * * * such proofs may not be obtained from those who are forbidden by law to give them. In regard to the obligation of an attorney to his client in this respect, our statutes are very explicit, making it his [the attorney's] duty to 'maintain inviolate the confidence, and at every peril to himself, to preserve the secrets of his client.' * * *

the facts existing here. Under those facts, an attorney cannot be compelled to state the names of clients who employed him to voluntarily mail sums of money to the government in payment of undetermined income taxes, unsued on, and with no government audit or investigation into that client's income tax liability pending.

*   *   *

The judgment of the lower court is reversed so far as it orders appellant Baird to reveal any information regarding the persons who employed him, and affirmed as to those questions which it held appellant Baird need not answer.

UPJOHN CO. v. UNITED STATES

Supreme Court of the United States, 1981.
— U.S. —, 101 S.Ct. 677, 66 L.Ed.2d 584.

Justice REHNQUIST delivered the opinion of the Court.

We granted certiorari in this case to address important questions concerning the scope of the attorney-client privilege in the corporate context and the applicability of the work-product doctrine in proceedings to enforce tax summonses. With respect to the privilege question the parties and various *amici* have described our task as one of choosing between two "tests" which have gained adherents in the courts of appeals. We are acutely aware, however, that we sit to decide concrete cases and not abstract propositions of law. We decline to lay down a broad rule or series of rules to govern all conceivable future questions in this area, even were we able to do so. We can and do, however, conclude that the attorney-client privilege protects the communications involved in this case from compelled disclosure and that the work-product doctrine does apply in tax summons enforcement proceedings.

I

Petitioner Upjohn manufactures and sells pharmaceuticals here and abroad. In January 1976 independent accountants conducting an audit of one of petitioner's foreign subsidiaries discovered that the subsidiary made payments to or for the benefit of foreign govern-

"*   *   *   We cannot escape the conclusion that, in view of the findings of the lower court, to require the petitioner [attorney] to answer any of the questions as to the name of the client who employed him to defend Higgins et al. would be to require him to divulge a confidential communication made to him by a client in the course of his employment—a communication tending to show, and, under the circumstances of this case, material only for the purpose of showing, an acknowledgment of guilt on the part of such client of the very offenses on account of which the attorney had been employed to defend him."

Ex parte McDonough, supra, 170 Cal. at pages 233, 236–237, 149 P. at page 566.

*   *   *

ment officials in order to secure government business. The accountants, so informed Mr. Gerard Thomas, petitioner's Vice-President, Secretary, and General Counsel. Thomas is a member of the Michigan and New York bars, and has been petitioner's General Counsel for 20 years. He consulted with outside counsel and R. T. Parfet, Jr., petitioner's Chairman of the Board. It was decided that the company would conduct an internal investigation of what were termed "questionable payments." As part of this investigation the attorneys prepared a letter containing a questionnaire which was sent to "all foreign general and area managers" over the Chairman's signature. The letter began by noting recent disclosures that several American companies made "possibly illegal" payments to foreign government officials and emphasized that the management needed full information concerning any such payments made by Upjohn. The letter indicated that the Chairman had asked Thomas, identified as "the company's General Counsel," "to conduct an investigation for the purpose of determining the nature and magnitude of any payments made by the Upjohn Company or any of its subsidiaries to any employee or official of a foreign government." The questionnaire sought detailed information concerning such payments. Managers were instructed to treat the investigation as "highly confidential" and not to discuss it with anyone other than Upjohn employees who might be helpful in providing the requested information. Responses were to be sent directly to Thomas. Thomas and outside counsel also interviewed the recipients of the questionnaire and some 33 other Upjohn officers or employees as part of the investigation.

On March 26, 1976, the company voluntarily submitted a preliminary report to the Securities and Exchange Commission on Form 8–K disclosing certain questionable payments. A copy of the report was simultaneously submitted to the Internal Revenue Service, which immediately began an investigation to determine the tax consequences of the payments. Special agents conducting the investigation were given lists by Upjohn of all those interviewed and all who had responded to the questionnaire. On November 23, 1976, the Service issued a summons pursuant to 26 U.S.C. § 7602 demanding production of:

> "All files relative to the investigation conducted under the supervision of Gerard Thomas to identify payments to employees of foreign governments and any political contributions made by the Upjohn Company or any of its affiliates since January 1, 1971 and to determine whether any funds of the Upjohn Company had been improperly accounted for on the corporate books during the same period.

> "The records should include but not be limited to written questionnaires sent to managers of the Upjohn Company's foreign affiliates, and memoranda or notes of the inter-

views conducted in the United States and abroad with officers and employees of the Upjohn Company and its subsidiaries."

The company declined to produce the documents specified in the second paragraph on the grounds that they were protected from disclosure by the attorney-client privilege and constituted the work product of attorneys prepared in anticipation of litigation. On August 31, 1977, the United States filed a petition seeking enforcement of the summons under 26 U.S.C. §§ 7402(b) and 7604(a) in the United States District Court for the Western District of Michigan. That court adopted the recommendation of a magistrate who concluded that the summons should be enforced. Petitioner appealed to the Court of Appeals for the Sixth Circuit which rejected the magistrate's finding of a waiver of the attorney-client privilege, but agreed that the privilege did not apply "to the extent the communications were made by officers and agents not responsible for directing Upjohn's actions in response to legal advice * * * for the simple reason that the communications were not the 'client's.' " The court reasoned that accepting petitioner's claim for a broader application of the privilege would encourage upper-echelon management to ignore unpleasant facts and create too broad a "zone of silence." Noting that petitioner's counsel had interviewed officials such as the Chairman and President, the Court of Appeals remanded to the District Court so that a determination of who was within the "control group" could be made. In a concluding footnote the court stated that the work-product doctrine "is not applicable to administrative summonses issued under 26 U.S.C. § 7602."

II

Federal Rule of Evidence 501 provides that "the privilege of a witness * * * shall be governed by the principles of the common law as they may be interpreted by the courts of the United States in light of reason and experience." The attorney-client privilege is the oldest of the privileges for confidential communications known to the common law. 8 Wigmore, Evidence § 2290 (McNaughton rev. 1961). Its purpose is to encourage full and frank communication between attorneys and their clients and thereby promote broader public interests in the observance of law and administration of justice. The privilege recognizes that sound legal advice or advocacy serves public ends and that such advice or advocacy depends upon the lawyer being fully informed by the client. As we stated last Term in Trammel v. United States, 445 U.S. 40, 51, 100 S.Ct. 906, 913, 63 L.Ed.2d 186 (1980), "The attorney-client privilege rests on the need for the advocate and counselor to know all that relates to the client's reasons for seeking representation if the professional mission is to be carried out." And in Fisher v. United States, 425 U.S. 391, 403, 96 S.Ct. 1569, 1577, 48 L.Ed.2d 39 (1976), we recognized the purpose of the privilege to be "to encourage clients to make full disclosures to their attorneys." This rationale for the privilege has long been recognized by the Court, see Hunt v. Blackburn, 128 U.S. 464, 470, 9 S.Ct. 125, 127, 32 L.Ed. 488 (1888) (privilege "is founded upon the necessity, in the interest and administration of justice, of the aid of persons having knowledge of the law and skilled in its practice, which assistance can only be safely and readily availed of when free from the consequences or the apprehension of disclosure"). Admittedly complications in the application of the privilege arise when the client is a corporation, which in theory is an artificial creature of the law, and not an individual; but this Court has assumed that the privilege applies when the client is a corporation. United States v. Louisville & Nashville R. Co., 236 U.S. 318, 336, 35 S.Ct. 363, 369, 59 L.Ed. 598 (1915), and the Government does not contest the general proposition.

The Court of Appeals, however, considered the application of the privilege in the corporate context to present a "different problem," since the client was an inanimate entity and "only the senior management, guiding and integrating the several operations, * * * can be said to possess an identity analogous to the corporation as a whole." The first case to articulate the so-called "control group test" adopted by the court below, City of Philadelphia v. Westinghouse Electric Corp., 210 F.Supp. 483, 485 (ED Pa.), petition for mandamus and prohibition denied, General Electric Company v. Kirkpatrick, 312 F.2d 742 (CA3 1962), cert. denied, 372 U.S. 943, 83 S.Ct. 937, 9 L.Ed. 2d 969 (1963), reflected a similar conceptual approach:

> "Keeping in mind that the question is, Is it the corporation which is seeking the lawyer's advice when the asserted privileged communication is made?, the most satisfactory solution, I think, is that if the employee making the communication, of whatever rank he may be, is in a position to control or even to take a substantial part in a decision about any action which the corporation may take upon the advice of the attorney, * * * then, in effect, *he is (or personifies) the corporation* when he makes his disclosure to the lawyer and the privilege would apply." (Emphasis supplied.)

Such a view, we think, overlooks the fact that the privilege exists to protect not only the giving of professional advice to those who can act on it but also the giving of information to the lawyer to enable him to give sound and informed advice. See *Trammel,* 445 U.S., at 51, 100 S.Ct., at 913; *Fisher,* 425 U.S., at 403, 96 S.Ct. at 1577. The first step in the resolution of any legal problem is ascertaining the factual background and sifting through the facts with an eye to the legally relevant. See ABA Code of Professional Responsibility, Ethical Consideration 4–1:

> "A lawyer should be fully informed of all the facts of the matter he is handling in order for his client to obtain the

full advantage of our legal system. It is for the lawyer in the exercise of his independent professional judgment to separate the relevant and important from the irrelevant and unimportant. The observance of the ethical obligation of a lawyer to hold inviolate the confidences and secrets of his client not only facilitates the full development of facts essential to proper representation of the client but also encourages laymen to seek early legal assistance."

See also Hickman v. Taylor, 329 U.S. 495, 511, 67 S.Ct. 385, 393–394, 91 L.Ed. 451 (1947).

In the case of the individual client the provider of information and the person who acts on the lawyer's advice are one and the same. In the corporate context, however, it will frequently be employees beyond the control group as defined by the court below—"officers and agents * * * responsible for directing [the company's] actions in response to legal advice"—who will possess the information needed by the corporation's lawyers. Middle-level—and indeed lower-level—employees can, by actions within the scope of their employment, embroil the corporation in serious legal difficulties, and it is only natural that these employees would have the relevant information needed by corporate counsel if he is adequately to advise the client with respect to such actual or potential difficulties. This fact was noted in Diversified Industries, Inc. v. Meredith, 572 F.2d 596 (CA8 1978) (en banc):

"In a corporation, it may be necessary to glean information relevant to a legal problem from middle management or non-management personnel as well as from top executives. The attorney dealing with a complex legal problem 'is thus faced with a "Hobson's choice." If he interviews employees not having "the very highest authority" their communications to him will not be privileged. If, on the other hand, he interviews *only* those employees with the "very highest authority," he may find it extremely difficult, if not impossible, to determine what happened.' " Id., at 608–609 (quoting Weinschel Corporate Employee Interviews and the Attorney-Client Privilege, 12 B.C.Ind. & Comm.L.Rev. 873, 876 (1970).

The control group test adopted by the court below thus frustrates the very purpose of the privilege by discouraging the communication of relevant information by employees of the client to attorneys seeking to render legal advice to the client corporation. The attorney's advice will also frequently be more significant to noncontrol group members than to those who officially sanction the advice, and the control group test makes it more difficult to convey full and frank legal advice to the employees who will put into effect the client corporation's policy. See, e. g., Duplan Corp. v. Deering Milliken,

Inc., 397 F.Supp. 1146, 1164 (DSC 1974) ("After the lawyer forms his or her opinion, it is of no immediate benefit to the Chairman of the Board or the President. It must be given to the corporate personnel who will apply it.").

The narrow scope given the attorney-client privilege by the court below not only makes it difficult for corporate attorneys to formulate sound advice when their client is faced with a specific legal problem but also threatens to limit the valuable efforts of corporate counsel to ensure their client's compliance with the law. In light of the vast and complicated array of regulatory legislation confronting the modern corporation, corporations, unlike most individuals, "constantly go to lawyers to find out how to obey the law," Burnham, The Attorney-Client Privilege in the Corporate Arena, 24 Bus.Law. 901, 913 (1969), particularly since compliance with the law in this area is hardly an instinctive matter, see, e. g., United States v. United States Gypsum Co., 438 U.S. 422, 440–441, 98 S.Ct. 2864, 2875–2876, 57 L. Ed.2d 854 (1978) ("the behavior proscribed by the [Sherman] Act is often difficult to distinguish from the gray zone of socially acceptable and economically justifiable business conduct").[2] The test adopted by the court below is difficult to apply in practice, though no abstractly formulated and unvarying "test" will necessarily enable courts to decide questions such as this with mathematical precision. But if the purpose of the attorney-client privilege is to be served, the attorney and client must be able to predict with some degree of certainty whether particular discussions will be protected. An uncertain privilege, or one which purports to be certain but results in widely varying applications by the courts, is little better than no privilege at all. The very terms of the test adopted by the court below suggest the unpredictability of its application. The test restricts the availability of the privilege to those officers who play a "substantial role" in deciding and directing a corporation's legal response. Disparate decisions in cases applying this test illustrate its unpredictability.

The communications at issue were made by Upjohn employees[3] to counsel for Upjohn acting as such, at the direction of corporate su-

2. The Government argues that the risk of civil or criminal liability suffices to ensure that corporations will seek legal advice in the absence of the protection of the privilege. This response ignores the fact that the depth and quality of any investigations, to ensure compliance with the law would suffer, even were they undertaken. The response also proves too much, since it applies to all communications covered by the privilege: an individual trying to comply with the law or faced with a legal problem also has strong incentive to disclose information to his lawyer, yet the common law has recognized the value of the privilege in further facilitating communications.

3. Seven of the 86 employees interviewed by counsel had terminated their employment with Upjohn at the time of the interview. Petitioner argues that the privilege should nonetheless apply to communications by these former employees concerning activities during their period of employment. Neither the District Court nor the Court of Appeals had occasion to address this issue, and we decline to decide it without the benefit of treatment below.

periors in order to secure legal advice from counsel. As the magistrate found, "Mr. Thomas consulted with the Chairman of the Board and outside counsel and thereafter conducted a factual investigation to determine the nature and extent of the questionable payments *and to be in a position to give legal advice to the company with respect to the payments.*" (Emphasis supplied.) Information, not available from upper-echelon management, was needed to supply a basis for legal advice concerning compliance with securities and tax laws, foreign laws, currency regulations, duties to shareholders, and potential litigation in each of these areas. The communications concerned matters within the scope of the employees' corporate duties, and the employees themselves were sufficiently aware that they were being questioned in order that the corporation could obtain legal advice. The questionnaire identified Thomas as "the company's General Counsel" and referred in its opening sentence to the possible illegality of payments such as the ones on which information was sought. A statement of policy accompanying the questionnaire clearly indicated the legal implications of the investigation. The policy statement was issued "in order that there be no uncertainty in the future as to the policy with respect to the practices which are the subject of this investigation." It began "Upjohn will comply with all laws and regulations," and stated that commissions or payments "will not be used as a subterfuge for bribes or illegal payments" and that all payments must be "proper and legal." Any future agreements with foreign distributors or agents were to be approved "by a company attorney" and any questions concerning the policy were to be referred "to the company's General Counsel." This statement was issued to Upjohn employees worldwide, so that even those interviewees not receiving a questionnaire were aware of the legal implications of the interviews. Pursuant to explicit instructions from the Chairman of the Board, the communications were considered "highly confidential" when made and have been kept confidential by the company.[5] Consistent with the underlying purposes of the attorney-client privilege, these communications must be protected against compelled disclosure.

The Court of Appeals declined to extend the attorney-client privilege beyond the limits of the control group test for fear that doing so would entail severe burdens on discovery and create a broad "zone of silence" over corporate affairs. Application of the attorney-client privilege to communications such as those involved here, however, puts the adversary in no worse position than if the communications had never taken place. The privilege only protects disclosure of com-

---

5. See magistrate's opinion: "The responses to the questionnaires and the notes of the interviews have been treated as confidential material and have not been disclosed to anyone except Mr. Thomas and outside counsel."

munications; it does not protect disclosure of the underlying facts by those who communicated with the attorney:

> "The protection of the privilege extends only to *communications* and not to facts. A fact is one thing and a communication concerning that fact is an entirely different thing. The client cannot be compelled to answer the question, 'What did you say or write to the attorney?' but may not refuse to disclose any relevant fact within his knowledge merely because he incorporated a statement of such fact into his communication to his attorney." City of Philadelphia v. Westinghouse Electric Corp., 205 F.Supp. 830, 831 (ED Pa. 1962).

Here the Government was free to question the employees who communicated with Thomas and outside counsel. Upjohn has provided the IRS with a list of such employees, and the IRS has already interviewed some 25 of them. While it would probably be more convenient for the Government to secure the results of petitioner's internal investigation by simply subpoenaing the questionnaires and notes taken by petitioner's attorneys, such considerations of convenience do not overcome the policies served by the attorney-client privilege. As Justice Jackson noted in his concurring opinion in Hickman v. Taylor, 329 U.S., at 516, 67 S.Ct., at 396: "Discovery was hardly intended to enable a learned profession to perform its functions * * * on wits borrowed from the adversary."

Needless to say, we decide only the case before us, and do not undertake to draft a set of rules which should govern challenges to investigatory subpoenas. Any such approach would violate the spirit of F.R.E. 501. While such a "case-by-case" basis may to some slight extent undermine desirable certainty in the boundaries of the attorney-client privilege, it obeys the spirit of the Rules. At the same time we conclude that the narrow "control group test" sanctioned by the Court of Appeals, in this case cannot, consistent with "the principles of the common law as * * * interpreted * * * in light of reason and experience," F.R.E. 501, govern the development of the law in this area.

III

Our decision that the communications by Upjohn employees to counsel are covered by the attorney-client privilege disposes of the case so far as the responses to the questionnaires and any notes reflecting responses to interview questions are concerned. The summons reaches further, however, and Thomas has testified that his notes and memoranda of interviews go beyond recording responses to his questions. To the extent that the material subject to the summons is not protected by the attorney-client privilege as disclosing communications between an employee and counsel, we must reach the rulings by the Court of Appeals that the work-product doctrine does not apply to summonses issued under 26 U.S.C. § 7602.[6]

The Government concedes, wisely, that the Court of Appeals erred and that the work-product doctrine does apply to IRS summonses. This doctrine was announced by the Court over 30 years ago in Hickman v. Taylor, 329 U.S. 495, 67 S.Ct. 385, 91 L.Ed. 451 (1947). In that case the Court rejected "an attempt, without purported necessity or justification, to secure written statements, private memoranda, and personal recollections prepared or formed by an adverse party's counsel in the course of his legal duties." Id., at 510, 67 S.Ct., at 393. The Court noted that "it is essential that a lawyer work with a certain degree of privacy" and reasoned that if discovery of the material sought were permitted

"much of what is now put down in writing would remain unwritten. An attorney's thoughts, heretofore inviolate, would not be his own. Inefficiency, unfairness and sharp practices would inevitably develop in the giving of legal advice and in the preparation of cases for trial. The effect on the legal profession would be demoralizing. And the interests of the clients and the cause of justice would be poorly served." Id., at 511, 67 S.Ct., at 393–394.

The "strong public policy" underlying the work-product doctrine was reaffirmed recently in United States v. Nobles, 422 U.S. 225, 236–240, 95 S.Ct. 2160, 2169–2171, 45 L.Ed.2d 141 (1975), and has been substantially incorporated in Federal Rule of Civil Procedure 26(b)(3).

As we stated last Term, the obligation imposed by a tax summons remains "subject to the traditional privileges and limitations." United States v. Euge, 444 U.S. 707, 714, 100 S.Ct. 874, 879–880, 63 L.Ed.2d 741 (1980). Nothing in the language of the IRS summons provisions or their legislative history suggests an intent on the part of Congress to preclude application of the work-product doctrine. Rule 26(b)(3) codifies the work-product doctrine, and the Federal Rules of Civil Procedure are made applicable to summons enforcement proceedings by Rule 81(a)(3). See Donaldson v. United States, 400 U.S. 517, 528, 91 S.Ct. 534, 541, 27 L.Ed.2d 580 (1971). While conceding the applicability of the work-product doctrine, the Government asserts that it has made a sufficient showing of necessity to overcome its protections. The magistrate apparently so found. The Government relies on the following language in Hickman:

"We do not mean to say that all written materials obtained or prepared by an adversary's counsel with an eye toward litigation are necessarily free from discovery in all cases.

6. The following discussion will also be relevant to counsels' notes and memoranda of interviews with the seven former employees should it be determined that the attorney-client privilege does not apply to them. See n. 3, supra.

> Where relevant and nonprivileged facts remain hidden in an attorney's file and where production of those facts is essential to the preparation of one's case, discovery may properly be had * * *. And production might be justified where the witnesses are no longer available or may be reached only with difficulty." 329 U.S., at 511, 67 S.Ct., at 394.

The Government stresses that interviewees are scattered across the globe and that Upjohn has forbidden its employees to answer questions it considers irrelevant. The above-quoted language from *Hickman,* however, did not apply to "oral statements made by witnesses * * * whether presently in the form of [the attorney's] mental impressions or memoranda." Id., at 512, 67 S.Ct., at 394. As to such material the Court did "not believe that any showing of necessity can be made under the circumstances of this case so as to justify production * * *. If there should be a rare situation justifying production of these matters petitioner's case is not of that type." Id., at 512–513, 67 S.Ct., at 394–395. See also *Nobles,* supra, 422 U.S., at 252–253, 95 S.Ct., at 2177 (WHITE, J., concurring). Forcing an attorney to disclose notes and memoranda of witnesses' oral statements is particularly disfavored because it tends to reveal the attorney's mental processes, 329 U.S., at 513, 67 S.Ct., at 394–395 ("what he saw fit to write down regarding witnesses' remarks"); id., at 516–517, 67 S.Ct., at 396 ("the statement would be his [the attorney's] language, permeated with his inferences") (Jackson, J., concurring).[8]

Rule 26 accords special protection to work product revealing the attorney's mental processes. The Rule permits disclosure of documents and tangible things constituting attorney work product upon a showing of substantial need and inability to obtain the equivalent without undue hardship. This was the standard applied by the magistrate. Rule 26 goes on, however, to state that "[i]n ordering discovery of such materials when the required showing has been made, the court shall protect against disclosure of the mental impressions, conclusions, opinions or legal theories of an attorney or other representative of a party concerning the litigation." Although this language does not specifically refer to memoranda based on oral statements of witnesses, the *Hickman* court stressed the danger that compelled disclosure of such memoranda would reveal the attorney's mental processes. It is clear that this is the sort of material the draftsmen of the Rule had in mind as deserving special protection.

Based on the foregoing, some courts have concluded that *no* showing of necessity can overcome protection of work product which

---

8. Thomas described his notes of the interviews as containing "what I consider to be the important questions, the substance of the responses to them, my beliefs as to the importance of these, my beliefs as to how they related to the inquiry, my thoughts as to how they related to other questions. In some instances they might even suggest other questions that I would have to ask or things that I needed to find elsewhere."

is based on oral statements from witnesses. See, e. g., In re Grand Jury Proceedings, 473 F.2d 840, 848 (CA8 1973) (personal recollections, notes and memoranda pertaining to conversation with witnesses); In re Grand Jury Investigation, 412 F.Supp. 943, 949 (ED Pa. 1976) (notes of conversation with witness "are so much a product of the lawyer's thinking and so little probative of the witness's actual words that they are absolutely protected from disclosure"). Those courts declining to adopt an absolute rule have nonetheless recognized that such material is entitled to special protection. See, e. g., In re Grand Jury Investigation, 599 F.2d, at 1231 ("special considerations * * * must shape any ruling on the discoverability of interview memoranda * * * such documents will be discoverable only in a 'rare situation' ").

We do not decide the issue at this time. It is clear that the magistrate applied the wrong standard when he concluded that the Government had made a sufficient showing of necessity to overcome the protections of the work-product doctrine. The magistrate applied the "substantial need" and "without undue hardship" standard articulated in the first part of Rule 26(b)(3). The notes and memoranda sought by the Government here, however, are work product based on oral statements. If they reveal communication, they are, in this case, protected by the attorney-client privilege. To the extent they do not reveal communications, they reveal the attorneys' mental processes in evaluating the communications. As Rule 26 and *Hickman* make clear, such work product cannot be disclosed simply on a showing of substantial need and inability to obtain the equivalent without undue hardship.

While we are not prepared at this juncture to say that such material is always protected by the work-product rule, we think a far stronger showing of necessity and unavailability by other means than was made by the Government or applied by the magistrate in this case would be necessary to compel disclosure. Since the Court of Appeals thought that the work-product protection was never applicable in an enforcement proceeding such as this, and since the magistrate whose recommendations the District Court adopted applied too lenient a standard of protection, we think the best procedure with respect to this aspect of the case would be to reverse the judgment of the Court of Appeals for the Sixth Circuit and remand the case to it for such further proceedings in connection with the work-product claim as are consistent with this opinion.

Accordingly, the judgment of the Court of Appeals is reversed, and the case remanded for further proceedings.

(2) ACCOUNTANTS

FALSONE v. UNITED STATES

205 F.2d 734 (5th Cir.), cert. denied,
346 U.S. 864, 74 S.Ct. 103, 98 L.Ed. 375 (1953).

RIVES, Circuit Judge.

An Internal Revenue agent acting under authority of 26 U.S.C.A. § 3614(a) [e], served appellant, a certified public accountant, with summons to appear before him and testify in the matter of the tax liability of Salvatore Italiano and his wife, Maria, for the years 1947 to 1951, inclusive, and to bring with him [certain] books and papers * * *.

[The accountant objected to the summons on the ground that, under Florida law, there was an accountant-client privilege analogous to the common law attorney-client privilege, and that the client had not waived the privilege. Hence, it was urged, production of documents and testimony which would violate the privilege could not be compelled, just as if there were a common law privilege involved. A summons enforcement proceeding was brought by the United States, and the District Court ordered the accountant to produce the documents requested and to give testimony pursuant to the summons.]

Appellant concedes, as he must, that at common law no privilege was attached to communications from "client" to accountant. If such a privilege exists, it can only arise from some federal or state statute. Appellant's insistence is based upon both. He contends: 1. that the attorney-client privilege extends to certified public accountants who, like appellant, are enrolled before the Treasury Department; and 2. that the State of Florida, by specific statute, has made privileged all communications between certified public accountants and their clients.

[The Court noted that the Treasury Department regulations permitting accountants to practice before the IRS could not be construed to create a privilege or to bring an accountant within the attorney-client privilege. The Court then considered the effect of the state statutory accountant-client privilege.]

We have heretofore noted that the power granted to the Commissioner by 26 U.S.C.A. § 3614 is inquisitorial in character and is similar to the power vested in federal grand juries. As said by the Eighth Circuit in Brownson v. United States, 32 F.2d at page 848, " * * * the statutes involved * * * should receive a like liberal construction in view of the like important ends sought by the government." Or as stated in United States v. Murdock, 284 U.S. 141, 149, 52 S.Ct. 63, 64, 76 L.Ed. 210, "Investigations for federal

e. The predecessor to 26 U.S.C.A. § 7602.

purposes may not be prevented by matters depending upon state law."
Or in the language of this Court, "These statutes, enacted to effectuate a constitutional power, are the supreme law of the land. If
they are in conflict with State law, constitutional or statutory, the
latter must yield." Shambaugh v. Scofield, 5 Cir., 132 F.2d 345, 346.

* * *

We find no error in the record, and the judgment or order of the
District Court is therefore affirmed.

UNITED STATES v. KOVEL

296 F.2d 918 (2d Cir. 1961).

FRIENDLY, Circuit Judge.

This appeal from a sentence for criminal contempt for refusing
to answer a question asked in the course of an inquiry by a grand
jury raises an important issue as to the application of the attorney-
client privilege to a non-lawyer employed by a law firm. * * *

Kovel is a former Internal Revenue agent having accounting
skills. Since 1943 he has been employed by Kamerman & Kamerman, a law firm specializing in tax law. A grand jury in the Southern District of New York was investigating alleged Federal income
tax violations by Hopps, a client of the law firm; Kovel was subpoenaed to appear on September 6, 1961, a few days before the date,
September 8, when the Government feared the statute of limitations
might run. The law firm advised the Assistant United States Attorney that since Kovel was an employee under the direct supervision of
the partners, Kovel could not disclose any communications by the
client or the result of any work done for the client, unless the latter
consented; the Assistant answered that the attorney-client privilege
did not apply to one who was not an attorney.

* * *

Decision under what circumstances, if any, the attorney-client
privilege may include a communication to a nonlawyer by the lawyer's client is the resultant of two conflicting forces. One is the general teaching that "The investigation of truth and the enforcement of
testimonial duty demand the restriction, not the expansion, of these
privileges," 8 Wigmore, Evidence (McNaughton Rev. 1961), § 2192,
p. 73. The other is the more particular lesson "That as, by reason of
the complexity and difficulty of our law, litigation can only be properly conducted by professional men, it is absolutely necessary that a
man * * * should have recourse to the assistance of professional
lawyers, and * * * it is equally necessary * * * that he
should be able to place unrestricted and unbounded confidence in the
professional agent, and that the communications he so makes to him
should be kept secret * * *," Jessel, M. R. in Anderson v. Bank, 2
Ch.D. 644, 649 (1876). Nothing in the policy of the privilege suggests

that attorneys simply by placing accountants, scientists or investigators on their payrolls and maintaining them in their offices should be able to invest all communications by clients to such persons with a privilege the law has not seen fit to extend when the latter are operating under their own steam. On the other hand, in contrast to the Tudor times when the privilege was first recognized, see 8 Wigmore, Evidence, § 2290, the complexities of modern existence prevent attorneys from effectively handling clients' affairs without the help of others; few lawyers could now practice without the assistance of secretaries, file clerks, telephone operators, messengers, clerks not yet admitted to the bar, and aides of other sorts. "The assistance of these agents being indispensable to his work and the communications of the client being often necessarily committed to them by the attorney or by the client himself, the privilege must include all the persons who act as the attorney's agents." 8 Wigmore, Evidence, § 2301.

Indeed, the Government does not here dispute that the privilege covers communications to non-lawyer employees with "a menial or ministerial responsibility that involves relating communications *to an attorney.*" We cannot regard the privilege as confined to "menial or ministerial" employees. Thus, we can see no significant difference between a case where the attorney sends a client speaking a foreign language to an interpreter to make a literal translation of the client's story; a second where the attorney, himself having some little knowledge of the foreign tongue, has a more knowledgeable non-lawyer employee in the room to help out; a third where someone to perform that same function has been brought along by the client; and a fourth where the attorney, ignorant of the foreign language, sends the client to a non-lawyer proficient in it, with instructions to interview the client on the attorney's behalf and then render his own summary of the situation, perhaps drawing on his own knowledge in the process, so that the attorney can give the client proper legal advice. All four cases meet every element of Wigmore's famous formulation, § 2292, "(1) Where legal advice of any kind is sought (2) from a professional legal adviser in his capacity as such, (3) the communications relating to that purpose, (4) made in confidence (5) by the client, (6) are at his instance permanently protected (7) from disclosure by himself or by the legal adviser, (8) except the protection be waived," save (7); literally, none of them is within (7) since the disclosure is not sought to be compelled from the client or the lawyer. Yet § 2301 of Wigmore would clearly recognize the privilege in the first case and the Government goes along to that extent; § 2301 would also recognize the privilege in the second case and § 2311 in the third unless the circumstances negated confidentiality. We find no valid policy reason for a different result in the fourth case, and we do not read Wigmore as thinking there is. Laymen consulting lawyers should not be expected to anticipate niceties perceptible only to judges—and not even to all of them.

This analogy of the client speaking a foreign language is by no means irrelevant to the appeal at hand. Accounting concepts are a foreign language to some lawyers in almost all cases, and to almost all lawyers in some cases. Hence the presence of an accountant, whether hired by the lawyer or by the client, while the client is relating a complicated tax story to the lawyer, ought not destroy the privilege, any more than would that of the linguist in the second or third variations of the foreign language theme discussed above; the presence of the accountant is necessary, or at least highly useful, for the effective consultation between the client and the lawyer which the privilege is designed to permit. By the same token, if the lawyer has directed the client, either in the specific case or generally, to tell his story in the first instance to an accountant engaged by the lawyer, who is then to interpret it so that the lawyer may better give legal advice, communications by the client reasonably related to that purpose ought fall within the privilege; there can be no more virtue in requiring the lawyer to sit by while the client pursues these possibly tedious preliminary conversations with the accountant than in insisting on the lawyer's physical presence while the client dictates a statement to the lawyer's secretary or is interviewed by a clerk not yet admitted to practice. What is vital to the privilege is that the communication be made *in confidence* for the purpose of obtaining *legal* advice *from the lawyer*. If what is sought is not legal advice but only accounting service, as in Olender v. United States, 210 F.2d 795, 805–806 (9 Cir. 1954), or if the advice sought is the accountant's rather than the lawyer's, no privilege exists. We recognize this draws what may seem to some a rather arbitrary line between a case where the client communicates first to his own accountant (no privilege as to such communications, even though he later consults his lawyer on the same matter, Gariepy v. United States, 189 F.2d 459, 463 (6 Cir. 1951),[4] and others, where the client in the first instance consults a lawyer who retains an accountant as a listening post, or consults the lawyer with his own accountant present. But that is the inevitable consequence of having to reconcile the absence of a privilege for accountants and the effective operation of the privilege of client and lawyer under conditions where the lawyer needs outside help. We realize also that the line we have drawn will not be so easy to apply as the simpler positions urged on us by the parties— the district judges will scarcely be able to leave the decision of such cases to computers; but the distinction has to be made if the privilege is neither to be unduly expanded nor to become a trap.

*   *   *

4. We do not deal in this opinion with the question under what circumstances, if any, such communications could be deemed privileged on the basis that they were being made to the accountant as the client's agent for the purpose of subsequent communication by the accountant to the lawyer; communications by the client's agent to the attorney are privileged, 8 Wigmore, Evidence, § 2317–1.

The judgment [of criminal contempt] is vacated and the cause remanded for further proceedings consistent with this opinion.

B. THE PRIVILEGE AGAINST SELF-INCRIMINATION

(1) INDIVIDUALS

COUCH v. UNITED STATES

Supreme Court of the United States, 1973.
409 U.S. 322, 93 S.Ct. 611, 34 L.Ed.2d 548.

Mr. Justice POWELL delivered the opinion of the Court.

On January 7, 1970, the Government filed a petition in the United States District Court for the Western District of Virginia, pursuant to 26 U.S.C. §§ 7402(b) and 7604(a), seeking enforcement of an Internal Revenue summons in connection with an investigation of petitioner's tax liability from 1964–1968. The summons was directed to petitioner's accountant for the production of:

> "All books, records, bank statements, cancelled checks, deposit ticket copies, workpapers and all other pertinent documents pertaining to the tax liability of the above taxpayer."

The question is whether the taxpayer may invoke her Fifth Amendment privilege against compulsory self-incrimination to prevent the production of her business and tax records in the possession of her accountant. Both the District Court and the Court of Appeals for the Fourth Circuit held the privilege unavailable.

Petitioner is the sole proprietress of a restaurant. Since 1955 she had given bank statements, payroll records, and reports of sales and expenditures to her accountant, Harold Shaffer, for the purpose of preparing her income tax returns. The accountant was not petitioner's personal employee but an independent contractor with his own office and numerous other clients who compensated him on a piecework basis. When petitioner surrendered possession of the records to Shaffer, she, of course, retained title in herself.

* * *

I

It is now undisputed that a special agent is authorized, pursuant to 26 U.S.C. § 7602, to issue an Internal Revenue summons in aid of a tax investigation with civil and possible criminal consequences. In Donaldson v. United States the Court upheld such a summons * * *.

The Court in *Donaldson* noted that the taxpayer there had attempted to intervene, pursuant to Fed.Rule Civ.Proc. 24(a) (2), to bar production of records "in which the taxpayer has no proprietary interest of any kind, which are owned by the third person, which are in his hands, and which relate to the third person's business transactions with the taxpayer." The Court quite properly concluded that, under those facts, no absolute right to intervene existed. The instant case, however, presents a different question. Here petitioner does own the business records which the Government seeks to review and the courts below did permit her to intervene. The essential inquiry is whether her proprietary interest further enables her to assert successfully a privilege against compulsory self-incrimination to bar enforcement of the summons and production of the records, despite the fact that the records no longer remained in her possession.

II

The importance of preserving inviolate the privilege against compulsory self-incrimination has often been stated by this Court and need not be elaborated. By its very nature, the privilege is an intimate and personal one. It respects a private inner sanctum of individual feeling and thought and proscribes state intrusion to extract self-condemnation. Historically, the privilege sprang from an abhorrence of governmental assault against the single individual accused of crime and the temptation on the part of the State to resort to the expedient of compelling incriminating evidence from one's own mouth. The Court has thought the privilege necessary to prevent any "recurrence of the Inquisition and the Star Chamber, even if not in their stark brutality," Ullmann v. United States, 350 U.S. 422, 428, 76 S.Ct. 497, 501, 100 L.Ed. 511 (1956).

* * *

It is important to reiterate that the Fifth Amendment privilege is a *personal* privilege: it adheres basically to the person, not to information that may incriminate him. As Mr. Justice Holmes put it: "A party is privileged from producing the evidence, but not from its production." Johnson v. United States, 228 U.S. 457, 458, 33 S.Ct. 572, 57 L.Ed. 919 (1913). The Constitution explicitly prohibits compelling an accused to bear witness "against himself": it necessarily does not proscribe incriminating statements elicited from another. Compulsion upon the person asserting it is an important element of the privilege, and "prohibition of compelling a man * * * to be witness against himself is a prohibition of the use of physical or moral compulsion to extort communications from *him*," Holt v. United States, 218 U.S. 245, 252–253, 31 S.Ct. 2, 6, 54 L.Ed. 1021 (1910) (emphasis added). It is extortion of information from the accused himself that offends our sense of justice.

In the case before us the ingredient of personal compulsion against an accused is lacking. The summons and the order of the

District Court enforcing it are directed against the accountant.[9] He, not the taxpayer, is the only one compelled to do anything. And the accountant makes no claim that he may tend to be incriminated by the production. Inquisitorial pressure or coercion against a potentially accused person, compelling her, against her will, to utter self-condemning words or produce incriminating documents is absent. In the present case, no "shadow of testimonial compulsion upon or enforced communication by the accused" is involved. Schmerber v. California, 384 U.S. 757, 765, 86 S.Ct. 1826, 1832, 16 L.Ed.2d 908 (1966).

The divulgence of potentially incriminating evidence against petitioner is naturally unwelcome. But petitioner's distress would be no less if the divulgence came not from her accountant but from some other third party with whom she was connected and who possessed substantially equivalent knowledge of her business affairs. The basic complaint of petitioner stems from the fact of divulgence of the possibly incriminating information, not from the manner in which or the person from whom it was extracted. Yet such divulgence, where it does not result from coercion of the suspect herself, is a necessary part of the process of law enforcement and tax investigation.

III

Petitioner's reliance on Boyd v. United States, 116 U.S. 616, 6 S. Ct. 524, 29 L.Ed. 746 (1886), is misplaced. In *Boyd,* the person asserting the privilege was in possession of the written statements in question. The Court in *Boyd* did hold that "any forcible and compulsory extortion of a man's own testimony, or of his private papers to be used as evidence to convict him of crime," violated the Fourth and Fifth Amendments. Id., at 630, 6 S.Ct., at 532. That case did not, however, address or contemplate the divergence of ownership and possession,[10] and petitioner concedes that court decisions applying *Boyd* have largely been in instances where possession and ownership conjoined.[12] In *Boyd,* the production order was directed against the

---

9. Technically the order to produce the records was directed to petitioner's attorney since, after the summons was served upon the accountant, he ignored it and surrendered the records to the attorney. But constitutional rights obviously cannot be enlarged by this kind of action. The rights and obligations of the parties became fixed when the summons was served, and the transfer did not alter them.

10. A later Court commenting on the *Boyd* privilege noted that "the papers and effects which the privilege protects must be the private property of the person claiming the privilege, or *at least in his possession in a purely*

personal capacity." United States v. White, 322 U.S. 694, 699, 64 S.Ct. 1248, 1251, 88 L.Ed. 1542 (1944). (Emphasis added.)

12. See also United States v. Cohen, 388 F.2d 464, 468 (CA9 1967), where the court, in upholding the right of a possessor, nonowner, to assert the privilege, noted that "it is possession of papers sought by the government, not ownership, which sets the stage for exercise of the governmental compulsion which it is the purpose of the privilege to prohibit." Though the instant case concerns the scope of the privilege for an owner, nonpossessor, the Ninth Circuit's linkage of possession to the purposes served

owner of the property who, by responding, would have been forced "to produce and authenticate any personal documents or effects that might incriminate him." United States v. White, 322 U.S., at 698, 64 S.Ct., at 1251. But we reiterate that in the instant case there was no enforced communication of any kind from any accused or potential accused.

Petitioner would, in effect, have us read *Boyd* to mark ownership, not possession, as the bounds of the privilege, despite the fact that possession bears the closest relationship to the personal compulsion forbidden by the Fifth Amendment. To tie the privilege against self-incrimination to a concept of ownership would be to draw a meaningless line. It would hold here that the business records which petitioner actually owned would be protected in the hands of her accountant, while business information communicated to her accountant by letter and conversations in which the accountant took notes, in addition to the accountant's own workpapers and photocopies of petitioner's records, would not be subject to a claim of privilege since title rested in the accountant. Such a holding would thus place unnecessary emphasis on the form of communication to an accountant and the accountant's own working methods, while diverting the inquiry from the basic purposes of the Fifth Amendment's protections.

Other precedents debated by the parties lend no support to petitioner's contention that ownership of documents should determine the availability of the privilege.[14] *   *   *

*   *   *

by the privilege was appropriate.

We do not, of course, decide what qualifies as rightful possession enabling the possessor to assert the privilege.

14. Burdeau v. McDowell, 256 U.S. 465, 41 S.Ct. 574, 65 L.Ed. 1048 (1921), also debated and cited in the briefs, held that the Government may retain for use against their owner in a criminal proceeding incriminating documents which were stolen by private individuals, without any governmental knowledge or complicity, and turned over to the Government. The Court, in denying the owner's privilege, alluded primarily to the absence of any governmental compulsion against the accused, the precise factor considered in the instant case. It is true, as petitioner argues, that the case turns somewhat on a discussion of governmental versus private compulsion and invasion, but it is equally true that the Court in *Burdeau* failed to find any impermissible public com-

pulsion on the owner absent his possession:

"We know of no constitutional principle which requires the government to surrender the papers under such circumstances. Had it learned that such incriminatory papers, tending to show a violation of federal law, were in the hands of a person other than the accused, it having had no part in wrongfully obtaining than, we know of no reason why a subpoena might not issue for the production of the papers as evidence. Such production would require no unreasonable search or seizure, nor would it amount to compelling the accused to testify against himself." Id., at 476, 41 S.Ct., at 576.

In Johnson v. United States, 228 U.S. 457, 33 S.Ct. 572, 57 L.Ed. 919 (1913), the Court held that the books and records of a bankrupt transferred to a trustee in bankruptcy could be used as evidence against the bankrupt in a prosecution for concealing money

Petitioner argues, nevertheless, that grave prejudice will result from a denial of her claim to equate ownership and the scope of the privilege. She alleges that "[i]f the IRS is able to reach her records the instant those records leave her hands and are deposited in the hands of her retainer whom she has hired for a special purpose then the meaning of the privilege is lost." That is not, however, the import of today's decision. We do indeed believe that actual possession of documents bears the most significant relationship to Fifth Amendment protections against governmental compulsions upon the individual accused of crime. Yet situations may well arise where constructive possession is so clear or the relinquishment of possession is so temporary and insignificant as to leave the personal compulsions upon the accused substantially intact.[16] But this is not the case before us. Here there was no mere fleeting divestment of possession: the records had been given to this accountant regularly since 1955 and remained in his continuous possession until the summer of 1969 when the summons was issued. Moreover, the accountant himself worked neither in petitioner's office nor as her employee. The length of his possession of petitioner's records and his independent status confirm the belief that petitioner's divestment of possession was of such a character as to disqualify her entirely as an object of any impermissible Fifth Amendment compulsion.

IV

Petitioner further argues that the confidential nature of the accountant-client relationship and her resulting expectation of privacy in delivering the records protect her, under the Fourth and Fifth Amendments, from their production. Although not in itself controlling, we note that no confidential accountant-client privilege exists under federal law, and no state-created privilege has been recognized in federal cases. Nor is there justification for such a privilege where

from the trustee. Unlike the instant case, both title and possession passed in that transfer and the records were, in one sense, "published" by it. But the Court, in denying the privilege, recognized that the transfer also succeeded in removing the important element of personal compulsion against the accused, id., at 459, 33 S.Ct., at 572, just as, in this case, the nature of the divestment of possession did.

16. See, e. g., Schwimmer v. United States, 232 F.2d 855 (CA8, 1956), which involved an attorney's partially successful motion to quash two subpoenas *duces tecum* issued in a grand jury proceeding against a corporation where the attorney had stored his office files. See also United States v. Guterma, 272 F.2d 344 (CA2 1959), concerning the storage of taxpayer's

personal records in a safe in offices of a corporation which the taxpayer had served as Chairman of the Board. Only the taxpayer and an indicted co-defendant knew the combination of the safe, and the corporation had no access to it. The Court of Appeals upheld the taxpayer's assertion of Fifth Amendment privilege as to his personal records in the face of a grand jury subpoena directed to the corporation.

Petitioner argues these cases support her position; the Government argues they can be distinguished from the instant case as involving mere custodial safekeeping of records, not disclosure of their information to a third person. We refrain from judging the merits of such distinctions today.

records relevant to income tax returns are involved in a criminal investigation or prosecution. In *Boyd,* a pre-income tax case, the Court spoke of protection of privacy, but there can be little expectation of privacy where records are handed to an accountant, knowing that mandatory disclosure of much of the information therein is required in an income tax return. What information is not disclosed is largely in the accountant's discretion, not petitioner's. Indeed, the accountant himself risks criminal prosecution if he willfully assists in the preparation of a false return. 26 U.S.C. § 7206(2). His own need for self-protection would often require the right to disclose the information given him. Petitioner seeks extensions of constitutional protections against self-incrimination in the very situation where obligations of disclosure exist and under a system largely dependent upon honest self-reporting even to survive. Accordingly, petitioner here cannot reasonably claim, either for Fourth or Fifth Amendment purposes, an expectation of protected privacy or confidentiality.

V

The criterion for Fifth Amendment immunity remains not the ownership of property but the " 'physical or moral compulsion' exerted." Perlman [v. United States,] 247 U.S., at 15, 38 S.Ct., at 420. We hold today that no Fourth or Fifth Amendment claim can prevail where, as in this case, there exists no legitimate expectation of privacy and no semblance of governmental compulsion against the person of the accused. It is important, in applying constitutional principles, to interpret them in light of the fundamental interests of personal liberty they were meant to serve. Respect for these principles is eroded when they leap their proper bounds to interfere with the legitimate interest of society in enforcement of its laws and collection of the revenues.

The judgment of the Court of Appeals is affirmed.

Mr. Justice DOUGLAS, dissenting.

* * *

The decision may have a more immediate impact which the majority does not consider. Our tax laws have become so complex that very few taxpayers can afford the luxury of completing their own returns without professional assistance. If a taxpayer now wants to insure the confidentiality and privacy of his records, however, he must forgo such assistance. To my mind, the majority thus attaches a penalty to the exercise of the privilege against self-incrimination. It calls for little more discussion than to note that we have not tolerated such penalties in the past.

* * *

One's privacy embraces what the person has in his home, his desk, his files, and his safe as well as what he carries on his person.

It also has a very meaningful relationship to what he tells any confi-
dant—his wife, his minister, his lawyer, or his tax accountant. The
constitutional fences of law are being broken down by an ever-in-
creasingly powerful Government that seeks to reduce every person to
a digit.

FISHER v. UNITED STATES

Supreme Court of the United States, 1976.
425 U.S. 391, 96 S.Ct. 1569, 48 L.Ed.2d 39.

Mr. Justice WHITE delivered the opinion of the Court.

In these two cases we are called upon to decide whether a summons directing an attorney to produce documents delivered to him by
his client in connection with the attorney-client relationship is enforceable over claims that the documents were constitutionally immune from summons in the hands of the client and retained that immunity in the hands of the attorney.

I

In each case, an Internal Revenue agent visited the taxpayer or
taxpayers and interviewed them in connection with an investigation
of possible civil or criminal liability under the federal income tax
laws. Shortly after the interviews—one day later in No. 74–611 and
a week or two later in No. 74–18—the taxpayers obtained from their
respective accountants certain documents relating to the preparation
by the accountants of their tax returns. Shortly after obtaining the
documents—later the same day in No. 74–611 and a few weeks later
in No. 74–18—the taxpayers transferred the documents to their lawyers—respondent Kasmir and petitioner Fisher, respectively—each of
whom was retained to assist the taxpayer in connection with the investigation. Upon learning of the whereabouts of the documents, the
Internal Revenue Service served summonses on the attorneys directing them to produce documents listed therein. In No. 74–611, the
documents were described as "the following records of Tannebaum
Bindler & Lewis [the accounting firm].

"1. Accountant's workpapers pertaining to Dr. E. J. Mason's books and records of 1969, 1970 and 1971.

"2. Retained copies of E. J. Mason's income tax returns for
1969, 1970 and 1971.

"3. Retained copies of reports and other correspondence
between Tannebaum Bindler & Lewis and Dr. E. J. Mason during
1969, 1970 and 1971."

In No. 74–18, the documents demanded were analyses by the accountant of the taxpayers' income and expenses which had been copied by
the accountant from the taxpayers' canceled checks and deposit receipts. In No. 74–611, a summons was also served on the accountant

directing him to appear and testify concerning the documents to be produced by the lawyer. In each case, the lawyer declined to comply with the summons directing production of the documents, and enforcement actions were commenced by the Government under 26 U. S.C. §§ 7402(b) and 7604(a). In No. 74–611, the attorney raised in defense of the enforcement action the taxpayer's accountant-client privilege, his attorney-client privilege, and his Fourth and Fifth Amendment rights. In No. 74–18, the attorney claimed that enforcement would involve compulsory self-incrimination of the taxpayers in violation of their Fifth Amendment privilege, would involve a seizure of the papers without necessary compliance with the Fourth Amendment, and would violate the taxpayers' right to communicate in confidence with their attorney. In No. 74–18 the taxpayers intervened and made similar claims.

* * *

II

All of the parties in these cases and the Court of Appeals for the Fifth Circuit have concurred in the proposition that if the Fifth Amendment would have excused a *taxpayer* from turning over the accountant's papers had he possessed them, the *attorney* to whom they are delivered for the purpose of obtaining legal advice should also be immune from subpoena. Although we agree with this proposition for the reasons set forth in Part III, infra, we are convinced that, under our decision in Couch v. United States, 409 U.S. 322, 93 S.Ct. 611, 34 L.Ed.2d 548 (1973), it is not the taxpayer's Fifth Amendment privilege that would excuse the *attorney* from production.

The relevant part of that Amendment provides:

"No person * * * shall be *compelled* in any criminal case to be a *witness against himself.*" (Emphasis added.)

The taxpayer's privilege under this Amendment is not violated by enforcement of the summonses involved in these cases because enforcement against a taxpayer's lawyer would not "compel" the taxpayer to do anything—and certainly would not compel him to be a "witness" against himself. The Court has held repeatedly that the Fifth Amendment is limited to prohibiting the use of "physical or moral compulsion" exerted on the person asserting the privilege. In Couch v. United States, supra, we recently ruled that the Fifth Amendment rights of a taxpayer were not violated by the enforcement of a documentary summons directed to her accountant and requiring production of the taxpayer's own records in the possession of the accountant. We did so on the ground that in such a case "the ingredient of personal compulsion against an accused is lacking."

Here, the taxpayers are compelled to do no more than was the taxpayer in *Couch*. The taxpayers' Fifth Amendment privilege is therefore not violated by enforcement of the summonses directed toward their attorneys. This is true whether or not the Amendment would have barred a subpoena directing the taxpayer to produce the documents while they were in his hands.

The fact that the attorneys are agents of the taxpayers does not change this result. *Couch* held as much, since the accountant there was also the taxpayer's agent, and in this respect reflected a long-standing view. In Hale v. Henkel, 201 U.S. 43, 69–70, 26 S.Ct. 370, 377, 50 L.Ed. 652, 663 (1906), the Court said that the privilege "was never intended to permit [a person] to plead the fact that some third person might be incriminated by his testimony, even though he were the agent of such person * * * *. [T]he Amendment is limited to a person who shall be compelled in any criminal case to be a witness against *himself*." (Emphasis in original.) "It is extortion of information from the accused himself that offends our sense of justice." Couch v. United States, supra, 409 U.S., at 328, 93 S.Ct., at 616, 34 L.Ed.2d, at 554. Agent or no, the lawyer is not the taxpayer. The taxpayer is the "accused," and nothing is being extorted from him.

Nor is this one of those situations, which *Couch* suggested might exist, where constructive possession is so clear or relinquishment of possession so temporary and insignificant as to leave the personal compulsion upon the taxpayer substantially intact. In this respect we see no difference between the delivery to the attorneys in these cases and delivery to the accountant in the *Couch* case. As was true in *Couch,* the documents sought were obtainable without personal compulsion on the accused.

* * *

The Court of Appeals for the Fifth Circuit suggested that because legally and ethically the attorney was required to respect the confidences of his client, the latter had a reasonable expectation of privacy for the records in the hands of the attorney and therefore did not forfeit his Fifth Amendment privilege with respect to the records by transferring them in order to obtain legal advice. It is true that the Court has often stated that one of the several purposes served by the constitutional privilege against compelled testimonial self-incrimination is that of protecting personal privacy. But the Court has never suggested that every invasion of privacy violates the privilege. Within the limits imposed by the language of the Fifth Amendment, which we necessarily observe, the privilege truly serves privacy interests; but the Court has never on any ground, personal privacy included, applied the Fifth Amendment to prevent the otherwise proper acquisition or use of evidence which, in the Court's view, did not involve compelled testimonial self-incrimination of some sort.[5]

The proposition that the Fifth Amendment protects private information obtained without compelling self-incriminating testimony is contrary to the clear statements of this Court that under appropriate safeguards private incriminating statements of an accused may be overheard and used in evidence, if they are not compelled at the time they were uttered, Katz v. United States, 389 U.S. 347, 354, 88 S.Ct. 507, 512, 19 L.Ed.2d 576, 583 (1967); Osborn v. United States, 385 U.S. 323, 329–330, 87 S.Ct. 429, 432–433, 17 L.Ed.2d 394, 399–400 (1966); and that disclosure of private information may be compelled if immunity removes the risk of incrimination. Kastigar v. United States, 406 U.S. 441, 92 S.Ct. 1653, 32 L.Ed.2d 212 (1972). If the Fifth Amendment protected generally against the obtaining of private information from a man's mouth or pen or house, its protections would presumably not be lifted by probable cause and a warrant or by immunity. The privacy invasion is not mitigated by immunity; and the Fifth Amendment's strictures, unlike the Fourth's, are not removed by showing reasonableness. The Framers addressed the subject of personal privacy directly in the Fourth Amendment. They struck a balance so that when the State's reason to believe incriminating evidence will be found becomes sufficiently great, the invasion of privacy becomes justified and a warrant to search and seize will issue. They did not seek in still another Amendment—the Fifth—to achieve a general protection of privacy but to deal with the more specific issue of compelled self-incrimination.

We cannot cut the Fifth Amendment completely loose from the moorings of its language, and make it serve as a general protector of privacy—a word not mentioned in its text and a concept directly addressed in the Fourth Amendment. We adhere to the view that the Fifth Amendment protects against "compelled self-incrimination, not [the disclosure of] private information." United States v. Nobles, 422 U.S. 225, 233 n. 7, 95 S.Ct. 2160, 2167, 45 L.Ed.2d 141 (1975).

Insofar as private information not obtained through compelled self-incriminating testimony is legally protected, its protection stems

---

5. There is a line of cases in which the Court stated that the Fifth Amendment was offended by the use in evidence of documents or property seized in violation of the Fourth Amendment. Gouled v. United States, 255 U.S. 298, 306, 41 S.Ct. 261, 264, 65 L.Ed. 647, 651 (1921); Mapp v. Ohio, 367 U.S. 643, 661, 81 S.Ct. 1684, 1694, 6 L.Ed.2d 1081, 1093 (1961) (Black, J., concurring). But the Court purported to find elements of compulsion in such situations. "In either case he is the unwilling source of the evidence, and the Fifth Amendment forbids that he shall be compelled to be a witness against himself in a criminal case." Gouled v. United States, supra, 255 U.S., at 306, 41 S.Ct., at 264, 65 L.Ed., at 651. In any event the predicate for those cases, lacking here, was a violation of the Fourth Amendment. Cf. Burdeau v. McDowell, 256 U.S. 465, 475–476, 41 S.Ct. 574, 576, 65 L.Ed. 1048, 1050–1051 (1921).

from other sources [6]—the Fourth Amendment's protection against seizures without warrant or probable cause and against subpoenas which suffer from "too much indefiniteness or breadth in the things required to be 'particularly described,' " Oklahoma Press Pub. Co. v. Walling, 327 U.S. 186, 208, 66 S.Ct. 494, 505, 90 L.Ed. 614, 629 (1946); the First Amendment, see NAACP v. Alabama, 357 U.S. 449, 462, 78 S.Ct. 1163, 1171, 2 L.Ed.2d 1488, 1499 (1958); or evidentiary privileges such as the attorney-client privilege.[7]

III

Our above holding is that compelled production of documents from an attorney does not implicate whatever Fifth Amendment privilege the taxpayer might have enjoyed from being compelled to produce them himself. The taxpayers in these cases, however, have from the outset consistently urged that they should not be forced to expose otherwise protected documents to summons simply because they have sought legal advice and turned the papers over to their attorneys. The Government appears to agree unqualifiedly. The difficulty is that the taxpayers have erroneously relied on the Fifth Amendment without urging the attorney-client privilege in so many words. They have nevertheless invoked the relevant body of law and policies that govern the attorney-client privilege. In this posture of the case, we feel obliged to inquire whether the attorney-client privilege applies to documents in the hands of an attorney which would have been privileged in the hands of the client by reason of the Fifth Amendment.

Confidential disclosures by a client to an attorney made in order to obtain legal assistance are privileged. The purpose of the privilege is to encourage clients to make full disclosure to their attorneys. As a practical matter, if the client knows that damaging information could more readily be obtained from the attorney following disclosure than from himself in the absence of disclosure, the client would be reluctant to confide in his lawyer and it would be difficult to obtain fully informed legal advice. However, since the privilege has the effect

6. In Couch v. United States, 409 U.S. 322, 93 S.Ct. 611, 34 L.Ed.2d 548 (1973), on which taxpayers rely for their claim that the Fifth Amendment protects their "legitimate expectation of privacy," the Court differentiated between the things protected by the Fourth and Fifth Amendments. "We hold today that no Fourth or Fifth Amendment claim can prevail where, as in this case, there exists no legitimate expectation of privacy and no semblance of governmental compulsion against the person of the accused." Id., 409 U.S., at 336, 93 S. Ct., at 620, 34 L.Ed.2d, at 558.

7. The taxpayers and their attorneys have not raised arguments of a Fourth Amendment nature before this Court and could not be successful if they had. The summonses are narrowly drawn and seek only documents of unquestionable relevance to the tax investigation. Special problems of privacy which might be presented by subpoena of a personal diary, United States v. Bennett, 409 F.2d 888, 897 (CA2 1969) (Friendly, J.), are not involved here.

First Amendment values are also plainly not implicated in these cases.

of withholding relevant information from the factfinder, it applies only where necessary to achieve its purpose. Accordingly it protects only those disclosures—necessary to obtain informed legal advice— which might not have been made absent the privilege. This Court and the lower courts have thus uniformly held that pre-existing documents which could have been obtained by court process from the client when he was in possession may also be obtained from the attorney by similar process following transfer by the client in order to obtain more informed legal advice. The purpose of the privilege requires no broader rule. Pre-existing documents obtainable from the client are not appreciably easier to obtain from the attorney after transfer to him. Thus, even absent the attorney-client privilege, clients will not be discouraged from disclosing the documents to the attorney, and their ability to obtain informed legal advice will remain unfettered. It is otherwise if the documents are not obtainable by subpoena *duces tecum* or summons while in the exclusive possession of the client, for the client will then be reluctant to transfer possession to the lawyer unless the documents are also privileged in the latter's hands. Where the transfer is made for the purpose of obtaining legal advice, the purposes of the attorney-client privilege would be defeated unless the privilege is applicable. "It follows, then, that *when the client himself would be privileged* from production of the document, either as a party at common law * * * or as exempt from self-incrimination, the attorney having possession of the document is not bound to produce." 8 Wigmore § 2307, p. 592. * * *

Since each taxpayer transferred possession of the documents in question from himself to his attorney in order to obtain legal assistance in the tax investigations in question, the papers, if unobtainable by summons from the client, are unobtainable by summons directed to the attorney by reason of the attorney-client privilege. We accordingly proceed to the question whether the documents could have been obtained by summons addressed to the taxpayer while the documents were in his possession. The only bar to enforcement of such summons asserted by the parties or the courts below is the Fifth Amendment's privilege against self-incrimination. * * *

IV

* * *

A subpoena served on a taxpayer requiring him to produce an accountant's workpapers in his possession without doubt involves substantial compulsion. But it does not compel oral testimony; nor would it ordinarily compel the taxpayer to restate, repeat, or affirm the truth of the contents of the documents sought. Therefore, the Fifth Amendment would not be violated by the fact alone that the papers on their face might incriminate the taxpayer, for the privilege protects a person only against being incriminated by his own compelled testimonial communications. The accountant's workpapers are not the taxpayer's. They were not prepared by the taxpayer, and they contain no testimonial declarations by him. Furthermore, as far as this record demonstrates, the preparation of all of the papers sought in these cases was wholly voluntary, and they cannot be said to contain compelled testimonial evidence, either of the taxpayers or of anyone else.[11] The taxpayer cannot avoid compliance with the subpoena merely by asserting that the item of evidence which he is required to produce contains incriminating writing, whether his own or that of someone else.

The act of producing evidence in response to a subpoena nevertheless has communicative aspects of its own, wholly aside from the contents of the papers produced. Compliance with the subpoena tacitly concedes the existence of the papers demanded and their possession or control by the taxpayer. It also would indicate the taxpayer's belief that the papers are those described in the subpoena. The elements of compulsion are clearly present, but the more difficult issues are whether the tacit averments of the taxpayer are both "testimonial" and "incriminating" for purposes of applying the Fifth Amendment. These questions perhaps do not lend themselves to categorical answers; their resolution may instead depend on the facts and circumstances of particular cases or classes thereof. In light of the records now before us, we are confident that however incriminating the contents of the accountant's workpapers might be, the act of producing them—the only thing which the taxpayer is compelled to do—would not itself involve testimonial self-incrimination.

It is doubtful that implicitly admitting the existence and possession of the papers rises to the level of testimony within the protection of the Fifth Amendment. The papers belong to the accountant, were prepared by him, and are the kind usually prepared by an accountant working on the tax returns of his client. Surely the Government is in no way relying on the "truth-telling" of the taxpayer to prove the existence of or his access to the documents. The existence and location of the papers are a foregone conclusion and the taxpayer adds little or nothing to the sum total of the Government's information by conceding that he in fact has the papers. Under these circumstances by enforcement of the summons "no constitutional rights are touched. The question is not of testimony but of surrender." In re Harris, 221 U.S. 274, 279, 31 S.Ct. 557, 558, 55 L.Ed. 732, 735 (1911).

---

11. The fact that the documents may have been written by the person asserting the privilege is insufficient to trigger the privilege. And, unless the Government has compelled the subpoenaed person to write the document, the fact that it was written by him is not controlling with respect to the Fifth Amendment issue. Conversations may be seized and introduced in evidence under proper safeguards, if not compelled. In the case of a documentary subpoena the only thing compelled is the act of producing the document and the compelled act is the same as the one performed when a chattel or document not authored by the producer is demanded.

When an accused is required to submit a handwriting exemplar he admits his ability to write and impliedly asserts that the exemplar is his writing. But in common experience, the first would be a near truism and the latter self-evident. In any event, although the exemplar may be incriminating to the accused and although he is compelled to furnish it, his Fifth Amendment privilege is not violated because nothing he has said or done is deemed to be sufficiently testimonial for purposes of the privilege. This Court has also time and again allowed subpoenas against the custodian of corporate documents or those belonging to other collective entities such as unions and partnerships and those of bankrupt businesses over claims that the documents will incriminate the custodian despite the fact that producing the documents tacitly admits their existence and their location in the hands of the possessor. E. g., Wilson v. United States, 221 U.S. 361, 31 S.Ct. 538, 55 L.Ed. 771 (1911); Bellis v. United States, 417 U.S. 85, 94 S.Ct. 2179, 40 L.Ed.2d 678 (1974). The existence and possession or control of the subpoenaed documents being no more in issue here than in the above cases, the summons is equally enforceable.

Moreover, assuming that these aspects of producing the accountant's papers have some minimal testimonial significance, surely it is not illegal to seek accounting help in connection with one's tax returns or for the accountant to prepare workpapers and deliver them to the taxpayer. At this juncture, we are quite unprepared to hold that either the fact of existence of the papers or of their possession by the taxpayer poses any realistic threat of incrimination to the taxpayer.

As for the possibility that responding to the subpoena would authenticate the workpapers, production would express nothing more than the taxpayer's belief that the papers are those described in the subpoena. The taxpayer would be no more competent to authenticate the accountant's workpapers or reports by producing them than he would be to authenticate them if testifying orally. The taxpayer did not prepare the papers and could not vouch for their accuracy. The documents would not be admissible in evidence against the taxpayer without authenticating testimony. Without more, responding to the subpoena in the circumstances before us would not appear to represent a substantial threat of self-incrimination. * * *

Whether the Fifth Amendment would shield the taxpayer from producing his own tax records in his possession is a question not involved here; for the papers demanded here are not his "private papers." We do hold that compliance with a summons directing the taxpayer to produce the accountant's documents involved in these cases would involve no incriminating testimony within the protection of the Fifth Amendment.

* * *

Affirmed in part; reversed in part.

(2) COLLECTIVE ENTITIES

BELLIS v. UNITED STATES

Supreme Court of the United States, 1974.
417 U.S. 85, 94 S.Ct. 2179, 40 L.Ed.2d 678.

Mr. Justice MARSHALL delivered the opinion of the Court.

The question presented in this case is whether a partner in a small law firm may invoke his personal privilege against self-incrimination to justify his refusal to comply with a subpoena requiring production of the partnership's financial records.

[Until 1969 Bellis was the senior partner in the firm of Bellis, Kolsby & Wolf. In late 1969 he left the firm, leaving the former partnership's financial records with Kolsby and Wolf, who continued in partnership together. In early 1973, shortly before issuance of the subpoena in this case, Bellis had the records moved to his new office. On May 1, 1973, Bellis was served with a federal grand jury subpoena, directing him to appear and testify and to bring with him "all partnership records currently in your possession for the partnership of Bellis, Kolsby & Wolf for the years 1968 and 1969." Bellis appeared, but refused to produce the records, claiming his Fifth Amendment privilege against compulsory self-incrimination. The district court ordered Bellis to produce the records but when he appeared before the grand jury a second time and again refused to produce the documents, the district court held him in civil contempt and released him on his own recognizance pending an expedited appeal. On July 9, 1973, the Third Circuit affirmed, relying on United States v. White, 322 U.S. 694, 64 S.Ct. 1248, 88 L.Ed. 1542 (1944).|

* * *

It has long been established, of course, that the Fifth Amendment privilege against compulsory self-incrimination protects an individual from compelled production of his personal papers and effects as well as compelled oral testimony. In Boyd v. United States, 116 U.S. 616, 6 S.Ct. 524, 29 L.Ed. 746 (1886), we held that "any forcible and compulsory extortion of a man's own testimony, or of his private papers to be used as evidence to convict him of crime" would violate the Fifth Amendment privilege. Id., at 630, 6 S.Ct., at 532; see also Wilson v. United States, 221 U.S. 361, 377, 31 S.Ct. 538, 543, 55 L.Ed. 771 (1911). The privilege applies to the business records of the sole proprietor or sole practitioner as well as to personal documents containing more intimate information about the individual's private life. Boyd v. United States, supra; Couch v. United States, 409 U.S. 322, 93 S.Ct. 611, 34 L.Ed.2d 548 (1973). As the Court explained in United States v. White, supra, 322 U.S. at 698, 64 S.Ct. at 1251, "[t]he constitutional privilege against self-incrimination * * * is designed to prevent the use of legal process to force from the lips of the accused individual the evidence necessary to convict him or to force him to produce and authenticate any personal documents or effects that might incriminate him.''

On the other hand, an equally long line of cases has established that an individual cannot rely upon the privilege to avoid producing the records of a collective entity which are in his possession in a representative capacity, even if these records might incriminate him personally. This doctrine was first announced in a series of cases dealing with corporate records. In Wilson v. United States, supra, the Court held that an officer of a corporation could not claim his privilege against compulsory self-incrimination to justify a refusal to produce the corporate books and records in response to a grand jury subpoena *duces tecum* directed to the corporation. A companion case, Dreier v. United States, 221 U.S. 394, 31 S.Ct. 550, 55 L.Ed. 784 (1911), held that the same result followed when the subpoena requiring production of the corporate books was directed to the individual corporate officer. In Wheeler v. United States, 226 U.S. 478, 33 S.Ct. 158, 57 L.Ed. 309 (1913), the Court held that no Fifth Amendment privilege could be claimed with respect to corporate records even though the corporation had previously been dissolved. And Grant v. United States, 227 U.S. 74, 33 S.Ct. 190, 57 L.Ed. 423 (1913), applied this principle to the records of a dissolved corporation where the records were in the possession of the individual who had been the corporation's sole shareholder.

To some extent, these decisions were based upon the particular incidents of the corporate form, the Court observing that a corporation has limited powers granted to it by the State in its charter, and is subject to the retained "visitorial power" of the State to investigate its activities. See, e. g., Wilson v. United States, supra, 221 U.S., at 382–385, 31 S.Ct., at 545–546. But any thought that the principle formulated in these decisions was limited to corporate records was put to rest in United States v. White, supra. In *White,* we held that an officer of an unincorporated association, a labor union, could not claim his privilege against compulsory self-incrimination to justify his refusal to produce the union's records pursuant to a grand jury subpoena. *White* announced the general rule that the privilege could not be employed by an individual to avoid production of the records of an organization, which he holds in a representative capacity as custodian on behalf of the group. Relying on *White,* we have since upheld compelled production of the records of a variety of organizations over individuals' claims of Fifth Amendment privilege. See, e. g., United States v. Fleischman, 339 U.S. 349, 357–358, 70 S.Ct. 739, 743–744, 94 L.Ed. 906 (1950) (Joint Anti-Fascist Refugee Committee); Rogers v. United States, 340 U.S. 367, 371–372, 71 S.Ct. 438, 440–442, 95 L.Ed. 344 (1951) (Communist Party of Denver); McPhaul v. United States, 364 U.S. 372, 380, 81 S.Ct. 138, 143, 5 L.Ed.2d 136 (1960) (Civil Rights Congress).

These decisions reflect the Court's consistent view that the privilege against compulsory self-incrimination should be "limited to its historic function of protecting only the natural individual from compulsory incrimination through his own testimony or personal records." United States v. White, supra, 322 U.S. at 701, 64 S.Ct. at 1252. *White* is only one of the many cases to emphasize that the Fifth Amendment privilege is a purely personal one, most recent among them being the Court's decision last Term in Couch v. United States, 409 U.S., at 327–328, 93 S.Ct., at 615–616. Relying on this fundamental policy limiting the scope of the privilege, the Court in *White* held that "the papers and effects which the privilege protects must be the private property of the person claiming the privilege, or at least in his possession in a purely personal capacity." 322 U.S., at 699, 64 S.Ct. at 1251. Mr. Justice Murphy reasoned that "individuals, when acting as representatives of a collective group, cannot be said to be exercising their personal rights and duties nor to be entitled to their purely personal privileges. Rather they assume the rights, duties and privileges of the artificial entity or association of which they are agents or officers and they are bound by its obligations." Ibid.

Since no artificial organization may utilize the personal privilege against compulsory self-incrimination, the Court found that it follows that an individual acting in his official capacity on behalf of the organization may likewise not take advantage of his personal privilege. In view of the inescapable fact that an artificial entity can only act to produce its records through its individual officers or agents, recognition of the individual's claim of privilege with respect to the financial records of the organization would substantially undermine the unchallenged rule that the organization itself is not entitled to claim any Fifth Amendment privilege, and largely frustrate legitimate governmental regulation of such organizations. Mr. Justice Murphy put it well:

> "The scope and nature of the economic activities of incorporated and unincorporated organizations and their representatives demand that the constitutional power of the federal and state governments to regulate those activities be correspondingly effective. The greater portion of evidence of wrongdoing by an organization or its representatives is usually to be found in the official records and documents of that organization. Were the cloak of the privilege to be thrown around these impersonal records and documents, effective enforcement of many federal and state laws would be impossible. The framers of the constitutional guarantee against compulsory self-disclosure, who were interested primarily in protecting individual civil liberties, cannot be said to have intended the privilege to be available to protect economic or other interests of such organizations so as to nulli-

fy appropriate governmental regulations." Id., at 700, 64 S. Ct., at 1251 (citations omitted).

The Court's decisions holding the privilege inapplicable to the records of a collective entity also reflect a second, though obviously interrelated, policy underlying the privilege, the protection of an individual's right to a " 'private enclave where he may lead a private life.' " Murphy v. Waterfront Comm'n, 378 U.S. 52, 55, 84 S.Ct. 1594, 1597, 12 L.Ed.2d 678 (1964). We have recognized that the Fifth Amendment "respects a private inner sanctum of individual feeling and thought"—an inner sanctum which necessarily includes an individual's papers and effects to the extent that the privilege bars their compulsory production and authentication—and "proscribes state intrusion to extract self-condemnation." Couch v. United States, supra, 409 U.S. at 327, 93 S.Ct. at 615. Protection of individual privacy was the major theme running through the Court's decision in *Boyd,* and it was on this basis that the Court in *Wilson* distinguished the corporate records involved in that case from the private papers at issue in *Boyd.*

But a substantial claim of privacy or confidentiality cannot often be maintained with respect to the financial records of an organized collective entity. Control of such records is generally strictly regulated by statute or by the rules and regulations of the organization, and access to the records is generally guaranteed to others in the organization. In such circumstances, the custodian of the organization's records lacks the control over their content and location and the right to keep them from the view of others which would be characteristic of a claim of privacy and confidentiality. Mr. Justice Murphy recognized the significance of this in *White*; he pointed out that organizational records "[u]sually, if not always, * * * are open to inspection by the members," that "this right may be enforced on appropriate occasions by available legal procedures," and that "[t]hey therefore embody no element of personal privacy." 322 U.S., at 699–700, 64 S.Ct., at 1251. And here lies the modern-day relevance of the visitorial powers doctrine relied upon by the Court in *Wilson* and the other cases dealing with corporate records; the Court's holding that no privilege exists "where, by virtue of their character and the rules of law applicable to them, the books and papers are held subject to examination by the [state]," 221 U.S., at 382, 31 S.Ct., at 545, can easily be understood as a recognition that corporate records do not contain the requisite element of privacy or confidentiality essential for the privilege to attach.

The analysis of the Court in *White,* of course, only makes sense in the context of what the Court described as "organized, institutional activity." 322 U.S., at 701, 64 S.Ct., at 1252. This analysis presupposes the existence of an organization which is recognized as an independent entity apart from its individual members. The group must be relatively well organized and structured and not merely a loose, informal association of individuals. It must maintain a distinct set of organizational records, and recognize rights in its members of control and access to them. And the records subpoenaed must in fact be organizational records held in a representative capacity. In other words, it must be fair to say that the records demanded are the records of the organization rather than those of the individual under *White*.

The Court in *White* had little difficulty in concluding that the demand for production of the official records of a labor union, whether national or local, in the custody of an officer of the union, met these tests. The Court observed that a union's existence in fact, if not in law, was "as perpetual as that of any corporation," id., at 701, 64 S.Ct., at 1252, that the union operated under formal constitutions, rules, and bylaws, and that it engaged in a broad scope of activities in which it was recognized as an independent entity. The Court also pointed out that the official union books and records were distinct from the personal books and records of its members, that the union restricted the permissible uses of these records, and that it recognized its members' rights to inspect them. Although the Court was aware that the individual members might legally hold title to the union records, the Court characterized this interest as a "nominal" rather than a significant personal interest in them.

We think it is similarly clear that partnerships may and frequently do represent organized institutional activity so as to preclude any claim of Fifth Amendment privilege with respect to the partnership's financial records. Some of the most powerful private institutions in the Nation are conducted in the partnership form. Wall Street law firms and stock brokerage firms provide significant examples. These are often large, impersonal, highly structured enterprises of essentially perpetual duration. The personal interest of any individual partner in the financial records of a firm of this scope is obviously highly attenuated. It is inconceivable that a brokerage house with offices from coast to coast handling millions of dollars of investment transactions annually should be entitled to immunize its records from SEC scrutiny solely because it operates as a partnership rather than in the corporate form. Although none of the reported cases has involved a partnership of quite this magnitude, it is hardly surprising that all of the courts of appeals which have addressed the question have concluded that *White's* analysis requires rejection of any claim of privilege in the financial records of a large business enterprise conducted in the partnership form. Even those lower courts which have held the privilege applicable in the context of a smaller partnership have frequently acknowledged that no absolute exclusion of the partnership form from the *White* rule generally applicable to unincorporated associations is warranted.

In this case, however, we are required to explore the outer limits of the analysis of the Court in *White*. Petitioner argues that in view of the modest size of the partnership involved here, it is unrealistic to consider the firm as an entity independent of its three partners; rather, he claims, the law firm embodies little more than the personal legal practice of the individual partners. Moreover, petitioner argues that he has a substantial and direct ownership interest in the partnership records, and does not hold them in a representative capacity.

Despite the force of these arguments, we conclude that the lower courts properly applied the *White* rule in the circumstances of this case. While small, the partnership here did have an established institutional identity independent of its individual partners. This was not an informal association or a temporary arrangement for the undertaking of a few projects of short-lived duration. Rather, the partnership represented a formal institutional arrangement organized for the continuing conduct of the firm's legal practice. The partnership was in existence for nearly 15 years prior to its voluntary dissolution. Although it may not have had a formal constitution or bylaws to govern its internal affairs, state partnership law imposed on the firm a certain organizational structure in the absence of any contrary agreement by the partners; for example, it guaranteed to each of the partners the equal right to participate in the management and control of the firm, Pa.Stat.Ann., Tit. 59, § 51(e) (1964), and prescribed that majority rule governed the conduct of the firm's business, § 51(h). The firm maintained a bank account in the partnership name, had stationery using the firm name on its letterhead, and, in general, held itself out to third parties as an entity with an independent institutional identity. It employed six persons in addition to its partners, including two other attorneys who practiced law on behalf of the firm, rather than as individuals on their own behalf. It filed separate partnership returns for federal tax purposes, as required by § 6031 of the Internal Revenue Code. State law permitted the firm to be sued, Pa.Rule Civ.Proc. 2128, and to hold title to property, Pa. Stat.Ann., Tit. 59, § 13(3), in the partnership name, and generally regarded the partnership as a distinct entity for numerous other purposes.

Equally important, we believe it is fair to say that petitioner is holding the subpoenaed partnership records in a representative capacity. The documents which petitioner has been ordered to produce are merely the financial books and records of the partnership. These reflect the receipts and disbursements of the entire firm, including income generated by and salaries paid to the employees of the firm, and the financial transactions of the other partners. Petitioner holds these records subject to the rights granted to the other partners by state partnership law. Petitioner has no direct ownership interest in the records; rather, under state law, they are partnership property, and petitioner's interest in partnership property is a derivative interest subject to significant limitations. Petitioner has no right to use this property for other than partnership purposes without the consent of the other partners. Pa.Stat.Ann., Tit. 59, § 72(2)(a). Petitioner is of course accountable to the partnership as a fiduciary, § 54(1), and his possession of the firm's financial records is especially subject to his fiduciary obligations to the other partners. Indeed, Pennsylvania law specifically provides that "every partner shall at all times have access to and may inspect and copy any of [the partnership books]." § 52. To facilitate this right of access, petitioner was required to keep these financial books and records at the firm's principal place of business, at least during the active life of the partnership. Ibid. The other partners in the firm were—and still are—entitled to enforce these rights through legal action by demanding production of the records in a suit for a formal accounting. § 55.

It should be noted also that petitioner was content to leave these records with the other members of the partnership at their principal place of business for more than three years after he left the firm. Moreover, the Government contends that the other partners in the firm had agreed to turn the records over to the grand jury before discovering that petitioner had removed them from their offices, and that they made an unavailing demand upon petitioner to return the records. Whether or not petitioner's present possession of these records is an unlawful infringement of the rights of the other partners, this provides additional support for our conclusion that it is the organizational character of the records and the representative aspect of petitioner's present possession of them which predominates over his belatedly discovered personal interest in them.

Petitioner relies heavily on language in the Court's opinion in *White* which suggests that the "test" for determining the applicability of the Fifth Amendment privilege in this area is whether the organization "has a character so impersonal in the scope of its membership and activities that it cannot be said to embody or represent the purely private or personal interests of its constituents, but rather to embody their common or group interests only." 322 U.S., at 701, 64 S.Ct., at 1252. We must admit our agreement with the Solicitor General's observation that "it is difficult to know precisely what situations the formulation in *White* was intended to include within the protection of the privilege." Brief for United States 21. The Court in *White*, after stating its test, did not really apply it, nor has any of the subsequent decisions of this Court. On its face, the test is not particularly helpful in the broad range of cases, including this one, where the organization embodies neither "purely * * * personal interests" nor "group interests only," but rather some combination of the two.

In any event, we do not believe that the Court's formulation in *White* can be reduced to a simple proposition based solely upon the size of the organization. It is well settled that no privilege can be claimed by the custodian of corporate records, regardless of how small the corporation may be. Every State has now adopted laws permitting incorporation of professional associations, and increasing numbers of lawyers, doctors, and other professionals are choosing to conduct their business affairs in the corporate form rather than the more traditional partnership. Whether corporation or partnership, many of these firms will be independent entities whose financial records are held by a member of the firm in a representative capacity. In these circumstances, the applicability of the privilege should not turn on an insubstantial difference in the form of the business enterprise.

This might be a different case if it involved a small family partnership, see United States v. Slutsky, 352 F.Supp. 1105 (S.D.N.Y. 1972); In re Subpoena Duces Tecum, 81 F.Supp., at 421, or, as the Solicitor General suggests, if there were some other pre-existing relationship of confidentiality among the partners. But in the circumstances of this case, petitioner's possession of the partnership's financial records in what can be fairly said to be a representative capacity compels our holding that his personal privilege against compulsory self-incrimination is inapplicable.

Affirmed.

QUESTION

In a case entitled Matter of Special Grand Jury No. 1, Impanelled December, 1977 Term, 465 F.Supp. 800 (D.Md.1978), two brothers were engaged in the practice of law from the same suite of offices. Although they did not have a written or oral partnership agreement, there was a holding out to the public, by virtue of their utilization of stationery of "X and X, Attorneys at Law", telephone directory listings, etc., that there was a partnership. Under state law the two were partners by estoppel and each would have been liable for the debts and obligations incurred by the other in the course of the practice of law. Should the court in this case have sustained an objection by one brother to the production of records relating to the law practice based upon his Fifth Amendment privilege against self-incrimination?

UNITED STATES v. O'HENRY'S FILM WORKS, INC.
598 F.2d 313 (2d Cir. 1979).

EDELSTEIN, District Judge:

* * *

In March 1976, an Internal Revenue Service (IRS) summons was served on Pergament as president of O'Henry's Film Works, Inc. (O'Henry's), which called upon him to produce certain corporate documents of O'Henry's and to give testimony in connection with an IRS investigation of the corporation's tax liability for fiscal years 1973, 1974, and 1975. On the return date of the summons, the corporation made available some of the documents demanded, but did not produce cash register tapes and cash register reconciliation statements called for by the summons. When Pergament appeared in response to the summons, he declined to answer any substantive questions asked by an IRS Special Agent, and claimed his Fifth Amendment privilege against self-incrimination.

A second IRS summons was served on Pergament as president of O'Henry's, in July 1976. It called for his testimony and for production of the cash register tapes and reconciliation statements that had not been produced in response to the previous summons. No such records were produced. When Pergament appeared in response to the summons on August 2, 1976, he again refused to answer any substantive questions on the ground that his answers might tend to incriminate him. Pergament's attorney stated that "[w]e have produced everything we can in response to this summons, and that is nothing," and made similar statements to the same effect.[1]

Nine months after Pergament's second appearance before IRS agents, in May 1977, Petitioners by order to show cause instituted a summary proceeding pursuant to 26 U.S.C. §§ 7402, 7604 to compel compliance with the second summons. An IRS Special Agent submitted an affidavit in support of the application stating his factual basis for believing the tapes still existed. Pergament submitted an affidavit in opposition to the application which, in relevant part, adopted his attorney's statements made on August 2, 1976, and stated further:

> I am not now, nor was I at the time I was served with the summons in question, in possession or in control of the documents called for in the summons. The same is and was true of O'Henry's Film Works, Inc. Moreover, I reaffirm that I respectfully decline on the advice of counsel to answer any further questions concerning these documents on the ground that the answers to such questions may tend to incriminate me.

By memorandum and order filed October 18, 1977, the district court found that Pergament had waived his Fifth Amendment privilege by filing the affidavit described above. However, on the issue of enforcement of the summons to produce records, the district court found that the IRS had not adequately established the existence of the records sought and therefore denied Petitioners' application without prejudice. The court stated that if the IRS could establish, through testimony of Pergament or other evidence, the existence of the records and Pergament's possession of them, the court would enforce the summons. * * *

---

1. Pergament's attorney also stated: "we have, so that the record will be clear, no records to produce in a re- sponse to this summons"; and "I am saying we cannot produce anything in response to this summons."

Pergament then was requested to appear to testify regarding the whereabouts of the cash register records by an Assistant United States Attorney. Pergament's attorney declined to produce Pergament unless a new IRS summons were issued. On April 27, 1978, Petitioners moved for an order directing Pergament to appear and answer questions about the tapes. The district court granted the motion by memorandum endorsement filed June 9, 1978, stating that its earlier memorandum and order of October 18, 1977, had denied enforcement only of the portion of the summons that called for production of documents, and that the portion of the summons that called for Pergament's testimony remained enforceable. Therefore, by order of July 5, 1978, the district court ordered Pergament to "respond to appropriate questions including ones concerning the whereabouts of the documents described in the summons," but stayed enforcement of the order pending this appeal.

* * *

It is well settled that the Fifth Amendment privilege against self-incrimination does not extend to corporations and similar organizations. An agent of such an organization has a duty to produce the organization's records, even where the records might incriminate the corporation or the agent, if a valid summons or subpoena has issued for those records. * * *

It is also well settled that an agent of an organization retains a personal privilege against self-incrimination. Curcio v. United States, 354 U.S. 118, 77 S.Ct. 1145, 1 L.Ed.2d 1225 (1957). Even a routine tax investigation is a situation in which answers to questions by an IRS agent might tend to incriminate, and thus Fifth Amendment rights apply to such answers. Of course, the Fifth Amendment protects a witness such as Pergament [2] only if it is raised in timely fashion. A witness who fails to invoke the Fifth Amendment against questions as to which he could have claimed it is deemed to have waived his privilege respecting all questions on the same subject matter. See Rogers v. United States, 340 U.S. 367, 71 S.Ct. 438, 95 L.Ed. 344 (1951).

The question whether Pergament made such a waiver depends upon whether his duty as an agent of a corporation rendered unprivileged, and therefore compulsory under valid process, certain statements he made when he failed to produce corporate records. If Pergament, as president of O'Henry's, was compelled at the time Petitioners applied to enforce the summons to state that he was not in possession of the cash register tapes and reconciliation statements

2. Different procedural rules might apply to a witness under other circumstances. For example, if a witness is "in custody" and unaccompanied by counsel, IRS agents would be required to follow the procedures set out in Miranda v. Arizona, 384 U.S. 436, 86 S.Ct. 1602, 16 L.Ed.2d 694 (1966). Mathis v. United States, 391 U.S. 1, 88 S.Ct. 1503, 20 L.Ed.2d 381 (1968).

called for, then the statement in his affidavit could not have been avoided by a claim of privilege, and no Fifth Amendment waiver occurred. If, on the other hand, Pergament was free to say nothing in response to Petitioners' application, then the statement in his affidavit might be deemed a voluntary waiver of his Fifth Amendment privilege. A resolution of this issue must begin with an examination of two United States Supreme Court cases, Curcio v. United States, 354 U.S. 118, 77 S.Ct. 1145, 1 L.Ed.2d 1225 (1957), and McPhaul v. United States, 364 U.S. 372, 81 S.Ct. 138, 5 L.Ed.2d 136 (1960).

Curcio v. United States, supra, reversed a contempt conviction of a union official who had refused to answer questions regarding the whereabouts of union records he had failed to produce to a grand jury. Joseph Curcio, secretary-treasurer of a union local, had testified "that the union had books and records; but that they were not then in his possession." He then refused to answer any further questions about the whereabouts of the records, on the ground that his answers might tend to incriminate him. A unanimous Court held that Curcio could not be compelled to testify regarding the whereabouts of corporate books and records because such testimony might lead to a criminal conviction. Although Curcio had stated that the records were not in his possession, the Court did not even consider whether that statement constituted a waiver of his Fifth Amendment privilege.

McPhaul v. United States, supra, upheld a contempt conviction against the putative executive secretary of an organization who had refused to answer any questions whatsoever regarding possession or custody of organizational records called for by a Congressional subpoena. McPhaul did not produce the records called for, then refused to answer even a question whether he was refusing to comply with the subpoena. At no point in the Congressional hearing, nor in proceedings before any court, did McPhaul claim that the records called for did not exist or were not in his possession. Although McPhaul could not have been convicted of contempt if he had satisfied the Court that he did not possess the records, his failure to make any statement regarding his nonproduction of the records led to his conviction. As to whether any statement by McPhaul would have been a waiver of his Fifth Amendment privilege, the Court stated: "[T]here is no merit in petitioner's argument that he could not have advised the Subcommittee that he was unable to produce the records without thereby inviting other questions respecting the records and thus risking waiver of his privilege against self-incrimination. See Curcio v. United States, 354 U.S. 118, [77 S.Ct. 1145, 1 L.Ed.2d 1225]." 364 U.S. at 380, 81 S.Ct. at 143.

A plain reading of *Curcio* and *McPhaul* leads to the conclusion that the duty of the putative custodian of an organization's records extends beyond mere production or nonproduction: when the agent fails to produce documents that are the subject of a valid summons or subpoena, if called before a court, he must give sworn testimony that he does not possess them. The agent's statement that he does not possess the records at issue is merely part of his duty to comply with a lawful demand for them. It might be called "testimony auxiliary to his nonproduction," by analogy to Judge Learned Hand's holding that an agent must identify the documents he does produce because "testimony auxiliary to the production is as unprivileged as are the documents themselves." United States v. Austin-Bagley Corp., 31 F. 2d 229, 234 (2d Cir. 1929). Just as an agent's identification of documents he has produced "merely makes explicit what is implicit in the production itself," *Curcio*, supra, 354 U.S. at 125, 77 S.Ct. at 1150, so does an agent's statement that he does not possess documents he has failed to produce make explicit what is implicit in the nonproduction. Because the agent's testimony is unprivileged, it is not a waiver of his privilege against self-incrimination as to other matters. The agent cannot be interrogated further unless, at this point, he voluntarily waives his Fifth Amendment privilege or is granted immunity. The Government is then free to attempt to establish by extrinsic evidence that the documents exist in the agent's custody or control, or that the agent destroyed the documents.

Accordingly, we hold that Pergament's statement in his affidavit that he did not possess the cash register tapes and reconciliation statements called for in the summons was compelled under *McPhaul* and was not a waiver of his Fifth Amendment privilege. Were we to conclude, however, that Pergament's statement was not strictly compelled by *McPhaul*, it would not necessarily follow that a waiver had occurred. The Supreme Court has taught us that the Fifth Amendment is a fundamental right that "must not be interpreted in a hostile or niggardly spirit," Ullman v. United States, 350 U.S. 422, 426, 76 S.Ct. 497, 500, 100 L.Ed. 511 (1956), and that courts must "indulge every reasonable presumption against waiver," Emspak v. United States, 349 U.S. 190, 198, 75 S.Ct. 687, 692, 99 L.Ed. 997 (1955).

The facts presented are that, in response to two IRS summonses, Pergament initially made broad and unequivocal claims of his Fifth Amendment privilege and refused to answer any substantive question. In his affidavit to the district court, his statement that he did not possess the documents called for immediately was followed, in the same numbered paragraph, by another assertion that he would not answer any further questions on Fifth Amendment grounds. Pergament thus attempted to navigate the perilous straits between contempt for not performing his duty as a corporate agent and waiver of his Fifth Amendment rights. Were we to find that Pergament's statement was not strictly compelled under our reading of the case law, a finding would not necessarily follow that a voluntary waiver had occurred. See Emspak v. United States, 349 U.S. 190, 75 S.Ct. 687, 99 L.Ed. 997 (1955); Smith v. United States, 337 U.S. 137 (1949).

Presser v. United States, 284 F.2d 233 (1960), cert. denied, 365 U.S. 816, 81 S.Ct. 694, 5 L.Ed.2d 696 (1961), is relied upon by Petitioners in their brief and cited by the district court in its memorandum and order of October 18, 1977, and its memorandum endorsement denying reargument of November 10, 1977. *Presser* is distinguishable, however, because it involved a subpoena for a union official's personal records. Presser was free not to answer all questions. Once he produced some of the records called for and testified that he had complied with the subpoena to the best of his ability, he was found to have waived his privilege against self-incrimination.

*   *   *

The order of the district court, filed July 5, 1978, is reversed.

SECTION 4.   THIRD–PARTY RECORDKEEPER SUMMONSES

In the Tax Reform Act of 1976 Congress provided that certain types of Internal Revenue Service summonses required special safeguards for taxpayers. Essentially, these "third-party recordkeeper" summonses are defined to include summonses issued to specified types of persons who ordinarily keep records of another. Thus, the statute brings within its definition summonses issued to most financial institutions, consumer reporting agencies, persons extending credit through credit cards, brokers, attorneys and accountants.[f] A summons issued to one of these "third-party recordkeepers" for records made or kept for a person identified in the summons is a third-party recordkeeper summons within the meaning of the statute. As described in the following decision, the service of such a summons requires notice and the opportunity for a peremptory stay of compliance to one named (as the taxpayer or person otherwise entitled to notice) in the summons. Hence, there can be a material difference in the rights of a taxpayer or named person if a third-party recordkeeper (as distinct from a regular) summons is served.

The wisdom of providing for a peremptory stay of compliance is questionable. At this writing, consideration is being given to eliminating the peremptory stay power and substituting for it a right on the part of a noticee to commence an action to restrain compliance only for good cause shown.

The utilization of the peremptory stay power by a taxpayer under investigation is not without its price. The cost to the taxpayer is the suspension of the statute of limitations (for both civil and criminal prosecution purposes) during the entire pendency (including appeals) of an action to enforce the summons.[g] This price is paid even

f. IRC § 7609(a)(3). For exceptions, see IRC §§ 7609(a)(4), (c)(2) and (g).

g. IRC § 7609(e).

if the taxpayer prevails and the summons is determined to be unenforceable.

UNITED STATES v. EXXON CO., U. S. A.

450 F.Supp. 472 (D.Md.1978).

HERBERT F. MURRAY, District Judge.

The United States and W. Donald Bell, a Special Agent of the Internal Revenue Service have filed a Petition under Sections 7402(b) and 7604(a) of the Internal Revenue Code of 1954 to enforce an Internal Revenue Service summons served on October 27, 1977 on the respondent, Exxon Company, U.S.A. (Exxon) which maintains offices in Maryland. * * *

The petition and supporting affidavit of Special Agent Bell state that he is conducting an investigation of the federal income tax liabilitites of Maryland Lumber Company, Fabian Kolker and M. Budd Kolker for the taxable years 1972 through 1974, inclusive, and that the documents requested relate to this investigation. The taxpayers filed a Joint Motion to Intervene as Parties Respondent on March 8, 1978. * * *

The motion to intervene is based on two asserted grounds: (1) that under Section 7609(b)(1) of the Internal Revenue Code of 1954 movants, as persons entitled to notice of the summons at issue in this case, are entitled to intervene as a matter of right in this summons enforcement proceeding; and (2) that movants are entitled to intervene in this action pursuant to Rule 24(a) and (b) of the Federal Rules of Civil Procedure.

I.

The court first will consider movants' first ground for intervention under Section 7609(b)(1). Subsection (b)(1) of this section provides:

> Notwithstanding any other law or rule of law, any person who is entitled to notice of a summons under subsection (a) shall have the right to intervene in any proceeding with respect to the enforcement of such summons under section 7604.

Thus, the right to intervene under this section exists only if movants are persons who were entitled to notice of the summons issued to Exxon by the Internal Revenue Service.

At this point, the court notes that respondent Exxon in its answer to the Order to Show Cause contends that its failure to comply with the summons is warranted because Maryland Lumber Company, Fabian Kolker and M. Budd Kolker, persons entitled to notice of the summons under 26 U.S.C. § 7609(a)(1), did not receive such notice from the Internal Revenue Service. * * *

The determination of whether, in fact, movants were entitled to notice of the summons to Exxon requires that the court examine the summons at issue in this case. The summons is a third-party summons under 26 U.S.C. § 7602(2) requiring Exxon to produce:

> Copies of all agreements, contracts and correspondence between you and the Maryland Lumber Company and/or Fabian Kolker and/or M. Budd Kolker which pertains [sic] to the rental of 2501 W. Franklin Street and all checks and record of payments made by you during the period from January 1, 1972 thru Dec. 31, 1974, to Maryland Lumber Co. and/or Fabian Kolker and/or M. Budd Kolker under said agreements, contracts and correspondence.

It appears to the court from the arguments of counsel and the pleadings filed in this case that Special Agent Bell is attempting to have Exxon produce its lease with movants for the service station property noted in the summons, its checks paid to movants pursuant to the lease agreement, and certain other of its financial records pertaining to its lease * * *.

Section 7609 outlines the procedures to be followed by the IRS in the issuance of certain third-party summonses, which procedures are made applicable to those summonses issued after February 28, 1977. If the summons is one issued under Section 7602(2), as is the case with the summons here at issue, notice is required to be given if the summons is served on a third-party recordkeeper and if the summons requires the production of records of business transactions of a person identified in the description of the records in the summons. Section 7609(a)(1). Maryland Lumber Company, Fabian Kolker and M. Budd Kolker were identified in the request for production in the summons and the summons does request records of certain business transactions in which the movants were involved. However, what is really at issue here is whether Exxon qualifies as a third-party recordkeeper so that this provison would be applicable to the instant summons. Movants assert that Exxon comes within the definition of a third-party recordkeeper under Section 7609(a)(3)(C) in that it extends credit through the use of credit cards. If Exxon is in fact a third-party recordkeeper under the above definition of the term, then the IRS would have been required to give written notice of the summons to movants on October 27, 1977, fourteen days prior to the date for compliance with the summons by Exxon. Further, if movants are entitled to notice under this section, they are entitled to intervene in the proceedings to enforce the summons under subsection (b) of this section and they also were entitled to stay compliance by Exxon with the summons by giving written notice to Exxon not to comply and by sending a copy of this notice to the IRS under conditions which would have been contained in the original notice of IRS to movants. In this case, the IRS did not provide notice to movants and notice of the issuance of the summons was received informally by means of a letter dated November 2, 1977 from Exxon to the movants. In turn, movants, by letter to Exxon dated November 4, 1977, sent notice not to comply, and sent a copy of this notice to Special Agent Bell. Exxon notified the IRS by letter dated November 7, 1977 of its position that it was a third-party recordkeeper under Section 7609, that it had been requested not to comply with the summons by the movants and that it would not, therefore, comply. As a result of this non-compliance by Exxon with the summons, the instant action was commenced.

The court must determine whether Exxon is a third-party recordkeeper within the meaning of Section 7609, as the notice issue turns on the outcome of that question. More broadly, the issue presented is whether, when a summons is issued for records which pertain to the taxpayer, the taxpayer has a statutory right to intervene in the enforcement proceedings against the third party on whom the summons was served when that third party is a third-party recordkeeper by reason of issuance of credit cards in an aspect of its business which is unrelated to the records sought in the summons.

The court has sought in vain to locate a case which has interpreted the Section 7609 notice requirements or the meaning to be given to the term "third-party recordkeeper." This lack of reported case law most probably is due to the fact that the notice requirement was not made to apply to IRS summonses until after February 28, 1977, a relatively short time ago. Counsel for the parties in this case have informed the court that they, likewise, have been unable to locate a reported case dealing with the question here presented and counsel for the IRS has further informed the court that, currently, two other cases involving this question are pending in other federal district courts but that those cases have not progressed to a point where a decision has been rendered on this question. Although there is no decided case interpreting the Tax Reform Act of 1976, which amended Section 7609 particularly with regard to the procedural requirements for third-party summonses, the legislative history of the Act does cast some light on its meaning.

The House Report mentions as one of the general reasons for the change in the law the need to balance the IRS's investigative tools with the concern for the privacy of individuals:

> The use of the administrative summons, including the third-party summons, is a necessary tool for the IRS in conducting many legitimate investigations concerning the proper determination of tax. The administration of the tax laws requires that the Service be entitled to obtain records, etc., without an advance showing of probable cause or other stan-

dards which usually are involved in the issuance of a search warrant. On the other hand, the use of this important investigative tool should not unreasonably infringe on the civil rights of taxpayers, including the right to privacy. H.R. Rep. No. 94–658, 94th Cong., 2nd Sess. 307, reprinted in [1976] U.S.Code Cong. & Admin.News, pp. 2897, 3203.

The House Report went on to state that the notice is to be sent to the person who is identified in the description of the records contained in the summons "as the person relating to whose business or transactions the books or records are kept." Id. at 3204. The implication is that notice is required when the person's records of his business transactions are kept by a third person. The Senate Report indicated what was felt to be the definition of this third-party recordkeeper when it stated:

> For purposes of these rules, a third party recordkeeper is generally to be a *person engaged in making or keeping the records involving transactions of other persons.* For example, an administrative summons served on a partnership, with respect to records of the partnership's own transactions, would not be subject to these rules. (emphasis supplied) S.Rep. No. 94–938, 94th Cong., 2nd Sess. 369, reprinted in [1976] U.S.Code Cong. & Admin.News, pp. 2897, 3798.

This definition was further clarified in the House Conference Report wherein it was stated:

> * * * the agreement clarifies the definition of a third-party recordkeeper, limiting this category to attorneys, accountants, banks, trust companies, credit unions, savings and loan institutions, credit reporting agencies, issuers of credit cards, and brokers in stock or other securities. H.R.Conf. Rep. No. 94–1515, 94th Cong., 2nd Sess. 486, reprinted in [1976] U.S.Code Cong. & Admin.News, pp. 2897, 4190.

Thus, although the list of third-party recordkeepers includes those who issue credit cards and Exxon surely falls within this category, in that it issues to consumers credit cards which are generally used for the purchase of gasoline and other automobile related services, the underlying rationale of the amendment and the definition of third-party recordkeepers is to protect a citizen against the invasion of his privacy when his records are maintained or made by another. A person's credit transactions using his Exxon credit card come within this rationale and had the summons in issue in this case been for the credit transaction records of movants, the court would have little difficulty in deciding that notice was required under Section 7609. However, the records sought by the instant summons are not the credit records of movants and do not appear to involve directly the type of business transactions contemplated in the statute. The records sought more directly involve the business transactions of Exxon —its lease of a property from movants and its payments of rent on the same property. Although Exxon does make and keep the records of the transactions of other persons in carrying out its functions as an issuer of credit cards, the records at issue here more properly involve Exxon's own transactions and would not be subject to the notice rule. For the court to hold otherwise would necessitate a determination on the part of this court that the fact that a person or company issues credit cards to some persons automatically places all records of any transactions of any nature of that person or company within the notice requirement of Section 7609. This would place a burden on IRS investigators which would far exceed the intent of the Congress as expressed in the legislative history of the amendment to Section 7609. In the absence of evidence of an express purpose on the part of Congress to place such a burden on the IRS, this court is not inclined to read Section 7609 so broadly as to find a notice requirement in the issuance of the present summons. Accordingly, the court finds that no notice to movants was required by the IRS when it issued the summons to Exxon. As Section 7609(b)(1) requires that a person be one who is entitled to notice of a summons before a right to intervene under that section exists, the court further finds that Maryland Lumber Company, Fabian Kolker and M. Budd Kolker have no right of intervention under Section 7909(b)(1) in the proceedings to enforce the IRS summons to Exxon.

II.

Movants' assertion that they are entitled to intervene in this enforcement proceeding under Rule 24(a) and (b) of the Federal Rules of Civil Procedure is based on the allegation that "the summoned records relate to them, they are the subject of the tax investigation pursuant to which the summons was purportedly issued, they have an interest in the subject matter of this action which would be affected adversely if they are not allowed to intervene to raise their defenses to the summonses and they have no other adequate remedy at law to contest the lawfulness of said summons." Movants have also asserted that their interests are not adequately represented by the parties to this action. * * *

Both movants and petitioners have referred the court to the Supreme Court's decision in Donaldson v. United States, 400 U.S. 517, 91 S.Ct. 534, 27 L.Ed.2d 580 (1970), as the authority on whether a taxpayer should be allowed to intervene in a proceeding to enforce an IRS summons which is issued pursuant to an investigation of that taxpayer. * * *

* * *

In the instant case, this court is confronted with a situation not only similar to that in *Donaldson,* but basically identical. The records of Exxon sought by the IRS are owned by Exxon and relate to Exxon's business transactions with movants with respect to the rental of certain of movants' property by Exxon. Thus, it cannot be said that movants have any proprietary interest in these records. At most, it can be said that movants' interest lies in the fact that these records contain information concerning payment of rent income to the movants by Exxon which may have some bearing on their tax liabilities for the years under investigation by the IRS. Further, the records sought by the IRS are not subject to any established privilege which would bring movants within the language of Rule 24(a). The court finds that movants have no "significantly protectable interest" in the records which are the subject of the summons at issue in this case and that movants are not entitled to intervene in this action under Rule 24(a).

As to movants' assertion that they are entitled to intervene in this action under Rule 24(b) which provides for permissive intervention "when an applicant's claim or defense and the main action have a question of law or fact in common," this court is guided by the Fifth Circuit Court of Appeals' decision in United States v. Newman, 441 F.2d 165 (1971). *Newman* involved a case wherein the IRS sought enforcement of certain third-party summonses issued in aid of the investigation of the tax liabilities of taxpayer Pollack. The district court issued an Order to Show Cause and the taxpayer sought leave to intervene in the enforcement proceedings. The response of the taxpayer to the Order to Show Cause alleged that the special agent who had issued the summons had acted in bad faith and that the agent was "simply looking for evidence to use in a criminal proceeding." The district court allowed the taxpayer to intervene and the circuit court reversed this decision of the district court, finding that the facts that the records sought by the summons related to the taxpayer's own tax liability and that a recommendation for criminal prosecution could result from the investigation were not sufficient to warrant either intervention of right or permissive intervention under Rule 24. In finding that intervention of right was precluded, the court relied on the decision of the Supreme Court in *Donaldson*, supra, having found that the case before it was identical to the *Donaldson* case in terms of the allegations presented by the taxpayer.

In considering the taxpayer's reliance on permissive intervention under Rule 24(b), the court in *Newman* found that the decision in the *Donaldson* case precluded this form of intervention although the Court had been concerned only with intervention of right:

> * * * *Donaldson*—upholding a denial of intervention— compels rejection of intervention on discretionary grounds. In the course of its analysis of the *Reisman* dictum and the limitation of it to "the situation of a pending criminal charge or, at most, of an investigation solely for criminal purposes," the Court makes this decisive declaration:

"Any other holding, of course, would thwart and defeat the appropriate investigatory powers which the Congress has placed in 'the Secretary or his delegate.' "

400 U.S. at 533, 91 S.Ct. at 544, 27 L.Ed. at 591.

Bearing in mind that the allegations here are the identical ones there, this is a flat holding that on charges of this kind intervention by a taxpayer in a summons proceeding against a third party witness would thwart and defeat the policies and mechanisms ordained by Congress. It is the *intervention* in such situation, not the technical basis—as of right or permissive—for permitting it which thwarts and defeats. Clearly the Court did not mean to allow a single District Judge in the exercise of a wide and often undefinable discretion to ignore if not judicially repeal policies prescribed by the Congress. [441 F.2d at 172–173.]

*   *   *

This court has found that the allegations of movants in this case are identical to those presented in the *Donaldson* case, and thus, identical to those presented in the *Newman* case. *   *   * Accordingly, this court will deny movants' motion for permissive intervention in this action under Rule 24(b).

During the course of oral argument on this motion, counsel for movants and Exxon indicated that the enactment of Section 7609 effectively overruled the Supreme Court's decision in *Donaldson,* supra. Although this court does not attempt to determine the extent, if any, to which Section 7609 overrules the *Donaldson* decision, the court notes that, in any event, the *Donaldson* decision remains good law for purposes of the instant motion. It is clear that Section 7609 has created a statutory right to intervention not previously existing for taxpayers; however, this right is a limited one in that it applies only to those taxpayers or persons who are entitled to notice of the summons under Section 7609(a). Thus, as to those taxpayers who are not entitled to notice under Section 7609(a), no right of intervention has been created under Section 7609(b) and the *Donaldson* decision remains as controlling as to any rights of intervention of such taxpayers under Rule 24. In turn, *Donaldson* and the cases interpreting *Donaldson,* such as *Newman,* supra, remain in full force and effect as to the movants in this case, as this court has found that movants were not entitled to notice of the IRS summons to Exxon under Section 7609(a).

*   *   *

SECTION 5.   THE "JOHN DOE" SUMMONS

UNITED STATES v. BISCEGLIA

Supreme Court of the United States, 1975.
420 U.S. 141, 95 S.Ct. 915, 43 L.Ed.2d 88.

Mr. Chief Justice BURGER delivered the opinion of the Court.

⁎   ⁎   ⁎

On November 6 and 16, 1970, the Commercial Bank of Middlesboro, Ky., made two separate deposits with the Cincinnati Branch of the Federal Reserve Bank of Cleveland, each of which included $20,000 in $100 bills.   The evidence is undisputed that the $100 bills were "paper thin" and showed signs of severe disintegration which could have been caused by a long period of storage under abnormal conditions.   As a result the bills were no longer suitable for circulation and they were destroyed by the Federal Reserve in accord with established procedures.   Also in accord with regular Federal Reserve procedures, the Cincinnati Branch reported these facts to the Internal Revenue Service.

It is not disputed that a deposit of such a large amount of high denomination currency was out of the ordinary for the Commercial Bank of Middlesboro   ⁎   ⁎   ⁎.

After interviewing some of the bank's employees, none of whom could provide him with information regarding the two $20,000 deposits, [an IRS] agent issued a "John Doe" summons directed to respondent, an executive vice president of the Commercial Bank of Middlesboro.   The summons called for production of "[t]hose books and records which will provide information as to the person(s) or firm(s) which deposited, redeemed or otherwise gave to the Commercial Bank $100 bills which the Commercial Bank sent in two shipments of (200) two hundred each $100 bills U.S. Currency to the Cincinnati Branch of the Federal Reserve Bank on or about November 6, 1970 and November 16, 1970."   This, of course, was simply the initial step in an investigation which might lead to nothing or might reveal that there had been a failure to report money on which federal estate, gift, or income taxes were due.   Respondent, however, refused to comply with the summons even though he has not seriously argued that compliance would be unduly burdensome.

In due course, proceedings were commenced in the United States District Court for the Eastern District of Kentucky to enforce the summons.   That court narrowed its scope to require production only of deposit slips showing cash deposits in the amount of $20,000 and deposit slips showing cash deposits of $5,000 or more which involved $100 bills, and restricted it to the period between October 16, 1970, and November 16, 1970.   Respondent was ordered to comply with the summons as modified.

The Court of Appeals reversed, holding that § 7602 of the Internal Revenue Code of 1954, pursuant to which the summons had been issued, "presupposes that the [Internal Revenue Service] has already identified the person in whom it is interested as a taxpayer before proceeding." We disagee, and reverse the judgment of the Court of Appeals.

* * *

We recognize that the authority vested in tax collectors may be abused, as all power is subject to abuse. However, the solution is not to restrict that authority so as to undermine the efficacy of the federal tax system, which seeks to asure that taxpayers pay what Congress has mandated and to prevent dishonest persons from escaping taxation thus shifting heavier burdens to honest taxpayers. Substantial protection is afforded by the provision that an Internal Revenue Service summons can be enforced only by the courts. Once a summons is challenged it must be scrutinized by a court to determine whether it seeks information relevant to a legitimate investigative purpose and is not meant "to harass the taxpayer or to put pressure on him to settle a collateral dispute, or for any other purpose reflecting on the good faith of the particular investigation." United States v. Powell, 379 U.S., at 58, 85 S.Ct., at 255, 13 L.Ed.2d 112. The cases show that the federal courts have taken seriously their obligation to apply this standard to fit particular situations, either by refusing enforcement or narrowing the scope of the summons. Indeed, the District Judge in this case viewed the demands of the summons as too broad and carefully narrowed them.

Finally, we note that the power to summon and inquire in cases such as the instant one is not unprecedented. For example, had respondent been brought before a grand jury under identical circumstances there can be little doubt that he would have been required to testify and produce records or be held in contempt. * * *

* * *

Against this background, we turn to the question whether the summons issued to respondent, as modified by the District Court, was authorized by the Internal Revenue Code of 1954. Of course, the mere fact that the summons was styled "In the matter of the tax liability of John Doe" is not sufficient ground for denying enforcement. The use of such fictitious names is common in indictments and other types of compulsory process. Indeed, the Courts of Appeals have regularly enforced Internal Revenue Service summonses which did not name a specific taxpayer who was under investigation. * * *

* * * Section 7601 permits the Internal Revenue Service to investigate and inquire after "*all* persons * * * who *may be* liable to pay *any* internal revenue tax * * *." To aid in this investigative function, § 7602 authorizes the summoning of "*any* * * * person" for the taking of testimony and examination of books which may be relevant for "ascertaining the correctness of *any* return, * * * determining the liability of *any* person * * * or collecting *any* such liability * * *." Plainly, this language is inconsistent with an interpretation that would limit the issuance of summonses to investigations which have already focused upon a particular return, a particular named person, or a particular potential tax liability.

Moreover, such a reading of the Internal Revenue Service's summons power ignores the fact that it has a legitimate interest in large or unusual financial transactions, especially those involving cash. The reasons for that interest are too numerous and too obvious to catalog. Indeed, Congress has recently determined that information regarding transactions with foreign financial institutions and transactions which involve large amounts of money is so likely to be useful to persons responsible for enforcing the tax laws that it must be reported by banks.

It would seem elementary that no meaningful investigation of such events could be conducted if the identity of the persons involved must first be ascertained, and that is not always an easy task. Fiduciaries and other agents are understandably reluctant to disclose information regarding their principals, as respondent was in this case. Moreover, if criminal activity is afoot the persons involved may well have used aliases or taken other measures to cover their tracks. Thus, if the Internal Revenue Service is unable to issue a summons to determine the identity of such persons, the broad inquiry authorized by § 7601 will be frustrated in this class of cases. Settled principles of statutory interpretation require that we avoid such a result absent unambiguous directions from Congress. No such congressional purpose is discernible in this case.

We hold that the Internal Revenue Service was acting within its statutory authority in issuing a summons to respondent for the purpose of identifying the person or persons who deposited 400 decrepit $100 bills with the Commercial Bank of Middlesboro within the space of a few weeks. Further investigation may well reveal that such person or persons have a perfectly innocent explanation for the transactions. It is not unknown for taxpayers to hide large amounts of currency in odd places out of a fear of banks. But on this record the deposits were extraordinary, and no meaningful inquiry can be made until respondent complies with the summons as modified by the District Court.

We do not mean to suggest by this holding that respondent's fears that the § 7602 summons power could be used to conduct "fishing expeditions" into the private affairs of bank depositors are trivial. However, as we have observed in a similar context:

> " 'That the power may be abused, is no ground for denying its existence. It is a limited power, and should be

kept within its proper bounds; and, when these are exceeded, a jurisdictional question is presented which is cognizable in the courts.' " McGrain v. Daugherty, 273 U.S. 135, 166, 47 S.Ct. 319, 326, 71 L.Ed. 580 (1927), quoting People ex rel. McDonald v. Keeler, 99 N.Y. 463, 482, 2 N.E. 615, 626 (1885).

So here, Congress has provided protection from arbitrary or capricious action by placing the federal courts between the Government and the person summoned. The District Court in this case conscientiously discharged its duty to see that a legitimate investigation was being conducted and that the summons was no broader than necessary to achieve its purpose.

The judgment of the Court of Appeals is reversed and the cause is remanded to it with directions to affirm the order of the District Court.

* * *

Mr. Justice BLACKMUN, with whom Mr. Justice POWELL joins, concurring.

I join the Court's opinion and its judgment, and add this word only to emphasize the narrowness of the issue at stake here. We decide today that the Internal Revenue Service has statutory authority to issue a summons to a bank in order to ascertain the identity of a person whose transactions with that bank strongly suggest liability for unpaid taxes. Under the circumstances here, there was an overwhelming probability, if not a certitude, that one individual or entity was responsible for the deposits. The uniformly deteriorated condition of the currency and the amount, combined with other unusual aspects, gave the Service good reason, and indeed, the duty to investigate. The Service's suspicion as to possible liability was more than plausible. The summons was closely scrutinized and appropriately narrowed in scope by the United States District Court.

The summons, in short, was issued pursuant to a genuine investigation. The Service was not engaged in researching some general problem; its mission was not exploratory. The distinction between an investigative and a more general exploratory purpose has been stressed appropriately by federal courts, see e. g., United States v. Humble Oil & Refining Co., 488 F.2d 953, 958 (CA5 1974), and that distinction is important to our decision here.

We need not decide in this case whether the Service has statutory authority to issue a "John Doe" summons where neither a particular taxpayer nor an ascertainable group of taxpayers is under investigation. At most, we hold that the Service is not always required to state a taxpayer's name in order to obtain enforcement of its summons, and that under the circumstances of this case it is definitely not required to do so. We do not decide that a "John Doe" summons is always enforceable where the name of an individual is lacking and the Service's purpose is other than investigative.

Upon this understanding, I join the Court's opinion.

Mr. Justice STEWART, with whom Mr. Justice DOUGLAS joins, dissenting.

*   *   *

The Court today completely obliterates the historic distinction between the general duties of the IRS, summarized in § 7601, and the limited purposes for which a summons may issue, specified in § 7602. Relying heavily on § 7601, and noting that the IRS "has a legitimate interest in large or unusual financial transactions, especially those involving cash," the Court approves enforcement of a summons having no investigative predicate. The sole premise for this summons was the Service's theory that the deposit of old wornout $100 bills was a sufficiently unusual and interesting transaction to justify compulsory disclosure of the identities of all the large-amount depositors at the respondent's bank over a one-month period. That the summons was not incident to an ongoing, particularized investigation, but was merely a shot in the dark to see if one might be warranted, was freely conceded by the IRS agent who served the summons.

*   *   *

*   *   * For this summons, there was absolutely no investigative predicate. The sole indication of this John Doe's tax liability was the unusual character of the deposit transaction itself. Any private economic transaction is now fair game for forced disclosure, if any IRS agent happens in good faith to want it disclosed. This new rule simply disregards the language of § 7602 and the body of established case law construing it.

*   *   *

I would affirm the judgment of the Court of Appeals.

UNITED STATES v. HUMBLE OIL & REFINING CO.

518 F.2d 747 (5th Cir. 1975).

PER CURIAM:

The Supreme Court of the United States on April 28, 1975 vacated the judgment of this court in the case of United States v. Humble Oil and Refining Company, 488 F.2d 953 (5th Cir. 1974) and remanded the case for further consideration in light of United States v. Bisceglia.

We have carefully considered *Bisceglia* and have concluded that it does not require a reversal of our decision in this case. Both cases involve the enforceability of a "John Doe" summons issued by the Internal Revenue Service. While the *Bisceglia* Court held the "John

Doe" summons before it to be enforceable, we decline to construe that holding as a blanket endorsement of the use of "John Doe" summonses in every situation without reference either to the purpose of the summons or to the factual circumstances which underlie its issuance.

At issue in *Bisceglia* was the enforceability of a "John Doe" summons issued by the IRS to a bank. The impetus behind the issuance of the summons was the deposit with the bank of some 400 badly deteriorated one hundred dollar bills by an unknown bank customer. This extraordinary transaction gave rise to a strong suspicion of unpaid taxes. An agent was assigned to investigate, and the issuance of the summons constituted the first step in the investigative process.

In the case now before us the IRS issued a "John Doe" summons in order to discover the identities of all lessors of mineral leases surrendered by Humble Oil in the calendar year 1970. The information sought did not relate to a specific, extraordinary transaction as in *Bisceglia*. Nor were there any factually demonstrable grounds to suggest the likelihood of unpaid taxes. The summons was not issued to facilitate any ongoing investigation. Rather, the information was sought from Humble to expedite research on an IRS project concerning compliance with the lease restoration requirements of the Internal Revenue Code. An adjustment of tax liabilities may have incidentally resulted from the project, but the primary purpose of the project was research. We do not believe that the provisions of 26 U. S.C. §§ 7601 and 7602 authorize the IRS to force private citizens to do its research. Nor do we believe that *Bisceglia* sanctions this use of the summons power. The judgment is therefore affirmed.

UNITED STATES v. BRIGHAM YOUNG UNIV.

485 F.Supp. 534 (D.Utah 1980).

WINDER, District Judge.

On November 5, 1979, the government filed a petition for leave to serve a third party John Doe summons in File No. C–79–0647. Thereafter, this court signed an order allowing the IRS to serve a John Doe summons upon Brigham Young University (BYU), in the matter of the tax liability of donors of charitable contributions in kind, excluding securities, to BYU during the years 1976, 1977, and 1978. The summons was served on BYU, who refused to produce the information requested. On December 21, 1979, the government filed a petition to enforce the IRS summons, File No. C–79–0753.

* * *

The pertinent facts are not seriously in dispute. BYU is a private institution of higher education located in Provo, Utah. As such, it is exempt from income taxation under 26 U.S.C. § 501(c)(3). Under § 170, gifts to BYU are charitable contributions that are deductible from the donor's income. A taxpayer who makes a charitable contribution in kind to BYU may deduct from income in the year of the gift the fair market value of the property contributed as of the time of the contribution, subject to the limitations set forth in § 170.

The IRS has audited some 162 federal income tax returns of persons who made charitable contributions in kind to BYU. Eighty-five of these returns were for taxable years ending before January 1, 1976. The remainder were for taxable years ending after December 31, 1975. The IRS has proposed deficiencies for all the returns for years ending before January 1, 1976, and has proposed or expects to propose deficiencies for all the returns for the years ending after December 31, 1975. The proposed deficiency in each case results from a determination by the IRS that the actual fair market value of the property contributed is substantially less than the amount claimed on the return. Because of these overvaluations, the IRS has commenced an investigation of the correct tax liability of all persons who made gifts in kind, excluding securities, to BYU during the years 1976, 1977, and 1978. By these proceedings it is seeking to obtain from BYU the names and addresses of all such donors. BYU has acknowledged their number totals approximately 300.

Of the overvaluations which the IRS has determined so far, all but fourteen deal with one group of donors of art objects and another group of donors of silver mining claims. BYU has offered to provide the IRS with the names and addresses of the individuals in these two groups. The members of each of these groups had certain common characteristics. The donors of the art objects participated in a transaction devised by an art dealer or dealers, part of which involved the dealer or dealers appraising the art objects for purposes of valuation. Similarly with the silver mining claims, one mining engineer had appraised all of the mining claims of that group of donors. There was no such common characteristic relating to the fourteen other donors investigated by the IRS and not within the art objects or silver mining claim groups. So far as the record discloses, these fourteen donors made their overvaluated gifts under circumstances where no relationship has been demonstrated between their gifts and that of any other gift in this group except, of course, that all made a gift in kind to BYU.

Both parties agree that the requirements of 26 U.S.C. § 7609(f) [h] govern the result in this case. That section states:

> Additional requirement in the case of a John Doe summons.—Any summons described in subsection (c) which does not identify the person with respect to whose liability the summons is issued may be served only after a court proceeding in which the Secretary establishes that—

h. Section 7609(f) was added to the Code by the Tax Reform Act of 1976.

(1) the summons relates to the investigation of a particular person or ascertainable group or class of persons,

(2) there is a reasonable basis for believing that such person or group or class of persons may fail or may have failed to comply with any provision of any internal revenue law, and

(3) the information sought to be obtained from the examination of the records (and the identity of the person or persons with respect to whose liability the summons is issued) is not readily available from other sources.

BYU argues that there is no ongoing investigation and that the requirements of subsection (1) of § 7609(f) have not been met by the IRS. It is clear from the record, however, that the summons does relate to an investigation of a class of persons within the meaning of § 7609(f)(1). Likewise, the court rejects BYU's objection that because the IRS already has technical possession of the records it seeks it therefore has not met the requirements of subsection (3). Several recent cases have held that the mere technical possession of records by the IRS where there is no method of practical retrieval does not defeat the subsection (3) requirement of § 7609(f). United States v. First National State Bank, 616 F.2d 668 (3d Cir. 1980); United States v. Reprints, Inc., 79–1 U.S.T.C. ¶ 9108 (N.D.Ga.1978). It would be most impractical and also unnecessary, under this subsection, to require the IRS to manually search through thousands or hundreds of thousands of tax returns for the three years in question to determine the identity of each donor in kind to BYU. That this would have to be done satisfies the court that such information is "not readily available."

Before discussing the requirements of subsection (2) of § 7609(f) there are two other issues that can be briefly resolved. Both the IRS and BYU agree that BYU is not a third-party recordkeeper pursuant to § 7609(a)(3). BYU argues that a John Doe summons may only be issued to third-party recordkeepers as enumerated in § 7609(a)(3). It appears clear from the language of § 7609 and the legislative history that such an interpretation is not correct. It also appears that the only court to rule on the issue did not restrict the issuance of John Doe summons to only the third parties enumerated in § 7609(a)(3). United States v. Reprints, Inc., supra. This court holds therefore that this summons would be properly issuable to BYU under these circumstances if the other requirements of § 7609(f) were met.

BYU's claim that the information demanded by the IRS may interfere with the donors' freedom of association under the First Amendment is also without merit. * * * Even assuming that the

IRS received the information on the donors and the flow of gifts in kind to BYU was thereafter reduced, there would still not be a violation of the associational rights of donors to BYU under the authority of these two cases.

Finally, and before reaching the determinative issue, there is one further point to consider. The government contends that BYU should not be allowed to challenge enforcement of the summons on the ground that the petitioners have failed to meet the requirements of § 7609(f). The rationale for this argument is that the court has already issued an order for leave to serve the summons and any attempt by BYU to challenge that order would be an attempt to relitigate a prior determination of the court. The court finds no merit to that contention. The order authorizing the summons was signed ex parte based on the petition and motion of the government and the affidavit of a representative of the IRS. It would be inappropriate to rule that because the court had signed an ex parte order, it should now refuse to consider in a contested proceeding the claim of a party that the requirements of the applicable statute were not fulfilled. This is particularly so where this court has heretofore had served upon BYU an order to show cause directing it to appear and show cause why it "should not be compelled to obey" the IRS summons. That is exactly what BYU is now attempting to show and it should be permitted to do so if it has a legitimate basis.

The critical issue thus becomes whether there is a reasonable basis for believing that the individuals in the unaudited class of donors in kind to BYU have overvalued their donations. BYU has objected to the statement in the magistrate's report that "[t]here is logic in saying that, because all known members of a group have overvalued, one or more of the unknown members of the group might likewise have overvalued." BYU argues that the 148 donors in the art object and silver mining groups, whose identity it has offered to furnish, must be distinguished from the other fourteen individuals whom the IRS has found to have overvalued. It further argues that there is no rational basis for concluding that because these fourteen did overvalue their gifts that other donors in kind to BYU have overvalued theirs.

The government argues that since every one of the returns of the 162 BYU donors in kind audited to date has shown overvaluation, there exists unusual or suspicious circumstances which create a likelihood that the other donors in kind to BYU have overvalued their donations. It points out, and correctly so, that the standard required to invoke the "reasonable basis for believing" requirement of § 7609(f)(2) is not mathematical certainty. What is required is some logical basis for believing that because some members of the class have been shown to have violated the revenue laws, there is reasonable likelihood others may have done so.

So far as it appears from the record, the only argument of the IRS in support of satisfying § 7609(f)(2) is that because every donor in kind to BYU who has been investigated to date has been found to have overvalued his or her gift, that this suggests or should make one suspicious that there has been overvaluation by other donors in kind. Implicit in this argument is that there is some characteristic common to donors in kind to BYU that causes them to overvalue their donations. The court rejects this contention and holds that there is no reasonable basis to believe that one or more BYU donors have overvalued their gifts simply because one or more other donors have overvalued theirs.

The court also rejects the notion that as the number of donors shown to have overvalued their gifts increases, there is a greater likelihood other donors (acting independently and with no unique or common characteristic) have overvalued their gifts.

There has been no showing that BYU donors have a uniform characteristic or that BYU exercises any influence over its donors to cause them to overvalue their donations. Unless this court is to conclude there is something inherently suspicious or unique about donors in kind to BYU, it is as logical to believe, based on the showing the IRS has made in this case, that donors in kind to other private universities or, for that matter, donors in kind to any charity, have overvalued their gifts as that the unaudited donors to BYU have overvalued theirs.

The cases relied upon by the IRS do not compel a different result. Those cases include United States v. Carter, 489 F.2d 413 (5th Cir. 1973); United States v. Turner, 480 F.2d 272 (7th Cir. 1973); United States v. Theodore, 479 F.2d 749 (4th Cir. 1973). Each of these cases involved the Tax Preparer's Project of the IRS in which undercover IRS agents would take a sample return to be prepared and then summons the records of the tax preparer if the return was wrongfully prepared. Either by direct holding or by the reasoning of these three cases, the IRS was allowed to obtain the names of all persons for whom the respondent had prepared tax returns when the respondent incorrectly prepared the IRS agent's tax return. Certainly there is some logic in believing that if a tax preparer prepared one return wrongfully he may have done so with other returns. However, that reasoning is not applicable to the present case.

The government also relies on the legislative history of § 7609 and particularly United States v. Bisceglia, 420 U.S. 141, 95 S.Ct. 915, 43 L.Ed.2d 88 (1975), for the proposition that if there exists unusual or possibly suspicious circumstances it is proper for the IRS to use a John Doe summons. The court agrees with that proposition, but does not agree this case presents facts "so suggestive of possible tax liability that the Service would be remiss in its duty of collection and enforcement of the Internal Revenue laws if it did not investigate." H.

R.Rep. No. 94–658, 94th Cong., 2d Sess. 311, reprinted in [1976] U.S. Code Cong. & Admin.News, pp. 2897, 3207.   To say that unrelated, independent donors to BYU present a suspicious circumstance, with nothing more, goes against the clear legislative history of § 7609 and the holding and facts of *Bisceglia*.

Under our voluntary tax reporting system where each citizen must pay his or her fair share of the tax, the court recognizes that in order to insure compliance, the IRS must be given the broadest latitude to investigate possible irregularities in the reporting of income and deductions.   Nevertheless, and as applied to the statute in question here, this does not mean the IRS may require a third party to furnish the names and addresses of all members of a class simply because the investigation of some members of that class has disclosed irregularities on their returns.   In order to satisfy the requirements of § 7609(f) in this case, it is not enough to state that because the BYU donors investigated to date have overvalued their gifts, there is a reasonable basis to believe that all such donors have overvalued their gifts.

Accordingly, the court holds that the requirements of § 7609(f)(2) have not been satisfied in this case and therefore the respondents are not required to comply with the summons.

SECTION 6.   THE SUMMONS ENFORCEMENT ACTION

UNITED STATES v. GARDEN STATE NAT'L BANK

607 F.2d 61 (3d Cir. 1979).

GARTH, Circuit Judge.

These appeals call upon us once again to review the enforcement procedures pertaining to Internal Revenue summonses.   In Nos. 79–1425 through 79–1428, taxpayers Shafer and Boot Strap, Ltd. appeal from the district court's order enforcing summonses issued to banks for the production of records relating to taxpayers' liability.   In No. 79–1681, Marilee Shafer, in addition to Shafer and Boot Strap, Ltd., appeals.   A similar appeal is presented by taxpayers Roger and Sandra Keech and Lakeville Fasteners, Inc. at No. 79–1682.

Benefiting from the instruction of United States v. LaSalle National Bank, 437 U.S. 298, 98 S.Ct. 2357, 57 L.Ed.2d 221 (1978); United States v. McCarthy, 514 F.2d 368 (3d Cir. 1975); United States v. Genser, 595 F.2d 146 (3d Cir. 1979) (*Genser II*); and our recently published opinions in United States v. Genser, 602 F.2d 69 (3d Cir. 1979) (per curiam) (*Genser III*), and United States v. Serubo, 604 F.2d 807 (3d Cir. 1979), we affirm the district court's enforcement of all summonses in both appeals   *   *   *.

I.

A.   Shafer and Boot Strap (Shafer)

In September, 1977, the Internal Revenue Service began investigating Shafer's tax liability for the years 1974, 1975, and 1976.   Appellee Special Agent Robert McCorry was assigned to the case at the outset and has since been in charge of the investigation.   A revenue agent was also assigned to the investigation in June 1978.   In July 1978, pursuant to I.R.C. §§ 7602, 7604, McCorry issued four summonses which are subjects of this appeal, one to each of four respondent banks.   On January 19, 1979, an additional summons was issued to United Jersey Bank.   The record does not reveal the issuance date of the last summons issued to the Columbia Savings and Loan Association, however, inasmuch as these last two summonses were treated as a unit by all parties and the district court, we will assume that the Columbia summons issued no later than January 19, 1979.   Each summons sought production of testimony, books, records, papers, and other data relating to Shafer.   Notice was given Shafer under I.R.C. § 7609(a), and Shafer immediately caused the summonses to be stayed under I.R.C. § 7609(b)(2).

On October 6, 1978 the Government applied for orders directing the banks to show cause why the first four summonses which had issued in July, should not be enforced.   Shafer intervened to oppose enforcement on the ground that the summonses were issued solely for purposes of a criminal investigation and were therefore unenforceable under United States v. LaSalle National Bank, 437 U.S. 298, 98 S.Ct. 2357, 57 L.Ed.2d 221 (1977).   The banks, which had been subpoenaed, took no position on enforcement.   An evidentiary hearing was held over the objection of the Government on January 11, 1979.   The Government contended that the issue of enforcement should have been disposed of on the pleadings.[5]   On January 22, 1979 the district court, by memorandum opinion and order, directed compliance with these four summonses.   United States v. Garden State National Bank, 465 F.Supp. 437 (D.N.J.1979).   In its opinion, the district court stated that the I.R.S.'s procedures were characterized by the "bad faith" condemned by *LaSalle*.   The district court based this characterization on testimony of I.R.S. witnesses.   That testimony purportedly established that the Service would not agree to negotiate a compromise on the civil aspects of a case until the issue of referral (to the Department of Justice) had been resolved.   In essence, the district court determined that once a special agent of the Criminal Investigation Division has been assigned, no compromise can be effected by I.R.S. even

5.   On April 5, 1979, enforcement was sought by the Government of the United Jersey summons, and apparently of the Columbia Savings and Loan Summons, both of which had issued in January.   On May 14, 1979, a hearing was held by the district court.   On that same day, enforcement was ordered.

though I.R.S. has not decided to refer the investigation to the Justice Department for criminal prosecution. Accordingly, the district court declared that, measured against its newly evolved "conference for compromise " standard, a taxpayer can show "institutional bad faith" on the part of I.R.S. if a conference looking toward a possible compromise is sought, and I.R.S. refuses to engage in such compromise negotiations. In such a situation, the district court would have held that "bad faith" had been established "in that the civil summons was being used solely as a means for deciding whether or not to refer for criminal prosecution, meanwhile [enabling the I.R.S. to gather] evidence in support," id. at 440. Despite this dictum, the district court enforced all four bank summonses on the ground that:

> [s]ince taxpayer has stated on the hearing record that no request for conference was made, the court finds that the problems which concern it are abstract, and concludes that taxpayer has not met the burden established by *LaSalle*.

Id. at 441.

Shafer appealed, and the Government consented to a stay pending determination of the appeal as to these four summonses. This court ordered a stay as to the summonses appealed at No. 79–1681, see note 5 supra.

B.   Keech and Lakeville (Keech)

The Keech investigation by I.R.S. began sometime prior to February 1977. Appellee Special Agent Alexander Dombroski issued summonses similar to those in the Shafer matter to two banks. One summons was issued in July 1977 and the other in September 1977. Compliance with both summonses was stayed pursuant to I.R.C. § 7609(b)(2). In February 1979, the Government obtained orders to show cause why the summonses should not be enforced, and Keech intervened. On April 23, 1979, oral argument, but no testimony, was heard before the district court. At its conclusion, Keech was denied an evidentiary hearing and discovery. An order was entered on May 8, 1979 enforcing the summonses. The district court's stated ground for these actions differed from the grounds upon which it relied in granting enforcement of the Shafer summonses. Here the district court held that inasmuch as I.R.S. always retains an ultimate residual interest in collecting tax money even after a taxpayer's criminal conviction for tax fraud, i. e., I.R.S. never abandons its civil interest, a taxpayer in Keech's position could *never* satisfy the *LaSalle* requirement of showing that the summons had been institutionally issued solely for purposes of a criminal investigation.

Keech moved for a stay of enforcement in this court, which we granted on June 1, 1979.

*   *   *

III.

* * * The procedures by which [summons enforcement] proceedings are to be conducted and by which they may be challenged have previously been set down in United States v. McCarthy, 514 F.2d at 372–77. More recently, *Genser I* has reaffirmed the *McCarthy* procedures as follows:

> In United States v. McCarthy, 514 F.2d 368 (3d Cir. 1975), this court carefully formulated procedural guidelines for use in enforcement proceedings and provided that an evidentiary hearing is an "integral part" of those proceedings. Under *McCarthy*, the IRS must be prepared to make a preliminary showing that the investigation has a legitimate purpose and that the inquiry may be relevant to that purpose, that the information sought is not already in the government's possession, and that the government has followed the procedural steps required by the Internal Revenue Code. The burden then shifts to the opposing party to establish any defenses or to prove that enforcement would constitute an abuse of the court's process.[15] If the district court con-

[15] The burden is on the taxpayer to negate the existence of a proper civil purpose. The Supreme Court has characterized this burden as "heavy." United States v. LaSalle National Bank, supra, [437] U.S. at [316], 98 S.Ct. 2357.

> cludes that it cannot fairly decide the case on the record before it, it may direct further proceedings, including discovery, if requested. Id. at 372–73. [Citations omitted].[16]

[16] The *McCarthy* court stated: "Although our proposed procedure for summons enforcement contemplates that provision for an evidentiary hearing be an integral part of the proceedings, implicit in our design is the realization that not every summons enforcement proceeding will require an evidentiary hearing. *Thus, if the person summoned neither puts in issue allegations of the complaint nor raises proper affirmative defenses, no evidentiary hearing will be required; the matter can be decided on the pleadings.*" 514 F.2d at 373.

582 F.2d at 302 (emphasis supplied).

Thus the Government, must make the *Powell prima facie* showing. Then the taxpayer has the burden "to negate the existence of a proper civil purpose," id. at 302 n. 15. To meet this burden, the taxpayer must "establish any defenses or * * * prove that enforcement would constitute an abuse of the court's process," id. at 302. In responding to the Government's showing, it is clear that a taxpayer must factually oppose the Government's allegations by affidavit. Legal conclusions or mere memoranda of law will not suffice. In the absence of such a response by the taxpayer, uncontested allegations in the Government's petition and affidavit must be accepted as admitted. Moreover, if at this stage the taxpayer cannot refute the government's *prima facie Powell* showing or cannot factually support a proper affirmative defense, the district court should dispose of the proceeding on the papers before it and without an evidentiary hearing.

Where, however, material Government allegations are factually refuted by the taxpayer, thus presenting a disputed factual issue, or where proper affirmative defenses, such as those alleging "bad faith" under the tests of *LaSalle* and *Genser II*, are factually supported by the taxpayer's affidavits, the taxpayer is entitled to an evidentiary hearing. *McCarthy,* 514 F.2d at 368. Allegations supporting a "bad faith" defense are, as we have stated, insufficient if conclusionary. The affidavit must particularize those specific facts from which an inference may be drawn that the conduct of the Service was the same as, or similar to, the hypothetical conduct condemned in *LaSalle* and *Genser II.* In those cases, as earlier noted, two examples were given: one, that a summons was issued at the request of the Justice Department; the other, that formal recommendations for prosecution were being delayed until a summons could be issued and enforced, solely to further a *criminal* prosecution.

The taxpayer is assisted in meeting his burden by the availability of certain basic discovery to which we have held he is entitled in *Genser II:*

[1] the identities of the investigating agents,

[2] the date the investigation began,

[3] the dates the agent or agents filed reports recommending prosecution,

[4] the date the district chief of the Intelligence Division or Criminal Investigation Division reviewed the recommendation,

[5] the date the Office of Regional Counsel referred the matter for prosecution,

[6] the dates of all summonses issued under 26 U.S.C. § 7602, [and]

[7] the nature of any contacts, relating to and during the investigation, between the investigating agents and officials of the Department of Justice.

595 F.2d at 152. If the taxpayer's evidence reveals:

(1) that the IRS issued summonses after the investigating agents recommended prosecution, (2) that inordinate and unexplained delays in the investigation transpired, or (3) that the investigating agents were in contact with the Department of Justice,

the district court must then permit further investigation. Id.[13]

---

13. If a hearing is authorized by *McCarthy,* additional discovery may be allowed *after* the hearing if the taxpayer shows at the hearing that the I.R.S. acted in "bad faith." *McCarthy,* 514 F.2d at 376 & n. 10. Indeed, as *Genser I* points out, 582 F.2d at 302, "[i]f the district court con-

IV.

Under the standards and procedures we have set forth above, the record reveals that neither Shafer nor Keech has met its burden of showing "bad faith" on the part of the Service, nor has either established a right to further discovery or to an evidentiary hearing.

A.

In *McCarthy*, the Government had failed to establish all elements of the *prima facie Powell* requirements. Thus the district court's order of enforcement was reversed on appeal. In remanding to the district court, however, the *McCarthy* court discussed considerations bearing on a defendant's required showing.

The defendant in *McCarthy* had alleged no more than that the summons was unenforceable since it was issued for criminal purposes and emphasized that the investigation was being conducted by the I.R.S. investigatory branch, and that no revenue agent was assigned to the case when the summons issued. These allegations in a pre-recommendation context were held insufficient.

The court in *McCarthy* also undertook consideration of the defendant's attack upon the Service's "good faith." That challenge was in terms of an alleged absence of civil purpose in the I.R.S.' investigation. While holding that the defendant's allegations were insufficient to raise the issue of criminal purpose, the *McCarthy* court, in light of the decisional law as it then was, held that the allegations "although not very strong, sufficiently raise the possibility that the IRS agents charged with the investigation of defendant-corporation had no intention of pursuing any civil remedies as to bring into question their good faith." The district court was thereupon ordered to conduct a hearing as to that issue.

Compared with the *McCarthy* allegations, Shafer's allegations are far less substantial. The affidavit filed on behalf of Shafer, in response to the Government's petitions, was not the affidavit of the taxpayer but was rather that of his counsel. The Government's petitions and affidavits, to which the Shafer affidavit responded, reveal that the *Powell* requirements were fully met, and that "no recommendation for prosecution of the taxpayer for the years and tax returns under investigation has been made to the United States Department of Justice." Despite this showing by the Government, Shafer's only "response" or "affirmative defense" to the Government's petition was couched in legal conclusions rather than in factual terms. For example, paragraph 2 alleged: "the summonses were not issued in good faith in that they have been issued solely for the purpose of criminal

cludes that it cannot fairly decide the case on the record before it, it may direct further proceedings, including discovery, if requested."

investigation as determined by an examination of the institutional posture of the I.R.S."

Paragraphs 3 and 4 of that same affidavit assert that the requirements of *LaSalle* were not met by the Government's petitions, and that the Government's petitions failed to satisfy the criteria for judicial enforcement of I.R.S. summonses. Moreover, Shafer has never disputed the fact that no recommendation for prosecution has ever been made by the Service to the Department of Justice. Indeed, not the slightest suggestion appears in the papers filed that any recommendation was ever made even *within* the I.R.S. Significantly, the Shafer affidavit nowhere disputes any allegations made in the Government's enforcement papers.

We are aware that paragraph 4 of the Shafer affidavit refers to a memorandum of law which was evidently submitted to the district court, but a legal memorandum or brief cannot substitute for evidence or for sworn facts in an affidavit. * * * Thus, even tested by the standards of pre-*LaSalle,* pre-*Genser,* and pre-*Serubo* jurisprudence, the showing made by Shafer was insufficient to warrant an evidentiary hearing.

Nevertheless the district court did afford Shafer the hearing Shafer sought. An examination of the record developed at that hearing, however, reveals little more than was disclosed by Shafer's initial papers. Only two Government witnesses testified; Shafer's only evidence was a page from the I.R.S. manual. Read charitably, the record merely establishes the following:

(1) as of the time the summonses issued, the I.R.S. under its own internal procedures would not have been willing to discuss compromise of Shafer's civil tax liability;

(2) nine months passed while a special agent investigated the cases before a revenue agent was assigned;

(3) nearly four months elapsed between issuance of the summonses and the Government's attempt to enforce them, during which time the district court found that referrals took place "up to and down from the regional level for clearance to proceed;" and

(4) Special Agent McCorry told his supervisor that this was "a real good criminal case."

These facts, even if accepted as true, neither singularly nor in combination rise to the level required to prove "bad faith," or to justify a hearing under the decisions of the Supreme Court and this court.

* * * [T]he refusal of the Service to enter into compromise negotiations, standing alone, does not amount to "bad faith." [In addition,] the type of agents used by I.R.S. to investigate a particular case does not characterize the case in any way as "civil" or "criminal." Nor is any inference of "bad faith" necessarily to be drawn

from the lapse of time between the issuance and enforcement of the summonses. In any event, the uncontradicted testimony of Special Agent McCorry was to the effect that the nine-month delay was partially attributable to his working on another matter. He also testified without contradiction that the referrals "up and down" the I.R.S. administrative chain, which delayed enforcement, were standard Service procedure. Finally, the charge made by Shafer that an agent had characterized the investigation as "a real good criminal case" is insufficient to amount to "bad faith," since the agent's personal intent is irrelevant to the institutional "good faith" of the Service.

Shafer additionally complains that he sought prehearing discovery which was improperly denied by the district court. We have stressed in this opinion, just as this court did in *McCarthy,* that conclusionary allegations cannot take the place of hard evidence or allegations in fact under oath. In this respect, Shafer's papers responding to the Government's petitions and seeking dismissal of those petitions, or alternatively an evidentiary hearing with appropriate prehearing discovery, do not satisfy our standard. As we have earlier held, Shafer had no right to a hearing under *McCarthy.* Notwithstanding, the district court accorded him a hearing, yet, despite that additional opportunity to bolster his case, the evidence adduced at that hearing did not meet the burden which the cases have placed on Shafer.

Without deciding whether *Genser II*, requiring "basic discovery," should ever be given retroactive effect, we are not persuaded that in light of this record any discovery should be permitted here. Our reading of the record discloses that the information which would normally be allowed a taxpayer under the basic discovery provided by *Genser II* came to light at the hearing. Furthermore, the two "delays" about which Shafer complains are neither inordinate nor are they unexplained within the meaning of *Genser II*.

We are satisfied therefore that Shafer's showing falls far short of defeating the presumption of validity of a pre-recommendation summons. He has not carried the "heavy" burden imposed by *La-Salle*, let alone the virtually insurmountable burden imposed by *Genser II*. Accordingly, since Shafer has failed to mount an effective challenge to the Government's *Powell* showing or to the institutional "good faith" of the Service, the Shafer subpoenas were properly enforced.

B.

Unlike the Shafer proceeding where an evidentiary hearing was afforded, the district court denied such a hearing to Keech. This ruling was appropriate in light of *LaSalle* and *Genser II* and *III*. We are mindful that the Keech affidavit in response to the Government's petition for enforcement is somewhat more factual than the Shafer affidavit. However, the facts to which Keech's attorney certified, even if accepted as true, cannot overcome the presumptively valid pre-recommendation summonses under the standards of *LaSalle, Genser II* and *III,* and *Serubo.* Our discussion in the *Shafer* appeal is dispositive of Keech's contentions.[19]

The only essential distinction between the Shafer and Keech cases is found in Keech's demand for discovery which was predicated on *Genser II* guidelines. That distinction, however, is not sufficient to require a result different from the one we have reached in the Shafer appeals.

Whereas *Genser II* had not been filed at the time the district court disposed of Shafer's initial objections to enforcement, it was referred to and relied upon in the Keech papers and at the time of the Keech oral argument. Our comparison, however, of that information to which Keech would be entitled under *Genser II's* basic discovery formula, with the information available to Keech * * * in the course of this litigation, satisfies us that ordering basic discovery would be meaningless and would amount to no more than an academic exercise. It is evident to us that Keech had virtually all the information which would have been afforded to him under *Genser II* basic discovery.[20]

V.

The orders of the district court enforcing all of the Shafer and Keech summonses, will be affirmed.

SECTION 7. THE FORMAL INTERVIEW ("Q & A")

The Internal Revenue Service summons literally calls for the summoned party to appear to produce documents and to give testimony. In situations in which the summons is utilized solely to obtain access to documents (for example, in most cases in which a summons is issued for bank records) the formality of an appearance and testimony is dispensed with. Compliance is accomplished by the summoned party making available the documents (originals or copies) for the Service.

In those cases in which information in addition to documents is desired, the agents frequently will seek to have an informal conversation with the summoned party in lieu of, or prior to, a formal inter-

---

19. Keech's affidavit alleges two delays in I.R.S.' attempt to enforce summonses; a special agent is claimed to have stated that I.R.S. was conducting a criminal investigation of the taxpayer; only the tax liability of Roger Keech was being investigated although joint returns had been filed; and the return for one of the years under investigation had been audited and the return accepted as filed.

20. The alleged delays asserted in the Keech affidavit would entitle Keech to no more than basic discovery.

view. A number of considerations (including the relationship between the summoned party and the subject of the investigation, the status of the summoned party as a potential subject, and the existence of possible objections to providing information) enter into the decision whether to agree to an informal interview. In the vast majority of instances the summoned party, either through ignorance of his options, lack of concern, or perhaps even due to an informed decision, will consent to an informal interview. However, it should be observed that there is no legal duty to provide information to the Service on an informal basis. Moreover, there can be circumstances in which it is unwise for the summoned party to discuss (except in a formal context) matters with the investigating agents.

The formal interview, commonly referred to as a "Q & A",[i] is essentially a deposition conducted by the agent. The witness must provide the answers to questions under oath.[j] The IRS normally will have the interview recorded by a reporter or electronically. The witness should always make his own recording of the interview for several reasons. When the witness has his own recording he can review it (or have it transcribed) and correct any inadvertent errors or omissions personally without waiting for the Service to get around to preparing the transcript and disclosing it to him. Moreover, the witness can, if he wishes, make the recording available to the taxpayer's representative for such assistance as it may provide in defending the case. A witness should not proceed (absent the most extraordinary circumstances) with a formal interview at which the Service refuses to permit him to make his own record of the interview.[k] The witness also must be given a chance to read and correct the transcript of the interview and provide any necessary explanation of his statements.[l]

There is no specific authority holding that the taxpayer under investigation has the right to insist upon being present (personally or through counsel) at the formal interview of third-party witnesses.[m] Normally, however, the witness (as distinct from the taxpayer under investigation) can insist upon the presence of an authorized representative of the taxpayer during the formal interview.[n]

The witness is entitled to be represented by counsel at the formal interview. Absent a conflict of interest, the witness can be represented by the same attorney who represents the taxpayer under

i.   This name derives from the standard "Q & A" (i. e. question and answer) format of the transcripts produced by the Internal Revenue Service.

j.   United States v. Lewis, 16 AFTR 2d 5244.1 (W.D.Tenn.1965).

k.   See Mott v. MacMahon, 214 F.Supp. 20 (N.D.Cal.1963).

l.   United States v. Lewis, 16 AFTR 2d 5244.1 (W.D.Tenn.1965).

m.   See United States v. Traynor, 611 F.2d 809 (10th Cir. 1979).

n.   See IRS Special Agents Handbook, § 343.6 (April 13, 1981), excerpted above at pages 63–66.

investigation.[o] It should be noted that there are circumstances in which it may not be wise for an attorney to represent both the subject of the investigation and a witness. Unforeseen future developments could create a situation in which the attorney might be disqualified from further representation of either (or both). However, in many instances there is no realistic chance of a conflict of interest; in fact, there may be a common interest on the part of the witness and the subject, or other practical reasons (for example, the cost of "educating" independent counsel) for one attorney to represent both the subject and a witness. In such circumstances, dual representation is common. However, where the witness is going to assert his own privilege against self-incrimination (as distinct from a privilege effectively on behalf of the taxpayer—for example the attorney-client privilege) it is advisable for the witness to be represented separately.

As noted above, the formal interview itself is roughly equivalent to a deposition. The summons requires the witness to appear and to have available (actually or constructively) the summoned documents in his possession or control. However, as held in Reisman v. Caplin,[p] the summons *per se* does not require the witness to answer questions or to produce documents if there is a good faith objection asserted. Hence, the witness (preferably through counsel) should place on the record objections to the production of documents which are in his possession or control and not produced. As to testimony, the witness should not simply state "blanket" objections (absent an agreement with the agent). The witness must respond to specific questions with appropriate objections so that a record can be made as to the validity of the objections in the event a summons enforcement action is brought.[q] Of course if the witness has some objections which, if sustained, would invalidate the entire formal interview, then such an objection should be stated at the commencement of the interview as the ground for refusing to answer any questions at all. Hence, in a case in which there was a bona fide contention that the summons was issued in bad faith, such an objection would justify (pending a ruling on the objection in a summons enforcement action) a good faith declination to produce any documents or to respond to any questions at all. Even where there is an overall objection stated, the witness should permit the agent to make whatever record he wishes, and should invite the agent to place on the record any specific questions upon which the agent wishes a ruling.

The formal interview will conclude with a standardized series of questions designed to establish that the witness testified freely, without being threatened or coerced by the agents. In appropriate cir-

o. Backer v. Commissioner, 275 F.2d 141 (5th Cir. 1960).

p. 375 U.S. 440, 84 S.Ct. 508, 11 L.Ed. 2d 459 (1964).

q. Colton v. United States, 306 F.2d 633 (2d Cir. 1962).

cumstances it may be noted on the record that the witness testified under legal compulsion and not voluntarily. The witness will also be given the opportunity to make any further statement that he wishes to have on the record. The witness, or his counsel, should be alert to the fact that the purpose of the formal interview is for the Service to make a formal record tying down the testimony of the witness. In this regard, some agents might omit from the formal interview subjects upon which testimony favorable to the taxpayer under investigation would be given. Similarly, the agents might fail to ask questions which would permit explanations of answers given during the course of the questioning. The witness (preferably through questions asked by his attorney) should consider taking the opportunity to complete or clarify the record if the agent's questioning might otherwise leave an incorrect or incomplete impression.

Following the formal interview (sometimes many months thereafter) the Internal Revenue Service will prepare a transcript and, eventually, present it to the witness for review and signing. The IRS transcript should be reviewed carefully before signing. Where there are errors (either due to transcription or due to mistakes made by the witness in responses to questions) they should be noted. Errors in transcription should be corrected on the transcript itself. If there is any doubt as to what actually was said, the witness should compare the transcript with a tape recording (hopefully, the one that he made) of the interview. If the agent refuses to permit such corrections then the witness should decline to sign the transcript but should submit, in writing, a statement of the changes which would have to be made to provide a correct transcript. Errors in statements made by the witness should be corrected by an addendum to the transcript submitted by the witness. It may be that the witness will have to undergo a further session in light of the necessary corrections. However, it is essential that any material mistake made by the witness be corrected so that no incorrect statement of the witness (even though inadvertently made) becomes a part of the formal record. Where there has been a mistake by the witness, the transcript can properly be signed, but the signature should be followed by a statement indicating that the transcript is acknowledged as correct subject to the addendum correcting inadvertent errors.

Chapter VII

CRIMINAL TAX MATTERS

Scope Note: The success of the federal system of self-assessment is attributable largely to the existence of a variety of sanctions designed to encourage the highest possible degree of voluntary compliance with the tax laws. Although the civil penalty provisions of the Code may help to encourage such compliance by making non-compliance costly, the deterrent effect of the criminal provisions is the real key to maintaining an effective system of internal revenue taxation.

This chapter begins with an overview of the basic tax offenses, followed by a discussion of the elements of each offense and the methods used by the government to prove violations. Also covered are some recurring issues involved in the representation of taxpayers who are suspected of tax violations, and a number of features peculiar to the trial of a criminal tax case. The final section deals with the problem of when may a taxpayer "take the Fifth" on a tax return.

SECTION 1. THE TAX CRIMES

The Internal Revenue Code contains a number of different criminal provisions.[a] In addition, a wide variety of general criminal offenses defined in Title 18 of the United States Code are pertinent to tax matters. Hence, it would be impractical (if not impossible) to provide a comprehensive discussion of the full range of what might fairly be described as tax crimes. However, the vast majority of criminal tax cases are concerned with four provisions of the Internal Revenue Code (and two related general criminal provisions).

Evasion (or more precisely, attempted evasion)[b] is a felony carrying a maximum penalty of 5 years in prison and/or a $10,000 fine. The elements of the crime are an attempt to evade or defeat tax (or payment of tax) in any manner, the existence of a tax deficiency (or tax due and owing in an evasion of payment case), an affirmative act of fraud, and willfulness.

---

a. IRC §§ 7201–7216, 7231, 7232, 7240, 7261, 7262, 7268–7273 and 7275.

b. IRC § 7201, Attempt to Evade or Defeat Tax, which provides:
    Any person who willfully attempts in any manner to evade or defeat any tax imposed by this title or the payment thereof shall, in addition to other penalties provided by law, be guilty of a felony and, upon conviction thereof, shall be fined not more than $10,000, or imprisoned not more than 5 years, or both, together with the costs of prosecution.

The false return charge [c] is a felony carrying a maximum penalty of 3 years in prison and/or a $5,000 fine. The elements of the offense are the making and subscribing of a return, statement or other document which states that it is signed under penalty of perjury, knowledge that the document is not true as to any material matter, and willfulness.

The charge of aiding or assisting in the preparation of a false return [d] is a felony carrying a maximum penalty of 3 years in prison and/or a $5,000 fine. The elements of the offense are aiding or assisting in the preparation or presentation of a return or other document which is fraudulent or false as to any material matter, and willfulness.

The "failure to file" charge [e] is a misdemeanor carrying a maximum penalty of 1 year in prison and/or a $10,000 fine. The elements of the offense are a duty to file a return, supply information or pay any tax or estimated tax, the failure to comply with the duty, and willfulness.

There is also a frequently discussed, but rarely used, misdemeanor charge for delivering or disclosing to the IRS a fraudulent return, statement or other document.[f] This offense carries a maximum pen-

---

c. IRC § 7206, Fraud and False Statements, which provides in pertinent part:

Any person who—

(1) **Declaration under penalties of perjury.**—Willfully makes and subscribes any return, statement, or other document, which contains or is verified by a written declaration that it is made under the penalties of perjury, and which he does not believe to be true and correct as to every material matter; or

(2) **Aid or assistance.**—Willfully aids or assists in, or procures, counsels, or advises the preparation or presentation under, or in connection with any matter arising under, the internal revenue laws, of a return, affidavit, claim, or other document, which is fraudulent or is false as to any material matter, whether or not such falsity or fraud is with the knowledge or consent of the person authorized or required to present such return, affidavit, claim, or document; * * *

* * *

shall be guilty of a felony and, upon conviction thereof, shall be fined not more than $5,000, or imprisoned not more than 3 years, or both, together with the costs of prosecution.

d. IRC § 7206(2), above.

e. IRC § 7203, Willful Failure to File Return, Supply Information, or Pay Tax, which provides:

Any person required under this title to pay any estimated tax or tax, or required by this title or by regulations made under authority thereof to make a return (other than a return required under authority of section 6015), keep any records, or supply any information, mated tax or tax, make such return, keep such records, or supply such information, at the time or times required by law or regulations, shall, in addition to other penalties provided by law, be guilty of a misdemeanor and, upon conviction thereof, shall be fined not more than $10,000, or imprisoned not more than 1 year, or both, together with the costs of prosecution.

f. IRC § 7207, Fraudulent Returns, Statements, or Other Documents, which provides:

Any person who willfully delivers or discloses to the Secretary any list, return, account, statement, or other document, known by him to be fraudulent or to be false as to any material matter, shall be

alty of 1 year in prison and/or a $1,000 fine. The elements of the offense are the delivery or disclosure to the IRS of a return, statement or other document known to be fraudulent or false as to any material matter, and willfulness.

In addition to crimes specified in the Internal Revenue Code, a criminal tax case may be cast in the form of a conspiracy prosecution.[g] A conspiracy conviction carries a maximum penalty of 5 years in prison and/or a $10,000 fine, except where the object of the conspiracy is a misdemeanor. The elements of the crime of conspiracy are an agreement between two or more persons to commit an offense against or to defraud the United States and an overt act in furtherance of the conspiracy.

A criminal tax case may also involve a false statement charge,[h] which carries the possibility of a 5 year prison sentence and/or a $10,000 fine. The elements of the offense are the falsification or concealment of a material fact or the making of a false statement or use of a false document, and willfulness.[i]

fined not more than $1,000, or imprisoned not more than 1 year, or both. Any person required pursuant to sections 6047(b) or (c), 6056, or 6104(d) to furnish any information to the Secretary or any other person who willfully furnishes to the Secretary or such other person any information known by him to be fraudulent or to be false as to any material matter shall be fined not more than $1,000, or imprisoned not more than 1 year, or both.

g. 18 U.S.C.A. § 371, Conspiracy to Commit Offense or to Defraud United States, which provides:
    If two or more persons conspire either to commit any offense against the United States, or to defraud the United States, or any agency thereof in any manner or for any purpose, and one or more of such persons do any act to effect the object of the conspiracy, each shall be fined not more than $10,000 or imprisoned not more than five years, or both.

If, however, the offense, the commission of which is the object of the conspiracy, is a misdemeanor only, the punishment for such conspiracy shall not exceed the maximum punishment provided for such misdemeanor.

h. 18 U.S.C.A. § 1001, Statements or Entries Generally, which provides:
    Whoever, in any matter within the jurisdiction of any department or agency of the United States knowingly and willfully falsifies, conceals or covers up by any trick, scheme, or device a material fact, or makes any false, fictitious or fraudulent statements or representations, or makes or uses any false writing or document knowing the same to contain any false, fictitious or fraudulent statement or entry, shall be fined not more than $10,000 or imprisoned not more than five years, or both.

i. Note that a perjury offense, 18 U.S.C.A. § 1621, may exist if the false statement was made under oath.

A. THE BASIC TAX OFFENSES

---

(1) SECTIONS 7201, 7203 AND 7207

SPIES v. UNITED STATES

Supreme Court of the United States, 1943.
317 U.S. 492, 63 S.Ct. 364, 87 L.Ed. 418.

Mr. Justice JACKSON delivered the opinion of the Court.

Petitioner has been convicted of attempting to defeat and evade income tax in violation of § 145(b) of * * * the Internal Revenue Code [of 1939].[j]

Petitioner admitted at the opening of the trial that he had sufficient income during the year in question to place him under a statutory duty to file a return and to pay a tax, and that he failed to do either. The evidence during nearly two weeks of trial was directed principally toward establishing the exact amount of the tax and the manner of receiving and handling income and accounting, which the Government contends shows an intent to evade and defeat tax. Petitioner's testimony related to his good character, his physical illness at the time the return became due, and lack of willfulness in his defaults, chiefly because of a psychological disturbance, amounting to something more than worry but something less than insanity.

Section 145(a)[k] makes, among other things, willful failure to pay a tax or make a return by one having petitioner's income at the time or times required by law a misdemeanor. Section 145(b) makes a willful attempt in any manner to evade or defeat any tax such as his a felony. Petitioner was not indicted for either misdemeanor. The indictment contained a single count setting forth the felony charge of willfully attempting to defeat and evade the tax, and recited willful failure to file a return and willful failure to pay the tax as the means to the felonious end.

* * * The Court refused a request to instruct that an affirmative act was necessary to constitute a willful attempt and charged that "Attempt means to try to do or accomplish. In order to find an attempt it is not necessary to find affirmative steps to accomplish the prohibited purpose. An attempt may be found on the basis of inactivity or on refraining to act, as well."

It is the Government's contention that a willful failure to file a return together with a willful failure to pay the tax may, without more, constitute an attempt to defeat or evade a tax within § 145(b). Petitioner claims that such proof establishes only two misdemeanors

j. The predecessor to § 7201 of the Internal Revenue Code of 1954.

k. The predecessor to § 7203 of the Internal Revenue Code of 1954.

under § 145(a) and that it takes more than the sum of two such misdemeanors to make the felony under § 145(b). The legislative history of the section contains nothing helpful on the question here at issue, and we must find the answer from the section itself and its context in the revenue laws.

The United States has relied for the collection of its income tax largely upon the taxpayer's own disclosures rather than upon a system of withholding the tax from him by those from whom income may be received. This system can function successfully only if those within and near taxable income keep and render true accounts. In many ways taxpayers' neglect or deceit may prejudice the orderly and punctual administration of the system as well as the revenues themselves. Congress has imposed a variety of sanctions for the protection of the system and the revenues. The relation of the offense of which this petitioner has been convicted to other and lesser revenue offenses appears more clearly from its position in this structure of sanctions.

The penalties imposed by Congress to enforce the tax laws embrace both civil and criminal sanctions. The former consist of additions to the tax upon determinations of fact made by an administrative agency and with no burden on the Government to prove its case beyond a reasonable doubt. The latter consist of penal offenses enforced by the criminal process in the familiar manner. Invocation of one does not exclude resort to the other.

The failure in a duty to make a timely return, unless it is shown that such failure is due to reasonable cause and not due to willful neglect, is punishable by an addition to the tax of 5 to 25 per cent thereof, depending on the duration of the default. But a duty may exist even when there is no tax liability to serve as a base for application of a percentage delinquency penalty; the default may relate to matters not identifiable with tax for a particular period; and the offense may be more grievous than a case for civil penalty. Hence the willful failure to make a return, keep records, or supply information when required, is made a misdemeanor, without regard to existence of a tax liability. § 145(a). Punctuality is important to the fiscal system, and these are sanctions to assure punctual as well as faithful performance of these duties.

Sanctions to insure payment of the tax are even more varied to meet the variety of causes of default. It is the right as well as the interest of the taxpayer to limit his admission of liability to the amount he actually owes. But the law is complicated, accounting treatment of various items raises problems of great complexity, and innocent errors are numerous, as appear from the number who make overpayments. It is not the purpose of the law to penalize frank difference of opinion or innocent errors made despite the exercise of reasonable care. Such errors are corrected by the assessment of the deficiency of tax and its collection with interest for the delay. If any part of the deficiency is due to negligence or intentional disregard of rules and regulations, but without intent to defraud, five per cent of such deficiency is added thereto; and if any part of any deficiency is due to fraud with intent to evade tax, the addition is 50 per cent thereof. Willful failure to pay the tax when due is punishable as a misdemeanor. § 145(a). The climax of this variety of sanctions is the serious and inclusive felony defined to consist of willful attempt in any manner to evade or defeat the tax. § 145(b). The question here is whether there is a distinction between the acts necessary to make out the felony and those which may make out the misdemeanor.

A felony may, and frequently does, include lesser offenses in combination either with each other or with other elements. We think it clear that this felony may include one or several of the other offenses against the revenue laws. But it would be unusual and we would not readily assume that Congress by the felony defined in § 145(b) meant no more than the same derelictions it had just defined in § 145(a) as a misdemeanor. Such an interpretation becomes even more difficult to accept when we consider this felony as the capstone of a system of sanctions which singly or in combination were calculated to induce prompt and forthright fulfillment of every duty under the income tax law and to provide a penalty suitable to every degree of delinquency.

The difference between willful failure to pay a tax when due, which is made a misdemeanor, and willful attempt to defeat and evade one, which is made a felony, is not easy to detect or define. Both must be willful, and willful, as we have said, is a word of many meanings, its construction often being influenced by its context. It may well mean something more as applied to nonpayment of a tax than when applied to failure to make a return. Mere voluntary and purposeful, as distinguished from accidental, omission to make a timely return might meet the test of willfulness. But in view of our traditional aversion to imprisonment for debt, we would not without the clearest manifestation of Congressional intent assume that mere knowing and intentional default in payment of a tax where there had been no willful failure to disclose the liability is intended to constitute a criminal offense of any degree. We would expect willfulness in such a case to include some element of evil motive and want of justification in view of all the financial circumstances of the taxpayer.

Had § 145(a) not included willful failure to pay a tax, it would have defined as misdemeanors generally a failure to observe statutory duties to make timely returns, keep records, or supply information—duties imposed to facilitate administration of the Act even if, because of insufficient net income, there were no duty to pay a tax. It would then be a permissible and perhaps an appropriate construction of § 145(b) that it made felonies of the same willful omissions when there was the added element of duty to pay a tax. The definition of such nonpayment as a misdemeanor we think argues strongly against such an interpretation.

The difference between the two offenses, it seems to us, is found in the affirmative action implied from the term "attempt," as used in the felony subsection. It is not necessary to involve this subject with the complexities of the common-law "attempt". The attempt made criminal by this statute does not consist of conduct that would culminate in a more serious crime but for some impossibility of completion or interruption or frustration. This is an independent crime, complete in its most serious form when the attempt is complete and nothing is added to its criminality by success or consummation, as would be the case, say, of attempted murder. Although the attempt succeed in evading tax, there is no criminal offense of that kind, and the prosecution can be only for the attempt. We think that in employing the terminology of attempt to embrace the gravest of offenses against the revenues Congress intended some willful commission in addition to the willful omissions that make up the list of misdemeanors. Willful but passive neglect of the statutory duty may constitute the lesser offense, but to combine with it a willful and positive attempt to evade tax in any manner or to defeat it by any means lifts the offense to the degree of felony.

Congress did not define or limit the methods by which a willful attempt to defeat and evade might be accomplished and perhaps did not define lest its effort to do so result in some unexpected limitation. Nor would we by definition constrict the scope of the Congressional provision that it may be accomplished "in any manner". By way of illustration, and not by way of limitation, we would think affirmative willful attempt may be inferred from conduct such as keeping a double set of books, making false entries or alterations, or false invoices or documents, destruction of books or records, concealment of assets or covering up sources of income, handling of one's affairs to avoid making the records usual in transactions of the kind, and any conduct, the likely effect of which would be to mislead or to conceal. If the tax-evasion motive plays any part in such conduct the offense may be made out even though the conduct may also serve other purposes such as concealment of other crime.

In this case there are several items of evidence apart from the default in filing the return and paying the tax which the Government claims will support an inference of willful attempt to evade or defeat the tax. These go to establish that petitioner insisted that certain income be paid to him in cash, transferred it to his own bank by armored car, deposited it, not in his own name but in the names of others of his family, and kept inadequate and misleading records. Petitioner claims other motives animated him in these matters. We intimate no opinion. Such inferences are for the jury. If on proper submission the jury found these acts, taken together with willful failure to file a return and willful failure to pay the tax, to constitute a willful attempt to defeat and evade tax, we would consider conviction of a felony sustainable. But we think a defendant is entitled to a charge which will point out the necessity for such an inference of willful attempt to defeat or evade tax from some proof in the case other than that necessary to make out the misdemeanors; and if the evidence fails to afford such an inference, the defendant should be acquitted.

The Government argues against this construction, contending that the milder punishment of a misdemeanor and the benefits of a short statute of limitation should not be extended to violators of the income tax laws such as political grafters, gamblers, racketeers, and gangsters. We doubt that this construction will handicap prosecution for felony of such flagrant violators. Few of them, we think, in their efforts to escape tax stop with mere omission of the duties put upon them by the statute, but if such there be, they are entitled to be convicted only of the offense which they have committed.

Reversed.

SANSONE v. UNITED STATES

Supreme Court of the United States, 1965.
380 U.S. 343, 85 S.Ct. 1004, 13 L.Ed.2d 882.

Mr. Justice GOLDBERG delivered the opinion of the Court.

Petitioner Sansone was indicted for willfully attempting to evade federal income taxes for the year 1957 in violation of § 7201 of the Internal Revenue Code of 1954. *   *   *

The following facts were established at trial. In March 1956 petitioner and his wife purchased a tract of land for $22,500 and simultaneously sold a portion of the tract for $20,000. In August 1957 petitioner sold another portion of the tract for $27,000. He did not report the gain on either the 1956 or 1957 sale in his income tax returns for those years. Petitioner conceded that the 1957 transaction was reportable and that, in not reporting it, he understated his tax liability for that year by $2,456.48. He contended, however, that this understatement was not willful since he believed at the time that extensive repairs on a creek adjoining a portion of the tract he retained might be necessary and that the cost of these repairs might wipe out his profit on the 1957 sale.

To counter this defense, the Government introduced the following signed statement made by petitioner during the Treasury investigation of his tax return:

"I did not report the 1957 sale in our joint income tax return for 1957 because I was burdened with a number of financial obligations and did not feel I could raise the money to pay any tax due. It was my intention to report all sales in a future year and pay the tax due. I knew that I should have reported the 1957 sale, but my wife did not know that it should have been reported. It was not my intention to evade the payment of our proper taxes and I intended to pay any additional taxes due when I was financially able to do so."

At the conclusion of the trial, petitioner requested that the jury be instructed that it could acquit him of the charged offense of willfully attempting to evade or defeat taxes in violation of § 7201, but still convict him of either or both of the asserted lesser-included offenses of willfully filing a fraudulent or false return, in violation of § 7207, or willfully failing to pay his taxes at the time required by law, in violation of § 7203. Section 7201 is a felony providing for a maximum fine of $10,000 and imprisonment for five years. Both §§ 7203 and 7207 are misdemeanors with maximum prison sentences of one year under each section, and maximum fines of $10,000 under § 7203 and $1,000 under § 7207.

* * *

We are faced with the threshold question as to whether or not § 7207, which proscribes the willful filing with a Treasury official of any known false or fraudulent "return," applies to the filing of an income tax return. If § 7207 does not apply to income tax returns, it is obvious that the defendant was not here entitled to a lesser-included offense charge based on that section. [The Court determined, however, that § 7207 would apply to the filing of a false income tax return.]

* * *

* * * Since there is no doubt that §§ 7201 and 7203 also apply to income tax violations, with obvious overlapping among them, there can be no doubt that the lesser-included offense doctrine applies to these statutes in an appropriate case.

The basic principles controlling whether or not a lesser-included offense charge should be given in a particular case have been settled by this Court. Rule 31(c) of the Federal Rules of Criminal Procedure provides in relevant part, that the "defendant may be found guilty of an offense necessarily included in the offense charged." Thus, "[i]n a case where some of the elements of the crime charged themselves constitute a lesser crime, the defendant, if the evidence justifie[s] it * * * [is] entitled to an instruction which would permit a finding of guilt of the lesser offense." Berra v. United States, 351 U.S. 131, 134, 76 S.Ct. 685, 688, 100 L.Ed. 1013 (1956). But a lesser-offense charge is not proper where, on the evidence presented, the factual issues to be resolved by the jury are the same as to both the lesser and greater offenses. In other words, the lesser offense must be included within but not, on the facts of the case, be completely encompassed by the greater. A lesser-included offense instruction is only proper where the charged greater offense requires the jury to find a disputed factual element which is not required for conviction of the lesser-included offense. We now apply the principles declared in these cases to the instant case.

The offense here charged was a violation of § 7201, which proscribes willfully attempting in any manner to evade or defeat any tax imposed by the Internal Revenue Code. As this Court has recognized, this felony provision is "the capstone of a system of sanctions which singly or in combination were calculated to induce prompt and forthright fulfillment of every duty under the income tax law and to provide a penalty suitable to every degree of delinquency." Spies v. United States, 317 U.S. at 497, 63 S.Ct. at 367. As such a capstone, § 7201 necessarily includes among its elements actions which, if isolated from the others, constitute lesser offenses in this hierarchical system of sanctions. Therefore, if on the facts of a given case there are disputed issues of fact which would enable the jury rationally to find that, although all the elements of § 7201 have not been proved, all the elements of one or more lesser offenses have been, it is clear that the defendant is entitled to a lesser-included offense charge as to such lesser offenses.

As has been held by this Court, the elements of § 7201 are willfulness; the existence of a tax deficiency; and an affirmative act constituting an evasion or attempted evasion of the tax. In comparison, § 7203 makes it a misdemeanor willfully to fail to perform a number of specified acts at the time required by law—the one here relevant being the failure to pay a tax when due. This misdemeanor requires only willfulness and the omission of the required act—here the payment of the tax when due. As recognized by this Court in Spies v. United States, 317 U.S. at 499, 63 S.Ct. at 368, the difference between a mere willful failure to pay a tax (or perform other enumerated actions) when due under § 7203 and a willful attempt to evade or defeat taxes under § 7201 is that the latter felony involves "some willful commission in addition to the willful omissions that make up the list of misdemeanors." Where there is, in a § 7201 prosecution, a disputed issue of fact as to the existence of the requisite affirmative commission in addition to the § 7203 omission, a defendant would, of course, be entitled to a lesser-included offense charge based on § 7203. In this case, however, it is undisputed that petitioner filed a tax return and that the petitioner's filing of a false tax return constituted a sufficient affirmative commission to satisfy that requirement of § 7201. The only issue at trial was whether petitioner's act was willful. Given this affirmative commission and the conceded tax deficiency, if petitioner's act was willful, that is, if the jury believed, as it obviously did, that he knew that the capital gain on the sale of the property was reportable in 1957, he was guilty of violating both

§§ 7201 and 7203. If his act was not willful, he was not guilty of violating either § 7201 or § 7203. Thus on the facts of this case, §§ 7201 and 7203 "covered precisely the same ground." Berra v. United States, supra, 351 U.S. at 134, 76 S.Ct. at 688. This being so, on the authorities cited, it is clear that petitioner was not entitled to a lesser-included offense charge based on § 7203.

Section 7207 requires the willful filing of a document known to be false or fraudulent in any material manner. The elements here involved are willfulness and the commission of the prohibited act. Section 7207 does not, however, require that the act be done as an attempt to evade or defeat taxes. Conduct could therefore violate § 7207 without violating § 7201 where the false statement, though material, does not constitute an attempt to evade or defeat taxation because it does not have the requisite effect of reducing the stated tax liability. This may be the case, for example, where a taxpayer understates his gross receipts and he offsets this by also understating his deductible expenses. In this example, if the Government in a § 7201 case charged tax evasion on the grounds that the defendant had understated his tax by understating his gross receipts, and the defendant contended that this was not so, as the misstatement of gross receipts had been offset by an understatement of deductible expenses, the defendant would be entitled to a lesser-included offense charge based on § 7207, there being this relevant disputed issue of fact. This would be so, for in such a case, if the jury believed that an understatement of deductible expenses had offset the understatement of gross receipts, while the defendant would have violated § 7207 by willfully making a material false and fraudulent statement on his return, he would not have violated § 7201 as there would not have been the requisite § 7201 element of a tax deficiency. Here, however, there is no dispute that petitioner's material misstatement resulted in a tax deficiency. Thus there is no disputed issue of fact concerning the existence of an element required for conviction of § 7201 but not required for conviction of § 7207. Given petitioner's material misstatement which resulted in a tax deficiency, if, as the jury obviously found, petitioner's act was willful in the sense that he knew that he should have reported more income than he did for the year 1957, he was guilty of violating both §§ 7201 and 7207. If his action was not willful, he was guilty of violating neither. As was true with § 7203, on the facts of this case §§ 7201 and 7207 "covered precisely the same ground," Berra v. United States, supra, and thus petitioner was not entitled to a lesser-included offense charge based on § 7207.

Petitioner makes one final contention. He argues that he could have been acquitted of attempting to evade or defeat his 1957 taxes, in violation of § 7201, but still have been convicted for willfully failing to pay his tax when due in violation of § 7203 or willfully filing a fraudulent return in violation of § 7207, if the jury believed his statement contained in the government-introduced affidavit, that, although he knew that profit on the sale in question was reportable for 1957 and that tax was due thereon, he intended to report the sale and pay the 1957 tax at some unspecified future date. The basic premise of this argument is that, although all three sections require willfulness, on the facts here, the contents of these willfulness requirements differ. The argument is made that while an intent to report and pay the tax in the future does not vitiate the willfulness requirements of §§ 7203 and 7207, it does constitute a defense to a willful attempt "in any manner to evade or defeat any tax imposed by" the Internal Revenue Code, in violation of § 7201. While we agree that the intent to report the income and pay the tax sometime in the future does not vitiate the willfulness required by §§ 7203 and 7207, we cannot agree that it vitiates the willfulness requirement of § 7201.

No defense to a § 7201 evasion charge is made out by showing that the defendant willfully and fraudulently understated his tax liability for the year involved but intended to report the income and pay the tax at some later time. As this Court has recognized, § 7201 includes the offense of willfully attempting to evade or defeat the *assessment* of a tax as well as the offense of willfully attempting to evade or defeat the *payment* of a tax. The indictment here charged an attempt to evade income taxes by defeating the assessment for 1957. The fact that petitioner stated to a revenue agent that he intended to report his 1957 income in some later year, even if taken at face value, would not detract from the criminality of his willful act defeating the 1957 assessment. That crime was complete as soon as the false and fraudulent understatement of taxes (assuming, of course, that there was in fact a deficiency) was filed.

In sum, it is clear here that there were no disputed issues of fact which would justify instructing the jury that it could find that petitioner had committed all the elements of either or both of the §§ 7203 and 7207 misdemeanors without having committed a violation of the § 7201 felony. This being the case, the petitioner was not entitled to a lesser-included offense charge and the judgment of the Court of Appeals is

Affirmed.

PAPPAS v. UNITED STATES

216 F.2d 515 (10th Cir. 1954).

HUXMAN, Circuit Judge.

Appellant, George Pappas, has appealed in Number 4809 and appellant, Harry Pappas, has appealed in Number 4810 from judgments of conviction on informations charging them with wilfully and knowingly failing to furnish to the Collector of Internal Revenue information as to partnership assets and liabilities as required under the Internal Revenue Code and Treasury Regulation No. 111 and specifically Schedule I of Partnership Return of Income, in violation of Section 145(a), Internal Revenue Code, for the year 1951. * * *

Appellants' quotation of Section 145(a) in their brief omits some of the essential parts of that Section. Section 145(a) so far as material requires taxpayers to make a return or declaration, keep records and supply information for the purpose of computation, assessment or collection of any estimated tax and provides that anyone who wilfully fails to pay such estimated tax, or make a return, or keep records, *"or supply such information * * * required by law or regulations"* shall be guilty of an offense.

On April 18, 1952 appellants filed the partnership return required of partners by 26 U.S.C.A. § 187, but did not include in the return the information required by Schedule I. Schedule I was adopted under Treasury Regulation No. 111 and called for beginning and ending balance sheets, showing the partnership assets, liabilities and net worth at the beginning and ending of the year. This schedule was left blank. Repeated efforts on the part of internal revenue agents to obtain this information were unavailing. Finally appellants were informed that criminal prosecution against them had been recommended. Even that failed to elicit the required information. They were given a final date of October 31, 1952, to supply the information. They did not furnish the required information and did not ask for extensions of time. The criminal information was filed April 22, 1953.

The first assignment of error urged for reversal is that the trial court erred in refusing to sustain appellants' motion to dismiss the information and appellants' motion for directed verdicts of acquittal.

In support of their contention that the information failed to state an offense, appellants merely cite the case of United States v. Carroll, 345 U.S. 457, 73 S.Ct. 757, 97 L.Ed. 1147, without pointing out in what manner that case is controlling. In that case Treasury Regulations required that, together with the income tax return form 1096, there be filed informational returns on forms 1099, showing payments to every person receiving $600 or more in any calendar year. Defendants were prosecuted for refusing to fill out the informational forms. The Supreme Court held that since the return specified in Section 145(a) was that provided in form 1096, failure to file 1099 which was not required by statute did not constitute a violation of Section 145(a). But here the basic law, Section 145(a), requires taxpayers to make a return and to supply all information required by the Act or properly promulgated regulations under the Act and makes wilful non-compliance a criminal offense. We think the information stated an offense.

* * *

(2) SECTION 7206(1)

The essence of the charge under § 7206(1) is that there is a false tax return. Typically, but not exclusively, the statute is applied in cases where there has been a false entry on the return which results in an understatement of tax liability. However, as noted below, § 7206(1) may also be utilized in cases in which a false item on the tax return does not affect tax liability or, perhaps, where the falsity lies in an omission.

UNITED STATES v. DiVARCO

343 F.Supp. 101 (N.D.Ill.1972),
aff'd, 484 F.2d 670 (7th Cir. 1973).

WILL, District Judge.

The government is prosecuting the defendants in this case pursuant to an indictment which charges each of them with having made "a false statement as to a material matter on their respective 1965 United States Individual Income Tax Return," in violation of 26 U.S. C. § 7206(1), in that each reported income from commissions paid them by Chemical Mortgage & Investment Corporation never having received any income from such a source, thereby falsely stating the source of their reported income. * * * The defendants have moved to dismiss the indictment on the ground that the source of one's income as distinguished from the amount of one's income is not a material matter which can be falsely stated within the meaning of 26 U.S.C. § 7206(1). Defendants' motion is denied inasmuch as we find the source of income to be such a material matter.

* * *

Defendants' essential argument is that the source of one's income is not a material matter within the meaning of 26 U.S.C. § 7206(1), and that a false statement of the source of income on one's tax return is not an indictable offense. They contend that the only material matter on a tax return that is indictable is the amount of one's taxable income. They continue that, since an overstatement of taxable income is not an indictable offense, citing Poonian v. United States, 294 F.2d 74 (9th Cir. 1961), no valid prosecution can be maintained under 26 U.S.C. § 7206(1) without a showing of understatement of the defendants' taxable income.

The question whether misstatement of the source of one's income alone without a misstatement of the amount of one's income is indictable under 26 U.S.C. § 7206(1) is one of first impression. The government has cited a number of cases in support of their position that an indictment for the misstatement of source of income alone is valid. See Gaunt v. United States, 184 F.2d 284 (1st Cir. 1950), cert. denied 340 U.S. 917, 71 S.Ct. 350, 95 L.Ed. 662 (1951); United States v.

Null, 415 F.2d 1178 (4th Cir. 1969); United States v. Rayor, 204 F. Supp. 486 (S.D.Cal.1962). The defendants have correctly noted that none of these cases involved an indictment solely for the false statement of the source of income. Technically, not one of the cases proffered by the government holds that a false statement as to the source of income alone in an indictable offense under 26 U.S.C. § 7206(1). Most of the government cases involved prosecution for the understatement of taxable income. In a few of the cases, it is unclear what material matter was falsely misstated.

The mere fact that the government cases are not strict precedents for the indictment in the instant case does not, however, render them useless in our analysis. Defendants' historical position that there have been no reported prosecutions under § 7206(1) for false statement as to source of income alone is not dispositive of the issue whether source of income is a material matter under the statute, the false statement of which is indictable. The reported cases, while involving fact patterns where there had been understatement of the amount of income, did not focus on the particular material matter which had been misstated. Rather, these courts found a more general rationale underlying the section.

One of the more basic tenents running through all the cases is that the purpose behind the statute is to prosecute those who intentionally falsify their tax returns regardless of the precise ultimate effect that such falsification may have. In the early and oft-cited *Gaunt* case, it was stated:

> It seems to us clear that the latter subsection [§ 145(c) of the 1939 Code, which is virtually identical to its successor § 7206(1)] makes it a felony merely to make and subscribe a tax return without believing it to be true and correct as to every material matter, whether or not the purpose in so doing was to evade or defeat the payment of taxes. That is to say, it seems to us that the subsection's purpose is to impose the penalties for perjury upon those who willfully falsify their returns regardless of the tax consequences of the falsehood. 184 F.2d at 288.

The *Gaunt* case has been followed and cited for this particular point in numerous subsequent cases.

Another basic rationale for prohibiting any falsity on the return is that without truthful representation as to all matters it becomes administratively more difficult, if not impossible, for the Internal Revenue Service (IRS) to compute the amount of tax due or to check on the accuracy of returns. In *Rayor*, the court borrowed a test for materiality from the D. C. Circuit in Weinstock v. United States, 97 U.S.App.D.C. 365, 231 F.2d 699 (1956), a prosecution under the federal false statement statute, 18 U.S.C. § 1001, for submitting an allegedly false affidavit to the Subversive Activities Control Board, where the D. C. Circuit stated:

> The test [for materiality] is whether the false statement has a natural tendency to influence, or was capable of influencing, the decision of the tribunal in making a determination required to be made. 231 F.2d at 701–702.

The idea that a matter is material under § 7206(1) if it would have a tendency to influence the IRS in its normal processing of tax returns was reiterated in *Null,* supra.

Each of these analyses of the statute and its purpose argues for validating the indictment in the instant case. It is alleged in the indictment that the defendants wilfully falsified their tax returns. So under *Gaunt* and its progeny, the indictment is valid. In addition, the indictment envisions no mere oversight or mistake. The W–2 forms defendants attached to their tax returns were allegedly fabricated. Certainly, such a scheme would impede the IRS in its quite proper role of auditing and investigating returns and would be material under *Rayor* and *Null.*

Even defendants' argument that there can be no prosecution except for understatement of income reflects the importance and *materiality* of the source of one's income as reported on the tax return. Without truthful representation of the source of income, it is impossible for the government to determine whether the amount paid is in fact understated, overstated, or correct. Surely, save the amount, there is no more material matter on the tax return than the source of income.

Moreover, the consequence of accepting defendants' position would be to open one of the widest loopholes in the tax structure. To allow taxpayers to wilfully misstate and fabricate the source of their income would thereby render virtually impossible the task of ascertaining whether the amount of income as reported is accurate. Evasion of income tax would become much easier. It is inconceivable that Congress could have intended that this statute be construed in a manner that would make it impossible for the IRS to verify and check the accuracy of the amounts reported.

In summary, we hold that the source of one's income as stated on the federal income tax return is a material matter within the meaning of 26 U.S.C. § 7206(1), and that, as such, the government may properly prosecute a taxpayer for falsely stating the source of his income on his federal income tax return. Accordingly, defendants' motion to dismiss the indictment is denied.

An appropriate order will enter.

SIRAVO v. UNITED STATES

377 F.2d 469 (1st Cir. 1967).

COFFIN, Circuit Judge.

Defendant appeals from judgments of conviction on three counts for wilfully making and subscribing false tax returns in 1958, 1959, and 1960, in violation of 26 U.S.C. § 7206(1)   *   *   *.

Defendant's returns during 1958–1960 showed as income only wages (not exceeding $7,500 in any of the tax years in question) paid by Siravo Motor Sales. In each year the tax due was less than tax withheld and refund was applied for. Evidence at trial showed that during these years defendant operated Trans-Lux Jewelry Co., which assembled jewelry components as a subcontractor for various manufacturers, receiving for this work the following amounts: 1958— $22,242.83; 1959—$28,976.22; 1960—$54,319.47; 1961—$71,362.73.

Defendant made no entry on his form 1040 opposite the heading "profit (or loss) from business from separate Schedule C", nor did he file a separate Schedule C ("Profit (or Loss) From Business or Profession"). He signed the customary declaration.

While the evidence indicated that the defendant's jewelry assembly work must have required a number of people, there was no evidence as to the amount of any costs or expenses, whether of materials, labor, or overhead.

The first three counts charged that defendant "did wilfully *   *   * make and subscribe   *   *   * a   *   *   * tax return *   *   * which was verified by a written declaration that it was made under the penalties of perjury, and which   *   *   * he did not believe to be true and correct as to every material matter in that *   *   * he failed and omitted to disclose   *   *   * substantial gross receipts from a business activity   *   *   *."

Defendant's principal contention is that 26 U.S.C. § 7206(1) describes a form of perjury, that a basic requirement of perjury is a false statement of fact, and that failure to attach a separate Schedule C reporting "gross receipts" is neither a constructive misrepresentation of taxable income nor a false statement. He therefore attacks the sufficiency of both the indictment and the evidence. The government denies that section 7206(1) is a perjury statute and that a false statement of facts is an essential element of this crime. It argues that a violation of the section can consist of the knowing and wilful omission of facts   *   *   *.

In our view it is unnecessary to resolve this dispute in semantics, for we hold that a return that omits material items necessary to the computation of income is not "true and correct" within the meaning of section 7206. If an affirmative false statement be required, it is supplied by the taxpayer's declaration that the return is true and correct, when he knows it is not. Therefore, the government has made out a violation of the section, whether it be labelled "a perjury statute", Kolaski v. United States, 5 Cir., 1966, 362 F.2d 847, or "similar in nature", Hoover v. United States, 5 Cir., 1966, 358 F.2d 87, cert. denied, 385 U.S. 822, 87 S.Ct. 50, 17 L.Ed.2d 59.

Our decision is grounded first on the language of the statute. If "true" and "correct" are not to be construed as precisely synonymous, therefore redundant, they must mean something more than that no false figures have been used and that the arithmetic is accurate. In fact, the two terms together are commonly construed as meaning that the document described is both accurate and complete.

Moreover, we think this construction is necessary to effect the statutory "self-assessing" approach to income taxation. As the Supreme Court said in United States v. Carroll, 1953, 345 U.S. 457, 460, 73 S.Ct. 757, 759, 97 L.Ed. 1147 (dictum), "The code and regulations must be construed in light of the purpose to locate and check upon recipients of income and the amounts they receive." In the context of this case, defendant's contrary construction comes down to this: The return of an employee who earned $10,000 a year and reported only $8,000 would not be "true and correct", while that of a corporation director who reported fees of $5,000 but omitted an accounting for the receipt of $1,000,000 in rents would be "true and correct". Or, to reverse the pattern in this case, defendant would have to say that a return showing an accounting for a taxpayer's business resulting in a net profit of $7,500 and omitting wage payments of $50,000 would also be "true and correct". We cannot conclude that Congress, in devising "a variety of sanctions for the protection of the system and the revenues", Spies v. United States, 1943, 317 U.S. 492, 495, 63 S.Ct. 364, 87 L.Ed. 418, intended to place such a premium on the telling of half truths.

Defendant argues also that another statute amply covers the wilful omission of information and that the principle of narrow construction of penal statutes compels us not to allow the application of section 7206(1) to defendant. Section 7203 of title 26 creates a misdemeanor for the wilful failure to keep required tax records or supply required information. But the fact that Congress has seen fit to classify wilful failure to supply information as a misdemeanor quite clearly does not preclude it from establishing a felony for falsely swearing under the penalties of perjury that a partial return is a whole one. The structure of sanctions, particularly in the tax field, is not one of mutually exclusive alternatives. While we respect the principle of narrow construction, we see no ambiguity in the words "true and correct". This is a far cry from the situation in Commissioner of Internal Revenue v. Acker, 1959, 361 U.S. 87, 80 S.Ct. 144, 4

L.Ed.2d 127, where the government sought to parlay a failure to file a declaration of estimated tax into a "substantial underestimate".

* * *

Affirmed.

QUESTION

Assume that an individual is charged with violating § 7206(1) by virtue of having filed federal income tax returns on which he failed to check either the "yes" or "no" box indicating whether he had an interest in or a signature or other authority over a foreign bank account. (See Form 1040, Schedule B, Part III). In such a case, would § 7206(1) apply at all under the holding in *Siravo*? Would the defendant be entitled to a lesser-included offense instruction under § 7203 or § 7207 according to the principles set forth in *Sansone*?

(3) SECTION 7206(2)

UNITED STATES v. KELLEY

105 F.2d 912 (2d Cir. 1939).

L. HAND, Circuit Judge.

The chief appeals are from a judgment of conviction of the three accused under two indictments, consolidated for trial, for assisting in the preparation and presentation of fraudulent income tax returns for the years 1929 to 1932, inclusive. One indictment concerned the partnership returns of Ringling Bros.-Barnum & Bailey Combined Shows; the other those of the estate of Charles E. Ringling, who died December 3, 1926. During the years in question the partners and the executors of some who were dead were the owners of this well-known circus, and Kelley was, and for many years had been, their legal adviser; to him was entrusted the preparation of the firm income tax returns from at least 1917 forward. In or about 1923 he employed as an assistant one, Rabner, at one time a Treasury agent; and in 1929 Greer, another Treasury agent. The frauds consisted of deductions taken from the gross income. They were of several kinds; one was for the depreciation or abandonment of the circus property; another was the write-off as a bad debt of a claim against one, Rickard; there were others which we shall not discuss. With the two indictments upon which the accused were convicted, the government consolidated two conspiracy indictments, charging, not only the three accused now before us, but five others in all, against whom the prosecution was severed at the beginning of the trial. The jury acquitted the accused upon the conspiracy indictments. The issues raised upon the appeals from the conviction are (1) that it was an error to consolidate the four indictments; (2) that the taxpayers (the representative of the partners, and the "estate" of Charles Ringling) were not proved to have been guilty of any fraud, without which the accused could not have been themselves found guilty; (3) that incompetent documents were admitted and the incompetent opinion of revenue agents received; (4) that the admission of the partners' books against Kelley was erroneous; and (5) that the evidence did not support the verdict.

* * *

* * * The returns took deductions for depreciation yearly from 1929 to 1932, based upon an inventory—Ex. 89—made by Kelley, either during or before the year 1923, but calculated as of 1918. He admitted to one of the Treasury officials in charge of the inquiry that this inventory had been made up from three others, found in a loft at Sarasota, Florida; two of which were made in 1913, and one, in 1911. Most of the items upon these three were contained in Ex. 89. The prosecution proved in a number of ways that this inventory (Ex. 89) was fabricated; one, by comparing it with the three inventories just mentioned; another, by comparing it with inventories of the estates of four dead partners, which had been filed in the probate proceedings, one in March 1911, another in January 1916, a third in October 1918, and the fourth in October 1919. The padding was both in the number of items contained—e. g. cars, wagons and animals— and in their value. Several witnesses, including some who had formerly been employed by the circus, testified to the number of animals and wagons which it had had while they were with it, and to their cost. The accused answer that this did not take into account the money used to repair the wagons and to train the animals, which should be added. But these were, or at least it was fair to argue that they were, expenses of the business, and were taken out of the gross in the year in which they were incurred. Certainly it was improper, having once been so taken, that they should be taken again as depreciation. Again, there had originally been an item of "Autos and trucks" of about $51,000, which by the end of 1928 had been substantially all written off through depreciation. Rabner wrote to Kelley in June and July of that year that it would be necessary that additional purchases should be shown in the inventory for 1927, in order to get proper depreciation charges. This was done. Again, Wadsworth, who became auditor at the beginning of 1930, prepared the depreciation schedule for that year (Ex. 380) based upon a similar schedule in 1929 which had been given him by either Kelley or Greer. This showed a total depreciation of about $49,000. Greer, raised this by exactly $100,000 and upon the witness stand, could not explain why this was done. In the same year Kelley instructed Greer to raise the gross of this inventory by $200,000 or $300,000, and Greer fabricated plausible items to fetch it up by about that much.

In 1929 one, Rickard, who owed the partners a debt of $50,000, died, and his estate was known to be insolvent. Kelley and Greer deducted the whole debt twice by elaborate concealment. One, De-Wolfe, had prepared a statement of the net income for the year, charging the partners with a total gross of about $4,000,000, and taking deductions which included accounts receivable of about $103,000. The accounts were obviously not proper deductions for income tax purposes and had to be deleted, but only $21,000 was subtracted instead of the full figure, $103,000. This resulted in taking as deductions the Rickard debt and an item of about $32,000, known as "J. M. K. Expense Account". From the income so computed the Rickard debt was a second time expressly deducted as a bad debt. In the year 1931, the Rickard estate paid half the debt, and, in the return for that year also, the difference, $25,000, was deducted as a bad debt. It is true that the deduction on the 1929 return of $50,000 as a bad debt was disallowed on July 15, 1930, because the debt had not been written off the books, but the attempted fraud was as great as though it had been successful. Moreover, the full amount of the debt having been deducted in that year in making up the net income, it was a second fraud to deduct one half of it again in 1931. By this chicanery a fraudulent credit was thus secured of $50,000.

There was other evidence that the returns were fraudulent, but it is not necessary to set it forth, because it is apparent from the foregoing recital that there was ample to justify a jury in so finding. There was also ample to connect the accused with their preparation and presentation. Greer was in charge of the books during the years in question and his complicity is too plain to justify any discussion; indeed his own testimony fastened his guilt upon him. It would be absurd to suppose that he should have originated the fraud himself; Kelley was in charge of all such matters for the partners and their estates, and was the only person at once capable of dealing with them, and having any motive to rig the returns. Moreover, Greer repeatedly said that he got figures from Kelley with instructions as to how to use them. As to Rabner, his letters to Kelley in June and July, 1928, about the necessity of fabricating a new item of $50,000 for autos and motor trucks to replace that which had been exhausted by previous depreciation, showed his complicity in the fraud. This was to swell the inventory which he knew was to be used in future years until by depreciation the new item should be exhausted as the old had been. Moreover in 1932 he was still concerned with the preparation of the returns as his letter—Ex. 234—disclosed, in which he advised Kelley how to make up the depreciation schedule from the 1926 purchases. Add to this his attendance at conferences in Washington in 1931 and 1932, when the Treasury officials were induced to pass some of the items, and it plainly appears that he was working with Kelley throughout the whole period. * * *

The next point is that the crime of assisting in the preparation of a fraudulent tax return presupposes that the taxpayer himself is a party to the fraud, and that this was not proved. Whatever embarrassment that might have caused, had the accused been charged as abettors of the partners and their executors, it is quite immaterial here, because the statute (section 1114(c) of the Revenue Act of 1926, 26 U.S.C.A. § 1693(b)(1)) expressly provides that the assistance shall be a crime "whether or not such falsity or fraud is with the knowledge or consent of the person authorized * * * to present such return." The purpose was very plainly to reach the advisers of taxpayers who got up their returns, and who might wish to keep down the taxes because of the credit they would get with their principals, who might be altogether innocent.

* * *

Convictions affirmed.

UNITED STATES v. CRUM

529 F.2d 1380 (9th Cir. 1976).

WRIGHT, Circuit Judge.

Crum was convicted on four counts of aiding and assisting in the preparation of false income tax returns [26 U.S.C. § 7206(2)] and on this appeal argues that (a) the indictment is infirm because Section 7206(2) is inapplicable to those not preparers of tax returns, [and] (b) the evidence was insufficient to sustain the verdict * * *. There being no merit to any contention, we affirm the conviction on all counts.

An attorney, Galas, devised a scheme of enticing high income taxpayers and physicians in particular to invest in domesticated beavers as a tax shelter device. Galas solicited the aid of Monroe, an accountant, and Crum, who bred and sold beavers. The scheme employed the fraudulent use of depreciation deductions by backdating beaver purchase contracts. As purchasers became involved, Galas and Monroe participated by preparing the doctors' income tax returns.

All three schemers were indicted. Their usual procedure was to visit a prospect, ask for his income figures for his yet unfiled tax return, then suggest how many beavers he would need to reduce his income tax by use of the depreciation deduction. Crum admits that he attended two such meetings with Drs. McAdams and Harris.

Crum advised Dr. McAdams that investment in beavers would provide a good depreciation deduction and Crum heard Galas and Monroe tell the doctor how much deduction would be needed. A backdated beaver purchase contract was then signed by Crum and McAdams.

Some months later, when an IRS agent was in Dr. McAdams' waiting room with an appointment to discuss the doctor's tax return, Galas, Monroe and Crum entered through a rear door and persuaded McAdams to sign a new backdated contract which could be exhibited to the agent. Crum also signed it.

We reject Crum's contention that Section 7206(2) applies only to preparers of tax returns. In United States v. Johnson, 319 U.S. 503, 518, 63 S.Ct. 1233, 1240, 87 L.Ed. 1546 (1943), the Court said: [1]

> The nub of the matter is that they aided and abetted if they consciously were parties to the concealment of [a taxable business] interest * * *.

In United States v. Maius, 378 F.2d 716, 718 (6th Cir. 1967), the court sustained a conviction under Section 7206(2) even though defendant was not a preparer. The court reasoned:

> There was sufficient evidence to support the conclusion of the jury that appellant was a party to the scheme of concealing the receipt of income and not reporting it on the corporate records, and this [sic] his knowledge of the use of such records in preparing the tax returns is sufficient * * *.

Accord United States v. Frazier, 365 F.2d 316, 318 (6th Cir. 1966).

Since the reach of Section 7206(2) is clearly not limited to acts of tax return "preparers," the indictment in this case encompasses Crum's conduct.[2]

As for the sufficiency of the evidence argument, we view the evidence in a light most favorable to the government. The facts as we have outlined them amply support the jury's conclusion that Crum fraudulently backdated the purchase contracts, knowing that the false information would be used in the preparation of tax returns. His complicity is beyond dispute.[4]

1. The court in *Johnson* was construing then 26 U.S.C. § 145(b) (53 Stat. 63, 1939 Code) (making it a felony for any person who, being subject to tax, "willfully attempts in any manner to evade or defeat any tax imposed by this chapter or the payment thereof"), together with then 18 U.S. C. § 550 (Section 332 of the Criminal Code) (the general aiding and abetting statute).

2. The indictment charged that the defendants Galas, Monroe, and Crum, on each of four counts, did "wilfully and knowingly aid and assist in, and counsel, procure, and advise the preparation and presentation to the Internal Revenue Service, of [false and fraudulent income tax returns] * * *."

The district court's instruction tracked the indictment and instructed that the government must establish three essential elements to prove the offense:

First: That the income tax return described * * * was fraudulent or false as to some material matter;

Second: That the defendant had aided or assisted in or procured or advised the preparation or filing of that return; and

Third: That the defendant did so wilfully.

4. The court instructed the jury as to the "aids or assists in" language in 26 U.S.C. § 7206(2):

"In order to aid and abet another to commit a crime it is necessary that the accused wilfully associate himself in some way with the criminal venture, and wilfully participates in it as he would in something he wishes to bring about; that is to say, that he wilfully seeks by some act or omission of his to make the criminal venture succeed.

"In making a determination as to whether the defendants aided or

We reject as frivolous Crum's argument that the evidence failed to show that the information on the returns was false as to any material matter under Section 7206(2). We can scarcely imagine anything more material than a false schedule designed to induce allowance of a wholly unwarranted depreciation deduction.

* * *

Affirmed.

B. THE WILLFULNESS ELEMENT

UNITED STATES v. BISHOP

Supreme Court of the United States, 1973.
412 U.S. 346, 93 S.Ct. 2008, 36 L.Ed.2d 941.

Mr. Justice BLACKMUN delivered the opinion of the Court.

* * *

Mr. Bishop is a lawyer who has practiced his profession in Sacramento, California, since 1951. During that period, he owned an interest in a walnut ranch he and his father operated. In 1960 his secretary, Louise, married his father. The father died, and thereafter respondent's stepmother managed the ranch.

Respondent periodically sent checks to Louise. These were used to run the ranch, to pay principal on loans, and to make improvements.

Louise maintained a record of ranch expenditures and submitted an itemized list of these disbursements to respondent at the end of each calendar year. In his 1963 return respondent asserted as business deductions all amounts paid to Louise and, in addition, all the expenses Louise listed. This necessarily resulted in a double deduction for all ranch expenditures in 1963. Moreover, some of these expenditures were for repayment of loans and for other personal items that did not qualify as income tax deductions. In his 1964 and 1965 returns respondent similarly included nondeductible amounts among the ranch figures that were deducted.

[Bishop was charged with felony violations of § 7206(1) with respect to his 1963, 1964 and 1965 returns. At trial he requested lesser-included offense instructions based on the misdemeanor statute, § 7207. This tax misdemeanor is committed by one "who willfully delivers or discloses" to the IRS any return or document "known by him to be fraudulent or to be false as to any material matter." Bishop argued that the word "willfully" in the misdemeanor statute

assisted in or procured or advised the preparation for filing of false income tax returns, the fact that the defendants did not sign the income tax returns in question is not material to your consideration."

There was no objection to the first paragraph of the above instruction. Indeed, it is proper. As to the second paragraph, we have determined that it is a proper statement of the law.

should be construed to require less scienter than the same word in the felony statute. With the state of the defendant's guilty knowledge in dispute, Bishop's proposed instructions would have allowed the jury to choose between a misdemeanor based on caprice or careless disregard and a felony requiring evil purpose. The trial judge declined to give the requested instructions and, instead, gave an instruction only on the felony, requiring a finding by the jury that the defendant intended "with evil motive or bad purpose either to disobey or to disregard the law." The jury convicted Bishop, but the Court of Appeals reversed the judgment of the District Court and remanded the case for a new trial. The Supreme Court granted certiorari in order to resolve a division in the circuits concerning the meaning of "willfully" as used in the tax crime statutes.]

The Court of Appeals relied upon and followed a series of its own cases, particularly Abdul v. United States, 9 Cir., 254 F.2d 292 (1958), enunciating the proposition that the word "willfully" has a meaning in tax felony statutes that is more stringent than its meaning in tax misdemeanor statutes. * * *

* * *

In the present case the Court of Appeals continued this *Abdul* distinction between willfulness in tax misdemeanor charges and willfulness in tax felony charges. Section 7207, it was said, requires only a showing of "unreasonable, capricious, or careless disregard for the truth or falsity of income tax returns filed," whereas § 7206(1) "requires proof of an evil motive and bad faith." The level of willfulness, thus, would create a disputed factual element that made appropriate a lesser-included-offense instruction.

The decisions of this Court do not support the holding in *Abdul*, and implicitly they reject the approach taken by the Court of Appeals. In Spies [v. United States, 317 U.S. 492, 63 S.Ct. 364, 87 L.Ed. 418 (1943)] the Court speculated that Congress could have distinguished between the regulatory aspects of the tax system, which call for compliance regardless of financial status, and the revenue-collecting aspects, which may place demands on a taxpayer he cannot meet. Since the antecedent of § 7203 (as does that section itself today) punished both failure to file and failure to pay as misdemeanors, the Court concluded that Congress had not drawn the line between felonies and misdemeanors on the basis of distinctions between the system's regulatory aspects and its revenue-collecting aspects. The reliance in *Abdul* on that hypothetical statutory scheme, discussed by this Court in *Spies* but found not in line with what Congress had actually done, was misplaced. Utilizing the unsupported *Abdul* distinction as a foundation, the Court of Appeals constructed the further general distinction between tax felonies and tax misdemeanors, a distinction also inconsistent with prior decisions of this Court.

* * *

It would be possible, of course, that the word "willfully" was intended by Congress to have a meaning in § 7206(1) different from its meaning in § 7207, and we turn now to that possibility.

We continue to recognize that context is important in the quest for the word's meaning. See United States v. Murdock, 290 U.S. 389, 394–395, 54 S.Ct. 223, 225, 78 L.Ed. 381 (1933). Here, as in *Spies*, the "legislative history of the section[s] contains nothing helpful on the question here at issue, and we must find the answer from the [sections themselves] and [their] context in the revenue laws." 317 U.S., at 495, 63 S.Ct., at 366. We consider first, then, the sections themselves.

A. Respondent argues that both §§ 7206(1) and 7207 apply to a fraudulent "return" and cover the same ground if the word "willfully" has the same meaning in both sections. Since "it would be unusual and we would not readily assume that Congress by the felony * * * meant no more than the same derelictions it had just defined * * * as a misdemeanor," 317 U.S., at 497, 63 S.Ct., at 367, respondent concludes that Congress must have intended to require a more willful violation for the felony than for the misdemeanor.

The critical difficulty for respondent is that the two sections have substantially different express terms. The most obvious difference is that § 7206(1) applies only if the document "contains or is verified by a written declaration that it is made under the penalties of perjury." No equivalent requirement is present in § 7207. Respondent recognizes this but then relies on the presence of perjury declarations on all federal income tax returns, a fact that effectively equalizes the sections where a federal tax return is at issue. See 26 U.S.C. § 6065(a).

This approach, however, is not persuasive for two reasons. First, the Secretary or his delegate has the power under § 6065(a) to provide that no perjury declaration is required. If he does so provide, then § 7207 immediately becomes operative in the area theretofore covered by § 7206(1). Second, the term "return" is not necessarily limited to a federal income tax return. A state or other non-federal return could be intended and might not contain a perjury warning. If this type of return were submitted in support of a federal return, or in the course of a tax audit, § 7207 could apply even if § 7206(1) could not.

There are other distinctions. The felony applies to a document that a taxpayer "[w]illfully makes and subscribes * * * and which he does not believe to be true and correct as to every material matter," whereas the misdemeanor applies to a document that a taxpayer "willfully delivers or discloses to the Secretary or his delegate * * * known by him * * * to be false as to any material matter." In the felony, then, the taxpayer must verify the return or document in writing, and he is liable if he does not affirmatively believe that the material statements are true. For the misdemeanor, however, a document prepared by another could give rise to liability on the part of the taxpayer if he delivered or disclosed it to the Service; additional protection is given to the taxpayer in this situation because the document must be known by him to be fraudulent or to be false.

These differences in the respective applications of §§ 7206(1) and 7207 provide solid evidence that Congress distinguished the statutes in ways that do not turn on the meaning of the word "willfully." Judge Hastie, in analyzing this Court's holding in *Spies*, appropriately described this distinction as follows:

> "However, this distinction is found in the additional misconduct which is essential to the violation of the felony statute * * * and not in the quality of willfulness which characterizes the wrongdoing." United States v. Vitiello, 363 F.2d 240, 243 (C.A.3, 1966).

Thus the word "willfully" may have a uniform meaning in the several statutes without rendering any one of them surplusage. We next turn to context.

B. The hierarchy of tax offenses set forth in §§ 7201–7207, inclusive, utilizes the mental state of the offender as a guide in establishing the penalty. Section 7201, relating to attempts to evade or defeat tax, has been described and recognized by the Court as the "climax of this variety of sanctions" and as the "capstone of a system of sanctions which singly or in combination were calculated to induce prompt and forthright fulfillment of every duty under the income tax law and to provide a penalty suitable to every degree of delinquency." *Spies*, 317 U.S., at 497, 63 S.Ct. 367; *Sansone*, 380 U.S., at 350–351, 85 S.Ct. at 1009. The actor's mental state is described both by the requirement that acts be done "willfully" and by the designation of certain express elements of the offenses. In § 7201, for example, the Court has held that, by requiring an attempt to evade, "Congress intended some willful commission in addition to the willful omissions that make up the list of misdemeanors." *Spies*, 317 U.S., at 499, 63 S.Ct. at 368. Similarly, in § 7207, the Government must show that the document was known by the taxpayer to be fraudulent or to be false as to a material matter.

All these offenses, except two subsections of § 7206, viz., subsections (3) and (4), require that acts be done "willfully." Although the described states of mind might be included in the normal meaning of the word "willfully," the presence of both an express designation and the simultaneous requirement that a violation be committed "willfully" is strong evidence that Congress used the word "willfully" to describe a constant rather than a variable in the tax penalty formula.

The Court, in fact, has recognized that the word "willfully" in these statutes generally connotes a voluntary, intentional violation of a known legal duty. It has formulated the requirement of willfulness as "bad faith or evil intent," *Murdock* 290 U.S., at 398, 54 S.Ct. at 226, or "evil motive and want of justification in view of all the financial circumstances of the taxpayer," *Spies,* 317 U.S., at 498, 63 S.Ct. at 368, or knowledge that the taxpayer "should have reported more income than he did." *Sansone,* 380 U.S., at 353, 85 S.Ct. at 1011.

This longstanding interpretation of the purpose of the recurring word "willfully" promotes coherence in the group of tax crimes. In our complex tax system, uncertainty often arises even among taxpayers who earnestly wish to follow the law. The Court has said, "It is not the purpose of the law to penalize frank difference of opinion or innocent errors made despite the exercise of reasonable care." *Spies,* 317 U.S., at 496, 63 S.Ct. at 367. Degrees of negligence give rise in the tax system to civil penalties. The requirement of an offense committed "willfully" is not met, therefore, if a taxpayer has relied in good faith on a prior decision of this Court. The Court's consistent interpretation of the word "willfully" to require an element of *mens rea* implements the pervasive intent of Congress to construct penalties that separate the purposeful tax violator from the well-meaning, but easily confused, mass of taxpayers.

Until Congress speaks otherwise, we therefore shall continue to require, in both tax felonies and tax misdemeanors that must be done "willfully," the bad purpose or evil motive described in *Murdock,* supra. We hold, consequently, that the word "willfully" has the same meaning in § 7207 that it has in § 7206(1). Since the only issue in dispute in this case centered on willfulness, it follows that a conviction of the misdemeanor would clearly support a conviction for the felony. Under these circumstances a lesser-included-offense instruction was not required or proper, for in the federal system it is not the function of the jury to set the penalty.

The judgment of the Court of Appeals is reversed, and the case is remanded for further proceedings. It is so ordered.

UNITED STATES v. POMPONIO

Supreme Court of the United States, 1976.
429 U.S. 10, 97 S.Ct. 22, 50 L.Ed.2d 12.

PER CURIAM.

After a jury trial, respondents were convicted of willfully filing false income tax returns in violation of 26 U.S.C. § 7206(1). Based on its reading of United States v. Bishop, the Court of Appeals held that the jury was incorrectly instructed concerning willfulness, and remanded for a new trial. The United States petitioned for certiorari. We reverse.

* * *

The jury was instructed that respondents were not guilty of violating § 7206(1) unless they had signed the tax returns knowing them to be false, and had done so willfully. A willful act was defined in the instructions as one done "voluntarily and intentionally and with the specific intent to do something which the law forbids, that is to say with [the] bad purpose either to disobey or to disregard the law." Finally, the jury was instructed that "[g]ood motive alone is never a defense where the act done or omitted is a crime," and that consequently motive was irrelevant except as it bore on intent. The Court of Appeals held this final instruction improper because "the statute at hand requires a finding of a bad purpose or evil motive." In so holding, the Court of Appeals incorrectly assumed that the reference to an "evil motive" in United States v. Bishop and prior cases meant something more than the specific intent to violate the law described in the trial judge's instruction.

In *Bishop* we held that the term "willfully" has the same meaning in the misdemeanor and felony sections of the Revenue Code, and that it requires more than a showing of careless disregard for the truth. We did not, however, hold that the term requires proof of any motive other than an intentional violation of a known legal duty. We explained the meaning of willfulness in § 7206 and related statutes:

> "The Court, in fact, has recognized that the word 'willfully' in these statutes generally connotes a voluntary, intentional violation of a known legal duty. It has formulated the requirement of willfulness as 'bad faith or evil intent,' *Murdock,* 290 U.S. 398, 54 S.Ct. at 226, or 'evil motive and want of justification in view of all the financial circumstances of the taxpayer,' *Spies,* 317 U.S. 498, 63 S.Ct. at 368, or knowledge that the taxpayer 'should have reported more income than he did.' *Sansone,* 380 U.S. 353, 85 S.Ct. at 1011.

Our references to other formulations of the standard did not modify the standard set forth in the first sentence of the quoted paragraph. On the contrary, as the other Courts of Appeals that have considered the question have recognized, willfulness in this context simply means a voluntary, intentional violation of a known legal duty. The trial judge in the instant case adequately instructed the jury on willfulness. An additional instruction on good faith was unnecessary.

* * *

UNITED STATES v. PHILLIPS

217 F.2d 435 (7th Cir. 1955).

MAJOR, Circuit Judge.

A six-count indictment was returned against defendant, George E. Phillips, on March 2, 1951. Each count charged that defendant "did wilfully and knowingly attempt to defeat and evade" taxes, in violation of Section 145(b) of the Internal Revenue Code. Count 1 charged a violation for the year 1944; count 2, for the year 1945; count 3, for the year 1946; count 4, for the year 1947; count 5 charged that defendant as president of a corporation, Phillips Company, Inc., wholly owned by defendant except for qualifying shares, caused the evasion of taxes due by the corporation for the year 1944, and count 6, that the defendant caused evasion of taxes of the same corporation for the period of January and February, 1945. * * * The trial commenced October 22, 1953, to a jury which returned a general verdict finding defendant guilty as charged. Upon such verdict the court, on November 16, 1953, entered judgment providing for defendant's imprisonment for a period of five years and imposing a fine in the sum of $10,000. From this judgment defendant appeals to this court.

* * *

During the years in question and prior thereto, defendant was engaged in the manufacture of jams, preserves and syrups, some of the time in his individual capacity and at other times by a corporation of which he was the owner and manager. Sales were made to restaurants in Chicago and its suburbs by truck driver-salesmen and to wholesale and retail customers throughout the midwest. Among his employees were William Freitag, his bookkeeper, and Blanche O'Donnell, an assistant bookkeeper, both of whom were called as government witnesses. The defendant also employed at intervals outside accountants and tax experts who made or assisted in making his returns for the years in question, including John Bertrand and Nels Tessem, also called as government witnesses.

The government relied upon two theories in proving its case, (1) that the defendant received a large amount of money from the sale of his products which was not included in his gross income as reported in his returns, and (2) the so-called net worth theory. The employees of defendant as government witnesses testified that acting under his instructions, a certain portion of income was not shown on the books from which the tax returns were prepared but that it was recorded in a special accounts receivable ledger, with the amount so recorded deposited in a special account in the bank, either in the name of defendant individually or in that of his corporation. The monies thus received and handled are referred to throughout the record as segregated business receipts. These so-called segregated receipts which were not reported resulted in the deficiency in gross income as reported. This segregated income was invested by defendant in real estate, the rental income from which was shown in his returns.

It was and is defendant's contention that this course was pursued in good faith on the advice of his attorney, George S. Porikos. Defendant did not testify and offered no evidence other than that of character witnesses. Thus, defendant relies upon evidence elicited from government witnesses, either on direct or cross-examination. Defendant does not claim, of course, that the asserted fact that he acted on the advice of counsel is a bar to the charge, but it is strenuously urged that it was a circumstance to be taken into consideration by the jury on the issue of defendant's good faith or, more accurately, that it was a circumstance which the jury was entitled to consider on the charge that he "did wilfully and knowingly attempt to defeat and evade" taxes. Notwithstanding, the court refused to instruct on the advice of counsel issue, which is here urged as prejudicial error.

In view of the concessions contained in the government's brief we think there is no occasion to relate in detail the evidence under discussion. Typical is the testimony of defendant's bookkeeper, Freitag, called as a government witness, who stated that the segregated business receipts were recorded in a special accounts receivable ledger kept by O'Donnell and that they were not reflected in the general ledger from which the tax returns were prepared. On direct examination, questions were asked and answered as follows:

"Q. Did you have a conversation with Mr. Phillips, Mr. Freitag, just about the time this practice of separating orders into these two categories began? A. Yes, I did.

"Q. Now, would you please state what Mr. Phillips told you about this practice? A. He said he was acting on the authority of his attorney and following his advice.

"Q. What else did he say? A. He said he was acting in his—that he had the authority, I mean he was acting on the attorney's statement that he could put that money in a special account and use it for the purpose of buying buildings.

"Q. What else did he say about it? A. He said that all of the money that was recorded in the special ledger would be picked up and deposited, and it would be reflected in his personal income tax.

"Q. Did he mention the name of the lawyer? A. Yes, he did.

"Q. What was the name? A. Mr. Porikos."

That government's counsel recognized this testimony as important is evidenced by the fact that at that point a request was made that the jury and the witness be excused. Thereupon, government's counsel represented that the testimony came as a surprise, that the witness was hostile and requested that the court call the witness as its own, with permission to the government to cross-examine. The record does not disclose any ruling by the court on this request but it is inferable that it was denied because the goverment proceeded with the examination of the witness as its own. On cross-examination the witness testified that the defendant said to him in substance that at about the time the special account and special ledger were segregated, he (defendant) was acting on the advice of an attorney named Porikos who had advised him that he could segregate some of his business sales, invest them in real estate and account for the proceeds of the real estate when sold.

Testimony to the same effect was given by other government witnesses and was admitted on the theory that it was a part of the *res gestae*. The testimony of the witness Tessem, also a government witness, falls in a different category insofar as concerns the reasons for its admission. Tessem was a tax expert who had formerly been employed for many years as an agent by the Treasury Department and who was employed by defendant in connection with his tax affairs and to prepare his tax return for 1947. The witness was informed by defendant regarding the segregation of business receipts in 1947 and earlier years, and was asked on cross-examination what the defendant had told him regarding the practice which had been followed. * * * He testified that the defendant told him in substance that since the year 1944, he had been separating or segregating a part of his income and had been investing the proceeds in real estate, reporting the income from the same on his personal returns, and that he had deferred reporting further income until he sold the buildings. Defendant followed this practice, so he told the witness, on the advice of attorney Porikos. The witness informed the defendant that these segregated accounts must be included in his tax return, which was done with defendant's consent for the year 1947.

Defendant's assistant bookkeeper, O'Donnell, at the request of the government was called as a court witness. For some reason not explained, the court sustained an objection by the government when it was sought to show on cross-examination that she had been told by defendant that he was acting under the advice of his lawyer. This was the same character of testimony which had been elicited from the witness Freitag by the government itself and from the witness Tessem on cross-examination, after the government's objection had been withdrawn. We need not dwell further upon this character of evidence emanating from government's witnesses because the government in its brief states, "The record is replete with references by Government witnesses concerning statements made to them by the defendant that he was following the advice of an attorney." In response to defendant's contention that much evidence of this character was suppressed, the government in its brief states, "The record to the contrary shows affirmatively that the Court, the defendant, and the jury were aware of the alleged advice." And again, the government in its brief states, "It is well to remember that the only evidence of defendant's reliance on advice adduced at the trial below was by Government witnesses. * * * The testimony of each uniformly was that the defendant told each of them he was acting on advice of counsel."

Defendant offered an instruction (referred to as No. 13), reading as follows:

"There is evidence in this trial that some business receipts were segregated from receipts used for ordinary business purposes, and that such receipts were invested in real estate, and that the net rental income from the said real estate was reported on the individual income tax returns of Mr. Phillips for the years in question, and that the segregated receipts were not reported on any tax returns in the taxable year when received because Mr. Phillips relied upon the legal advice of Attorney George Porikos in deferring the reporting of segregated receipts until after he had sold the real estate.

"You are advised that the defendant, Mr. Phillips, was entitled to act in good faith upon the advice of his attorney to such effect, whether or not such advice was correct as a matter of law.

"You are further advised that unless you find from the evidence beyond a reasonable doubt that the defendant was not acting upon such legal advice and in good faith, then you must find the defendant not guilty as to each and every count of the indictment."

The sole reason given by the court for its refusal was, "I will refuse No. 13, and my reason for doing it is in the court's opinion there is nothing in the record to support the instruction. If the defendant wanted to avail himself of that defense, he should have called Mr. Porikos and had him testify to that effect, as his own witness." Thus it is inherent in this statement, given as the reason for denying the instruction, that the defendant was not entitled to an instruction based upon favorable testimony given by government's witnesses, but that as a prerequisite to his right to such an instruction, there must be testimony coming from his side of the case. We think this was clearly an erroneous idea, the effect of which was to shift the burden of proof.

* * *

We think the government's contention, apparently embraced by the trial court, that a defendant is not entitled to an instruction embodying a theory merely because it is predicated upon proof adduced by the government, is not the law. * * *

* * *

We can think of no more important circumstance as bearing upon the crucial issue in a criminal prosecution for tax evasion than that the defendant acted in good faith upon the advice of an attorney. And where there is proof that he did so, irrespective of whether it comes from the witnesses of the government or those of the defendant, he is entitled to have the issue of his asserted good faith reliance submitted to the jury, under instruction, to be considered with all the other circumstances in proof in arriving at a decision as to whether the defendant "did wilfully and knowingly attempt to defeat and evade" taxes. It is not the province of this court, and neither was it that of the trial court, to appraise the reasonableness or unreasonableness of the evidence relative to the advice of counsel theory. * * *

Inasmuch as the judgment must be reversed, we need not discuss in detail the criticism directed at the court's charge to the jury. The argument in the main is that by the instructions the burden was shifted from the prosecution to the defendant. We think there is some merit in the criticism. For instance, it is stated in the instructions, "Even though you should believe from the evidence that the returns filed by the defendant were incorrect, if you further believe that he acted in good faith in making such returns, then the defendant is not guilty of the offenses charged in the indictment." This statement standing alone undoubtedly would indicate to the jury that the burden was upon the defendant to establish good faith as a basis for acquittal. As previously shown, however, no such burden was upon the defendant. On the contrary, the burden was upon the government to prove defendant's bad faith, or, in other words, to prove wilfulness and knowledge on his part, beyond a reasonable doubt. When the charge is considered as a whole, however, as it must be, we think much of defendant's criticism evaporates. At any rate, we need not under the circumstances give any further consideration to this phase of the situation.

* * *

The judgment appealed from is, therefore, reversed, and the cause remanded for a new trial.

NOTE

It must be borne in mind that the reliance defense to willfulness is not available to a taxpayer who is less than candid with the professional upon whom he purportedly relied. Thus, the following instruction to the jury was approved in United States v. Cox, 348 F.2d 294, 296 (4th Cir. 1965):

However, effectiveness of [the reliance] defense requires not only that the advice be sought from a person believed to be competent to give advice, but also that the taxpayer make full disclosure to that person of all pertinent facts, in order that the advice given may be in response to the true situation and not to one from which material facts have been withheld.

UNITED STATES v. GARBER

607 F.2d 92 (5th Cir. 1979).

CHARLES CLARK, Circuit Judge:

Dorothy Clark Garber was indicted for willfully and knowingly attempting to evade a portion of her income tax liability for the years 1970, 1971, and 1972 by filing a false and fraudulent income tax return on behalf of herself and her husband. A jury found her innocent of the charges for 1970 and 1971 but convicted her under 26 U. S.C.A. § 7201 for knowingly misstating her income on her 1972 tax return. She was sentenced to 18 months imprisonment—all but 60 days of which was suspended—placed on probation for 21 months, and fined $5,000 exclusive of any civil tax liability. The taxability of the money received by Garber presents a unique legal question. Because of trial errors which deprived defendant of her defense on the element of willfulness, we reverse the conviction.

Some time in the late 1960's after the birth of her third child, Dorothy Garber was told that her blood contained a rare antibody useful in the production of blood group typing serum. Dade Reagents, Inc. (Dade Reagents), a manufacturer of diagnostic reagents used in clinical laboratories and blood banks, had made the discovery and in 1967 induced her to enter into a contract for the sale of her blood plasma. * * *

* * *

In exchange for Garber's blood plasma, Dade Reagents agreed to ·pay her for each bleed on a sliding scale dependent on the titre or strength of the plasma obtained. Dade Reagents then marketed the substance for the production of blood group typing serum.

Because Garber's blood is so rare—she is one of only two or three known persons in the world with this antibody—she was approached by other laboratories which lured her away from Dade Reagents by offering an increasingly attractive price for her plasma. By 1970, 1971, and 1972, the three years covered in the indictment, she was receiving substantial sums of money in exchange for her plasma.[1] For two of those years she was selling her blood under separate contract to Associated Biologicals, Inc. (Associated) and to Biomedical Industries, Inc. (Biomedical), in both cases receiving in exchange a sum of money dependent on the strength of the antibody

1. Sale of her plasma allegedly brought her $80,200 in 1970, $71,400 in 1971, and $87,200 in 1972.

in each unit sold. In addition, Biomedical offered a weekly salary of
$200, provided a leased automobile, and in 1972 added a $25,000 bo-
nus. In that last year Garber sold her plasma to Biomedical exclusively, producing the coveted body fluid as often as six times a
month.

For all three years involved, Biomedical had treated the regular
$200 weekly payments as a salary subject to withholding taxes and
provided Garber with a yearly W-2 form noting the taxes withheld.
Every year, Garber attached those W-2 forms to her income tax return (which was filed jointly with her husband whom she has since
divorced), declared the $200 per week as income, and paid the taxes
due. All other payments, both from Biomedical and from Associated,
had been paid directly to defendant by check. No income taxes were
withheld by the companies; she received no W-2 forms, and paid no
taxes on the money received. Biomedical did, however, file a Form
1099 Information Return with the IRS which showed a portion of
Garber's donor fees not subject to withholding. Garber was provided
a copy of each 1099, which plainly states that it is for information
only and is not to be attached to the income tax return. She had
never before received Information Returns, and, while she was receiving checks from both Biomedical and Associated, only Biomedical
provided this information.

In this prosecution for the felony of willful evasion of income
taxes the government had the burden of proving every element of the
crime beyond a reasonable doubt. Holland v. United States, 348 U.S.
121, 75 S.Ct. 127, 99 L.Ed. 150 (1954). This required proof of a tax
deficiency, an affirmative act constituting evasion or attempted evasion of the tax due, and willfulness. The element we find lacking
here was willfulness.

At trial, outside the presence of the jury, the government proffered the testimony of Jacquin Bierman, a professor of law and practicing attorney in the City of New York, who stated his opinion that
Garber had made available her bodily functions or products for a consideration which constituted taxable gross income. His conclusion
was based on section 61(a) of the Internal Revenue Code * * *.

The defense proffered to the court the testimony of Daniel Nall,
a Certified Public Accountant and former revenue agent, who concluded that the money received by Garber was not within the legal
definition of income in section 61(a) and that she had therefore participated in tax-free exchanges. * * *

The district court heard the testimony of these two experts but
refused to admit either opinion in the evidence which went to the
jury because it considered the question of taxability to be one of law
for the court and not the jury to decide. However, the court did permit the government to introduce testimony by an Internal Revenue
Service agent who qualified as an expert in the field of accounting

and taxation. This agent offered his opinion that additional taxable income was due but not reported in the years in question. His testimony was received over defense objection that it was based on his conclusion that the compensation received was income and taxable. During cross examination, the witness conceded that the taxability of money received for giving up a part of one's body is a unique and undecided question in tax law. He also agreed that money received as a return on a capital product is not subject to tax. Yet, he based his calculations on his opinion that the blood plasma donations here were taxable personal services. His view, was, in turn, based solely on a Revenue Ruling which declared donations of whole blood to be a service for purposes of determining the deductibility of a charitable contribution. The court sustained objections to the relevancy of further inquiry regarding the nature or value of blood plasma.

The defense argued to the court that the expert testimony of Daniel Nall should be presented to the jury to rebut the government's expert IRS agent, to show that doubt existed as to whether a tax was due because it was incapable of being computed, and to demonstrate the vagueness of the law, which would preclude a willful intent to violate it. The court recognized that Nall's theory could be relevant to its judicial resolution of the legal conflict. It ruled however that since Nall had never discussed his opinion of the law with the defendant, it had no relevancy to the fact issue of Garber's intent. The jury never heard the testimony. It did, however, hear considerable factual evidence relating to Garber's actual intent.

After hearing all the evidence, the court ruled as a matter of law that the moneys Garber received for her blood plasma, whether considered a personal service or a product, were income subject to federal income taxation. Consistent with that ruling the jury was instructed that the funds Garber received from the sale of her blood plasma were taxable income. The court also instructed the jury extensively on good faith and willfulness but refused the instructions requested by defense to the effect that a misunderstanding as to defendant's liability for the tax is a valid defense to the charge of income tax evasion * * *.

We hold that the combined effect of the trial court's evidentiary rulings excluding defendant's proffered expert testimony and its requested jury charge prejudicially deprived the defendant of a valid theory of her defense. No court has yet determined whether payments received by a donor of blood or blood components are taxable as income. * * *

* * * However, we need not and do not undertake the complex task of resolving what the law should be, nor is it necessary to decide whether, as the trial court concluded, the question is purely one of law for the court and not the jury to resolve. Rather, because the district court refused to permit Bierman, the expert for the gov-

ernment, and Nall, the expert for the defense, to testify and because it reserved to itself the job of unriddling the tax law, thus completely obscuring from the jury the most important theory of Garber's defense—that she could not have willfully evaded a tax if there existed a reasonable doubt in the law that a tax was due—her trial was rendered fundamentally unfair.

A tax return is not criminally fraudulent simply because it is erroneous. Willfulness is an essential element of the crime charged. As such, the government must prove beyond a reasonable doubt that the defendant willfully and intentionally attempted to evade and defeat income taxes for each year in question by filing with the IRS tax returns which she knew were false. It is not enough to show merely that a lesser tax was paid than was due. Nor is a negligent, careless, or unintentional understatement of income sufficient. The government must demonstrate that the defendant willfully concealed and omitted from her return income which she knew was taxable.

When the taxability of unreported income is problematical as a matter of law, the unresolved nature of the law is relevant to show that defendant may not have been aware of a tax liability or may have simply made an error in judgment. Furthermore, the relevance of a dispute in the law does not depend on whether the defendant actually knew of the conflict. In United States v. Critzer, 498 F.2d 1160 (4th Cir. 1974), the Fourth Circuit reversed a criminal tax fraud conviction against an Eastern Cherokee Indian who failed to report a portion of her income derived from land held by the United States in trust for the Eastern Cherokee Band. The evidence clearly established that the underreporting was intentional. Whether the income was taxable, however, was a disputed question dependent on the interpretation of certain land allotment statutes, which the court did not resolve. Instead, it reversed the conviction because of the absence of authority definitively governing the situation. The court's language is particularly apt here:

> As a matter of law, defendant cannot be guilty of willfully evading and defeating income taxes on income, the taxability of which is so uncertain that even co-ordinate branches of the United States Government plausibly reach directly opposing conclusions. As a matter of law, the requisite intent to evade and defeat income taxes is missing. *The obligation to pay is so problematical that defendant's actual intent is irrelevant. Even if she had consulted the law and sought to guide herself accordingly, she could have had no certainty as to what the law required.*

498 F.2d at 1162 (emphasis added).

Critzer differs from this case in that the defendant there had been advised by the Bureau of Indian Affairs that the income received from the transactions on the Reservation was exempt from taxation. The fact that Garber did not have the benefit of such official advice does not persuade us that the result here should be different. The *Critzer* court did not so limit its holding:

> It is settled that when the law is vague or highly debatable, a defendant—actually or imputedly—lacks the requisite intent to violate it.

498 F.2d at 1162. To hold otherwise would advocate convicting an unsophisticated taxpayer who failed to seek expert advice as to whether certain income was taxable while setting free a wise taxpayer who could find advice that taxes were not due on the identical type of debatably taxable income.

That *Critzer* was not decided on the basis of the defendant's actual intent is further evidenced by the reasoning of the court and its reliance on James v. United States, 366 U.S. 213, 81 S.Ct. 1052, 6 L. Ed.2d 246 (1961). In *James*, the Supreme Court put to rest a dispute over the taxability of embezzled funds. Fifteen years before *James*, the Court had held such funds non-taxable. CIR v. Wilcox, 327 U.S. 404, 66 S.Ct. 546, 90 L.Ed. 752 (1946). Subsequently a realigned Court undermined the viability of *Wilcox* by deciding that extortion money was taxable, distinguishing *Wilcox* on tenuous grounds. Rutkin v. United States, 343 U.S. 130, 72 S.Ct. 571, 96 L.Ed. 833 (1952). When the taxability of embezzled funds again reached the Court in *James,* it decided that *Rutkin* had in effect overruled *Wilcox* and that embezzled monies were taxable. Nevertheless, the court reversed James' conviction for willfully failing to report embezzled funds in violation of section 7201 because of the uncertainty of the law created by *Wilcox*. Significantly, neither *James* nor the cases following *James* required actual reliance on *Wilcox* to negate willful intent.

As noted in *Critzer*:

> the uncertainty created by *Wilcox* as a matter of law precluded a demonstration of "willfulness," without regard to the defendant's actual state of mind with respect to his knowledge or reliance on *Wilcox*.

498 F.2d at 1163.

Both *Critzer* and *James* involved disagreements among recognized authorities which were more clearly documented than the theories presented here. *James* involved conflicting Supreme Court decisions, and in *Critzer* the Bureau of Indian Affairs and the Internal Revenue Service strongly disagreed on the taxability of the income. In the case presently before us, as conceded by all the experts who testified, there is a dearth of authority directly supporting either argument. However, the fact that the question has never before evoked anything more than theories on either side adds to rather than detracts from the critical conflict upon which defendant's criminal liability hinges. Neither position is frivolous, and the fact that both are urged without clear precedential support in law demonstrates that the court should not have restricted the evidence or instructed as it did.

The tax treatment of earnings from the sale of blood plasma or other parts of the human body is an uncharted area in tax law. The parties in this case presented divergent opinions as to the ultimate taxability by analogy to two legitimate theories in tax law. The trial court should not have withheld this fact, and its powerful impact on the issue of Garber's willfulness, from the jury. In a case such as this where the element of willfulness is critical to the defense, the defendant is entitled to wide latitude in the introduction of evidence tending to show lack of intent. United States v. Brown, 411 F.2d 1134 (10th Cir. 1969). The defendant testified that she subjectively thought that proceeds from the sale of part of her body were not taxable. By disallowing Nall's testimony that a recognized theory of tax law supports Garber's feelings, the court deprived the defendant of evidence showing her state of mind to be reasonable.

This error was compounded by the court's instructions to the jury which took from them the question of the validity of the tax. In effect, the court adopted the government's position that a tax was owing as a matter of law. Garber admitted receiving unreported money and disclosed its source; the defense in this case rested entirely on a denial of the necessary criminal intent to evade taxes. The court erred by refusing to instruct the jury that a reasonable misconception of the tax law on her part would negate the necessary intent. By withholding this theory, the court left the jury with the impression that a tax was clearly due and that Garber simply refused to pay it. * * *

* * * [I]n the case before us, the government presented persuasive evidence showing that the defendant knowingly and willfully evaded her taxes. She received a significant amount of money over a three year period, but reported none of it. The proof also showed that those with whom she dealt advised her that they thought the proceeds were taxable. Nevertheless, the tax question was completely novel and unsettled by any clearly relevant precedent. A criminal proceeding pursuant to section 7201 is an inappropriate vehicle for pioneering interpretations of tax law. The conviction is reversed and the cause is remanded for retrial.

REVERSED and REMANDED.

TJOFLAT, Circuit Judge, with whom AINSWORTH and ALVIN B. RUBIN, Circuit Judges, join dissenting:

* * *

The case before us involves three distinct issues that are present in every tax evasion prosecution. The threshold issue is whether the "income" in question is subject to federal income taxation. If the "income" is taxable, the trial court next must determine whether the civil obligation to pay taxes was sufficiently clear to support a criminal prosecution for tax evasion. Finally there arises the factual issue whether the defendant acted with the willfulness that is an essential element of the crime. The majority's analysis goes astray, in my view, by confusing the legal issues of taxability and sufficiency of notice with the factual issue of intent. For the court to dispose of this appeal properly, it is essential that these three issues be sorted out and considered individually.

I.

Dorothy Garber was charged under section 7201 of the Internal Revenue Code with willfully attempting to evade her obligation to pay taxes on "income" she received for her blood plasma. This allegation is premised on the notion that Garber actually had such an obligation. Of course, section 7201 does not itself create any duty to pay taxes; it merely sets out criminal sanctions that enforce the tax liability imposed by other sections of the Internal Revenue Code. Whether Garber was actually liable for taxes on the sums in question depends on whether those sums are a part of her "gross income" within the meaning of section 61(a) of the Internal Revenue Code. This question of the meaning of "gross income" is purely a legal one, a matter of statutory construction. Such a question of law is for the court alone, although the court would certainly be free to consider the opinions of the parties' experts or any other sources of authority in making this threshold determination.

* * *

II

After ruling on the taxability issue, the district court was confronted with a second question of law: whether, at the time of the alleged tax evasions, the taxability of the monies was so uncertain as to make it fundamentally unfair to prosecute Garber. Due process requires that the language of a criminal statute convey "sufficiently definite warning as to the proscribed conduct when measured by common understanding and practices." Jordan v. De George, 341 U.S. 223, 231–32, 71 S.Ct. 703, 708, 95 L.Ed. 886 (1951). At the commencement of trial, Garber's attorney argued to the court that the taxability of the monies is "so uncertain" that "defendant cannot be guilty of willfully evading and defeating taxes on income." This argument contained the essential elements of the vagueness challenge, although it was not put squarely in those terms or in the form of a motion to dismiss the indictment. Here the vagueness issue is whether the obligation to pay taxes on monies received for plasmapheresis was too uncertain to give notice that a taxpayer who willfully evaded such taxes would be subject to prosecution under section 7201. The question narrows to the consideration whether it was or should have been reasonably clear to Garber that those monies were a part of her "gross income" within the meaning of section 61(a). Although "common understanding and practices" are the standards by which the adequacy of the notice given by a criminal statute is to be measured, it is settled that the question of vagueness is for the court rather than the jury. The question is separate from the court's threshold inquiry whether the monies are taxable at all. The court might well have held that although the monies are taxable, their taxability was so uncertain at the times when Garber filed her returns that she did not have constitutionally sufficient notice of the conduct proscribed by section 7201. If this had been the court's conclusion, the proper disposition of the case would   *   *   *   have been to have dismissed the indictment under rule 12(b)(2). Whereas the trial judge did not rule specifically that the obligation to pay taxes was not unconstitutionally vague, he effectively rejected any vagueness challenge when he sent the case to the jury.

United States v. Critzer, 498 F.2d 1160 (4th Cir. 1974), relied on by the majority, suggests what is essentially another approach to the vagueness issue. *Critzer* is premised on the proposition that "when the law is vague or highly debatable, a defendant—actually or imputedly—lacks the requisite intent to violate it." Id. at 1162.   *   *   *

  *   *   *   While I agree that *Critzer* says that the clarity of the law has an impact on Garber's willfulness, *Critzer* does not support the suggestion that confusion in the tax laws is a "defense" that should be considered by the jury. The *Critzer* court reiterates that the impact of any vagueness of the law on the defendant's intent is a matter of law—a determination to be made by the court alone.

Under either the conventional vagueness analysis or the *Critzer* analysis, the question on appeal is whether Judge Fulton *should* have dismissed the indictment on the ground that the taxability of the monies was too unclear to support criminal liability. My view is that the monies were so clearly a part of Garber's "gross income" that no reasonable person could have supposed otherwise. The majority, on the other hand, appears to give much credence to Garber's contention that she reasonably supposed the monies to be nontaxable. If this is the majority's persuasion, the proper resolution of the case would be to dismiss the charges as the court did in *Critzer*, not to remand for a new trial. Since the certainty of the law would be assessed as of a past date, a dismissal on this ground would be perfectly consistent with a ruling that money received for blood plasma is indeed taxable. Thus, no future defendant in Garber's position could escape under the same vagueness challenge.

The majority's mysterious refusal to follow the logic of its reasoning and dismiss the indictment leads to certain inconsistencies. The opinion, like the opinion in the *Critzer* case, ends with the observation that "[a] criminal proceeding pursuant to section 7201 is an inappropriate vehicle for pioneering interpretations of tax law."

This conclusion makes sense in *Critzer*, but in the present case it is blatantly inconsistent with the court's decision that there should be a *new* "criminal proceeding" that will allow the jury to hear evidence concerning the certainty of the tax laws.

III

The court need consider the propriety of Judge Fulton's refusal to admit the testimony of Nall, Garber's expert, only if we find that Judge Fulton correctly declined to dismiss the indictment. Assuming that the indictment *is* sufficient, the critical issue in the case becomes a factual one: whether Garber acted with the requisite willfulness in failing to pay taxes on the sums in question. To be admissible, the proffered testimony must be relevant to this issue, Fed.R.Evid. 402, and its probative value must outweigh the danger of unfair prejudice, confusion of the issues, or misleading the jury. Fed.R.Evid. 403. I conclude that Nall's testimony is not relevant to Garber's intent, and that it certainly fails the weighing test. I would hold, therefore, that Judge Fulton properly excluded the evidence. It is necessary to examine closely this relevance issue to show the dangers created by the majority opinion.

A

The factual question for the jury, narrowly stated, was whether Garber had an honest belief that the money she had received for her blood plasma was nontaxable. The inquiry is a subjective one. Garber's belief does not have to have been reasonable; in fact, if her asserted belief *had been* reasonable, presumably the indictment should be dismissed for failure to charge an offense. The majority opinion obscures the subjective nature of the issue: "The court erred by refusing to instruct the jury that a *reasonable misconception* of the tax law on her part would negate the necessary intent." By drawing the notion of reasonableness into the inquiry, the majority improperly broadens the scope of relevancy, causing certain evidence to appear admissible although it would be excluded if the factual issue were correctly identified.

Fed.R.Evid. 401 defines relevant evidence as evidence "having any tendency to make the existence of any fact that is of consequence to the determination of the action more probable or less probable than it would be without the evidence." Garber sought to introduce expert testimony that the taxability of the plasma sales proceeds was in doubt. Conceivably, there are two ways in which such testimony might be relevant. It might provide evidence of the defendant's state of mind, or it might indirectly buttress her explanation of her actions. Concededly, there was never any communication between Garber and Nall. Since Nall neither influenced Garber's opinion nor learned of her opinion, it follows that he could have nothing to say that would bear directly on Garber's intent. So if Nall's proffered testimony is relevant at all, it can only be relevant through reinforcing the credibility of Garber's explanation.

* * *

In deciding the relevancy of this testimony, the trial judge should have, in essence, asked himself whether a reasonable juror could believe that the proffered testimony makes it more probable that Garber actually believed no tax was due on the money. I am certain that what this professional accountant concluded after studying the law could not make one whit more or less probable the truth of Garber's explanation that she had not paid taxes on what she had received for plasmapheresis because "in my heart I did not feel it was taxable * * *." Therefore, the proffer does not pass the rule 401 test, and the testimony should be excluded.

* * *

B

Even if the relevancy of this hypothetical testimony is established, the testimony should still not be admitted into evidence because the danger of prejudice and confusion manifestly outweighs the mere scintilla of probative value. The process of impeachment and rehabilitation before the jury would be just as wide-ranging as in the voir dire hearing on relevancy. In fact, even if the problem could be escaped in the voir dire hearing, it would certainly surface in the presence of the jury. The trial would no longer be focused on the defendant's intent * * *. The case would quickly become untriable.

* * *

An even more serious problem results from the jury's being asked to assess the *merits* of Nall's legal opinion. In essence, Nall's testimony is that Garber's asserted belief is reasonable. Presumably, the more meritorious Nall's opinion, the greater the number of people likely to share the opinion and the greater the probability that Garber is telling the truth. But however persuasive Nall may be, the court has already concluded in deciding the vagueness issue that the belief Nall is defending is *not* reasonable. The risk is that the jurors, who lack the training necessary to assess legal arguments, will too willingly accept the expert's opinion. To permit the jury to base its verdict on an interpretation of the law that is at odds with the court's will inevitably create the appearance of injustice. Assuming that the testimony is relevant, I believe that it would be foolhardy to lead the jury onto such treacherous ground when the possible benefits are so miniscule.

IV

Expert testimony about the state of the law will not only befuddle the jury; it will, in my view, utterly undermine the usual constraints on expert testimony, creating the potential for intolerable abuses. Until today, there has been a requirement that expert opinion testimony be founded on facts or data that comprise the context of the alleged offense. See Fed.R.Evid. 703. Under the majority's approach, however, the expert may ignore the factual context and say nearly anything he desires about the legal issues in the case. Opposing counsel will find it impossible to lock him into a particular interpretation of the law because the range of his interpretation is practically infinite. The bestowal of such freedom on expert witnesses creates the opportunity for a well-coached expert to "manufacture" testimony while he is on the stand, shaping his testimony to fit the facts that counsel has succeeded in eliciting from the defendant.

I think it manifest that the danger of prejudice and confusion that would result from the admission of testimony like that proffered by Nall outweighs any probative value. But even if this court should weigh the probative value and prejudice elements differently, we should affirm Judge Fulton's ruling as clearly within the broad discretion a trial judge has under rule 403. Unfortunately, however, the majority has avoided the rule 403 weighing process altogether.

A further difficulty with the majority's holding is that it apparently *requires* the district court in a case like this to permit practically anyone professing expertise in the subject to give his opinion about the law. The trial is likely to degenerate into a confused battle among experts. Such a situation can benefit no one but the experts themselves.

* * *

Because I conclude that the district court correctly decided the issues of law before it and properly excluded "expert" testimony concerning the state of the law, I would affirm Garber's conviction.[l]

C. CONSPIRACY

UNITED STATES v. TARNOPOL

561 F.2d 466 (3d Cir. 1977).

MARIS, Circuit Judge.

The appellants, Nat Tarnopol, Peter Garris, Irving Wiegan and Lee Shep, appeal from their convictions of violations of the federal mail fraud statute, 18 U.S.C. § 1341 and of conspiracy to commit mail fraud in violation of 18 U.S.C. § 1341, wire fraud in violation of 18 U.S.C. § 1343, and fraud against the United States in violation of 18 U.S.C. § 371.

l. The government dismissed the indictment against Mrs. Garber on remand.

The facts of the case as they appear from the evidence viewed in the light most favorable to the government may be briefly summarized. Brunswick Record Corporation (herein "Brunswick"), a New York corporation with offices in New York City, New York and Chicago, Illinois, and Dakar Records, Inc. (herein "Dakar"), a Pennsylvania corporation also with offices in New York City and Chicago, from 1971 to 1975, the period relevant to the criminal charges against the appellants, were engaged in the business of producing, marketing and selling phonograph records featuring artists' renditions of "soul" and "rhythm and blues" music. Columbia Record Productions (herein "Columbia") a division of CBS, Inc., at its record pressing plant and distribution center located in Pitman, New Jersey, manufactured records from original recordings produced by Brunswick and Dakar. Columbia shipped records thus manufactured to customers according to instructions received from Brunswick and Dakar.

Nat Tarnopol was president and controlling stockholder of Brunswick and sole stockholder of Dakar. Peter Garris was executive vice-president, sales manager and a stockholder of Brunswick. Irving Wiegan was secretary-treasurer of the two corporations and a stockholder of Brunswick. Lee Shep was production manager for the corporations in charge of placing and processing customers' orders with Columbia. Carl Davis, Melvin Moore and Carmine De Noia, also known as "Doc Wassel", were acquitted co-defendants of the appellants. Davis was a vice-president and stockholder of Brunswick in charge of operations at Brunswick's recording studio in Chicago. Moore was in charge of promoting Brunswick and Dakar recordings with distributors and disc jockeys. De Noia, although not employed by Brunswick or Dakar, allegedly used their facilities from time to time and was engaged in the sale of records including those produced by Brunswick and Dakar.

It was the government's contention that sales of over $350,000 worth of Brunswick and Dakar records were not recorded on the corporations' books, that the proceeds of the sales in the form of cash or merchandise were retained by the defendants or used to create a fund out of which improper payments were made to disc jockeys and program directors of radio stations to secure favored treatment of Brunswick and Dakar recordings, and that the transactions were used to defraud the United States by impeding the functions of the Internal Revenue Service, and to defraud artists, song writers and publishers to whom the corporations were obligated to pay royalties based on sales as well as radio stations and the listening public who were deprived of the honest services of the radio stations' employees. Three of the government's witnesses were Brunswick employees, Edward Hurley, an unindicted participant in the alleged criminal activities, who was employed by Brunswick to solicit sales from the military and the export market, and Martha Archie and Anita Campbell,

Brunswick bookkeepers. Other government witnesses included recording artists under contract to Brunswick, representatives of record
distributors and retailers, a disc jockey and program directors for radio stations located in Cleveland, Ohio and Chicago, Illinois.

Sales of Brunswick and Dakar records were processed as follows.
Garris informed Shep of customers' orders for records. Shep directed Columbia, by telephone, to fill the orders. This Columbia did out
of its stock of records. If the stock was depleted, Columbia manufactured the required quantity and made shipment directly to the customer. A shipping document known as a "packing slip" accompanied
each shipment, Columbia retaining one copy of the shipping document and mailing a second copy to the Brunswick offices in New
York, attention of Shep, to confirm the fact of shipment. Wiegan,
who opened the mail at Brunswick, channeled to Shep these confirmation slips, the Brunswick copies of the packing slips.

With the exception of sales made for cash or in exchange for
merchandise, Shep, after noting on the slip the number, type and
price of the records, passed it on to the billing department where
Mrs. Archie entered the sale in the sales journal, posted it to the customer's card in the accounts receivable ledger which she maintained,
and prepared an invoice for billing purposes. The sales for cash or
merchandise were not recorded in these books.

In the case of sales of records—usually at substantial discounts
—for cash or merchandise, where the buyer received delivery from
Columbia, Shep retained the confirmation slips instead of transmitting them to the billing department, and the transactions were not recorded by Mrs. Archie. Some sales for cash were made out of a large
stockpile of records kept in Tarnopol's New York office. These
transactions were also unrecorded on the books kept by Mrs. Archie.
Various other artifices were employed by the defendants and adjustments made to Brunswick's sales records to conceal the nature of the
payments made for records received from Brunswick or to eliminate
the purchaser's obligation appearing on the books.

When Cardinal Export Corporation demanded payment of the
value of merchandise delivered to the defendants in excess of the value of the Brunswick records it had received, false invoices were prepared by a Brunswick employee purporting to have been sent to
Brunswick by Cardinal Export Corporation for recording equipment
never actually ordered or received by Brunswick and costing an
amount equaling that owed Cardinal Export Corporation. Cardinal
Export was then paid out of Brunswick's funds.

Tarnopol arranged with Joseph Voynow, president and owner of
Carol Distributing Company, to purchase a new Cadillac Eldorado automobile which Voynow had recently acquired. Payment by Brunswick for the car was reflected on Brunswick's books by a "correction" to Carol Distributing Company's account with Brunswick re-

sulting in a credit to that company in the amount of the cost of the car.

Other instances of false documentation and false entries made in Brunswick's books to conceal payments received by the defendants for records furnished by Brunswick were letters falsely stating that a customer's orders for records had been cancelled and credits entered in the books of Brunswick for returned records which, in fact, had not been returned.

[The court decided that the convictions on the substantive mail fraud charges should be reversed because the use of the mails was not sufficiently related to the alleged fraudulent scheme.]

The conspiracy count of the indictment, however, included broader charges of mail fraud as well as charges of wire fraud and of defrauding the United States by impeding, impairing and obstructing the functions of the Internal Revenue Service. Since all the appellants were convicted on this count also, it requires further discussion.

The conspiracy count, as we have seen, alleged that the conspiracy had three objectives, (1) to defraud the United States in violation of 18 U.S.C. § 371 by impeding the functions of the Internal Revenue Service, (2) to use the mails, in violation of 18 U.S.C. § 1341, to defraud (a) artists, writers and publishers, (b) radio stations and the listening public, and (c) the Internal Revenue Service, and (3) to use the wires, in violation of 18 U.S.C. § 1343, to defraud the same three groups. The jury rendered a general verdict of guilty on the conspiracy count under instructions by the trial judge that the defendants could be found guilty on this count if the jury found that the defendants had engaged in any one or more of the illegal activities alleged in the count as objectives of the conspiracy. Under these circumstances, it is impossible to determine whether or not the jury based its verdict upon less than all three of these activities and, if so, upon which ones the verdict was founded. In this situation, the verdict of guilty on Count 1 cannot stand if the indictment was insufficient in law in that any one of the three objectives of the conspiracy did not constitute a crime or if the evidence was insufficient to sustain a finding by the jury that any one of these activities had been engaged in. To this question, therefore, we now turn.

The first objective of the conspiracy alleged in Count 1 is to "Defraud the United States by impeding, impairing, obstructing and defrauding the lawful governmental functions of the Internal Revenue Service * * * in the ascertainment, computation, assessment and collection of income taxes due and owing and to be due and owing from" Tarnopol, Brunswick and Dakar in violation of 18 U.S.C. § 371. The appellants urge that 18 U.S.C. § 371, which proscribes in general terms conspiracies to defraud the United States has been superseded with respect to conspiracies involving violations of the internal revenue laws by the penal provisions of the Internal Revenue

Code, which, as the Supreme Court pointed out in Spies v. United States, 317 U.S. 492, 497, 63 S.Ct. 364, 87 L.Ed. 418 (1943), comprehensively cover every duty under the income tax law and provide a penalty suitable to every degree of delinquency. However this may be, and there is support for the appellants' position, United States v. Henderson, 386 F.Supp. 1048, 1053–1054 (S.D.N.Y.1974), we are satisfied, in any event, that the government's evidence was insufficient to support a finding that the appellants did in fact wilfully impede or obstruct the Internal Revenue Service in the ascertainment, assessment and collection of income taxes due and owing from Tarnopol, Brunswick and Dakar. The trial judge properly instructed the jury that merely omitting transactions from the corporate books was in itself insufficient to establish a crime. The jury, he told them, must go further and find that this was done with an intent to impede and obstruct the functions of the Internal Revenue Service in the manner charged. This was as the indictment alleged, with respect to the income tax liability of Tarnopol, Brunswick and Dakar.

We think that in submitting to the jury on the evidence in this case the question of criminal intent to defraud the United States the trial judge erred. For our examination of the entire transcript of testimony fails to disclose any evidence, other than the mere fact that numerous sales were not entered in the books, upon which a finding of such intent could be based. And this, as the trial judge properly told the jury, was not enough without more to establish a crime. There was no evidence that Brunswick, Dakar or Tarnopol filed inaccurate income tax returns or omitted gross income therefrom for the years involved; that they evaded income taxes for those years; or that an Internal Revenue Service examination or audit was pending, expected or contemplated by the defendants. Moreover, there was no evidence, oral or documentary, which established or hinted at the evading or avoiding of the tax liability of Tarnopol, Brunswick or Dakar or which even mentioned the subject of tax liability, let alone any misrepresentation to the Internal Revenue Service or any of its agents.

It thus appears that the finding of conspiracy to defraud the United States by impeding the functions of the Internal Revenue Service rests at bottom solely on the failure to record certain sales for cash or merchandise on the sales journal and accounts receivable ledger or to falsify those records. We are clear, as was the trial judge, that this was not enough. In United States v. Klein, 247 F.2d 908 (2d Cir. 1957), cert. denied, 355 U.S. 924, 78 S.Ct. 365, 2 L.Ed.2d 354 (1958), which involved a similar charge of conspiracy to defraud the United States and in which there was evidence, *inter alia*, of false returns and false statements to treasury officials, the Court of Appeals for the Second Circuit, while affirming the defendants' conviction, took occasion to say (p. 916):

"Mere failure to disclose income would not be sufficient to show the crime charged of defrauding the United States under 18 U.S.C. § 371."

It follows that there was a failure of proof with respect to this particular alleged objective of the conspiracy. Accordingly, since we cannot know whether or not the jury based its verdict upon this objective alone, the verdict of guilty on Count 1 cannot stand. The question remains, however, whether the judgment entered on it should be reversed or whether it must be vacated and the case remanded for further proceedings on Count 1. This in turn depends on whether the evidence offered by the government was sufficient to support a verdict of guilty on that count based on either the mail fraud or the wire fraud allegations or both.

* * *

As we have seen, Count 1 of the indictment charged use of both the mails and the wires for the purpose of executing the alleged scheme to defraud (1) artists, writers and publishers of royalties and (2) radio stations and the listening public of the loyal service of disc jockeys and other employees. Since there was evidence from which a jury might find that the defendants, as members of a conspiracy, engaged in both the activities mentioned as well as in the use of the mails and the wires in furtherance of them, we conclude that the case must be remanded for a new trial which will be limited to those two activities alone, excluding the third activity originally alleged, namely, the defrauding of the United States by impeding the functions of the Internal Revenue Service.

* * *

THE SANDMAN COMETH: CONSPIRACY PROSECUTIONS AND TAX PRACTITIONERS

Sheldon M. Sisson
31 Tax Lawyer 805 (1978).

The Department of Justice has recently shown aroused interest in the prosecution of "white-collar" crime. Although this fact may have little effect on the average attorney, the tax practitioner is faced with a serious problem: the predicates of a conspiracy prosecution are present in his daily activities. At least two people are involved whenever a tax practitioner services a client through tax planning or tax litigation; thus, a conspiracy charge based upon "throwing sand in the government's eyes" is easy to maintain. This article will examine the responsibilities of the tax practitioner, the concept of a tax crime, and the relationship between tax planning or litigation and the crime of tax conspiracy.

* * *

In recent years * * * there have been a number of indictments of tax practitioners charging, at least in part, a "Conspiracy to Commit an Offense to Defraud the United States" under Title 18, section 371 of the United States Code. Although there are no readily available statistics on the number of indictments brought against tax practitioners under this section, there has been widespread publicity given to certain of those indictments.

The origin, historical development and shortcomings of section 371 are related in Professor Goldstein's outstanding article, *"Conspiracy to Defraud the United States."*[102] The author suggests that, in combination, the terms "conspiracy" and "defraud" assume such broad and imprecise proportions as to violate the constitutional prohibition against vagueness in a criminal charge and the prohibition against double jeopardy. * * *

Shortcomings in the conspiracy statute itself, however, are of little comfort to a defendant. The government's willingness to employ conspiracy prosecutions, and the concomitant likelihood of an increased number of such prosecutions, may be the result of several tactical advantages which accrue to the prosecutor who seeks a conspiracy indictment.

* * *

The amount of money alleged to have been saved in a tax conspiracy, or the wealth or identity of the defendants, may taint a juror's attitude. For example, assume that the members of the jury consist of twelve working class persons. Their income is withheld and reported to the government on a Form W–2. They are subject to the ravages of inflation and the inability to engage in "imaginative" planning. The defendants' tax plan, which calls for the imaginative exploitation of a situation is presented. When the large dollar amounts involved in the case are combined with the tendency of the prosecutor to use terms that are colored or loaded (such as "manipulation" or "sham"), the predicates for a hostile reaction on the part of the jurors are present.

* * *

A recent case, United States v. Rosenblatt,[116] criticized the government's attempt to proceed with a "conspiracy to defraud" indictment under Title 18, section 371. Rabbi Rosenblatt was the Dean of the Rabbinical College of Queens. At the request of Morris D. Brooks, who worked for the Postal Service, the Rabbi "laundered" eight checks through the College's bank account. The checks totaled over $180,000 and were obtained through false entries in the "ac-

---

102. Goldstein, "Conspiracy to Defraud the United States", 68 Yale L.J. 405 (1959).

116. 554 F.2d 36 (2d Cir. 1977).

counts payable" records at the Manhattan Postal Service headquarters. The Rabbi was told that Brooks was helping some payees evade taxes and helping other payees conceal kickbacks on government contracts. Brooks actually was defrauding the Post Office. The Rabbi kept ten percent for his services. Brooks pled guilty to conspiracy and to one count of making false entries; he then testified against the Rabbi. Brooks was sentenced to five years imprisonment, but was placed on probation for five years. The Rabbi was sentenced to six months imprisonment and fined $8000. The prime mover went free; the accomplice was sent to jail.

The Rabbi argued that proof of an agreement to defraud, without further explanation or proof of the nature of the fraud, is insufficient to support a conviction under section 371. The court stated the government's primary argument as follows: " 'the statute does not require the setting out of any particular type or form of fraud or scheme on which the defendants have agreed.' * * * As a fallback position the government suggests that the fraud pled and proved here was 'a classic one for pecuniary gain.' "

The Court held that:

> [W]hen the government proceeds under the conspiracy-to-defraud clause it must plead and prove an agreement with respect to the essential nature of the alleged fraud. Thus, just as the particular offense must be specified under the "offense" branch * * * the fraudulent scheme must be alleged and proved under the conspiracy-to-defraud clause.

The court found that although both men had agreed to defraud the United States, they had not reached an agreement as to the type of fraud to commit. A general agreement to engage in unspecified criminal conduct is not sufficient to identify the nature of the conspiracy. It is therefore essential to determine what agreement or understanding existed as to each defendant. Since the punishment that may be imposed under Section 371 depends on whether the object of the conspiracy is a felony or a misdemeanor, specificity in the object of the conspiracy is essential.

* * *

United States v. Klein [150] is the leading case concerning a conspiracy involving taxes. It is the source of the slogan that "throwing sand in the government's eyes" is a crime. Yet a careful reading of the case establishes that the conspiracy consisted of lying to the government during the investigation, and not artful or clever tax planning.

In 1944, liquor was purchased from a Canadian distiller by a Cuban corporation. It was shipped directly by the distiller to an Ameri-

---

150. 139 F.Supp. 135 (S.D.N.Y.1955), aff'd, 247 F.2d 908 (2d Cir. 1957), cert. denied, 355 U.S. 924, 78 S.Ct. 365, 2 L.Ed.2d 354 (1958).

can wholesaler, a customer of an American importer. When the Canadian distiller's invoice for the purchase was received with the necessary shipping papers at the corporation's Baltimore office, that corporation would bill, at an increased price, the American importer to whose wholesale customer the shipment had been made. The employee would then present the shipping documents at the New York bank of the American importer and collect against an irrevocable letter of credit. The Cuban corporation then would pay the Canadian distiller.

In 1945 and 1946 the procedure was slightly different. In those years a Panamanian corporation was inserted between the distiller and the Cuban corporation. The transaction was structured in the following manner. Liquor was purchased from a Canadian distiller by the Panamanian corporation. The liquor was shipped, as it had been before, directly by the distributor to an American wholesaler, who again was a customer of an American importer. When the Canadian distiller's invoice for the purchase was received with the necessary shipping papers at the Baltimore office of the Panamanian corporation, an employee of the Panamanian corporation would bill the Cuban corporation at an increased price, and simultaneously, on behalf of the Cuban corporation, would bill the American importer, to whose wholesale customer the shipment had been made, at a further increase in price. The employee would then present the shipping documents at the New York bank of the American importer and collect against an irrevocable letter of credit. The Cuban corporation then would pay the Panamanian corporation (or another Panamanian corporation) its share of the proceeds and the Panamanian corporation would then pay the Canadian distiller the amount of its original invoice. The Panamanian corporation and/or the Cuban corporation later transferred the profits to yet another Panamanian corporation, where the funds remained until the liquidation of the final Panamanian corporation.

The obvious result of the amended plan adopted in 1945 and 1946 was to shift profits to the Panamanian corporation. In 1947 the Panamanian corporation which served as the final depository of the diverted funds was liquidated. Klein, the principal shareholder of that liquidated Panamanian corporation and the moving force in the entire transaction, was a resident of the United States and paid a capital gains tax as a result of the liquidation. The government charged that Klein had attempted to evade his individual income taxes for 1944, 1945 and 1946.

The court observed that if the Cuban and Panamanian corporations were doing business and were not a sham, then the substantive counts of the indictment must fail. The court reasoned that if these corporations were recognized, then the income at issue was not that of Klein (and his three Canadian associates) in this particular venture. The test, giving the government the benefit of all reasonable inferences that might logically flow from the evidence, was whether a reasonable man could conclude that the defendant was guilty.

The test required a number of assumptions: that the Panamanian/Cuban structure of the transaction in 1944, 1945 and 1946 was created as a tax maneuver and further that the contracts were drafted and supplemented so as to shift the profits away from United States taxation; that the agreement reserved to Klein (and his associates) control over the approval and selection of salesmen for the American importer and wholesalers, as well as allocation of the quantities of whiskey to be sold; that Klein (and his associates) were the dominant figures; that Klein and his associates) dictated the policies of the 17 Panamanian and Cuban corporations involved; and finally, that the structure and operations in the United States and elsewhere for the entire period were specifically designed to gain a tax advantage suggested by tax counsel (one of the defendants). Even granting the government the benefit of all the assumptions, the court found the government's position to be untenable. Submitting the tax planning aspects of this case to the jury, according to the court, would "in effect, have the jury pass on a question of law, namely, whether for tax purposes, any or all of the constituent corporations had an independent personality, 'a vexed question at best.' "

The court was troubled with submitting to a lay jury the issue of whether a closely held corporation or a "one-man" corporation should be recognized as a corporate entity for tax and other purposes. The opinions of Judge Learned Hand were relied upon for the proposition that the corporate entities will be respected if the corporations are engaged in "some industrial, commercial, or other activity besides avoiding taxation."

The government's proof established that five of the seventeen Cuban and Panamanian corporations paid the Canadian distillers over $17,000,000 for the liquor purchased, and four of the seventeen Cuban and Panamanian corporations received from the American importers for the same whiskey in excess of $38,000,000. (The government had limited itself in its Bill of Particulars to the income of four corporations which sold to the American market.) The court concluded that a reasonable person could not hold that these corporations were a sham. The corporations observed formalities and structure in functioning. They billed the American distributors for the whiskey. They collected for it. They paid their suppliers for it. They maintained active bank accounts in Cuba, New York, and Canada, in their own names, and deposited and withdrew large sums of money in many transactions. In fact, the corporations did everything normally to be expected in the sale of over $38,000,000 worth of whiskey at wholesale in the three years at issue. Even if the Bill of Particulars had included more of the seventeen corporations, the result would not have been different. Even if all seventeen corporations considered together were subjected to the test, the court concluded that they had some industrial, commercial, or other activity besides avoiding taxation. The attempt of the government to disregard the corporations which clearly met the test and to focus upon those which functioned to a lesser degree was scorned:

> [The government] would have a lay jury in a criminal prosecution in essence make the type of allocation heretofore reserved for the technical skill of the Secretary of the Treasury in determining a civil liability for tax deficiency. So novel and unconscionable a procedure, this Court summarily rejects. Even the technical skill of the Secretary has been repeatedly successfully challenged and the decisions still leave the question far from resolved.

The court held that the seventeen corporations were viable entities for tax purposes. They were not a sham. The income of the corporations was their own, not that of Klein and his three Canadian associates. Those counts which charged an attempt to evade individual income taxes in 1944, 1945 and 1946 by means of reporting a capital gain in 1947 were dismissed. Count four was a charge that there was a conspiracy to evade taxes for 1944, 1945 and 1946. Since there were no taxes owed, this count was also dismissed. The dismissal of this count is especially important. Since there may be an illegal attempt to perform a legal act, such as the reduction of taxes, the court in effect said there was nothing illegal about the Cuban/Panamanian planning involving the seventeen entities and the revision of the structure in 1945.

The fifth count of the indictment presented a different problem; it charged that Klein and others violated section 371 of Title 18. This charge required examination of events that took place in January 1947 and thereafter. Klein and his associates wound up the activities of the liquor venture by transferring funds into and among the four Panamanian corporations which were the depositories. The three Canadians retained three of these depositories and Klein retained the fourth, Tivoli Trading Company.

On March 27, 1947, at Klein's direction, checks, each in excess of $250,000, were drawn on Tivoli's funds payable to Panamanian corporations as nominees for Alprin, a defendant, and Koerner and Roer, co-conspirators. The checks were delivered with instructions from Klein, which Klein denied, that the drafts were not to be cashed. The proceeds did not reach Roer until 1950 and Koerner and Alprin until 1952. Roer in 1950 and Koerner and Alprin in 1952 reported the proceeds as capital gains from the liquidation of Tivoli. Klein, however, insisted that the stock subscriptions of Alprin, Koerner and Roer had long before been cancelled. Klein alleged that these payments were in the nature of a bonus or gift for services in 1945 and 1946. The books of Tivoli, the Panamanian corporation, characterized the payments as commissions or expenses.

The government charged in count five that there was a concealment of the nature and source of the income from Tivoli that was designed to impede, impair, obstruct and defeat the Treasury Department in its collection of revenue, namely, that the parties lied during the course of the investigation. The court held that there was enough evidence to permit this issue to be determined by the jury.

The court viewed the possibilities as follows: (1) the funds were the proceeds of the liquidation of Tivoli owed to Koerner, Alprin and Roer for their stock in Tivoli; or, (2) the funds were additional income by way of commissions, bonuses, or even gifts to Koerner, Alprin and Roer for their services; or, (3) the funds were neither. A reasonable person, the court concluded, could find the funds were in fact the proceeds of the liquidation, as claimed by Koerner, Alprin and Roer. If that were correct, then Klein and one other co-conspirator conspired to falsely label these funds as commissions on the books of Tivoli. The second hypothesis was that the funds were not a liquidating dividend, but were additional ordinary income paid to Koerner, Alprin and Roer for their services in the liquor venture. In that event, Alprin, Koerner and Roer would have fraudulently stated that these funds were other than ordinary income when Roer filed his return in 1950, and Koerner and Alprin filed their returns in 1952. The third hypothesis also seemed possible. The drafts were issued at a time when Klein was in income tax difficulties. There was a conflict of testimony between those who claimed the payments to have been ordinary income and those who claimed the funds to have been a liquidating distribution. The length of time that the funds had been held and not been negotiated might lead to the conclusion that a purpose other than that claimed by either side was the truth. In other words, the funds were to be given the appearance of a legitimate expenditure by Tivoli until the conclusion of Klein's income tax difficulties.

Klein is significant. Insofar as the charges concerned aggressive tax planning, even to the extent of changing horses in mid-stream (the insertion of the Panamanian corporation in 1945), the Court dismissed the charges. Machinations during the course of an examination are a different matter. Throwing sand in the government's eyes means lying, not planning.

* * *

CONCLUSION

The lesson of the *Klein* case cannot be over-emphasized. Tax planning, regardless whether that planning is advanced, novel, unorthodox or enters uncharted areas, is not a conspiracy or any other crime. White-collar crime, however, currently is a favorite preoccupation, and a prime target, of the Department of Justice. Further emphasis on the conspiracy prosecution as well as prosecution under inventive interpretations of other statutes can therefore be anticipated. The practitioner, especially the tax practitioner, is a highly visible target for a conspiracy investigation and prosecution, and is well advised to be on his guard when his practice leads to inventive tax planning.

D. STATUTE OF LIMITATIONS

For most tax prosecutions there is a six-year statute of limitations, although a three-year limitations period is applicable to certain offenses.[m] The period of limitations commences with the date of commission of the charged offense—a date which is frequently, but not always, the due date of the relevant tax return. The running of the statute of limitations is suspended for any period during which the accused is outside the United States or is a fugitive from justice.

m. IRC § 6531, Periods of Limitation on Criminal Prosecutions, which provides in pertinent part:

No person shall be prosecuted, tried, or punished for any of the various offenses, arising under the internal revenue laws unless the indictment is found or the information instituted within 3 years next after the commission of the offense, except that the period of limitation shall be 6 years—

(1) for offenses involving the defrauding or attempting to defraud the United States or any agency thereof, whether by conspiracy or not, and in any manner;

(2) for the offense of willfully attempting in any manner to evade or defeat any tax or the payment thereof;

(3) for the offense of willfully aiding or assisting in, or procuring, counseling, or advising, the preparation or presentation under, or in connection with any matter arising under, the internal revenue laws, of a false or fraudulent return, affidavit, claim, or document (whether or not such falsity or fraud is with the knowledge or consent of the person authorized or required to present such return, affidavit, claim or document);

(4) for the offense of willfully failing to pay any tax, or make any return (other than a return required under authority of part III of subchapter A of chapter 61) at the time or times required by law or regulations;

(5) for offenses described in sections 7206(1) and 7207 (relating to false statements and fraudulent documents);

(6) for the offense described in section 7212(a) (relating to intimidation of officers and employees of the United States);

(7) for offenses described in section 7214(a) committed by officers and employees of the United States; and

(8) for offenses arising under section 371 of Title 18 of the United States Code, where the object of the conspiracy is to attempt in any manner to evade or defeat any tax or the payment thereof.

The time during which the person committing any of the various offenses arising under the internal revenue laws is outside the United States or is a fugitive from justice within the meaning of section 3290 of Title 18 of the United States Code, shall not be taken as any part of the time limited by law for the commencement of such proceedings. * * * For the purpose of determining the periods of limitation on criminal prosecutions, the rules of section 6513 shall be applicable.

UNITED STATES v. HABIG

Supreme Court of the United States, 1968.
390 U.S. 222, 88 S.Ct. 926, 19 L.Ed.2d 1055.

Mr. Justice FORTAS delivered the opinion of the Court.

Appellees were indicted for crimes relating to allegedly false income tax returns. The District Court dismissed Counts 4 and 6 of the indictment, charging an attempt to evade taxes by filing of a false return (26 U.S.C. § 7201) and aiding in the preparation and presentation of a false return (26 U.S.C. § 7206(2)), on the ground that the six-year statute of limitations, 26 U.S.C. § 6531, barred prosecution under those counts. * * *

The question presented is the construction of §§ 6531 and 6513(a) of the Internal Revenue Code of 1954. It is squarely raised by the facts of this case. The indictment was filed on August 12, 1966. The income tax returns involved in Counts 4 and 6 were filed on August 12, and 15, 1960. Section 6531 limits the time when indictments may be filed for the charged offenses to six years "next after the commission of the offense."

The offenses involved in Counts 4 and 6 are committed at the time the return is filed. Six years had not quite elapsed from the commission of the crimes in the present case to the filing of the indictment. Appellees do not contest the chronological calculation. But because of § 6513(a) of the Code, they say that the critical date here is not the date when the returns were actually filed but the date when they were initially due to be filed, *viz.*, May 15, and not August 15, 1960.

The basis for this contention is as follows: Section 6531, which prescribes the six-year period of limitations, also says that "[f]or the purpose of determining [such] periods of limitation * * * the rules of section 6513 shall be applicable." Instead of filing on the due date of May 15, 1960, the corporations obtained extensions of time to August 15, 1960. Accordingly, if the six-year period of limitations runs not from the date of actual filing (August 12 and 15, 1960) but from the original due date of the returns (May 15, 1960), the indictment, having been filed on August 12, 1966, was several months too late.

Section 6513(a) reads as follows:

"SECTION 6513. TIME RETURNED DEEMED AND TAX CONSIDERED PAID.

"(a) *Early Return or Advance Payment of Tax.*—For purposes of section 6511 [relating to claims for credit or refund], any return filed before the last day prescribed for the filing thereof shall be considered as filed on such last day. For purposes of section 6511(b)(2) and (c) and section 6512 [relating to suits in the Tax Court], payment of any portion of the tax made before the last day prescribed for the payment of the tax shall be considered made on such last day. For purposes of this subsection, the last day prescribed for filing the return or paying the tax shall be determined without regard to any extension of time granted the taxpayer and without regard to any election to pay the tax in installments."

Appellees' argument is that by reason of the third sentence of § 6513(a), the starting date for computing the six-year limitations period is to be determined by the original due date of the return, May 15, 1960, "without regard to any extension of time granted the taxpayer." The District Court agreed.   *   *   *

On the other hand, the Government argues that appellees' contention, despite its support in the decisions of several courts, is necessarily based upon the surprising assertion that Congress intended the limitations period to begin to run before appellees committed the acts upon which the crimes were based. It argues that this result cannot be squared with the language of the Code or the intent of Congress. We perforce agree with the Government's analysis.

Section 6513(a), as its title clearly indicates, was designed to apply when a return is filed or a tax is paid before the statutory deadline. The first two sentences provide that the limitations periods on claims for refunds and tax suits (26 U.S.C. §§ 6511, 6512), when the return has been filed or payment made in advance of the date "prescribed" therefor, shall not begin to run on the early date, but on the "prescribed" date. The third sentence states that, for "purposes of [the] subsection," the date "prescribed" for filing or payment shall be determined on the basis fixed by statute or regulations, without regard to any extension of time. The net effect of the language is to prolong the limitations period when, and only when, a return is filed or tax paid in advance of the statutory deadline.

There is no reason to believe that § 6531, by reference to the "rules of section 6513" expands the effect and operation of the latter beyond its own terms so as to make it applicable to situations other than those involving early filing or advance payment. The reference to § 6513 in § 6531 extends the period within which criminal prosecution may be begun only when the limitations period would also be extended for the refunds and tax suits expressly dealt with in § 6513— only when there has been early filing or advance payment. In other words, if a taxpayer anticipates the April 15 filing date by filing his return on January 15, the six-year limitations period for prosecutions under § 6531 commences to run on April 15. Practically, the effect of the reference to § 6513 in § 6531 is to give the Government the administrative assistance, for purposes of its criminal tax investigations, of a uniform expiration date for most taxpayers, despite variations in the dates of actual filing.

The legislative history supports this reading. The first predecessor of § 6513(a) was enacted in 1942. See § 332(b)(4) of the 1939 Code. This section applied only to civil income tax refund proceedings. The Report of the House Ways and Means Committee (H.R. Rep. No. 2333, 77th Cong., 2d Sess., 119) states:

> "If the taxpayer files his return before the last day on which it is due, the period in which he can file a claim for refund under the provisions of section 322(b)(1), measured from the date the return was filed, will expire sooner than would be the case if he waited until such last day. Section 150 of the bill adds paragraph (4) to section 322(b) to provide that the period of limitations with respect to credit or refund is measured from the last day prescribed for the filing of the return in cases where the return is filed before such last day. *This provision does not apply to taxpayers who are given the benefit of an extension of time in which to file their returns, and file the return before the last day of the extended period* * * * " (Emphasis added.)

Then, in adopting the 1954 Code, the contested reference to § 6513 was added to § 6531. The House and Senate Reports expressly confirmed that § 6513 still encompassed "the existing * * * rule *as to early returns and advance payment.*" H.R.Rep. No. 1337, 83d Cong., 2d Sess., A. 416; S.Rep. No. 1622, 83d Cong., 2d Sess., 587. (Emphasis added.)

The language of § 6513(a) does not purport to apply when a return is filed during an extension of time. The legislative history is to the same effect. Accordingly, although we reiterate the principle that criminal limitations statutes are "to be liberally interpreted in favor of repose," United States v. Scharton, 285 U.S. 518, 522, 52 S. Ct. 416, 417, 76 L.Ed. 917 (1932), we cannot read the statute as appellees urge.

The judgment of the District Court is reversed and the case is remanded for further proceedings.

Reversed and remanded.

QUESTION

The *Habig* case involved the crime of filing false returns, which is committed at the time that the tax returns in question are filed. It should be noted that in a charge under § 7201 (attempted evasion) the crime may be committed by virtue of actions other than, or in addition to, the filing of the subject tax return. Hence, an act of fraud committed after the filing of the tax return may be construed as an event which commences a six-year period of limitations. The crime of willfully failing to file a tax return is committed when the required return is not filed on the due date. However, assuming continued willfulness, is the crime also committed on each day thereafter that the failure to file continues?

UNITED STATES v. LOWDER

492 F.2d 953 (4th Cir.), cert. denied,
419 U.S. 1092, 95 S.Ct. 685, 42 L.Ed.2d 685 (1974).

PER CURIAM.

W. Horace Lowder was convicted in January, 1973, in a trial by jury, of one count of conspiracy to defraud the United States by obstructing the Internal Revenue Service in its task of computing and collecting revenue (18 U.S.C. § 371) and two counts of knowingly filing false corporate income tax returns (26 U.S.C. § 7206(1)). Lowder was sentenced to two years' imprisonment on each count and was fined $10,000 on the conspiracy count and $5,000 on each of the other two counts.

The government's case was based on the theory that Lowder utilized his intimate connection with six family-owned corporations to foster an intricate scheme whereby their tax liability would be obscured and evaded, in the years 1961–65.   *   *   *

Lowder throughout the relevant years was the active manager of the affairs of each corporation. He held, among others, the position of secretary-treasurer in each, was in charge of the overall business and financial operations for all, including bookkeeping, and signed each of the corporate tax returns. That Lowder was responsible for the practices alleged to have constituted a scheme to cover up tax liability was not disputed by him; the other shareholders and officers apparently gave him a free hand in decision-making.

*   *   *

The conspiracy conviction is assailed as barred by the applicable statute of limitations. We do not agree and, therefore, we affirm.

Lowder and the six corporations were charged with conspiring, from January, 1961, up through the date of the indictment, October 8, 1971, to defraud the United States "by impeding, impairing and obstructing the lawful functions of the Internal Revenue Service,   *   *   * in the ascertainment, computation, assessment and collection of revenue" from the four active corporations.

As alleged and proved the essence of the government's case was that: (1) each corporation had a different accounting year—Mills was on a calendar year basis and the other five were each on different fiscal years; (2) the transfers of money, ostensibly paid for supplies such as feed, would usually occur in large amounts towards the close of the fiscal year for the transferor/"purchaser"; (3) these transfers, treated as expenses, would in virtually every instance wipe out then-existing profits which had been accumulating to the transferor during its taxable year; (4) the "seller"/transferee would in turn eliminate the effect these amounts had on its books as receipts (and potential profits) when its taxable year closed a few months later by another transfer similarly expensed, and so on, in a process denoted as "rolling" by the investigating agent; (5) the transfers of money, in the aggregate, overstated the value of the goods actually changing hands, i. e., Mills did sell feed to Hatcheries, but not nearly in the quantities which would justify the amounts expensed on the books; (6) the fact that Mills and Farms were on an accrual basis method of accounting and Hatcheries and Foods were on a cash basis method was utilized by Lowder to obscure the real transactions; and (7) the underlying documents—invoices, ledger cards, etc.—against which the validity of these transfers could have been checked were deliberately destroyed or concealed.

Of the eighteen alleged overt acts, all of which were corporate income tax filings for the years in question, the latest occurred on *March 14, 1966,* the date of the filing of Mills' return for the previous calendar year. The date of the indictment is *October 8, 1971,* approximately five years and seven months after the date of the last overt act alleged therein.

Before the trial, the court ruled that the six-year statute of limitations specified in 26 U.S.C. § 6531(1) applied to the conspiracy count as well as to the fraudulent filing charges. Lowder asserts that the first count, charging a conspiracy to defraud under 18 U.S.C. § 371, was governed by the general five-year limitation period specified in 18 U.S.C. § 3282, but we think the six-year limitation period in 26 U.S.C. § 6531 governs. The general conspiracy statute, 18 U.S. C. § 371, contains no period of limitations. Limitations, for indictments under § 371, are those supplied by other provisions of law, or where there are none, by 18 U.S.C. § 3282 which is a general statute of limitations applicable "[e]xcept as otherwise expressly provided by law." Thus, § 3282 applies where no other statute is applicable, and, stated conversely, its application is ousted when there is a special limitation period prescribed for a specific offense.

In the case of prosecutions of violations of the tax laws, 26 U.S. C. § 6531 provides, in relevant part:

> No person shall be prosecuted * * * for any of the various offenses arising under the internal revenue laws unless the indictment is found or the information instituted within 3 years next after the commission of the offense, except that *the period of limitation shall be 6 years—*
>
>> (1) *for offenses involving the defrauding* or attempting to defraud *the United States* or any agency thereof, *whether by conspiracy or not,* and in any manner * * *.

It thus appears that for a conspiracy to defraud the United States by filing false and fraudulent tax returns—the crime charged against Lowder, § 6531 prescribes a six-year period of limitations and, as part of the overall statutory scheme, § 3282, by its terms, is inapplicable.

Two authorities do apparently stand opposed to what seems to be this fairly obvious statutory scheme: Grunewald v. United States, 353 U.S. 391, 77 S.Ct. 963, 1 L.Ed.2d 931 (1957); and United States v. Klein, 247 F.2d 908 (2 Cir. 1957), cert. denied, 355 U.S. 924, 78 S.Ct. 365, 2 L.Ed.2d 354 (1958).

In *Klein,* on an indictment charging a § 371 conspiracy to defraud in language virtually identical to that contained in count one here, the court, as a prelude to its discussion of the evidence showing the period that the conspiracy continued, stated that 18 U.S.C. § 3282 was applicable. In *Grunewald,* on an indictment charging a conspiracy " 'to defraud the United States in the exercise of its governmental functions of administering the internal revenue laws' " the Court stated that the "first question before us is whether [the § 371 count] was barred by the applicable three-year statute of limitations." 353 U.S. at 396, 77 S.Ct. at 969. The footnote was to § 3282 (amended in 1954 to provide for the present five-year period).

The government argues that the language in both cases represents not holding, but dicta, since the precise issue here was not contested by the parties. Especially in *Grunewald,* we do not think that the language was dicta. On the other hand, the language was not part of the main holdings in either case; it was not with respect to any issue which was fully briefed and pressed; and it seems nothing more than mere inadvertence on the part of both courts that the specific language of § 6351, and its predecessors, was overlooked. We, therefore, conclude to follow the specific statutory language, rather than the contrary statements in *Grunewald* and *Klein* and hold that the applicable limitation period was six years. The prosecution against Lowder   *   *   *   was not barred.

*   *   *

SECTION 2.   METHODS OF PROOF OF INCOME

A.   DIRECT PROOF: THE SPECIFIC ITEMS METHOD

In most tax prosecutions the government will be required to prove the taxpayer's income for the years in issue. Proof of income, like proof of any other ultimate fact, may be presented by direct or circumstantial evidence. In the jargon of tax fraud, direct evidence of income is presented by what is known as the "specific items" method. Circumstantial proof of income may be accomplished through what are commonly referred to as the "indirect" methods of proof, such as the net worth, cash expenditures, bank deposits, percentage mark-up or other methods.

The specific items method of proof of income is simple to describe. In brief, the prosecution will establish the taxpayer's income by proof of every item of income which the taxpayer realized (or, more accurately, which the IRS could find) for the period in issue. The specific items method is useful only to the extent that there are provable income producing transactions. For example, this method frequently is used in cases in which the taxpayer failed to report interest or dividend income or the income arising from specific provable transactions. In such a case the prosecution would introduce the tax returns (with supporting evidence) to prove the income reported thereon, and establish through the payors of interests or dividends, or other persons, the specific items of income received but not reported.

The specific items method is available, of course, only in a case in which the taxpayer's precise sources of income can be located by an investigating agent. The method is of little, if any, use in the investigation and prosecution of a taxpayer engaged in a cash business (i. e., one in which there are substantial receipts in currency). Imagine, for example, a specific items investigation of a gambler, a bartender, a cab driver or a drug dealer. The specific items method is also of limited value in cases in which a taxpayer has a substantial number of customers, clients or patients.

In view of the difficulty (and frequent impossibility) of proving income through the specific items method, the IRS will often utilize indirect methods of proof of income. As discussed more fully below, the indirect methods are inherently less precise than the specific items method. However, when the pertinent standards are met, the indirect methods can result in the requisite proof of income beyond a reasonable doubt.

B. INDIRECT PROOF

(1) THE NET WORTH METHOD

HOLLAND v. UNITED STATES

Supreme Court of the United States, 1955.
348 U.S. 121, 75 S.Ct. 127, 99 L.Ed. 150.

Mr. Justice CLARK delivered the opinion of the Court.

Petitioners, husband and wife, stand convicted under § 145 of the Internal Revenue Code of an attempt to evade and defeat their income taxes for the year 1948. The prosecution was based on the net worth method of proof * * *.

In recent years, * * * tax-evasion convictions obtained under the net worth theory have come here with increasing frequency and left impressions beyond those of the previously unrelated petitions. We concluded that the method involved something more than the ordinary use of circumstantial evidence in the usual criminal case. Its bearing, therefore, on the safeguards traditionally provided in the administration of criminal justice called for a consideration of the entire theory. * * *

In a typical net worth prosecution, the Government, having concluded that the taxpayer's records are inadequate as a basis for determining income tax liability, attempts to establish an "opening net worth" or total net value of the taxpayer's assets at the beginning of a given year. It then proves increases in the taxpayer's net worth for each succeeding year during the period under examination and calculates the difference betwen the adjusted net values of the taxpayer's assets at the beginning and end of each of the years involved. The taxpayer's nondeductible expenditures, including living expenses, are added to these increases, and if the resulting figure for any year is substantially greater than the taxable income reported by the taxpayer for that year, the Government claims the excess represents unreported taxable income. In addition, it asks the jury to infer willfulness from this understatement, when taken in connection with direct evidence of "conduct, the likely effect of which would be to mislead or to conceal." Spies v. United States, 317 U.S. 492, 499, 63 S. Ct. 364, 368, 87 L.Ed. 418.

Before proceeding with a discussion of these cases, we believe it important to outline the general problems implicit in this type of litigation. In this consideration we assume, as we must in view of its widespread use, that the Government deems the net worth method useful in the enforcement of the criminal sanctions of our income tax laws. Nevertheless, careful study indicates that it is so fraught with danger for the innocent that the courts must closely scrutinize its use.

One basic assumption in establishing guilt by this method is that most assets derive from a taxable source, and that when this is not true the taxpayer is in a position to explain the discrepancy. The application of such an assumption raises serious legal problems in the administration of the criminal law. Unlike civil actions for the recovery of deficiencies, where the determinations of the Commissioner have *prima facie* validity, the prosecution must always prove the criminal charge beyond a reasonable doubt. This has led many of our courts to be disturbed by the use of the net worth method, particularly in its scope and the latitude which it allows prosecutors.

But the net worth method has not grown up overnight. It was first utilized in such cases as Capone v. United States, 7 Cir., 1931, 51 F.2d 609 and Guzik v. United States, 7 Cir., 1931, 54 F.2d 618, to corroborate direct proof of specific unreported income. In United States v. Johnson, [319 U.S. 503, 63 S.Ct. 1233, 87 L.Ed. 1546 (1943)] this Court approved of its use to support the inference that the taxpayer, owner of a vast and elaborately concealed network of gambling houses upon which he declared no income, had indeed received unreported income in a "substantial amount." It was a potent weapon in establishing taxable income from undisclosed sources when all other efforts failed. Since the *Johnson* case, however, its horizons have been widened until now it is used in run-of-the-mine cases, regardless of the amount of tax deficiency involved. In each of the four cases decided today the allegedly unreported income comes from the same disclosed sources as produced the taxpayer's reported income and in none is the tax deficiency anything like the deficiencies in *Johnson, Capone* or *Guzik*. The net worth method, it seems, has evolved from the final volley to the first shot in the Government's battle for revenue, and its use in the ordinary income-bracket cases greatly increases the chances for error. This leads us to point out the dangers that must be consciously kept in mind in order to assure adequate appraisal of the specific facts in individual cases.

1.   Among the defenses often asserted is the taxpayer's claim that the net worth increase shown by the Government's statement is in reality not an increase at all because of the existence of substantial cash on hand at the starting point. This favorite defense asserts that the cache is made up of many years' savings which for various reasons were hidden and not expended until the prosecution period. Obviously, the Government has great difficulty in refuting such a contention. However, taxpayers too encounter many obstacles in convincing the jury of the existence of such hoards. This is particularly so when the emergence of the hidden savings also uncovers a fraud on the taxpayer's creditors.

In this connection, the taxpayer frequently gives "leads" to the Government agents indicating the specific sources from which his cash on hand has come, such as prior earnings, stock transactions, real estate profits, inheritances, gifts, etc. Sometimes these "leads" point back to old transactions far removed from the prosecution period. Were the Government required to run down all such leads it would face grave investigative difficulties; still its failure to do so might jeopardize the position of the taxpayer.

2.   As we have said, the method requires assumptions, among which is the equation of unexplained increases in net worth with unreported taxable income. Obviously such an assumption has many weaknesses. It may be that gifts, inheritances, loans and the like account for the newly acquired wealth. There is great danger that the jury may assume that once the Government has established the figures in its net worth computations, the crime of tax evasion automatically follows. The possibility of this increases where the jury, without guarding instructions, is allowed to take into the jury room the various charts summarizing the computations; bare figures have a way of acquiring an existence of their own, independent of the evidence which gave rise to them.

3.   Although it may sound fair to say that the taxpayer can explain the "bulge" in his net worth, he may be entirely honest and yet

unable to recount his financial history. In addition, such a rule would tend to shift the burden of proof. Were the taxpayer compelled to come forward with evidence, he might risk lending support to the Government's case by showing loose business methods or losing the jury through his apparent evasiveness. Of course, in other criminal prosecutions juries may disbelieve and convict the innocent. But the courts must minimize this danger.

4. When there are no books and records, willfulness may be inferred by the jury from that fact coupled with proof of an understatement of income. But when the Government uses the net worth method, and the books and records of the taxpayer appear correct on their face, an inference of willfulness from net worth increases alone might be unjustified, especially where the circumstances surrounding the deficiency are as consistent with innocent mistake as with willful violation. On the other hand, the very failure of the books to disclose a proved deficiency might indicate deliberate falsification.

5. In many cases of this type, the prosecution relies on the taxpayer's statements, made to revenue agents in the course of their investigation, to establish vital links in the Government's proof. But when a revenue agent confronts the taxpayer with an apparent deficiency, the latter may be more concerned with a quick settlement than an honest search for the truth. Moreover, the prosecution may pick and choose from the taxpayer's statement, relying on the favorable portion and throwing aside that which does not bolster its position. The problem of corroboration * * * therefore becomes crucial.

6. The statute defines the offense here involved by individual years. While the Government may be able to prove with reasonable accuracy an increase in net worth over a period of years, it often has great difficulty in relating that income sufficiently to any specific prosecution year. While a steadily increasing net worth may justify an inference of additional earnings, unless that increase can be reasonably allocated to the appropriate tax year the taxpayer may be convicted on counts of which he is innocent.

While we cannot say that these pitfalls inherent in the net worth method foreclose its use, they do require the exercise of great care and restraint. The complexity of the problem is such that it cannot be met merely by the application of general rules. Trial courts should approach these cases in the full realization that the taxpayer may be ensnared in a system which, though difficult for the prosecution to utilize, is equally hard for the defendant to refute. Charges should be especially clear, including, in addition to the formal instructions, a summary of the nature of the net worth method, the assumptions on which it rests, and the inferences available both for and against the accused. Appellate courts should review the cases, bearing constantly in mind the difficulties that arise when circumstantial evidence as to guilt is the chief weapon of a method that is itself only an approximation.

With these considerations as a guide, we turn to the facts.

The indictment returned against the Hollands embraced three counts. The first two charged Marion L. Holland, the husband, with attempted evasion of his income tax for the years 1946 and 1947. He was found not guilty by the jury on both of these counts. The third count charged Holland and his wife with attempted evasion in 1948 of the tax on $19,736.74 not reported by them in their joint return. The jury found both of them guilty. Mrs. Holland was fined $5,000, while her husband was sentenced to two years' imprisonment and fined $10,000.

The Government's opening net worth computation shows defendants with a net worth of $19,152.59 at the beginning of the indictment period. Shortly thereafter, defendants purchased a hotel, bar and restaurant, and began operating them as the Holland House. Within three years during which they reported $31,265.92 in taxable income, their apparent net worth increased by $113,185.32. The Government's evidence indicated that, during 1948, the year for which defendants were convicted, their net worth increased by some $32,000, while the amount of taxable income reported by them totaled less than one-third that sum.

Use of Net Worth Method Where Books Are Apparently Adequate

As we have previously noted, this is not the first net worth case to reach this Court. In United States v. Johnson, supra, the Court affirmed a tax-evasion conviction on evidence showing that the taxpayer's expenditures had exceeded his "available declared resources." Since Johnson and his concealed establishments had destroyed the few records they had, the Government was forced to resort to the net worth method of proof. This Court approved on the ground that "To require more * * * would be tantamount to holding that skilful concealment is an invincible barrier to proof", 319 U.S. at 517–518, 63 S.Ct. at 1240. Petitioners ask that we restrict the *Johnson* case to situations where the taxpayer has kept no books. They claim that § 41 of the Internal Revenue Code, expressly limiting the authority of the Government to deviate from the taxpayer's method of accounting, confines the net worth method to situations where the taxpayer has no books or where his books are inadequate. Despite some support for this view among the lower courts, we conclude that this argument must fail. The provision that the "net income shall be computed * * * in accordance with the method of accounting regularly employed in keeping the books of such taxpayer", refers to methods such as the cash receipts or the accrual method, which allocate income and expenses between years. The net worth technique, as used in this case, is not a method of accounting different from the one employed by defendants. It is not a method of accounting at all, except insofar as it calls upon taxpayers to account for their unexplained income. Petitioners' accounting system was appropriate for their business purposes; and, admittedly, the Government did not detect any specific false entries therein. Nevertheless, if we believe the Government's evidence, as the jury did, we must conclude that the defendants' books were more consistent than truthful, and that many items of income had disappeared before they had even reached the recording stage. Certainly Congress never intended to make § 41 a set of blinders which prevents the Government from looking beyond the self-serving declarations in a taxpayer's books. "The United States has relied for the collection of its income tax largely upon the taxpayer's own disclosures * * *. This system can function successfully only if those within and near taxable income keep and render true accounts." Spies v. United States, 317 U.S. 495, 63 S.Ct. 366. To protect the revenue from those who do not "render true accounts", the Government must be free to use all legal evidence available to it in determining whether the story told by the taxpayer's books accurately reflects his financial history.

Establishing a Definite Opening Net Worth

We agree with petitioners that an essential condition in cases of this type is the establishment, with reasonable certainty, of an opening net worth, to serve as a starting point from which to calculate future increases in the taxpayer's assets. The importance of accuracy in this figure is immediately apparent, as the correctness of the result depends entirely upon the inclusion in this sum of all assets on hand at the outset. The Government's net worth statement included as assets at the starting point stock costing $29,650 and $2,153.09 in cash. The Hollands claim that the Government failed to include in its opening net worth figure an accumulation of $113,000 in currency and "hundreds and possibly thousands of shares of stock" which they owned at the beginning of the prosecution period. They asserted that the cash had been accumulated prior to the opening date, $104,000 of it before 1933, and the balance between 1933 and 1945. They had kept the money, they claimed, mostly in $100 bills and at various times in a canvas bag, a suitcase, and a metal box. They had never dipped into it until 1946, when it became the source of the apparent increase in wealth which the Government later found in the form of a home, a ranch, a hotel and other properties. This was the main issue presented to the jury. The Government did not introduce any direct evidence to dispute this claim. Rather it relied on the inference that anyone who had had $104,000 in cash would not have undergone the hardship and privation endured by the Hollands all during the late 20's and throughout the 30's. During this period they lost their cafe business; accumulated $35,000 in debts which were never paid; lost their household furniture because of an unpaid balance of $92.20; suffered a default judgment for $506.66; and were forced to separate for some eight years because it was to their "economical advantage." During the latter part of this period, Mrs. Holland was obliged to support herself and their son by working at a motion picture house in Denver while her husband was in Wyoming. The evidence further indicated that improvements to the hotel, and other assets acquired during the prosecution years, were bought in installments and with bills of small denominations, as if out of earnings rather than from an accumulation of $100 bills. The Government also negatived the possibility of petitioners' accumulating such a sum by checking Mr. Holland's income tax returns as far back as 1913, showing that the income declared in previous years was insufficient to enable defendants to save any appreciable amount of money. The jury resolved this question of the existence of a cache of cash against the Hollands, and we believe the verdict was fully supported.

* * *

The Government's Investigation of Leads

So overwhelming, indeed, was the Government's proof on the issue of cash on hand that the Government agents did not bother to check petitioners' story that some of the cash represented proceeds from the sales of two cafes in the 20's; and that in 1933 an additional portion of this $113,000 in currency was obtained by exchanging some $12,000 in gold at a named bank. While sound administration of the criminal law requires that the net worth approach—a powerful method of proving otherwise undetectable offenses—should not be denied the Government, its failure to investigate leads furnished by the taxpayer might result in serious injustice. It is, of course, not for us to prescribe investigative procedures, but it is within the province of the courts to pass upon the sufficiency of the evidence to convict. When the Government rests its case solely on the approximations and circumstantial inferences of a net worth computation, the cogency of its proof depends upon its effective negation of reasonable explanations by the taxpayer inconsistent with guilt. Such refutation might fail when the Government does not track down relevant leads furnished by the taxpayer—leads reasonably susceptible of being checked, which, if true, would establish the taxpayer's innocence. When the Government fails to show an investigation into the validity of such leads, the trial judge may consider them as true and the Government's case insufficient to go to the jury. This should aid in forestalling unjust prosecutions, and have the practical advantage of eliminating the dilemma, especially serious in this type of case, of the accused's being forced by the risk of an adverse verdict to come forward to substantiate leads which he had previously furnished the Government. It is a procedure entirely consistent with the position long espoused by the Government, that its duty is not to convict but to see that justice is done.

In this case, the Government's detailed investigation was a complete answer to the petitioners' explanations. Admitting that in cases of this kind it "would be desirable to track to its conclusion every conceivable line of inquiry," the Government centered its inquiry on the explanations of the Hollands and entered upon a detailed investigation of their lives covering several states and over a score of years. The jury could have believed that Mr. Holland had received moneys from the sale of cafes in the twenties and that he had turned in gold in 1933 and still it could reasonably have concluded that the Hollands lacked the claimed cache of currency in 1946, the crucial year. Even if these leads were assumed to be true, the Government's evidence was sufficient to convict. The distant incidents relied on by petitioners were so remote in time and in their connection with subsequent events proved by the Government that, whatever petitioners' net worth in 1933, it appears by convincing evidence that on January 1, 1946, they had only such assets as the Government credited to them in its opening net worth statement.

Net Worth Increases Must be Attributable to Taxable Income

Also requisite to the use of the net worth method is evidence supporting the inference that the defendant's net worth increases are attributable to currently taxable income.

The Government introduced evidence tending to show that although the business of the hotel apparently increased during the years in question, the reported profits fell to approximately one-quarter of the amount declared by the previous management in a comparable period; that the cash register tapes, on which the books were based, were destroyed by the petitioners; and that the books did not reflect the receipt of money later withdrawn from the hotel's cash register for the personal living expenses of the petitioners and for payments made for restaurant supplies. The unrecorded items in this latter category totaled over $12,500 for 1948. Thus there was ample evidence that not all the income from the hotel had been included in its books and records. In fact, the net worth increase claimed by the Government for 1948 could have come entirely from the unreported income of the hotel and still the hotel's total earnings for the year would have been only 73% of the sum reported by the previous owner for the comparable period in 1945.

But petitioners claim the Government failed to adduce adequate proof because it did not negative all the possible nontaxable sources of the alleged net worth increases—gifts, loans, inheritances, etc. We cannot agree. The Government's proof, in our view, carried with it the negations the petitioners urge. Increases in net worth, standing alone, cannot be assumed to be attributable to currently taxable income. But proof of a likely source, from which the jury could reasonably find that the net worth increases sprang, is sufficient. In the *Johnson* case, where there was no direct evidence of the source of the taxpayer's income, this Court's conclusion that the taxpayer "had large, unreported income was reinforced by proof * * * that [for certain years his] private expenditures * * * exceeded his available declared resources." This was sufficient to support "the finding that he had some unreported income which was properly attributable to his earnings * * *." There the taxpayer was the owner of an undisclosed business capable of producing taxable income; here the disclosed business of the petitioners was proven to be capable of producing much more income than was reported and in a quantity sufficient to account for the net worth increases. Any other rule would burden the Government with investigating the many possible nontaxable sources of income, each of which is as unlikely as it is difficult to disprove. This is not to say that the Government may disregard explanations of the defendant reasonably susceptible of being checked. But where relevant leads are not forthcoming, the Government is not required to negate every possible source of nontaxable income, a matter peculiarly within the knowledge of the defendant.

The Burden of Proof Remains on the Government

Nor does this rule shift the burden of proof. The Government must still prove every element of the offense beyond a reasonable doubt though not to a mathematical certainty. The settled standards of the criminal law are applicable to net worth cases just as to prosecutions for other crimes. Once the Government has established its case, the defendant remains quiet at his peril. The practical disadvantages to the taxpayer are lessened by the pressures on the Government to check and negate relevant leads.

Willfulness Must be Present

A final element necessary for conviction is willfulness. The petitioners contend that willfulness "involves a specific intent which must be proven by independent evidence and which cannot be inferred from the mere understatement of income." This is a fair statement of the rule. Here, however, there was evidence of a consistent pattern of underreporting large amounts of income, and of the failure on petitioners' part to include all of their income in their books and records. Since, on proper submission, the jury could have found that these acts supported an inference of willfulness, their verdict must stand. * * *

In the light of these considerations the judgment is affirmed.

(2) THE CASH EXPENDITURES METHOD

TAGLIANETTI v. UNITED STATES

398 F.2d 558 (1st Cir. 1968).

COFFIN, Circuit Judge.

* * *

Appellant filed joint tax returns with his wife for the years in prosecution, showing income from two sources: his employment as a "locations" man for a cigarette vending machine company and his net winnings from parimutuel betting. * * * The government's evidence at trial showed substantially larger amounts of income and tax due.

The government proceeded on a "cash expenditure" theory. This is a variant of the net worth method of establishing unreported taxable income. Both proceed by indirection to overcome the absence of direct proof. The net worth method involves the ascertaining of a taxpayer's net worth positions at the beginning and end of a tax period, and deriving that part of any increase not attributable to reported income. This method, while effective against taxpayers who channel their income into investment or durable property, is unavailing against the taxpayer who consumes his self-determined tax free dollars during the year and winds up no wealthier than before. The cash expenditure method is devised to reach such a taxpayer by establishing the amount of his purchases of goods and services which are not attributable to the resources at hand at the beginning of the year or to non-taxable receipts during the year. The beginning and ending net worth positions must be identified with sufficient particularity to rule out or account for the use of a taxpayer's capital to pay for his purchases. If the end-of-year net worth position is equal to that at the beginning of the year, and if there are no non-taxable sources of income during the year, such as gifts or inheritances, the totality of the year's expenditures reflects total taxable income. If ending net worth shows an increase, the increase reflects an added component of income. If ending net worth shows a diminution, the decrease reduces pro tanto the extent to which expenditures reflect income.

* * *

Appellant's contention that there was a failure of proof in the government's case is, to follow his position as stated in his brief, " * * * that even assuming, *arguendo*, that the evidence adduced shows he spent more money during the indictment years than his reported gross income, there is not one scintilla of evidence to show that said expenditures came out of current receipts *only* and not out of available assets acquired in prior years. This is so because there is absolutely no competent evidence which, in any way suffices to clearly and accurately establish the extent of defendant's prior assets at the beginning of any or all the indictment years; i. e., there is no opening net worth for January 1, 1956, 1957 or 1958."

Appellant mistakes form for substance. In this case, the prosecution presented evidence to support the conclusion that the assets owned by appellant and his wife either remained at a static level, or instead increased over the taxable years, and in any event made no contribution to the expenditures shown. The jury was entitled to accept appellant's statement that he did not touch his loan proceeds for other than betting and to reject the testimony of payments received from Merola. There is no suggestion that cars, boats, furniture, jewels, or other property were disposed of to finance current purchases. The expense items excluded by appellant's accountant presented issues of fact which the jury obviously resolved against appellant.

This state of the proof fully satisfies the requirement in Holland v. United States of "the establishment, with reasonable certainty, of an opening net worth, to serve as a starting point from which to calculate future increases in the taxpayer's assets." In a typical net worth case, as *Holland,* precise figures would have to be attached to opening and closing net worth positions for each of the taxable years to provide a basis for the critical subtraction. In a cash expenditures case reasonable certainty may be established without such a presentation, as long as the proof—as in this case—makes clear the extent of any contribution which beginning resources or a diminution of resources over time could have made to expenditures. We recognize that courts occasionally blur the distinction between the two approaches and use language implying that they are subject not only to the same principle of excluding the availability of nontaxable resources but also to the same method of implementing that principle, i. e., establishing net worth figures. Appellant has cited several cash expenditure cases for the latter proposition. A careful review of the language used and the problems addressed in these opinions indicates that they cannot be fairly read as embracing such an inflexible formal requirement.

In the case at bar it is apparent that while the jury may not have been apprised of the dollar value of each of the assets comprising appellant's opening net worth, it was so informed as to his cash on hand and the few non-liquid items which were disposed of or acquired during the course of each prosecution year. A running series of net worth statements would not have added to the jury's understanding. We therefore hold that the proof adduced here was sufficient to allow the jury an intelligent determination of the single relevant issue; whether any expenditures found to be in excess of reported income can be accounted for by assets available at the outset of the prosecution period or non-taxable receipts during the period.

United States v. Johnson, 319 U.S. 503, 63 S.Ct. 1233, 87 L.Ed. 1546 (1943).

* * *

Affirmed.

(3) THE BANK DEPOSITS METHOD

UNITED STATES v. ESSER

520 F.2d 213 (7th Cir. 1975).

BAUER, Circuit Judge.

Appellant-defendant, Dr. Charles Esser, a veterinarian, was indicted on three counts of willful evasion of income taxes for the years 1967, 1968 and 1969 in violation of 26 U.S.C. § 7201.

* * *

Appellant argues that the trial court should have granted motions for judgment of acquittal based upon the government's failure to conduct a thorough examination and analysis of defendant's bank deposits. We do not accept appellant's argument and find that the trial judge had sufficient grounds for denial of the motion for acquittal.

I.R.S. Agent Hoak testified that deposit slips and underlying items of deposit are customarily introduced to demonstrate the nature of the deposits. However, in this instance it was virtually impossible to introduce the deposit slips due to their poor quality, unreliability, and unavailability. The government introduced the bank statements and pass books as the most reliable evidence available. Though appellant attempted on cross-examination to establish that the slips and items were capable of retrieval, the question was left as one of fact for the jury.

Defendant argues also that the bank deposits theory requires an analysis of the bank deposit items themselves. He contends that the government's duty to specifically identify and analyze the defendant's deposit slips and the underlying items is mandated by the "bank deposits cases"; and that failure to do so is fatal to the government's case. On examination the authorities reveal no such duty.

These cases establish that the bank deposits theory requires the government to prove that the defendant was engaged in an income producing business and that regular deposits of funds having the appearance of income were in fact made to bank accounts during the course of business. The total deposits figure serves as the starting point for further analysis of the taxpayer's accounts. The government must do everything that is reasonable and fair under the circumstances to identify any non-income transactions and deduct them from total deposits. Further, all proper deductions and credits must be subtracted. However, the government's investigators are not obliged to track down every conceivable lead offered by the taxpayer to justify the non-income designation of a particular item.

After the government proves that deposits having the appearance of income were made the defendant has the burden to explain as far as possible the deposits. With this done the jury is entitled to infer that the difference between the balance of deposited items and reported income constitutes unreported income.[2]

* * *

Appellant seeks to attack the testimony of the government's summary witness predicated on the argument heretofore decided; that the deposits proof was insufficient. The nature of a summary witness' testimony requires that he draw conclusions from the evidence presented at trial. In the instant case the record shows that the summary witness relied only upon the evidence received during the trial and that he was available for full cross-examination. Consequently the evidence was properly admitted for the jury's consideration and the judge properly denied defendant's motion.

* * *

In short, the government proved by clear, reliable evidence that defendant had enormous bank deposits and that after deducting all non-income sources of deposits, the business receipts far exceeded the amounts shown on his income tax returns. This evidence was more than sufficient to support the jury verdict below.

* * *

Accordingly it is the decision of this Court that the conviction should be affirmed.

Affirmed.

---

(4) THE PERCENTAGE MARK–UP METHOD

The percentage mark-up method of proof of income is rarely used as the principal method in a criminal prosecution. However, this method may be utilized to support or corroborate proof of income by another indirect method.

In essence, under the percentage mark-up method, the taxpayer's cost of goods sold or merchandise purchases are "marked up" to establish gross profit. The method is useful in cases in which the taxpayer has one (or only a few) sources of supply, and the taxpayer's

---

2. The government explained in detail the method employed to analyze the defendant's bank deposits during the years in question. Total deposits were determined by examination of the defendant's bank statements. From that total, all interbank deposits, re-deposits of cash, proceeds of inheritance and gifts and all other non-taxable sources of income were deducted.

mark-up can be established to a reasonable degree of certainty. The method is most accurately applied in those industries in which pricing is regulated, as is the liquor industry in certain states. The percentage mark-up method is typically attacked on the basis of the inaccuracy of the percentage used due to the taxpayer's deviation from the comparable operations used by the investigating agent. The defense also frequently argues that the Service has failed properly to take into account such factors as spillage, breakage and theft. Hence, as noted above, one will rarely, if ever, see a criminal tax prosecution based solely upon this method of proof.

WEBB v. COMMISSIONER

394 F.2d 366 (5th Cir. 1968).

GOLDBERG, Circuit Judge.

* * *

In September of 1961 Revenue Agent Larry Kelley was assigned to investigate the Webbs' 1958, 1959, and 1960 returns. He found Webb's books and records to be totally inadequate. Likewise, after examining Webb's canceled checks and his primary bank's microfilm of Webb's canceled checks, bank statements, and deposit slips, Agent Kelley was no more enlightened. He thus estimated Webb's liquor income by the percentage mark-up method * * * .

* * *

(1) Use of the Percentage Mark-up Method sans Net Worth
   Considerations

It is conceded that Webb had no adequate books and records to reflect his income during the contested years. Webb contends, however, that a net worth analysis of his financial status in 1958, 1959, and 1960 shows that he could not possibly have earned $96,444.48, which the Commissioner, using the percentage mark-up method, determined to be his total liquor business income. In Webb's brief he states in part, "Ignoring the undisputed testimony as to Petitioner's net worth was clear error. * * * In no other percentage mark-up case have considerations of net worth been totally disregarded."

Our analysis starts with the basic principle that Webb, along with every taxpayer, must maintain accounting records which enable him to file a correct tax return. Because Webb's records did not clearly reflect his income, the Commissioner was authorized to use such methods as in his opinion clearly reflected that income.

* * *

Webb's broad assertion that net worth determinations are always considered is not supported by the cases. In Kurnick v. C. I. R., 6 Cir. 1956, 232 F.2d 678, for example, the Sixth Circuit affirmed a deficiency and fraud assessment under the percentage mark-up method without mentioning net worth considerations. Eleven years later the same Circuit upheld a deficiency and fraud assessment despite the taxpayer's contention that his net worth computations had successfully countered the Commissioner's percentage mark-up estimate. The Tax Court had dismissed the contention by noting that "the petitioners did not introduce any evidence to show the correctness of the items contained therein." Carmine Bollella, 24 T.C.M. 858 (1965), aff'd., Bollella v. C.I.R., 6 Cir. 1967, 374 F.2d 96. Although in the case at bar Webb did introduce "testimonial evidence" as to his net worth, we question whether his self-serving statements satisfy the quest of the *Bollella* courts. We refer to Miller v. C. I. R., 5 Cir. 1956, 237 F.2d 830, where the Commissioner's reconstruction of income under the "bank deposit method" was challenged by a net worth attack. As in this case, the taxpayer's integrity had been placed in doubt, and we concluded as follows:

> "The taxpayer complains that the agent should have followed the increase in net worth method of computation. * * * There can be no requirement that the Commissioner use for his calculation of income a method which depends absolutely for its accuracy on the taxpayer's voluntary disclosure of his assets at the end of the period in a case where the court rejected his contention that he had a large amount of cash at the beginning of the period and when he overlooked a bank account of $5,000 at the end of the period." 237 F.2d at 838.

For Webb the percentage mark-up method was the most reasonable means of computing income because his cost of sales in each taxable year was known with certainty. In comparison, net worth or bank deposit computations would lack any known figure because Webb transacted a substantial amount of his liquor business in cash, and he readily commingled cash flowing to and from personal and business expenses. The supposed disparity between the percentage mark-up and net worth determinations is based almost exclusively on Webb's own testimony concerning his property, expenses, and money hoards. Moreover, the Commissioner did disclose possible unreported income drains in the elimination of certain debts and the purchase in 1959 of two new air-conditioned Cadillacs.

We recognize that the absence of adequate tax records does not give the Commissioner carte blanche for imposing Draconian absolutes. But such absence does weaken any critique of the Commissioner's methodology.

Arithmetic precision was originally and exclusively in Webb's hands, and he had a statutory duty to provide it. He did not have to add or subtract; rather, he had simply to keep papers and data for others to mathematicize. Having defaulted in his duty, he cannot frustrate the Commissioner's reasonable attempts by compelling investigation and recomputation under every means of income determination. Nor should he be overly chagrined at the Tax Court's reluctance to credit every word of his negative wails.

(2) Mark-up Percentage of 25% for Determining Gross Sales

Predictably, Webb claims that the Commissioner's mark-up percentage of 25% is arbitrary and unreasonably high. His major argument is that shelf prices, upon which the mark-up percentage was based, are not reliable representations of selling prices because his stores regularly granted liberal discounts. He adds that even selling prices do not accurately report income because of the magnitude of business inefficiency and theft in his stores. The Tax Court considered all of Webb's contentions and found that a mark-up of 25% was fair and reasonable for Webb's business during the years 1958 through 1960. After a brief recitation of the relevant facts, we will discuss the * * * specific areas in which Webb challenges the 25% mark-up figure. In doing so, however, we emphasize that the same presumptions of verity are accorded to Commissioner and Tax Court determinations here as in Section (1) of this opinion, supra.

Revenue Agent Kelley began his investigation of Webb's 1958, 1959, and 1960 income tax returns in September of 1961. * * * Kelley computed the cost of sales by obtaining accurate records from Webb's suppliers. To arrive at a mark-up percentage, he first averaged the 1959 and 1960 shelf prices of what, according to Webb, were the eighteen best selling items. Based on these shelf prices, the average mark-up on all of Webb's most popular brands in all sizes was computed to be 34.25% over cost for 1959 and 30.50% for 1960. The average mark-up on these brands in the most frequently sold half-pint sizes was 36.68% and 32.64% for 1959 and 1960, respectively. Kelley reduced the average mark-up to 25% to account for "any possible discounts or losses for breakage, theft, minor changes of price during the year." Using this mark-up of 25%, Kelley reconstructed Webb's sales for each of the three years and deducted therefrom the costs of sales and business expenses.

The * * * specific challenges will be considered separately.

* * *

Quantity discounts. Webb asserts in his brief: "Every person who ever sold liquor in Petitioner's store testified that he gave large discounts on quantity sales. * * * " We need not attack the verity of that statement; we will instead analyze its persuasive power. Both Bolen and Cornelia Webb testified that they granted five to twenty-cent discounts on quantity sales (more than five bottles). Jewel Jackson, a store manager, corroborated the Webbs and added that he often sold a twelve-bottle case of Thunderbird wine for $7.50 (by 1960 wholesale prices, only a 7.59% mark-up). J. T. Lightner testified that he occasionally made quantity sales at a discount, but only after calling Webb for his approval. J. D. Cooper, who managed a store which was open only six months during the three-year period involved, testified that he "sold a lot of whiskey to bootleggers" without telling Webb. However, he also testified that some of his shelf prices were higher than those used by Kelley in determining Webb's mark-up. None of the above stated what percentage of their business was in quantity discount sales.

Especially as to the testimony of Lightner and Cooper, the Commissioner's allowance for discounts seems generous enough. As to the testimony of the Webbs and Jackson, even if substantial discounting can be inferred, the Tax Court was justified in "discounting" the testimony due to an interest in the proceedings. Jackson, for instance, was still employed by the Webbs at the time of the Tax Court hearing, and his testimony was impeached by Revenue Agent Kelley's recitation of a prior conversation with Jackson.

General discounting procedures. It is true that all witnesses testified to the practice of discounting from five to twenty-five cents on certain sales to meet the competition of other stores. Webb's testimony on this regard is typical:

> "Sometime—well, people would come in often and say I am short and would like a nickel having and sometimes fifteen cents having the price and I would say let them have it."

The same problems of frequency and credibility plagued Webb in this challenge as they did concerning the quantity sales. Moreover, Webb himself testified twice that in more than half his sales no discounts were given. In its appellate brief the government has computed the mark-up percentages (1) if all sales were discounted ten cents from shelf prices and (2) if half of the sales were discounted ten cents from shelf prices. The * * * computations show that the 25% general mark-up was a reasonable one * * * .

* * *

Inefficiency and theft. Webb asserts that the 25% mark-up does not provide for substantial losses caused by inefficient operations, employee thefts, and credit losses. We note that Webb claimed on his returns, and was allowed, the following deductions from gross profits for bad check losses: $902.46 for 1958, $943.80 for 1959, and $522.96 for 1960. These allowed losses, therefore, could have no effect on the Commissioner's determination of gross profit or net income. As to other, purely testimonial, evidence of reduced income due to inefficient operations and credit losses, we find no clear error in the Tax Court's failure to be convinced.

Webb claimed employee theft in the cases of Lightner and Cooper. Having no direct evidence as to Lightner, he attempted to reconstruct Lightner's income and expenditures to show that Lightner was taking from the till. Webb's enthusiasm and diligence in this income determination would have been appreciated in the determination of his own income. However, even here there are substantial gaps, and Webb's willingness to keep Lightner in his employ through the end of 1962 weakens his argument considerably. As to Cooper, Webb presented more direct evidence, the fact that police arrested Cooper for coming out of his store with whiskey "before day." But this incident occurred in 1964. There is no evidence that Cooper stole substantial amounts during the first six months of his employment, June through December of 1960.

* * *

Comparison with other businesses. Bill Barnes, whose bookkeeping services were solicited by Webb in 1962, testified that a reasonable mark-up for liquor stores in the area was less than twelve per cent. The testimony mentioned no specific period of time, and, as the Tax Court found, Webb presented no evidence of prices charged in other stores or of a similarity of pricing and discount practices among liquor dealers. Webb's own shelf prices indicated a much higher mark-up, and he testified that he sold at shelf prices more than half the time. The Tax Court was not clearly erroneous in disregarding Barnes' testimony.

* * *

The Commissioner's 25% base, while perhaps not overly generous, was neither arbitrary nor capricious. Discounts, losses, theft—all the elements claimed by Webb—were taken into consideration. Webb has failed to supply us with the factual primates [sic] of further reduction, even in retrospective analysis.

* * *

Affirmed.

SECTION 3. CRIMINAL TAX INVESTIGATIONS

A criminal tax case usually develops from an investigation by the Criminal Investigation (formerly Intelligence) Division (CID) of the Internal Revenue Service. The investigation itself can be triggered in many different ways. A large number of criminal tax investigations result from referrals from the civil (particularly Examination and Collection) divisions of the Service upon the suspicion of fraud in matters within their jurisdiction. However, the Service's informant [n] and information gathering system, other law enforcement agencies, the daily newspapers and countless other sources all yield "information items" which can result in a criminal tax investigation.

The criminal tax investigation, conducted by a Special Agent of the CID (often with the assistance of a civil agent and advice from

n. IRC § 7623 authorizes (but does not require) the payment of rewards to informants at the discretion of the Service. See also Reg. § 301.7623–1.

IRS counsel), will result in either the referral of the case for civil disposition or a recommendation for prosecution. Should the Special Agent recommend prosecution, the taxpayer under investigation is entitled, upon request, to a conference at the CID level,[o] with the Chief of the pertinent section of the Division.

These conferences normally (if not invariably) are followed by the referral of a recommendation for prosecution [p] to a division of the Office of Chief Counsel, IRS, usually the District Counsel for the district in which the investigation was conducted. The precise review steps prior to an indictment vary depending upon the characteristics of the case.[q] Hence, a definitive and universally applicable "flow chart" of the progress of a criminal tax case cannot be provided without extensive and detailed discussion. However, it should be noted that there will be a review of the case by an IRS attorney, often one in the office of the District Counsel. The taxpayer usually will be afforded a conference at this level, if one is requested, and will have the opportunity at the conference to present reasons why prosecution is not appropriate. The IRS attorney's consideration (and internal review) will conclude with either a termination of the criminal case and a referral for civil disposition, a referral back to the Criminal Investigation Division for further investigation, or a referral to the Department of Justice with a recommendation for prosecution.

At the Department of Justice, criminal tax cases are referred to the Criminal Section of the Tax Division. The Tax Division, in some cases, may refer the matter to a United States Attorney without further review. However, in many cases (in prior years, in all cases) a substantive review will take place at the Tax Division. The Tax Division usually will provide the taxpayer the opportunity for a conference in Washington, D.C., if one is requested. At the conference, the taxpayer can attempt to persuade the Justice Department attorney assigned to the case that prosecution is not appropriate. The Tax Division's consideration of a criminal tax case can result in a declination of prosecution and a referral back to the IRS or a referral to a United States Attorney. The referral to the United States Attorney can be with an authorization and direction to prosecute, with discretion to prosecute or decline and refer for civil disposition, or with directions to conduct further investigation through a grand jury.[r]

o. Proc.Rules § 601.107(b)(2). See also Short v. Murphy, 512 F.2d 374 (6th Cir. 1975) (taxpayer cannot compel IRS to disclose specifics of its case at CID conference); United States v. Goldstein, 342 F.Supp. 661 (E.D.N.Y.1972) (conference opportunity is for benefit of Service, cannot be demanded as a matter of right by taxpayer).

p. Since they are provided after the Special Agent's decision to recommend prosecution has been reached, a decision which has doubtlessly been cleared with his Chief, it is most unlikely that a taxpayer will be able to stop a criminal case at the CID conference level.

q. See Internal Revenue Manual—Administration § 9600 et seq.

r. A referral back to the IRS for further investigation is theoretically possible. However, there is some ques-

The United States Attorney, upon receipt of a criminal tax case, normally will afford a pre-indictment conference to the taxpayer. The taxpayer may be able to persuade the United States Attorney to decline prosecution (in those cases in which he has the discretion to do so) or to refer the case back to the Justice Department for reconsideration. On the other hand, the taxpayer may be able only to obtain a "plea bargain" for consideration in lieu of proceeding to trial on the charges.

It should be noted that a criminal tax case may arise out of an investigation conducted by a grand jury assisted by IRS agents. In such a case, there will be IRS and Tax Division review of the use of the agents in the grand jury investigation and of any charges prior to indictment. The taxpayer's ability to have conferences with the Service and the Tax Division may be limited (or perhaps even nonexistent) in the context of a grand jury investigation.[s]

A. REPRESENTATION OF TAXPAYERS

DIAGNOSIS OF TAX FRAUD INVESTIGATIONS

Marvin J. Garbis and Sylvan H. Sack
55 A.B.A. Journal 441 (1969).

Our brothers in the medical profession, in carrying out their Hippocratic obligations, have long recognized the benefits of an early diagnosis of the more serious of human ills. And the physicians have found it helpful to advise their patients of the various symptoms which may call for immediate professional attention.

In our own profession as well there are problems for which an early diagnosis can often be the *sine qua non* for cure. We too may consider initiating an educational program to make known some of the early symptoms of various legal woes. Finding the ailment with which to commence the campaign may be the easiest of our problems.

Probably more business and professional men are seriously injured by tax fraud investigations and their side effects than by any other legal disease. Each year hundreds of taxpayers are "totally disabled" for terms ranging from months to years as the direct result of criminal tax cases. The annual toll in terms of time (both kinds), effort, anxiety and money from tax fraud investigations is staggering. Yet the sad results of many fraud investigations are not always necessary. Far too often taxpayers fatally infect their own case before they or their counsel are even aware that a case exists.

In the tax fraud field an early diagnosis of the existence of an investigation can make all the difference in the prognosis. Early

---

tion as to the propriety of utilizing an IRS summons once a case has been referred to Justice. See United States v. LaSalle Nat'l Bank, excerpted above at pages 391–400.

s. See Internal Revenue Manual—Administration § 9267, for the internal IRS procedures incident to the use of IRS agents in a grand jury investigation.

professional attention to provide the correct prescription of co-operation, assertion of constitutional rights and use of other available remedies can yield a good rate of cures and remissions.

The problem of diagnosing a tax fraud investigation can be acute. The malignant criminal investigation can appear to the layman (and even to the practiced observer) as nothing more than a benign civil audit. Worse yet, the minor irritation of an ordinary civil audit can suddenly turn malignant without the taxpayer's being aware of or appreciating the significance of this dangerous metamorphosis. In this day of legal internships, neighborhood legal clinics and annual legal checkups, the time may well be ripe to steal another page from the doctors' book and make known the symptoms which may indicate that a tax fraud investigation is under way. There are seven principal danger signs of a tax fraud investigation.

1. Diplopia—If You See Double, You've Got Trouble

Most civil tax audits (whether office or field audits) are conducted by a single internal revenue agent. However, criminal tax investigations are generally conducted by a special agent and an internal revenue agent and occasionally by two or more special agents. It must be noted that in certain instances civil audits are conducted by more than one internal revenue agent. For example, in the case of taxpayers who pay very large taxes there are "team audits" in which several agents work together on a complex return. Also, there are occasions when a new agent receives on-the-job training from his supervisor or a more experienced internal revenue agent. However, unless the presence of two or more agents on a case is readily explained, the possibility that one of them is a special agent bent on making a fraud case is a real and present danger.

2. Overdose of Man-Hours

If an audit appears to be consuming far more of an internal revenue agent's time than appears normal, a closer look at the course of the audit may be warranted. Even if a fraud case is not likely, a whopping deficiency may be. And an early appreciation of this possibility can be helpful.

3. Diarrhea of the Copying Machine

The copying of key documents such as contracts, leases, wills, deeds, trusts, financial reports and the like is a normal attribute of many civil tax audits. However, the extensive copying of basic evidentiary financial records is not and may provide the clue to the existence of a present or potential tax fraud case. Therefore, an unduly large amount of copying or borrowing of the taxpayer's records, although frequently consistent with a civil audit, can indicate trouble and should be examined by taxpayer's counsel.

4. Infectious Publicity

Many tax fraud investigations are sparked by newspaper articles or other publicity tending to indicate that a taxpayer has large sums of unexplained cash or an illegal or unreported source of income. Therefore, the appearance of the Internal Revenue Service on the heels of publicity of this type can point to a fraud investigation.

5. Peripheral Deterioration

Many tax fraud investigations commence with the gathering of evidence from sources remote from the taxpayer. Frequently, the taxpayer starts to hear about this "encircling" Internal Revenue Service action from friends or business associates long before he himself is confronted by an internal revenue agent. It must be noted that this peripheral investigation technique is often used in purely civil investigations. Thus, the fact that "the Internal Revenue Service has been asking about" a taxpayer does not require the conclusion that a fraud case is being made or contemplated. But the possibility should not be overlooked.

6. Persistent Sore Spots

If an internal revenue agent conducting an ordinary civil audit discovers the possibility of tax fraud the case will be referred to the intelligence division as a potential tax fraud matter. The taxpayer will not necessarily be notified of this referral and may not be aware of what is happening until he is fully enmeshed in a tax fraud investigation. Probably the best clue that a fraud referral may be made is the appearance of a persistent sore spot in the course of the civil audit, i. e., a matter or series of matters tending to lead to a conclusion that there may be a fraud case. Thus, if there should appear an undisclosed source of income or a series of grossly improper deductions or omissions from income which cannot be explained satisfactorily to the agent, the taxpayer's counsel should investigate to determine whether a fraud referral may be, or already has been, made. Similarly, probing by an auditing agent into such matters as the taxpayer's net worth, cost of living and bank deposits can indicate that a case has taken a turn for the worse.

7. Tinnitus—Echoes of Miranda

In Miranda v. Arizona, 384 U.S. 456 (1966), the Supreme Court declared that law enforcement officers must warn a person deprived of his freedom of his right to remain silent and his right to counsel before subjecting him to questioning about matters which may tend to incriminate him. The precise manner in which the Miranda case principles will affect criminal tax investigations has not yet been resolved. And a discussion of the intricate problems in this area would be beyond the scope of this note. However, one echo of Miranda provides definite evidence of a tax fraud investigation. Special agents of the Internal Revenue Service are now required, upon their first contact with a taxpayer being investigated, to advise him that they are special agents and "have the function of investigating the possibility of tax fraud" and that anything he says may be used against him. The special agents must also tell the taxpayer that he cannot be compelled to incriminate himself by answering any questions or producing any documents and that he has the right to seek the assistance of an attorney before responding. (I. R. S. News Release No. 949, November 26, 1968). These warnings require the immediate attention of counsel to the fact that a fraud investigation is (and, unfortunately, probably has been for some time) under way. In brief, if the taxpayer is advised of his right to counsel, he needs one, fast.

Although written in a light vein, this article is intended to convey a serious message. In handling a tax fraud case, as in many other areas of our practice, ultimate results can be significantly affected by action or inaction in the early stages. The general practitioner and the tax specialist should both always be alert to the chance that a tax audit can create significant problems, whether civil or criminal, for his client. One of the above noted "danger signs", or some other clue which tends to indicate that something more than a normal tax audit is under way, requires immediate attention by the taxpayer's counsel. In the tax area, as in other fields of the law, the earlier the diagnosis the more likely the cure.

CRIMINAL TAX FRAUD—REPRESENTING THE TAXPAYER BEFORE TRIAL

George D. Crowley and Richard L. Manning

* * *

OVERVIEW OF DEFENSE STRATEGY

The Commissioner's Enforcement Program is perhaps the most integrated and selective program ever to utilize criminal sanctions. It is a part of an overall system of collecting taxes that may invoke civil audits, assert substantial civil fines, require extensive recordkeeping, collect delinquent taxes almost without legal opposition, or, if it chooses, attempt to send the best and the brightest to jail as a public reminder to file accurate returns. When it chooses to prosecute, it does so without passion, carefully weighing the facts, selecting only the best cases, investigating only the most promising leads, arriving at the District Court with almost undefeatable cases, and, after they have been won, asking the Court to send the victim to jail not because it will help him but only because it will help the program.

Over 100,000 information items are screened annually for fraud potential. About 8,000 of these are selected for an investigation. Of the cases investigated, approximately 2,500 will become full scale investigations, some 1200 will be recommended for prosecution by the

Intelligence Division, and about 1,000 will result in an indictment. Once the indictment is returned, 90 percent of the taxpayers who have survived all of the prior opportunities for escape will be convicted and 50 percent of these will be sent to jail. The first and most profound observation that can be made about defending a taxpayer who is the subject of a tax fraud investigation is that the quicker a taxpayer avails himself of the services of a qualified attorney, the better his chances will be to escape disaster.

The second observation that can be made is that the suspicions of the special agent are absolutely irrelevant. Taxpayers will not hire an attorney, will make statements to the special agent, and will give the agent free access to their books because they fear that, if they hire an attorney or refuse to cooperate, the agent will believe something is wrong. There is not a special agent alive who is not naturally suspicious of every taxpayer he investigates. In fact, by the time the taxpayer knows he is the subject of an investigation, the special agent will have already investigated an information item by reviewing other Internal Revenue Service information which indicates the case has fraud potential. Allaying his suspicions is pointless.

When he comes to see the taxpayer, he is after evidence. If he obtains the evidence, he will refer the case whether the taxpayer has been cooperative or not. If he does not obtain the evidence, he will not refer the case whether the taxpayer has been cooperative or not. It is just that simple and bloodless. The suspicions will always be there; the only real, important question is whether the evidence is there and whether the agent can obtain it. It is the job of the lawyers to know what the evidence is, what evidence is needed, whether the taxpayer is obliged to supply it, whether certain evidence can be suppressed, impeached, contradicted, or diluted, what evidence constitutes a defense, how slightly irrelevant evidence (the taxpayer's health, reputation, education, etc.) can be made relevant, and how to manage a case generally. A lawyer is as vital in an investigation as he is at a trial, and in the tax fraud field, he will have a statistically better chance to be more effective.

The third observation that can be made, and the most important in determining specific tactics, is that defense counsel must conduct the investigation as if he were preparing a case that is certain to go to trial. The special agent is gathering evidence; he is constantly assessing the "reasonable probability of conviction" formula. The most common failing in these cases is the tendency of taxpayers and inexperienced counsel to treat these investigations like civil audits, where negotiations begin early and often proceed issue by issue and day by day. There is only one issue in a tax fraud case: Is the evidence gathered sufficient to conclude that the taxpayer will be found guilty in the district court? That issue does not permit a lot of give and take. There is no way to split it down the middle. Advocacy skills and a refined sense of evidence will decide the case, not negotiating talent. These cases must be beaten. They cannot be settled.

* * *

LIMITING THE OPEN-ENDED QUALITY OF A TAX FRAUD INVESTIGATION

When a man is charged with murder, the focus of the investigation is directed immediately to a limited historical event. Questions of where the defendant was on the night in question, what his relationship was to the victim, whether he had any motive to kill the victim, can be pursued immediately by both the prosecution and the defense. Tax fraud cases are different. Most criminal investigations start with a defendant and seek a crime. Any crime against the revenues will do, whether it was committed yesterday or five years ago. If the initial suspicion that precipitated the investigation proves worthless, it does not mean the taxpayer is free. There are other years, other transactions, other criminal sections, other means of proof.

A tax fraud investigation is the nearest thing to an inquisition known to modern times. The question is not whether the taxpayer did something wrong; it is whether he did anything wrong. There are probably very few doctors, lawyers, small businessmen, accountants, etc. who could afford to permit a special agent free range over the multitude of transactions they have been involved in during the last several years without experiencing at least a solid scare.

This is why the universal position of experienced tax fraud practitioners is to withhold all of the information possible from the special agent in the early stages of an investigation. The immediate effort is to reduce the investigation to manageable limits. The special agent will usually have a specific reason for being there. Often it will be because of a particular series of transactions, such as evidence of unrecorded cash receipts, excessive cash purchases, allegations of bookkeeping improprieties by a former employee, or specific irregularities that precipitated a group or chain investigation. Notwithstanding the specific nature of the inquiry, the special agent will usually ask to see all of the taxpayer's records for a three-year period, partly because it is often necessary to have the books to tie out the fact that a particular transaction was not included in income and partly because he knows from prior investigations that where there is smoke there is fire.

If counsel can withhold vital evidence and does so, he can call the special agent in, advise him that he will not permit a gambol through the taxpayer's books to find whatever can be found, but if there are specific questions, counsel will make a determination of whether it would be in the taxpayer's interest to supply any information concerning them. At this point, if the special agent is really only inquiring into certain transactions and he needs the taxpayer's cooperation to determine if anything is there, he will tell the attorney what his specific questions are. Counsel then initially at least, has limited the inquiry, and if it is possible to answer the questions without opening up other transactions, the special agent's investigation may be still-born.

* * *

SILENCING THE TAXPAYER OR "BLESSED IS HE WHO SAYS NOTHING FOR HE SHALL HAVE AN EVEN CHANCE"

Special agents usually give little warning of their initial visit, and they do this for a reason: to trap the taxpayer. On occasion, they will call to try to set up an immediate meeting. Sometimes they will simply arrive at the taxpayer's office or home and ask to see him. In any event, most taxpayers are taken by surprise when the special agent advises them of their constitutional rights.

The result of these warnings seems to be in direct opposition to their intended effect. They are an invitation to remain silent. Most taxpayers, however, * * * are extraordinarily reluctant to remain silent. Whether they have never been accused before, whether they are not accustomed to being treated with anything but respect and honor, or whether they have been accustomed to viewing the fifth amendment as the refuge of low-level hoodlums and inarticulate Mafiosos, they tend to treat the warning as a challenge to speak or be thought guilty. They are invariably confident of their ability to make answers,[16] especially in what they view to be the safe harbor of faulty recollection. Any answer to a question by a special agent, with the sole exception of an assertion of the fifth amendment, is admissible as a statement of the taxpayer. "I don't know," and "I can't recall," are answers to question. As answers, they are subject to proof of their truthfulness or falsity. If the taxpayer has just reviewed the transaction inquired about with his accountant or bookkeeper, his accountant or bookkeeper can be a witness to the fact that he lied to the special agent when he said, "I can't recall." If the transaction inquired about is the largest or most unusual of his business career,

---

16. When a special agent interviews a taxpayer it is a classic "pro-am confrontation." The agent is a highly trained, experienced criminal investigator who has obtained and reviewed some basic information before he has arrived at the taxpayer's office. * * * [H]e has timed his interview with the taxpayer, selected the place of interview, and has specific objectives in mind. The taxpayer usually has no training in tax matters and no familiarity with Service procedure. In all likelihood, he has never had *Miranda* warnings directed at him and is in a state of shock at hearing them. He will not know what questions the agent will ask; he will usually not review any records before trying to answer, and he will wrongly believe he must answer if a full-scale investigation is to be avoided. Submitting to such a one-sided interview is like wagering one's liberty on a golf match with the club pro.

proof of its uniqueness is sufficient for a jury to conclude the taxpayer lied when he said he did not remember it. Any statement, no matter how innocent or "safe" it might sound, is subject to further proof.

If a taxpayer has the common sense to ask his attorney to be present at the interview, the attorney should immediately call the special agent, advise him that he has just gotten into the case, ask about the nature of the inquiry and, particularly, whether any specific questions or transactions are being investigated, and set up another date sufficiently in the future to provide the attorney an opportunity to familiarize himself with the case. If the special agent is persistent, advise him that the taxpayer will not meet with him at all. The agent will then become far more tractable. As mentioned above, time is seldom of the essence in tax fraud cases, and an attorney should never be reluctant to ask for all he needs.

* * *

PROTECTING THE EVIDENCE: CONSTITUTIONAL AND PROCEDURAL RIGHTS

The investigative stage of a tax fraud case can best be described as a contest for evidence between the taxpayer's counsel and the special agent. In this contest, the agent is armed with awesome investigatory authority; he can compel the production of documentary evidence from the taxpayer and third parties; he can require witnesses to appear and give testimony under oath; he can avail himself of the Commissioner's Summons by merely executing and serving it; with the cooperation of the local United States Attorney's office, he can seek grand jury subpoenaes ad testificandum or duces tecum and the issuance of search warrants;[4] with the approval of the Department of Justice, immunity or other concessions can be granted to vital witnesses;[5] and, by merely exhibiting his badge and describing his function, he can obtain the voluntary cooperation of most individuals and institutions.

Against this Goliath, the taxpayer's counsel has the constitutional rights of the taxpayer to refuse to speak and, under certain circumstances, to refuse to produce records. He also has the right to seek suppression of evidence obtained in violation of the taxpayer's constitutional rights. He may constitutionally and procedurally challenge how, why and when such compulsory process as the Commissioner's Summons and grand jury subpoenaes were served and what they may

---

4. 26 U.S.C. §§ 7302, 7321 and 7608 contain the statutory authority pertinent to searches and seizures by special agents. Rule 41 of the Federal Rules of Criminal Procedure must also be complied with. Rule 17 of the Federal Rules of Criminal Procedure authorizes grand jury subpoenaes.

5. 18 U.S.C. §§ 6002 and 6003 authorize the Department of Justice to grant immunity to witnesses. This power has been widely used in political cases involving income tax charges.

lawfully require. These are important rights and can well make the difference between a criminal conviction in the district court and an administrative acquittal within the Service.

Arrayed against the power of the Service, however, these rights of the taxpayer are like a slingshot, whose effectiveness is determined by the timing of its use and the accuracy of its aim. The agent will easily obtain a volume of evidence without ever coming into counsel's range, but, invariably, to procure the evidence sought to prove the crime effectively, the agent must come close to the taxpayer, must seek his statements, his personal records, the documentary evidence under his direct control, what he wrote, what he did, what he said. When the agent thus approaches, then the battle must be joined.

* * *

B. VOLUNTARY DISCLOSURE

CRIMINAL TAX FRAUD—REPRESENTING THE TAXPAYER BEFORE TRIAL

George D. Crowley and Richard L. Manning

VOLUNTARY DISCLOSURE

From 1946 to 1952, the Internal Revenue Service had a formal policy regarding voluntary disclosure. The policy provided that if a taxpayer voluntarily disclosed to a responsible official of the Internal Revenue Service, prior to any audit or investigation, either that he had wilfully failed to file his return or had filed a false return, the criminal phase of the case would be forgiven. This policy was officially withdrawn by the Service on January 10, 1952, after the King Subcommittee of the House Ways and Means Committee developed information that the policy was an "apt vehicle for some corruption in high places." A great deal of litigation also had arisen concerning the policy, which had never been reduced to precise guidelines. The initial purpose of the policy was an attempt to collect taxes from black marketing operations during the war years; these operations were so widespread that insufficient manpower existed to stop them by means of the criminal process alone. By 1952, the pressing nature of this problem had been substantially relieved. Whatever the precise reasons for the withdrawal of the policy, the fact is that it has been withdrawn, and, despite the urgings of the American Bar Association and other groups, has never been reinstated.

An informal voluntary disclosure policy does, however, exist. The outlines of it have never been discussed by the Service except in the chilling formulation of the Commissioner on August 23, 1959: [12]

---

12. Remarks of Commissioner of Internal Revenue Latham before the Section of Taxation, ABA, August 23, 1959 (Bulletin of Section of Taxation, October, 1959, at 16).

But in any event, it should be borne in mind that in determining whether or not an evader should be prosecuted, the existence of a true voluntary disclosure is an important element taken into consideration by Regional Counsel, Intelligence, and the Department of Justice. The Department of Justice has learned by what may be termed the "hard way" that evidence of a truly penitent spirit weighs heavily with a jury * * *. This does not mean that no evader who has made a voluntary disclosure will not be prosecuted. But it is, nevertheless, a very important element to be considered by you as practitioners * * *.

This statement appears to say that if the existence of the voluntary disclosure presents a substantial trial problem, the taxpayer might not be prosecuted. Confessions seldom present trial problems to the prosecution. It is certainly possible that voluntarily disclosing a failure to file tax returns, followed by prompt filing of those returns might make "wilfulness" difficult to prove under 26 USC 7203. As to tax evasion, however, voluntary disclosure may well amount to a confession, placing the taxpayer totally at the mercy of the special agent and other reviewers.

The experience of many practitioners in making voluntary disclosures, in both failure-to-file and evasion situations, indicates the policy is broader than the Commissioner's statement would indicate. * * * The Commissioner's statement may be somewhat of a bureaucratic hedge; it does not require him to make his determination on that basis only, but it may well preclude a taxpayer from demanding that he consider more than he announced he would consider.

* * *

VOLUNTARY DISCLOSURE—GENERALLY
* * *

The first question is whether what the taxpayer proposes to do constitutes, in fact, a voluntary disclosure. The Service has never specifically formulated a definition of voluntary disclosure. Under the policy as it existed between 1946 to 1952, it was reasonably clear that a voluntary disclosure, to be considered as such, had to be made prior to an audit or an investigation. The idea was that a taxpayer would come forth on his own, without any specific prompting by a Service action or Service personnel, and correct either his failure to file or his fraudulent filing. Once an action was directly taken by the Service either by notifying the taxpayer that he had been selected for audit, or by a contact by a revenue officer, revenue agent, or special agent, a voluntary disclosure was simply cooperation in the audit or investigation.

In interviewing the taxpayer, the circumstances of his recent motivation to set himself straight with the Service should be fully explored. If he has specific notice of an impending audit, for example, if he is a corporate officer who has been advised by the revenue agent conducting an audit of the corporation that his returns will be picked up when the corporate audit is completed, counsel should [not rely] upon a voluntary disclosure. If, however, the taxpayer has merely experienced sleepless nights, as is often the case in failure-to-file cases, he is in a position to make a voluntary disclosure.

Voluntary Disclosure—Failure to File a Return

Whether a taxpayer who has not filed his returns is in a position to make a voluntary disclosure or not, he must be advised to file his returns as quickly as possible. Even when the taxpayer receives a Notice of the Nonreceipt of Tax Return or a visit from a revenue officer, it is still possible to avoid a criminal investigation by the prompt filing of the returns. If the special agent is already in the case, the filing of the returns will still affect his determination of whether to recommend prosecution or not, because defenses to the criminal charge are obviously enhanced by prompt and accurate filing; arguments of negligence, inadvertence, mistake, disability, etc. are far more compelling if there has been prompt attention to correcting the problem. Instruction to spend whatever time or money is required to put the return together, whatever the status of the case, is the first and best advice in a failure-to-file case.

If the taxpayer has not been contacted by the Service, a voluntary disclosure of failure to file is almost always effective in preventing a criminal prosecution. The manner of making the voluntary disclosure is a source of some dispute among tax practitioners. Some suggest that the taxpayer should merely prepare returns and file the latest return in question, as soon as it is completed, with the Service, followed by the remaining returns when they are finished. This advice is practical if the returns are relatively simple and can be completed in a matter of a few weeks. Under such circumstances, counsel's notation of the date of the taxpayer's initial visit, his statement of his intention to file his returns and his request for counsel's advice as to the best manner of doing it, should be sufficient to preserve the voluntary disclosure, even though it is not technically made to the Service.

However, in our view, if the returns are complex or, as often happens, the taxpayer's records are incomplete, confused or scattered, some protection must be sought immediately to preserve a voluntary disclosure. It may be impossible to file accurate returns for months and the possibility of a revenue officer or a special agent contacting the taxpayer in the interim must be dealt with. We have made voluntary disclosures to a Group Chief of Intelligence, advising him that we are representing a taxpayer who has failed to file returns, that every effort will be made to file them as quickly as possible and that because we wish the returns to be as accurate as possible we will require a period of time to file them. We do not mention the taxpayer's name in so doing, but we advise the Group Chief that when the returns are completed, they will be filed with the Service and we will disclose the taxpayer's name to him.

Filing will usually result in an audit by a revenue agent with a special agent overseeing the work. If the returns are accurate, which they must be in any failure-to-file case, no prosecution will ordinarily be recommended, in our experience.

Voluntary Disclosure—Fraudulent Returns

"Wilfulness" in failing to file a return is obviously favorably affected by a voluntary disclosure and the filing of the returns. It indicates that the taxpayer was late, but at least willing to discharge his obligations; his failure to discharge the obligation would be the basis of the criminal charge. "Wilfulness" is much less affected by the voluntary disclosure and correction of a fraudulent return. Such cases seem more a confession with contrition. This type of disclosure constitutes a much weaker defense at trial, because whatever jury sympathy might be evoked, the facts disclosed may easily overcome the sympathy created. From the point of view of the Service, a confession of filing a false return confers more advantage than disadvantage in securing a conviction.

These cases require much more judgment than failure-to-file cases. However clean the voluntary disclosure was, if the taxpayer was a gambler, an underworld figure, or a politician who failed to report a bribe, or if the evasion was substantial or flagrant, the attractiveness of the case to the Service may outweigh any bureaucratic desire to leave the door open to contrite taxpayers. If, on the other hand, the taxpayer was a low-profile citizen who failed to report dividends or interest income, the Service's prosecution of such a man would be viewed as administratively self-defeating and probably not very palatable to a jury in any case.

In either situation, caution must be exercised. If a voluntary disclosure is made, it should contain only an admission as to the tax liability. It should remain silent on the question of "wilfulness." The best vehicle for making the disclosure is an amended return, rather than a formal contact with the Intelligence Division or any other Service personnel. The fact that an amended return was filed prior to any contact by the Service would create as many trial problems for the Service as a contrite confession and would avoid creating the adverse evidence engendered by a confession. Nor does it insure an audit or an investigation, because an amended return declaring more tax might be routinely processed. If it is routinely processed, the mere passage of time will tend to make it coalesce with the original return, if not in law, at least in the eyes of a special agent determining the trial problems of a particular case.

In preparing the amended return, accuracy and completeness are essential. An audit or an investigation may well result, and if it is determined that only half of the errors were corrected, the amended return is not simply useless, it is both another false return and a partial confession of the falsity of the original. We insist that a complete audit of the taxpayer's books and records be made prior to filing any amended return. The taxpayer himself must also be impressed with the grave dangers of any inaccuracy in filing such a return, because he may be the only one in a position to know whether a thorough review of his books and records will, in fact, give an accurate picture of his tax liability.

The classification of income in an amended return of this type is also a problem, if a confession is to be avoided. If the taxpayer has received bribes, it will not be helpful to return them as "proceeds from bribes." On the other hand, the proceeds cannot be added to other income categories, such as dividend or interest income, or attributed to a wholly fictitious category like "finder's fees," because such classifications would be or could be a violation of § 7206, Filing False and Fraudulent Returns. The most sensible category is "Miscellaneous Income," with the fifth amendment as a protection against further inquiry.

Quite often, classification will not be a problem, because the evasion will simply be an understatement of some category of income or an overstatement of some category of deductions. If an accurate but neutral category is difficult to find, or if the sums put into "Miscellaneous Income" begin to dwarf the original reported gross income, the question of making a voluntary disclosure in the first place should be actively reconsidered. The first consideration of a lawyer in a voluntary disclosure case must be maximizing the taxpayer's opportunities to escape criminal prosecution. If the objectives cannot be achieved by confessing the error and paying the tax, these should not be done, whatever the taxes owed may be.

A possible alternative to the amended return is the undisclosed taxpayer tax payment. After the taxpayer's tax liability is calculated, an attorney can make a payment to any District Director against the tax liability of an "undisclosed taxpayer" for the years in question. Such a payment constitutes the payment of the tax, and if the taxpayer is subsequently discovered and prosecuted, he can demonstrate that he has paid the tax in question. This is not as effective as an amended return, because proof of the manner of payment would carry with it the implication of a confession. Nevertheless, the fact would remain that the taxpayer voluntarily paid the tax without prompting from the Service, sought out an attorney qualified in the field to advise him as to the best manner of doing so, and followed his advice. In the meantime, the Service has the problem of finding out who the taxpayer is,[t] how and to what extent and in what categories he filed an inaccurate return, and in what manner the understatement was wilful.

*   *   *

NOTE

It is, at least as of the date of this writing, generally recognized in the tax field that a consistent "voluntary disclosure" practice has been applied by the government in declining to prosecute tax offenses in which a "true" voluntary disclosure was made. As noted in R. Fink, Tax Fraud, § 14.03 (Matthew Bender & Company, 1980):

> Despite the fact that the Service has withdrawn its "official" voluntary disclosure policy, an informal voluntary disclosure policy, albeit anemic, does survive.

> In its published statement regarding voluntary disclosure, the Service is careful to state that voluntary disclosure does not necessarily preclude prosecution. But there is, however, a substantial discrepancy between what the government says about a voluntary disclosure policy and what it has done in practice regarding "true" voluntary disclosures.

> What is a "true" voluntary disclosure? Absent a published policy, one cannot state with certainty the precise distinction between a disclosure which is voluntary and one which is not. As stated in Fink, supra:

> > *   *   * Until 1974, section 707 of the Regional Counsel Enforcement Division Manual entitled "Voluntary Disclosure" stated:

> > > Our initial inquiry is, of course, whether the disclosure was *timely*. We view a disclosure as timely if it is communicated to an officer or representative of the Service at a time when the Service is not actively considering information which is virtually certain to lead to evidence that the taxpayer committed a tax crime involving the matters disclosed *   *   *. A timely good faith disclosure will ordinarily be dispositive of a prosecution recommendation *   *   *.

> > Under this section, the timing of the disclosure was the crucial factor in determining whether the disclosure was voluntary. If the disclosure was made prior to an inquiry by the Internal Revenue Service, by definition, it was "voluntary." This time test had the advantages of simplicity and objectivity; what came first, the audit or the disclosure? However, in 1974, section 707 of the Regional Counsel Enforcement Manual was withdrawn and, although not formally announced, its objective definition of the term "voluntary" appears to have been replaced by a subjective standard which looks to both timeliness and motivation. Under such a definition, a disclosure by the taxpayer that preceded any inquiry from the

---

t. See Baird v. Koerner, excerpted above at pages 428–430, and Tillotson v. Boughner, 350 F.2d 663 (7th Cir. 1965), applying the attorney-client privilege in barring enforcement of IRS summonses which sought to obtain the identities of taxpayers who made anonymous tax payments through counsel.

Service would nevertheless not be deemed voluntary if it was "triggered" by an outside event which in effect forced the taxpayer to disclose his tax situation to the Service.

Even under this restrictive definition of the term "voluntary," the taxpayer need not be motivated by pure altruism for his disclosure to be deemed voluntary. Rather, the Service looks to whether or not the information disclosed would have otherwise come to its attention from another source and whether knowledge of this fact caused the taxpayer to come forth with his disclosure. What remains unclear is the nature of the requisite triggering event and the necessary degree of certainty that the event would have come to the Service's attention. While most practitioners agree that an investigation by another branch of the government is a negating event, it is much less certain whether a threat by a third party to become an informant against the taxpayer would qualify as such an event.

Can a taxpayer who makes a "true" voluntary disclosure be assured that he will not be prosecuted? After all, the taxpayer might well be making such a disclosure (which includes the filing of amended or delinquent tax returns containing admissions usable against him in any prosecution) in reliance upon the advice of a practitioner who was guided himself by the Service's consistent practice of nonprosecution. Perhaps significantly, as of this writing, the issue has not been decided by any court—a fact which may well indicate that there has not been a prosecution in such a case. But see, Plunkett v. Commissioner, 465 F.2d 299 (7th Cir. 1972) (alluding to a prosecution following a "voluntary disclosure"; however, the facts of the case indicate that the disclosure involved therein was far from a "true" voluntary disclosure).

C. MIRANDA–TYPE WARNINGS

MATHIS v. UNITED STATES

Supreme Court of the United States, 1968.
391 U.S. 1, 88 S.Ct. 1503, 20 L.Ed.2d 381.

Mr. Justice BLACK delivered the opinion of the Court.

Petitioner was convicted by a jury in a United States District Court on two counts charging that he knowingly filed false claims against the Government in violation of 18 U.S.C. § 287 and sentenced to 30 months' imprisonment on each count, the sentences to run concurrently. The frauds charged were claims for tax refunds growing out of petitioner's individual income taxes for 1960 and 1961. * * * A part of the evidence on which the conviction rested consisted of documents and oral statements obtained from petitioner by a government agent while petitioner was in prison serving a state sentence. Before eliciting this information, the government agent did not warn petitioner that any evidence he gave the Government could be used against him, and that he had a right to remain silent if he desired as well as a right to the presence of counsel and that if he was unable to afford counsel one would be appointed for him. At trial petitioner sought several times without success to have the judge hold hearings out of the presence of the jury to prove that his statements to the revenue agent were given without these warnings and should therefore not be used as evidence against him. For this contention he relied exclusively on our case of Miranda v. State of Arizona, 384 U.S. 436, 86 S.Ct. 1602, 16 L.Ed.2d 694 (1966). * * *

* * * The Government here seeks to escape application of the *Miranda* warnings on two arguments: (1) that these questions were asked as a part of a routine tax investigation where no criminal proceedings might even be brought, and (2) that the petitioner had not been put in jail by the officers questioning him, but was there for an entirely separate offense. These differences are too minor and shadowy to justify a departure from the well-considered conclusions of *Miranda* with reference to warnings to be given to a person held in custody.

It is true that a "routine tax investigation" may be initiated for the purpose of a civil action rather than criminal prosecution. To this extent tax investigations differ from investigations of murder, robbery, and other crimes. But tax investigations frequently lead to criminal prosecutions, just as the one here did. In fact, the last visit of the revenue agent to the jail to question petitioner took place only eight days before the full-fledged criminal investigation concededly began. And as the investigating revenue agent was compelled to admit, there was always the possibility during his investigation that his work would end up in a criminal prosecution. We reject the contention that tax investigations are immune from the *Miranda* requirements for warnings to be given a person in custody.

The Government also seeks to narrow the scope of the *Miranda* holding by making it applicable only to questioning one who is "in custody" in connection with the very case under investigation. There is no substance to such a distinction, and in effect it goes against the whole purpose of the *Miranda* decision which was designed to give meaningful protection to Fifth Amendment rights. We find nothing in the *Miranda* opinion which calls for a curtailment of the warnings to be given persons under interrogation by officers based on the reason why the person is in custody. In speaking of "custody" the language of the *Miranda* opinion is clear and unequivocal:

> "To summarize, we hold that when an individual is taken into custody or otherwise deprived of his freedom by the authorities in any significant way and is subjected to questioning, the privilege against self-incrimination is jeopardized." 384 U.S., at 478, 86 S.Ct., at 1630.

And the opinion goes on to say that the person so held must be given the warnings about his right to be silent and his right to have a lawyer.

Thus, the courts below were wrong in permitting the introduction of petitioner's self-incriminating evidence given without warning of his right to be silent and right to counsel. The cause is reversed and remanded for further proceedings consistent with this opinion. It is so ordered.

Reversed and remanded.

Mr. Justice WHITE, with whom Mr. Justice HARLAN and Mr. Justice STEWART join, dissenting.

*   *   *

*   *   * Although petitioner was confined, he was at the time of interrogation in familiar surroundings. Neither the record nor the Court suggests reasons why petitioner was "coerced" into answering Lawless' questions any more than is the citizen interviewed at home by a revenue agent or interviewed in a Revenue Service office to which citizens are requested to come for interviews. *   *   *

UNITED STATES v. HEFFNER

420 F.2d 809 (4th Cir. 1970).

WINTER, Circuit Judge.

*   *   *

Defendant assails his convictions, *inter alia,* upon the ground that they were obtained in part by the use of statements which had been obtained from him without compliance with Miranda v. Arizona, 384 U.S. 436, 86 S.Ct. 1602, 16 L.Ed.2d 799 (1966). We need not decide that issue, however, for we perceive a narrower ground which requires reversal.

[The defendant, described as "uneducated and emotionally disturbed", claimed a "ridiculously large number of exemptions" in order to prod the government into taking action to redress his grievance about an alleged conspiracy between various state and local officials and a business associate.] *   *   * In order to insure that the significance of this action was not missed, he wrote to the Internal Revenue Service (IRS) to notify them of his action and the reason for it.

Although his previous attempts to communicate with the government had gone without reply, this action evoked a response from IRS. Sometime in early 1967, Special Agents of the Intelligence Division of the IRS made a preliminary investigation, which disclosed that defendant was not entitled to the number of exemptions which he had claimed. The agents then arranged for an interview with defendant at a local IRS office. Defendant appeared voluntarily, without counsel, on February 19, 1967. He was advised by the agents that he was not required to furnish any information which might tend to incriminate him, and that anything he said could be used against him. Defendant, however, was not warned that the function of Special Agents of the Intelligence Division was to investigate the possibility of a criminal prosecution for tax fraud. Nor was he advised that he could retain counsel to assist him in the interview. There followed a question-and-answer interview which was recorded and subsequently transcribed. In this interview defendant seriously incriminated himself.

There followed a delay of over nine months. Then, on November 30, 1967, defendant was again invited to the IRS local office. Again, however, he was neither warned of the purpose of the investigation nor advised that he could retain counsel. Upon request, he signed a transcribed version of the interview of the previous February.

Over timely objection, the Special Agent's testimony concerning defendant's incriminating statements in the February interview was admitted at trial. We hold that this was reversible error.

On October 3, 1967, the IRS issued instructions to all Special Agents of the Intelligence Division. These instructions were reported in "IRS News Release No. 897, Oct. 3, 1967," reprinted in 7 CCH 1967 Stand.Fed.Tax Rep. § 6832:

> "In response to a number of inquiries, the Internal Revenue Service today described its procedure for protecting the Constitutional rights of persons suspected of criminal tax fraud, during all phases of its investigations.
>
> "Investigation of suspected criminal tax fraud is conducted by Special Agents of the IRS Intelligence Division. This function differs from the work of Revenue Agents and Tax Technicians who examine returns to determine the correct tax liability.
>
> "Instructions issued to IRS Special Agents go beyond most legal requirements to assure that persons are advised of their Constitutional rights.
>
> "On initial contact with a taxpayer, IRS Special Agents are *instructed* to produce their credentials and state: *'As a special agent, I have the function of investigating the possibility of criminal tax fraud.'*
>
> "If the potential criminal aspects of the matter are not resolved by preliminary inquiries and further investigation becomes necessary, the Special Agent is *required* to advise the taxpayer of his Constitutional rights to remain silent and to *retain counsel.*
>
>   *   *   *
>
> "IRS said although many Special Agents had in the past advised *persons, not in custody,* of their privilege to remain silent and retain counsel, the recently adopted procedures *insure uniformity in protecting the Constitutional rights of all persons."* (emphasis supplied.)

Thus, voluntarily IRS took upon itself the obligation to give taxpayers, before interrogation, notice that they were suspected of criminal tax fraud and the further obligation to give the full *Miranda* warnings before seeking incriminating statements.

The November 30 interview with defendant occurred almost two months after these instructions had been announced. Yet in two particulars the Special Agent failed to comply with them. First, he never warned the defendant that "[a]s a special agent, I have the function of investigating the possibility of criminal tax fraud." Second, the defendant was never advised that he could "retain counsel."

An agency of the government must scrupulously observe rules, regulations, or procedures which it has established. When it fails to do so, its action cannot stand and courts will strike it down. This doctrine was announced in United States ex rel. Accardi v. Shaughnessy, 347 U.S. 260, 74 S.Ct. 499, 98 L.Ed. 681 (1954). There, the Supreme Court vacated a deportation order of the Board of Immigration because the procedure leading to the order did not conform to the relevant regulations. The failure of the Board and of the Department of Justice to follow their own established procedures was held a violation of due process. The *Accardi* doctrine was subsequently applied by the Supreme Court in Service v. Dulles, 354 U.S. 363, 77 S. Ct. 1152, 1 L.Ed.2d 1403 (1959), and Vitarelli v. Seaton, 359 U.S. 535, 79 S.Ct. 968, 3 L.Ed.2d 1012 (1959), to vacate the discharges of government employees. And the *Accardi* doctrine has been utilized by the courts of appeal.

It is of no significance that the procedures or instructions which the IRS has established are more generous than the Constitution requires. In Service v. Dulles, supra, the Supreme Court vitiated the discharge of a foreign service officer because of the State Department's failure to follow its own procedures. The Court concluded that it made no difference that the State Department had no statutory or constitutional obligation to establish the procedure in question:

> While it is of course true that * * * the Secretary was not obligated to impose upon himself these more rigorous substantive and procedural standards, * * * having done so he could not, so long as the Regulations remained unchanged, proceed without regard to them.

354 U.S. at 388, 77 S.Ct. at 1165.

Nor does it matter that these IRS instructions to Special Agents were not promulgated in something formally labeled a "Regulation" or adopted with strict regard to the Administrative Procedure Act; the *Accardi* doctrine has a broader sweep. * * *

These cases are consistent with the doctrine's purpose to prevent the arbitrariness which is inherently characteristic of an agency's violation of its own procedures. As the Second Circuit said in Hammond v. Lenfest, 398 F.2d at 715, cited with approval in United States ex rel. Brooks v. Clifford, 409 F.2d at 706, departures from an agency's procedures "cannot be reconciled with the fundamental principle that ours is a government of laws, not men." The arbitrary character of such a departure is in no way ameliorated by the fact that the ignored procedure was enunciated as an instruction in a "News Release." The document purports to establish certain procedures which Special Agents are "required" to follow. Undoubtedly, a failure to comply is a rare event within the Intelligence Division—a fact which highlights the apparently inadvertent failure to give the required warnings here. Furthermore, a reversal here would not only have the salutary effect of encouraging IRS agents to observe their own procedures, but would assist the IRS in fulfilling its own important stated purpose in requiring that the warnings be given. For the announcement of the instructions was coupled with the justification that they would insure *uniformity* in protecting the Constitutional rights of all persons."

* * *

It matters not that part of the interrogation which produced defendant's admissions occurred in February before the IRS instructions were promulgated. As the IRS News Release stated, the purpose of the instruction was to "insure uniformity" in protecting all persons from unknowledgeable relinquishment of their rights. The obligation to fulfull this purpose by giving the *Miranda* warnings arose on November 30 when defendant was asked to sign the written transcript —and thus to create indisputable proof—of his previous damaging admissions. If given the warnings, perhaps defendant would have decided to sign without the advice of counsel. An equal possibility is that defendant, alerted to the prosecutorial purpose of the interview, would have requested counsel. In either event the uniformity which the IRS sought would have been achieved.

* * *

Reversed and remanded.

BECKWITH v. UNITED STATES

Supreme Court of the United States, 1976.
425 U.S. 341, 96 S.Ct. 1612, 48 L.Ed.2d 1.

Mr. Chief Justice BURGER delivered the opinion of the Court.

The important issue presented in this case is whether a special agent of the Internal Revenue Service, investigating potential criminal income tax violations, must, in an interview with a taxpayer, not in custody, give the warnings called for by this Court's decision in Miranda v. Arizona. * * *

* * *

Petitioner contends that the "entire starting point" for the criminal prosecution brought against him was secured from his own statements and disclosures during the interview with the Internal Revenue agents from the Intelligence Division. He correctly points out that cases are assigned to the Intelligence Division only when there is some indication of criminal fraud and that, especially since tax offenses rarely result in pretrial custody, the taxpayer is clearly the "focus" of a criminal investigation when a matter is assigned to the Intelligence Division. Given the complexity of the tax structure and the confusion on the part of taxpayers between the civil and criminal function of the Internal Revenue Service, such a confrontation, argues petitioner, places the taxpayer under "psychological restraints" which are the functional, and, therefore, the legal, equivalent of custody.

[Special Agents of the IRS investigating the defendant interviewed him at a private home where he occasionally stayed. While some warnings were given to the defendant, he was not given the actual *Miranda* warnings. The statements by the defendant were the subject of a suppression motion, which was denied, and were introduced at trial, leading to his conviction for attempted evasion. The Court of Appeals affirmed.|

An interview with Government agents in a situation such as the one shown by this record simply does not present the elements which the *Miranda* Court found so inherently coercive as to require its holding. Although the "focus" of an investigation may indeed have been on Beckwith at the time of the interview in the sense that it was his tax liability which was under scrutiny, he hardly found himself in the custodial situation described by the *Miranda* Court as the basis for its holding. *Miranda* implicitly defined "focus," for its purposes, as "questioning initiated by law enforcement officers *after* a person has been taken into custody or otherwise deprived of his freedom of action in any significant way." 384 U.S., at 444, 86 S.Ct., at 1612. (Emphasis supplied.) It may well be true, as petitioner contends that the "starting point" for the criminal prosecution was the information obtained from petitioner and the records exhibited by him. But this amounts to no more than saying that a tax return signed by a taxpayer can be the "starting point" for a prosecution.

We recognize, of course, that noncustodial interrogation might possibly in some situations, by virtue of some special circumstances, be characterized as one where "the behavior of * * * law enforcement officials was such as to overbear petitioner's will to resist and bring about confessions not freely self-determined * * *." Rogers v. Richmond, 365 U.S. 534, 544, 81 S.Ct. 735, 741, 5 L.Ed.2d 760, 768 (1961). * * * In the present case, however, as Chief

Judge Bazelon noted, "[t]he entire interview was free of coercion," 510 F.2d, at 743 (footnote omitted).

Accordingly, the judgment of the Court of Appeals is

Affirmed.

D. SEARCHES AND SEIZURES

LORD v. KELLEY

223 F.Supp. 684 (D.Mass.1963).

WYZANSKI, District Judge.

*   *   *

[Special Agent Flattery of the Internal Revenue Service went to the taxpayer's accountant (Donald R. Lord) and demanded production of the taxpayer's records in the accountant's possession. Lord complied as a result of threats by Flattery that a failure to produce the documents immediately would subject him to investigation or other proceedings initiated by the government.]

When he turned the records over to Flattery, Lord asked for some evidence to show his clients that he had yielded to compulsory process. Then, for the first time, Flattery served upon Lord the summons which, of course, was merely a command that at a date 12 days thereafter Lord should produce the records in Boston.

*   *   *

In the instant case no adequate basis for the seizure of the clients' records existed. There was no search warrant. The summons does not purport to be a warrant or its equivalent; and in any event it only commands Lord to bring the records with him to another city 12 days later than the date the records were seized. There is no statutory or common law authority under which Flattery claims, or ever did claim, the right to seize the records. There was no arrest to which the seizure could be incidental. Nor was consent effectively given to the taking of those records.

If it were necessary to decide the point, this Court would hold that Lord himself never gave consent. Intimidated by Flattery's statements and implied threats, Lord did not regard himself as having a free choice whether to allow Flattery to remove the records. When a special agent of the Internal Revenue Service tells an accountant who, so far as appears, is quite innocent of wrongdoing, that unless he turns over his clients' records and cooperates with the Internal Revenue Service the accountant will be in trouble, the agent is close to extortion. That Flattery did exercise unlawful pressure is proved by Lord's credible testimony.

But even if Lord had freely consented to allow Flattery to remove the records, that consent would have been of no significance.

Lord was an agent to whom the clients had entrusted their records for the sole purpose of preparing their tax returns. He lacked, and Flattery, as an experienced special agent familiar with the usual scope of an accountant's authority, could infer that Lord had not been given, express or implied power to deliver those records to third persons. Indeed Lord initially told Flattery that he had no authority from his clients to hand over documents. Yet, with this awareness, Flattery induced Lord in breach of his duty to his principals to deliver to the Internal Revenue Service their records.

Even if Flattery had not known of the limitation on Lord's authority, inasmuch as the delivery by Lord on Flattery's demand was beyond the scope of Lord's actual or apparent authority, such delivery was without the consent of the clients and the taking by Flattery constituted an unlawful seizure violative of the clients' rights under the Fourth Amendment.

A fortiori, inasmuch as Flattery was aware of the limitation of Lord's authority, Flattery's conduct amounted to a tortious conversion of the clients' records and a tortious inducement of breach of confidential contractual relations between the clients and the accountant. Hence, on that further ground, Flattery's acquisition of the clients' records was an unlawful seizure violative of the clients' rights under the Fourth Amendment.

Defendants make much of the asserted relevance of their statutory right as delegates of the Secretary of the Treasury "[t]o examine any books * * * material to such inquiry" in a tax matter. 26 U.S.C. § 7602. No doubt, by proper application to a Court of competent jurisdiction, the agents of the Internal Revenue Service could have that right enforced, even if the taxpayers' or clients' records were in the hands of an accountant. But here the suggestion is that, unarmed with any judicial or administrative order, without the consent of a taxpayer, and without giving him a chance to be heard, an Internal Revenue Service agent may examine any of the taxpayer's records, even those in the hands of an independent professional agent for a limited purpose. There is no need for this Court to rule upon that suggestion in the case at bar, for here the complaint is not against looking at the records before taking them, but at taking them and then looking.

The seizures having been unlawful, this Court must grant the prayer that there shall be returned to the clients, or, rather, their agent, Lord, their records. But it does not automatically follow that it is appropriate for this Court to suppress the use of these records in evidence at any future criminal or other trial.

It is to be recalled that Flattery knew of these records before they were delivered to him. More significantly, he had already signed a summons covering those records. Had he waited patiently, the records, no doubt, would have been produced in response either to the administrative summons or to a judicial order enforcing such administrative summons—for it is difficult to imagine any excuse for non-production of records so obviously relevant to a standard administrative procedure.

The only ground for suppressing the use of these records in evidence is not to allow the Government to gain advantage from violating the Bill of Rights and those high standards of fair play which should govern men entrusted with official power. The owner of the records is entitled to be as well off as if Flattery had not unlawfully seized those papers, but he is not entitlted to be any better off. He is not entitled to gain perpetual immunity from ever responding, in any future criminal proceeding or civil suit or administrative, tax inquiry, to an appropriate summons to produce those records which the tax statute require him to keep and which before the unlawful seizure the Government knew he had.

If it be argued that the Internal Revenue Service should be taught a lesson and penalized for Flattery's misconduct, there are many answers, of which the best is that exclusionary rules of evidence are designed not as punishment but to prevent the public prosecutor from using "dirty hands" to achieve a conviction. Moreover, Flattery has acknowledged his error in open court, and it is unlikely that, at least in this District, Internal Revenue Service special agents will soon again, without a warrant, subpoena, or summons, take from accountants their clients' records unless the Internal Revenue Service has proof that the accountants are acting with the express or implied authority of their principals.

So that the complainants may be as well off as, but not better off than, before the unlawful seizures, this Court's order will enjoin any defendant or any federal agent in concert with him from using in any proceeding, criminal, civil, or administrative, federal or state, information or clues derived from the records while Flattery and his associates in the Internal Revenue Service were holding them. But nothing in that injunction shall preclude the United States or its agents from requiring, by appropriate warrant, subpoena, summons, or other due process of law, a complainant to produce any record covered by the summons which Flattery signed before he made the unlawful seizure, or shall preclude the United States or its agents from using the contents of or clues furnished by a production later than November 19, 1963. If it be said that this Court's order calls to mind Southey's poem on the Battle of Blenheim,[u] the only response is that while the complainants may be disappointed that they have not won immunity, they have vindicated the right of an independent accountant's clients not to have their papers taken by arbitrary, high-handed methods of tax enforcement.

*   *   *

---

u. But what good came of it at last?   "Why that I cannot tell," said he
Quoth little Peterkin.   "But 'twas a famous victory."

RENTEX CORP. v. MESSINGER

570 F.2d 913 (10th Cir. 1978).

PER CURIAM.

The plaintiffs sought money damages, the return of personal property seized by the Internal Revenue Service, and to enjoin the use of the documents seized in any future criminal proceeding. The individual and the corporate plaintiffs assert a violation of Fourth Amendment rights.

The IRS was conducting an income tax investigation of plaintiff Rentex Corporation and also of plaintiff Larry Glist who was the "principal officer" of Rentex. The plaintiffs were in the business of selling lists of available residential rental property to persons looking for apartments or houses. The place of business of Mr. Glist was in Denver. The plaintiffs also sold franchises to persons wishing to engage in the same business. The office in Denver had four rooms including the private office of Mr. Glist. The business was a perfectly legitimate one, and no fraud or unfair dealing is asserted.

However, the IRS stated that it had information, apparently from former employees, that Mr. Glist kept a separate ledger at the Denver office as to payments received from franchisees. This was referred to as a "skim book," and was apparently used to record transactions not reported or not fully reported to the IRS. In any event, the IRS decided to put one of its agents in an undercover capacity into the Denver office as an employee. Thus Agent Messinger obtained employment at the Rentex office as a "rental counselor." He reported regularly to his superior in the IRS as to what he observed, heard, and read in the office. It is not necessary to describe this in detail as he had free access to the entire office. He read material on or in the desk and apparently elsewhere in the office. He asked questions of the other employees and of Mr. Glist as to how the business was conducted and how the franchises were handled. Mr. Messinger acted as an employee at Denver from October 18th until November 20th. He was then assigned to Boulder but "quit" on November 20th, and went to Denver to get his pay check. The next day he and Agent Kilpatrick filed affidavits with a magistrate and procured a search warrant for the Rentex office which was executed the same day. The agents thereby seized books and records.

As to the claim for damages, the record does not contain any evidence upon which a judgment for damages could be based. We thus agree with the conclusion reached on this point by the trial court. The personal property was returned to the plaintiffs, and the claim for return is moot.

The claim for injunctive relief to prevent the use of the material seized, or information derived from it at any criminal proceedings in the future must also fail. Such a matter cannot properly be litigated in a civil action under the circumstances here present. It was a premature claim and the matter had not yet reached the status of a justiciable controversy. There were, as we read the record, only possibilities. The claim could not be considered in the context of a particular indictment or information, and the impact of the search was thus speculative. The nature and scope of the criminal proceedings were not formed. If the criminal proceeding had proceeded to a point where the issue could be considered with reference to the particular charge, then the proper remedy would be a motion to suppress. This civil suit cannot be used in place of a motion to suppress nor to anticipate such a motion in advance of charges.

This opinion should not be taken in any way as an approval or disapproval of the use of undercover agents in legitimate businesses. Quite different considerations are there present which are not present in the drug cases, and we have not evaluated them.

Affirmed.

NOTE

Following the foregoing decision in Rentex Corp. v. Messinger, there was a conspiracy prosecution based upon the evidence derived from the undercover activity and the resulting search warrant. The trial court determined that the issues relating to the suppression of evidence could best be decided after a trial on the merits in which the substantive evidence could be placed in context and rulings could be made as to specific sources of evidence and any taint traced to particular evidence. As the trial progressed into its sixth day it became apparent that no reliable record could ever be made, and the trial court dismissed the conspiracy charge. As stated by the Tenth Circuit, in rejecting the government appeal and affirming the district court's dismissal of the conspiracy count:

Despite statements made by the judge to the jury and counsel defending the government prosecutors, we construe his remarks to find fault with the governmental agents' handling of the investigation and the prosecution of this case. He stated this was a "shambles of a trial," the government investigative files were scattered among many people and offices, the IRS lead agent was no longer with the government and there was not "the kind of disciplined development of the facts that is required." * * * Government agents had not listened to tapes which arguably contained exculpatory statements by defendants, and these had been represented to defense counsel and to the court as duplicates of tapes which contained no such material. The incident which seemed to precipitate the court finally granting the motion to dismiss due to preindictment delay involved the government providing tape recordings of the company meeting where the tax fraud scheme was discussed together with a written transcript which purportedly contained all pertinent remarks made at the meeting about the conspiracy. After five days of trial it was revealed that a government agent had cut off the transcription 82 seconds before a clearly exculpatory statement by one of the defendants.

Our examination of the record demonstrates that while there may have been no deliberate intention on the part of government agents to deceive, there was substantial fault by government representatives, enough to support dismissal for preindictment delay under the standards of [United States v.] Lovasco, [431 U.S. 783, 97 S.Ct. 2044, 52 L.Ed.2d 752 (1977)] and [United States v.] Marion, [404 U.S. 307, 92 S.Ct. 455, 30 L.Ed.2d 468 (1971)].

United States v. Glist, 594 F.2d 1374, 1378 (10th Cir. 1979).

ANDRESEN v. MARYLAND

Supreme Court of the United States, 1976.
427 U.S. 463, 96 S.Ct. 2737, 49 L.Ed.2d 627.

Mr. Justice BLACKMUN delivered the opinion of the Court.

This case presents the issue whether the introduction into evidence of a person's business records, seized during a search of his offices, violates the Fifth Amendment's command that "[n]o person * * * shall be compelled in any criminal case to be a witness against himself." We also must determine whether the particular searches and seizures here were "unreasonable" and thus violated the prohibition of the Fourth Amendment.

[State investigators concluded that there was probable cause to believe that an attorney specializing in real estate settlements had committed a fraud in connection with the sale of a specific lot in Montgomery County, Maryland. A warrant was applied for and obtained, permitting a search of the law office of the attorney and the office of his wholly-owned corporation for specified documents relating to the sale of the lot in question. The documents seized from the law office included drafts of documents and memoranda in the attorney's handwriting. The attorney was convicted on evidence including the seized documents.]

The Fifth Amendment, made applicable to the States by the Fourteenth Amendment, provides that "[n]o person * * * shall be compelled in any criminal case to be a witness against himself." As the Court often has noted, the development of this protection was in part a response to certain historical practices, such as ecclesiastical inquisitions and the proceedings of the Star Chamber, "which placed a premium on compelling subjects of the investigation to admit guilt from their own lips." Michigan v. Tucker, 417 U.S. 433, 440, 94 S.Ct. 2357, 2362, 41 L.Ed.2d 182 (1974). The "historic function" of the privilege has been to protect a " 'natural individual from compulsory incrimination through his own testimony or personal records.' " Bellis v. United States, 417 U.S. 85, 89–90, 94 S.Ct. 2179, 2184, 40 L.Ed. 2d 678 (1974), quoting from United States v. White, 322 U.S. 694, 701, 64 S.Ct. 1248, 1252, 88 L.Ed. 1542 (1944).

There is no question that the records seized from petitioner's offices and introduced against him were incriminating. Moreover, it is undisputed that some of these business records contain statements made by petitioner. The question, therefore, is whether the seizure of these business records, and their admission into evidence at his trial, compelled petitioner to testify against himself in violation of the Fifth Amendment. This question may be said to have been reserved in Warden v. Hayden, 387 U.S. 294, 302–303, 87 S.Ct. 1642, 1647–1648, 18 L.Ed.2d 782 (1967), and it was adverted to in United States v. Miller, 425 U.S. 435, 441 n. 3, 96 S.Ct. 1619, 1623, 48 L.Ed. 2d 71 (1976).

Petitioner contends that "the Fifth Amendment prohibition against compulsory self-incrimination applies as well to personal business papers seized from his offices as it does to the same papers being required to be produced under a subpoena." He bases his argument, naturally, on dicta in a number of cases which imply, or state, that the search for and seizure of a person's private papers violate the privilege against self-incrimination. Thus, in Boyd v. United States, 116 U.S. 616, 633, 6 S.Ct. 524, 534, 29 L.Ed. 746 (1886), the Court said: "[W]e have been unable to perceive that the seizure of a man's private books and papers to be used in evidence against him is substantially different from compelling him to be a witness against himself." And in Hale v. Henkel, 201 U.S. 43, 76, 26 S.Ct. 370, 379, 50 L.Ed. 652 (1906), it was observed that "the substance of the offense is the compulsory production of private papers, whether under a search warrant or a *subpoena duces tecum,* against which the person * * * is entitled to protection."

We do not agree, however, that these broad statements compel suppression of this petitioner's business records as a violation of the Fifth Amendment. In the very recent case of Fisher v. United States, 425 U.S. 391, 96 S.Ct. 1569, 48 L.Ed.2d 39 (1976), the Court held that an attorney's production, pursuant to a lawful summons, of his client's tax records in his hands did not violate the Fifth Amendment privilege of the taxpayer "because enforcement against a taxpayer's lawyer would not 'compel' the taxpayer to do anything—and certainly would not compel him to be a 'witness' against himself." Id., at 397, 96 S.Ct., at 1573. We recognized that the continued validity of the broad statements contained in some of the Court's earlier cases had been discredited by later opinions. In those earlier cases, the legal predicate for the inadmissibility of the evidence seized was a violation of the Fourth Amendment; the unlawfulness of the search and seizure was thought to supply the compulsion of the accused necessary to invoke the Fifth Amendment.[6] Compulsion of the accused

6. In Boyd v. United States, 116 U.S. 616, 6 S.Ct. 524, 29 L.Ed. 746 (1886), for example, it was held that the Government could not, consistently with the Fourth Amendment, obtain "mere evidence" from the accused; accordingly, a subpoena seeking "mere evidence" constituted compulsion of the accused against which he could invoke the Fifth Amendment. The "mere evidence" rule was overturned in Warden v. Hayden, 387 U. S. 294, 301–302, 87 S.Ct. 1642, 1647, 18 L.Ed.2d 782 (1967).

was also absent in Couch v. United States, 409 U.S. 322, 93 S.Ct. 611, 34 L.Ed.2d 548 (1973), where the Court held that a summons served on a taxpayer's accountant requiring him to produce the taxpayer's personal business records in his possession did not violate the taxpayer's Fifth Amendment rights.[7]

Similarly, in this case, petitioner was not asked to say or to do anything. The records seized contained statements that petitioner had voluntarily committed to writing. The search for and seizure of these records were conducted by law enforcement personnel. Finally, when these records were introduced at trial, they were authenticated by a handwriting expert, not by petitioner. Any compulsion of petitioner to speak, other than the inherent psychological pressure to respond at trial to unfavorable evidence, was not present.

This case thus falls within the principle stated by Mr. Justice Holmes: "A party is privileged from producing the evidence but not from its production." Johnson v. United States, 228 U.S. 457, 458, 33 S.Ct. 572, 57 L.Ed. 919 (1913). This principle recognizes that the protection afforded by the Self-Incrimination Clause of the Fifth Amendment "adheres basically to the person, not to information that may incriminate him." Couch v. United States, 409 U.S., at 328, 93 S.Ct. at 616. Thus, although the Fifth Amendment may protect an individual from complying with a subpoena for the production of his personal records in his possession because the very act of production may constitute a compulsory authentication of incriminating information, see Fisher v. United States, supra, a seizure of the same materials by law enforcement officers differs in a crucial respect—the individual against whom the search is directed is not required to aid in the discovery, production, or authentication of incriminating evidence.

A contrary determination that the seizure of a person's business records and their introduction into evidence at a criminal trial violates the Fifth Amendment, would undermine the principles an-

The "convergence theory" of the Fourth and Fifth Amendments is also illustrated by Agnello v. United States, 269 U.S. 20, 46 S.Ct. 4, 70 L. Ed. 145 (1925), where the seizure of contraband pursuant to a search not incident to arrest and otherwise unlawful in violation of the Fourth Amendment was held to permit the accused to invoke the Fifth Amendment when the Government sought to introduce this evidence in a criminal proceeding against him.

7. Petitioner relies on the statement in Couch that "possession bears the closest relationship to the personal compulsion forbidden by the Fifth Amendment," 409 U.S., at 331, 93 S. Ct. at 617, in support of his argument that possession of incriminating evidence itself supplies the predicate for invocation of the privilege. Couch, of course, was concerned with the production of documents pursuant to a summons directed to the accountant where there might have been a possibility of compulsory self-incrimination by the principal's implicit or explicit "testimony" that the documents were those identified in the summons. The risk of authentication is not present where the documents are seized pursuant to a search warrant.

nounced in earlier cases. Nearly a half century ago, in Marron v. United States, 275 U.S. 192, 48 S.Ct. 74, 72 L.Ed. 231 (1927), the Court upheld, against both Fourth and Fifth Amendment claims, the admission into evidence of business records seized during a search of the accused's illegal liquor business. And in Abel v. United States, 362 U.S. 217, 80 S.Ct. 683, 4 L.Ed.2d 668 (1960), the Court again upheld, against both Fourth and Fifth Amendment claims, the introduction into evidence at an espionage trial of false identity papers and a coded message seized during a search of the accused's hotel room. These cases recognize a general rule: "There is no special sanctity in papers, as distinguished from other forms of property, to render them immune from search and seizure, if only they fall within the scope of the principles of the cases in which other property may be seized, and if they be adequately described in the affidavit and warrant." Gouled v. United States, 255 U.S. 298, 309, 41 S.Ct. 261, 265, 65 L.Ed. 647 (1921).

Moreover, a contrary determination would prohibit the admission of evidence traditionally used in criminal cases and traditionally admissible despite the Fifth Amendment. For example, it would bar the admission of an accused's gambling records in a prosecution for gambling; a note given temporarily to a bank teller during a robbery and subsequently seized in the accused's automobile or home in a prosecution for bank robbery; and incriminating notes prepared, but not sent, by an accused in a kidnaping or blackmail prosecution.

We find a useful analogy to the Fifth Amendment question in those cases that deal with the "seizure" of oral communications. As the Court has explained, " '[t]he constitutional privilege against self-incrimination * * * is designed to prevent the use of legal process to force from the lips of the accused individual the evidence necessary to convict him or to force him to produce and authenticate any personal documents or effects that might incriminate him.' " Bellis v. United States, 417 U.S. at 88, 94 S.Ct. at 2183, quoting United States v. White, 322 U.S., at 698, 64 S.Ct. at 1251. The significant aspect of this principle was apparent and applied in Hoffa v. United States, 385 U.S. 293, 87 S.Ct. 408, 17 L.Ed.2d 374 (1966), where the Court rejected the contention that an informant's "seizure" of the accused's conversation with him, and his subsequent testimony at trial concerning that conversation, violated the Fifth Amendment. The rationale was that, although the accused's statements may have been elicited by the informant for the purpose of gathering evidence against him, they were made voluntarily. We see no reasoned distinction to be made between the compulsion upon the accused in that case and the compulsion in this one. In each, the communication, whether oral or written, was made voluntarily. The fact that seizure was contemporaneous with the communication in *Hoffa* but subsequent to the communication here does not affect the question whether the accused was compelled to speak.

Finally, we do not believe that permitting the introduction into evidence of a person's business records seized during an otherwise lawful search would offend or undermine any of the policies undergirding the privilege. Murphy v. Waterfront Comm'n, 378 U.S. 52, 55, 84 S.Ct. 1594, 1596, 12 L.Ed.2d 678 (1964).[8]

In this case, petitioner, at the time he recorded his communication, at the time of the search, and at the time the records were admitted at trial, was not subjected to "the cruel trilemma of self-accusation, perjury or contempt." Ibid. Indeed, he was never required to say or to do anything under penalty of sanction. Similarly, permitting the admission of the records in question does not convert our accusatorial system of justice into an inquisitorial system. "The requirement of specific charges, their proof beyond a reasonable doubt, the protection of the accused from confessions extorted through whatever form of police pressures, the right to a prompt hearing before a magistrate, the right to assistance of counsel, to be supplied by government when circumstances make it necessary, the duty to advise an accused of his constitutional rights—these are all characteristics of the accusatorial system and manifestations of its demands." Watts v. Indiana, 338 U.S. 49, 54, 69 S.Ct. 1347, 1350, 93 L.Ed. 1801 (1949). None of these attributes is endangered by the introduction of business records "independently secured through skillful investigation." Ibid. Further, the search for and seizure of business records pose no danger greater than that inherent in every search that evidence will be "elicited by inhumane treatment and abuses." 378 U.S., at 55, 84 S.Ct. at 1597. In this case, the statements seized were voluntarily committed to paper before the police arrived to search for them, and petitioner was not treated discourteously during the search. Also, the "good cause" to "disturb," ibid., petitioner was independently determined by the judge who issued the warrants; and the State bore the burden of executing them. Finally, there is no chance in this case, of petitioner's statements being self-deprecatory and untrustworthy because they were extracted from him—they were already in existence and had been made voluntarily.

8. "The privilege against self-incrimination * * * reflects many of our fundamental values and most noble aspirations: our unwillingness to subject those suspected of crime to the cruel trilemma of self-accusation, perjury or contempt; our preference for an accusatorial rather than an inquisitorial system of criminal justice; our fear that self-incriminating statements will be elicited by inhumane treatment and abuses; our sense of fair play which dictates 'a fair state-individual balance by requiring the government to leave the individual alone until good cause is shown for disturbing him and by requiring the government in its contest with the individual to shoulder the entire load' * * *; our respect for the inviolability of the human personality and of the right of each individual 'to a private enclave where he may lead a private life' * * *; our distrust of self-deprecatory statements; and our realization that the privilege, while sometimes 'a shelter to the guilty,' is often 'a protection to the innocent.' "

We recognize, of course, that the Fifth Amendment protects privacy to some extent. However, "the Court has never suggested that every invasion of privacy violates the privilege." Fisher v. United States, 425 U.S., at 399, 96 S.Ct., at 1575. Indeed, we recently held that unless incriminating testimony is "compelled," any invasion of privacy is outside the scope of the Fifth Amendment's protection, saying that "the Fifth Amendment protects against 'compelled self-incrimination, not [the disclosure of] private information.'" Id., at 401, 96 S.Ct., at 1576. Here, as we have already noted, petitioner was not compelled to testify in any manner.

Accordingly, we hold that the search of an individual's office for business records, their seizure, and subsequent introduction into evidence do not offend the Fifth Amendment's proscription that "[n]o person * * * shall be compelled in any criminal case to be a witness against himself."

We turn next to petitioner's contention that rights guaranteed him by the Fourth Amendment were violated because the descriptive terms of the search warrants were so broad as to make them impermissible "general" warrants, and because certain items were seized in violation of the principles of Warden v. Hayden, 387 U.S. 294, 87 S. Ct. 1642, 18 L.Ed.2d 782 (1967).

The specificity of the search warrants. Although petitioner concedes that the warrants for the most part were models of particularity, he contends that they were rendered fatally "general" by the addition, in each warrant, to the exhaustive list of particularly described documents, of the phrase "together with other fruits, instrumentalities and evidence of crime at this [time] unknown." The quoted language, it is argued, must be read in isolation and without reference to the rest of the long sentence at the end of which it appears. When read "properly," petitioner contends, it permits the search for and seizure of any evidence of any crime.

General warrants of course, are prohibited by the Fourth Amendment. "[T]he problem [posed by the general warrant] is not that of intrusion *per se*, but of a general, exploratory rummaging in a person's belongings * * *. [The Fourth Amendment addresses the problem] by requiring a 'particular description' of the things to be seized." Coolidge v. New Hampshire, 403 U.S. 443, 467, 91 S.Ct. 2022, 2038, 29 L.Ed.2d 564 (1971). This requirement "'makes general searches * * * impossible and prevents the seizure of one thing under a warrant describing another. As to what is to be taken, nothing is left to the discretion of the officer executing the warrant.'" Stanford v. Texas, 379 U.S. 476, 485, 85 S.Ct. 506, 512, 13 L.Ed. 2d 431 (1965), quoting Marron v. United States, 275 U.S., at 196, 48 S.Ct. at 76.

In this case we agree with the determination of the Court of Special Appeals of Maryland that the challenged phrase must be read as

authorizing only the search for and seizure of evidence relating to "the crime of false pretenses with respect to Lot 13T." The challenged phrase is not a separate sentence. Instead, it appears in each warrant at the end of a sentence containing a lengthy list of specified and particular items to be seized, all pertaining to Lot 13T. We think it clear from the context that the term "crime" in the warrants refers only to the crime of false pretenses with respect to the sale of Lot 13T. The "other fruits" clause is one of a series that follows the colon after the word "Maryland." All clauses in the series are limited by what precedes that colon, namely, "items pertaining to-
* * * lot 13, block T." The warrants, accordingly, did not authorize the executing officers to conduct a search for evidence of other crimes but only to search for and seize evidence relevant to the crime of false pretenses and Lot 13T.

*   *   *

The judgment of the Court of Special Appeals of Maryland is affirmed.

UNITED STATES v. CACERES

Supreme Court of the United States, 1979.
440 U.S. 741, 99 S.Ct. 1465, 59 L.Ed.2d 733.

Mr. Justice STEVENS delivered the opinion of the Court.

The question we granted certiorari to decide is whether evidence obtained in violation of Internal Revenue Service (IRS) regulations may be admitted at the criminal trial of a taxpayer accused of bribing an IRS agent.

*   *   *

I

Neither the Constitution nor any Act of Congress requires that official approval be secured before conversations are overheard or recorded by Government agents with the consent of one of the conversants. Such "consensual electronic surveillance" between taxpayers and IRS agents is, however, prohibited by Internal Revenue Service regulations unless appropriate prior authorization is obtained.

The Internal Revenue Service Manual sets forth in detail the procedures to be followed in obtaining such approvals. *   *   *

II

[On March 14, 1974, Agent Yee, auditing the Caceres' 1971 income tax returns, was offered a bribe by Mr. Caceres, reported the offer to his superiors, and prepared an affidavit describing it. In a further audit session on January 27, 1975, the bribe offer was repeated. Subsequent telephone conversations (properly monitored) led to a meeting on January 31, 1975. The IRS obtained "emergency approval" under its regulations to monitor that meeting. Similarly, on February 5, 1975, "emergency approval" was obtained to monitor a February 6, 1975 meeting. On February 11, 1975, the IRS obtained approval to monitor conversations for thirty days, which covered a meeting of that date. The District Court and the Court of Appeals both held that the two earlier meetings had not been monitored in accordance with IRS regulations.]

The Government does not challenge that conclusion. We are therefore presented with the question whether the tape recordings, and the testimony of the agents who monitored the January 31st and February 6th conversations, should be excluded because of the violation of the IRS regulations.

III

A court's duty to enforce an agency regulation is most evident when compliance with the regulation is mandated by the Constitution or federal law. In Bridges v. Wixon, 326 U.S. 135, 152–153, 65 S.Ct. 1443, 1451–1452, 89 L.Ed. 2103, for example, this Court held invalid a deportation ordered on the basis of statements which did not comply with the Immigration Service's rules requiring signatures and oaths, finding that the rules were designed "to afford [the alien] due process of law" by providing "safeguards against essentially unfair procedures."

In this case, however, unlike Bridges v. Wixon, the agency was not required by the Constitution or by statute to adopt any particular procedures or rules before engaging in consensual monitoring and recording. While Title III of the Omnibus Crime Control and Safe Streets Act of 1968, 18 U.S.C. § 2510 et seq., regulates electronic surveillance conducted without the consent of either party to a conversation, federal statutes impose no restrictions on recording a conversation with the consent of one of the conversants.

Nor does the Constitution protect the privacy of individuals in respondent's position. In Lopez v. United States, 373 U.S. 427, 439, 83 S.Ct. 1381, 1388, 10 L.Ed.2d 462, we held that the Fourth Amendment provided no protection to an individual against the recording of his statements by the IRS agent to whom he was speaking. In doing so, we repudiated any suggestion that the defendant had a "constitutional right to rely on possible flaws in the agent's memory, or to challenge the agent's credibility without being beset by corroborating evidence that is not susceptible of impeachment," concluding instead that "the risk that the petitioner took in offering a bribe to [the IRS agent] fairly included the risk that the offer would be accurately reproduced in court, whether by faultless memory or mechanical recording." The same analysis was applied in United States v. White, 401 U.S. 745, 91 S.Ct. 1122, 28 L.Ed.2d 453, to consensual monitoring and recording by means of a transmitter concealed on an informant's person, even though the defendant did not know that he was speaking with a government agent * * *.

Our decisions in *Lopez* and *White* demonstrate that the IRS was not required by the Constitution to adopt these regulations.[14] It is equally clear that the violations of agency regulations disclosed by this record do not raise any constitutional questions.

[The Court stated that there was no denial of equal protection just because others would be monitored only in compliance with the regulations. Moreover, the IRS officials' erroneous interpretation of the regulations in this case was not obviously wrong, so that there was no error of constitutional dimension. |

Nor is this a case in which the Due Process Clause is implicated because an individual has reasonably relied on agency regulations promulgated for his guidance or benefit and has suffered substantially because of their violation by the agency. Respondent cannot reasonably contend that he relied on the regulation, or that its breach had any effect on his conduct. He did not know that his conversations with Yee was being recorded without proper authority. He was, of course, prejudiced in the sense that he would be better off if all monitoring had been postponed until after the Deputy Assistant Attorney General's approval was obtained on February 11, 1975, but precisely the same prejudice would have ensued if the approval had been issued more promptly. For the record makes it perfectly clear that a delay in processing the request, rather than any doubt about its propriety or sufficiency, was the sole reason why advance authorization was not obtained before February 11.

Finally, the Administrative Procedure Act provides no grounds for judicial enforcement of the regulation violated in this case. The APA authorizes judicial review and invalidation of agency action that is arbitrary, capricious, an abuse of discretion or not in accordance

---

14. It does not necessarily follow, however, as a matter of either logic or law, that the agency had no duty to obey them. "Where the rights of individuals are affected, it is incumbent upon agencies to follow their own procedures. This is so even where the internal procedures are possibly more rigorous than otherwise would be required." Morton v. Ruiz, 415 U.S. 199, 235, 94 S.Ct. 1055, 1074, 39 L.Ed.2d 270. See, e. g., United States ex rel. Accardi v. Shaughnessy, 347 U.S. 260, 74 S.Ct. 499, 98 L.Ed. 681 (holding habeas corpus relief proper where government regulations "with the force and effect of law" governing the procedure to be followed in processing and passing upon an alien's application for suspension of deportation were not followed); Service v. Dulles, 354 U.S. 363, 77 S.Ct. 1152, 1 L.Ed.2d 1403 (invalidating Secretary of State's dismissal of an employee where regulations requiring approval of the Deputy Undersecretary and consultation of full record were not satisfied); Vitarelli v. Seaton, 359 U.S. 535, 79 S.Ct. 968, 3 L.Ed.2d 1012 (invalidating dismissal of Interior Department employee where regulations governing hearing procedures for national security dismissals were not followed). See also Yellin v. United States, 374 U.S. 109, 83 S.Ct. 1828, 10 L.Ed.2d 778 (reversing contempt conviction where congressional committee had not complied with its rules requiring it to consider a witness' request to be heard in executive session).

with law, as well as action taken "without observance of procedure required by law." Agency violations of their own regulations, whether or not also in violation of the Constitution, may well be inconsistent with the standards of agency action which the APA directs the courts to enforce. Indeed, some of our most important decisions holding agencies bound by their regulations have been in cases originally brought under the APA.

But this is not an APA case, and the remedy sought is not invalidation of the agency action. Rather, we are dealing with a criminal prosecution in which respondent seeks judicial enforcement of the agency regulations by means of the exclusionary rule. That rule has primarily rested on the judgment that the importance of deterring police conduct that may invade the constitutional rights of individuals throughout the community outweighs the importance of securing the conviction of the specific defendant on trial. In view of our conclusion that none of respondent's constitutional rights has been violated here, either by the actual recording or by the agency violation of its own regulations, our precedents enforcing the exclusionary rule to deter constitutional violations provide no support for the rule's application in this case.

IV

Respondent argues that the regulations concerning electronic eavesdropping, even though not required by the Constitution or by statute, are of such importance in safeguarding the privacy of the citizenry that a rigid exclusionary rule should be applied to all evidence obtained in violation of any of their provisions. We do not doubt the importance of these rules. Nevertheless, without pausing to evaluate the Government's challenge to our power to do so, we decline to adopt any rigid rule requiring federal courts to exclude any evidence obtained as a result of a violation of these rules.

* * * In the long run, it is far better to have rules like those contained in the IRS Manual, and to tolerate occasional erroneous administration of the kind displayed by this record, than either to have no rules except those mandated by statute, or to have them framed in a mere precatory form.

Nor can we accept respondent's further argument that even without a rigid rule of exclusion, his is a case in which evidence secured in violation of the agency regulation should be excluded on the basis of a more limited, individualized approach. Quite the contrary, this case exemplifies those situations in which evidence would *not* be excluded if a case-by-case approach were applied. The two conversations at issue here were recorded with the approval of the IRS officials in San Francisco and Washington. In an emergency situation, which the agents thought was present, this approval would have been sufficient. The agency action, while later found to be in violation of the regulations, nonetheless reflected a reasonable, good-faith attempt to comply in a situation in which no one questions that monitoring was appropriate and would have certainly received Justice Department authorization, had the request been received more promptly. In these circumstances, there is simply no reason why a court should exercise whatever discretion it may have to exclude evidence obtained in violation of the regulations.

The judgment of the Court of Appeals is

Reversed.

QUESTION

What effect, if any, does the Supreme Court's decision in *Caceres* have upon the principle enunciated in United States v. Heffner, page 599, above?

UNITED STATES v. PAYNER

Supreme Court of the United States, 1980.
447 U.S. 727, 100 S.Ct. 2439, 65 L.Ed.2d 468.

Mr. Justice POWELL delivered the opinion of the Court.

The question is whether the District Court properly suppressed the fruits of an unlawful search that did not invade the respondent's Fourth Amendment rights.

I

Respondent Jack Payner was indicted in September 1976 on a charge of falsifying his 1972 federal income tax return in violation of 18 U.S.C. § 1001. The indictment alleged that respondent denied maintaining a foreign bank account at a time when he knew that he had such an account at the Castle Bank and Trust Company of Nassau, Bahama Islands. The Government's case rested heavily on a loan guarantee agreement dated April 28, 1972, in which respondent pledged the funds in his Castle Bank account as security for a $100,000 loan.

Respondent waived his right to jury trial and moved to suppress the guarantee agreement. With the consent of the parties, the United States District Court for the Northern District of Ohio took evidence on the motion at a hearing consolidated with the trial on the merits. The court found respondent guilty as charged on the basis of all the evidence. The court also found, however, that the Government discovered the guarantee agreement by exploiting a flagrantly illegal search that occurred on January 15, 1973. The court therefore suppressed "all evidence introduced in the case by the Government with the exception of Jack Payner's 1972 tax return * * * and the related testimony." As the tax return alone was insufficient to demonstrate knowing falsification, the District Court set aside respondent's conviction.

The events leading up to the 1973 search are not in dispute. In 1965, the Internal Revenue Service launched an investigation into the financial activities of American citizens in the Bahamas. The project, known as "Operation Trade Winds," was headquartered in Jacksonville, Fla. Suspicion focused on the Castle Bank in 1972, when investigators learned that a suspected narcotics trafficker had an account there. Special Agent Richard Jaffe of the Jacksonville office asked Norman Casper, a private investigator and occasional informant, to learn what he could about the Castle Bank and its depositors. To that end, Casper cultivated his friendship with Castle Bank vice-president Michael Wolstencroft. Casper introduced Wolstencroft to Sybol Kennedy, a private investigator and former employee. When Casper discovered that the banker intended to spend a few days in Miami in January of 1973, he devised a scheme to gain access to the bank records he knew Wolstencroft would be carrying in his briefcase. Agent Jaffe approved the basic outline of the plan.

Wolstencroft arrived in Miami on January 15 and went directly to Kennedy's apartment. At about 7:30 p. m., the two left for dinner at a Key Biscayne restaurant. Shortly thereafter, Casper entered the apartment using a key supplied by Kennedy. He removed the briefcase and delivered it to Jaffe. While the agent supervised the copying of approximately 400 documents taken from the briefcase, a "lookout" observed Kennedy and Wolstencroft at dinner. The observer notified Casper when the pair left the restaurant, and the briefcase was replaced. The documents photographed that evening included papers evidencing a close working relationship between the Castle Bank and the Bank of Perrine, Fla. Subpoenas issued to the Bank of Perrine ultimately uncovered the loan guarantee agreement at issue in this case.

The District Court found that the United States, acting through Jaffe, "knowingly and willfully participated in the unlawful seizure of Michael Wolstencroft's briefcase. * * *" According to that court, "the Government affirmatively counsels its agents that the Fourth Amendment standing limitation permits them to purposefully conduct an unconstitutional search and seizure of one individual in order to obtain evidence against third parties * * *." The District Court also found that the documents seized from Wolstencroft provided the leads that ultimately led to the discovery of the critical loan guarantee agreement. Although the search did not impinge upon the respondent's Fourth Amendment rights, the District Court believed that the Due Process Clause of the Fifth Amendment and the inherent supervisory power of the federal courts required it to exclude evidence tainted by the Government's "knowing and purposeful *bad faith hostility* to any person's fundamental constitutional rights."

The Court of Appeals for the Sixth Circuit affirmed in a brief order endorsing the District Court's use of its supervisory power.

The Court of Appeals did not decide the due process question. We granted certiorari, and we now reverse.

II

This Court discussed the doctrine of "standing to invoke the [Fourth Amendment] exclusionary rule" in some detail last Term. Rakas v. Illinois, 439 U.S. 128, 138, 99 S.Ct. 421, 427–28, 58 L.Ed.2d 387 (1978). We reaffirmed the established rule that a court may not exclude evidence under the Fourth Amendment unless it finds that an unlawful search or seizure violated the defendant's own constitutional rights. And the defendant's Fourth Amendment rights are violated only when the challenged conduct invaded *his* legitimate expectation of privacy rather than that of a third party.

The foregoing authorities establish, as the District Court recognized, that respondent lacks standing under the Fourth Amendment to suppress the documents illegally seized from Wolstencroft. The Court of Appeals did not disturb the District Court's conclusion that "Jack Payner possessed no privacy interest in the Castle Bank documents that were seized from Wolstencroft." Nor do we. United States v. Miller, 425 U.S. 435, 96 S.Ct. 1619, 48 L.Ed.2d 71 (1976), established that a depositor has no expectation of privacy and thus no "protectable Fourth Amendment interest" in copies of checks and deposit slips retained by his bank. Nothing in the record supports a contrary conclusion in this case.[4]

The District Court and the Court of Appeals believed, however, that a federal court should use its supervisory power to suppress evidence tainted by gross illegalities that did not infringe the defendant's constitutional rights. The United States contends that this approach—as applied in this case—upsets the careful balance of interests embodied in the Fourth Amendment decisions of this Court. In the Government's view, such an extension of the supervisory power would enable federal courts to exercise a standardless discretion in their application of the exclusionary rule to enforce the Fourth Amendment. We agree with the Government.

III

We certainly can understand the District Court's commendable desire to deter deliberate intrusions into the privacy of persons who are unlikely to become defendants in a criminal prosecution. No court should condone the unconstitutional and possibly criminal behavior of those who planned and executed this "briefcase caper."[5]

4. We are not persuaded by respondent's suggestion that the Bahamian law of bank secrecy creates an expectation of privacy not present in United States v. Miller, 425 U.S. 435, 96 S.Ct. 1619, 48 L.Ed.2d 71 (1976). * * *

5. "The security of persons and property remains a fundamental value which law enforcement officers must respect. Nor should those who flout the rules escape unscathed." Alderman v. United States, 394 U.S. 165, 175, 89 S.Ct. 961, 967, 22 L.Ed.2d 176

Indeed, the decisions of this Court are replete with denunciations of willfully lawless activities undertaken in the name of law enforcement. But our cases also show that these unexceptional principles do not command the exclusion of evidence in every case of illegality. Instead, they must be weighed against the considerable harm that would flow from indiscriminate application of an exclusionary rule.

Thus, the exclusionary rule "has been restricted to those areas where its remedial objectives are most efficaciously served." United States v. Calandra, 414 U.S. 338, 348, 94 S.Ct. 613, 620, 38 L.Ed.2d 561 (1974). The Court has acknowledged that the suppression of probative but tainted evidence exacts a costly toll upon the ability of courts to ascertain the truth in a criminal case. E. g., Rakas v. Illinois, supra, 439 U.S., at 137–138, 99 S.Ct., at 427–28; Stone v. Powell, 428 U.S. 465, 489–491, 96 S.Ct. 3037, 3050–51, 49 L.Ed.2d 1067 (1976). Our cases have consistently recognized that unbending application of the exclusionary sanction to enforce ideals of governmental rectitude would impede unacceptably the truth-finding functions of judge and jury. E. g., Stone v. Powell, supra, 428 U.S., at 485–489, 96 S.Ct., at 3048–3050. After all, it is the defendant, and not the constable, who stands trial.

The same societal interests are at risk when a criminal defendant invokes the supervisory power to suppress evidence seized in violation of a third party's constitutional rights. The supervisory power is applied with some caution even when the defendant asserts a violation of his own rights.[7] In United States v. Caceres, 440 U.S. 741, 754–757, 99 S.Ct. 1465, 1473–74, 59 L.Ed.2d 733 (1979), we refused to exclude all evidence tainted by violations of an executive department's rules. And in Elkins v. United States, 364 U.S. 206, 216, 80 S.Ct.

(1969). We note that in 1976 Congress investigated the improprieties revealed in this record. * * * As a result, the Commissioner of Internal Revenue "called off" Operation Trade Winds. The Commissioner also adopted guidelines that require agents to instruct informants on the requirements of the law and to report known illegalities to a supervisory officer, who is in turn directed to notify appropriate state authorities. IRS Manual Supp. 9–21, §§ 9373.3(3), 9373.4 (Dec. 27, 1977). Although these measures appear on their face to be less positive than one might expect from an agency charged with upholding the law, they do indicate disapproval of the practices found to have been implemented in this case. We cannot assume that similar lawless conduct, if brought to the attention of responsible officials, would not be dealt with appropriately. To require in addition the suppression of highly probative evidence in a trial against a third party would penalize society unnecessarily.

7. Federal courts may use their supervisory power in some circumstances to exclude evidence taken from the *defendant* by "willful disobedience of law." McNabb v. United States, 318 U.S. 332, 345, 63 S.Ct. 608, 615, 87 L. Ed. 819 (1943). This Court has never held, however, that the supervisory power authorizes suppression of evidence obtained from third parties in violation of Constitution, statute or rule. The supervisory power merely permits federal courts to supervise "the administration of criminal justice" among the parties before the bar. McNabb v. United States, supra, 318 U.S., at 340, 63 S.Ct. 612.

1437, 1443, 4 L.Ed.2d 1669 (1960), the Court called for a restrained application of the supervisory power.

> "[A]ny apparent limitation upon the process of discovering truth in a federal trial ought to be imposed only upon the basis of considerations which outweigh the general need for untrammeled disclosure of competent and relevant evidence in a court of justice." 364 U.S., at 216, 80 S.Ct., at 1443.

We conclude that the supervisory power does not authorize a federal court to suppress otherwise admissible evidence on the ground that it was seized unlawfully from a third party not before the court. Our Fourth Amendment decisions have established beyond any doubt that the interest in deterring illegal searches does not justify the exclusion of tainted evidence at the instance of a party who was not the victim of the challenged practices. Rakas v. Illinois, supra, 439 U.S., at 137, 99 S.Ct., at 427. The values assigned to the competing interests do not change because a court has elected to analyze the question under the supervisory power instead of the Fourth Amendment. In either case, the need to deter the underlying conduct and the detrimental impact of excluding the evidence remain precisely the same.

The District Court erred, therefore, when it concluded that "society's interest in deterring [bad faith] conduct by exclusion outweigh[s] society's interest in furnishing the trier of fact with all relevant evidence." This reasoning, which the Court of Appeals affirmed, amounts to a substitution of individual judgment for the controlling decisions of this Court.[9] Were we to accept this use of the supervisory power, we would confer on the judiciary discretionary power to disregard the considered limitations of the law it is charged with enforcing. We hold that the supervisory power does not extend so far.

The judgment of the Court of Appeals is

Reversed.

Mr. Chief Justice BURGER, concurring.

I join the Court's opinion because Payner—whose guilt is not in doubt—cannot take advantage of the Government's violation of the constitutional rights of Wolstencroft, for he is not a party to this

---

9. The same difficulty attends respondent's claim to the protections of the Due Process Clause of the Fifth Amendment. The Court of Appeals expressly declined to consider the Due Process Clause. But even if we assume that the unlawful briefcase search was so outrageous as to offend fundamental " 'canons of decency and fairness,' " Rochin v. California, 342 U.S. 165, 169, 72 S.Ct. 205, 208, 96 L.Ed. 183 (1952), quoting Malinski v. New York, 324 U.S. 401, 417, 65 S.Ct. 781, 789, 89 L.Ed. 1029 (1945) (opinion of Frankfurter, J.), the fact remains that "[t]he limitations of the Due Process Clause * * * come into play only when the Government activity in question violates some protected right of the *defendant*," Hampton v. United States, 425 U.S., at 490, 96 S.Ct., at 1650 (plurality opinion).

case. The Court's opinion makes clear the reason for that sound rule.

Orderly government under our system of separate powers calls for internal self-restraint and discipline in each Branch; this Court has no general supervisory authority over operations of the Executive Branch, as it has with respect to the federal courts. I agree fully with the Court that the Exclusionary Rule is inapplicable to a case of this kind, but that should not be read as condoning the conduct of the IRS "private investigators" as disclosed by this record, or as approval of their evidence-gathering methods.

Mr. Justice MARSHALL, with whom Mr. Justice BRENNAN and Mr. Justice BLACKMUN join, dissenting.

The Court today holds that a federal court is unable to exercise its supervisory powers to prevent the use of evidence in a criminal prosecution in that court, even though that evidence was obtained through intentional illegal and unconstitutional conduct by agents of the United States, because the defendant does not satisfy the standing requirement of the Fourth Amendment. That holding effectively turns the standing rules created by this Court for assertions of Fourth Amendment violations into a sword to be used by the Government to permit it deliberately to invade one person's Fourth Amendment rights in order to obtain evidence against another person. Unlike the Court, I do not believe that the federal courts are unable to protect the integrity of the judicial system from such gross government misconduct.

* * *

Since the supervisory powers are exercised to protect the integrity of the *court,* rather than to vindicate the constitutional rights of the defendant, it is hard to see why the Court today bases its analysis entirely on Fourth Amendment standing rules. The point is that the federal judiciary should not be made accomplices to the crimes of Casper, Jaffe and others. The only way the IRS can benefit from the evidence it chose to obtain illegally is if the evidence is admitted at trial against persons such as Payner; that was the very point of the criminal exercise in the first place. If the IRS is permitted to obtain a conviction in federal court based almost entirely on that illegally obtained evidence and its fruits, then the judiciary has given full effect to the deliberate wrongdoings of the government. The federal court does indeed become the accomplice of the government lawbreaker, an accessory after the fact, for without judicial use of the evidence the "caper" would have been for nought. Such a pollution of the federal courts should not be permitted.[14]

14. It is simply not a sufficient cure for the Court to denounce the actions of the IRS while at the same time rewarding the Government for this conduct by permitting the IRS to use the evidence in the very manner which was the purpose of the illegal and unconstitutional activities.

It is particularly disturbing that the Court today chooses to allow the IRS deliberately to manipulate the standing rules of the Fourth Amendment to achieve its ends. As previously noted, the District Court found that "the Government affirmatively counsels its agents that the Fourth Amendment standing limitation permits them to purposefully conduct an unconstitutional search and seizure of one individual in order to obtain evidence against third parties, who are the real targets of the governmental intrusion, and that the IRS agents in this case acted, *and will act in the future,* according to that counsel." Whatever role those standing limitations may play, it is clear that they were never intended to be a sword to be used by the Government in its deliberate choice to sacrifice the constitutional rights of one person in order to prosecute another.

The Court's decision to engraft the standing limitations of the Fourth Amendment onto the exercise of supervisory powers is puzzling not only because it runs contrary to the major purpose behind the exercise of the supervisory powers—to protect the integrity of the court—but also because it appears to render the supervisory powers superfluous. In order to establish that suppression of evidence under the supervisory powers would be proper, the Court would also require Payner to establish a violation of his Fourth or Fifth Amendment rights, in which case suppression would flow directly from the Constitution. This approach is totally unfaithful to our prior supervisory power cases, which, contrary to the Court's suggestion, are not constitutional cases in disguise.

I also do not understand the basis for the Court's assertion that this is not a case in which the District Court was supervising the administration of justice "among the parties before the bar," ante, at n. 7, and therefore supervisory powers are inapplicable. Clearly the Government is before the bar. Equally clearly, the Government embarked on this deliberate pattern of lawless behavior for the express purpose of gaining evidence against persons such as Payner, so there can be no legitimate claim that the illegal actions are only tangentially related to the present prosecution. Instead, the Government misconduct is at the very heart of this case; without the evidence produced by the illegal conduct, there would have been no case at all, and Payner would never have been brought before the bar. This is simply not a case in which a federal court has attempted to exercise "general supervisory authority over operations of the Executive Branch," ante (BURGER, C. J., concurring). Rather, this is a case where the District Court refused to be made an accomplice to illegal conduct by the IRS by permitting the agency to use the proceeds of its crimes for the very purpose for which they were committed—to convict persons such as Payner.

Contrary to the Court's characterization, this is also not a case in which there has been "indiscriminate" or "unbending" application of the exclusionary rule. The District Court noted that "exclusion on the basis of supervisory power is only done as a last resort." That court concluded that suppression was proper only where there had been "purposefully illegal" conduct by the Government to obtain the evidence or where the Government's conduct was "motivated by an intentional bad faith hostility to a constitutional right." In this case, both those threshold requirements were met, and the District Court in addition concluded that absent suppression there was no deterrent to continued lawless conduct undertaken by the IRS to facilitate these types of prosecutions.[16] This is not "a 'chancellor's foot' veto [by the District Court] over law enforcement practices of which it did not approve," United States v. Russell, 411 U.S. 423, 435, 93 S.Ct. 1637, 36 L.Ed.2d 366 (1973); Hampton v. United States, 425 U.S. 484, 490, 96 S.Ct. 1646, 1650, 48 L.Ed.2d 113 (1976) (plurality opinion). As my Brother POWELL noted on a prior occasion, "[t]he fact that there is sometimes no sharply defined standard against which to make these judgments [of fundamental fairness] is not itself a sufficient reason to deny the federal judiciary's power to make them when warranted by the circumstances * * * * Nor do I despair of our ability in an appropriate case to identify appropriate standards for police practices without relying on the 'chancellor's' 'fastidious squeamishness or private sentimentalism.' " Hampton v. United States, supra, at 495, n. 6, 96 S.Ct., at 1652 (POWELL, J., concurring). That appropriate case has arrived, and the Court should prevent the Government from profiting by use in the federal courts of evidence deliberately obtained by illegal actions taken in bad-faith hostility to constitutional rights.

I would affirm the judgment of the Court of Appeals and suppress the fruits of the Government's illegal action under the Court's supervisory powers. Accordingly, I dissent.

E. GRAND JURY PROCEEDINGS

The federal grand jury, composed of 23 individuals, has an accusatory role in all felony tax prosecutions since, absent a waiver, the United States may prosecute a felony charge only upon an indictment returned by a grand jury.[v] The accusatory function of the grand jury in a tax case takes place at the termination of the investigation and after the various review procedures are concluded with a decision

---

16. There is no suggestion by the Government that any action has been taken against Casper, Jaffe or others for the conduct exposed in this case. The Court admits that the corrective measures taken by the IRS "appear on their face to be less positive than one might expect from an agency charged with upholding the law," ante, at n. 5. The District Court specifically found that the Government agents knew they were violating the Constitution at the time and that continued manipulation of the standing limitations of the Fourth Amendment by the IRS could be deterred only by suppression of the evidence.

v. I. e., voted for by at least twelve grand jurors.

to prosecute.   The grand jury may, however, have a material role during the investigative phase of a tax case.

A grand jury is utilized to investigate criminal tax offenses in essentially three categories of situations:

(1) Where the government attorney conducting a grand jury investigation of non-tax criminal violations uncovers during the course of that investigation evidence indicating that tax violations may also have been committed. The government attorney thus seeks to investigate jointly, through the grand jury, these alleged tax offenses, together with the non-tax violations that initially gave rise to the grand jury inquiry.

(2) Where the IRS has reached an impasse in its administrative investigation and recommends that a tax grand jury investigation be undertaken to develop evidence regarding the alleged criminal tax violations.

(3) Where the IRS has referred a case to the Department of Justice recommending prosecution and the Tax Division's evaluation affirms prosecution potential, but discloses the need for additional investigation.

When a tax investigation is conducted by a grand jury, IRS personnel act as "agents of the grand jury" in connection with the investigation. There will then be imposed upon the IRS personnel various safeguards to separate the Service (in its civil capacity) from the grand jury (a purely criminal investigatory body). The procedural safeguards imposed include the following: ʷ

(1) IRS personnel assisting in the investigation may not use administrative summonses.

(2) If a revenue agent is assigned to assist the government attorney conducting the grand jury investigation, he has no civil tax function. Neither special agents nor revenue agents may seek information for other than criminal purposes while assisting the grand jury.

(3) No disclosure may be made of information gathered during the grand jury process by IRS personnel for other than criminal purposes, and then only to IRS personnel who are assisting the government attorney conducting the grand jury investigation.

(4) All information gathered during the course of the grand jury investigation remains under the custody and control of the grand jury, the United States Attorney's Office (or Strike Force office) or the Tax Division—including, for example, documentary evidence and copies, information obtained from witnesses,

w.   See Internal Revenue Manual—Administration § 9267.3.

and information gathered from discussions with the government attorney conducting the investigation.

(5) All IRS personnel—even those on the highest management levels—who have had access to information obtained through the grand jury process must exclude themselves from involvement in non-grand jury matters concerning the individuals, entities, and subject matter of the grand jury investigation.

(6) Information gathered during the grand jury investigation may not be used for civil purposes without a court order pursuant to Rule 6(e) of the Federal Rules of Criminal Procedure specifically authorizing such civil use.

The procedures incident to a grand jury investigation are far more efficient for the prosecution and far more burdensome for the defense than those incident to an IRS investigation. There is no requirement that notice of any grand jury subpoena be provided to the subject of the investigation.[x] Witnesses must testify before the grand jury without the presence of their attorney and can consult with counsel only by leaving the room for this purpose. Objections to subpoenas and to questions asked of witnesses can be brought immediately to the attention of a district judge for prompt ruling, rather than made the subject of a separately instituted summons enforcement action. The investigation is controlled directly by government counsel rather than by agents of the IRS.

Because of the procedural differences, and because of the generally greater intensity and impact of a grand jury investigation, taxpayers frequently consider the possibility of objecting to the use of a grand jury to conduct what they argue is an administrative investigation. However, as noted by the following case, there is little that the subject of an investigation can do to tell the government how it must investigate his allegedly criminal activities.

IN RE GRAND JURY SUBPOENAS, APRIL, 1978, AT BALTIMORE

581 F.2d 1103 (4th Cir. 1978).

WINTER, Circuit Judge.

A corporation, currently under investigation by a federal grand jury for possible federal income tax violations, appeals from an order of the district court denying its motion to quash eight grand jury subpoenas and to terminate the grand jury proceedings. Alternatively, the corporation seeks a writ of mandamus directing the district court to hold an evidentiary hearing into allegations that the grand jury process has been abused by the Internal Revenue Service (IRS) and the Justice Department.

*   *   *

---

x. Compare IRC § 7609 regarding third-party recordkeeper summonses.

After actively auditing petitioner's tax returns for more than seven years, the Intelligence Division of the IRS, in May, 1977, initiated a criminal investigation of petitioner's tax returns for the years 1971–1975. At some point prior to April, 1978, the decision was made to discontinue the administrative investigation into petitioner's possible criminal liability and to rely instead on the investigatory powers of the federal grand jury. The decision to resort to a grand jury was made at or about the time that petitioner was successful in resisting judicial enforcement of several administrative summonses, but the record does not establish whether before or after. The grand jury investigation is currently proceeding, with five IRS agents who were previously involved in the administrative investigation (including one that has also been involved in the civil audits) now assisting the government attorney responsible for the grand jury investigation.

* * *

Petitioner contends that the powers of the grand jury have been purposely abused by the government and that, because of the government's improper motives, petitioner should not be subjected to the grand jury's process and the grand jury's investigation should be terminated. Briefly stated, petitioner alleges that IRS has had a history of using grand jury powers to further administrative investigations that have otherwise become stymied.[9]

Coupled with its allegation of historical abuse, petitioner points out that, in the instant case, IRS was conducting a joint civil and criminal investigation during which petitioner was served with a number of administrative summons with which it refused to comply, and this refusal was subsequently vindicated in an enforcement action in the district court. Shortly after IRS lost its court battle to enforce the summons, the grand jury investigation began, with several agents previously involved in the administrative investigation being deputized for the grand jury probe. The subpoenas then served by the grand jury sought the same materials which the IRS had unsuccessfully attempted to obtain administratively. Petitioner's inference, which it wants the district court to investigate, is that the

---

9. Petitioner attempts to substantiate this allegation by citing an IRS practice commonly known as an "open-ended grand jury" proceeding. As the relevant section (now withdrawn) of the Internal Revenue Manual states, it was established IRS practice, until recently, to recommend a grand jury investigation when an administrative *criminal* investigation had become stymied. The expectation was that the grand jury could develop evidence, unobtainable by administrative procedures, which would allow IRS to make a better informed recommendation to the Justice Department concerning whether or not to prosecute. See § 9267.4, Internal Revenue Manual (withdrawn November, 1977). While we express no opinion as to the propriety of this practice, we do not think that it lends support to the allegation that IRS regularly engaged in the use of the grand jury process for *civil* law enforcement purposes. Petitioner's other attempts at buttressing its suspicions of official wrongdoing are equally unconvincing.

grand jury is being used as a subterfuge for gaining access to documents IRS needs in its pending civil and criminal investigation of petitioner.

The district court refused to conduct the investigation into the government's motives and purposes which petitioner sought. Instead it relied on an affidavit by a Department of Justice attorney attesting to the government's good faith in utilizing the grand jury. We agree with the district court that no further inquiry is required at this juncture and that petitioner is subjected to no risk of substantial injury by allowing the grond jury to run its course.

A grand jury is convened to determine "if there is probable cause to believe that a crime has been committed * * *." Branzburg v. Hayes, 408 U.S. 665, 686, 92 S.Ct. 2646, 2659, 33 L.Ed.2d 626 (1972). If the powers of the grand jury, including the power to subpoena documents, are used, not for the purpose of criminal investigation but rather to gather evidence for civil enforcement, there exists an abuse of the grand jury process. United States v. Proctor & Gamble, 356 U.S. 677, 683, 78 S.Ct. 983, 2 L.Ed.2d 1077 (1958); Robert Hawthorne, Inc. v. Director of Internal Revenue, 406 F.Supp. 1098, 1118 (E.D.Pa.1976). This is the abuse alleged by petitioner. The precise question for decision is whether a district court is obliged to conduct a full evidentiary hearing at the time such abuse is alleged or whether it is sufficient, during the course of the grand jury's proceedings, to rely on the government's own affirmations of good faith.

We begin with the well-recognized principle that courts should not intervene in the grand jury process absent compelling reason. United States v. Dionisio, 410 U.S. 1, 16–18, 93 S.Ct. 764, 35 L.Ed.2d 67 (1973). Clearly, to hold an evidentiary hearing into prosecutorial motivation with an eye toward quashing otherwise lawfully issued subpoenas and even terminating the entire process would be substantial judicial intervention. Nonetheless, such intervention might well be required if it were the only means of protecting petitioner from the abuse he alleges. There is, however, a less drastic remedy in F. R.Crim.P. 6(e). The district court made clear that it considered Rule 6(e) to be adequate protection of petitioner's interests. We agree.

Rule 6(e), as recently amended, provides generally that materials secured by the grand jury in the course of its investigation shall not be disclosed except as authorized in subsection (2). As relevant here, subsection (2) allows disclosure to "an attorney for the government for use in the performance of [his] duty" and to "such government personnel as are deemed necessary by an attorney for the government to assist an attorney for the government in the performance of such attorney's duty to enforce Federal criminal law." In the instant case, the government attorney in charge of the grand jury investigation deemed it necessary to secure the assistance of several special agents with some knowledge of petitioner's business and tax affairs. Subsection (2) also imposes certain obligations with respect to disclosure to these necessary government personnel. Their names and a description of the materials disclosed must be provided to the district court. Each is under a duty not to "utilize that grand jury material for any purpose other than assisting the attorney for the government in the performance of such attorney's duty to enforce Federal criminal law." Each of the special agents involved in the instant case has been advised of his duty not to disclose grand jury material and that a breach of this duty is punishable by contempt.

This is not to say that the Audit Division, which is charged with civil enforcement of federal tax law, has no legitimate interest in the materials secured by the grand jury. "The Government does not sacrifice its interest in unpaid taxes just because a criminal prosecution begins." United States v. LaSalle Nat'l Bank, 437 U.S. 298, 311–312, 98 S.Ct. 2357, 2365, 57 L.Ed.2d 221 (1978). Congress recognized this in amending Rule 6(e) and, accordingly, authorized judicially supervised disclosure of grand jury materials to government agency personnel for civil law enforcement purposes.

Very recently one of the district courts in this circuit had occasion to supervise such a disclosure and in so doing developed certain criteria which the government must meet in order to secure a disclosure order under Rule 6(e)(2)(C)(i), where the purpose of such disclosure is to aid civil tax enforcement. *First,* the government must provide a general description of the materials sought in order to allow the court intelligently to determine if such materials are rationally related to an existing or contemplated civil proceeding. *Second,* and of particular importance to the instant case, the government must satisfy the court that "the grand jury proceeding has not been used as a subterfuge for obtaining records for a civil investigation or proceeding." In re December 1974 Term Grand Jury Investigation, 449 F.Supp. 743, 751 (D.Md.1978).

We fully agree that the government should be required to demonstrate its *bona fides* prior to obtaining a Rule 6(e)(2)(C) order. This showing is particularly important where the grand jury fails to return an indictment. In such case, the likelihood of improper use of the grand jury process is substantially greater, and an evidentiary hearing of the type now sought by petitioner might be necessary before disclosure is ordered.[15]

In sum, we are of the opinion that petitioner's legitimate interests are fully protected by Rule 6(e). Disclosure to the IRS for civil

---

15. The district court in In re December 1974 Term Grand Jury Investigation, supra, concluded that Congress intended that the government's application for a disclosure order be *ex parte* in the interests of grand jury secrecy. However, it is our view that the district court proceeding *ex parte* is not precluded from holding as extensive a hearing as is required to satisfy it that the government's use of the grand jury process has been proper.

enforcement purposes requires a court order predicated on a demonstration of good faith. Unauthorized disclosure is deterred by the threat of contempt.[16]

We emphasize that the extent of petitioner's legitimate interest is that the grand jury process not be used for the primary purpose of obtaining materials relevant only to civil liability. We do not think that petitioner has alleged a case entitling it to the issuance of a writ of mandamus; and, because of the safeguards contained in Rule 6(e) and the government's representations as to motivation, we conclude that an evidentiary hearing at this juncture is neither warranted nor required in order to protect this interest. A hearing of the sort sought by petitioner at this stage in the proceedings would result in both an unwarranted breach of grand jury secrecy and an unnecessary delay in its proceedings. Particularly with a limitations period soon to run, we agree with the district court that the proper course is to let the grand jury process continued unimpeded. If there does exist evidence of criminal liability, it is in society's interest that this be made available to the grand jury before limitations have run. Any abuse of the grand jury process can be dealt with effectively at another time and in another manner.

SECTION 4. CRIMINAL TAX PROSECUTIONS

A criminal tax prosecution is neither more nor less than a federal criminal case in which the alleged violation happens to pertain to the internal revenue laws. There are, nevertheless, a number of aspects of federal criminal practice which are of particular interest in the context of tax prosecutions. In this section, a sampling of these subjects is provided.

A. VENUE

The basic rule is that venue for a federal criminal prosecution lies in the district in which the offense was committed.[y] Hence, when the prosecution is for a failure to file returns, the prosecution may be brought in the district in which the return should have been filed. This could be either the district in which the legal residence or principal place of business of the taxpayer was located, or the district in which the IRS service center serving the accused taxpayer was located.[z] When the offense is attempted evasion, the filing of a false return or conspiracy, there may be more than one district in which

---

16. While we do not decide the issue, it may well be argued in an appropriate case that fairness would require exclusion of any evidence in a civil proceeding which had been improperly obtained from the grand jury.

y. Fed.R.Crim.P. 18.

z. See IRC § 6091.

the prosecution may be brought. Thus, in an evasion case, the prosecution might properly be brought in the district in which the false return was filed, signed or prepared, or in which some other affirmative act of fraud was committed. Moreover, in a conspiracy prosecution, proper venue lies in any district in which any overt act in furtherance of the conspiracy was committed.

Once a prosecution is brought in a district of proper venue, the defendant may seek to transfer the case to another district. As in all federal criminal cases, transfer in a tax case can be sought for plea and sentencing,[a] for prejudice in the district,[b] or "for the convenience of parties and witnesses, and in the interest of justice." [c] However, in certain tax prosecutions there is a special statutory provision which gives the defendant the right to have the case transferred to the district in which he was residing at the time the alleged offense was committed.[d] In cases in which the statute is applicable, the defendant's right to transfer is absolute.

UNITED STATES v. DeMARCO

394 F.Supp. 611 (D.D.C.1975).

GASCH, District Judge.

This matter came on for consideration on defendants' motion to transfer this cause to the district of defendants' residence, namely, in the case of Mr. DeMarco, Los Angeles (Central District of California), and Chicago, in the case of Mr. Newman (Northern District of Illinois).

Both defendants rely upon 18 U.S.C. § 3237(b), which reads as follows:

> (b) Notwithstanding subsection (a), where an offense is described in section 7203 of the Internal Revenue Code of 1954, or where an offense involves use of the mails and is an offense described in section 7201 or 7206(1), (2), or (5) of such Code (whether or not the offense is also described in another provision of law), and prosecution is begun in a judicial district other than the judicial district in which the defendant resides, he may upon motion filed in the district in which the prosecution is begun, elect to be tried in the district in which he was residing at the time the alleged offense was committed: *Provided,* That the motion is filed within twenty days after arraignment of the defendant upon indictment or information.

Eligibility for transfer thus depends on *four* conditions: (1) It must appear that the offense involves use of the mails; (2) and is an

a. Fed.R.Crim.P. 20(a).

b. Fed.R.Crim.P. 21(a).

c. Fed.R.Crim.P. 21(b).

d. 18 U.S.C.A. § 3237(b).

offense described in § 7201 or § 7206(1), (2), or (5) of the Internal Revenue Code of 1954 (Title 26, United States Code); (3) that prosecution was commenced in a district other than the district of defendant's residence; and (4) that the transfer motion was filed within twenty days after arraignment. As to conditions (3) and (4) there is no issue.

In an 18-page four-count indictment filed in this district by the Special Prosecutor of the Watergate Special Prosecution Force on the 19th of February, 1975, these defendants are charged with assisting former President Nixon and Mrs. Nixon in the preparation of certain false and fraudulent income tax returns, in that certain deductions claimed were based upon deductions allowable prior but not subsequent to July 26, 1969, and in an effort to claim such deductions, the date of the charitable contribution by Mr. Nixon of his papers was claimed to have been prior to that date. Mr. DeMarco was alleged to have been Mr. Nixon's tax attorney and Mr. Newman is alleged to have appraised the pre-Presidential papers which were the subject of the contribution.

Focusing, as we must, on Section 3237 of Title 18, it appears, insofar as Mr. Newman is concerned, that the offense described in Count One of the indictment involves use of the mails as follows. Overt acts 6 and 7 pertaining to Mr. Newman alleged

> 6. On or about April 6, 1970, RALPH G. NEWMAN had a telephone conversation with Mary Walton Livingston, who was then at the National Archives Building in the District of Columbia, in which RALPH G. NEWMAN stated that his March 27, 1970, letter to her would be the only deed of gift reflecting Richard M. Nixon's alleged 1969 gift of pre-Presidential papers which GSA would receive.

> 7. On or about April 6, 1970, RALPH G. NEWMAN caused an affidavit to be mailed to FRANK DEMARCO, JR. in which RALPH G. NEWMAN stated he had examined the pre-Presidential papers, described as "The Papers of Richard M. Nixon, Part II," from April 6 to April 8, 1969.

Other overt acts, in the conspiracy count, 3, 8, 12, 14 and 23 refer to the use of the mails.

The charging paragraph, numbered 12 of Count One of the indictment, alleges that Mr. Newman, Mr. DeMarco and another "did combine, conspire, confederate, and agree together and with each other to defraud the United States and an agency thereof by impairing, impeding, defeating, and obstructing the proper and lawful governmental functions and rights of the IRS to ascertain, compute, levy, assess, and collect Federal income taxes due and owing from Richard M. and Patricia R. Nixon."

The next charging paragraph, numbered 13, alleges in substance that the conspirators would cause to be made and transmitted false and fraudulent verbal and written statements and documents to IRS for the purpose of representing that prior to July 26, 1969, the effective date of legislation which reduced and restricted charitable tax deductions, that the gift of Mr. Nixon had occurred prior to the effective date of the act, whereas the gift occurred subsequent to the effective date of the act.

Paragraph 14, in substance, charges the conspirators with aiding, assisting, and counselling in matters arising under the Internal Revenue laws and advising in the preparation of documents, affidavits and returns which were fraudulent and false as to material matters. As the government concedes, this language charges a violation of 26 U. S.C. § 7206(2).

Thus it is plain that the thrust of the conspiracy count of the indictment is that these defendants are charged with aiding, assisting and counselling in the making of false and fraudulent income tax returns which had the effect of defrauding the United States of income taxes owed by Mr. and Mrs. Nixon.

Mr. Newman is charged with predating the appraisal and it would appear that the acts charged in the indictment fall under the eumerated Sections 7201 or 7206(2) of Title 26, United States Code, or both sections. Since Mr. Newman, a resident of Chicago, Illinois, has, through counsel, moved for transfer to his home district within the time prescribed by law, it appears that he is entitled to such transfer. As previously pointed out, one of the requirements of eligibility for transfer under Section 3237(b) is use of the mails. The government argues for a restricted interpretation of the phrase: "where the offense involves use of the mails." The government's contention is that this phrase means the mailing by the taxpayer of his return to IRS. The cases do not support such an interpretation. Section 7201 of Title 26, United States Code, refers to "any person" who willfully attempts in any manner to evade or defeat any tax imposed by this section. "Any" means all persons, not just the taxpayer whose returns are in issue. Likewise, the second enumerated section, 7206, refers to "any person" and subsection (2) specifically includes those who willfully aid or assist.

It is noted that Count Two charges Mr. Newman with the substantive violation of Section 7206(2) in that he "did aid and assist in the preparation and presentation of a document which was fraudulent and false as to a material matter, to wit, the aforesaid affidavit * * *." In overt acts 7, 8, 9, and 10 of Count One, the government alleges the mailing of this affidavit as well as its attachment to the Nixon 1969 tax return and the presentation to IRS.

Cases cited by counsel support his contention that under the circumstances alleged in this indictment, Mr. Newman is entitled to a transfer. United States v. Rosenberg, 226 F.Supp. 199 (S.D.Fla. 1964), like the instant case, included a count charging conspiracy under 18 U.S.C. § 371. The government argued there, as it argues here, that transfer to the district of Rosenberg's residence was not within the contemplation of Section 3237(b) for the reason that 18 U.S.C. § 371 (conspiracy) is not one of the enumerated offenses under the transfer section, 3237(b). In *Rosenberg,* as in the instant case, the substantive count did charge a violation of one of the enumerated sections, namely, Section 7201 of Title 26. The *Rosenberg* Court, at page 201, concluded:

> This Court concludes that said section 3237(b) gives each defendant the right to require the transfer of the conspiracy count, along with the substantive counts, to the judicial district of his residence. This result will make it possible for each defendant to be tried in a single prosecution in the judicial district where he resides. It will prevent dual or triple prosecutions at different times and places. Such a result appears to fulfill, rather than frustrate, the purpose of Congress. Moreover, such a result accords with reason, and facilitates the administration of justice.

In United States v. Kimble, 186 F.Supp. 616 (S.D.N.Y.1960), the indictment was in two counts, each charging a violation of Internal Revenue laws, but neither count specified one of the enumerated sections of the Internal Revenue Code. On the motion to transfer under the provisions of Section 3237(b) of Title 18, Judge McGohey of the Southern District of New York ruled, at page 618, that defendant was entitled to a transfer:

> Accordingly, the first test of availability must be, and I hold it is, the *nature and effect* of the acts alleged. If these would support a charge under one of the specified provisions of the Internal Revenue Code, it is immaterial that the charge is laid under another applicable provision of law. (Emphasis supplied.)

In United States v. Dalitz, 248 F.Supp. 238 (S.D.Cal., C.D.1965), as in the instant case, defendant was charged under the conspiracy statute, 18 U.S.C. § 371. This was a one-count indictment in which this was the only charge, but as the Court pointed out, the real offense concerns a violation of Section 7201 of the Internal Revenue Code, one of the enumerated sections set forth in 3237(b) of Title 18. In granting defendant's motion to transfer to the district of his residence, the Court noted at page 241:

> Since the real offense concerns a violation of Section 7201, the application of 18 U.S.C. § 3237(b) would appear appropriate to allow defendant Dalitz to undergo trial in Nevada, the state of his residence. The Indictment under the con-

spiracy section should not circumvent the intent of Congress in the circumstances.

The government relies on the *Wortman* case, 26 F.R.D. 183 (E. D.Ill.1960), which involved a conspiracy count under 18 U.S.C. § 371 and several substantive counts brought under enumerated sections. The substantive counts were ordered transferred to the district of the defendant's residence; however, the Court refused to transfer the conspiracy count, thus necessitating separate trials. The doctrine of the *Wortman* case was rejected in the *Rosenberg* case, supra. See also United States v. Dalitz, supra.

* * * To the extent that the *Wortman* case is contra to the result reached, the Court declines to follow it.

* * *

Count Two of the indictment charges Mr. Newman with violating Section 7206(2) of Title 26, in that the government contends that his appraisal and examination of the pre-Presidential papers occurred after July 26, 1969, and not before, as his affidavit states. Count One of the indictment, the conspiracy count, previously discussed, charges that Mr. Newman mailed this false affidavit to the defendant DeMarco in Los Angeles.

From the indictment itself, as well as the plain language of Section 3237 of Title 18, it appears that Mr. Newman is entitled to be tried in the district of his residence, namely, the Northern District of Illinois.

Mr. DeMarco has also moved for transfer to the district of his residence, the Central District of California. He, likewise, relies upon the plain meaning of Section 3237(b) of Title 18. The indictment, in overt act 23 of Count One, conspiracy, charges him with causing a memorandum to be mailed to the Joint Committee in which he stated that on April 21, 1969, Edward L. Morgan had signed a deed purporting to relate to the 1969 gift of papers by Richard M. Nixon. While it is clear that much of the conduct described in the indictment is alleged to have occurred in this district, the indictment does specify in overt act 8 that defendant DeMarco did cause the Newman affidavit, described in overt act 7, which had been mailed to DeMarco, to be affixed to the 1969 Nixon tax return.

The first count, which involves both Mr. DeMarco and Mr. Newman, and another, is a conspiracy count. Under the rules of conspiracy, once conspiracy is proved, the acts of each conspirator is attributable to the other. Therefore, any mailings attributable to other conspirators become the responsibility of the particular conspirator whose case the jury is considering. This may be considered by the Court in evaluating whether Section 3237(b) provides Mr. DeMarco with an appropriate basis for his motion. Mailings are either mentioned specifically or involved in overt acts numbered 3, 6, 7, 8, 9, 12,

14 and 23. Count Three charges Mr. DeMarco with making a false official statement in connection with the preparation of the Nixon tax returns in that it did represent that the charitable gift of Mr. Nixon was made in 1969 whereas it was made subsequent thereto and under conditions considerably more stringent which would have allowed a materially smaller tax deduction. Count Four involves the alleged actions by Mr. DeMarco calculated to influence, obstruct and impede and endeavor to influence, obstruct, and impede the investigation by the Joint Committee on Internal Revenue Taxation of the Congress of the United States. Count One clearly involves matters within the purview of Section 3237(b). Count Three involves matters within the purview of Section 3237(b) but Count Four does not. Since Mr. DeMarco has timely moved for a transfer of all counts to his home district, it seems to the Court that such action would be more clearly consonant with the interests of justice than to sever Count Four for trial in this district and transfer the other two counts for trial in Los Angeles. Accordingly, the three counts, One, Three, and Four involving Mr. DeMarco will be transferred to the Central District of California and Counts One and Two, involving Mr. Newman, will be transferred to the Northern District of Illinois.

So ordered.

B. SUPPRESSION OF EVIDENCE OBTAINED BY SUMMONS

UNITED STATES v. GENSER (GENSER I)

582 F.2d 292 (3d Cir. 1978).

BIGGS, Circuit Judge.

The appellants, defendants below, Genser and Forman, appeal from their convictions by a jury for violations of 18 U.S.C. §§ 2, 371, and 26 U.S.C. §§ 7201, 7206(1). *   *   *

The appellants assert *   *   * that the United States procured some of its evidence illegally by administrative summonses pursuant to 26 U.S.C. § 7602, and that the district court erred in not granting an evidentiary hearing. They contend that such a hearing would have demonstrated that the administrative summonses were issued after the United States had formed an intention to prosecute the appellants for income tax evasion and fraud, and that therefore the evidence procured by the summonses was tainted and should have been suppressed, and a new trial granted.

*   *   *

The question of whether or not a taxpayer has standing at trial to attack the validity of a § 7602 summons issued to third parties who voluntarily complied and to have the fruits of an improper summons excluded from evidence has never been addressed directly by this court or by the Supreme Court insofar as we are aware.   Previous decisions, of course, have established that the person to whom a summons is issued, whether the taxpayer or a third party, may refuse to comply with the summons, thereby triggering judicial enforcement proceedings at which the legality of the summons can be determined.   Reisman v. Caplin, [375 U.S. 440, 84 S.Ct. 508, 11 L. Ed.2d 459 (1964)]; Donaldson v. United States, [400 U.S. 517, 91 S. Ct. 534, 27 L.Ed.2d 580 (1971)].   Where an administrative summons is issued to a third party, such as the taxpayer's bank, the taxpayer may attempt to restrain voluntary compliance by the third party, assuming that he is aware of the issuance of the summons prior to compliance, and he may challenge the validity of the summons by attempting to intervene in the ensuing enforcement proceedings.

* * *

In United States v. McCarthy, 514 F.2d 368 (3d Cir. 1975), this court carefully formulated procedural guidelines for use in enforcement proceedings and provided that an evidentiary hearing is an "integral part" of those proceedings.   Under *McCarthy,* the IRS must be prepared to make a preliminary showing that the investigation has a legitimate purpose and that the inquiry may be relevant to that purpose, that the information sought is not already in the government's possession, and that the government has followed the procedural steps required by the Internal Revenue Code.   The burden then shifts to the opposing party to establish any defenses or to prove that enforcement would constitute an abuse of the court's process.   If the district court concludes that it cannot fairly decide the case on the record before it, it may direct further proceedings, including discovery, if requested.   Other courts have established similar procedures.

* * *

To make available the remedy of suppression to taxpayers in cases such as the present is merely to ensure governmental compliance with the principles enunciated in *Reisman, Donaldson,* [United States v.] LaSalle [Nat'l Bank, 437 U.S. 298, 98 S.Ct. 2357, 57 L.Ed.2d 221 (1977)], and the decisions of this circuit: the IRS, in issuing administrative summonses under § 7602, may not act outside its statutory authority by garnering evidence in furtherance of a solely criminal investigation.   If a court determines in the context of enforcement proceedings that a summons was illegally issued, it will deny enforcement of the summons.   That summons is no less illegal merely because it escapes detection at the investigatory stage.   The prophylactic principles which operate at the enforcement level are equally appropriate to the trial stage, and suppression is the only practical remedy at that point to cure the statutory abuse.

* * *

In sum, although § 7602 does not expressly restrict the power to issue a summons thereunder as long as the purpose is to ascertain the correctness of any return and the material sought is relevant to such inquiry, *LaSalle, Donaldson,* [United States v.] *Friedman,* [532 F.2d 928 (3d Cir. 1976)] and the other cited decisions have promulgated a judicial policy, binding on the IRS, to protect a taxpayer from any attempt on the part of the IRS to obtain evidence by use of § 7602 summonses after the IRS recommends prosecution to the Department of Justice or after the IRS has abandoned, in an institutional sense, the pursuit of civil tax determination or collection. The only effective remedy for violation of that policy is to require suppression of the evidence obtained as the evidentiary fruits of an illegal summons.

The government, however, contends that even if the remedy of suppression is theoretically available to taxpayers, it is an inappropriate remedy under the circumstances of this particular case. First, the government implies that appellants have "waived" any opportunity to seek suppression of evidence at trial because they knew of the issuance of at least some of the summonses prior to the third parties' compliance and failed to request the court to stay such compliance or to seek other judicial relief at that earlier stage. * * *

The record in the present case is unclear as to the precise extent of appellants' knowledge of the issuance of the summons. However, assuming *arguendo* that appellants were aware, prior to compliance, that summonses had been issued to third parties, and that they failed, intentionally or otherwise, to institute judicial proceedings at that point in time, we do not think this would necessarily bar them from asserting a claim of abuse of process at trial. *Donaldson* indicated that the taxpayer can attack the validity of the summons at trial even though he has sought and been denied intervention, and it nowhere suggests that the taxpayer must exhaust his pre-indictment remedies before proceeding at the trial level. We note, in addition, that the Senate Report accompanying 26 U.S.C. § 7609, added by the Tax Reform Act of 1976, which gives taxpayers the statutory right to stay voluntary compliance and intervene in enforcement proceedings, states that where the taxpayer *"does not request* the third party witness not to comply at this stage, *he would still be permitted to assert such defenses* as may be available to him with respect to any evidence obtained pursuant to the summons in any later court action in which the [taxpayer] was directly involved (i. e., affecting his tax liability or any criminal charges which might be brought) *to the same extent as may be permitted under present law."* Senate Report No. 94–938, 94th Cong., 2d Sess. 370 (1976) (emphasis added).[31]

31. Similarly, one 1975 Congressional report, summarizing the administrative procedures of the IRS prior to the 1976 Tax Reform Act, states that "a taxpayer who *either does not attempt to intervene or restrain or who fails in his attempt* may assert his rights when the government subsequently attempts to use the material against him." Report on Administrative Procedures of the Internal Revenue Service to the Administrative Conference of the United States (October 1975), 94th Cong., 2d Sess. 755 (emphasis added).

Finally, the government asserts that as a practical matter suppression would gain the appellants nothing in the case. According to the government, grand jury subpoenas were issued to many, if not all, of the same parties who received administrative summonses. The only "taint" which the appellants can claim, urges the government, is that the "identities" of the subpoenaed third parties were learned by way of the summonses and that the subpoenas were therefore fatally infected. The government stresses that this claim is without merit because the fact that the summonses themselves were served on the third parties demonstrates that their identities were already known prior to the issuance of the summonses. However, the present record contains no complete accounting of the dates of the subpoenas or the summonses or of the parties on whom they were served. While the government may well be able to establish an independent, "taint-free" basis for its evidence, see Wong Sun v. United States, 371 U.S. 471, 83 S.Ct. 407, 9 L.Ed.2d 441 (1963), we are unable to so conclude on the record before us. * * *

We thus conclude that the trial judge erred in ruling that as a matter of law appellants lacked standing to attack the validity of the summonses and to suppress the illegally obtained evidentiary fruits thereof. Accordingly, in light of the allegations of governmental impropriety raised by appellants, we shall remand this case to the district court with instructions to conduct an evidentiary hearing and to certify to this court its findings of fact and conclusions of law as to whether the government fully complied with the requirements of 26 U.S.C. § 7602, as judicially interpreted, and if not, whether suppression is required. * * *

* * *

C. THE USE OF SUMMARY WITNESSES

A criminal tax trial is, or should be, both a criminal and a tax trial. In many ways, however, the trial of a criminal tax charge is different from the run of the mill federal case. For example, there usually is no issue as to "who did it", or even as to what the defendant did or failed to do. Rather, the focus is normally upon the intention of the defendant in performing or failing to perform the acts in question. Moreover, the issue as to the defendant's state of mind frequently is directed to a broad period of time (usually years) rather than to a specific time and place.

While a criminal tax trial presents many (if not potentially all) of the situations which can arise in any complex criminal case, there is perhaps one circumstance which is characteristic of tax prosecutions. That is the appearance (generally at the conclusion of the government's case) of the summary expert witness.

UNITED STATES v. JOHNSON

Supreme Court of the United States, 1943.
319 U.S. 503, 63 S.Ct. 1233, 87 L.Ed. 1546.

Mr. Justice FRANKFURTER delivered the opinion of the Court.

* * *

* * * The court below held that the admission of the testimony of an expert witness regarding Johnson's income and expenditures during the disputed period invaded the jury's province. The witness gave computations based on substantially the entire evidence in the record as to Johnson's income. The Circuit Court of Appeals held that while undoubtedly "a proper hypothetical question could have been framed and propounded", in fact the witness was not giving answers on the basis of any assumption or hypothesis but as testimony on the "controverted issue" in the case. We do not so read the meaning of this testimony. No issue was withdrawn from the jury. The correctness or credibility of no materials underlying the expert's answers was even remotely foreclosed by the expert's testimony or withdrawn from proper independent determination by the jury. The judge's charge was so clear and correct that no objection was made, though, of course, there were exceptions to the refusal to grant the usual requests for charges that were either redundant or unduly particularized items of testimony. The worth of our jury system is constantly and properly extolled, but an argument such as that which we are rejecting tacitly assumes that juries are too stupid to see the drift of evidence. The jury in this case could not possibly have been misled into the notion that they must accept the calculations of the government expert any more than that they were bound by the calculations made by the defense's expert based on the defendants' assumptions of the case. So long as proper guidance by a trial court leaves the jury free to exercise its untrammeled judgment upon the worth and weight of testimony, and nothing is done to impair its freedom to bring in its verdict and not someone else's, we ought not be too finicky or fearful in allowing some discretion to trial judges in the conduct of a trial and in the appropriate submission of evidence within the general framework of familiar exclusionary rules.

* * *

STEELE v. UNITED STATES

222 F.2d 628 (5th Cir. 1955).

HUTCHESON, Chief Judge.

Found guilty on three counts of an indictment charging income tax evasion, * * * defendant is here with seven specifications of error, urging upon us that the judgment was so affected with prejudicial error that it may not stand.

* * *

Of these, in our opinion, the most egregious and prejudicial are those under the first specification of error, dealing with the two government exhibits. Government Exhibit 58 purports to be a computation of the Steeles' income on a net worth basis, and Government Exhibit 59 purports to be a computation of such income on the expenditures-available funds basis. These exhibits were the work of Travis Howard, a special agent of the Bureau of Internal Revenue. He was permitted to stay in the courtroom during the entire proceeding, heard all of the testimony of all of the Government witnesses, and was the last witness for the Government. He testified that he had not only heard all of the testimony of the Government witnesses but that he had examined all of the exhibits introduced by the Government and that Exhibits 58 and 59 were computations based upon all of the Government's case.

Since the computations contained in these exhibits purport to be a computation of all of the evidence of the government's witnesses, one of appellant's contentions against them is that there are omissions, interpretations and discrepancies between the record and these exhibits and a considerable portion of the testimony of the witnesses Jimmie Lim, Frank Garrett, Lawrence M. Curry, W. L. Bridges, Jr., and Mary Elizabeth Swanson. The exhibits were admitted in evidence over the objections of the defendant, and after the jury had retired for deliberation, the United States Attorney requested that Exhibits 58 and 59 be sent to the jury room. Defendant's counsel objected on the ground: that the exhibits were offered and accepted in evidence in a restricted manner; that they were essentially argumentative; and counsel's thought was that to send them to the jury would be to send there the argument and the interpretation of how Agent Howard felt each witness had testified; that, therefore, the exhibits were not really evidence which had gone before the jury but special pleas of the government and its witness. The objections were overruled and defendant excepted.

Recognizing that the Supreme Court, in United States v. Johnson, 319 U.S. 503, 63 S.Ct. 1233, 87 L.Ed. 1546, has held that in a prosecution for income tax evasion, an expert witness such as Howard purported to be may give testimony of his computation based upon substantially the entire evidence in the record as to the defendant's income, the defendant contends that the admission of these exhibits, their offer and reception in evidence, and their sending in to the jury room, were something entirely different from what was authorized in the *Johnson* case; that agent Howard did not merely attempt to summarize the testimony; that, on the contrary, he undertook to evaluate it, endeavoring to pass upon the reliability and credibility of certain witnesses and to determine what weight should be given their testimony, so that, by his testimony as to the exhibits and their sending to the jury, the Government, through its witness Howard, was enabled to invade, indeed to take over the province of, the jury.

* * *

For its answer to this specification, the Government first seeks to minimize the discrepancies between the testimony of the witnesses and the summaries of them set down in the exhibits, and, second, rests its case on United States v. Johnson, supra. We do not think that this will do, for this is not at all the *Johnson* case.

Putting aside the question of the significance and importance of the claimed discrepancies, we think that it was as clear error to admit to the so-called exhibits as it was to admit the seven charts prepared in the *Elder* case, Elder v. United States, 5 Cir., 213 F.2d 876, by and under the directions of the government witness, Buol, an agent of the Federal Bureau of Investigation. It is true that in that case, involving theft of automobiles, we held that the error, though a clear one, was not so prejudicial as to be reversible, but, as was carefully pointed out in the opinion, this was because of the nature of the case, the admitted accuracy of the charts, the simple and uncomplicated nature of the evidence attempted to be summarized, and the explicit and careful instructions given by the district judge.

Here, this is an entirely different kind of case, a prosecution under the net worth and expenditures method attended * * * with great difficulties and problems in reconciling the right of the government to convict on substantial evidence with the rights of the defendant to a fair trial in accordance with law, and the overall effect of the exhibits and their handling was far more clearly prejudicial.

The Government's reliance on the statement quoted in its brief from United States v. Johnson, supra [319 U.S. 503, 63 S.Ct. 1241], " * * * but an argument such as that which we are rejecting tacitly assumes that juries are too stupid to see the drift of evidence * * * ", is vain in this case. For the argument accepted here is very different from the one rejected there. Besides the quotation is no more than a more or less aimless and glittering generality having little, if any, real bearing upon the decision in that case and certainly none here.

* * *

The judgment is reversed and the cause is remanded for further and not inconsistent proceedings.

———

An introduction to criminal tax trials should not be limited to excerpts from appellate opinions. There must be some exposure to the trial itself. For this purpose, the authors have selected the examination of the prosecution summary witness in the case of United States v. Glist, et al., (Criminal Action No. 77–CR–29, D.Colo.1977) (indictment on conspiracy counts dismissed, mistrial declared on substantive tax counts).[e]

The effective criminal tax practitioner must combine the skills of an aggressive criminal defense lawyer with those of a sophisticated tax practitioner. There are precious few who have both of these talents, and none who combined them better than did Leslie H. Wald of Denver, Colorado, during his distinguished career. In the following excerpt from the trial transcript [f] one can observe the unique skill with which Mr. Wald effectively undermined the foundation of the prosecution's case.

The case involved allegations of income tax evasion by a corporation and its sole shareholder. The final prosecution witness was the summary expert through whom the government sought to introduce charts establishing corporate and individual income greatly in excess of the amounts reported on the tax returns in issue. The following excerpts from the voir dire and cross examination question three actions taken by the summary witness in preparing the Government's exhibits. First, the witness had considered the interest earned on funds deposited into a personal bank account as being interest income to both the corporation and the individual. Second, the witness assumed that certain funds deposited into the individual taxpayer's personal bank accounts were actually income of the corporate taxpayer. Third, the witness had neglected to take into account (as a non-taxable source of funds) some $40,000 of alleged loans which were reflected on balance sheets included on the corporate tax returns in issue.

UNITED STATES v. GLIST

Transcript of Trial Proceedings.
Criminal Action No. 77–CR–29 (D.Colo. April 8, 1977).

* * *

VOIR DIRE EXAMINATION

BY MR. WALD:

Q. In preparing these exhibits, was your approach to try to be completely neutral in putting all of the evidence in, whether it was favorable to the Government or favorable to the defense?

A. That was my approach.

Q. Where there was ambiguity or conflict in the testimony or in the documents, did you attempt in this exhibit to give the benefit of the doubt to the Government or to the taxpayer?

e. See United States v. Glist, 594 F.2d 1374 (10th Cir. 1979) (affirming dismissal of conspiracy counts).

f. The excerpt has been edited by the authors due to space limitations, but is fairly representative of the full transcript.

A.   To the taxpayer.

Q.   In all instances?

A.   Well I strived—as well as I could, to determine all the facts that were available. If there was a gray area or a doubtful area, I would have resolved it in favor of the taxpayer.

Q. Thank you. In going through or sitting here in the courtroom listening to the testimony, did you, in preparing these exhibits, pick and choose which to use and which to ignore?

A.   No, I think I examined all of them with the same degree of care.

Q.   I am troubled, Mr. [Expert], and I would like to pursue on voir dire whether we should have an either/or situation of admissibility of these exhibits. Either [the corporate chart] or [the personal chart] rather than both. Without going into the specifics of the exhibits which are not in evidence, but just as an example, which I feel is pervasive of both exhibits, you do have the bank deposits in the personal account of Chase Manhattan Bank listed in both exhibits; am I correct?

A.   That's true.

Q.   And you have the same figure for total deposits in the Chase Manhattan Bank's saving account, personal account for both the corporate income tax computation and the personal income tax computation?

A.   That is true.

Q.   Included in that figure, Mr. [Expert]—correct me if I am wrong—is interest earned on that account?

A.   Yes, that is true. The interest is included in the deposits.

Q.   As a CPA and/or lawyer, can you explain how both the corporation and the individual can earn interest income out of the same bank account?

A.   Well, all the bank deposits in the personal bank accounts are treated in these computations as corporation's income. That's the gross deposits including any interest that accumulated in the savings account. To the extent that the money was ultimately lodged in accounts which were in Mr. Glist's name as an individual, those deposits are being treated as distributions from the corporation to Mr. Glist, so that the money that Mr. Glist would have received as a result of that interest would come to him not in the form of interest but in dividends.

Q.   I don't think I am communicating sufficiently to have a responsive answer. Let me try again. I will do it in a hypothetical:

Assume $100 is deposited in the first personal savings account at Chase Manhattan Bank on April 1. Now, at that point in time, it's included in both [the corporate chart] and [the personal chart] as simultaneous income of the corporation and the individual, that same $100.

A.   The computations would have been made as of the end of the year. I don't think it is necessary to reach the precise time when that $100 income would have arisen.

Q.   I will rephrase it, because I think this is vital to whether it's either/or, or both. At the end of the year, you have an adding machine total of deposits in that account. At some point in time, it must be your representation that it was corporate income which was distributed to the individual in the form of a dividend; is that correct?

A.   Yes.

Q.   Okay. At what point in time, at the end of the year or as the deposit is made? Which?

A.   As the deposit is made.

Q.   All right. If a deposit of $100 then is made on April 1, and it is your concept that at that point it is corporate income coming in which is transmuted into a dividend to the individual, at that point in time it's an individual's money; isn't it?

A.   Yes.

Q.   Yes. Then, do you charge the corporation with interest on that $100 for the rest of the year?

A.   Well, the corporation isn't being charged with interest. This is interest income.

Q.   If the corporation owns it, I can understand your saying interest income attributable as taxable income to the corporation. If the corporation has made a dividend of it to the individual, I can understand you saying it's individual interest, taxable income of the individual. What I don't understand and what I am asking you to explain is how it could be both.

A.   I would just have to repeat the explanation I previously made.

Q.   All right. Let me ask this, to try to help out: Can you have dividend income to an individual without title to those funds passing from the corporation to the individual?

A.   When the distribution is made, you treat the title of the funds as passing to the individual.

Q.   All right. In your exhibit haven't you treated the corporation as earning interest income on those funds after you have treated it as passing to the individual?

A.   Well, no, I cannot—I cannot state that I have done that.

Q.   Well, explain how you haven't done it.

A.   The computations are made as of the end of the year.

Q. All right, sir. And as of the end of the year—and I am right with you and I will stay with you—as for the end of the year, you say that there were "X" dollars total deposited in that savings account?

A. Yes.

Q. And aren't you doubling up and saying with your left hand or the left side of your position, that the corporation owned all that money during the year and, therefore it was interest income to the corporation which we are going to tax them on, and with your right hand saying when that money went in there, it was the individual's income because the corporation transferred it to the individual as a dividend and therefore we are going to tax the individual with it? Isn't that what you have done?

A. Well, I think so.

Q. Is that right?

A. I think it is consistent with the whole computation.

MR. WALD: If Your Honor please, I would object to the admission of both [the corporate and the personal charts]. I would have no objection to the admission of either of them.

THE COURT: What's your position on the objection?

THE PROSECUTOR: I would oppose it.

THE COURT: [The personal chart] is excluded and [the corporate chart] is what we will talk about first. I don't know if we will ever get to [the personal chart]. Proceed on [the corporate chart].

DIRECT EXAMINATION (resumed)

BY THE PROSECUTOR:

Q. Mr. [Expert], I ask you to refer to [the corporate chart] which has been admitted into evidence and I will ask you now to explain to the jurors what that is, what that represents, how you arrive at it and state how you arrived at the final figures.

A. The bank deposits method which we have employed here starts out at Step 1 by adding up the total deposits into the bank accounts. And after you get the bank deposits added up you also have to add on any income which the taxpayer may have received, which did not get deposited into his bank account.

Then when you get total additions, it is necessary to go through everything, as painstakingly as possible, to determine anything which might be included in that gross amount which is not really subject to income treatment. For example, if there are transfers from one bank account to another, it's necessary to subtract out that transaction from the gross deposits.

Likewise, if the corporation had borrowed money during the year and deposited the loan proceeds into its bank account, we would have those loan proceeds but it would not be proper to treat the loan proceeds as income. So they have to be subtracted out. Similarly, if the corporation had received repayment during the taxable year of loans which it had made, those repayments would have to be taken out because they would be included in the bank deposits, assuming they had been deposited in the bank account, but would not be properly included in the corporation's income.

You also have to search for non-taxable sources of income and several of many, many examples are gifts, inheritance, bequeaths and these things have to be eliminated from the computation.

Then you have to allow the corporation the deductions which it would ordinarily be entitled to under the law, in order to arrive at the corporation's taxable income as we have determined it here.

Q. And is it your statement then that the summary which you just read from is based upon the evidence that was presented in this case; is that correct?

A. Yes.

*   *   *

CROSS EXAMINATION ON BEHALF OF DEFENDANT
GLIST

BY MR. WALD:

Q. In counting the deposits in the Wheat Ridge National Bank checking account in the name of the corporation, and the savings account in the name of the corporation, are you not making two assumptions, one on top of the other? One that all of these deposits are taxable income and, two, they are the corporation's taxable income.

A. I testified as a starting point to a bank deposit computation method, you add up the gross bank deposits and then you eliminate those things that you determine should not be included.

Q. Mr. [Expert], I understand the bank deposit method of computing or reconstructing income. What I am getting at is that that method bears no relation to the other question of who is the taxable entity that you are counting income against. Now, your witness that you have opposite the bank deposits is [the Special Agent], but didn't he testify, sir, that for the majority of the deposits, in the checking account and the savings account in the Wheat Ridge National Bank, that he didn't know what they were?

A. Well, I have examined enough of the exhibits myself, including the bank deposit slips, to know that that is a fact, that you cannot determine from looking at the bank deposits.

Q. Okay. And then all the exhibits do is to summarize or total the deposits and how much of them were in turn in currency and how much were in checks and that's where we stop and [the Special

Agent], as a witness, could not add any identification; is that correct?

A. In those instances, you cannot determine anything additional from the exhibits.

Q. Now, we go to that next column or paragraph, "Add on deposit receipts and cash expenditures," and this is where the question of who is the taxpayer that we are talking about deserves scrutiny by you. If you left out that area of amounts deposited to personal bank account, it would be quite a chunk out of this computation wouldn't it?

A. It would make a substantial change.

Q. Now, you did state on voir dire earlier this morning, that in looking at all the evidence, you didn't pick and choose. If it was a gray area, you resolved the benefit of the doubt for the taxpayer. How did you resolve the gray area, if it is a gray area, of amounts deposited to personal bank accounts or cash used to buy traveler's checks? Why didn't you resolve the benefit of the doubt that this was not the corporation's money?

A. I made a determination that that was not a gray area to me.

Q. I see. In spite of the fact that the accounts were in the name of the individual, and in spite of the fact that the traveler's checks were in the name of the individual?

A. Yes. That's right.

Q. And in spite of the fact that there is no evidence before this Court and jury that there was corporate money going into those personal accounts or that there was corporate money going into the traveler's checks? Am I correct?

A. I cannot agree with your contention that there is no evidence before the jury at this time.

Q. Well, I am using your witness that you cite for these personal accounts and traveler's checks. Who were your witnesses on the personal bank accounts? [The Special Agent]. And certainly he testified that he couldn't identify the nature or the source of the money in these accounts; the exhibits themselves that you have there do not do more than just give a transcript and the summary of what went into that bank account without any characterization. So neither your exhibits nor your witnesses support a determination that [the deposits into the personal account are] corporate money. Am I correct?

A. I will not agree that there is no evidence in the exhibits or in the testimony. As a matter of fact, it is my belief that there is evidence to support that.

Q. I will let the jury decide that. But it is your testimony that you resolved the personal accounts giving the benefit of the doubt to the corporate taxpayer?

A. I don't know—could you repeat that, please? I am sorry.

Q. I will pass. Let's go on to your second page, the first item and this is very important, Mr. [Expert], so listen carefully. You have allowed as non-taxable sources of deposits loans from the Wheat Ridge National Bank totaling $5,700, right?

A. Yes.

Q. Pick up Exhibit 21, please. I think you have that before you. That's the '72 corporate return.

A. Yes.

Q. Would you turn to page four of that return, the corporate balance sheet?

A. Yes.

Q. You have two columns, have you not, assets and liabilities of the corporation at the end of 1971 and at the end of '72, right?

A. Yes.

Q. Does it not show that there were $40,064 in new liabilities still outstanding at the end of '72 that weren't there at the beginning of '72?

A. Yes.

Q. Okay. And you have allowed in your computations less than $6,000 of loans and the corporate return which is in evidence reflects loans of $40,000. Are you picking and choosing which evidence to use in your computation, Mr. [Expert]?

A. I don't—I don't have any evidence of any loans being made to the corporation during 1972 other than these two from the Wheat Ridge National Bank. And I do not have any support or any idea as to what makes up this $40,000 figure.

Q. The $40,000 figure is on a return which is in evidence, isn't it?

A. Well—

Q. Isn't that as good evidence as some bank documents on two particular small loans and the testimony of [the Special Agent] that he found those?

A. I haven't been able to—I think—I should qualify this by saying with few exceptions, but with few exceptions, I haven't been able to determine where any of the figures on this return came from.

Q. Mr. [Expert], are you testifying as an investigator or as a summary and expert witness? If you are collating the testimony and evidence in this trial to present in a computation, why didn't you use that $40,000 figure as a liability available for redeposit rather than the less than $6,000 figure that you had in your computation.

A. Because I didn't have any idea what the $40,000 represented and I didn't see any evidence at all that there had been loans to the corporation in the amount of $40,000 during 1972 other than that one entry on the return.

Q. Mr. [Expert], this is a Government exhibit, isn't it?

A. It's the return that was filed by the taxpayer.

Q. But it is a Government exhibit?

A. Yes.

Q. All right. Let me summarize some areas that we covered and some areas that we haven't covered. You have made your own decision, I take it, that personal accounts should be counted as corporate income; is that correct or not correct?

A. My computation here treats the deposits into the personal bank accounts as income to [the corporation].

Q. And can you point to any evidence, documentary or testimonial, other than the citations that you have in your computations?

A. Well, the primary evidence goes to the fact that we do know that the corporation was realizing income from all over the country. We had the testimony—

Q. Oh, do we, Mr. [Expert]? Let me refresh your memory of the witnesses. Dealer after dealer on the witness stand, was he not asked by [the Prosecutor]: "And did you remit 10 percent to Mr. Glist?" And the answer was: "Yes, I remitted 10 percent to Mr. Glist." I heard no question or answer that referred to remitting 10 percent to the corporation, from these dealers, that I recall. Do you recall any that so testified?

A. Well, the income is taxable to the taxpayer that earned the money—

Q. And my question? Answer my question.

THE PROSECUTOR: Your Honor, I think the witness is trying. He keeps interrupting.

THE COURT: No. The witness is not answering the question.

BY MR. WALD:

Q. The witness testified he paid 10 percent to Mr. Glist. You end up attributing that to the corporation.

A. That's correct.

Q. Okay. The evidence says this, and then you make a judgment: "I am going to put it over here in the corporate end." Isn't that your judgment rather than the evidence?

A. I would have determined those remittances payable to Mr. Glist to be income to the corporation.

Q. Isn't that fact finding, which this jury is supposed to make?

A. Well, that is the way the computation is. The income is taxable to the earner of the income, not necessarily to who receives and deposits the money.

MR. WALD: If your honor please, on the basis of the answers elicited on cross-examination, I move to strike [the corporate chart], unless it's submitted in a corrected form. I don't believe that the witness has supported that this exhibit is a summary of the evidence in this trial. He has substituted his fact finding for that of the jury, and I move that the exhibit be stricken.

THE COURT: Obviously [the corporate chart] is based on an assumption, and that assumption is that all of the receipts and all of the deposits are corporate, right?

THE PROSECUTOR: Right.

THE COURT: And that assumption is an assumption, it is not in evidence.

THE PROSECUTOR: I don't know.

THE COURT: It is clear that the witness has gone beyond the evidence. It is clear that the witness has made findings of fact. What I am saying is that it is apparent that the witness had to make an assumption, and that assumption is not directly supported in the evidence. He assumed that everything, every dollar that was going into those accounts except for the ones that he deducted were corporate dollars, and where is that in the evidence? It's an assumption. It's one thing to present it in terms of: If you treat it this way, on that assumption, this could be the result. If you treat it as personal income, that's another result. And it is also clear that your summary witness had made interpretive findings as, for example, with respect to Exhibit 21 in saying, because there is no evidence to support $40,000 of new loans, you have to disregard it.

THE PROSECUTOR: Surely, the bank deposits method of proof is in essence an assumption. It is an indirect method of proof in which you gather as much as you can and, based upon that gathering, you make—

THE COURT: I know what it is. The [corporate chart] is stricken from evidence.

* * *

D. SENTENCING

The prosecution "party line" is to request some period of incarceration in virtually every tax case. It is urged that a mere fine and a period of probation is an ineffective deterrent to future potential tax violators. The hypothetical potential tax evader will be deterred, it is argued, only by fear of the loss of liberty. A fine, like a civil fraud penalty, is said to be considered an acceptable risk by those contemplating the commission of an economic crime.

The convicted tax offender, on the other hand, is frequently an individual with a spotless (sometimes exemplary) record, a pillar of the community and one who needs neither punishment nor rehabilitation. Moreover, when the offender is an attorney, accountant or other professional, the conviction alone may cause the forfeiture of his professional license. In any event, the defendant invariably has endured years of extensive investigation, anxiety and expense with the prospect of civil tax penalties and deficiencies in the immediate future. Defense counsel, normally, has a great deal on which to base an argument that there should be no period of incarceration.

Ultimately, of course, it is the judge who must determine the appropriate sentence to impose. The difficulty of the court's task and the element of fortuity inherent in the sentencing process are illustrated by the following two decisions by Judge Marvin Frankel of the Southern District of New York.

UNITED STATES v. PATERNO

375 F.Supp. 647 (S.D.N.Y.1974).

MEMORANDUM ON SENTENCING

FRANKEL, District Judge.

The two defendants have come on for sentencing upon a jury's solidly grounded verdict finding them guilty of cheating on taxes in substantial amounts over a period of years.

The defendants have lived to middle age with unblemished—indeed, highly respectable—reputations. They have been industrious. They have employed their business and professional skills for socially constructive ends. They were endowed with above average talents for the acquisition of money. Their community has rewarded them with esteem and with material blessings considerably more lavish than those fated for the common run. Nevertheless, though they were surely not driven to crime by the goads of want, these defendants found it agreeable to engage, over at least several years, in a knowing, wilful, blatant scheme to defraud their fellow citizens by defrauding the Treasury of the United States.

This is, in short, a species of criminal case sorrowfully familiar to everyone.

The sad question now, acknowledging our imperfect understanding and our still primitive instruments of criminal justice, has been the determination of a just sentence. Justice is owed, certainly, to the defendants themselves. We are not permitted, however, to overlook that the community for which the judge is commissioned to speak ultimately decides and demands and is owed justice too.

We start, if only fleetingly, with the sentencing provisions of the laws defendants have violated. Defendant Michael Paterno has been convicted on eight counts carrying, in literal but fantastic terms, total sentences of 34 years' imprisonment and $65,000 in fines. The comparably astronomic numbers for defendant George Denti are 28 years and $55,000. Paterno's corporation has also been convicted, and it faces theoretical fines totaling $50,000. Although our newspapers delight in publishing numbers like these, nobody supposes seriously that cumulative sentences remotely approaching them will actually be imposed.

The largest single question, faced at the threshold, is whether the individual defendants are to be imprisoned at all. Judges, armed with too much discretion in such matters, are sharply divided on this question. Many eschew prison sentences in such cases as unnecessary and cruelly retributive. Others, in seemingly growing numbers, recoil from the evident premise that "respectable" criminals—who have lived seemingly ordered lives, well groomed and well spoken, so much like ourselves after all—should be immunized for all that against the law's harsher sanctions.

The arguments against imprisonment cover a familiar gamut and include, at this particular time in our history, a special, if passing, supplement. The latter, to dispose of it first, runs this way: How can we condemn and imprison relatively obscure men for mere fraud upon their government when so many near the pinnacles of power have been discovered lately perjuring themselves, obstructing justice, burglarizing, spying, criminally giving and receiving forbidden monies for campaign uses, taking bribes, and otherwise betraying their trust? The question is not frivolous. But it has—it must have while we survive as what we mean to be—a clear answer.

We are, for much more than a slogan, a government "of the people." We are not led by any permanent or sacred aristocracy, anointed to do its will and pronounce our standards, good or evil, from on high. To be sure, we look for leadership to those we select. But we select them. And in the end it is we who govern them, not they who govern us. The Supreme Court recalled a while ago, and we do well never to forget, two bedrock propositions as James Madison declared them for us:

> "The people, not the government, possess the absolute sovereignty."

* * *

> "If we advert to the nature of Republican Government, we shall find that the censorial power is in the people over the Government, and not in the Government over the people." [1]

It follows that the missteps of people in power are no excuse, and should be no cause, for our breaking faith with ourselves.

1. New York Times Co. v. Sullivan, 376 U.S. 254, 274, 275, 84 S.Ct. 710, 723, 11 L.Ed.2d 686 (1964).

Wrongdoers in high places and low must be brought to justice. Whether or not that ideal is always achieved, our standards of law and morality are rooted in the people. If the poet may be paraphrased without disrespect, it is to ourselves, not the occasionally fallen star, that we must look for the preservation and steady renewal of our deepest values.

We come, then, to the more familiar appeals for leniency in cases like those here considered. The defendants, as has been mentioned, have led exemplary lives—at least so far as anyone knew until now. They have built stable families and a stable business. People of distinction and more humble workers in their enterprise write letters of sincere praise, devotion, and appreciation on their behalf. The defendants have not been ungenerous in dealing with friends, employees, family members, and charitable agencies. It may be predicted with reasonable confidence that neither defendant will ever run afoul of the law again. The fall from untarnished eminence in their communities has been an irreparably grievous blow. The defendants, in the frequently heard but still pertinent appeal, "have been punished enough already." It is urged earnestly that a sentence of imprisonment would serve ends only of vengeance.

These arguments, however familiar, have been weighed solemnly and attentively, as they deserve to be. But they are outweighed finally by the compelling premise that crimes of greed may be deterred in some measure only if the law's sanctions are seen to be genuine. It must be acknowledged that our belief in the possibility of general deterrence is far from a certainty.[2] The fact remains that this objective—the hope of discouraging others from criminal behavior by announcing credible threats of punishment—remains among the few widely accepted justifications for sending people to prison. The consensus tends to be especially strong with respect to deliberate, calculated crimes prompted by avarice. Common experience and introspective reports, from judges among others, support the view that the taxpayer may be expected in at least many cases to weigh the joys of freedom in the early springtime against the financial rewards of deceiving the tax collector. So-called crimes of passion are different, of course, and raise problems of different orders.

Thus, our acceptance of the prediction that the specific defendants here involved have "learned their lesson" is not enough to eliminate altogether the penalty of imprisonment contemplated and authorized by Congress. But it does not follow that the terms should be long ones. The defendants are in the eyes of the law first offenders. First offenders of all kinds, from the ghetto or anywhere else, are always serious candidates for non-custodial sentences. If, as the court holds, the goal of general deterrence plays a large role here, it is a

2. For a sensitive and enlightening appraisal of the subject, including the array of unresolved doubts, see F. Zimring and G. Hawkins, Deterrence (1973).

goal served by a sentence sufficient to be painful without being savage. It is pertinent to opine that the vision of closed penitentiary gates and cell doors for periods of months rather than years should be horror enough for the people at whom this deterrent message is aimed. ·

The point is a suitable one at which to note some of the excessively simple-minded things heard these days about distinctions between "white collar" and "ghetto" offenders. The danger of unfair discrimination is real, as this opinion has already noted. On the other hand, the subject is not usefully or justly treated by hasty sloganeering. It is not nearly fair to compare the businessman sent away for six months with the burglar given five years and to decide instantly that this exposes the venom of race or class or other outrageous prejudice. That prejudice too often exists as a matter not to be doubted. But the bare facts of the suggested contrast are scarcely enough to demonstrate it. A sentence for a crime ought to reflect a compendious judgment. Is the businessman a first offender and the burglar a fifth? Is the defendant dangerous—i. e., likely to repeat? Is there need and hope of rehabilitation? How frightening to the community is the particular crime? Such questions only suggest the range of proper inquiry before the court may pronounce judgment or that judgment may in turn be judged. Easy slogans and labels disserve the cause of understanding and fairness.

In the specific cases before us, the court has sought to reckon with every relevant circumstance. The defendants have been considered separately and together. The court has reviewed their evidently deep family commitments and the inevitably tragic impact of a prison sentence upon the innocent people who love and need the defendant. Attention has been paid to questions of health, of relative culpability, of seeming shares in illicit gains. An effort has been made, but without success, to divine mitigating factors explaining or in some measure lessening the enormity of the offenses. Defendants' crimes involved a calculated course of fraud extending over a period of years and involving substantial sums of money. In the final analysis, the case seems to be one of undiluted cupidity, not rendered more appealing by the bizarre theories of factual "explanation" defendants evidently gave to their counsel in attempts to obscure the brutal truths from court and jury.

Weighing all the facts together, the court has concluded that sentences must be imposed as follows:

(1) Michael Paterno, on each of Counts 1–8, a sentence of nine months in prison, the prison sentences to run concurrently. In addition, on each of said eight counts a fine of $2,500, to be cumulated, for a total fine of $20,000.

(2) For George Denti, a similar prison sentence—namely, on each of Counts 1–5 and 9, a sentence of nine months in prison to run

concurrently. In addition, on each of Counts 1–5, a fine of $2,000, to be cumulated, for a total fine of $10,000.

(3) For defendant corporation, Paterno & Sons, Inc., on each of Counts 1–5, a fine of $5,000, to be cumulated, for a total fine of $25,000.

UNITED STATES v. B_____

34 AFTR 2d 74–5968 (S.D.N.Y.1974).

FRANKEL, District Judge:

Memorandum On Reconsideration Of Sentence

On September 4, 1974, the defendant in this case, a young, perhaps excessively ambitious businessman was sentenced to a relatively short term of imprisonment for attempted tax evasion. Four days later, on Sunday, September 8, 1974, the 38th President of the United States granted "a full, free, and absolute pardon unto" the 37th President of the United States "for all offenses against the United States which he, Richard Nixon, has committed or may have committed or taken part in during the period from January 20, 1969, through August 9, 1974." The Court has been driven to consider whether these events may be thought to have any meaningful relationship to each other.

The defendant before us, who has moved for a reduction of sentence, is a man of 35. He has no prior criminal record. He is talented, gainfully employed, earnest in the discharge of family obligations, and entitled to hope for a bright, if unsung future. He needs no "rehabilitation" our prisons can offer. The likelihood that he will transgress again is as close to nil as we are ever able to predict. Vengeance, the greatest texts tell us, is not for mortal judges. Why, then, should such a man be sentenced to imprisonment at all?

That question, always the hardest at the time of sentencing, was not made easier by the fact that the crime in question (to which this defendant made a full public confession of guilt without a trial) occurred over six years ago. The court is told—and knows in any event—that the defendant has suffered terribly in the intervening years of investigation, uncertainty, legitimate efforts to avoid indictment, the awful decision to plead guilty, and the tortured wait for the day of sentence. This particular defendant, we learned on impressive professional opinion, has experienced some unique agonies under the emotional stress of criminal prosecution. "The defendant has suffered enough already" is a familiar refrain to sentencing judges. But the familiar is not necessarily contemptible. The refrain tells a true and moving story. Prison sentences are imposed in spite of it, for presumably weightier reasons, not because the griefs of a convicted defendant before sentence are unreal or trivial.

Why, indeed, then, a prison term for the defendant before us? The grounds, for better or worse, may be recalled briefly: First, *general deterrence,* to make good the law's threats in the hope or belief that others will be discouraged from evading their taxes by the force of this example among many others. Second, *denunciation*—the recording of society's outraged disapproval in a case so serious that, in the words of a classic statement, a lesser penalty would "depreciate the seriousness of the defendant's crime." [1]   Third, the demands of *equal justice;* increasingly, the courts recognize that "respectable" or so-called "white-collar" crimes must not be treated with benign understanding while our less privileged (and more driven) criminals serve long terms of imprisonment.[2]

But how do we reconcile the application of these factors to our unknown defendant with the pardon granted last Sunday? In the case at bar, the defendant's crime may have involved as much as $22,000 or as little as $2,500 in evaded taxes. The alleged crimes embraced by the recent pardon may have included among the lesser items tax evasion to the extent of several hundreds of thousands of dollars. This was, of course, a matter of relative insignificance in the course of conduct for which impeachment had been recommended. Comparison of the cases in terms of what might "depreciate the seriousness" of the crimes would, obviously, be ludicrous. And whatever is meant when we say comparisons are "odious," comparisons are the daily essence of our efforts to be fair and just.

As for "deterrence," the cases of the former President and of our defendant are different, to be sure, but scarcely in any way that makes it comfortable to be harsher here. We are entitled to hope that motivations loftier than the threat of prison will prompt our Presidents to execute the laws faithfully, to promote rather than obstruct justice, and to pay their taxes. But it remains a source of queasiness to realize that deterrence means "making examples" of people (despite the moral and philosophic questions that raises); that our relatively anonymous defendant adds at most to a mass of indistinguishable examples; and that the alleged example of a topmost leader has been declared immune by the pardoning power.

There remains, among others, the question whether and when a defendant has "suffered enough." Attempts to measure relative suffering must commonly be, and would be in the present case, grossly inexact and unsatisfactory. The agonies of a President, exposed to the glare of daily publicity and the thunder of daily attack, are surely unparalleled by the travails of inconspicuous people caught in the

1.   Model Penal Code § 7.01(1)(c).

2.   A lawyer-like concern for accuracy compels an aside to say that some current generalities about "white-collar" versus "blue-collar" crime are swift and uncritical. The armed robber and the embezzling bank official are likely to be dissimilar in an array of respects relevant to sentencing. But all of that is not vital for today's concerns in the case at hand.

criminal process. On the other hand, fairness would demand a huge discount for the corollary facts that a President has sought the spotlight, won it along with the trust and hopes of the people, and therefore became exposed to what he and everyone would expect when charges of betrayal were brought. A President falls from, because he has been raised to, a dizzying height. Except to know that the qualities of many experiences are magnified and deepened by his position, we have no scale on which to weigh his sorrows against those of others.

The question about "equal justice" continues to demand an answer. (The quoted phrase is essentially redundant, however familiar. The word "justice" must entail "equality," though that does not exhaust its meaning.) The ideal is not easily reached. It is not achieved by treating everyone alike. The objectives are to treat "like" people alike while taking account of meaningful differences. Where differences are discerned—between people or their crimes or both—they are to be justly appraised. The armed robber is different from the shoplifter, the impoverished thief from the rich embezzler, the professional from the passionate offender, the petty miscreant from the violator of high trust. The differences suggest value judgments as to where the weight of severity should fall.

Making the comparison thrust upon us by recent events, it is difficult to tip the balance against the defendant before us. And yet the answer must in the long run be clear: if people in high (or even the highest) places may on occasion have been dealt with too easily, the remedy is not to loosen the bonds of law and decency for all of us. It is to resolve that we shall strive more earnestly, at every level, to enforce the rule of equality under the law.

* * *

We adhere to those views for the long run. But the defendant before the court neither lives nor pleads in a long run. He is here short days after Sunday, September 8, 1974. Sentencing, as reflected in the title of a recent and valuable book,[3] is still an exceedingly "human process"—variable, disorderly, riddled with the uncertainties produced by the differences among well-meaning judges. The judges of this Circuit, assembled in annual conference, spent much of last weekend brooding together over the grim subject of "disparities" in sentencing. Many were driving home from those sessions when the pardon of last Sunday was announced. We may pretend, but can never manage entirely, to ignore such juxtapositions of events in the imposition of sentence. Certainly the people sentenced cannot be expected to ignore them. And we must pay attention to their sense of justice too—not least of all on the ground taught by Saint Thomas Aquinas, that the person punished must, if possible, be moved to "accept" his affliction as the joint consequence of a just system.

3. J. Hogarth, Sentencing as a Human Process (1971).

Having tried to review the many pertinent factors, and having recorded some major portions of the effort, the court concludes that in the particular case at bar, at this particular time, the prison sentence cannot justly be executed. Accordingly, the motion for reconsideration will be granted, execution of the prison sentence will be suspended, and defendant will be placed on probation for a period of one year in addition to paying the fine of $1,000 heretofore imposed.

SECTION 5. THE FIFTH AMENDMENT CLAIM ON TAX RETURNS

UNITED STATES v. SULLIVAN

Supreme Court of the United States, 1927.
274 U.S. 259, 47 S.Ct. 607, 71 L.Ed. 1037.

Mr. Justice HOLMES delivered the opinion of the Court.

The defendant in error was convicted of willfully refusing to make a return of his net income as required by the Revenue Act of 1921. The judgment was reversed by the Circuit Court of Appeals. A writ of certiorari was granted by this Court.

We may take it that the defendant had sufficient gross income to require a return under the statute unless he was exonerated by the fact that the whole or a large part of it was derived from business in violation of the National Prohibition Act (Comp.St. § 10138¼ et seq.). The Circuit Court of Appeals held that gains from illicit traffic in liquor were subject to the income tax, but that the Fifth Amendment to the Constitution protected the defendant from the requirement of a return.

The Court below was right in holding that the defendant's gains were subject to the tax. By section 213(a), gross income includes "gains, profits, and income derived from * * * the transaction of any business carried on for gain or profit, or gains or profits and income derived from any source whatever." * * * We see no reason to doubt the interpretation of the Act, or any reason why the fact that a business is unlawful should exempt it from paying the taxes that if lawful it would have to pay.

As the defendant's income was taxed, the statute of course required a return. In the decisions that this was contrary to the Constitution we are of opinion that the protection of the Fifth Amendment was pressed too far. If the form of return provided called for answers that the defendant was privileged from making he could have raised the objection in the return, but could not on that account refuse to make any return at all. We are not called on to decide what, if anything, he might have withheld. Most of the items warranted no complaint. It would be an extreme if not an extravagant application of the Fifth Amendment to say that it authorized a man to refuse to state the amount of his income because it had been made in crime. But if the defendant desired to test that or any other point he should have tested it in the return so that it could be passed upon. He could not draw a conjurer's circle around the whole matter by his own declaration that to write any word upon the government blank would bring him into danger of the law. In this case the defendant did not even make a declaration, he simply abstained from making a return.

It is urged that if a return were made the defendant would be entitled to deduct illegal expenses such as bribery. This by no means follows but it will be time enough to consider the question when a taxpayer has the temerity to raise it.

Judgment reversed.

GARNER v. UNITED STATES

Supreme Court of the United States, 1976.
424 U.S. 648, 96 S.Ct. 1178, 47 L.Ed.2d 370.

Mr. Justice POWELL delivered the opinion of the Court.

This case involves a nontax criminal prosecution in which the Government introduced petitioner's income tax returns to prove the offense against him. The question is whether the introduction of this evidence, over petitioner's Fifth Amendment objection, violated the privilege against compulsory self-incrimination when petitioner made the incriminating disclosures on his returns instead of then claiming the privilege.

*   *   *

II

In United States v. Sullivan, 274 U.S. 259, 47 S.Ct. 607, 71 L.Ed. 1037 (1927), the Court held that the privilege against compulsory self-incrimination is not a defense to prosecution for failing to file a return at all. But the Court indicated that the privilege could be claimed against specific disclosures sought on a return *   *   *.

Had Garner invoked the privilege against compulsory self-incrimination on his tax returns in lieu of supplying the information used against him, the Internal Revenue Service could have proceeded in either or both of two ways. First, the Service could have sought to have Garner criminally prosecuted under § 7203 of the Internal Revenue Code of 1954 (Code), 26 U.S.C. § 7203, which proscribes, among other things, the willful failure to make a return. Second, the Service could have sought to complete Garner's returns administratively "from [its] own knowledge and from such information as [it could] obtain through testimony or otherwise." 26 U.S.C. § 6020(b)(1). Section 7602(2) of the Code authorizes the Service in such circumstances to summon the taxpayer to appear and to produce records or give testimony. 26 U.S.C. § 7602(2). If Garner had persisted in his claim when summoned, the Service could have sued for enforcement in district court, subjecting Garner to the threat of the court's contempt power. 26 U.S.C. § 7604.

Given *Sullivan,* it cannot fairly be said that taxpayers are "volunteers" when they file their tax returns. The Government compels the filing of a return much as it compels, for example, the appearance of a "witness" [7] before a grand jury. The availability to the Service of § 7203 prosecutions and the summons procedure also induces taxpayers to disclose unprivileged information on their returns. The question, however, is whether the Government can be said to have compelled Garner to incriminate himself with regard to specific disclosures made on his return when he could have claimed the Fifth Amendment privilege instead.

III

We start from the fundamental proposition:

"[A] witness protected by the privilege may rightfully refuse to answer unless and until he is protected at least against the use of his compelled answers and evidence derived therefrom in any subsequent criminal case in which he is a defendant. * * * Absent such protection, if he is nevertheless compelled to answer, his answers are inadmissible against him in a later criminal prosecution. * * * " Lefkowitz v. Turley, 414 U.S. 70, 78, 94 S.Ct. 316, 322, 38 L.Ed. 2d 274, 282 (1973).

Because the privilege protects against the use of compelled statements as well as guarantees the right to remain silent absent immunity, the inquiry in a Fifth Amendment case is not ended when an incriminating statement is made in lieu of a claim of privilege. Nor, however, is failure to claim the privilege irrelevant.

* * *

* * * Despite its cherished position, the Fifth Amendment addresses only a relatively narrow scope of inquiries. Unless the government seeks testimony that will subject its giver to criminal liability, the constitutional right to remain silent absent immunity does not arise. An individual therefore properly may be compelled to give testimony, for example, in a noncriminal investigation of himself. Unless a witness objects, a government ordinarily may assume that its compulsory processes are not eliciting testimony that he deems to be incriminating. Only the witness knows whether the apparently in-

---

7. The term "witness" is used herein to identify one who, at the time disclosures are sought from him, is not a defendant in a criminal proceeding. The more frequent situations in which a witness' disclosures are compelled, subject to Fifth Amendment rights, include testimony before a grand jury, in a civil or criminal case or proceeding, or before a legislative or administrative body possessing subpoena power.

nocent disclosure sought may incriminate him, and the burden appropriately lies with him to make a timely assertion of the privilege. If, instead, he discloses the information sought, any incriminations properly are viewed as not compelled.

* * *

IV

The information revealed in the preparation and filing of an income tax return is, for purposes of Fifth Amendment analysis, the testimony of a "witness," as that term is used herein. Since Garner disclosed information on his returns instead of objecting, his Fifth Amendment claim would be defeated by an application of the general requirement that witnesses must claim the privilege. Garner, however, resists the application of that requirement, arguing that incriminating disclosures made in lieu of objection are "compelled" in the tax-return context. He relies specifically on three situations in which incriminatory disclosures have been considered compelled despite a failure to claim the privilege. * * *

A

Garner relies first on cases dealing with coerced confessions, e. g., Miranda v. Arizona, 384 U.S. 436, 86 S.Ct. 1602, 16 L.Ed.2d 694 (1966) * * *.

It is evident that these cases have little to do with disclosures on a tax return. The coerced-confession cases present the entirely different situation of custodial interrogation. It is presumed that without proper safeguards the circumstances of custodial interrogation deny an individual the ability freely to choose to remain silent. * * * Nothing in this case suggests the need for a similar presumption that a taxpayer makes disclosures on his return rather than claims the privilege because his will is overborne. In fact, a taxpayer, who can complete his return at leisure and with legal assistance, is even less subject to the psychological pressures at issue in *Miranda* than a witness who has been called to testify in judicial proceedings.

B

Garner relies next on Mackey v. United States, 401 U.S. 667, 91 S.Ct. 1160, 28 L.Ed.2d 404 (1971), the relevance of which can be understood only in light of Marchetti v. United States, 390 U.S. 39, 88 S.Ct. 697, 19 L.Ed.2d 889 (1968), and Grosso v. United States, 390 U. S. 62, 88 S.Ct. 709, 19 L.Ed.2d 906 (1968). In the latter cases the Court considered whether the Fifth Amendment was a defense in prosecutions for failure to file the returns required of gamblers in connection with the federal occupational and excise taxes on gambling. The Court found that any disclosures made in connection with the payment of those taxes tended to incriminate because of the pervasive criminal regulation of gambling activities. Since submitting a claim of privilege in lieu of the returns also would incriminate, the Court held that the privilege could be exercised by simply failing to file.

In *Mackey,* the disclosures required in connection with the gambling excise tax had been made before *Marchetti* and *Grosso* were decided. Mackey's returns were introduced in a criminal prosecution for income tax evasion. Although a majority of the Court considered the disclosures on the returns to have been compelled incriminations, Mackey was not immunized against their use because *Marchetti* and *Grosso* were held nonretroactive. Garner assumes that if Mackey had made his disclosures after *Marchetti* and *Grosso,* they could not have been used against him. He then concludes that since Mackey would have been privileged to file no returns at all, *Mackey* stands for the proposition that an objection at trial always suffices to preserve the privilege even if disclosures have been made previously.

Assuming that Garner otherwise reads *Mackey* correctly, we do not think that case should be applied in this context. The basis for the holdings in *Marchetti* and *Grosso* was that the occupational and excise taxes on gambling required disclosures only of gamblers, the great majority of whom were likely to incriminate themselves by responding. Therefore, as in the coerced-confession cases, any compulsion to disclose was likely to compel self-incrimination. Garner is differently situated. Although he disclosed himself to be a gambler, federal income tax returns are not directed at those " 'inherently suspect of criminal activities.' " *Marchetti*, supra, 390 U.S. at 52, 88 S.Ct., at 704, 19 L.Ed.2d, at 900. As noted in Albertson v. SACB, 382 U.S. 70, 79, 86 S.Ct. 194, 199, 15 L.Ed.2d 165, 172 (1965), "the questions in [an] income tax return [are] neutral on their face and directed at the public at large." The great majority of persons who file income tax returns do not incriminate themselves by disclosing their occupation. The requirement that such returns be completed and filed simply does not involve the compulsion to incriminate considered in *Mackey.*

C

Garner's final argument relies on Garrity v. New Jersey, 385 U. S. 493, 87 S.Ct. 616, 17 L.Ed.2d 562 (1967). There policemen summoned during an investigation of police corruption were informed that they could claim the privilege but that they would be discharged for doing so. The disclosures they made were introduced against them in subsequent criminal prosecutions. The Court held that the penalty of discharge for reliance on the privilege foreclosed a free choice to remain silent, and therefore had the effect of compelling the incriminating testimony given by the policemen. Garner notes that a taxpayer who claims the privilege on his return faces the possibility of a criminal prosecution under § 7203 for failure to make a return.

He argues that the possibility of prosecution, like the threat of discharge in *Garrity,* compels a taxpayer to make incriminating disclosures rather than claim the privilege. This contention is not entirely without force, but we find it unpersuasive.

The policemen in *Garrity* were threatened with punishment for a concededly valid exercise of the privilege, but one in Garner's situation is at no such disadvantage. A § 7203 conviction cannot be based on a valid exercise of the privilege. This is implicit in the dictum of United States v. Sullivan, 274 U.S. 259, 47 S.Ct. 607, 71 L.Ed. 1037 (1927), that the privilege may be claimed on a return. Furthermore, the Court has held that an individual summoned by the Service to provide documents or testimony can rely on the privilege to defend against a § 7203 prosecution for failure to "supply any information." See United States v. Murdock, 284 U.S. 141, 52 S.Ct. 63, 76 L.Ed. 210 (1931) *(Murdock I),* disapproved on other grounds, Murphy v. Waterfront Comm'n, 378 U.S. 52, 84 S.Ct. 1594, 12 L.Ed.2d 678 (1964). The Fifth Amendment itself guarantees the taxpayer's insulation against liability imposed on the basis of a valid and timely claim of privilege, a protection broadened by § 7203's statutory standard of "willfulness."

Since a valid claim of privilege cannot be the basis for a § 7203 conviction, Garner can prevail only if the possibility that a claim made on the return will be tested in a criminal prosecution suffices in itself to deny him freedom to claim the privilege. He argues that it does so, noting that because of the threat of prosecution under § 7203 a taxpayer contemplating a claim of privilege on his return faces a more difficult choice than does a witness contemplating a claim of privilege in a judicial proceeding. If the latter claims the protection of the Fifth Amendment, he receives a judicial ruling at that time on the validity of his claim, and he has an opportunity to reconsider it before being held in contempt for refusal to answer. A § 7203 prosecution, however, may be brought without a preliminary judicial ruling on a claim of privilege that would allow the taxpayer to reconsider.

In essence, Garner contends that the Fifth Amendment guarantee requires such a preliminary-ruling procedure for testing the validity of an asserted privilege. It may be that such a procedure would serve the best interests of the Government as well as of the taxpayer, but we certainly cannot say that the Constitution requires it. The Court previously has considered Fifth Amendment claims in the context of a criminal prosecution where the defendant did not have the benefit of a preliminary judicial ruling on a claim of privilege. It has never intimated that such a procedure is other than permissible. Indeed, the Court has given some measure of endorsement to it. In *Murdock I,* supra, an individual was prosecuted under predecessors of § 7203 for refusing to make disclosures after being summoned by the Bureau of Internal Revenue. In this Court he contended, apparently on statutory grounds, that there could be no prosecution without a prior judicial enforcement suit to allow presentation of his claim of privilege to a court for a preliminary ruling. The Court said:

> "While undoubtedly the right of a witness to refuse to answer lest he incriminate himself may be tested in proceedings to compel answer, there is no support for the contention that there must be such a determination of that question before prosecution for the willful failure so denounced." 284 U.S., at 148, 52 S.Ct., at 64, 76 L.Ed., at 213.

We are satisfied that *Murdock I* states the constitutional standard. What is at issue here is principally a matter of timing and procedure. As long as a valid and timely claim of privilege is available as a defense to a taxpayer prosecuted for failure to make a return, the taxpayer has not been denied a free choice to remain silent merely because of the absence of a preliminary judicial ruling on his claim. We therefore do not agree that Garner was deterred from claiming the privilege in the sense that was true of the policemen in *Garrity*.

V

In summary, we conclude that since Garner made disclosures instead of claiming the privilege on his tax returns his disclosures were not compelled incriminations.[21] He therefore was foreclosed from invoking the privilege when such information was later introduced as evidence against him in a criminal prosecution.

The judgment is

Affirmed.

Mr. Justice MARSHALL, with whom Mr. Justice BRENNAN joins, concurring in the judgment.

* * *

I accept the proposition that a preliminary ruling is not a prerequisite to a § 7203 prosecution. But it does not follow, and *Murdock I* does not hold, that the absence of a preliminary ruling is of no import in considering whether a defense of good-faith assertion of the privilege is constitutionally required. It is one thing to deny a good-faith defense to a witness who is given a prompt ruling on the validity of his claim of privilege and an opportunity to reconsider his refusal to testify before subjecting himself to possible punishment for

---

21. No language in this opinion is to be read as allowing a taxpayer desiring the protection of the privilege to make disclosures concurrently with a claim of privilege and thereby to immunize himself against the use of such disclosures. If a taxpayer desires the protection of the privilege, he must claim it instead of making disclosures. Any other rule would deprive the Government of its choice between compelling the evidence from the claimant in exchange for immunity and avoiding the burdens of immunization by obtaining the evidence elsewhere.

contempt. It would be quite another to deny a good-faith defense to someone like petitioner, who may be denied a ruling on the validity of his claim of privilege until his criminal prosecution, when it is too late to reconsider. If, contrary to the undisputed fact, a taxpayer had no assurance of either a preliminary ruling or a defense of good-faith assertion of the privilege, he could claim the privilege only at the risk that an erroneous assessment of the law of self-incrimination would subject him to criminal liability. In that event, I would consider the taxpayer to have been denied the free choice to claim the privilege, and would view any incriminating disclosures on his tax return as "compelled" within the meaning of the Fifth Amendment. Only because a good-faith erroneous claim of privilege entitles a taxpayer to acquittal under § 7203 can I conclude that petitioner's disclosures are admissible against him.

UNITED STATES v. PAEPKE

550 F.2d 385 (7th Cir. 1977).

[On October 26, 1971 the Marin County, California police arrested Arnold Paepke and seized $12,725 from him. State narcotics charges against Paepke were later dropped after the state court suppressed the evidence (including the money) seized from Paepke. The seized money was turned over to the IRS which terminated Paepke's tax year in October, 1971, assessed a deficiency of approximately $26,000 and levied upon the funds seized. On April 3, 1972 Paepke filed his 1971 tax return, showing an adjusted gross income of $3,275 from "golf playing" and a tax due of $234. The return further claimed a refund of $12,491 of the money seized in 1971. Following receipt of the return, the IRS referred the matter for criminal investigation. About two years later, Paepke filed another claim for refund of the $12,491 and, obtaining no relief, filed a refund suit in the District Court. The United States then indicted Paepke under § 7206(1) for understating his income in 1971 and misrepresenting its source. The District Court for the Western District of Wisconsin granted Paepke's motion to suppress and barred the government from using any documents related to Paepke's efforts to retrieve the money in the federal tax fraud trial. A majority of the Seventh Circuit panel decided for the government on Fourth Amendment principles. Judge Tone, concurring, reaches the same result "by a narrower path":]

* * *

The defendant was not faced with the dilemma of either not filing and being prosecuted for that omission or filing and being prosecuted for tax fraud. If the seized money was 1971 income he could have included it and declined to state its source if such a statement would incriminate him. He could also, I believe, have declined to state even the amount of his income if that fact alone might have tended to incriminate him, cf. Garner v. United States, 424 U.S. 648, 96 S.Ct. 1178, 1186–1187, 47 L.Ed.2d 370 (1976), although it is doubtful that such a possibility existed in view of the dismissal of the state charges. The one course that was not open to defendant was to make a false statement in his income tax return.

If he did make a false statement, which remains to be determined, he is in the same position as a witness who testifies falsely. Illegally obtained evidence that would not otherwise be admissible, becomes admissible for the purpose of proving the falsity of the statement under oath The illegality of the seizure does not allow him to commit with impunity the new crime of perjury or false statement.

* * *

QUESTION

Under what circumstances, if any, could you advise a client to claim the privilege against self-incrimination with regard to the amount of income reported on a federal tax return?

UNITED STATES v. CARLSON

617 F.2d 518 (9th Cir. 1980).

WALLACE, Circuit Judge.

Carlson was convicted of willful failure to file income tax returns in violation of 26 U.S.C. § 7203. On appeal he seeks reversal by claiming that his failure to file proper returns constituted a valid exercise of his Fifth Amendment privilege against self-incrimination. We affirm the conviction.

I

Carlson, a factory worker, earned $9,346.21 in 1974 and $13,053.-53 in 1975. Although he had filed complete tax returns for previous years, Carlson did not do so for 1974 and 1975. Instead, as part of a tax protest movement, he utilized the following tax-evasion scheme for each of those years. In 1974, Carlson claimed 99 withholding exemptions on the withholding tax form (form W–4) that he submitted to his employer, although he was not married and had no dependents. This form W–4 remained effective through 1975, and resulted in no federal income taxes being withheld from Carlson's wages in either 1974 or 1975. Carlson thereafter asserted the Fifth Amendment in his 1974 and 1975 year-end tax returns (form 1040) in lieu of providing any information from which his tax liability could be calculated. He appended to the 1974 return tax protest material claiming that federal reserve notes were unconstitutional, that he therefore had not received enough constitutionally valid money to require filing a tax return, and that all rules promulgated by the Secretary of the Treasury were also unconstitutional.

The result of Carlson's submission of the false withholding form and his subsequent assertion of the Fifth Amendment in his year-end returns was that Carlson paid no federal income taxes for 1974 or 1975. Carlson claims that he validly asserted the Fifth Amendment to avoid incriminating himself for having previously filed the false withholding forms. After hearing all of the evidence, however, the district judge, sitting without a jury, found that Carlson "did not have a good-faith claim or reasonable ground for [asserting the] privilege, as he was a tax protestor and his activities and his actions and methods of submitting his returns were those of a tax protestor only." He held, therefore, that Carlson's Fifth Amendment claim did not constitute defense to his prosecution, pursuant to section 7203, for failure to file a tax return.

II

This case presents a question of first impression: can the privilege against self-incrimination constitute a defense to a section 7203 prosecution when it is asserted to avoid incrimination for a past violation of income tax laws? * * *

* * *

An examination of the facts of this case reveals that Carlson did assert the privilege at the time he filed his return, and did so while facing a real and appreciable hazard of prosecution for having previously filed a false withholding form. In addition, there is little doubt that a truthfully completed tax return, stating his gross income, the lack of federal income taxes actually withheld, and the true number of available deductions would have provided " 'a lead or clue' to evidence having a tendency to incriminate" Carlson. It is equally certain that a trial judge examining these facts would find a substantial threat of incrimination. Thus, it appears that Carlson satisfies those indicia of validity previously considered by us in cases where the privilege has been asserted to avoid self-incrimination other than under the tax laws.

When the privilege is asserted to avoid incrimination for past tax crimes, however, additional complications arise. If Carlson's assertion of the privilege were valid, it would license a form of conduct that would undermine the entire system of personal income tax collection. The essence of Carlson's plan was to claim 99 withholding exemptions so that no federal income tax would be withheld by his employer, and then to assert the Fifth Amendment privilege in lieu of a properly completed tax return, thus attempting to avoid both prosecution for the false withholding claim and payment of required income taxes. The widespread use of such a scheme would emasculate the present system of revenue collection which, by virtue of its scope alone, necessarily depends upon personal reporting by wage earners. We are thus confronted with the collision of two critical interests:

the privilege against self-incrimination, and the need for public revenue collection by a process necessarily reliant on self-reporting.

To decide which of these two interests prevails, we follow Supreme Court guidance:

> Tension between the State's demand for disclosures and the protection of the right against self-incrimination is likely to give rise to serious questions. Inevitably these must be resolved in terms of balancing the public need on the one hand, and the individual claim to constitutional protections on the other; neither interest can be treated lightly.

California v. Byers, 402 U.S. 424, 427, 91 S.Ct. 1535, 1537, 29 L.Ed.2d 9 (1971). * * *

* * *

In the case before us, Carlson has attempted to take advantage of the privilege's protective capacity to further a calculated effort to avoid the payment of taxes. Although it is true that Carlson actually seeks protection against self-incrimination for his prior tax crime, he does so only as part of an overall plan to evade taxes. The first step of that plan—submitting a false withholding form to his employer—was concealed from the Service by assertion of the Fifth Amendment on Carlson's year-end returns; and the very act of asserting the Fifth Amendment also effectuated the second step of the plan—failing to file meaningful returns that would divulge both his prior misstatement and his overall year-end tax liabilities. In other words, the Fifth Amendment was the linchpin of Carlson's plan to evade the payment of taxes. He used the privilege more as a sword than as a shield. The history and purpose of the privilege do not, in light of such circumstances, weigh heavily in favor of extending its coverage to Carlson.

At the same time, the character and urgency of the public interest in raising revenue through self-reporting weighs heavily against affording the privilege to Carlson. The federal government's power to raise revenue is its lifeblood. Were taxpayers permitted to employ Carlson's scheme, they could avoid filing completed tax returns and thereby severely impair the government's ability to determine tax liability. * * *

Another factor in our weighing process is that the requirement of filing an annual income tax return is primarily designed to facilitate revenue collection, not criminal prosecution. "[T]he questions in the income tax return [are] neutral on their face and directed at the public at large." Albertson v. SACB, 382 U.S. 70, 79, 86 S.Ct. 194, 199, 15 L.Ed.2d 165 (1965). * * *

After weighing the appropriate factors, we conclude that the purpose and history of the privilege against self-incrimination do not compel protection of Carlson's actions, and that the character and urgency of the opposing revenue interests require that his scheme not be permitted. We therefore hold that an individual who seeks to frustrate the tax laws by claiming too many withholding exemptions, with an eye to covering that crime and evading the tax return requirement by assertion of the Fifth Amendment, is not entitled to the amendment's protection.

III

In spite of our holding that Carlson is not entitled to protection of the Fifth Amendment, we still must review the district court's finding that Carlson did not assert his claim in "good faith." * * * In prosecutions of the kind before us, * * * a defendant's assertion of even an invalid Fifth Amendment claim in "good faith" would defeat the section 7203 requirement that a failure to file income tax returns be "willful." Someone who thinks he is complying with the law cannot be said to be "willfully" violating it. Therefore, we must review the trial court's finding that Carlson did not make his claim in good faith.

The trial judge's determination was a finding of fact. "[U]pon appeal of a conviction in a criminal case the evidence must be considered in a light most favorable to the government and the findings of fact of a trial judge (or jury) may not be set aside unless clearly erroneous." United States v. Glover, 514 F.2d 390, 391 (9th Cir.), cert. denied, 423 U.S. 857, 96 S.Ct. 108, 46 L.Ed.2d 83 (1975). The record clearly discloses that Carlson was a tax protestor who attempted to frustrate the tax laws by use of the Fifth Amendment. We cannot say that the trial judge's conclusion that Carlson failed to assert the privilege in good faith was clearly erroneous.

Affirmed.

UNITED STATES v. NEFF

615 F.2d 1235 (9th Cir. 1980).

WALLACE, Circuit Judge:

* * *

I

During 1974 and 1975, Neff was employed as a police officer and received wages from the City of San Jose, California. During 1974 he also received capital gains from dealings in gold and silver coins. His community property share of income from employment and investments exceeded $14,000 in 1974 and $8,500 in 1975. During each of these years, Neff, who had previously filed proper returns, submitted to the IRS a standard individual income tax return form (form 1040) on which Neff provided no financial information from which his tax liabilities could be calculated. As returned by Neff, the forms contained only essential identification information and Neff's signature. In response to more than 25 questions about his financial and tax status, Neff had printed the words "Object: Self-Incrimination." Remaining questions had been answered either "None" or "Unknown." Neff also appended to the forms, in each of these years, over 100 pages of general protest material challenging, among other things, the national monetary system, government spending, and federal reserve notes.

The Internal Revenue Service (IRS) responded by letter to Neff, explaining that the forms as he filled them out were not acceptable tax returns and providing additional blank forms for proper completion. Neff refused to comply, claiming that by doing so he would waive his Fifth Amendment privilege against self-incrimination. The government filed an information charging Neff with two counts of willful failure to file income tax returns, and a jury found him guilty of both counts.

* * *

We are here faced with a case in which the taxpayer did assert his privilege in response to specific questions in the tax return form, but did so on such a wholesale basis as to deny the IRS any useful financial or tax information. Other circuits, faced with similar wholesale assertions of the privilege against self-incrimination, have concluded that a tax return form which contains no information from which tax liability can be calculated does not constitute a tax return within the meaning of the IRS laws. Once these courts determine that the taxpayer has filed no return, simple application of the *Sullivan* precedent, [United States v. Sullivan, 274 U.S. 259, 47 S.Ct. 607, 71 L.Ed. 1037 (1927),] which states that the Fifth Amendment will never justify a complete failure to file a return, invalidates the Fifth Amendment defense. E. g., United States v. Irwin, 561 F.2d 198, 201 (10th Cir. 1977), cert. denied, 434 U.S. 1012, 98 S.Ct. 725, 54 L.Ed.2d 755 (1978).

Although we recognize the ease with which the logic used in these cases would resolve the issue before us, we conclude that such reliance upon the definition of a tax return is inappropriate, because it lacks independent Fifth Amendment analysis. Moreover, the usefulness of this definitional approach is too limited because it is confined to facts such as those presented here: the wholesale assertion, albeit in response to specific questions, of the privilege against self-incrimination. In settings in which the Fifth Amendment right has been more discretely asserted, it would be difficult to conclude that no return has been filed, and, therefore, inappropriate to apply this definitional analysis. We therefore choose not to follow the lead of the cited cases. We believe that the better approach to this and future Fifth Amendment tax return cases is to apply more traditional Fifth Amendment analysis.

* * *

To claim the privilege validly a defendant must be faced with " 'substantial hazards of self-incrimination,' " California v. Byers, 402 U.S. at 429, 90 S.Ct. at 1538, that are " 'real and appreciable' and not merely 'imaginary and unsubstantial.' " Marchetti v. United States, 390 U.S. at 48, 88 S.Ct. at 702. Moreover, he must have "reasonable cause to apprehend [such] danger from a direct answer" to questions posed to him. Hoffman v. United States, 341 U.S. 479, 486, 71 S.Ct. 814, 818, 95 L.Ed. 1118 (1951). The information that would be revealed by direct answer need not be such as would itself support a criminal conviction, however, but must simply "furnish a link in the chain of evidence needed to prosecute the claimant for a federal crime." Id. See also Hashagen v. United States, 283 F.2d 345, 348 (9th Cir. 1960). Indeed, it is enough if the responses would merely "provide a lead or clue" to evidence having a tendency to incriminate. Id. at 348.

* * *

Applying these principles to the facts before us, we conclude that the trial judge correctly decided that Neff had no valid Fifth Amendment defense to the section 7203 prosecution. The questions asked of Neff on the income tax form did not, of themselves, suggest that the response would be incriminating; nor did the setting in which they were asked—a general inquiry about Neff's financial and tax status, to be completed in the privacy of his own home—alter the non-incriminatory nature of those questions. Moreover, the peculiarities of the case did not strengthen Neff's claim. If anything, the tax protest nature of defense witness Holmes' testimony and of the materials that Neff appended to his returns suggest that Neff's refusal to complete the forms was motivated by a desire to protest taxes, rather than a fear of self-incrimination. In short, the whole circumstance was "innocuous and thus unprotected absent some positive disclosure by the witness of its hidden dangers * * *." Hashagen v. United States, supra, 283 F.2d at 350. Neff made no such disclosure. At no point during the trial, including when Neff testified, was the district judge presented with any indicia of potential incrimination. On the contrary, Neff's counsel argued that Neff's sincerity of belief was sufficient to validate his assertion of the privilege, and that Neff alone should be the final arbiter of the assertion's validity. As we have seen, that is not the law. Neff did not show that his response to the tax form questions would have been self-incriminating. He cannot, therefore, prevail on his Fifth Amendment claim.

* * *

Affirmed.

QUESTION

A client has failed to report income taxable to him derived from annual payments into a foreign bank account of the receipts from his sale, three years earlier, of property located offshore. He is under a criminal tax investigation with regard to the failure to report this income. He seeks your advice as to the reporting of these continuing payments on his income tax return for the current year. In light of the decisions in *Carlson* and *Neff*, what can you advise him to do?

Chapter VIII

COLLECTION OF THE TAX

Scope Note: The final step in the administration of the federal tax laws is collection of the tax determined to be due by the Service or the courts. Chapter VIII contains a general discussion of the broad powers of the IRS Collection Division, and the means available to the Service to assist it in the collection of the tax, including the federal tax lien and jeopardy and termination assessments. The materials that follow also cover some recurring problems relating to collection of taxes from persons who might be described as "secondarily liable" for the taxes of another, including liability for withholding taxes by responsible persons, lenders and providers of wages; transferee and fiduciary liability; and the "innocent spouse" provisions of the Code. Section 7 is devoted to a discussion of the means available to taxpayers and others, in appropriate cases, to prevent the Service from assessing or collecting taxes alleged to be due; and the final section contains a brief description of the rules applicable to administration of the tax laws in the context of a proceeding under the federal Bankruptcy Code.

SECTION 1. THE IRS COLLECTION DIVISION: POWERS AND PROCEDURES

WHAT CAN A TAXPAYER DO WHEN A CASE HAS BEEN TURNED OVER FOR COLLECTION: ADMINISTRATIVE AND LEGAL REMEDIES: POWERS OF THE AGENT

Marvin J. Garbis
29 N.Y.U. Institute on Federal Taxation 909 (1971).

* * *

POWERS OF THE COLLECTION DIVISION

The Collection Division of the Service, and the Revenue Officer within the Division, has legal powers which can only be described as awesome. In our nation there is probably no other public servant who has the legal power (subject to virtually no external review) given the Revenue Officer over the property, reputation and often health of a taxpayer who is behind in his tax payments. The Revenue Officer has the legal power to find property and property rights of the taxpayer, to levy upon and seize such assets and to sell the seized assets to satisfy the tax debt. There is, perhaps, good reason for the Service to have this power available to it provided it is not misused. As noted by the great bard: [38]

38. Shakespeare, Measure for Measure, Act II, Scene I.

O, it is excellent
To have a giant's strength;
But it is tyrannous
To use it like a giant.

In most instances the Revenue Officer uses his powers with reasonable restraint. However, there are inevitably cases of excessive zeal in "protecting the revenue."

Taxpayer's Practical Relief

Unfortunately, the taxpayer who is the victim of the excessive action of a Revenue Officer usually has no practical or legal remedy except the bittersweet satisfaction which might result from the exposure of the "horror story" in the popular press. In this context it must be noted that the various District Directors and Chiefs of the Collection Division field officers are highly sensitive to charges of unreasonably harsh action or proposed action by Revenue Officers.

Where there has been, or there is threatened, a truly unreasonable step by the Revenue Officer, the taxpayer's representative will have a chance to present his side of the picture to the higher levels within the Service. If the taxpayer is right, practical relief very often will be granted in the form of a withholding of excessive action or the granting of some administrative remedy.

It is important, in this area, for the taxpayer to be correct in his position and quick to bring it to the attention of the Revenue Officer's superiors. Hence, unlike almost any other phase of tax practice, a representative dealing with a Revenue Officer must be ready to seek immediate relief "over his head" on short notice.

Power to Find Property Subject to Levy

The federal tax lien is a broad security device, attaching to all of the taxpayer's property and rights to property and even to certain property owned by others.[39] Any property subject to the tax lien (with minor exemptions) [40] is subject to levy.

The Collection Division's Revenue Officer has wide powers for the discovery of property subject to the tax lien securing payment of the tax debt. He has available to him the vast investigative resources of the Service to ascertain the existence and location of property or rights to property which can be levied upon. He has the authority to use the Service's administrative summons in his quest for property.[41] He can issue a summons to any person and compel the production of documents or the giving of testimony under oath which will, or may, aid in the collection of taxes.[42] Moreover, by a special statutory provision, the Revenue Officer, if a levy has been, or is

---

39. I.R.C. § 6321. * * *

40. I.R.C. § 6334.

41. I.R.C. § 7602.

42. Subject, of course, to constitutional and other defenses.

about to be, made can summarily demand the production of documents containing evidence or statements relating to the property or right to property subject to levy.[43]

Power to Levy Upon and Sell Property

Once property or rights to property subject to the tax lien are located the Revenue Officer has the power to levy on the assets.[44] This power is mitigated only by an Internal Revenue Code provision providing very limited exemptions from levy for such items as clothes, school books, undelivered mail, books and tools of the taxpayer's trade (not exceeding $250 in value) and furniture, fuel and personal effects (not exceeding $500 in value).[45] The Code definitely states that nothing other than the property specified in Section 6334(a) is exempt from levy, rendering ineffective any other federal or state exemptions.[46]

A levy is effected by serving a notice of levy on any person in possession of, or obligated with respect to, property subject to levy.[47] The Code further specifies that the term "levy" includes the power of "distraint and seizure" by any means.[48] In practice, the power of distraint and seizure is taken to include the power to take physical possession of specific property and to padlock a building or part thereof and take custody over its contents.

With limited exceptions,[49] any person in possession of, or obligated with respect to, property or rights to property subject to levy upon which a levy has been made must, on demand by the Internal Revenue Service, surrender the property or rights or satisfy the obligation.[50] Any failure to comply with a levy subjects the defaulting party to personal liability in the amount of the lesser of the value of the property or rights not surrendered, or the tax liability which was sought to be collected, together with costs and interest at [an annual rate established under § 6621] from the date of levy.[51] Moreover, a failure to surrender property or rights in response to a levy without reasonable cause renders the defaulting party liable for a

---

43. I.R.C. § 6333.

44. I.R.C. § 6331(a).

45. I.R.C. § 6334(a). [Section 1209(a) of the Tax Reform Act of 1976 (P.L. 94–455) added new subsections 6634(a)(9) and (d) to the Code, granting an additional exemption from levy to a limited amount of an individual taxpayer's wages or salary for personal services, or income derived from other sources.]

46. Reg. § 301.6334–1(c).

47. Reg. § 301.6331–1(a)(1).

48. I.R.C. § 6331(b).

49. The exception relates to property which is, at the time of the levy, subject to an attachment or execution under any judicial process. I.R.C. § 6332(a). Special rules apply with respect to life insurance and endowment contracts. I.R.C. § 6332(b).

50. I.R.C. § 6332(a).

51. I.R.C. § 6332(c)(1).

penalty equal to 50 percent of the principal amount for which he is personally liable.[52]

Limitation on Levy

One minor limitation on the scope of a levy warrants particular note. The Federal Tax Lien Act of 1966[53] modified the Internal Revenue Code by providing that "a levy shall extend only to property possessed and obligations existing at the time thereof."[54] The legislative history makes it clear that, after 1966 at least, a levy is not of continuing effect. Rather it "catches" only property or rights to property then in existence.[55]

Therefore, if a bank is served with a levy with respect to the account of a delinquent taxpayer, the levy will be satisfied if the bank surrenders to the Internal Revenue Service the amount of the taxpayer's balance as of the time the levy was made. The levy has no effect on subsequent deposits which may be made by the taxpayer. These may be reached only by a subsequent levy.

[The Tax Reform Act of 1976, P.L. 94–455, added a new § 6331(d)(3) to the Code. Under § 6331(d)(3)(A), levies on wages and salaries made after February 28, 1977 are to have a continuing effect that will make them apply to future earnings. Section 6331(d)(3)(B) requires the IRS to " * * * promptly release the levy when the liability * * * is satisfied or becomes unenforceable by reason of lapse of time * * *", which would normally be at the expiration of six years after assessment of the liability out of which the levy arose.|

Disposition of Seized Property

After property has been taken by levy, the Service may proceed to sell the seized assets and to apply the proceeds against the taxpayer's liability. The Code and Regulations contain detailed provisions relating to the notice requirements and terms and conditions of tax sales.[56] While a full discussion of these provisions is beyond the scope of this article several points may serve to illustrate the kind of safeguards which are provided by the law.

As soon as practical after a seizure of property, the Internal Revenue Service must give the owner (and with respect to personal property, the possessor) notice of the seizure.[57] Similarly, as soon as practical after seizure, the Service must give the owner of seized

---

52. I.R.C. § 6332(c)(2).

53. By Section 104(a) of the Act.

54. I.R.C. § 6331(b).

55. Committee Report, Federal Tax Lien Act of 1966, P.L. 89–719, House Technical Explanation.

56. I.R.C. § 6335 et seq. and Regulations issued thereunder.

57. I.R.C. § 6335(a).

property, and must by publication give the public, notice of the sale of the property.[58]

Any owner of property that has been levied upon, may halt the sale and regain the property prior to sale, by paying the full tax liability (together with the costs of proceeding) with respect to which the levy was made.[59] Moreover, the owner of property which has been wrongfully levied upon has specific statutory rights, including the right to halt the tax sale by injunction.[60]

As to real estate, the Code has a special provision allowing redemption after sale. The owner of real estate which has been levied upon and sold has a right to redeem the property within 120 days after sale by paying the person who was the purchaser at the tax sale the amount which he paid for the realty plus interest at the rate of 20 percent per annum.[61]

* * *

Judicial Proceedings to Collect

The Government is not limited to administrative levy to collect its taxes. It can, where it finds it advantageous to do so, utilize judicial procedures in its quest for the taxpayer's assets.

The most frequent Government resort to the judiciary is in an action to foreclose the tax lien on specific property.[77] Another commonly used action by the Government is a personal action against the taxpayer based upon the underlying tax liability.[78] The purpose of this type of suit is to reduce the tax lien to a judgment, thereby extending the period within which collection is possible.

It should be noted that the limitation on collection on an assessment expires six years after the tax assessment (subject to extension by agreement).[79] Although the power of the Collection Division to collect by levy is not extended by the obtaining of a judgment,[80] the Service has the power to sue to enforce its judgment or to foreclose its tax lien,[81] even after the time for collection by levy has expired. It must be borne in mind that the obtaining of a judgment on the tax assessment will keep the time for collection (albeit by judicial procedures rather than administrative levy) open indefinitely and will concomitantly extend the life of the tax lien.

In addition to lien foreclosure actions and actions to reduce the tax claim to judgment, the Internal Revenue Service can also utilize

58. I.R.C. § 6335(b).

59. I.R.C. § 6337(a).

60. I.R.C. § 7426(a).

61. I.R.C. § 6337(b).

77. I.R.C. § 7403(a).

78. I.R.C. § 6502. * * *

79. I.R.C. § 6502(a).

80. I.R.C. § 6502(a). Added by § 113(b), Federal Tax Lien Act of 1966.

81. I.R.C. §§ 6322, 6502(a).

any type of legal action which may be available to creditors generally. It may furthermore find itself more or less involuntarily in court suing on its tax claim, for example as a counterclaimant in a tax refund suit, or a claimant in a probate or bankruptcy proceeding.

Offset of Government Liability to Taxpayer

In addition to its right to take property or rights to property from the taxpayer or third parties, the Collection Division can take, by offset, any tax refund which the Service may owe the taxpayer.[83] Moreover, the Government even has the right to set off against a tax liability amounts which it may owe the taxpayer on contracts to the potential detriment of third parties who acquired rights in the taxpayer's contract claim.[84]

ADMINISTRATIVE REMEDIES

The Collection Division is given broad discretion to ease the pain of the collection process. The very flexible administrative remedies potentially available to the delinquent taxpayer often make it possible, although it is generally not a matter of right, to work out a reasonable method for payment of his tax debt.

Informal Collection Moratorium

A taxpayer can possibly work out an informal collection moratorium or "gentleman's" agreement with the Collection Division in appropriate circumstances. If he can establish to the satisfaction of the Revenue Officer and his Chief that (1) there is a good reason for delaying any drastic collection action and (2) there will be no likelihood of diminution of collectability, he may be able to obtain a reasonable withholding of the seizure and sale of assets.

The relief available, and the conditions imposed as a prerequisite to the relief, necessarily depend upon the facts and circumstances of the case and upon the discretion of the Collection Division. There is no publication setting forth the criteria considered in determining whether a taxpayer can obtain this relief. Necessarily, therefore, the existence and extent of availability of this informal relief will vary from district to district due to the varying concepts of duty and moral judgment of the respective District Directors and Chiefs of Collection Division field offices.

Extension of Time to Pay Tax

The Code authorizes the Service to extend the time for payment of a tax shown due on an income, estate or gift tax return or of an

---

83. I.R.C. § 6402.

84. United States v. Munsey Trust Co., 332 U.S. 234, 67 S.Ct. 1599, 91 L.Ed. 2d 2022 (1947). See 31 U.S.C. § 203 authorizing the inclusion, in defense contracts, of a prohibition of the Government's right to set off taxes and other debts in respect to contract proceeds.

assessment of a tax deficiency.[85] The maximum period of the extension varies from six months in most cases to ten years in the case of estate taxes. The granting of this relief depends primarily upon a finding by the Service (subject to no external review) that the payment of the tax when due would result in "undue hardship" to the taxpayer. The relief is not authorized in cases in which a deficiency is due to negligence, intentional disregard of rules and regulations, or fraud with intent to evade tax.[86]

Release of Levy

The Service may release a levy upon all or part of property or rights to property levied upon where it determines that such action will facilitate ultimate collection of the liability.[87] Hence, for example, the Service may (but need not) release a levy on funds earmarked for a payroll or business purchase where the effect of the levy will be to put the taxpayer out of business.

The Treasury Regulations provide that a levy shall be released only where the taxpayer has complied with such conditions for release as the Collection Division may choose to require.[88] These conditions can include an escrow arrangement, an installment payment agreement or even an agreement to extend the statute of limitations for collection.

Substitution of Proceeds of Sale for Property

Where the Collection Division feels that the practicalities of a situation require it, the Service may discharge specific property from the federal tax lien in order to facilitate a sale.[89] The sale must divest the delinquent taxpayer of all right, title and interest in the subject property.

In order to obtain a discharge of the property from the lien, the delinquent taxpayer (or other interested party) must enter into a written agreement with the Service whereby the proceeds of sale are to be held subject to the Government's claims and liens to the same extent, and with the same priorities, as the original property.[90]

Certificate of Discharge of Specific Property From Lien

Where appropriate, the Service may issue a Certificate of Discharge of Specific Property from Federal Tax Lien. The effect of the Certificate is conclusively to establish that the specific property named in the Certificate is discharged from the federal tax lien until such time as it may be reacquired by the delinquent taxpayer.[91]

85. I.R.C. § 6161 et seq.

86. I.R.C. § 6161(b)(3).

87. I.R.C. § 6343(a).

88. Reg. § 301.6343–1(a).

89. I.R.C. § 6325(b)(3).

90. [Reg. § 301.6325–1(b)(3).]

91. I.R.C. § 6325(f)(1)(B).

To obtain the Certificate the taxpayer must provide proof (satisfactory to the Service) that other property subject to the federal tax lien is worth double the tax liability plus any prior liens.[92]   Alternatively, the taxpayer may prove to the satisfaction of the Service that the Government's interest in the specific property is worthless, or make a payment equal to the value (as determined by the Service) of the Government's interest in the property.[93]

Certificate of Subordination of Tax Lien

The Internal Revenue Service is authorized to issue a Certificate of Subordination of Federal Tax Lien. This Certificate conclusively will establish that the specific lien or interest described in the Certificate is superior to the federal tax lien.[94]   To obtain the Certificate the taxpayer (or other interested party) must either pay an amount equal to the amount or value of the lien or interest which will be given superiority over the tax lien or must prove to the satisfaction of the Service that the issuance of the Certificate will increase the amount ultimately collected on the tax liability and will facilitate its collection.

Certificate of Release of Tax Lien

The Service may issue a Certificate of Release of Federal Tax Lien which will conclusively establish that the federal tax lien is extinguished with respect to the specified taxpayer and tax liability until such time as the Certificate may be revoked.[95]   The Service will, of course, release the tax lien if the underlying tax obligation together with all interest thereon is paid in full.[96]   Where the taxpayer can post a bond, acceptable to the Service, guaranteeing the payment of the full tax liability plus interest the Certificate will be issued.[97]

The tax lien may be released if the taxpayer can satisfy the Internal Revenue Service that the tax liability upon which it is based has become legally unenforceable.[98]   The term "legally unenforceable" is construed by the Service to mean unenforceable as a matter of law and not either uncollectible or unenforceable as a matter of fact.[99]   Therefore, proof that the taxpayer presently has no assets would not be sufficient.

Presumably, a clear showing that the period of limitations on collection has expired would be sufficient to obtain the Certificate. Perhaps a clear and undeniable showing that the underlying assessment was made after the period of limitations for assessment would

92. I.R.C. § 6325(b)(1).

93. I.R.C. § 6325(b)(2).

94. I.R.C. § 6325(f)(1)(C).

95. I.R.C. § 6325(f)(1)(A).

96. I.R.C. § 6325(a)(1).

97. I.R.C. § 6325(a)(2).

98. I.R.C. § 6325(a)(1).

99. Reg. § 301.6325–1(a).

suffice. However, the determination of whether the taxpayer's showing on this point is adequate is left solely to the discretion of the Service.[100] Of course, if the assessment were in fact undeniably improper the Service might be subject to an injunction against collection.

Compromise of the Tax Liability

The Internal Revenue Service has statutory authority to compromise a taxpayer's liability based on a doubt as to the collectability of the full tax liability assessment.[101] In substance the Service, through the Collection Division, will make a thorough examination of the delinquent taxpayer's present and prospective financial information. If it appears clear that there is no prospect of realizing payment in full, and if the Service in its sole discretion decides to do so, it can compromise the outstanding tax liability for the immediate or deferred payment of some fraction of the total tax debt.

Offer in Compromise

Procedurally, a taxpayer seeking to work out a compromise must file an "Offer in Compromise" on Treasury Form 656 [102] together with a Statement of Financial Condition on Treasury Form 433.[103] As a practical matter there will normally be some negotiation with the Collection Division field office handling the taxpayer's account prior to the formal submission of the offer and financial statement.

The Regulations require that, generally, an offer in compromise should be accompanied by full or part payment of the proposed compromised liability.[104] This amount is to be refunded in the event the offer is not accepted.[105] The requirement of payment with the offer is sometimes flexibly applied and sometimes waived. It is often a negotiable point in dealing with the Collection Division in view of the financial circumstances of the taxpayer.

Deferral of Collection Pending Compromise

Another important consideration in connection with the compromise offer is whether the Service will cease making collection efforts while the taxpayer's offer in compromise is being considered. It is clear Service policy that the submission of an offer in compromise does not automatically operate to stay the collection of the tax liability.[106] However, if the Collection Division feels that the inter-

---

100. I.R.C. § 6325(a)(1).

101. I.R.C. § 7122; Reg. § 301.7122–1(a)(2).

102. Statement of Procedural Rules § 601.203(b), Rev.Proc. [80–6, 1980–1 C.B. 586].

103. Statement of Procedural Rules § 601.203(b), Rev.Proc. [80–6, supra].

104. Reg. § 301.7122(d)(1).

105. Reg. § 301.7122(d)(4).

106. Reg. § 301.7122–1(d)(2).

ests of the Government will not be jeopardized by so doing, it can halt any collection efforts during the pendency of the offer.

Collateral Agreement

As a condition to the acceptance of an offer in compromise the Internal Revenue Service may require the taxpayer to enter into a collateral agreement.[107]   By such an agreement the taxpayer is committed to make additional payments on the compromised liability if his "annual income" should exceed designated amounts over the term of the agreement (sometimes ten years or longer).[108]

For purposes of the collateral agreement "annual income" is defined much more broadly than is taxable income for income tax purposes.[109]   Hence, depending on the specific collateral agreement entered into, "annual income" may include such items as inheritances, returns of capital and other items generally treated as nontaxable receipts for tax purposes.

Review of Offer in Compromise

There are various internal levels of review through which an offer in compromise must pass prior to acceptance by the Internal Revenue Service.[110]   Moreover, except in a few specified instances, an investigation (normally performed by a Revenue Officer) is required of the basis of the offer.[111]   In terms of procedures it should be noted that [both before and] after an offer in compromise is filed, the taxpayer, if his case is one over which the district director has processing jurisdiction,[112] may have conferences with the Collection Division [and, if agreement is not reached at such conferences, the taxpayer may request consideration of his case by the Appeals Office].[113]

Binding Effect of Compromise

An offer in compromise is accepted only when the taxpayer is notified of the acceptance in writing.[114]   Once accepted, a compromise is binding unless it can be shown that it resulted from a mutual mistake of fact, fraud, misrepresentation or duress.[115]   In this context it has been held that "duress" is not present merely because economic circumstances would make the full payment of the asserted tax liabil-

---

107.   Reg. § 301.7122–1(d)(3).

108.   See Treasury Form 2261.

109.   See Treasury Form 2261.

110. See Statement of Procedural Rules § 601.203(c)(1). [Cf. Rev.Proc. 80–6, supra.]

111. Statement of Procedural Rules § 601.203(c)(1). [Cf. Rev.Proc. 80–6, supra.]

112. Statement of Procedural Rules § 601.203(c)(1). [Cf. Rev.Proc. 80–6, supra.]

113. Statement of Procedural Rules § 601.203(d). [Cf. Rev.Proc. 80–6, supra.]

114.   Reg. § 301.7122–1(d)(3).

115.   Reg. § 301.7122–1(c).

ity a hardship,[116] or because the Service threatened to seize and sell the taxpayer's property if a suitable compromise was not agreed upon.[117]

Conceptually, an offer in compromise may be thought of as a "tax bankruptcy" which is discretionary with the Internal Revenue Service.

* * *

NOTE

The Fourth Amendment protects taxpayers from unreasonable searches conducted pursuant to an IRS levy. For example, in G.M. Leasing Corp. v. United States, 429 U.S. 338, 97 S.Ct. 619, 50 L.Ed.2d 530, on remand, 560 F.2d 1011 (10th Cir. 1977), the IRS made a jeopardy assessment against the taxpayer and proceeded to seize the property of G.M. Leasing Corp., determined to be the taxpayer's alter ego. Acting without a warrant, IRS agents seized automobiles belonging to the corporation and broke into the corporation's office, seizing books and papers. The Supreme Court ruled that IRC § 6331(b), which authorizes "distraint and seizure by any means", does not sanction unconstitutional searches. Thus, under normal Fourth Amendment principles, the warrantless search of the office was illegal, while the seizure of the automobiles (from premises in which the taxpayer had no interest) was constitutional, there being no invasion of privacy.

The remedies available to taxpayers whose constitutional rights have been infringed in levy proceedings are rarely satisfactory, however. Although the property wrongfully searched and seized must be returned, the IRS generally can reacquire the property by obtaining a search warrant prior to executing a second search and seizure. In certain circumstances, a motion to suppress may be appropriate. If it can be shown that the agents in bad faith violated the taxpayer's constitutional rights, a suit for damages may be brought against the agents in their individual capacities. See G.M. Leasing Corp., supra; see generally Bivens v. Six Unknown Federal Narcotics Agents, 403 U.S. 388, 91 S.Ct. 1999, 29 L.Ed.2d 619 (1971), on remand, 456 F.2d 1339 (2d Cir. 1972).

116. E. g., Cooper Agency v. United States, 301 F.Supp. 871 (D.S.C.1969), aff'd per curiam on opinion of district court 422 F.2d 1131 (4th Cir. 1970).

117. E. g. Walker v. Alamo Foods Co., 16 F.2d 694 (5th Cir. 1927).

SECTION 2.   THE FEDERAL TAX LIEN

TAX PROCEDURE AND INTERNAL REVENUE SERVICE PRACTICE

Michael I. Saltzman

THE GENERAL TAX LIEN

When and how the general tax lien arises

The general rule is that "If any person liable to pay any tax neglects or refuses to pay the same after demand, the amount * * * shall be a lien in favor of the United States * * *." [1] The demand referred to is obviously the demand the Service is required to make of the taxpayer "as soon as practicable" and in no event later than 60 days after an assessment. [2] The notice and demand used by the Service accords the taxpayer 10 days to make payment, presumably drawing on the levy provision which prohibits a levy within 10 days after the notice and demand. [3] Consequently, a tax lien arises when three events have happened: (1) a tax assessment has been made; (2) the taxpayer has been given notice of the assessment stating the amount and demanding its payment; and (3) the taxpayer has failed to pay the amount assessed within 10 days after the notice and demand. When, and only when, these three events have occurred, the tax lien which arises is enforceable against "all property and rights to property, whether real or personal, belonging to the [taxpayer]" as of the date the assessment was made. [4] Because the lien arises only after assessment and attaches to "all property and rights to property," it is called the assessment or general tax lien to distinguish it from the special gift and estate tax liens which arise without any assessment having been made and which attach to a limited class of property. [a]

The general tax lien arises automatically on the happening of the three prerequisites of assessment, demand and nonpayment. Nothing more is required to make the lien valid as against the taxpayer, and to subject property belonging to the taxpayer to seizure by levy. Moreover, nothing more need be done to establish the government's interest in the taxpayer's property as against other creditors of the taxpayer and persons having dealings with or claims against the taxpayer, although the lien will not be valid unless notice of the lien is filed as against certain persons (purchasers, holders of security interests, judgment lien creditors and mechanic lienors) and even though

1. I.R.C. § 6321.

2. I.R.C. § 6303(a).

3. I.R.C. § 6331(a).

4. I.R.C. §§ 6321, 6322.

a. The special estate and gift tax liens are discussed at pages 694–696 below.

a notice is filed, [it] will not be valid as against a limited class of "superpriority" interests.[b] Because the general tax lien has such a substantial impact on the taxpayer and those having dealings with the taxpayer—it literally is the basis for the collection process—the three prerequisites for the lien will be examined separately.

Assessment. It is not the act of assessment but its timing which is generally significant to a taxpayer because assessment is merely the official act of recording on a list the liability of a taxpayer.[5] * * *

* * *

Demand. Once the formal act of assessment takes place, the Service must "as soon as practicable, and within 60 days, after the making of an assessment of a tax, give notice to each person liable for the unpaid tax, stating the amount and demanding payment thereof * * * " by leaving the notice and demand "at the dwelling or usual place of business of such person" or mailing it to his "last known address."[6] [The initial notice customarily used by the Service provides a 10-day grace period for making payment.]

* * *

Nonpayment. * * * [S]ince the Service uses a series of notices, the 10-day grace period for making payment provided for in the initial notice and demand may, as a practical matter, be far longer than 10 days. Practical delay aside, on the expiration of the 10 days without payment (the statute literally requires "neglect or refusal to pay"), the general assessment lien attaches to all the taxpayer's property as of the date the assessment was made.[7]

Duration of lien

The duration of the general tax lien is tied to the statute of limitations on collection. Once the tax lien arises, it continues until the liability for the amount assessed (or a judgment against the taxpayer arising out of the liability) is satisfied or "becomes unenforceable by reason of lapse of time."[8] Generally, an assessed tax must be collected by levy or by a proceeding in court within 6 years after the date of assessment.[9] This means that the general tax lien exists for the 6-year statutory period of collection. Unless the tax has been collected by levy or the government has commenced a proceeding in court to collect the tax before the end of the 6-year period, the lien terminates at the end of that period. But the same rules that apply to the statute of limitations on collection apply to the duration of the tax

---

b. I.R.C. § 6223. See discussion at pages 700–701, below.

5. I.R.C. § 6203.

6. I.R.C. § 6303(a). * * *

7. I.R.C. § 6322. * * *

8. I.R.C. § 6322.

9. I.R.C. § 6502(a).

lien. Thus, if the 6-year period for collection is extended by agreement or by one of the circumstances of suspension described in § 6503, the period of the lien is extended as well. *   *   *

If a proceeding in court is begun before the expiration of the 6-year period, and a judgment against the taxpayer is obtained, whether before or after the 6-year period, the general assessment lien continues independently of any judgment until the underlying tax liability is satisfied or becomes unenforceable by reason of lapse of time. *   *   *

Once a judgment against the taxpayer is obtained, the assessment lien does not merge with the judgment. Section 6322 provides that the assessment lien continues until the liability "(or a judgment against the taxpayer arising out of such liability)" is satisfied or becomes unenforceable by reason of lapse of time. The effect of § 6322 is illustrated by a case where an assessment lien arose in 1949, a proceeding in court was commenced on the day before the 6-year period of limitations expired in 1955, and a judgment obtained in 1962 was foreclosed in 1971. Since the life of the lien was extended by the court proceeding, the tax lien continued to have priority over competing creditors who might have acquired liens on the taxpayer's property between the date of assessment (1949) and the date of the judgment (1962).[10]

State statutes of limitations do not affect the assessment lien, nor do they run against a judgment obtained by the Service.[11] However, a judgment lien arising from an action to reduce the tax assessment to judgment, is subject to state statutes as to duration.[12] Once a judgment is obtained, moreover, the assessment lien may not be enforced by administrative action such as levy after the period of limitations on collection would have run but for the action in court by the government. *   *   * [T]here comes a time when it is inappropriate for the government to collect by administrative levy action without court supervision.

The scope of the general tax lien

After assessment, demand and failure to pay, the general tax lien attaches automatically to "all property and rights to property, whether real or personal, belonging to the [taxpayer]".[13] The types of property subject to the general lien are unlimited, but there are certain principles which apply to the general tax lien irrespective of the type of property involved:

---

10. Moyer v. Mathas, et al., 71–2 U.S. T.C. ¶ 9533 (M.D.Fla.1971), aff'd 458 F.2d 431 (5th Cir. 1972).

11. United States v. Overman, 424 F. 2d 1142 (9th Cir. 1970). [But see United States v. Home Beneficial Life Ins. Co., Inc., 31 AFTR 2d 73–1085 (E.D.Tenn.), discussed below at page 709.]

12. See 28 U.S.C.A. § 1962.

13. I.R.C. § 6321.

1. *The government's interest is derivative.* While the tax lien attaches to all a taxpayer's property and rights to property, the security of the lien is derivative—that is, it is only as good as the taxpayer's interest in the property. Thus, it is said that the government as lienor "stands in the shoes" of the taxpayer. This means that while the tax lien attaches to and encumbers the taxpayer's property, it is subject to the same restrictions, conditions and disabilities the taxpayer has with respect to the property. * * *

[However,] there are certain restrictions which might operate to limit the right of a taxpayer but which do not limit the general tax lien; e. g., a state statute of limitations which runs against the taxpayer does not run against the government; [14] and an insurance clause requiring the insured-taxpayer to surrender the policy in order to receive its surrender value does not affect the operation of the lien.[15]

2. *The lien encumbers after-acquired property.* The general tax lien which attaches to all property of the taxpayer as of the assessment date continues until the liability is satisfied or becomes unenforceable by lapse of time.[16] Accordingly, the tax lien attaches not only to property belonging to the taxpayer on the assessment date, but also to property acquired after that date ("after-acquired property") until the tax is paid or collection becomes barred by the statute of limitations.[17]

3. *The lien only attaches to property belonging to the taxpayer on the assessment date.* The general tax lien does not attach to property the taxpayer has completely transferred before the assessment date because the transferred property does not "belong" to him as of that date. The transfer must be *bona fide.* A mere formal transfer will be ineffective to defeat the attachment of the lien; e. g., where a taxpayer transfers title but retains proceeds from the transferred property. Similarly, the tax lien will attach to property of a taxpayer even if it is held by an alter ego.[18]

4. *There are no exemptions from the effect of the lien.* The general tax lien attaches to literally all property belonging to the taxpayer as of the assessment date or acquired by him during the time the lien is in effect. No exemptions are provided for in the Code with respect to the general tax lien, although certain types and amounts of property are exempt from levy.[19] This means that the

14. United States v. Polan Industries, Inc., 196 F.Supp. 333 (S.D.W.Va. 1961).

15. Equitable Life Assur. Soc'y of the United States v. United States, 331 F.2d 29 (1st Cir. 1964).

16. I.R.C. § 6322.

17. Glass City Bank v. United States, 326 U.S. 265, 66 S.Ct. 108, 90 L.Ed. 56 (1945).

18. G.M. Leasing Corp. v. United States, 429 U.S. 338, 97 S.Ct. 619, 50 L.Ed.2d 530 (1977).

19. I.R.C. §§ 6321, 6334.

tax lien technically could be foreclosed even against exempt property, although it could not be administratively seized by levy. * * * Any exemption from the effect of the lien (to the extent one exists at all), must be found in the federal not the state law. * * *

The general tax lien attaches to property of the taxpayer wherever located and thus would encumber property outside the United States. While the lien may attach to property outside the United States, enforcement of the lien is quite another matter. Generally, foreign jurisdictions have not enforced tax claims absent treaty. Cooperation of a foreign government may not be necessary if a court in the United States has jurisdiction over the taxpayer.[20] * * *

5. *State law determines whether a taxpayer has "property" for purposes of the lien.* The Code in § 6321 may create the general tax lien which attaches to all property and rights to property of the taxpayer, but it does not create the rights, powers and privileges, or interests, the sum of which is called "property"; state law does. Consequently, state law controls the determination of the nature of the legal interest which the taxpayer had in property sought to be reached by the general tax lien.[21] Federal law attaches the consequences to the determination, or as the Supreme Court has said, "[The predecessor of § 6321] creates no property rights but merely attaches consequences, federally defined, to rights created under state law * * *."[22] In other words, whether and to what extent the taxpayer had a property interest is one of state law, but whether the state-created property interest constitutes "property or rights to property" and the consequences of that determination (such as lien priority or sale) is one of federal law.[23]

* * *

Government suits involving liens

* * *

There appears to be no limitation on the kinds of actions the Service may bring to effect collection of a tax, nor on the jurisdiction of district courts to hear such actions. District courts are granted jurisdiction "to make and issue in civil actions, writs and orders of injunction, and of *ne exeat republica,* orders appointing receivers, and such other orders as may be necessary and appropriate for the en-

20. United States v. Ross, 302 F.2d 831 (2nd Cir. 1962), aff'g 196 F.Supp. 243 (S.D.N.Y.1961); United States v. McNulty, 446 F.Supp. 90 (N.D.Cal. 1978) (taxpayer who won Irish sweepstakes ordered to repatriate from the Island of Jersey assets sufficient to satisfy taxes owed).

21. Aquilino v. United States, 363 U.S. 509, 80 S.Ct. 1277, 4 L.Ed.2d 1365 (1960).

22. United States v. Bess, 357 U.S. 51, 55, 78 S.Ct. 1054, 1057, 2 L.Ed.2d 1135 (1958).

23. See, Fidelity & Deposit Co. v. New York City Housing Auth., 241 F.2d 142, 144 (2d Cir. 1957). * * *

forcement of the internal revenue laws." [24]   The grant of jurisdiction is obviously very broad indeed, but this "all writs" jurisdiction of the district courts is "in addition to and not exclusive of any and all other remedies of the United States in such courts or otherwise to enforce such [internal revenue] laws."   *   *   *   What follows is a summary of the more common collection actions brought by the government.

1.   *Suit to reduce tax assessment to judgment.*   A suit to reduce a tax assessment to judgment is generally instituted to prevent the statute of limitations for collection from running where collection cannot be accomplished by administrative methods (levy and sale) within the normal collection period.[25]   In order to reduce a tax assessment to judgment, the government has the burden of proving that the assessment and collection suit is timely and the period of limitations has not expired.   *   *   *

2.   *Foreclosure of tax liens.*   Where there has been a refusal or neglect to pay any tax, and it is not feasible to seize and sell the delinquent taxpayer's real or personal property administratively to satisfy the tax liability, an action may be commenced in a federal district court to foreclose the tax lien against specific property.[26]   All persons having liens upon or claiming any interest in the property involved must be made parties.[27]   The form of action is a proceeding *in rem,* so that venue is determined by the location of the property, and a jury trial is not available.[28]   After the parties have been "duly notified of the action," the court proceeds to adjudicate all matters involved and finally determines the merits of all claims to and liens on the property.   If the claim or interest of the United States is established, the court may order that the property be sold and the proceeds of the sale be distributed according to the court's findings. *   *   *   At a judicial sale, the purchaser can expect a good marketable title without the necessity of further litigation [and, therefore, will generally pay a higher price for the property sold than at a sale following administrative seizure].   The practical difference in result between an administrative seizure and sale and a lien foreclosure suit presents the government with an option which is generally resolved in favor of judicial sale, thus cutting off the statutory right of redemption afforded the taxpayer and others when administrative collection action is taken.

---

24.   I.R.C. § 7403.

25.   Authority for this type of action is found in I.R.C. § 7403(a).

26.   I.R.C. §§ 7402(a) and 7403(a).   A suit to enforce or foreclose a tax lien is generally initiated when title to property claimed to be subject to the lien is in dispute   *   *   *.

27.   I.R.C. § 7403(b).

28.   *   *   *   [However,] if a personal judgment for taxes owed is sought, then personal jurisdiction over the taxpayer must be obtained.

3. *Appointment of a receiver.* At the request of the government, the court may appoint a receiver to (a) enforce the tax lien or, (b) during the pendency of the proceeding, upon certification of the Commissioner that it is in the public interest, appoint a receiver with all the powers of a receiver in equity.[29] *   *   *

4. *Intervention.* If the United States is not a party to a civil action or suit, it may intervene in the action or suit to assert any tax lien on the property which is the subject of the action or suit.[30] [Although the court need not grant the government's motion to intervene,] if the government's motion *   *   * is denied, the proceedings have no effect on the tax lien. The government could enforce the lien against property by foreclosure.

5. *Action to open safe deposit box.* If a taxpayer refuses to cooperate and voluntarily consent to the opening of his safe deposit box, the government can make an application in a district court for a court order directing the keeper of the box to open it for inspection or seizure of the contents by the government.[31] *   *   *

6. *Warrants of entry.* In the same manner as it proceeds to open a safe deposit box, the Service believes it can make an *ex parte* application to a federal district court for authorization to enter a taxpayer's premises to seize property for tax collection purposes.[32] *   *   *

7. *Miscellaneous actions.* To collect a tax the United States may bring any suit available to creditors generally. The government may obtain a court order restraining the taxpayer from leaving the country (a writ *"ne exeat republica"*).[33] Where a third party holds a taxpayer's "property or rights to property" subject to a tax lien, the government can sue the third party even though no levy has been served, for tortious conversion of the government's "collateral". The United States may also institute a suit under the fraudulent conveyance statutes of the various states to set aside transfers of property by a taxpayer which are fraudulent or which are without adequate consideration at a time when the transferor is insolvent or rendered insolvent by the transfer.

Any portion of any internal revenue tax which has been erroneously refunded to a taxpayer may be recovered by administrative action or a suit in court.[34] While assessment and collection may be used to collect the tax due and erroneously refunded to a taxpayer, a suit is generally used because the statute of limitations on assessment

29. I.R.C. § 7403(d).

30. I.R.C. § 7424.

31. I.R.C. § 6402. At one time, the action was considered to be one to enforce a levy, but in United States v. First Nat'l City Bank, 321 F.2d 14 (1963), the Second Circuit found jurisdiction under the "all writs" statute, I.R.C. § 7402.

32. *   *   * See In re Carlson, 580 F.2d 1365 (10th Cir. 1978).

33. I.R.C. § 7402(a).

34. I.R.C. § 7405.

has run. However, there is a relatively short period within which the suit for erroneous refund must be brought—within 2 years from the making of the refund or within 5 years if any part of the refund was induced by fraud or misrepresentation of material fact.[35] The 2-year period begins to run from the date of delivery of the refund check.[36]

SPECIAL ESTATE AND GIFT TAX LIENS

The special estate tax lien—in general

The general tax lien attaches to all property belonging to a taxpayer after assessment, demand and nonpayment of the tax. This general lien secures payment of all types of federal taxes, including estate taxes. To secure payment of estate taxes, a second type of lien called the "special estate tax lien" also exists in favor of the government. Without assessment or notice and demand, the special estate tax lien comes into existence automatically on the date of death. It continues for 10 years unless, before the end of the 10-year period, the estate tax is paid in full or becomes unenforceable by expiration of the statute of limitations on collection.[37]   *   *   *

*   *   *

The general tax and the special estate tax liens are cumulative security devices to ensure payment of an estate tax. Either or both liens may be available to the government in a particular situation. The different liens operate independently of each other in the sense that each lien comes into existence when the conditions precedent to creation of the lien (general or special) are met and continue according to the facts and the applicable statutory provisions.   *   *   *

Despite their independence, there is some relationship between the two liens. While the special lien has a duration of no more than 10 years, it terminates before the expiration of the 10-year period if the general lien has been extinguished. If the general lien securing an assessed estate tax liability becomes unenforceable because of the expiration of the 6-year statutory period of collection (without commencement of a collection action, for example), then the special lien also becomes unenforceable "by reason of the lapse of time."[38]
*   *   *

Operation of the special estate tax lien

The special estate tax lien attaches to property includible in the gross estate of a decedent. The term "gross estate" is a creation of the estate tax provisions (§§ 2031–2044) of the Code. Since the general lien attaches only to property or rights to property owned by the

35. I.R.C. § 6532(b).

36. United States v. Wurts, 303 U.S. 414, 58 S.Ct. 637, 82 L.Ed. 932 (1938).

37. I.R.C. § 6324(a).

38. I.R.C. § 6324(a)(1).

decedent at the time of death and thus passing through probate, the special lien is far broader than the general lien. Accordingly, the property subject to the special estate tax lien may be divided into two categories: property belonging to the decedent or his estate (i. e., probate property), and other property included in the gross estate under §§ 2034–2042 (i. e., nonprobate property). The special lien attaches to such nonprobate property as dower or curtesy interests (§ 2034), property transferred in contemplation of death (§ 2035), transfers with a retained life estate (§ 2036), transfers taking effect at death (§ 2037), revocable transfers (§ 2038), annuities (§ 2039), joint interests (§ 2040), powers of appointment (§ 2041), and the proceeds of life insurance (§ 2042).

* * *

There is [a] discharge provision peculiar to the special tax lien called the "shifting" lien. Certain third parties are protected against the effect of the general lien by the requirement that the lien be publicly filed in order to be valid against them. No notice of the special lien need be filed for it to be effective, however. Rather, property sold or transferred to a "purchaser" or "holder of a security interest" is automatically discharged or divested from the effect of the lien, but the lien shifts to the consideration received from the purchaser or the secured lender.[39] * * *

* * *

The special gift tax lien

There is a special gift tax lien which attaches to any and all gifts made during the period for which the donor filed a return and continues for ten years from the date the gifts are made, unless the gift tax is sooner paid in full or becomes unenforceable by reason of lapse of time.[40] If the tax is not paid when due, the donee of any gift becomes personally liable for the tax to the extent of the value of the gift. This personal liability exists so long as there is any gift (including one to another donee) during the year, the tax on which is owing.[41] * * * The limit of a donee's liability, however, is the value of the gift received.[42]

The same shifting lien procedure used with respect to the special estate tax lien is found where the special gift tax lien is involved. If any part of the property comprised in the gift is transferred by the donee (or by a transferee of the donee) to a purchaser or a holder of a security interest, the property sold or secured is divested of the lien, but the lien to the extent of the value of the gift attaches to all the property (including after-acquired property) of the donee (or the transferee) except the part transferred to the purchaser or a holder

39. I.R.C. § 6324(a)(3). * * *   41. I.R.C. § 6324(b). * * *

40. I.R.C. § 6324(a).   42. Id.

of a security interest. As with the special estate tax lien, the gift tax lien is not effective as against a mechanic lienor or the lien or security interest of a person having "superpriority" over a filed tax lien.[43]

* * *

* * *

PRIORITY OF TAX CLAIMS

Determining the issue of priority: general principles

As a general rule, when a tax lien is competing with another secured creditor, the first lien to arise has priority (first-in-time, first-in-right). This general rule is only a starting point in resolving priority questions involving tax liens, however. To determine the priority of a tax lien and a competing interest, the nature of the competing interest, the property involved and the form of the transaction between the taxpayer and the interest competing with the tax lien must be taken into acount. Determination of the priority of interests competing with the tax lien also depends upon the resolution of three other issues:

1. On the date the tax lien arose, as a matter of state law, did the taxpayer own "property" which could be encumbered by a tax lien;

2. [As of] the date the tax lien arose, had the taxpayer completely transferred the property to a third person * * * (considering the creation of a lien a transfer); and

3. Is the third person competing with the tax lien protected from its effect by the statutory provisions of § 6323.

* * *

* * *

The protection of § 6323

Prior to 1966, the predecessor version of § 6323 provided that, although the tax lien arises on the date of assessment, purchasers and certain categories of secured creditors had priority over the tax lien up to the time a notice of tax lien was filed in the appropriate local office designated by state law. Mortgagees, pledgees, purchasers and judgment lien creditors were given this status. The Federal Tax Lien Act of 1966 (FTLA) was the first comprehensive revision and modernization of the provision of the Code dealing with the relationship of Federal tax liens to the interests of other creditors. Briefly, the revised § 6323: (1) expanded the categories of creditors protected against a nonfiled tax lien to include a mechanic lienor; (2) substituted "holder of a security interest" for "mortgagee" and "pledg-

---

43. The statutory definitions of these superpriority interests are found at I.R.C. § 6323(b). [See discussion below.]

ee" with a view to giving the various types of interests defined by the term priority over a nonfiled tax lien "whether or not in all other regards they are definite and complete at the time the tax lien is filed"; (3) increased from two to ten the categories of interests in properties which have priority even though notice of the lien has been filed; (4) provided priority status for interests arising under three types of financing agreements entered into before tax lien filing even though funds are advanced or property comes into existence after tax lien filing; and (5) gave a limited priority with respect to disbursements made within 45 days after tax lien filing and for interest and expenses attributable to interests having priority over a tax lien.

* * *

Protection of transactions occurring before tax lien filing—§ 6323(a)

Section 6323(a) lists certain categories of persons whose interests arise after the general tax lien exists but before notice of the lien is filed and provides that the interests of those persons have priority over the unfiled tax lien. The persons listed in § 6323 are purchasers, holders of security interests, judgment lien creditors and mechanic lienors. Until a notice of tax lien is filed, transactions of these persons with the taxpayer are protected although a tax lien may already be in existence on all the taxpayer's "property and rights to property." The definitions of the four interests included in the protected class are discussed in subparagraphs [1] through [4] and the filing rules in subparagraph [5].

[1] *Purchasers.* * * * A "purchaser" entitled to notice of a federal tax lien, means a person who (1) for adequate and full consideration in money or money's worth, (2) acquires an interest (other than a lien or security interest) in property and (3) whose interest in the property is valid under local law against subsequent purchasers without actual notice.[44] * * *

[2] *Holder of a security interest.* The "holder of a security interest" as used in § 6323(a) was meant to include the terms "mortgagee" and "pledgee" under the pre-1966 law and to bring the tax lien statute in line with the Uniform Commercial Code (UCC) now adopted in all states except Louisiana. The definition of security interest is not identical with the UCC definition, however. Under § 6323 a "security interest" means any interest (including a chattel mortgage or pledge) acquired by contract for the purpose of securing payment, performance of an obligation or indemnifying against loss or liability.[45] * * *

* * * The § 6323 definition of a security interest * * * states that a security interest exists when (1) the property is "in existence" (not that the debtor-taxpayer has "rights in the collateral");

44. I.R.C. § 6323(h)(6).   45. I.R.C. § 6323(h)(1). Treas.Reg. § 301.6323(h)–1(a).

(2) the interest has become protected under local law against a "subsequent judgment lien arising out of an unsecured obligation" (not a person who becomes a "lien creditor before the security interest was perfected"); and (3) to the extent that the holder has parted with money or money's worth.[46]

* * *

[3] *Judgment lien creditor.* * * * A judgment lien creditor under present law is a person who has obtained a valid judgment in a court of record and of competent jurisdiction for the recovery of specific property or a sum of money.[47]

The regulations defining the term "judgment lien creditor" [48] [state that w]here a judgment for a sum of money is involved, a judgment lien creditor is a person who has *perfected* a lien under the judgment on the property involved.[49] Thus, a judgment lien creditor does not include an attachment or garnishment lien or lien lis pendens until that lien has ripened into judgment, even though under local law the lien of the judgment related back to an earlier date. * * *

* * *

[4] *Mechanic lienor.* A mechanic's lien is conferred by state statutes and gives those furnishing labor or materials in improving land a lien on the land to secure payment for the work and material furnished.[50] * * * Under the statutory definition of the term, § 6323(f)(2), a mechanic lienor is a person who under local law has a lien on real property (or on the proceeds of a contract relating to real property) for services, labor or materials furnished in connection with the construction or improvement of real property. * * *

The Code definition goes on to say, however, that "a person has a lien on the earliest date such lien became valid under local law against subsequent purchasers without actual notice, but not before he begins to furnish the services, labor or materials." Consequently, a mechanic must take appropriate steps under local law to perfect his lien against subsequent purchasers without notice if he is to have priority over a later [filed] tax lien.[51] But * * * a mechanic need not have "perfected" his lien by filing or securing a judgment unless state law requires it. Under most state laws and § 6323, the mechanic's lien arises when the mechanic commences his labor or begins

---

46. I.R.C. § 6323(h)(1).

47. Treas.Reg. § 301.6323(h)–1(g).

48. Ibid.

49. Ibid.

50. Brown, Personal Property (3d ed. 1975), p. 393; see also, UCC § 9–104(C).

51. Jitney-Jungle Stores of America, Inc. v. United States, 1977–2 U.S.T.C. ¶ 9751 (S.D.Miss.).

supplying material, even though he does not perfect his lien until long after this time. *   *   *

*   *   *

[5] *The requirement of a filed notice of tax lien.* A notice of tax lien must be filed if the lien is to be effective (that is, to have priority) over a protected class of creditors and transferees comprised of purchasers, holders of security interests, judgment lien creditors and mechanic's lienors. The kind of notice referred to is record notice—that is, the tax lien is not perfected or "valid" against this protected class until notice of the lien has been filed (1) in the proper place and (2) form, § 6323(f), and (3) to continue its effectiveness against this protected class, refiled within a specified time, § 6323(g).

Place of filing. Since 1966, the Code has adopted a "single office" rule for filing tax liens. This means that if the law of the state in which the real or personal property is situated provides for the filing of liens in a single office, the federal tax lien must also be filed in that office.[52] If state law designates more than one office, however, the federal tax lien must be filed with the Clerk of the United States District Court for the judicial district in which the property subject to the lien is situated.[53] *   *   *

There is an additional requirement in order for the notice of lien to be considered filed for the purposes of § 6323. In the case of real property, a notice of tax lien must be entered and recorded in a public index at the place of filing maintained by a state.[54] Consequently, a notice of tax lien filed in accordance with the state's single office rule is not "filed" unless it has also been entered and recorded in the public index at the appropriate state office.

Where is property situated? Real property is situated at its physical location. Personal property, whether tangible or intangible, is situated at the residence of the taxpayer at the time the notice of lien is filed. This means that if state law designates the county clerk's office of the county in which the debtor resides as the office for filing liens on personal property, a tax lien filed in that office is validly filed, even if the taxpayer-debtor subsequently moves to another county within the state or to another state.[55] The place of resi-

---

52. I.R.C. § 6323(f)(1)(A).

53. I.R.C. § 6323(f)(1)(B). The statute says filing with the Clerk of the federal district court is required when a state has "not by law designated one office" for filing notices of liens. *   *   *

54. I.R.C. § 6323(f)(4). This indexing of the tax lien is required if (1) state law provides that a deed is not valid against a purchaser of the realty without actual notice or knowledge of the existence of the deed unless the filing of the deed has been entered and recorded in a public index for filing so that a reasonable inspection will reveal the existence of the deed and (2) at this office an adequate system for the public indexing of federal tax liens is maintained.

55. Treas.Reg. § 301.6323(f)–1(d) Ex. (1) and (2).

dence of a corporation or a partnership is the place its principal executive office is located.[56] The residence of an individual probably means his domicile (roughly speaking, his place of permanent residence to which he returns or intends to return). The residence of a taxpayer whose residence is not within the United States is considered to be in the District of Columbia.[57] * * *

In general, once a tax lien is filed, it is effective for a period of six years which is the limitations period for collection. But the period of collection may be extended beyond six years by agreement or by periods of suspension of the statutory period. Because of this possibility, a creditor might mistakenly assume that a tax lien which is older than six years is no longer effective and extend credit to a taxpayer. To protect creditors against a lien which is still enforceable after the six-year period, the Service is required to refile the notice of lien within the one-year period ending 30 days after the expiration of the six-year period after the assessment of the tax.[58] Failure to file within this required refiling period has the effect of nullifying the original tax lien filing as to interests in property arising at any time after the original tax lien filing.[59] * * *

* * *

Persons protected against filed tax liens—superpriorities: § 6323(b)

Prior to 1966, even if a federal tax lien was filed, it was not valid against a mortgagee, pledgee or purchaser of a security, or certain purchasers of motor vehicles, if the transfer was made for adequate or full consideration in money or money's worth and without notice or knowledge of the existence of the tax lien. These interests were said to be "superpriorities." In 1966, eight other superpriorities were added to the superpriorities for securities and motor vehicles. Some of these superpriorities are casual or common transactions (such as purchases of personal property at retail or in casual sale, or those of securities or of a motor vehicle) where it could not reasonably be expected that the purchaser check for filed tax liens. Others are transactions which tend to increase the value of the taxpayer's property (such as possessory liens attaching to repaired personal property or mechanic's liens for certain repairs and improvements to residential property). [On the theory that an attorney's action in prosecuting a claim or cause of action for the taxpayer tends to increase the amount available for collection, a superpriority to the extent of reasonable compensation is provided attorneys with respect to a settle-

---

56. Treas.Reg. § 301.6323(f)–1(b).

57. Ibid.

58. I.R.C. § 6323(g). * * *

59. Treas.Reg. § 301.6323(g)–1(a)(3). The Treasury Regulations state two

exceptions to this rule: (1) property which is the subject matter of a suit to which the United States is party, commenced prior to the expiration of the 6-year period and (2) property which has been levied upon prior to the end of the 6-year period. Ibid.

ment or judgment except in certain cases involving suits against the United States.| Others (such as policy and premium loans or passbook loans) do not easily fit into any category, except perhaps transfers of a debtor's funds where checking for liens would be commercially infeasible. [A complete listing of the ten superpriority interests is located at § 6323(b)(1)–(10).|

[Although it is not the purpose of this discussion to examine each of the ten superpriority interests, it should be noted that most of these interests will be defeated if the person claiming the protection of § 6323(b) had "actual notice or knowledge" of the existence of the tax lien at the time of his or her dealings with the taxpayer.|

* * *

NOTES

1. The priority of a lien competing with a tax lien depends upon whether (and when) the competing lien is deemed to have become choate. To be choate, a lien must be identified as to lienor, the amount of lien and property subject to lien. United States v. Equitable Life Assur. Soc'y, 384 U.S. 323, 86 S.Ct. 1561, 16 L.Ed.2d 593 (1966) (federal tax lien afforded priority over mortgagee's claim for attorney's fee, where notice of tax lien was filed prior to default by the mortgagor). The continued viability of the choate lien doctrine has been brought into question by the enactment of the Federal Tax Lien Act of 1966. Compare, e. g., Texas Oil & Gas Corp. v. United States, 466 F.2d 1040 (5th Cir. 1977) (applying the choate lien test) with Donald v. Madison Indus., Inc., 483 F.2d 837 (10th Cir. 1973) (choate-ness criteria "inappropriate and out-of-date" and "totally obsolete"). Saltzman suggests that Congress intended that § 6323 replace the choate lien test only where the statute specifically applies. Tax Procedure and Internal Revenue Service Practice at § 16.01[3]. In certain contexts, (consider, for example, the requirement that a judgment lien creditor *perfect* his interest under state law) the test applied under § 6323 is essentially the same as that applied under the choate lien doctrine.

2. Sections 6323(c) and (d) afford priority to interests arising under certain types of commercial financing agreements even though these interests arise after tax lien filing. Security interests which: (1) are in "qualified property", (2) arise under specified financing agreements (commercial transactions financing agreements, real property construction or improvement financing agreements and obligatory disbursement agreements) entered into before tax lien filing, and (3) are protected under local law against a judgment lien arising at the time of tax lien filing, are given priority over the tax lien although funds are advanced to the taxpayer after the tax lien has been filed. IRC § 6323(c)(1)–(4). Section 6323(d) states that, under certain conditions, a lender may, for 45 days after the filing of notice of tax lien, make additional advances to the taxpayer (upon a written agreement entered into before tax lien filing₁ and still retain priority for these advances despite the filing of the lien.

3. In addition to § 6323 of the Code, there are other statutory provisions which ensure priority for tax claims against debtors. The Bankrupt-

cy Code, at 11 U.S.C.A. § 507(a)(6), states that most types of tax liabilities have sixth-level priority over the claims of other creditors. Priority is also given to tax claims in collective creditors proceedings (which have not resulted in bankruptcy) under 31 U.S.C.A. §§ 191, 192, commonly referred to by their Revised Statutes designations, §§ 3466 and 3467. Proceedings under §§ 3466 and 3467 involve claims against the insolvent estate of a deceased taxpayer, or against a fiduciary having possession and control of the property of an insolvent living taxpayer.

REVENUE RULING 68–57

1968–1 C.B. 553

The Federal Tax Lien Act of 1966, C.B. 1966–2, 623, does not refer to a purchase money security interest or mortgage. However, the General Explanation of the Act, as set forth in House of Representatives Report No. 1884, C.B. 1966–2, at page 817, states as follows:

> Although so-called purchase money mortgages are not specifically referred to under present law, it has generally been held that these interests are protected whenever they arise. This is based upon the concept that the taxpayer has acquired property or a right to property only to the extent that the value of the whole property or right exceeds the amount of the purchase money mortgage. This concept is not affected by the bill.

In view of the legislative history of the Federal Tax Lien Act of 1966, the Internal Revenue Service will consider that a purchase money security interest or mortgage valid under local law is protected even though it may arise after a notice of Federal tax lien has been filed.

AQUILINO v. UNITED STATES

Supreme Court of the United States, 1960.
363 U.S. 509, 80 S.Ct. 1277, 4 L.Ed.2d 1365.

Mr. Chief Justice WARREN delivered the opinion of the Court.

In this case we are asked to determine which of two competing claimants—the Federal Government by virtue of its tax lien, or certain petitioning subcontractors by virtue of their rights under Section 36-a of the New York Lien Law—is entitled to a sum of money owed under a general construction contract which was performed by the taxpayer.

The taxpayer, Fleetwood Paving Corporation, is a general contractor, which in July or August 1952, agreed to remodel a restaurant belonging to one Ada Bottone, herein referred to as the owner. The petitioners in August and September of that year entered into a subcontract with the taxpayer to supply labor and materials for the remodeling job. Shortly thereafter, the petitioners performed their obligations under the subcontract, but were not fully compensated by the contractor-taxpayer. Therefore on November 3, 1952, and on November 10, 1952, they filed notices of their mechanic's liens on the owner's realty in the office of the Clerk of Westchester County. In June 1953, they instituted actions in the New York Supreme Court to foreclose those liens.

By order of court, the owner was permitted to deposit with the Clerk of the court the $2,200 which she still owed under the original construction contract, and she was thereafter dismissed as a defendant in the action. The Government, having previously levied upon the owner's alleged indebtedness to the taxpayer, was permitted by the court to enter the case as a party defendant.

The Government asserted precedence over the claims of petitioners because of the following facts: The Director of Internal Revenue in December 1951 and March 1952 received assessment lists containing assessments against the taxpayer for unpaid federal withholding and social security taxes. On October 31, 1952, the Director filed a notice of federal tax liens in the office of the Clerk of the City of Mount Vernon, New York, which is the city wherein the taxpayer maintained its principal place of business. The Government claimed priority for its tax lien under Sections 3670 and 3671 of the Internal Revenue Code of 1939, 26 U.S.C.A. §§ 3670, 3671.[1] The petitioners contended that since the contractor-taxpayer owed them more than $2,200 for labor and materials supplied to the job, under the New York Lien Law, Section 36–a, he had no property interest in the $2,200 which the owner still owed under the original remodeling contract.

The New York Supreme Court, Special Term, granted petitioners' motion for summary judgment. * * * On appeal, the Appellate Division affirmed, * * * on the ground that there was no debt due from the owner to the taxpayer to which the Government's lien could attach. The court reasoned that the fund deposited by the owner was a substitute for her realty to which the mechanic's liens had attached; and that since the Government had no lien on the owner's property, it could have no lien on the fund substituted for that property. On appeal, the New York Court of Appeals held that the tax lien had taken effect prior to the petitioners' claims. It therefore reversed the lower New York courts, and ruled that the motion of the United States for summary judgment, rather than that of petitioners, should have been granted by the Supreme Court, Special Term. We granted certiorari.

The threshold question in this case, as in all cases where the Federal Government asserts its tax lien, is whether and to what ex-

1. * * * These provisions also appear in the 1954 Code. Int.Rev.Code of 1954, §§ 6321, 6322, 26 U.S.C.A. §§ 6321, 6322.

tent the taxpayer had "property" or "rights to property" to which the tax lien could attach. In answering that question, both federal and state courts must look to state law, for it has long been the rule that "in the application of a federal revenue act, state law controls in determining the nature of the legal interest which the taxpayer had in the property * * * sought to be reached by the statute." Morgan v. Commissioner, 309 U.S. 78, 82, 60 S.Ct. 424, 426, 84 L.Ed. 585. Thus, as we held only two Terms ago, Section 3670 "creates no property rights but merely attaches consequences, federally defined, to rights created under state law * * *." United States v. Bess, 357 U.S. 51, 55, 78 S.Ct. 1054, 1057, 2 L.Ed.2d 1135. However, once the tax lien has attached to the taxpayer's state-created interests, we enter the province of federal law, which we have consistently held determines the priority of competing liens asserted against the taxpayer's "property" or "rights to property." United States v. Vorreiter, 355 U.S. 15, 78 S.Ct. 19, 2 L.Ed.2d 23, reversing 134 Colo. 543, 307 P. 2d 475. The application of state law in ascertaining the taxpayer's property rights and of federal law in reconciling the claims of competing lienors is based both upon logic and sound legal principles. This approach strikes a proper balance between the legitimate and traditional interest which the State has in creating and defining the property interest of its citizens, and the necessity for a uniform administration of the federal revenue statutes.

Petitioners contend that the New York Court of Appeals did not make its determination in the light of these settled principles. Relying upon the express language of Section 36–a of the Lien Law and upon a number of lower New York court decisions interpreting that statute, petitioners conclude that the money actually received by the contractor-taxpayer and his right to collect amounts still due under the construction contract constitute a direct trust for the benefit of subcontractors, and that the only property rights which the contractor-taxpayer has in the trust are bare legal title to any money actually received and a beneficial interest in so much of the trust proceeds as remain after the claims of subcontractors have been settled. The Government, on the other hand, claims that Section 36–a merely gives the subcontractors an ordinary lien, and that the contractor-taxpayer's property rights encompass the entire indebtedness of the owner under the construction contract.

This conflict should not be resolved by this Court, but by the highest court of the State of New York. We cannot say from the opinion of the Court of Appeals that it has been satisfactorily resolved. * * * We therefore vacate the judgment of the Court of Appeals, and remand the case to that court so that it may ascertain the property interests of the taxpayer under state law and then dispose of the case according to established principles of law.

Vacated and remanded.

NOTE

On remand, the New York Court of Appeals concluded that, under New York law, "a contractor does not have a sufficient beneficial interest in the moneys, due or to become due from the owner under the contract, to give him a property right in them, except insofar as there is a balance remaining after all subcontractors and other statutory beneficiaries [under Section 36–a of the New York Lien Law] have been paid." Aquilino v. United States, 10 N.Y.2d 271, 282, 176 N.E.2d 826, 832 (1961). Therefore the government's lien was ineffective in reaching the monies owing to the general contractor-taxpayer for the benefit of the subcontractors under the construction contract.

UNITED STATES v. OVERMAN

424 F.2d 1142 (9th Cir. 1970).

HUFSTEDLER, Circuit Judge.

This interlocutory appeal raises novel questions about the creation and enforcement of federal tax liens levied on Washington community property to secure payment of a husband's premarital income tax liability.

In 1954 the Internal Revenue Service levied deficiency assessments against the taxpayer in respect of his income taxes for the years 1946 and 1947. The taxpayer married Marie Overman in 1948. When the taxpayer failed to meet the deficiency demand, a notice of federal tax liens was filed with the proper Washington state officials. The Government sued in 1960 to recover judgment against the taxpayer for the tax liabilities underlying the assessments, and a judgment for $109,709.56 in favor of the Government was rendered in 1961. The judgment recited that it was "individually only, and not against his marital community." The Government brought the present action on August 2, 1967, under section 7403 of the Internal Revenue Code to enforce the liens, joining as defendants the taxpayer, his wife, and certain other persons claiming an interest in the property attached.

In the order from which this appeal has been taken the district court decided that the Government had a valid lien on the taxpayer's undivided one-half interest in the marital community, that the lien was enforceable against the community assets as to which foreclosure was sought, and that the Government was not precluded from enforcing its lien by limitations or laches, or by the doctrines of res judicata, estoppel, or waiver. We affirm the order.

I.

Section 6321 of the Internal Revenue Code provides that the amount of the delinquent taxpayer's liability "shall be a lien in favor of the United States upon all property and rights to property, whether real or personal, belonging to such person." The statute incorporates state law for the limited purpose of ascertaining whether or not the taxpayer's interest is "property" or "rights to property." If state law raises the taxpayer's interest to the status of property or rights to property, federal law will cause a lien to attach to that interest. We must thus turn to Washington law to determine whether the taxpayer's interest in the community property constitutes "property" or "rights to property" belonging to him. We believe that it does.

* * *

The taxpayer contends, however, that his interest in the community is made nonattachable by the Washington rule that the community is generally immune from liability for a husband's premarital debt. While admitting that a state rule of exemption is ineffective against a United States tax lien, the taxpayer argues that the Washington rule is more than that. He contends that the rule is one of property law, and creates a limitation on the extent and quality of his ownership rights under state law. Even assuming that this characterization of Washington law is correct, all that section 6321 requires is that the interest be "property" or "rights to property." It is of no statutory moment how extensive may be those rights under state law, or what restrictions exist on the enjoyment of those rights. Similarly, taxpayer's reliance on the "entity theory" of community property is misplaced. Early Washington cases suggest that neither spouse has title to the assets of the community, but our concern here is with the taxpayer's *interest* in the community. Whatever may be said with regard to his interest in particular assets in the community, Washington law has never suggested that his interest in the community is nonexistent or valueless. Thus, neither the rule of nonliability nor the entity theory negates our conclusion that the taxpayer's interest constitutes "rights to property."

The attachment of a tax lien under section 6321 and the enforcement of the lien under section 7403 of the Code present different questions. From the conclusion that a lien attaches, the further conclusion that these particular liens may be foreclosed or otherwise enforced in a particular manner does not automatically follow.

We agree with the Government that the right of the United States to enforce its liens on Washington community property does not depend on Washington law regulating the rights of creditors generally. The result is sometimes reached by labeling as an "exemption" state law immunizing some kinds of property against the claims of some kinds of creditors and by concluding that such law does not bind the United States. Labels aside, state law regulating creditors' rights does not apply to the United States because the United States has not looked to state law to decide how to enforce federal tax liens and nothing in section 7403, under which this action was brought, suggests that Congress intended to change that rule.

Section 7403 provides that the Government in an action to enforce its tax lien may "subject any property, of whatever nature, of the delinquent, or in which he has any right, title, or interest, to the payment of such tax or liability." It requires joinder of all parties having an interest in the property, and, if a claim of the United States is established, "the court   *   *   *   may decree a sale of such property   *   *   *   and a distribution of the proceeds of such sale according to the findings of the court in respect to the interests of the parties and of the United States."

Once the lien has been established, the statute empowers the district court to subject the whole of the property in which the delinquent taxpayer has an interest to a forced sale. The power is not limited to the sale of only the delinquent taxpayer's interest. Thus, the statute contemplates that the district court may subject the interests of persons other than the taxpayer to an involuntary conversion during the course of enforcing the Government's lien on the delinquent taxpayer's interest in the same property. The owners other than the taxpayer, however, are entitled to just compensation from the proceeds of the sale for that "taking."

We emphasize that Section 7403 is cast in mandatory terms only in respect of the establishment of the Government's lien, the joinder of all persons interested in the property involved, and the determination of their respective interests. The remainder of the section confers broad discretionary powers upon the court in shaping a decree designed to work substantial justice among all interested persons. *   *   *

In shaping its decree the court, however, must turn to state law to define the property interests involved. Under Washington law, as we have earlier stated, each spouse has an undivided one-half interest in the marital community. The Government cannot claim from the proceeds of sale more than that share of the proceeds attributable to the taxpayer's half of the community interest in the asset. It cannot reach the proceeds attributable to the wife's interest. Her interest was not subject to attachment for her husband's premarital tax debt, and the Government's right to share in the proceeds of sale does not exceed the taxpayer's interest in the property subjected to the lien.

We therefore conclude that the district court correctly held that the taxpayer's undivided one-half interest in the community was subject to the tax liens, and that those liens could be enforced by foreclosure against assets of the community. From the proceeds of the sale, the Government should receive such share attributable to the taxpayer's interest, due regard being given to the compensation of those persons, including the taxpayer's wife, whose interests have been established in the property.

The district court has not shaped a final decree. Nothing in the record before us on this interlocutory appeal suggests that the court has abused its discretion in causing a forced sale of the property or in allocating the proceeds of a sale to the persons having interests in such property.

II.

Enforcement of the Goverment's liens on the taxpayer's interest in the community is not barred by limitations, laches, or equitable estoppel.

The tax liens that the Government seeks to enforce in the present action arose in 1954, when taxpayer failed to respond to a notice of assessment issued by the District Director of Internal Revenue. (26 U.S.C. § 6321.) Under section 6322 of the Code, those liens were to continue until the underlying liability was satisfied or became "unenforceable by reason of lapse of time." The Government brought suit to recover judgment upon the liability underlying the assessments before the expiration of the six-year statute of limitations upon the collection of an assessment. (26 U.S.C. § 6502(a).) The life of the liens was thereby extended beyond the initial six-year period. The 1961 judgment entered in the suit again extended the enforceability of the liability and thus the life of the liens. Although a lien based on that judgment is subject to state-created limitations (28 U. S.C. § 1962; Fed.R.Civ.Proc. 69(a)), the judgment itself is not subject to limitations and is enforceable at any time. The tax liens are merged neither into the judgment nor into the judgment liens; they continue to exist independently of either. The tax liens are enforceable at any time, because the underlying liability has been merged into the 1961 judgment and that liability cannot become "unenforceble by reason of lapse of time."

The United States is not subject to the defense of laches in enforcing its rights. No case has been made out by the appellants for the application of the doctrine of equitable estoppel, even if the doctrine were otherwise applicable to the Government.

The appellants claim that the assertion of the Government's lien against taxpayer's interest in the community is foreclosed by the recitation in the 1961 judgment that it was "individually only, and not against his marital community."

Under Washington law a personal judgment against a married man is presumed to be against the community. The purpose of the recitation was to make clear that the judgment was against the taxpayer for a separate, not a community, debt. No greater sigificance can be attributed to the recitation.

The interlocutory is affirmed, and the cause is remanded for further proceedings.

QUESTION

The case law is unsettled regarding the applicability of state statutes of limitations to judgments obtained by the Service against delinquent taxpayers. The *Overman* decision and the decision in United States v. Ettelson, 159 F.2d 193 (7th Cir. 1947), are cited for the proposition that as long as the court proceeding reducing the assessment lien to judgment is commenced within six years of the date of assessment (pursuant to IRC § 6502(a)), the resulting judgment can be enforced at any time. However, a contrary result was reached in the case of United States v. Home Beneficial Life Ins. Co., Inc., 31 AFTR 2d 73–1085 (E.D.Tenn.1973). In that case, the court held that the government was barred from enforcing a judgment against the taxpayer's estate where the enforcement proceeding was commenced after the running of both the six-year period under § 6502(a) and the ten-year period of limitations applicable to judgments of the state courts of Tennessee. Which view is best supported by the language of §§ 6322 and 6502? Would the applicability of a state statute of limitations depend upon whether the judgment sought to be enforced was rendered by a federal district court instead of by a state court? See 28 U.S.C.A. § 1962.

SECTION 3. JEOPARDY AND TERMINATION ASSESSMENTS

The Internal Revenue Service must be able to prevent a taxpayer from rendering his tax liabilities uncollectable by dissipating, hiding or removing his assets from the country. Once the subject tax has been assessed there is, as discussed above, ample power to accomplish this objective. However, a taxpayer may seek to place assets outside the reach of the Service prior to the conclusion of the administrative and/or judicial proceedings which normally must precede the assessment of a tax liability. Therefore, the Internal Revenue Code consistently has permitted the IRS to make an immediate assessment of tax in "jeopardy" situations, so that the collection powers can be utilized to secure the payment of taxes without delay.

As discussed in the followng cases, the Service is permitted to make a jeopardy assessment for a tax period for which a tax return has been filed or is due. In addition, for a taxable period which is not yet completed, or for which a return is not yet due, the Service is permitted to terminate the taxable period or accelerate the due date of the return and make a jeopardy assessment. The *Schreck* case was the first, and the *Laing* case the last, of a series of decisions questioning the long-standing provisions of the Code relating to termination assessments. As a reaction to this litigation, and to concomitant concerns regarding the effectively unrestricted discretion of the Service in the jeopardy area, the jeopardy and termination provisions were revised by the Tax Reform Act of 1976.

SCHRECK v. UNITED STATES

301 F.Supp. 1265 (D.Md.1969).

FRANK A. KAUFMAN, District Judge.

The facts of this case are simple and undisputed. The legal issue, however, impels research into the depths of statutory history and case law development involving the Tax Court of the United States and its predecessor, the Board of Tax Appeals.

On November 8, 1967, the Internal Revenue Service (IRS) sent to the plaintiff, William Schreck, a letter advising him that, acting under Section 6851 of the Internal Revenue Code (the Code), the IRS had terminated his taxable year as of October 25, 1967, and that his income tax for the short taxable year of January 1, 1967 to October 25, 1967 was immediately due and payable. In that letter, Schreck was notified that "an assessment has been made against you for the income taxes due from you for such taxable period in the following amount"—

Taxable Period	Tax Due
January 1, 1967 to October 25, 1967	$20,7300.00

and was also notified that demand was made for the immediate payment of those taxes.

On November 9, 1967, one day after the date of that notice and demand letter, a Notice of Federal Tax Lien was filed by the IRS against Schreck. That notice stated that it was based on the assessment of November 8th. Further, on November 9, 1967, a Notice of Levy was filed by the IRS. It also stated that it was based on the November 8th assessment, and was served on Irving Machiz in his official capacity as District Director of Internal Revenue for the District of Maryland. That official had in his possession on November 9, 1967 certain of Schreck's property—including $13,749.35 in cash and other personal property—which had been seized from Schreck by agents of the federal government the preceding October 23rd. The notice and demand letter of November 8, 1967 is the only document that Schreck has received from the IRS concerning the assessment of that same date.

Schreck has instituted this present action under section 6213(a) of the Code, seeking an injunction ordering the defendants to return the property which they have seized from him and now hold under the Notice of Levy. * * *

Reduced to essentials, section 6213(a) makes injunctive relief available against the assessment, levy or collection of a tax when the IRS does not send to the taxpayer a deficiency notice as required by the tax laws. The plaintiff's position in this case is that the IRS was required by section 6861 to send him a deficiency notice within 60 days of the November 8th assessment, and, since it did not do so, he may now obtain the equitable relief provided for in section 6213(a). The Government admits that no such deficiency notice was sent to Schreck and concedes that if it were under a legal obligation to send such a notice, an injunction should now issue under section 6213(a). But the Government vigorously argues that neither the Code nor the Treasury Regulations require a deficiency notice to be sent to Schreck and that the Government is therefore justified in declining to provide such a notice.

It would appear that the parties have joined issue on whether or not a certain letter must be sent by the IRS to Schreck, which would, at first blush, appear to pose a wholly uninteresting, technical issue. What saves it from this fate is that the deficiency notice is a jurisdictional prerequisite to adjudication in the Tax Court; it is, as the Ninth Circuit has pointed out, a "ticket to the tax court," see Corbett v. Frank, 293 F.2d 501, 502, 503 (9 Cir. 1961). Thus, the real issue in this case is whether a taxpayer has a right to have adjudicated in the Tax Court the validity of an assessment in a jeopardy situation made for a short-year period. The resolution of this basic issue must be made within the confines of "the harmony of our carefully structured twentieth century system of tax litigation."

The enactment of the Revenue Acts of 1916 and 1918 followed close on the heels of the ratification of the Sixteenth Amendment. Neither Act provided for a procedure by which a taxpayer could challenge, prior to payment, the validity of an assessment by the IRS. The only remedy prescribed was a suit for refund following payment of the tax.

Section 250(g) of the 1918 Act gave the IRS the power to terminate the taxable year before its completion and to declare taxes, for the truncated period, immediately due and payable, once the IRS had found that there existed certain prejudicial activity by the taxpayer which threatened the future collectibility of taxes. That section, which has been repeatedly reenacted in essentially identical language ever since, now stands as section 6851 of the Code * * *.

As far as remedies under the 1918 Act were concerned, the short-period taxpayer was in the same position as any other taxpayer against whom an assessment was made—he had to pay the tax first and then bring a suit for refund. The IRS's authority to assess income taxes for both the full-year period and the short-year period was found in the general authorizing statute, section 3176 of the Revised Statutes.

The inherent harshness of the pay first-litigate later scheme led Congress in 1924 to establish a non-prepayment forum, the Board of Tax Appeals. The 1924 Board of Tax Appeals was given limited jurisdiction, however, since section 274(b) and section 279(b) of the Revenue Act of 1924 gave a dissatisfied party—be it the taxpayer or the Government—the right to a further suit in the district courts.

Even though this meant that the Board was more or less an advisory body, the Government's power of immediate income tax assessment in the normal (as opposed to jeopardy) case was sharply curtailed by the deficiency notice provision of section 274(a). That section required the IRS to send the taxpayer a deficiency notice of the IRS's finding that a deficiency was due and of the intention of the IRS to assess and to collect the deficiency. But, for sixty days following that notification, the IRS could take no action, and the taxpayer could petition the Board for a redetermination of the income tax deficiency. § 274(a) and (c). The power of the IRS was left virtually unaffected in those cases in which it believed that the assessment or collection of a deficiency would be jeopardized by delay. In the event of a jeopardy assessment under section 274(d), no deficiency notice was required; the only way the taxpayer could get to the Board was by filing a claim in abatement and posting a bond. § 279(a) and (b). Thus, if the taxpayer could not post bond, his only available remedy was, again, to pay first and sue for a refund later.

The structure of tax litigation was brought to its basic, present form with the passage of the Revenue Act of 1926. The 1926 Act changed the rights and remedies of both the normal and the jeopardy income taxpayer. With respect to the normal income taxpayer, the deficiency notice requirement was retained, with the Board of Tax Appeals (later called the Tax Court of the United States) given expanded jurisdiction. No recourse could be had to a federal district court by either the disappointed taxpayer or by the Government after proceedings before the Board; instead, direct appeal from the Board was provided to the circuit courts of appeals. The normal taxpayer was thus given his choice of two routes to judicial review of the tax assessment—going directly to the Board of Tax Appeals without first paying the tax, or paying first and then suing for a refund in the appropriate district court.

The 1926 Revenue Act also made a fundamental change in the rights and remedies of the jeopardy income taxpayer. Whereas previously he was barred from the Board of Tax Appeals unless he could post adequate bond, he was now given the absolute right to a redetermination of the jeopardy assessment by the Board of Tax Appeals, albeit after the assessment took effect. The Government was authorized, by the predecessor of present section 6861, "immediately [to] assess" an income tax deficiency, the assessment or collection of which it "believes * * * will be jeopardized by delay." § 279(a), Revenue Act of 1926. At the same time, the Government was required to give notice of and to make demand for payment *and*, if the jeopardy assessment preceded in time the notice of deficiency, to send a deficiency notice within 60 days after making the assessment. § 279(b) of the 1926 Act. This enabled the jeopardy taxpayer, under section 274(a), to petition for an adjudication by the Board of Tax Appeals within 60 days of the mailing of the deficiency notice. That procedure has been carried over to the present with slight changes and is now set forth in sections 6861, 6212(a) and 6213(a) of the 1954 Code. *   *   *

In sum, then, both the normal and jeopardy income taxpayer were given the right, through the deficiency notice technique, to judicial review by the Board of Tax Appeals (now the Tax Court). The only difference—and, as the subsequent discussion will make clear, a very important one—was that the normal taxpayer had the right to petition for and receive a determination by the Board before the assessment, while the IRS had the power to make the jeopardy taxpayer wait as long as 60 days after the jeopardy assessment for a similar right to petition to and obtain review by the Board. Furthermore, if the Government did not send the deficiency notice as required, both the normal and jeopardy income taxpayer were given the right to obtain injunctive relief in the district courts under present section 6213(a). That is precisely what the plaintiff seeks in this suit in a short-year jeopardy tax assessment situation.

The plaintiff's argument is at once simple and powerful: The careful development of the structure of tax litigation sketched above shows, he urges, a definite congressional intent to mitigate the harshness of the pay first-litigate later rule by making available to all income taxpayers—normal and jeopardy alike—the Tax Court as a non-prepayment forum. Viewed as either a normal or jeopardy assessment, the Government's refusal to give him a "ticket to the Tax Court" violates that congressional intent.

*   *   *

As this Court has already pointed out, the real focus of the present case is what rights, if any, this plaintiff has to litigate, without prepayment, the validity of the assessment and levy made against him. That issue must be considered against the background of congressional intent.

In the normal case, after the IRS has determined that there is a deficiency, Congress requires the IRS to send a deficiency notice, or "ninety-day letter," informing the taxpayer of that determination and of the IRS's intention to assess and collect the deficiency. During the ninety-day period, the IRS is barred from action by way of assessment or levy. The taxpayer may obtain a further unconditional respite from assessment or collection action if he petitions the Tax Court for a redetermination of the deficiency, since the IRS cannot act during the pendency of the Tax Court litigation. All this is set forth in section 6213(a) of the 1954 Code, has been in effect from 1926, and is still in effect today.

In comparison to a "normal" case in which summary governmental enforcement action is virtually proscribed by section 6213(a), the enforcement power of the Government in a section 6861 "jeopardy" case is rather awesome. Whenever the IRS "believes" that delay will jeopardize the assessment or collection of a deficiency, it is authorized immediately to assess (section 6861), immediately to send notice and demand for payment (ibid.), and immediately to levy upon all the taxpayer's property (section 6331). The courts have consistently refused, although sometimes reluctantly,[20] to review whether the IRS's determination of jeopardy had any substance whatsoever. Only when "extraordinary and exceptional circumstances" exist will the courts in an injunction proceeding examine into the validity of the underlying assessment. And even that narrow review standard may have been eroded by the opinion in Enochs v. Williams Packing Co., 370 U.S. 1, 82 S.Ct. 1125, 8 L.Ed.2d 292 (1962).

Nevertheless, even with this unquestioned statutory power of immediate assessment and seizure, the statutory safeguards superimposed upon the jeopardy assessment system contain restraints. The following four protections are now afforded to the section 6861 jeopardy taxpayer:

1. The IRS is required to send a deficiency notice within sixty days after the assessment, thus enabling the jeopardy taxpayer to litigate in the Tax Court. § 6861(b). If the IRS does not comply with this requirement, the assessment and levy (or seizure) may be enjoined by the federal courts. § 6213(a);

2. The jeopardy taxpayer can stay all collection action pending the Tax Court's decision if he is able to post an adequate bond. § 6863(a).

3. Property seized pursuant to the assessment may not, in general, be sold during the pendency of litigation in the Tax Court. § 6863(b)(3)(A).[23]

4. The IRS "may" abate the jeopardy assessment if it "finds" that jeopardy does not exist. § 6861(g).

When applied to any given factual situation, those procedural safeguards may or may not give real protection to a taxpayer who has been subjected to an erroneous assessment and seizure. To a taxpayer who does not have assets far in excess of the assessment, the right to file a bond is an "illusory" remedy; to one whose entire assets have been seized pursuant to the assessment, it "would seem to be mere mockery."[25] The provision that the IRS "may" abate an er-

20. See Kimmel v. Tomlinson, 151 F. Supp. 901 (S.D.Fla.1957).

23. The three exceptions to that general prohibition on sale are: (a) if the taxpayer consents to the sale; (b) if the property is perishable; and (c) if the IRS "determines that the expenses of conservation and maintenance will greatly reduce the net proceeds." § 6863(b)(3)(B).

25. Kimmel v. Tomlinson, supra 151 F.Supp. at 902:
In the instant case every bit of property (inclusive of bank accounts) of both taxpayers (and their wives) has been seized; it would seem to be mere mockery to say they, after they have been stripped of all assets, are protected in that they may either post a bond or pay the three hundred odd thousand dollars of taxes and pen-

roneous jeopardy assessment was enacted in 1953 because the IRS believed that it needed explicit statutory authority to do so. Whether or not the IRS does abate in a given case depends entirely on the persuasiveness of the taxpayer to convince the IRS that it has erred; there is no right to a formal hearing, and the courts have declined to review the IRS's refusal to abate. The only meaningful safeguards are the right to litigation in the Tax Court and the restrictions on sale of most types of property during that litigation. And it is apparent that if the IRS follows its assessment with a levy upon, or seizure of, a large part (or even all) of the taxpayer's property, and refuses to allow him access to that property, then even those provisions may not prevent the destruction of the taxpayer's business and his financial ruin—losses which cannot be remedied by a subsequent favorable judicial decision. This is a risk that Congress has decided must be taken in those rare cases in which the collection of the revenues may be jeopardized by delay. But in making that decision, Congress has at the same time sought to mute that risk by affording in section 6861 itself a prompt opportunity for litigation in the Tax Court.

If the Government's view of the law is correct, then those taxpayers who have been subjected to a jeopardy assessment for a short-year period are deprived of the prompt opportunity for litigation in the Tax Court which Congress has given to all other jeopardy income taxpayers. The question then arises, what judicial form *is* available for the taxpayer to contest the assessment and the seizure of his property? If, as the Government says, a litigable deficiency cannot arise until at least the end of the full year, then the taxpayer has absolutely no remedy until then. At that time, a "deficiency" may be determined by the IRS, but the Government has three years in which to do so under the statute of limitations (or six years if the return omits more than twenty-five percent of property includible in gross income, or forever if no return is filed or there is a willful attempt to evade taxes). § 6501(a), (e), (c). Until the IRS decides to determine what full-year deficiency, if any, exists and then sends a notice of deficiency to the taxpayer, he cannot institute suit in the Tax Court. Furthermore, if the Government's view is correct, the taxpayer in this situation may not ever be able to institute a refund suit. For, if the Government levies upon all of his property but does not take action to apply any of it to the tax allegedly due, then the taxpayer cannot sue for a refund for the simple reason that he has not paid anything. Even if the property is physically seized and applied to the jeopardy assessment by the IRS, the taxpayer cannot bring a refund suit unless the value of the seized property is at least as great as the amount of the assessment; otherwise, he is barred by the full-payment rule of Flora v. United States. Finally, even if enough is physically seized to satisfy the full-payment rule, the IRS

alties assessed in order to stay the waste of a forced sale of their as-

sets and the certain destruction of their business.

may not, for one reason or another, apply the seized property to the assessment (e. g., because the property may be subject to a forfeiture proceeding). And, of course, there may be other factual situations in which a refund suit is impossible. These hypothetical possibilities are far from fanciful. In this case, Schreck cannot bring a refund suit because: (a) $13,749.35 worth of property was seized, whereas the assessment was $20,730.00 and, alternatively, (b) the property seized was not applied to plaintiff's taxes because it has been held for a forfeiture proceeding. In sum, then, the plaintiff herein has no available judicial forum in which he can challenge the legality of the Government's assessment and seizure. And, given the prohibition of suits to restrain the assessment or collection of taxes set forth in section 7421 of the Code, a suit by the taxpayer for equitable relief will almost surely be dismissed.

In essence, the Government asks this Court to hold that Congress has constitutionally authorized the IRS to seize and sell all of a person's property and has also provided that that person has no right to institute *any* court proceedings, for perhaps longer than three years, in which to litigate the validity of the underlying assessment and the seizure, while at the same time all jeopardy income taxpayers, other than short-year jeopardy income taxpayers, have the right to begin a judicial proceeding within 60 days of the assessment. That proposition on its face of course raises constitutional questions of equal protection and due process.

* * *

* * * This Court has found nothing in the legislative history of the relevant statutes nor any other reason which compels this Court to accept the result urged here by the Government and to face head-on the constitutional issues raised by it.[32] The words of the

---

32. The Government correctly points out that a jeopardy taxpayer assessed under the provisions of section 6862 (which relates to the jeopardy assessment of taxes other than income, estate and gift taxes) has none of the procedural safeguards set forth in section 6861. The reason is simply that Congress has specifically limited the jurisdiction of the Tax Court to cases involving income, estate and gift taxes. Thus, the Tax Court has no statutory authority to redetermine, for example, an excise tax deficiency. This Court does not in any way suggest that section 6862 is unconstitutional; indeed, for the purposes of this opinion this Court assumes its constitutionality. But it does not follow that because Congress may rationally decide, as it has, that the expertise of the Tax Court does not ex-

tend to certain types of taxes, that congressional intent to discriminate among taxpayers paying the same type of tax is necessarily to be inferred. This Court has found no suggestion in the legislative history that such a latter discrimination has, at any time, been intended by the Congress, nor does there appear to be any clear rational basis on which to infer such an intention. Moreover, as the Supreme Court stated in Flora v. United States, 362 U.S. at 175 n. 38, 80 S.Ct., at 646, the effect of section 6862 on a taxpayer's judicial remedies is mitigated inasmuch as "excise tax assessments may be divisible into a tax on each transaction or event, so that the full-payment rule would probably require no more than payment of a small amount."

statutes do not irresistably lead to either of the conflicting construc-
tions urged in this case. But fairness, the pattern of congressional
intent, and the avoidance of not inconsequential constitutional issues
all weigh heavily in favor of the contentions of the taxpayer. Nor
has the Government presented to this Court any reason to believe
that the rejection of its position will in any way hamper its enforcement of the tax laws and its collection of the revenue.

For the reasons stated hereinabove, this Court holds that section
6851 does not confer upon the Government independent assessment
authority. The Government may, under that section, terminate a
taxpayer's taxable year and may declare income taxes for the short-
year period immediately due and payable. But any jeopardy assessment made for the short-year period must have as its source section
6861, and the requirements of that section may not be circumvented.
Since the Government has not complied with those requirements and
has failed to send the plaintiff a notice of deficiency which would enable him promptly to litigate in the Tax Court, an injunction will issue under section 6213(a), enjoining the Government from continuing
in force and effect its assessment and levy against the plaintiff unless
it promptly sends a deficiency notice to the plaintiff.

This holding will not in any way fasten upon the Government in
this or in any other case an obligation which it cannot practically
meet. The Government can (as it has in the past) utilize exactly the
same techniques to determine a deficiency as it does in any case of a
jeopardy assessment. The only import of this holding is that a
short-year jeopardy taxpayer such as this plaintiff has the same access to the courts as every other jeopardy income taxpayer.

The basic purpose for creating the Board of Tax Appeals as a
non-prepayment forum was succinctly stated in 1924:

> The right of appeal after payment of the tax is an incom-
> plete remedy, and does little to remove the hardship occa-
> sioned by an incorrect assessment. The payment of a large
> additional tax on income received several years previous and
> which may have, since its receipt, been either wiped out by
> subsequent losses, invested in nonliquid assets, or spent,
> sometimes forces taxpayers into bankruptcy, and often caus-
> es great financial hardship and sacrifice. These results are
> not remedied by permitting the taxpayer to sue for the re-
> covery of the tax after this payment. He is entitled to an
> appeal and to a determination of his liability for the tax prior
> to its payment. [H.R.Rep. No. 179, 68th Cong., 1st Sess.
> (1924).]

That statement still has controlling force today.

Counsel will prepare an appropriate order.

LAING v. UNITED STATES

Supreme Court of the United States, 1976.
423 U.S. 161, 96 S.Ct. 473, 46 L.Ed.2d 416.

Mr. Justice MARSHALL delivered the opinion of the Court.

These companion cases involve two taxpayers whose taxable years were terminated by the Internal Revenue Service (IRS) prior to their normal expiration date pursuant to the jeopardy termination provisions of § 6851(a)(1) of the Internal Revenue Code of 1954 (Code). Section 6851(a)(1) allows the IRS immediately to terminate a taxpayer's taxable period when it finds that the taxpayer intends to do any act tending to prejudice or render ineffectual the collection of his income tax for the current or preceding taxable year. Upon termination the tax is immediately owing and, after notice, the IRS may, and usually does, levy upon the taxpayer's property under § 6331(a) of the Code to assure payment.

We must decide whether the IRS, when assessing and collecting the unreported tax due after the termination of a taxpayer's taxable period, must follow the procedures mandated by § 6861 et seq. of the Code for the assessment and collection of a deficiency whose collection is in jeopardy. The answer, as we shall see, depends on whether the unreported tax due upon such a termination is a "deficiency" as defined in § 6211(a) of the Code. The Government argues that the tax liability that arises after a § 6851 termination cannot be a "deficiency," and that the procedures for the assessment and collection of deficiencies in jeopardy are therefore inapplicable. We reject this argument. We agree with the taxpayers that any tax owing, but unreported, after a § 6851 termination is a deficiency, and that the assessment of that deficiency is subject to the provisions of § 6861 et seq.
* * *

I

[In the *Laing* case, customs officials in Vermont searched a car in which Mr. Laing and three other persons were traveling. They found over $300,000 in currency and notified the IRS, which "orally asserted" a termination deficiency of $310,000 against each of the individuals and seized the cash. The assessment against Mr. Laing subsequently was abated to $195,985.55 when a formal letter-notice of termination and demand for payment and the filing of a tax return were sent. In the companion case, United States v. Hall, the Respondent-taxpayer's husband was arrested on drug-related charges and the Respondent's house subsequently was searched by state police, who found controlled substances there. The next day, Mrs. Hall received notice from the IRS that a termination assessment of $52,680.-25 had been made against her. In neither case was the taxpayer provided with a deficiency notice under § 6861(b), or otherwise given any specific information as to how the tax was determined.]

II

In these cases, the taxpayers seek the protection of certain procedural safeguards that the Government claims were not intended to apply to jeopardy terminations. Specifically, the taxpayers argue that the procedures mandated by § 6861 et seq. for assessing and collecting deficiencies whose collection is in jeopardy also govern assessments of taxes owing, but not reported, after the termination of a taxpayer's taxable period under § 6851. Resolution of this claim requires analysis of the interplay between these two basic jeopardy provisions—§ 6851, the jeopardy-termination provision, and § 6861, the jeopardy-assessment provision.

The initial workings of the jeopardy-termination provision, which essentially permits the shortening of a taxable year, are not in dispute. When the District Director determines that the conditions of § 6851(a) are met—generally, that the taxpayer is preparing to do something that will endanger the collection of his taxes—the District Director may declare the taxpayer's current tax year terminated. The tax for the shortened period and any unpaid tax for the preceding year become due and payable immediately, § 6851(a), and the taxpayer must file a return for the shortened year. § 443(a)(3).

The disagreement between the taxpayers and the Government focuses on the applicability of the jeopardy-assessment procedures of § 6861 et seq. to the assessment and collection of taxes that become due upon a § 6851 termination. Section 6861(a) provides for the immediate assessment of a deficiency, as defined in § 6211(a), whenever the assessment or collection of the deficiency would be "jeopardized by delay." By allowing an immediate assessment, § 6861(a) provides an exception to the general rule barring an assessment until the taxpayer has been sent a notice of deficiency and has been afforded an opportunity to seek resolution of his tax liability in the Tax Court. Certain procedural safeguards are provided, however, to the taxpayer whose deficiency is assessed immediately under § 6861(a). Within 60 days after the jeopardy assessment, the District Director must send the taxpayer a notice of deficiency, § 6861(b), which enables the taxpayer to file a petition with the Tax Court for a redetermination of the deficiency. The taxpayer can stay the collection of the amount assessed by posting an equivalent bond, § 6863(a). Any property seized for the collection of the tax cannot be sold until a notice of deficiency is issued and the taxpayer is afforded an opportunity to file a petition in the Tax Court. If the taxpayer does seek a redetermination of the deficiency in the Tax Court, the prohibition against sale extends until the Tax Court decision becomes final. § 6863(b)(3)(A).

The taxpayers view the provisions of § 6861 et seq. as complementary to those of § 6851. They contend that to the extent the tax owing upon a jeopardy termination has not been reported, it is a "deficiency" as that term is defined in § 6211(a) and used in § 6861(a), and that the deficiency, being of necessity one whose assessment or collection is in jeopardy, must be assessed and collected in accordance with the procedures of § 6861 et seq.

Under the Government's view, on the other hand, §§ 6851 and 6861 are aimed at distinct problems and have no bearing on each other. "Section 6851," according to the Government, "advances the date when taxes are due and payable, while Section 6861 advances the time for collection of taxes which are already overdue [i. e., already owing for a prior, normally expiring taxable year]." The validity of this distinction rests on the Government's claim that a deficiency can arise only with respect to a nonterminated taxable year, so that no deficiency can be created by a § 6851 termination. If there is no deficiency to assess, of course, the provisions of § 6861 et seq. cannot apply.

Thus, under the Government's reading of the Code, the procedures for assessment and collection of a tax owing, but not reported, after the termination of a taxable period are not governed by § 6861 et seq. The Government argues that, with the single exception of the bond provision of § 6851(e), the taxpayer's only remedy upon a jeopardy termination is to pay the tax, file for a refund, and, if the refund is refused, bring suit in the district court or the Court of Claims. Since the IRS has up to six months to act on a request for a refund, the taxpayer, under the Government's theory, may have to wait up to half a year before gaining access to any judicial forum.

The Government does not seriously challenge the taxpayers' conclusion that if the termination of their taxable periods created a deficiency whose assessment or collection was in jeopardy, the assessments and collections in these cases should have been pursuant to the procedures of § 6861 et seq. The question, then, is whether the tax owing, but not reported, upon a jeopardy termination is a deficiency within the meaning of § 6211(a).

III

In essence, a deficiency as defined in the Code is the amount of tax imposed less any amount that may have been reported by the taxpayer on his return. § 6211(a). Where there has been no tax return filed, the deficiency is the amount of tax due. Treas.Reg. § 301.6211–1(a). As we have seen, upon terminating a taxpayer's taxable year under § 6851, the District Director makes a demand for the payment of the unpaid tax for the terminated period and for the preceding taxable year. The taxpayer is then required to file a return for the truncated taxable year. § 443(a)(3). The amount due, of course, must be determined according to ordinary tax principles, as applied to the abbreviated reporting period. The amount properly assessed upon a § 6851 termination is thus the amount of tax imposed under the Code for the preceding year and the terminated short year, less any amount that may already have been paid. To the extent this sum has not been reported by the taxpayer on a return, it fits precisely the statutory definition of a deficiency.

The Government resists this conclusion by reading the definition of "deficiency" restrictively to include only those taxes due at the end of a full taxable year when a return has been or should have been made. It argues that a "deficiency" cannot be determined before the close of a taxable year. Of course, we agree with the Government that a deficiency does not arise until the tax is actually due and the taxable year is complete. The fact is, however, that under § 6851 the tax is due immediately upon termination. Moreover, upon a § 6851 termination, the taxpayer's taxable year has come to a close. Section 441(b)(3) defines as a "taxable year" the terminated taxable period on which a return is due under § 443(a)(3). See also § 7701(a)(23). Under the statutory definition of § 6211(a), the tax owing and unreported after a jeopardy termination, which in these cases and in most § 6851 terminations is the full tax due, is clearly a deficiency. We see nothing in the definition to suggest that a deficiency can arise only at the conclusion of a 12-month taxable year; it is sufficient that the taxable period in question has come to an end and the tax in question is due and unreported.

Besides conflicting with the plain language of the Code provisions directly before us, the Government's position in these cases would, for no discernible purpose, isolate the taxpayer subjected to a jeopardy termination from most other income-tax payers. If the unreported tax due after a jeopardy termination is not a deficiency, the IRS need not issue the taxpayer a deficiency notice and accord him access to the Tax Court for a redetermination of his tax. Denial of an opportunity to litigate in the Tax Court is out of keeping with the thrust of the Code, which generally allows income-tax payers access to that court. Where exceptions are intended, the Code is explicit on the matter. See, e. g., § 6871(b). Denying a Tax Court forum to a particular class of taxpayers is sufficiently anomalous that an intention to do so should not be imputed to Congress when the statute does not expressly so provide. This is particularly so in view of the Government's concession that the jeopardy-assessment procedures of § 6861 et seq. are sufficient to protect its interests, and that providing taxpayers with the limited protections of those procedures would not impair the collection of the revenues.

IV

While the plain language of the provisions at issue here and their place in the legislative scheme suggest that the unreported tax due upon a § 6851 termination is a deficiency and that the deficiency, its collection being in jeopardy, must be assessed and collected according to the procedures of § 6861 et seq., the Government attempts to undercut this conclusion by pointing to the legislative history of the several provisions at issue in this case. We are unpersuaded. The jeopardy-assessment and jeopardy-termination provisions have long been treated in a closely parallel fashion, and nothing that the Government points to in the early codification suggests the contrary.

* * *

* * * [T]o the extent that it sheds any light on the question at all, the legislative history seems to help the taxpayers rather than the Government. In the course of the development of a prepayment remedy and a jeopardy exception to that remedy between 1918 and 1926, taxpayers subjected to jeopardy terminations and those subjected to jeopardy assessments for nonterminated taxable years were consistently treated alike. In 1921, when the administrative remedy was first created, neither those subjected to a jeopardy assessment for a nonterminated year nor those subjected to a termination could avail themselves of that remedy. In 1924, those terminated and those subjected to jeopardy assessments for nonterminated years were similarly denied access to the Board of Tax Appeals, unless they filed a bond in the amount of the claim. And in 1926, when the scheme assumed its current form, there was no indication that Congress intended for the first time to treat the two groups separately by granting direct access to the Board of Tax Appeals to those subjected to a jeopardy assessment for a nonterminated year, but denying it to those subjected to an assessment following a jeopardy termination.

V

Based on the plain language of the statutory provisions, their place in the legislative scheme, and the legislative history, we agree with the taxpayers' reading of the pertinent sections of the Code.[26] Under that reading, the tax owing, but not reported, at the time of a § 6851 termination is a deficiency whose assessment and collection are subject to the procedures of § 6861 et seq. Section 6861(b) re-

26. As a final reason for adopting their construction of the Code, the taxpayers argue that the Government's reading would violate the Due Process Clause of the Fifth Amendment. The basis for this claim is that under the assessment procedures of § 6861 et seq. the taxpayer is guaranteed access to the Tax Court within 60 days, while under the procedures suggested by the Government the taxpayer in a termination case could be denied access to a judicial forum for up to six months. Moreover, the taxpayers argue, under the procedures of § 6861 et seq. the property seized may not be sold until after a final determination by the Tax Court, § 6863, while under the Government's theory the property seized in a jeopardy termination may be immediately subject to sale. Because we agree with the taxpayers' construction of the Code, we need not decide whether the procedures available under the Government's theory would, in fact, violate the Constitution.

The taxpayers do not question here, and we do not consider whether, even if the jeopardy-assessment procedures of § 6861 et seq. are followed, due process demands that the taxpayer in a jeopardy-assessment situation be afforded a prompt post-assessment hearing at which the Government must make some preliminary showing in support of the assessment.

quires a notice of deficiency to be mailed to a taxpayer within 60 days after the jeopardy assessment. Section 6863 bars the offering for sale of property seized until the taxpayer has had an opportunity to litigate in the Tax Court. Because the District Director failed to comply with these requirements in these cases, the taxpayers' suits were not barred by the Anti-Injunction Act, § 7421(a) of the Code. The judgment of the United States Court of Appeals for the Sixth Circuit in No. 74–75 is affirmed. The judgment of the United States Court of Appeals for the Second Circuit in No. 73–1808 is reversed, and the case is remanded to that court for further proceedings consistent with this opinion.

It is so ordered.

Mr. Justice BRENNAN, concurring.

I join the Court's opinion, and the statutory construction that makes unnecessary the Court's addressing the claims of Mr. Laing and Mrs. Hall that they were denied procedural due process secured by the Fifth Amendment. Decision of that question is therefore expressly reserved, ante, at n. 26. I write only to state my views of the considerations raised by the due process claim.

The Court's construction of the relevant statutes permits the IRS to seize a taxpayer's assets upon a finding by the Commissioner in compliance with § 6851(a)(1). No hearing is required, judicial or administrative, prior to the seizure. But it cannot be gainsaid that the risk of erroneous determinations by the Commissioner with consequent possibility of irreparable injury to a taxpayer is very real. This suffices to bring due process requirements into play.

The "root requirement" of the Due Process Clause is "that an individual be given an opportunity for a hearing *before* he is deprived of any significant property interest, except for extraordinary situations where some valid governmental interest is at stake that justifies postponing the hearing until after the event." Boddie v. Connecticut, 401 U.S. 371, 379, 91 S.Ct. 780, 786, 28 L.Ed.2d 113 (1971) (emphasis in original). The precise timing and attributes of the due process requirement, however, depend upon accommodating the competing interests involved.

Governmental seizures without a prior hearing have been sustained where (1) the seizure is necessary to protect an important governmental or public interest, (2) there is a "special need for very prompt action," and (3) "the standards of a narrowly drawn statute" require that an official determine that the particular seizure is both necessary and justified. See Fuentes v. Shevin, 407 U.S. 67, 91, 92 S. Ct. 1983, 2000, 32 L.Ed.2d 556 (1972). Seizures pursuant to jeopardy assessments are clearly necessary to protect important governmental interests and there is a "special need for very prompt action." But § 6851(a)(1), although requiring an official determination that the particular seizure is both necessary and justified, nevertheless falls short, in my view, of meeting due process requirements. This is because present law denies an affected taxpayer access to any forum for review of jeopardy assessments for up to 60 days.

* * *

* * * However expeditiously the Tax Court handles the claim, that court is not required to decide the merits within any specified time, and no provision is made for a prompt preliminary evaluation of the basis for the assessment. In my view, such delay would be constitutionally permissible only if there were some overriding governmental interest at stake, and the IRS suggested none in either of these cases. But even if delay in judicial review on the merits were justifiable, due process would at least require some supporting rationale for denying taxpayers the opportunity for a prompt preliminary determination by an unbiased tribunal on the validity of the basis for the assessment. Again, none was offered in either of these cases.

The Tax Reform Act of 1976, in addition to providing for expedited administrative and judicial review of the *propriety* of jeopardy and termination assessments (as discussed in the following case),[c] also explicitly provided a *prepayment forum* for those who received termination assessments. To solve the problems recognized in the *Schreck-Laing* line of cases, Congress provided that if a termination assessment is made, the IRS must issue a statutory notice of deficiency for the full taxable year with respect to which the termination assessment was made. This notice must be issued within 60 days after the later of the due date of the taxpayer's return for the full taxable year or the date the return is actually filed.[d] Thus, a taxpayer receiving a terminated year assessment, in addition to his rights to immediate review under § 7429, will have the opportunity to petition the Tax Court for a determination of the merits of the assessment relatively promptly. Nevertheless, there remains a difference (perhaps unavoidable) between the two types of assessments. The jeopardy assessment made under § 6861 requires a notice and opportunity to petition the Tax Court *within 60 days of the assessment*. The delay between a termination assessment under § 6851 and the required issuance of a deficiency notice, on the other hand, will be 60 days plus the time between the assessment and the due date or filing of the return for the full taxable year. The delay could thus extend for as long as seventeen and one-half months (or more, if the return for the full taxable year is not filed on time).[e]

c. I.R.C. § 7429.

d. I.R.C. § 6851(b).

e. Assuming a termination assessment on January 2, 1984, the deficiency notice would be due on June 15, 1985, i. e., 60 days after April 15, 1985 (the due date for the full year return for 1984).

FIDELITY EQUIPMENT LEASING CORP. v. UNITED STATES

462 F.Supp. 845 (N.D.Ga.1978).

HAROLD L. MURPHY, District Judge.

On October 23, 1978, the plaintiffs filed a complaint to determine the reasonableness and appropriateness of two jeopardy assessments for income tax levied against them by the Internal Revenue Service on August 9, 1978. Jurisdiction of the Court was invoked pursuant to 26 U.S.C. § 7429(b).

* * *

1. Section 7429(a)(1) of the Internal Revenue Code requires that within 5 days after an assessment is made pursuant to 26 U.S.C. § 6861(a), "the Secretary shall provide the taxpayer with a written statement of the information upon which the Secretary relies in making such assessment." Apparently attempting to comply with this notice requirement the defendant included the following paragraph in the letters of August 11, 1978, notifying the plaintiffs of the jeopardy assessment:

> Under section 6861 of the Internal Revenue Code, you are notified that I have found you to be designing quickly to place your property beyond the reach of the Government either by removing it from the United States, by concealing it, by transferring it to other persons, or by dissipating it, thereby tending to prejudice or render ineffectual collection of income tax for the taxable years ended as shown below. Accordingly, based on information available at this time, I have approved assessment of tax and additional amounts determined to be due as reflected in the attached computations:

The plaintiff correctly argues that such conclusionary statements do not fulfill the requirements of the statute. The Government should have informed the plaintiff of the information which led to these conclusions, rather than merely the conclusions.

However, the Government's failure to satisfy the notice requirement of section 7429 will not serve to invalidate these proceedings. The legislative history of this section indicates that both the notice and administrative review requirements were included simply to facilitate the subsequent Court proceedings. Through the process of discovery the taxpayers have been informed of the information relied upon by the Government. Any deficiency in the notice issued by the Government is now immaterial. The plaintiffs were not prejudiced by the lack of information contained in the notification letters.

2. The plaintiffs contend that this proceeding should be declared illegal and void because of inadequate administrative review. The

only deficiency raised by the plaintiffs is again the Government's failure to supply adequate information. Without determining the adequacy of the administrative review, the Court holds that any possible inadequacy has been corrected through full use of the discovery process and the *de novo* review of plaintiffs' claims provided by this Court.

3. In order to support its determination of a jeopardy assessment the Government must show that the assessment is "reasonable under the circumstances * * *" 26 U.S.C. § 7429(b)(2). The burden of proof in such a showing rests upon the Government. 26 U.S.C. § 7429(g)(1). In determining the reasonableness of the assessment, this Court is not limited to information available to the IRS at the time of the assessment, but may also consider relevant information gathered after that date.

In determining "reasonableness" the Court is given little guidance by the statute. A jeopardy assessment may be levied by the IRS if it believes that the collection of a deficiency will be "jeopardized by delay". 26 U.S.C. § 6861(a). The Internal Revenue Manual suggests that a jeopardy assessment should not be made unless one of the following three conditions is met:

(1) The taxpayer is or appears to be designing quickly to depart from the United States or to conceal himself;

(2) The taxpayer is or appears to be designing quickly to place his property beyond the reach of the Government either by removing it from the United States, or by concealing it, or by transferring it to other persons, or by dissipating it; or

(3) The taxpayer's financial solvency appears to be imperiled.

The legislative history of section 7429 indicates Congressional approval of the standards set forth in the IRS manual. The Court agrees that a finding of any one of the three conditions listed would support the Government's determination. However, the Court's consideration is in no way limited to the factors delineated in the IRS manual.

[The Government's evidence established that the corporate taxpayer was attempting to liquidate its real estate holdings, was engaging in "skimming" operations, and was insolvent.]

The factors outlined above support the Government's decision to seek a jeopardy assessment. The apparent attempt to sell substantial amounts of real property, the evidence of past skimming of income and the likelihood of its continuation, and the significant evidence of plaintiffs' insolvency make the assessment rendered pursuant to 26 U.S.C. § 6861, reasonable under the circumstances.

* * *

5. The plaintiffs argue that the statutory scheme enacted in 26 U.S.C. §§ 6861 and 7429 is unconstitutional because it does not provide for adequate post-seizure review as required by the Fifth Amendment to the Constitution. The Court does not agree. The statutory scheme provides a taxpayer with notice of the governmental action. The judicial review afforded allows the taxpayer to examine witnesses, present evidence and receive a *de novo* review from an uninterested impartial party.

The jeopardy assessment procedures can be used only in circumstances which indicate that the collection of taxes would be adversely affected by the delay inherent in normal deficiency collection procedures. The collection of tax is of the very highest priority to any government. The importance of revenue collection justifies the extraordinary procedures Congress has provided for in sections 6861 and 7429 of the Internal Revenue Code. The statutory procedures available in the case of a jeopardy assessment are constitutionally valid.

6. The final question to be passed on by the Court concerns the propriety of the amount of the assessment. 26 U.S.C. § 7429(b)(2)(B). The taxpayer bears the burden of proving that the amount assessed is not appropriate. 26 U.S.C. § 7429(g)(2).

The assessment against Fidelity Equipment Leasing Corporation and its subsidiaries for the taxable year ending November 30, 1975, equaled $1,207,405.12. * * * The total amount assessed against [co-plaintiff] Global equaled $10,718,553.07. The amounts assessed against the plaintiffs included substantial penalties levied pursuant to 26 U.S.C. § 6653(b) and interest.

While it is unable to specify any incorrect determination by the Government, the Court cannot hold that the amount assessed is appropriate under the circumstances. The Internal Revenue Service, in determining the assessed deficiencies, relied on findings that this Court, with the evidence now before it, cannot uphold nor deny. For example, while the Court has before it copies of the sales agreement and promissory notes executed between Fidelity and Michael G. Thevis, the Internal Revenue Service determined that the transaction was a sham and disallowed deductions for interest paid on the notes. Further, a substantial portion of the assessment constituted addition to the tax, under 26 U.S.C. § 6653(b), as a result of the Government's decision that the underpayment resulted from fraud. This Court is not able to presently make such a finding. While the IRS apparently used the best available means of determining the deficiency, the unreliability of its methods combined with the Government's other holdings, compels this Court to deny the Government's request for a finding that the amount of liability assessed was appropriate.

Pursuant to 26 U.S.C. § 7429(b)(3), when the Court finds that the amount assessed is inappropriate, authority is granted to take such action, "as the court finds appropriate." Accordingly, the Court will fashion a remedy which protects the Government's ability to collect its revenue, allows an accurate determination of the plaintiffs' deficiency and does not subject the plaintiffs to irreparable injury. The Court orders the following:

1. The liens imposed by the IRS as a result of their jeopardy assessment will be allowed to stay in effect, however the enforcement of those liens by seizure or sale is stayed until such time as the actual deficiencies owed by the plaintiffs may be determined by the Tax Court.

2. The plaintiffs are ordered to immediately retain the services of a reputable accounting firm (the choice will be subject to this Court's approval). This firm will be retained in order to establish an acceptable method of business procedures for the accounting and bookkeeping obligations of the plaintiffs. The large daily flow of cash now a part of plaintiffs' operation must be stopped. All of plaintiffs' dealings must be by check, draft, or other documentary means. Each of plaintiffs' subsidiaries must strictly maintain accurate records of all sales, purchases, or other transactions. All "peep shows" or theaters must maintain accurate meter or ticket readings, which are to be recorded and stored. Any operation which is not susceptible to some reliable method of record keeping will be halted immediately. All procedures for documenting income and expenses must have the approval of the retained accounting firm.

Upon completion of procedures to assure accurate bookkeeping and accounting procedures for plaintiffs, the accounting firm instituting such procedures shall file a report with this Court as to the methods and procedures utilized to assure accuracy of the plaintiffs' records, and complete reporting as to all income and expenses, with a copy of such report being furnished to the Internal Revenue Service.

All of this action shall be taken at plaintiffs' expense and plaintiffs must commence implementing this order immediately.

Additionally, Agents of the Internal Revenue Service shall be allowed continuing reasonable access to the current books and records of plaintiffs to assure compliance with this order and to determine if plaintiffs are maintaining correct records of all income and expenses and are otherwise complying with this order.

In order to facilitate any future interpretations of this order, the Court notes that the collection of revenue by the Government is the primary purpose of this order. If at any time the plaintiffs jeopardize that purpose through skimming, dissipation of assets, inadequate or inaccurate record keeping, the Government may seek an immediate lifting of the stay and execution of their liens. The Court retains jurisdiction of the present action in order to insure compliance with these instructions and for such other action as may hereafter be appropriate.

So ordered, this the 20th day of December, 1978.

NOTE

In the case of an assessment under IRC §§ 6851, 6861 or 6862, the Service may levy immediately upon the taxpayer's property, without regard to the 10-day notice period provided by § 6331(a). IRC § 6331(a). In addition to the preliminary review procedure provided by § 7429, the taxpayer may wish to stay collection of the assessment by filing a bond pursuant to IRC § 6863. This section provides that "[w]hen an assessment has been made under section 6851, 6861 or 6862 * * * the collection of the whole or any amount of such assessment may be stayed by filing with the Secretary * * * a bond in an amount equal to the amount as to which the stay is desired * * *." It is a rare case, however, in which the taxpayer against whom a jeopardy assessment has been made will be able to file a bond to secure the payment of the *full* asserted liability.

SECTION 4. TRUST FUND TAXES (WITHHOLDINGS)

There is no area of tax practice more depressing to the practitioner and client than the problem of unpaid withholding taxes. The business entity involved is invariably in the process of failing or (worse yet) has collapsed already, owing substantial amounts in withholding taxes. The Internal Revenue Service, armed with the ability to seek payment from any "responsible person" and certain others, stands ready to unleash the full force of its collection arsenal to recoup the taxes owed by the business.

A. RESPONSIBLE PERSONS' LIABILITY

---

(1) THE BASIC TESTS

BAUER v. UNITED STATES

543 F.2d 142 (Ct.Cl.1976).

OPINION

PER CURIAM.

* * * Since the court agrees with the trial judge's recommended decision (with the modification requested by defendant), as hereinafter set forth, it hereby affirms and adopts the same as the basis for its judgment in this case. * * *

OPINION OF TRIAL JUDGE

SPECTOR, Trial Judge: This is a tax refund suit to recover the sum of $421.35, plus interest, paid by plaintiff in partial satisfaction of a 100 percent penalty of $69,022.39 assessed by the Internal Revenue Service. The defendant has counterclaimed for the balance of the assessment, plus interest, and a lien fee.

Resolution of the case hinges upon application of the relevant facts, to the following pertinent provisions of the Internal Revenue Code of 1954:

RULES FOR APPLICATION OF ASSESSABLE PENALTIES

(a) *Penalty Assessed as Tax.*—The penalties and liabilities provided by this subchapter shall be paid upon notice and demand by the Secretary or his delegate, and shall be assessed and collected in the same manner as taxes. Except as otherwise provided, any reference in this title to "tax" imposed by this title shall be deemed also to refer to the penalties and liabilities provided by this subchapter.

(b) *Person Defined.*—The term "person", as used in this subchapter, includes an officer or employee of a corporation, or a member or employee of a partnership, who as such officer, employee, or member *is under a duty to perform the act in respect of which the violation occurs.* [26 U.S.C. § 6671. Emphasis supplied.]

FAILURE TO COLLECT AND PAY OVER TAX OR ATTEMPT TO EVADE OR DEFEAT TAX

Any person *required to collect, truthfully account for, and pay over any tax imposed by this title who willfully fails to collect such tax, or truthfully account for and pay over such tax, or willfully attempts in any manner to evade or defeat any such tax or the payment thereof*, shall, in addition to other penalties provided by law, be liable to a penalty equal to the total amount of the tax evaded, or not collected, or not accounted for and paid over. No penalty shall be imposed under section 6653 for any offense to which this section is applicable. [26 U.S.C. § 6672. Emphasis supplied.]

Plaintiff's former employer, Management and Technology, Inc. (hereinafter MATI), failed to pay over withholding taxes with respect to wages paid to employees of MATI during the last two calendar quarters of 1970. The 100 percent penalty has been levied by IRS against plaintiff individually on the grounds that he was a person, within the contemplation of the code above-quoted, under a *duty* to collect and pay over these withholding taxes, but that he *willfully* failed to do so. This case, therefore, has essentially two issues—was plaintiff's position with MATI during the pertinent period such that he had the *duty* to collect and pay over taxes within the meaning of the code; and, if such a duty is found to exist, was plaintiff's failure to discharge that duty *willful.*

* * *

This type of case is especially dependent upon its facts. Prior decisions are principally useful for comparison on their facts and to illustrate the type of facts which are ordinarily highlighted and emphasized. In White v. United States, [372 F.2d 513, 517 (Ct.Cl.1967),] for example, it was observed that:

> Since the courts are looking for the person who could have seen to it that the taxes were paid, sometimes they just speak more generally about general policy-making authority or *fiscal* control, instead of pointing more explicitly to authority to direct payment of creditors. Thus, in United States v. Strebler, 313 F.2d 402 (8th Cir. 1963), the court decided that the corporation's president was the person responsible for collecting and paying over taxes withheld because he had the authority to act, and did act, as *fiscal* manager of that company's affairs, and exercised authority over the general policy, affairs, and *finances* of the corporation.

> Both approaches would seem to amount to the same thing—*a search for a person with ultimate authority over expenditures of funds* since such a person can fairly be said to be responsible for the corporation's failure to pay over its taxes. In Bloom v. United States, 272 F.2d 215, the court tied the two together in holding the president of the corporation involved there to be the responsible person, since he was in charge of the entire operation, made the final decisions, and decided what creditors were, or were not, to be paid. [Emphasis supplied.]

Plaintiff does not fit these definitions. He was at best only a nominal figure of authority in the fiscal area. Mere office holding of and by itself does not render one responsible for the collection and paying over of employee withholding taxes.

In each case in this court in which a person was found to possess the requisite "duty" under section 6672 of the code, it has been established by the evidence that he actually signed or cosigned corporate checks. Aside from the fact that this plaintiff's "authority" to sign checks was not in accordance with the company's by-laws, the evidence establishes that he never had custody of nor control over the corporate checkbook, and never in fact signed a corporate check.

Another important factor is to determine who was responsible for preparation and payment of the payroll. This function was performed only by Rodgers, or by persons under his supervision. The payroll clerk specifically testified that when there were insufficient funds to pay employee withholding taxes and other debts, she would on occasion be directed by Rodgers to apply the withholding taxes to other debts. Plaintiff had nothing to do with payroll. He was not authorized in the by-laws or in actual practice to act in that area.

Rodgers, furthermore, signed and filed quarterly employment tax returns, and reported directly to Williams on such matters. As a former treasurer and comptroller, Williams was also conversant with fiscal affairs, in contrast with plaintiff whose experience, skills and duties were and always had been technical in nature. The meetings with IRS representatives were with Williams and Rodgers, not with plaintiff, and he was dependent on the president and treasurer for information about, and the resolution of those tax problems.

Nor did plaintiff have "the final word as to what bills or creditors should or should not be paid and when." All bills were paid by a clerk under Rodgers' supervision, and it was he who directed the priorities when funds became insufficient. Nowhere in the record is it suggested that Williams or Rodgers asked plaintiff whether the bills of specific suppliers should or should not be paid, and plaintiff did not have that utimate decision-making authority. He would be consulted if supplies for his division were involved, in the hope that he could settle for less and still maintain production. Significantly the largest supplier, Kodak, sought out Williams and Rodgers, not plaintiff, when they had a problem.

In short, plaintiff was an outsider with respect to the financial and fiscal affairs of the company. He did not meet with representatives of the bank which was principally concerned with MATI's financial condition and, without plaintiff's approval, Williams sold major corporate assets and obtained a loan by granting rights to acquire MATI stock.

The courts recognize the normal division of and limitations on authority exercised by various representatives of a particular business, as illustrated in Bernardi v. United States.[6] There the 100 percent penalty was asserted against three persons but one of these (Lutz) whose authority in fiscal affairs, incidentally, was greater than that of plaintiff's in this case, was held not responsible. He was a vice president, director, and shareholder of a corporation, and in charge of operations. He had no responsibility for payroll nor in determining creditor priorities. He had nothing to do with keeping tax records or making out tax returns. Lutz was, however, authorized to sign corporate checks, and did so. He actually signed the employer's quarterly tax returns for the quarters at issue, had intimate knowledge of the corporation's financial problems and met with the accounts receivable factor to discuss credit arrangements.

6. 74-1 U.S.T.C. ¶ 9170 (N.D.Ill.1973), aff'd 507 F.2d 682 (7th Cir. 1974), cert. denied, 422 U.S. 1042, 95 S.Ct. 2656, 45 L.Ed.2d 693 (1975).

In *Bernardi*, the court held that Bernardi, the treasurer, and one Richter, the chairman of the board, had the requisite duty to pay the taxes, but not Lutz. As to the latter, the court observed:

> * * * If Lutz had decided that withheld taxes should be segregated or paid over to the Government immediately, he could have implemented that decision only by persuading Bernardi or Richter, or both, to segregate funds or to pay the taxes.

That observation would be even more appropriate in this case where plaintiff had comparatively less knowledge and actual authority in the financial and tax affairs of MATI.

It should perhaps be further noted that even if it were assumed, *arguendo*, that plaintiff in this case had the requisite "duty" within the contemplation of the code, his failure to discharge that duty must also have been "willful," if he is to be held liable for the penalty. It has been held that "[f]or the purposes of the statute, the individual must be responsible and his failure willful. Responsibility without willfulness is not enough." [McCarty v. United States, 437 F.2d 961, 967 (Ct.Cl.1971).] The facts fall far short of demonstrating the requisite "willfulness" on plaintiff's part even if it were found (which it is not) that he was chargeable with the requisite "duty." Mere negligence in failing to ascertain facts regarding a tax delinquency is insufficient to constitute willfulness under the code.

On the basis of the evidence, it is concluded that judgment should be entered for plaintiff, and that defendant's counterclaim should be dismissed.

*   *   *

BLOOM v. UNITED STATES

272 F.2d 215 (9th Cir. 1959).

JERTBERG, Circuit Judge.

This is an appeal from a judgment against an officer of a corporation for the amount of income taxes and social security taxes withheld from wages of employees of the corporation but not paid over to the United States.

*   *   *

Appellant's final and fourth assertion of error is that the trial court applied an improper definition of "willfully" in concluding that appellant willfully failed to pay over the amount of taxes withheld or deducted from the wages of employees of the corporation under the terms of Section 2707(a).[f] This contention is based on the claim that

---

f.   Internal Revenue Code of 1939, 26 U.S.C.A. § 2707(a), the predecessor to § 6672(a) of the 1954 Code.

he was prevented from paying the taxes by the financing bank, and that proof of a criminal intent or motive or purpose to violate the law was necessary to establish civil liability in this case. We have already disposed of appellant's contention that the withheld taxes were not paid over because of the financing bank's purported interference into the internal affairs of the corporation.

It must be borne in mind that the action instituted against appellant was not designed to impose criminal sanctions, but is a civil action to insure payment to the United States of a tax already collected or deducted by an employer, whose employees have already received credit for the withheld taxes in their individual returns. Section 2707(a) does not provide for a "double" penalty. In our view there need not be present an intent to defraud or deprive the United States of the taxes collected or withheld for its account, nor need bad motives be present in order to invoke the sanctions of Section 2707(a). The decision of appellant as the responsible officer of the corporation not to have the corporation pay over to the government the withheld taxes was a voluntary, conscious, and intentional act to prefer other creditors of the corporation over the United States. In our view such conduct was willful within the meaning of Section 2707(a).

Appellant relies on Cushman v. Wood, [149 F.Supp. 644 (D.Ariz. 1956),] as standing for the proposition that "willfully" in Section 2707(a) requires criminal conduct and means "without reasonable cause." The court there held, 149 F.Supp. at page 646, "Thus, the basic elements of willfulness are evil motive, lack of justification, bad purpose, or something done or not done without justifiable excuse." We are unable to agree with the views thus expressed.

The judgment of the district court is affirmed.

NOTES

1.   The willfulness requirement in a § 6672 case is satisfied by "showing that the responsible person recklessly disregarded his duty to collect, account for, and pay over the trust fund taxes or by showing that the responsible person ignored an obvious and known risk that the trust fund might not be remitted." Feist v. United States, 607 F.2d 954, 961 (Ct.Cl.1979); see also Teel v. United States, 529 F.2d 903, 905–906 (9th Cir. 1976). However, as the *Bauer* opinion excerpted above notes, "[m]ere negligence in failing to ascertain facts regarding a tax delinquency is insufficient to constitute willfulness under the code." The burden of proving a lack of willfulness is on the responsible person. Anderson v. United States, 561 F.2d 162, 165 (8th Cir. 1977).

2.   Section 6672(b), added to the Code in 1979 by P.L. 95–628 and effective with respect to penalties assessed after January 9, 1979, permits an individual to stay collection of the 100% penalty if, within 30 days of the date on which notice and demand for payment of the penalty is made, he pays the minimum amount necessary to invoke the jurisdiction of a court in a refund suit, files a claim for refund of the amount paid, and posts a bond equal to one and one-half times the amount of the balance of the unpaid as-

sessment. The stay of collection expires automatically, however, if the alleged responsible person fails to file suit in a district court or the Court of Claims within 30 days after the date on which his claim for refund is denied.

Prior to the enactment of § 6672(b) there was no statutory provision for obtaining a stay of collection of the 100% penalty. The Service could institute collection proceedings 10 days after notice and demand for payment was made, and any stay had to be worked out with the Collection Division on an informal basis. Although § 6672(b) now makes a stay a matter of statutory right if a bond is posted, the provision is not intended to *require* an individual to post a bond in order to have his liability adjudicated in a district court or the Court of Claims prior to collection. Thus, in appropriate cases, the IRS and the taxpayer can agree to an informal stay pending a court decision on the taxpayer's liability for the penalty. In such a case, the alleged responsible person still would have to pay the minimum jurisdictional amount and file a claim for refund before instituting proceedings in a district court or the Court of Claims.

(2) LIABILITY FOR PRIOR PERIODS

SLODOV v. UNITED STATES

Supreme Court of the United States, 1978.
436 U.S. 238, 98 S.Ct. 1778, 56 L.Ed.2d 251.

Mr. Justice BRENNAN delivered the opinion of the Court.

Petitioner, an orthodontist by profession, on January 31, 1969, purchased the stock and assumed the management of three corporations engaged in the food vending business. The corporations were indebted at the time of the purchase for approximately $250,000 of taxes, including federal wage and Federal Insurance Contribution Act (FICA) taxes withheld from employees' wages prior to January 31. The sums withheld had not been paid over when due, however, but had been dissipated by the previous management before petitioner acquired the businesses. After petitioner assumed control, the corporations acquired funds sufficient to pay the taxes, but petitioner used the funds to pay employees' wages, rent, suppliers and other creditors, and to meet other day-to-day expenses incurred in operating the businesses. * * *

I

* * * When he bought the stock, petitioner understood, and the purchase agreement reflected, that the corporations had an outstanding obligation for taxes in the amount of $250,000 due for payment on January 31, including withheld employee wage and FICA taxes (hereinafter trust-fund taxes). During the purchase negotiations, the sellers represented to petitioner that balances in the various corporate checking accounts were sufficient to pay these taxes as well as bills due other creditors. Relying on the representation, petition-

er, on Saturday, February 1, sent four checks to the IRS in payment of the taxes. On Monday, February 3, petitioner discovered that the accounts were overdrawn and stopped payment on the checks. Thus, at the time that petitioner assumed control, the corporations had no liquid assets, and whatever trust-fund taxes had been collected prior to petitioner's assumption of control had been dissipated.

Petitioner immediately advised the IRS that the corporations had no funds with which to pay the taxes, and solicited guidance concerning how the corporations should proceed. There was evidence that IRS officials advised petitioner that they had no objection to his continuing operations so long as current tax obligations were met, and that petitioner agreed to do so and to endeavor to pay the arrearages as soon as possible. The IRS never represented that it would hold petitioner harmless under § 6672 for the back taxes, however.

To continue operations, petitioner deposited personal funds in the corporate account, and, to obtain inventory, agreed with certain suppliers to pay cash upon delivery. During petitioner's tenure, from January 31 to July 15, 1969, the corporations' gross receipts approximated $130,000 per week for the first few months but declined thereafter. The corporations "established a system of segregating funds for payment of withheld taxes and did, in fact, pay withheld taxes during the period February 1, 1969, to July 15, 1969." The bankruptcy judge found, and the IRS concedes, that the $249,212 in taxes paid during this period was approximately sufficient to defray current tax obligations. No taxes owing for periods prior to February 1, were paid, however, and in July 1969 the corporations terminated operations and filed for bankruptcy.

II

Several provisions of the Internal Revenue Code require third persons to collect taxes from the taxpayer. Among the more important are 26 U.S.C. §§ 3102(a) and 3402(a) which respectively require deduction from wages paid to employees of the employees' share of FICA taxes, and the withholding tax on wages applicable to individual income taxes. The withheld sums are commonly referred to as "trust fund taxes," reflecting the Code's provision that such withholdings or collections are deemed to be a "special fund in trust for the United States." 26 U.S.C. § 7501(a). There is no general requirement that the withheld sums be segregated from the employer's general funds, however, or that they be deposited in a separate bank account until required to be paid to the Treasury. Because the Code requires the employer to collect taxes as wages are paid, § 3102(a), while requiring payment of such taxes only quarterly, the funds accumulated during the quarter can be a tempting source of ready cash to a failing corporation beleaguered by creditors. Once net wages are paid to the employee, the taxes withheld are credited to the employee regardless of whether they are paid by the employer, so that the IRS has recourse only against the employer for their payment.

An employer who fails to pay taxes withheld from its employees' wages is, of course, liable for the taxes which should have been paid, §§ 3102(b) and 3403. The IRS has several means at its disposal to effect payment of the taxes so withheld. First, once it has been determined that an employer has been inexcusably delinquent, the IRS, upon giving hand-delivered notice, may require the employer, thereafter, and until further notice, to deposit withheld taxes in a special bank trust account within two banking days after collection, to be retained there until required to be paid to the Treasury at the quarter's end. § 7512. Second, with respect to trust funds past due prior to any such notification, the amount collected or withheld "shall be held to be a special fund in trust for the United States [and] [t]he amount of such fund shall be assessed, collected, and paid in the same manner and subject to the same provisions and limitations (including penalties) as are applicable with respect to the taxes from which such fund arose." 26 U.S.C. § 7501. Thus there is made applicable to employment taxes withheld but not paid the full range of collection methods available for the collection of taxes generally. After assessment, notice, and demand, the IRS may, therefore, create a lien upon the property of the employer, § 6321, and levy, distrain, and sell the employer's property in satisfaction. §§ 6331 to 6344.

Third, penalties may be assessed against the delinquent employer. Section 6656 of the Code imposes a penalty of 5% of the underpayment of any tax required to be deposited, and 26 U.S.C. §§ 7202 and 7215 provide criminal penalties respectively for willful failure to "collect or truthfully account for and pay over" trust-fund taxes, and for failure to comply with the requirements of § 7512, discussed *supra,* regarding special accounting requirements upon notice by the Secretary.

Finally, as in this case, the officers or employees of the employer responsible for effectuating the collection and payment of trust-fund taxes who willfully fail to do so are made personally liable to a "penalty" equal to the amount of the delinquent taxes. Section 6672 provides, *inter alia*:

> "Any person required to collect, truthfully account for, and pay over any tax imposed by this title who willfully fails to collect such tax, or truthfully account for and pay over such tax, or willfully attempts in any manner to evade or defeat any such tax or the payment thereof, shall, in addition to other penalties provided by law, be liable to a penalty equal to the total amount of the tax evaded, or not collected, or not accounted for and paid over * * *."

Section 6671(b) defines "person," for purposes of § 6672, as including "an officer or employee of a corporation, or a member or employee of a partnership, who as such officer, employee, or member is under a duty to perform the act in respect of which the violation occurs." Also, § 7202 of the Code, which tracks the wording of § 6672, makes a violation punishable as a felony subject to a fine of $10,000, and imprisonment for 5 years. Thus, an employer-official or other employee responsible for collecting and paying taxes who willfully fails to do so is subject to both a civil penalty equivalent to 100% of the taxes not collected or paid, and to a felony conviction. Only the application to petitioner of the civil penalty provision, § 6672, is at issue in this case.

III

When the same individual or individuals who caused the delinquency in any tax quarter are also the "responsible persons" at the time the Government's efforts to collect from the employer have failed, and it seeks recourse against the "responsible employees," there is no question that § 6672 is applicable to them. It is the situation that arises when there has been a change of control of the employer enterprise, here corporations, prior to the expiration of a tax quarter, or at a time when a tax delinquency for past quarters already exists that creates the question for our decision. In this case, petitioner assumed control at a time when a delinquency existed for unpaid trust-fund taxes, while the specific funds withheld but not paid had been dissipated by predecessor officers and when the corporations had no liquid assets with which to pay the overdue taxes.

A

Petitioner concedes that he was subject to personal liability under § 6672 as a person responsible for the collection, accounting, and payment of employment taxes required to be withheld between January 31, 1969, when he assumed control of the corporations and July 15, 1969, when he resigned. His contention is that he was not, however, a responsible person within § 6672 with respect to taxes withheld prior to his assumption of control and that § 6672 consequently imposed no duty upon him to pay the taxes collected by his predecessors. Petitioner argues that this construction of § 6672 follows necessarily from the statute's limitation of personal liability to "[a]ny person required to collect, truthfully account for *and* pay over any tax imposed by this title," who willfully fails to discharge those responsibilities (emphasis added). He argues that since the obligations are phrased in the conjunctive, a person can be subject to the section only if all three duties—(1) to collect, (2) truthfully account for, *and* (3) pay over—were applicable to him with respect to the tax dollars in question. See McCullough v. United States, 462 F.2d 588 (CA 5 1972). On the other hand, as the Government argues, the language could be construed as describing, in terms of their general responsibilities, the persons potentially liable under the statute, without regard to whether those persons were in a position to perform all of the duties with respect to the specific tax dollars in question. Although neither construction is inconsistent with the language of the statute, we reject petitioner's as inconsistent with its purpose.

Sections 6672 and 7202 were designed to assure compliance by the employer with its obligation to withhold and pay the sums withheld, by subjecting the employer's officials responsible for the employer's decisions regarding withholding and payment to civil and criminal penalties for the employer's delinquency. If § 6672 were given petitioner's construction, the penalties easily could be evaded by changes in officials' responsibilities prior to the expiration of any quarter. Because the duty to *pay over* the tax arises only at the quarter's end, a "responsible person" who willfully failed to *collect* taxes would escape personal liability for that failure simply by resigning his position, and transferring to another the decisionmaking responsibility prior to the quarter's end. Obversely, a "responsible person" assuming control prior to the quarter's end could, without incurring personal liability under § 6672, willfully dissipate the trust funds collected and segregated by his predecessor.

That this result, obviously at odds with the statute's purpose to assure payment of withheld taxes, was not intended is buttressed by the history of the provision. The predecessor of § 6672, § 1308(c), Revenue Act of 1918, provided, *inter alia*: "Any person who willfully refuses to pay, collect, or truly account for and pay over [taxes enumerated in § 1308(a)] shall * * * be liable to a penalty of the amount of the tax evaded or not paid, collected, or accounted for and paid over * * *." The statute remained unchanged in this respect until 1954 when the successor section to § 1308(c) was revised to its present form. Both before and after the 1954 revision the "person" potentially liable under the statute was defined in a separate provision, § 1308(d), succeeded by present § 6671(b), as, including "an officer or employee of a corporation or a member or employer of a partnership, who as such officer, employee, or member is under a duty to perform the act in respect of which the violation occurs." When, in 1954, Congress added the phrase modifying "person"—"Any person required to collect, truthfully account for, and pay over any tax imposed by this title"—it was not seeking further to describe the class of persons defined in § 6671(b) upon whom fell the responsibility for collecting taxes, but was attempting to clarify the type of tax to which the penalty section was applicable. Since under the 1954 amendment the penalty would otherwise be applicable to "any tax imposed by this title," the phrase modifying "person" was necessary to insure that the penalty provided by that section would be read as applicable only to failure to pay taxes which *require collection*, that is, third-party taxes, and not failure to pay "*any* tax imposed by this title," which, of course, would include *direct* taxes such as employer

FICA and income taxes. As both the House and Senate Committees expressed it, "the application of this penalty is limited only to the collected or withheld taxes which are imposed on some person other than the person who is required to collect, account for and pay over, the tax." Thus, by adding the phrase modifying "person," Congress was attempting to clarify the type of tax to which the penalty section was applicable, perhaps inartfully, by reference to the duty of the person required to collect them. This view is supported by the fact that the Commissioner of Internal Revenue issued a regulation shortly after the amendment, limiting the application of the § 6672 penalty to third-party taxes.

We conclude therefore that the phrase "[a]ny person required to collect, truthfully account for, and pay over any tax imposed by this title" was meant to limit § 6672 to persons responsible for collection of third-party taxes and not to limit it to those persons in a position to perform all three of the enumerated duties with respect to the tax dollars in question.

We turn then to the Government's contention that petitioner was subject to personal liability under § 6672 when during the period in which he was a responsible person, the corporations generated gross receipts sufficient to pay the back taxes, but used the funds for other purposes.

B

Although at the time petitioner became a responsible person the trust-fund taxes had been dissipated and the corporations had no liquid assets, the Government contends that § 6672 imposed civil liability upon petitioner because sums received from sales in carrying on the businesses after January 31, 1969, were impressed with a trust in favor of the United States for the satisfaction of overdue employment taxes, and petitioner's willful use of those funds to pay creditors other than the United States, violated the obligation to "pay over" imposed by § 6672. The Government does not argue that the statute requires a "responsible person," to liquidate corporate assets to pay the back taxes upon assuming control, however; it argues only that a trust was impressed on all cash received by the corporations. We think that that construction of § 6672 would not advance the statute's purpose and, moreover, is inconsistent with the context and legislative history of the provision and its relation to the Code's priority rule applicable to collection of back taxes.

(1)

The Government argues that its construction of the statute is necessary to effectuate the congressional purpose to assure collection and payment of taxes. Although that construction might in this case

garner tax dollars otherwise uncollectable, its long-term effect arguably would more likely frustrate than aid the IRS's collection efforts.

At the time petitioner assumed control, the corporations owed
back taxes, were overdue on their supplier accounts, and had no cash.
To the extent that the corporations had assets unencumbered by
liens superior to a tax lien, the IRS could satisfy its claim by levy
and sale. But as will often be the case, the corporations here apparently did not have such assets. The Government admits that in such
circumstances, the IRS's practice is to be "flexible," and does not insist that the corporation discontinue operations, thereby substituting
for certain loss at least the potential of recovering back taxes if the
corporation makes a financial recovery. It argues nevertheless that
the "responsible person" renders himself personally liable to the §
6672 penalty by using gross receipts to purchase inventory or pay
wages, or even by using personal funds for those purposes, so long as
any third-party employment tax bill remains unpaid.

Thus, although it is in the IRS's interest to encourage the responsible person to continue operation with the hope of receiving
payment of the back taxes, if the attempt fails and the taxes remain
unpaid, the IRS insists that the § 6672 personal-liability penalty attached upon payment of the first dollar to a supplier. The practical
effect of that construction of the statute would be that a well-coun-
seled person contemplating assuming control of a financially beleaguered corporation owing back employment taxes would recognize
that he could do so without incurring personal civil and criminal en-
alties only if there were available sufficient borrowed or personal
funds fully to pay all back employment taxes before doing *any* business. If that course is unattractive or unavailable to the corporation,
the Government will be remitted to its claim in bankruptcy. When
an immediate filing for bankruptcy means a total loss, the Government understandably, as it did here, does not discourage the corporation from continuing to operate so long as current taxes are paid. As
soon as the corporation embarks upon that course, however, the "responsible person" is potentially liable to heavy civil and criminal penalties not for doing anything which compromised the Government's
collection efforts, but for doing what the Government regards as
maximizing its chances for recovery. As construed by the Government, § 6672 would merely discourage changes of ownership and
management of financially troubled corporations and the infusion of
equity or debt funding which might accompany it without encouraging employer compliance with tax obligations or facilitating collection
of back taxes. Thus, recovery of employer taxes would likely be limited to the situation in which the prospective purchaser or management official is ignorant of § 6672.

(2)

As noted in the previous section, § 6672 as construed by the Government would, in effect, make the responsible person assuming con-

trol of a business a guarantor for payment of the delinquent taxes simply by undertaking to continue operation of the business. That construction is precluded by the history and context of § 6672 and cognate provisions of the Code.

Section 6672 cannot be read as imposing upon the responsible person an absolute duty to "pay over" amounts which should have been collected and withheld. The fact that the provision imposes a "penalty" and is violated only by a "willful failure" is itself strong evidence that it was not intended to impose liability without personal fault. Congress, moreover, has not made corporate officers personally liable for the corporation's tax obligations generally, and § 6672 therefore should be construed in a way which respects that policy choice. The Government's concession—that § 6672 does not impose a duty on the responsible officer to use personal funds or even to liquidate corporate assets to satisfy the tax obligations—recognizes that the "pay over" requirement does not impose an absolute duty on the responsible person to pay back taxes.

Recognizing that the statute cannot be construed to impose liability without fault, the Government characterizes petitioner's use of gross receipts for payment of operating expenses as a breach of trust, arguing that a trust was impressed on all after-acquired cash. Nothing whatever in § 6672 or its legislative history suggests that the effect of the requirement to "pay over" was to impress a trust on the corporation's after-acquired cash, however. Moreover, the history of a related section, 26 U.S.C. § 7501, makes clear that it was not. Section 7501 of the Code provides, *inter alia,* that the "amount of tax * * * collected or withheld shall be held to be a special fund in trust for the United States [which] shall be assessed, collected, and paid in the same manner and subject to the same provisions and limitations (including penalties) as are applicable with respect to the taxes from which such fund arose." This section was enacted in 1934. The provision was added to H.R. 7835, 73d Cong., 2d Sess., by the Senate Finance Committee, which explained:

> "Under existing law the liability of the person collecting and withholding the taxes to pay over the amount is merely a debt, and he cannot be treated as a trustee or proceeded against by distraint. Section [607] of the bill as reported impresses the amount of taxes withheld or collected with a trust and makes applicable for the enforcement of the Government's claim the administrative provisions for assessment and collection of taxes." S.Rep. No. 558, 73d Cong., 2d Sess., 53 (1934).

Since the very reason for adding § 7501 was, as the Senate Report states, that "the liability of the person collecting and withholding the taxes * * * is *merely a debt*" (emphasis added), § 6672, whose predecessor section was enacted in 1919 while the *debt* concept prevailed, hardly could have been intended to impose a *trust* on after-acquired cash.

We further reject the argument that § 7501, whose trust concept may be viewed as having modified the duty imposed under § 6672, can be construed as establishing a fiduciary obligation to pay over after-acquired cash unrelated to the withholding taxes. The language of § 7501 limits the trust to "the amount of the taxes *withheld* or *collected*." (Emphasis added.) Comparing that language with § 6672, which imposes liability for a willful failure to *collect* as well as failure to pay over, makes clear that under § 7501 there must be a nexus between the funds collected and the trust created. That construction is consistent with the accepted principle of trust law requiring tracing of misappropriated trust funds into the trustee's estate in order for an impressed trust to arise. Finally, for the reasons discussed in the next section, a construction of § 7501 or § 6672 as imposing a trust on all after-acquired corporate funds without regard to the interests of others in those funds would conflict with the priority rules applicable to the collection of back taxes.

(3)

We developed in Part II, *supra,* that the Code affords the IRS several means to collect back taxes, including levy, distraint, and sale. But the IRS is not given the power to levy on property in the hands of the taxpayer beyond the extent of the taxpayer's interest in the property, and the Code specifically subordinates tax liens to the interests of certain others in the property, generally including those with a perfected security interest in the property. For example, the Code and established decisional principles subordinate the tax lien to perfected security interests arising before the filing of the tax lien, to certain perfected security interests in certain collateral, including inventory, arising after the tax lien filing when pursuant to a security agreement entered into before the filing, and to collateral which is the subject of a purchase money mortgage regardless of whether the agreement was entered into before or after filing of the tax lien. As a consequence, secured parties often will have interests in certain proceeds superior to the tax lien, and it is unlikely, moreover, that corporations in the position of those involved here could continue in operation without making some payments to secured creditors under the terms of security agreements. Those payments may well take the form of cash or accounts receivable, which like other property may be subject to a security interest, when, for example, the security agreement covers the proceeds of inventory the purchase of which is financed by the secured party, or the security agreement requires the debtor to make payments under a purchase-money mortgage by assigning accounts receivable which are the proceeds of inventory financed by the mortgage. Thus, although the IRS is powerless to attach assets in which a secured party has a superior interest, it would impose a penalty under § 6672 if the responsible person fails to divert the secured party's proceeds to the Treasury without regard to whether the secured party's interests are superior to those of the Government. Surely Congress did not intend § 6672 to hammer the responsible person with the threat of heavy civil and criminal penalties to pay over proceeds in which the Code does not assert a priority interest.

IV

We hold that a "responsible person" under § 6672 may violate the "pay over" requirement of that statute by willfully failing to pay over trust funds collected prior to his accession to control when at the time he assumed control the corporation has funds impressed with a trust under § 7501, but that § 7501 does not impress a trust on after-acquired funds, and that the responsible person consequently does not violate § 6672 by willfully using employer funds for purposes other than satisfaction of the trust-fund tax claims of the United States when at the time he assumed control there were no funds with which to satisfy the tax obligation and the funds thereafter generated are not directly traceable to collected taxes referred to by that statute. * * *

Mr. Justice WHITE, with whom THE CHIEF JUSTICE and Mr. Justice BLACKMUN join, dissenting.

* * *

* * * The Court holds that a person who assumes control must satisfy the business' pre-existing trust-fund tax obligations if the concern has funds available at the time he assumes control. Apparently, neither it nor the IRS would require the sale of the business' assets in order to meet such obligations. It is clear, however, that there will be a great number of companies which do not have cash available at the time of a change in ownership and management but are nevertheless viable, ongoing enterprises not in need of Government subsidization. Furthermore, any businessman with a minimum of acumen could in most circumstances make sure that the financial affairs of the company are so arranged that there are no uncommitted funds available at the moment of his accession to control. Finally, there can be little doubt that the Court's ruling today will result in changes in management and ownership which are in fact nothing but subterfuges to avoid using the company's funds to pay outstanding trust-fund tax obligations. The investors in any corporation seriously in arrears will also have a strong incentive to arrange changes of management, whether sham or real, in order to permit funds acquired by the corporation to be used for purposes other than satisfying its tax obligations without exposing its managers to personal liability. In addition, changes of ownership, often more formal than real, will frequently be arranged for no purpose other than to

permit the concern to use future funds without regard to its pre-existing tax obligations.

* * *

Because I believe that the Court has without justification, created yet another means of impeding the collection of taxes for purposes designated by Congress, I dissent from Parts III–B and IV of the Court's opinion.

NOTE

What are the obligations of a responsible person of a business who discovers, just prior to the sale of the company, that there are withholding taxes owed to the government? Generally, the responsible person's liability would continue despite the subsequent sale of the business. In Feist v. United States, 607 F.2d 954 (Ct.Cl.1979), however, a rather extreme set of circumstances led the Court of Claims to a different conclusion. The responsible person in *Feist* discovered, on the day of the planned sale of the business, that the company's taxes for its most recent quarter were delinquent. Rather than postpone the sale and gather the cash necessary to pay the tax from the company's several hundred cash registers scattered throughout various retail outlets, the responsible person elected to proceed with the sale after receiving oral assurances from the buyer that it would pay the tax immediately after the sale. However, just after the sale one of the principals of the buyer illegally appropriated the company's funds and two weeks later the company was adjudicated bankrupt. In an action against the responsible person/seller for payment of the tax, the court seized upon the Supreme Court's statement in *Slodov*, that section 6672 "was not intended to impose liability without personal fault", and found the failure to pay the tax not willful, as the seller had taken reasonable precautions to see that the tax was paid, given the nature of the surrounding circumstances.

(3) JOINT AND SEVERAL LIABILITY

BROWN v. UNITED STATES

591 F.2d 1136 (5th Cir. 1979).

ALVIN B. RUBIN, Circuit Judge.

Section 6672 of the Internal Revenue Code of 1954 provides that responsible persons who "willfully" fail to ensure that their corporation pays federal withholding taxes are liable for a penalty in the amount not paid. This case involves questions concerning the liability of two officers, Ralph H. Brown and Don R. Sibley, of Sibwin, Inc. for penalties under § 6672 because of Sibwin's failure to pay withholding taxes for the first quarter of 1972. Each asserts that the other was the only person responsible for seeing that the liability was paid, and is, therefore, the only one liable for a § 6672 penalty. In addition, each asserts that, even if he was a responsible person during the first quarter, he did not "willfully" fail to ensure that the taxes were paid because the corporation had no unencumbered funds available to pay the tax. We conclude, however, that both of them were responsible officers, that they both willfully failed to ensure that Sibwin paid its withholding tax obligation for the first quarter, and that they, therefore, are each liable for the Section 6672 penalty.

* * *

Because we conclude that both Brown and Sibley are liable for § 6672 penalties, the issue arises whether their indebtedness is joint and several or whether they are each only severally liable, and therefore owe only a pro rata portion of the total penalty. The Eighth Circuit has held that liability under § 6672 is joint and several, Hartman v. United States, 8 Cir. 1976, 538 F.2d 1336, 1340, but this circuit has never decided the question. For reasons set forth below, we agree that the liability of responsible officers for the penalty provided in § 6672 is joint and several; therefore, it is unnecessary for an apportionment of liability to be made in this case.

The language of § 6672 indicates that each responsible person is liable for a penalty equal to the total amount of the withholding tax not paid to the government; it provides:

> "*Any person* required to collect, truthfully account for, and pay over any tax imposed by this title who willfully fails to collect such tax * * * shall * * * be liable to a penalty equal to the total amount of the tax evaded, or not collected, or not accounted for and paid over."

26 U.S.C. § 6672 (emphasis added). If Congress had intended § 6672 to impose only several liability, it would have provided that all of the responsible persons, *together*, were to be liable for the total amount of tax evaded. The legislative history of § 6672 does not touch upon this question, but joint and several liability is more consistent with the intent of Congress to ensure that withholding trust funds are turned over to the government; the government is more likely to recover the total taxes owed and the expected cost of such recovery will be less if liability is joint and several. It would be unduly burdensome for the government to have to sue each responsible officer in order to recover withholding taxes not paid voluntarily. In addition, there would be the risk that the government would not be able to recover the total amount owed if some responsible persons were judgment proof or if the number of officers found to be responsible varied from one suit to the next. Our conclusion that § 6672 liability is joint and several is also consistent with cases that have held that the existence of other responsible persons does not affect or preclude recovery of a § 6672 penalty in the amount of the entire tax owed from one of the persons responsible for a corporation's payment of withholding taxes, and with a Fifth Circuit case that held two officers liable for a § 6672 penalty for the same period without apportioning lia-

bility, see Moore v. United States, 5 Cir. 1972, 465 F.2d 514, cert. denied, 1973, 409 U.S. 1108, 93 S.Ct. 907, 34 L.Ed.2d 688.

Because the government has stated that its policy is to collect the total penalty only once, and that it will not attempt to exact that penalty separately and cumulatively from each responsible person, it is unnecessary for us to decide whether it would be entitled to multiple collections of that liability. However, we note that the Eighth Circuit has held that the government is entitled to only one satisfaction, Kelly v. Lethert, 8 Cir. 1966, 362 F.2d 629, 635, and that this court has previously stated:

> While the penalty imposed by section 6672 is distinct from and not in substitution of the liability for taxes owed by the employer, it brings to the government only the same amount to which it was entitled by way of the tax.

Newsome v. United States, 431 F.2d at 745 (footnote omitted). Double recovery by the government is not necessary to fulfill § 6672's primary purpose—protection of government revenues.

* * *

More than one person can properly be assessed as a responsible person under § 6672, and all who are held liable for the taxes are jointly and severally liable. The Service will collect the penalty amount once, and is not required to allocate in any manner its collection from the several responsible persons. Indeed, it is common practice for the Service to effect collection from the deepest or most convenient pocket available.

It is generally agreed by tax practitioners from both private and government practice that the fairest and most equitable practice would be to spread the liability among those persons determined to be liable. However, there is in reality no procedure by means of which this laudatory result can be imposed upon unwilling (much less impecunious) parties. Hence, multi-party responsible person disputes can be complicated and bitter affairs in which each party seeks to reduce the payment burden to the maximum extent possible.

One salutary procedural posture, not always possible to achieve, is for all potentially responsible persons to be brought before the same court for a single determination of responsibility. Where A and B have both been assessed as responsible persons and A brings a refund suit to test his liability,[g] the government will counterclaim against A for the unpaid balance of the assessment. The government usually will seek to bring in B also, as a third-party defendant.[h]

---

g. A will have to pay a divisible portion of the assessed liability and file a claim for refund before bringing the suit.

h. It is doubtful that A would be able to state a cause of action against B that would permit A (as distinct from the government) to bring B in as a party.

However, there can be procedural problems (for example venue or the ability to effect service of process) which can prevent the government (or *A*) from bringing *B* into the lawsuit. Moreover, there are cases in which the IRS has not assessed a person whom *A* contends should be held responsible. In such a case, *A* cannot force the IRS to assess, and cannot get this putatively responsible person before the court even if there were no procedural impediments to jurisdiction.

It should be noted, further, that there appears to be little, if any, possibility for the responsible person who pays a penalty for which another is jointly and severally liable to obtain contribution from the other. Therefore, absent an agreement among the responsible persons, the burden of payment falls arbitrarily upon those unfortunate, rich or available enough to be vulnerable to IRS collection efforts.

Due to the foregoing problems, one who is a potential responsible person is well advised to aid the Service in collecting the underlying liability from the assets of the business entity, and to advise the Service of facts indicating that others may be properly assessed as responsible persons.

(4) BANKRUPTCY AND RESPONSIBLE PERSONS

UNITED STATES v. SOTELO

Supreme Court of the United States, 1978.
436 U.S. 268, 98 S.Ct. 1795, 56 L.Ed.2d 275.

Mr. Justice MARSHALL delivered the opinion of the Court.

This case involves the interaction of sections of the Internal Revenue Code of 1954 and the Bankruptcy Act. Respondent Onofre J. Sotelo was found personally liable to the Government for his failure to pay over taxes withheld from employees of the corporation in which he was the principal officer. The question presented is whether this liability is dischargeable in bankruptcy.

*   *   *

Section 17a of the Bankruptcy Act provides in pertinent part:

"A discharge in bankruptcy shall release a bankrupt from all of his provable debts, * * * except such as

"(1) are taxes which became legally due and owing by the bankrupt to the United States or to any State * * * within three years preceding bankruptcy: *Provided, however*, That a discharge in bankruptcy shall not release a bankrupt from any taxes * * * (e) which the bankrupt has collected or withheld from others as required by the laws of the United States or any State * * * but has not paid over * * *." 11 U.S.C. § 35(a) (1976 ed.).

Relying on this statutory language, the Government presents what it views as two independent grounds for holding the § 6672 liability of

Onofre Sotelo (hereinafter respondent) to be nondischargeable. The Government's primary argument is based on the specific language relating to withholding in § 17a(1)(e); alternatively, it argues that respondent's liability, although called a "penalty," IRC § 6672, is in fact a "tax" as that term is used in § 17a(1).

Regardless of whether these two grounds are in fact independent, § 17a(1)(e) leaves no doubt as to the nondischargeability of "taxes * * * which the bankrupt has collected or withheld from others as required by the laws of the United States or any State * * * but has not paid over." The Court of Appeals viewed this provision as inapplicable here for two reasons: first, because "it was not Sotelo himself, but his employer-corporation, that was obligated by law to collect and withhold the taxes"; and second, because in any event the money involved constituted a "penalty," whereas § 17a(1)(e) "renders only 'taxes' nondischargeable." We believe that the first reason is inconsistent with the Court of Appeals' recognition of respondent's undisputed liability under Internal Revenue Code § 6672, and that the second is inconsistent with the language of § 17a(1)(e).

The fact that respondent was found liable under § 6672 necessarily means that he was "required to collect, truthfully account for, and pay over" the withholding taxes, and that he willfully failed to meet one or more of these obligations. Since the § 6672 "require-[ment]" of collection presumably derives from federal or state law, both of which are referred to in Bankruptcy Act § 17a(1)(e), it is difficult to understand how the court below could have recognized respondent's § 6672 liability and nonetheless have concluded that he was not "obligated by law to collect * * * the taxes." It is undisputed here, moreover, that the taxes in question were "collected or withheld" from the corporation's employees and that the taxes, though collected, have not been "paid over" to the Government. It is therefore clear that the § 6672 liability was not imposed for a failure on the part of respondent to collect taxes, but was rather imposed for his failure to pay over taxes that he was required both to collect and to pay over. Under these circumstances, the most natural reading of the statutory language leads to the conclusion that respondent "collected or withheld" the taxes within the meaning of Bankruptcy Act § 17a(1)(e).

We also cannot agree with the Court of Appeals that the "penalty" language of Internal Revenue Code § 6672 is dispositive of the status of respondent's debt under Bankruptcy Act § 17a(1)(e). The funds here involved were unquestionably "taxes" at the time they were "collected or withheld from others." § 17a(1)(e); see IRC §§ 3102(a), 3402(a). It is this time period that § 17a(1)(e), with its modification of "taxes" by the phrase "collected or withheld," treats as the relevant one. That the funds due are referred to as a "penalty" when the Government later seeks to recover them does not alter their essential character as taxes for purposes of the Bankruptcy Act, at least in a case in which, as here, the § 6672 liability is predicated on a failure to pay over, rather than a failure initially to collect, the taxes.

*   *   *

In terms of statutory language and legislative history, then the liability of respondent under Internal Revenue Code § 6672 must be held nondischargeable under Bankruptcy Act § 17a(1)(e). The judgment of the Court of Appeals is, accordingly,

Reversed and remanded.

Mr. Justice REHNQUIST, with whom Mr. Justice BRENNAN, Mr. Justice STEWART, and Mr. Justice STEVENS join, dissenting.

The Government undoubtedly needs the revenues it receives from taxes, but great as that need may be I cannot join the Court's thrice-twisted analysis of this particular statute to gratify it. The issue involved is the dischargeability in the corporate officer's bankruptcy proceedings of taxes which the corporation is obligated to collect and pay over to the Government. In order to conclude that the corporate officer remains liable for this corporate obligation the Court turns to an unlikely source indeed: a 1966 amendment to the Bankruptcy Act, the only apparent purpose of which was to ameliorate the lot of at least some bankrupts. The Court then proceeds to slog its way to its illogical conclusion by reading a proviso obviously intended to *limit* dischargeability of the debts of a bankrupt so as to *expand* that category of debts. *   *   *

*   *   *

While the lifelong liability which the Court imposes today falls on the shoulders of one who was the chief executive officer of a small family business, there is unfortunately nothing in the Court's reasoning which would prevent the same liability from surviving bankruptcy in the case of a comptroller, accountant, or bookkeeper who reaped none of the fruits of entrepreneurial success other than continued employment in the corporation, and in some cases possibly not even that. So long as the Government in its zeal for the collection of the revenue may persuade a bankruptcy court that a corporate employee comes within the Court's Delphic construction of 26 U.S.C. § 6672 and 11 U.S.C. § 35(a)(1)(e) (1976 ed.), such a person will be denied the "fresh start" which Congress clearly intended to enhance by the 1966 amendments to the Bankruptcy Act. Before the Government may randomly sweep such persons into a net whereby they are denied a discharge, not of their own tax liability but of a penalty imposed upon them for failure to pay over taxes which had been withheld by another, I would at least insist on a statute which seemed to point in that direction, rather than in the opposite one.

NOTE

The rule that liabilities arising under § 6672 are not dischargeable in bankruptcy remains unaffected by the enactment of the Bankruptcy Reform Act of 1978, P.L. 95–598. Under 11 U.S.C.A. § 523(a)(1)(A), a discharge under the Bankruptcy Code does not discharge an individual debtor from any debt for taxes which receive a sixth priority under 11 U.S.C.A. § 507(a)(6), which includes the liability of a responsible person under § 6672. See also IRC § 6658(b) (added to the Code by the Bankruptcy Tax Act of 1980, P.L. 96–589).

(5) DESIGNATION OF PAYMENTS

Section 6672 provides for the assessment against a responsible person of the *tax* not withheld or collected and paid over. The assessment is limited to this tax and is not coextensive with the tax obligation of the business entity with respect to which it is assessed. In common parlance, the responsible person is held liable for the "trust fund" portion of the business liability, i. e., the employees' share of FICA taxes and the withholding tax on wages applicable to individual income taxes.

By way of example, assume that Ajax, Inc. has failed to meet its full obligations for the relevant quarters, and that Mr. A is a responsible person of Ajax, Inc. The corporation owes the following amounts as of the date the responsible person assessment is made:

Withholding Tax on Wages	$10,000 (Balance)
Late Filing Penalty	5,000
Employer's Share FICA	1,000
Employees' Share FICA	1,000
Interest	3,000
	$20,000

The section 6672 assessment against Mr. A will be in the amount of $11,000, consisting of the withholding tax of $10,000 and the employees' share of FICA (withheld), but will exclude the penalty, the employer's share of FICA and the interest due from the corporation. Interest (and a late payment penalty) due from Mr. A will accrue on *his* liability only after an assessment is made against him.

In light of Mr. A's exposure for the trust fund portion only of the liabilities of Ajax, Inc., there is great significance to the precise application of any corporate funds collected by the IRS. Assume, for example, that $5,000 of Ajax funds are paid to the Service or collected by means of a levy or seizure and sale of corporate assets. If the funds are allocated to the corporate late filing penalty, the total corporate obligation would be reduced by $5,000, but the liability of Mr. A would remain the full $11,000. On the other hand, if the funds were allocated to withholding taxes, the corporation would still owe $15,000, but Mr. A's liability also would be reduced to $6,000.

It is well established that the IRS must allocate a payment as directed by the payor.[i] Therefore, if Ajax, Inc. submits a check to the Service and designates the payment "to be applied to the trust fund portion of Form 941 liability" for the relevant period, Mr. A will receive the maximum personal benefit. In the absence of a specific direction, the Service can allocate the payment as it sees fit—generally not to maximize the benefit to a responsible person. Moreover, where a payment is effected involuntarily (by levy or seizure and sale) the Service does not consider itself obligated to apply the collection as designated by the taxpayer.

In view of the foregoing, it greatly behooves a potential (or assessed) responsible person who has control over corporate assets to see to it that payments are made to the Service on the corporation's tax liabilities and that the payments are appropriately designated. It should also be noted that the designation of payments as among several taxable periods may also be important. For example, one usually would wish to designate payments to a period for which he is clearly liable, rather than to a period for which he may have a defense to responsibility.

The key point to be considered in the context of any payments to the Internal Revenue Service is that one should always precisely designate the application of a payment so as to maximize the benefit of the payment to the client.

B. LIABILITY OF PROVIDERS OF WAGES

UNITED STATES v. FRED A. ARNOLD, INC.

573 F.2d 605 (9th Cir. 1978).

PER CURIAM:

The United States brought this action under § 3505(a) of the Internal Revenue Code, seeking to collect from Fred A. Arnold, Inc., a general contractor, the withholding and F.I.C.A. taxes which its subcontractor, Pannell Brothers Construction Co., failed to pay on behalf of its employees. Arnold appeals from the district court's grant of the government's motion for summary judgment. This court has jurisdiction under 28 U.S.C. § 1291.

*   *   *

We question whether this case was an appropriate one for summary judgment. It is well-settled in this circuit and others that the filing of cross-motions for summary judgment, both parties asserting that there are no uncontested issues of material fact, does not vitiate the court's responsibility to determine whether disputed issues of ma-

---

i. Rev.Rul. 79–284, 1979–2 C.B. 83, modifying Rev.Rul. 73–305, 1973–2 C.B. 43.

terial fact are present. A summary judgment cannot be granted if a genuine issue as to any material fact exists.

*   *   *

This case presents a situation surely not uncommon in the construction industry. On a contract for the United States Navy, Arnold subcontracted the framing work to Pannell. Pannell eventually requested that progress payments be made weekly so as to alleviate cash flow problems, rather than biweekly or monthly, as had been the case up to that point. Arnold agreed to the proposed payment schedule, provided the funds were expended on Arnold's project rather than on other Pannell jobs. A special checking account was set up in the name of Pannell Brothers. The funds advanced were to be deposited to this account and an Arnold supervisor was to cosign all withdrawals to ensure that the funds were not diverted to other Pannell jobs. Arnold paid amounts sufficient to cover more than the net payroll. Pannell drew on the account for purposes other than payroll, including the partnership draw. Arnold's supervisors apparently never refused to countersign a withdrawal.

Eventually, Pannell defaulted on the contract and went into bankruptcy. At that point Arnold learned that the bank signature card permitted funds to be withdrawn on the signature of the two Arnold supervisors. They withdrew $4,400, using it to pay wages to Pannell employees for the payroll period ending on the day of default. The taxes owing on those wages were paid, and from that point on, Arnold paid workers to finish the subcontract work, remitting withholding and F.I.C.A. taxes to the government on the wages it paid. The only taxes in question are those related to the wages paid out of the special account prior to Pannell's default.

Before 1966 only "employers" were liable for withholding taxes. This lead to problems, especially in the construction industry. A financially-strapped subcontractor would go to a lender, often his general contractor, for interim financing. The lender, wishing to minimize costs, would supply only the net payroll funds. The employees received credit as if the withholding taxes had been paid. The subcontractor-employer remained liable under 26 U.S.C. §§ 3102(b) and 3402, but recourse against him frequently proved fruitless.

In 1966, Congress enacted § 3505 of the Code.[2] It provides that

---

2. "(a) Direct payment by third parties—For purposes of sections 3102, 3202, 3402, and 3403, if a lender, surety, or other person, who is not an employer under such sections with respect to any employee or group of employees, pays wages directly to such an employee or group of employees, employed by one or more employers, or to an agent on behalf of such employee or employees, such lender, surety, or other person shall be liable in his own person and estate to the United States in a sum equal to the taxes (together with interest) required to be deducted and withheld from such wages by such employer."

"(b) Personal liability where funds are supplied.—If a lender, surety, or other person supplies

a surety, lender, or other person who directly or indirectly pays another's employees is secondarily liable for F.I.C.A. and withholding taxes.

Under § 3505(b), when a surety, lender, or other person advances funds to the employer, he is liable for the employer's withholding taxes if he knows that the funds are to be used specifically for the payment of wages and if he has actual notice or knowledge that the employer does not intend to, or will not be able to, make payment of the withholding taxes.

In contrast, under § 3505(a), a person is automatically liable, whatever his knowledge or notice, if he "directly" pays the employees. The intention of Congress was to prevent sureties, lenders, or other persons from assuming responsibility for net wages, excluding taxes. If payroll responsibility is assumed, it must include responsibility for the taxes tied to the wages.

To decide this appeal we must determine what constitutes "direct payment" for the purposes of § 3505(a). In our opinion, in order to be direct payment the payor must have (1) the ability to control the funds, and (2) the right and legal authority to exercise that control.

With respect to the first prong: "the ability to control the funds", the inferences which might be drawn from the evidence are conflicting. It is not clear whether Arnold sent checks to Pannell Brothers, and left it to the good faith of the payee to deposit the checks in the restricted account, or whether Arnold itself deposited the checks. The depositions indicate that the deposit books were kept in the Arnold field office, an assertion which finds support in the defendant's admission that, at the time the plaintiff's interrogatories were propounded, it had possession of the deposit books. This fact alone is not dispositive, because Pannell Brothers did not maintain an office at the worksite, but worked out of the Arnold field office there. Nor are the deposit slips, reproduced in Exhibit 11 to the deposition of Fred A. Arnold, particularly helpful. Most were standard slips, bearing the printed name of Pannell Brothers Construction Co. One was a counter-deposit slip which bears the name of "Fred A. Arnold" as the depositor, rather than the usual Pannell Brothers designation. Of the seventeen Arnold checks deposited, only three

funds to or for the account of an employer for the specific purpose of paying wages of the employees of such employer, with actual notice or knowledge (within the meaning of section 6323(i)(l)) that such employer does not intend to or will not be able to make timely payment or deposit of the amounts of tax required by this subtitle to be deducted and withheld by such employer from such wages, such lender, surety, or other person shall be liable in his own person and estate to the United States in a sum equal to the taxes (together with interest) which are not paid over to the United States by such employer with respect to such wages. However, the liability of such lender, surety, or other person shall be limited to an amount equal to 25 percent of the amount so supplied to or for the account of such employer for such purpose."

appear to have been endorsed by a Pannell Brothers' representative. In addition, the depositions of John and Jesse Pannell both intimate that Arnold employees were the ones who carried the checks to the bank. Each check also carries a typewritten "for deposit only Account # 011183" (number of Del Monte account) notation on its back. Nowhere in the depositions or the record have the parties developed the information of who placed this endorsement on the checks. The typeface appears to be the same as that which appears on the face of the checks. A disputed issue of material fact thus exists with respect to whether Arnold retained and maintained the ability to control the funds.

Also disputed is whether Arnold had "the right and legal authority to exercise that control." At the time Arnold took over the work and the bank account it learned that under the bank signature card funds could be withdrawn under the signature of two Arnold employees without Pannell participation. It is important to a proper disposition of the case to know whether the agreement between Arnold and Pannell did require both an Arnold and a Pannell signature for withdrawals. Also, the exact purpose of the restricted account under the agreement of the parties is important. If it was contemplated that Arnold signatories would "rubber stamp" checks prepared by Pannell which on their face were for job connected expenses, that is one thing, but if it was contemplated that Arnold would have a more pervasive control of the disbursements, albeit by the reservation of a veto power, the situation would be different.

The action is remanded for trial.

C. LENDERS' LIABILITY

FIDELITY BANK, N. A. v. UNITED STATES

616 F.2d 1181 (10th Cir. 1980).

LOGAN, Circuit Judge.

CDI Homes, Inc., a construction company, failed to pay $36,150.-42 in income and Federal Insurance Contribution Act (FICA) taxes it withheld from wages paid to its employees during the second quarter of 1973. The Commissioner assessed against Fidelity Bank, N.A., a lender to CDI, a penalty in the amount of one hundred percent of the withholding taxes owed by CDI, relying upon I.R.C. § 6672. Fidelity paid $381.23 of the amount assessed and brought this refund suit. The government counterclaimed for the unpaid balance and also alleged that Fidelity was liable for a sum equal to the taxes under I.R.C. § 3505(b). The jury found in favor of Fidelity and against the government on the refund claim and counterclaims. * * *

* * *

Viewing the facts and reasonable inferences drawn therefrom in a light most favorable to Fidelity, the record shows the following.

Beginning in 1971, CDI built prefabricated homes for the Kiowa Housing Authority (KHA), which apparently is affiliated with the Department of Housing and Urban Development. This contract was acquired from another construction company, and pursuant to the acquisition agreement contract payments owed by KHA to CDI were sent directly to an escrow account maintained at Fidelity. Under the terms of the escrow contract, a certain portion of the funds received were distributed to the old construction company and other specified entities, and the balance was available to CDI.

In order to be able to perform the construction contract, CDI obtained from Fidelity a one million dollar revolving credit line. This loan was used by CDI for construction of a prefabrication plant and for general working capital. In conjunction with the extension of credit, CDI assigned to the bank the proceeds from the KHA construction contract, CDI's only source of income, and granted to the bank a security interest in all CDI's assets.

In January 1973 financial difficulties forced CDI to shut down its operations. At that time the bank requested financial information from the company and discovered the company had lost a substantial amount of money. After securing additional collateral, the bank agreed to provide the funds necessary for resuming operations. Since CDI had by that time exceeded the $1,000,000 line of credit, the bank allowed CDI to overdraw its account, but only when a sale of homes to KHA was imminent. From January 1973 until June 26, 1973, the CDI account was overdrawn in amounts generally of $60,000 to $80,000 and as much as $180,000.

The procedure followed for approving the overdrafts was as follows. An officer of CDI would contact Mickey Johnson, the bank officer in charge of monitoring the CDI account, apprise Johnson that a sale was forthcoming and that certain creditors must be paid to complete the transaction, and request that the bank extend sufficient credit by honoring checks drawn in excess of the credit line. CDI would then draft checks and when they came to the bank through normal banking channels, Johnson would examine each; if the payee appeared to be a bona fide CDI creditor connected with the KHA project, Johnson initialled the check, which was then honored. These additional extensions of credit, although made separately, were secured by the same security agreements and assignments of contract proceeds that applied to the original extension of credit. Until June 26, the bank honored all CDI checks.

In conjunction with the reopening of the plant in January, and at the bank's request, CDI closed its payroll account maintained in a bank in Anadarko, Oklahoma; thereafter all payroll checks were paid through the general account at Fidelity. Payroll checks paid through this account were easily identifiable; the word "payroll" was prominently printed on the upper left hand corner of the face of the check.

These checks were for net wages only. CDI withheld income and FICA taxes and, because it had no other funds, depended on the bank to honor checks drawn in the amount of the withholdings and deposited with the bank.

During a part of the second quarter of 1973, officials at the bank thought CDI's financial situation would improve and CDI would be able to complete the contract on a profitable basis. But KHA did not continue to provide CDI with work orders sufficient to justify continued production. On June 26 the bank dishonored all CDI checks presented on June 25 through the normal banking channels. Among those checks was one for the taxes withheld from wages paid in April, the first month of the second quarter. Thereafter, the bank returned all CDI checks unprocessed, among them checks for taxes withheld from wages paid during May and June. On June 29 the bank shut the company down, foreclosing on its security interests, and began to liquidate the assets.

Thereafter, some homes built by CDI before its operations were shut down were sold to KHA. In connection with this transaction, KHA demanded that the bank honor payroll checks that had been dishonored during the second quarter. Had the bank refused to pay these wages, KHA would have paid them and would have sent to the bank the net proceeds, if any. Fidelity acceded, honoring some of those checks and issuing cashier's checks drawn by the bank for the remainder. Proceeds from the sale were used by the bank to reduce the overdraft status of CDI's account. Taxes withheld from these, as well as the prior payroll checks, were not paid, the only exception being those paid by the bank in order to initiate this refund suit.

I

To be held liable under I.R.C. § 3505(b), Fidelity must have supplied funds for the specific purpose of paying wages and must have had actual knowledge that CDI did not intend to or would not be able to timely deposit or pay the income and FICA taxes required to be withheld from the wages of its employees. Notwithstanding the verdict of the jury, we believe the evidence conclusively establishes liability in this case.

The bank supplied funds for the specific purpose of paying wages by honoring payroll checks that were drawn in excess of the credit line. It is true, as the bank argues, that a lender making an ordinary working capital loan with knowledge that some funds may be used for payroll purposes does not violate section 3505(b). See Treas.Reg. § 31.3505–1(b)(3). In this case, however, each check honored after the $1,000,000 lending limit was exceeded and the account was in an overdraft position constituted a separate loan. Each check was individually initialled and approved for payment by Mickey Johnson, the bank's loan officer; each payroll check prominently bore the notation "payroll" on its face and was known by the bank to be for the specific purpose of paying wages; and each was an overdraft. Although the overdrafts were secured by the agreements relating to the general credit line, the bank, through Mickey Johnson, see I.R.C. § 6323(i)(1), knew it was supplying funds specifically for wages.

The bank had actual notice that CDI would not be able to make timely deposit or payment of the taxes due for the second quarter. At least after January 1973, when CDI's payroll account at Anadarko was closed and all creditors were paid from the general account with Fidelity, that bank had to know that without loans from it CDI would be unable to pay taxes due. All assets of CDI were pledged to the bank; but more importantly, the bank had control of all CDI's income. The KHA contract proceeds, CDI's only income, were sent directly to the bank, which applied them to the reduction of the company's indebtedness. Thus, every time the bank supplied funds for payment of wages it had to know it would be requested to supply the funds for paying the withholding taxes. This, we believe, fits well within the situations envisioned for application of section 3505(b).

It is thus clear that the trial court should have entered judgment in favor of the United States on this issue. Because section 3505(b) limits the penalty to 25% of the amount of funds supplied for payment of wages, however, further proceedings to determine the amount of the penalty recoverable by the government will be necessary before judgment in favor of the government can be entered.

II

The government also asserts that the evidence conclusively shows the bank to be liable under I.R.C. § 6672 for the unpaid withholding taxes. Section 6672 imposes a one hundred percent penalty in the amount of unpaid withholding taxes on any person, other than the employer, who was responsible for the collection and payment of these taxes, but who willfully fails to perform any of these acts. Thus, for liability to attach, the bank must have been a "responsible person" "willfully" failing to perform.

The administrative practice, at least, is that once net wages are paid to the employee, taxes withheld are credited to that employee for income and social security tax purposes, whether or not the employer pays them over to the Internal Revenue Service (IRS). Thus section 6672 was enacted to impose personal liability upon those responsible for transmitting these trust funds should they divert the money to pay other pressing creditors. The section is applied to persons who have sufficient control to divert the funds away from the IRS, usually officers and supervisory employees. But the courts have fashioned a functional definition of "responsible person" to include some who do not hold any official position with the company. Lenders and employees of lenders have been considered liable under section 6672 in particular circumstances. Adams v. United States, 504

F.2d 73 (7th Cir. 1974). Contra, United States v. Hill, 368 F.2d 617 (5th Cir. 1966).

Considering the infinite degrees of control that might be exercised by a lender, we cannot agree with the apparent holding of United States v. Hill, supra, that a bank lender may never come under the ambit of section 6672. But we do believe that the emphasis of the section upon the persons whose duty to the employer is "to collect * * * account for, and pay over" the tax but who "willfully" fail to do so, requires more control by a bona fide lender for liability than does I.R.C. § 3505(b).

Viewed in the light most favorable to the bank, the evidence in the instant case shows no more than an arrangement by which Fidelity made a series of loans to CDI for specific purposes. It does not show that the bank decided which creditors were to be paid, or that it initiated payment decisions. Thus, the jury was entitled to conclude the bank was not a responsible person within the meaning of section 6672.

In reaching this conclusion, we are mindful that because of CDI's complete financial dependence on the bank, Fidelity could have coerced CDI into fulfilling its withholding tax obligations. But we are unwilling to hold that the bank had a duty to do so when it had not otherwise intruded into the financial or operational aspects of CDI's business; such a holding would effectively extend the scope of section 6672 to precisely duplicate the coverage of I.R.C. § 3505, specifically passed by Congress to impose liability upon lenders of funds to be used for payrolls.

* * *

We do not understand the government to argue it is entitled to recover twice for CDI's unpaid taxes—once each under sections 3505(b) and 6672. In view of our holding on section 3505(b) liability it may be unnecessary to try the case again; but if the 25% limitation in that section will not cover the entire sum claimed by the government, a retrial on section 6672 liability may be necessary. There was before the jury sufficient evidence to raise factual questions concerning liability under section 6672; we will not speculate how the jury would have resolved those questions had it been properly instructed. Thus, remand is required on this issue.

* * *

The judgments are reversed and the case is remanded for proceedings consistent herewith.

UNITED STATES v. DIXIELINE FINANCIAL, INC.

594 F.2d 1311 (9th Cir. 1979).

MERRILL, Circuit Judge.

Section 3505(b) of the Internal Revenue Code of 1954 (the Code) imposes liability on one who supplies funds to an employer to enable him to meet a payroll, knowing that the employer does not intend to, or will be unable to pay the taxes required to be withheld and paid to the government. The liability imposed is equal to the amount of tax due and unpaid. The Code, § 6501(a), requires that "the amount of any tax imposed by this title shall be assessed within 3 [three] years after the return was filed * * * and no proceeding in court without assessment for the collection of such tax shall be begun after expiration of such period."

The question presented here is whether § 6501(a) applies to the liability created by § 3505(b) and requires, as a condition to suit, that that liability be assessed within three years against the supplier of funds.

* * * The district court held that assessment against Dixieline as supplier was required and that the suit was barred by failure to assess within the period of three years. Summary judgment was entered in favor of Dixieline and the government has taken this appeal. We reverse.

Assessment of tax as defined consists of no more than the ascertainment of the amount due and the formal entry of that amount on the books of the secretary. As was stated by the court in United States v. Walker, 217 F.Supp. 888, 890 (W.D.S.C.1963); "The Commissioner is required to assess the tax * * * rather than assess the taxpayer." Here, when the assessment against the employer was made, the amount of the only sum in question was ascertained and was entered. Section 3505 does not require the supplier to file a withholding return. * * * Section 3505(b) does not impose a tax on the supplier the amount of which remains to be ascertained. Nor does it impose a penalty in addition to the tax the amount of which must be fixed. It imposes a liability "in a sum equal to the taxes" due from the employer, these taxes having already been ascertained as to amount and assessed by entry. Further independent assessment would accomplish nothing.

Dixieline argues that Bloom v. United States, 272 F.2d 215 (9th Cir. 1960), supports the district court decision. That case, however, is distinguishable. It involved the duty of the employer to withhold and pay tax due from the employees and the liability of the president of the employer for the willful failure to pay the withholding taxes due. The court quoted from § 2707(a) of the Internal Revenue Code of 1939 (a similar provision is now covered by 26 U.S.C. § 6672). It stated: "While this liability is denominated 'penalty,' it is 'to be assessed and collected in the same manner as taxes are assessed and collected.'" 272 F.2d at 221. The Code in many other instances where penalties are imposed makes the same express provision respecting assessment. In most instances the penalty remains to be fixed and is in addition to the tax due. Assessment plays a useful role in such cases. No such role is played here and the code does not provide for independent assessment of the § 3505 (b) liability against the supplier.

Dixieline protests that without requiring this liability to be assessed against it, it would not have due notice of the fact that the government is looking to it for payment. This is not so. 26 U.S.C. § 6303 requires that notice of the assessment be given within 60 days "to each person liable for the unpaid tax." If Dixieline was not given notice of the assessment against the employer of the tax for which it is being held liable, then the case may present a question as to the consequences that flow from that fact. However, dismissal by the district court was not based on failure to give notice but on failure to assess against Dixieline a tax already assessed against the employer.

We conclude that the assessment of the tax against Framing Systems, the employer, met the requirements of § 6501 (a); no assessment of the § 3505 (b) liability of Dixieline was required.

Summary judgment is reversed. The case is remanded for further proceedings.

SECTION 5.   TRANSFEREE AND FIDUCIARY LIABILITY

COMMENT—SECTION 6901: TRANSFEREE LIABILITY

Jerome Borison
30 Tax Lawyer 433 (1977).

INTRODUCTION

The Service's power to reach assets which are in the taxpayer's hands when a deficiency is assessed against him is well known and frequently exercised. Less widely understood is the power of the Government to reach assets disposed of by the taxpayer prior to assessment (and, therefore, not subject to a federal tax lien) by imposing liability for the taxes owed by the taxpayer on the recipient, or transferee, of these assets. To appreciate the impact of transferee liability, one need only consider the reaction of a donee or legatee who, having disposed of the gift or bequest, receives a deficiency notice not for "his" taxes, but for taxes that his donor or testator never paid.

* * *

BACKGROUND

The doctrine of transferee liability [2] predates enactment of the concept into positive law in the Revenue Act of 1926. Prior to that

---

2. Generally, transferee liability requires that when one party transfers property to another, the transferee will be held liable for the taxes of the transferor where the transferor cannot pay. The transferee's liability may be imposed because he has contracted for all of the transferor's liabilities (e. g., merger), or because a statute so requires (e. g., the liability

statutory enactment, when a taxpayer transferred away his assets to avoid payment of a tax the Government's exclusive remedy was to proceed against the transferee of the delinquent taxpayer by a bill of equity under the "trust fund doctrine." [4]   Because this procedure was found to be burdensome and frequently ineffective, Congress provided the Commissioner, in what is now section 6901, a summary procedure similar to that which is available against the original taxpayer.[5]   It should be stressed that section 6901 is only a procedural statute which provides a new remedy for the collection of an existing debt, either at law or in equity or by use of the "trust fund doctrine."   It does not create any new financial obligations.

* * *

REQUIREMENTS FOR ESTABLISHING TRANSFEREE LIABILITY

There are two principal methods by which the United States may proceed where assets have been transferred to defraud creditors. The first is to file suit in a United States district court to have the transfer set aside and the asset subjected to collection of the transferor's debt.   The other method is to issue a statutory notice of transferee liability pursuant to section 6901, which could lead to a hearing in Tax Court.

Because the first method generally requires the employment of a state's Uniform Fraudulent Conveyance Act, it is brought in the na-

of the distributee of an estate for the estate's taxes), or because the transfer worked a fraud on creditors, one of which is the Government.

4. This doctrine was first enunciated in the United States in Wood v. Dummer, 30 F.Cas. 435 (No. 17,944) (C.C.D.Me.1824).   It states that the corporate assets constitute a fund for the benefit of creditors, and should the corporation be stripped of its assets by its shareholders without first satisfying the claims of the corporation's creditors, the creditors could follow the trust fund into the hands of the shareholders for payment.

5. H.R.Rep. No. 356, 69th Cong., 1st Sess. (1926), 1939–1 (pt. 2) C.B. 361, 371, stated:

"Without in any way changing the extent of such liability of the transferee under existing law, the amendment enforces such liability * * * in the same manner as liability for a tax deficiency is enforced * * *."   The procedure requires the issuance of a notice of transferee liability to the trans-

feree, determination of such liability in the Tax Court, and collection of the assessed liability, subject to review by a district court.

While the procedures for collection from transferees and from original taxpayers are similar, they are not identical.   The statute of limitations for the assessment of the deficiency against the transferee is, as provided in § 6901(c)(1), one additional year from the expiration of the period of assessment against the original taxpayer, which is usually three years, absent fraud.   Another year (up to an additional three years) is granted for each successive transferee.

The other major difference is that of the burden of proof.   As provided in § 6902(a), the Commissioner must prove, in a Tax Court proceeding, that the transferee is liable as such, but the transferee has the burden of establishing that the taxpayer-transferor was not liable for the tax in the first instance.

ture of an in rem action. The summary procedure provided by section 6901, on the other hand, results in an in personam judgment against the transferee, thus making him primarily liable for the tax. Instead of merely bringing back the transferred assets by setting the transaction aside, the latter method subjects any and all of the transferee's assets to collection. The liability can be enforced either at law or in equity.

Before the Government can collect the taxes, however, it must prove several substantive elements and comply with various procedural guidelines. Some of these requirements are common to both an action at law and a suit in equity, while others are elements to only one of these theories.

A.   Requirements Common to Actions at Law and Suits in Equity

Whether a proceeding is brought at law or in equity, the Commissioner must establish three elements: (1) the transferee has received assets of value from the transferor; [18] (2) the transferor has primary liability for the tax; and (3) the tax has not been paid. In addition, the Commissioner must proceed against the transferee within the statutory limitations period.[21]

B.   Requirements at Law

When an action is brought at law, the Government most frequently proceeds under the "assumption by contract" theory. Transferee liability under this theory is predicated upon the common law "third-party beneficiary doctrine," with the Commissioner asserting himself as a creditor of the transferor for the unpaid taxes. To succeed under this theory, the Service must prove that there was a valid contract between the vendor and vendee and that the transferee-vendee assumed the liabilities of the vendor.

In addition to the "assumption by contract" theory, transferee liability at law may be imposed by federal statute [24] or by state statute, the latter being effectuated generally under the merger provisions of the Model Business Corporation Act or the notification provisions of the Bulk Transfers Act. If the Government attempts to enforce transferee liability using one or more of these statutory bases, its burden of proof is limited to those requirements common to an action at law or in equity.

C.   Requirements in Equity

The primary theory of recovery in equity is that of fraud—constructive or actual. When the basis is constructive fraud, the trans-

---

18. I.R.C. § 6901(a)(1)(A). * * *
The transfer of assets need not be direct or actual, but may be indirect or constructive.

21. I.R.C. § 6901(c).

24. I.R.C. § 6324. Under this approach the Government must prove that: (a) the transferee received from the transferor property which was the subject of the estate or gift; (b) the transferor owed the taxes; and (c) the tax remains unpaid.

fer is considered fraudulent without regard to the transferor's actual intent; instead, it is deemed fraudulent by law. In proving actual fraud, however, the Government must prove that there was an actual *intent* to hinder, delay, or defraud creditors. Even though the law has recognized certain types of actions from which an intent to defraud can be inferred, actual fraud is a more difficult theory to prove and, therefore, is a less commonly used method of recovery. Where the Government is not an existing creditor at the time of the transfer, however, proving actual fraud may be its only means of recovery.

The Government must prove the following substantive elements in order to establish transferee liability in equity: (1) that the transfer of assets was without full and adequate consideration; (2) that the transfer of assets was made subsequent to or contemporaneous with the accrual of the tax liability (i. e., the Government is a present creditor); and (3) where the basis is constructive fraud, that the transferor was insolvent (in the bankruptcy sense) when the transfer was made or was made insolvent by the transfer. However, regardless of which theory of fraud is used to impose liability, the Government must exhaust all reasonable procedural remedies against the taxpayer before proceeding against the transferee.

EXTENT OF TRANSFEREE LIABILITY

Transferee liability at law is established in two ways. The liability exists either because a statute specifically imposes such an obligation or because the transferee expressly assumes the liabilities of the transferor by contract. The extent of the transferee's liability, therefore, will be the amount specified in the statute or the amount for which he has contracted.

When transferee liability arises in equity, however, the amount for which one may be liable is limited to the value of the assets received as of the date of the transfer. This is reduced by: (1) the fair market value of the consideration paid to the transferor; (2) the amount of the encumbrances on the property received where such encumbrances have priority over the Government's tax claim; and (3) the value of any assets returned to the transferor prior to the issuance of a statutory notice of transferee liability.

WHO IS A TRANSFEREE?

The Code defines a transferee as a "donee, heir, legatee, devisee, and distributee, and with respect to estate taxes, also includes any person who, under section 6324(a)(2), is personally liable for any part of such tax." [40] The regulations include a "distributee of an estate of a deceased person, the shareholder of a dissolved corporation, the assignee or donee of an insolvent person, the successor of a corporation, a party to a reorganization as defined in section 368, and all other classes of distributees." [41] In addition, the courts have defined

---

40. I.R.C. § 6901(h).   **41.** Reg. § 301.6901–1(b).

a transferee as "one who takes or receives property of another without full, fair and adequate consideration to the prejudice of creditors." [42]   The above definitions are not all-inclusive and are not meant to limit the meaning of who is a transferee. Rather, their purpose is to eliminate any doubt as to those classes specifically mentioned. As will be discussed below, the phrase "all other classes of distributees" has been broadly interpreted by the courts, thus extending liability to others, including life insurance beneficiaries and stockholders receiving loans from a corporation.

A. *Donee*

Section 6901 provides that a donee of an inter vivos gift from an insolvent taxpayer is liable for the donor's unpaid income taxes, and section 6324(b) imposes liability upon the donee for the donor's unpaid gift taxes.

An action to recover the donor's unpaid *income* taxes from the donee is brought in equity and, as such, must satisfy those requirements previously mentioned. *   *   *

Where the Government seeks to impose liability upon a transferee-donee for the donor's unpaid *gift* taxes, the action is at law. As such, it requires different proof and imposes different limits on liability. At law, a finding of transferee liability is neither dependent upon the donor's insolvency,[50] nor upon the Commissioner's exhaustion of remedies against the donor. Furthermore, one court [52] has held that under section 6324(b) the donees are liable to the extent of their individual gifts for the unpaid tax resulting from *all* gifts made by the donor during the same calendar year, even if the deficiency was the result of gifts to individuals other than the transferee.

B. *Estate and Trusts*

The distributee of a decedent's estate is liable as a transferee for the decedent's unpaid income taxes and estate taxes. Like a donee, a transferee of a decedent is liable for income taxes in equity and for estate taxes at law. Accordingly, it has been held that where the taxpayer was not shown to have been insolvent when he transferred assets to an inter vivos trust, thereby eliminating one of the key equity requirements, the trustee was not liable as a transferee for the deceased's unpaid *income taxes*.[54]

On the other hand, the trustee of an inter vivos trust—includable in the decedent's gross taxable estate—was held liable as a trans-

42. United States v. Floersch, 276 F.2d 714, 717 (10th Cir.), cert. denied, 364 U.S. 816 (1960) (footnote omitted); *accord* First Nat'l Bank v. Commissioner, 255 F.2d 759 (7th Cir. 1958); Louis Costanzo, 16 B.T.A. 1294 (1929).

50. Reg. § 301.6901–1(b).

52. La Fortune Trust v. Commissioner, 263 F.2d 186 (10th Cir. 1959).

54. American Trust Co., 18 B.T.A. 580 (1929).

feree for the *estate taxes* attributable to the trust, even though the deceased was not insolvent when the transfer was made.[55] This result was reached because the liability was imposed by section 6324(a)(1); hence, it was enforceable at law.

When a taxpayer dies, there are several potential transferees, each of whom will be discussed separately.

1. *Fiduciaries*

Initially, it is important to distinguish between transferee liability and fiduciary liability.[56] Though section 6901 provides a summary assessment and collection procedure to the United States against both a transferee and a fiduciary, these two parties have separate and distinct liabilities. While a transferee is defined by section 6901(h) as a "donee, heir, legatee, devisee, [or] distributee," a fiduciary according to section 7701(a)(6), is a "guardian, trustee, executor, administrator, receiver, conservator, or any person acting in any fiduciary capacity for any person." Further, whereas transferee liability is imposed because one is the recipient of assets, fiduciary liability is imposed because one pays on behalf of the debtor or estate debts which do not have priority over the "debts" due to the United States." [58]

*   *   *

    *   *   *

An estate and its executors remain liable as transferees until the estate is closed and the executors are dismissed under local law. Despite the executors' dismissal, the estate will not be relieved of liability until the Service issues a notice of the transferee liability to the estate *prior to* the dismissal of the executors. The executors, however, can relieve themselves of personal liability imposed upon fiduciaries by complying with the provisions of section 6905.

2. *Distributee's and Beneficiaries' Liability for the Decedent's or Trust's Income Taxes*

When an estate is insolvent or has been completely distributed, the Government has a right, enforceable in equity, to pursue the estate's assets into the hands of an heir, devisee, legatee or distributee in order to collect the decedent's unpaid income taxes. For example, in one case the deceased taxpayer's brother and sister were held liable for his unpaid income taxes to the extent of the value of the property they had received, despite the fact that the deficiency assessment was made in the name of the decedent instead of the transferees.[66]

    *   *   *

55. Equitable Trust Co., 13 T.C. 731 (1949).

56. See Miller, The Fiduciary's Personal Liability for Deficiencies in Federal Income, Estate and Gift Taxes of a Decedent or Decedent's Estate, 11 Gonz.L.Rev. 431 (1976).

58. 31 U.S.C. §§ 191, 192.

66. Viles v. Commissioner, 233 F.2d 376, 379 (6th Cir. 1956).

3. *Distributee's Liability for the Decedent's Estate Taxes*

The Code provides in sections 6324(a)(1) and (2) that if the estate taxes of a deceased are not paid in full, a lien attaches to the entire gross estate for a ten-year period. In addition, secondary liability will be imposed upon several persons, including the spouse, transferee, trustee and surviving tenant. Furthermore, persons in possession of the property not subject to probate but otherwise includable in the decedent's gross estate for tax purposes are liable either to the executor or to the Commissioner for their pro rata share of those estate taxes.[70]

Because liability for estate taxes is at law, rather than in equity, it is unnecessary for the Commissioner to prove that the estate was insolvent or that there was inadequate consideration given for the assets received. He is also not required to first exhaust the assets in the hands of the executor before proceeding against a transferee, or to first mail a deficiency notice to the executor.[71]

* * *

WHO IS NOT A TRANSFEREE?

In order to understand when a concept or doctrine applies, it is often helpful to outline when it does not. This section will attempt to do that. Since the discussion of most of the following classes of persons to whom transferee liability does *not* attach has already been included in previous sections, discussion of those persons at this time will be limited * * *.

Those persons who are not transferees would include: (1) beneficiaries of life insurance policies when there has been no prior federal tax lien imposed upon the insured and where state law so provides; (2) other exemptions provided by state law; (3) the surviving joint tenant, tenant by the entirety, or spouse in a community property state; (4) the seller of corporate stock; (5) creditors of a delinquent taxpayer; and (6) the reorganized company when such reorganization was entered into for the benefit of creditors.

In addition to the above list, one who is not a beneficial owner of the property that he receives from a transferor is not liable as transferee. For example, an individual receiving stock so that he may act as a voting agent of the transferor at corporate meetings will not be liable as a transferee. Neither will the registered owner of stock or the holder of legal title to realty, be liable as a transferee when he is merely a "nominee" acting as a conduit to the beneficial owner of any income or assets of the transferor which he received. Nor will an insurance company be liable as a transferee where, upon the death

---

70. I.R.C. §§ 2206, 2207.

71. Equitable Trust Co., 13 T.C. 731 (1949).

of the insured taxpayer, it merely holds life insurance proceeds or serves as a depository of the proceeds of life insurance policies.

* * *

COMMISSIONER v. STERN

Supreme Court of the United States, 1958.
357 U.S. 39, 78 S.Ct. 1047, 2 L.Ed.2d 1126.

Mr. Justice BRENNAN delivered the opinion of the Court.

Respondent petitioned the Tax Court for redetermination of the liability assessed against her for her deceased husband's unpaid income tax deficiencies. The Tax Court held that, as beneficiary of proceeds of her husband's life insurance exceeding the amount of the deficiencies, the respondent was liable for the full amount of the deficiencies. The Court of Appeals reversed, holding that the respondent was not liable even to the extent of the amount of the cash surrender values of the policies, which was less than the amount of the deficiencies. We granted certiorari.

Dr. Milton J. Stern died a resident of Lexington, Kentucky, on June 12, 1949. Nearly six years later the Tax Court held that Dr. Stern had been deficient in his income taxes for the years 1944 through 1947 and was liable for the amount, including interest and penalties, of $32,777.51. Because the assets of the estate were insufficient to meet this liability, the Commissioner proceeded under § 311 of the Internal Revenue Code of 1939 [j] against respondent, Dr. Stern's widow, as the beneficiary of life insurance policies held by him. The proceeds and the cash surrender value of these policies at Dr. Stern's death totaled $47,282.02 and $27,259.68 respectively. The right to change the beneficiary and to draw down the cash surrender value of each policy had been retained until death by Dr. Stern. There were no findings that Dr. Stern paid any premiums with intent to defraud his creditors or that he was insolvent at any time prior to his death.

* * *

First. Section 311(a) provides that "The liability, at law or in equity, of a transferee of property of a taxpayer, in respect of the tax * * * imposed upon the taxpayer by this chapter" shall be "assessed, collected, and paid in the same manner and subject to the same provisions and limitations as in the case of a deficiency in a tax imposed by this chapter * * *." The decisions of the Court of Appeals and the Tax Court have been in conflict on the question whether the substantive liability enforced under § 311 is to be determined by state or federal law. This Court has expressly left the

j. The predecessor to § 6901 of the 1954 Code.

question open. Phillips v. Commissioner, 283 U.S. 589, 602, 51 S.Ct. 608, 613, 75 L.Ed. 1289.

The courts have repeatedly recognized that § 311 neither creates nor defines a substantive liability but provides merely a new procedure by which the Government may collect taxes. Prior to the enactment of § 280 of the Revenue Act of 1926, the predecessor of § 311, the rights of the Government as creditor, enforceable only by bringing a bill in equity or an action at law, depended upon state statutes or legal theories developed by the courts for the protection of private creditors, as in cases where the debtor had transferred his property to another. This procedure proved unduly cumbersome, however, in comparison with the summary administrative remedy allowed against the taxpayer himself. The predecessor section of § 311 was designed "to provide for the enforcement of such liability to the Government by the procedure provided in the act for the enforcement of tax deficiencies." S.Rep. No. 52, 69th Cong., 1st Sess. 30. "Without in any way changing the extent of such liability of the transferee under existing law, * * * [this section] enforces such liability * * * in the same manner as liability for a tax deficiency is enforced; that is, notice by the commissioner to the transferee and opportunity either to pay and sue for refund or else to proceed before the Board of Tax Appeals, with review by the courts. Such a proceeding is in lieu of the present equity proceeding * * *." H.R. Conf.Rep. No. 356, 69th Cong., 1st Sess. 43–44. Therefore, since § 311 is purely a procedural statute we must look to other sources for definition of the substantive liability. Since no federal statute defines such liability, we are left with a choice between federal decisional law and state law for its definition.

Second. The Government urges that, to further "uniformity of liability," we reject the applicability of Kentucky law in favor of having the federal courts fashion governing rules. But a federal decisional law in this field displacing state statutes as determinative of liability would be a sharp break with the past. Federal courts, in cases where the Government seeks to collect unpaid taxes from persons other than the defaulting taxpayer, have applied state statutes, and the Government itself has urged reliance upon such statutes in similar cases. The Congress was aware of the use of state statutes when the enactment of the predecessor section to § 311 was under consideration, for the Congress in disclaiming any intention "to define or change existing liability," S.Rep. No. 52, 69th Cong., 1st Sess. 30, identified "existing liability" as liability ensuing "[b]y reason of the trust fund doctrine and various State statutory provisions * * *." H.R.Conf.Rep. No. 356, supra, at 43.

It is true that, in addition to reliance upon state statutes, the Government invoked principles judicially developed for the protection of private creditors, in cases where the debtor had transferred his property to another and been left insolvent. In such cases the federal courts applied a "general law" which did not distinguish between federal and state decisional law. But the fact remains that the varying definitions of liability under state statutes resulted in an absence of uniformity of liability. Yet Congress, with knowledge that this was "existing law" at the time the predecessor section to § 311 was enacted, has refrained from disturbing the prevailing practice. Uniformity is not always the federal policy. * * * What is a good transfer in one jurisdiction might not be so in another.

Since Congress has not manifested a desire for uniformity of liability, we think that the creation of a federal decisional law would be inappropriate in these cases. In diversity cases, the federal courts must now apply state decisional law in defining state-created rights, obligations, and liabilities. They would, of course, do so in diversity actions brought by private creditors. Since the federal courts no longer formulate a body of federal decisional law for the larger field of creditors' rights in diversity cases, any such effort for the small field of actions by the Government as a creditor would be necessarily episodic. That effort is plainly not justified when there exists a flexible body of pertinent state law continuously being adapted to changing circumstances affecting all creditors. Accordingly we hold that, until Congress speaks to the contrary, the existence and extent of liability should be determined by state law.

Third. The Court of Appeals held in this case that under the applicable Kentucky law the beneficiary of a life insurance policy is not liable to the insured's creditors, at least where, as here, the premiums have not been paid in fraud of creditors, and that therefore no liability of the respondent exists under state law to any creditor, including the Government. The parties do not contest this construction of local law.

The Government, however, argues in its brief, "Just as in the situation where a tax lien has attached it is held that state law may not destroy that lien, so here, where a tax liability is imposed by Congress, the state may not provide exemptions." We agree that state law may not destroy a tax lien which has attached in the insured's lifetime. We held today in United States v. Bess, 357 U.S. 51, 78 S. Ct. 1054, that a New Jersey statute, similar to the Kentucky statutes, could not defeat the attachment in the insured's lifetime of a federal tax lien under § 3670 against the cash surrender value of the policy, or prevent enforcement of the lien out of the proceeds received by the beneficiary on the insured's death. We might also agree that a State may not provide exemptions from a tax liability imposed by Congress. The fallacy in the Government's argument is in the premise that Congress has imposed a tax liability against the beneficiary. We have concluded that Congress has not seen fit to define that liability and that none exists except such as is imposed by state law. Thus there is no problem here of giving effect to state exemption provisions when federal law imposes such liability. The Government's substantive rights in this case are precisely those which other creditors would have under Kentucky law. The respondent is not liable to the Government because Kentucky law imposes no liability against respondent in favor of Dr. Stern's other creditors.

Affirmed.

GRIEB v. COMMISSIONER

36 T.C. 156 (1961).

FISHER, Judge.

Respondent determined a fiduciary liability against petitioner under section 311(a)(2)[k] of the 1939 Code resulting from the distribution to him of the assets of Victory Builders, Inc., upon its liquidation, and the subsequent payment of some of its debts without first satisfying a liability of that company for unpaid income taxes of $560.37 for the year 1949. Respondent has also determined against petitioner an addition to tax in the amount of $61.88 under section 293(a), I.R.C. 1939, and $177.75 for interest which was also determined against the company.

Petitioner, having failed to contest the propriety of the determination of the tax liability against Victory, either in pleading or on brief, has apparently conceded the corporate liability. The significant question for our determination is whether petitioner is liable as a fiduciary of the company for its tax liability, any transferee liability being barred by limitations.

* * *

OPINION

Pursuant to the provisions of section 311(a)(2) of the Internal Revenue Code of 1939, which provides for enforcement of Government priority and fiduciary liability imposed under sections 3466 and 3467 of the Revised Statutes,[l] the respondent has determined that petitioner was a fiduciary of the company and, as such, is liable for the unpaid balance of the deficiency in income tax determined against the company for the year 1949, additions to tax, and interest.

Section 311 of the 1939 Code provides for two separate liabilities, one against a transferee, and another against a fiduciary. A transferee is defined in section 311(f) as an "heir, legatee, devisee, and distributee." The regulation under this section also includes the shareholder of a dissolved corporation, the assignee or donee of an insolvent person, and the successor of a corporation. A transferee may be liable to the full amount which he received from the debtor irre-

k. The predecessor to § 6901(a)(1)(B)   l. 31 U.S.C.A. §§ 191 and 192.
   of the 1954 Code.

spective of any payments of debts he made on behalf of the debtor transferor. It is a defense, however, if any of the debts so paid, or his own debt, had priority over that of the Government.

Transferee liability covers the situation where one takes complete title to property from an insolvent debtor without full, fair, and adequate consideration to the prejudice of the rights of the creditors of the transferor. The transfer is void against existing creditors. The rights and priorities of the Government, however, as any other creditor, against the transferee is determined under State law. The rationale for this liability is that a transferee, not having priority over the Government, holds the property in trust for the Government. Commissioner v. Stern, 357 U.S. 39.

A fiduciary, on the other hand, is defined in the Code as "a guardian, trustee, executor, administrator, receiver, conservator, or any person acting in any fiduciary capacity for any person." Sec. 3797(a)(6), I.R.C. 1939.[m] Unlike a transferee, a fiduciary can be liable under the provisions of Revised Statutes, section 3467, supra, only to the extent of debts he pays on behalf of the debtor which do not have priority over the Government. Thus, when a fiduciary retains assets for himself absolutely or distributes them to persons not creditors of the transferor, although he may be subject to transferee liability, he is not subject to fiduciary liability within the meaning of section 3467.

The basis of fiduciary liability in the Code rests solely upon the provisions of sections 3466 and 3467 of the Revised Statutes. It is not a liability attaching to one receiving funds without fair consideration which is based upon any equitable principles of constructive trust, but rather a liability to enforce the prior claim of the Government to the fund he so received over general creditors of the debtor.

Fiduciary liability has been summarized in Bush v. United States, 14 F. 321, 323 (D.Ore.1882), as follows:

> The latter [sec. 3467] is only applicable to cases where the debtor's estate, either by his death, legal bankruptcy, or insolvency, has passed into the hands of an administrator or assignee for the benefit of his creditors, or where the debtor himself has voluntarily made such disposition of it. It does not apply, then, to a conveyance, assignment, or transfer, by whatever means accomplished, to a real or pretended creditor or creditors in payment or satisfaction of a debt or claim. There must be in some way an assignment of the debtor's property to a third person for distribution among his creditors before the statute can be invoked, and then it operates directly upon the assignee by requiring him to pay

m. See § 7701(a)(6) of the 1954 Code.

the claim of the United States first, and making him person-ally liable therefor if he does not.   *   *   *

The payments made by the fiduciary to creditors not having pri-ority over the Government are not avoided or set aside. Unlike the transferee's liability which is limited to the value of the property which he has unjustly received, the fiduciary may be liable to the full extent of debts he paid for the transferor, irrespective of any benefit, and notwithstanding that he has received none.

A case illustrating the fine distinction between a fiduciary and a transferee within the meaning of the Code is Bell v. Commissioner, 82 F.2d 499 (C.A. 3, 1936), affirming a Memorandum Opinion of this Court. In that case the executors under a will were also the legatees. It was held that initially, while they held the assets as executors, they could have been liable as fiduciaries, but upon the court order transferring the assets to them under the will, they became trans-ferees, and thus subject to a different liability for the tax owing by the estate.

*   *   *

From the above analysis it is clear that transferee and fiduciary liability attaches to persons holding different interests in property for different purposes, and imposes different standards of liability. While we have seen that one person may hold the same property in both capacities at different times, and one person may hold different properties in both capacities at the same time, from the very nature of the two capacities, one person may not hold the same property in both capacities at the same time.

It has long been established that stockholders receiving the as-sets of a corporation upon liquidation are liable to the Government for unpaid taxes of the corporation under the broader transferee lia-bility section of the Code, since it is presumed that they received them absolutely for their own benefit. This liability is imposed even in situations when a stockholder in fact subsequently distributes all of the proceeds to liquidate corporate debts. We find no authority for the view that a stockholder, receiving the assets of his liquidated cor-poration, is liable as a fiduciary rather than a transferee.

*   *   *

Petitioner, as sole stockholder, received all of the assets of the company at a time when it was liable for income taxes. These facts would indicate liability as a transferee rather than as a fiduciary. The respondent, conceding that the burden lies with him to go for-ward with the evidence in this respect, maintains that petitioner took the assets of the company under an express trust for the benefit of creditors. If such a trust was, in fact, created, petitioner would be a fiduciary under the Code.

*   *   *

Respondent has offered no evidence of an express trust created over all of the assets of the company. On the basis of what we have before us, we are unable to find as a fact that any such express trust was ever created between petitioner and the company.

We next must see whether petitioner is included under section 311(a)(2) in a capacity other than an express trustee. From the definition of "fiduciary" we must eliminate, as not applying to petitioner, a guardian, trustee, executor, administrator, receiver, or conservator. The only remaining position is "any person acting in any fiduciary capacity for any person."

The word "fiduciary" used in the Internal Revenue Code is not mentioned in the Revised Statutes. It is, however, descriptive of the types of persons intended to be covered under the statute. The statute provides that the person covered is executor, administrator, assignee, or other person who pays a debt due by the person "for whom or for which he acts."

The mere payment of a debt for another person will not automatically cause one to be included under this section. The crucial test, therefore, looking at both the Internal Revenue Code and the Revised Statutes, is whether the payment of the debts were made by one who is acting for the debtor in a fiduciary or representative capacity.

Petitioner can only be liable as a fiduciary if he, in fact, received the assets from the company as an officer or director for the purpose of liquidating the corporate debts rather than as a stockholder, and that he paid these debts in his capacity as a representative of the company.

*   *   *

A stockholder receiving all of the assets of a corporation is one of the clearest cases of one receiving assets in his own behalf, and he will be presumed to be acting on his own behalf as a transferee unless there is a clear showing to the contrary. In the absence of such proof, we cannot find that petitioner was acting as a fiduciary upon receipt and distribution of the corporate assets.

Under Wisconsin Statutes when a corporation distributes its assets without first satisfying its creditors, the directors and stockholders may be liable only to the corporation. There is no provision for direct liability on their part to creditors thus defrauded, nor is there any trust created for creditors upon these assets. Respondent, nevertheless, relies on two Wisconsin cases which hold that, upon insolvency of a corporation, the assets become, by equitable conversion, a trust fund for the benefit of creditors. Therefore, respondent concludes that petitioner, as an equitable trustee under Wisconsin law, is a fiduciary within the meaning of the Code. Respondent contends, then, that all persons who hold property impressed with an equitable trust are liable as fiduciaries. This contention has been rejected by this Court in Bond, Incorporated, 12 B.T.A. 339, 341 (1928), where we said (p. 341):

> * * * The Act itself * * * defines a fiduciary in such manner as to make it clear that it refers to one *acting in a representative capacity; a true fiduciary and not merely the holder of property which may, under certain circumstances, be impressed with a trust.* * * * [Emphasis supplied.]

The sole basis for transferee liability is that the recipient of the funds is, under certain circumstances, deemed to hold them in constructive trust for certain creditors. If everyone who is held to hold funds in trust for another is deemed to be a fiduciary under the Code, as respondent contends, it would completely eliminate the basis for the distinction between the two liabilities. Respondent has failed to recognize that in order to be a fiduciary, petitioner must have, in fact, *acted* as such, rather than on his own behalf.

The existence of an *actual* fiduciary relationship is indispensable in placing one within the provisions of fiduciary liability. This fiduciary capacity must be established from the very nature of the transaction rather than through the equitable "trust fund" doctrine. This distinction was well illustrated in the case of *Jessie Smith, Executrix*, [24 B.T.A. 807 (1931)]. In this case a wife, upon the death of her husband, received the assets of her husband's estate as executrix, and she received complete title to real estate which was held jointly by her husband and herself. It was held that since the real estate was not a part of the estate she did not receive it as executrix and, therefore, she did not hold it in a fiduciary capacity. Section 3467 was held to relate only to the payment of debts out of the funds or assets *coming into her hands as executrix* and not to the real estate. It was added that if it were found that the real estate was burdened with the tax liability of the decedent, under the *trust fund* doctrine, she would be liable as a transferee of the real estate, albeit not as a fiduciary.

The mere finding of a "trust fund," then, is insufficient to deem the holder a fiduciary under the statute. If a trust is created out of the nature of the transfer, such as the transfer of assets for the benefit of another, then the holder is a fiduciary. On the other hand, if a trust arises because the person receiving the assets was not rightfully entitled to them, he is a transferee. In the latter situation, the debtor has divested himself completely of the assets to another and this transfer, if prejudicial to other creditors, can be avoided. In the former situation, on the other hand, the debtor by placing his assets with a representative has not divested himself completely of the assets to defraud creditors, inasmuch as his creditors have a beneficial interest in them pursuant to the very nature of the assignment. The transfer to a fiduciary cannot be avoided, and liability attaches to the fiduciary only if he fails to recognize legal priorities in discharging his obligation under the trust.

The distinction between the two different types of trusts was also recognized in Hollins v. Brierfield Coal & Iron Co., 150 U.S. 371, 378 (1893), where it was said (p. 383):

> Becoming insolvent, the equitable interest of the stockhold-
> ers in the property, together with their conditional liability
> to the creditors, places the property in a condition of trust,
> first, for the creditors, and then for the stockholders.
> Whatever of trust there is arises from the peculiar and di-
> verse equitable rights of the stockholders as against the cor-
> poration in its property and their conditional liability to its
> creditors. It is rather a trust in the administration of the
> assets after possession by a court of equity than a trust at-
> taching to the property, as such, for the direct benefit of ei-
> ther creditor or stockholder.

An analogous situation to the one before us concerns a provision in the Bankruptcy Act which exempts persons "acting in any fiduciary capacity." The issue arose as to whether one placed in a fiduciary capacity by operation of equity was included under this section. It was held that to include such equitable trustees would nullify the provision, since almost all insolvent debtors were also equitable trustees. The term was held to include only trusts actually created in law, rather than implied or constructive trusts.

The above reasoning also applies to our situation. The sole basis for transferee liability is that a trust is created in equity for the benefit of creditors. Wherein would lie the distinction if we were to hold that such equitable trustees were fiduciaries rather than transferees? This would completely nullify the difference between the two liabilities, and, indeed, eliminate transferee liability.

* * *

One of the main objectives of the provisions for transferee liability in the Code is to provide an effective remedy for such a situation as that presented in the instant case. To accept respondent's contention that such persons are fiduciaries rather than transferees would create the anomalous result of providing a statutory remedy only to the extent of the corporate debts they pay with the corporate assets but providing no statutory remedy for recovery of the assets they retain for themselves.

Respondent has failed to show any evidence that petitioner ever received the assets impressed with an express trust or that he received them as a representative or an agent for the corporation. This cannot be presumed from the transfer of assets and the subsequent payment of corporate debts or by the operation of equity.

We have not closed our eyes to the obvious fact that the company was liquidated with the full knowledge on the part of petitioner of the pending tax liability, but this is clearly one of the situations sought to be remedied by proceeding on the basis of transferee liability.

The statute of limitations has obviously barred transferee liability which appears to be the reason why respondent relies solely on a claim of fiduciary liability because, if his contention were well grounded, he would get the benefit of a longer period of limitations. Since we have held that the provisions of section 311(a)(2) relating to fiduciary liability do not apply upon the record before us, we must hold for petitioner.

Decision will be entered for the petitioner.

SECTION 6.   THE INNOCENT SPOUSE PROVISIONS

SONNENBORN v. COMMISSIONER

57 T.C. 373 (1971).

*   *   *

RAUM, Judge.

Petitioners are husband and wife, who filed joint returns for the years 1965, 1966, and 1967. Together they owned, in equal shares, all of the stock of Monodon corporation. During the taxable years, Monodon made various payments, which the Commissioner treated as dividends or constructive dividends to petitioners. He accordingly determined deficiencies in tax against both petitioners, whose liability is joint and several as a consequence of the filing of joint returns (sec. 6013(d)(3), I.R.C. 1954). The husband has already conceded that he is liable for these deficiencies. Moreover, the wife, now the only remaining litigant contesting the Commissioner's action (and referred to herein for convenience as the petitioner), does not challenge the correctness of the Commissioner's determination. She seeks to be relieved of liability only on the narrow ground that she comes within the so-called innocent spouse provisions of the recently enacted addition to section 6013 of the Internal Revenue Code of 1954 *   *   *.[n]

n.   IRC § 6013 reads, in part, as follows:
  (e) Spouse Relieved of Liability in Certain Cases.—
    (1) In general.—Under regulations prescribed by the Secretary, if—
    (A) a joint return has been made under this section for a taxable year and on such return there was omitted from gross income an amount properly includable therein which is attributable to one spouse and which is in excess of 25 percent of the amount of gross income stated in the return,
    (B) the other spouse establishes that in signing the return he or she did not know of, and had no reason to know of, such omission, and
    (C) taking into account whether or not the other spouse significantly benefited directly or indirectly from the items omitted from gross income and taking into account all other facts and circumstances, it is

It is important that these provisions be kept in proper perspective. The filing of a joint return is a highly valuable privilege to husband and wife since the resulting tax liability is generally substantially less than the combined taxes that would be due from both spouses if they had filed separate returns. This circumstance gives particular emphasis to the statutory rule that liability with respect to tax is joint and several, regardless of the source of the income or of the fact that one spouse may be far less informed about the contents of the return than the other, for both spouses ordinarily benefit from the reduction in tax that ensues by reason of the joint return. However, some highly inequitable results were called to the attention of Congress, particularly where a wife had been divorced or separated or abandoned after the tax year, where she was saddled with a disproportionately high tax liability as a consequence of having filed a joint return, where such liability grew out of income attributable only to the husband, unknown to the wife, and where she had not enjoyed any benefit therefrom. It was in an effort to eliminate the unfairness of the joint and several liability provisions in such circumstances that section 6013(e) was enacted. To be sure, section 6013(e) is not limited to precisely such narrow situations. But it must be kept in mind that Congress still regards joint and several liability as an important adjunct to the privilege of filing joint returns, and that if there is to be any relaxation of that rule the taxpayer must comply with the carefully detailed conditions set forth in section 6013(e). We hold that petitioner has not brought herself within those provisions here.

The Government argues that there has been a failure to meet all three conditions of paragraph (e)(1). Without pausing to consider whether its position is correct in respect of (e)(1)(A) to the effect that petitioner has failed to establish that the income omitted from the joint return was "attributable" to her husband, we are satisfied that petitioner did not carry her burden of proof in respect of both (e)(1)(B) and (e)(1)(C).

1. *Condition (B)*.—Section 6013(e)(1)(B) requires that the spouse seeking relief must establish that "in signing the return he or she did not know of, and had no reason to know of" the omission from gross income on the joint return. In this case the record af-

inequitable to hold the other spouse liable for the deficiency in tax for such taxable year attributable to such omission, then the other spouse shall be relieved of liability for tax (including interest, penalties, and other amounts) for such taxable year to the extent that such liability is attributable to such omission from gross income.

(2) **Special rules.—For purposes of paragraph (1)—**

(A) the determination of the spouse to whom items of gross income (other than gross income from property) are attributable shall be made without regard to community property laws, and

(B) the amount omitted from gross income shall be determined in the manner provided by section 6501(e)(1)(A).

firmatively establishes that petitioner herself received weekly checks of $900 each issued by Monodon during each of the 3 years in issue, or an aggregate of $46,800 each year. In addition, the returns that she signed disclosed withholdings from salary on behalf of herself and her husband in the amounts of $5,067.20, $6,226.70, and $11,088.60 for the years 1965, 1966, and 1967, respectively. Adding these amounts to the Monodon checks received by petitioner, she either knew or had reason to know that the reportable amounts of income from Monodon were at the very least $51,867.20 for 1965, $53,026.70 for 1966, and $57,888.60 for 1967. Each of these figures is substantially greater than the income appearing on the returns which could have had their source in Monodon, namely, salaries of $39,520, $39,-520, and $53,920 for the years 1965, 1966, and 1967, respectively. It thus appears affirmatively on this record that petitioner knew or should reasonably have known that her joint returns underreported income from Monodon in at least the differences between the last two sets of figures.

Moreover, the largest single component of unreported income from Monodon charged to petitioners by the Commissioner was an item designated "Payments charged to loan account." These payments aggregated $34,038.59, $52,510.38, and $7,710.02 for the years 1965, 1966, and 1967, respectively. By their present failure to challenge the classification of these payments as income petitioners must be taken to have conceded the correctness of the Commissioner's determination in this regard. Yet petitioner has offered no evidence whatever to establish that she had no reason to know that such amounts should have been included in the income reported as having been received from Monodon. It must be recalled that petitioner was an officer of Monodon—indeed, its compensated treasurer—and there is no showing whatever in this case that the books and records of Monodon were unavailable to her, or that she had no reason to make inquiry about these payments. The burden of proof was upon her, and that burden cannot be carried by remaining silent. Although her counsel at the trial carefully led her through nearly all the expenditures relating to "entertainment" and "selling and travel"—expenditures of a lower order of magnitude—he put not a single question to her about the so-called payments charged to loan account. We must conclude on this state of the record, taking into account not only the unreported income of which petitioner was shown affirmatively to have been on notice but also the glaring failure of proof in respect of the payments charged to loan account, that there has been a failure to satisfy condition (B) of paragraph (e)(1) of section 6013.

2. *Condition (C).*—Paragraph (e)(1)(C) requires us to take into account whether petitioner "significantly benefited directly or indirectly" from the unreported income. The burden of proof is upon her in respect of this condition, and what we have said above about

the "Payments charged to loan account" item is equally applicable here.

The record is tantalizingly silent as to the nature of these payments and the use to which they were put. Conceivably, they were used by petitioner's husband in one or more enterprises in which they had a joint or common interest. The funds may have been invested in Northland Paper Mill, the stock ownership of which was not disclosed on this record. We do not know, and these suggestions are mere speculations. The point is, however, that the burden was upon petitioner and it has not been discharged. Her husband could have been called as a witness to offer clarifying evidence, but he did not appear, nor was any explanation offered as to his absence. * * *

In the circumstances, we cannot assume that petitioner did not benefit significantly from these payments, and we must hold for this reason as well that petitioner has failed to satisfy the requirements of section 6013(e).

Decision will be entered for the respondent.

NOTES

1. In determining whether the taxpayer's spouse had reason to know of the omissions from income, the courts generally look to the spouse's awareness of unusual or lavish expenditures, or of other facts which might indicate the existence of unreported income. Mysse v. Commissioner, 57 T. C. 680 (1972). In some situations there may be a duty to question one's spouse about the correctness of the figures on the return. For example, in Adams v. Commissioner, 60 T.C. 300 (1973), the Tax Court held that the failure of the taxpayer, a successful businesswoman, to be forthright about the family income put her husband on notice that their income tax returns were incorrect. Compare, Terzian v. Commissioner, 72 T.C. 1164 (1979), where the Tax Court concluded that the taxpayer's wife had no reason to know of her husband's omissions from income, even though the wife signed the returns without looking at them. In *Terzian,* the husband's dominance in family financial matters, coupled with the absence of any lavish expenditures which would have alerted the wife to the existence of unreported income, led to the conclusion that the wife qualified as an innocent spouse.

The innocent spouse claiming the protection of § 6013(e) must prove that he or she was completely ignorant of the omissions from income. Ignorance or misapprehension of the legal tax consequences of transactions, the facts of which are known to the spouse, is not sufficient to relieve one of liability. McCoy v. Commissioner, 57 T.C. 732 (1972).

2. The legislative history underlying the "significantly benefited" test of § 6013(e)(1)(C) indicates that the term "benefit" does not include ordinary support payments to the spouse claiming to be an innocent spouse. S. Rept. 91–1537, 91st Cong., 2d Sess. 1971–1 C.B. 606, 608. Thus, in Terzian v. Commissioner, supra, the Tax Court concluded that a one-time transfer of $155,000 from the taxpayer to his spouse was a support payment incidental to an informal agreement to separate which did not disqualify the spouse from the protection of § 6013.

3. Section 6653(b) of the Code provides that the spouse of a taxpayer is not liable for a fraud penalty assessed against the taxpayer unless it can be shown that the spouse was also guilty of fraud. In contrast to the situation under § 6013, the Commissioner bears the burden of proving the spouse is liable for the amount of the fraud penalty. See Stone v. Commissioner, 56 T.C. 213 (1971).

QUESTIONS

In the Internal Revenue Code the 25% omission test is stated in the same terms for both innocent spouse and extension of limitations purposes. It is debatable whether this symmetry in the Code is wise.

With regard to extensions of limitations, the purpose of the test is to allow additional time for the IRS to catch one who omits a substantial amount of gross receipts. In this context, it would appear sound to provide that the Service should be deemed to be on notice of everything that is filed with the IRS which discloses the gross income in question—including partnership returns. On the other hand, the purpose of the innocent spouse provision is to avoid saddling a truly innocent spouse from tax liability for omitted amounts of income of which the spouse was not aware and from which the spouse did not benefit. What do you think is the purpose (if any) of the 25% test in the innocent spouse context? To the extent that you feel that some worthy policy is being forwarded by the utilization of a 25% test in an innocent spouse context, does it really make sense to have the determination of the innocence of the spouse affected in any way by what may or may not have been disclosed on partnership returns of which the spouse is totally unaware? Reread Estate of Klein v. Commissioner, pages 176–180, above.

SECTION 7. RESTRAINING TAX COLLECTION

The Anti-Injunction Act, § 7421 of the Internal Revenue Code, provides that " * * * no suit for the purpose of restraining the assessment or collection of any tax shall be maintained in any court by any person * * *." There are, however, limited exceptions to the general prohibition against injunctions. The Code itself expressly permits injunctions to restrain assessment and/or collection in the following circumstances:

1. When deficiency notice requirements have not been met or a prohibited deficiency notice is issued.[o]

2. When a responsible person assessment has been made and an appropriate bond is furnished to secure collection pending litigation of the liability.[p]

3. When certain income tax return preparer penalties have been assessed, 15% of the amount of the assessment is paid and the preparer pursues litigation to determine liability.[q]

o. I.R.C. §§ 6212(a) and (c); 6213(a).   q. I.R.C. § 6694(c).

p. I.R.C. § 6672(b).

4.   When there has been a wrongful levy.[r]

5.   When there has been an improper termination or jeopardy assessment.[s]

There is also a judicially recognized exception to the general prohibition against injunctions to restrain assessment or collection. In this section the scope of the non-statutory exception to the Anti-Injunction is examined, as well as the statutory exceptions for failure to comply with deficiency notice requirements and for wrongful levy.

NOTE

Congress has provided that most types of tax penalties shall be assessed and collected "in the same manner as taxes." IRC §§ 6659(a) and 6671. Thus, the Anti-Injunction Act applies to bar taxpayer suits to restrain the assessment or collection of such penalties. See, e. g., Crouch v. Commissioner, 447 F.Supp. 385 (N.D.Cal.1978) (tax return preparer penalty imposed under § 6695(c) for failure to include preparer's social security number on return held "tax" within meaning of Anti-Injunction Act). Sections 6659(a) and 6671 render inapplicable an old line of cases holding that the Anti-Injunction Act does not bar suits to restrain the assessment or collection of tax penalties which are truly penal in nature. See, e. g., Pool v. Walsh, 282 F. 620 (9th Cir. 1922); Tovar v. Jarecki, 173 F.2d 449 (7th Cir. 1949).

A.   NONSTATUTORY EXCEPTION TO THE ANTI-INJUNCTION ACT

MILLER v. STANDARD NUT MARGARINE CO. OF FLORIDA

Supreme Court of the United States, 1932.
284 U.S. 498, 52 S.Ct. 260, 76 L.Ed. 422.

Mr. Justice BUTLER delivered the opinion of the Court.

Respondent, a manufacturer of "Southern Nut Product," brought this suit in the Southern district of Florida to restrain petitioner from collecting from respondent, or from dealers selling its product, any tax purporting to be levied under the Oleomargarine Act of August 2, 1886.[t] Petitioner answered denying the essential allegations of the complaint. Respondent applied for a temporary injunction; the court found that it would suffer irreparable injury unless petitioner be restrained pending the final disposition of the case, and granted the application. At the trial, respondent introduced oral and documentary evidence, together with specimens of the product sought to be taxed. The court found that the material allegations of the complaint were established by the evidence, and granted permanent injunction. * * * The Circuit Court of Appeals * * * held

---

r.   I.R.C. §§ 7426(a) and (b)(1).

s.   I.R.C. § 7429(b).

t.   The Oleomargarine Act of 1886 levied an excise tax upon certain butter substitutes and other products intended to be sold as or for butter.

Rev.St. § 3224 (26 USCA § 154),[u] does not apply and affirmed the decree.

That section declares (26 U. S. Code, § 154 [26 U.S.C.A. § 154]): "No suit for the purpose of restraining the assessment or collection of any tax shall be maintained in any court." This suit was commenced December 26, 1929. The complaint, the evidence contained in the record, and documents of which judicial notice may be taken show [that the product in question was not, in fact, oleomargarine].

* * *

In 1928, pursuant to instructions sent him by the deputy commissioner stating that respondent's product was held taxable as colored oleomargarine, the petitioner demanded and threatened to collect a tax of ten cents a pound upon respondent's product. But petitioner made no effort to collect the tax on "Nut-Z-All," [a comparable product marketed by a competitor,] which at the time of the trial was being sold in Florida. Excluding the tax from cost, respondent's net profit was approximately three cents per pound. The enforcement of the Oleomargarine Act against respondent would impose a tax that respondent would be unable to pay, would subject it to heavy penalties and the forfeiture of its plant, together with the materials and manufactured product on hand, and would destroy its business.

* * *

Petitioner does not here assign as error the finding below that respondent's product was not oleomargarine. He seeks reversal upon the grounds that the statute forbids injunction against the collection of the tax even if erroneously assessed; that this assessment was made by the Commissioner under color of his office, was not arbitrary or capricious and that, if there is any exception to the application of section 3224, this case is not within it.

* * *

Independently of, and in cases arising prior to, the enactment of the provision which became Rev.St. § 3224, this court, in harmony with the rule generally followed in courts of equity, held that a suit will not lie to restrain the collection of a tax upon the sole ground of its illegality. The principal reason is that, as courts are without authority to apportion or equalize taxes or to make assessments, such suits would enable those liable for taxes in some amount to delay payment or possibly to escape their lawful burden, and so to interfere with and thwart the collection of revenues for the support of the government. And this court likewise recognizes the rule that, in cases where complainant shows that in addition to the illegality of an exaction in the guise of a tax there exist special and extraordinary circumstances sufficient to bring the case within some acknowledged

---

u. The predecessor to § 7421(a) of the 1954 Code.

head of equity jurisprudence, a suit may be maintained to enjoin the collector. Section 3224 is declaratory of the principle first mentioned and is to be construed as near as may be in harmony with it and the reasons upon which it rests. The section does not refer specifically to the rule applicable to cases involving exceptional circumstances. The general words employed are not sufficient, and it would require specific language undoubtedly disclosing that purpose, to warrant the inference that Congress intended to abrogate that salutary and well-established rule. This court has given effect to section 3224 in a number of cases. It has never held the rule to be absolute, but has repeatedly indicated that extraordinary and exceptional circumstances render its provisions inapplicable.

This is not a case in which the injunction is sought upon the mere ground of illegality because of error in the amount of the tax. The article is not covered by the act. A valid oleomargarine tax could by no legal possibility have been assessed against respondent, and therefore the reasons underlying § 3224 apply, if at all, with little force. Respondent commenced business after the product it proposed to make had repeatedly been determined by the Commissioner and adjudged in courts not to be oleomargaine or taxable under the act and upon the assurance from the Bureau that its product would not be taxed. For more than a year and a half respondent sold its product relying that it was not subject to tax. If required to pay the tax, its loss would be seven cents per pound. Before the Commissioner's latest ruling, [which reversed the Service's prior position and held products like "Southern Nut Product" taxable under the act,] respondent had made and sold so much that the tax would have amounted to more than it could pay. Petitioner acquiesced in the injunctions granted in Rhode Island and the District of Columbia and did not assess any tax upon identical products contemporaneously being made by complainants in such suits, and directed enforcement against respondent's entire product. Such discrimination conflicts with the principle underlying the constitutional provision directing that excises laid by Congress shall be uniform throughout the United States. It requires no elaboration of the facts found to show that the enforcement of the act against respondent would be arbitrary and oppressive, would destroy its business, ruin it financially, and inflict loss for which it would have no remedy at law. It is clear that, by reason of the special and extraordinary facts and circumstances, section 3224 does not apply. The lower courts rightly held respondent entitled to the injunction.

* * *

ENOCHS v. WILLIAMS PACKING & NAVIGATION CO.

Supreme Court of the United States, 1962.
370 U.S. 1, 82 S.Ct. 1125, 8 L.Ed.2d 292.

Mr. Chief Justice WARREN delivered the opinion of the Court.

Fearing that the District Director of Internal Revenue for Mississippi would attempt to collect allegedly past due social security and unemployment taxes for the years 1953, 1954 and 1955, respondent, in late 1957, brought suit in the District Court, maintaining that it was not liable for the exactions and seeking an injunction prohibiting their collection. The District Director, petitioner herein, made no objection to the issuance of a preliminary restraining order but resisted a permanent injunction, asserting that the provisions of § 7421(a) of the Internal Revenue Code of 1954 barred any such injunctive proceeding. That section provides:

"Except as provided in sections 6212(a) and (c), and 6213(a), no suit for the purpose of restraining the assessment or collection of any tax shall be maintained in any court."

The exception for Tax Court proceedings created by §§ 6212(a) and (c) and 6213(a), 26 U.S.C.A. §§ 6212(a, c), 6213(a) was not applicable because that body is without jurisdiction over taxes of the sort here in issue. Nevertheless, on July 14, 1959, the court, relying upon Miller v. Standard Nut Margarine Co., 284 U.S. 498, 52 S.Ct. 260, 76 L.Ed. 422, permanently enjoined collection of the taxes on the ground that they were not, in fact, payable and because collection would destroy respondent's business. On June 14, 1961, the Court of Appeals for the Fifth Circuit affirmed, one judge dissenting. We granted certiorari to determine whether the case came within the scope of this Court's holding in *Nut Margarine* which indicated that § 7421(a) was not, in the "special and extraordinary facts and circumstances" of that case, intended to apply.

Respondent corporation (hereinafter referred to as Williams) is engaged in the business of providing trawlers to fishermen who take shrimp, oysters and fish off the Louisiana and Mississippi coasts. It is the Government's position that these fishermen are the corporation's employees * * *. If, under the involved circumstances of this case, the fishermen were employees, respondent Williams is admittedly liable for social security and unemployment taxes for the years in question.

* * *

The object of § 7421(a) is to withdraw jurisdiction from the state and federal courts to entertain suits seeking injunctions prohibiting the collection of federal taxes. In Miller v. Standard Nut Margarine Co., supra, this Court was confronted with the question whether a manufacturer of "Southern Nut Product" could enjoin the collection of federal oleomargarine taxes on its goods. Prior to the assessment in issue three lower federal court cases had held that similar products were nontaxable and, by letter, the collector had informed the manufacturer that "Southern Nut Product" was not subject to the tax. This Court found that "[a] valid oleomargarine tax could by no legal possibility have been assessed against [the manufacturer], and therefore the reasons underlying [§ 7421(a)] apply, if at all, with little force." Noting that collection of the tax "would destroy its business, ruin it financially and inflict loss for which it would have no remedy at law," the Court held that an injunction could properly issue. The courts below seem to have found that *Nut Margarine* decides that § 7421(a) does not bar suit for an injunction against the collection of taxes not due if the legal remedy is inadequate. We cannot agree.

The enactment of the comparable Tax Injunction Act of 1937, 50 Stat. 738, now, as amended, 28 U.S.C.A. § 1341, forbidding the federal courts to entertain suits to enjoin collection of state taxes "where a plain, speedy, and efficient remedy may be had at law or in equity in the courts of such State," throws light on the proper construction to be given § 7421(a). It indicates that if Congress had desired to make the availability of the injunctive remedy against the collection of federal taxes not lawfully due depend upon the adequacy of the legal remedy, it would have said so explicitly. Its failure to do so shows that such a suit may not be entertained merely because collection would cause an irreparable injury, such as the ruination of the taxpayer's enterprise. This is not to say, of course, that inadequacy of the legal remedy need not be established if § 7421(a) is inapplicable; indeed, the contrary rule is well established. However, since we conclude that § 7421(a) bars any suit for an injunction in this case, we need not determine whether the taxpayer would suffer irreparable injury if collection were effected.

The manifest purpose of § 7421(a) is to permit the United States to assess and collect taxes alleged to be due without judicial intervention, and to require that the legal right to the disputed sums be determined in a suit for refund. In this manner the United States is assured of prompt collection of its lawful revenue. Nevertheless, if it is clear that under no circumstances could the Government ultimately prevail, the central purpose of the Act is inapplicable and, under the *Nut Margarine* case, the attempted collection may be enjoined if equity jurisdiction otherwise exists. In such a situation the exaction is merely in "the guise of a tax."

We believe that the question of whether the Government has a chance of ultimately prevailing is to be determined on the basis of the information available to it at the time of suit. Only if it is then apparent that, under the most liberal view of the law and the facts, the United States cannot establish its claim, may the suit for an injunction be maintained. Otherwise, the District Court is without jurisdiction, and the complaint must be dismissed. To require more than good faith on the part of the Government would unduly interfere with a collateral objective of the Act—protection of the collector from litigation pending a suit for refund. And to permit even the maintenance of a suit in which an injunction could issue only after the taxpayer's nonliability had been conclusively established might "in every practical sense operate to suspend collection of the * * * taxes until the litigation is ended." Great Lakes Dredge & Dock Co. v. Huffman, 319 U.S. 293, 299, 63 S.Ct. 1070, 1073, 87 L.Ed. 1407. Thus, in general, the Act prohibits suits for injunctions barring the collection of federal taxes when the collecting officers have made the assessment and claim that it is valid.

The record before us clearly reveals that the Government's claim of liability was not without foundation. Therefore, we reverse the judgment of the Court of Appeals and remand the case to the District Court with directions to dismiss the complaint.

Reversed.

NOTE

In Bob Jones Univ. v. Simon, 416 U.S. 725, 94 S.Ct. 2038, 40 L.Ed.2d 496 (1974), the taxpayer sought an order enjoining the IRS from revoking a ruling letter which stated that the university qualified for tax-exempt status. The IRS had proposed taking this action because of the school's racially discriminatory admissions policy. The Supreme Court, applying the *Williams Packing* standard, which it described as the "capstone of judicial construction of the Act", refused to grant the injunction. The Court held that the test for issuance of an injunction is two-pronged—in addition to proving that equity jurisdiction exists, (i. e., the taxpayer, threatened with irreparable injury, has no adequate remedy at law), the taxpayer must also establish that the Service's action is clearly without legal basis. See also Alexander v. "Americans United" Inc., 416 U.S. 752, 758–759, 94 S.Ct. 2053, 2057–2058, 40 L.Ed.2d 518 (1974) ("the constitutional nature of a taxpayer's claim, as distinct from its probability of success", is of no consequence in overcoming the barrier of § 7421(a)). Note that much of the hardship inherent in situations involving the revocation of an organization's tax-exempt status has been eliminated by the enactment of IRC § 7428(a), which authorizes the Tax Court, the Court of Claims and the United States District Court for the District of Columbia to issue declaratory judgments relating to an organization's qualification for tax-exempt treatment. See pages 303–305, above.

COMMISSIONER v. SHAPIRO

Supreme Court of the United States, 1976.
424 U.S. 614, 96 S.Ct. 1062, 47 L.Ed.2d 278.

Mr. Justice WHITE delivered the opinion of the Court.

* * *

Normally, the Internal Revenue Service may not "assess" a tax or collect it, by levying on or otherwise seizing a taxpayer's assets, until the taxpayer has had an opportunity to exhaust his administrative remedies, which include an opportunity to litigate his tax liability fully in the Tax Court, 26 U.S.C. §§ 6212, 6213; and if the Internal Revenue Service does attempt to collect the tax by levy or otherwise, before such exhaustion of remedies in violation of § 6213, the collection is not protected by the Anti-Injunction Act and may be restrained by a United States district court at the instance of the taxpayer. §§ 6213(a), 7421(a). The rule is otherwise when the Commissioner proceeds under § 6861 and finds that collection of a tax due and owing from a taxpayer will be "jeopardized by delay" in collection. In such a case, the Commissioner may immediately assess the tax and, upon "notice and demand * * * for payment thereof" followed by the taxpayer's "failure or refusal to pay such tax," may immediately levy on the taxpayer's assets. §§ 6861, 6331. When the Commissioner follows this procedure, the Anti-Injunction Act applies in full force and "no suit for the purpose of restraining the assessment or collection of any tax shall be maintained in any court by any person." § 7421(a).

In this case, the Commissioner found, on December 6, 1973, that the imminent departure of respondent Samuel Shapiro (hereinafter Shapiro or respondent) for Israel and the probable departure with him of the assets in his New York bank accounts and safe-deposit boxes jeopardized the collection of income taxes claimed to be due and owing by him for the tax years 1970 and 1971. Accordingly, he assessed income taxes against respondent in the amount of $92,726.41 for the tax years 1970 and 1971. On the same day, he filed liens against respondent and served notices of levy upon various banks in New York State in which respondent maintained accounts or had safe-deposit boxes. These notices of levy effectively froze the money in the accounts—totaling about $35,000—and the contents of the safe-deposit boxes.

At that time respondent Shapiro was under a final order of extradition to Israel, for trial on criminal fraud charges * * *.

Upon learning of the notices of levy, respondent obtained the consent of the State of Israel to postpone his extradition date until December 16, 1973; and then on December 13, 1973, he initiated the instant lawsuit. Claiming that he owed no taxes; that he could not litigate the issue with the Internal Revenue Service while in jail in Israel; that he would be in jail in Israel, unless he could use the frozen $35,000 as bail money; and that the Internal Revenue Service had deliberately and in bad faith waited until December 6, 1973, before filing its notices of levy precisely in order to place him in this predicament, respondent requested in his complaint an order enjoining his extradition until he had an opportunity to litigate the question whether he owed the Internal Revenue Service any taxes or, in the alternative, an order directing the Internal Revenue Service to lift the notices of levy.

[The District Court dismissed the complaint on the ground of the Anti-Injunction Act. The Court of Appeals] concluded that the District Court should not have dismissed the complaint without further inquiry into the factual foundation for the jeopardy assessment and that further proceedings were necessary before finally determining whether upon viewing the law and the facts most favorably to the Government there was "no factual foundation" for the Government's claim that Shapiro was a tax-delinquent narcotics dealer during 1971 and thus no basis for the assessment. Accordingly, the court remanded in order to "allow the District Court * * * to develop a record" and to determine in light of it whether the asserted deficiency was "so arbitrary and excessive" as to be an exaction in the guise of a tax.

* * *

In Enochs v. Williams Packing Co., the Court held that an injunction may be obtained against the collection of any tax if (1) it is "clear that under no circumstances could the government ultimately prevail" and (2) "equity jurisdiction" otherwise exists, i. e., the taxpayer shows that he would otherwise suffer irreparable injury. 370 U.S. at 7, 82 S.Ct. at 1129, 8 L.Ed.2d at 296. The Court also said that "the question of whether the Government has a chance of ultimately prevailing is to be determined on the basis of the information available to it at the time of the suit," ibid. The Government's claim that the Court of Appeals placed on it the burden of justifying its assessment and thereby erroneously applied the *Williams Packing* rule is wrong. *Williams Packing* did not hold that the taxpayer's burden of persuading the District Court that the Government will under no circumstances prevail must be accomplished without any disclosure of information by the Government. It says instead that the question will be resolved on the basis of the information available to the Government at the time of the suit. Since it is absolutely impossible to determine what information is available to the Government at the time of the suit, unless the Government discloses such information in the District Court pursuant to appropriate procedures, it is obvious that the Court in *Williams Packing* intended some disclosure by the Government. Although the Government casts its argument in terms of "burden of proof," the Court of Appeals did not place any technical burden of producing evidence on the Government and it would appear to matter little whether the Government discloses such information because it is said to have the burden of producing evidence on the question or whether it discloses such evidence by responding to a discovery motion made or interrogatories served by the taxpayer—in which case the burden of producing evidence may be said to have rested with the taxpayer. Thus the Court of Appeals cannot be said to have erred in declining to specify the precise manner in which the relevant facts would be revealed on remand. In either event, under *Williams Packing* the relevant facts are those in the Government's possession and they must somehow be obtainable from the Government.[10]

* * *

Our conclusion that the Court of Appeals correctly reversed the judgment of the District Court and remanded for further proceedings is fortified by the fact that construing the Act to permit the Government to seize and hold property on the mere good-faith allegation of an unpaid tax would raise serious constitutional problems in cases, such as this one, where it is asserted that seizure of assets pursuant to a jeopardy assessment is causing irreparable injury. This Court has recently and repeatedly held that, at least where irreparable injury may result from a deprivation of property pending final adjudication of the rights of the parties, the Due Process Clause requires that the party whose property is taken be given an opportunity for some kind of predeprivation or prompt post-deprivation hearing at which some showing of the probable validity of the deprivation must be made. Here the Government seized respondent's property and contends that it has absolutely no obligation to prove that the seizure has any basis in fact no matter how severe or irreparable the injury to the taxpayer and no matter how inadequate his eventual remedy in the Tax Court.

* * *

* * * At the time the District Court dismissed the complaint, the Government had done little more than assert that respondent owed taxes in an amount greater than the value of the property levied—it had alleged that respondent had made an unexplained bank deposit of $18,000 in 1970 and, in a wholly conclusory fashion, that he had received $137,280 in income from selling hashish. Before the taxpayer had an opportunity to inquire into the factual basis for this conclusory allegation, it was not possible to tell whether the Government had any chance of ultimately prevailing. Accordingly, the

10. We believe that it is consistent with *Williams Packing* to place the burden of producing evidence with the taxpayer, and to require, if the Government insists, that facts in its sole possession be obtained through discovery. However, nothing we say here should prevent the Government from voluntarily and immediately disclosing the basis for its assessment, which, if sufficient, would terminate discovery proceedings and justify judgment for the Government.

Court of Appeals properly concluded that the Anti-Injunction Act did not require dismissal of the taxpayer's complaint.

* * * The Government may defeat a claim by the taxpayer that its assessment has no basis in fact—and therefore render applicable the Anti-Injunction Act—without resort to oral testimony and cross-examination. Affidavits are sufficient so long as they disclose basic facts from which it appears that the Government may prevail. The Constitution does not invariably require more and we would not hold that it does where collection of the revenues is involved.

* * *

The judgment of the Court of Appeals is Affirmed.

QUESTION

The Anti-Injunction Act was amended by the Tax Reform Act of 1976 to provide an explicit exception to the general prohibition against injunctions in cases falling under § 7429(b) of the Code, which provides taxpayers with the right to a prompt judicial determination of (1) whether an assessment under §§ 6851, 6861 or 6862 is reasonable under the circumstances, and (2) whether the amount so assessed is appropriate under the circumstances. Section 7429(a) also requires the Service, within 5 days after such an assessment is made, to "provide the taxpayer with a written statement of the information upon which the Secretary relies in making such assessment." Do the provisions of § 7429 address adequately the constitutional problems in the jeopardy and termination assessment area which the Supreme Court perceived in the *Shapiro* case? What additional reforms do you think may be necessary? See generally Fidelity Equipment Leasing Corp. v. United States, pages 725–729, above.

NOTE

Where the Service has failed to adhere to express statutory procedures applicable to the collection process, injunctive relief may be appropriate. For example, in Mrizek v. Long, 187 F.Supp. 830 (N.D.Ill.1959), the Service's failure to comply with the 10-day notice and demand period required by § 6331(a) before a levy may be made upon the taxpayer's property was held grounds for the issuance of an injunction against collection. Where the procedural irregularity complained of is not a violation of a statutory command, but merely a violation of a regulation or procedure which the IRS has itself promulgated, it is less clear that collection may be enjoined. See Cleveland Trust Co. v. United States, 421 F.2d 475 (6th Cir. 1970) (injunction denied, revenue procedure pertaining to IRS rejection of informal conference agreement held not mandatory). But see, generally, Morton v. Ruiz, 415 U.S. 199, 235, 94 S.Ct. 1055, 39 L.Ed.2d 270 (1974) ("Where the rights of individuals are affected, it is incumbent upon agencies to follow their own procedures. This is so even where the internal procedures are possibly more rigorous than otherwise would be required."); Accardi v. Shaughnessy, 347 U.S. 260, 74 S.Ct. 499, 98 L.Ed. 681 (1954) (habeas corpus relief proper where the government failed to follow regulations "with the force and effect of law" governing the procedure to be followed in processing and passing upon an alien's application for suspension of deportation); cf. United States v. Caceres, excerpted above at page 615.

B. DEFICIENCY NOTICE DEFECTS (PREMATURE ASSESSMENTS)

AN INQUIRY INTO THE ASSESSMENT PROCESS

Alan R. Johnson
35 Tax Law Review 285 (1980).

* * *

Premature Assessments

Section 6213 and corresponding provisions of prior revenue acts contain restrictions on the time during which assessments may be made. The sections provide that an assessment cannot be made until 90 (60 in the case of some predecessor sections) days after the issuance of a notice of deficiency and, if the taxpayer files a petition with the Tax Court, not until the Tax Court decision has become final. The Service has, from time to time, mistakenly made assessments during the prohibited period, and a number of cases discuss the effect of such a mistake. Most of the law arises in the context of a refund suit, i. e., the taxpayer has paid the premature assessment and later sues for a refund on the ground that the assessment was invalid. A smaller number of cases arise from taxpayer injunction suits, or government collection actions. The decisions in the area are in conflict and, once again, the least favorable decisions to the taxpayer are from the Court of Claims.

The leading Court of Claims case is Lehigh Portland Cement Co. v. United States.[28] In that case, a notice of deficiency was sent to the taxpayer and, within the then applicable 60-day period for petitioning the Board of Tax Appeals, an assessment was made and the tax paid. The taxpayer did not file a petition with the Board. The court rejected the taxpayer's refund suit, giving seven numbered reasons. The court stated specifically that it was not considering or discussing the question of when or under what circumstances an injunction might be appropriate; indeed, the first of the seven stated reasons was that the taxpayer took no action to enjoin the making of the assessment or the collection.

The thrust of the *Lehigh* decision is that a premature assessment is voidable rather than void. The reasoning of the decision is not beyond criticism and some of it—particularly the portions revolving around the fact that if Congress had meant a premature assessment to be void it easily could have said so—seem quite farfetched. More impressive is the treatment of estoppel which runs throughout the case though, strangely, it is not listed as a reason in itself. In this connection, the court noted that the taxpayer had stated that its payment of the tax was under protest but failed to make any reference

28. 30 F.Supp. 217 (Ct.Cl.1939).

to the assessment being premature, and had such an objection been raised the Commissioner could, within about eight months, have made a proper assessment. The court also noted that courts of equity always have refused to aid parties who have slept on their rights. * * * However, the court's most important statement, which is of general applicability, was:

> Harmless procedural errors or deviations from the general plan which work no hardship upon the taxpayer, or to which he does not object to the manner specified in this statute, nor which in any way deprive him of any substantive right, privileges or protection afforded and intended to be secured by the plan outlined, cannot be made the basis for avoiding the payment of a just tax because the taxpayer did not at any time avail himself of the specific remedy given which, if invoked, would go not to the validity of the tax nor the right to collect it, but only to the time when it may be collected.[31]

Finally, the court discusses United States v. Yellow Cab Co., Ventura Consolidated Oil Fields v. Rogan, and United States v. Barber,[32] all to the contrary. Although the court's discussion of these cases is lengthy—consuming nearly seven columns of small type—nearly the entire discussion consists of description and none of it enlightenment as to where those decisions might have gone wrong. Rather, at the end of the description, there is simply a statement that the Court of Claims thinks its own reasoning is right and that it therefore is unable to concur in the other courts' conclusions.

On the same day it decided *Lehigh*, the Court of Claims decided two similar cases, each of which consists of a fairly short opinion relying upon *Lehigh*. In the first of these, Champion Rivet Co. v. United States,[33] the assessment took place after entry of a stipulated Board of Tax Appeals decision, but before the decision became final. The court noted that there were reasons in addition to *Lehigh* why the taxpayer could not recover. The first was that a stipulation contained a statement that "the taxpayer hereby consents to the assessment appealed from." The court felt this was a consent to immediate assessment and collection. The court also noted that the taxpayer did not at any time seek to enjoin collection, "even if it might have done so in the circumstances." It is interesting that the court mentioned this, apparently as an additional reason, despite the fact that it was clearly stated in *Lehigh*. The clear inference is that notions of waiver or estoppel are of great im-

31. 30 F.Supp. at 233.

32. United States v. Yellow Cab Co., 90 F.2d 699 (7th Cir. 1937); Ventura Consolidated Oil Fields v. Rogan, 86 F.2d 149 (9th Cir. 1936), cert. denied, 300 U.S. 672 (1937); United States v. Barber, 24 F.Supp. 229 (D.Md.1938), discussed in the text accompanying Ns. 37–43 infra.

33. 30 F.Supp. 234 (Ct.Cl.1939).

portance in this area, but can be avoided by seeking to enjoin collection.

In the second case, Dunnington v. United States,[34] an assessment was made before a Board decision had become final, which decision had been entered after the Board had granted the taxpayer's motion to dismiss his appeal. The motion papers, as in the case of the stipulation in *Champion Rivet*, contained a statement that the taxpayer consented to the assessment of the deficiency set forth in the notice. The opinion consists of two paragraphs, the first of which describes the facts and the second of which reads:

> On these facts it is clear that plaintiff is not entitled to recover. The plaintiff specifically consented on November 5, 1927 to assessment of the deficiency determined by the Commissioner. This consent justified the Commissioner in assessing and collecting the tax. The taxpayer's consent to assessment of the deficiency as determined by the Commissioner carried with it the right to collect. He specifically agreed to the deficiency and there was therefore no basis for any objection by him to its assessment and collection. No objection was made to the assessment or collection until March 1931. See Lehigh Portland Company v. United States, decided this date.[35]

Ryan v. Alexander,[36] which follows *Lehigh*, is to the same basic effect. In that case, the court held that a letter forwarding a check in payment of an assessment made while the taxpayer's case was before the Board constituted a waiver. The court also noted that the United States was entitled to retain money which it collected and could have assessed but did not.

Of the contrary cases cited in *Lehigh*, one is particularly favorable to taxpayers: United States v. Yellow Cab Co.[37] The chronology of events in that case was: the Commissioner sent a proper notice of deficiency and the taxpayer filed a petition with the Board of Tax Appeals. While the case was pending, the tax was assessed and, over taxpayer's protest, collected. Subsequently, the Board held against the taxpayer. The taxpayer then sued for refund of the amount paid on the ground that the assessment was invalid. The court first rejected the government's contention that no court had jurisdiction since the Board had passed on the matter; the court stated that to sustain the government's position would ignore the mandate of present section 6212 and would give the Commissioner an unintended arbitrary power. The court also rejected an estoppel argument based on the fact that the taxpayer could have obtained an injunction but

---

34. 30 F.Supp. 236 (Ct.Cl.1939).

35. Id. at 239.

36. 118 F.2d 744 (10th Cir.), cert. denied, 314 U.S. 622 (1941).

37. 90 F.2d 699 (7th Cir. 1937).

did not. In doing so, it held that the specific statutory authorization for an injunction in such circumstances was an additional remedy which did not preclude a refund suit. The meat of this two-page opinion, however, is contained in the following paragraph:

> We see no difference in principle whether the statute prohibiting the assessment and collection of a tax is a limitation statute or one evidently designed to protect the taxpayer until he has had the opportunity to litigate his dispute with the Government in the form and manner prescribed. Appellant cites authorities holding that irregularities in the collection of a tax are not sufficient to entitle the taxpayer to a refund. These cases are clearly distinguishable for the reason that the question with which we are confronted is not a mere irregularity but an assessment which was made contrary to the statute and was therefore illegal.[38]

The question, of course, is what is a "mere irregularity," as distinguished from the fatal error in *Yellow Cab*. Although the distinction is far from clear, what is clear is that a technical error in assessment cost the government a tax, even though it won its case before the Board.

In the injunction area another circuit court had already reached the same result. In Ventura Consolidated Oil Fields v. Rogan,[39] the taxpayer obtained an injunction where a proper notice of deficiency had not been sent. The court leaned heavily on the fact that the taxpayer had been deprived of its right to petition the Board of Tax Appeals. The court also noted that even assuming the notice was proper, the assessment was prohibited because it was made within 60 days of mailing the letter in question. Perhaps the most interesting aspect of the case is its complete rejection of the Commissioner's plea that since the time to assess had expired, the granting of an injunction would cost the government the tax, which, in this case, was quite large. To these contentions the court stated:

> We are unable to discover any difference in the applications of the rules of law or equity in tax cases, whether the government's claim be for $100 or $10,000,000.

> Nor are we able to discover anything in the record to warrant finding that the statutory period in which the Commissioner can assess is not extended by the customary waivers for which the statute makes provision. But presuming the Commissioner's claim is sustained by the record and that he has failed in his duty either to obtain the waivers or to make the assessment in the period provided by Congress, such failure on his part cannot be made the basis of a claim

38. Id. at 701.   **39.** 86 F.2d 149 (9th Cir. 1936).

in equity that it has created a power in the court to make good his dereliction.[40]

A more recent case from the same circuit, Bromberg v. Ingling,[41] throws some interesting light on *Ventura*, as well as being of interest itself. There, the taxpayer sought and obtained an injunction against collection based upon an assessment made simultaneously with the issuance of a notice of deficiency. The taxpayer never filed a petition with the Tax Court. The question of the notice's invalidity was viewed as being settled by *Ventura*. The court stated specifically that it was not holding that if the tax had been paid the taxpayer necessarily would be entitled to get it back: "If such a case lurks in Guam, it will be time enough to decide when it comes here." [42] The court also noted that though some of the Court of Claims' language in *Lehigh* and Lyddon & Co. (America) Inc. v. United States [43] seemed to be contrary to *Ventura*, perhaps those cases were consistent on other grounds, and added that the Ninth [Circuit] was not yet in conflict with the Court of Claims.

Similar is Dierks v. United States,[44] where the taxpayer obtained an injunction against collection on an assessment made after entry of a Tax Court decision entered pursuant to a stipulation, the validity of which was contested, but before the time to appeal had expired. It is unclear whether the injunction would expire with the expiration of the time to appeal.

The issue has arisen also in the context of a collection suit. As with the injunction cases, the results generally have been favorable to taxpayers. In United States v. Barber,[45] the Commissioner had sent the defendant a notice of deficiency and the defendant, one day late, filed a petition with the Board. The Commissioner then assessed the tax. Subsequently, the Board dismissed the petition as untimely. The court held, first, that the restrictions on assessments contained in the predecessor of section 6213 relating to "if a petition has been filed" [46] meant any petition, even if apparently untimely, for it was up to the Board and not the Commissioner to determine that the petition did not confer jurisdiction.[47] The court then went on to hold that the assessment was void, relying upon a case which, as the court itself noted, was not directly in point, and also citing *Ventura*. The government's bill of complaint thus was dismissed.

---

40. Id. at 156.

41. 300 F.2d 859 (9th Cir. 1962).

42. Id. at 862.

43. 158 F.Supp. 951 (Ct.Cl.), cert. denied, 358 U.S. 852 (1958) * * *.

44. 215 F.Supp. 338 (S.D.N.Y.1963).

45. 24 F.Supp. 229 (D.Md.1938).

46. Revenue Act of 1928, § 272(a).

47. This result is, incidentally, the opposite of that reached in Ryan v. Alexander, 118 F.2d 744 (10th Cir.), cert. denied, 314 U.S. 622 (1941), n. 36 supra.

United States v. Walker [48] reached a similar result. The assessments there were made after a judgment against the taxpayer in the Tax Court, but within the appeal period. The court referred to the doctrine of the first *Anderson* [v] case and *First Huntington*,[w] that the Commissioner assesses the tax rather than the taxpayer, but noted that the court in *First Huntington* had stated that a valid assessment of tax was necessary. Citing *Ventura, Yellow Cab,* and *Barber,* the court held that because they were made within the prohibited period, the assessments were void, and accordingly granted the defendant's motion for summary judgment. The court noted that by the time the government brought the proceeding, the time to assess had long since expired. The opinion in *Walker* contains no mention of *Lehigh* or the cases following it.

To the contrary is United States v. Teti.[49] There, citing *Lehigh* and *Lyddon* (with a "but see" for *Bromberg*), the court, in the context of a government collection suit, held a premature assessment to be effective upon the expiration of the taxpayer's period to petition the Tax Court. Two companion cases, both entitled United States v. Paschen,[50] also reached the same conclusion. Without discussion or citation of authority, the court held that an assessment was valid and that the United States should prevail in its collection suit where the assessment was made while the case was before the Board which subsequently, pursuant to stipulation, entered its decision.

*   *   *

DIERKS v. UNITED STATES

215 F.Supp. 338 (S.D.N.Y.1963).

DAWSON, District Judge.

This is a motion brought on by an order to show cause to restrain the defendant, its officers, agents and employees from taking any steps to enforce the collection of certain Internal Revenue taxes against the estate of John Dierks, deceased, and for an order quashing, nullifying and setting aside a certain assessment against the said estate.

It appears, apparently without controversy, that on or about October 5, 1960, the Commissioner of Internal Revenue issued a deficiency letter addressed to John Dierks, assessing deficiencies in income taxes and penalties for the tax years 1949 through 1955, inclu-

---

48. 217 F.Supp. 888 (W.D.S.C.1963).

v. 15 F.Supp. 216 (Ct.Cl.1936), cert. denied, 300 U.S. 675 (1937).

w. 34 F.Supp. 578 (S.D.W.Va.1940), aff'd without opinion, 117 F.2d 376 (4th Cir. 1941).

49. 75–2 U.S.T.C. ¶ 9709 (D.Conn. 1975).

50. 40–2 U.S.T.C. ¶¶ 9679, 9680 (N.D. Ill.1940).

sive, aggregating a total of $208,519.10. Thereupon Mr. Dierks filed a petition for a review of this deficiency in the Tax Court. On November 30, 1962, the tax case was called for trial before the Tax Court. On that occasion counsel for Mr. Dierks handling the Tax Court proceedings entered into a written stipulation with representatives of the Internal Revenue Service for entry of a decision in said tax case, amounting to a deficiency in internal revenue taxes, fraud penalties, additions to the tax and statutory interest in the approximate sum of $247,996.19. In the stipulation it was provided that any and all restrictions contained in the Internal Revenue laws regarding the assessment and collection of the tax deficiencies were waived.

The attorney for the plaintiffs maintains that at the time this stipulation was entered into Mr. Dierks, who was then approximately eighty years of age, was in a coma; that he did not know about the stipulation and did not authorize it; and that his counsel entered into the stipulation knowing of his physical condition without getting the approval of his client. Apparently Mr. Dierks shortly thereafter died. Counsel for the plaintiffs therefore contends that the stipulation is without binding effect upon Mr. Dierks or his estate. This, of course, is a question which properly should be decided in the Tax Court where the stipulation was filed. It is not an issue now before this Court.

However, the representatives of the Bureau of Internal Revenue have proceeded promptly to collect the taxes, having levied an assessment upon the estate and having served notices of liens upon various depositaries of funds of the estate. It is to restrain these collection activities that this order to show cause has been brought.

The basis upon which the order to show cause is sought is contained in Section 6213, Title 26 United States Code, which provides in part as follows:

"Except as otherwise provided in section 6861 [jeopardy assessments] no assessment of a deficiency in respect of any tax imposed by subtitle A or B and no levy or proceeding in court for its collection shall be made, begun, or prosecuted until * * * nor, if a petition has been filed with the Tax Court, until the decision of the Tax Court has become final. * * *"

Plaintiffs contend that the decision of the Tax Court has not become final and that therefore under this provision of the act no proceedings for the levying of the tax can be made at the present time. Plaintiffs contend that the decision of the Tax Court does not become final, under the provisions of Section 7481 of Title 26 U.S.C., until the expiration of the time allowed for filing a petition for review, and that this time does not expire, under Section 7483, Title 26 U.S.C., until three months after the decision is rendered. This is correct. It is not disputed in this case that the decision of the Tax Court was rendered on December 10, 1962, which would mean that it would not become final until March 10, 1963. In the meantime it may be presumed that proceedings can be brought in the Tax Court to set aside the stipulation on the grounds hereinabove mentioned, or that a petition to review can be sought.

The Government objects to the issuance of any injunction on the ground that Section 7421 of Title 26 U.S.C., provides that no suit for the purpose of restraining the assessment or collection of any tax shall be maintained in any court. This section of the statute, however, specifically provides:

> "Except as provided in sections 6212(a) and (c), and 6213(a), * * * no suit for the purpose of restraining the assessment or collection of any tax shall be maintained in any court."

Therefore, one of the excepted situations is that contained in Section 6213(a). This section, which is the one restricting collection activities until the decision of the Tax Court has become final, also provides in part:

> "Notwithstanding the provisions of section 7421(a), the making of such assessment or the beginning of such proceeding or levy during the time such prohibition is in force may be enjoined by a proceeding in the proper court."

Reading these sections together it becomes obvious that Congress intended that no levy or proceeding in court for the collection of tax shall be made, begun or prosecuted until after the decision of the Tax Court has become final, and that until that time has expired the beginning of such tax collection proceedings or the making of a levy may be enjoined by a proceeding in the proper court. This is the proper court. If the well established rule prohibiting the courts from enjoining tax collections was applicable to this situation Congress would not have put the exception in Section 6213(a). Congress obviously intended that until the Tax Court decision had become final the collection authorities would not begin collection activities or making levies to collect the tax, and that if they did they could be enjoined.

The Government contends in this case that the stipulation on which the decision was entered specifically waived any restrictions contained in the Internal Revenue laws regarding the assessment and collection of the tax deficiencies. However, the very validity of the stipulation itself is in question. In order to sustain its position the Government must show that the stipulation was a valid stipulation, and this is the issue which may still have to be determined by the Tax Court. Until this is done the decision of the Tax Court has not become final and any collection activities or levy must be restrained.

The motion for a preliminary injunction is granted. Submit interlocutory decree in accordance herewith.

So ordered.

UNITED STATES v. TETI

36 AFTR 2d 75–5762 (D.Conn.1975).

NEWMAN, District Judge:

MEMORANDUM OF DECISION

In this tax lien-foreclosure action the Government seeks judgment against defendant Harold T. Teti, individually, in the amount of $26,775.48, plus accrued, unassessed interest, and against defendants Harold T. Teti and Ann B. Teti, individually and jointly, in the additional amount of $15,519.13, plus accrued, unassessed interest. The Government also requests that the Court order the sale of certain real property at 50 High Meadow Road, Hamden, for the purpose of satisfying these tax deficiencies. * * *

The amount alleged due from both Harold and Ann Teti ("Harold" and "Ann") represents a joint personal income tax deficiency for the years 1967–69. The Government's proof consisted of Internal Revenue Service Certificates of Assessments and Payments (Forms 4340), which reflected transactions on the Tetis' account for the relevant time periods.

* * *

Ann's * * * argument is that the assessment was prematurely made and therefore void. Title 26, U.S.C. § 6213(a) provides in part that no income tax deficiency assessment shall be made before ninety days have elapsed from the mailing to the taxpayer of the notice of deficiency provided for in § 6212. Section 6213(d) provides, inter alia, for the waiver of the notice and time restriction. In the present case it appears that no formal § 6212 notice was sent, probably because the I.R.S. had obtained waivers from both Tetis. The waivers are not in evidence, although defendants concede that Harold executed one. In light of the assessments' presumed validity, the defendants have the burden of putting in issue whether Ann waived § 6213's restrictions. Ann never testified that she did not execute a waiver, and the burden therefore never shifted to the Government. This alone would allow the Court to reject the claim. In any event, the parties seem agreed that the conference report provided adequate notice. The conference report was dated October, 1971, and the assessments were made on November 26, 1971, within the prohibited ninety-day period. They urge that this conflict with the terms of § 6213 renders the assessments void and deprives the Government of the right to use the certificates of assessment as evidence of Ann's 1040 liability.

Defendants misconstrue the purpose of § 6213. Congress intended, by establishing the ninety-day period during which no assessment may be made, to provide the taxpayer with the opportunity to seek redetermination of the claimed deficiency in the Tax Court, see Lehigh Portland Cement Co. v. United States, 30 F.Supp. 217 (Ct.Cl. 1939), and perhaps to allow the taxpayer time to arrange payment, see Bromberg v. Ingling, 300 F.2d 859 (9th Cir. 1962). See also, Lyddon & Co. v. United States, 158 F.Supp. 951 (Ct.Cl.1958). The Tetis sought neither Tax Court relief nor an injunction against enforcement of the assessment pending such review,[7] and the assessment, while originally premature, became valid and enforceable some time in February, 1972, at the expiration of the ninety-day period. Lyddon & Co. v. United States, supra; Lehigh Portland Cement Co. v. United States, supra. But see Bromberg v. Ingling, supra.

The wording of the statute is also inconsistent with the contention that a premature assessment is void. Section 6213 provides that "the beginning of such [enforcement] proceeding * * * • *during the time such prohibition is in force* may be enjoined by a proceeding in the proper court." [Emphasis added.] The limiting language, underscored in the preceding excerpt, would have been entirely unnecessary if Congress had intended that a premature assessment be void.

* * *

* * * The Government will serve and submit, within twenty days, an appropriate form of judgment ordering sale of the High Meadow Road property and distribution of the proceeds in a manner consistent with the Court's conclusions.

NOTE

Many of the cases involving failure of the Service to comply with the deficiency notice requirements are based upon the allegedly erroneous mailing address used by the Service on the 90-day letter. The issue of the validity of the mailing of a deficiency notice can arise in the context of an action to enjoin collection or in the context of a Tax Court motion for dismissal due to lack of jurisdiction. See page 249, above. In those relatively rare cases in which the Service simply issues no deficiency notice, an injunction against collection will be granted if a deficiency notice was in fact required.

7. Failure to take advantage of the remedies provided by § 6213(a) may amount to laches, and may preclude assertion of any claim based on that section. Compare Ventura Consolidated Oil Fields v. Rogan, 86 F.2d 149, 156 (9th Cir. 1936).

C. WRONGFUL LEVY

WHAT CAN A TAXPAYER DO WHEN A CASE HAS BEEN TURNED OVER FOR COLLECTION: ADMINISTRATIVE AND LEGAL REMEDIES: POWERS OF THE AGENT

Marvin J. Garbis
29 N.Y.U. Institute on Federal Taxation 909 (1971).

*   *   *

Third Party Remedies for Wrongful Levy

On occasion, the power to levy and sell property is incorrectly used, typically by virtue of an identification error, and occasionally by virtue of a Revenue Officer's determination to levy and "protect the Revenue." Despite a possibility that the property or rights to property seized may not be those of the delinquent taxpayer, a Revenue Officer will sometimes levy upon the assets of others which are not properly subject to levy. The injured party, not a delinquent taxpayer, who has seen his property (or what he contends to be his property) taken and advertised for sale (or, perhaps even sold) does have substantial legal rights under the Internal Revenue Code as amended by the Federal Tax Lien Act of 1966.

Action for Injunction and/or Damages

Under the Code any person (other than the delinquent taxpayer) claiming an interest in, or lien on, property levied upon or sold pursuant to a tax levy has the right to bring an action in a United States District Court for relief. The plaintiff in such an action can seek to establish that there was a wrongful levy,[62] that his interest or lien, although junior to the tax lien, entitles him to the surplus proceeds of the tax sale,[63] or that he is entitled to all or part of the proceeds of a sale of property which have, by agreement [64] been substituted for the sold property.[65] If the third party plaintiff files suit prior to sale he may obtain an injunction prohibiting sale or enforcement of the levy.[66] In addition, the court may order the Internal Revenue Service to return the specific property to him.[67]

To the extent appropriate, the court may award the plaintiff a money judgment against the United States of America in an amount equal to:

(a) The amount of any money levied upon,[68]

62. I.R.C. § 7426(a)(1).

63. I.R.C. § 7426(a)(2).

64. I.R.C. § 6325(b)(3).

65. I.R.C. § 7426(a)(3).

66. I.R.C. § 7426(b)(1).

67. I.R.C. § 7426(b)(2)(A).

68. I.R.C. § 7426(b)(2)(B).

(b) An amount not greater than the amount the Government received from the sale of the property,[69]

(c) All or part of the amount of any surplus proceeds of the sale of the seized property [70] or

(d) All or part of the amount of any fund which has by agreement been substituted for the property levied upon.[71]

Any such money judgment will bear interest at the rate [established under § 6621] from the date the Government took possession in the case of a levy upon money, or from the date of the sale of property in the case of a sale.[72]

Statutes of Limitation

The third party who seeks to protect his rights in the case of a levy must act within a relatively short limitations period. He must file his suit after the levy or agreement for substitution of proceeds in question but not later than nine months after such levy or agreement.[73] The period for suit is extended if, within the nine month period, an administrative request for relief (analogous to a claim for refund) is filed.

If a timely administrative request is filed, the period for filing suit will be extended to the earlier of 12 months after the filing of the administrative request or 6 months after formal notice of disallowance of the request.[74] The action must be filed against the United States of America and not any employee or officer thereof.[75] Venue for the action lies in the judicial district in which the property was situated at the time of levy or (in the absence of a levy) in the district in which occurred the event giving rise to the cause of action.[76]

* * *

AMERICAN PAC. INV. CORP. v. NASH

342 F.Supp. 797 (D.N.J.1972).

CLARKSON S. FISHER, District Judge.

American Pacific Investment Corporation (APIC), a mortgagee in possession of the property owned by its mortgagor, Carlson's Point Pleasant Fisheries, Inc., has filed suit to enjoin the Internal Revenue Service, Roland Nash Jr., District Director, from interfering with its conduct of the business of the mortgaged property. The fear of interference is the result of the presence of tax liens filed by the Inter-

69. I.R.C. § 7426(b)(2)(C).

70. I.R.C. § 7426(b)(3).

71. I.R.C. § 7426(b)(4).

72. I.R.C. § 7426(g).

73. I.R.C. § 6532(c)(1).

74. I.R.C. §§ 6532(c)(2), 6342, 6343.

75. I.R.C. § 7426(d).

76. 28 U.S.C. § 1402(c).

nal Revenue Service against the Fisheries plant on April 12, 1971 and October 15, 1971 in conjunction with alleged threats by the IRS Officer in charge of the nearby Toms River Office to close down the Fishery. The Government has moved to dismiss the suit citing 26 U.S.C. § 7421(a), a statute prohibiting suits to restrain the assessment or collection of any tax, as authority. It is only the motion to dismiss which is presently before this Court.

Plaintiff, APIC, argues that its lien is senior to that of the Government and that by levying against the Fisheries the Government would be, in essence, taxing their interests in order to satisfy the liability of APIC's mortgagor. This, plaintiff contends, would be a wrongful levy.

Numerous cases have held that both 26 U.S.C. § 7421 and its predecessor 26 U.S.C. § 3653 do not prohibit judicial interposition to prevent a collector for taking the property of one person to satisfy the tax obligation of another. E. g., Logan Planing Mill Co. v. Fidelity and Casualty Co. of N. Y., 212 F.Supp. 906 (D.W.Va.1962). As was stated by the Court in *Logan,* supra, the cases support the position that the purpose of Section 7421 is to prevent suits by a taxpayer to contest the taxability and bar collection of the tax asserted; but that the prohibitions of Section 7421 have no applicability to suits to protect the property of a non-taxpayer which the government has seized to satisfy a taxpayer's liability.

This exception to the prohibitions of Section 7421 was codified by Congress as Section 7426(a)(1) and (b)(1) of Title 26 [2] in 1966, as part of the Federal Tax Lien Act of 1966. Thus, now, by statute, a non-taxpayer can sue in Federal Court to prevent his property from being levied upon to satisfy the tax liabilities of another.

The Government argues that plaintiff is seeking an injunction prematurely and thus does not fit within this exception to Section 7421. Section 7426(a)(1) permits actions where a levy "has been made", not one in the future. However, plaintiff points to Section

---

2. 26 U.S.C. 7426(a)(1)—
"WRONGFUL LEVY—If a levy has been made on property or property has been sold pursuant to a levy, any person (other than the person against whom is assessed the tax out of which such levy arose) who claims an interest in or lien on such property and that such property was wrongfully levied upon may bring a civil action against the United States in a district court of the United States. Such action may be brought without regard to whether such property has been surrendered to or sold by the Secretary or his delegate.
* * *

"(b) Adjudication—The district court shall have jurisdiction to grant only such of the following forms of relief as may be appropriate in the circumstances:
"(1) Injunction—If a levy or sale would irreparably injure rights in property which the court determines to be superior to rights of the United States in such property, the court may grant an injunction to prohibit the enforcement of such levy or to prohibit such sale."
* * *

7426(b)(1) which grants a District Court jurisdiction to issue an injunction where a levy "would irreparably injure rights in property * * * ", suggesting the ability of the Court to prevent a levy at the outset. Plaintiff further argues that to require physical seizure of plaintiff's property before the statute may be invoked requires plaintiff to suffer the very injury from which the legislation was designed to save him.

However sensible the plaintiff's position may be, a strict reading of the statute and its legislative history requires that the suit be dismissed until such time as an actual levy is made.

Section 7426(b)(1) allows a Court to "grant an injunction to prohibit the enforcement of such (wrongful) levy." This clause implies that the Court can act only once a levy is in existence. It can prevent the enforcement of a levy, not the institution of one. The Statute is not authority for the Court to act upon a threatened levy, only upon one in existence and it is clear that a threatened levy does not constitute an actual levy. Freeman v. Mayer, 152 F.Supp. 383 (D.N.J.1957).[4]

A view at the statute's legislative history, as is required when construing a federal taxing statute, further convinces me of the necessity for an actual levy. In Mertons' Law of Federal Income Taxation, the Editors cite from House Report No. 1704, 89th Congress, 2nd Session, p. 74 and say:

"The action may be brought without regard to whether the property has been surrendered to or sold by the Government but it may not be brought before the levy is made by the Government." Ch. 54 at p. 339.

As there is presently no jurisdiction in this Court the suit will be dismissed without prejudice to the plaintiffs right to renew the action if and when a levy has been made and it is so ordered.

NOTE

In United Pac. Ins. Co. v. United States, 320 F.Supp. 450 (D.Or.1970), it was held that a notice of lien entitled "Tax Levy" was in fact the equivalent of a levy for purposes of invoking jurisdiction under § 7426.

---

4. Judge Modarelli said, "A 'levy' requires that property be brought into legal custody through seizure, actual or constructive, levy being an absolute appropriation in law of the property levied on, and mere notice of intent to levy is insufficient (to constitute a levy)."

26 U.S.C. § 7701(a)(21) defines levy as including "the power of distraint and seizure by any means". Some actual action, not threatened action, is necessary for levy.

SHANNON v. UNITED STATES

521 F.2d 56 (9th Cir. 1975).

EUGENE A. WRIGHT, Circuit Judge.

The government appeals from two orders by which the district court (1) denied the defendant's motion to dismiss for lack of jurisdiction and (2) granted a preliminary injunction against the Internal Revenue Service (IRS) enjoining the enforcement of a levy against Shannon's assets. * * *

FACTS

On August 1, 1973 a jeopardy assessment was made against C. Arnholt Smith for over $22.8 million for unpaid 1969 income taxes. On October 3 of that year a notice of levy was served upon Carol Smith Shannon, appellee, as the alleged nominee, agent, or transferee of Mr. Smith.

The notice of levy for approximately $23.3 million sought to attach all of Smith's interest in $478,366.35 allegedly withdrawn by Shannon from an account in the United California Bank about August 3, 1973.

About October 19, 1973, pursuant to 26 U.S.C. §§ 6861(a) and 6901, a jeopardy transferee assessment was made against Shannon for over $2.6 million, a notice of levy was served and a lien filed against Shannon's property in the county recorder's office. The amount of the transferee assessment was later reduced to $630,635.90 and on December 11 a statutory notice of deficiency in the amount of the transferee assessment was issued to Shannon.

She then sought an injunction against the enforcement of the levy and other relief. The United States, appellant, moved for dismissal. The district court denied the motion to dismiss and granted the preliminary injunction pending a determination of the action on its merits.

ISSUES

(1) Did the district court have jurisdiction under 28 U.S.C. § 1346(e)?

* * *

DISCUSSION

The provisions of 26 U.S.C. § 7421 provide the backdrop against which both issues must be discussed.[3] Section 7421 not only prohib-

---

3. Applicable portions of § 7421 provide:

"(a) *Tax.*—Except as provided in section * * * 7426(a) and (b)(1), * * * no suit for the purpose of restraining the assessment or collection of any tax shall be maintained in any court by any person, whether or not such person is the person against whom such tax was assessed.

its suits to restrain the assessment or collection of a tax, but also prevents the district court from granting such equitable relief. Unless one seeking to enjoin the IRS brings herself within a statutory or judicially-created exception to § 7421, the district court has no jurisdiction and the suit for injunction is barred.

The district court based jurisdiction on 28 U.S.C. § 1346(e), the jurisdictional counterpart of U.S.C. § 7426. Applicable provisions of § 7426 give a civil action against the United States to third persons whose assets have been wrongfully levied against by the IRS.

Shannon argues that despite being assessed as a transferee she comes within the provisions of § 7426 and the district court thus has jurisdiction under § 1346(e). She reasons that: the prohibition of § 7421(b)(1) applies only to an actual transferee; the IRS was wrong in assessing her as such and the district court should therefore find that she is not a transferee; and once found not to be a transferee the injunction should be granted under § 7421(a) with its § 7426 exception.

The fatal flaw in this analysis is that it fails to take into account the literal language of § 7426. Clearly, the section was not intended for those assessed as transferees.

First, the § 7426 remedies are denied to "the person against whom is assessed the tax out of which such levy arose." The undeniable fact is that the October 19 jeopardy transferee assessment was made against Shannon herself. That assessment is the one out of which the levy arose.

Shannon argues that it is Smith, not she, contemplated by § 7426 when it speaks of "the person against whom is assessed the tax * * * *" This may have been true at the time of the first levy (October 3).[7] It certainly was not true of the second (October 23), made after she was assessed in her own right as a transferee. One who has been assessed as a transferee cannot argue that the assessment was not made against her.

Second, one who sues under § 7426 cannot challenge the validity of the assessment. 26 U.S.C. § 7426(c). Shannon sought to enjoin the levy as wrongful under § 7426 because she was "not the trans-

---

"(b) *Liability of transferee* * * * *—No suit shall be maintained in any court for the purpose of restraining the assessment or collection * * * of—

    (1) the amount of the liability, at law or in equity, of a transferee of property of a taxpayer in respect of any internal revenue tax * * * *."

7. We do not decide whether Shannon could have brought her § 7426 action at that time. Shannon argues that she could have and assuming that fact, argues that the IRS should not be allowed to destroy the § 7426 remedies by "utilizing the mechanical * * * provisions of § 6901." This ignores the fact the section was intended for the relatively "remedy-less" third person, not for transferees who have the same remedies as tax-payers.

feree of C. Arnholt Smith," i. e., she had been improperly assessed as such. She was thus challenging the validity of the transferee assessment which is foreclosed by § 7426(c).

Finally, legislative history indicates that it was not the intent of Congress to make § 7426 available to persons assessed as transferees.

Our decision does not leave Shannon without a remedy. On the contrary, a transferee has available the same avenues as a taxpayer who seeks judicial review to challenge the government's collection efforts against him. She may bring a refund suit in district court or a petition to the Tax Court for a redetermination of the deficiency. Philips v. Commissioner, 283 U.S. 589, 597–598, 51 S.Ct. 608, 75 L.Ed. 1289 (1931).

Having decided that § 7426 is not available to a transferee, we conclude that the district court did not have jurisdiction under § 1346(e).

* * *

* * * The order granting the preliminary injunction is reversed and the cause is remanded to the district court to dismiss the complaint for want of jurisdiction.

NOTE

A spouse who signs a joint return with respect to which a tax liability is asserted is not a third-party within the meaning of § 7426 and cannot enjoin the Service from collecting upon separately owned property. Moreover, the innocent spouse provision of § 6013(e) provides no independent source of jurisdiction for such action. Kirtley v. Bickerstaff, 488 F.2d 768 (10th Cir. 1973), cert. denied, 419 U.S. 828, 95 S.Ct. 47, 42 L.Ed.2d 52 (1974).

SECTION 8. BANKRUPTCY

Bankruptcy proceedings started after September 30, 1979 are governed by the provisions of the Bankruptcy Reform Act of 1978, P.L. 95–598 (commonly referred to as the Bankruptcy Code) and the Bankruptcy Tax Act of 1980, P.L. 96–589 (which is intended to coordinate the provisions of the Internal Revenue Code of 1954 with those of the new Bankruptcy Code).

Automatic Stay of Assessment and Collection Activity. The Bankruptcy Code provides for an automatic stay of the assessment and/or collection of any taxes owed by the debtor.[x] It prohibits the commencement or continuation of both judicial and administrative proceedings (including collection activities) against the debtor or with respect to property of the debtor.[y] The Bankruptcy Code does

---

x. 11 U.S.C.A. § 362(a)(6).   **y.** 11 U.S.C.A. § 362(a)(1)–(a)(5).

not, however, stay the commencement or continuation of any criminal proceedings,[z] or any proceedings over which the Bankruptcy Court has jurisdiction. Nor does the Bankruptcy Code prohibit the issuance of a notice of deficiency.[a]

The running of the limitations period for the assessment and collection of tax is suspended for the time during which the stay is in effect, plus (i) for assessments, 60 days thereafter, and (ii) for collection, 6 months thereafter.[b] This rule provides the IRS adequate time to collect nondischargeable taxes following the end of Title 11 proceedings.

Judicial Resolution of Tax Claims During Bankruptcy. Once bankruptcy proceedings have been instituted, the Bankruptcy Court has jurisdiction over any new tax claim arising against the individual debtor or the bankruptcy estate involving unpaid taxes, fines, penalties or additions to tax, whether or not previously assessed,[c] and upon a determination by the Bankruptcy Court, the Service may assess the tax immediately.[d] The Bankruptcy Court will not have jurisdiction to rule on the merits of any tax claim which has been previously adjudicated in a contested proceeding before a court of competent jurisdiction.[e] For this purpose, a proceeding in the Tax Court is to be considered "contested" if the debtor filed a petition in the Tax Court and the IRS answered the petition by the time of the commencement of the bankruptcy case. The Bankruptcy Court can, under certain conditions, determine the amount of a tax refund claim by the trustee. If the refund results from an offset or counterclaim to a claim or request for payment by the IRS, the trustee would not first have to file an administrative claim for refund with the Service. However, if the trustee requests a refund in other situations, he would first have to submit an administrative claim for the refund. If the IRS does not rule on the refund claim within 120 days (rather than the usual six months), then the Bankruptcy Court may rule on the merits of the refund claim.[f]

If there is no proceeding pending in the Tax Court at the time the bankruptcy petition is filed, the Service has two procedural options in asserting a pre-petition deficiency. It may file a claim against the bankruptcy estate,[g] in which case the claim will be adjudicated in Bankruptcy Court and the taxpayer will not be allowed to petition the Tax Court. If the Service fails to present the claim to the Bankruptcy Court, the debtor or trustee may enter the claim. Note, however, that jurisdiction in the Bankruptcy Court is discretion-

z. 11 U.S.C.A. § 362(b)(1).

a. 11 U.S.C.A. § 362(b)(8).

b. IRC § 6503(i); 11 U.S.C.A. § 108(c).

c. 11 U.S.C.A. § 505(a)(1).

d. 11 U.S.C.A. § 505(c); IRC § 6871(b).

e. 11 U.S.C.A. § 505(a)(2)(A).

f. 11 U.S.C.A. § 505(a)(2)(B).

g. IRC § 6871(c)(1).

ary with respect to the tax issues.[h]   Alternatively, the Service may follow regular procedures by issuing a notice of deficiency. Since the Bankruptcy Code imposes an automatic stay, the taxpayer may not petition the Tax Court for a redetermination of the deficiency until the stay is lifted, a discharge is granted or denied, or the bankruptcy proceeding terminates.[i]   (The stay also applies if a deficiency notice which had been issued prior to the bankruptcy proceeding had not yet been petitioned to the Tax Court, and the time for filing a petition had not expired at the commencement of the bankruptcy case.) If the stay is lifted, the taxpayer may then file a petition in the Tax Court.[j]

Where a proceeding is pending in the Tax Court at the time the bankruptcy petition is filed, further action is stayed unless the stay is lifted by order of the Bankruptcy Court. The stay may be lifted at the request of the trustee, who may wish to intervene in the Tax Court action on behalf of the bankruptcy estate,[k] or at the request of either the individual debtor or the Service, in which case the decision of the Tax Court will be res judicata for purposes of the bankruptcy action. If the stay is not lifted, the Tax Court will determine the debtor's liability for any nondischargeable taxes at the close of the bankruptcy proceeding.

Provisions for Accelerating Determination of the Tax Liability of the Bankruptcy Estate. The Bankruptcy Code accelerates the procedures for determining the bankruptcy estate's tax liability so that the trustee may distribute expeditiously the assets of the estate. The trustee may request a prompt determination of the estate's liability for any tax incurred during the administration of the estate by submitting a tax return and a request for a determination of the tax.[l] The IRS must notify the trustee within sixty days after the request if it intends to audit any return filed by the trustee with respect to the estate's tax liability.[m] Furthermore, the examination must be completed and the trustee notified of any tax deficiency within 180 days of the request for determination.[n] If the Service fails either to notify the trustee of its intention to audit, or to complete the audit, within the required time, the trustee, the debtor, and any successor to the

---

h. 28 U.S.C.A. § 1471(d).

i. 11 U.S.C.A. § 362(c)–(f).

j. IRC § 6213(f) provides that the running of the normal 90 or 150 day period for filing a petition in the Tax Court under § 6213(a) is suspended during the period the bankruptcy stay is in effect and for 60 days thereafter. Note, also, that the Bankruptcy Tax Act of 1980 amended IRC § 6871 to delete language which previously had prevented taxpayers from

filing Tax Court petitions during the pendency of bankruptcy proceedings.

k. Pursuant to IRC § 7464, added to the Code by the Bankruptcy Tax Act of 1980.

l. 11 U.S.C.A. § 505(b).

m. 11 U.S.C.A. § 505(b)(1)(A).

n. 11 U.S.C.A. § 505(b)(1)(B).

debtor are discharged from any liability for the tax upon payment of the amount shown due on the return (unless the return filed by the trustee was materially false or fraudulent).[o] Otherwise, the trustee and the debtor receive such a discharge upon payment of the tax as determined by the Bankruptcy Court after notice and a hearing on the correctness of the determination made by the Service.[p]

As noted above, if the trustee files a claim for refund he need wait only 120 days for IRS approval or disapproval of the claim before submitting the claim for refund for adjudication by the Bankruptcy Court.

Priorities of Tax Claims in Bankruptcy. Tax liabilities incurred during the administration of the bankruptcy estate are given first priority, along with other expenses of administration.[q] The bulk of the remaining federal, state and local tax liabilities are accorded sixth level priority behind administrative expenses, wages, contributions to employee bnfit plans, and certain narrowly defined unsecured claims.[r] The sixth level priority claims include:

1. Income taxes for which the due date of the return, including any extensions, occurred within three years preceding the filing of the bankruptcy petition.[s]

2. Income taxes assessed within 240 days preceding the filing of the petition, except that a submission of an offer in compromise for payment of the assessed amount may toll the running of the 240-day period.[t]

3. Income taxes not assessed prior to the filing of the bankruptcy petition, but which may be assessed under applicable law or by agreement after the commencement of the case.[u]

4. Taxes required to be collected or withheld and for which the debtor is liable in any capacity.[v] This would include taxes for which the debtor is liable as an employer, as a responsible person under § 6672 of the Code, or as a lender or provider of wages under § 3505 of the Code.

5. The employer's share of employment taxes for returns due within three years preceding the filing of the petition.[w]

6. Excise taxes for returns due or transactions occurring within three years preceding the filing of the petition.[x]

Discharge of Tax Liabilities. The Bankruptcy Code provides that no individual debtor shall be discharged from any of the taxes

o. 11 U.S.C.A. § 505(b)(1).

p. 11 U.S.C.A. § 505(b)(2).

q. 11 U.S.C.A. § 507(a)(1).

r. See generally 11 U.S.C.A. § 507(a).

s. 11 U.S.C.A. § 507(a)(6)(A)(i).

t. 11 U.S.C.A. § 507(a)(6)(A)(ii).

u. 11 U.S.C.A. § 507(a)(6)(A)(iii).

v. 11 U.S.C.A. § 507(a)(6)(C).

w. 11 U.S.C.A. § 507(a)(6)(D).

x. 11 U.S.C.A. § 507(a)(6)(E).

accorded sixth level priority under section 507.[y]   Also excepted from discharge are taxes from any period in which the debtor willfully attempted to evade or defeat tax, subscribed to a false return, or failed to file a return.[z]   Penalties which are punitive in nature and which relate to a nondischargeable tax liability are similarly excepted from discharge.[a]

A plan of reorganization under Chapter 13 of the Bankruptcy Code (Adjustment of Debts of an Individual with Regular Income) must provide for full payment of all § 507 priority debts.[b] Thus, tax liabilities incurred within the three years preceding the petition generally may not be discharged in any bankruptcy proceeding.[c]

Tax Liens and Bankruptcy. As a general rule, taxes will be accorded their sixth level priority in liquidation proceedings regardless of whether the government perfects its tax lien by filing. Payment of the debt secured by a perfected tax lien is effectively postponed until the first through fifth priorities have been satisfied, without prejudice to other parties having an interest in the assets.[d] Thus, perfecting a tax lien would merely give the tax lien priority over other sixth level claims.

A tax lien which has not been perfected by filing prior to bankruptcy may be voidable, under certain circumstances, by the trustee.[e] It is, however, merely the lien which may be extinguished, and not the underlying tax liability. The liability would remain as an unsecured claim which would be entitled to general sixth level priority.

Miscellaneous Provisions of the Bankruptcy Tax Act of 1980. The Bankruptcy Tax Act of 1980 is concerned with the application of the internal revenue laws to bankruptcy and insolvency proceedings. The Act sets forth the permissible means of accounting for any discharged debt.[f] The Act also gives an individual debtor the option of terminating his or her taxable year on the day before Chapter 7 or 11 proceedings are filed.[g] The debtor's taxable year can thus be split into two "short" taxable years, with the tax liability for the first period becoming an allowable claim against the bankruptcy estate. If this election is made, the debtor is required to annualize his or her taxable income in accordance with IRC § 1398(d)(2)(F). This election is not available to a debtor filing under Chapter 13.

---

y. 11 U.S.C.A. § 523(a)(1)(A).

z. 11 U.S.C.A. § 523(a)(1)(B) and (C).

a. 11 U.S.C.A. § 523(a)(7).

b. 11 U.S.C.A. § 1322(a)(2).

c. Note, however, that the section 523 exceptions from discharge do not apply to a discharge under § 1328(a) of the Bankruptcy Code. Thus, under 11 U.S.C.A. § 1328(a), a Chapter 13 debtor will receive a discharge "as soon as practicable after completion * * * of all payments under the plan" for taxes and penalties, even if incurred in connection with the filing of fraudulent returns or the failure to file returns.

d. 11 U.S.C.A. § 724(b).

e. 11 U.S.C.A. § 544(a)(1).

f. See IRC § 108.

g. IRC § 1398(d).

APPENDIX A

FORMAL OPINION 346
of the American Bar Association
Standing Committee on Ethics and
Professional Reponsibility

Tax Law Opinions in Tax Shelter Investment Offerings
June 1, 1981

67 A.B.A.J. 1057 (1981) *

An opinion by an expert tax attorney analyzing the tax effects of a tax shelter investment is frequently of critical importance in a tax shelter offering.[1] The promoter of the offering may depend upon the recommendations of the tax lawyer on structuring the venture and often publishes the opinion in the offering circular as a marketing device. The offerees may be expected to rely upon the tax shelter tax opinion in determining whether to invest in the venture. It is often uneconomic for the individual offeree to pay for a separate tax analysis of the offering because of the relatively small sum each offeree may invest.[2]

In response to mass marketing of tax shelter investments over the past decade, regulatory agencies and Congress have sought to eliminate what is termed the "abusive tax shelter." An abusive tax shelter has been described by the general counsel of the Treasury Department as "a transaction without any economic purpose other than the generation of tax benefits that typically employs exaggerated valuation of assets and otherwise mischaracterizes critical aspects of the transaction."

Because the successful marketing of tax shelters frequently involves tax opinions issued by lawyers, concerns have been expressed by the organized bar, regulatory agencies, and others over the need to articulate ethical standards applicable to a lawyer who prepares an opinion letter which the lawyer knows will be included among the tax shelter offering materials and relied upon by offerees.[4] Among

---

* Reprinted with permission from the American Bar Association Journal.

1. A "tax shelter" is an investment that succeeds in generating a mismatching of income and deductions to reduce or defer taxable income. Through the use of tax credits, non-cash deductions, the expenditures of borrowed money, and sometimes by recharacterizing ordinary income to long-term capital gain, the current tax burden is diminished.

2. In the event the tax consequences prove less favorable than those set out in a tax shelter tax opinion, claims may be made by offerees against the lawyer for negligence or for violating federal or state securities laws. The civil liability incurred by a lawyer who writes a tax shelter tax opinion is beyond the scope of an ethics opinion.

4. The Treasury Department proposed a rule which would require lawyers

the responsibilities of this committee is the responsibility to express its opinion on proper professional conduct of lawyers and to do so by a formal opinion where the subject is of widespread interest. Accordingly, the committee expresses its opinion as to the ethical standards applicable to lawyers who issue tax shelter tax opinions.[5]

The concerns have been directed at three types of tax shelter tax opinions: (1) the *false opinion,* which ignores or minimizes serious legal risks or misstates facts or the law, knowingly or through gross incompetence; (2) the *assumed facts opinion* which does not speak to the actual facts, either by disclaiming knowledge of the accuracy of the facts, by discussing legal issues without relating the law to the facts, by failing to analyze the critical facts, or by discussing purely hypothetical facts; and (3) the *reasonable basis opinion* which points out that there is reasonable basis for claiming certain tax benefits but fails to express an opinion of a likelihood that the promoted tax benefits will be sustained by a court if attacked by the Internal Revenue Service.

The lawyer who gives a false opinion, including one which is intentionally or recklessly misleading, commits serious violations of the disciplinary rules of the Model Code of Professional Responsibility. Quite clearly, the lawyer exceeds the duty to represent the client zealously within the bounds of the law. See D.R. 7–101; E.C. 7–10. Knowingly misstating facts or law violates D.R. 7–102(A)(5) and is "conduct involving dishonesty, fraud, deceit, or misrepresentation," a violation of D.R. 1–102(A)(4). The lawyer also violates D.R. 7–102(A) by counseling or assisting the offeror "in conduct that the lawyer knows to be illegal or fraudulent." In addition, the lawyer's conduct may involve the concealment or knowing nondisclosure of matters which the lawyer is required by law to reveal, a violation of D.R. 7–102 (A)(3).

The lawyer who accepts as true the facts which the promoter tells him, when the lawyer knows that a further inquiry would likely disclose that these facts are untrue, also gives a false opinion. It has been said that lawyers cannot "escape criminal liability on a plea of ignorance when they have shut their eyes to what was plainly to be seen." United States v. Benjamin, 328 F.2d 854, 863 (2d Cir. 1964).

who provide tax opinions to comply with standards of due diligence, disclosure, and judgmental determinations. Proposed rule adding a new regulation § 10.33 and amending Regulations §§ 10.51 and 10.52, relating to standards for providing opinions regarding tax shelters. 45 Fed.Reg. 58,594 (1980).

5. The standards developed here would apply to any tax opinion issued with the intention that the opinion be relied upon by taxpayers other than the client who engages the lawyer to issue the opinion. These standards, however, would not necessarily apply to tax opinions where the investors other than the immediate client will rely upon their own tax counsel to make a thorough investigation and to advise them.

Recklessly and consciously disregarding information strongly indicating that material facts expressed in the tax opinion are false or misleading involves dishonesty as does assisting the offeror in conduct the lawyer knows to be fraudulent. Such conduct violates D.R. 1–102 (A)(4) and D.R. 7–102(A). We equate the minimum extent of the knowledge required for the lawyer's conduct to have violated these disciplinary rules with the knowledge required to sustain a Rule 10b–5 recovery, see Ernst & Ernst v. Hochfelder, 425 U.S. 185 (1976), rather than the lesser negligence standard required to sustain a cause of action under Section 17(a) of the Securities Act.

But even if the lawyer lacks the knowledge required to sustain a Rule 10b–5 recovery, the lawyer's conduct nevertheless may involve gross incompetence, or indifference, inadequate preparation under the circumstances, and consistent failure to perform obligations to the client. If so, the lawyer will have violated D.R. 6–101(A).

The lawyer who issues a tax shelter tax opinion also should follow the axiomatic norms in the canons and the ethical considerations of the model code.[7] A.B.A. Formal Opinion 335 (1974) establishes guidelines which a lawyer should follow when furnishing an assumed facts opinion in connection with the sale of unregistered securities. The same guidelines describe the extent to which a lawyer should verify the facts presented to him as the basis for a tax shelter tax opinion:

> "[T]he lawyer should, in the first instance, make inquiry of his client as to the relevant facts and receive answers. If any of the alleged facts, or the alleged facts taken as a whole, are incomplete in a material respect; or are suspect; or are inconsistent; or either on their face or on the basis of other known facts are open to question, the lawyer should make further inquiry. The extent of this inquiry will depend in each case upon the circumstances; for example, it would be less where the lawyer's past relationship with the client is sufficient to give him a basis for trusting the client's probity than where the client has recently engaged the lawyer, and less where the lawyer's inquiries are answered fully than when there appears a reluctance to disclose information.

> "Where the lawyer concludes that further inquiry of a reasonable nature would not give him sufficient confidence as to all the relevant facts, or for any other reason he does not make the appropriate further inquiries, he should refuse to give an opinion. However, assuming that the alleged facts are not incomplete in a material respect, or suspect, or in any way inherently inconsistent, or on their face or on the basis of other known facts open to question, the lawyer may prop-

---

7. Canon 1 says "[a] lawyer should assist in maintaining the integrity and competence of the legal profession." Canon 6 says "[a] lawyer should represent a client competently." * * *

erly assume that the facts as related to him by his client, and checked by him by reviewing such appropriate documents as are available, are accurate.

* * *

"The essence of this opinion   *   *   *   is that, while a lawyer should make adequate preparation including inquiry into the relevant facts that is consistent with the above guidelines, and while he should not accept as true that which he should not reasonably believe to be true, he does not have the responsibility to 'audit' the affairs of his client or to assume, without reasonable cause, that a client's statement of the facts cannot be relied upon."

For instance, where essential underlying information, such as an appraisal or financial projection, makes little common sense, or where the reputation or expertise of the person who has prepared the appraisal or projection is dubious, further inquiry clearly is required. If this further inquiry reveals that the appraisal or projection is reasonably well supported and complete, the lawyer is justified in relying upon the material facts which the underlying information supports.

The lawyer also should inquire preliminarily into all relevant matters of law, even if the lawyer originally has not been asked to address some of the issues in the tax opinion.   The lawyer also should ascertain that adequate effort has been expended to comply with laws other than those which are the subject of the lawyer's tax opinion.   Tax counsel need not re-examine the conclusions of other counsel rendering opinions in other specialized areas of law, such as the exemption of the transaction or securities from registration or the validity of a patent. Tax counsel nevertheless should ascertain that competent professional advice on these and similar matters has been obtained where relevant to the offering.

In writing a tax opinion for a tax shelter offering, the lawyer also should relate the law to the facts.   Moreover, each material tax issue should be fully addressed.   Since the term "opinion" connotes a prediction of outcome if the issue is challenged and litigated, wherever possible the lawyer also should state the lawyer's opinion of the probable outcome on the merits.

However, given the complexity and lack of authority respecting many tax issues which must be addressed in the tax opinion issued for a tax shelter offering, it often is not possible for the lawyer to state an opinion that every tax issue addressed will result in a favorable outcome if litigated.   Absent clear authority, the lawyer may state that there are "substantial grounds for arguing" for a position necessitated by a phase of the contemplated operations of the venture. Nevertheless, this and similar statements should be made only if the lawyer in good faith concludes, after a careful factual and legal analysis, that a reasonable basis exists for the position taken.

It also is incumbent upon the lawyer who issues a tax shelter tax opinion, especially an opinion which does not contain a prediction of a favorable outcome, to assure that the offerees, who can be expected to rely on the opinion, will not be misled. The prospectus or offering circular always should be reviewed by the lawyer to make certain that the tax risks are clearly disclosed and that the offering materials, taken as a whole, make it clear that the lawyer's opinion is not a prediction of a favorable outcome, of the tax issues concerning which no favorable prediction is made. The risks and uncertainties of the tax issues should be referred to in a summary statement at the very outset of the opinion. If the lawyer disagrees with the course of conduct the client insists upon, the lawyer may and should withdraw from the employment. See E.C. 7–8; A.B.A. Formal Opinion 335, supra.

In addition, the lawyer should not assist in a tax shelter offering unless, in the lawyer's good faith judgment, there is a reasonable likelihood that the major tax consequences used to promote the venture would be resolved in favor of the taxpayer, if litigated. This admonition would apply, for instance, where there is not a reasonable likelihood that the venture would be treated as the owner for tax purposes of property that is the subject of a sale-leaseback transaction, if this ownership is the foundation of the tax sheltering effect. The lawyer should never participate in the offering if a prerequisite to obtaining the tax benefits is nondiscovery of the arrangement and should not issue an opinion solely for the purpose of assisting in avoiding penalties which might be imposed absent an opinion.

E.C. 7–22 says "a litigant or his lawyer may, in good faith and within the framework of the law, take steps to test the correctness of a ruling of a tribunal." See also E.C. 7–25. Principles similar to these are applied where the lawyer represents a client in adversarial proceedings before the Internal Revenue Service. The lawyer has a duty not to mislead the service by any misstatement, not to further any misrepresentations made by the client, and to deal candidly and fairly. A.B.A. Formal Opinion 314 (1965).

However, the lawyer rendering a tax shelter tax opinion which he knows will be relied upon by third persons functions more as an adviser than as an advocate. See E.C. 7–3, distinguishing these roles. Since the model code was adopted in 1969, the differing functions of the adviser and advocate have become more widely recognized.[10]

---

10. See * * * preamble to Discussion Draft of Model Rules of Professional Conduct (A.B.A. Commission on Evaluation of Professional Standards, January 30, 1980) at 1:

"As adviser, a lawyer should provide a client with an informed understanding of the client's legal rights and their practical implications. A lawyer's advice should include considerations of the client's legal obligations and the interests of other persons who may be affected in the circumstances. A lawyer should seek to dissuade clients from conduct wrongful to others and should not lend assistance to such purposes."

"As advocate, a lawyer should diligently assert the client's position

The proposed model rules would also specifically recognize the ethical considerations applicable where a lawyer undertakes an evalution for the use of third persons other than a client. These third persons have an interest in the integrity of the evaluation. The legal duty of the lawyer therefore "goes beyond the obligations a lawyer normally has to third persons." Model Rules, supra, Discussion Draft at 102.

Because the lawyer who issues a tax shelter tax opinion occupies an advisory role and third persons may rely on the tax advice, the principles announced in A.B.A. Formal Opinion 314 have only partial applicability. For instance, in a tax shelter tax opinion a lawyer may question the correctness of an Internal Revenue Service ruling or the reasoning in a lower court opinion. But in the opinion the lawyer should also explain his questions, should state the position the service is likely to take on the issue and an analysis of why the position is wrong, and should explain the risks of an adversarial proceeding if one is likely to occur. In the opinion, the lawyer should take a position only with honest intent to advance the objective of the taxpayer and on a basis that is reasonable and not frivolous; otherwise, the opinion lacks requisite good faith.

In the committee's view, the general ethical guidelines that a lawyer issuing a tax shelter tax opinion should follow are:

1. Establish in the beginning the lawyer's relationship with the offeror, making clear that in order to issue the opinion the lawyer requires from the client a full disclosure of the structure and intended operations of the venture and access to all relevant information.

2. Adequately investigate underlying facts to assure accuracy and completeness of the material facts.

3. Ascertain that adequate effort has been made to address important legal issues other than the tax issues addressed in the opinion.

4. Address facts that are actual and not ones that are hypothetical or unsupportable.

5. Address all material tax issues in relation to the facts.

6. Where practicable, predict the outcome of each material tax issue on the merits if challenged.

7. Be sure that the prospectus or offering circular does not misrepresent the nature or extent of the opinion.

8. Do not issue a tax shelter tax opinion unless there is reasonable likelihood that the major tax objectives used to promote the venture would, if litigated, be resolved in favor of the taxpayer.

while being honest with the tribunal and showing proper respect for the interests of opposing parties and other concerned persons."

APPENDIX B

THE ECONOMIC RECOVERY TAX ACT OF 1981

The Economic Recovery Tax Act of 1981, Pub.L.No. 97–34 (enacted August 13, 1981), made important changes to the administrative and procedural provisions of the Internal Revenue Code. Several of these changes were a reaction to the tremendous increase in the volume of tax controversies, particularly in the United States Tax Court. The increase in tax controversies resulted from a combination of circumstances, including: a long period in which the interest rate on tax liabilities was significantly lower than the market rate; the widespread utilization of tax shelters in which tax benefits were dependent upon allegedly inflated property valuations; and the IRS emphasis on partnership audits (largely in cases involving allegedly "abusive" tax shelters) in which adjustments can affect many taxpayers. Hence, the 1981 Act was designed to create a "downside risk" for those purchasing tax shelters (by the valuation overstatement penalty) and to eliminate the financial advantage in delaying the resolution of tax controversies for as long as possible (by the annually revised "market" interest rate on deficiencies and the additional negligence penalty). The principal administrative and procedural provisions of the 1981 Act are summarized below.

INTEREST ON DEFICIENCIES AND OVERPAYMENTS

The 1981 Act amended section 6621 of the Code, which provides for the periodic adjustment of the interest rate applicable to deficiencies and overpayments of taxes. Previously, the interest rate was set by the Secretary of the Treasury at 90% of the average prime rate charged by banks during the previous September. The rate became effective the following February, and could not be adjusted again for the next 23 months. Under the 1981 Act, commencing February 1, 1982, the interest rate is set at 100% of the prime rate and is adjusted annually. Beginning in 1983, the adjustments are effective each January 1.

ADDITIONAL NEGLIGENCE PENALTY

Code section 6653(a) [a] was amended to add a new penalty (in addition to the traditional 5% "negligence" penalty) applicable to

---

a. IRC § 6653(a), as amended by the Economic Recovery Tax Act of 1981, Pub.L. No. 97–34, § 722(b)(1), reads as follows:

SEC. 6653. FAILURE TO PAY TAX

(a) Negligence or Intentional Disregard of Rules and Regulations With Respect to Income, Gift, or Windfall Profit Taxes.—

(1) IN GENERAL.—If any part of any underpayment (as defined in subsection (c)(1) of any tax imposed by subtitle A, by chapter 12 of subtitle B, or by

underpayments of taxes resulting from negligence or intentional disregard of rules and regulations (but not due to fraud). This penalty, applied only to that portion of the underpayment attributable to the negligence or disregard, is in an amount equal to 50% of the interest payable with respect to the "tainted" underpayment. The penalty, although accruing contemporaneously with interest, is not deductible.

INCOME TAX VALUATION OVERSTATEMENT PENALTY

The 1981 Act added a new civil penalty to the Code for income tax "valuation overstatements" resulting in an underpayment of tax. IRC § 6659.[b] A "valuation overstatement" exists if the value or adjusted basis of any property claimed on a return exceeds 150% of

---

chapter 45 (relating to windfall profit tax) is due to negligence or intentional disregard of rules or regulations (but without intent to defraud), there shall be added to the tax an amount equal to 5 percent of the underpayment.

(2) ADDITIONAL AMOUNT FOR PORTION ATTRIBUTABLE TO NEGLIGENCE, ETC.—There shall be added to the tax (in addition to the amount determined under paragraph (1)) an amount equal to 50 percent of the interest payable under section 6601—

(A) with respect to the portion of the underpayment described in paragraph (1) which is attributable to the negligence or intentional disregard referred to in paragraph (1), and

(B) for the period beginning on the last date prescribed by law for payment of such underpayment (determined without regard to any extension) and ending on the date of the assessment of the tax.

*   *   *

The penalty is applicable to taxes the last day prescribed for payment of which is after December 31, 1981.

b. IRC § 6659, added to the Code by the Economic Recovery Tax Act of 1981, Pub.L.No. 97–34, § 722(a)(1), provides in part as follows:

SEC. 6659. ADDITION TO TAX IN THE CASE OF VALUATION OVERSTATEMENTS FOR PURPOSES OF THE INCOME TAX

(a) Addition to the tax.—If—

(1) an individual, or

(2) a closely held corporation or a personal service corporation,

has an underpayment of the tax imposed by chapter 1 for the taxable year which is attributable to a valuation overstatement, then there shall be added to the tax an amount equal to the applicable percentage of the underpayment so attributable.

(b) Applicable Percentage Defined.—

For purposes of subsection (a), the applicable percentage shall be determined under the following table:

If the valuation claimed is the following percent of the correct valuation—	The applicable percentage is—
150 percent or more but not more than 200 percent	10
More than 200 percent but not more than 250 percent	20
More than 250 percent	30

(c) Valuation Overstatement Defined.—

(1) IN GENERAL.—For purposes of this section, there is a valuation overstatement if the value of any property, or the adjusted basis of any property, claimed on any return exceeds 150 percent of the amount determined to be the correct amount of such valuation or adjusted basis (as the case may be).

the determined correct amount. The amount of the penalty is a percentage of the amount of the underpayment attributable to the overvaluation, determined under § 6659(b).

The penalty, which may be assessed in addition to the negligence penalty, applies only to taxpayers who are individuals, "closely held corporations" c or "personal service corporations." d The penalty is not applicable to property acquired more than five years preceding the close of the tax year at issue. The penalty also is not applicable if the underpayment attributable to the valuation overstatement is less than $1,000. Further, the IRS has the discretionary authority to waive all or any part of the penalty if it is found that the overvaluation was made on a reasonable basis and in good faith.

MISCELLANEOUS PROVISIONS

Penalties for False Withholding Allowance Certificate. The 1981 Act increased the civil and criminal penalties for claiming withholding allowances based upon false information. IRC §§ 6682, 7205. The civil penalty was increased from $50 to $500. The maximum criminal penalty for willfully failing to supply information, or for willfully supplying false or fraudulent information, was raised to a fine of $1,000 and/or a year of imprisonment.

Information Returns. Code sections 6041, 6652 and 6678 were amended to increase the civil penalty for failing to file information returns with the IRS (up to $10 per return from $1), and to add the requirement (subject to a $10 penalty) that a copy of the information return be furnished to the person to whom the information relates.

Tax Court Filing Fee. The Tax Court filing fee was increased to $60 (from $10) to bring it in line with the United States District Court filing fee.

---

(2) PROPERTY MUST HAVE BEEN ACQUIRED WITHIN LAST 5 YEARS. —This section shall not apply to any property which, as of the close of the taxable year for which there is a valuation overstatement, has been held by the taxpayer for more than 5 years.

(d) Underpayment Must Be at Least $1,000.—
   This section shall not apply if the underpayment for the taxable year attributable to the valuation overstatement is less than $1,000.

(e) Authority To Waive.—
   The Secretary may waive all or any part of the addition to the tax provided by this section on a showing by the taxpayer that there was a reasonable basis for the valuation or adjusted basis claimed on the return and that such claim was made in good faith.

* * *

The penalty is applicable to returns filed after December 31, 1981.

c. A "closely held corporation" is one in which more than 50% in value of the outstanding stock is owned by, or for, five or fewer individuals, applying the attribution rules of IRC § 318. IRC § 6659(f)(2).

d. A "personal service corporation" is a corporation "the principal business of which is the performance of services." IRC § 6659(f)(3).

IRS Disclosure of Audit-Selection Criteria. In response to several cases under the Freedom of Information Act seeking disclosure of IRS standards relating to the selection of returns for audit, the 1981 Act amended IRC § 6103 to provide that audit-selection standards need not be disclosed if the Secretary of the Treasury determines that their disclosure will seriously impair the assessment, collection or enforcement of the internal revenue laws.

INDEX

References are to Pages

†